DUN & BRADSTREET/ GALE GROUP

Industry Handbook

1521-6640

DUN & BRADSTREET/ GALE GROUP

Industry Handbook

Chemicals and Pharmaceuticals

Jennifer Zielinski, Editor

GALE GROUP

Detroit
San Francisco
London
Boston
Woodbridge, CT

Mary Alampi and Jennifer Zielinski, *Editors*
Erin E. Braun, *Managing Editor*

Wendy Blurton, *Buyer*
Dorothy Maki, *Manufacturing Manager*

Cynthia Baldwin, *Product Design Manager*
Michelle DiMercurio, *Senior Art Director*

ISBN 0-7876-3623-1
ISBN 0-7876-4909-0 (5 volume set)

Printed in the United States of America

CONTENTS

INTRODUCTION

This section presents a general introduction to the contents of *Dun & Bradstreet/Gale Industry Handbook: Chemicals and Pharmaceuticals*. In addition to presenting information on the book's contents, sources, organization, indices, and appendix, special explanations are provided for (1) the statistical tables and the projections used for some years of data and (2) the industry norms and ratios used in the Dun & Bradstreet, Inc. data. Information for contacting the editors completes the introduction.

Dun & Bradstreet/Gale Industry Handbook: Chemicals and Pharmaceuticals is a timely compilation of information on companies, associations, consultants, trade publications, and trade shows participating in or supporting these two industries. Recent statistics from corporate and government sources highlight financial, employment, and other trends. Descriptive materials are included on major industry issues (Foreword), industry history and trends (Industry Overview) and on recent mergers and acquisitions (Mergers & Acquisitions). Overall, *Chemicals and Pharmaceuticals* provides an up-to-date and comprehensive guide to these industries for all—the analyst, investor, planner, marketeer, benchmarker, student, or interested member of the public.

CONTENTS AND SOURCES

Chemicals and Pharmaceuticals is divided into two parts, with Part I featuring *Chemicals* and Part II featuring *Pharmaceuticals*. Each part has the same structure but different content.

Part I - Chemicals covers 25 industries and *Part II - Pharmaceuticals* covers four industries as defined in the Standard Industrial Classification (SIC) system. The SIC system is presently undergoing a major revision, with SIC codes in the process of being replaced by North American Industry Classification System (NAICS) codes. This book is still organized by SIC code because most data providers still use the "old" system. However, an SIC to NAICS and a NAICS to SIC conversion table is provided in the appendix. Data provided in *Chemicals and Pharmaceuticals*, shown here in chapter order, include the following categories—

Description and Context. The Foreword presents an expert view of each industry at the beginning of each part. In each part, Chapter 1 features an overview of the industry, including its history, important participants, current trends, and future directions.

Statistics. Chapter 2 presents federal government statistics and projections from 1987 to 1998. These data include establishments, employment, compensation, revenues, and ratios. Data in this chapter are drawn from the most recent edition of *Manufacturing USA*.

Company Information. Chapter 3 shows financial norms and ratios for 1996, 1997 and 1998. A full discussion of norms and ratios is presented, below, under the heading **Industry Norms and Ratios**. Chapter 4 presents company capsules for leading participants in each industry in directory format, including company name, parent, address, telephone, sales, employment, company type, SIC classification, description, and name and title of the leading company officer. Chapter 5 shows companies in rank order, first by sales volume and then by employment. The data in Chapters 3-5 in each part were prepared by and are shown by special arrangement with Dun & Bradstreet, Inc. Chapter 6 presents a summary of recent merger and acquisition activity in each industry.

Association Data. Chapter 7 presents a listing of domestic and international associations directly involved in each industry or in support of their activities. Information provided includes name of the organization, electronic access (url and/or e-mail), address, contact person, telephone and fax number, and a full description of the organization's activities, including such categories as founding date, membership, staff. Data shown are adapted from Gale's *Encyclopedia of Associations*.

Consultants. Information on industry consultants is shown in Chapter 8, adapted from Gale's *Consultants and Consulting Organizations Directory*. Categories shown include the name of the organization, e-mail and/or url for electronic access, address, leading officer, telephone and fax numbers, and a full description, including founding date and staff.

Trade Information Sources. Chapter 9 features publications offering trade information for each of the industries covered. The entries are adapted from Gale's *Encyclopedia of Business Information Sources* and include name of the book, periodical, or database, publisher, electronic contact (e-mail, url), complete address, telephone and fax numbers, and a description.

Trade Show Information. Chapter 10 presents information needed by all those planning to visit or to participate in trade shows for the chemicals or pharmaceutical sectors. Data are drawn from Gale's *Trade Shows Worldwide*. Entries include the name of the show, sponsoring organization, electronic access (e-mail, url), address, telephone and fax numbers, and a description including such categories as frequency of the event, audience, and principal exhibits.

ORGANIZATION

Chemicals and Pharmaceuticals is divided into two parts and organized by chapter. A common Master Index, Geographical Index, and an SIC Index follow Part II. The Appendix presents an SIC to NAICS and a NAICS to SIC lookup guide. Each chapter in each part begins with a brief description of contents and formats (if required). Additional explanatory materials are provided in this Introduction to *Chapter 2, Industry Statistics & Performance Indicators* (see **Statistics and Projections**, below) and *Chapter 3, Financial Norms and Ratios* (see **Industry Norms and Ratios**, below). The formats of these chapters are the same in both parts.

Chapter 1	Industry Overview
Chapter 2	Industry Statistics & Performance Indicators
Chapter 3	Financial Norms and Ratios
Chapter 4	Company Directory
Chapter 5	Rankings and Companies
Chapter 6	Mergers & Acquisitions
Chapter 7	Associations
Chapter 8	Consultants
Chapter 9	Trade Information Sources
Chapter 10	Trade Shows

INDEXES AND APPENDIX

Chemicals and Pharmaceuticals features three indexes. Each index provides combined coverage of Parts I and II. The **Master Index** shows company, organization, topical terms, and personal names in alphabetical order, with page references. Also included, in alphabetical order, are industry names followed by SIC codes in parentheses. The **Geographical Company Index** shows companies arranged by state and then in alphabetical order, with page references to each part's Chapter 4. The **Company Index by SIC** presents the Chapter 4 company information arranged numerically by SIC codes.

The Appendix, **SIC/NAICS Conversion Guide**, is a two part look-up facility featuring SIC to NAICS conversions in the first part and NAICS to SIC conversions in the second part. The first part is organized by SIC codes in ascending order; the second part is sorted by NAICS codes in ascending order.

STATISTICS AND PROJECTIONS

The tables presented in each part's Chapter 2 are drawn from federal government sources. Federal surveys are comprehensive and accurate, but they are published at some significant delay from the time of data collection. For this reason, projections were used to show data for more recent or future years in the tables in Chapter 2. In this section, terminology used in government data sources is briefly explained and the methods used in making the projections are outlined.

Terminology. Federal data make use of two terms subject to some misunderstanding. These are *establishments* and *value of shipments*.

- **Establishments** are physical locations where economic activity takes place. The establishment count for an industry is rarely the same as a census of the number of *companies* participating. There are typically more establishments than companies in an industry: many companies have multiple locations.

- **Value of Shipments** includes all products shipped from a plant, including primary and secondary products, transfers of goods to another plant, miscellaneous receipts (including contact work and work not related to the SIC at all), sales of scrap, and sales of purchased and resold products. Value of shipments, therefore, includes more than is normally associated with the concept of industry *sales*. The government makes a distinction between value of shipments and value of *product* shipments. In some SICs, the two values are very close (with value of shipments typically slightly higher). In others, there is a significant spread between the two.

Projections. The projections shown in the tables of Chapter 2 are footnoted to indicate that values are estimates. Projections are based on a curve-fitting algorithm using the least-squares method. In essence, the algorithm calculates a trend line for the data using existing data points (survey data). The trend line is the best "straight" line that can be laid over the existing points. Once the trend line has been established, it can be extended into the future. Estimated values, therefore, are points on the extended trend line indicated by past information.

INDUSTRY NORMS AND RATIOS

For each industry, as denoted by SIC, two tables are presented in each part's Chapter 3. The first, entitled **D&B Industry Norms**, presents financial norms for that industry. The second, entitled **D&B Key Business Ratios**, presents ratios. In what follows, each type of table is explained in some detail.

INDUSTRY NORMS

This table shows data for the years 1996-1998. Each table is entitled *D&B Industry Norms* followed by the SIC code and industry name of the industry featured. Next to each year, in parenthesis, is shown the number of companies in the sample used. The "typical" balance-sheet figures are in the first column and the "common-size" balance-sheet figures (in percent) are in the second.

The Common-Size Financial Statement. The common-size balance-sheet and income statement present each item of the financial statement (e.g., *Cash*) as a percentage of its respective aggregate total (e.g., *Total Assets*). Common-size percentages are computed for all statement items for each company in the industry sample. An average for each item is then calculated and presented as the industry norm. This enables the analyst to examine the current composition of assets, liabilities and sales of a particular industry.

The Typical Financial Statement. The typical balance-sheet figures are the result of translating the common-size percentages into dollar figures. They permit, for example, a quick check of the relative size of assets and liabilities between one's own company and that company's own line of business.

Typical values are computed as follows: after the common-size percentages have been calculated for the sample, the actual financial statements are sorted by both total assets and total sales, with the median, or

mid-point figure in both of these groups serving as the "typical" amount. Next, the typical balance-sheet and income statement dollar figures are computed by multiplying the item totals by the common-size percentages.

For example, if the median *Total Assets* for an SIC category is $669,599 and the common-size figure for *Cash* is 9.2 percent, then multiplying the two produces a cash figure of $61,603 for the typical balance sheet (669,559 x 0.092).

KEY BUSINESS RATIOS

This table shows data for the years 1996-1998. For each year, data are provided for the upper quartile, median, and lower quartile of the sample, providing the analyst with an even more refined set of figures. These ratios cover critical areas of business performance with indicators of solvency, efficiency and profitability.

The data serve as the basis for a profound and well-documented insight into all aspects of performance for anyone interested in the financial workings of business—executives and managers, credit executives, bankers, lenders, investors, academicians and students. An explanation of the ratios follows.

In the ratio tables shown, the figures are broken down into the median, upper, and lower quartiles. The *median* is the midpoint of all companies in the sample. The *upper* quartile shows the midpoint of the upper half, the *lower* quartile the midpoint of the lower half of the total sample.

Upper quartile figures are not always the highest numerical value, nor are lower quartile figures always the lowest numerical value. The quartile listings reflect *judgmental ranking*, thus the upper quartile represents the best condition for any given ratio and is not necessarily the highest numerical value. For example, a low numerical value is *better* for such ratios as Total Liabilities-to-Net Worth or Collection Period, indicating low liabilities and rapid collection of receivables.

Each of the 14 ratios is calculated individually for every company in the sample. These individual figures are then sorted for each ratio according to condition (best to worst). The value that falls in the middle of this series becomes the median (or mid-point) for that ratio in that line of business. The figure halfway between the median and the best condition of the series becomes the upper quartile; and the number halfway between the median and the least favorable condition of the series is the lower quartile.

In a statistical sense, each median is considered the *typical* ratio figure for a concern in a given category.

SOLVENCY RATIOS

Quick Ratio

$$\frac{Cash + Accounts\ Receivable}{Current\ Liabilities}$$

The Quick Ratio is computed by dividing cash plus accounts receivable by total current liabilities. Current liabilities are all the liabilities that fall due within one year. This ratio reveals the protection afforded short-term creditors in cash or near-cash assets. It shows the number of dollars of liquid assets available to cover each dollar of current debt. Any time this ratio is as much as 1 to 1 (1.0) the business is said to be in a liquid condition. The larger the ratio the greater the liquidity.

Current Ratio

$$\frac{Current\ Assets}{Current\ Liabilities}$$

Total current assets are divided by total current liabilities. Current assets include cash, accounts and notes receivable (less reserves for bad debts), advances on inventories, merchandise inventories and marketable securities. This ratio measures the degree to which current assets cover current liabilities. The higher the ratio the more assurance exists that the retirement of current liabilities can be made. The current ratio measures the margin of safety available to cover any possible shrinkage in the value of current assets. Normally a ratio of 2 to 1 (2.0) or better is considered good.

Current Liabilities to Net Worth

$$\frac{Current\ Liabilities}{Net\ Worth}$$

Current Liabilities to Net Worth is derived by dividing current liabilities by net worth. This contrasts the funds that creditors are risking temporarily with the funds permanently invested by the owners. The smaller the net worth and the larger the liabilities, the less security is afforded the creditors. Care should be exercised when selling any firm with current liabilities exceeding two-thirds (66.6 percent) of net worth.

Current Liabilities to Inventory

$$\frac{Current\ Liabilities}{Inventory}$$

Dividing current liabilities by inventory yields another indication of the extent to which the business relies on funds from disposal of unsold inventories to meet its debts. This ratio combines with Net Sales to Inventory to indicate how management controls inventory. It is possible to have decreasing liquidity while maintaining consistent sales-to-inventory ratios. Large increases in sales with corresponding increases in inventory levels can cause an inappropriate rise in current liabilities if growth isn't managed wisely.

Total Liabilities to Net Worth

$$\frac{Total\ Liabilities}{Net\ Worth}$$

This ratio is obtained by dividing total current plus long-term and deferred liabilities by net worth. The effect of long-term (funded) debt on a business can be determined by comparing this ratio with Current Liabilities to Net Worth. The difference will pinpoint the relative size of long-term debt, which, if sizable, can burden a firm with substantial interest charges. In general, total liabilities should not exceed net worth (100 percent) since in such cases creditors have more at stake than owners.

Fixed Assets to Net Worth

$$\frac{Fixed\ Assets}{Net\ Worth}$$

Fixed assets are divided by net worth. The proportion of net worth that consists of fixed assets will vary greatly from industry to industry, but generally a smaller proportion is desirable. A high ratio is unfavorable because heavy investment in fixed assets indicates that either the concern has a low net working capital and is overtrading or has utilized large funded debt to supplement working capital. Also, the larger the fixed assets, the bigger the annual depreciation charge that must be deducted from the income statement. Normally, fixed assets above 75 percent of net worth indicate possible over-investment and should be examined with care.

EFFICIENCY RATIOS

Collection Period

$$\frac{Accounts\ Receivable}{Sales\ x\ 365}$$

Accounts receivable are divided by sales and then multiplied by 365 days to obtain this figure. The quality of the receivables of a company can be determined by this relationship when compared with selling terms and industry norms. In some industries where credit sales are not the normal way of doing business, the percentage of cash sales should be taken into consideration. Generally, where most sales are for credit, any collection period more than one-third over normal selling terms (40.0 for 30-day terms) is indicative of some slow-turning receivables. When comparing the collection period of one concern with that of another, allowances should be made for possible variations in selling terms.

Sales to Inventory

$$\frac{Sales}{Inventory}$$

Obtained by dividing annual net sales by inventory. Inventory control is a prime management objective since poor controls allow inventories to become costly to store, obsolete, or insufficient to meet demands. The sales-to-inventory relationship is a guide to the rapidity at which merchandise is being moved and the effect on the flow of funds into the business. This ratio varies widely between lines of business, and a company's figure is only meaningful when compared with industry norms. Individual figures that are outside either the upper or lower quartiles for a given industry should be examined with care. Although low figures are usually the biggest problem, as they indicate excessively high inventories, extremely high turnovers might reflect insufficient merchandise to meet customer demand and result in lost sales.

Asset to Sales

$$\frac{Total\ Assets}{Net\ Sales}$$

Assets to sales are calculated by dividing total assets by annual net sales. This ratio ties in sales and the total investment that is used to generate those sales. While figures vary greatly from industry to industry, by comparing a company's ratio with industry norms it can be determined whether a firm is overtrading (handling an excessive volume of sales in relation to investment) or undertrading (not generating sufficient sales to warrant the assets invested). Abnormally low percentages (above the upper quartile) can indicate overtrading which may lead to financial difficulties if not corrected. Extremely high percentages (below the lower quartile) can be the result of overly conservative or poor sales management, indicating a more aggressive sales policy may need to be followed.

Sales to Net Working Capital

Sales

—

Net Working Capital

Net sales are divided by net working capital (net working capital is current assets minus current liabilities). This relationship indicates whether a company is overtrading or conversely carrying more liquid assets than needed for its volume. Each industry can vary substantially and it is necessary to compare a company with its peers to see if it is either overtrading on its available funds or being overly conservative. Companies with substantial sales gains often reach a level where their working capital becomes strained. Even if they maintain an adequate total investment for the volume being generated (Assets to Sales), that investment may be so centered in fixed assets or other noncurrent items that it will be difficult to continue meeting all current obligations without additional investment or reducing sales.

Accounts Payable to Sales

Accounts Payable

———

Annual Net Sales

Computed by dividing accounts payable by annual net sales. This ratio measures how the company is paying its suppliers in relation to the volume being transacted. An increasing percentage, or one larger than the industry norm, indicates the firm may be using suppliers to help finance operations. This ratio is especially important to short-term creditors since a high percentage could indicate potential problems in paying vendors.

PROFITABILITY RATIOS

Return on Sales (Profit Margin)

Net Profit After Taxes

———

Annual Net Sales

Obtained by dividing net profit after taxes by annual net sales. This reveals the profits earned per dollar of sales and therefore measures the efficiency of the operation. Return must be adequate for the firm to be able to achieve satisfactory profits for its owners. This ratio is an indicator of the firm's ability to withstand adverse conditions such as falling prices, rising costs and declining sales.

Return on Assets

Net Profit After Taxes

———

Total Assets

Net profit after taxes divided by total assets. This ratio is the key indicator of profitability for a firm. It matches operating profits with the assets available to earn a return. Companies efficiently using their assets will have a relatively high return while less well-run businesses will be relatively low.

Return on Net Worth (Return on Equity)

Net Profit After Taxes

———

Net Worth

Obtained by dividing net profit after tax by net worth. This ratio is used to analyze the ability of the firm's management to realize an adequate return on the capital invested by the owners of the firm. Tendency is to look increasingly to this ratio as a final criterion of profitability. Generally, a relationship of at least 10 percent is regarded as a desirable objective for providing dividends plus funds for future growth.

USING INDUSTRY NORMS FOR FINANCIAL ANALYSIS

The principal purpose of financial analysis is to identify irregularities that require explanations to completely understand an industry's or company's current status and future potential. Comparing the industry norms with the figures of specific companies (comparative analysis) can identify these irregularities. D&B's Industry Norms are specifically formatted to accommodate this analysis.

Relative Position

Common-size and typical balance sheets provide an excellent picture of the makeup of the industry's assets and liabilities. Are assets concentrated in inventories or accounts receivable? Are payables to the trade or bank loans more important as a method for financing operations? The answers to these and other important questions are clearly shown by the Industry Norms, its common-size balance sheet approach and is then further crystallized by the typical balance sheets.

Financial Ratio Trends

Key Business Ratio changes indicate trends in the important relationships between key financial items, such as the relationship between Net Profits and Net Sales (a common indicator of profitability). Ratios that reflect short and long-term liquidity, efficiency in managing assets and controlling debt, and different measures of profitability are all included in the Key Business Ratios sections of the Industry Norms.

Comparative Analysis

Comparing a company with its peers is a reliable method for evaluating financial status. The key to this technique is the composition of the peer group and the timeliness of the data. The D&B Industry Norms are unique in scope for sample size and in level of detail.

Sample Size

The number of firms in the sample must be representative or they will be unduly influenced by irregular figures from relatively few companies. The more than one million companies used as a basis for the Industry Norms allow for more than adequate sample sizes in most cases.

Key Business Ratios Analysis

Valuable insights into an industry's performance can be obtained by equating two related statement items in the form of a financial ratio. For really effective ratio analysis, the items compared must be meaningful and the comparison should reflect the combined effort of two potentially diverse trends. While dozens of different ratios can be computed from financial statements, the fourteen included in the Industry Norms and Key Business Ratio books are those most commonly used and were rated as the most significant as shown in a survey of financial analysts. Many of the other ratios in existence are variations on these fourteen.

The 14 Key Business Ratios are categorized into three major groups:

Solvency, or liquidity, measurements are significant in evaluating a company's ability to meet short and long-term obligations. These figures are of prime interest to credit managers of commercial companies and financial institutions.

Efficiency ratios indicate how effectively a company uses and controls its assets. This is critical information for evaluating how a company is managed. Studying these ratios is useful for credit, marketing and investment purposes.

Profitability ratios show how successfully a business is earning a return to its owners. Those interested in mergers and acquisitions consider this key data for selecting candidates.

Recent research efforts have revealed that the use of financial analysis (via Industry Norms) is very useful in several functional areas. To follow are only a few of the more widely used applications of this unique data.

Credit

Industry Norm data has proven to be an invaluable tool in determining minimum acceptable standards for risk. The credit worthiness of an existing or potential account is immediately visible by ranking its solvency status and comparing its solvency trends to that of the industry. Short term solvency gauges, such as the quick and current ratios, are ideal indicators when evaluating an account. Balance sheet comparisons supplement this qualification by allowing a comparison of the make-up of current assets and liability items. Moreover, leverage ratios such as current liability to net worth and total liability to net worth provide valuable benchmarks to spot potential problem accounts while profitability and collection period figures provide cash flow comparisons for an overall evaluation of accounts.

In addition to evaluating individual accounts against industry standards, internal credit policies also benefit from Industry Norm data. Are receivables growing at an excessive rate as compared to the industry? If so, how does your firm's collections stack up to the industry?

Finance

Here exists a unique opportunity for financial executives to rank their firm, or their firm's subsidiaries and divisions, against its peers. Determine the efficiency of management via ratio quartile breakdowns which provides you the opportunity to pinpoint your firm's profitability position versus the industry. For example, are returns on sales and gross profit margins comparatively low thereby indicating that pricing per unit may be too low or that the cost of goods is unnecessarily high?

In much the same way, matching the firm's growth and efficiency trends to that of the industry reveals conditions which prove to be vital in projecting budgets. If asset expansion exceeds the industry standard while asset utilization (as indicated by the asset to sales ratio) is sub par, should growth be slowed?

Investment executives have also utilized this diverse information when identifying optimal investment opportunities. By uncovering which industries exhibit the strongest sales growth while maintaining adequate returns, risk is minimized.

Corporate Planning

Corporate plans, competitive strategies and merger & acquisition decisions dictate a comprehensive analysis of the industry in question. Industry Norm data provides invaluable information in scrutinizing the performance of today's highly competitive, and sometimes unstable, markets. Does the liquidity of an industry provide a sufficient cushion to endure the recent record-high interest levels or is it too volatile to risk an entry? Are the profitability and equity conditions of an acquisition candidate among the best in the industry thereby qualifying it as an ideal acquisition target?

Industry Norm data provide these all-important benchmarks for setting strategic goals and measuring overall corporate performance.

Marketing and Sales

Attaining an in-depth knowledge of a potential or existing customer base is a key factor when developing successful marketing strategies and sales projections. Industry Norm data provide a competitive edge when determining market potential and market candidates. Identify those industries that meet or exceed your qualifications and take it one step further by focusing in on the specific region or size category that exhibits the greatest potential. For example, isolate the industries which have experienced the strongest growth trends in sales and inventory turnover and then fine tune marketing and sales strategies by identifying the particular segment which is the most attractive (such as firms with assets of $1 million or more).

This information can also be used in a different context by examining the industries of existing accounts. If an account's industry shows signs of faltering profitability and stagnating sales, should precautionary measures be taken? Will the next sale be profitable for your company or will it be written-off? Industry Norm data assist in answering these and many other important questions.

COMMENTS AND SUGGESTIONS

Comments on or suggestions for improvement of the usefulness, format, and coverage of *Dun & Bradstreet/ Gale Industry Handbook* are always welcome. Although every effort is made to maintain accuracy, errors may occasionally occur; the editors will be grateful if these are called to their attention. Please contact—

Editors

Dun & Bradstreet/Gale Industry Handbook
27500 Drake Rd.
Farmington Hills, MI 48331-3535
248-699-GALE

PART I
CHEMICALS

THE CHEMICAL INDUSTRY:
PAST, PRESENT, AND FUTURE

Roy Atkins

The use of chemicals can be traced back to ancient civilization, and although generally not identified as such, they have played an increasing part in the development of civilization as we know it. The simple arts of preparing foods, making bricks for building, lighting a fire all involve the manipulation of molecules, although our ancestors were unaware of such detail. As men came together in cities the collection of simple manufacturing techniques began to grow. Trades such as potting, metalworking, weaving and brewing became established and eventually primitive industries became identifiable in cities in the Middle East prior to Babylon. Archaeological evidence strongly supports this and particularly striking is the evidence of products obtained by the action of fire on special materials. Such are artifacts in gold, copper, and bronze with glass ornaments from the colored slags associated with winning the metals. From the earliest times seven metals came to dominate at different times, they were iron, copper and tin, gold, silver, mercury, and lead. The prominence of the first three over time were so important that they are used to label those periods. These seven metals represented the limit of knowledge of chemical elements if we include the non-metallic elements sulphur and carbon until the sixteenth century. This limited knowledge nonetheless made possible the foundations of the later Industrial Revolution in the nineteenth century.

The chemical industry began to emerge in the early industrial revolution in Europe around 1800 AD. Inorganic chemicals, such as bleaching powder for use in the cotton industry, and alkali for soap making, were early examples. The demand for larger scale supply and consistency in quality, acted as the incentive for industrialization of what had been local cottage industries. Improvement in transport systems, changes in the political climate for taxation were also incentives. These often followed closely upon the heels of discoveries in chemistry and the physical sciences, and the process innovations which resulted had sometimes profound social, as well as economic, implications. Organic chemicals, compounds containing carbon, came later when the pioneering work of Perkin was exploited in the large-scale manufacture of the first synthetic dyestuff Mauve, or aniline purple, in the 1860's. This led to the proliferation of the synthetic dyestuff industry. The modern chemical industry is a worldwide activity of enormous size and complexity, which provides much of the material basis for the wealth and

lifestyle of developed and developing nations. It contributes in a major way to world trade and to the myriad of technological miracles we all take for granted in modern life. The total sales of the world industry are probably around one trillion U.S. Dollars per annum. This includes not only a relatively small number of well known and very large multi-national companies, but also over 95% of the industry in companies that employ less 500 people, which in the European Union alone total 33,000.

The prime function of the chemicals industry is to convert raw materials into products that are usually the starting point for other industrial and consumer products. The petrochemical industry for instance, takes its feedstock from oil and gas processing and makes polymers for plastic products, solvents and intermediates. These and other products of the industry are used for making dyestuffs, drugs, fertilizers, food preservatives and flavorings, glass, metal alloys and paper products. The whole industry can be described either by dividing it into functional groups:

Petrochemicals
Polymers
Dyestuffs
Agrochemicals
Pharmaceuticals
Chlor-alkali
Sulphur
Fertilizers
Phosphorus

or by product end-use categories:

Pharmaceuticals
Specialized chemicals
Organics
Soap & toiletries
Paints & inks
Plastics, resins & rubbers
Dyestuffs & pigments
Inorganics
Fertilizers

Whichever way, its impact is so obviously wide and profound that it affects almost every aspect of our everyday lives. This intimate and complex linking is often misunderstood not least because of the very technical nature of the underlying science. In this regard the hitherto reluctance of many chemical corporations to explain their activities, policies and even products has only added to the mystery and suspicion surrounding newsworthy events. Greater transparency in the industry is a commonly sought goal, but this has to be achieved within the ever present need to protect highly sensitive commercial information on processes and products. A combination of increasingly stringent legislation on environmental and safety issues and the general availability of information is accelerating this trend to the benefit of all.

The worldwide chemical industry was for much of this century concentrated in the USA, Europe and Japan with total sales in 1991 of:

USA	$285 billion
W Europe	$265
Japan	$180

During the last two decades the increasing trend to globalize production in many sectors of the industry, has been coincident with the explosive growth in the Pacific Rim countries. Contrary to popular belief, this has not been the result of companies rushing away headlong from draconian legislation or spiraling costs at home into joint-ventures and the like abroad. It has rather been a trend to minimize transport costs, and make full use of raw material availability and investment opportunities. The industry is one where, in the case of commodity chemicals, capital investment in plants largely dominates its financial structure and labor costs are a small proportion of manufacturing overheads. The reverse is true for the equally large pharmaceutical industry where research and development activity dominates the financial structure of the companies and the intellectual capital of highly skilled people is paramount. The cost of raw materials, energy and transportation dominate all parts of the industry, and economies of scale have enormous impact. The industry is highly sensitive to macro-economic fluctuations and has been ravaged many times in the recent past by cyclical demand. Globalization is seen as affording some protection in this respect whilst increasing corporate influence in world markets for the really big players, hence the prominence of ever larger mergers. To put some idea of investment scale to the trend of the 1990's, during the period 1995 to 2000, $100 billion is being spent world-wide on new chemical plant

of which roughly half will be concentrated in the Asia-Pacific region.

Chemical products are developed as a result of a complex mix of market-pull, technical feasibility, raw material availability, cost reduction and environmental pressures. The market's desire for more effective products at lower cost is a universal one. It has been met consistently by the chemical industry with innovation that has largely gone unnoticed by the public at large. In this industry, as in many others, these pressures are matched by political considerations that can extend from climate change to the toxicological impact of new materials. It is an ironic fact of life that detrimental effects elsewhere so often accompany innovative improvements, which were quite unforeseen at the time. Such was the case with the use of chemicals known as CFCs (chlorofluorocarbons), which were developed in the 1940's in the US as improved refrigerants, solvents and aerosol propellants. Only recently they have been shown to massively contribute to stratospheric ozone depletion due to their chlorine component. This is a particular case in point where the chemical industry reacted with admirable speed and innovative flair to find acceptable alternatives. HCFCs, (hydrochlorofluorocarbons) were found and commercial processes for their manufacture developed within two years. These are compounds that have only one tenth the depletion effect of CFCs. Later other substitutes known as HFCs have been discovered which contain no chlorine at all, but which may present longer-term human health hazards. This change-uncertainty relationship is a feature of all highly complex systems. It cannot be avoided short of abandoning all innovative progress, and thus a system of vigilant monitoring will always be required. A promising feature of international cooperation in recent years has been the establishment and global coordination of governmental bodies to undertake this monitoring role.

A HIGHLY PROFESSIONAL INDUSTRY

The professional roles involved in the industry obviously major on the supporting sciences of chemistry, chemical engineering and biochemistry. These, together with a mix of disciplines composed of mechanical, electrical, instrumentation, and construction engineering with a large compliment of IT support, make up the staff component. The largest functional group is of course the production operation comprising large groups of highly trained process operatives with management drawn from the professions. The history of those professions is intimately linked with the growth of the chemical industry and none more than Chemistry. This is the study of substances, their properties and how they behave under different conditions. Chemists attempt to explain this by reference to the structure and composition of the substance and to account for chemical changes by the alteration in the chemical makeup. Beginning with substances that occur in nature, the science grew out of the practice of Alchemy that had its roots in Egypt in the first century AD and developed across Europe to a peak in the 1600's. Progress during the mid 1700's featured fundamental work on the identification of gases. Carbon Monoxide by Joseph Black and Hydrogen by Henry Cavendish in 1766 was followed by the identification of Oxygen by Joseph Priestley in 1774. Lavoisier's contribution to the science, his Law of the Conservation of Mass was a crucial step. This together with his experiments in collaboration with the Marquis de Laplace on respiration in animals, the first experiments in Biochemistry, lead to his *Elementary Treatise on Chemistry* published in 1789. This was the first modern textbook of chemistry.

In 1803 an English chemist, John Dalton developed an atomic theory which had each chemical element with its own composition of atoms. He postulated that all atoms of a particular element had the same mass and chemical properties. His theory held that a fixed number of atoms of one substance always combine with a fixed number of atoms of another forming a compound. This meant that substances must combine in the same proportions by weight as the weight proportions of their atoms. This had been observed with pure substances according to the established Law of Constant Proportions. Dalton's theory explained the Law. He was the first to calculate the weights of the atoms of several elements, and he began the practice of using letters of the alphabet as symbols for elements. The way in which these elements fit into a table based upon their atomic weights is the basis for the Periodic Table discovered by the Russian chemist Mendeleev. The periods arise when elements with similar properties are arranged in columns and he predicted correctly that the gaps left would be filled with elements of certain properties when they were eventually discovered. The modern periodic table summarizes the chemistry of all known elements.

In the early 1800's, chemists believed that organic substances, those found in plants and animals, could only be produced with the help of a "vital force." They were especially resistant to any form of analysis and so all chemical knowledge was obtained by the study of simpler inorganic substances. However, in 1824, the German chemist Wohler mixed two inorganic substances, heated them and obtained urea—an organic compound found in urine. He thus made the first synthetic organic compound from inorganic materials and disproved the vitalism theory. When chemists isolated organic substances during the 1800's they discovered that most consisted of carbon combined with oxygen, hydrogen and nitrogen in various proportions. Also that in some cases separate organic compounds with different properties were composed of the same elements in the same proportions. The German chemist Berzelius explained this by coining the term "isomers" which indicates molecules having the same kinds and numbers of atoms but differ in the way they are joined together. In the mid 1800's molecular structure theories began to appear and valency theory formed the basis for explaining the way atoms combine to form molecules. By 1900 organic chemistry had become a major branch of the science and eventually developed into the now separate field of Biochemistry. During the 1800's chemists and physicists investigating the properties and energy changes that accompany chemical reactions were pursuing a parallel path. This field eventually became Physical Chemistry which is amongst other things a vital plank in the scaling-up of chemical reactions for industrial production.

Chemical Engineers first came upon the scene in an identifiable way at the turn of the twentieth century. The American Society was founded in 1908 and the British Institution incorporated in 1922. Formal education in Chemical Engineering began in the US in 1915 with Arthur D. Little at Massachusetts Institute of Technology and it is he who is credited with inventing the term "unit operation." Prior to 1915 flow charts and descriptions of chemical processes had dominated industrial chemistry. Later came the concepts of material and energy balances and industrial reaction kinetics. After the first World War chemical engineers in America took the petroleum industry by the scruff of the neck and revolutionized it. Pot stills became a thing of the past whereas in Europe they were in use until the 1950's. American industry welcomed the new profession with open arms and it grew rapidly, whereas in Europe the largest companies, I G Farben and Imperial Chemical Industries did not recognize the profession through the first half of the century! Newman defined the profession in 1938 as the branch of engineering concerned with the development and application of manufacturing processes in which chemical and certain physical changes in materials are involved. He went on to mention the coordination of series of unit operations into processes, and concluded that chemistry, physics and mathematics were the underlying sciences with economics as its guide in practice. That was certainly true then and in the 1950's a more fundamental definition was adopted by the American Institute of Chemical Engineers, that restated the main thrust of that earlier one. Given that the underlying sciences and technologies have progressed to an astonishing degree during the latter half of this century, it remains no less true today for the modern chemical engineer and technician.

Biochemistry is concerned with the study of chemical processes that take place in living things. All living organisms contain compounds such as carbohydrates, lipids, nucleic acids and proteins. The molecules of these compounds help form the various structures in a living cell and provide mechanisms for functional control. Biochemistry is of course closely associated with the sciences of Biology and Medicine. The fields of study become ever more close and overlapping when the more recent science of Molecular Biology is considered. In 1938 the American mathematician Warren Weaver defined it as "involving those areas in which physics and chemistry merge with biology." It is the study of those molecules that direct molecular processes in living cells. It includes the study of the large molecules that store genetic information known collectively as macromolecules. The best known, DNA (deoxyribonucleic acid) is the chief constituent in chromosomes, the cell structures that control heredity. Research in this area has only just begun to find industrial application with what has become known as "genetic engineering." It is now possible to study gene regulation in the cells of plants and animals, and this has greatly added to our understanding of many biological processes. It is now possible to genetically modify plants and animals to obtain benefits not previously possible. These are finding their way into human and animal food and healthcare but the longer-term effects are not known causing great concern in many quarters.

THE PRODUCTS

PLASTICS

To understand the range of uses to which products of the chemical industry are put it is useful to look at major groupings of common materials. The word plastic has good and bad connotations depending upon the context. Globally it describes man-made materials that can be shaped into almost any form and can thus be said to be one of the most useful classes of compounds ever created. The range of possibilities covers materials as soft as silk or rigid as steel, and stronger. The basic molecular structure of plastics is the polymer, and these are linked together in chains of repeating units of polymer molecules. In some plastics these chains are rigid and lined up whereas in others they are flexibly linked. These different structural systems give rise to the variety of properties of the plastic and its ability to be shaped. Engineers have created hundreds of plastics each with its own properties. There are plastics to replace metals, paper, wood, stone, glass and ceramics and natural fibers. These often are stronger, lighter, easier to maintain and cheaper to produce. There are now plastic products that could not have been made using any other material.

Plastic parts now replace metals in the construction of airplanes, and automobiles saving on weight and benefiting from a marked resistance to corrosion. Pipes made from polymers are becoming universal in buildings replacing copper, steel and iron. The surgical use of plastics to mend bones and joints minimizes rejection complications and tooth fillings benefit from similar properties together with color matching to the patient's natural teeth. We are all now so familiar with artificial fibers being used in clothing, giving our garments the look and feel of silk, cotton or wool or whatever. Not so obvious perhaps are the additional advantages such as stain resistance, and durability and even fire proofing which for furniture coverings is a lifesaver. Much of the paper, which in the past would have been used for wrapping and packaging, is now made from plastic materials specially designed for the purpose. Polymeric foam which is made in truly enormous amounts, not only protects boxed goods better than any other system but has excellent insulating properties with very low weight. It can thus be found insulating vehicles, homes and even whole building foundations, as well as the cups we use for fast food.

Lamination of plastic films to a substrate such as plywood, provides the ubiquitous worktop which is strong, durable and can be made to look like many natural materials which could themselves never now satisfy world demand.

The chemistry of plastics is very complex, but in simple terms the starting substances made by chemical manufacturers are called synthetic resins. These are sold to companies that make the plastic products.

The resins are composed of polymer chains containing hundreds, thousands or even millions of links composed of monomers that are the fundamental chemical components. Some polymers are made of the same links repeated over and over again. Others are mixtures of two or more different monomers that may be linked randomly or in alternating sequence, some are even organized into blocks that are linked together. The polymer chains may have branches in them, which may be on one side or both. The chains may be packed together in straight rows that make stiff crystalline solids or be tangled and spread out making soft rubbery material. The properties of the final plastics are determined by these factors together with the length of the chains and with the use of mixtures of polymers, lubricants and fillers.

Polymer technicians can produce blends with ideal properties for nearly any task. However, all these benefits are balanced by a major problem: most of these materials do not readily decompose (in the environment) into simpler compounds in the normal course of events. They therefore represent a major waste disposal problem at the end of their useful life, but however they are generally ideal candidates for some kind of segregated recycling.

The history of the invention of plastics materials is a fascinating story of necessity indeed being the mother of invention. From very early times people have used natural gums and resins with properties similar to plastics. The earliest probably being Amber which was used in Roman times, and later shellac was used to coat objects.

In the late 1860's John W. Hyatt of New York developed a synthetic replacement for ivory used to make billiard balls. He treated Cellulose from cotton with nitric acid and obtained pyroxylin that he then reacted with Camphor. This was known as Celluloid and gained rapid and wide commercial use. Its major drawback was its flammability and at the turn of the twentieth century was modified to Cellulose Acetate.

The first thermosetting plastic, which is one that can be heated and set only once, was invented by Leo Baekeland in New York in 1909. This was a reaction between phenol and formaldehyde which being very exothermic, that is given off lots of heat rapidly, was very difficult to control. He was looking for a synthetic shellac but found the first Phenolic Resin, which he called Bakelite.

During the following decades plastics chemistry developed very important compounds called thermoplastics, that is materials that can be melted and reformed, which included acrylics, nylon, polystyrene and polyvinyl chloride (PVC). After the second World War the very important thermosetting polyesters were developed and the equally important thermoplastics; polyethylene, silicones and epoxy resins were developed. The latter have grown into a very widely used range of adhesives. The major source of the raw materials for most plastics is now the petrochemical industry with production into millions of tons per year.

PHARMACEUTICALS

These are chemical compounds obtained either from natural sources or synthetically produced and used to treat or prevent diseases. Most drugs are taken orally, but may also be injected into the bloodstream, inhaled or applied to the skin. The simplest way to administer a drug is to swallow it, however this is not always possible because the stomach juices destroy some materials very rapidly. Most drugs act after they have entered the bloodstream by travelling around the body and reacting with the target tissue by altering particular cell activity. The specific action of a particular drug relates to its effect on the cell chemistry concerned, this is known as the Receptor Theory. Specific receptor molecules attach themselves to each cell and alter the controlling reactions. This is not however a one-way process because the body changes most drugs into one or more new substances which are weaker than the original drug compound. This process is known as biotransformation and is the body's way of protecting itself. The liver is the main organ involved, which makes liver disease more complex to treat. All drugs have both good and bad effects on the body and the relative balance of these underlies the critical requirement to get the dose taken by the patient at the right level. Side reactions are manifestations of the bad effect of drugs, which are mainly due to active molecules effecting other parts of the body than that intended. This effect is increased with the strength of the dose. However not everyone is effected to the same extent by a given drug dose.

There is a vast range of pharmaceutical compounds, and their development is a major undertaking by the companies concerned. The financial investment in these companies—for research and development of new drugs—is a major proportion of their turnover and far greater than in any other branch of the chemical industry. Drug discovery sometimes happens by accident and there have been many well-documented stories of such serendipity. However, the vast majority are the result of an idea pursued by the company chemist.

The company having invented the new compound must test it and develop it into a safe and useable form. The registration and approval by the regulatory authorities, together with patent protection and the investment in production and marketing, can be a very expensive and long process which can take up to ten years to complete. Large initial profit margins on new drugs are absolutely essential in order for these companies to continue to explore new and more effective ways to treat illness and improve human and animal welfare.

Drugs have at least two names, the chemical one and its generic name and it may also have a trade name specific to the producing company. Hence generic drugs may be available around the world under a variety of different trade names but essentially contain the same active chemical ingredients.

The main classification of drugs is in the beneficial way they effect the body. The most important four are: drugs that fight bacteria, those that prevent infection, those that affect the heart and blood vessels, and those that affect the nervous system. Drugs are made from a variety of starting materials such as plants and moulds, animals, minerals and bacteria. Medicines such as antibiotics that kill bacteria, cardiotonics which strengthen the heartbeat, and certain analgesics which relieve pain, are all made from plants and molds. A number of important drugs including hormones are obtained from the cells and tissues of animals, whilst the minerals iodine and silver nitrate, prevent infection and stop bleeding. The most complex developments involve techniques such as the growth of human genes inside bacterial cells to make the same chemicals humans make in their own cells. Insulin and interferons are made in this way thus allowing the treatment of diabetes, many viral infections and some forms of cancer.

AGROCHEMICALS

These are mainly chemicals to control or eliminate pests such as insects, fungi, weeds and rats, and are commonly known as Pesticides. Insects are probably the largest group of pests and are capable of destroying valuable crops in a variety of ways. They can also be a problem in urban areas where, for instance, mosquitoes can spread malaria and moths, cockroaches and termites can inflict damage on buildings and other property. Pesticides can be selective, toxic only the target pests whilst others are non-selective and should only be used when no other method of control is available.

Herbicides help control weeds, or eliminate plants that grow where they are unwanted. They are used extensively by farmers and also by the general public in gardens and recreational areas. Fungicides are designed to control plant diseases caused by pathogenic fungi. These can be infections on fruit crops, cereals and beans amongst many. Most disinfectants used in hospitals, homes and food preparation areas contain fungicides. Rodenticides are used to eliminate rats and other rodents that present a health risk. Rabies and typhus are just two of the many infectious diseases carried by rats who also destroy large amounts of grain and other foodstuffs under storage.

Agrochemicals vary greatly in composition having specific active ingredients for the purpose for which they are intended. Most are designed to last only long enough in the environment to control the target. However some others are persistent and can enter the biological cycle known as the food chain. This involves a persistent compound that is absorbed by organisms at a low level in the food chain, they are in turn eaten by organisms at a higher level who retain the compound. The process continues and the contamination increases as it moves up the chain, reeking havoc in mammals and birds and eventually man. The best known example is DDT which is now completely banned in many parts of the world, or very seriously restricted.

FUELS

Most of the useable energy released in the world is the result of the oxidation of hydrocarbons with oxygen from air. Overwhelmingly fossil fuels such as coal, petroleum and natural gas are the primary source, with a small but slowly increasing proportion of biomass sources emerging. These involve the generation of methane from the breakdown of organic materials such as wood, rubbish and animal manure. The remaining proportion is accounted for by nuclear fission in which atoms of Uranium are split under controlled conditions generating massive amounts of heat for each kilo of fuel, and as yet tiny amounts of energy are generated from wind, sun and wave sources. Coal is the predominant world source of fuel for electrical generation. Burning the coal in furnaces produces steam and the steam driving mechanical turbines generates electrical energy in turn. The overall thermal efficiency of such arrangements is around 30-40% conversion of the energy available, this can be improved upon radically by substituting the solid fuel with natural or synthetic gas and burning that directly in the turbine. This allows efficiencies of more than double conventional steam stations with considerable reduction in capital costs and very much less environmental impact.

The world fuel industry attracts more concern from environmentalists than any other. These mostly involve the consequences of global warming associated with the release of carbon dioxide from the burning of fossil and other hydrocarbon fuels. The insatiable demand for energy by the developed and developing world means that the industry continues to expand whilst finding great difficulty in addressing the net increases in emissions. These can only be controlled by improvements in efficiency of energy conversion to which there are strong practical limits. Reductions in total demand, that are sustainable, can only come from political decisions affecting the lifestyle of nations. The increasing and seemingly irreversible demand for liquid fuels for automobiles throughout the world is the principle market for the petroleum corporations that form the largest sector of fuel processors. Chemical industry unit operations feature strongly in the production of gasoline and aviation fuels. Primarily

distillation and thermal cracking, often with the help of catalysts, produces the sophisticated fuels for modern engines and turbines whilst product stream integration ensures the simultaneous production of feedstocks for petrochemical operations. It is true to say that no part of the crude oil extracted from the ground or seabed is unused, with gases and liquids for fuels and chemical processes, solid residues for greases, waxes and road-making asphalt. The industry is highly efficient and uses the all skills familiar in other sectors of the chemical industry albeit in sometimes very specialized ways, whilst having unique skill requirements at the exploration end of the business.

PAINTS

Paint has been known since the earliest times, mainly comprising vegetable and earth pigments mixed with water and animal fats. These were applied to walls, tombs etc. with examples of cave painting in Europe dating from over 20,000 years ago. The ancient Egyptians used sophisticated paint systems not greatly different from some still used today. The Italian Renaissance artists and craftsmen developed very complex paints but because of the trade secrecy of the day the formulas died with the inventor.

The commercial manufacture of paint began in Europe and the United States in 1700's. Paints comprise one or more finely ground pigments for color and a liquid vehicle. Extenders such as clay, mica and talc are added to improve wear characteristics. The early manufacturers used, in addition to naturally occurring pigments, eggs, coffee grounds and skimmed milk, which they ground on stone wheels and thinned down with water. During the early Industrial Revolution more sophisticated grinding machines were developed which allowed greater volumes to be produced. New pigments, extenders and solvent vehicles were developed with advances in chemistry. In the present century, in addition to synthetic pigments, resin and solvents have been used to modify adhesive qualities, drying times, the degree of gloss produced and the hardness of the final finish. Various modes of curing are possible in addition to the common drying by evaporation of the solvent. Some form a solid film only after a reaction triggered by a catalyst causes the resin particles to bond together. Oil based paints cure by oxidation of the resin film after most of the solvent has evaporated.

PETROCHEMICALS

The chemicals manufactured using feedstocks from petroleum or natural gas are called petrochemicals and are a quite separate operation from the oil refinery. The companies may well be the same as the oil refiners but the operations have a significantly different culture and purpose. The major operations in petrochemicals are the synthesis of compounds using primary gas streams from the refinery together with other chemical compounds not associated with refining and producing products that are not fuels. The major application areas for the products include detergents, fertilizers, medicines, paint, plastics, synthetic fibers and rubbers.

The basic products can be divided into three major groups:

Olefins: ethylene, propylene and butadiene; used in industrial chemicals, plastics and synthetic rubber

Aromatics: benzene, toluene, xylenes; and synthesis gas; used in dyestuffs, detergents, explosives, plastics and synthetic fibers.

Synthesis gas: used to make basic petrochemicals ammonia and methanol which in turn make fertilizers and as a source of other chemicals.

The first petrochemical product was made in the United States in 1872. Carbon Black was made from natural gas and now has wide use as a reinforcing material in vehicle tires. The proportion of oil and gas used for petrochemicals has increased dramatically during the period 1970-1990's.

THE ENVIRONMENT

Wastes are produced by all industrial activity, from the trivial, such as wood shavings from furniture manufacture to the serious pollutants from heavy chemical operations. The chemical industry is carefully regulated by statutory provision in the way that it treats its wastes. Most are dealt with firstly by reduction techniques since all waste is lost revenue, then treatment processes using chemical and biological techniques with recycle wherever possible. Only when the stage is reached of minimum environmental impact does the waste leave the chemical production facility for

landfill etc. Wastes, which are considered hazardous, receive special consideration and control, with emphasis on minimization and replacement. Hazardous wastes are nonetheless produced throughout the world in alarmingly large amounts of the order of 400 million metric tons annually, mostly from industrialized countries. They are any unwanted chemicals, usually byproducts that may endanger human health if released into the environment. The commonest such wastes are arsenic, lead and mercury and their compounds. Together with chlorinated solvents, organochlorine pesticides and asbestos these materials remain poisonous for an indefinite time and are not rendered harmless by natural agents in the environment. Their transportation across national boundaries is regulated by international treaty and their disposal by landfill carefully regulated by national governments. Some compounds can be rendered harmless by the action of bacteria, oxidation at high temperature or under special chemical regimes. Of special concern to environmentalists is the waste created by nuclear activity. Unlike toxic chemicals this material is capable of contaminating its surroundings outside its containment and with which it never comes into direct contact. This radiation hazard can create physical changes that can increase the total contamination load many times over and can last for thousands of years.

THE FUTURE

The future will be at least as eventful and exciting as the past has been in the chemical industry. As we enter the twenty-first century, developments such as the application of life sciences to the petrochemicals area is already set to start. Biotechnology can revolutionize sequential reactions by the use of appropriate microorganisms and soon on a scale appropriate to the sector. This can have advantages such as greater reaction selectivity and the ability to operate at ambient temperature thus greatly improving energy efficiency whilst offering significant implications in areas such as reduced waste production and co-product developments. The largely aqueous systems present problems with product separation, these will however be solved in due time. Biotechnology can provide not only the possibilities of biosynthesis of chemicals but also genetically engineered plants that will provide for the production of materials such as vitamins, flavors and fragrances. This latter development when used in the area of Chemurgy, that is the use of farm and forest products for raw materials for chemical manufacturing, already established, offers sustainable possibilities beyond our present ken. The distant future will need to be based on sustainable feedstocks and much greater recycling, the journey to which may already have started.

—Roy Atkins B.Sc. C.Eng. MIChemE, FInstD MIMC. Managing Director, Innovia Ltd.

Roy Atkins has over twenty-five years in the chemical, process, and equipment manufacturing industries. Clean technologies, air and gas filtration are areas of specialist knowledge, with experience in Europe, the Far East and Africa. Atkins is a Registered Environmental Auditor.

Additional experience includes four years as national council member and as regional chairman of the Institute of Directors. He has published on environmental issues and is the consulting editor for an international process industry yearbook. Atkins is a member of the Chemical & Industrial Consultants Association (UK).

CHAPTER 1 - PART I

INDUSTRY OVERVIEW

This chapter presents a comprehensive overview of the Chemicals industry. Major topics covered include an Industry Snapshot, Organization and Structure, Background and Development, Pioneers in the Industry, Current Conditions and Future Projections, Industry Leaders, Work Force, North America and the World, and Research and Technology. A suggested list for further reading, including web sites to visit, completes the chapter. Additional company information is presented in Chapter 6 - Mergers & Acquisitions.

Chemistry is one of the world's oldest pursuits. Prehistoric humans used early versions of paint on cave walls. Perfumes and cosmetics were used in religious ceremonies and embalming treatments. Gold was valued as a medical remedy. Philosophers theorized about the chemical nature of the world around them. These seemingly unrelated practices, which developed separately and at varying paces, came together in the last few centuries as a new science—chemistry. Since then, advances and discoveries have occurred so rapidly that the discipline has spun off new fields, including pharmaceuticals, biochemistry, electrochemistry, and chemical engineering.

The commercial application of chemistry gave birth to the chemicals industry. (The pharmaceuticals industry, closely related to chemicals, is covered in a Part II of this handbook.) Our discussion of the chemicals industry is limited to the following 25 SICs (Standard Industrial Classifications): **2812, Alkalies and Chlorine; 2813, Industrial Gases; 2816, Inorganic Pigments; 2819, Industrial Inorganic Chemicals, Not Elsewhere Classified; 2821, Plastics Materials, Synthetic Resins, and Nonvulcanizable Elastomers; 2822, Synthetic Rubber (Vulcanizable Elastomers); 2823, Cellulosic Manmade Fibers; 2824, Manmade Organic Fibers, Except Cellulosic; 2841, Soap and Other Detergents, Except Specialty Cleaners; 2842, Specialty Cleaning, Polishing, and Sanitation Preparations; 2843, Surface Active Agents, Finishing Agents, Sulfonated Oils, and Assistants; 2844, Perfumes, Cosmetics, and Other Toilet Preparations; 2851, Paints, Varnishes, Lacquers, Enamels, and Allied Products; 2861, Gum and Wood Chemicals; 2865, Cyclic Organic Crudes and Intermediates, and Organic Dyes and Pigments; 2869, Industrial Organic Chemicals, Not Elsewhere Classified; 2873, Nitrogenous Fertilizers; 2874, Phosphatic Fertilizers; 2875, Fertilizers, Mixing Only; 2879, Pesticides and Agricultural Chemicals, Not Elsewhere Classified; 2891, Adhesives and Sealants; 2892, Explosives; 2893, Printing Ink; 2895, Carbon Black; and 2899, Chemicals and Chemical Preparations, Not Elsewhere Classified.**

Organization and Structure

The chemicals industry is unique in that it does not typically manufacture products for direct consumption.

Rather, its products are used by other industries in the manufacture of their own products. As a supplier, the industry is broken down into two main types: basic and specialty.

Basic

Basic, or commodity, chemicals are mass-produced and shipped in high volumes at low prices. This segment is subject to cyclical economics due to its close relationship with the manufacturing, automobile, housing, and agricultural industries. Its manufacturing plants are large and concentrated with huge pieces of equipment, but few personnel. In the U.S., basic chemical manufacturers are located in every state, but about 60% of total production comes from only ten states, so distribution is a significant concern. Shipping by trucks is the primary distribution channel, followed by rail and marine shipping. Pipelines are sometimes used to transport petrochemicals a short distance to the customer.

Specialty

Specialty chemicals are custom-designed chemicals that are sold in low volumes at high prices. Although about 50% of its chemicals serve the large, commodity-driven industries, specialty chemicals serve a specific purpose, usually involved in the manufacturing process or quality of end product. Since they are necessary components of these industries, they are less subject than basic chemicals to economic fluctuations. Manufacturers usually obtain raw materials from basic chemical suppliers. The manufacturing plants are small- or medium-sized, and employ various stainless steel pieces of equipment and numerous personnel. Since the plants are smaller than those of basic chemical producers, they can be built at a lower cost, making this industry segment more appealing to newcomers. On the other hand, its custom design nature requires the additional expense for close customer contact as well as research and development. Distribution costs are higher than for the basic chemical segment because products are typically shipped in low volumes.

Both the basic and specialty segments are heavily regulated by federal and state laws, and must answer to the Environmental Protection Agency (EPA), the Department of Labor, and the Food & Drug Administration (FDA). The specialty segment comes under closer scrutiny than its counterpart because it transforms existing chemicals into a variety of others through complex processes.

Industrial Chemicals

The industrial chemicals industry is broken down by organic and inorganic chemicals. Both types are commodity-based products usually comprised of petrochemicals. They are used as the raw materials for a variety of industries, among them the production of fuels, plastics, fibers, fertilizers, detergents, explosives, and pharmaceuticals. The difference between the two is that inorganic chemicals do not contain carbon, while organic do.

Inorganic

Alkalines and Chlorine, or Chlor-alkalies, include chlorine and caustic soda. These two chemicals are produced simultaneously through the same chemical process, so they are usually sold as a set. Chlorine has a variety of uses, including incorporation into polyvinyl chloride plastics and pigments, as well as in paper production and water and sewage treatment.

Because chlorine gas is dangerous, it is expensive to store and transport. It is therefore produced on demand, and the production of caustic soda, chlorine's co-product, depends on the demand for chlorine. The primary use of caustic soda is in the production of other chemicals, pulp and paper manufacturing, and soap and detergents.

Soda ash, or sodium carbonate, is an alkali used primarily in the manufacture of glass, followed by other chemicals, soap, and pulp and paper.

Inorganic chemicals comprise a long list of chemicals, and include sulfur and sulfuric acid. Sulfur is extracted from the earth during oil refining and natural gas processing. Its largest producer and consumer is the U.S., where about 60% of its total production has an end-use in agricultural chemicals. Sulfuric acid is produced from about 90% of the sulfur used in the U.S. This acid is derived through the oxidation of sulfur, and is used primarily for the manufacture of fertilizer.

The best-selling **inorganic pigment** is titanium dioxide, which is used primarily in the paint and coatings industry, followed by paper coatings and plastics manufacturing.

Industrial gases are produced through two methods. Air separation derives nitrogen, oxygen and other gases from the atmosphere, while chemical processes create hydrogen, carbon dioxide, and acetylene. Their main markets are chemical processing, metallurgy, and electronics.

Organic

Aliphatics are a class of organic chemicals that are extracted from natural gas as hydrocarbons. Ethylene is the largest-volume organic chemical, finding its main market in the plastics industry, as well as the manufacture of antifreeze, synthetic textiles, and detergents. Ethylene is followed in volume by propylene, used in polypropylene resins, and then by butadiene, most of which goes into the production of synthetic rubber.

Aromatics are obtained from petroleum refining, and as a result, their production is highly dependent upon gasoline production. They are used in a variety of products, particularly plastic resins, fibers, and rubber, as well as to increase gasoline's octane level.

Methanol, or methyl alcohol, is a **gum and wood chemical** derived from a combination of natural gas and steam. It is used primarily in polymers and gasoline.

Plastic Resins

Synthetic resins have almost entirely replaced natural resins in industrial use. This class of resin is divided into two subgroups: thermoplastics and thermosets. Thermoplastics, which make up 90% of the plastic resin industry, can be heated to return to their original state, while thermosets cannot be resoftened.

The largest-selling thermoplastics are: polyethylene and polystyrene, used in packaging; polyvinyl chloride, for housing and construction; polypropylene, for automobiles and durable goods; and polyester plastics, for food and beverage containers. Thermosets are used primarily in the housing and construction industries; its two main types are phenolics and polyurethane.

Manmade fibers are chemically altered during manufacturing. There are two main types: cellulosic and organic. Cellulosic fibers are obtained from wood-pulp operations, then modified and regenerated into cellulose-based fibers. Acetate and rayon are examples of such fibers.

Manmade organic fibers are derived from synthetic polymers that are produced as a by-product of petroleum or natural gas production. Examples include acrylic, nylon, polyester, and polyvinyl.

Soaps and Detergents

Soaps and detergents are comprised of a number of chemical components. Bar soaps combine the acids of organic fats and oils with an alkali, usually either sodium hydroxide (caustic soda) or potassium hydroxide (caustic potash). Soaps made from the alkali sodium hydroxide are hard bar soaps, while those made from potassium hydroxide are soft and used in liquid hand soaps and shaving products.

Soaps are usually manufactured by the saponification method, in which the acids are heated and then reacted with the liquid alkali. Liquid, or neat, soap is produced along with glycerin, a by-product that is used in cosmetics and drugs. A bar of soap is then manufactured by drying the neat soap, mixing it with fragrances and coloring, and then rolling and cutting it into the desired shape.

Like soaps, detergents contain fats and alkalis, but they also contain several types of chemicals. One such ingredient is the surfactant, or surface active agent, which loosens the soil from the surface of the material and then holds it in the water until it is rinsed away. Surfactants are typically produced from petrochemicals, which can be designed to perform in a variety of circumstances. Detergents are produced by combining the ingredients into a slurry, which is then sprayed under high pressure. The resulting droplets are dried into powder granules by passing them through a current of hot air.

The cleansers and cosmetic industries have recently been impacted by consumer demand for environmentally safe ingredients. Manufacturers are responding by offering biodegradable or concentrated products, sometimes packaged in refillable containers. These industries are also instituting more direct contact with the consumer by increasingly inviting comments and suggestions on company Web pages.

Paints and Coatings

Paints and coatings are specialty chemicals that are used for decorative or protective purposes. As a whole, this industry is increasingly called upon to reduce environmental impact by limiting emissions and solvents. There are four categories of paints and coatings: architectural, including general-purpose paints and varnishes; original equipment manufacturer (OEM), for use by manufacturers on their end-products, including automobiles, appliances, and furniture; and special-purpose, designed for specific environments or applications, such as industrial construction, traffic markings, and roof coatings. The fourth category includes paint removers and thinners, wood treatments, and putties.

Fertilizers

Fertilizers are commodity chemicals that are applied to the soil to facilitate agricultural growth by supplementing the soil's nutrients. Since their use depends heavily on the agriculture industry, which in turn fluctuates based on grain prices, weather conditions, and farming practices, the demand for fertilizer is volatile. The crops that require the most fertilizer are corn, wheat, and soybeans.

They are offered in two basic types: nitrogenous and phosphatic. Nitrogenous is the largest-selling type of fertilizer because nitrogen is the most readily absorbed by crops, requiring reapplication each year. Nitrogen comprises nearly 80% of the earth's atmosphere, and is derived in the form of ammonia.

Phosphatic fertilizer is derived from phosphoric acid, which is produced by combining phosphate rock with sulfuric acid. Like nitrogen, phosphate is usually applied to the soil annually.

Pesticides

Pesticides are specialty agricultural chemicals that deter or destroy unwanted plants and animals. There are four main types, the largest of which is herbicides, which eliminate weeds. Insecticides control insect infestation and fungicides prevent the growth of fungi. Other pesticides include rodenticides and fumigants.

Adhesives and Sealants

Adhesives are specialty chemicals that bond two different materials, called substrates. Primarily serving the packaging industry, adhesives are made from either organic products, usually starch and dextrin, or synthetic polymers, which account for about 60% of all adhesives. Adhesives come in three main types. Nonwovens are flexible materials comprised of synthetic materials, and include diapers, feminine napkins, and incontinence products. Pressure-sensitive adhesives require only light pressure for application, and include such products as self-adhesive postage stamps and clear plastic labels. The largest adhesives segment is packaging adhesives. Used for product packaging, they primarily have paper and cardboard applications, but are increasingly finding demand in flexible plastic packaging.

Sealants are specialty chemicals that are utilized to fill a gap between two surfaces. This application requires them to be flexible and capable of withstanding various environmental conditions. Their primary end-markets are the construction and transportation industries.

Background and Development

The history of the chemical industry follows, in essence, the history of chemistry itself. This discipline has its roots not in the pursuit of scientific knowledge, but in art, religion, and the accumulation of wealth.

Esthetic Beginnings

Chemistry's earliest application was in paint, a product that extends back about 10,000 years to ancient Egypt. These crude forms of paint had a limited range of color, as they were obtained from charcoal, iron carbonate, and calcium carbonate. In 6000 B.C., Chinese were preparing organic compounds—from gum arabic, egg whites, and beeswax—fired, or calcinated, with pigments. By 3000 B.C., Egyptians produced the first synthetic pigment, Egyptian blue, and within one thousand years, their palette had expanded to include red and green. Egypt also offers the first record of perfumery, the forerunner of cosmetics. Tombs dating back to 3500 B.C. contain vessels for aromatics, and perfumes were used as offerings for the deities and as embalming fluids.

Ancient Babylon provides evidence that soapmaking dates to 2800 B.C. These early substances were fashioned by boiling fats with ashes, a recipe that survived into modern times. By 312 B.C., luxurious Roman baths popularized bathing. However, with the fall of the Roman Empire in 467 A.D., bathing, and with it the market for soap, fell into a decline until the 17th century.

Ancient Science

Archaeological classifications of the Bronze Age, the Copper Age, and the Iron Age in the last centuries B.C. were based on each era's respective development of the smelting of metal ore. Craftspeople were usually employed by religious leaders, who promoted magic or divine intervention as the force behind such observable changes in materials.

Greek philosophers were the first to speculate on more earthly causes for such changes. Around 440 B.C., Democritus proposed that all matter is composed of minute, indestructible particles existing in a vacuum. Aristotle suggested that nature has four components—heat, cold, moisture, and dryness—that, when combined in various measures, form all matter. This belief implied that one substance could be changed into another by adding or eliminating a proportion of these elements, a school of thought known as alchemy.

Alchemy, or the art of transmutation, held that all substances gradually turned into gold, the perfect metal. Contemporary Chinese also strove to achieve gold, but for medicinal, rather than monetary, purposes. Although experiments in making gold were, of course, unsuccessful, they did contribute to knowledge of chemicals and chemical processes.

Fall and Rise

The decline of the Roman Empire brought alchemy to an end in the West until Arab conquerors translated Greek texts in the 7th century. These, along with observation of its continued practice in China, revitalized alchemy. Philosophy and science had spread to Europe by the 11th century. By then, the store of knowledge included practical subjects, including distillation, and the manufacture of glass and gunpowder, as well as theories of nature, which sought physical explanations of transmutation.

The invention (in 1450) of movable type increased the number and proliferation of texts on alchemy. Widespread practice soon necessitated precision in measurement, especially in the field of medicine. The physician Paracelsus adamantly promoted chemical methods of preparing medicine as superior to the orthodox herbal methods. He founded the field of iatrochemistry, the precursor of pharmacology, as the science of chemical medicine. By the end of the 16th century, the first textbook of chemistry, *Alchema*, was published.

17th Century

The seventeenth century produced the first experimental studies of chemical reactions for the sake of science rather than for the promotion of other disciplines. In 1662, Boyle's Law, advanced by Robert Boyle, showed that the volume of a gas is an inverse of its pressure. Georg Ernst Stahl proposed the phlogiston theory, which would dominate chemistry for a century. This theory asserted that when a substance is burned, its phlogiston, or combustible portion, is given off and absorbed by plants.

18th Century

As new chemicals and components were discovered, scientists noted that substances had varying affinities with other substances, and tables were created to chart these attractions. This led to improvements in quantitative and qualitative analytical methods, thereby creating the field of analytical chemistry.

Antoine-Laurent Lavosier's experiments falsified Stahl's theory. Lavosier showed that heated metals gained weight, the opposite of the expected reaction if such substances were losing matter by emitting phlogiston. This chemist also contributed to chemistry by devising the modern nomenclature of chemicals, advancing the theory of the conservation of mass, and defining elements as substances that cannot be decomposed. By 1786, scientists had rejected the phlogiston theory in favor of Lavosier's.

The chemical industry experienced growth as a result of these scientific discoveries as well as the demands of the Industrial Revolution. The Revolution's primary demand was sulfuric acid, the basis for the production of dyestuffs and alkali salts. The Lead-Chamber Method of producing this chemical was introduced in 1749, and required air, water, sulfur dioxide, and nitrate.

In 1789, Nicolas Leblanc developed the Leblanc process for producing soda ash, or sodium carbonate, from common salt. Soda ash was used in such products as soap, glass, and textiles. Commercial development of this process was delayed by the French Revolution, and did not occur until 1823, in England. Dangerous byproducts (including hydrochloric acid) of this process resulted in damage to vegetation surrounding manufacturing sites, and a petition in 1839 called for an improved process.

Early 19th Century

The chemical industry by now primarily consisted of Britain's soda industry and Germany's dyestuff industry. By mid-century, soapmaking was a fast-growing industry, as soap was perceived as a necessity rather than a luxury.

The first professional chemists were trained in the early 19th century. Prior to this, wealthy amateurs pursued the science, often relying on assistants who did not have the means or the desire to continue its pursuit after their employment came to an end. Germany established the first university chemistry program, research center, and teaching laboratory, and attracted students internationally. Organized education gave graduates the foundation to advance the Industrial Revolution in the laboratories of commercial plants.

Late 19th Century

The 19th century marked a change in focus from natural products to synthetic products, which could be produced more efficiently. In 1869 John Wesley Hyatt produced celluloid, the first synthetic plastic to be a commercial success. By 1886, France's Chardonnet had a daily production of 125 pounds of nitrocellulose textile filament, known as "artificial silk;" in less than ten years, this daily total jumped to 3,500 pounds.

In 1873, the Leblanc process was finally replaced by a safer method. The Solvay Process, invented by Ernest Solvay, produced sodium bicarbonate within an enclosed tower, thereby eliminating the escape of dangerous gases.

Increasingly complex production methods and growing competition between manufacturers gave rise to the need for a new branch of science, that of chemical engineering, which combined the fields of applied chemistry and traditional engineering. In 1888 the Massachusetts Institute of Technology (MIT) offered the first chemical engineering program in the U.S.

As the century drew to a close, Germany had established itself as a significant presence in the dyestuffs and pharmaceutical industries.

Early 20th Century

In the early 20th century, synthetics occupied much of the industry's attention, and discoveries occurred at a rapid pace. Among the most notable were the discovery of cellophane in 1908; the first production of synthetic ammonia in 1910; the development of isopropyl alcohol, the first commercial petrochemical, in 1920; the discovery of polyethylene in 1933; and the discovery of teflon in 1944.

World War I

The First World War gave rise to increased industrial development. With their traditional avenues of supply closed, countries were forced to become self-reliant on domestic raw materials and technologies. For example, a shortage of fats and oils during the war prompted Germany to develop a synthetic cleansing product, the first detergent.

In the U.S., another force spurred innovation—the automobile industry. The demand for petroleum-based products gave rise to new technologies and manufacturing plants. Leo Baekeland's synthetic resin, the first synthetic plastic, opened an era of synthetics. The so-called Bakelite found use in the 1920s in such products as steering wheels, battery terminals, and spark plugs, as well as in the newly invented radio set. The war also cut off U.S. textile manufacturers from Germany's dye industry, forcing the U.S. to develop a domestic dye industry.

Although U.S. firms successfully filled the nation's demand for dyes, pharmaceuticals, and fertilizers, they had not yet developed the processes to do so as efficiently as the Germans. The end of the war, however, brought Germany's industrial secrets to light. The federal government expropriated Germany's processes and patents, and then sold them to the Chemical Foundation for $270,000. Nearly every U.S. chemical company held a stake in that foundation, and greatly benefited from the sale.

After the war, German chemical companies combined to form Interessengemeinschaft Farbenindustrie Aktiengesellschaft, or I.G. Farben. This company, whose name literally means the "community of interests of the dye industry corporation," was organized to allow German companies to share technology, reduce bureaucracy, and recover from the war.

Synthetic rubber was discovered and developed by Bayer during the war. At the war's conclusion, less expensive organic materials eliminated much of the need for synthetic rubber, but I.G. Farben continued to develop it during the 1920s and 30s in the event that another war again shut Germany off from organic supplies.

By now, two branches of industrial chemistry were arising. Coal-based processes were continuing in Western Europe, while in North America petroleum-based processes were under development.

World War II

Just as Germany experienced the need to develop synthetic detergents during World War I, so did the U.S. during World War II. This demand was further spurred by the military's demand for a cleanser that would work in cold water.

The war created heightened demand for synthetic rubber and fibers. Wallace Carothers, a DuPont employee, invented the first commercial synthetic fiber, nylon, in 1935. DuPont built the first nylon plant three years later. It was immediately put to use in fashioning parachutes for the war, but consumer demand for nylon stockings was intense. In 1940, crowds lined up to purchase such stockings, and in just a few hours had bought four million pairs.

The automobile industry and the war effort drove demand for higher-octane gasoline. Standard Oil's 1940 development of catalytic reformers produced a high-octane fuel, allowing Allied vehicles to outperform their German counterparts.

Post War

In 1951, the Allies dismantled I.G. Farben, forcing member companies to return to their original operations. The Allies again expropriated Germany's chemical patents and processes.

By the 1950s, most chemical producers recognized petroleum and gas as the most versatile and efficient of raw materials. Europe, which had been dependent on countries in the Persian Gulf for its supplies, became more self-reliant when an oil source was discovered off the Dutch coastline. By the 1960s, more than half of U.S. chemical production was in polymers.

The Arab oil embargo of the 1970s prompted Eastman Chemical to produce coal-based acetyl chemicals, of which it started production in 1983. The embargo also forced many U.S. chemical companies to consolidate or divest themselves of overly diverse operations.

In the 1980s the industry started to diverge between commodity and specialty chemical production.

Environmental Matters

On April 16, 1947, the chemical industry experienced its first disaster when the *S.S. Grandcamp*, a freighter carrying 2,500 tons of ammonium nitrate, exploded at a Texas dock, killing 512 people. In 1962, Rachel Carson published *Silent Spring*, a book criticizing the chemical industry for its reckless promotion of pesticides at the expense of the environment.

Public concern over environmental matters prompted the U.S. to pass the Water Quality Act in 1965; the Clean Air Act of 1970; the Occupational Safety & Health Act of 1970; the Clean Water Act in 1972; the Federal Insecticide, Fungicide, & Rodenticide Act of 1972; the Safe Drinking Water Act of 1974; the Resource Conservation & Recovery Act of 1976; the Toxic Substances Control Act of 1976; and the Pollution Prevention Act of 1990. These measures addressed the industry's product lines as well as its production processes and waste treatment methods.

The Environmental Protection Agency (EPA) was formed in 1970, and in 1980 it established the $1.6 billion Superfund for the clean-up of pollution sites.

The U.S. federal government has banned or limited the sale of several products and chemicals due to their damaging impact on the population or the environment. In 1975, emissions standards for automobiles brought about the introduction of catalytic converters; in 1976 chloroform was banned from pharmaceuticals and cosmetics; in 1978 chlorofluorcarbons were banned to protect the ozone layer; and in 1980 lead-based paints were banned.

In response to public outcry against the chemical industry for its negative impact on the environment, the industry formed the Responsible Care program in 1985. Modeled after a Canadian program, Responsible Care addresses safeguards for employees, users, and transporters of chemicals, not only for humanitarian reasons, but also to protect the industry against legal action. A string of product liability lawsuits against chemical companies began in the 1970s in response to side effects experienced by soldiers exposed to Agent Orange. One of the most famous product liability suits was the 1994 suit brought against Dow Corning by women with silicone gel breast implants. As a result, several large chemical manufacturers, including Dow, Hoechst, and DuPont, will no longer sell polymers for use in the human body.

Pioneers and Newsmakers in the Industry

Leo Hendrik Baekeland

Baekeland was born on November 14, 1863, in Ghent, Belgium. His parents, both illiterate, saw to it that Leo was well-educated. He had a gift for chemistry, earning a doctorate in that field only four years after graduating from high school. His hobby was photography, and he formed a partnership with a friend to develop dry plates as a replacement for the current messy wet plate photographic system. He moved to the U.S. to offer his technology to American photographic suppliers in 1889.

In 1892 he invented Velox, the first photography paper that could be developed under artificial light. Shunned by professional photographers, it was an instant hit with amateurs. Eastman Kodak Co. took notice of its success and bought Baekeland's invention for $750,000. Baekeland was suddenly wealthier than he had ever imagined, especially since he had intended to set its asking price at $50,000, but come down to $25,000 if necessary.

No longer driven by the financial need to work, he nonetheless continued to develop chemical innovations. After perusing scientific literature for ideas, he decided to try to invent a synthetic shellac for use by the growing electrical industry. In 1906 he discovered Bakelite, the first thermosetting plastic. This resin rapidly and permanently hardened into any molded shape, finding an immediate use in a variety of industries outside of electronics.

In 1939 Baekeland sold his company, Bakelite General, to Union Carbide. The following year, he received the Franklin Medal for his life-long contributions to science. On February 23, 1944, Baekeland died, having become the founder of the modern plastics industry.

Wallace Hume Carothers

Carothers was born on April 27, 1896, in Burlington, Iowa. A propensity for electronics earned him the nickname "Doc" from his elementary school classmates. He graduated from business school and obtained a teaching job in that field. Meanwhile, he enrolled in an undergraduate chemistry program, and in two years, while only a junior, was offered a position as a chemistry teaching assistant.

He earned his doctorate in 1924 and took a post in Harvard's chemistry department. He left that institution to accept a position as director of research in Du-Pont's new organic chemistry unit. He pursued research in an area of interest to him, that of substances having high molecular weights. In 1930 Carothers and his team discovered the material that would become known as nylon, the first purely synthetic fiber. The original material, however, was brittle, and only after several years of additional research and experimentation was it discovered to be flexible enough to produce economically. In 1934 Carothers strode into his mana-

ger's office, squirted a bit of the solution onto the desk, and said, "There's your synthetic fiber," before turning and walking out of the office.

Carothers had been plagued nearly his entire life with depression. In June 1936, he had a severe nervous breakdown and was confined to a mental institution for five weeks. Subsequent treatments proved ineffectual, and in April 1937, just days after filing the nylon patent application, Carothers committed suicide by ingesting cyanide.

Antoine Laurent Lavoisier

Antoine Laurent Lavoisier was born on August 26, 1743, in Paris, France. Although he received a law degree in 1764, he opted instead for a career in science. After having presented several research papers in various disciplines, he was elected to the Academy of Science as an assistant chemist in 1768.

He refuted the century-old phlogiston theory when he showed that combustion occurs when a substance reacts with oxygen, not due to that substance's emission of a flammable component. His discovery was soon accepted by the scientific community.

Lavoisier's contribution to chemistry did not end there. He dispelled the belief that water is converted to earth. He formulated the principle of the conservation of matter. He defined elements as those substances that cannot be decomposed. He contributed to a revision of chemical nomenclature. He was one of the first chemists whose experiments were quantitative, and he published a paper outlining proper procedures for scientific pursuit.

The chemist was also very active in politics and public service. He was appointed a director of the gunpowder administration, he attempted to introduce methods of scientific agriculture to farmers, and he was a member of the committee of weights and measures that would eventually establish the metric system.

Despite these achievements, Lavoisier was put to death on the guillotine on May 8, 1794 by a French Revolutionary tribunal.

Nicolas Leblanc

Nicolas Leblanc was born in France in 1742. He studied medicine and became a private surgeon in 1780. His medical background gave him an education in chemistry, which he put to use in his participation in a contest of the Academy of Sciences. The challenge offered a prize to the developer of a process for deriving soda ash from salt. Soda ash, or sodium carbonate, was used in a variety of industries for the manufacture of such products as paper, glass, and soap. The only process available at the time was expensive and complex, as it involved the extraction of soda ash from wood or seaweed ash.

In 1790 Leblanc won that contest with the development of the Leblanc process. With it, salt cake was obtained by treating salt with sulfuric acid, then roasting it to produce black ash, from which soda ash could be separated.

The French Revolution interrupted its commercial implementation, and Leblanc's factory was seized by Napoleon. In 1800, the factory was restored to Leblanc, but he lacked the capital to reopen it. The inventor of one of the most important processes in the chemical industry committed suicide on January 16, 1806.

Current Conditions, Future Projections

Biotechnology

Biotechnology—the use of organisms to manufacture products, or the modification of organisms to carry desired traits—is a growing field that is impacting the chemicals industry. In the late 1970s and early 1980s the U.S. began to produce new pharmaceuticals through genetic manipulation. These new techniques soon expanded into other chemical fields, including herbicides and seed development. This science is an answer to stiffer environmental regulations on pesticides, the increasing resistance of insects to traditional insecticides, and farmers' expectations of enhanced productivity. In 1996, more than 1,300 U.S. companies were involved in biotechnology.

Promising new biotechnological advances have spurred a recent wave of change in the chemicals industry. This relatively new field offers greater growth potential than that of traditional chemicals. A new business classification, life sciences, has emerged in the industry. This classification can include such fields as agrichemicals, animal health, seeds, food ingredients, and specialty chemicals—in short, the areas of health, agriculture, and nutrition. To many companies, these fields complement each other, as agriculture impacts nutrition, which has a direct relationship on overall health.

The move to life sciences has many chemical and pharmaceutical companies shedding other operations. Novartis, formed by the merger of the pharmaceutical companies Sandoz and Ciba in 1996, exited from much of its previous chemical businesses. In September 1997, Monsanto spun off its chemical operations as a new company, Solutia, in order to focus on agriculture and human health. Hoechst announced plans in 1997 to restructure as a life sciences company by the year 2000. Rhone-Poulenc spun off its chemicals and polymers operations in 1998 as a new company, Rhodia.

Some integrated chemical companies, such as Bayer, BASF, and DuPont, disagree with the logic of separating life sciences businesses, asserting that life sciences and traditional chemicals are a natural combination due to their similarities in manufacturing, marketing, and technology. They also believe that innovation in biotechnology will bring about developments in chemicals. Some companies are even using biotechnology to develop chemicals from plants. For example, Dow produces polymers made from the lactic acid derived from cornstarch.

Aside from the life sciences business, another chemical business to benefit from biotechnology is detergents. Enzymes, key ingredients in the destruction and removal of soil, are expensive to produce synthetically. Biotechnology has provided a method of producing them economically. Some industry experts predict that genetically engineered enzymes will account for most industrial enzymes by 2005.

Consolidation

Merger and acquisition activity is also driven by the procurement of additional manufacturing plants. Distribution can be a problem for manufacturers of certain chemicals that may be difficult, and therefore expensive, to store and transport. For this reason, chemical companies benefit by maintaining plants near their customers.

Other companies are consolidating in order to gain access to new technologies and processes. Still others engage in mergers and acquisitions to offer "one-stop shopping" for customers, who seek long-term relationships with chemical suppliers in order to reduce costs and improve research and development.

Conversely, some companies are divesting themselves of non-core businesses. The primary reason for doing so is to reduce the high costs of the research and development that is necessary for staying competitive, particularly in the specialty chemicals segment. Another reason to slim down is to become more appealing to Wall Street, which tends to assign lower valuations to diverse companies.

Globalization

The basic, or commodity, chemicals market in the U.S. is considered mature. Its principal markets of manufacturing, automobile, and housing are expected to experience only modest domestic growth. The specialty chemical segment, which supplies about half of its total production to the basic chemicals segment, will also be slightly affected by the domestic market, although it is not entirely dependent on the commodity segment's sales performance. Specialty chemicals are usually vital to the manufacturing process of commodity chemicals, and will therefore probably continue to be required in set volumes regardless of sales of those basic chemicals.

The geographic areas that are expected to provide the most rapid growth for chemicals overall are Asia and Latin America. These areas should have the largest markets for new industries due to increases in their population, living standards, and industrialization.

In response to, or anticipation of, these developing markets, Western chemical companies are moving production into these areas to facilitate distribution to their customers, the manufacturing, construction, and automobile industries that have done likewise. As reported in *Chemical & Engineering News*, William S. Stavropoulos, chairman of Dow, predicts that "55% of

global economic growth will take place in Asia over the next ten years."

Industry Leaders

BASF AG

Badische Anilin- & Soda-Fabrik (BASF) AG was founded in Mannheim, Germany, in 1865 for the production of synthetic dyes. After 17 years of research, BASF was the first to produce synthesized indigo dye. The company entered the fertilizer industry in the early 20th century by developing a method for synthesizing nitrogen.

By this time, Germany's major chemical companies had formed cartels to control the industry. In 1925 these cartels formally merged as Interessengemeinschaft Farbenindustrie, or I.G. Farben. In addition to supporting the Nazi party financially, the new company erected chemical plants near Jewish concentration camps in order to utilize slave labor. At the conclusion of World War II, each member of I.G. Farben's board of directors was sentenced to less than four years in prison for his participation in war crimes. Allied forces dismantled the company in 1952, forcing BASF, Bayer, and Hoechst to return to their original operations. As they had done at the end of World War I, the Allies seized Germany's chemical patents and processes.

BASF began production of plastics during the 1950s, and it diversified into coatings and pharmaceuticals the following decade. In 1969 it acquired Wintershall, producer of 25% of Germany's natural gas and 50% of its potash supplies. In 1994 BASF became Europe's second-largest producer of polypropylene by purchasing Imperial Chemical's operations in that business. It entered the plant biotechnology business in 1998 by establishing two joint ventures: Metanomics and SunGene.

Bayer AG

Bayer AG was founded in 1863 by Friedrich Bayer in Wuppertal, Germany, to produce a synthetic magenta dye. The company soon expanded into other chemical industries, producing a synthetic pesticide in 1892 and discovering aspirin in 1899. This pharmaceutical product proved tremendously successful, and the company invested in further pharmaceutical research and development. After World War I, Sterling Winthrop Inc. purchased the U.S. rights to Bayer's name and products. In 1925, Bayer merged with other German chemical companies to form I.G. Farben. (*see BASF*)

After I.G. Farben was dismantled in 1952, Bayer returned to its previous organization, and began work in insecticides, fibers, and synthetic plastic. One decade later, the company had agrichemical and pharmaceutical operations in eight countries. In 1978, after purchasing Miles Laboratories, the U.S.-based manufacturer of Alka-Seltzer and daily vitamins, 65% of Bayer's sales originated outside Germany. Its 1990 purchase of the polysar rubber operations of Nova Corp. made it a world leader in synthetic rubber products. In 1994, it regained the U.S. rights to the Bayer name.

Bayer instituted plans to focus on its healthcare, agriculture, polymer, and specialty chemical operations. In 1998 it announced its intention to spin off Agfa, its imaging technology subsidiary, in 1999. The company also joined with Millennium Pharmaceuticals to conduct research in the field in genomics.

Dow Chemical Co.

Midland Chemical Co. was formed by Herbert Dow and J.H. Osborn in 1890 to manufacture ferric bromide from brine. Five years later it formed the Dow Process Co. for the production of bleach; in 1897 this operation was incorporated as Dow Chemical Co. In 1900 Dow Chemical absorbed its parent, Midland Chemical. The next decade, it entered the agrichemical business, and soon thereafter discontinued the production of bleach. Expansion and diversification continued in the following decades, into such areas as coatings and plastics.

In 1943 Dow joined with Corning Glass Works to form a joint venture, Dow Corning Co., for the production of organosilicon compounds and materials. The following year, Dow Chemical introduced Styrofoam. In 1953 it released its first consumer product, Saran Wrap. By 1974, having expanded into medical products, Dow Chemical was the world's largest chemical company.

Dow acquired the pharmaceutical company Merrell in 1981, thereby ranking its human health business the

20th-largest worldwide. In 1985 it acquired the polymer chemical business of the Upjohn Co., and the following year it became the world's largest producer of thermoplastics. Dow joined with Eli Lilly & Co. in 1989 to form DowElanco, an agricultural company holding its parents' plant sciences and pest control operations. That year, Marion Laboratories, Inc. joined Merrell and Dow to form Marion Merrell Dow Inc.; Dow sold its share in this company to Hoechst in 1995.

In 1998 Dow Corning paid $3.2 billion to settle a class action suit for its silicone breast implants, and Dow Corning exited from Chapter 11 bankruptcy protection. Despite this setback, Dow Chemical continued to grow its chemical and plastics businesses, agreeing to purchase the European general-purpose rubber business of Shell Chemical Co. In January 1998, it sold its consumer products subsidiary, DowBrands, to S.C. Johnson & Son.

DuPont

E. I. duPont de Nemours and Co. was founded in 1802 near Wilmington, Delaware, for the production of gunpowder. In 1902, after one hundred years in the production of explosives, the company reorganized as a corporation and began research into new product lines. In response to an anti-trust lawsuit of 1912, DuPont divested itself of some of its explosives businesses, spinning off Hercules Powder Co. and Atlas Powder Co.

Over the course of World War I, duPont diversified into plastics, rubber, and dyes, and its 1917 acquisition of Harrison Bros. & Co. gave it entry into the production of acids, heavy chemicals, pigments, and paints. In 1931 it introduced the Freon refrigerant and the Neoprene general-purpose synthetic rubber. Other synthetic innovations include nylon, Teflon, and Butacite resin sheeting. Diversification and expansion continued through the following decades, and by 1970 its operations included more than 20 international subsidiaries and joint ventures.

In 1981 DuPont purchased Conoco, Inc., a leading fossil fuel company, for $8 billion. By the late 1980s it had expanded into many diverse businesses, and it began to refocus on its core businesses—petroleum, specialty, healthcare, and electronics chemicals. By 1991 it had withdrawn from the electronics and pharmaceuticals businesses. It soon began to build on its life sciences business by increasing its interests in agrichemicals and biotechnology. A recent purchase in this field was its July 1997 acquisition of a 20% stake in Pioneer Hi-Bred International, a producer of genetically enhanced seeds.

In 1998 it announced plans to exit the energy business by divesting itself of Conoco. That same year, it strengthened its pharmaceutical operations by purchasing the stake held by Merck & Co. in the DuPont-Merck Pharmaceutical Co., a joint venture formed in 1990.

Eastman Kodak Co.

George Eastman and Henry Strong formed the Eastman Dry Plate Co. in 1881 to produce Eastman's invention, dryplate photographic film. Within two years, the company introduced gelatin-coated roll film, and in 1884 it changed its name to Eastman Dry Plate and Film Co. It introduced the first transparent negative and expanded internationally the following year.

It trademarked the brand name "Kodak" in 1888, the same year that it introduced the first portable camera. The success of the Kodak name prompted the company to change its name to Eastman Kodak Co. of New York in 1892. Four years later it introduced the first film specially coated for motion picture use. The company produced the first commercially practical safe film for still photography in 1908, replacing the highly flammable cellulose nitrate base with a cellulose acetate base. During World War I, it furnished the U.S. military with this material for use on airplane wings and gas masks.

Kodacolor Film was introduced in 1928, enabling amateurs to produce color motion pictures. The following year, Eastman Kodak introduced film for sound motion pictures. Numerous film and camera innovations continued during the following decades. In 1950 it received its first Academy Award, for its 35mm tri-acetate safety base film, which replaced the flammable film previously used by the motion picture industry. The widely successful Instamatic camera was introduced in 1963.

Its Tennessee Eastman subsidiary began marketing cellulose acetate yarn for the textiles industry in 1931,

and the following year it began production of its first plastic. Expanding further into the chemicals trade, Kodak formed Texas Eastman in 1952 to manufacture alcohol and aldehydes, and formed Arkansas Eastman in 1977 for the commercial production of organic chemicals. The company introduced its first digital camera for the home consumer market in 1996, and soon expanded on its line of computer products.

W.R. Grace & Co.

In order to transport organic fertilizers to California, William R. Grace founded W.R. Grace & Co. in Peru, in 1954. Eleven years later, the company moved to New York City and established three-way trade with South America and Europe. Investing further in transportation, it joined with Pan American Airways in 1928 to found Panagra Airlines, the first carrier to serve the west coast of South America; Grace sold its interest in this venture in 1967.

The company diversified into agrichemicals in 1952. Two years later, it diversified further by acquiring Davison Chemical Co. and the Dewey & Almy Chemical Co., thereby gaining entry into packaging, silica, and construction businesses. Continuing this expansion program, in 1970 it acquired Baker & Taylor, supplier of books to libraries; F.A.O. Schwarz, toy retailer; and Herman's World of Sporting Goods. It backed away from diversification in 1974, and it began selling off peripheral businesses to focus on the areas of consumer goods, chemicals, and natural resources. In 1988 it divested itself of its agricultural and fertilizer interests, and three years later it reorganized around specialty chemicals and healthcare operations. In 1994 it became the world's leading specialty chemicals company.

Grace spun off its healthcare subsidiary, National Medical Care, in 1996, and the following year it sold its specialty polymer business to National Starch & Chemicals Co. In 1998, Grace merged its Cryovac flexible packaging unit with Sealed Air Corp. As of September of that year, Grace had become a specialty chemicals business comprised of three operations: Grace Davison, petrochemical and silica products; Grace Construction Products, specialty construction chemicals and building materials; and Darex Container Products, container sealants and coatings.

Hoechst AG

Theerfarbenfabrik Meister, Lucius & Co. was founded in Hoechst am Main, Germany, in 1863 as a dye manufacturer. In 1880 it changed its name to Farbwerke vorm. Meister Lucius & Bruning. The following year it diversified its chemical operations by beginning production of inorganic acids, followed by pharmaceuticals. It expanded overseas and formed alliances with other German chemical companies. In 1925 it joined these operations in forming I.G. Farben. (*see BASF*)

The company reemerged from I.G. Farben as Farbwerke Hoechst AG vorm. Meister Lucius & Bruning. During the following decades, it expanded into new businesses such as petrochemicals, plastics, films, and fibers. Among its many acquisitions was Celanese Corp., the eighth-largest U.S. chemical company, purchased for $2.8 billion. Its U.S. presence was further strengthened with its 1995 purchase of Marion Merrell Dow for $7.1 billion, becoming the world's third-largest pharmaceuticals company. In 1994 it underwent dramatic reorganization to focus on pharmaceutical, agricultural, and industrial chemicals, and in 1997 it announced plans to reorganize as a life sciences company by 2000.

The company, which had shortened its unwieldy name to Hoechst AG in 1974, had six chemical operations as of 1998: AgrEvo, agrichemicals; Celanese, basic chemicals and cellulose acetate; Trevina, polyesters; Ticona, technical polymers; Messer, industrial gases; and Herberts, paints and coatings. In 1998 it announced plans to sell its synthetic resins business in order to focus on the life sciences business, and to purchase the North American seed business of Cargill Inc.

S.C. Johnson & Son, Inc.

Samuel Curtis Johnson purchased the parquet floor business of the Racine Hardware Co. in 1886. He invented a specialty floor wax two years later, and its success prompted him to experiment in wood dye, crack filler, and car wax. Sales of these products soon surpassed those of the parquet floors. In 1906 the company changed its name to S.C. Johnson & Son to reflect a partnership with his son. In 1932, having established several overseas branches, the company incorporated.

In 1956 it diversified outside household cleansers by introducing Raid House & Garden Bug Killer and Glade Air Freshener. Two years later, it introduced Pledge furniture polish. Johnson entered the personal care market with Edge Shaving Gel in 1970. In 1982 its marketing division reorganized into three groups—personal care, insect control, and home care—thereby indicating the company's primary product lines.

In January 1998, Johnson acquired Dow Chemical's consumer products subsidiary, DowBrands Inc. With this purchase it augmented its home cleaning product line, as well as gained access to a new business, that of plastic bags and wraps.

Novartis AG

In 1996 Sandoz AG and Ciba-Geigy AG merged, forming Novartis. This $36 billion merger combined the two Swiss pharmaceutical manufacturers to create the world's largest life sciences company. Upon formation, the new company divested itself of non-core businesses to focus on three areas—healthcare, agrichemicals, and nutrition.

In July 1997, Novartis acquired the crop protection business of Merck & Co. for $910 million. The following year it merged its over-the-counter (OTC) drug operation with its nutrition business into a new Consumer Health division, which became one of the leading three OTC drug and specialty nutrition companies.

For the year 1997, its first full year of operation, Novartis had total revenues of 31.1 billion Swiss francs and net income of 5.2 billion Swiss francs. By segment, its healthcare division, comprising pharmaceuticals, consumer health, generics, and CIBA Vision, contributed most to those sales, 18.7 billion Swiss francs. Agribusiness, made up of crop protection, seeds, and animal health operations, accounted for 8.3 billion Swiss francs. The Nutrition division, its healthcare and baby food businesses, contributed 4.1 billion Swiss francs to the company's total sales.

Sherwin-Williams Co.

Sherwin-Williams & Co. was founded in 1870 to manufacture paste paints, oil colors, and putty. In 1877 it patented the resealable paint can, revolutionizing the manner in which paint could be used. It also developed paint that no longer required constant stirring, thus allowing the shipment of paints over long distances. By the turn of the century, Sherwin-Williams offered specialty paints for a variety of uses, such as roofs, floors, metal bridges, and automobiles.

The company embarked on a period of acquisition and innovation. In 1922 it introduced nitrocellulose lacquer and synthetic enamel for automobile finishes, reducing their drying time from 21 days to just a few hours. Similarly, it introduced Kem-Tone, the first fast-drying paint for the consumer market, in 1941.

In 1972 it expanded its retail offerings to include home decorating items such as carpeting and draperies. The following decade, it sold its chemical operations to PMC Specialties Group. In 1996 it acquired the water sealer and wood stains company Thompson Minwax, thereby becoming the largest supplier of wood coatings.

Sherwin-Williams is the largest U.S. paint manufacturer. Its 1997 net income was $260.6 million on sales of $4.9 billion, and it had more than 20,000 employees worldwide.

Work Force

Employment in the chemical industry is strong, despite a slight annual decrease, and most related professions are expected to grow as fast as the average U.S. employment rate. The demand for chemistry-related professionals occurs in a diverse range of industries, from chemical manufacturing to food processing, and in a variety of arenas, including industry, academia, and government.

The industry is experiencing a trend—the focus is shifting away from workers possessing narrow and limited training and experience to those with a broader base of knowledge, as well as intangible qualities such as interpersonal skills. This is not to say that formal education in science, particularly in chemistry, is no longer required, it just means that a job candidate must supplement his or her academic degree with other skills, qualities, and knowledge.

Among these secondary characteristics and skills is a broader knowledge of science across disciplines, as well as a general understanding of business. Computer skills are becoming increasingly important, as are interpersonal and communication skills. In the chemical industries, professionals are often expected to function within teams, a distinction from the individual-based work performed during college. New graduates, therefore, must quickly adapt to and work well in a different environment.

Chemists

Chemists research and develop applications for chemicals. This profession is broken down by segment based on the type of work involved. Aside from management and sales/marketing positions, chemists work in one of two segments: basic research or applied research and development. Those in basic research advance the field of chemistry, investigating the structure, composition, properties, and reactions of elements and the laws governing them. Chemists involved in applied research are charged with the development or improvement of products and processes.

Within these two segments are four specialties. Analytical chemists examine the composition and structure of substances. Organic chemists study carbon compounds, while inorganic chemists study those compounds lacking carbon. Physical chemists examine the physical characteristics of molecules and atoms, and observe chemical reactions.

In 1996 U.S. chemists numbered 91,000, about half of which worked in the industrial sector. Chemists employed in academia hold faculty positions at colleges and universities. Others work in the government, mostly for Health and Human Services (incorporates the Food & Drug Administration, the National Institute of Health, and the Center for Disease Control), the Department of Defense, the Department of Agriculture, and the Environmental Protection Agency.

A bachelor's degree in chemistry is the minimal educational requirement for chemists. The degree should be supplemented with courses in mathematics, business, and computers, as well as other sciences. Internships are also valuable, as they impart practical experience to students. Employers usually provide additional training and education for new hires. Many employers prefer recruits possessing master's or PhDs, and for some research and administrative positions, PhDs are required.

Aside from job prerequisites, salaries rise decidedly with the level of degree. According to a survey conducted by the American Chemical Society, the median salary for chemists overall, as of March 1, 1998, was $65,000. Considered by education, the median for PhDs was $73,300; for master's, $57,700; and for bachelor's, $49,600. The salary drawn also depends on the work sector. For chemists employed in industry, the median was $69,500; in government, $64,100; and in academia, $54,000. Of the various combinations, the highest median, $80,000, went to PhDs working in the industrial sector, while the lowest, $37,300, was for bachelor's employed in academia.

Analysis of median salaries by gender reveals a marked distinction. The median for male chemists overall, as of March 1, 1998, was $69,500, while for women it was only $51,000. However, this figure may not present an entirely accurate picture. A trend among women in the industry is to resign by the time they turn 50, thereby vacating the presumably higher-paying positions.

The job market for chemists is expected to grow as fast as the national average through the year 2006, and it will be strongest in biotechnology and pharmaceuticals. Research and development will remain solid markets, as competition and environmental concerns continually spur the need for new or improved products and processes.

The unemployment rate for chemists, while lower than the nation's overall rate, continues to fall. The rates over the past two decades seem to indicate a fairly regular pattern. The industry undergoes a period of gradual decline followed by a period of gradual increase, and then repeats the cycle. The unemployment rate for chemists as of March 1, 1996 was 3%, followed by a sharp drop in 1997 that seemed to indicate the beginning of the downward cycle. By March 1, 1998, however, unemployment again rose, climbing from 2% in 1997 to 2.3%, despite a drop in the national rate from 5.1% to 4.5% over the same period.

Chemical Engineers

Chemical engineers apply the fields of chemistry and engineering to the design and operation of chemical manufacturing processes, equipment, and plants. They are involved in research, design, construction, operation, management, and sales, or any combination of these six. They design equipment, develop and test processes, and oversee production.

This work requires a strong background in chemistry, physics, and mathematics. Additionally, chemical engineers must be versed in economics, as that field applies to world resources and plant operating costs. Computer science has an even more direct application in this field than in other chemical professions, as computers are heavily utilized in the design and test processes, as well as in quality control. A bachelor's degree is usually the minimal educational requirement for chemical engineers, and many institutions across the U.S. offer chemical engineering programs.

The job market for chemical engineers is expected to grow as fast as the national average, especially in the areas of specialty chemicals, pharmaceuticals, and plastics materials. In 1996 more than 49,000 chemical engineers were employed in the nation, and about 2/3 of them were in the manufacturing industries.

As of March 1, 1998, chemical engineers with a bachelor's degree earned a median salary in the industrial sector of $60,000, compared with $50,000 for chemists at the same level. This gap between the professions continued for those holding master's degrees, but it became nearly non-existent at the PhD level.

Chemical Technicians

These science technicians assist chemists in the research and development of products and processes. They set up and monitor experiments, and record observations and results. They may even participate in the interpretation of data, the formation of conclusions, and the devising of solutions. In the chemical manufacturing sector, where they are also called process technicians, they may operate equipment and monitor processes.

Of the total 228,000 science technicians employed in the U.S. in 1996, about 35% were involved in the man-

ufacturing segment, mostly of chemicals. The job outlook for technicians overall is expected to grow as fast
as the national average through 2006. The median salary in 1996 for chemical technicians was $31,100,
compared with the median of $27,000 for science tech-
nicians in general.

The educational minimum is an associate's degree in
science or two years of specialized training. Some employers seek recruits with a bachelor's in chemistry,
but many such employees find themselves over-
qualified for the tasks that the job entails. As with chemists, strong computer and communications skills are
vital, as technicians will work closely with chemists
and probably with larger teams as well.

North America and the World

U.S. Trade

The chemical industry can be defined in various ways,
depending on a number of factors. Therefore, overall
1997 trade data for the chemical industry are not useful, as they may encompass areas that are outside the
scope of our discussion. Instead, we will look at the industry sectors individually. One statement, however,
can be made in general—all but one, photographic
equipment, experienced a trade surplus in 1997.

- Industrial Inorganic Chemicals, comprising SIC
  2812, Alkalies and chlorine; 2813, Industrial gases;
  2816, Inorganic pigments; and 2819, Industrial inorganic chemicals, not elsewhere classified: U.S.
  imports totaled $6.8 billion while exports totaled
  $8.3 billion, creating a trade surplus of $1.5 billion,
  a 112% increase from 1996.

- SIC 2821, Plastics materials, synthetic resins, and
  nonvulcanizable elastomers; 2822 Synthetic rubber;
  2823 Cellulosic manmade fibers; and 2824, Manmade organic fibers, except cellulosic: U.S. imports
  amounted to $6.9 billion and exports amounted to
  $15.4 billion, representing a surplus of $8.5 billion,
  a 6.6% increase from the previous year.

- SIC 2841, Soap and other detergents, except specialty cleaners; 2842, Specialty cleaning, polishing,
  and sanitation preparations; 2843, Surface active
  agents, finishing agents, sulfonated oils and assis-

tants; and 2844, Perfumes, cosmetics, and other toilet preparations: The U.S. imported $2.5 billion
worth while exporting $4.9 billion. This trade sur-
plus was $2.4 billion, a 22.6% increase from 1996.

- SIC 2851, Paints, varnishes, lacquers, enamels, and
  allied products: U.S. imports totaled $440 million
  and exports were $1.3 billion, resulting in a surplus
  of $892 million, a 25% increase from the previous
  year.

- Industrial Organic Chemicals, comprising SIC
  2861, Gum and wood chemicals; 2865, Cyclic organic crudes and intermediates, and organic dyes
  and pigments; 2869, Industrial organic chemicals,
  not elsewhere classified: The U.S. imported $12.1
  billion and exported $16 billion, resulting in a trade
  surplus of $3.9 billion, a 9% increase from 1996.

- Agricultural Chemicals, including SIC 2873, Nitrogenous fertilizers; 2874, Phosphatic fertilizers;
  2875, Fertilizers, mixing only; and 2879, Pesticides
  and agricultural chemicals, not elsewhere classified:
  U.S. imports were $2.7 billion and exports were
  $5.7 billion, creating a surplus of $3 billion, a
  15.4% increase from 1996.

- SIC 3861, Photographic equipment and supplies:
  The U.S. imported $9.5 billion and exported $5.3
  billion, creating a trade deficit of $4.2 billion, an in-
  crease of 9.3% from 1996.

Trade data was available only for standard industrial
groupings as a whole, not for SICs individually. Therefore, three SICs that were discussed earlier are not represented here, as they are part of industrial groupings
that were not considered in their entirety: SIC 2891,
Adhesives and sealants; 2899, Chemicals and chemical
preparations, not elsewhere classified; and 5191, Farm
supplies.

Globalization

Chemical companies must increasingly look beyond
their countries' shores to stay competitive. Alliances
are a practical method of penetrating new markets. Industry analysts predict that alliances will increase in
importance in upcoming years. As reported in *Chemical Market Reporter*, alliances accounted for 5-15% of
the revenues of the world's 30 largest chemical com-

panies, and are expected to increase that contribution to 20-40% by the year 2010.

Experts warn that merely participating in alliances, while an important step toward globalization, is not enough for success. Management tactics must also be modified from the status quo, where international operations must filter organizational issues through central management. Instead, global sites should be staffed with senior-level managers capable of making strategic decisions themselves, thereby functioning more efficiently.

Another factor in globalization concerns intellectual property protection. Countries interpret intellectual property differently. The Patent Cooperation Treaty (PCT), administered by the World Intellectual Property Organization in Geneva, Switzerland, assists companies in filing global patents. The PCT enables a company to file a single patent application for patent protection in 94 countries simultaneously. It issues data on related patents, allowing the applicant to determine if the application requires modification to distinguish it from an existing patent. The PCT then copies and sends the application to the national offices of the countries selected by the applicant. The effect is the same as if the application had been submitted to each country individually.

Research and Technology

University Partnerships

Chemical companies routinely use universities as research partners, funding projects of their own design. The relationship is symbiotic, with each partner deriving benefit. The industrial sector regards universities as a replacement for the funding and staffing of their own research and development (R&D) departments. They are also attracted to the university's track record of discovering inventions. The Association of University Technology Managers reports that before 1980, U.S. universities received fewer than 250 patents per year. By the mid-1990s, that number had leapt to 1,500.

On the university's part, it is interested in the funding granted by the industry, which accounts for 6% of university research. The federal government is the university's largest sponsor, funding 66% of the research. The guarantee of the government's contribution is shaky, however, as it is more likely to decrease in upcoming years than to increase. In order to stay in business, university research departments must look to other sectors for supplemental funding.

In negotiations between the company and the university, one of the most difficult barriers is the issue of intellectual property, or the rights to the fruits of the research. Both partners believe that they have claim for part, or very often all, of the rights to discoveries. Companies believe that if a technology is discovered through research that they funded, it naturally belongs to them, the sponsor. The university is an extension of the company's R&D department, in other words, hired on a contract basis. They also point out the utter injustice of funding the development of a technology that the university can then sell to the sponsor's competition.

From the university's standpoint, any technology developed by its staff at its facilities is its property. This attitude was reinforced by the 1980 Bayh-Dole Act, which granted universities the rights to all technology developed under federal funding. Universities also believe that in holding the rights, they are more apt than the commercial sector to serve the public's best interest.

These positions, as well as the issue of research fees, make negotiations a challenge. Yet while some discussions do reach an impasse, most negotiations are met by compromise. Both the industry and the university realize that their collaboration must continue for the sake of both parties.

R&D Spending

For the fifth straight year, R&D spending for U.S. chemical companies decreased in 1997. In an analysis by *Chemical & Engineering News* of 16 large U.S. chemical companies (including Dow Chemical, Solutia, and W.R. Grace), R&D expenditures totaled $1.95 billion, a 3% decrease from 1996. This trend in decreased spending is a drastic change from the trend that began a decade ago and continued into the early 1990s. R&D was not only increased each year, it increased in double-digit percentages—up 11% in both 1988 and 1989, and up 18% in 1990.

In contrast, the R&D spending of 13 large U.S. pharmaceutical and diverse chemicals companies (including DuPont, Monsanto, and Proctor & Gamble), continued its decade-long increase. Spending in 1997 reached $13.9 billion, an 11% increase over 1996. This total more than doubled 1987's expenditures of $6.3 billion.

Computer Labs

An emerging computer technology has the potential to revolutionize the chemicals, pharmaceuticals, forensic, and biotechnology fields. Researchers are working on designing computer microchips and semiconductors to replace some of the traditional laboratory work. These tiny laboratories, made of glass, plastic, or silicon, allow a scientist to place a minuscule amount of liquid onto a chip and then simply wait for the results. The analysis is quick and, because there is no human intervention, accurate.

The chips use electricity and chemicals to control the movement of the fluid through a series of valves, pumps, and filters. Electric charges can push the liquid, separate its components, and bring about change in those components.

An example of an application of this technology is in DNA analysis. A blood sample injected onto the chip is treated electrically so that the blood cells are separated from the bacteria. The bacteria are then broken down by an electric current, exposing the protein within their cells. An enzyme removes the protein, leaving behind the DNA and RNA.

The first markets for these chips are the scientific and commercial laboratories. However, the consumer market may not be far behind. Perhaps home-health testing devices will one day find themselves in every home.

Further Reading

1998-99 Occupational Outlook Handbook. Bureau of Labor Statistics: January 1998.

ACS Career Services—Workforce Report. October 1998. Available from the American Chemical Society, http://www.acs.org/careers/empres/workforc.htm

"Agrochemicals." *Chemical & Engineering News*. 23 March 1998.

All about Grace. October 1998. Available from W.R. Grace & Co., http://www.grace.com/html/compro.html

"Baekeland, Leo Hendrik." *Britannica CD 98 Multimedia Edition, 1994-1998*.Encyclopedia Britannica, Inc.

"Carothers, Wallace Hume." *Britannica CD 98 Multimedia Edition, 1994-1998*.Encyclopedia Britannica, Inc.

Cleaning Products Overview. October 1998. Available from the Soap and Detergent Association, http://sdahq.org/sdalatest/html/cleaning_products. html

"Corporate Overview." October 1998. Available from Bayer AG, http://www.bayer.com/bayer/ueberblick_e. htm

Dutton, Gail. "Protecting Intellectual Property." *Chemical Market Reporter*. 23 March 1998.

Facts & Figures for the Chemical Industry." *Chemical & Engineering News*. 29 July 1998.

Fenichell, Stephen. *Plastic: The Making of a Synthetic Century*. New York: HarperCollins, 1996.

Haber, L.F. *The Chemical Industry, 1900-1930*. London: Oxford University Press, 1971.

Heylin, Michael. "More Money but without Job Gains." *Chemical & Engineering News*. 27 July 1998.

"History of DuPont." October 1998. Available from http://www.dupont.com/corp/gbl-company/hist1800. html.

Hunt, Kimberly N., and AnnaMarie L. Sheldon, eds. *Notable Corporate Chronologies*. 2nd ed. Detroit: Gale Research, 1999.

Kirschner, Elisabeth M. "Soaps & Detergents." *Chemical & Engineering News*. 26 January 1998.

"Lavoisier, Antoine-Laurent." *Britannica CD 98 Multimedia Edition, 1994-1998.*Encyclopedia Britannica, Inc.

Layman, Patricia. "Global Top 50 Chemical Producers." *Chemical & Engineering News.* 20 July 1998.

"Leblanc, Nicolas." *Britannica CD 98 Multimedia Edition, 1994-1998.*Encyclopedia Britannica, Inc.

Morrow, David J. "Deal Settles Battle over Implants." *Bakersfield Californian.* 9 July 1998.

Morse, Paige Marie. "Adhesives." *Chemical & Engineering News.* 20 April 1998.

"Novartis Posts 43% Surge in Net on 19% Sales Gain." *Wall Street Journal Europe.* 18 March 1998.

Poucher, W.A. *The Production, Manufacture, and Application of Perfumes.* 8th ed. Vol. 2 of *Perfumes, Cosmetics, and Soap.* London: Chapman and Hall, 1974.

Reisch, Marc S. "From Coal Tar to Crafting: A Wealth of Diversity." *Chemical & Engineering News.* 12 January 1998.

Rogers, Ronald S. "Prickly Research Partnerships." *Chemical & Engineering News.* 21 September 1998.

"SC Johnson Wax Completes DowBrands Acquisition." 23 January 1998. Available from http://www.scjohnsonwax.com/news.html

Sherwin-Williams 1997 Annual Report. October 1998. Available from http://www.sherwin-williams.com/Investor_Relations/index.html.

Standard & Poor's Industry Surveys. New York: Standard & Poor's, 1998.

Storck, William J. "Top 100: Few Changes at the Top." *Chemical & Engineering News.* 4 May 1998.

U.S. Industry and Trade Outlook 1998. Springfield, VA.: U.S. Department of Commerce, International Trade Administration, 1998.

U.S. International Trade Administration. *U.S. Aggregate Foreign Trade Data.* October 1998. Available from http://www.ita.doc.gov/industry/otea/usfth/tabcon.html

Van Arnum, Patricia. "Global Strategies at Work." *Chemical Market Reporter.* 23 March 1998.

Wall, Joseph Frazier. *Alfred I du Pont: The Man and His Family.* New York: Oxford University Press, 1990.

W.R. Grace 1997 Annual Report. October 1998. Available from http://www.grace.com

Wu, Corinna. "The Incredible Shrinking Laboratory." *Science News.* 15 August 1998.

Zilg, Gerard Colby. *DuPont: Behind the Nylon Curtain.* Englewood Cliffs, NJ: Prentice-Hall, 1974.

—Deborah J. Untener

INDUSTRY STATISTICS & PERFORMANCE INDICATORS

This chapter presents statistical information on the Chemicals industry. This view of the industry is through the lens of federal statistics. All the data shown are drawn from government sources, including the 100 percent surveys of the Economic Census and the partial surveys of manufacturing and other industries conducted annually by the U.S. Department of Commerce. Tables include general statistics, indices of change, and selected ratios.

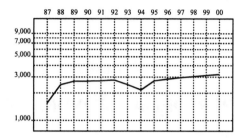

Revenues ($ millions)

SIC 2812 ALKALIES AND CHLORINE: GENERAL STATISTICS

| Year | Estab-lish-ments | Employment | | | Compensation | | Production ($ mil.) | | |
| | | Total (000) | Production | | Payroll ($ mil.) | Wages ($/hr) | Cost of Materials | Value of Shipments | Capital Inves. |
			Workers (000)	Hours (mil.)					
1987	45	5.0	3.5	7.3	165.3	15.07	809.0	1,547.9	68.4
1988	50	6.5	4.4	9.4	237.5	16.90	1,159.9	2,469.3	104.2
1989	47	5.2	4.6	10.0	248.7	16.67	1,309.9	2,699.0	155.6
1990	46	5.0	4.7	10.1	263.3	17.40	1,265.8	2,709.8	127.0
1991	52	7.5	5.2	11.0	303.5	18.15	1,347.6	2,728.9	144.6
1992	51	8.0	5.4	11.3	353.3	20.53	1,393.4	2,786.9	176.2
1993	51	7.7	5.3	11.1	351.6	20.95	1,425.2	2,480.9	181.5
1994	48	6.2	4.2	8.9	287.2	21.70	1,121.8	2,171.1	126.5
1995	45	6.1	4.2	8.4	295.0	23.63	1,156.4	2,729.6	199.3
1996	48[1]	5.9	4.0	8.4	300.3	23.42	1,212.9	2,849.7	215.2
1997	48[1]	6.1[1]	4.4[1]	9.4[1]	331.3[1]	23.67[1]	1,260.2[1]	2,960.8[1]	175.1[1]
1998	48[1]	6.1[1]	4.4[1]	9.4[1]	339.7[1]	24.40[1]	1,295.9[1]	3,044.7[1]	177.9[1]
1999	48[1]	6.0[1]	4.3[1]	9.3[1]	348.1[1]	25.13[1]	1,331.6[1]	3,128.7[1]	180.8[1]
2000	47[1]	5.9[1]	4.3[1]	9.3[1]	356.5[1]	25.86[1]	1,367.4[1]	3,212.6[1]	183.7[1]

Source: 1987 and 1992 Economic Census; *Annual Survey of Manufactures,* 88-91, 93-96. Establishment counts for non-Census years are from *County Business Patterns.* Extracted from *Manufacturing USA,* 6th Edition, Gale, 1998. Note: 1. Projections by the editors.

SIC 2812 ALKALIES AND CHLORINE: INDICES OF CHANGE

| Year | Estab-lish-ments | Employment | | | Compensation | | Production ($ mil.) | | |
| | | Total (000) | Production | | Payroll ($ mil.) | Wages ($/hr) | Cost of Materials | Value of Shipments | Capital Inves. |
			Workers (000)	Hours (mil.)					
1987	88	63	65	65	47	73	58	56	39
1988	98	81	81	83	67	82	83	89	59
1989	92	65	85	88	70	81	94	97	88
1990	90	63	87	89	75	85	91	97	72
1991	102	94	96	97	86	88	97	98	82
1992	100	100	100	100	100	100	100	100	100
1993	100	96	98	98	100	102	102	89	103
1994	94	78	78	79	81	106	81	78	72
1995	88	76	78	74	83	115	83	98	113
1996	94[1]	74	74	74	85	114	87	102	122
1997	94[1]	77[1]	82[1]	83[1]	94[1]	115[1]	90[1]	106[1]	99[1]
1998	94[1]	76[1]	81[1]	83[1]	96[1]	119[1]	93[1]	109[1]	101[1]
1999	93[1]	75[1]	80[1]	82[1]	99[1]	122[1]	96[1]	112[1]	103[1]
2000	93[1]	74[1]	80[1]	82[1]	101[1]	126[1]	98[1]	115[1]	104[1]

Source: Same as General Statistics. Values reflect change from the base year, 1992. Values above 100 mean greater than 1992, values below 100 mean less than 1992, and a value of 100 in the 1982-91 or 1993-2000 period means same as 1992. Note: 1. Projections by the editors.

SIC 2812 ALKALIES AND CHLORINE: SELECTED RATIOS

For 1996	Average of All Manufacturing	Analyzed Industry	Index
Employees per Establishment	49	123	253
Payroll per Establishment	1,574,035	6,264,856	398
Payroll per Employee	32,350	50,898	157
Production Workers per Establishment	34	83	244
Wages per Establishment	890,687	4,104,138	461
Wages per Production Worker	26,064	49,182	189
Hours per Production Worker	2,055	2,100	102
Wages per Hour	12.68	23.42	185
Value Added per Establishment	4,932,584	34,238,698	694
Value Added per Employee	101,376	278,169	274
Value Added per Production Worker	144,340	410,300	284
Cost per Establishment	5,569,059	25,303,508	454
Cost per Employee	114,457	205,576	180
Cost per Production Worker	162,965	303,225	186
Shipments per Establishment	10,422,474	59,450,413	570
Shipments per Employee	214,207	483,000	225
Shipments per Production Worker	304,989	712,425	234
Investment per Establishment	394,953	4,489,500	1,137
Investment per Employee	8,117	36,475	449
Investment per Production Worker	11,557	53,800	466

Source: Same as General Statistics. The 'Average of All Manufacturing' column represents the average of all manufacturing industries reported for the most recent complete year available. The Index shows the relationship between the Average and the Analyzed Industry. For example, 100 means that they are equal; 500 that the Analyzed Industry is five times the average; 50 means that the Analyzed Industry is half the national average. The abbreviation 'na' is used to show that data are 'not available'.

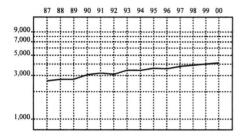

Revenues ($ millions)

SIC 2813 INDUSTRIAL GASES: GENERAL STATISTICS

Year	Estab-lish-ments	Employment Total (000)	Production Workers (000)	Production Hours (mil.)	Compensation Payroll ($ mil.)	Compensation Wages ($/hr)	Production ($ mil.) Cost of Materials	Production ($ mil.) Value of Shipments	Production ($ mil.) Capital Inves.
1987	594	8.1	4.0	8.5	241.4	13.56	1,052.9	2,617.8	104.3
1988	573	8.1	4.4	9.4	245.3	13.51	1,134.4	2,721.2	73.0
1989	576	9.9	4.7	10.0	261.4	14.00	1,087.2	2,731.5	121.0
1990	587	9.9	4.8	9.7	282.8	14.56	1,154.2	3,058.1	177.8
1991	650	9.2	4.9	10.4	300.2	14.33	1,148.9	3,193.9	289.7
1992	592	7.7	4.2	9.1	261.8	14.65	1,012.2	3,095.7	146.3
1993	616	7.8	4.1	8.9	275.2	15.02	1,092.7	3,435.7	163.7
1994	600	8.0	4.2	9.2	289.3	15.72	1,013.2	3,415.7	174.5
1995	595	8.1	4.2	9.6	301.0	15.40	1,096.7	3,605.7	279.5
1996	618[1]	8.6	4.4	9.8	329.9	16.61	1,039.8	3,559.6	341.7
1997	622[1]	8.7[1]	4.4[1]	9.5[1]	331.9[1]	17.07[1]	1,105.0[1]	3,782.8[1]	237.1[1]
1998	627[1]	8.8[1]	4.4[1]	9.5[1]	341.7[1]	17.51[1]	1,139.1[1]	3,899.5[1]	243.4[1]
1999	631[1]	8.8[1]	4.4[1]	9.5[1]	351.6[1]	17.96[1]	1,173.1[1]	4,016.1[1]	249.7[1]
2000	636[1]	8.9[1]	4.4[1]	9.5[1]	361.4[1]	18.41[1]	1,207.2[1]	4,132.7[1]	256.0[1]

Source: 1987 and 1992 Economic Census; *Annual Survey of Manufactures,* 88-91, 93-96. Establishment counts for non-Census years are from *County Business Patterns.* Extracted from *Manufacturing USA,* 6th Edition, Gale, 1998. Note: 1. Projections by the editors.

SIC 2813 INDUSTRIAL GASES: INDICES OF CHANGE

Year	Estab-lish-ments	Employment Total (000)	Production Workers (000)	Production Hours (mil.)	Compensation Payroll ($ mil.)	Compensation Wages ($/hr)	Production ($ mil.) Cost of Materials	Production ($ mil.) Value of Shipments	Production ($ mil.) Capital Inves.
1987	100	105	95	93	92	93	104	85	71
1988	97	105	105	103	94	92	112	88	50
1989	97	129	112	110	100	96	107	88	83
1990	99	129	114	107	108	99	114	99	122
1991	110	119	117	114	115	98	114	103	198
1992	100	100	100	100	100	100	100	100	100
1993	104	101	98	98	105	103	108	111	112
1994	101	104	100	101	111	107	100	110	119
1995	101	105	100	105	115	105	108	116	191
1996	104[1]	112	105	108	126	113	103	115	234
1997	105[1]	113[1]	105[1]	104[1]	127[1]	116[1]	109[1]	122[1]	162[1]
1998	106[1]	114[1]	105[1]	104[1]	131[1]	120[1]	113[1]	126[1]	166[1]
1999	107[1]	114[1]	105[1]	104[1]	134[1]	123[1]	116[1]	130[1]	171[1]
2000	107[1]	115[1]	106[1]	104[1]	138[1]	126[1]	119[1]	133[1]	175[1]

Source: Same as General Statistics. Values reflect change from the base year, 1992. Values above 100 mean greater than 1992, values below 100 mean less than 1992, and a value of 100 in the 1982-91 or 1993-2000 period means same as 1992. Note: 1. Projections by the editors.

SIC 2813 INDUSTRIAL GASES: SELECTED RATIOS

For 1996	Average of All Manufacturing	Analyzed Industry	Index
Employees per Establishment	49	14	29
Payroll per Establishment	1,574,035	533,838	34
Payroll per Employee	32,350	38,360	119
Production Workers per Establishment	34	7	21
Wages per Establishment	890,687	263,404	30
Wages per Production Worker	26,064	36,995	142
Hours per Production Worker	2,055	2,227	108
Wages per Hour	12.68	16.61	131
Value Added per Establishment	4,932,584	4,096,909	83
Value Added per Employee	101,376	294,395	290
Value Added per Production Worker	144,340	575,409	399
Cost per Establishment	5,569,059	1,682,584	30
Cost per Employee	114,457	120,907	106
Cost per Production Worker	162,965	236,318	145
Shipments per Establishment	10,422,474	5,760,075	55
Shipments per Employee	214,207	413,907	193
Shipments per Production Worker	304,989	809,000	265
Investment per Establishment	394,953	552,932	140
Investment per Employee	8,117	39,733	489
Investment per Production Worker	11,557	77,659	672

Source: Same as General Statistics. The 'Average of All Manufacturing' column represents the average of all manufacturing industries reported for the most recent complete year available. The Index shows the relationship between the Average and the Analyzed Industry. For example, 100 means that they are equal; 500 that the Analyzed Industry is five times the average; 50 means that the Analyzed Industry is half the national average. The abbreviation 'na' is used to show that data are 'not available'.

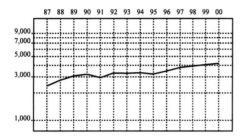

Revenues ($ millions)

SIC 2816 INORGANIC PIGMENTS: GENERAL STATISTICS

Year	Estab-lish-ments	Employment Total (000)	Employment Production Workers (000)	Employment Production Hours (mil.)	Compensation Payroll ($ mil.)	Compensation Wages ($/hr)	Production ($ mil.) Cost of Materials	Production ($ mil.) Value of Shipments	Production ($ mil.) Capital Inves.
1987	92	8.3	5.1	10.5	266.8	14.18	1,001.6	2,388.3	115.3
1988	91	8.9	5.3	11.4	295.2	14.12	1,189.6	2,764.3	145.4
1989	95	9.2	5.1	10.0	287.2	15.03	1,247.5	3,072.8	357.0
1990	97	8.8	5.3	11.3	298.9	14.65	1,282.6	3,203.9	353.5
1991	95	8.4	5.1	11.0	324.1	16.06	1,285.1	2,939.0	223.2
1992	89	8.6	5.6	12.4	347.7	17.03	1,326.0	3,305.6	508.9
1993	90	8.7	5.6	12.1	336.2	17.13	1,323.2	3,275.7	149.1
1994	94	8.6	5.7	12.0	340.4	18.13	1,437.0	3,320.9	156.9
1995	87	8.6	5.6	11.5	356.4	19.97	1,480.2	3,213.4	359.2
1996	86[1]	8.7	5.8	12.3	373.6	19.50	1,583.9	3,469.5	180.2
1997	85[1]	8.0[1]	5.2[1]	11.4[1]	366.4[1]	19.96[1]	1,732.9[1]	3,796.0[1]	322.2[1]
1998	84[1]	7.8[1]	5.2[1]	11.3[1]	373.9[1]	20.55[1]	1,795.4[1]	3,932.8[1]	337.1[1]
1999	82[1]	7.7[1]	5.1[1]	11.3[1]	381.3[1]	21.15[1]	1,857.9[1]	4,069.6[1]	352.0[1]
2000	81[1]	7.5[1]	5.0[1]	11.2[1]	388.8[1]	21.75[1]	1,920.3[1]	4,206.4[1]	366.9[1]

Source: 1987 and 1992 Economic Census; *Annual Survey of Manufactures*, 88-91, 93-96. Establishment counts for non-Census years are from *County Business Patterns*. Extracted from *Manufacturing USA*, 6th Edition, Gale, 1998. Note: 1. Projections by the editors.

SIC 2816 INORGANIC PIGMENTS: INDICES OF CHANGE

Year	Estab-lish-ments	Employment Total (000)	Employment Production Workers (000)	Employment Production Hours (mil.)	Compensation Payroll ($ mil.)	Compensation Wages ($/hr)	Production ($ mil.) Cost of Materials	Production ($ mil.) Value of Shipments	Production ($ mil.) Capital Inves.
1987	103	97	91	85	77	83	76	72	23
1988	102	103	95	92	85	83	90	84	29
1989	107	107	91	81	83	88	94	93	70
1990	109	102	95	91	86	86	97	97	69
1991	107	98	91	89	93	94	97	89	44
1992	100	100	100	100	100	100	100	100	100
1993	101	101	100	98	97	101	100	99	29
1994	106	100	102	97	98	106	108	100	31
1995	98	100	100	93	103	117	112	97	71
1996	97[1]	101	104	99	107	115	119	105	35
1997	96[1]	93[1]	93[1]	92[1]	105[1]	117[1]	131[1]	115[1]	63[1]
1998	94[1]	91[1]	92[1]	91[1]	108[1]	121[1]	135[1]	119[1]	66[1]
1999	93[1]	89[1]	91[1]	91[1]	110[1]	124[1]	140[1]	123[1]	69[1]
2000	91[1]	88[1]	90[1]	91[1]	112[1]	128[1]	145[1]	127[1]	72[1]

Source: Same as General Statistics. Values reflect change from the base year, 1992. Values above 100 mean greater than 1992, values below 100 mean less than 1992, and a value of 100 in the 1982-91 or 1993-2000 period means same as 1992. Note: 1. Projections by the editors.

SIC 2816 INORGANIC PIGMENTS: SELECTED RATIOS

For 1996	Average of All Manufacturing	Analyzed Industry	Index
Employees per Establishment	49	101	207
Payroll per Establishment	1,574,035	4,324,294	275
Payroll per Employee	32,350	42,943	133
Production Workers per Establishment	34	67	196
Wages per Establishment	890,687	2,776,183	312
Wages per Production Worker	26,064	41,353	159
Hours per Production Worker	2,055	2,121	103
Wages per Hour	12.68	19.50	154
Value Added per Establishment	4,932,584	21,748,792	441
Value Added per Employee	101,376	215,977	213
Value Added per Production Worker	144,340	323,966	224
Cost per Establishment	5,569,059	18,333,109	329
Cost per Employee	114,457	182,057	159
Cost per Production Worker	162,965	273,086	168
Shipments per Establishment	10,422,474	40,158,293	385
Shipments per Employee	214,207	398,793	186
Shipments per Production Worker	304,989	598,190	196
Investment per Establishment	394,953	2,085,754	528
Investment per Employee	8,117	20,713	255
Investment per Production Worker	11,557	31,069	269

Source: Same as General Statistics. The 'Average of All Manufacturing' column represents the average of all manufacturing industries reported for the most recent complete year available. The Index shows the relationship between the Average and the Analyzed Industry. For example, 100 means that they are equal; 500 that the Analyzed Industry is five times the average; 50 means that the Analyzed Industry is half the national average. The abbreviation 'na' is used to show that data are 'not available'.

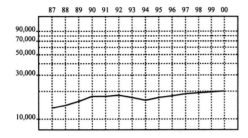

Revenues ($ millions)

SIC 2819 INDUSTRIAL CHEMICALS, NEC: GENERAL STATISTICS

| Year | Estab-lish-ments | Employment | | | Compensation | | Production ($ mil.) | | |
| | | Total (000) | Production | | Payroll ($ mil.) | Wages ($/hr) | Cost of Materials | Value of Shipments | Capital Inves. |
			Workers (000)	Hours (mil.)					
1987	662	72.2	37.5	75.2	2,425.2	15.14	5,639.5	13,211.6	506.1
1988	659	72.2	38.0	83.3	2,485.8	13.40	5,920.7	14,154.8	515.8
1989	645	73.4	39.1	78.7	2,694.4	15.18	6,201.1	15,654.2	703.9
1990	685	77.5	40.0	83.4	2,998.1	15.69	6,955.7	17,719.0	670.6
1991	705	78.9	41.0	88.5	3,156.7	16.10	7,078.9	17,648.9	718.9
1992	697	79.1	39.8	87.5	3,270.5	16.28	6,962.9	18,169.1	722.5
1993	719	69.5	34.7	75.9	2,920.6	16.53	6,634.1	17,146.7	684.9
1994	717	64.6	32.7	71.2	2,751.9	17.38	6,267.2	16,032.2	844.7
1995	698	58.9	31.9	70.7	2,623.9	19.05	6,798.4	17,173.6	869.2
1996	721[1]	57.0	31.0	66.3	2,744.8	21.24	7,461.1	17,861.9	1,264.9
1997	728[1]	62.4[1]	31.5[1]	70.9[1]	3,079.5[1]	19.65[1]	7,865.3[1]	18,829.5[1]	995.4[1]
1998	735[1]	61.0[1]	30.6[1]	69.7[1]	3,134.5[1]	20.17[1]	8,049.9[1]	19,271.5[1]	1,037.0[1]
1999	742[1]	59.7[1]	29.7[1]	68.4[1]	3,189.6[1]	20.70[1]	8,234.5[1]	19,713.4[1]	1,078.5[1]
2000	749[1]	58.3[1]	28.8[1]	67.2[1]	3,244.6[1]	21.23[1]	8,419.1[1]	20,155.3[1]	1,120.0[1]

Source: 1987 and 1992 Economic Census; *Annual Survey of Manufactures*, 88-91, 93-96. Establishment counts for non-Census years are from *County Business Patterns*. Extracted from *Manufacturing USA*, 6th Edition, Gale, 1998. Note: 1. Projections by the editors.

SIC 2819 INDUSTRIAL CHEMICALS, NEC: INDICES OF CHANGE

| Year | Estab-lish-ments | Employment | | | Compensation | | Production ($ mil.) | | |
| | | Total (000) | Production | | Payroll ($ mil.) | Wages ($/hr) | Cost of Materials | Value of Shipments | Capital Inves. |
			Workers (000)	Hours (mil.)					
1987	95	91	94	86	74	93	81	73	70
1988	95	91	95	95	76	82	85	78	71
1989	93	93	98	90	82	93	89	86	97
1990	98	98	101	95	92	96	100	98	93
1991	101	100	103	101	97	99	102	97	100
1992	100	100	100	100	100	100	100	100	100
1993	103	88	87	87	89	102	95	94	95
1994	103	82	82	81	84	107	90	88	117
1995	100	74	80	81	80	117	98	95	120
1996	103[1]	72	78	76	84	130	107	98	175
1997	104[1]	79[1]	79[1]	81[1]	94[1]	121[1]	113[1]	104[1]	138[1]
1998	105[1]	77[1]	77[1]	80[1]	96[1]	124[1]	116[1]	106[1]	144[1]
1999	106[1]	75[1]	75[1]	78[1]	98[1]	127[1]	118[1]	108[1]	149[1]
2000	107[1]	74[1]	72[1]	77[1]	99[1]	130[1]	121[1]	111[1]	155[1]

Source: Same as General Statistics. Values reflect change from the base year, 1992. Values above 100 mean greater than 1992, values below 100 mean less than 1992, and a value of 100 in the 1982-91 or 1993-2000 period means same as 1992. Note: 1. Projections by the editors.

SIC 2819 INDUSTRIAL CHEMICALS, NEC: SELECTED RATIOS

For 1996	Average of All Manufacturing	Analyzed Industry	Index
Employees per Establishment	49	79	162
Payroll per Establishment	1,574,035	3,805,543	242
Payroll per Employee	32,350	48,154	149
Production Workers per Establishment	34	43	126
Wages per Establishment	890,687	1,952,423	219
Wages per Production Worker	26,064	45,426	174
Hours per Production Worker	2,055	2,139	104
Wages per Hour	12.68	21.24	167
Value Added per Establishment	4,932,584	14,578,024	296
Value Added per Employee	101,376	184,467	182
Value Added per Production Worker	144,340	339,181	235
Cost per Establishment	5,569,059	10,344,482	186
Cost per Employee	114,457	130,896	114
Cost per Production Worker	162,965	240,681	148
Shipments per Establishment	10,422,474	24,764,728	238
Shipments per Employee	214,207	313,367	146
Shipments per Production Worker	304,989	576,190	189
Investment per Establishment	394,953	1,753,727	444
Investment per Employee	8,117	22,191	273
Investment per Production Worker	11,557	40,803	353

Source: Same as General Statistics. The 'Average of All Manufacturing' column represents the average of all manufacturing industries reported for the most recent complete year available. The Index shows the relationship between the Average and the Analyzed Industry. For example, 100 means that they are equal; 500 that the Analyzed Industry is five times the average; 50 means that the Analyzed Industry is half the national average. The abbreviation 'na' is used to show that data are 'not available'.

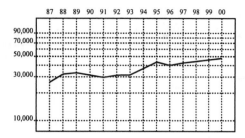

Revenues ($ millions)

SIC 2821 PLASTICS MATERIALS AND RESINS: GENERAL STATISTICS

Year	Estab-lish-ments	Employment			Compensation		Production ($ mil.)		
		Total (000)	Production		Payroll ($ mil.)	Wages ($/hr)	Cost of Materials	Value of Shipments	Capital Inves.
			Workers (000)	Hours (mil.)					
1987	480	56.3	34.9	75.6	2,005.8	15.24	15,410.4	26,245.5	1,247.2
1988	487	58.3	36.0	79.8	2,169.9	15.37	19,333.8	32,109.9	1,605.8
1989	498	61.4	37.8	83.7	2,383.2	15.92	20,292.9	33,256.7	1,966.2
1990	510	61.8	37.9	82.5	2,485.7	16.88	19,390.9	31,325.8	2,436.6
1991	519	60.5	36.7	80.8	2,479.9	17.25	18,593.4	29,565.8	2,251.7
1992	449	60.4	35.9	78.5	2,671.6	18.71	18,839.8	31,303.9	1,707.3
1993	501	62.2	36.6	80.9	2,799.3	18.75	19,500.6	31,545.6	1,925.9
1994	499	69.2	40.6	90.0	3,150.0	19.37	21,937.8	36,964.6	2,554.9
1995	558	69.7	41.5	91.8	3,309.0	19.97	26,209.1	43,528.7	2,336.8
1996	528[1]	58.6	36.3	80.6	2,864.1	20.50	24,829.0	40,097.2	2,783.6
1997	534[1]	66.7[1]	39.9[1]	89.9[1]	3,332.1[1]	21.17[1]	26,357.0[1]	42,564.9[1]	2,810.8[1]
1998	540[1]	67.7[1]	40.4[1]	91.4[1]	3,460.1[1]	21.77[1]	27,416.2[1]	44,275.4[1]	2,947.3[1]
1999	545[1]	68.6[1]	40.9[1]	92.8[1]	3,588.1[1]	22.37[1]	28,475.4[1]	45,985.8[1]	3,083.9[1]
2000	551[1]	69.5[1]	41.4[1]	94.3[1]	3,716.1[1]	22.97[1]	29,534.5[1]	47,696.3[1]	3,220.4[1]

Source: 1987 and 1992 Economic Census; *Annual Survey of Manufactures,* 88-91, 93-96. Establishment counts for non-Census years are from *County Business Patterns.* Extracted from *Manufacturing USA*, 6th Edition, Gale, 1998. Note: 1. Projections by the editors.

SIC 2821 PLASTICS MATERIALS AND RESINS: INDICES OF CHANGE

Year	Estab-lish-ments	Employment			Compensation		Production ($ mil.)		
		Total (000)	Production		Payroll ($ mil.)	Wages ($/hr)	Cost of Materials	Value of Shipments	Capital Inves.
			Workers (000)	Hours (mil.)					
1987	107	93	97	96	75	81	82	84	73
1988	108	97	100	102	81	82	103	103	94
1989	111	102	105	107	89	85	108	106	115
1990	114	102	106	105	93	90	103	100	143
1991	116	100	102	103	93	92	99	94	132
1992	100	100	100	100	100	100	100	100	100
1993	112	103	102	103	105	100	104	101	113
1994	111	115	113	115	118	104	116	118	150
1995	124	115	116	117	124	107	139	139	137
1996	118[1]	97	101	103	107	110	132	128	163
1997	119[1]	110[1]	111[1]	115[1]	125[1]	113[1]	140[1]	136[1]	165[1]
1998	120[1]	112[1]	113[1]	116[1]	130[1]	116[1]	146[1]	141[1]	173[1]
1999	121[1]	114[1]	114[1]	118[1]	134[1]	120[1]	151[1]	147[1]	181[1]
2000	123[1]	115[1]	115[1]	120[1]	139[1]	123[1]	157[1]	152[1]	189[1]

Source: **Same as General Statistics.** Values reflect change from the base year, 1992. Values above 100 mean greater than 1992, values below 100 mean less than 1992, and a value of 100 in the 1982-91 or 1993-2000 period means same as 1992. Note: 1. Projections by the editors.

SIC 2821 PLASTICS MATERIALS AND RESINS: SELECTED RATIOS

For 1996	Average of All Manufacturing	Analyzed Industry	Index
Employees per Establishment	49	111	228
Payroll per Establishment	1,574,035	5,422,400	344
Payroll per Employee	32,350	48,875	151
Production Workers per Establishment	34	69	201
Wages per Establishment	890,687	3,128,184	351
Wages per Production Worker	26,064	45,518	175
Hours per Production Worker	2,055	2,220	108
Wages per Hour	12.68	20.50	162
Value Added per Establishment	4,932,584	28,986,111	588
Value Added per Employee	101,376	261,270	258
Value Added per Production Worker	144,340	421,774	292
Cost per Establishment	5,569,059	47,007,011	844
Cost per Employee	114,457	423,703	370
Cost per Production Worker	162,965	683,994	420
Shipments per Establishment	10,422,474	75,913,228	728
Shipments per Employee	214,207	684,253	319
Shipments per Production Worker	304,989	1,104,606	362
Investment per Establishment	394,953	5,269,995	1,334
Investment per Employee	8,117	47,502	585
Investment per Production Worker	11,557	76,683	664

Source: Same as General Statistics. The 'Average of All Manufacturing' column represents the average of all manufacturing industries reported for the most recent complete year available. The Index shows the relationship between the Average and the Analyzed Industry. For example, 100 means that they are equal; 500 that the Analyzed Industry is five times the average; 50 means that the Analyzed Industry is half the national average. The abbreviation 'na' is used to show that data are 'not available'.

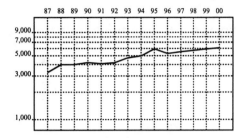

Revenues ($ millions)

SIC 2822 SYNTHETIC RUBBER: GENERAL STATISTICS

Year	Estab- lish- ments	Employment			Compensation		Production ($ mil.)		
		Total (000)	Production		Payroll ($ mil.)	Wages ($/hr)	Cost of Materials	Value of Shipments	Capital Inves.
			Workers (000)	Hours (mil.)					
1987	68	10.4	6.7	14.4	394.6	15.88	2,082.5	3,283.0	170.5
1988	115	11.3	7.1	14.8	428.8	16.36	2,508.9	3,995.5	216.4
1989	76	11.7	7.1	15.1	443.6	16.78	2,403.1	4,007.8	265.5
1990	86	12.3	7.2	15.0	474.9	17.91	2,533.7	4,210.3	378.6
1991	92	11.5	7.4	15.6	491.2	17.79	2,234.6	4,088.3	360.0
1992	92	11.7	7.5	15.9	513.1	18.74	2,342.6	4,184.1	318.2
1993	109	12.2	7.7	16.4	551.0	19.27	2,592.1	4,738.6	255.8
1994	113	11.9	7.7	16.6	552.5	19.62	2,759.8	4,983.6	230.0
1995	126	12.0	8.0	16.7	576.7	20.61	3,231.0	5,942.2	268.3
1996	115[1]	12.0	7.9	16.7	573.9	20.68	3,009.3	5,290.6	279.3
1997	118[1]	12.2[1]	7.9[1]	17.0[1]	609.3[1]	21.21[1]	3,143.9[1]	5,527.2[1]	
1998	121[1]	12.4[1]	7.9[1]	17.3[1]	629.6[1]	21.72[1]	3,252.5[1]	5,718.1[1]	
1999	125[1]	12.5[1]	8.0[1]	17.5[1]	649.9[1]	22.23[1]	3,361.0[1]	5,909.0[1]	
2000	128[1]	12.6[1]	8.1[1]	17.8[1]	670.2[1]	22.74[1]	3,469.6[1]	6,099.9[1]	

Source: 1987 and 1992 Economic Census; *Annual Survey of Manufactures*, 88-91, 93-96. Establishment counts for non-Census years are from *County Business Patterns*. Extracted from *Manufacturing USA*, 6th Edition, Gale, 1998. Note: 1. Projections by the editors.

SIC 2822 SYNTHETIC RUBBER: INDICES OF CHANGE

Year	Estab- lish- ments	Employment			Compensation		Production ($ mil.)		
		Total (000)	Production		Payroll ($ mil.)	Wages ($/hr)	Cost of Materials	Value of Shipments	Capital Inves.
			Workers (000)	Hours (mil.)					
1987	74	89	89	91	77	85	89	78	54
1988	125	97	95	93	84	87	107	95	68
1989	83	100	95	95	86	90	103	96	83
1990	93	105	96	94	93	96	108	101	119
1991	100	98	99	98	96	95	95	98	113
1992	100	100	100	100	100	100	100	100	100
1993	118	104	103	103	107	103	111	113	80
1994	123	102	103	104	108	105	118	119	72
1995	137	103	107	105	112	110	138	142	84
1996	125[1]	103	105	105	112	110	128	126	88
1997	128[1]	105[1]	105[1]	107[1]	119[1]	113[1]	134[1]	132[1]	
1998	132[1]	106[1]	106[1]	109[1]	123[1]	116[1]	139[1]	137[1]	
1999	135[1]	107[1]	107[1]	110[1]	127[1]	119[1]	143[1]	141[1]	
2000	139[1]	108[1]	108[1]	112[1]	131[1]	121[1]	148[1]	146[1]	

Source: Same as General Statistics. Values reflect change from the base year, 1992. Values above 100 mean greater than 1992, values below 100 mean less than 1992, and a value of 100 in the 1982-91 or 1993-2000 period means same as 1992. Note: 1. Projections by the editors.

SIC 2822 SYNTHETIC RUBBER: SELECTED RATIOS

For 1996	Average of All Manufacturing	Analyzed Industry	Index
Employees per Establishment	49	104	215
Payroll per Establishment	1,574,035	4,991,389	317
Payroll per Employee	32,350	47,825	148
Production Workers per Establishment	34	69	201
Wages per Establishment	890,687	3,003,670	337
Wages per Production Worker	26,064	43,716	168
Hours per Production Worker	2,055	2,114	103
Wages per Hour	12.68	20.68	163
Value Added per Establishment	4,932,584	19,818,570	402
Value Added per Employee	101,376	189,892	187
Value Added per Production Worker	144,340	288,443	200
Cost per Establishment	5,569,059	26,172,828	470
Cost per Employee	114,457	250,775	219
Cost per Production Worker	162,965	380,924	234
Shipments per Establishment	10,422,474	46,014,011	441
Shipments per Employee	214,207	440,883	206
Shipments per Production Worker	304,989	669,696	220
Investment per Establishment	394,953	2,429,160	615
Investment per Employee	8,117	23,275	287
Investment per Production Worker	11,557	35,354	306

Source: Same as General Statistics. The 'Average of All Manufacturing' column represents the average of all manufacturing industries reported for the most recent complete year available. The Index shows the relationship between the Average and the Analyzed Industry. For example, 100 means that they are equal; 500 that the Analyzed Industry is five times the average; 50 means that the Analyzed Industry is half the national average. The abbreviation 'na' is used to show that data are 'not available'.

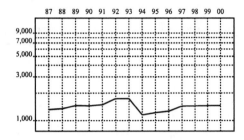

Revenues ($ millions)

SIC 2823 CELLULOSIC MANMADE FIBERS: GENERAL STATISTICS

Year	Estab-lish-ments	Employment Total (000)	Production Workers (000)	Production Hours (mil.)	Compensation Payroll ($ mil.)	Compensation Wages ($/hr)	Production ($ mil.) Cost of Materials	Production ($ mil.) Value of Shipments	Production ($ mil.) Capital Inves.
1987	7	10.5	7.9	16.5	280.7	10.95	669.7	1,319.7	23.8
1988	10	10.2	7.7	16.9	287.1	10.74	737.4	1,352.4	113.2
1989	9	10.5	7.6	15.8	297.2	11.63	786.0	1,469.4	104.9
1990	10	9.3	7.2	15.0	302.4	12.28	786.3	1,456.7	71.5
1991	13	10.5	7.7	15.6	349.1	13.50	818.3	1,496.7	105.3
1992	7	11.0	7.8	16.7	372.8	13.11	950.3	1,748.1	92.8
1993	10	9.3	7.2	15.4	301.2	13.23	800.8	1,744.6	207.5
1994	13	6.2	5.0	10.7	181.7	11.91	426.9	1,153.5	137.5
1995	12	6.1	4.9	10.2	192.4	13.42	527.5	1,222.1	113.2
1996	10[1]	6.0	4.8	10.7	196.2	12.99	588.7	1,267.2	
1997	10[1]	5.9[1]	4.6[1]	10.3[1]	236.3[1]	13.91[1]	670.2[1]	1,442.6[1]	
1998	10[1]	5.3[1]	4.2[1]	9.6[1]	229.9[1]	14.19[1]	673.8[1]	1,450.5[1]	
1999	10[1]	4.7[1]	3.8[1]	8.9[1]	223.6[1]	14.48[1]	677.5[1]	1,458.4[1]	
2000	9[1]	4.2[1]	3.4[1]	8.2[1]	217.2[1]	14.76[1]	681.2[1]	1,466.3[1]	

Source: 1987 and 1992 Economic Census; *Annual Survey of Manufactures*, 88-91, 93-96. Establishment counts for non-Census years are from *County Business Patterns*. Extracted from *Manufacturing USA*, 6th Edition, Gale, 1998. Note: 1. Projections by the editors.

SIC 2823 CELLULOSIC MANMADE FIBERS: INDICES OF CHANGE

Year	Estab-lish-ments	Employment Total (000)	Production Workers (000)	Production Hours (mil.)	Compensation Payroll ($ mil.)	Compensation Wages ($/hr)	Production ($ mil.) Cost of Materials	Production ($ mil.) Value of Shipments	Production ($ mil.) Capital Inves.
1987	100	95	101	99	75	84	70	75	26
1988	143	93	99	101	77	82	78	77	122
1989	129	95	97	95	80	89	83	84	113
1990	143	85	92	90	81	94	83	83	77
1991	186	95	99	93	94	103	86	86	113
1992	100	100	100	100	100	100	100	100	100
1993	143	85	92	92	81	101	84	100	224
1994	186	56	64	64	49	91	45	66	148
1995	171	55	63	61	52	102	56	70	122
1996	145[1]	55	62	64	53	99	62	72	
1997	143[1]	53[1]	59[1]	62[1]	63[1]	106[1]	71[1]	83[1]	
1998	140[1]	48[1]	53[1]	58[1]	62[1]	108[1]	71[1]	83[1]	
1999	137[1]	43[1]	48[1]	53[1]	60[1]	110[1]	71[1]	83[1]	
2000	134[1]	38[1]	43[1]	49[1]	58[1]	113[1]	72[1]	84[1]	

Source: Same as General Statistics. Values reflect change from the base year, 1992. Values above 100 mean greater than 1992, values below 100 mean less than 1992, and a value of 100 in the 1982-91 or 1993-2000 period means same as 1992. Note: 1. Projections by the editors.

SIC 2823 CELLULOSIC MANMADE FIBERS: SELECTED RATIOS

For 1996	Average of All Manufacturing	Analyzed Industry	Index
Employees per Establishment	49	590	1,212
Payroll per Establishment	1,574,035	19,280,994	1,225
Payroll per Employee	32,350	32,700	101
Production Workers per Establishment	34	472	1,380
Wages per Establishment	890,687	13,659,139	1,534
Wages per Production Worker	26,064	28,957	111
Hours per Production Worker	2,055	2,229	108
Wages per Hour	12.68	12.99	102
Value Added per Establishment	4,932,584	67,670,194	1,372
Value Added per Employee	101,376	114,767	113
Value Added per Production Worker	144,340	143,458	99
Cost per Establishment	5,569,059	57,852,808	1,039
Cost per Employee	114,457	98,117	86
Cost per Production Worker	162,965	122,646	75
Shipments per Establishment	10,422,474	124,530,454	1,195
Shipments per Employee	214,207	211,200	99
Shipments per Production Worker	304,989	264,000	87
Investment per Establishment	394,953	0	0
Investment per Employee	8,117	0	0
Investment per Production Worker	11,557	0	0

Source: Same as General Statistics. The 'Average of All Manufacturing' column represents the average of all manufacturing industries reported for the most recent complete year available. The Index shows the relationship between the Average and the Analyzed Industry. For example, 100 means that they are equal; 500 that the Analyzed Industry is five times the average; 50 means that the Analyzed Industry is half the national average. The abbreviation 'na' is used to show that data are 'not available'.

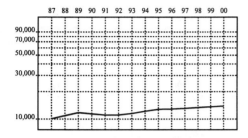

Revenues ($ millions)

SIC 2824 ORGANIC FIBERS, NONCELLULOSIC: GENERAL STATISTICS

Year	Estab-lish-ments	Employment			Compensation		Production ($ mil.)		
		Total (000)	Production		Payroll ($ mil.)	Wages ($/hr)	Cost of Materials	Value of Shipments	Capital Inves.
			Workers (000)	Hours (mil.)					
1987	72	45.7	34.4	70.5	1,347.4	12.70	5,154.1	10,111.6	460.0
1988	81	45.8	34.6	69.5	1,399.2	13.34	5,514.4	10,930.3	632.6
1989	71	46.7	36.3	72.5	1,500.7	13.84	5,881.2	11,796.3	690.6
1990	74	46.3	36.1	72.7	1,539.3	13.90	5,486.6	11,427.1	814.7
1991	78	46.9	35.0	70.4	1,568.7	14.67	4,915.9	11,083.8	810.1
1992	71	44.4	33.9	71.1	1,545.2	14.48	5,337.1	11,113.7	721.3
1993	88	42.3	32.6	67.2	1,474.9	14.95	5,548.0	11,548.4	921.4
1994	83	40.7	31.6	68.3	1,417.2	14.37	5,778.9	12,212.6	563.9
1995	89	38.6	30.1	65.6	1,438.2	15.09	6,367.6	12,813.3	681.3
1996	84[1]	38.5	30.3	64.8	1,451.9	15.66	6,170.9	12,911.7	865.1[1]
1997	85[1]	36.6[1]	29.3[1]	64.6[1]	1,503.1[1]	15.98[1]	6,269.1[1]	13,117.1[1]	902.9[1]
1998	86[1]	35.3[1]	28.5[1]	63.7[1]	1,510.2[1]	16.28[1]	6,405.2[1]	13,401.9[1]	940.6[1]
1999	87[1]	34.0[1]	27.7[1]	62.9[1]	1,517.3[1]	16.59[1]	6,541.3[1]	13,686.7[1]	978.4[1]
2000	88[1]	32.7[1]	27.0[1]	62.0[1]	1,524.4[1]	16.89[1]	6,677.4[1]	13,971.5[1]	1,016.1[1]

Source: 1987 and 1992 Economic Census; *Annual Survey of Manufactures,* 88-91, 93-96. Establishment counts for non-Census years are from *County Business Patterns.* Extracted from *Manufacturing USA,* 6th Edition, Gale, 1998. Note: 1. Projections by the editors.

SIC 2824 ORGANIC FIBERS, NONCELLULOSIC: INDICES OF CHANGE

Year	Estab-lish-ments	Employment			Compensation		Production ($ mil.)		
		Total (000)	Production		Payroll ($ mil.)	Wages ($/hr)	Cost of Materials	Value of Shipments	Capital Inves.
			Workers (000)	Hours (mil.)					
1987	101	103	101	99	87	88	97	91	64
1988	114	103	102	98	91	92	103	98	88
1989	100	105	107	102	97	96	110	106	96
1990	104	104	106	102	100	96	103	103	113
1991	110	106	103	99	102	101	92	100	112
1992	100	100	100	100	100	100	100	100	100
1993	124	95	96	95	95	103	104	104	128
1994	117	92	93	96	92	99	108	110	78
1995	125	87	89	92	93	104	119	115	94
1996	118[1]	87	89	91	94	108	116	116	120[1]
1997	120[1]	82[1]	86[1]	91[1]	97[1]	110[1]	117[1]	118[1]	125[1]
1998	121[1]	80[1]	84[1]	90[1]	98[1]	112[1]	120[1]	121[1]	130[1]
1999	122[1]	77[1]	82[1]	88[1]	98[1]	115[1]	123[1]	123[1]	136[1]
2000	124[1]	74[1]	80[1]	87[1]	99[1]	117[1]	125[1]	126[1]	141[1]

Source: Same as General Statistics. Values reflect change from the base year, 1992. Values above 100 mean greater than 1992, values below 100 mean less than 1992, and a value of 100 in the 1982-91 or 1993-2000 period means same as 1992. Note: 1. Projections by the editors.

SIC 2824 ORGANIC FIBERS, NONCELLULOSIC: SELECTED RATIOS

For 1996	Average of All Manufacturing	Analyzed Industry	Index
Employees per Establishment	49	458	941
Payroll per Establishment	1,574,035	17,268,710	1,097
Payroll per Employee	32,350	37,712	117
Production Workers per Establishment	34	360	1,055
Wages per Establishment	890,687	12,069,519	1,355
Wages per Production Worker	26,064	33,491	128
Hours per Production Worker	2,055	2,139	104
Wages per Hour	12.68	15.66	123
Value Added per Establishment	4,932,584	80,253,888	1,627
Value Added per Employee	101,376	175,260	173
Value Added per Production Worker	144,340	222,690	154
Cost per Establishment	5,569,059	73,395,883	1,318
Cost per Employee	114,457	160,283	140
Cost per Production Worker	162,965	203,660	125
Shipments per Establishment	10,422,474	153,570,082	1,473
Shipments per Employee	214,207	335,369	157
Shipments per Production Worker	304,989	426,129	140
Investment per Establishment	394,953	10,289,570	2,605
Investment per Employee	8,117	22,471	277
Investment per Production Worker	11,557	28,552	247

Source: Same as General Statistics. The 'Average of All Manufacturing' column represents the average of all manufacturing industries reported for the most recent complete year available. The Index shows the relationship between the Average and the Analyzed Industry. For example, 100 means that they are equal; 500 that the Analyzed Industry is five times the average; 50 means that the Analyzed Industry is half the national average. The abbreviation 'na' is used to show that data are 'not available'.

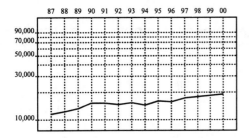

Revenues ($ millions)

SIC 2841 SOAPS AND OTHER DETERGENTS: GENERAL STATISTICS

Year	Estab- lish- ments	Employment Total (000)	Employment Production Workers (000)	Employment Production Hours (mil.)	Compensation Payroll ($ mil.)	Compensation Wages ($/hr)	Production ($ mil.) Cost of Materials	Production ($ mil.) Value of Shipments	Production ($ mil.) Capital Inves.
1987	764	31.7	19.3	39.2	955.7	13.81	5,673.4	11,558.5	338.7
1988	749	33.3	21.0	41.4	1,011.8	13.85	5,995.9	12,306.3	368.3
1989	731	31.6	22.0	39.8	1,093.1	14.36	6,790.8	13,280.7	396.0
1990	715	31.5	22.8	42.7	1,197.7	14.65	7,509.8	15,373.4	475.8
1991	686	36.6	23.1	44.1	1,220.7	14.67	7,158.9	15,298.5	630.8
1992	710	32.9	20.0	41.0	1,175.9	14.85	6,960.1	14,760.9	571.4
1993	704	31.2	17.9	38.1	1,144.3	15.06	7,174.4	15,457.7	513.8
1994	685	31.3	18.5	38.8	1,166.9	14.92	7,077.0	14,527.7	454.4
1995	674	32.1	18.3	39.1	1,231.6	15.33	6,917.2	16,131.8	363.6
1996	692[1]	30.3	16.8	35.4	1,172.5	15.68	6,708.5	15,778.5	426.9
1997	688[1]	31.0[1]	18.6[1]	38.2[1]	1,290.0[1]	16.33[1]	7,392.3[1]	17,386.7[1]	536.2[1]
1998	685[1]	30.7[1]	18.5[1]	37.9[1]	1,319.0[1]	16.64[1]	7,633.8[1]	17,954.9[1]	553.4[1]
1999	682[1]	30.5[1]	18.3[1]	37.7[1]	1,347.9[1]	16.95[1]	7,875.4[1]	18,523.0[1]	570.6[1]
2000	679[1]	30.3[1]	18.1[1]	37.4[1]	1,376.9[1]	17.25[1]	8,116.9[1]	19,091.2[1]	587.8[1]

Source: 1987 and 1992 Economic Census; *Annual Survey of Manufactures*, 88-91, 93-96. Establishment counts for non-Census years are from *County Business Patterns*. Extracted from *Manufacturing USA*, 6th Edition, Gale, 1998. Note: 1. Projections by the editors.

SIC 2841 SOAPS AND OTHER DETERGENTS: INDICES OF CHANGE

Year	Estab- lish- ments	Employment Total (000)	Employment Production Workers (000)	Employment Production Hours (mil.)	Compensation Payroll ($ mil.)	Compensation Wages ($/hr)	Production ($ mil.) Cost of Materials	Production ($ mil.) Value of Shipments	Production ($ mil.) Capital Inves.
1987	108	96	96	96	81	93	82	78	59
1988	105	101	105	101	86	93	86	83	64
1989	103	96	110	97	93	97	98	90	69
1990	101	96	114	104	102	99	108	104	83
1991	97	111	116	108	104	99	103	104	110
1992	100	100	100	100	100	100	100	100	100
1993	99	95	90	93	97	101	103	105	90
1994	96	95	93	95	99	100	102	98	80
1995	95	98	91	95	105	103	99	109	64
1996	97[1]	92	84	86	100	106	96	107	75
1997	97[1]	94[1]	93[1]	93[1]	110[1]	110[1]	106[1]	118[1]	94[1]
1998	97[1]	93[1]	92[1]	93[1]	112[1]	112[1]	110[1]	122[1]	97[1]
1999	96[1]	93[1]	91[1]	92[1]	115[1]	114[1]	113[1]	125[1]	100[1]
2000	96[1]	92[1]	91[1]	91[1]	117[1]	116[1]	117[1]	129[1]	103[1]

Source: Same as General Statistics. Values reflect change from the base year, 1992. Values above 100 mean greater than 1992, values below 100 mean less than 1992, and a value of 100 in the 1982-91 or 1993-2000 period means same as 1992. Note: 1. Projections by the editors.

SIC 2841 SOAPS AND OTHER DETERGENTS: SELECTED RATIOS

For 1996	Average of All Manufacturing	Analyzed Industry	Index
Employees per Establishment	49	44	90
Payroll per Establishment	1,574,035	1,695,549	108
Payroll per Employee	32,350	38,696	120
Production Workers per Establishment	34	24	71
Wages per Establishment	890,687	802,688	90
Wages per Production Worker	26,064	33,040	127
Hours per Production Worker	2,055	2,107	103
Wages per Hour	12.68	15.68	124
Value Added per Establishment	4,932,584	13,046,254	264
Value Added per Employee	101,376	297,746	294
Value Added per Production Worker	144,340	537,006	372
Cost per Establishment	5,569,059	9,701,143	174
Cost per Employee	114,457	221,403	193
Cost per Production Worker	162,965	399,315	245
Shipments per Establishment	10,422,474	22,817,244	219
Shipments per Employee	214,207	520,743	243
Shipments per Production Worker	304,989	939,196	308
Investment per Establishment	394,953	617,339	156
Investment per Employee	8,117	14,089	174
Investment per Production Worker	11,557	25,411	220

Source: Same as General Statistics. The 'Average of All Manufacturing' column represents the average of all manufacturing industries reported for the most recent complete year available. The Index shows the relationship between the Average and the Analyzed Industry. For example, 100 means that they are equal; 500 that the Analyzed Industry is five times the average; 50 means that the Analyzed Industry is half the national average. The abbreviation 'na' is used to show that data are 'not available'.

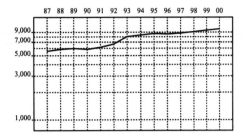

Revenues ($ millions)

SIC 2842 POLISHES AND SANITATION GOODS: GENERAL STATISTICS

| Year | Estab-lish-ments | Employment | | | Compensation | | Production ($ mil.) | | |
| | | Total (000) | Production | | Payroll ($ mil.) | Wages ($/hr) | Cost of Materials | Value of Shipments | Capital Inves. |
			Workers (000)	Hours (mil.)					
1987	726	20.6	13.2	26.5	500.4	9.89	1,943.8	5,593.9	117.7
1988	683	20.5	13.4	27.0	502.2	10.06	2,109.8	5,857.7	71.7
1989	643	21.3	13.4	26.7	555.6	10.24	2,299.5	5,987.4	141.1
1990	636	21.4	12.3	24.4	532.2	10.63	2,167.9	5,847.9	95.0
1991	656	19.6	12.2	24.4	573.4	11.09	2,283.9	6,171.5	137.2
1992	749	22.0	13.4	27.2	662.4	11.84	2,463.4	6,676.2	121.5
1993	732	22.8	13.8	27.2	707.7	11.94	2,963.8	8,078.6	130.4
1994	713	21.2	12.9	25.6	649.0	11.17	2,912.2	8,371.7	123.5
1995	693	23.0	14.0	27.7	702.3	11.49	3,203.3	8,700.3	154.7
1996	667[1]	24.2	14.2	28.6	737.1	11.49	3,154.0	8,601.7	172.8
1997	661[1]	22.4[1]	13.3[1]	26.4[1]	741.6[1]	12.37[1]	3,226.9[1]	8,800.6[1]	161.2[1]
1998	655[1]	22.5[1]	13.3[1]	26.3[1]	764.4[1]	12.63[1]	3,344.3[1]	9,120.7[1]	167.4[1]
1999	648[1]	22.6[1]	13.3[1]	26.2[1]	787.3[1]	12.89[1]	3,461.6[1]	9,440.7[1]	173.6[1]
2000	642[1]	22.7[1]	13.3[1]	26.2[1]	810.1[1]	13.16[1]	3,579.0[1]	9,760.8[1]	179.8[1]

Source: 1987 and 1992 Economic Census; *Annual Survey of Manufactures*, 88-91, 93-96. Establishment counts for non-Census years are from *County Business Patterns*. Extracted from *Manufacturing USA*, 6th Edition, Gale, 1998. Note: 1. Projections by the editors.

SIC 2842 POLISHES AND SANITATION GOODS: INDICES OF CHANGE

| Year | Estab-lish-ments | Employment | | | Compensation | | Production ($ mil.) | | |
| | | Total (000) | Production | | Payroll ($ mil.) | Wages ($/hr) | Cost of Materials | Value of Shipments | Capital Inves. |
			Workers (000)	Hours (mil.)					
1987	97	94	99	97	76	84	79	84	97
1988	91	93	100	99	76	85	86	88	59
1989	86	97	100	98	84	86	93	90	116
1990	85	97	92	90	80	90	88	88	78
1991	88	89	91	90	87	94	93	92	113
1992	100	100	100	100	100	100	100	100	100
1993	98	104	103	100	107	101	120	121	107
1994	95	96	96	94	98	94	118	125	102
1995	93	105	104	102	106	97	130	130	127
1996	89[1]	110	106	105	111	97	128	129	142
1997	88[1]	102[1]	99[1]	97[1]	112[1]	104[1]	131[1]	132[1]	133[1]
1998	87[1]	102[1]	99[1]	97[1]	115[1]	107[1]	136[1]	137[1]	138[1]
1999	87[1]	103[1]	99[1]	96[1]	119[1]	109[1]	141[1]	141[1]	143[1]
2000	86[1]	103[1]	99[1]	96[1]	122[1]	111[1]	145[1]	146[1]	148[1]

Source: Same as General Statistics. Values reflect change from the base year, 1992. Values above 100 mean greater than 1992, values below 100 mean less than 1992, and a value of 100 in the 1982-91 or 1993-2000 period means same as 1992. Note: 1. Projections by the editors.

SIC 2842 POLISHES AND SANITATION GOODS: SELECTED RATIOS

For 1996	Average of All Manufacturing	Analyzed Industry	Index
Employees per Establishment	49	36	75
Payroll per Establishment	1,574,035	1,104,333	70
Payroll per Employee	32,350	30,459	94
Production Workers per Establishment	34	21	62
Wages per Establishment	890,687	492,334	55
Wages per Production Worker	26,064	23,142	89
Hours per Production Worker	2,055	2,014	98
Wages per Hour	12.68	11.49	91
Value Added per Establishment	4,932,584	8,127,060	165
Value Added per Employee	101,376	224,153	221
Value Added per Production Worker	144,340	382,007	265
Cost per Establishment	5,569,059	4,725,366	85
Cost per Employee	114,457	130,331	114
Cost per Production Worker	162,965	222,113	136
Shipments per Establishment	10,422,474	12,887,185	124
Shipments per Employee	214,207	355,442	166
Shipments per Production Worker	304,989	605,754	199
Investment per Establishment	394,953	258,891	66
Investment per Employee	8,117	7,140	88
Investment per Production Worker	11,557	12,169	105

Source: Same as General Statistics. The 'Average of All Manufacturing' column represents the average of all manufacturing industries reported for the most recent complete year available. The Index shows the relationship between the Average and the Analyzed Industry. For example, 100 means that they are equal; 500 that the Analyzed Industry is five times the average; 50 means that the Analyzed Industry is half the national average. The abbreviation 'na' is used to show that data are 'not available'.

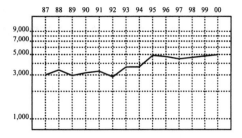

Revenues ($ millions)

SIC 2843 SURFACE ACTIVE AGENTS: GENERAL STATISTICS

Year	Estab-lish-ments	Employment Total (000)	Production Workers (000)	Production Hours (mil.)	Compensation Payroll ($ mil.)	Compensation Wages ($/hr)	Production ($ mil.) Cost of Materials	Production ($ mil.) Value of Shipments	Production ($ mil.) Capital Inves.
1987	217	9.1	4.7	10.0	289.8	13.37	1,683.7	3,002.2	103.4
1988	204	9.0	4.8	10.2	296.5	13.70	2,045.4	3,398.5	191.7
1989	196	9.0	4.6	10.3	311.8	13.32	1,771.8	2,959.2	129.3
1990	197	8.8	4.6	10.2	332.1	13.71	1,945.7	3,168.3	165.0
1991	200	9.3	4.8	10.7	339.5	14.28	2,024.8	3,298.8	157.4
1992	205	8.2	4.2	9.0	320.3	14.94	1,689.5	2,864.0	92.4
1993	199	8.6	4.3	9.4	358.0	15.95	2,087.8	3,660.5	203.4
1994	197	8.0	3.9	8.8	347.1	16.57	2,080.6	3,678.3	204.5
1995	199	8.0	4.0	9.2	343.4	16.35	2,422.7	4,886.6	122.4
1996	196[1]	8.8	4.5	10.6	400.3	16.55	2,532.4	4,741.3	161.1
1997	195[1]	8.3[1]	4.4[1]	10.1[1]	393.4[1]	17.53[1]	2,396.6[1]	4,487.0[1]	186.3[1]
1998	194[1]	8.2[1]	4.4[1]	10.2[1]	404.3[1]	18.04[1]	2,483.4[1]	4,649.6[1]	193.4[1]
1999	193[1]	8.2[1]	4.4[1]	10.2[1]	415.3[1]	18.54[1]	2,570.3[1]	4,812.2[1]	200.6[1]
2000	192[1]	8.1[1]	4.4[1]	10.3[1]	426.2[1]	19.04[1]	2,657.1[1]	4,974.8[1]	207.8[1]

Source: 1987 and 1992 Economic Census; *Annual Survey of Manufactures*, 88-91, 93-96. Establishment counts for non-Census years are from *County Business Patterns*. Extracted from *Manufacturing USA*, 6th Edition, Gale, 1998. Note: 1. Projections by the editors.

SIC 2843 SURFACE ACTIVE AGENTS: INDICES OF CHANGE

Year	Estab-lish-ments	Employment Total (000)	Production Workers (000)	Production Hours (mil.)	Compensation Payroll ($ mil.)	Compensation Wages ($/hr)	Production ($ mil.) Cost of Materials	Production ($ mil.) Value of Shipments	Production ($ mil.) Capital Inves.
1987	106	111	112	111	90	89	100	105	112
1988	100	110	114	113	93	92	121	119	207
1989	96	110	110	114	97	89	105	103	140
1990	96	107	110	113	104	92	115	111	179
1991	98	113	114	119	106	96	120	115	170
1992	100	100	100	100	100	100	100	100	100
1993	97	105	102	104	112	107	124	128	220
1994	96	98	93	98	108	111	123	128	221
1995	97	98	95	102	107	109	143	171	132
1996	96[1]	107	107	118	125	111	150	166	174
1997	95[1]	101[1]	104[1]	112[1]	123[1]	117[1]	142[1]	157[1]	202[1]
1998	95[1]	101[1]	104[1]	113[1]	126[1]	121[1]	147[1]	162[1]	209[1]
1999	94[1]	100[1]	104[1]	114[1]	130[1]	124[1]	152[1]	168[1]	217[1]
2000	94[1]	99[1]	104[1]	114[1]	133[1]	127[1]	157[1]	174[1]	225[1]

Source: Same as General Statistics. Values reflect change from the base year, 1992. Values above 100 mean greater than 1992, values below 100 mean less than 1992, and a value of 100 in the 1982-91 or 1993-2000 period means same as 1992. Note: 1. Projections by the editors.

SIC 2843 SURFACE ACTIVE AGENTS: SELECTED RATIOS

For 1996	Average of All Manufacturing	Analyzed Industry	Index
Employees per Establishment	49	45	92
Payroll per Establishment	1,574,035	2,039,831	130
Payroll per Employee	32,350	45,489	141
Production Workers per Establishment	34	23	67
Wages per Establishment	890,687	893,948	100
Wages per Production Worker	26,064	38,984	150
Hours per Production Worker	2,055	2,356	115
Wages per Hour	12.68	16.55	131
Value Added per Establishment	4,932,584	11,210,662	227
Value Added per Employee	101,376	250,000	247
Value Added per Production Worker	144,340	488,889	339
Cost per Establishment	5,569,059	12,904,491	232
Cost per Employee	114,457	287,773	251
Cost per Production Worker	162,965	562,756	345
Shipments per Establishment	10,422,474	24,160,505	232
Shipments per Employee	214,207	538,784	252
Shipments per Production Worker	304,989	1,053,622	345
Investment per Establishment	394,953	820,926	208
Investment per Employee	8,117	18,307	226
Investment per Production Worker	11,557	35,800	310

Source: Same as General Statistics. The 'Average of All Manufacturing' column represents the average of all manufacturing industries reported for the most recent complete year available. The Index shows the relationship between the Average and the Analyzed Industry. For example, 100 means that they are equal; 500 that the Analyzed Industry is five times the average; 50 means that the Analyzed Industry is half the national average. The abbreviation 'na' is used to show that data are 'not available'.

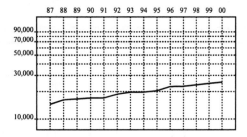

87 88 89 90 91 92 93 94 95 96 97 98 99 00

Revenues ($ millions)

SIC 2844 TOILET PREPARATIONS: GENERAL STATISTICS

Year	Estab-lish-ments	Employment Total (000)	Production Workers (000)	Production Hours (mil.)	Compensation Payroll ($ mil.)	Compensation Wages ($/hr)	Production ($ mil.) Cost of Materials	Production ($ mil.) Value of Shipments	Production ($ mil.) Capital Inves.
1987	694	57.9	35.1	69.9	1,352.8	9.22	3,881.6	14,592.9	225.5
1988	687	64.9	40.5	78.1	1,551.3	9.08	4,445.1	16,293.6	292.6
1989	676	63.6	39.4	75.4	1,615.5	9.69	4,758.2	16,641.9	313.7
1990	682	63.6	38.1	74.3	1,620.6	10.14	4,904.6	17,048.4	280.4
1991	674	57.4	35.6	69.8	1,616.3	10.81	5,046.3	17,085.4	299.5
1992	756	60.1	37.2	75.6	1,783.3	10.82	5,611.3	18,753.5	507.3
1993	778	61.7	38.6	79.7	1,857.8	10.59	6,152.6	19,706.4	472.6
1994	767	57.6	35.3	72.8	1,796.6	10.93	6,482.1	19,736.0	490.6
1995	760	59.5	37.4	75.2	1,871.5	11.49	7,023.2	20,438.9	410.0
1996	775[1]	62.9	39.1	78.5	2,078.7	11.89	7,537.4	22,687.5	542.7
1997	786[1]	60.7[1]	38.3[1]	78.4[1]	2,073.7[1]	12.09[1]	7,590.2[1]	22,846.5[1]	513.1[1]
1998	797[1]	60.7[1]	38.5[1]	79.1[1]	2,139.3[1]	12.38[1]	7,870.4[1]	23,689.7[1]	534.7[1]
1999	808[1]	60.7[1]	38.7[1]	79.9[1]	2,204.9[1]	12.67[1]	8,150.5[1]	24,532.9[1]	556.2[1]
2000	819[1]	60.7[1]	38.9[1]	80.6[1]	2,270.5[1]	12.97[1]	8,430.6[1]	25,376.1[1]	577.8[1]

Source: 1987 and 1992 Economic Census; *Annual Survey of Manufactures*, 88-91, 93-96. Establishment counts for non-Census years are from *County Business Patterns*. Extracted from *Manufacturing USA*, 6th Edition, Gale, 1998. Note: 1. Projections by the editors.

SIC 2844 TOILET PREPARATIONS: INDICES OF CHANGE

Year	Estab-lish-ments	Employment Total (000)	Production Workers (000)	Production Hours (mil.)	Compensation Payroll ($ mil.)	Compensation Wages ($/hr)	Production ($ mil.) Cost of Materials	Production ($ mil.) Value of Shipments	Production ($ mil.) Capital Inves.
1987	92	96	94	92	76	85	69	78	44
1988	91	108	109	103	87	84	79	87	58
1989	89	106	106	100	91	90	85	89	62
1990	90	106	102	98	91	94	87	91	55
1991	89	96	96	92	91	100	90	91	59
1992	100	100	100	100	100	100	100	100	100
1993	103	103	104	105	104	98	110	105	93
1994	101	96	95	96	101	101	116	105	97
1995	101	99	101	99	105	106	125	109	81
1996	103[1]	105	105	104	117	110	134	121	107
1997	104[1]	101[1]	103[1]	104[1]	116[1]	112[1]	135[1]	122[1]	101[1]
1998	105[1]	101[1]	103[1]	105[1]	120[1]	114[1]	140[1]	126[1]	105[1]
1999	107[1]	101[1]	104[1]	106[1]	124[1]	117[1]	145[1]	131[1]	110[1]
2000	108[1]	101[1]	104[1]	107[1]	127[1]	120[1]	150[1]	135[1]	114[1]

Source: Same as General Statistics. Values reflect change from the base year, 1992. Values above 100 mean greater than 1992, values below 100 mean less than 1992, and a value of 100 in the 1982-91 or 1993-2000 period means same as 1992. Note: 1. Projections by the editors.

SIC 2844 TOILET PREPARATIONS: SELECTED RATIOS

For 1996	Average of All Manufacturing	Analyzed Industry	Index
Employees per Establishment	49	81	167
Payroll per Establishment	1,574,035	2,682,003	170
Payroll per Employee	32,350	33,048	102
Production Workers per Establishment	34	50	148
Wages per Establishment	890,687	1,204,257	135
Wages per Production Worker	26,064	23,871	92
Hours per Production Worker	2,055	2,008	98
Wages per Hour	12.68	11.89	94
Value Added per Establishment	4,932,584	19,553,065	396
Value Added per Employee	101,376	240,933	238
Value Added per Production Worker	144,340	387,588	269
Cost per Establishment	5,569,059	9,724,988	175
Cost per Employee	114,457	119,831	105
Cost per Production Worker	162,965	192,772	118
Shipments per Establishment	10,422,474	29,272,118	281
Shipments per Employee	214,207	360,692	168
Shipments per Production Worker	304,989	580,243	190
Investment per Establishment	394,953	700,208	177
Investment per Employee	8,117	8,628	106
Investment per Production Worker	11,557	13,880	120

Source: Same as General Statistics. The 'Average of All Manufacturing' column represents the average of all manufacturing industries reported for the most recent complete year available. The Index shows the relationship between the Average and the Analyzed Industry. For example, 100 means that they are equal; 500 that the Analyzed Industry is five times the average; 50 means that the Analyzed Industry is half the national average. The abbreviation 'na' is used to show that data are 'not available'.

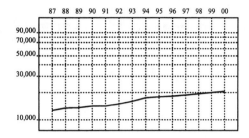

Revenues ($ millions)

SIC 2851 PAINTS AND ALLIED PRODUCTS: GENERAL STATISTICS

| Year | Estab-lish-ments | Employment | | | Compensation | | Production ($ mil.) | | |
| | | Total (000) | Production | | Payroll ($ mil.) | Wages ($/hr) | Cost of Materials | Value of Shipments | Capital Inves. |
			Workers (000)	Hours (mil.)					
1987	1,426	55.2	28.3	56.3	1,491.3	11.16	6,508.9	12,702.4	275.1
1988		56.9	28.3	57.0	1,564.7	11.20	7,088.6	13,531.7	252.7
1989	1,409	55.0	27.7	55.8	1,607.5	11.69	7,291.5	13,656.3	240.8
1990		53.9	27.2	55.6	1,627.6	11.89	7,461.2	14,238.7	271.3
1991		51.1	25.2	52.1	1,568.2	12.09	7,434.7	14,254.9	255.7
1992	1,418	51.2	25.7	53.2	1,711.4	12.72	7,806.2	14,973.7	290.2
1993		50.3	25.9	53.4	1,697.7	13.00	8,293.3	16,030.3	256.3
1994		50.1	27.0	55.7	1,911.1	13.98	9,125.4	17,544.4	279.5
1995		52.4	27.7	57.3	1,981.1	13.88	9,585.4	17,942.6	417.1
1996		51.1	27.9	57.9	1,939.8	14.61	9,849.3	18,257.4	403.7
1997		50.6[1]	26.5[1]	55.8[1]	2,016.9[1]	14.73[1]	10,129.5[1]	18,776.8[1]	334.9[1]
1998		50.2[1]	26.4[1]	55.8[1]	2,072.9[1]	15.11[1]	10,466.8[1]	19,402.1[1]	340.4[1]
1999		49.9[1]	26.2[1]	55.8[1]	2,129.0[1]	15.48[1]	10,804.1[1]	20,027.3[1]	345.9[1]
2000		49.5[1]	26.1[1]	55.8[1]	2,185.0[1]	15.86[1]	11,141.4[1]	20,652.5[1]	351.4[1]

Source: 1987 and 1992 Economic Census; *Annual Survey of Manufactures*, 88-91, 93-96. Establishment counts for non-Census years are from *County Business Patterns*. Extracted from *Manufacturing USA*, 6th Edition, Gale, 1998. Note: 1. Projections by the editors.

SIC 2851 PAINTS AND ALLIED PRODUCTS: INDICES OF CHANGE

| Year | Estab-lish-ments | Employment | | | Compensation | | Production ($ mil.) | | |
| | | Total (000) | Production | | Payroll ($ mil.) | Wages ($/hr) | Cost of Materials | Value of Shipments | Capital Inves. |
			Workers (000)	Hours (mil.)					
1987	101	108	110	106	87	88	83	85	95
1988		111	110	107	91	88	91	90	87
1989	99	107	108	105	94	92	93	91	83
1990		105	106	105	95	93	96	95	93
1991		100	98	98	92	95	95	95	88
1992	100	100	100	100	100	100	100	100	100
1993		98	101	100	99	102	106	107	88
1994		98	105	105	112	110	117	117	96
1995		102	108	108	116	109	123	120	144
1996		100	109	109	113	115	126	122	139
1997		99[1]	103[1]	105[1]	118[1]	116[1]	130[1]	125[1]	115[1]
1998		98[1]	103[1]	105[1]	121[1]	119[1]	134[1]	130[1]	117[1]
1999		97[1]	102[1]	105[1]	124[1]	122[1]	138[1]	134[1]	119[1]
2000		97[1]	102[1]	105[1]	128[1]	125[1]	143[1]	138[1]	121[1]

Source: Same as General Statistics. Values reflect change from the base year, 1992. Values above 100 mean greater than 1992, values below 100 mean less than 1992, and a value of 100 in the 1982-91 or 1993-2000 period means same as 1992. Note: 1. Projections by the editors.

SIC 2851 PAINTS AND ALLIED PRODUCTS: SELECTED RATIOS

For 1996	Average of All Manufacturing	Analyzed Industry	Index
Employees per Establishment	46	36	79
Payroll per Establishment	1,332,320	1,206,911	91
Payroll per Employee	29,181	33,426	115
Production Workers per Establishment	31	18	58
Wages per Establishment	734,496	477,224	65
Wages per Production Worker	23,390	26,331	113
Hours per Production Worker	2,025	2,070	102
Wages per Hour	11.55	12.72	110
Value Added per Establishment	3,842,210	5,048,449	131
Value Added per Employee	84,153	139,818	166
Value Added per Production Worker	122,353	278,549	228
Cost per Establishment	4,239,462	5,505,078	130
Cost per Employee	92,853	152,465	164
Cost per Production Worker	135,003	303,743	225
Shipments per Establishment	8,100,800	10,559,732	130
Shipments per Employee	177,425	292,455	165
Shipments per Production Worker	257,966	582,634	226
Investment per Establishment	278,244	204,654	74
Investment per Employee	6,094	5,668	93
Investment per Production Worker	8,861	11,292	127

Source: Same as General Statistics. The 'Average of All Manufacturing' column represents the average of all manufacturing industries reported for the most recent complete year available. The Index shows the relationship between the Average and the Analyzed Industry. For example, 100 means that they are equal; 500 that the Analyzed Industry is five times the average; 50 means that the Analyzed Industry is half the national average. The abbreviation 'na' is used to show that data are 'not available'.

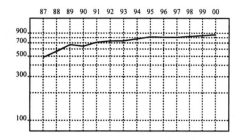

Revenues ($ millions)

SIC 2861 GUM AND WOOD CHEMICALS: GENERAL STATISTICS

Year	Estab-lish-ments	Employment			Compensation		Production ($ mil.)		
		Total (000)	Production						
			Workers (000)	Hours (mil.)	Payroll ($ mil.)	Wages ($/hr)	Cost of Materials	Value of Shipments	Capital Inves.
1987	77	2.6	2.1	4.1	57.4	10.24	275.4	486.5	35.2
1988	75	2.7	2.2	4.3	61.1	10.37	299.8	566.2	19.8
1989	75	2.8	2.1	4.3	65.9	10.79	345.9	668.9	24.7
1990	76	2.7	2.0	3.8	59.9	10.89	304.9	642.9	40.2
1991	79	2.5	2.0	4.0	63.6	11.02	360.9	711.4	19.8
1992	76	2.5	1.9	4.0	67.8	11.75	352.1	734.6	42.8
1993	73	2.6	2.0	4.2	72.1	11.36	373.7	738.8	33.4
1994	79	2.8	2.2	4.5	76.5	11.69	367.2	774.1	42.1
1995	77	2.9	2.3	4.9	89.2	12.63	338.3	816.9	31.8
1996	70[1]	2.9	2.2	5.1	88.4	11.86	379.1	808.7	26.6
1997	68[1]	2.3[1]	1.8[1]	3.7[1]	73.9[1]	12.65[1]	378.2[1]	806.8[1]	33.4[1]
1998	66[1]	2.2[1]	1.7[1]	3.6[1]	74.1[1]	12.91[1]	387.0[1]	825.5[1]	33.8[1]
1999	65[1]	2.1[1]	1.6[1]	3.5[1]	74.3[1]	13.18[1]	395.8[1]	844.2[1]	34.1[1]
2000	63[1]	2.0[1]	1.6[1]	3.3[1]	74.5[1]	13.44[1]	404.5[1]	863.0[1]	34.5[1]

Source: 1987 and 1992 Economic Census; *Annual Survey of Manufactures*, 88-91, 93-96. Establishment counts for non-Census years are from *County Business Patterns*. Extracted from *Manufacturing USA*, 6th Edition, Gale, 1998. Note: 1. Projections by the editors.

SIC 2861 GUM AND WOOD CHEMICALS: INDICES OF CHANGE

Year	Estab-lish-ments	Employment			Compensation		Production ($ mil.)		
		Total (000)	Production						
			Workers (000)	Hours (mil.)	Payroll ($ mil.)	Wages ($/hr)	Cost of Materials	Value of Shipments	Capital Inves.
1987	101	104	111	102	85	87	78	66	82
1988	99	108	116	108	90	88	85	77	46
1989	99	112	111	108	97	92	98	91	58
1990	100	108	105	95	88	93	87	88	94
1991	104	100	105	100	94	94	102	97	46
1992	100	100	100	100	100	100	100	100	100
1993	96	104	105	105	106	97	106	101	78
1994	104	112	116	113	113	99	104	105	98
1995	101	116	121	123	132	107	96	111	74
1996	92[1]	116	116	127	130	101	108	110	62
1997	90[1]	90[1]	93[1]	94[1]	109[1]	108[1]	107[1]	110[1]	78[1]
1998	87[1]	86[1]	89[1]	90[1]	109[1]	110[1]	110[1]	112[1]	79[1]
1999	85[1]	82[1]	86[1]	86[1]	110[1]	112[1]	112[1]	115[1]	80[1]
2000	83[1]	78[1]	82[1]	83[1]	110[1]	114[1]	115[1]	117[1]	81[1]

Source: Same as General Statistics. Values reflect change from the base year, 1992. Values above 100 mean greater than 1992, values below 100 mean less than 1992, and a value of 100 in the 1982-91 or 1993-2000 period means same as 1992. Note: 1. Projections by the editors.

SIC 2861 GUM AND WOOD CHEMICALS: SELECTED RATIOS

For 1996	Average of All Manufacturing	Analyzed Industry	Index
Employees per Establishment	49	42	85
Payroll per Establishment	1,574,035	1,266,436	80
Payroll per Employee	32,350	30,483	94
Production Workers per Establishment	34	32	92
Wages per Establishment	890,687	866,534	97
Wages per Production Worker	26,064	27,494	105
Hours per Production Worker	2,055	2,318	113
Wages per Hour	12.68	11.86	94
Value Added per Establishment	4,932,584	6,310,690	128
Value Added per Employee	101,376	151,897	150
Value Added per Production Worker	144,340	200,227	139
Cost per Establishment	5,569,059	5,431,061	98
Cost per Employee	114,457	130,724	114
Cost per Production Worker	162,965	172,318	106
Shipments per Establishment	10,422,474	11,585,595	111
Shipments per Employee	214,207	278,862	130
Shipments per Production Worker	304,989	367,591	121
Investment per Establishment	394,953	381,077	96
Investment per Employee	8,117	9,172	113
Investment per Production Worker	11,557	12,091	105

Source: Same as General Statistics. The 'Average of All Manufacturing' column represents the average of all manufacturing industries reported for the most recent complete year available. The Index shows the relationship between the Average and the Analyzed Industry. For example, 100 means that they are equal; 500 that the Analyzed Industry is five times the average; 50 means that the Analyzed Industry is half the national average. The abbreviation 'na' is used to show that data are 'not available'.

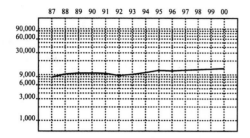

Revenues ($ millions)

SIC 2865 CYCLIC CRUDES AND INTERMEDIATES: GENERAL STATISTICS

Year	Estab-lish-ments	Employment			Compensation		Production ($ mil.)		
		Total (000)	Production		Payroll ($ mil.)	Wages ($/hr)	Cost of Materials	Value of Shipments	Capital Inves.
			Workers (000)	Hours (mil.)					
1987	186	22.8	13.4	27.6	786.6	15.76	5,502.7	8,859.4	378.8
1988	186	23.9	13.9	29.5	877.8	16.01	6,121.7	10,301.9	428.3
1989	181	23.3	13.9	29.5	873.6	16.34	7,020.7	10,812.0	584.9
1990	185	23.4	13.9	29.6	910.9	16.84	7,027.7	10,892.6	954.9
1991	190	23.5	14.1	30.9	962.0	16.96	6,796.4	10,651.8	713.9
1992	206	22.2	13.2	29.1	934.6	17.10	6,311.4	9,572.8	540.7
1993	213	23.3	13.4	28.9	1,028.1	18.27	6,457.2	10,177.0	669.5
1994	210	22.7	13.1	28.9	1,017.6	18.17	6,954.1	11,151.5	564.6
1995	209	22.6	13.2	28.6	1,023.5	18.54	7,157.2	12,419.0	844.6
1996	208[1]	22.8	13.2	29.4	1,086.7	18.90	7,366.5	12,123.9	1,032.9
1997	210[1]	21.9[1]	12.8[1]	28.8[1]	1,102.2[1]	19.69[1]	7,618.0[1]	12,537.8[1]	875.7[1]
1998	212[1]	21.7[1]	12.6[1]	28.8[1]	1,130.4[1]	20.14[1]	7,838.7[1]	12,901.0[1]	912.8[1]
1999	214[1]	21.5[1]	12.5[1]	28.7[1]	1,158.7[1]	20.59[1]	8,059.4[1]	13,264.2[1]	950.0[1]
2000	217[1]	21.3[1]	12.4[1]	28.7[1]	1,186.9[1]	21.04[1]	8,280.0[1]	13,627.4[1]	987.1[1]

Source: 1987 and 1992 Economic Census; *Annual Survey of Manufactures,* 88-91, 93-96. Establishment counts for non-Census years are from *County Business Patterns.* Extracted from *Manufacturing USA,* 6th Edition, Gale, 1998. Note: 1. Projections by the editors.

SIC 2865 CYCLIC CRUDES AND INTERMEDIATES: INDICES OF CHANGE

Year	Estab-lish-ments	Employment			Compensation		Production ($ mil.)		
		Total (000)	Production		Payroll ($ mil.)	Wages ($/hr)	Cost of Materials	Value of Shipments	Capital Inves.
			Workers (000)	Hours (mil.)					
1987	90	103	102	95	84	92	87	93	70
1988	90	108	105	101	94	94	97	108	79
1989	88	105	105	101	93	96	111	113	108
1990	90	105	105	102	97	98	111	114	177
1991	92	106	107	106	103	99	108	111	132
1992	100	100	100	100	100	100	100	100	100
1993	103	105	102	99	110	107	102	106	124
1994	102	102	99	99	109	106	110	116	104
1995	101	102	100	98	110	108	113	130	156
1996	101[1]	103	100	101	116	111	117	127	191
1997	102[1]	99[1]	97[1]	99[1]	118[1]	115[1]	121[1]	131[1]	162[1]
1998	103[1]	98[1]	96[1]	99[1]	121[1]	118[1]	124[1]	135[1]	169[1]
1999	104[1]	97[1]	95[1]	99[1]	124[1]	120[1]	128[1]	139[1]	176[1]
2000	105[1]	96[1]	94[1]	99[1]	127[1]	123[1]	131[1]	142[1]	183[1]

Source: Same as General Statistics. Values reflect change from the base year, 1992. Values above 100 mean greater than 1992, values below 100 mean less than 1992, and a value of 100 in the 1982-91 or 1993-2000 period means same as 1992. Note: 1. Projections by the editors.

SIC 2865 CYCLIC CRUDES AND INTERMEDIATES: SELECTED RATIOS

For 1996	Average of All Manufacturing	Analyzed Industry	Index
Employees per Establishment	49	110	225
Payroll per Establishment	1,574,035	5,221,760	332
Payroll per Employee	32,350	47,662	147
Production Workers per Establishment	34	63	186
Wages per Establishment	890,687	2,670,032	300
Wages per Production Worker	26,064	42,095	162
Hours per Production Worker	2,055	2,227	108
Wages per Hour	12.68	18.90	149
Value Added per Establishment	4,932,584	22,703,390	460
Value Added per Employee	101,376	207,228	204
Value Added per Production Worker	144,340	357,939	248
Cost per Establishment	5,569,059	35,397,164	636
Cost per Employee	114,457	323,092	282
Cost per Production Worker	162,965	558,068	342
Shipments per Establishment	10,422,474	58,257,202	559
Shipments per Employee	214,207	531,750	248
Shipments per Production Worker	304,989	918,477	301
Investment per Establishment	394,953	4,963,243	1,257
Investment per Employee	8,117	45,303	558
Investment per Production Worker	11,557	78,250	677

Source: Same as General Statistics. The 'Average of All Manufacturing' column represents the average of all manufacturing industries reported for the most recent complete year available. The Index shows the relationship between the Average and the Analyzed Industry. For example, 100 means that they are equal; 500 that the Analyzed Industry is five times the average; 50 means that the Analyzed Industry is half the national average. The abbreviation 'na' is used to show that data are 'not available'.

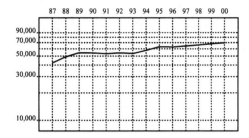

Revenues ($ millions)

SIC 2869 INDUSTRIAL ORGANIC CHEMICALS, NEC: GENERAL STATISTICS

Year	Estab-lish-ments	Employment			Compensation		Production ($ mil.)		
		Total (000)	Production		Payroll ($ mil.)	Wages ($/hr)	Cost of Materials	Value of Shipments	Capital Inves.
			Workers (000)	Hours (mil.)					
1987	699	100.3	57.9	122.4	3,696.4	16.03	24,226.0	42,189.1	1,986.9
1988	685	97.1	56.9	122.3	3,717.2	16.62	27,102.2	49,103.6	2,753.6
1989	651	100.0	58.3	125.1	3,944.8	17.17	29,433.1	54,512.4	3,484.2
1990	648	103.2	58.8	126.2	4,216.3	17.93	30,091.0	54,160.0	4,156.2
1991	661	101.0	58.4	125.0	4,403.0	18.61	30,671.3	53,069.3	4,537.6
1992	705	100.1	57.4	126.3	4,504.8	19.07	31,860.6	54,254.2	4,216.6
1993	695	97.5	57.5	127.0	4,503.0	19.01	30,666.7	53,364.2	3,358.3
1994	691	89.3	52.6	116.2	4,501.0	20.74	33,449.2	57,670.5	2,958.9
1995	698	92.1	53.9	118.3	4,801.0	21.10	35,357.9	63,303.1	4,063.8
1996	695[1]	100.3	59.3	128.7	5,589.9	22.22	39,189.6	62,739.3	5,209.5
1997	697[1]	94.5[1]	55.7[1]	123.3[1]	5,333.4[1]	22.47[1]	40,227.6[1]	64,401.1[1]	4,767.0[1]
1998	700[1]	93.9[1]	55.5[1]	123.3[1]	5,505.4[1]	23.13[1]	41,359.3[1]	66,212.8[1]	4,966.0[1]
1999	703[1]	93.2[1]	55.2[1]	123.2[1]	5,677.3[1]	23.79[1]	42,491.0[1]	68,024.6[1]	5,165.0[1]
2000	705[1]	92.6[1]	54.9[1]	123.1[1]	5,849.3[1]	24.45[1]	43,622.7[1]	69,836.3[1]	5,364.0[1]

Source: 1987 and 1992 Economic Census; *Annual Survey of Manufactures*, 88-91, 93-96. Establishment counts for non-Census years are from *County Business Patterns*. Extracted from *Manufacturing USA*, 6th Edition, Gale, 1998. Note: 1. Projections by the editors.

SIC 2869 INDUSTRIAL ORGANIC CHEMICALS, NEC: INDICES OF CHANGE

Year	Estab-lish-ments	Employment			Compensation		Production ($ mil.)		
		Total (000)	Production		Payroll ($ mil.)	Wages ($/hr)	Cost of Materials	Value of Shipments	Capital Inves.
			Workers (000)	Hours (mil.)					
1987	99	100	101	97	82	84	76	78	47
1988	97	97	99	97	83	87	85	91	65
1989	92	100	102	99	88	90	92	100	83
1990	92	103	102	100	94	94	94	100	99
1991	94	101	102	99	98	98	96	98	108
1992	100	100	100	100	100	100	100	100	100
1993	99	97	100	101	100	100	96	98	80
1994	98	89	92	92	100	109	105	106	70
1995	99	92	94	94	107	111	111	117	96
1996	99[1]	100	103	102	124	117	123	116	124
1997	99[1]	94[1]	97[1]	98[1]	118[1]	118[1]	126[1]	119[1]	113[1]
1998	99[1]	94[1]	97[1]	98[1]	122[1]	121[1]	130[1]	122[1]	118[1]
1999	100[1]	93[1]	96[1]	98[1]	126[1]	125[1]	133[1]	125[1]	122[1]
2000	100[1]	93[1]	96[1]	97[1]	130[1]	128[1]	137[1]	129[1]	127[1]

Source: Same as General Statistics. Values reflect change from the base year, 1992. Values above 100 mean greater than 1992, values below 100 mean less than 1992, and a value of 100 in the 1982-91 or 1993-2000 period means same as 1992. Note: 1. Projections by the editors.

SIC 2869 INDUSTRIAL ORGANIC CHEMICALS, NEC: SELECTED RATIOS

For 1996	Average of All Manufacturing	Analyzed Industry	Index
Employees per Establishment	49	144	297
Payroll per Establishment	1,574,035	8,046,559	511
Payroll per Employee	32,350	55,732	172
Production Workers per Establishment	34	85	250
Wages per Establishment	890,687	4,116,506	462
Wages per Production Worker	26,064	48,225	185
Hours per Production Worker	2,055	2,170	106
Wages per Hour	12.68	22.22	175
Value Added per Establishment	4,932,584	34,145,228	692
Value Added per Employee	101,376	236,496	233
Value Added per Production Worker	144,340	400,008	277
Cost per Establishment	5,569,059	56,412,715	1,013
Cost per Employee	114,457	390,724	341
Cost per Production Worker	162,965	660,870	406
Shipments per Establishment	10,422,474	90,312,080	867
Shipments per Employee	214,207	625,516	292
Shipments per Production Worker	304,989	1,057,998	347
Investment per Establishment	394,953	7,498,980	1,899
Investment per Employee	8,117	51,939	640
Investment per Production Worker	11,557	87,850	760

Source: Same as General Statistics. The 'Average of All Manufacturing' column represents the average of all manufacturing industries reported for the most recent complete year available. The Index shows the relationship between the Average and the Analyzed Industry. For example, 100 means that they are equal; 500 that the Analyzed Industry is five times the average; 50 means that the Analyzed Industry is half the national average. The abbreviation 'na' is used to show that data are 'not available'.

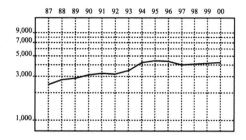

Revenues ($ millions)

SIC 2873 NITROGENOUS FERTILIZERS: GENERAL STATISTICS

Year	Estab-lish-ments	Employment Total (000)	Production Workers (000)	Production Hours (mil.)	Compensation Payroll ($ mil.)	Compensation Wages ($/hr)	Production ($ mil.) Cost of Materials	Production ($ mil.) Value of Shipments	Production ($ mil.) Capital Inves.
1987	164	7.4	4.5	9.6	222.8	13.04	1,503.5	2,447.2	36.9
1988	159	7.2	4.4	9.6	222.0	12.96	1,626.4	2,761.1	48.1
1989	157	6.8	4.4	9.7	231.6	14.03	1,724.4	2,866.0	122.7
1990	151	7.2	4.8	10.4	253.6	13.80	1,905.3	3,113.4	99.4
1991	155	7.3	4.7	10.3	260.2	14.77	1,982.1	3,238.1	220.1
1992	152	7.0	4.7	10.1	257.6	15.65	1,871.7	3,174.6	208.8
1993	166	7.0	4.7	10.3	270.4	16.11	2,118.8	3,467.1	186.0
1994	159	8.0	5.4	11.8	308.1	16.69	2,251.2	4,246.1	174.6
1995	164	7.3	5.1	11.7	300.2	16.37	1,998.4	4,445.9	175.8
1996	168[1]	7.5	5.1	11.6	313.6	16.95	2,109.8	4,375.7	304.7
1997	170[1]	6.6[1]	4.7[1]	10.7[1]	295.5[1]	17.23[1]	1,930.0[1]	4,002.9[1]	234.2[1]
1998	173[1]	6.5[1]	4.7[1]	10.7[1]	300.4[1]	17.61[1]	1,971.6[1]	4,089.1[1]	246.3[1]
1999	175[1]	6.4[1]	4.7[1]	10.7[1]	305.3[1]	17.98[1]	2,013.2[1]	4,175.3[1]	258.5[1]
2000	178[1]	6.3[1]	4.6[1]	10.7[1]	310.2[1]	18.36[1]	2,054.7[1]	4,261.5[1]	270.7[1]

Source: 1987 and 1992 Economic Census; *Annual Survey of Manufactures*, 88-91, 93-96. Establishment counts for non-Census years are from *County Business Patterns*. Extracted from *Manufacturing USA*, 6th Edition, Gale, 1998. Note: 1. Projections by the editors.

SIC 2873 NITROGENOUS FERTILIZERS: INDICES OF CHANGE

Year	Estab-lish-ments	Employment Total (000)	Production Workers (000)	Production Hours (mil.)	Compensation Payroll ($ mil.)	Compensation Wages ($/hr)	Production ($ mil.) Cost of Materials	Production ($ mil.) Value of Shipments	Production ($ mil.) Capital Inves.
1987	108	106	96	95	86	83	80	77	18
1988	105	103	94	95	86	83	87	87	23
1989	103	97	94	96	90	90	92	90	59
1990	99	103	102	103	98	88	102	98	48
1991	102	104	100	102	101	94	106	102	105
1992	100	100	100	100	100	100	100	100	100
1993	109	100	100	102	105	103	113	109	89
1994	105	114	115	117	120	107	120	134	84
1995	108	104	109	116	117	105	107	140	84
1996	110[1]	107	109	115	122	108	113	138	146
1997	112[1]	95[1]	100[1]	106[1]	115[1]	110[1]	103[1]	126[1]	112[1]
1998	114[1]	93[1]	100[1]	106[1]	117[1]	112[1]	105[1]	129[1]	118[1]
1999	115[1]	91[1]	99[1]	106[1]	119[1]	115[1]	108[1]	132[1]	124[1]
2000	117[1]	89[1]	99[1]	106[1]	120[1]	117[1]	110[1]	134[1]	130[1]

Source: Same as General Statistics. Values reflect change from the base year, 1992. Values above 100 mean greater than 1992, values below 100 mean less than 1992, and a value of 100 in the 1982-91 or 1993-2000 period means same as 1992. Note: 1. Projections by the editors.

SIC 2873 NITROGENOUS FERTILIZERS: SELECTED RATIOS

For 1996	Average of All Manufacturing	Analyzed Industry	Index
Employees per Establishment	49	45	92
Payroll per Establishment	1,574,035	1,869,479	119
Payroll per Employee	32,350	41,813	129
Production Workers per Establishment	34	30	89
Wages per Establishment	890,687	1,172,121	132
Wages per Production Worker	26,064	38,553	148
Hours per Production Worker	2,055	2,275	111
Wages per Hour	12.68	16.95	134
Value Added per Establishment	4,932,584	13,824,369	280
Value Added per Employee	101,376	309,200	305
Value Added per Production Worker	144,340	454,706	315
Cost per Establishment	5,569,059	12,577,255	226
Cost per Employee	114,457	281,307	246
Cost per Production Worker	162,965	413,686	254
Shipments per Establishment	10,422,474	26,085,077	250
Shipments per Employee	214,207	583,427	272
Shipments per Production Worker	304,989	857,980	281
Investment per Establishment	394,953	1,816,423	460
Investment per Employee	8,117	40,627	501
Investment per Production Worker	11,557	59,745	517

Source: Same as General Statistics. The 'Average of All Manufacturing' column represents the average of all manufacturing industries reported for the most recent complete year available. The Index shows the relationship between the Average and the Analyzed Industry. For example, 100 means that they are equal; 500 that the Analyzed Industry is five times the average; 50 means that the Analyzed Industry is half the national average. The abbreviation 'na' is used to show that data are 'not available'.

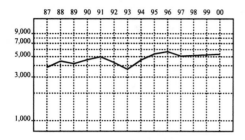

Revenues ($ millions)

SIC 2874 PHOSPHATIC FERTILIZERS: GENERAL STATISTICS

Year	Estab-lish-ments	Employment Total (000)	Production Workers (000)	Production Hours (mil.)	Compensation Payroll ($ mil.)	Compensation Wages ($/hr)	Production ($ mil.) Cost of Materials	Production ($ mil.) Value of Shipments	Production ($ mil.) Capital Inves.
1987	77	9.4	6.2	13.2	286.2	12.94	2,612.4	3,819.3	63.6
1988	75	10.4	7.1	15.8	324.7	13.10	2,882.2	4,474.2	133.7
1989	77	11.2	7.4	16.1	348.5	13.55	3,035.7	4,187.3	132.2
1990	75	11.0	7.5	17.0	364.0	13.70	3,462.4	4,636.2	137.5
1991	71	10.3	7.3	16.4	368.4	14.65	3,619.4	4,983.9	197.1
1992	75	9.5	6.7	15.8	342.1	13.82	3,076.4	4,332.8	307.7
1993	84	9.4	6.6	14.5	332.6	14.70	2,625.9	3,648.0	149.9
1994	74	8.5	6.2	13.7	339.0	16.69	3,006.8	4,596.5	159.3
1995	75	8.6	6.5	14.8	359.9	16.70	3,489.5	5,358.3	194.9
1996	63[1]	7.8	5.8	13.2	336.4	17.30	3,602.2	5,684.4	199.5
1997	60[1]	7.5[1]	5.6[1]	13.2[1]	352.8[1]	17.28[1]	3,213.4[1]	5,070.9[1]	194.7[1]
1998	57[1]	7.1[1]	5.3[1]	12.8[1]	354.8[1]	17.74[1]	3,268.0[1]	5,157.0[1]	197.8[1]
1999	54[1]	6.7[1]	5.1[1]	12.4[1]	356.9[1]	18.19[1]	3,322.5[1]	5,243.1[1]	201.0[1]
2000	51[1]	6.3[1]	4.9[1]	12.1[1]	358.9[1]	18.65[1]	3,377.1[1]	5,329.2[1]	204.2[1]

Source: 1987 and 1992 Economic Census; *Annual Survey of Manufactures*, 88-91, 93-96. Establishment counts for non-Census years are from *County Business Patterns*. Extracted from *Manufacturing USA*, 6th Edition, Gale, 1998. Note: 1. Projections by the editors.

SIC 2874 PHOSPHATIC FERTILIZERS: INDICES OF CHANGE

Year	Estab-lish-ments	Employment Total (000)	Production Workers (000)	Production Hours (mil.)	Compensation Payroll ($ mil.)	Compensation Wages ($/hr)	Production ($ mil.) Cost of Materials	Production ($ mil.) Value of Shipments	Production ($ mil.) Capital Inves.
1987	103	99	93	84	84	94	85	88	21
1988	100	109	106	100	95	95	94	103	43
1989	103	118	110	102	102	98	99	97	43
1990	100	116	112	108	106	99	113	107	45
1991	95	108	109	104	108	106	118	115	64
1992	100	100	100	100	100	100	100	100	100
1993	112	99	99	92	97	106	85	84	49
1994	99	89	93	87	99	121	98	106	52
1995	100	91	97	94	105	121	113	124	63
1996	84[1]	82	87	84	98	125	117	131	65
1997	80[1]	79[1]	83[1]	83[1]	103[1]	125[1]	104[1]	117[1]	63[1]
1998	76[1]	75[1]	80[1]	81[1]	104[1]	128[1]	106[1]	119[1]	64[1]
1999	72[1]	71[1]	76[1]	79[1]	104[1]	132[1]	108[1]	121[1]	65[1]
2000	68[1]	67[1]	73[1]	76[1]	105[1]	135[1]	110[1]	123[1]	66[1]

Source: Same as General Statistics. Values reflect change from the base year, 1992. Values above 100 mean greater than 1992, values below 100 mean less than 1992, and a value of 100 in the 1982-91 or 1993-2000 period means same as 1992. Note: 1. Projections by the editors.

SIC 2874 PHOSPHATIC FERTILIZERS: SELECTED RATIOS

For 1996	Average of All Manufacturing	Analyzed Industry	Index
Employees per Establishment	49	123	253
Payroll per Establishment	1,574,035	5,309,122	337
Payroll per Employee	32,350	43,128	133
Production Workers per Establishment	34	92	268
Wages per Establishment	890,687	3,604,017	405
Wages per Production Worker	26,064	39,372	151
Hours per Production Worker	2,055	2,276	111
Wages per Hour	12.68	17.30	136
Value Added per Establishment	4,932,584	32,596,497	661
Value Added per Employee	101,376	264,795	261
Value Added per Production Worker	144,340	356,103	247
Cost per Establishment	5,569,059	56,850,538	1,021
Cost per Employee	114,457	461,821	403
Cost per Production Worker	162,965	621,069	381
Shipments per Establishment	10,422,474	89,712,175	861
Shipments per Employee	214,207	728,769	340
Shipments per Production Worker	304,989	980,069	321
Investment per Establishment	394,953	3,148,543	797
Investment per Employee	8,117	25,577	315
Investment per Production Worker	11,557	34,397	298

Source: Same as General Statistics. The 'Average of All Manufacturing' column represents the average of all manufacturing industries reported for the most recent complete year available. The Index shows the relationship between the Average and the Analyzed Industry. For example, 100 means that they are equal; 500 that the Analyzed Industry is five times the average; 50 means that the Analyzed Industry is half the national average. The abbreviation 'na' is used to show that data are 'not available'.

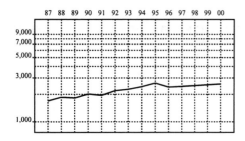

87 88 89 90 91 92 93 94 95 96 97 98 99 00

Revenues ($ millions)

SIC 2875 FERTILIZERS, MIXING ONLY: GENERAL STATISTICS

Year	Estab-lish-ments	Employment			Compensation		Production ($ mil.)		
		Total (000)	Production		Payroll ($ mil.)	Wages ($/hr)	Cost of Materials	Value of Shipments	Capital Inves.
			Workers (000)	Hours (mil.)					
1987	452	7.5	4.7	9.6	145.2	7.48	1,240.4	1,701.1	26.3
1988	415	7.5	4.7	9.5	145.9	7.72	1,375.2	1,864.2	16.2
1989	397	7.4	4.1	8.6	138.0	8.01	1,373.2	1,831.7	26.6
1990	400	7.3	4.3	9.5	163.6	7.86	1,465.3	2,018.8	31.2
1991	394	6.7	4.1	9.1	157.4	7.96	1,443.8	1,954.3	26.4
1992	401	6.9	4.2	9.4	181.9	8.90	1,562.7	2,188.8	43.7
1993	413	6.7	4.3	9.5	179.2	9.26	1,574.5	2,272.9	33.9
1994	458	7.8	5.1	11.0	202.7	9.42	1,592.3	2,420.7	38.1
1995	463	8.4	5.2	10.4	263.6	10.90	1,583.4	2,641.1	90.4
1996	388[1]	7.7	5.0	9.7	272.8	11.96	1,525.2	2,393.1	57.3
1997	378[1]	6.9[1]	4.3[1]	9.2[1]	232.1[1]	10.88[1]	1,553.7[1]	2,437.7[1]	54.4[1]
1998	369[1]	6.7[1]	4.2[1]	9.1[1]	239.4[1]	11.21[1]	1,585.0[1]	2,486.9[1]	56.8[1]
1999	360[1]	6.6[1]	4.2[1]	9.0[1]	246.8[1]	11.54[1]	1,616.3[1]	2,536.0[1]	59.2[1]
2000	351[1]	6.5[1]	4.1[1]	8.9[1]	254.1[1]	11.87[1]	1,647.5[1]	2,585.1[1]	61.5[1]

Source: 1987 and 1992 Economic Census; *Annual Survey of Manufactures*, 88-91, 93-96. Establishment counts for non-Census years are from *County Business Patterns*. Extracted from *Manufacturing USA*, 6th Edition, Gale, 1998. Note: 1. Projections by the editors.

SIC 2875 FERTILIZERS, MIXING ONLY: INDICES OF CHANGE

Year	Estab-lish-ments	Employment			Compensation		Production ($ mil.)		
		Total (000)	Production		Payroll ($ mil.)	Wages ($/hr)	Cost of Materials	Value of Shipments	Capital Inves.
			Workers (000)	Hours (mil.)					
1987	113	109	112	102	80	84	79	78	60
1988	103	109	112	101	80	87	88	85	37
1989	99	107	98	91	76	90	88	84	61
1990	100	106	102	101	90	88	94	92	71
1991	98	97	98	97	87	89	92	89	60
1992	100	100	100	100	100	100	100	100	100
1993	103	97	102	101	99	104	101	104	78
1994	114	113	121	117	111	106	102	111	87
1995	115	122	124	111	145	122	101	121	207
1996	97[1]	112	119	103	150	134	98	109	131
1997	94[1]	99[1]	102[1]	98[1]	128[1]	122[1]	99[1]	111[1]	125[1]
1998	92[1]	97[1]	101[1]	97[1]	132[1]	126[1]	101[1]	114[1]	130[1]
1999	90[1]	96[1]	99[1]	96[1]	136[1]	130[1]	103[1]	116[1]	135[1]
2000	88[1]	94[1]	97[1]	95[1]	140[1]	133[1]	105[1]	118[1]	141[1]

Source: Same as General Statistics. Values reflect change from the base year, 1992. Values above 100 mean greater than 1992, values below 100 mean less than 1992, and a value of 100 in the 1982-91 or 1993-2000 period means same as 1992. Note: 1. Projections by the editors.

SIC 2875 FERTILIZERS, MIXING ONLY: SELECTED RATIOS

For 1996	Average of All Manufacturing	Analyzed Industry	Index
Employees per Establishment	49	20	41
Payroll per Establishment	1,574,035	703,970	45
Payroll per Employee	32,350	35,429	110
Production Workers per Establishment	34	13	38
Wages per Establishment	890,687	299,373	34
Wages per Production Worker	26,064	23,202	89
Hours per Production Worker	2,055	1,940	94
Wages per Hour	12.68	11.96	94
Value Added per Establishment	4,932,584	2,303,902	47
Value Added per Employee	101,376	115,948	114
Value Added per Production Worker	144,340	178,560	124
Cost per Establishment	5,569,059	3,935,833	71
Cost per Employee	114,457	198,078	173
Cost per Production Worker	162,965	305,040	187
Shipments per Establishment	10,422,474	6,175,479	59
Shipments per Employee	214,207	310,792	145
Shipments per Production Worker	304,989	478,620	157
Investment per Establishment	394,953	147,865	37
Investment per Employee	8,117	7,442	92
Investment per Production Worker	11,557	11,460	99

Source: Same as General Statistics. The 'Average of All Manufacturing' column represents the average of all manufacturing industries reported for the most recent complete year available. The Index shows the relationship between the Average and the Analyzed Industry. For example, 100 means that they are equal; 500 that the Analyzed Industry is five times the average; 50 means that the Analyzed Industry is half the national average. The abbreviation 'na' is used to show that data are 'not available'.

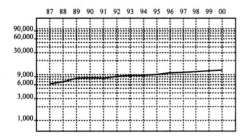

Revenues ($ millions)

SIC 2879 AGRICULTURAL CHEMICALS, NEC: GENERAL STATISTICS

| Year | Estab-lish-ments | Employment | | | Compensation | | Production ($ mil.) | | |
| | | Total (000) | Production | | Payroll ($ mil.) | Wages ($/hr) | Cost of Materials | Value of Shipments | Capital Inves. |
			Workers (000)	Hours (mil.)					
1987	277	16.1	9.1	18.5	518.3	13.69	2,442.9	6,299.7	234.1
1988	254	15.9	8.9	18.5	531.7	13.98	2,761.6	6,977.6	331.6
1989	243	16.6	9.8	20.1	621.3	15.08	3,451.5	8,327.2	503.0
1990	237	17.0	10.2	21.1	664.1	16.27	3,414.9	8,538.9	557.7
1991	249	16.4	9.1	20.1	619.6	15.15	3,399.3	8,345.5	481.0
1992	263	16.9	9.6	20.2	670.2	15.59	3,645.8	9,151.4	428.4
1993	258	16.3	9.2	19.8	665.5	16.41	3,515.8	9,553.8	356.1
1994	253	15.3	8.8	18.4	700.2	18.40	3,695.2	9,636.1	299.3
1995	242	14.8	8.7	17.7	672.2	19.85	3,959.6	10,079.3	317.6
1996	226[1]	13.8	7.8	17.3	670.1	19.45	3,892.7	10,902.5	463.0
1997	220[1]	15.5[1]	8.8[1]	19.2[1]	757.0[1]	19.75[1]	3,982.5[1]	11,154.0[1]	470.9[1]
1998	214[1]	15.5[1]	8.8[1]	19.3[1]	781.0[1]	20.34[1]	4,139.9[1]	11,594.8[1]	488.1[1]
1999	208[1]	15.5[1]	8.7[1]	19.4[1]	805.1[1]	20.94[1]	4,297.2[1]	12,035.5[1]	505.3[1]
2000	202[1]	15.4[1]	8.7[1]	19.4[1]	829.1[1]	21.54[1]	4,454.6[1]	12,476.3[1]	522.5[1]

Source: 1987 and 1992 Economic Census; *Annual Survey of Manufactures*, 88-91, 93-96. Establishment counts for non-Census years are from *County Business Patterns*. Extracted from *Manufacturing USA*, 6th Edition, Gale, 1998. Note: 1. Projections by the editors.

SIC 2879 AGRICULTURAL CHEMICALS, NEC: INDICES OF CHANGE

| Year | Estab-lish-ments | Employment | | | Compensation | | Production ($ mil.) | | |
| | | Total (000) | Production | | Payroll ($ mil.) | Wages ($/hr) | Cost of Materials | Value of Shipments | Capital Inves. |
			Workers (000)	Hours (mil.)					
1987	105	95	95	92	77	88	67	69	55
1988	97	94	93	92	79	90	76	76	77
1989	92	98	102	100	93	97	95	91	117
1990	90	101	106	104	99	104	94	93	130
1991	95	97	95	100	92	97	93	91	112
1992	100	100	100	100	100	100	100	100	100
1993	98	96	96	98	99	105	96	104	83
1994	96	91	92	91	104	118	101	105	70
1995	92	88	91	88	100	127	109	110	74
1996	86[1]	82	81	86	100	125	107	119	108
1997	84[1]	92[1]	92[1]	95[1]	113[1]	127[1]	109[1]	122[1]	110[1]
1998	81[1]	92[1]	91[1]	96[1]	117[1]	130[1]	114[1]	127[1]	114[1]
1999	79[1]	92[1]	91[1]	96[1]	120[1]	134[1]	118[1]	132[1]	118[1]
2000	77[1]	91[1]	91[1]	96[1]	124[1]	138[1]	122[1]	136[1]	122[1]

Source: Same as General Statistics. Values reflect change from the base year, 1992. Values above 100 mean greater than 1992, values below 100 mean less than 1992, and a value of 100 in the 1982-91 or 1993-2000 period means same as 1992. Note: 1. Projections by the editors.

SIC 2879 AGRICULTURAL CHEMICALS, NEC: SELECTED RATIOS

For 1996	Average of All Manufacturing	Analyzed Industry	Index
Employees per Establishment	49	61	125
Payroll per Establishment	1,574,035	2,962,739	188
Payroll per Employee	32,350	48,558	150
Production Workers per Establishment	34	34	101
Wages per Establishment	890,687	1,487,714	167
Wages per Production Worker	26,064	43,139	166
Hours per Production Worker	2,055	2,218	108
Wages per Hour	12.68	19.45	153
Value Added per Establishment	4,932,584	30,948,931	627
Value Added per Employee	101,376	507,239	500
Value Added per Production Worker	144,340	897,423	622
Cost per Establishment	5,569,059	17,210,946	309
Cost per Employee	114,457	282,080	246
Cost per Production Worker	162,965	499,064	306
Shipments per Establishment	10,422,474	48,203,649	462
Shipments per Employee	214,207	790,036	369
Shipments per Production Worker	304,989	1,397,756	458
Investment per Establishment	394,953	2,047,080	518
Investment per Employee	8,117	33,551	413
Investment per Production Worker	11,557	59,359	514

Source: Same as General Statistics. The 'Average of All Manufacturing' column represents the average of all manufacturing industries reported for the most recent complete year available. The Index shows the relationship between the Average and the Analyzed Industry. For example, 100 means that they are equal; 500 that the Analyzed Industry is five times the average; 50 means that the Analyzed Industry is half the national average. The abbreviation 'na' is used to show that data are 'not available'.

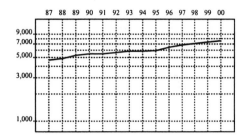

87 88 89 90 91 92 93 94 95 96 97 98 99 00

Revenues ($ millions)

SIC 2891 ADHESIVES AND SEALANTS: GENERAL STATISTICS

Year	Estab-lish-ments	Employment			Compensation		Production ($ mil.)		
		Total (000)	Production		Payroll ($ mil.)	Wages ($/hr)	Cost of Materials	Value of Shipments	Capital Inves.
			Workers (000)	Hours (mil.)					
1987	714	20.9	11.8	24.2	552.8	10.59	2,694.8	4,678.1	111.7
1988	722	21.2	11.8	23.9	579.0	11.05	2,875.6	4,859.9	118.4
1989	729	22.1	12.3	25.6	612.7	11.02	3,128.8	5,285.7	136.2
1990	710	22.1	11.9	24.6	633.3	11.50	3,167.9	5,485.1	127.1
1991	706	20.9	11.7	25.1	645.5	11.43	3,181.3	5,483.4	139.4
1992	685	21.1	11.6	24.5	677.8	12.41	3,016.9	5,659.0	189.6
1993	680	20.9	11.5	24.6	684.0	12.57	3,131.2	5,859.3	182.8
1994	673	19.2	11.3	23.7	687.1	13.41	3,338.5	5,848.9	204.2
1995	654	18.8	11.2	23.6	644.6	13.40	3,505.0	5,934.7	197.0
1996	689[1]	17.3	11.1	23.4	657.1	14.04	3,831.5	6,465.5	188.2
1997	689[1]	20.3[1]	11.6[1]	25.2[1]	759.0[1]	14.33[1]	4,057.7[1]	6,847.3[1]	222.4[1]
1998	689[1]	20.4[1]	11.6[1]	25.4[1]	783.8[1]	14.74[1]	4,206.7[1]	7,098.7[1]	234.2[1]
1999	689[1]	20.4[1]	11.6[1]	25.6[1]	808.7[1]	15.15[1]	4,355.8[1]	7,350.2[1]	246.0[1]
2000	689[1]	20.5[1]	11.6[1]	25.8[1]	833.6[1]	15.55[1]	4,504.8[1]	7,601.6[1]	257.8[1]

Source: 1987 and 1992 Economic Census; *Annual Survey of Manufactures*, 88-91, 93-96. Establishment counts for non-Census years are from *County Business Patterns*. Extracted from *Manufacturing USA*, 6th Edition, Gale, 1998. Note: 1. Projections by the editors.

SIC 2891 ADHESIVES AND SEALANTS: INDICES OF CHANGE

Year	Estab-lish-ments	Employment			Compensation		Production ($ mil.)		
		Total (000)	Production		Payroll ($ mil.)	Wages ($/hr)	Cost of Materials	Value of Shipments	Capital Inves.
			Workers (000)	Hours (mil.)					
1987	104	99	102	99	82	85	89	83	59
1988	105	100	102	98	85	89	95	86	62
1989	106	105	106	104	90	89	104	93	72
1990	104	105	103	100	93	93	105	97	67
1991	103	99	101	102	95	92	105	97	74
1992	100	100	100	100	100	100	100	100	100
1993	99	99	99	100	101	101	104	104	96
1994	98	91	97	97	101	108	111	103	108
1995	95	89	97	96	95	108	116	105	104
1996	101[1]	82	96	96	97	113	127	114	99
1997	101[1]	96[1]	100[1]	103[1]	112[1]	116[1]	134[1]	121[1]	117[1]
1998	101[1]	96[1]	100[1]	104[1]	116[1]	119[1]	139[1]	125[1]	124[1]
1999	101[1]	97[1]	100[1]	105[1]	119[1]	122[1]	144[1]	130[1]	130[1]
2000	101[1]	97[1]	100[1]	105[1]	123[1]	125[1]	149[1]	134[1]	136[1]

Source: Same as General Statistics. Values reflect change from the base year, 1992. Values above 100 mean greater than 1992, values below 100 mean less than 1992, and a value of 100 in the 1982-91 or 1993-2000 period means same as 1992. Note: 1. Projections by the editors.

SIC 2891 ADHESIVES AND SEALANTS: SELECTED RATIOS

For 1996	Average of All Manufacturing	Analyzed Industry	Index
Employees per Establishment	49	25	52
Payroll per Establishment	1,574,035	954,325	61
Payroll per Employee	32,350	37,983	117
Production Workers per Establishment	34	16	47
Wages per Establishment	890,687	477,142	54
Wages per Production Worker	26,064	29,598	114
Hours per Production Worker	2,055	2,108	103
Wages per Hour	12.68	14.04	111
Value Added per Establishment	4,932,584	3,849,251	78
Value Added per Employee	101,376	153,202	151
Value Added per Production Worker	144,340	238,775	165
Cost per Establishment	5,569,059	5,564,597	100
Cost per Employee	114,457	221,474	193
Cost per Production Worker	162,965	345,180	212
Shipments per Establishment	10,422,474	9,390,030	90
Shipments per Employee	214,207	373,728	174
Shipments per Production Worker	304,989	582,477	191
Investment per Establishment	394,953	273,328	69
Investment per Employee	8,117	10,879	134
Investment per Production Worker	11,557	16,955	147

Source: Same as General Statistics. The 'Average of All Manufacturing' column represents the average of all manufacturing industries reported for the most recent complete year available. The Index shows the relationship between the Average and the Analyzed Industry. For example, 100 means that they are equal; 500 that the Analyzed Industry is five times the average; 50 means that the Analyzed Industry is half the national average. The abbreviation 'na' is used to show that data are 'not available'.

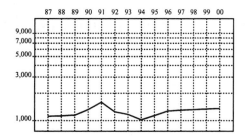

Revenues ($ millions)

SIC 2892 EXPLOSIVES: GENERAL STATISTICS

Year	Estab-lish-ments	Employment			Compensation		Production ($ mil.)		
		Total (000)	Production		Payroll ($ mil.)	Wages ($/hr)	Cost of Materials	Value of Shipments	Capital Inves.
			Workers (000)	Hours (mil.)					
1987	132	13.8	9.2	17.9	349.2	11.45	362.6	1,117.8	22.6
1988	126	13.6	9.1	17.8	359.1	11.83	361.6	1,128.4	26.8
1989	116	13.1	8.9	17.3	342.8	11.85	383.4	1,151.0	49.3
1990	129	12.3	9.4	17.6	380.2	13.10	454.1	1,324.6	43.6
1991	135	14.0	9.2	16.9	401.2	13.70	573.7	1,592.4	84.3
1992	123	11.4	7.5	13.4	338.6	14.83	402.1	1,252.0	31.7
1993	119	10.0	6.8	13.2	314.7	13.78	385.2	1,172.6	49.1
1994	119	9.1	6.4	12.6	303.1	14.49	421.0	1,023.4	52.6
1995	117	8.7	6.2	12.7	299.6	14.61	518.0	1,138.3	52.7
1996	124[1]	8.5	6.1	12.1	293.4	14.23	560.4	1,276.0	46.5
1997	125[1]	9.4[1]	6.7[1]	13.1[1]	340.4[1]	15.44[1]	572.8[1]	1,304.1[1]	56.5[1]
1998	125[1]	9.1[1]	6.6[1]	12.8[1]	342.4[1]	15.81[1]	581.1[1]	1,323.1[1]	58.3[1]
1999	126[1]	8.8[1]	6.4[1]	12.5[1]	344.4[1]	16.18[1]	589.4[1]	1,342.1[1]	60.2[1]
2000	126[1]	8.5[1]	6.2[1]	12.2[1]	346.4[1]	16.55[1]	597.7[1]	1,361.0[1]	62.0[1]

Source: 1987 and 1992 Economic Census; *Annual Survey of Manufactures*, 88-91, 93-96. Establishment counts for non-Census years are from *County Business Patterns*. Extracted from *Manufacturing USA*, 6th Edition, Gale, 1998. Note: 1. Projections by the editors.

SIC 2892 EXPLOSIVES: INDICES OF CHANGE

Year	Estab-lish-ments	Employment			Compensation		Production ($ mil.)		
		Total (000)	Production		Payroll ($ mil.)	Wages ($/hr)	Cost of Materials	Value of Shipments	Capital Inves.
			Workers (000)	Hours (mil.)					
1987	107	121	123	134	103	77	90	89	71
1988	102	119	121	133	106	80	90	90	85
1989	94	115	119	129	101	80	95	92	156
1990	105	108	125	131	112	88	113	106	138
1991	110	123	123	126	118	92	143	127	266
1992	100	100	100	100	100	100	100	100	100
1993	97	88	91	99	93	93	96	94	155
1994	97	80	85	94	90	98	105	82	166
1995	95	76	83	95	88	99	129	91	166
1996	101[1]	75	81	90	87	96	139	102	147
1997	101[1]	83[1]	90[1]	98[1]	101[1]	104[1]	142[1]	104[1]	178[1]
1998	102[1]	80[1]	88[1]	95[1]	101[1]	107[1]	145[1]	106[1]	184[1]
1999	102[1]	77[1]	85[1]	93[1]	102[1]	109[1]	147[1]	107[1]	190[1]
2000	102[1]	75[1]	83[1]	91[1]	102[1]	112[1]	149[1]	109[1]	196[1]

Source: Same as General Statistics. Values reflect change from the base year, 1992. Values above 100 mean greater than 1992, values below 100 mean less than 1992, and a value of 100 in the 1982-91 or 1993-2000 period means same as 1992. Note: 1. Projections by the editors.

SIC 2892 EXPLOSIVES: SELECTED RATIOS

For 1996	Average of All Manufacturing	Analyzed Industry	Index
Employees per Establishment	49	68	140
Payroll per Establishment	1,574,035	2,359,229	150
Payroll per Employee	32,350	34,518	107
Production Workers per Establishment	34	49	144
Wages per Establishment	890,687	1,384,524	155
Wages per Production Worker	26,064	28,227	108
Hours per Production Worker	2,055	1,984	97
Wages per Hour	12.68	14.23	112
Value Added per Establishment	4,932,584	5,795,953	118
Value Added per Employee	101,376	84,800	84
Value Added per Production Worker	144,340	118,164	82
Cost per Establishment	5,569,059	4,506,177	81
Cost per Employee	114,457	65,929	58
Cost per Production Worker	162,965	91,869	56
Shipments per Establishment	10,422,474	10,260,316	98
Shipments per Employee	214,207	150,118	70
Shipments per Production Worker	304,989	209,180	69
Investment per Establishment	394,953	373,907	95
Investment per Employee	8,117	5,471	67
Investment per Production Worker	11,557	7,623	66

Source: Same as General Statistics. The 'Average of All Manufacturing' column represents the average of all manufacturing industries reported for the most recent complete year available. The Index shows the relationship between the Average and the Analyzed Industry. For example, 100 means that they are equal; 500 that the Analyzed Industry is five times the average; 50 means that the Analyzed Industry is half the national average. The abbreviation 'na' is used to show that data are 'not available'.

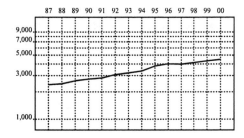

Revenues ($ millions)

SIC 2893 PRINTING INK: GENERAL STATISTICS

Year	Estab-lish-ments	Employment Total (000)	Employment Production Workers (000)	Employment Production Hours (mil.)	Compensation Payroll ($ mil.)	Compensation Wages ($/hr)	Production ($ mil.) Cost of Materials	Production ($ mil.) Value of Shipments	Production ($ mil.) Capital Inves.
1987	504	11.1	6.2	13.0	310.9	11.76	1,410.5	2,391.7	37.8
1988	484	11.1	6.4	13.5	336.7	12.91	1,511.8	2,447.2	32.7
1989	498	12.2	6.3	13.1	356.8	12.61	1,602.5	2,637.2	46.6
1990	491	11.5	6.2	12.9	354.4	12.64	1,727.2	2,754.4	44.3
1991	495	10.8	5.9	12.5	358.1	12.92	1,761.7	2,825.7	29.2
1992	519	12.3	6.5	13.1	407.4	14.12	1,973.0	3,075.1	46.0
1993	517	12.2	6.8	14.2	404.9	13.85	2,084.1	3,209.9	55.8
1994	518	13.2	7.8	16.0	458.5	13.92	2,110.0	3,366.0	55.4
1995	534	14.2	8.4	17.7	506.6	13.67	2,179.9	3,805.6	58.0
1996	527[1]	13.1	7.4	16.4	492.4	14.26	2,300.6	4,022.6	82.7
1997	531[1]	13.8[1]	7.8[1]	16.5[1]	513.8[1]	15.14[1]	2,281.3[1]	3,988.8[1]	66.1[1]
1998	534[1]	14.1[1]	7.9[1]	16.9[1]	534.9[1]	15.50[1]	2,378.4[1]	4,158.6[1]	68.9[1]
1999	538[1]	14.4[1]	8.1[1]	17.3[1]	555.9[1]	15.86[1]	2,475.5[1]	4,328.4[1]	71.8[1]
2000	542[1]	14.7[1]	8.3[1]	17.7[1]	576.9[1]	16.22[1]	2,572.6[1]	4,498.2[1]	74.7[1]

Source: 1987 and 1992 Economic Census; *Annual Survey of Manufactures,* 88-91, 93-96. Establishment counts for non-Census years are from *County Business Patterns.* Extracted from *Manufacturing USA*, 6th Edition, Gale, 1998. Note: 1. Projections by the editors.

SIC 2893 PRINTING INK: INDICES OF CHANGE

Year	Estab-lish-ments	Employment Total (000)	Employment Production Workers (000)	Employment Production Hours (mil.)	Compensation Payroll ($ mil.)	Compensation Wages ($/hr)	Production ($ mil.) Cost of Materials	Production ($ mil.) Value of Shipments	Production ($ mil.) Capital Inves.
1987	97	90	95	99	76	83	71	78	82
1988	93	90	98	103	83	91	77	80	71
1989	96	99	97	100	88	89	81	86	101
1990	95	93	95	98	87	90	88	90	96
1991	95	88	91	95	88	92	89	92	63
1992	100	100	100	100	100	100	100	100	100
1993	100	99	105	108	99	98	106	104	121
1994	100	107	120	122	113	99	107	109	120
1995	103	115	129	135	124	97	110	124	126
1996	102[1]	107	114	125	121	101	117	131	180
1997	102[1]	112[1]	119[1]	126[1]	126[1]	107[1]	116[1]	130[1]	144[1]
1998	103[1]	114[1]	122[1]	129[1]	131[1]	110[1]	121[1]	135[1]	150[1]
1999	104[1]	117[1]	125[1]	132[1]	136[1]	112[1]	125[1]	141[1]	156[1]
2000	104[1]	119[1]	127[1]	135[1]	142[1]	115[1]	130[1]	146[1]	162[1]

Source: Same as General Statistics. Values reflect change from the base year, 1992. Values above 100 mean greater than 1992, values below 100 mean less than 1992, and a value of 100 in the 1982-91 or 1993-2000 period means same as 1992. Note: 1. Projections by the editors.

SIC 2893 PRINTING INK: SELECTED RATIOS

For 1996	Average of All Manufacturing	Analyzed Industry	Index
Employees per Establishment	49	25	51
Payroll per Establishment	1,574,035	934,267	59
Payroll per Employee	32,350	37,588	116
Production Workers per Establishment	34	14	41
Wages per Establishment	890,687	443,728	50
Wages per Production Worker	26,064	31,603	121
Hours per Production Worker	2,055	2,216	108
Wages per Hour	12.68	14.26	112
Value Added per Establishment	4,932,584	3,295,171	67
Value Added per Employee	101,376	132,573	131
Value Added per Production Worker	144,340	234,689	163
Cost per Establishment	5,569,059	4,365,101	78
Cost per Employee	114,457	175,618	153
Cost per Production Worker	162,965	310,892	191
Shipments per Establishment	10,422,474	7,632,380	73
Shipments per Employee	214,207	307,069	143
Shipments per Production Worker	304,989	543,595	178
Investment per Establishment	394,953	156,913	40
Investment per Employee	8,117	6,313	78
Investment per Production Worker	11,557	11,176	97

Source: Same as General Statistics. The 'Average of All Manufacturing' column represents the average of all manufacturing industries reported for the most recent complete year available. The Index shows the relationship between the Average and the Analyzed Industry. For example, 100 means that they are equal; 500 that the Analyzed Industry is five times the average; 50 means that the Analyzed Industry is half the national average. The abbreviation 'na' is used to show that data are 'not available'.

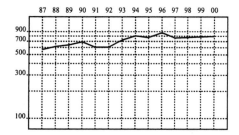

Revenues ($ millions)

SIC 2895 CARBON BLACK: GENERAL STATISTICS

Year	Estab-lish-ments	Employment Total (000)	Employment Production Workers (000)	Employment Production Hours (mil.)	Compensation Payroll ($ mil.)	Compensation Wages ($/hr)	Production ($ mil.) Cost of Materials	Production ($ mil.) Value of Shipments	Production ($ mil.) Capital Inves.
1987	22	1.8	1.4	3.0	64.7	15.40	306.8	569.6	39.2
1988	26	1.8	1.3	3.0	67.4	16.03	284.0	615.7	49.0
1989	23	1.9	1.3	2.7	71.1	17.33	325.8	640.3	50.6
1990	22	1.8	1.2	2.7	70.1	17.33	316.3	691.9	60.1
1991	23	2.0	1.2	2.8	72.0	17.18	282.7	604.3	53.3
1992	23	1.9	1.2	2.7	73.7	17.07	286.8	606.8	28.7
1993	22	1.9	1.3	2.8	76.4	18.57	312.6	723.8	33.3
1994	22	1.9	1.2	2.8	77.0	17.50	311.2	804.7	45.7
1995	22	1.8	1.0	2.7	75.9	17.44	306.9	772.3	65.9
1996	22[1]	1.9	1.1	2.7	87.4	19.89	379.9	871.8	299.1
1997	21[1]	1.8[1]	1.0[1]	2.6[1]	83.9[1]	19.59[1]	333.2[1]	764.7[1]	119.4[1]
1998	21[1]	1.8[1]	1.0[1]	2.6[1]	85.7[1]	20.01[1]	337.7[1]	774.9[1]	126.8[1]
1999	21[1]	1.8[1]	1.0[1]	2.6[1]	87.6[1]	20.43[1]	342.1[1]	785.1[1]	134.2[1]
2000	20[1]	1.8[1]	1.0[1]	2.5[1]	89.5[1]	20.85[1]	346.6[1]	795.3[1]	141.6[1]

Source: 1987 and 1992 Economic Census; *Annual Survey of Manufactures,* 88-91, 93-96. Establishment counts for non-Census years are from *County Business Patterns.* Extracted from *Manufacturing USA,* 6th Edition, Gale, 1998. Note: 1. Projections by the editors.

SIC 2895 CARBON BLACK: INDICES OF CHANGE

Year	Estab-lish-ments	Employment Total (000)	Employment Production Workers (000)	Employment Production Hours (mil.)	Compensation Payroll ($ mil.)	Compensation Wages ($/hr)	Production ($ mil.) Cost of Materials	Production ($ mil.) Value of Shipments	Production ($ mil.) Capital Inves.
1987	96	95	117	111	88	90	107	94	137
1988	113	95	108	111	91	94	99	101	171
1989	100	100	108	100	96	102	114	106	176
1990	96	95	100	100	95	102	110	114	209
1991	100	105	100	104	98	101	99	100	186
1992	100	100	100	100	100	100	100	100	100
1993	96	100	108	104	104	109	109	119	116
1994	96	100	100	104	104	103	109	133	159
1995	96	95	83	100	103	102	107	127	230
1996	94[1]	100	92	100	119	117	132	144	1,042
1997	92[1]	97[1]	87[1]	97[1]	114[1]	115[1]	116[1]	126[1]	416[1]
1998	91[1]	96[1]	85[1]	96[1]	116[1]	117[1]	118[1]	128[1]	442[1]
1999	90[1]	96[1]	82[1]	95[1]	119[1]	120[1]	119[1]	129[1]	468[1]
2000	89[1]	96[1]	80[1]	93[1]	121[1]	122[1]	121[1]	131[1]	493[1]

Source: Same as General Statistics. Values reflect change from the base year, 1992. Values above 100 mean greater than 1992, values below 100 mean less than 1992, and a value of 100 in the 1982-91 or 1993-2000 period means same as 1992. Note: 1. Projections by the editors.

SIC 2895 CARBON BLACK: SELECTED RATIOS

For 1996	Average of All Manufacturing	Analyzed Industry	Index
Employees per Establishment	49	88	182
Payroll per Establishment	1,574,035	4,064,078	258
Payroll per Employee	32,350	46,000	142
Production Workers per Establishment	34	51	150
Wages per Establishment	890,687	2,497,176	280
Wages per Production Worker	26,064	48,821	187
Hours per Production Worker	2,055	2,455	119
Wages per Hour	12.68	19.89	157
Value Added per Establishment	4,932,584	23,305,672	472
Value Added per Employee	101,376	263,789	260
Value Added per Production Worker	144,340	455,636	316
Cost per Establishment	5,569,059	17,665,253	317
Cost per Employee	114,457	199,947	175
Cost per Production Worker	162,965	345,364	212
Shipments per Establishment	10,422,474	40,538,477	389
Shipments per Employee	214,207	458,842	214
Shipments per Production Worker	304,989	792,545	260
Investment per Establishment	394,953	13,908,074	3,521
Investment per Employee	8,117	157,421	1,939
Investment per Production Worker	11,557	271,909	2,353

Source: Same as General Statistics. The 'Average of All Manufacturing' column represents the average of all manufacturing industries reported for the most recent complete year available. The Index shows the relationship between the Average and the Analyzed Industry. For example, 100 means that they are equal; 500 that the Analyzed Industry is five times the average; 50 means that the Analyzed Industry is half the national average. The abbreviation 'na' is used to show that data are 'not available'.

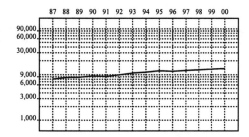

Revenues ($ millions)

SIC 2899 CHEMICAL PREPARATIONS, NEC: GENERAL STATISTICS

Year	Estab-lish-ments	Employment Total (000)	Production Workers (000)	Production Hours (mil.)	Compensation Payroll ($ mil.)	Compensation Wages ($/hr)	Production ($ mil.) Cost of Materials	Production ($ mil.) Value of Shipments	Production ($ mil.) Capital Inves.
1987	1,529	37.9	22.4	46.2	1,020.7	11.30	3,767.6	8,023.9	234.3
1988	1,462	37.0	21.8	44.6	1,040.7	12.11	4,248.6	8,726.7	258.6
1989	1,371	40.1	23.2	48.5	1,094.5	11.39	4,376.7	8,838.3	341.3
1990	1,329	40.3	23.9	49.3	1,205.0	12.11	4,540.4	9,418.0	352.2
1991	1,338	39.4	22.5	46.8	1,201.6	12.35	4,418.4	9,175.9	453.4
1992	1,486	37.1	21.4	44.0	1,227.7	13.62	4,933.0	9,965.8	441.1
1993	1,410	36.8	20.6	43.3	1,265.8	14.09	5,419.8	10,885.1	468.6
1994	1,392	36.5	20.1	44.1	1,364.6	14.77	5,683.2	11,370.4	378.7
1995	1,396	38.0	20.8	45.0	1,445.2	14.74	6,168.1	12,199.0	433.5
1996	1,404[1]	35.1	19.3	42.3	1,389.1	15.07	6,012.3	11,872.2	389.8
1997	1,406[1]	36.6[1]	20.2[1]	43.7[1]	1,472.3[1]	15.62[1]	6,280.2[1]	12,401.2[1]	456.5[1]
1998	1,408[1]	36.4[1]	20.0[1]	43.4[1]	1,516.8[1]	16.07[1]	6,494.1[1]	12,823.7[1]	470.4[1]
1999	1,409[1]	36.2[1]	19.8[1]	43.1[1]	1,561.4[1]	16.52[1]	6,708.1[1]	13,246.2[1]	484.3[1]
2000	1,411[1]	36.0[1]	19.5[1]	42.8[1]	1,605.9[1]	16.97[1]	6,922.1[1]	13,668.7[1]	498.1[1]

Source: 1987 and 1992 Economic Census; *Annual Survey of Manufactures*, 88-91, 93-96. Establishment counts for non-Census years are from *County Business Patterns*. Extracted from *Manufacturing USA*, 6th Edition, Gale, 1998. Note: 1. Projections by the editors.

SIC 2899 CHEMICAL PREPARATIONS, NEC: INDICES OF CHANGE

Year	Estab-lish-ments	Employment Total (000)	Production Workers (000)	Production Hours (mil.)	Compensation Payroll ($ mil.)	Compensation Wages ($/hr)	Production ($ mil.) Cost of Materials	Production ($ mil.) Value of Shipments	Production ($ mil.) Capital Inves.
1987	103	102	105	105	83	83	76	81	53
1988	98	100	102	101	85	89	86	88	59
1989	92	108	108	110	89	84	89	89	77
1990	89	109	112	112	98	89	92	95	80
1991	90	106	105	106	98	91	90	92	103
1992	100	100	100	100	100	100	100	100	100
1993	95	99	96	98	103	103	110	109	106
1994	94	98	94	100	111	108	115	114	86
1995	94	102	97	102	118	108	125	122	98
1996	94[1]	95	90	96	113	111	122	119	88
1997	95[1]	99[1]	94[1]	99[1]	120[1]	115[1]	127[1]	124[1]	103[1]
1998	95[1]	98[1]	93[1]	99[1]	124[1]	118[1]	132[1]	129[1]	107[1]
1999	95[1]	98[1]	92[1]	98[1]	127[1]	121[1]	136[1]	133[1]	110[1]
2000	95[1]	97[1]	91[1]	97[1]	131[1]	125[1]	140[1]	137[1]	113[1]

Source: Same as General Statistics. Values reflect change from the base year, 1992. Values above 100 mean greater than 1992, values below 100 mean less than 1992, and a value of 100 in the 1982-91 or 1993-2000 period means same as 1992. Note: 1. Projections by the editors.

SIC 2899 CHEMICAL PREPARATIONS, NEC: SELECTED RATIOS

For 1996	Average of All Manufacturing	Analyzed Industry	Index
Employees per Establishment	49	25	51
Payroll per Establishment	1,574,035	989,233	63
Payroll per Employee	32,350	39,575	122
Production Workers per Establishment	34	14	40
Wages per Establishment	890,687	453,961	51
Wages per Production Worker	26,064	33,029	127
Hours per Production Worker	2,055	2,192	107
Wages per Hour	12.68	15.07	119
Value Added per Establishment	4,932,584	4,228,255	86
Value Added per Employee	101,376	169,157	167
Value Added per Production Worker	144,340	307,637	213
Cost per Establishment	5,569,059	4,281,595	77
Cost per Employee	114,457	171,291	150
Cost per Production Worker	162,965	311,518	191
Shipments per Establishment	10,422,474	8,454,659	81
Shipments per Employee	214,207	338,239	158
Shipments per Production Worker	304,989	615,140	202
Investment per Establishment	394,953	277,592	70
Investment per Employee	8,117	11,105	137
Investment per Production Worker	11,557	20,197	175

Source: Same as General Statistics. The 'Average of All Manufacturing' column represents the average of all manufacturing industries reported for the most recent complete year available. The Index shows the relationship between the Average and the Analyzed Industry. For example, 100 means that they are equal; 500 that the Analyzed Industry is five times the average; 50 means that the Analyzed Industry is half the national average. The abbreviation 'na' is used to show that data are 'not available'.

FINANCIAL NORMS AND RATIOS

Industry-specific financial norms and ratios are shown in this chapter for sixteen industries in the Chemicals sector. For each industry in the sector, balance sheets are presented for the years 1996 through 1998, with the most recent year shown first. As part of each balance sheet, additional financial averages for net sales, gross profits, net profits after tax, and working capital are shown. The number of establishments used to calculate the averages are shown for each year.

The second table in each display shows D&B Key Business Ratios for the SIC-denominated industry. These data, again, are for the years 1996 through 1998. Ratios measuring solvency (e.g., Quick ratio), efficiency (e.g., Collection period, in days), and profitability (e.g. % return on sales) are shown. A total of 14 ratios are featured. Ratios are shown for the upper quartile, median, and lowest quartile of the D&B sample.

This product includes proprietary data of Dun & Bradstreet Inc.

D&B INDUSTRY NORMS: SIC 2819 - INDUSTRIAL INORGANIC CHEMICALS, NEC

	1998 (79) Estab.		1997 (103) Estab.		1996 (85) Estab.	
	$	%	$	%	$	%
Cash	563,806	13.8	344,316	12.2	223,333	10.4
Accounts Receivable	968,275	23.7	742,254	26.3	586,249	27.3
Notes Receivable	36,770	.9	11,289	.4	4,295	.2
Inventory	665,945	16.3	474,140	16.8	416,602	19.4
Other Current Assets	236,962	5.8	152,402	5.4	152,468	7.1
Total Current Assets	2,471,758	60.5	1,724,401	61.1	1,382,947	64.4
Fixed Assets	1,250,178	30.6	883,367	31.3	609,871	28.4
Other Non-current Assets	363,614	8.9	214,492	7.6	154,615	7.2
Total Assets	4,085,550	100.0	2,822,260	100.0	2,147,433	100.0
Accounts Payable	502,523	12.3	409,228	14.5	302,788	14.1
Bank Loans	-	-	-	-	-	-
Notes Payable	57,198	1.4	59,267	2.1	70,865	3.3
Other Current Liabilities	547,464	13.4	375,361	13.3	326,410	15.2
Total Current Liabilities	1,107,185	27.1	843,856	29.9	700,063	32.6
Other Long Term	727,228	17.8	417,694	14.8	319,967	14.9
Deferred Credits	8,171	.2	25,400	.9	15,032	.7
Net Worth	2,242,967	54.9	1,535,309	54.4	1,112,370	51.8
Total Liabilities & Net Worth	4,085,551	100.0	2,822,259	100.0	2,147,432	100.0
Net Sales	9,843,660	100.0	3,735,798	100.0	3,956,349	100.0
Gross Profits	3,622,467	36.8	1,464,433	39.2	1,479,675	37.4
Net Profit After Tax	551,245	5.6	123,281	3.3	272,988	6.9
Working Capital	1,364,574	-	880,545	-	682,883	-

Source: Dun & Bradstreet. Data in this table are copyright (c) 1999 of Dun & Bradstreet. Reprinted by special arrangement with D&B. *Notes:* Values in parentheses above columns indicate the number of establishments in the sample. Data shown are for all companies.

D&B KEY BUSINESS RATIOS: SIC 2819

	1998			1997			1996		
	UQ	MED	LQ	UQ	MED	LQ	UQ	MED	LQ
Solvency									
Quick ratio	2.4	1.2	.8	2.6	1.2	.8	1.6	1.1	.6
Current ratio	4.3	2.2	1.6	4.2	2.2	1.4	2.9	2.0	1.3
Current liabilities/Net worth (%)	19.4	35.5	108.2	18.2	42.3	114.9	17.7	49.3	92.1
Current liabilities/Inventory (%)	74.0	132.9	219.7	77.3	143.5	289.8	82.5	123.8	215.4
Total liabilities/Net worth (%)	30.9	81.3	151.3	25.3	79.2	173.5	29.8	71.2	134.4
Fixed assets/Net worth (%)	21.8	55.8	106.4	24.9	59.7	111.1	17.8	40.2	84.8
Efficiency									
Collection period (days)	37.6	50.4	70.1	37.6	48.6	57.3	36.9	44.5	54.6
Sales to Inventory	12.3	8.3	4.7	20.9	10.5	7.2	16.0	8.1	5.6
Assets/Sales (%)	49.6	77.3	130.4	28.3	48.8	81.6	31.9	50.6	71.0
Sales/Net Working Capital	9.2	4.2	2.3	13.7	7.8	4.4	8.1	4.7	3.4
Accounts payable/Sales (%)	4.2	6.6	10.7	3.4	6.1	9.3	3.9	5.6	9.0
Profitability									
Return - Sales (%)	8.8	4.4	.2	7.5	3.7	.7	7.5	4.1	.8
Return - Assets (%)	13.8	6.4	1.7	13.1	7.1	1.5	12.1	6.2	1.1
Return - Net Worth (%)	29.2	12.4	4.7	34.0	14.0	4.3	27.6	13.1	3.0

Source: Dun & Bradstreet. Data in this table are copyright (c) 1999 of Dun & Bradstreet. Reprinted by special arrangement with D&B. *Note:* UQ stands for "Upper Quartile" and represents the top 25 percent of sample; MED stands for "Median"; and LQ stands for "Lower Quartile" and represents the lowest 25 percent.

D&B INDUSTRY NORMS: SIC 2821 - PLASTICS MATERIALS AND RESINS

	1998 (97) Estab.		1997 (118) Estab.		1996 (107) Estab.	
	$	%	$	%	$	%
Cash	370,379	8.9	211,238	12.6	92,459	9.2
Accounts Receivable	1,152,753	27.7	502,949	30.0	320,591	31.9
Notes Receivable	79,070	1.9	15,088	.9	3,015	.3
Inventory	732,435	17.6	279,975	16.7	182,907	18.2
Other Current Assets	149,816	3.6	51,971	3.1	53,264	5.3
Total Current Assets	2,484,453	59.7	1,061,221	63.3	652,236	64.9
Fixed Assets	1,315,054	31.6	467,742	27.9	286,421	28.5
Other Non-current Assets	362,056	8.7	147,532	8.8	66,329	6.6
Total Assets	4,161,563	100.0	1,676,495	100.0	1,004,986	100.0
Accounts Payable	541,003	13.0	276,622	16.5	184,917	18.4
Bank Loans	-	-	-	-	-	-
Notes Payable	133,170	3.2	63,707	3.8	58,289	5.8
Other Current Liabilities	611,750	14.7	241,415	14.4	138,688	13.8
Total Current Liabilities	1,285,923	30.9	581,744	34.7	381,894	38.0
Other Long Term	782,374	18.8	301,769	18.0	157,783	15.7
Deferred Credits	16,646	.4	1,676	.1	3,015	.3
Net Worth	2,076,620	49.9	791,306	47.2	462,294	46.0
Total Liabilities & Net Worth	4,161,563	100.0	1,676,495	100.0	1,004,986	100.0
Net Sales	4,953,433	100.0	3,809,002	100.0	3,610,937	100.0
Gross Profits	1,520,704	30.7	1,165,555	30.6	1,112,169	30.8
Net Profit After Tax	232,811	4.7	198,068	5.2	198,602	5.5
Working Capital	1,198,530	-	479,477	-	270,341	-

Source: Dun & Bradstreet. Data in this table are copyright (c) 1999 of Dun & Bradstreet. Reprinted by special arrangement with D&B. *Notes:* Values in parentheses above columns indicate the number of establishments in the sample. Data shown are for all companies.

D&B KEY BUSINESS RATIOS: SIC 2821

	1998			1997			1996		
	UQ	MED	LQ	UQ	MED	LQ	UQ	MED	LQ
Solvency									
Quick ratio	2.2	1.1	.7	2.4	1.2	.7	1.8	1.0	.7
Current ratio	3.1	2.0	1.3	3.3	1.9	1.3	2.8	1.8	1.2
Current liabilities/Net worth (%)	26.5	54.4	103.5	24.3	58.6	140.9	27.4	59.9	129.5
Current liabilities/Inventory (%)	104.7	166.9	257.3	113.5	175.1	262.5	118.0	200.6	319.9
Total liabilities/Net worth (%)	39.7	115.5	199.2	49.0	126.3	208.8	40.5	99.2	185.2
Fixed assets/Net worth (%)	31.3	70.5	120.0	21.2	51.4	107.2	23.4	62.2	109.7
Efficiency									
Collection period (days)	41.1	50.7	66.6	37.1	48.2	59.0	34.0	44.2	55.5
Sales to Inventory	16.2	10.8	6.8	20.7	11.0	7.4	30.1	12.1	7.7
Assets/Sales (%)	34.6	60.7	107.1	29.0	52.0	80.2	24.4	43.6	68.9
Sales/Net Working Capital	11.4	7.4	4.4	15.4	7.8	4.8	17.2	8.7	5.8
Accounts payable/Sales (%)	3.6	6.2	10.4	4.2	6.8	9.6	4.2	6.5	10.0
Profitability									
Return - Sales (%)	9.1	4.1	1.3	8.6	4.4	1.4	9.4	5.3	1.6
Return - Assets (%)	15.3	7.7	3.1	20.8	8.0	2.4	20.8	9.1	3.8
Return - Net Worth (%)	28.6	16.4	8.3	38.7	18.5	5.9	35.6	20.6	11.4

Source: Dun & Bradstreet. Data in this table are copyright (c) 1999 of Dun & Bradstreet. Reprinted by special arrangement with D&B. *Note:* UQ stands for "Upper Quartile" and represents the top 25 percent of sample; MED stands for "Median"; and LQ stands for "Lower Quartile" and represents the lowest 25 percent.

D&B INDUSTRY NORMS: SIC 2822 - SYNTHETIC RUBBER

	1998 (15) Estab.		1997 (15) Estab.		1996 (10) Estab.	
	$	%	$	%	$	%
Cash	575,772	10.8	387,043	8.8	431,681	10.7
Accounts Receivable	1,274,163	23.9	967,607	22.0	1,101,392	27.3
Notes Receivable	-	-	26,389	.6	4,034	.1
Inventory	964,952	18.1	725,705	16.5	867,397	21.5
Other Current Assets	325,205	6.1	197,920	4.5	161,376	4.0
Total Current Assets	3,140,092	58.9	2,304,664	52.4	2,565,880	63.6
Fixed Assets	1,727,317	32.4	1,684,516	38.3	1,258,734	31.2
Other Non-current Assets	463,817	8.7	409,034	9.3	209,789	5.2
Total Assets	5,331,226	100.0	4,398,214	100.0	4,034,403	100.0
Accounts Payable	613,091	11.5	536,582	12.2	786,709	19.5
Bank Loans	-	-	-	-	-	-
Notes Payable	122,618	2.3	290,282	6.6	246,099	6.1
Other Current Liabilities	725,047	13.6	413,432	9.4	399,406	9.9
Total Current Liabilities	1,460,756	27.4	1,240,296	28.2	1,432,214	35.5
Other Long Term	954,289	17.9	813,670	18.5	451,853	11.2
Deferred Credits	10,662	.2	-	-	-	-
Net Worth	2,905,518	54.5	2,344,249	53.3	2,150,337	53.3
Total Liabilities & Net Worth	5,331,225	100.0	4,398,215	100.0	4,034,404	100.0
Net Sales	4,130,981	100.0	7,200,000	100.0	10,149,166	100.0
Gross Profits	1,470,629	35.6	3,088,800	42.9	3,562,357	35.1
Net Profit After Tax	165,239	4.0	446,400	6.2	679,994	6.7
Working Capital	1,679,336	-	1,064,368	-	1,133,667	-

Source: Dun & Bradstreet. Data in this table are copyright (c) 1999 of Dun & Bradstreet. Reprinted by special arrangement with D&B. *Notes:* Values in parentheses above columns indicate the number of establishments in the sample. Data shown are for all companies.

D&B KEY BUSINESS RATIOS: SIC 2822

	1998			1997			1996		
	UQ	MED	LQ	UQ	MED	LQ	UQ	MED	LQ
Solvency									
Quick ratio	1.9	1.1	.8	2.5	1.0	.6	1.6	1.2	.8
Current ratio	2.9	2.2	1.7	3.8	2.3	1.3	2.7	2.2	1.4
Current liabilities/Net worth (%)	33.2	38.4	56.5	19.6	37.5	136.9	31.7	39.2	162.1
Current liabilities/Inventory (%)	98.2	178.7	306.0	78.4	148.1	370.7	92.5	146.3	151.4
Total liabilities/Net worth (%)	41.2	57.3	125.5	21.0	79.4	341.5	33.3	76.3	216.4
Fixed assets/Net worth (%)	30.4	37.7	89.1	37.7	76.9	145.6	35.7	62.6	94.3
Efficiency									
Collection period (days)	35.7	47.6	62.4	37.3	44.5	52.4	37.6	48.6	59.2
Sales to Inventory	16.0	10.7	6.9	19.1	13.5	8.4	12.1	9.0	4.7
Assets/Sales (%)	36.1	52.4	89.0	54.7	67.6	82.7	38.5	56.9	93.8
Sales/Net Working Capital	4.9	4.4	4.2	5.7	4.9	4.1	4.1	3.9	3.2
Accounts payable/Sales (%)	1.9	5.4	9.6	5.8	11.0	12.4	5.2	11.1	13.4
Profitability									
Return - Sales (%)	6.5	4.3	1.7	4.9	4.3	.4	6.4	4.1	1.0
Return - Assets (%)	11.1	9.9	1.9	15.6	6.5	1.0	10.7	7.5	3.3
Return - Net Worth (%)	18.0	12.9	3.5	27.1	16.1	-6.2	23.0	17.3	14.3

Source: Dun & Bradstreet. Data in this table are copyright (c) 1999 of Dun & Bradstreet. Reprinted by special arrangement with D&B. *Note:* UQ stands for "Upper Quartile" and represents the top 25 percent of sample; MED stands for "Median"; and LQ stands for "Lower Quartile" and represents the lowest 25 percent.

D&B INDUSTRY NORMS: SIC 2841 - SOAP AND OTHER DETERGENTS

	1998 (40) Estab.		1997 (54) Estab.		1996 (44) Estab.	
	$	%	$	%	$	%
Cash	99,264	14.1	77,259	12.0	67,491	10.8
Accounts Receivable	221,056	31.4	190,572	29.6	188,099	30.1
Notes Receivable	704	.1	5,794	.9	2,500	.4
Inventory	153,472	21.8	149,367	23.2	151,229	24.2
Other Current Assets	38,016	5.4	17,383	2.7	12,498	2.0
Total Current Assets	512,512	72.8	440,375	68.4	421,817	67.5
Fixed Assets	136,576	19.4	140,354	21.8	134,981	21.6
Other Non-current Assets	54,912	7.8	63,095	9.8	68,116	10.9
Total Assets	704,000	100.0	643,824	100.0	624,914	100.0
Accounts Payable	110,528	15.7	82,409	12.8	83,114	13.3
Bank Loans	6,336	.9	-	-	-	-
Notes Payable	23,232	3.3	7,082	1.1	6,874	1.1
Other Current Liabilities	71,808	10.2	84,985	13.2	78,739	12.6
Total Current Liabilities	211,904	30.1	174,476	27.1	168,727	27.0
Other Long Term	91,520	13.0	102,368	15.9	85,613	13.7
Deferred Credits	-	-	1,931	.3	1,875	.3
Net Worth	400,576	56.9	365,048	56.7	368,699	59.0
Total Liabilities & Net Worth	704,000	100.0	643,823	100.0	624,914	100.0
Net Sales	1,892,208	100.0	1,397,760	100.0	1,300,000	100.0
Gross Profits	883,661	46.7	595,446	42.6	574,600	44.2
Net Profit After Tax	102,179	5.4	46,126	3.3	41,600	3.2
Working Capital	300,608	-	265,900	-	253,090	-

Source: Dun & Bradstreet. Data in this table are copyright (c) 1999 of Dun & Bradstreet. Reprinted by special arrangement with D&B. *Notes:* Values in parentheses above columns indicate the number of establishments in the sample. Data shown are for all companies.

D&B KEY BUSINESS RATIOS: SIC 2841

	1998			1997			1996		
	UQ	MED	LQ	UQ	MED	LQ	UQ	MED	LQ
Solvency									
Quick ratio	3.6	1.4	.7	3.2	1.7	.8	3.4	1.9	.7
Current ratio	5.1	2.3	1.5	5.1	2.7	1.7	5.7	2.7	1.5
Current liabilities/Net worth (%)	17.0	63.5	88.3	16.1	32.0	82.6	17.2	32.7	79.9
Current liabilities/Inventory (%)	69.1	134.5	263.2	62.5	104.7	205.7	59.8	111.5	207.0
Total liabilities/Net worth (%)	19.0	63.5	152.1	26.3	48.9	134.3	29.5	60.3	194.1
Fixed assets/Net worth (%)	12.7	26.9	79.1	14.6	26.9	65.2	15.4	37.4	76.4
Efficiency									
Collection period (days)	28.7	40.0	49.3	28.0	40.7	49.8	27.4	37.2	50.4
Sales to Inventory	15.4	11.9	9.0	17.9	11.0	7.4	14.3	9.9	6.4
Assets/Sales (%)	27.5	33.6	53.8	27.4	36.5	76.7	36.6	40.9	79.3
Sales/Net Working Capital	13.0	6.9	4.8	10.4	5.9	4.0	7.4	5.5	3.7
Accounts payable/Sales (%)	4.0	6.8	7.9	4.4	5.5	8.0	4.8	5.6	7.9
Profitability									
Return - Sales (%)	8.3	3.5	1.7	9.3	5.3	1.9	6.9	3.5	1.9
Return - Assets (%)	15.4	9.1	4.5	21.5	9.4	5.2	16.5	8.8	3.5
Return - Net Worth (%)	31.5	16.7	9.0	38.5	19.8	7.6	26.0	12.0	4.5

Source: Dun & Bradstreet. Data in this table are copyright (c) 1999 of Dun & Bradstreet. Reprinted by special arrangement with D&B. *Note:* UQ stands for "Upper Quartile" and represents the top 25 percent of sample; MED stands for "Median"; and LQ stands for "Lower Quartile" and represents the lowest 25 percent.

D&B INDUSTRY NORMS: SIC 2842 - POLISHES AND SANITATION GOODS

	1998 (95) Estab.		1997 (133) Estab.		1996 (144) Estab.	
	$	%	$	%	$	%
Cash	125,850	14.5	138,288	13.7	87,476	11.0
Accounts Receivable	246,492	28.4	274,558	27.2	225,846	28.4
Notes Receivable	8,679	1.0	7,066	.7	5,567	.7
Inventory	210,907	24.3	260,426	25.8	202,785	25.5
Other Current Assets	42,529	4.9	53,498	5.3	46,124	5.8
Total Current Assets	634,457	73.1	733,836	72.7	567,798	71.4
Fixed Assets	176,190	20.3	191,787	19.0	155,866	19.6
Other Non-current Assets	57,283	6.6	83,781	8.3	71,571	9.0
Total Assets	867,930	100.0	1,009,404	100.0	795,235	100.0
Accounts Payable	129,321	14.9	155,448	15.4	137,575	17.3
Bank Loans	2,604	.3	1,009	.1	795	.1
Notes Payable	27,774	3.2	60,564	6.0	40,557	5.1
Other Current Liabilities	85,057	9.8	130,213	12.9	97,019	12.2
Total Current Liabilities	244,756	28.2	347,234	34.4	275,946	34.7
Other Long Term	125,850	14.5	86,809	8.6	93,042	11.7
Deferred Credits	-	-	1,009	.1	-	-
Net Worth	497,323	57.3	574,351	56.9	426,245	53.6
Total Liabilities & Net Worth	867,929	100.0	1,009,403	100.0	795,233	100.0
Net Sales	1,910,998	100.0	1,876,235	100.0	1,903,667	100.0
Gross Profits	728,090	38.1	786,142	41.9	793,829	41.7
Net Profit After Tax	57,330	3.0	73,173	3.9	60,917	3.2
Working Capital	389,700	-	386,602	-	291,851	-

Source: Dun & Bradstreet. Data in this table are copyright (c) 1999 of Dun & Bradstreet. Reprinted by special arrangement with D&B. *Notes:* Values in parentheses above columns indicate the number of establishments in the sample. Data shown are for all companies.

D&B KEY BUSINESS RATIOS: SIC 2842

	1998			1997			1996		
	UQ	MED	LQ	UQ	MED	LQ	UQ	MED	LQ
Solvency									
Quick ratio	3.0	1.5	.8	2.5	1.1	.7	2.4	1.1	.7
Current ratio	4.8	2.7	1.6	4.2	2.2	1.4	4.0	2.1	1.3
Current liabilities/Net worth (%)	19.4	39.8	114.5	19.6	58.7	123.2	23.6	45.5	100.7
Current liabilities/Inventory (%)	76.0	124.4	176.0	65.8	136.2	205.6	68.5	125.1	258.7
Total liabilities/Net worth (%)	21.0	58.9	178.4	25.3	67.0	153.8	26.5	63.9	142.8
Fixed assets/Net worth (%)	13.5	28.2	67.9	13.0	30.1	60.6	14.3	33.5	64.8
Efficiency									
Collection period (days)	28.5	40.0	53.5	31.6	40.9	51.1	28.4	41.8	52.8
Sales to Inventory	15.6	12.6	8.3	15.0	10.6	7.0	15.9	10.2	6.9
Assets/Sales (%)	26.9	35.6	65.0	30.1	39.8	59.9	29.9	38.4	61.8
Sales/Net Working Capital	12.0	6.9	4.0	11.4	5.7	3.5	13.8	7.0	3.5
Accounts payable/Sales (%)	3.4	5.6	8.6	3.4	5.7	9.5	3.4	5.5	8.4
Profitability									
Return - Sales (%)	4.6	2.1	.3	6.0	2.2	.5	6.0	2.4	.9
Return - Assets (%)	10.5	6.5	.5	11.1	5.6	1.6	11.1	6.2	2.0
Return - Net Worth (%)	19.6	8.7	1.7	22.3	10.3	2.9	29.0	12.1	3.7

Source: Dun & Bradstreet. Data in this table are copyright (c) 1999 of Dun & Bradstreet. Reprinted by special arrangement with D&B. *Note:* UQ stands for "Upper Quartile" and represents the top 25 percent of sample; MED stands for "Median"; and LQ stands for "Lower Quartile" and represents the lowest 25 percent.

D&B INDUSTRY NORMS: SIC 2843 - SURFACE ACTIVE AGENTS

	1998 (20) Estab.		1997 (19) Estab.		1996 (16) Estab.	
	$	%	$	%	$	%
Cash	139,260	13.3	272,116	10.8	250,118	8.3
Accounts Receivable	332,968	31.8	970,042	38.5	819,663	27.2
Notes Receivable	1,047	.1	15,118	.6	6,027	.2
Inventory	258,626	24.7	491,320	19.5	699,125	23.2
Other Current Assets	25,130	2.4	108,342	4.3	286,279	9.5
Total Current Assets	757,031	72.3	1,856,938	73.7	2,061,212	68.4
Fixed Assets	224,073	21.4	582,025	23.1	795,556	26.4
Other Non-current Assets	65,965	6.3	80,627	3.2	156,700	5.2
Total Assets	1,047,069	100.0	2,519,590	100.0	3,013,468	100.0
Accounts Payable	234,543	22.4	473,683	18.8	455,034	15.1
Bank Loans	2,094	.2	-	-	-	-
Notes Payable	84,813	8.1	131,019	5.2	162,727	5.4
Other Current Liabilities	101,566	9.7	377,939	15.0	497,222	16.5
Total Current Liabilities	423,016	40.4	982,641	39.0	1,114,983	37.0
Other Long Term	70,154	6.7	259,518	10.3	319,428	10.6
Deferred Credits	8,377	.8	12,598	.5	6,027	.2
Net Worth	545,523	52.1	1,264,834	50.2	1,573,030	52.2
Total Liabilities & Net Worth	1,047,070	100.0	2,519,591	100.0	3,013,468	100.0
Net Sales	2,088,991	100.0	8,015,963	100.0	10,000,426	100.0
Gross Profits	643,409	30.8	2,557,092	31.9	3,060,130	30.6
Net Profit After Tax	56,403	2.7	384,766	4.8	510,022	5.1
Working Capital	334,015	-	874,298	-	946,229	-

Source: Dun & Bradstreet. Data in this table are copyright (c) 1999 of Dun & Bradstreet. Reprinted by special arrangement with D&B. *Notes:* Values in parentheses above columns indicate the number of establishments in the sample. Data shown are for all companies.

D&B KEY BUSINESS RATIOS: SIC 2843

	1998			1997			1996		
	UQ	MED	LQ	UQ	MED	LQ	UQ	MED	LQ
Solvency									
Quick ratio	1.5	1.2	.9	1.7	1.3	1.0	1.4	1.0	.7
Current ratio	2.2	1.9	1.8	2.9	1.9	1.4	2.7	2.2	1.5
Current liabilities/Net worth (%)	45.7	60.1	92.9	40.1	68.4	150.2	39.2	70.2	94.0
Current liabilities/Inventory (%)	126.7	161.8	193.3	133.5	151.8	280.1	99.1	128.1	165.5
Total liabilities/Net worth (%)	46.9	95.5	124.5	42.5	115.1	177.7	46.5	98.6	139.9
Fixed assets/Net worth (%)	22.2	46.0	84.1	12.9	31.5	80.3	23.7	36.2	75.6
Efficiency									
Collection period (days)	22.3	50.7	57.3	45.5	49.6	63.2	38.0	50.2	57.9
Sales to Inventory	14.9	11.1	7.1	14.6	10.7	8.6	14.1	9.7	7.6
Assets/Sales (%)	29.7	41.0	60.1	36.9	47.4	66.2	40.9	55.3	72.8
Sales/Net Working Capital	8.8	7.3	5.8	7.6	5.7	3.9	11.5	5.3	4.3
Accounts payable/Sales (%)	5.2	6.7	13.2	5.9	7.4	9.8	4.2	8.2	9.9
Profitability									
Return - Sales (%)	5.2	3.3	1.4	9.2	4.3	1.9	10.7	4.0	2.3
Return - Assets (%)	9.6	7.1	3.4	36.2	6.2	4.2	12.9	5.7	4.4
Return - Net Worth (%)	17.5	14.8	7.8	69.5	17.7	11.1	61.4	13.9	12.7

Source: Dun & Bradstreet. Data in this table are copyright (c) 1999 of Dun & Bradstreet. Reprinted by special arrangement with D&B. *Note:* UQ stands for "Upper Quartile" and represents the top 25 percent of sample; MED stands for "Median"; and LQ stands for "Lower Quartile" and represents the lowest 25 percent.

D&B INDUSTRY NORMS: SIC 2844 - TOILET PREPARATIONS

	1998 (99) Estab.		1997 (123) Estab.		1996 (114) Estab.	
	$	%	$	%	$	%
Cash	410,599	7.9	156,819	11.0	97,776	9.6
Accounts Receivable	1,366,931	26.3	337,874	23.7	245,459	24.1
Notes Receivable	25,987	.5	5,703	.4	2,037	.2
Inventory	1,533,250	29.5	402,028	28.2	290,274	28.5
Other Current Assets	384,612	7.4	84,112	5.9	65,184	6.4
Total Current Assets	3,721,379	71.6	986,536	69.2	700,730	68.8
Fixed Assets	914,752	17.6	275,147	19.3	202,682	19.9
Other Non-current Assets	561,325	10.8	163,947	11.5	115,091	11.3
Total Assets	5,197,456	100.0	1,425,630	100.0	1,018,503	100.0
Accounts Payable	867,975	16.7	191,034	13.4	144,628	14.2
Bank Loans	5,197	.1	2,851	.2	1,019	.1
Notes Payable	150,726	2.9	65,579	4.6	45,833	4.5
Other Current Liabilities	769,224	14.8	228,101	16.0	174,164	17.1
Total Current Liabilities	1,793,122	34.5	487,565	34.2	365,644	35.9
Other Long Term	1,060,281	20.4	250,911	17.6	187,405	18.4
Deferred Credits	5,197	.1	5,703	.4	4,074	.4
Net Worth	2,338,856	45.0	681,451	47.8	461,382	45.3
Total Liabilities & Net Worth	5,197,456	100.0	1,425,630	100.0	1,018,505	100.0
Net Sales	7,162,806	100.0	2,262,984	100.0	1,747,888	100.0
Gross Profits	3,094,332	43.2	1,068,128	47.2	821,507	47.0
Net Profit After Tax	343,815	4.8	79,204	3.5	106,621	6.1
Working Capital	1,928,256	-	498,971	-	335,088	-

Source: Dun & Bradstreet. Data in this table are copyright (c) 1999 of Dun & Bradstreet. Reprinted by special arrangement with D&B. *Notes:* Values in parentheses above columns indicate the number of establishments in the sample. Data shown are for all companies.

D&B KEY BUSINESS RATIOS: SIC 2844

	1998			1997			1996		
	UQ	MED	LQ	UQ	MED	LQ	UQ	MED	LQ
Solvency									
Quick ratio	1.7	.9	.6	1.9	1.0	.7	1.6	.9	.6
Current ratio	3.2	2.2	1.5	3.7	2.1	1.4	3.5	1.8	1.4
Current liabilities/Net worth (%)	37.8	59.8	168.6	26.0	51.9	116.6	24.7	66.7	151.6
Current liabilities/Inventory (%)	81.8	118.2	165.5	73.8	129.8	192.3	75.1	119.0	197.1
Total liabilities/Net worth (%)	53.5	93.2	266.4	41.4	93.5	171.5	52.5	116.2	231.7
Fixed assets/Net worth (%)	14.6	36.1	79.1	11.7	35.9	70.0	12.6	38.2	73.6
Efficiency									
Collection period (days)	36.0	51.3	72.3	33.4	52.9	72.0	29.5	49.1	64.0
Sales to Inventory	9.5	6.1	4.7	9.1	6.4	3.8	10.5	6.6	3.7
Assets/Sales (%)	38.8	55.4	86.0	42.4	59.1	100.6	35.4	54.2	81.7
Sales/Net Working Capital	10.3	5.8	2.9	9.4	4.9	2.6	9.2	6.3	3.6
Accounts payable/Sales (%)	5.3	8.2	11.5	4.1	6.8	10.9	3.4	5.9	10.3
Profitability									
Return - Sales (%)	7.7	4.9	1.8	6.8	3.8	1.3	9.5	4.6	1.5
Return - Assets (%)	14.3	8.5	2.5	11.8	6.2	1.7	15.6	7.0	2.4
Return - Net Worth (%)	44.1	21.0	8.3	30.8	13.0	7.1	40.7	18.5	8.7

Source: Dun & Bradstreet. Data in this table are copyright (c) 1999 of Dun & Bradstreet. Reprinted by special arrangement with D&B. *Note:* UQ stands for "Upper Quartile" and represents the top 25 percent of sample; MED stands for "Median"; and LQ stands for "Lower Quartile" and represents the lowest 25 percent.

D&B INDUSTRY NORMS: SIC 2851 - PAINTS AND ALLIED PRODUCTS

	1998 (131) Estab.		1997 (173) Estab.		1996 (174) Estab.	
	$	%	$	%	$	%
Cash	179,022	10.4	157,308	10.4	135,021	11.4
Accounts Receivable	478,539	27.8	431,085	28.5	335,185	28.3
Notes Receivable	8,607	.5	6,050	.4	9,475	.8
Inventory	478,539	27.8	429,573	28.4	334,000	28.2
Other Current Assets	75,740	4.4	62,016	4.1	45,007	3.8
Total Current Assets	1,220,447	70.9	1,086,032	71.8	858,688	72.5
Fixed Assets	399,356	23.2	314,617	20.8	229,773	19.4
Other Non-current Assets	101,560	5.9	111,931	7.4	95,936	8.1
Total Assets	1,721,363	100.0	1,512,580	100.0	1,184,397	100.0
Accounts Payable	277,139	16.1	266,214	17.6	200,163	16.9
Bank Loans	1,721	.1	-	-	-	-
Notes Payable	55,084	3.2	42,352	2.8	42,638	3.6
Other Current Liabilities	194,514	11.3	183,022	12.1	133,837	11.3
Total Current Liabilities	528,458	30.7	491,588	32.5	376,638	31.8
Other Long Term	246,155	14.3	205,711	13.6	146,865	12.4
Deferred Credits	-	-	6,050	.4	3,553	.3
Net Worth	946,750	55.0	809,230	53.5	657,341	55.5
Total Liabilities & Net Worth	1,721,363	100.0	1,512,579	100.0	1,184,397	100.0
Net Sales	3,889,107	100.0	3,365,198	100.0	3,007,246	100.0
Gross Profits	1,384,522	35.6	1,167,724	34.7	1,046,522	34.8
Net Profit After Tax	116,673	3.0	104,321	3.1	114,275	3.8
Working Capital	691,988	-	594,443	-	482,050	-

Source: Dun & Bradstreet. Data in this table are copyright (c) 1999 of Dun & Bradstreet. Reprinted by special arrangement with D&B. *Notes:* Values in parentheses above columns indicate the number of establishments in the sample. Data shown are for all companies.

D&B KEY BUSINESS RATIOS: SIC 2851

	1998			1997			1996		
	UQ	MED	LQ	UQ	MED	LQ	UQ	MED	LQ
Solvency									
Quick ratio	2.1	1.3	.8	2.0	1.2	.8	2.1	1.3	.8
Current ratio	4.0	2.4	1.6	4.1	2.4	1.6	4.1	2.3	1.6
Current liabilities/Net worth (%)	25.1	52.3	87.3	25.4	50.3	101.0	26.2	50.6	103.8
Current liabilities/Inventory (%)	67.8	102.7	166.3	62.2	111.1	177.5	61.4	103.2	166.3
Total liabilities/Net worth (%)	35.6	76.9	146.9	40.0	74.5	159.5	31.6	77.7	144.4
Fixed assets/Net worth (%)	19.3	37.4	69.0	17.2	36.9	67.3	15.9	30.8	54.2
Efficiency									
Collection period (days)	34.3	44.2	55.9	33.2	43.4	59.1	33.6	44.5	61.8
Sales to Inventory	12.0	7.9	6.3	13.2	8.6	5.8	10.6	8.1	6.1
Assets/Sales (%)	30.5	42.9	56.8	31.8	42.8	54.4	33.2	44.5	57.3
Sales/Net Working Capital	9.3	5.8	4.2	10.4	5.7	3.8	8.9	5.8	4.0
Accounts payable/Sales (%)	4.0	6.3	10.2	3.7	6.8	10.3	3.9	7.1	9.8
Profitability									
Return - Sales (%)	5.5	2.9	.8	6.8	2.5	.4	5.8	2.4	.7
Return - Assets (%)	10.9	5.9	2.5	12.7	5.1	.6	11.0	5.9	1.4
Return - Net Worth (%)	21.8	12.5	4.3	25.5	10.1	2.0	21.2	9.5	2.9

Source: Dun & Bradstreet. Data in this table are copyright (c) 1999 of Dun & Bradstreet. Reprinted by special arrangement with D&B. *Note:* UQ stands for "Upper Quartile" and represents the top 25 percent of sample; MED stands for "Median"; and LQ stands for "Lower Quartile" and represents the lowest 25 percent.

D&B INDUSTRY NORMS: SIC 2865 - CYCLIC CRUDES AND INTERMEDIATES

	1998 (23) Estab.		1997 (27) Estab.		1996 (25) Estab.	
	$	%	$	%	$	%
Cash	680,293	7.4	253,728	8.7	77,659	5.7
Accounts Receivable	2,059,265	22.4	781,598	26.8	392,381	28.8
Notes Receivable	9,193	.1	17,498	.6	1,362	.1
Inventory	1,930,561	21.0	694,106	23.8	311,997	22.9
Other Current Assets	367,726	4.0	113,740	3.9	54,497	4.0
Total Current Assets	5,047,038	54.9	1,860,670	63.8	837,896	61.5
Fixed Assets	3,088,898	33.6	819,511	28.1	404,643	29.7
Other Non-current Assets	1,057,212	11.5	236,229	8.1	119,894	8.8
Total Assets	9,193,148	100.0	2,916,410	100.0	1,362,433	100.0
Accounts Payable	1,130,757	12.3	463,709	15.9	246,601	18.1
Bank Loans	-	-	-	-	-	-
Notes Payable	257,408	2.8	34,997	1.2	9,537	.7
Other Current Liabilities	1,617,994	17.6	440,378	15.1	162,130	11.9
Total Current Liabilities	3,006,159	32.7	939,084	32.2	418,268	30.7
Other Long Term	2,914,228	31.7	454,960	15.6	174,392	12.8
Deferred Credits	-	-	14,582	.5	4,087	.3
Net Worth	3,272,761	35.6	1,507,784	51.7	765,688	56.2
Total Liabilities & Net Worth	9,193,148	100.0	2,916,410	100.0	1,362,435	100.0
Net Sales	15,813,010	100.0	6,507,857	100.0	5,624,917	100.0
Gross Profits	4,569,960	28.9	2,056,483	31.6	1,456,854	25.9
Net Profit After Tax	869,716	5.5	390,471	6.0	269,996	4.8
Working Capital	2,040,879	-	921,586	-	419,630	-

Source: Dun & Bradstreet. Data in this table are copyright (c) 1999 of Dun & Bradstreet. Reprinted by special arrangement with D&B. *Notes:* Values in parentheses above columns indicate the number of establishments in the sample. Data shown are for all companies.

D&B KEY BUSINESS RATIOS: SIC 2865

	1998			1997			1996		
	UQ	MED	LQ	UQ	MED	LQ	UQ	MED	LQ
Solvency									
Quick ratio	1.6	.9	.6	2.1	1.4	.9	1.6	1.3	1.1
Current ratio	2.9	1.9	1.2	3.7	2.3	1.5	3.6	2.3	1.7
Current liabilities/Net worth (%)	28.1	79.8	439.9	23.0	45.8	130.9	17.4	29.4	97.4
Current liabilities/Inventory (%)	100.8	133.7	176.0	73.1	158.9	226.2	66.8	123.3	201.8
Total liabilities/Net worth (%)	37.6	103.0	365.7	27.6	66.2	308.3	26.8	65.1	111.0
Fixed assets/Net worth (%)	38.3	65.2	114.2	35.1	58.3	136.0	20.4	65.0	88.9
Efficiency									
Collection period (days)	45.9	52.2	69.3	36.6	45.5	58.5	39.6	45.9	54.8
Sales to Inventory	11.7	8.0	5.4	18.3	10.7	7.8	18.7	9.1	6.5
Assets/Sales (%)	39.9	70.5	113.8	31.2	40.9	71.6	33.5	58.2	81.6
Sales/Net Working Capital	7.8	5.4	3.4	11.2	6.7	3.9	8.4	5.6	3.6
Accounts payable/Sales (%)	4.4	7.9	12.6	3.1	8.4	9.4	3.9	6.7	8.6
Profitability									
Return - Sales (%)	9.2	3.7	1.1	8.6	3.1	2.2	10.3	4.7	.4
Return - Assets (%)	13.1	4.8	1.6	18.2	8.5	3.8	26.8	8.8	.6
Return - Net Worth (%)	38.9	21.4	6.0	49.3	26.2	15.2	42.3	16.0	2.7

Source: Dun & Bradstreet. Data in this table are copyright (c) 1999 of Dun & Bradstreet. Reprinted by special arrangement with D&B. *Note:* UQ stands for "Upper Quartile" and represents the top 25 percent of sample; MED stands for "Median"; and LQ stands for "Lower Quartile" and represents the lowest 25 percent.

D&B INDUSTRY NORMS: SIC 2869 - INDUSTRIAL ORGANIC CHEMICALS, NEC

	1998 (79) Estab.		1997 (89) Estab.		1996 (72) Estab.	
	$	%	$	%	$	%
Cash	853,437	8.3	502,598	9.0	566,241	13.4
Accounts Receivable	2,272,406	22.1	1,256,494	22.5	942,327	22.3
Notes Receivable	10,282	.1	5,584	.1	4,226	.1
Inventory	1,552,639	15.1	1,055,455	18.9	878,942	20.8
Other Current Assets	421,578	4.1	228,961	4.1	164,802	3.9
Total Current Assets	5,110,342	49.7	3,049,092	54.6	2,556,538	60.5
Fixed Assets	3,670,809	35.7	1,747,923	31.3	1,267,705	30.0
Other Non-current Assets	1,501,227	14.6	787,403	14.1	401,440	9.5
Total Assets	10,282,378	100.0	5,584,418	100.0	4,225,683	100.0
Accounts Payable	1,521,792	14.8	742,728	13.3	481,728	11.4
Bank Loans	-	-	-	-	-	-
Notes Payable	349,601	3.4	161,948	2.9	135,222	3.2
Other Current Liabilities	1,233,885	12.0	731,559	13.1	667,658	15.8
Total Current Liabilities	3,105,278	30.2	1,636,235	29.3	1,284,608	30.4
Other Long Term	2,087,323	20.3	1,005,195	18.0	566,241	13.4
Deferred Credits	102,824	1.0	27,922	.5	8,451	.2
Net Worth	4,986,954	48.5	2,915,067	52.2	2,366,382	56.0
Total Liabilities & Net Worth	10,282,379	100.0	5,584,419	100.0	4,225,682	100.0
Net Sales	9,830,591	100.0	6,921,129	100.0	6,214,132	100.0
Gross Profits	3,578,335	36.4	2,477,764	35.8	2,628,578	42.3
Net Profit After Tax	717,633	7.3	318,372	4.6	422,561	6.8
Working Capital	2,005,064	-	1,412,858	-	1,271,931	-

Source: Dun & Bradstreet. Data in this table are copyright (c) 1999 of Dun & Bradstreet. Reprinted by special arrangement with D&B. *Notes:* Values in parentheses above columns indicate the number of establishments in the sample. Data shown are for all companies.

D&B KEY BUSINESS RATIOS: SIC 2869

	1998			1997			1996		
	UQ	MED	LQ	UQ	MED	LQ	UQ	MED	LQ
Solvency									
Quick ratio	1.4	.9	.5	1.6	.9	.6	1.8	1.1	.8
Current ratio	2.4	1.7	1.1	3.0	1.7	1.2	3.4	1.9	1.6
Current liabilities/Net worth (%)	27.6	47.7	89.2	22.6	52.2	103.1	20.7	45.5	94.9
Current liabilities/Inventory (%)	95.0	166.9	294.2	85.9	144.0	236.9	87.9	128.6	182.4
Total liabilities/Net worth (%)	44.5	97.3	151.8	40.1	89.9	166.6	33.2	80.9	138.3
Fixed assets/Net worth (%)	29.6	75.6	134.3	29.8	51.1	96.4	31.2	45.6	97.5
Efficiency									
Collection period (days)	28.7	46.7	62.4	32.7	43.8	58.6	31.6	42.0	54.2
Sales to Inventory	21.8	11.2	6.8	17.2	10.5	6.9	13.3	9.4	6.8
Assets/Sales (%)	37.0	68.1	103.0	42.6	71.8	121.9	37.4	65.3	106.5
Sales/Net Working Capital	17.9	7.7	3.5	22.4	7.3	4.2	10.6	6.8	3.7
Accounts payable/Sales (%)	3.6	6.3	9.1	3.9	6.2	8.7	3.8	5.3	6.9
Profitability									
Return - Sales (%)	15.1	7.2	2.7	8.8	4.6	1.0	11.9	5.3	1.1
Return - Assets (%)	17.6	8.1	4.5	12.6	7.5	2.2	17.4	7.1	2.6
Return - Net Worth (%)	36.9	19.4	7.6	26.7	16.0	5.5	30.4	13.0	5.3

Source: Dun & Bradstreet. Data in this table are copyright (c) 1999 of Dun & Bradstreet. Reprinted by special arrangement with D&B. *Note:* UQ stands for "Upper Quartile" and represents the top 25 percent of sample; MED stands for "Median"; and LQ stands for "Lower Quartile" and represents the lowest 25 percent.

D&B INDUSTRY NORMS: SIC 2873 - NITROGENOUS FERTILIZERS

	1998 (36) Estab.		1997 (39) Estab.		1996 (39) Estab.	
	$	%	$	%	$	%
Cash	589,936	8.6	173,751	11.0	163,015	11.6
Accounts Receivable	1,419,963	20.7	314,330	19.9	275,438	19.6
Notes Receivable	6,860	.1	3,159	.2	-	-
Inventory	1,186,732	17.3	314,330	19.9	243,117	17.3
Other Current Assets	281,249	4.1	82,137	5.2	89,939	6.4
Total Current Assets	3,484,740	50.8	887,707	56.2	771,509	54.9
Fixed Assets	2,730,170	39.8	573,377	36.3	497,475	35.4
Other Non-current Assets	644,814	9.4	118,466	7.5	136,314	9.7
Total Assets	6,859,724	100.0	1,579,550	100.0	1,405,298	100.0
Accounts Payable	699,692	10.2	165,853	10.5	185,499	13.2
Bank Loans	-	-	-	-	7,026	.5
Notes Payable	27,439	.4	60,023	3.8	84,318	6.0
Other Current Liabilities	939,782	13.7	284,319	18.0	202,363	14.4
Total Current Liabilities	1,666,913	24.3	510,195	32.3	479,206	34.1
Other Long Term	1,502,279	21.9	325,387	20.6	289,491	20.6
Deferred Credits	54,878	.8	4,739	.3	1,405	.1
Net Worth	3,635,653	53.0	739,229	46.8	635,195	45.2
Total Liabilities & Net Worth	6,859,723	100.0	1,579,550	100.0	1,405,297	100.0
Net Sales	40,343,651	100.0	6,701,698	100.0	6,064,857	100.0
Gross Profits	10,449,006	25.9	1,682,126	25.1	1,910,430	31.5
Net Profit After Tax	3,267,836	8.1	462,417	6.9	351,762	5.8
Working Capital	1,817,826	-	377,512	-	292,302	-

Source: Dun & Bradstreet. Data in this table are copyright (c) 1999 of Dun & Bradstreet. Reprinted by special arrangement with D&B. *Notes:* Values in parentheses above columns indicate the number of establishments in the sample. Data shown are for all companies.

D&B KEY BUSINESS RATIOS: SIC 2873

	1998			1997			1996		
	UQ	MED	LQ	UQ	MED	LQ	UQ	MED	LQ
Solvency									
Quick ratio	1.8	1.1	.8	1.6	1.1	.5	1.5	1.0	.6
Current ratio	2.7	2.1	1.5	2.8	1.9	1.1	2.6	1.6	1.2
Current liabilities/Net worth (%)	17.0	42.9	95.3	24.1	48.0	184.6	28.4	70.2	169.4
Current liabilities/Inventory (%)	93.0	120.8	230.4	103.8	148.9	272.9	132.5	179.6	239.1
Total liabilities/Net worth (%)	24.6	73.3	134.2	32.6	82.0	180.1	40.1	114.2	158.2
Fixed assets/Net worth (%)	43.3	82.0	130.8	40.4	70.9	116.6	35.7	66.1	143.2
Efficiency									
Collection period (days)	18.5	42.0	59.2	14.5	36.0	53.0	26.7	42.7	71.5
Sales to Inventory	11.5	7.2	6.1	15.2	9.5	6.8	14.8	9.8	5.8
Assets/Sales (%)	52.6	81.9	110.4	34.9	65.0	87.3	41.2	71.8	92.7
Sales/Net Working Capital	9.3	5.7	3.4	13.1	6.0	4.1	11.8	5.3	4.1
Accounts payable/Sales (%)	3.2	5.7	12.7	2.4	6.5	9.2	3.0	5.6	9.7
Profitability									
Return - Sales (%)	10.9	5.3	2.6	7.2	3.1	.8	4.5	3.4	1.4
Return - Assets (%)	17.7	11.0	2.9	15.9	7.3	1.7	15.9	4.9	1.3
Return - Net Worth (%)	34.5	21.1	10.7	58.1	20.8	7.1	25.7	9.3	1.4

Source: Dun & Bradstreet. Data in this table are copyright (c) 1999 of Dun & Bradstreet. Reprinted by special arrangement with D&B. *Note:* UQ stands for "Upper Quartile" and represents the top 25 percent of sample; MED stands for "Median"; and LQ stands for "Lower Quartile" and represents the lowest 25 percent.

D&B INDUSTRY NORMS: SIC 2875 - FERTILIZERS, MIXING ONLY

	1998 (39) Estab.		1997 (50) Estab.		1996 (49) Estab.	
	$	%	$	%	$	%
Cash	406,792	12.2	214,689	10.6	227,208	13.8
Accounts Receivable	803,581	24.1	514,442	25.4	411,609	25.0
Notes Receivable	6,669	.2	14,178	.7	14,818	.9
Inventory	660,204	19.8	427,352	21.1	347,398	21.1
Other Current Assets	193,393	5.8	74,938	3.7	65,857	4.0
Total Current Assets	2,070,639	62.1	1,245,599	61.5	1,066,890	64.8
Fixed Assets	1,033,652	31.0	646,091	31.9	477,466	29.0
Other Non-current Assets	230,071	6.9	133,674	6.6	102,079	6.2
Total Assets	3,334,362	100.0	2,025,364	100.0	1,646,435	100.0
Accounts Payable	420,130	12.6	267,348	13.2	220,622	13.4
Bank Loans	-	-	-	-	-	-
Notes Payable	180,056	5.4	105,319	5.2	95,493	5.8
Other Current Liabilities	360,111	10.8	315,957	15.6	274,954	16.7
Total Current Liabilities	960,297	28.8	688,624	34.0	591,069	35.9
Other Long Term	593,516	17.8	346,337	17.1	265,076	16.1
Deferred Credits	-	-	4,051	.2	4,939	.3
Net Worth	1,780,549	53.4	986,352	48.7	785,349	47.7
Total Liabilities & Net Worth	3,334,362	100.0	2,025,364	100.0	1,646,433	100.0
Net Sales	4,687,713	100.0	4,404,430	100.0	4,453,692	100.0
Gross Profits	1,321,935	28.2	1,286,094	29.2	1,166,867	26.2
Net Profit After Tax	168,758	3.6	118,920	2.7	93,528	2.1
Working Capital	1,110,343	-	556,975	-	475,819	-

Source: Dun & Bradstreet. Data in this table are copyright (c) 1999 of Dun & Bradstreet. Reprinted by special arrangement with D&B. *Notes:* Values in parentheses above columns indicate the number of establishments in the sample. Data shown are for all companies.

D&B KEY BUSINESS RATIOS: SIC 2875

	1998			1997			1996		
	UQ	MED	LQ	UQ	MED	LQ	UQ	MED	LQ
Solvency									
Quick ratio	1.8	1.2	.9	1.6	.9	.6	1.3	.8	.6
Current ratio	2.9	1.9	1.6	2.7	1.9	1.3	2.3	1.4	1.2
Current liabilities/Net worth (%)	29.9	58.2	127.5	34.8	61.1	166.8	30.7	59.6	122.9
Current liabilities/Inventory (%)	91.5	136.1	226.5	94.4	140.8	237.7	77.1	124.8	188.1
Total liabilities/Net worth (%)	38.5	102.5	228.1	37.2	132.2	221.0	43.7	94.5	187.0
Fixed assets/Net worth (%)	41.5	58.0	87.4	39.5	63.2	117.8	32.6	59.8	85.4
Efficiency									
Collection period (days)	25.5	33.6	57.3	19.2	32.9	57.4	17.8	34.9	45.4
Sales to Inventory	28.6	14.7	7.0	22.0	14.5	6.8	11.1	7.2	4.5
Assets/Sales (%)	32.0	44.2	58.1	30.9	45.2	62.4	32.7	45.8	66.7
Sales/Net Working Capital	15.4	10.9	5.5	20.5	12.1	5.4	10.0	7.4	4.6
Accounts payable/Sales (%)	3.3	6.0	8.4	3.2	4.8	7.6	3.9	6.0	7.8
Profitability									
Return - Sales (%)	4.4	2.5	1.3	4.6	2.0	.2	3.5	2.5	.6
Return - Assets (%)	9.5	5.5	2.9	10.8	3.6	.4	7.4	4.2	1.5
Return - Net Worth (%)	18.8	13.1	6.2	26.4	10.8	3.2	14.1	10.7	2.6

Source: Dun & Bradstreet. Data in this table are copyright (c) 1999 of Dun & Bradstreet. Reprinted by special arrangement with D&B. *Note:* UQ stands for "Upper Quartile" and represents the top 25 percent of sample; MED stands for "Median"; and LQ stands for "Lower Quartile" and represents the lowest 25 percent.

D&B INDUSTRY NORMS: SIC 2879 - AGRICULTURAL CHEMICALS, NEC

	1998 (34) Estab.		1997 (34) Estab.		1996 (35) Estab.	
	$	%	$	%	$	%
Cash	435,968	11.9	359,144	11.5	391,696	6.3
Accounts Receivable	732,719	20.0	608,983	19.5	1,877,653	30.2
Notes Receivable	73,272	2.0	-	-	99,478	1.6
Inventory	798,663	21.8	605,860	19.4	1,137,783	18.3
Other Current Assets	150,207	4.1	224,855	7.2	453,870	7.3
Total Current Assets	2,190,829	59.8	1,798,842	57.6	3,960,480	63.7
Fixed Assets	1,040,461	28.4	933,774	29.9	1,716,001	27.6
Other Non-current Assets	432,304	11.8	390,374	12.5	540,913	8.7
Total Assets	3,663,594	100.0	3,122,990	100.0	6,217,394	100.0
Accounts Payable	490,922	13.4	515,293	16.5	1,056,957	17.0
Bank Loans	-	-	-	-	-	-
Notes Payable	194,170	5.3	96,813	3.1	304,652	4.9
Other Current Liabilities	472,604	12.9	480,940	15.4	926,392	14.9
Total Current Liabilities	1,157,696	31.6	1,093,046	35.0	2,288,001	36.8
Other Long Term	718,064	19.6	402,866	12.9	1,007,218	16.2
Deferred Credits	7,327	.2	9,369	.3	55,957	.9
Net Worth	1,780,507	48.6	1,617,709	51.8	2,866,219	46.1
Total Liabilities & Net Worth	3,663,594	100.0	3,122,990	100.0	6,217,395	100.0
Net Sales	4,935,781	100.0	5,520,445	100.0	3,129,106	100.0
Gross Profits	2,102,643	42.6	2,108,810	38.2	1,257,901	40.2
Net Profit After Tax	162,881	3.3	160,093	2.9	-18,775	-
Working Capital	1,033,133	-	705,795	-	1,672,480	-

Source: Dun & Bradstreet. Data in this table are copyright (c) 1999 of Dun & Bradstreet. Reprinted by special arrangement with D&B. *Notes:* Values in parentheses above columns indicate the number of establishments in the sample. Data shown are for all companies.

D&B KEY BUSINESS RATIOS: SIC 2879

	1998			1997			1996		
	UQ	MED	LQ	UQ	MED	LQ	UQ	MED	LQ
Solvency									
Quick ratio	1.4	.8	.6	1.5	.9	.5	1.8	1.0	.5
Current ratio	3.3	2.0	1.1	2.9	1.8	1.0	3.2	1.7	1.1
Current liabilities/Net worth (%)	20.8	76.9	118.9	24.2	55.4	127.1	27.8	78.2	222.9
Current liabilities/Inventory (%)	76.7	143.6	257.6	91.5	130.3	275.0	84.1	203.9	320.7
Total liabilities/Net worth (%)	48.7	128.2	198.2	29.5	87.8	184.8	38.6	135.4	304.9
Fixed assets/Net worth (%)	24.5	57.2	86.4	25.7	57.5	115.7	15.6	55.4	123.0
Efficiency									
Collection period (days)	23.0	42.7	88.3	24.2	42.4	61.4	43.8	56.4	72.5
Sales to Inventory	16.4	6.7	4.7	18.3	6.6	4.4	29.6	9.6	6.4
Assets/Sales (%)	48.3	62.2	101.8	44.1	69.6	91.2	41.1	57.9	84.9
Sales/Net Working Capital	10.9	6.9	3.6	6.0	3.8	2.6	5.9	3.9	2.8
Accounts payable/Sales (%)	3.0	6.6	11.2	4.4	6.1	16.2	4.1	6.5	8.4
Profitability									
Return - Sales (%)	5.0	2.5	-	3.8	1.6	.4	5.2	2.0	.8
Return - Assets (%)	9.1	3.1	.7	7.2	3.4	.9	7.2	3.0	.1
Return - Net Worth (%)	26.1	8.5	.2	19.2	9.7	.9	17.6	5.3	.4

Source: Dun & Bradstreet. Data in this table are copyright (c) 1999 of Dun & Bradstreet. Reprinted by special arrangement with D&B. *Note:* UQ stands for "Upper Quartile" and represents the top 25 percent of sample; MED stands for "Median"; and LQ stands for "Lower Quartile" and represents the lowest 25 percent.

D&B INDUSTRY NORMS: SIC 2891 - ADHESIVES AND SEALANTS

	1998 (75) Estab.		1997 (101) Estab.		1996 (95) Estab.	
	$	%	$	%	$	%
Cash	149,809	13.5	180,209	11.6	137,229	13.5
Accounts Receivable	302,948	27.3	448,968	28.9	293,771	28.9
Notes Receivable	4,439	.4	20,196	1.3	7,116	.7
Inventory	243,024	21.9	360,417	23.2	232,781	22.9
Other Current Assets	54,375	4.9	79,230	5.1	37,611	3.7
Total Current Assets	754,595	68.0	1,089,020	70.1	708,508	69.7
Fixed Assets	264,108	23.8	326,240	21.0	217,533	21.4
Other Non-current Assets	90,995	8.2	138,264	8.9	90,469	8.9
Total Assets	1,109,698	100.0	1,553,524	100.0	1,016,510	100.0
Accounts Payable	142,041	12.8	237,689	15.3	156,543	15.4
Bank Loans	1,110	.1	-	-	2,033	.2
Notes Payable	17,755	1.6	45,052	2.9	42,693	4.2
Other Current Liabilities	170,893	15.4	180,209	11.6	105,717	10.4
Total Current Liabilities	331,799	29.9	462,950	29.8	306,986	30.2
Other Long Term	156,467	14.1	198,851	12.8	125,031	12.3
Deferred Credits	3,329	.3	3,107	.2	2,033	.2
Net Worth	618,102	55.7	888,615	57.2	582,460	57.3
Total Liabilities & Net Worth	1,109,697	100.0	1,553,523	100.0	1,016,510	100.0
Net Sales	2,678,049	100.0	3,279,516	100.0	2,738,172	100.0
Gross Profits	910,537	34.0	967,457	29.5	917,288	33.5
Net Profit After Tax	107,122	4.0	111,504	3.4	109,527	4.0
Working Capital	422,795	-	626,070	-	401,521	-

Source: Dun & Bradstreet. Data in this table are copyright (c) 1999 of Dun & Bradstreet. Reprinted by special arrangement with D&B. *Notes:* Values in parentheses above columns indicate the number of establishments in the sample. Data shown are for all companies.

D&B KEY BUSINESS RATIOS: SIC 2891

	1998			1997			1996		
	UQ	MED	LQ	UQ	MED	LQ	UQ	MED	LQ
Solvency									
Quick ratio	2.5	1.4	.9	2.5	1.4	.8	3.0	1.5	.8
Current ratio	4.2	2.5	1.6	4.0	2.7	1.7	5.2	2.4	1.6
Current liabilities/Net worth (%)	17.2	47.1	81.8	23.7	43.0	96.6	16.1	43.1	96.9
Current liabilities/Inventory (%)	67.9	120.8	170.9	72.0	112.9	172.2	65.6	113.1	192.7
Total liabilities/Net worth (%)	29.6	69.0	125.4	27.0	58.0	141.2	24.9	60.7	147.4
Fixed assets/Net worth (%)	14.1	30.9	78.1	16.3	33.2	66.4	15.6	34.0	65.9
Efficiency									
Collection period (days)	34.0	47.8	61.0	33.6	43.1	55.9	34.3	49.3	62.4
Sales to Inventory	13.6	9.1	7.1	13.3	9.3	7.7	14.0	9.9	7.0
Assets/Sales (%)	33.8	47.4	67.5	32.9	44.8	60.1	33.3	43.3	58.0
Sales/Net Working Capital	7.6	5.5	3.3	8.4	5.7	3.2	8.6	4.8	3.5
Accounts payable/Sales (%)	3.6	5.4	8.2	3.9	6.9	10.1	4.0	6.5	9.7
Profitability									
Return - Sales (%)	8.1	4.0	1.3	7.2	3.2	1.0	6.2	2.7	.8
Return - Assets (%)	15.0	6.3	2.5	15.6	5.4	3.3	11.2	4.3	1.7
Return - Net Worth (%)	27.1	15.1	4.8	22.0	12.6	5.2	19.1	9.3	3.2

Source: Dun & Bradstreet. Data in this table are copyright (c) 1999 of Dun & Bradstreet. Reprinted by special arrangement with D&B. *Note:* UQ stands for "Upper Quartile" and represents the top 25 percent of sample; MED stands for "Median"; and LQ stands for "Lower Quartile" and represents the lowest 25 percent.

D&B INDUSTRY NORMS: SIC 2893 - PRINTING INK

	1998 (16) Estab.		1997 (30) Estab.		1996 (21) Estab.	
	$	%	$	%	$	%
Cash	140,151	12.7	118,220	9.6	118,030	9.8
Accounts Receivable	242,781	22.0	304,170	24.7	327,594	27.2
Notes Receivable	12,139	1.1	1,231	.1	-	-
Inventory	258,230	23.4	279,541	22.7	293,871	24.4
Other Current Assets	70,627	6.4	96,054	7.8	71,059	5.9
Total Current Assets	723,928	65.6	799,216	64.9	810,554	67.3
Fixed Assets	286,923	26.0	322,642	26.2	319,163	26.5
Other Non-current Assets	92,698	8.4	109,600	8.9	74,672	6.2
Total Assets	1,103,549	100.0	1,231,458	100.0	1,204,389	100.0
Accounts Payable	169,947	15.4	189,645	15.4	207,155	17.2
Bank Loans	-	-	12,315	1.0	-	-
Notes Payable	70,627	6.4	67,730	5.5	79,490	6.6
Other Current Liabilities	88,284	8.0	171,173	13.9	115,621	9.6
Total Current Liabilities	328,858	29.8	440,863	35.8	402,266	33.4
Other Long Term	94,905	8.6	105,905	8.6	143,322	11.9
Deferred Credits	3,311	.3	3,694	.3	-	-
Net Worth	676,476	61.3	680,997	55.3	658,800	54.7
Total Liabilities & Net Worth	1,103,550	100.0	1,231,459	100.0	1,204,388	100.0
Net Sales	6,134,026	100.0	2,813,851	100.0	2,317,479	100.0
Gross Profits	2,146,909	35.0	996,103	35.4	825,023	35.6
Net Profit After Tax	435,516	7.1	185,714	6.6	90,382	3.9
Working Capital	395,070	-	358,355	-	408,287	-

Source: Dun & Bradstreet. Data in this table are copyright (c) 1999 of Dun & Bradstreet. Reprinted by special arrangement with D&B. *Notes:* Values in parentheses above columns indicate the number of establishments in the sample. Data shown are for all companies.

D&B KEY BUSINESS RATIOS: SIC 2893

	1998			1997			1996		
	UQ	MED	LQ	UQ	MED	LQ	UQ	MED	LQ
Solvency									
Quick ratio	2.2	1.6	1.1	1.9	1.2	.7	2.1	1.2	.9
Current ratio	4.4	3.0	1.9	4.4	2.3	1.0	3.7	2.4	1.5
Current liabilities/Net worth (%)	27.1	35.5	69.0	25.9	56.1	150.2	27.6	53.4	104.2
Current liabilities/Inventory (%)	58.7	119.9	182.9	72.8	129.2	196.1	79.6	141.3	205.2
Total liabilities/Net worth (%)	31.5	62.4	92.4	35.3	89.6	165.4	39.2	98.7	140.2
Fixed assets/Net worth (%)	25.3	33.8	56.8	27.5	45.5	78.2	23.5	43.7	62.0
Efficiency									
Collection period (days)	24.5	33.3	46.1	25.4	39.8	49.0	17.1	38.7	54.9
Sales to Inventory	18.5	11.4	6.1	15.6	10.3	6.2	13.9	9.1	6.6
Assets/Sales (%)	23.1	45.4	72.4	23.8	45.0	60.6	24.6	41.1	50.7
Sales/Net Working Capital	11.7	6.9	4.5	9.4	6.4	4.0	9.6	8.2	5.5
Accounts payable/Sales (%)	3.9	5.2	6.9	3.4	5.5	10.8	3.5	6.7	10.6
Profitability									
Return - Sales (%)	16.7	8.6	2.6	14.2	7.6	2.3	8.7	2.1	1.2
Return - Assets (%)	20.9	10.7	6.6	26.7	10.3	4.7	33.3	6.2	2.7
Return - Net Worth (%)	66.2	18.0	8.6	45.7	22.6	12.2	43.7	12.6	5.2

Source: Dun & Bradstreet. Data in this table are copyright (c) 1999 of Dun & Bradstreet. Reprinted by special arrangement with D&B. *Note:* UQ stands for "Upper Quartile" and represents the top 25 percent of sample; MED stands for "Median"; and LQ stands for "Lower Quartile" and represents the lowest 25 percent.

D&B INDUSTRY NORMS: SIC 2899 - CHEMICAL PREPARATIONS, NEC

	1998 (129) Estab.		1997 (164) Estab.		1996 (166) Estab.	
	$	%	$	%	$	%
Cash	159,031	10.9	114,237	10.3	108,387	11.9
Accounts Receivable	421,652	28.9	323,857	29.2	281,442	30.9
Notes Receivable	5,836	.4	12,200	1.1	6,376	.7
Inventory	284,505	19.5	225,147	20.3	175,787	19.3
Other Current Assets	78,786	5.4	57,673	5.2	46,452	5.1
Total Current Assets	949,810	65.1	733,114	66.1	618,444	67.9
Fixed Assets	360,373	24.7	288,365	26.0	228,615	25.1
Other Non-current Assets	148,818	10.2	87,619	7.9	63,757	7.0
Total Assets	1,459,001	100.0	1,109,098	100.0	910,816	100.0
Accounts Payable	202,801	13.9	177,456	16.0	138,444	15.2
Bank Loans	1,459	.1	-	-	-	-
Notes Payable	51,065	3.5	46,582	4.2	20,949	2.3
Other Current Liabilities	182,375	12.5	170,801	15.4	116,584	12.8
Total Current Liabilities	437,700	30.0	394,839	35.6	275,977	30.3
Other Long Term	250,948	17.2	160,819	14.5	125,693	13.8
Deferred Credits	2,918	.2	1,109	.1	911	.1
Net Worth	767,435	52.6	552,331	49.8	508,235	55.8
Total Liabilities & Net Worth	1,459,001	100.0	1,109,098	100.0	910,816	100.0
Net Sales	2,496,605	100.0	3,146,342	100.0	2,800,623	100.0
Gross Profits	1,138,452	45.6	1,365,512	43.4	1,212,670	43.3
Net Profit After Tax	154,790	6.2	176,195	5.6	168,037	6.0
Working Capital	512,109	-	338,275	-	342,467	-

Source: Dun & Bradstreet. Data in this table are copyright (c) 1999 of Dun & Bradstreet. Reprinted by special arrangement with D&B. *Notes:* Values in parentheses above columns indicate the number of establishments in the sample. Data shown are for all companies.

D&B KEY BUSINESS RATIOS: SIC 2899

	1998			1997			1996		
	UQ	MED	LQ	UQ	MED	LQ	UQ	MED	LQ
Solvency									
Quick ratio	2.4	1.2	.8	2.2	1.1	.7	3.0	1.4	.8
Current ratio	4.2	2.3	1.3	3.9	1.9	1.3	4.7	2.4	1.4
Current liabilities/Net worth (%)	21.1	49.2	105.2	21.4	48.7	116.8	19.4	46.8	112.3
Current liabilities/Inventory (%)	84.2	146.3	284.3	91.2	169.7	306.4	72.1	124.4	283.1
Total liabilities/Net worth (%)	34.8	93.3	182.3	33.4	75.8	168.5	26.7	59.7	154.3
Fixed assets/Net worth (%)	23.2	50.6	85.6	21.5	53.7	94.7	19.2	43.4	92.4
Efficiency									
Collection period (days)	32.5	49.3	64.2	30.6	46.0	58.5	31.4	45.3	55.5
Sales to Inventory	22.1	11.0	7.0	20.8	12.7	7.9	22.5	11.4	7.9
Assets/Sales (%)	35.1	47.5	71.4	30.8	41.2	67.1	31.9	39.4	66.3
Sales/Net Working Capital	10.6	6.4	4.2	15.5	7.4	4.4	11.5	5.9	4.0
Accounts payable/Sales (%)	3.3	6.2	8.7	3.4	5.6	8.5	2.8	5.0	7.9
Profitability									
Return - Sales (%)	9.8	5.0	1.8	9.9	3.6	1.6	11.4	4.5	1.3
Return - Assets (%)	14.4	8.2	3.5	14.3	8.4	3.9	18.9	9.1	2.3
Return - Net Worth (%)	34.5	16.2	7.2	33.3	18.9	6.8	31.3	18.0	6.6

Source: Dun & Bradstreet. Data in this table are copyright (c) 1999 of Dun & Bradstreet. Reprinted by special arrangement with D&B. *Note:* UQ stands for "Upper Quartile" and represents the top 25 percent of sample; MED stands for "Median"; and LQ stands for "Lower Quartile" and represents the lowest 25 percent.

CHAPTER 4 - PART I

COMPANY DIRECTORY

This chapter presents brief profiles of 1,400 companies in the Chemicals sector. Companies are public, private, and elements of public companies ("public family members").

Each entry features the *D-U-N-S* access number for the company, the company name, its parent (if applicable), address, telephone, sales, employees, the company's primary SIC classification, a brief description of the company's business activity, and the name and title of its chairman, president, or other high-ranking officer. If the company is an exporter, importer, or both, the fact is indicated by the abbreviations EXP, IMP, and IMP EXP shown facing the *D-U-N-S* number.

Rankings of these companies are shown in Chapter 5. Additional financial data—on an aggregated, industry level—are shown in Chapter 3.

This product includes proprietary data of Dun & Bradstreet, Inc.

D-U-N-S 00-910-4381
3V INC.
888 Woodstock St, Georgetown, SC 29440
Phone: (843) 546-8556
Sales: $70,000,000   *Employees:* 260
Company Type: Private   *Employees here:* 20
SIC: 2869
   Mfg specialty organic industrial chemicals
John Centioni, Executive Vice-President

D-U-N-S 00-328-4353
A B C COMPOUNDING COMPANY INC.
6970 Jonesboro Rd, Morrow, GA 30260
Phone: (770) 968-9222
Sales: $19,100,000   *Employees:* 150
Company Type: Private   *Employees here:* 125
SIC: 2842
   Mfg sanitary supplies
Steve R Walker, President

D-U-N-S 00-531-9157   EXP
A M TODD COMPANY
   (Parent: A M Todd Group Inc)
1717 Douglas Ave, Kalamazoo, MI 49007
Phone: (616) 343-2603
Sales: $200,000,000   *Employees:* 275
Company Type: Private   *Employees here:* 50
SIC: 2899
   Mfg essential oils & whol vanilla beans & mfg seasonings
A J Todd III, President

D-U-N-S 83-827-4009
A M TODD GROUP, INC.
1717 Douglas Ave, Kalamazoo, MI 49007
Phone: (616) 343-2603
Sales: $50,000,000   *Employees:* 355
Company Type: Private   *Employees here:* 80
SIC: 2899
   Mfg essential oils & whol vanilla beans & mfg seasonings
A J Todd III, President

D-U-N-S 00-699-8413
A SCHULMAN INC.
3550 W Market St, Akron, OH 44333
Phone: (330) 666-3751
Sales: $996,466,000   *Employees:* 2,250
Company Type: Public   *Employees here:* 77
SIC: 2821
   Mfg proprietary plastic compounds & whol plastic &
      synthetic resins
Terry L Haines, President

D-U-N-S 07-135-2058   EXP
A-VEDA CORPORATION
   (Parent: Estee Lauder Companies Inc)
4000 Pheasant Ridge Dr NE, Minneapolis, MN 55449
Phone: (612) 783-4000
Sales: $50,600,000   *Employees:* 430
Company Type: Public Family Member   *Employees here:* 300
SIC: 2844
   Mfg hair shampoos conditioners rinses skin creams lipsticks
      and natural perfumes and fragrances
Horst Rechelbacher, Chairman of the Board

D-U-N-S 04-122-8990
AABA PLASTIC SALES ASSOCIATES
101 W 31st St, Ste 1802, New York, NY 10001
Phone: (212) 967-6077
Sales: $15,100,000   *Employees:* 80
Company Type: Private   *Employees here:* 4
SIC: 2821
   Manufactures raw plastics and plastic consultant
Fay Kaiser, Owner

D-U-N-S 05-108-3632
AABBITT ADHESIVES INC.
2403 N Oakley Ave, Chicago, IL 60647
Phone: (773) 227-2700
Sales: $25,000,000   *Employees:* 95
Company Type: Private   *Employees here:* 60
SIC: 2891
   Mfg adhesives
Benjamin B Sarmas, President

D-U-N-S 18-638-8476   EXP
AARBOR INTERNATIONAL CORP
9434 Maltby Rd, Brighton, MI 48116
Phone: (810) 220-0080
Sales: $15,813,000   *Employees:* 17
Company Type: Private   *Employees here:* 17
SIC: 2865
   Mfg organic pigments & exports chemical equipment
David Lee, President

D-U-N-S 78-645-7424
ABCO INDUSTRIES INCORPORATED
   (Parent: Eastman Chemical Company)
200 Railroad St, Roebuck, SC 29376
Phone: (864) 576-6821
Sales: $55,000,000   *Employees:* 125
Company Type: Public Family Member   *Employees here:* 125
SIC: 2843
   Mfg specialty chemicals
Edward E Page, President

D-U-N-S 04-342-0082   EXP
ABELL CORPORATION
2500 Sterlington Rd, Monroe, LA 71203
Phone: (318) 345-2600
Sales: $70,000,000   *Employees:* 377
Company Type: Private   *Employees here:* 40
SIC: 2875
   Mfg liquid fertilizer rotationally molds polyethylene plastic
      parts including plastic tanks
Nelson D Abell Jr, Chairman of the Board

D-U-N-S 87-317-4361
ABITEC CORPORATION
   (Parent: Gwh Investments Inc)
501 W 1st Ave, Columbus, OH 43215
Phone: (614) 429-6464
Sales: $32,000,000   *Employees:* 52
Company Type: Private   *Employees here:* 52
SIC: 2844
   Mfg specialty chemicals
Michael J O Neill, Vice-President

D-U-N-S 00-847-4652   EXP
ABLESTIK LABORATORIES
   (Parent: Ici Americas Inc)
20021 S Susana Rd, Compton, CA 90221
Phone: (310) 764-4600
Sales: $35,800,000   *Employees:* 230
Company Type: Private   *Employees here:* 230
SIC: 2891
   Mfg adhesives
James C Richards, President

D-U-N-S 06-311-2122   EXP
AC PRODUCTS, INC.
   (Parent: Quaker Chemical Corporation)
172 E La Jolla St, Placentia, CA 92870
Phone: (714) 630-7311

Sales: $15,000,000 *Employees:* 32
Company Type: Public Family Member *Employees here:* 32
SIC: 2891
   Mfg adhesives & coatings & roof coatings
Thomas Campbell, President

D-U-N-S 00-811-0181
ACETYLENE OXYGEN CO.
711 W Jackson St, Harlingen, TX 78550
Phone: (956) 423-4237
Sales: $25,000,000 *Employees:* 200
Company Type: Private *Employees here:* 25
SIC: 2813
   Mfg compressed acetylene gas & whol welding supplies
Albert Wolf III, President

D-U-N-S 00-815-0617 EXP
ACORDIS CELLULOSE FIBER INC.
   (Parent: Akzo Nobel Courtaulds Us Inc)
Hwy 43 N, Axis, AL 36505
Phone: (334) 679-2200
Sales: $81,200,000 *Employees:* 750
Company Type: Private *Employees here:* 730
SIC: 2823
   Mfg rayon and tencel staple fibers
D T Duthie, Chairman of the Board

D-U-N-S 00-301-0345 EXP
ADHESIVES RESEARCH, INC.
400 Seaks Run Rd, Glen Rock, PA 17327
Phone: (717) 235-7979
Sales: $60,000,000 *Employees:* 350
Company Type: Private *Employees here:* 310
SIC: 2891
   Mfg adhesive materials
Erwin W Huber, Chairman of the Board

D-U-N-S 02-579-7408
ADVANCED AROMATICS, LP
4600 Post Oak Place Dr, Houston, TX 77027
Phone: (713) 296-7500
Sales: $20,000,000 *Employees:* 39
Company Type: Private *Employees here:* 4
SIC: 2869
   Mfg industrial organic & inorganic chemicals
Peter R Buenz, President

D-U-N-S 05-973-5761 EXP
ADVANCED CHEMICAL COMPANY
105 Bellows St, Warwick, RI 02888
Phone: (401) 785-3434
Sales: $24,724,000 *Employees:* 41
Company Type: Private *Employees here:* 31
SIC: 2899
   Mfg plating compounds & refines precious metals
Gerald A Smith Sr, Chairman of the Board

D-U-N-S 18-057-1994 EXP
ADVANCED CHEMICAL SYSTEMS INTERNATIONAL
510 Alder Dr, Milpitas, CA 95035
Phone: (408) 321-8900
Sales: $21,452,000 *Employees:* 94
Company Type: Private *Employees here:* 44
SIC: 2819
   Mfg specialty chemicals & processing equipment
Richard Brewer, President

D-U-N-S 62-138-3942 EXP
ADVANCED ELASTOMER SYSTEMS LP
388 S Main St, Ste 600, Akron, OH 44311
Phone: (330) 849-5000

Sales: $260,504,000 *Employees:* 660
Company Type: Private *Employees here:* 230
SIC: 2822
   Mfg thermoplastic elastomers
Graham Wildsmith, President

D-U-N-S 04-085-8300
ADVANCED POLYMER ALLOYS, LLC
3521 Silverside Rd, Wilmington, DE 19810
Phone: (302) 478-8989
Sales: $18,000,000 *Employees:* 5
Company Type: Private *Employees here:* 5
SIC: 2822
   Thermal plastic rubber mfg
W R Abell III, President

D-U-N-S 10-209-9843
ADVANCED POLYMER SYSTEMS INC.
123 Saginaw Dr, Redwood City, CA 94063
Phone: (650) 366-2626
Sales: $18,333,000 *Employees:* 94
Company Type: Public *Employees here:* 45
SIC: 2822
   Mfg polymers consumer health care products &
     pharmaceutical ingredients
John J Meakem Jr, Chairman of the Board

D-U-N-S 00-204-5615
ADVANCED TECHNICAL PRODUCTS
200 E Mansell St, Ste 505, Roswell, GA 30076
Phone: (770) 993-0291
Sales: $119,433,000 *Employees:* 1,200
Company Type: Public *Employees here:* 60
SIC: 2821
   Manufactures composite products
Alan W Baldwin, Chairman of the Board

D-U-N-S 06-292-2133 EXP
AEROPRES CORPORATION
1324 N Hearne Ave, Ste 200, Shreveport, LA 71107
Phone: (318) 221-6282
Sales: $60,000,000 *Employees:* 140
Company Type: Private *Employees here:* 24
SIC: 2813
   Mfr hydrocarbon aerosol propellants whol liquefied
     petroleum gas & ret propane gas
Bill C Mc Keever, Chairman of the Board

D-U-N-S 96-897-4238
AEROSOL COMPANIES HOLDING
2030 Old Candler Rd, Gainesville, GA 30507
Phone: (770) 534-0300
Sales: $44,900,000 *Employees:* 382
Company Type: Private *Employees here:* 2
SIC: 2844
   Holding company
Sam Garretson, President

D-U-N-S 07-083-0617 EXP
AERVOE PACIFIC COMPANY, INC.
1198 Sawmill Rd, Gardnerville, NV 89410
Phone: (775) 782-0100
Sales: $25,000,000 *Employees:* 125
Company Type: Private *Employees here:* 125
SIC: 2851
   Mfg paints coatings cleaners & lubricating oils
David Williams, President

D-U-N-S 00-417-4819
AGA GAS INC.
   (Parent: Aga Inc)
6055 Rockside Woods Blvd, Cleveland, OH 44131
Phone: (216) 642-6600

Sales: $136,400,000
Company Type: Private
SIC: 2813
Employees: 1,200
Employees here: 150
Mfg industrial & medical gases & whol industrial welding
equipment
Patrick Murphy, President

D-U-N-S 15-727-8631
AGA INC.
6055 Rockside Woods Blvd, Cleveland, OH 44131
Phone: (216) 642-6600
Sales: $136,600,000
Company Type: Private
SIC: 2813
Employees: 1,202
Employees here: 2
Mfg industrial gases
Marcus Storch, Chairman of the Board

D-U-N-S 87-862-7298
AGREVO U S A COMPANY
2711 Centerville Rd, Wilmington, DE 19808
Phone: (302) 892-3000
Sales: $101,200,000
Company Type: Private
SIC: 2879
Employees: 494
Employees here: 194
Develops manufactures & markets agricultural & specialty
chemicals
Maurice Delage, President

D-U-N-S 08-216-5655
AGRI-EMPRESA INC.
6001 W Industrial Ave, Midland, TX 79706
Phone: (915) 694-1994
Sales: $18,000,000
Company Type: Private
SIC: 2899
Employees: 45
Employees here: 35
Mfg drilling mud
Steve Goree, President

D-U-N-S 80-895-7229
AGRIUM U.S. INC.
(Parent: Agrium Inc)
4582 S Ulster St, Ste 1400, Denver, CO 80237
Phone: (303) 804-4400
Sales: $1,937,900,000
Company Type: Private
SIC: 2873
Employees: 2,450
Employees here: 35
Mfg nitrogenous fertilizers
John Van Brunt, President

D-U-N-S 05-904-1707
AGSCO INC.
1168 12th St NE, Grand Forks, ND 58201
Phone: (701) 775-5325
Sales: $41,873,000
Company Type: Private
SIC: 2879
Employees: 125
Employees here: 45
Mfg & whol agricultural chemicals
Randy Brown, President

D-U-N-S 00-300-1070
AIR PRODUCTS AND CHEMICALS
7201 Hamilton Blvd, Allentown, PA 18195
Phone: (610) 481-4911
Sales: $4,933,800,000
Company Type: Public
SIC: 2813
Employees: 16,400
Employees here: 3,800
Mfg industrial gases chemicals & related industrial process
equipment & environmental and energy services
Harold A Wagner, Chairman of the Board

D-U-N-S 80-794-9912
AIR PRODUCTS, INCORPORATED
(Parent: Air Products And Chemicals)
7201 Hamilton Blvd, Allentown, PA 18195
Phone: (610) 481-4911
Sales: $454,500,000
Company Type: Public Family Member
SIC: 2813
Employees: 4,000
Employees here: 4,000
Mfg industrial gases
Joseph J Kaminski, President

D-U-N-S 19-897-6359
AIRGAS - NORTH CENTRAL INC.
(Parent: Airgas Inc)
10 W 4th St, Waterloo, IA 50701
Phone: (319) 287-3157
Sales: $60,000,000
Company Type: Public Family Member
SIC: 2813
Employees: 200
Employees here: 40
Mfg whol & ret industrial gases & welding supplies
Jeff Allen, President

D-U-N-S 04-113-8371
AIRGAS CARBONIC, INC.
(Parent: Airgas Inc)
3700 Crestwood Pkwy NW, Duluth, GA 30096
Phone: (770) 717-2200
Sales: $31,200,000
Company Type: Public Family Member
SIC: 2813
Employees: 275
Employees here: 25
Mfg carbon dioxide dry ice also leases co2 equipment & whol
related parts
Ted Schulte, N/A

D-U-N-S 18-965-4171
AIRGAS DRY ICE
(Parent: Airgas Inc)
4754 Shavano Oak, Ste 102, San Antonio, TX 78249
Phone: (210) 479-0100
Sales: $15,000,000
Company Type: Public Family Member
SIC: 2813
Employees: 125
Employees here: 15
Mfg liquid carbon dioxide & dry ice
Clifford H Collen, President

D-U-N-S 01-971-4331
AIRGAS INTERMOUNTAIN INC.
(Parent: Airgas Inc)
1118 NE Frontage Rd, Ste A, Fort Collins, CO 80524
Phone: (970) 490-7701
Sales: $37,500,000
Company Type: Public Family Member
SIC: 2813
Employees: 330
Employees here: 25
Mfg industrial gases & whol welding supplies
Jim Johnston, President

D-U-N-S 80-632-7102   EXP
AKCROS CHEMICALS AMERICA
500 Jersey Ave, New Brunswick, NJ 08901
Phone: (732) 247-2202
Sales: $19,600,000
Company Type: Private
SIC: 2869
Employees: 85
Employees here: 85
Mfg chemicals
Ralph Carbone, Controller

D-U-N-S 18-397-7487
AKZO NOBEL CHEMICALS INC.
(Parent: Akzo Nobel Inc)
300 S Riverside Plz, Fl 21, Chicago, IL 60606
Phone: (312) 906-7500

Sales: $783,018,000   *Employees:* 2,100
Company Type: Private   *Employees here:* 250
SIC: 2869
    Mfg specialty chemicals industrial & organic and fluid
      cracking catalysts
Conrad S Kent, Chairman of the Board

D-U-N-S 05-987-5567
AKZO NOBEL COURTAULDS US INC.
2 Manhattanville Rd, Purchase, NY 10577
Phone: (914) 642-8000
Sales: $645,900,000   *Employees:* 4,200
Company Type: Private   *Employees here:* 9
SIC: 2851
    Mfg coatings plastic performance & packaging films &
      packaging materials sealants adhesives & rayon fibers
Sipko Huismans, President

D-U-N-S 17-343-0927
AKZO NOBEL FORTAFIL FIBERS
    (Parent: Akzo Nobel Inc)
121 Old Cardiff Rd, Rockwood, TN 37854
Phone: (423) 354-4120
Sales: $45,000,000   *Employees:* 163
Company Type: Private   *Employees here:* 160
SIC: 2824
    Mfg carbon fibers
Rodger Prescott, Vice-President

D-U-N-S 06-299-9347   EXP
AKZO NOBEL INC.
300 S Riverside Plz, Chicago, IL 60606
Phone: (312) 906-7500
Sales: $2,567,600,000   *Employees:* 10,540
Company Type: Private   *Employees here:* 300
SIC: 2869
    Mfg indust organic chem paints & coatings mfr
      pharmaceuticals lab analytical equipment poultry vaccines
Piet P Kluit, President

D-U-N-S 60-607-1751   EXP
AL AMERICA HOLDINGS, INC.
    (Parent: American Air Liquide Inc)
2700 Post Oak Blvd, Houston, TX 77056
Phone: (713) 869-2100
Sales: $488,600,000   *Employees:* 4,300
Company Type: Private   *Employees here:* 4
SIC: 2813
    Mfg industrial gases
Gerard Levy, Chairman of the Board

D-U-N-S 88-309-2215
AL-CORN CLEAN FUEL
Hwy 14 W, Claremont, MN 55924
Phone: (507) 528-2494
Sales: $21,947,000   *Employees:* 28
Company Type: Private   *Employees here:* 28
SIC: 2869
    Mfg ethanol and dry distillers grain
Randall J Doyal, General Manager

D-U-N-S 09-872-9502
ALBAUGH INC.
121 NE 18th St, Ankeny, IA 50021
Phone: (515) 964-9444
Sales: $50,000,000   *Employees:* 40
Company Type: Private   *Employees here:* 5
SIC: 2879
    Mfg herbicides
Dennis R Albaugh, President

D-U-N-S 82-508-0096   EXP
ALBEMARLE CORPORATION
451 Florida St, Fl 16th, Baton Rouge, LA 70801
Phone: (225) 388-8011
Sales: $829,850,000   *Employees:* 2,700
Company Type: Public   *Employees here:* 450
SIC: 2821
    Mfg specialty chemicals
Floyd D Gottwald Jr, Chairman of the Board

D-U-N-S 00-507-1378
ALBERTO-CULVER COMPANY
2525 Armitage Ave, Melrose Park, IL 60160
Phone: (708) 450-3000
Sales: $1,834,711,000   *Employees:* 12,700
Company Type: Public   *Employees here:* 1,100
SIC: 2844
    Mfg whol & ret personal care pdts household & grocery pdts
      & food pdts
Leonard H Lavin, Chairman of the Board

D-U-N-S 61-504-1282
ALBERTO-CULVER INTERNATIONAL INC.
    (Parent: Alberto-Culver Company)
2525 Armitage Ave, Melrose Park, IL 60160
Phone: (708) 450-3000
Sales: $119,000,000   *Employees:* 1,000
Company Type: Public Family Member   *Employees here:* 1,000
SIC: 2844
    Mfg toilet preparations
Paul H Stoneham, President

D-U-N-S 61-504-1167
ALBERTO-CULVER U S A INC.
    (Parent: Alberto-Culver Company)
2525 Armitage Ave, Melrose Park, IL 60160
Phone: (708) 450-3000
Sales: $215,000,000   *Employees:* 1,800
Company Type: Public Family Member   *Employees here:* 1,350
SIC: 2844
    Mfg toilet preparations mfg food preparations
Carol L Bernick, President

D-U-N-S 04-575-5865   EXP
ALBIS CORPORATION
445 Highway 36, Rosenberg, TX 77471
Phone: (281) 342-3311
Sales: $34,400,000   *Employees:* 190
Company Type: Private   *Employees here:* 165
SIC: 2821
    Mfg and distributes plastic resins
Harry Meijer, President

D-U-N-S 13-139-7085
ALBRIGHT & WILSON AMERICAS
4851 Lake Brook Dr, Glen Allen, VA 23060
Phone: (804) 968-6300
Sales: $375,000,000   *Employees:* 1,400
Company Type: Private   *Employees here:* 150
SIC: 2819
    Mfg inorganic & organic industrial chemicals
Paul F Rocheleau, Chief Executive Officer

D-U-N-S 05-552-6982
ALCOA MINERALS OF JAMAICA INC.
    (Parent: Alcoa Inc)
425 6th Ave, Pittsburgh, PA 15219
Phone: (412) 553-4545
Sales: $161,000,000   *Employees:* 1,000
Company Type: Public Family Member   *Employees here:* 8
SIC: 2819
    Bauxite mining & refining
Paul H O Niell, President

D-U-N-S 00-516-8596
ALDEN & OTT PRINTING INKS CO.
616 E Brook Dr, Arlington Heights, IL 60005
Phone: (847) 956-6830
Sales: $20,000,000 | *Employees:* 150
Company Type: Private | *Employees here:* 100
SIC: 2893
   Mfg printing ink
Joseph G Alden, Chief Executive Officer

D-U-N-S 05-244-2118
ALDEN LEEDS INC.
55 Jacobus Ave, Kearny, NJ 07032
Phone: (973) 589-3544
Sales: $27,300,000 | *Employees:* 65
Company Type: Private | *Employees here:* 62
SIC: 2899
   Manufactures water treatment compounds
Mark Epstein, President

D-U-N-S 00-611-3906
ALDRICH CHEMICAL COMPANY INC.
   (Parent: Sigma-Aldrich Corporation)
1001 W Saint Paul Ave, Milwaukee, WI 53233
Phone: (414) 273-3850
Sales: $250,000,000 | *Employees:* 884
Company Type: Public Family Member | *Employees here:* 655
SIC: 2869
   Mfg organic & inorganic chemicals & lab products
Dr Jai Nagarkatti, President

D-U-N-S 07-738-0335
ALL-PURE CHEMICAL CO.
   (Parent: Pioneer Americas Inc)
2185 N California Blvd, Walnut Creek, CA 94596
Phone: (925) 280-2600
Sales: $39,200,000 | *Employees:* 250
Company Type: Public Family Member | *Employees here:* 40
SIC: 2812
   Mfg chlorine bleach
Ron Zirora, President

D-U-N-S 09-442-5048
ALLIANCE AGRONOMICS INC.
7104 Mechanicsville Tpke, Mechanicsville, VA 23111
Phone: (804) 730-2900
Sales: $28,000,000 | *Employees:* 90
Company Type: Private | *Employees here:* 8
SIC: 2875
   Mfg fertilizer
G W Garrett, Chairman of the Board

D-U-N-S 80-270-5038
ALLIED INDUSTRIAL GROUP INC.
120 S Central Ave, Ste 750, Saint Louis, MO 63105
Phone: (314) 725-0888
Sales: $45,000,000 | *Employees:* 62
Company Type: Private | *Employees here:* 2
SIC: 2819
   Manufactures industrial fluoride chemicals and distributes
      industrial chemicals
William E Cooper, President

D-U-N-S 04-904-9463
ALOE VERA OF AMERICA INC.
9660 Dilworth Rd, Dallas, TX 75243
Phone: (214) 343-5700
Sales: $112,561,000 | *Employees:* 250
Company Type: Private | *Employees here:* 100
SIC: 2844
   Mfg cosmetics including skin treatments
Rex G Maughan, Chairman of the Board

D-U-N-S 00-211-5889
ALOX CORPORATION
   (Parent: Kop-Coat Inc)
3943 Buffalo Ave, Niagara Falls, NY 14303
Phone: (716) 282-1295
Sales: $20,708,000 | *Employees:* 55
Company Type: Public Family Member | *Employees here:* 53
SIC: 2899
   Mfg corrosion preventive lubricants
Thomas C Sullivan, Chairman of the Board

D-U-N-S 07-534-2907   EXP
ALPER HOLDINGS USA, INC.
800 3rd Ave, Fl 24, New York, NY 10022
Phone: (212) 750-0200
Sales: $36,600,000 | *Employees:* 300
Company Type: Private | *Employees here:* 20
SIC: 2893
   Mfg water based inks real estate developers residential
      construction & investments in securities investment
      partnerships
Nicolas W Combemale, President

D-U-N-S 09-743-4484   EXP
ALPHA GARY CORPORATION
170 Pioneer Park, Leominster, MA 01453
Phone: (978) 537-8071
Sales: $77,400,000 | *Employees:* 370
Company Type: Private | *Employees here:* 200
SIC: 2821
   Mfg plastic & rubber compounds
Robert Gingue, President

D-U-N-S 00-214-7502   EXP
ALPINE AROMATICS INTERNATIONAL
51 Ethel Rd W, Piscataway, NJ 08854
Phone: (732) 572-5600
Sales: $17,000,000 | *Employees:* 45
Company Type: Private | *Employees here:* 45
SIC: 2869
   Mfg fragrance materials
John G Yorey, President

D-U-N-S 08-865-1617
ALUCHEM INC.
1 Landy Ln, Cincinnati, OH 45215
Phone: (513) 733-8519
Sales: $25,000,000 | *Employees:* 94
Company Type: Private | *Employees here:* 87
SIC: 2899
   Mfr fire retardant chemical fillers & processes non-clay
      refractory minerals
Ronald P Zapletal, President

D-U-N-S 06-871-1514
ALZO INC.
6 Gulfstreem Blvd, Matawan, NJ 07747
Phone: (732) 254-1901
Sales: $25,000,000 | *Employees:* 21
Company Type: Private | *Employees here:* 21
SIC: 2869
   Chemicals
Albert A Zofchak, President

D-U-N-S 06-707-8519   EXP
AMAX METALS RECOVERY INC.
   (Parent: Cyprus Amax Minerals Company)
1501 W Fountainhead Pkwy, Tempe, AZ 85282
Phone: (602) 929-4400

Sales: $28,800,000   *Employees:* 163
Company Type: Public Family Member   *Employees here:* 6
SIC: 2819
   Industrial waste recycling and maintenance and
   environmental clean up services
L H Morse, Vice-President

D-U-N-S 00-132-6388
AMCO PLASTIC MATERIALS INC.
595 Broadhollow Rd, Farmingdale, NY 11735
Phone: (516) 293-1600
Sales: $35,000,000   *Employees:* 50
Company Type: Private   *Employees here:* 50
SIC: 2821
   Manufactures plastic raw materials & color concentrates &
   dry color
Arthur Metzger, Chairman of the Board

D-U-N-S 01-094-4221
AMERCHOL CORPORATION
   (Parent: Union Carbide Corporation)
136 Talmadge Rd, Edison, NJ 08817
Phone: (732) 248-6000
Sales: $88,000,000   *Employees:* 150
Company Type: Public Family Member   *Employees here:* 110
SIC: 2841
   Manufactures lanolin and other specialty chemicals such as
   fatty acids glucose derivatives and sunscreens
Thomas Malafronte, President

D-U-N-S 60-606-7130   EXP
AMERICAN AIR LIQUIDE INC.
2700 Post Oak Blvd, Houston, TX 77056
Phone: (713) 624-8000
Sales: $2,000,000,000   *Employees:* 4,350
Company Type: Private   *Employees here:* 50
SIC: 2813
   Mfg industrial gases whol welding equipment mfg oil & gas
   drilling equipment cogeneration of electricity & steam
Alain Joly, Chairman of the Board

D-U-N-S 00-526-7588   EXP
AMERICAN CARBIDE & CARBON CORP
   (Parent: Airgas Inc)
365 Carbide Ln, Keokuk, IA 52632
Phone: (319) 524-6510
Sales: $35,000,000   *Employees:* 140
Company Type: Public Family Member   *Employees here:* 60
SIC: 2819
   Mfg calcium carbide & electrode soderburg paste
Ronald H Scott, President

D-U-N-S 00-623-3910   EXP
AMERICAN CHEMET CORPORATION
400 Lake Cook Rd, Ste 223, Deerfield, IL 60015
Phone: (847) 948-0800
Sales: $41,933,000   *Employees:* 94
Company Type: Private   *Employees here:* 8
SIC: 2819
   Mfg copper & zinc oxides
W W Shropshire Jr, President

D-U-N-S 07-758-5024
AMERICAN PACIFIC CORPORATION
3770 Howard Hughes Pkwy, Las Vegas, NV 89109
Phone: (702) 735-2200
Sales: $52,339,000   *Employees:* 218
Company Type: Public   *Employees here:* 27
SIC: 2819
   Mfg specialty chemicals
John R Gibson, Chairman of the Board

D-U-N-S 00-810-6205
AMERICAN PLANT FOOD CORP.
903 Mayo Shell Rd, Galena Park, TX 77547
Phone: (713) 675-2231
Sales: $81,905,000   *Employees:* 100
Company Type: Private   *Employees here:* 61
SIC: 2875
   Mfg (blends) fertilizer
Donald R Ford, President

D-U-N-S 11-738-6540
AMERICAN POLYMERS INC.
53 Millbrook St, Worcester, MA 01606
Phone: (508) 756-1010
Sales: $70,000,000   *Employees:* 42
Company Type: Private   *Employees here:* 42
SIC: 2821
   Mfg polystyrene resins compounding of plastic resins and
   distributes plastic resins
Harold E Doherty, President

D-U-N-S 36-076-4922
AMERICAN SILICONES INC.
420 N Taylor Rd, Garrett, IN 46738
Phone: (219) 357-6161
Sales: $15,000,000   *Employees:* 60
Company Type: Private   *Employees here:* 60
SIC: 2822
   Mfg custom silicone rubber
Tom Lapsley, President

D-U-N-S 00-638-2857   EXP
AMERICAN SYNTHETIC RUBBER CORP
   (Parent: Michelin Corporation)
4500 Camp Ground Rd, Louisville, KY 40216
Phone: (502) 449-8300
Sales: $27,900,000   *Employees:* 390
Company Type: Private   *Employees here:* 390
SIC: 2822
   Mfg synthetic rubber
Paul Serridge, President

D-U-N-S 96-381-4942
AMERICAN UNITED DISTILLING CO. LLC
301 4th Ave S, Ste 480, Minneapolis, MN 55415
Phone: (612) 371-3433
Sales: $300,000,000   *Employees:* 8
Company Type: Private   *Employees here:* 8
SIC: 2869
   Distills & whol bottled alcohol products
Douglas Mangine, Chief Executive Officer

D-U-N-S 04-934-3924   EXP
AMERICAN VANGUARD CORP.
4695 Macarthur Ct, Newport Beach, CA 92660
Phone: (949) 260-1200
Sales: $67,701,000   *Employees:* 206
Company Type: Public   *Employees here:* 128
SIC: 2879
   Holding company
Eric G Wintemute, President

D-U-N-S 00-446-7387
AMERICHEM INC.
225 Broadway St E, Cuyahoga Falls, OH 44221
Phone: (330) 929-4213
Sales: $85,600,000   *Employees:* 425
Company Type: Private   *Employees here:* 175
SIC: 2865
   Mfg organic & inorganic plastic color concentrates &
   specialty compounds & dispersions
Richard C Juve, Chief Executive Officer

D-U-N-S 79-720-5515
AMERIPOL SYNPOL CORPORATION
(*Parent:* G V C Holdings Inc)
1215 Main St, Port Neches, TX 77651
Phone: (409) 722-8321
Sales: $475,000,000 — *Employees:* 1,190
Company Type: Private — *Employees here:* 850
SIC: 2822
Mfg synthetic rubber
Mahendra Parekh, President

D-U-N-S 60-653-9682 — EXP
AMETHYST INVESTMENT GROUP
1000 E 87th St, Chicago, IL 60619
Phone: (773) 978-0700
Sales: $41,000,000 — *Employees:* 350
Company Type: Private — *Employees here:* 15
SIC: 2844
Mfg hair care products publishes magazines and advertising
agency
Betty A Gardner, Chairman of the Board

D-U-N-S 87-632-0185 — EXP
AMFIBE INC.
420 Industrial Park Rd, Ridgeway, VA 24148
Phone: (540) 638-2434
Sales: $19,000,000 — *Employees:* 200
Company Type: Private — *Employees here:* 200
SIC: 2824
Mfg nylon
W L Mcdorman, President

D-U-N-S 00-512-3195 — EXP
AMOCO CHEMICAL COMPANY
(*Parent:* Amoco Company)
200 E Randolph St, Chicago, IL 60601
Phone: (312) 856-3200
Sales: $3,222,800,000 — *Employees:* 14,700
Company Type: Private — *Employees here:* 260
SIC: 2821
Mfg polypropylene resins industrial organic chemicals
broadwoven synthetic fabrics & fibers & inorganic
chemicals
Enrique J Sosa, President

D-U-N-S 05-665-6259 — EXP
AMOCO FABRICS AND FIBERS CO
(*Parent:* Amoco Chemical Holding Co)
900 Circle 75 Pkwy SE, Atlanta, GA 30339
Phone: (770) 956-9025
Sales: $1,093,700,000 — *Employees:* 5,000
Company Type: Private — *Employees here:* 150
SIC: 2821
Mfg carpet backing and threads
Frank G Andrusko, President

D-U-N-S 14-831-1582 — EXP
AMOCO POLYMERS INC.
(*Parent:* Amoco Chemical Holding Co)
4500 McGinnis Ferry Rd, Alpharetta, GA 30005
Phone: (770) 772-8200
Sales: $200,000,000 — *Employees:* 2,000
Company Type: Private — *Employees here:* 465
SIC: 2824
Mfg man-made organic plastic fibers
Steven K Welch, President

D-U-N-S 79-310-3862
AMPAC INC.
(*Parent:* American Pacific Corporation)
10622 W 6400 N, Cedar City, UT 84720
Phone: (435) 865-5000

Sales: $20,000,000 — *Employees:* 190
Company Type: Public Family Member — *Employees here:* 185
SIC: 2873
Mfg ammonium perchlorate
John R Gibson, President

D-U-N-S 05-101-0429
AMREP, INC.
(*Parent:* Dawn Chemical Company Inc)
990 Industrial Park Dr, Marietta, GA 30062
Phone: (770) 422-2071
Sales: $27,100,000 — *Employees:* 230
Company Type: Private — *Employees here:* 195
SIC: 2842
Mfg specialty sanitary automotive chemicals and lubricating
greases
Kevin J Gallagher, Chief Executive Officer

D-U-N-S 10-141-5842 — EXP
AMSPEC CHEMICAL CORPORATION
(*Parent:* Antimony Products Of America)
751 Water St, Gloucester City, NJ 08030
Phone: (609) 456-3930
Sales: $25,000,000 — *Employees:* 90
Company Type: Private — *Employees here:* 60
SIC: 2819
Mfg industrial chemicals
John Gustavsen, President

D-U-N-S 09-722-2772
ANCHOR/LITH-KEM-KO, INC.
(*Parent:* Fuji Hunt Phtographic Chem Inc)
50 Industrial Loop N, Orange Park, FL 32073
Phone: (904) 264-3500
Sales: $45,000,000 — *Employees:* 150
Company Type: Private — *Employees here:* 95
SIC: 2899
Mfg chemicals for printing industry
Steven Zunde, General Manager

D-U-N-S 00-722-1880
ANCHOR PAINT MANUFACTURING CO.
6707 E 14th St, Tulsa, OK 74112
Phone: (918) 836-4626
Sales: $25,000,000 — *Employees:* 150
Company Type: Private — *Employees here:* 76
SIC: 2851
Mfg paint
Wanda Fowler, President

D-U-N-S 00-328-3199
ANDERSON CHEMICAL COMPANY INC.
1840 Waterville Rd, Macon, GA 31206
Phone: (912) 745-0466
Sales: $30,100,000 — *Employees:* 200
Company Type: Private — *Employees here:* 60
SIC: 2899
Mfg water treatment chemicals
Richard K Anderson, President

D-U-N-S 00-293-1228 — EXP
ANDERSON DEVELOPMENT COMPANY
(*Parent:* Mitsui Chemicals America Inc)
1415 E Michigan St, Adrian, MI 49221
Phone: (517) 263-2121
Sales: $50,000,000 — *Employees:* 130
Company Type: Private — *Employees here:* 110
SIC: 2821
Mfg chemical additives
K Hoshi, Chairman of the Board

D-U-N-S 00-425-1617
THE ANDREW JERGENS COMPANY
2535 Spring Grove Ave, Cincinnati, OH 45214
Phone: (513) 421-1400
Sales: $400,000,000   *Employees:* 500
Company Type: Private   *Employees here:* 425
SIC: 2844
    Mfr soap & cosmetic preparations
William Gentner, President

D-U-N-S 09-815-0535
ANZON INC.
    (Parent: Great Lakes Chemical Corp)
2545 Aramingo Ave, Philadelphia, PA 19125
Phone: (215) 427-3000
Sales: $50,000,000   *Employees:* 110
Company Type: Public Family Member   *Employees here:* 110
SIC: 2899
    Mfg flame retardant chemicals & plastic additives
Undetermin Principal, N/A

D-U-N-S 00-839-9263
APACHE NITROGEN PRODUCTS INC.
Apache Powder Rd, Benson, AZ 85602
Phone: (520) 720-2217
Sales: $40,344,000   *Employees:* 105
Company Type: Private   *Employees here:* 105
SIC: 2873
    Mfg ammonium nitrate & whol explosives
Robert D Willis, President

D-U-N-S 93-964-6113
APEX SPECIALTY MATERIALS INC.
100 W Commons Blvd, Ste 204, New Castle, DE 19720
Phone: (302) 323-1660
Sales: $70,000,000   *Employees:* 450
Company Type: Private   *Employees here:* 1
SIC: 2824
    Mfg synthetic fibers
Bradley A Yount, President

D-U-N-S 04-242-3087
APOLLO CHEMICAL CORP.
1105 Southerland Dr, Graham, NC 27253
Phone: (336) 226-1161
Sales: $25,000,000   *Employees:* 72
Company Type: Private   *Employees here:* 55
SIC: 2819
    Manufacturing specialty textile chemicals
Dexter R Barbee Sr, Chairman of the Board

D-U-N-S 04-757-8331
APOLLO COLORS INC.
1401 Mound Rd, Joliet, IL 60436
Phone: (815) 741-2588
Sales: $56,186,000   *Employees:* 210
Company Type: Private   *Employees here:* 14
SIC: 2865
    Mfg organic printing ink pigments
Thomas Rogers, President

D-U-N-S 05-102-1285
APOLLO INDUSTRIES INC.
1850 S Cobb Industrial Blvd, Smyrna, GA 30082
Phone: (770) 433-0210
Sales: $17,000,000   *Employees:* 120
Company Type: Private   *Employees here:* 75
SIC: 2813
    Mfg aerosol products
Maria Callas, President

D-U-N-S 18-114-4742
APPLE PLASTICS INC.
3100 E Harcourt St, Compton, CA 90221
Phone: (310) 609-1320
Sales: $15,200,000   *Employees:* 70
Company Type: Private   *Employees here:* 65
SIC: 2821
    Mfg plastic & polyethylene products
Gary Duboff, President

D-U-N-S 87-917-6329   EXP
APT ADVANCED POLYMER TECH CORP.
109 Conica Ln, Harmony, PA 16037
Phone: (724) 452-1330
Sales: $18,800,000   *Employees:* 32
Company Type: Private   *Employees here:* 32
SIC: 2851
    Mfg paints polyurethane coatings varnishes adhesives
       elastomers enamels industrial concrete protection & acrylic
       coatings
Michael Beyer, President

D-U-N-S 08-357-9995
AQUA CLEAR INDUSTRIES, LLC
2550 9th Ave, Watervliet, NY 12189
Phone: (518) 274-9777
Sales: $41,000,000   *Employees:* 90
Company Type: Private   *Employees here:* 77
SIC: 2899
    Mfg swimming pool spa water treatment & industrial
       chemicals
John Stiglmeier Jr, President

D-U-N-S 15-272-8887   EXP
AQUALON COMPANY
1313 N Market St, Wilmington, DE 19801
Phone: (302) 594-6600
Sales: $441,148,000   *Employees:* 2,000
Company Type: Private   *Employees here:* 200
SIC: 2869
    Mfg industrial organic chemicals
R J Frazier, Vice-President

D-U-N-S 06-459-3833
ARCAR GRAPHICS, LLC
    (Parent: Alper Holdings Usa Inc)
450 Wegner Dr, West Chicago, IL 60185
Phone: (630) 231-7313
Sales: $15,000,000   *Employees:* 96
Company Type: Private   *Employees here:* 94
SIC: 2893
    Mfg printing ink
Scott Billings, President

D-U-N-S 04-942-2509
ARCH CHEMICAL INC.
501 Merritt 7, Norwalk, CT 06851
Phone: (203) 229-2900
Sales: $862,800,000   *Employees:* 3,000
Company Type: Private   *Employees here:* 3,000
SIC: 2819
    Mfg chemical and allied product
Michael E Campbell, Chairman of the Board

D-U-N-S 07-290-6399
ARIA, PARVIZ
150 S Los Robles Ave, Pasadena, CA 91101
Phone: (626) 795-7720
Sales: $102,400,000   *Employees:* 500
Company Type: Private   *Employees here:* 6
SIC: 2879
    Oil co retail grocery mfg
Parviz Aria, Owner

D-U-N-S 00-215-4545   EXP
ARISTECH ACRYLICS LLC
7350 Empire Dr, Florence, KY 41042
Phone: (606) 283-1501
Sales: $61,000,000   *Employees:* 300
Company Type: Private   *Employees here:* 300
SIC: 2821
  Manufactures acrylic sheeting
Gary G Layne, President

D-U-N-S 16-166-9049
ARISTECH CHEMICAL CORPORATION
600 Grant St, Ste 1100, Pittsburgh, PA 15219
Phone: (412) 433-2747
Sales: $314,500,000   *Employees:* 1,450
Company Type: Private   *Employees here:* 200
SIC: 2821
  Mfg polymers basic & industrial chemicals
Masatake Bando, Chief Executive Officer

D-U-N-S 13-930-5197   EXP
ARIZONA CHEMICAL COMPANY
  (Parent: International Paper Company)
1001 E Bus Hwy 98, Panama City, FL 32401
Phone: (850) 785-6700
Sales: $300,000,000   *Employees:* 1,030
Company Type: Public Family Member   *Employees here:* 80
SIC: 2861
  Distillate refinery
Jim Caderna, General Manager

D-U-N-S 06-108-7508
ARIZONA NATURAL RESOURCES INC.
2525 E Beardsley Rd, Phoenix, AZ 85050
Phone: (602) 569-6900
Sales: $30,542,000   *Employees:* 275
Company Type: Private   *Employees here:* 200
SIC: 2844
  Mfg cosmetics toiletries and candles
George F Dembow Jr, President

D-U-N-S 17-553-3934
ARMAND PRODUCTS COMPANY
469 N Harrison St, Princeton, NJ 08540
Phone: (609) 683-7090
Sales: $40,000,000   *Employees:* 3
Company Type: Private   *Employees here:* 3
SIC: 2812
  Mfr potassium carbonate & potassium bicarbonate
W P Fiedler, President

D-U-N-S 05-979-5468
ARNCO
5141 Firestone Pl, South Gate, CA 90280
Phone: (323) 249-7500
Sales: $22,000,000   *Employees:* 45
Company Type: Private   *Employees here:* 25
SIC: 2822
  Mfg synthetic rubber
Larry Carapellotti, President

D-U-N-S 18-004-8803
AROMATIC TECHNOLOGIES, INC.
130 Industrial Pkwy, Somerville, NJ 08876
Phone: (908) 707-0707
Sales: $15,000,000   *Employees:* 50
Company Type: Private   *Employees here:* 50
SIC: 2844
  Manufacturer of perfume bases
Gary Bruno, President

D-U-N-S 09-298-3139
ARR-MAZ PRODUCTS, LP
621 Snively Ave, Winter Haven, FL 33880
Phone: (941) 293-7884
Sales: $58,000,000   *Employees:* 102
Company Type: Private   *Employees here:* 83
SIC: 2869
  Mfg specialty chemicals
William Holt, President

D-U-N-S 04-842-1247
ARTEVA SPECIALITIES SARL
2300 Archdale Dr, Charlotte, NC 28210
Phone: (704) 554-2000
Sales: $2,410,700,000   *Employees:* 11,000
Company Type: Private   *Employees here:* NA
SIC: 2821
  Mfg polyester products
Pedro Haas, Chief Executive Officer

D-U-N-S 00-500-3264
ASHLAND INC.
50 E Rivercenter Blvd, Covington, KY 41011
Phone: (606) 815-3333
Sales: $6,933,000,000   *Employees:* 21,200
Company Type: Public   *Employees here:* 250
SIC: 2819
  Petroleum refining & mfr chemicals
Paul W Chellgren, Chairman of the Board

D-U-N-S 60-439-3355   EXP
ASHTA CHEMICALS INC.
3509 Middle Rd, Ashtabula, OH 44004
Phone: (440) 997-5221
Sales: $63,000,000   *Employees:* 100
Company Type: Private   *Employees here:* 95
SIC: 2812
  Mfg caustic potash chlorine chlorpicrin & potassium
    carbonate
Reginald Baxter, President

D-U-N-S 78-559-7402
ASI INVESTMENT HOLDING CO.
  (Parent: A Schulman Inc)
3550 W Market St, Akron, OH 44333
Phone: (330) 666-3751
Sales: $17,600,000   *Employees:* 115
Company Type: Public Family Member   *Employees here:* 115
SIC: 2821
  Investment holding company
Terry L Haines, President

D-U-N-S 02-210-8005   EXP
ATLAS PRODUCTS, INC.
2124 Valley Dr, Des Moines, IA 50321
Phone: (515) 288-0231
Sales: $23,972,000   *Employees:* 45
Company Type: Private   *Employees here:* 45
SIC: 2851
  Mfg hardwood floor finishes
Lyle Middleton, Chairman of the Board

D-U-N-S 00-215-3344
ATLAS REFINERY INC.
142 Lockwood St, Newark, NJ 07105
Phone: (973) 589-2002
Sales: $15,869,000   *Employees:* 40
Company Type: Private   *Employees here:* 37
SIC: 2843
  Manufactures leather & textile oils & assistants & paper
    chemicals
Steven B Schroeder, President

D-U-N-S 79-078-3765   EXP
ATOHAAS AMERICAS INC.
    (Parent: Rohm And Haas Company)
Independence Mall W, Philadelphia, PA 19105
Phone: (215) 592-3000
Sales: $300,000,000   *Employees:* NA
Company Type: Public Family Member   *Employees here:* NA
SIC: 2821
    Mfg pmma products acrylic sheet & resins
A H Caesar, President

D-U-N-S 96-647-1815
ATOHAAS MEXICO INC.
830 W Price Rd, Brownsville, TX 78520
Phone: (956) 544-4055
Sales: $16,400,000   *Employees:* NA
Company Type: Private   *Employees here:* 100
SIC: 2821
    Mfg pmma products acrylic sheet & resins & polycarbonate
    sheets
Paul Blanco, Plant Manager

D-U-N-S 80-018-5910   EXP
ATOTECH USA INC.
    (Parent: Elf Atochem North America Inc)
1750 Overview Dr, Rock Hill, SC 29730
Phone: (803) 817-3500
Sales: $123,300,000   *Employees:* 570
Company Type: Private   *Employees here:* 130
SIC: 2899
    Mfg electroplating chemistry and equipment
William Wasulko, Vice-President

D-U-N-S 03-784-0212   EXP
AURO TECH INC.
    (Parent: Interntonal Flavors Fragrances)
14224 Anthony Ave, Menomonee Falls, WI 53051
Phone: (414) 251-0086
Sales: $16,000,000   *Employees:* 51
Company Type: Public Family Member   *Employees here:* 51
SIC: 2869
    Mfg dairy flavors
David Haase, Operations

D-U-N-S 18-350-0396
AUSIMONT FINANCIAL CORP.
    (Parent: Ausimont Industries Inc)
10 Leonard Ln, Thorofare, NJ 08086
Phone: (609) 853-8119
Sales: $35,800,000   *Employees:* 230
Company Type: Private   *Employees here:* 5
SIC: 2891
    Mfg industrial adhesives & specialty chemicals
Vittorio Cianchini, President

D-U-N-S 19-507-9512   EXP
AUSIMONT INDUSTRIES INC.
10 Leonard Ln, Thorofare, NJ 08086
Phone: (609) 853-8119
Sales: $64,300,000   *Employees:* 310
Company Type: Private   *Employees here:* 100
SIC: 2821
    Holding company
Vittorio Cianchini, President

D-U-N-S 00-415-9653
AUSTIN POWDER COMPANY
    (Parent: Austin Powder Holdings Co)
25800 Science Park Dr, Cleveland, OH 44122
Phone: (216) 464-2400

Sales: $138,900,000   *Employees:* 1,200
Company Type: Private   *Employees here:* 75
SIC: 2892
    Mfg explosives
David M Gleason, President

D-U-N-S 93-264-1988
AUSTIN POWDER HOLDINGS CO.
    (Parent: Davis Mining & Manufacturing)
25800 Science Park Dr, Cleveland, OH 44122
Phone: (216) 464-2400
Sales: $127,300,000   *Employees:* 1,100
Company Type: Private   *Employees here:* 75
SIC: 2892
    Mfg explosives
David M Gleason, President

D-U-N-S 00-736-3799   EXP
AUTO WAX COMPANY INC.
1275 Round Table Dr, Dallas, TX 75247
Phone: (214) 631-4000
Sales: $17,000,000   *Employees:* 60
Company Type: Private   *Employees here:* 50
SIC: 2842
    Mfg auto waxes & specialty cleaners
P D Miller III, Chairman of the Board

D-U-N-S 04-886-9767
AUTOLIGN MANUFACTURING GROUP INC.
620 S Platt Rd, Milan, MI 48160
Phone: (734) 439-4200
Sales: $30,000,000   *Employees:* 150
Company Type: Private   *Employees here:* 150
SIC: 2821
    Manufacturing of molding compounds plastic
Phillip Storm, Chief Executive Officer

D-U-N-S 62-648-2145   EXP
AVON INTERNATIONAL OPERATIONS
    (Parent: Avon Products Inc)
1345 Avenue Of The Americas, New York, NY 10105
Phone: (212) 282-7000
Sales: $59,000,000   *Employees:* 500
Company Type: Public Family Member   *Employees here:* 250
SIC: 2844
    Mfg and marketing of cosmetics fragrances toiletries fashion
    jewelry & giftware
James E Preston, Chairman of the Board

D-U-N-S 00-146-8693   EXP
AVON PRODUCTS, INC.
1345 Avenue Of The Americas, New York, NY 10105
Phone: (212) 282-5000
Sales: $5,212,700,000   *Employees:* 34,995
Company Type: Public   *Employees here:* 250
SIC: 2844
    Mfg & mkts cosmetics fragrances toiletries giftware fashion
    jewelry intimate apparel & casual clothing for women
Jose Ferreira Jr, President

D-U-N-S 08-593-7753
AWARE PRODUCTS INC.
9250 Mason Ave, Chatsworth, CA 91311
Phone: (818) 993-7215
Sales: $38,000,000   *Employees:* 325
Company Type: Private   *Employees here:* 325
SIC: 2844
    Mfg hair preparations including shampoo
Joe Pender, President

D-U-N-S 15-142-6616
AXIM CONCRETE TECHNOLOGIES
 (Parent: Essroc Corp)
8282 Middlebranch Rd NE, Middlebranch, OH 44652
Phone: (330) 966-0444
Sales: $15,000,000   *Employees:* 46
Company Type: Private   *Employees here:* 35
SIC: 2899
 Mfg chemical add mixtures for concrete
Don Lane, Vice-President

D-U-N-S 80-989-0924
AZTEC PEROXIDES, INC.
 (Parent: Laporte Inc)
7600 W Tidwell Rd, Ste 500, Houston, TX 77040
Phone: (713) 895-2000
Sales: $19,100,000   *Employees:* 115
Company Type: Private   *Employees here:* 15
SIC: 2819
 Mfg chemical catalysts
Jack L Kulasa, President

D-U-N-S 00-335-5344
THE B F GOODRICH COMPANY
Tanner Dr, Taylors, SC 29687
Phone: (864) 244-4831
Sales: $25,000,000   *Employees:* 160
Company Type: Private   *Employees here:* 80
SIC: 2843
 Mfg textile dyes and chemicals
Thomas J Reardon, Business Manager

D-U-N-S 80-789-1783
B F GOODRICH FREEDOM CHEMICAL CO.
 (Parent: The B F Goodrich Company)
9911 Brecksville Rd, Cleveland, OH 44141
Phone: (216) 447-5000
Sales: $300,000,000   *Employees:* 1,200
Company Type: Public Family Member   *Employees here:* 4
SIC: 2865
 Mfg organic color pigments & synthetic organic dyes & whol
   textile chemicals & natural additives & pharmaceutical
   intermediates
David B Price, President

D-U-N-S 78-849-7220   EXP
B F GOODRICH TEXTILE CHEMICALS
 (Parent: B F Goodrich Freedom Chem Co)
8309 Wilkinson Blvd, Charlotte, NC 28214
Phone: (704) 393-0089
Sales: $42,100,000   *Employees:* 266
Company Type: Public Family Member   *Employees here:* 215
SIC: 2819
 Mfg textile chemicals
John A Weaver, President

D-U-N-S 61-000-1984
BAERLOCHER USA
3676 Davis Rd NW, Dover, OH 44622
Phone: (330) 364-6000
Sales: $25,000,000   *Employees:* 30
Company Type: Private   *Employees here:* 30
SIC: 2819
 Mfg specialty chemicals
Phil Levy, General Manager

D-U-N-S 00-835-2387
BAKER PETROLITE INCORPORATED
 (Parent: Baker Hughes Oilfld Operations)
12645 W Airport Blvd, Sugar Land, TX 77478
Phone: (281) 276-5400

Sales: $146,900,000   *Employees:* 1,031
Company Type: Public Family Member   *Employees here:* 450
SIC: 2899
 Mfg specialty chemicals
Glen Bassett, President

D-U-N-S 04-199-2728   EXP
BALCHEM CORPORATION
Rr 284, Slate Hill, NY 10973
Phone: (914) 355-5300
Sales: $28,619,000   *Employees:* 117
Company Type: Public   *Employees here:* 96
SIC: 2869
 Mfg industrial specialty encapsulet organic chemicals
Dino A Rossi, President

D-U-N-S 00-130-7032
BASF CORPORATION
 (Parent: Basfin Corporation)
3000 Continental Dr N, Budd Lake, NJ 07828
Phone: (973) 426-2600
Sales: $3,546,000,000   *Employees:* 14,400
Company Type: Private   *Employees here:* 1,000
SIC: 2869
 Mfg chemicals pharmaceuticals consumer products dyestuffs
   coatings & plastics
Peter Oakley, Chairman of the Board

D-U-N-S 06-496-0248   EXP
BAYER CORPORATION
100 Bayer Rd Bldg 4, Pittsburgh, PA 15205
Phone: (412) 777-2000
Sales: $9,257,028,000   *Employees:* 24,300
Company Type: Private   *Employees here:* 1,800
SIC: 2821
 Mfg resins pesticides chemicals pharmaceuticals medical
   instruments bio-products perfumes & flavors
Helge H Wehmeier, President

D-U-N-S 03-722-8087
BAYSHORE INDUSTRIAL INC.
 (Parent: I C O Inc)
1300 McCabe Rd, La Porte, TX 77571
Phone: (281) 471-8397
Sales: $35,000,000   *Employees:* 120
Company Type: Public Family Member   *Employees here:* 120
SIC: 2821
 Mfg plastic additive concentrates and compounds
Roy W Cabler Jr, President

D-U-N-S 05-741-9814   EXP
BEAUTICONTROL COSMETICS INC.
2121 Midway Rd, Carrollton, TX 75006
Phone: (972) 458-0601
Sales: $69,421,000   *Employees:* 280
Company Type: Public   *Employees here:* 140
SIC: 2844
 Mfg cosmetics & appearance consulting service
Jinger L Heath, Chairman of the Board

D-U-N-S 06-618-6107
BECKER UNDERWOOD INC.
801 Dayton Ave, Ames, IA 50010
Phone: (515) 232-5907
Sales: $20,000,000   *Employees:* 70
Company Type: Private   *Employees here:* 70
SIC: 2865
 Mfg cyclic crudes/intermediates/dyes
Roger Underwood, President

D-U-N-S 10-573-9148
BECKMAN NAGUABO, INC.
  (*Parent:* Beckman Coulter Inc)
4 St Rr 971, Naguabo, PR 00718
Phone: (787) 874-2635
Sales: $43,022,000   *Employees:* 80
Company Type: Public Family Member   *Employees here:* 80
SIC: 2869
  Mfg organic laboratory chemicals
Jorge Escobar, Chairman of the Board

D-U-N-S 00-522-9448
BEE CHEMICAL COMPANY
  (*Parent:* Autoliv Asp Inc)
2701 E 170th St, Lansing, IL 60438
Phone: (708) 474-7000
Sales: $60,700,000   *Employees:* 402
Company Type: Public Family Member   *Employees here:* 304
SIC: 2851
  Mfg paints/allied products mfg cyclic crudes/intermediates/
    dyes mfg inorganic pigments
John Harigan, President

D-U-N-S 00-204-0793
BEHR HOLDINGS CORPORATION
3400 W Segerstrom Ave, Santa Ana, CA 92704
Phone: (714) 545-7101
Sales: $103,600,000   *Employees:* 680
Company Type: Private   *Employees here:* 5
SIC: 2851
  Holding company which through subsidiary mfg paints stains
    and varnishes
John V Croul, Co-Chairman of the Board

D-U-N-S 00-838-7524   EXP
BEHR PROCESS CORPORATION
  (*Parent:* Behr Holdings Corporation)
3400 W Segerstrom Ave, Santa Ana, CA 92704
Phone: (714) 545-7101
Sales: $103,600,000   *Employees:* 680
Company Type: Private   *Employees here:* 100
SIC: 2851
  Mfg paints stains & varnishes
Ron Lazof, President

D-U-N-S 00-117-7906
BEIERSDORF INC.
187 Danbury Rd, Wilton, CT 06897
Phone: (203) 563-5800
Sales: $250,000,000   *Employees:* 2,000
Company Type: Private   *Employees here:* 110
SIC: 2844
  Mfg & whol skin care products surgical bandages dressings
    and wound care prod specialty soaps and compression
    stockings
Ronald B Gordon, Chief Executive Officer

D-U-N-S 04-390-9600
BELAE BRANDS INC.
15458a N 28th Ave, Phoenix, AZ 85053
Phone: (602) 889-4800
Sales: $100,000,000   *Employees:* 300
Company Type: Private   *Employees here:* 100
SIC: 2844
  Mfg & sell consumer products
Andrew S Patti, President

D-U-N-S 04-317-3590
BELMAY COMPANY, INC.
200 Corporate Blvd S, Yonkers, NY 10701
Phone: (914) 376-1515

Sales: $29,000,000   *Employees:* 250
Company Type: Private   *Employees here:* 65
SIC: 2844
  Mfg fragrance oils
Alan Kesten, President

D-U-N-S 00-102-5865   EXP
BEMIS ASSOCIATES, INC.
1 Bemis Way, Shirley, MA 01464
Phone: (978) 425-6761
Sales: $33,000,000   *Employees:* 170
Company Type: Private   *Employees here:* 170
SIC: 2891
  Mfg thermoplastic adhesives & coatings & custom coating
    with adhesives
Stephen Howard, President

D-U-N-S 14-851-1553
BENCKISER CONSUMER PRODUCTS
5 American Ln, Greenwich, CT 06831
Phone: (203) 618-5200
Sales: $57,600,000   *Employees:* 451
Company Type: Private   *Employees here:* 100
SIC: 2841
  Mfg consumer cleaning products
Douglas Meyer, President

D-U-N-S 61-498-2197
BENCYN INC.
100 Creasy Ct, Lafayette, IN 47905
Phone: (765) 447-8767
Sales: $15,000,000   *Employees:* 51
Company Type: Private   *Employees here:* 30
SIC: 2899
  Mfg specialty chemicals
Don Benedyk, Vice-President

D-U-N-S 00-628-2727
THE BENJAMIN ANSEHL CO.
1555 Page Industrial Blvd, Saint Louis, MO 63132
Phone: (314) 429-4300
Sales: $50,000,000   *Employees:* 230
Company Type: Private   *Employees here:* 180
SIC: 2844
  Mfg health and beauty care products
W L Edwards III, President

D-U-N-S 00-121-0715   EXP
BENJAMIN MOORE & CO.
51 Chestnut Ridge Rd, Montvale, NJ 07645
Phone: (201) 573-9600
Sales: $666,294,000   *Employees:* 1,900
Company Type: Public   *Employees here:* 130
SIC: 2851
  Mfg coatings
Richard Roob, Chairman of the Board

D-U-N-S 62-787-9968
BERWIND INDUSTRIES, INC.
  (*Parent:* Berwind Corporation)
1 Lakeview Pl, Ste 305, Nashville, TN 37214
Phone: (615) 872-0199
Sales: $472,300,000   *Employees:* 3,300
Company Type: Private   *Employees here:* 5
SIC: 2899
  Mfg chemical specialties electronic test & measurement
    instruments security control equip bridge expansion joints
    auto parts
James L Hamling, President

D-U-N-S 00-505-0158   EXP
BETCO CORPORATION
1001 Brown Ave, Toledo, OH 43607

Phone: (419) 241-2156
Sales: $38,000,000   *Employees:* 160
Company Type: Private   *Employees here:* 145
SIC: 2841
   Mfg cleaning detergents
Paul C Betz, President

D-U-N-S 06-902-8637   EXP
BETZ INTERNATIONAL INC.
   (Parent: Hercules Incorporated)
4636 Somerton Rd, Langhorne, PA 19053
Phone: (215) 953-5754
Sales: $34,200,000   *Employees:* 190
Company Type: Public Family Member   *Employees here:* 20
SIC: 2899
   Mfg specialty chemical products for water treatment
Richard A Heberle, President

D-U-N-S 00-972-2265   EXP
BETZDEARBORN INC.
   (Parent: Hercules Incorporated)
4636 Somerton Rd, Langhorne, PA 19053
Phone: (215) 355-3300
Sales: $1,294,800,000   *Employees:* 5,300
Company Type: Public Family Member   *Employees here:* 600
SIC: 2899
   Mfg specialty chemicals chemical analyzer kits & whol pumps
Larry V Rankin, Senior Vice-President

D-U-N-S 02-792-5023
BEVERLY GIORGIO HILLS INC.
   (Parent: The Procter & Gamble Company)
2400 Broadway, Fl 3, Santa Monica, CA 90404
Phone: (310) 453-0711
Sales: $100,000,000   *Employees:* 325
Company Type: Public Family Member   *Employees here:* 125
SIC: 2844
   Mfg and distributes perfume
Paul Jongstra, President

D-U-N-S 13-964-2623   EXP
BF GOODRICH HILTON DAVIS INC.
   (Parent: The B F Goodrich Company)
2235 Langdon Farm Rd, Cincinnati, OH 45237
Phone: (513) 841-4000
Sales: $80,500,000   *Employees:* 400
Company Type: Public Family Member   *Employees here:* 400
SIC: 2865
   Mfr organic color pigments & synthetic organic dyes
John Fitzwater, President

D-U-N-S 00-328-6218
BIO-LAB INC.
   (Parent: Great Lakes Chemical Corp)
627 E College Ave, Decatur, GA 30030
Phone: (404) 378-1753
Sales: $400,000,000   *Employees:* 900
Company Type: Public Family Member   *Employees here:* 300
SIC: 2812
   Mfg swimming pool chemicals and related products
Marshall Bloom, Chairman of the Board

D-U-N-S 78-515-0947
BIOZYME
6010 Stock Yard Expy, Saint Joseph, MO 64504
Phone: (816) 238-3326
Sales: $16,400,000   *Employees:* 93
Company Type: Private   *Employees here:* 93
SIC: 2879
   Mfg agricultural chemicals
Merrill Ehlart, President

D-U-N-S 00-122-0359
BLOCK DRUG COMPANY INC.
257 Cornelison Ave, Jersey City, NJ 07302
Phone: (201) 434-3000
Sales: $863,057,000   *Employees:* 3,380
Company Type: Public   *Employees here:* 870
SIC: 2844
   Mfg dental & o-t-c consumer products
James A Block, Chairman of the Board

D-U-N-S 04-235-8619   EXP
BLUE CORAL-SLICK 50 LTD
1215 Valley Belt Rd, Cleveland, OH 44131
Phone: (216) 351-3000
Sales: $25,300,000   *Employees:* 215
Company Type: Private   *Employees here:* 118
SIC: 2842
   Mfg car appearance products & under the hood engine and
     fuel treatments
Brian Sokol, President

D-U-N-S 83-640-0879
BLUE WATER MOLDED SYSTEMS INC.
2000 Christian B Haas Dr, Saint Clair, MI 48079
Phone: (810) 329-7272
Sales: $15,000,000   *Employees:* 100
Company Type: Private   *Employees here:* 100
SIC: 2891
   Mfg plastics
Carl C Haas, President

D-U-N-S 00-136-8141
BOC GROUP INC.
   (Parent: Boc Inc)
575 Mountain Ave, New Providence, NJ 07974
Phone: (908) 665-2400
Sales: $1,090,900,000   *Employees:* 9,600
Company Type: Private   *Employees here:* 1,000
SIC: 2813
   Mfg gases & related pdts health care products high vacuum
     technology & distribution svcs
F D Rosenkranz, President

D-U-N-S 14-463-6503   EXP
BOC GROUP INC.
575 Mountain Ave, New Providence, NJ 07974
Phone: (908) 665-2400
Sales: $1,549,522,000   *Employees:* 8,000
Company Type: Private   *Employees here:* 1,000
SIC: 2813
   Mfr gases & related pdts & health care pdts & svcs & high
     vacuum technology
F D Rosenkranz, President

D-U-N-S 36-116-5509
BOCCHI LABORATORIES, INC.
20465 E Walnut Dr N, Walnut, CA 91789
Phone: (909) 598-1951
Sales: $47,000,000   *Employees:* 400
Company Type: Private   *Employees here:* 250
SIC: 2844
   Mfr hair & cosmetic preparations
Robert Bocchi, President

D-U-N-S 04-505-7155   EXP
BOEHME-FILATEX INC.
209 Watlington Industrial, Reidsville, NC 27320
Phone: (336) 342-6631
Sales: $30,700,000   *Employees:* 140
Company Type: Private   *Employees here:* 88
SIC: 2869
   Mfg industrial organic chemicals
Rene A Eckert, President

D-U-N-S 00-418-9809   IMP EXP
BONNE BELL INC.
18519 Detroit Ave, Cleveland, OH 44107
Phone: (216) 221-0800
Sales: $64,300,000   *Employees:* 544
Company Type: Private   *Employees here:* 345
SIC: 2844
   Mfg cosmetics toiletries & cologne preparations
Jesse A Bell, Chairman of the Board

D-U-N-S 00-194-1079   EXP
BONTEX INC.
1 Bontex Dr, Buena Vista, VA 24416
Phone: (540) 261-2181
Sales: $43,483,000   *Employees:* 196
Company Type: Public   *Employees here:* 96
SIC: 2824
   Manufactures elastomeric impregnated fiber board products
James C Kostelni, Chairman of the Board

D-U-N-S 14-783-9070   EXP
BORDEN CHEMICAL & PLASTIC, LP
Highway 73, Geismar, LA 70734
Phone: (225) 673-6121
Sales: $737,129,000   *Employees:* 800
Company Type: Public   *Employees here:* 465
SIC: 2821
   Mfg pvc polymer pdts methanol & nitrogen chemical pdts
Joseph M Saggese, Chairman of the Board

D-U-N-S 94-220-0932   EXP
BORDEN CHEMICAL INC.
   (Parent: Borden Inc)
180 E Broad St, Fl 32, Columbus, OH 43215
Phone: (614) 225-4000
Sales: $1,290,809,000   *Employees:* 3,000
Company Type: Private   *Employees here:* 300
SIC: 2869
   Mfg industrial organic chemicals
Joseph Saggese, Chief Executive Officer

D-U-N-S 00-573-4660   EXP
BORDEN HOLDINGS, INC.
   (Parent: Bw Holdings Llc)
180 E Broad St, Columbus, OH 43215
Phone: (614) 225-4000
Sales: $1,769,500,000   *Employees:* 11,200
Company Type: Private   *Employees here:* 10
SIC: 2891
   Mfg adhesives milk & dairy products and wallcoverings
C R Kidder, Chairman of the Board

D-U-N-S 00-133-8797
BORDEN INC.
   (Parent: Borden Holdings Inc)
180 E Broad St, Columbus, OH 43215
Phone: (614) 225-4000
Sales: $1,487,700,000   *Employees:* 8,000
Company Type: Private   *Employees here:* 1,200
SIC: 2869
   Mfg formaldehyde melamine resins and adhesives and
      management services
C R Kidder, Chairman of the Board

D-U-N-S 60-865-0164   EXP
BOSTIK INC.
   (Parent: Total America Inc)
211 Boston St, Middleton, MA 01949
Phone: (978) 777-0100

Sales: $120,000,000   *Employees:* 460
Company Type: Private   *Employees here:* 280
SIC: 2891
   Mfg specialty industrial adhesives & sealants
John L Fox, President

D-U-N-S 00-398-3483
BP CHEMICALS INC.
   (Parent: The Standard Oil Company)
200 Public Sq, Cleveland, OH 44114
Phone: (216) 586-4141
Sales: $637,000,000   *Employees:* 2,600
Company Type: Private   *Employees here:* 150
SIC: 2869
   Mfg organic chemicals polyester resins fiberglass panels
      missile & space components
Gary C Greve, President

D-U-N-S 07-462-3968   EXP
BPI BY-PRODUCT INDUSTRIES
612 S Trenton Ave, Pittsburgh, PA 15221
Phone: (412) 371-8554
Sales: $18,341,000   *Employees:* 28
Company Type: Private   *Employees here:* 8
SIC: 2899
   Mfg inorganic solid oxides
Joseph Quigley, President

D-U-N-S 00-419-8933   EXP
THE BRADEN-SUTPHIN INK CO.
3650 E 93rd St, Cleveland, OH 44105
Phone: (216) 271-2300
Sales: $40,000,000   *Employees:* 250
Company Type: Private   *Employees here:* 130
SIC: 2893
   Mfg printing inks
Ted Zelek, Chairman of the Board

D-U-N-S 02-575-8475
BRANDT CONSOLIDATED, INC.
Rr 125 Box West, Pleasant Plains, IL 62677
Phone: (217) 626-1123
Sales: $41,610,000   *Employees:* 85
Company Type: Private   *Employees here:* 30
SIC: 2875
   Mixes & whol fertilizer
Rick Brandt, President

D-U-N-S 06-067-7689   EXP
BRENT AMERICA HOLDINGS, INC.
16961 Knott Ave, La Mirada, CA 90638
Phone: (714) 739-2821
Sales: $16,200,000   *Employees:* 127
Company Type: Private   *Employees here:* 4
SIC: 2842
   Mfg cleaning preparations
K Hutchings, President

D-U-N-S 00-825-8295   EXP
BRENT AMERICA, INC.
   (Parent: Brent America Holdings Inc)
16961 Knott Ave, La Mirada, CA 90638
Phone: (714) 739-2821
Sales: $27,000,000   *Employees:* 120
Company Type: Private   *Employees here:* 60
SIC: 2869
   Mfg industrial specialty chemicals
Malcolm S Stopps, President

D-U-N-S 01-968-9330
BREWER SCIENCE, INC.
2401 Brewer Dr, Rolla, MO 65401
Phone: (573) 364-0300

Sales: $25,600,000   Employees: 180
Company Type: Private   Employees here: 175
SIC: 2851
   Mfg specialty coating chemicals and electronic research
Terry Brewer, Chairman of the Board

D-U-N-S 10-453-7022
BRONNER BROTHERS INC.
2141 Powers Ferry Rd SE, Marietta, GA 30067
Phone: (770) 988-0015
Sales: $17,096,000   Employees: 275
Company Type: Private   Employees here: 190
SIC: 2844
   Mfg whol & ret hair care products
Bernard Bronner, President

D-U-N-S 11-627-4572   EXP
BROOKS INDUSTRIES INC.
70 Tyler Pl, South Plainfield, NJ 07080
Phone: (908) 561-5200
Sales: $20,195,000   Employees: 65
Company Type: Private   Employees here: 45
SIC: 2869
   Producer of cosmetic ingredients used in the mfg of
   cosmetics
Ivar Malmstrom, President

D-U-N-S 04-876-3031   EXP
BROTECH CORP.
150 Monument Rd, Bala Cynwyd, PA 19004
Phone: (610) 668-9090
Sales: $149,900,000   Employees: 700
Company Type: Private   Employees here: 130
SIC: 2821
   Mfg ion exchange resins
Stephan Brodie, President

D-U-N-S 00-641-4692
BRULIN & COMPANY INC.
2920 Dr Andrew J Brown Av, Indianapolis, IN 46205
Phone: (317) 923-3211
Sales: $15,000,000   Employees: 160
Company Type: Private   Employees here: 140
SIC: 2842
   Mfg commercial floor cleaning preparations industrial
   cleaning preparations
Charles Pollnow, President

D-U-N-S 09-543-0948
BRUNING PAINT COMPANY
601 S Haven St, Baltimore, MD 21224
Phone: (410) 342-3636
Sales: $30,400,000   Employees: 205
Company Type: Private   Employees here: 100
SIC: 2851
   Mfg paints varnishes & enamels
Doug S Ramer, President

D-U-N-S 07-713-2280   EXP
BUCKEYE INTERNATIONAL INC.
2700 Wagner Pl, Maryland Heights, MO 63043
Phone: (314) 291-1900
Sales: $30,000,000   Employees: 180
Company Type: Private   Employees here: 100
SIC: 2842
   Mfg specialty cleaning preparations
Gilbert G Kosup, President

D-U-N-S 18-895-3434
BUCKMAN LABORATORIES, INC.
   (Parent: Bulab Holdings Inc)
1256 N Mclean Blvd, Memphis, TN 38108
Phone: (901) 278-0330

Sales: $158,981,000   Employees: 442
Company Type: Private   Employees here: 442
SIC: 2869
   Mfg industrial organic & inorganic chemicals
Steven B Buckman, Chairman of the Board

D-U-N-S 06-078-3552   EXP
BUFFALO COLOR CORPORATION
959 Route 46, Parsippany, NJ 07054
Phone: (973) 316-5600
Sales: $55,000,000   Employees: 250
Company Type: Private   Employees here: 8
SIC: 2865
   Mfg synthetic organic dyes industrial organic chemicals &
   medicinal chemicals
Kenneth W Mc Court, President

D-U-N-S 00-702-3658   EXP
BULAB HOLDINGS, INC.
1256 N Mclean Blvd, Memphis, TN 38108
Phone: (901) 278-0330
Sales: $160,996,000   Employees: 1,250
Company Type: Private   Employees here: 4
SIC: 2869
   Mfg industrial organic & inorganic chemicals
Robert H Buckman, Chairman of the Board

D-U-N-S 08-522-8377   EXP
BULK MOLDING COMPOUNDS, INC.
1600 Powis Ct, West Chicago, IL 60185
Phone: (630) 377-1065
Sales: $27,400,000   Employees: 130
Company Type: Private   Employees here: 71
SIC: 2821
   Mfg polyester molding compounds
Larry E Nunnery Jr, President

D-U-N-S 01-881-8971
BURTIN URETHANE CORPORATION
2550 S Garnsey St, Santa Ana, CA 92707
Phone: (714) 850-1370
Sales: $28,000,000   Employees: 55
Company Type: Private   Employees here: 25
SIC: 2821
   Mfg polyurethane resins
Carlos Burtin, President

D-U-N-S 00-187-5426   EXP
BUSH BOAKE ALLEN INC.
   (Parent: Union Camp Corporation)
7 Mercedes Dr, Montvale, NJ 07645
Phone: (201) 391-9870
Sales: $490,585,000   Employees: 1,964
Company Type: Public   Employees here: 150
SIC: 2869
   Mfg flavors fragrances & aroma chemicals
Julian W Boyden, Chairman of the Board

D-U-N-S 00-103-0535   EXP
THE BUTCHER COMPANY INC.
67 Forest St, Marlborough, MA 01752
Phone: (508) 481-5700
Sales: $65,000,000   Employees: 230
Company Type: Private   Employees here: 65
SIC: 2842
   Mfg floor finishes strippers & cleaners
Charles Butcher, Chairman of the Board

D-U-N-S 00-573-5469   EXP
BW HOLDINGS, LLC
180 E Broad St, Columbus, OH 43215
Phone: (614) 225-4000

Sales: $1,769,500,000   *Employees:* 11,200
Company Type: Private   *Employees here:* 10
SIC: 2891
    Holding company
Henry R Kravis, General Partner

D-U-N-S 86-118-4968
C & I HOLDINGS, INC.
1180 Central Industrial A, Saint Louis, MO 63110
Phone: (314) 771-6600
Sales: $15,000,000   *Employees:* 150
Company Type: Private   *Employees here:* 80
SIC: 2842
    Mfg fllor waxes disinfectants cleaning products soap &
        detergents
Leo A Epstein, President

D-U-N-S 00-311-9054   EXP
C B FLEET COMPANY INCORPORATED
4615 Murray Pl, Lynchburg, VA 24502
Phone: (804) 528-4000
Sales: $110,274,000   *Employees:* 432
Company Type: Private   *Employees here:* 290
SIC: 2844
    Manufactures personal hygiene products & pharmaceutical
        preparations
Brian Duffy, President

D-U-N-S 79-016-1756
C B FLEET INTERNATIONAL INC.
    (Parent: C B Fleet Company Incorporated)
4615 Murray Pl, Lynchburg, VA 24502
Phone: (804) 528-4000
Sales: $25,000,000   *Employees:* 140
Company Type: Private   *Employees here:* 50
SIC: 2844
    Holding co for overseas mfg of personal hygiene products
Doug Bellaire, President

D-U-N-S 14-766-7307
C H OXY CORPORATION
    (Parent: Oxy Chemical Corporation)
5005 LBJ Fwy, Dallas, TX 75244
Phone: (972) 404-3800
Sales: $1,845,000,000   *Employees:* 7,500
Company Type: Public Family Member   *Employees here:* 5
SIC: 2869
    Mfg chemicals plastics fertilizers & metal finishing chemicals
J R Hirl, President

D-U-N-S 18-316-7246
C P I PACKAGING INC.
240 Boundary Rd, Marlboro, NJ 07746
Phone: (732) 431-3500
Sales: $15,300,000   *Employees:* 74
Company Type: Private   *Employees here:* 35
SIC: 2821
    Mfg of plastic packaging materials
Harry Bussey III, President

D-U-N-S 00-214-1190   EXP
C P S CHEMICAL CO. INC.
    (Parent: Ciba Specialty Chemicals Corp)
900 Route 9 N, Woodbridge, NJ 07095
Phone: (732) 607-2700
Sales: $94,700,000   *Employees:* 400
Company Type: Private   *Employees here:* 150
SIC: 2869
    Mfg specialty and crosslinking monomers flocculants
        coagulants & specialty polymers organic chemicals &
        intermediates
Robert W Bohny, President

D-U-N-S 00-101-3580
CABOT CORPORATION
75 State St, Ste 13, Boston, MA 02109
Phone: (617) 345-0100
Sales: $410,300,000   *Employees:* 4,800
Company Type: Public   *Employees here:* 140
SIC: 2895
    Mfg carbon black polyethylene film silica electronic materials
        & whol liquid natural gas & coal
Kennett F Burnes, President

D-U-N-S 18-155-7794
CAESARS WORLD MERCHANDISING
    (Parent: Caesars World Inc)
3570 Las Vegas Blvd S, Las Vegas, NV 89109
Phone: (702) 866-1210
Sales: $22,000,000   *Employees:* 180
Company Type: Public Family Member   *Employees here:* 140
SIC: 2844
    Mfg & retail perfumes
Michael Wilkins, Administration

D-U-N-S 02-624-0267   EXP
CALABRIAN CHEMICAL CORPORATION
    (Parent: Calabrian Corporation)
1521 Green Oak Pl, Ste 200, Kingwood, TX 77339
Phone: (281) 348-2303
Sales: $20,000,000   *Employees:* 110
Company Type: Private   *Employees here:* 70
SIC: 2869
    Mfg inorganic chemicals
Charles E Cogliandro, President

D-U-N-S 07-327-4359   IMP EXP
CALABRIAN CORPORATION
1521 Green Oak Pl, Ste 200, Kingwood, TX 77339
Phone: (281) 348-2303
Sales: $20,000,000   *Employees:* 124
Company Type: Private   *Employees here:* 14
SIC: 2819
    Manufactures inorganic chemicals wholesales plastic
        materials and inorganic chemicals
Charles A Cogliandro, Chairman of the Board

D-U-N-S 00-431-9810   EXP
CALGON CARBON CORPORATION
400 Calgon Carbon Dr, Pittsburgh, PA 15205
Phone: (412) 787-6700
Sales: $327,500,000   *Employees:* 1,341
Company Type: Public   *Employees here:* 255
SIC: 2819
    Mfg activated carbon (charcoal) providing related services
        and mfg purification equipment
Thomas A Mcconomy, Chairman of the Board

D-U-N-S 80-904-4761
CALGON CORPORATION
    (Parent: English China Clays Inc)
Hc 60 Box West, Pittsburgh, PA 15205
Phone: (412) 494-8000
Sales: $139,600,000   *Employees:* 980
Company Type: Private   *Employees here:* 768
SIC: 2899
    Mfg chemical preparations
James H Heagle, President

D-U-N-S 00-102-7861
CALIFORNIA PRODUCTS CORP.
169 Waverly St, Cambridge, MA 02139
Phone: (617) 547-5300

Sales: $44,000,000   *Employees:* 162
Company Type: Private   *Employees here:* 115
SIC: 2851
    Mfg paints
Joseph S Junkin, President

D-U-N-S 10-387-1950   EXP
CALIFORNIA SULPHUR
2509 E Grant St, Wilmington, CA 90744
Phone: (562) 437-0768
Sales: $15,000,000   *Employees:* 15
Company Type: Private   *Employees here:* 15
SIC: 2819
    Mfg & whol (exports) pelletized sulphur
Jack Babbitt, General Partner

D-U-N-S 94-554-7388   EXP
CALLAWAY CHEMICALS COMPANY
    (Parent: Vulcan Materials Company)
6003 Veterans Pkwy, Columbus, GA 31909
Phone: (706) 576-2000
Sales: $175,000,000   *Employees:* 450
Company Type: Public Family Member   *Employees here:* 45
SIC: 2819
    Mfg industrial specialty chemicals
Daniel Mc Caul, President

D-U-N-S 01-175-9875
CAMBRIDGE ISOTOPE LABORATORIES
    (Parent: Otsuka America Inc)
50 Frontage Rd, Andover, MA 01810
Phone: (978) 749-8000
Sales: $27,500,000   *Employees:* 100
Company Type: Private   *Employees here:* 85
SIC: 2869
    Mfg industrial organic chemicals
Dr Joel Bradley, President

D-U-N-S 00-423-8366
CAMCO CHEMICAL COMPANY INC.
8150 Holton Dr, Florence, KY 41042
Phone: (606) 727-3200
Sales: $26,000,000   *Employees:* 100
Company Type: Private   *Employees here:* 100
SIC: 2842
    Contract blending of chemical sanitation preparations and
      lubricants
Thomas E Cropper, President

D-U-N-S 06-808-0621
CANBERRA CORP.
3610 N Holland Sylvania R, Toledo, OH 43615
Phone: (419) 841-6616
Sales: $20,816,000   *Employees:* 200
Company Type: Private   *Employees here:* 200
SIC: 2842
    Mfg chemical cleaning specialty products
R B Yacko, President

D-U-N-S 00-217-5636
CANNING GUMM, INC.
538 Forest St, Kearny, NJ 07032
Phone: (201) 991-4171
Sales: $25,000,000   *Employees:* 102
Company Type: Private   *Employees here:* 40
SIC: 2899
    Manufactures industrial metal treating compounds and
      polishing preparations and wholesales industrial metal
      finishing machinery
Frederick J Gumm, President

D-U-N-S 08-129-2070   EXP
CAPITAL RESIN CORPORATION
324 Dering Ave, Columbus, OH 43207
Phone: (614) 445-7177
Sales: $25,000,000   *Employees:* 70
Company Type: Private   *Employees here:* 70
SIC: 2821
    Mfg resins
Judith Hansen, Chief Executive Officer

D-U-N-S 08-229-5197
CAR BRITE, INC.
1910 S State Ave, Indianapolis, IN 46203
Phone: (317) 788-9925
Sales: $19,000,000   *Employees:* 65
Company Type: Private   *Employees here:* 60
SIC: 2842
    Mfg automotive cleaning products cleansers polishing agents
      and wares
John Campbell, President

D-U-N-S 00-222-5209
CAR-FRESHNER CORP.
203 N Hamilton St, Watertown, NY 13601
Phone: (315) 788-6250
Sales: $45,900,000   *Employees:* 387
Company Type: Private   *Employees here:* 200
SIC: 2842
    Mfg non-personal air fresheners
Richard Flechtner, President

D-U-N-S 00-628-2347   EXP
CARBOLINE COMPANY
    (Parent: Rpm Inc)
350 Hanley Industrial Ct, Saint Louis, MO 63144
Phone: (314) 644-1000
Sales: $60,400,000   *Employees:* 400
Company Type: Public Family Member   *Employees here:* 175
SIC: 2851
    Mfg protective coatings
Sherwin L Steinberg, President

D-U-N-S 93-252-7005   EXP
CARDINAL COMPANIES, LP
2010 S Beltline Blvd, Columbia, SC 29201
Phone: (803) 799-7190
Sales: $40,000,000   *Employees:* 125
Company Type: Private   *Employees here:* 125
SIC: 2869
    Mfg chemicals
Dennie Wetherley, Controller

D-U-N-S 00-829-7574
CARDINAL INDUSTRIAL FINISHES
1329 Potrero Ave, El Monte, CA 91733
Phone: (626) 444-9274
Sales: $31,100,000   *Employees:* 210
Company Type: Private   *Employees here:* 100
SIC: 2851
    Mfg paint and powder coatings
Stanley W Ekstrom, President

D-U-N-S 12-214-7564
CARDOLITE CORPORATION
500 Doremus Ave, Newark, NJ 07105
Phone: (973) 344-5015
Sales: $22,600,000   *Employees:* 91
Company Type: Private   *Employees here:* 90
SIC: 2869
    Mfg specialty industry organic chemicals & resins
Anthony Stonis, President

D-U-N-S 06-469-6107   EXP
CARGILL FERTILIZER INC.
  (*Parent:* Cargill Incorporated)
8813 Hwy 41 S, Riverview, FL 33569
Phone: (813) 677-9111
Sales: $750,000,000   *Employees:* 1,100
Company Type: Private   *Employees here:* 400
SIC: 2874
  Mfg phosphatic fertilizer
Ray Larson, Finance

D-U-N-S 01-814-8973   EXP
CARROLL SCIENTIFIC INC.
  (*Parent:* Lubrizol Corporation)
5401 Dansher Rd, La Grange, IL 60525
Phone: (708) 579-8000
Sales: $20,000,000   *Employees:* 65
Company Type: Public Family Member   *Employees here:* 65
SIC: 2899
  Mfg chemical preparations for printing inks
John R Carroll, President

D-U-N-S 96-319-0285
CARSON INC.
64 Ross Rd, Savannah, GA 31405
Phone: (912) 651-3400
Sales: $109,631,000   *Employees:* 372
Company Type: Public   *Employees here:* 200
SIC: 2844
  Mfg and markets ethnic hair care products
Malcolm Yesner, President

D-U-N-S 00-329-3073   EXP
CARSON PRODUCTS COMPANY
  (*Parent:* Carson Inc)
64 Ross Rd, Savannah, GA 31405
Phone: (912) 651-3400
Sales: $80,000,000   *Employees:* 400
Company Type: Public Family Member   *Employees here:* 400
SIC: 2844
  Mfg ethnic hair care products
Leroy Keith, Chairman of the Board

D-U-N-S 00-122-3445   EXP
CARTER-WALLACE INC.
1345 Avenue Of The Americ, New York, NY 10105
Phone: (212) 339-5000
Sales: $662,229,000   *Employees:* 3,360
Company Type: Public   *Employees here:* 175
SIC: 2844
  Mfg toiletries pharmaceuticals diagnostic specialties
    proprietary drugs & pet products
Thomas G Gerstmyer, President

D-U-N-S 00-246-0772
CARTRIDGE ACTUATED DEVICES
123 Clinton Rd, Fairfield, NJ 07004
Phone: (973) 575-1312
Sales: $18,200,000   *Employees:* 128
Company Type: Private   *Employees here:* 55
SIC: 2892
  Mfg explosive devices
Ralph P Dodd, President

D-U-N-S 00-547-7666
CARUS CORPORATION
315 5th St, Peru, IL 61354
Phone: (815) 223-1500
Sales: $46,845,000   *Employees:* 214
Company Type: Private   *Employees here:* 100
SIC: 2819
  Mfg industrial chemicals
M B Carus, Chairman of the Board

D-U-N-S 02-926-0833
CASCHEM INC.
  (*Parent:* Cambrex Corporation)
40 Avenue A, Bayonne, NJ 07002
Phone: (201) 858-7900
Sales: $55,000,000   *Employees:* 135
Company Type: Public Family Member   *Employees here:* 135
SIC: 2869
  Manufactures specialty organic chemicals
John Van Hulle, President

D-U-N-S 01-626-8658
CAST PRODUCTS CORP.
58263 Charlotte Ave, Elkhart, IN 46517
Phone: (219) 294-2684
Sales: $30,466,000   *Employees:* 140
Company Type: Private   *Employees here:* 48
SIC: 2891
  Mfg putty tapes caulks & adhesives also shutters & building
    supplies
Bruce A Mckibbin, President

D-U-N-S 88-477-8879
CATALYTICA PHARMACEUTICALS
  (*Parent:* Catalytica Inc)
U S Hwy 13 State Rd 1590, Greenville, NC 27834
Phone: (252) 758-3436
Sales: $360,000,000   *Employees:* 1,300
Company Type: Public Family Member   *Employees here:* 1,250
SIC: 2869
  Mfg chemicals
Gabriel R Cipau, President

D-U-N-S 05-516-3885
CATAWBA-CHARLAB INC.
5046 Old Pineville Rd, Charlotte, NC 28217
Phone: (704) 523-4242
Sales: $26,025,000   *Employees:* 123
Company Type: Private   *Employees here:* 123
SIC: 2869
  Mfg organic textile chemicals & colors
H M Thompson Jr, President

D-U-N-S 05-344-4667   EXP
CBI LABORATORIES INC.
  (*Parent:* Thermolase Corporation)
2055 Luna Rd, Ste C, Carrollton, TX 75006
Phone: (972) 241-7546
Sales: $20,900,000   *Employees:* 190
Company Type: Public Family Member   *Employees here:* 190
SIC: 2844
  Mfg & whol skin hair & body care products
Mary Frost, President

D-U-N-S 10-677-1041
CCA INDUSTRIES, INC.
200 Murray Hill Pkwy, East Rutherford, NJ 07073
Phone: (201) 330-1400
Sales: $41,402,000   *Employees:* 135
Company Type: Public   *Employees here:* 134
SIC: 2844
  Mfg health & beauty aids & dietary supplements
David Edell, President

D-U-N-S 84-864-7657
CCL CUSTOM MANUFACTURING, INC.
  (*Parent:* Ccl Industries Corporation)
6133 N River Rd, Ste 800, Des Plaines, IL 60018
Phone: (847) 823-0060

Sales: $257,300,000   *Employees:* 2,000
Company Type: Private   *Employees here:* 10
SIC: 2841
     Custom contract manufacturer of personal & household
     products
Paul Cummings, President

D-U-N-S 55-648-4640
CEDA INTERNATIONAL, INC.
3665 John F Kennedy Pkwy, Fort Collins, CO 80525
Phone: (970) 229-0202
Sales: $21,819,000   *Employees:* 150
Company Type: Private   *Employees here:* 9
SIC: 2819
     Holding company
Ernie P Koop, President

D-U-N-S 14-825-3156   EXP
CEDAR CHEMICAL CORPORATION
     (Parent: Nine West Corporation)
5100 Poplar Ave, Ste 2414, Memphis, TN 38137
Phone: (901) 685-5348
Sales: $140,000,000   *Employees:* 250
Company Type: Private   *Employees here:* 32
SIC: 2873
     Mfg potassium nitrate fertilizers organic chemicals &
     agricultural herbicides
Tom Hardy, President

D-U-N-S 02-519-0997
CELGARD, LLC
13800 S Lakes Dr, Charlotte, NC 28273
Phone: (704) 587-8459
Sales: $53,300,000   *Employees:* 260
Company Type: Private   *Employees here:* 260
SIC: 2821
     Mfg plastic materials
Milo A Hassloch, President

D-U-N-S 19-867-4293
CEMEDINE U.S.A., INC.
7655 S 6th St, Oak Creek, WI 53154
Phone: (414) 764-9544
Sales: $20,000,000   *Employees:* 56
Company Type: Private   *Employees here:* 56
SIC: 2891
     Mfg adhesives & sealants
Peter Barry, President

D-U-N-S 05-109-1528   EXP
CENTRAL INK CORPORATION
1100 Harvester Rd, West Chicago, IL 60185
Phone: (630) 231-6500
Sales: $35,564,000   *Employees:* 97
Company Type: Private   *Employees here:* 88
SIC: 2893
     Mfg web offset printing ink
Richard E Breen, President

D-U-N-S 87-875-4472
CENTRAL MN ETHANOL CO-OP, INC.
17936 Heron Rd, Little Falls, MN 56345
Phone: (320) 632-1614
Sales: $30,000,000   *Employees:* 31
Company Type: Private   *Employees here:* 31
SIC: 2869
     Mfg ethanol
Robin Wells, General Manager

D-U-N-S 80-279-7084   EXP
CERDEC CORPORATION
W Wylie Ave, Washington, PA 15301
Phone: (724) 223-5900

Sales: $70,000,000   *Employees:* 340
Company Type: Private   *Employees here:* 335
SIC: 2865
     Manufactures pigments and glass enamels
Robert W Martel, President

D-U-N-S 00-896-6632   EXP
CF INDUSTRIES, INC.
1 Salem Lake Dr, Lake Zurich, IL 60047
Phone: (847) 438-9500
Sales: $1,431,649,000   *Employees:* 1,652
Company Type: Private   *Employees here:* 290
SIC: 2873
     Mfg nitrogenous & phosphatic fertilizers
Robert C Liuzzi, President

D-U-N-S 00-802-4580   EXP
CHAMPION TECHNOLOGIES, INC.
     (Parent: Permian Mud Service Inc)
3355 W Alabama St, Ste 400, Houston, TX 77098
Phone: (713) 627-3303
Sales: $150,000,000   *Employees:* 725
Company Type: Private   *Employees here:* 75
SIC: 2819
     Mfg industrial inorganic chemicals
W S White, President

D-U-N-S 00-193-0254
CHANEL INC.
9 W 57th St, Fl 44, New York, NY 10019
Phone: (212) 688-5055
Sales: $119,000,000   *Employees:* 1,000
Company Type: Private   *Employees here:* 50
SIC: 2844
     Mfg cosmetics preparations & perfumes
A Kopelman, President

D-U-N-S 09-219-7466
CHARM SCIENCES INC.
36 Franklin St, Malden, MA 02148
Phone: (781) 322-1523
Sales: $15,000,000   *Employees:* 90
Company Type: Private   *Employees here:* 90
SIC: 2899
     Mfg food & milk contamination screening kits
Dr Stanley E Charm, President

D-U-N-S 93-813-7163
CHATTEM CHEMICALS, INC.
     (Parent: Elcat Inc)
3708 Saint Elmo Ave, Chattanooga, TN 37409
Phone: (423) 822-5000
Sales: $20,000,000   *Employees:* 60
Company Type: Private   *Employees here:* 60
SIC: 2869
     Mfg industrial organic chemicals
Rodney Sergent, Managing Director

D-U-N-S 02-106-8325
CHEM COMP SYSTEMS INC.
11065 Nott Ave, Cypress, CA 90630
Phone: (714) 379-8260
Sales: $15,000,000   *Employees:* 31
Company Type: Private   *Employees here:* 12
SIC: 2891
     Mfg cement
Edward K Rice, President

D-U-N-S 00-214-4673
CHEM FLEUR INC.
     (Parent: Firmenich Incorporated)
150 Firmench Way, Newark, NJ 07114
Phone: (973) 589-4266

Sales: $90,000,000   *Employees:* 140
Company Type: Private   *Employees here:* 110
SIC: 2899
   Mfg chemical preparations
Hans P Van Houten, Chairman of the Board

D-U-N-S 09-737-0803   EXP
CHEM POLYMER CORPORATION
   (Parent: Advent International Corp)
2443 Rockfill Rd, Fort Myers, FL 33916
Phone: (941) 337-0400
Sales: $20,000,000   *Employees:* 65
Company Type: Private   *Employees here:* 65
SIC: 2821
   Mfg nylon resin compounds
John Lee, President

D-U-N-S 15-370-1883   EXP
CHEMDAL CORPORATION
   (Parent: Chemdal International Corp)
1530 E Dundee Rd, Ste 350, Palatine, IL 60074
Phone: (847) 705-5600
Sales: $100,000,000   *Employees:* 125
Company Type: Public Family Member   *Employees here:* 55
SIC: 2821
   Mfg polymers
Gary Castagna, President

D-U-N-S 80-821-9562
CHEMDAL INTERNATIONAL CORP.
   (Parent: Amcol International Corp)
1530 E Dundee Rd, Ste 350, Palatine, IL 60074
Phone: (847) 705-5600
Sales: $62,100,000   *Employees:* 300
Company Type: Public Family Member   *Employees here:* 2
SIC: 2821
   Holding company
John Hughes, Chairman of the Board

D-U-N-S 10-676-8625   EXP
CHEMDESIGN CORPORATION
   (Parent: Bayer Corporation)
310 Authority Dr, Fitchburg, MA 01420
Phone: (978) 345-9999
Sales: $80,000,000   *Employees:* 390
Company Type: Private   *Employees here:* 260
SIC: 2869
   Mfg custom & specialty fine chemicals
Rolf Loewer, President

D-U-N-S 09-180-8246
CHEMETALS INCORPORATED
   (Parent: Comilog Us Inc)
610 Pittman Rd, Baltimore, MD 21226
Phone: (410) 789-8800
Sales: $65,000,000   *Employees:* 285
Company Type: Private   *Employees here:* 151
SIC: 2819
   Mfg manganese chemicals electrolytic manganese dioxide &
     manganese alloys
Richard L Mulholland, President

D-U-N-S 00-896-6418   EXP
CHEMFIRST INC.
700 North St, Jackson, MS 39202
Phone: (601) 948-7550
Sales: $445,821,000   *Employees:* 1,175
Company Type: Public   *Employees here:* 60
SIC: 2865
   Mfg industrial chemicals gas/liquid incinerators & steel
     ingots
J K Williams, Chairman of the Board

D-U-N-S 78-849-9853   EXP
CHEMICAL PACKAGING CORP.
300 State St, Paducah, KY 42003
Phone: (502) 443-4578
Sales: $21,200,000   *Employees:* 150
Company Type: Private   *Employees here:* 30
SIC: 2899
   Provides customized formulation blending & packaging of
     dry chemicals
C W Golightly, President

D-U-N-S 84-070-3144   EXP
CHEMICAL PRODUCTS TECHNOLOGIES
108 Old Mill Rd, Cartersville, GA 30120
Phone: (770) 606-8166
Sales: $18,000,000   *Employees:* 12
Company Type: Private   *Employees here:* 12
SIC: 2819
   Whol & mfg additives for the paper industry
John Olsen, General Manager

D-U-N-S 07-013-9068
CHEMICAL SPECIALISTS & DEV.
2210 Hackberry Ln, Conroe, TX 77306
Phone: (409) 756-1065
Sales: $23,281,000   *Employees:* 55
Company Type: Private   *Employees here:* 47
SIC: 2851
   Mfg & whol paint lacquer thinners contract packaging service
     & whol petroleum products
Stephen R Cooke, Chairman of the Board

D-U-N-S 04-297-3313
CHEMICAL SPECIALTIES INC.
   (Parent: Laporte Inc)
1 Wdlawn Grn, Ste 250, Charlotte, NC 28217
Phone: (704) 522-0825
Sales: $33,300,000   *Employees:* 212
Company Type: Private   *Employees here:* 20
SIC: 2819
   Mfg industrial inorganic chemicals (wood preservatives) and
     wood preserving equipment
Stephen B Ainscough, President

D-U-N-S 00-656-0999
CHEMONICS INDUSTRIES, INC.
   (Parent: Erly Industries Inc)
734 E Southern Pacific Dr, Phoenix, AZ 85034
Phone: (602) 262-5401
Sales: $74,508,000   *Employees:* 440
Company Type: Private   *Employees here:* 15
SIC: 2899
   Mfg chemical preparations
Gerald D Murphy, Chairman of the Board

D-U-N-S 08-390-1033   EXP
CHEMRON CORPORATION
3115 Propeller Dr, Paso Robles, CA 93446
Phone: (805) 239-1550
Sales: $15,600,000   *Employees:* 80
Company Type: Private   *Employees here:* 50
SIC: 2843
   Mfg surface active agents
William Frost, President

D-U-N-S 04-546-9160
CHEMTALL INCORPORATED
Chemical Plant Rd, Riceboro, GA 31323
Phone: (912) 884-3366

Sales: $39,300,000   *Employees:* 175
Company Type: Private   *Employees here:* 175
SIC: 2869
  Mfg industrial organic chemicals
Hubert Issaurat, President

D-U-N-S 80-265-9029   EXP
CHEMTECH PRODUCTS, INC.
  (Parent: Allied Industrial Group Inc)
1630 Des Peres Rd, Ste 210, Saint Louis, MO 63131
Phone: (314) 965-7100
Sales: $40,000,000   *Employees:* 62
Company Type: Private   *Employees here:* 14
SIC: 2819
  Mfg and distributor of industrial chemicals
Wayne E Brasser, President

D-U-N-S 06-538-6906   EXP
CHEMTREAT INC.
4301 Dominion Blvd, Glen Allen, VA 23060
Phone: (804) 965-0505
Sales: $90,000,000   *Employees:* 400
Company Type: Private   *Employees here:* 70
SIC: 2899
  Mfg water treatment chemicals and waste water treatment
    chemicals
Harrison Tyler, President

D-U-N-S 17-566-3699
CHEMTRUSION INC.
  (Parent: Intersystems Inc)
7115 Clinton Dr, Houston, TX 77020
Phone: (713) 675-1616
Sales: $15,000,000   *Employees:* 119
Company Type: Private   *Employees here:* 57
SIC: 2821
  Manufacturer of thermoplastic resins
Scott Owens, President

D-U-N-S 13-138-2012
CHESEBROUGH-PONDS INTERNATIONAL CAPITAL
  (Parent: Conopco Inc)
800 Sylvan Ave, Englewood Cliffs, NJ 07632
Phone: (201) 567-8000
Sales: $42,700,000   *Employees:* 364
Company Type: Private   *Employees here:* 3
SIC: 2844
  Holding company through subsidiaries mfg & whol cosmetics
    & mfg packaged foods
David Hamilton, President

D-U-N-S 09-104-3653
CHESEBROUGH-PONDS MANUFACTURING CO.
  (Parent: Conopco Inc)
Km 21 Hm 2 Rr 183, Las Piedras, PR 00771
Phone: (787) 783-7900
Sales: $94,256,000   *Employees:* 360
Company Type: Private   *Employees here:* 360
SIC: 2844
  Mfg cosmetics
Armando G Villa, General Manager

D-U-N-S 00-915-1051   EXP
CHEVRON CHEMICAL COMPANY, LLC
6001 Bollinger Canyon Rd, San Ramon, CA 94583
Phone: (925) 842-5500
Sales: $918,100,000   *Employees:* 4,200
Company Type: Private   *Employees here:* 450
SIC: 2821
  Mfr aromatic hydrocarbon-based intermediates and
    polystyrene olefins and derivatives and fuel additives
John E Peppercorn, President

D-U-N-S 80-808-8751   EXP
CHICAGO SPECIALTIES INC.
  (Parent: Pmc Specialties Group Inc)
735 E 115th St, Chicago, IL 60628
Phone: (773) 660-4000
Sales: $60,000,000   *Employees:* 130
Company Type: Private   *Employees here:* 130
SIC: 2869
  Mfg organic chemicals
Robert Prast, President

D-U-N-S 93-770-4138
CHIREX INC.
1 Apple Hl, Ste 316, Natick, MA 01760
Phone: (508) 652-0880
Sales: $74,615,000   *Employees:* 504
Company Type: Public   *Employees here:* 504
SIC: 2899
  Mfr fine chemicals & generic drugs
Alan R Clark, President

D-U-N-S 02-040-8837
CHRISTIAN DIOR PERFUMES INC.
9 W 57th St, Fl 39, New York, NY 10019
Phone: (212) 759-1840
Sales: $50,000,000   *Employees:* 198
Company Type: Private   *Employees here:* 30
SIC: 2844
  Manufactures & distributes perfumes and cosmetics
Robert Brady, President

D-U-N-S 00-121-1952   EXP
CHURCH & DWIGHT CO. INC.
469 N Harrison St, Princeton, NJ 08540
Phone: (609) 683-5900
Sales: $574,906,000   *Employees:* 1,137
Company Type: Public   *Employees here:* 350
SIC: 2812
  Mfg sodium bicarbonate ammonium bicarbonate detergents
    bleaches fabric softeners deodorants toothpaste & tooth
    powder
Robert A Davies III, President

D-U-N-S 96-425-3439
CIBA SPECIALTY CHEMICALS CORP.
560 White Plains Rd, Tarrytown, NY 10591
Phone: (914) 785-2000
Sales: $1,560,000,000   *Employees:* 4,000
Company Type: Private   *Employees here:* 600
SIC: 2819
  Development & manufacture of innovative material that
    provide color performance & care for plastics coating
Stanley Sherman, President

D-U-N-S 94-287-6681
CINCINNATI SPECIALTIES, INC.
  (Parent: Pmc Specialties Group Inc)
501 Murray Rd, Cincinnati, OH 45217
Phone: (513) 242-3300
Sales: $30,000,000   *Employees:* 200
Company Type: Private   *Employees here:* 200
SIC: 2819
  Mfr specialty chemicals
James Mckenna, President

D-U-N-S 00-150-2731
CITRUS AND ALLIED ESSENCES
3000 Marcus Ave, Ste 3E11, New Hyde Park, NY 11042
Phone: (516) 354-1200

Sales: $58,000,000   *Employees:* 95
Company Type: Private   *Employees here:* 29
SIC: 2899
   Processors dealers importers & exporters of flavor and
     fragrance ingredients
Richard C Pisano Sr, President

D-U-N-S 00-121-5557
CLAIROL INCORPORATED
   (Parent: Bristol-Myers Squibb Company)
345 Park Ave, New York, NY 10154
Phone: (212) 546-5000
Sales: $275,000,000   *Employees:* 2,300
Company Type: Public Family Member   *Employees here:* 450
SIC: 2844
   Mfg hair preparations & hand & body creams
Sadove Stephen I, President

D-U-N-S 10-870-6425   EXP
CLARIANT CORPORATION
4000 Monroe Rd, Charlotte, NC 28205
Phone: (704) 331-7000
Sales: $233,800,000   *Employees:* 1,150
Company Type: Private   *Employees here:* 250
SIC: 2865
   Mfg industrial dyes & chemicals & masterbatch color
     concentrates
Kenneth Golder, President

D-U-N-S 85-849-4909
CLEAN CONTROL CORPORATION
2954 Moody Rd, Bonaire, GA 31005
Phone: (912) 922-5340
Sales: $25,000,000   *Employees:* 500
Company Type: Private   *Employees here:* 500
SIC: 2842
   Mfg janitorial chemicals
Stephen Davison, President

D-U-N-S 92-886-9098
CLEARON CORP.
   (Parent: Clearon Holdings Inc)
52 Vanderbilt Ave, New York, NY 10017
Phone: (212) 867-5711
Sales: $85,000,000   *Employees:* 200
Company Type: Private   *Employees here:* 4
SIC: 2812
   Mfg chlorine dry bleach
Joshua Gecht, President

D-U-N-S 93-291-7651
CLEARON HOLDINGS INC.
52 Vanderbilt Ave, New York, NY 10017
Phone: (212) 867-5711
Sales: $76,733,000   *Employees:* 200
Company Type: Private   *Employees here:* 3
SIC: 2812
   Holding company
Shaul Ben-Zeev, President

D-U-N-S 01-208-1449
CLEARWATER HOLDINGS INC.
5605 Grand Ave, Pittsburgh, PA 15225
Phone: (412) 264-1100
Sales: $22,000,000   *Employees:* 100
Company Type: Private   *Employees here:* 8
SIC: 2819
   Holding company
Kevin Smith, Chief Executive Officer

D-U-N-S 17-345-8605
CLEARWATER, INC.
   (Parent: Clearwater Holdings Inc)
5605 Grand Ave, Pittsburgh, PA 15225
Phone: (412) 264-1100
Sales: $20,000,000   *Employees:* 55
Company Type: Private   *Employees here:* 53
SIC: 2819
   Mfg specialty chemicals
Kevin Smith, Chief Executive Officer

D-U-N-S 19-075-5298
CLINITEX HOLDINGS, INC.
11515 Vanstory Dr, Ste 100, Huntersville, NC 28078
Phone: (704) 875-0806
Sales: $15,000,000   *Employees:* 47
Company Type: Private   *Employees here:* 7
SIC: 2842
   Mfg disinfectants anti-microbial soaps & lotions long-term
     patient care products filtration devices & spec coatings for
     metal
Glenn Cueman, President

D-U-N-S 10-925-4961
CLO WHITE COMPANY INC.
75 Pineview Dr, Hampton, GA 30228
Phone: (770) 946-4216
Sales: $15,300,000   *Employees:* 130
Company Type: Private   *Employees here:* 95
SIC: 2842
   Mfg household products
Irwin Mazo, Chairman of the Board

D-U-N-S 00-913-8033   EXP
THE CLOROX COMPANY
1221 Broadway, Fl 13, Oakland, CA 94612
Phone: (510) 271-7000
Sales: $2,741,270,000   *Employees:* 6,600
Company Type: Public   *Employees here:* 775
SIC: 2842
   Mfg household cleaning pdts cat box filler charcoal briquets
     lighter fluid salad dressings & insecticides
Gerald E Johnston, President

D-U-N-S 78-135-5847
CLOROX INTERNATIONAL CO. INC.
   (Parent: The Clorox Company)
1221 Broadway, Fl 22, Oakland, CA 94612
Phone: (510) 271-7000
Sales: $162,100,000   *Employees:* 1,360
Company Type: Public Family Member   *Employees here:* 75
SIC: 2842
   Mfg cleaning products & insecticides
Richard T Conti, President

D-U-N-S 94-877-4013
CLOROX PRODUCTS MANUFACTURING CO.
   (Parent: The Clorox Company)
1319 Perryman Rd, Aberdeen, MD 21001
Phone: (410) 273-5136
Sales: $147,800,000   *Employees:* 1,240
Company Type: Public Family Member   *Employees here:* 180
SIC: 2842
   Mfg household cleaning proudcts
Jim Berger, Chairman of the Board

D-U-N-S 07-416-2207
COASTAL CHEM INC.
   (Parent: Coastal Corporation)
8305 Otto Rd, Cheyenne, WY 82001
Phone: (307) 637-2700

Sales: $160,000,000
Company Type: Public Family Member
SIC: 2873
Employees: 244
Employees here: 200
Mfg nitrogen based fertilizers and methyl tertiary butyl ether mtbe
David A Arledge, Chairman of the Board

D-U-N-S 15-054-9566
COATES BROTHERS INC.
(Parent: Total America Inc)
909 Fannin St, Ste 2200, Houston, TX 77010
Phone: (713) 793-3000
Sales: $35,400,000
Company Type: Private
SIC: 2893
Employees: 290
Employees here: 3
Holding company through subsidiaries manufactures printing inks resins & related items
Paul Eckhoff, President

D-U-N-S 83-497-0337
COATES SCREEN INC.
(Parent: Coates Brothers Inc)
180 E Union Ave, East Rutherford, NJ 07073
Phone: (201) 933-6100
Sales: $24,200,000
Company Type: Private
SIC: 2893
Employees: 152
Employees here: 80
Mfg screen printer's ink
Michael Cockett, Chairman of the Board

D-U-N-S 17-820-5670   EXP
COATING AND ADHESIVES CORP.
1901 Popular St NE, Leland, NC 28451
Phone: (910) 371-3184
Sales: $18,000,000
Company Type: Private
SIC: 2891
Employees: 41
Employees here: 36
Mfg adhesives & coatings
Richard Pasin, President

D-U-N-S 00-512-4672
COATINGS & CHEMICALS CORP.
521 Santa Rosa Dr, Des Plaines, IL 60018
Phone: (847) 759-0000
Sales: $18,000,000
Company Type: Private
SIC: 2851
Employees: 40
Employees here: 40
Mfg industrial paints and coatings
Kanti Gandhi, President

D-U-N-S 00-134-4381   EXP
COLGATE-PALMOLIVE COMPANY
300 Park Ave, Fl 8, New York, NY 10022
Phone: (212) 310-2000
Sales: $9,056,700,000
Company Type: Public
SIC: 2844
Employees: 37,800
Employees here: 1,000
Mfg oral personal & household care & pet nutrition pdts
Reuben Mark, Chairman of the Board

D-U-N-S 79-868-7794
COLGATE-PALMOLIVE (PR) INC.
(Parent: Colgate-Palmolive Company)
Km 144 Hm 7 Rr 3, Guayama, PR 00784
Phone: (787) 723-5625
Sales: $62,298,000
Company Type: Public Family Member
SIC: 2842
Employees: 200
Employees here: 200
Mfg specialty cleaning household disinfectants & toothpaste
Angel Vizcarrondo, General Manager

D-U-N-S 78-126-7943
COLLABORATIVE LABORATORIES
(Parent: Collaborative Group Ltd)
3 Technology Dr, East Setauket, NY 11733
Phone: (516) 689-0200
Sales: $20,000,000
Company Type: Private
SIC: 2844
Employees: 140
Employees here: 132
Research & development & manufacturer of raw materials & finished goods for the pharmaceutical & consumer products industries
James Hayward Phd, President

D-U-N-S 07-809-6732
COLOR CONVERTING INDUSTRIES CO.
11229 Aurora Ave, Des Moines, IA 50322
Phone: (515) 263-6500
Sales: $50,000,000
Company Type: Private
SIC: 2893
Employees: 225
Employees here: 130
Mfg printing ink
Ronald Barry, President

D-U-N-S 00-406-5256
COLOR WHEEL PAINT MANUFACTURING CO.
2814 Silver Star Rd, Orlando, FL 32808
Phone: (407) 293-6810
Sales: $26,467,000
Company Type: Private
SIC: 2851
Employees: 230
Employees here: 80
Mfg paint
Steven Strube, President

D-U-N-S 00-623-3332
COLUMBIA PAINT & COATINGS
104 S Freya St, Ste 206, Spokane, WA 99202
Phone: (509) 535-6311
Sales: $33,000,000
Company Type: Private
SIC: 2851
Employees: 195
Employees here: 15
Mfg & ret paints coatings & supplies
H H Larison, President

D-U-N-S 18-054-4702   EXP
COLUMBIAN CHEMICALS COMPANY
(Parent: Phelps Dodge Corporation)
1800 W Oak Commons Ct, Marietta, GA 30062
Phone: (770) 792-9400
Sales: $500,000,000
Company Type: Public Family Member
SIC: 2895
Employees: 1,400
Employees here: 170
Mfg carbon black raw material for rubber
John T Walsh, President

D-U-N-S 82-675-9011   EXP
COMALLOY INTERNATIONAL COMPANY
(Parent: A Schulman Inc)
481 Allied Dr, Nashville, TN 37211
Phone: (615) 333-3453
Sales: $40,000,000
Company Type: Public Family Member
SIC: 2821
Employees: 117
Employees here: 117
Mfg thermoplastic materials
Henry Muck, General Manager

D-U-N-S 00-240-6502   EXP
COMBE INCORPORATED
1101 Westchester Ave, White Plains, NY 10604
Phone: (914) 694-5454

Sales: $250,000,000   *Employees:* 600
Company Type: Private   *Employees here:* 200
SIC: 2844
   Mfg proprietary drugs veterinary pharmaceutical products &
   toiletries
Ivan D Combe, Chairman

D-U-N-S 78-749-1307   EXP
COMILOG US, INC.
610 Pittman Rd, Baltimore, MD 21226
Phone: (410) 789-8800
Sales: $100,000,000   *Employees:* 400
Company Type: Private   *Employees here:* 11
SIC: 2819
   Mfg manganese chemicals electrolytic manganese dioxide &
   manganese metals
Richard Mulholland, President

D-U-N-S 61-041-6802   EXP
COMPOSITES COOK & POLYMERS CO.
820 E 14th Ave, Kansas City, MO 64116
Phone: (816) 391-6000
Sales: $320,572,000   *Employees:* 1,120
Company Type: Private   *Employees here:* 251
SIC: 2821
   Mfg gelcoat resins polymers emulsions & industrial cleaners
Charles E Bennett, Chief Executive Officer

D-U-N-S 88-479-8166
CONAGRA FERTILIZER COMPANY
   (Parent: Conagra Inc)
1 Conagra Dr, Omaha, NE 68102
Phone: (912) 598-8392
Sales: $206,100,000   *Employees:* 1,000
Company Type: Public Family Member *Employees here:* 10
SIC: 2879
   Mfg & whol agricultural chemicals & fertilizers
Marty Collins, Controller

D-U-N-S 10-681-2555   EXP
CONAP INC.
   (Parent: Cytec Industries Inc)
1405 Buffalo St, Olean, NY 14760
Phone: (716) 372-9650
Sales: $22,646,000   *Employees:* 122
Company Type: Public Family Member *Employees here:* 115
SIC: 2821
   Mfg formulated urethane resins systems
Gerret M Peters, President

D-U-N-S 10-266-6872   EXP
CONDEA VISTA COMPANY
900 Threadneedle St, Houston, TX 77079
Phone: (281) 588-3000
Sales: $847,956,000   *Employees:* 1,400
Company Type: Private   *Employees here:* 250
SIC: 2821
   Mfg polyvinyl chloride resins industrial alcohols & detergent
   alkylate
William C Knodel, President

D-U-N-S 00-102-5535
CONNOISSEURS PRODUCTS CORP.
17 Presidential Dr, Woburn, MA 01801
Phone: (781) 932-3949
Sales: $19,600,000   *Employees:* 150
Company Type: Private   *Employees here:* 80
SIC: 2842
   Mfg jewelry & silver care products
Douglas Dorfman, President

D-U-N-S 13-197-0212   EXP
CONSEP INC.
213 SW Columbia St, Bend, OR 97702
Phone: (541) 388-3688
Sales: $39,204,000   *Employees:* 150
Company Type: Public   *Employees here:* 50
SIC: 2879
   Mfg pest control products
Volker Oakey, Chairman of the Board

D-U-N-S 00-807-6697   EXP
CONTINENTAL CARBON COMPANY
   (Parent: Csrc Usa Corp)
333 Cypress Run, Ste 100, Houston, TX 77094
Phone: (281) 647-3700
Sales: $100,000,000   *Employees:* 315
Company Type: Private   *Employees here:* 55
SIC: 2895
   Mfg black carbon
Peter T Wu, Vice-Chairman

D-U-N-S 07-069-4989
CONTINENTAL CARBONIC PRODUCTS INC.
3985 E Harrison Ave, Decatur, IL 62526
Phone: (217) 428-2068
Sales: $17,000,000   *Employees:* 130
Company Type: Private   *Employees here:* 40
SIC: 2813
   Mfg industrial gases
Robert O Wiesemann Sr, Chairman of the Board

D-U-N-S 05-031-2008   EXP
CONTRAN CORPORATION
   (Parent: Harold C Simmons Family Trust)
5430 LBJ Fwy, Ste 1700, Dallas, TX 75240
Phone: (972) 233-1700
Sales: $1,241,172,000   *Employees:* 12,000
Company Type: Private   *Employees here:* 50
SIC: 2816
   Mfg chemicals sugar and steel products
Harold C Simmons, Chairman of the Board

D-U-N-S 93-363-6011
COOK & DUNN ENTERPRISES, LLC
40 Industrial Rd, Lodi, NJ 07644
Phone: (973) 473-0050
Sales: $20,000,000   *Employees:* 72
Company Type: Private   *Employees here:* 65
SIC: 2851
   Mfg paints varnishes & enamels
Arthur Clemente, President

D-U-N-S 92-616-0391
COPOLYMER HOLDING COMPANY INC.
   (Parent: Dsm Elastomers Holding Co Inc)
5955 Scenic Hwy, Baton Rouge, LA 70805
Phone: (225) 267-3400
Sales: $51,100,000   *Employees:* 715
Company Type: Private   *Employees here:* 75
SIC: 2822
   Holding company to manufacture synthetic rubber
Larry R Powell, President

D-U-N-S 09-944-8466
CORDOVA LABS
   (Parent: International Academy Of Fin)
13177 Foothill Blvd, Sylmar, CA 91342
Phone: (818) 361-7724
Sales: $23,100,000   *Employees:* 122
Company Type: Private   *Employees here:* 122
SIC: 2879
   Mfg research & development mosquito & flea repellents
Sam Cordova, General Partner

D-U-N-S 06-198-0744
CORONADO LABORATORIES INC.
(*Parent:* Macklanburg-Duncan Co)
703 South St, New Smyrna Beach, FL 32168
Phone: (904) 428-8888
Sales: $22,100,000
Company Type: Private   *Employees:* 75
SIC: 2891   *Employees here:* 65
   Mfg caulking compounds sealants & elastomeric coatings
Kenneth G May, Chairman of the Board

D-U-N-S 08-240-0441   EXP
CORONADO PAINT CO. INC.
(*Parent:* Wattyl (us) Limited)
308 S Old County Rd, Edgewater, FL 32132
Phone: (904) 428-6461
Sales: $61,385,000
Company Type: Private   *Employees:* 275
SIC: 2851   *Employees here:* 165
   Mfg paints & industrial coatings
Christian Bosset, President

D-U-N-S 78-377-2353
COROPLAST INC.
(*Parent:* Great Pacific Enterprises (us))
4501 Spring Valley Rd, Dallas, TX 75244
Phone: (972) 392-2241
Sales: $25,000,000
Company Type: Private   *Employees:* 160
SIC: 2821   *Employees here:* 110
   Mfg plastic materials/resins
William Prowse, President

D-U-N-S 03-669-3984   EXP
CORSICANA TECHNOLOGIES INC.
(*Parent:* Permian Mud Service Inc)
3355 W Alabama St, Ste 400, Houston, TX 77098
Phone: (903) 874-9500
Sales: $15,000,000
Company Type: Private   *Employees:* 20
SIC: 2869   *Employees here:* 20
   Mfg organic chemicals
Tom Kowalski, General Manager

D-U-N-S 18-617-3662   EXP
CORTEC CORPORATION
4119 White Bear Pkwy, Saint Paul, MN 55110
Phone: (651) 429-1100
Sales: $16,777,000
Company Type: Private   *Employees:* 130
SIC: 2899   *Employees here:* 70
   Mfg environmentally safe corrosion chemical and packaging
       protection products and does film extruding
Boris Miksic, President

D-U-N-S 05-734-4079
COSMAIR CARIBE INC.
(*Parent:* Cosmair Inc)
Km 4 Hm 8 Rr 21, San Juan, PR 00921
Phone: (787) 793-3737
Sales: $29,000,000
Company Type: Private   *Employees:* NA
SIC: 2844   *Employees here:* NA
   Mfg toilet preparations
Gerard Bonenberger, President

D-U-N-S 15-078-5038
COSMAR CORPORATION
(*Parent:* Renaissance Cosmetics Inc)
11700 Monarch St, Garden Grove, CA 92841
Phone: (714) 848-0411

Sales: $22,200,000   *Employees:* 150
Company Type: Private   *Employees here:* 150
SIC: 2844
   Mfg and distributor of cosmetic products
Norbert Becker, President

D-U-N-S 00-417-7648   EXP
COSMETIC ESSENCE INC.
200 Clearview Rd, Edison, NJ 08837
Phone: (732) 225-2031
Sales: $50,001,000   *Employees:* 500
Company Type: Private   *Employees here:* 200
SIC: 2844
   Mfg cosmetic products
John F Croddick, President

D-U-N-S 00-798-0266
COSMETIC MNFCTRING RSURCES LLC
11312 Penrose St, Sun Valley, CA 91352
Phone: (818) 767-2889
Sales: $35,000,000   *Employees:* 300
Company Type: Private   *Employees here:* 100
SIC: 2844
   Manufactures perfumes cosmetics or other toilet
       preparations
Michael Baker, Chief Financial Officer

D-U-N-S 14-763-8787
COSMOLAB INC.
(*Parent:* Koh-I-Noor Inc)
1100 Garrett Pkwy, Lewisburg, TN 37091
Phone: (931) 359-6253
Sales: $143,000,000   *Employees:* 1,200
Company Type: Private   *Employees here:* 750
SIC: 2844
   Mfg toilet preparations
Robert Lasater Sr, Chairman of the Board

D-U-N-S 95-866-2223
COTY INC.
1325 Avenue Of The Americas, New York, NY 10019
Phone: (212) 479-4300
Sales: $158,600,000   *Employees:* 1,330
Company Type: Private   *Employees here:* 30
SIC: 2844
   Mfg fragrances & cosmetics
Peter Harf, Chairman of the Board

D-U-N-S 78-957-3201
COTY US INC.
(*Parent:* Coty Inc)
237 Park Ave, Fl 19, New York, NY 10017
Phone: (212) 850-2300
Sales: $405,458,000   *Employees:* 1,573
Company Type: Private   *Employees here:* 130
SIC: 2844
   Mfg fragrances & cosmetics
Jean-Andre Rougeot, Chief Executive Officer

D-U-N-S 04-560-5615
CPAC INC.
2364 Leicester Rd, Leicester, NY 14481
Phone: (716) 382-3223
Sales: $106,098,000   *Employees:* 662
Company Type: Public   *Employees here:* 50
SIC: 2842
   Mfg specialty cleaning products soaps shampoos & skin care
       items & prepackaged chemical formulations & supplies
Thomas J Weldgen, Chief Financial Officer

D-U-N-S 18-390-0182
CPH HOLDING CORP.
311 S Wacker Dr, Ste 4700, Chicago, IL 60606

Phone: (312) 554-7400
Sales: $46,600,000
Company Type: Private
SIC: 2869
   Mfg & whol industrial organic chemicals
George A Vincent, Chairman of the Board
Employees: 205
Employees here: 40

D-U-N-S 62-157-4300   EXP
CPS CORP.
   (Parent: The Inx Group Limited)
3257 Middle Rd, Dunkirk, NY 14048
Phone: (716) 366-6010
Sales: $50,000,000
Company Type: Private
SIC: 2893
   Mfg printing ink
Frank Moravec, President
Employees: 140
Employees here: 139

D-U-N-S 04-482-5909   EXP
CREANOVA INC.
   (Parent: Huls Corporation)
220 Davidson Ave, Somerset, NJ 08873
Phone: (732) 560-6800
Sales: $551,544,000
Company Type: Private
SIC: 2869
   Mfrs colorants & coatings chemicals plastics and
     performance products
Wolfgang Minnerup, President
Employees: 1,000
Employees here: 161

D-U-N-S 19-727-9490
CREST-HOOD FOAM COMPANY, INC.
   (Parent: Crest-Foam Corp)
122 Parker St, Newburyport, MA 01950
Phone: (978) 462-5400
Sales: $18,900,000
Company Type: Public Family Member
SIC: 2851
   Mfg polyurethane foam
Duane W Potter, President
Employees: 112
Employees here: 112

D-U-N-S 18-628-3909   EXP
CRITERION CATALYST COMPANY, LP
16825 Northchase Dr, Houston, TX 77060
Phone: (281) 874-2600
Sales: $71,900,000
Company Type: Private
SIC: 2819
   Mfg of chemical catalyst
Richard H Stade, President
Employees: 450
Employees here: 85

D-U-N-S 80-812-6452
CRODA ADHESIVES INC.
1000 Hollywood Ave, Itasca, IL 60143
Phone: (630) 773-1400
Sales: $27,300,000
Company Type: Private
SIC: 2891
   Mfg adhesives
Frank Bozich, President
Employees: 78
Employees here: 35

D-U-N-S 00-133-1032
CRODA INC.
7 Century Dr, Ste 303, Parsippany, NJ 07054
Phone: (973) 644-4900
Sales: $65,000,000
Company Type: Private
SIC: 2869
   Manufactures specialty chemicals and chemical surfactants
Kevin Gallagher, President
Employees: 278
Employees here: 40

D-U-N-S 94-724-5882
CROMPTON & KNOWLES COLORS INC.
   (Parent: Crompton & Knowles Corporation)
3001 N Graham St, Charlotte, NC 28206
Phone: (704) 372-5890
Sales: $190,000,000
Company Type: Public Family Member
SIC: 2899
   Mfg dyes
James Conway, President
Employees: 800
Employees here: 80

D-U-N-S 05-281-3136   EXP
CROMPTON & KNOWLES CORPORATION
1 Station Pl Metro Ctr, Stamford, CT 06902
Phone: (203) 353-5400
Sales: $1,796,119,000
Company Type: Public
SIC: 2865
   Mfg specialty chemicals & specialty process equipment &
     electrical controls
Vincent A Calarco, Chairman of the Board
Employees: 5,519
Employees here: 35

D-U-N-S 00-131-6116
CROWLEY TAR PRODUCTS CO. INC.
261 Madison Ave, Fl 14, New York, NY 10016
Phone: (212) 682-1200
Sales: $20,000,000
Company Type: Private
SIC: 2865
   Manufactures coal tar naval stores & petroleum products
William J Jennings, President
Employees: 45
Employees here: 39

D-U-N-S 04-837-3153
CRUCIBLE CHEMICAL CO. INC.
10 Crucible Ct, Greenville, SC 29605
Phone: (864) 277-1284
Sales: $25,000,000
Company Type: Private
SIC: 2842
   Mfg silicone defoamers and anti-foam agents and textile
     specialty products
Robert B Wilson, President
Employees: 40
Employees here: 40

D-U-N-S 94-141-9194
CRYSTAL INC.-PMC
601 W 8th St, Lansdale, PA 19446
Phone: (215) 368-1661
Sales: $23,000,000
Company Type: Private
SIC: 2899
   Mfg specialty chemicals & waxes
Paritosh Chakrabarti, President
Employees: 57
Employees here: 56

D-U-N-S 05-302-6019
CRYSTAL SPRINGS WATER COMPANY
   (Parent: Suntory Water Group Inc)
5331 NW 35th Ter 200, Fort Lauderdale, FL 33309
Phone: (954) 733-6880
Sales: $56,400,000
Company Type: Private
SIC: 2899
   Mfg distilled water and retail drinking water
Christophe White, General Manager
Employees: 400
Employees here: 21

D-U-N-S 96-548-0767
CSRC USA CORP.
333 Cypress Run, Ste 100, Houston, TX 77094
Phone: (281) 647-3700
Sales: $62,300,000
Company Type: Private
SIC: 2895
   Mfg carbon black
D T Norman, President
Employees: 315
Employees here: 4

D-U-N-S 02-143-3537   EXP
CULTOR FOOD SCIENCE, INC.
430 Saw Mill River Rd, Ardsley, NY 10502
Phone: (914) 674-6300
Sales: $500,000,000   *Employees:* 500
Company Type: Private   *Employees here:* 80
SIC: 2869
   Mfg diverse line of food ingredients including specialty
     sweeteners
Hakan Lauren, President

D-U-N-S 14-753-0000
CULTOR US INC.
430 Saw Mill River Rd, Ardsley, NY 10502
Phone: (914) 674-6300
Sales: $88,500,000   *Employees:* 375
Company Type: Private   *Employees here:* 2
SIC: 2869
   Holding company
Ilkka Suominen, Chief Executive Officer

D-U-N-S 00-165-0274
CUMBERLAND PACKING CORP.
2 Cumberland St, Brooklyn, NY 11205
Phone: (718) 858-4200
Sales: $60,000,000   *Employees:* 400
Company Type: Private   *Employees here:* 375
SIC: 2869
   Mfg sugar salt & butter substitutes
Marvin Eisenstadt, President

D-U-N-S 05-756-0914
CUTLER CORPORATION
1250 NW Overton St, Portland, OR 97209
Phone: (503) 223-9700
Sales: $46,900,000   *Employees:* 300
Company Type: Private   *Employees here:* 2
SIC: 2891
   Mfg filler sealers & non-motorized materials handling
     equipment
James N Cutler Jr, President

D-U-N-S 09-106-5102   EXP
CYANAMID AGRICULTURAL DE PR
   (Parent: American Cyanamid Company)
Rr 2, Manati, PR 00674
Phone: (787) 854-1666
Sales: $256,993,000   *Employees:* 180
Company Type: Public Family Member   *Employees here:* 180
SIC: 2879
   Mfg agricultural chemicals
W J Murray, President

D-U-N-S 06-080-9647
CYRO INDUSTRIES
100 Enterprise Dr, Rockaway, NJ 07866
Phone: (973) 442-6000
Sales: $200,000,000   *Employees:* 700
Company Type: Private   *Employees here:* 100
SIC: 2821
   Manufactures acrylic plastic polymers and sheets
Matthew A Taylor, President

D-U-N-S 80-974-9948   EXP
CYTEC INDUSTRIES INC.
5 Garret Mountain Plz, West Paterson, NJ 07424
Phone: (973) 357-3100
Sales: $1,290,600,000   *Employees:* 5,200
Company Type: Public   *Employees here:* 250
SIC: 2899
   Mfg & mktg specialty chemicals & materials
David Lilley, President

D-U-N-S 09-717-8834   EXP
D & K GROUP, INC.
1795 Commerce Dr, Elk Grove Village, IL 60007
Phone: (847) 956-0160
Sales: $54,800,000   *Employees:* 350
Company Type: Private   *Employees here:* 50
SIC: 2891
   Mfg laminating film compounds and equipment
Karl Singer, President

D-U-N-S 15-343-6100   EXP
D & K INTERNATIONAL, INC.
   (Parent: D & K Group Inc)
525 Crossen Ave, Elk Grove Village, IL 60007
Phone: (847) 956-0160
Sales: $18,400,000   *Employees:* 130
Company Type: Private   *Employees here:* 130
SIC: 2891
   Mfg laminating film compounds
Karl Singer, President

D-U-N-S 60-274-0144   EXP
D B J ENTERPRISES INC.
   (Parent: Stoller Group Inc)
8580 Katy Fwy, Ste 200, Houston, TX 77024
Phone: (713) 461-1493
Sales: $50,000,000   *Employees:* 150
Company Type: Private   *Employees here:* 5
SIC: 2879
   Mfg fertilizer chemicals
Jerry H Stoller, President

D-U-N-S 61-740-1625
D H COMPOUNDING COMPANY
1260 Carden Farm Dr, Clinton, TN 37716
Phone: (423) 457-1200
Sales: $30,918,000   *Employees:* 140
Company Type: Private   *Employees here:* 140
SIC: 2821
   Mfg plastic molding compounds
Paul Whitmire, President

D-U-N-S 96-040-3202
D K USA LTD.
600 Old Country Rd, Rm 333, Garden City, NY 11530
Phone: (516) 222-2250
Sales: $17,500,000   *Employees:* 135
Company Type: Private   *Employees here:* 135
SIC: 2844
   Mfg fragrances & cosmetics
Cheryl Borkes, VP Operations

D-U-N-S 04-804-4762   EXP
D S M ENGINEERING PLASTIC PRODUCTS
   (Parent: D S M Engrg Plastic Pdts Holdg)
2120 Fairmont Ave, Reading, PA 19605
Phone: (610) 320-6600
Sales: $185,000,000   *Employees:* 650
Company Type: Private   *Employees here:* 390
SIC: 2824
   Mfg cast nylon fiber & extruded various types of plastic
     materials
Jerry L Thurston, President

D-U-N-S 07-770-7461   EXP
DAICOLOR-POPE INC.
33 6th Ave, Paterson, NJ 07524
Phone: (973) 278-5170
Sales: $45,000,000   *Employees:* 125
Company Type: Private   *Employees here:* 120
SIC: 2816
   Mfg pigments flushes & dispersions imports & whol pigments
Takashi Kataoka, President

D-U-N-S 19-721-2954
DALLAS GROUP OF AMERICA INC.
374 Rte 22, Whitehouse, NJ 08888
Phone: (908) 534-7800
Sales: $26,000,000   *Employees:* 90
Company Type: Private   *Employees here:* 15
SIC: 2819
   Mfg specialty industrial chemicals
David Dallas, Chief Executive Officer

D-U-N-S 00-123-5746
DANA PERFUMES CORP.
   (Parent: Renaissance Cosmetics Inc)
3 Landmark Sq, Fl 5, Stamford, CT 06901
Phone: (203) 316-9800
Sales: $110,000,000   *Employees:* 200
Company Type: Private   *Employees here:* 50
SIC: 2844
   Mfg perfumes
Al De Chellis, President

D-U-N-S 00-702-2486   EXP
DAP PRODUCTS INC.
2400 Boston St, Baltimore, MD 21224
Phone: (410) 675-2100
Sales: $240,000,000   *Employees:* 550
Company Type: Private   *Employees here:* 150
SIC: 2891
   Mfr caulking glazing adhesives paints water repellents &
      wood preservatives
John J Mc Laughlin, President

D-U-N-S 06-465-2266   EXP
DASH MULTI-CORP, INC.
2500 Adie Rd, Maryland Heights, MO 63043
Phone: (314) 432-3200
Sales: $110,053,000   *Employees:* 403
Company Type: Private   *Employees here:* 70
SIC: 2821
   Mfg plastic raw materials & rubber mats and owns and
      operates commercial buildings
Marvin S Wool, President

D-U-N-S 00-625-1656
DAVIS-FROST, INC.
1209 Tyler St NE, Minneapolis, MN 55413
Phone: (612) 789-8871
Sales: $25,000,000   *Employees:* 105
Company Type: Private   *Employees here:* 40
SIC: 2851
   Mfg industrial finishes & varnishes retail home decorating
      stores
Calvin C Henning, Chief Executive Officer

D-U-N-S 15-179-9111
DAVIS MINING & MANUFACTURING
Miners Professional Bldg, Coeburn, VA 24230
Phone: (540) 395-3354
Sales: $185,200,000   *Employees:* 1,600
Company Type: Private   *Employees here:* 10
SIC: 2892
   Mfg explosives
William J Davis, Chairman of the Board

D-U-N-S 05-899-5614
DAVLYN INDUSTRIES INC.
   (Parent: Shiseido International Corp)
7 Fitzgerald Ave, Cranbury, NJ 08512
Phone: (609) 655-5600

Sales: $26,000,000   *Employees:* 250
Company Type: Private   *Employees here:* 250
SIC: 2844
   Mfg cosmetics
Masayoshi Hanafusa, President

D-U-N-S 14-760-8129
DAWN CHEMICAL COMPANY INC.
990 Industrial Dr, Marietta, GA 30069
Phone: (770) 422-2071
Sales: $53,000,000   *Employees:* 287
Company Type: Private   *Employees here:* 3
SIC: 2842
   Holding company
Kevin J Gallagher, President

D-U-N-S 00-419-7257   EXP
DAY-GLO COLOR CORP.
   (Parent: Rpm Inc)
4515 Saint Clair Ave, Cleveland, OH 44103
Phone: (216) 391-7070
Sales: $47,000,000   *Employees:* 175
Company Type: Public Family Member   *Employees here:* 140
SIC: 2816
   Mfg fluorescent inorganic pigment products
Charles G Pauli, President

D-U-N-S 60-409-1504
DE LA RUE CARD SYSTEMS INC.
   (Parent: De La Rue Inc)
523 James Hance Ct, Exton, PA 19341
Phone: (610) 524-2410
Sales: $73,000,000   *Employees:* 350
Company Type: Private   *Employees here:* 340
SIC: 2821
   Mfg plastic credit cards
David Stonely, President

D-U-N-S 06-764-6737   EXP
DECOART INC.
Jct Hwy 27 & 150, Stanford, KY 40484
Phone: (606) 365-3193
Sales: $20,000,000   *Employees:* 100
Company Type: Private   *Employees here:* 100
SIC: 2851
   Mfg acrylic paint
Stanley Clifford, President

D-U-N-S 00-825-4195   EXP
DEFT INCORPORATED
17451 Von Karman Ave, Irvine, CA 92614
Phone: (949) 474-0400
Sales: $38,528,000   *Employees:* 135
Company Type: Private   *Employees here:* 100
SIC: 2851
   Mfg paints/allied products
William A Desmond, President

D-U-N-S 06-820-9295
DEGUSSA CORPORATION
65 Challenger Rd, Ridgefield Park, NJ 07660
Phone: (201) 641-6100
Sales: $2,373,000,000   *Employees:* 2,027
Company Type: Private   *Employees here:* 200
SIC: 2869
   Mfg organic industrial chemicals inorganic chemicals dental
      equipment & supplies & fabricates & refines precious
      metals
Andrew J Burke, President

D-U-N-S 00-129-3166   EXP
DEL LABORATORIES, INC.
178 Eab Plz, Uniondale, NY 11556

Phone: (516) 844-2020
Sales: $263,010,000   Employees: 2,300
Company Type: Public   Employees here: 630
SIC: 2844
     Mfg cosmetics & proprietary pharmaceuticals
Dan K Wassong, Chairman of the Board

D-U-N-S 00-850-5679   IMP EXP
DELTA TECHNICAL COATINGS, INC.
     (Parent: Edward Keller Holding Ltd)
2550 Pellissier Pl, Whittier, CA 90601
Phone: (562) 695-7969
Sales: $40,000,000   Employees: 140
Company Type: Private   Employees here: 140
SIC: 2851
     Mfg paints & glue
Ronald A La Rosa, President

D-U-N-S 36-170-2756
DELTECH CORP.
     (Parent: Deltech Holdings Corp)
16 S Jefferson Rd, Whippany, NJ 07981
Phone: (973) 428-4500
Sales: $17,600,000   Employees: 100
Company Type: Private   Employees here: 6
SIC: 2899
     Manufactures specialty chemicals
Robert P Elefante, Chairman of the Board

D-U-N-S 62-388-4087
DELTECH HOLDINGS CORP.
16 S Jefferson Rd, Whippany, NJ 07981
Phone: (973) 428-4500
Sales: $59,000,000   Employees: 135
Company Type: Private   Employees here: 5
SIC: 2821
     Mfg polystyrene
Robert P Elefante, Chairman of the Board

D-U-N-S 62-334-8547
DELTECH POLYMERS CORPORATION
     (Parent: Deltech Holdings Corp)
1250 Union St, Troy, OH 45373
Phone: (937) 339-3150
Sales: $20,000,000   Employees: 40
Company Type: Private   Employees here: 40
SIC: 2821
     Mfg polystyrene
Robert Elefante, Chairman of the Board

D-U-N-S 04-756-9991   EXP
DENA CORPORATION
850 Nicholas Blvd, Elk Grove Village, IL 60007
Phone: (847) 593-3041
Sales: $20,000,000   Employees: 70
Company Type: Private   Employees here: 70
SIC: 2844
     Mfg hair care products & cosmetics
Hasan M Khatib, President

D-U-N-S 09-047-4024
DENTCO INC.
     (Parent: Block Drug Company Inc)
Km 76 Hm 9 Rr 3, Humacao, PR 00791
Phone: (787) 852-3400
Sales: $77,011,000   Employees: 180
Company Type: Public Family Member   Employees here: 180
SIC: 2844
     Mfg toothpaste
Luis R Acevedo, General Manager

D-U-N-S 00-531-7599   EXP
DETREX CORPORATION
24901 Northwestern Hwy, Southfield, MI 48075

Phone: (248) 358-5800
Sales: $95,757,000   Employees: 353
Company Type: Public   Employees here: 20
SIC: 2842
     Mfg specialty chemicals and equipment dry-cleaning
          equipment and degreasing equipment
William C King, Chairman of the Board

D-U-N-S 00-510-6083   EXP
DEVRO-TEEPAK, INC.
3 Westbrook, Westchester, IL 60154
Phone: (708) 409-3000
Sales: $200,000,000   Employees: 1,500
Company Type: Private   Employees here: 45
SIC: 2823
     Mfg synthetic cellulose meat casings
M W Paquette, President

D-U-N-S 55-696-3940
DEXCO POLYMERS
12012 Wickchester Ln, Houston, TX 77079
Phone: (281) 754-5800
Sales: $19,700,000   Employees: 100
Company Type: Private   Employees here: 10
SIC: 2821
     Mfg plastics
Tom Brewer, General Manager

D-U-N-S 00-115-5761   EXP
DEXTER CORPORATION
1 Elm St, Windsor Locks, CT 06096
Phone: (860) 627-9051
Sales: $1,147,055,000   Employees: 4,800
Company Type: Public   Employees here: 59
SIC: 2891
     Mfg specialty material products
K G Walker, Chairman of the Board

D-U-N-S 00-693-0366   EXP
DIAL CORPORATION
15501 N Dial Blvd, Scottsdale, AZ 85260
Phone: (602) 754-3425
Sales: $1,362,606,000   Employees: 3,716
Company Type: Public   Employees here: 775
SIC: 2841
     Mfg personal care detergents household & food products
Malcolm Jozoff, Chairman of the Board

D-U-N-S 06-783-7435
DIAMOND R FERTILIZER CO. INC.
     (Parent: Pioneer Ag-Chem Inc)
4100 Glades Rd, Fort Pierce, FL 34981
Phone: (561) 464-7237
Sales: $26,900,000   Employees: 100
Company Type: Private   Employees here: 40
SIC: 2873
     Mfg nitrogenous fertilizer
E H Sullivan, Chairman of the Board

D-U-N-S 92-673-7412
DIEFENTHAL INVESTMENTS, LLC
     (Parent: Southern Holdings Inc)
4801 Florida Ave, New Orleans, LA 70117
Phone: (504) 944-3371
Sales: $64,500,000   Employees: 311
Company Type: Private   Employees here: 40
SIC: 2821
     Plastics materials or resins, nec
James R Diefenthal, Chief Executive Officer

D-U-N-S 18-316-5596
DIHOMA CHEMICAL & MANUFACTURING
195 Drew Rd, Mullins, SC 29574
Phone: (843) 423-7799

Sales: $32,000,000   *Employees:* 7
Company Type: Private   *Employees here:* 7
SIC: 2869
  Mfg chemicals
Cynthia D Faulk, President

D-U-N-S 87-432-5715
DISPENSING CONTAINERS CORP.
62 Anthony Rd, Glen Gardner, NJ 08826
Phone: (908) 832-7882
Sales: $20,000,000   *Employees:* 100
Company Type: Private   *Employees here:* 60
SIC: 2813
  Mfg misc fabricated metal products
George B Diamond, Chairman of the Board

D-U-N-S 94-145-4639
DIVERSEY LEVER INC.
  (*Parent:* Unilever United States Inc)
14496 N Sheldon Rd, Plymouth, MI 48170
Phone: (734) 414-1725
Sales: $166,900,000   *Employees:* 1,400
Company Type: Private   *Employees here:* 300
SIC: 2842
  Mfr specialty chemicals
Arwyn Hughes, Vice-President

D-U-N-S 05-334-6508
DIVERSIFIED CHEMICAL TECH
15477 Woodrow Wilson St, Detroit, MI 48238
Phone: (313) 867-5444
Sales: $49,234,000   *Employees:* 145
Company Type: Private   *Employees here:* 25
SIC: 2891
  Mfg sealants hot melt glue epoxy adhesives & whol
    duplicating paper
George H Hill, President

D-U-N-S 00-808-8247   EXP
DIXIE CHEMICAL COMPANY, INC.
  (*Parent:* Dx Holding Company Inc)
300 Jackson Hill St, Houston, TX 77007
Phone: (713) 863-1947
Sales: $36,400,000   *Employees:* 179
Company Type: Private   *Employees here:* 46
SIC: 2869
  Mfg industrial chemicals organic & inorganic and whol
    drilling mud & related oil field chemicals
S R Morian, Chairman of the Board

D-U-N-S 00-104-5517
DODGE COMPANY INC.
165 Cambridge Park Dr, Cambridge, MA 02140
Phone: (617) 661-0500
Sales: $16,000,000   *Employees:* 105
Company Type: Private   *Employees here:* 55
SIC: 2869
  Mfg embalming fluids & whol funeral equipment & supplies
Arnold J Dodge, President

D-U-N-S 03-272-6226
DOUGLASS FERTILIZER & CHEMICAL
1180 Spring Centre South, Altamonte Springs, FL 32714
Phone: (407) 682-6100
Sales: $20,656,000   *Employees:* 70
Company Type: Private   *Employees here:* 8
SIC: 2875
  Mfg mixed liquid fertilizer
Spencer G Douglass, Chief Executive Officer

D-U-N-S 00-421-0563
DOVER CHEMICAL CORPORATION
  (*Parent:* Icc Industries Inc)
3676 Davis Rd NW, Dover, OH 44622
Phone: (330) 343-7711
Sales: $50,000,000   *Employees:* 153
Company Type: Private   *Employees here:* 150
SIC: 2819
  Mfg industrial inorganic & organic chemicals
C J Fette, President

D-U-N-S 60-548-2694   EXP
DOW AGROSCIENCES LLC
  (*Parent:* Rofan Services Inc)
9330 Zionsville Rd, Indianapolis, IN 46268
Phone: (317) 337-3000
Sales: $2,000,000,000   *Employees:* 3,100
Company Type: Public Family Member   *Employees here:* 1,100
SIC: 2879
  Mfg agricultural chemicals herbicides insecticides &
    fungicides & mkts planting seed & crop protection svcs
A C Fischer, President

D-U-N-S 00-138-1581   EXP
THE DOW CHEMICAL COMPANY
2030 Willard H Dow Center, Midland, MI 48674
Phone: (517) 636-1000
Sales: $18,441,000,000   *Employees:* 40,289
Company Type: Public   *Employees here:* 3,000
SIC: 2821
  Mfg plastics specialty chemicals & consumer specialties
Frank P Popoff, Chairman of the Board

D-U-N-S 00-535-3487   IMP EXP
DOW CORNING CORPORATION
2200 Salzburg St, Midland, MI 48640
Phone: (517) 496-4000
Sales: $2,643,500,000   *Employees:* 9,100
Company Type: Private   *Employees here:* 1,129
SIC: 2869
  Mfg silicone fluids resins rubber sealants and molybdenum
    silicon
Richard A Hazleton, Chairman of the Board

D-U-N-S 01-161-4286
DRAGOCO INC.
10 Gordon Dr, Totowa, NJ 07512
Phone: (973) 256-3850
Sales: $61,932,000   *Employees:* 240
Company Type: Private   *Employees here:* 234
SIC: 2869
  Mfg fragrances and flavors
Daniel E Stebbins, President

D-U-N-S 92-720-6508
DRAKE EXTRUSION INC.
  (*Parent:* Readicut Holdings Inc)
790 Industrial Park Rd, Ridgeway, VA 24148
Phone: (540) 632-0159
Sales: $22,200,000   *Employees:* 124
Company Type: Private   *Employees here:* 124
SIC: 2821
  Manufacture polymer extrusion
Geoff Schofield, Chief Executive Officer

D-U-N-S 07-352-4555
DREXEL CHEMICAL COMPANY
1700 Channel Ave, Memphis, TN 38106
Phone: (901) 774-4370

Sales: $80,000,000   *Employees:* 180
Company Type: Private   *Employees here:* 70
SIC: 2879
    Mfg agricultural chemicals
Leigh Shockey, Chairman of the Board

D-U-N-S 78-739-4873
DRI-KLEEN INC.
3930 W Ali Baba Ln, Las Vegas, NV 89118
Phone: (702) 262-5555
Sales: $25,952,000   *Employees:* 100
Company Type: Private   *Employees here:* 70
SIC: 2842
    Mfg cleaning hair & skin products nutritional supplements
       and pet care products
Rod Yanke, Chairman of the Board

D-U-N-S 62-055-8866
DRYVIT HOLDINGS, INC.
    (Parent: Rpm Inc)
1 Turks Head Pl, Ste 1550, Providence, RI 02903
Phone: (401) 822-4100
Sales: $27,500,000   *Employees:* 170
Company Type: Public Family Member   *Employees here:* 170
SIC: 2899
    Mfg exterior wall insulating compound
Peter Balint, President

D-U-N-S 04-897-3150   EXP
DRYVIT SYSTEMS INC.
    (Parent: Rpm Inc)
1 Energy Way, West Warwick, RI 02893
Phone: (401) 822-4100
Sales: $30,600,000   *Employees:* 159
Company Type: Public Family Member   *Employees here:* 80
SIC: 2899
    Mfr exterior wall insulating compound
Paul H Hill, President

D-U-N-S 05-101-1609   EXP
DSM CHEMICALS NORTH AMERICA
    (Parent: Dsm Finance Usa Inc)
1 Columbia Nitrogen Dr, Augusta, GA 30901
Phone: (706) 849-6600
Sales: $55,400,000   *Employees:* 348
Company Type: Private   *Employees here:* 348
SIC: 2819
    Mfg caprolactam and ammonium sulfate
J W Price, President

D-U-N-S 00-818-2990
DSM COPOLYMER, INC.
    (Parent: Copolymer Holding Company Inc)
5955 Scenic Hwy, Baton Rouge, LA 70805
Phone: (225) 267-3400
Sales: $333,926,000   *Employees:* 700
Company Type: Private   *Employees here:* 100
SIC: 2822
    Mfr synthetic rubber
Larry R Powell, President

D-U-N-S 60-823-3961
DSM FINANCE USA INC.
1201 Market St, Ste 1002, Wilmington, DE 19801
Phone: (302) 429-8942
Sales: $352,400,000   *Employees:* 2,233
Company Type: Private   *Employees here:* 2
SIC: 2891
    Mfg liquid resins adhesives pigments synthetic resins &
       thermoplastics & whol intermediate chemicals &
       petrochemicals
F J Pistorius, President

D-U-N-S 06-749-1936   EXP
DSM RESINS US INC.
    (Parent: Dsm Finance Usa Inc)
1 10th St, Ste 580, Augusta, GA 30901
Phone: (706) 849-6700
Sales: $35,000,000   *Employees:* 35
Company Type: Private   *Employees here:* 10
SIC: 2821
    Mfr synthetic resins
Gerard Hardeman, President

D-U-N-S 00-389-2986
DU PONT AG CARIBE INDUSTRIES
    (Parent: Du Pont Agrichemicals Caribe)
Km 2/3 Rr 686, Manati, PR 00674
Phone: (787) 854-1030
Sales: $27,000,000   *Employees:* 150
Company Type: Public Family Member   *Employees here:* 150
SIC: 2879
    Mfg agricultural chemicals
Carlos Avella, President

D-U-N-S 09-056-5631
DU PONT AGRICHEMICALS CARIBE
    (Parent: Du Pont E I De Nemours And Co)
Km 2 Hm 3 Rr 686, Manati, PR 00674
Phone: (787) 854-1030
Sales: $598,166,000   *Employees:* 150
Company Type: Public Family Member   *Employees here:* 150
SIC: 2879
    Mfg herbicides
Jerry Brown, President

D-U-N-S 80-442-2368
DU PONT-KANSAI AUTO COATINGS
    (Parent: Du Pont E I De Nemours And Co)
950 Stephenson Hwy, Troy, MI 48083
Phone: (248) 583-8008
Sales: $16,800,000   *Employees:* 106
Company Type: Public Family Member   *Employees here:* 100
SIC: 2851
    Mfg paint chemicals
John Vonwald, President

D-U-N-S 00-910-3672   EXP
DUNCAN ENTERPRISES
    (Parent: Duncan Financial Corporation)
5673 E Shields Ave, Fresno, CA 93727
Phone: (559) 291-4444
Sales: $41,300,000   *Employees:* 276
Company Type: Private   *Employees here:* 276
SIC: 2851
    Mfg ceramic colors & related products
Larry R Duncan, President

D-U-N-S 00-823-6648
DUNN-EDWARDS CORPORATION
4885 E 52nd Pl, Los Angeles, CA 90040
Phone: (323) 771-3330
Sales: $209,200,000   *Employees:* 1,257
Company Type: Private   *Employees here:* 400
SIC: 2851
    Mfg paint products
Robert E Mitchell, Chairman of the Board

D-U-N-S 00-506-7632   EXP
DUPLI-COLOR PRODUCTS CO.
    (Parent: Diversified Brands)
1601 Nicholas Blvd, Elk Grove Village, IL 60007
Phone: (847) 439-0600

Sales: $28,900,000   *Employees:* 200
Company Type: Public Family Member   *Employees here:* 200
SIC: 2851
    Mfg paint
Joseph Scamainace, President

D-U-N-S 93-319-4151
DUPONT DOW ELASTOMERS LLC
300 Bellevue Pkwy, Wilmington, DE 19809
Phone: (302) 792-4200
Sales: $1,086,932,000   *Employees:* 3,300
Company Type: Private   *Employees here:* 3,300
SIC: 2822
    Mfg elastomer products
Donald Duncan, President

D-U-N-S 96-633-9293
DUPONT DOW ELASTOMERS LLC
4200 Campground Rd, Louisville, KY 40216
Phone: (502) 569-3232
Sales: $26,200,000   *Employees:* NA
Company Type: Private   *Employees here:* 400
SIC: 2822
    Mfg elastomer products
Mike Sticklen, Branch Manager

D-U-N-S 62-331-4515
DX HOLDING COMPANY, INC.
300 Jackson Hill St, Houston, TX 77007
Phone: (713) 863-1947
Sales: $107,000,000   *Employees:* 450
Company Type: Private   *Employees here:* 50
SIC: 2869
    Mfg & whol chemicals
S R Morian, Chairman of the Board

D-U-N-S 06-795-2994   EXP
DYMON, INC.
    (Parent: Illinois Tool Works Inc)
805 E Old 56 Hwy, Olathe, KS 66061
Phone: (913) 397-8778
Sales: $22,763,000   *Employees:* 150
Company Type: Public Family Member   *Employees here:* 150
SIC: 2842
    Mfg specialty janitorial cleaning chemicals
Daniel J Schrock, Chief Operating Officer

D-U-N-S 00-909-1257   EXP
DYNO NOBEL INC.
    (Parent: Dyno Industries Usa Inc)
50 S Main St, Ste 1100, Salt Lake City, UT 84144
Phone: (801) 364-4800
Sales: $500,000,000   *Employees:* 2,700
Company Type: Private   *Employees here:* 100
SIC: 2892
    Mfg explosives
Douglas J Jackson, President

D-U-N-S 09-316-3418
DYNO NOBEL MIDWEST, INC.
    (Parent: Dyno Nobel Inc)
510 Maine St, Ste 906, Quincy, IL 62301
Phone: (217) 222-4806
Sales: $21,000,000   *Employees:* 95
Company Type: Private   *Employees here:* 10
SIC: 2892
    Mfg explosives
Bill Lytle, General Manager

D-U-N-S 83-867-6625
DYSTAR LP
9844-A Suthern Pines Blvd, Charlotte, NC 28273
Phone: (704) 561-3000

Sales: $200,000,000   *Employees:* 164
Company Type: Private   *Employees here:* 90
SIC: 2865
    Produces dyes and pigments
Herbert Klein, President

D-U-N-S 60-614-7403
E L C TECHNOLOGY, INC.
4410 N State Road 7, Fort Lauderdale, FL 33319
Phone: (954) 484-5300
Sales: $25,000,000   *Employees:* 209
Company Type: Private   *Employees here:* 209
SIC: 2819
    Manufacturer of organic chemicals and industrial parts
A M Appel, Finance

D-U-N-S 02-252-8553
E Q HOLDING COMPANY
36255 Michigan Ave, Wayne, MI 48184
Phone: (734) 329-8000
Sales: $76,700,000   *Employees:* 327
Company Type: Private   *Employees here:* 4
SIC: 2869
    Holding company
Michael Ferrantino, President

D-U-N-S 07-270-9231   EXP
E T BROWNE DRUG CO. INC.
140 Sylvan Ave, Englewood Cliffs, NJ 07632
Phone: (201) 947-3050
Sales: $60,000,000   *Employees:* 175
Company Type: Private   *Employees here:* 40
SIC: 2844
    Mfg cosmetic & toilet preparations & pharmaceutical creams
        & specialty chemicals
Arnold H Neis, President

D-U-N-S 02-928-5087
EAGLEBROOK INTERNATIONAL GROUP
4801 Southwick Dr, Fl 2, Matteson, IL 60443
Phone: (708) 747-5038
Sales: $28,900,000   *Employees:* 200
Company Type: Private   *Employees here:* 20
SIC: 2899
    Waste recycling and reconstitution
Ronald Tenny, President

D-U-N-S 80-889-8381   EXP
EASTMAN CHEMICAL COMPANY
100 N Eastman Rd, Kingsport, TN 37660
Phone: (423) 229-2000
Sales: $4,678,000,000   *Employees:* 16,100
Company Type: Public   *Employees here:* 10,000
SIC: 2821
    Mfg plastic materials acetate tow industrial intermediates &
        specialty chemicals
Allan R Rothwell, Chief Financial Officer

D-U-N-S 00-220-7546
EASTMAN GELATINE CORPORATION
    (Parent: Eastman Kodak Company)
227 Washington St, Peabody, MA 01960
Phone: (978) 531-1700
Sales: $81,572,000   *Employees:* 200
Company Type: Public Family Member   *Employees here:* 190
SIC: 2899
    Mfg gelatin
Wayne C Jones, President

D-U-N-S 83-635-4621
EASTWIND GROUP, INC.
100 4 Falls Corporate Ctr, West Conshohocken, PA 19428
Phone: (610) 828-6860

Sales: $23,633,000   *Employees:* 505
Company Type: Public   *Employees here:* 6
SIC: 2821
    Investment holding company
Paul A Dejuliis, Chief Executive Officer

D-U-N-S 11-261-4664   EXP
ECOGEN INC.
2005 Cabot Blvd W, Langhorne, PA 19047
Phone: (215) 757-1590
Sales: $16,398,000   *Employees:* 60
Company Type: Public   *Employees here:* 45
SIC: 2879
    Mfg pesticides & agricultural chemicals & environmental
    research laboratory
James P Reilly Jr, Chairman of the Board

D-U-N-S 00-615-4611   EXP
ECOLAB INC.
370 Wabasha St N, Saint Paul, MN 55102
Phone: (651) 293-2233
Sales: $1,640,352,000   *Employees:* 10,210
Company Type: Public   *Employees here:* 1,000
SIC: 2841
    Mfg detergents & sanitizers specialty cleaners pest control &
    janitorial pdts
Allan L Schuman, President

D-U-N-S 17-723-9498   EXP
ECOSCIENCE CORPORATION
10 Alvin Ct, East Brunswick, NJ 08816
Phone: (732) 257-4000
Sales: $22,317,000   *Employees:* 70
Company Type: Public   *Employees here:* 4
SIC: 2879
    Commercialization of natural pest control products for
    biological & ecological use and distributes greenhouse
    growing systems
Michael A Degiglio, President

D-U-N-S 19-625-6960   EXP
EDLON, INC.
    (Parent: Robbins & Myers Inc)
117 W State St, Avondale, PA 19311
Phone: (610) 268-3101
Sales: $15,000,000   *Employees:* 134
Company Type: Public Family Member   *Employees here:* 60
SIC: 2821
    Mfg fluoropolymers products
William Flannery, President

D-U-N-S 18-966-3206
EFTEC NORTH AMERICA LLC
    (Parent: H B Fuller Company)
31601 Research Park Dr, Madison Heights, MI 48071
Phone: (248) 585-2200
Sales: $100,000,000   *Employees:* 343
Company Type: Public Family Member   *Employees here:* 100
SIC: 2891
    Mfg sealants & adhesives
Jim Conaty, President

D-U-N-S 10-665-4973
EKA CHEMICALS INC.
    (Parent: Nobel Industries Usa Inc)
1775 W Oak Commons Ct, Marietta, GA 30062
Phone: (770) 578-0858
Sales: $225,000,000   *Employees:* 450
Company Type: Private   *Employees here:* 88
SIC: 2899
    Mfg sodium chlorate and hydrogen peroxide
Borje Andersson, President

D-U-N-S 06-884-5163   EXP
EKC TECHNOLOGY INC.
    (Parent: Chemfirst Inc)
2520 Barrington Ct, Hayward, CA 94545
Phone: (510) 784-9105
Sales: $28,500,000   *Employees:* 159
Company Type: Public Family Member   *Employees here:* 115
SIC: 2899
    Mfg specialty chemicals
P J Coder, President

D-U-N-S 18-730-6428
EKO SYSTEMS INC.
5490 W 13th Ave, Lakewood, CO 80214
Phone: (303) 232-2611
Sales: $19,300,000   *Employees:* 88
Company Type: Private   *Employees here:* 3
SIC: 2879
    Mfg soil conditioners & organic fertilizer
Thomas Pawlish, President

D-U-N-S 10-397-0307   EXP
EL DORADO CHEMICAL COMPANY
    (Parent: Lsb Chemical Corp)
16 S Pennsylvania Ave, Oklahoma City, OK 73107
Phone: (405) 235-4546
Sales: $131,762,000   *Employees:* 325
Company Type: Public Family Member   *Employees here:* 2
SIC: 2819
    Mfg industrial acids blasting products & ammonium nitrate
    based fertilizer
Jack Golsen, Chairman of the Board

D-U-N-S 04-289-5680   EXP
ELAN CHEMICAL COMPANY
268 Doremus Ave, Newark, NJ 07105
Phone: (973) 344-8014
Sales: $23,663,000   *Employees:* 85
Company Type: Private   *Employees here:* 84
SIC: 2869
    Mfg industrial organic chemicals mfg flavor extracts/syrup
David R Weisman, Chief Executive Officer

D-U-N-S 09-757-6862   EXP
ELASCO, INC.
11377 Markon Dr, Garden Grove, CA 92841
Phone: (714) 891-1795
Sales: $38,400,000   *Employees:* 180
Company Type: Private   *Employees here:* 180
SIC: 2821
    Mfg polyurethane products and sealant
Dan Walters, Chief Executive Officer

D-U-N-S 61-667-2325   EXP
ELECTROCHEMICALS, INC.
    (Parent: Laporte Inc)
5630 Pioneer Creek Dr, Maple Plain, MN 55359
Phone: (612) 479-2008
Sales: $23,000,000   *Employees:* 75
Company Type: Private   *Employees here:* 75
SIC: 2899
    Mfg proprietary chemicals for electroplating printed circuit
    boards
Moenes Elias, President

D-U-N-S 09-881-8339   EXP
ELEMENTIS CHROMIUM INC.
    (Parent: Elementise America Inc)
3800 Buddy Lawrence Dr, Corpus Christi, TX 78407
Phone: (361) 883-6421

Sales: $75,000,000   *Employees:* 190
Company Type: Private   *Employees here:* 190
SIC: 2819
    Mfg chromium chemicals
Jon L Moon, President

D-U-N-S 61-210-3564   EXP
ELEMENTIS PIGMENTS INC.
    (Parent: Elementise America Inc)
11 Executive Dr, Ste 1, Fairview Heights, IL 62208
Phone: (618) 628-2300
Sales: $26,900,000   *Employees:* 194
Company Type: Private   *Employees here:* 194
SIC: 2816
    Mfg inorganic pigments
Gerald Linnenbringer, President

D-U-N-S 79-867-3844   EXP
ELEMENTIS SPECIALTIES
400 Claremont Ave, Jersey City, NJ 07304
Phone: (201) 432-0800
Sales: $35,000,000   *Employees:* 108
Company Type: Private   *Employees here:* 108
SIC: 2851
    Mfg colorants and additives
Scott T Becker, President

D-U-N-S 00-229-0773   EXP
ELF ATOCHEM NORTH AMERICA INC.
    (Parent: Elf Atochem North America Del)
2000 Market St, Ste 2200, Philadelphia, PA 19103
Phone: (215) 419-7000
Sales: $1,903,600,000   *Employees:* 4,500
Company Type: Private   *Employees here:* 750
SIC: 2812
    Mfg inorganic and organic chemicals specialty chemicals and
        plastics
Bernard Azoulay, President

D-U-N-S 83-942-1633
ELMERS PRODUCTS INC.
    (Parent: Borden Inc)
180 E Broad St, Columbus, OH 43215
Phone: (614) 225-2000
Sales: $125,000,000   *Employees:* 250
Company Type: Private   *Employees here:* 50
SIC: 2891
    Mfg consumer adhesives & glue
Brian Schnabel, President

D-U-N-S 07-869-6721   EXP
EM INDUSTRIES, INC.
7 Skyline Dr, Hawthorne, NY 10532
Phone: (914) 592-4660
Sales: $191,670,000   *Employees:* 670
Company Type: Private   *Employees here:* 120
SIC: 2869
    Mfg high purity organic & inorganic chemicals & whol
        organic & inorganic chemicals
Peter A Wriede, President

D-U-N-S 00-334-3126
EMBERS CHARCOAL COMPANY INC.
385 French Collins Rd, Conway, SC 29526
Phone: (843) 347-3600
Sales: $18,000,000   *Employees:* 155
Company Type: Private   *Employees here:* 154
SIC: 2861
    Mfg charcoal
T S Ragsdale III, President

D-U-N-S 88-401-3913   EXP
EMERSON CMING COMPOSITE METALS INC.
59 Walpole St, Canton, MA 02021
Phone: (781) 821-4250
Sales: $22,398,000   *Employees:* 160
Company Type: Private   *Employees here:* 152
SIC: 2819
    Mfg syntactic foam microballoons & composite parts
Brian Barer, General Manager

D-U-N-S 13-077-6487   EXP
EMS-GRILON HOLDING INC.
2060 Corporate Way, Sumter, SC 29154
Phone: (803) 481-9173
Sales: $75,650,000   *Employees:* 106
Company Type: Private   *Employees here:* 106
SIC: 2821
    Holding company mfg & whol engineering nylon thermo
        plastic adhesives whol technical fibers
Karl Imhof, Treasurer

D-U-N-S 10-632-0005   IMP EXP
EMSCO INC.
306 Shenango St, Girard, PA 16417
Phone: (814) 774-3137
Sales: $16,000,000   *Employees:* 125
Company Type: Private   *Employees here:* 125
SIC: 2842
    Mfg household and industrial cleaning products lawn and
        garden tools poly furniture and christmas tree stands
David B Oas, President

D-U-N-S 09-929-0629   EXP
ENGELHARD CORPORATION
101 Wood Ave S, Iselin, NJ 08830
Phone: (732) 205-5000
Sales: $3,630,653,000   *Employees:* 6,872
Company Type: Public   *Employees here:* 925
SIC: 2819
    Mfr precious metal pdts & precious metal refining dealing &
        management mfr chem catalysts & pigments
Barry W Perry, President

D-U-N-S 92-630-3553   EXP
ENGINEERED CARBONS, INC.
    (Parent: Ameripol Synpol Corporation)
1215 Main St, Port Neches, TX 77651
Phone: (409) 722-8321
Sales: $56,200,000   *Employees:* 284
Company Type: Private   *Employees here:* 9
SIC: 2895
    Produces carbon black
W D Spence, President

D-U-N-S 05-850-9712
THE ENSIGN-BICKFORD COMPANY
    (Parent: Ensign-Bickford Industries)
660 Hopmeadow St, Simsbury, CT 06070
Phone: (860) 843-2000
Sales: $127,300,000   *Employees:* 345
Company Type: Private   *Employees here:* 100
SIC: 2892
    Mfr initiators & blasting accessories for explosives
Herman J Fonteyne, Chairman of the Board

D-U-N-S 05-850-9654
ENSIGN-BICKFORD INDUSTRIES
10 Mill Pond Ln, Simsbury, CT 06070
Phone: (860) 843-2000

Sales: $185,200,000	*Employees:* 2,278
Company Type: Private	*Employees here:* 600

SIC: 2892
   Mfg explosive initiation systems caulking compounds &
     polypropylene films
Ralph H Harnett, President

D-U-N-S 15-125-5155   EXP
ENZYME BIO SYSTEMS LTD.
   (*Parent:* Corn Products International)
2600 Kennedy Dr, Beloit, WI 53511
Phone: (608) 365-1112

Sales: $36,000,000	*Employees:* 84
Company Type: Public Family Member	*Employees here:* 84

SIC: 2869
   Mfg food grade enzymes
Michael J Friesema, President

D-U-N-S 62-465-3218   EXP
ENZYME DEVELOPMENT CORPORATION
2 Penn Plz, Rm 2439, New York, NY 10121
Phone: (212) 736-1580

Sales: $21,712,000	*Employees:* 25
Company Type: Private	*Employees here:* 10

SIC: 2869
   Mfg & markets enzymes & bio-chemical systems
Wallace Chavkin, Chairman of the Board

D-U-N-S 00-827-6545   EXP
EPOXYLITE CORPORATION
9400 Toledo Way, Irvine, CA 92618
Phone: (949) 951-3231

Sales: $19,100,000	*Employees:* 109
Company Type: Private	*Employees here:* 35

SIC: 2851
   Mfg epoxy resin coatings & paste adhesives
Peter R Dorsa, President

D-U-N-S 61-250-1460
EPSILON PRODUCTS CO, JV
Post Rd & Blueball Ave, Marcus Hook, PA 19061
Phone: (610) 497-8850

Sales: $130,000,000	*Employees:* 148
Company Type: Private	*Employees here:* 148

SIC: 2821
   Mfg polypropoleyne
Phil Jardine, President

D-U-N-S 96-955-7263
EQUISTAR CHEMICALS, LP
1221 Mckinney St, Ste 1600, Houston, TX 77010
Phone: (713) 652-7300

Sales: $365,800,000	*Employees:* 1,500
Company Type: Private	*Employees here:* 50

SIC: 2869
   Petrochemicals
Dan F Smith, Chief Executive Officer

D-U-N-S 11-849-5126
EQUISTAR CHEMICALS, LP
13 Miles S Of Hwy 60, Bay City, TX 77414
Phone: (409) 245-1225

Sales: $33,500,000	*Employees:* NA
Company Type: Private	*Employees here:* 180

SIC: 2869
   Mfg inorganic chemicals
Lonny Lindsey, Manager

D-U-N-S 00-654-5511
ESCO COMPANY, LP
2340 Roberts St, Muskegon, MI 49444
Phone: (616) 726-3106

Sales: $17,800,000	*Employees:* 85
Company Type: Private	*Employees here:* 80

SIC: 2865
   Mfg color former
Bruce Rice, President

D-U-N-S 00-437-8261   EXP
ESM II INC.
   (*Parent:* Skw Americas Inc)
300 Corporate Pkwy, Amherst, NY 14226
Phone: (716) 446-8800

Sales: $129,239,000	*Employees:* 186
Company Type: Private	*Employees here:* 15

SIC: 2819
   Mfg reagents
Meinholf Pousset, President

D-U-N-S 07-710-0469
ESSEX SPECIALTY PRODUCTS INC.
   (*Parent:* The Dow Chemical Company)
1250 Harmon Rd, Auburn Hills, MI 48326
Phone: (248) 391-6300

Sales: $72,200,000	*Employees:* 460
Company Type: Public Family Member	*Employees here:* 150

SIC: 2891
   Manufactures sealants and adhesives
W R Donberg, President

D-U-N-S 79-080-2086   EXP
ESTEE LAUDER COMPANIES INC.
767 5th Ave, New York, NY 10153
Phone: (212) 572-4200

Sales: $3,618,000,000	*Employees:* 15,300
Company Type: Public	*Employees here:* 1,000

SIC: 2844
   Mfg & ret cosmetics & fragrance products
Leonard A Lauder, Chairman of the Board

D-U-N-S 00-591-4387   EXP
ESTEE LAUDER INC.
   (*Parent:* Estee Lauder Companies Inc)
767 5th Ave, New York, NY 10153
Phone: (212) 572-4200

Sales: $1,199,100,000	*Employees:* 10,000
Company Type: Public Family Member	*Employees here:* 700

SIC: 2844
   Mfg & ret cosmetics & fragrance products
Leonard A Lauder, Chairman of the Board

D-U-N-S 93-394-7699
ESTEE LAUDER INTERNATIONAL INC.
   (*Parent:* Estee Lauder Inc)
767 5th Ave, New York, NY 10022
Phone: (212) 572-4200

Sales: $3,381,600,000	*Employees:* 620
Company Type: Public Family Member	*Employees here:* 7

SIC: 2844
   Mfg cosmetics
Patrick Bousquet-Chavan, President

D-U-N-S 05-506-3077   EXP
ETHOX CHEMICALS, LLC
   (*Parent:* Piedmont Chemical Industries)
1801 Perimeter Rd, Greenville, SC 29605
Phone: (864) 277-1620

Sales: $50,000,000	*Employees:* 120
Company Type: Private	*Employees here:* 120

SIC: 2843
   Mfg surface active wetting & finishing agents
Fred E Wilson Jr, Chairman of the Board

D-U-N-S 00-313-2222
ETHYL CORPORATION
330 S 4th St, Richmond, VA 23219
Phone: (804) 788-5000
Sales: $1,063,615,000   *Employees:* 1,800
Company Type: Public   *Employees here:* 242
SIC: 2869
   Mfr and whol fuel and lubricant additives mfr antioxidants
     corrosion inhibitors and petroleum dyes and detergents
Bruce C Gottwald, Chief Executive Officer

D-U-N-S 05-396-9234   EXP
ETHYL PETROLEUM ADDITIVES INC.
   (Parent: Ethyl Corporation)
330 S 4th St, Richmond, VA 23219
Phone: (804) 788-5000
Sales: $64,300,000   *Employees:* 455
Company Type: Public Family Member   *Employees here:* 194
SIC: 2899
   Mfgs fuel and lubricant additives
Thomas E Gottwald, President

D-U-N-S 00-420-1042   EXP
THE EUCLID CHEMICAL COMPANY
   (Parent: Rpm Inc)
19218 Redwood Rd, Cleveland, OH 44110
Phone: (216) 531-9222
Sales: $45,000,000   *Employees:* 20
Company Type: Public Family Member   *Employees here:* 2
SIC: 2899
   Mfg chemical adhesives & interstate trucking
Kenneth W Korach, President

D-U-N-S 61-854-5214
EVAL COMPANY OF AMERICA
   (Parent: Kuraray America Inc)
1001 Warrenville Rd, Lisle, IL 60532
Phone: (630) 719-4610
Sales: $15,800,000   *Employees:* 86
Company Type: Private   *Employees here:* 19
SIC: 2821
   Mfg evoh plastic resins
Thomas W Mchugh, President

D-U-N-S 00-428-1283
EVANS ADHESIVE CORPORATION
925 Old Henderson Rd, Columbus, OH 43220
Phone: (614) 451-2665
Sales: $17,000,000   *Employees:* 80
Company Type: Private   *Employees here:* 45
SIC: 2891
   Mfg adhesives
James A Fellows, President

D-U-N-S 62-624-3117
EVODE USA INC.
Pioneer Industrial Park, Leominster, MA 01453
Phone: (978) 537-8071
Sales: $31,500,000   *Employees:* 140
Company Type: Private   *Employees here:* 140
SIC: 2821
   Mfg plastic and rubber compounds textile finishing agents
     coatings adhesives and extruder of cove based products
Mike Funderburg, Chief Financial Officer

D-U-N-S 61-531-9886   EXP
EXXON CHEMICAL AMERICAS
12875 Scenic Hwy, Baton Rouge, LA 70807
Phone: (225) 775-4330

Sales: $500,000,000   *Employees:* 450
Company Type: Private   *Employees here:* 450
SIC: 2821
   Mfg polyethylene resins
Doug Connor, Plant Manager

D-U-N-S 00-219-4017
FABRICOLOR MANUFACTURING CORP
160 E 5th St, Paterson, NJ 07524
Phone: (973) 742-3900
Sales: $16,500,000   *Employees:* 80
Company Type: Private   *Employees here:* 4
SIC: 2865
   Manufactures dyestuffs & pigments
Walter Perron, Chairman of the Board

D-U-N-S 04-517-1766   EXP
FAIRFIELD PROCESSING CORP.
88 Rose Hill Ave, Danbury, CT 06810
Phone: (203) 744-2090
Sales: $24,000,000   *Employees:* 240
Company Type: Private   *Employees here:* 180
SIC: 2824
   Mfr polyester fibers
Roy Young, Chairman of the Board

D-U-N-S 10-389-2493
FALCON MANUFACTURING OF CALIF INC.
   (Parent: Falcon Foam Corporation)
14104 Towne Ave, Los Angeles, CA 90061
Phone: (310) 515-7102
Sales: $20,900,000   *Employees:* 100
Company Type: Public Family Member   *Employees here:* 100
SIC: 2821
   Mfg block molded eps foam
Tom Dorger, Principal

D-U-N-S 02-129-1133
THE FANNING CORPORATION
2450 W Hubbard St, Chicago, IL 60612
Phone: (312) 563-1234
Sales: $20,000,000   *Employees:* 26
Company Type: Private   *Employees here:* 26
SIC: 2899
   Mfg and whol chemical raw materials
Francis G Fanning, President

D-U-N-S 03-923-1261
FARMERS PLANT FOOD, INC.
205 Railroad Ave, Garretson, SD 57030
Phone: (605) 594-2121
Sales: $19,606,000   *Employees:* 12
Company Type: Private   *Employees here:* 8
SIC: 2873
   Mfg plant food
Kevin Baum, President

D-U-N-S 78-391-9780
FARMLAND HYDRO, LP
County Rd 640, Bartow, FL 33830
Phone: (941) 533-1141
Sales: $300,000,000   *Employees:* 306
Company Type: Private   *Employees here:* 306
SIC: 2874
   Mfg phosphate chemicals
Merle Farris, Vice-President

D-U-N-S 13-759-8132   EXP
FAROUK SYSTEMS INC.
250 Pennbright Dr, Ste 150, Houston, TX 77090
Phone: (281) 876-2000

Sales: $24,000,000   *Employees:* 150
Company Type: Private   *Employees here:* 150
SIC: 2844
   Mfg hair care products
Farouk Shami, President

D-U-N-S 06-771-1176
FARRELL-CALHOUN INC.
221 E Carolina Ave, Memphis, TN 38126
Phone: (901) 526-2211
Sales: $20,136,000   *Employees:* 100
Company Type: Private   *Employees here:* 47
SIC: 2851
   Mfr paint
John A Ward Jr, President

D-U-N-S 00-769-8368
FASHION LABORATORIES INC.
   (Parent: Azurel Ltd)
20-10 Maple Ave, Fair Lawn, NJ 07410
Phone: (973) 423-1515
Sales: $29,100,000   *Employees:* 251
Company Type: Public Family Member   *Employees here:* 251
SIC: 2844
   Mfg toilet preparations
Michael Assante, President

D-U-N-S 00-712-8135   EXP
FAULTLESS STARCH/BON AMI CO.
1025 W 8th St, Kansas City, MO 64101
Phone: (816) 842-1230
Sales: $62,359,000   *Employees:* 150
Company Type: Private   *Employees here:* 130
SIC: 2842
   Mfg laundry starch & cleaning preparations
Gordon T Beaham III, Chairman of the Board

D-U-N-S 84-704-1225   EXP
FERMPRO MANUFACTURING, LP
Hwy 52 N, Kingstree, SC 29556
Phone: (843) 382-8485
Sales: $19,500,000   *Employees:* 114
Company Type: Private   *Employees here:* 114
SIC: 2869
   Mfg industrial enzymes
James Godfrey, Purchasing

D-U-N-S 00-416-1477   EXP
FERRO CORPORATION
1000 Lakeside Ave, Cleveland, OH 44114
Phone: (216) 641-8580
Sales: $1,381,280,000   *Employees:* 6,851
Company Type: Public   *Employees here:* 90
SIC: 2899
   Mfr coatings colorings and industrial ceramics plastics and
     specialty chemicals
Albert C Bersticker, Chief Executive Officer

D-U-N-S 02-165-0189
FERTILIZER COMPANY ARIZONA INC.
2850 S Peart Rd, Casa Grande, AZ 85222
Phone: (520) 836-7477
Sales: $24,500,000   *Employees:* 132
Company Type: Private   *Employees here:* 50
SIC: 2875
   Whol agricultural fertilizers
James R Compton Jr, President

D-U-N-S 18-337-1574
FIBER INDUSTRIES INC.
   (Parent: Wellman Inc)
5146 Parkway Plaza Blvd, Charlotte, NC 28217
Phone: (704) 357-2000

Sales: $66,000,000   *Employees:* 660
Company Type: Public Family Member   *Employees here:* 100
SIC: 2824
   Mfg synthetic fibers and pet polymers
Thomas M Duff, President

D-U-N-S 80-658-8646
FIBERVISIONS, INCORPORATED
7101 Alcovy Rd NE, Covington, GA 30014
Phone: (770) 786-7011
Sales: $95,000,000   *Employees:* 450
Company Type: Private   *Employees here:* 450
SIC: 2821
   Mfg polypropylene fibers
John E Montgomery, President

D-U-N-S 18-856-0007   EXP
FILTROL CORPORATION
   (Parent: Akzo Nobel Inc)
3492 E 26th St, Los Angeles, CA 90023
Phone: (323) 260-8800
Sales: $44,300,000   *Employees:* 280
Company Type: Private   *Employees here:* 30
SIC: 2819
   Mfg fluid cracking catalysts
J K Day, Chairman of the Board

D-U-N-S 80-526-4785
FINE FRAGRANCES DISTRIBUTIONS
   (Parent: Prod Parfums Cosmetique Univer)
720 5th Ave, Fl 8, New York, NY 10019
Phone: (212) 333-7700
Sales: $47,000,000   *Employees:* 129
Company Type: Private   *Employees here:* 2
SIC: 2844
   Holding company
Erich Fayer, President

D-U-N-S 00-139-2174   EXP
FINETEX INC.
418 Falmouth Ave, Elmwood Park, NJ 07407
Phone: (201) 797-4686
Sales: $15,900,000   *Employees:* 75
Company Type: Private   *Employees here:* 28
SIC: 2869
   Mfg industrial organic chemicals textile finishing agents
     emulsifiers & softeners
Roger Porter, President

D-U-N-S 05-713-0965
FINNAREN & HALEY INC.
901 Washington St, Conshohocken, PA 19428
Phone: (610) 825-1900
Sales: $20,000,000   *Employees:* 170
Company Type: Private   *Employees here:* 80
SIC: 2851
   Mfg & dist & ret paints enamels varnishes lacquers & related
     products
Robert A Haley, Chairman of the Board

D-U-N-S 04-122-5509   EXP
FIRST CHEMICAL CORPORATION
   (Parent: Chemfirst Inc)
700 North St, Jackson, MS 39202
Phone: (601) 948-7550
Sales: $174,334,000   *Employees:* 235
Company Type: Public Family Member   *Employees here:* 3
SIC: 2865
   Manufactures aniline & other nitrated aromatic industrial &
     agricultural organic chemicals
G M Simmons, President

D-U-N-S 00-914-0054   EXP
FLECTO COMPANY INC.
  (Parent: Rpm Inc)
1000 45th St, Oakland, CA 94608
Phone: (510) 655-2470
Sales: $77,000,000   *Employees:* 80
Company Type: Public Family Member   *Employees here:* 70
SIC: 2851
  Mfg clear wood finishes stains enamels & sanders
Richard C Swanson, President

D-U-N-S 09-929-3250
FLEXIBLE COMPONENTS INC.
  (Parent: Sybron International Corp)
460 Milltown Rd, Bridgewater, NJ 08807
Phone: (908) 218-8888
Sales: $15,000,000   *Employees:* 48
Company Type: Public Family Member   *Employees here:* 48
SIC: 2821
  Mfr teflon and fabricates flexible metal hose assemblies
Michael Gioseffi, President

D-U-N-S 00-535-5854   EXP
FLINT INK CORPORATION
4600 Arrowhead Dr, Ann Arbor, MI 48105
Phone: (734) 622-6000
Sales: $757,062,000   *Employees:* 2,600
Company Type: Private   *Employees here:* 200
SIC: 2893
  Mfg printing ink pigments dispersions press blankets &
    graphic arts supplies
H H Flint Jr, Chairman of the Board

D-U-N-S 61-759-4601
FLO KAY INDUSTRIES INC.
1919 Grand Ave, Sioux City, IA 51106
Phone: (712) 277-2011
Sales: $44,000,000   *Employees:* 115
Company Type: Private   *Employees here:* 2
SIC: 2873
  Mfg fertilizer feed supplements & zinc chemicals
Royal Lohry, President

D-U-N-S 18-794-3477
FLOR QUIM INC.
  (Parent: Chem Fleur Inc)
Km 111 Int Grdarraya Rr 3, Patillas, PR 00723
Phone: (787) 839-2710
Sales: $15,000,000   *Employees:* 27
Company Type: Private   *Employees here:* 27
SIC: 2869
  Mfg aromatic chemical products
Hans P Van Housten, President

D-U-N-S 00-512-6453   EXP
FLORALIFE, INC.
751 Thunderbolt Dr, Walterboro, SC 29488
Phone: (843) 538-3839
Sales: $15,000,000   *Employees:* 65
Company Type: Private   *Employees here:* 25
SIC: 2899
  Mfg chemicals & whol floral supplies
James Sykora Jr, President

D-U-N-S 94-341-6610
FLUOR DANIEL HANFORD INC.
  (Parent: Fluor Daniel Inc)
2420 Stevens Dr, Richland, WA 99352
Phone: (509) 376-7411

Sales: $80,000,000   *Employees:* 500
Company Type: Public Family Member   *Employees here:* 450
SIC: 2819
  Nuclear power disposal engineering & research
    environmental cleanup
Ronald Hanson, President

D-U-N-S 00-914-6945   EXP
FMC CORPORATION
200 E Randolph St, Chicago, IL 60601
Phone: (312) 861-6000
Sales: $4,259,000,000   *Employees:* 16,805
Company Type: Public   *Employees here:* 250
SIC: 2812
  Mfg machinery & equipment performance chemicals &
    industrial chemicals
Larry D Brady, President

D-U-N-S 11-340-4719   EXP
FMC WYOMING CORPORATION
  (Parent: Fmc Corporation)
Westvaco Rd, Green River, WY 82935
Phone: (307) 875-2580
Sales: $174,600,000   *Employees:* 1,115
Company Type: Public Family Member   *Employees here:* 1,040
SIC: 2812
  Mfg soda ash
William G Walter, President

D-U-N-S 06-243-0756   EXP
FOAM SUPPLIES INC.
4387 Rider Trl N, Earth City, MO 63045
Phone: (314) 344-3330
Sales: $18,000,000   *Employees:* 48
Company Type: Private   *Employees here:* 22
SIC: 2821
  Mfg liquid polyurethane foam
David G Keske, President

D-U-N-S 10-623-8223
FORMOSA PLASTICS CORP.
  (Parent: Formosa Plastics Corp Usa)
9 Peach Tree Hill Rd, Livingston, NJ 07039
Phone: (973) 992-2090
Sales: $56,578,000   *Employees:* 117
Company Type: Private   *Employees here:* 117
SIC: 2821
  Manufactures polyvinyl chloride resins
Y C Wang, Chairman of the Board

D-U-N-S 10-623-8108   EXP
FORMOSA PLASTICS CORP. LOUISIANA
  (Parent: Formosa Plastics Corp Usa)
9 Peach Tree Hill Rd, Livingston, NJ 07039
Phone: (973) 992-2090
Sales: $350,000,000   *Employees:* 321
Company Type: Private   *Employees here:* 5
SIC: 2821
  Mfg polyvinyl chloride resins vinyl chloride monomers &
    caustic soda
Y C Wang, Chairman of the Board

D-U-N-S 10-623-8165   EXP
FORMOSA PLASTICS CORP. TEXAS
  (Parent: Formosa Plastics Corp Usa)
9 Peach Tree Hill Rd, Livingston, NJ 07039
Phone: (973) 992-2090
Sales: $960,000,000   *Employees:* 300
Company Type: Private   *Employees here:* 5
SIC: 2821
  Mfg polyvinyl chloride resins
Y C Wang, Chairman of the Board

D-U-N-S 03-994-4004   EXP
FORMOSA PLASTICS CORP. USA
9 Peach Tree Hill Rd, Livingston, NJ 07039
Phone: (973) 992-2090
Sales: $1,500,000,000   *Employees:* 3,800
Company Type: Private   *Employees here:* 400
SIC: 2821
    Through subsidiaries manufactures polyvinyl chloride resins
      vinyl chloride monomers caustic soda and pvc pipe
C T Lee, President

D-U-N-S 00-953-3704
FORMULABS, INC.
    (Parent: Kimberly-Clark Corporation)
529 W 4th Ave, Escondido, CA 92025
Phone: (760) 741-2345
Sales: $18,500,000   *Employees:* 105
Company Type: Public Family Member   *Employees here:* 48
SIC: 2899
    Mfg ink
Bruce Nichols, President

D-U-N-S 06-342-7306
FORREST PAINT CO.
1011 Mckinley St, Eugene, OR 97402
Phone: (541) 342-1821
Sales: $16,660,000   *Employees:* 75
Company Type: Private   *Employees here:* 75
SIC: 2851
    Mfg paint
Richard S Forrest, President

D-U-N-S 08-881-3480
FOSECO HOLDING INC.
20200 Sheldon Rd, Cleveland, OH 44142
Phone: (440) 826-4548
Sales: $113,800,000   *Employees:* 800
Company Type: Private   *Employees here:* 280
SIC: 2899
    Mfg metal treating exothermic compounds & fluxes chemical
      compounds magnesium oxide & resin cartridges
Anthony Money, President

D-U-N-S 00-415-7541
FOSECO INC.
    (Parent: Georgetown Holding Company)
20200 Sheldon Rd, Cleveland, OH 44142
Phone: (440) 826-4548
Sales: $70,800,000   *Employees:* 500
Company Type: Private   *Employees here:* 320
SIC: 2899
    Mfg exothermic compounds fluxes and ceramic filters
Lee Plutshack, Chairman of the Board

D-U-N-S 18-183-4532   EXP
FRAGRANCE RESOURCES INC.
620 Route 3, Clifton, NJ 07014
Phone: (973) 777-2979
Sales: $50,000,000   *Employees:* 100
Company Type: Private   *Employees here:* 45
SIC: 2899
    Mfg fragrance compounds aroma chemicals essential oils and
      floral absolutes
Richard T Carraher, President

D-U-N-S 86-770-1401
FRAMATOME COGEMA FUELS
Mount Athos Rd, Lynchburg, VA 24504
Phone: (804) 832-3000

Sales: $63,800,000   *Employees:* 400
Company Type: Private   *Employees here:* 400
SIC: 2819
    Mfg fuel assemblies for nuclear power plant
Bob Hoffman, President

D-U-N-S 01-112-1589
FRANKLIN-BURLINGTON PLASTICS
    (Parent: Spartech Corporation)
113 Passaic Ave, Kearny, NJ 07032
Phone: (201) 998-8002
Sales: $37,000,000   *Employees:* 87
Company Type: Public Family Member   *Employees here:* 56
SIC: 2821
    Mfg polyvinyl chloride compounds
Bradley B Buechler, President

D-U-N-S 04-433-1155
FRAZEE INDUSTRIES INC.
    (Parent: Williams Paint Holdings Inc)
6625 Miramar Rd, San Diego, CA 92121
Phone: (619) 276-9500
Sales: $129,700,000   *Employees:* 850
Company Type: Private   *Employees here:* 200
SIC: 2851
    Mfg paint and whol paint painting supplies and wall coverings
Edmund W Lanctot, President

D-U-N-S 05-081-1231   EXP
FREEMAN COSMETIC CORPORATION
    (Parent: Dial Corporation)
10000 Santa Monica Blvd, Los Angeles, CA 90067
Phone: (310) 286-0101
Sales: $57,375,000   *Employees:* 250
Company Type: Public Family Member   *Employees here:* 55
SIC: 2844
    Mfg hair preparations face creams & lotions
Larry J Freeman, President

D-U-N-S 96-947-6472
FREEPORT-MCMORAN SULPHUR, INC.
1615 Poydras St, New Orleans, LA 70112
Phone: (504) 528-4000
Sales: $211,945,000   *Employees:* 200
Company Type: Public   *Employees here:* 200
SIC: 2819
    Mines & produces sulphur
Robert M Wohleber, President

D-U-N-S 00-625-9485
FREMONT INDUSTRIES, INC.
4400 Valley Industrial Blvd, Shakopee, MN 55379
Phone: (612) 445-4121
Sales: $17,500,000   *Employees:* 120
Company Type: Private   *Employees here:* 50
SIC: 2819
    Mfg industrial inorganic chemicals & water treating
      compounds
Mark L Gruss, President

D-U-N-S 79-433-7337   EXP
FRENCH FRAGRANCES, INC.
14100 NW 60th Ave, Hialeah, FL 33014
Phone: (305) 818-8000
Sales: $215,487,000   *Employees:* 190
Company Type: Private   *Employees here:* 98
SIC: 2844
    Mfg & whol fragrances & related cosmetic products
E S Beattie, President

D-U-N-S 60-570-0897
FRIT INC.
Jodie Parker Rd, Ozark, AL 36360

Phone: (334) 774-2515
Sales: $69,884,000   *Employees:* 345
Company Type: Private   *Employees here:* 10
SIC: 2873
    Holding company
Shelton E Allred, Chairman of the Board

D-U-N-S 06-114-8631
FRIT INDUSTRIES INC.
    (*Parent:* Frit Inc)
Jodie Parker Rd, Ozark, AL 36360
Phone: (334) 774-2515
Sales: $18,011,000   *Employees:* 120
Company Type: Private   *Employees here:* 30
SIC: 2873
    Mfg micronutrients
Shelton E Allred, Chairman of the Board

D-U-N-S 00-732-0229   EXP
FRITZ INDUSTRIES INC.
500 N Sam Houston Rd, Mesquite, TX 75149
Phone: (972) 285-5471
Sales: $58,341,000   *Employees:* 170
Company Type: Private   *Employees here:* 90
SIC: 2899
    Mfg chemicals mfg floor & wall tile mfg concrete admixtures
        and pet supplies
C F Weisend, President

D-U-N-S 60-208-9161
THE FULLER BRUSH COMPANY
    (*Parent:* Cpac Inc)
1 Fuller Way, Great Bend, KS 67530
Phone: (316) 792-1711
Sales: $59,400,000   *Employees:* 500
Company Type: Public Family Member   *Employees here:* 350
SIC: 2842
    Mfg specialty cleaning products
Robert C Isaacs, President

D-U-N-S 06-836-9214
G & W ENTERPRISES, INC.
1800 Park Place Ave, Fort Worth, TX 76110
Phone: (817) 926-6811
Sales: $16,000,000   *Employees:* 71
Company Type: Private   *Employees here:* 70
SIC: 2851
    Mfg paints & coatings
W M Gardner, Chief Executive Officer

D-U-N-S 61-681-3853
G-I HOLDINGS INC.
    (*Parent:* Gaf Corporation)
1361 Alps Rd, Wayne, NJ 07470
Phone: (973) 628-3000
Sales: $851,967,000   *Employees:* 4,300
Company Type: Private   *Employees here:* 5
SIC: 2869
    Manufactures specialty chemicals
Samuel J Heyman, Chairman of the Board

D-U-N-S 61-681-3861   EXP
G INDUSTRIES CORP.
    (*Parent:* G-I Holdings Inc)
1361 Alps Rd, Wayne, NJ 07470
Phone: (973) 628-3000
Sales: $1,000,600,000   *Employees:* 4,075
Company Type: Private   *Employees here:* 1
SIC: 2869
    Manufactures specialty chemicals and roofing materials
Samuel J Heyman, Chairman of the Board

D-U-N-S 92-843-8233
G P C SALES INC.
    (*Parent:* Quality King Distributors Inc)
1095 Long Island Ave, Deer Park, NY 11729
Phone: (516) 254-9330
Sales: $20,000,000   *Employees:* 12
Company Type: Private   *Employees here:* 12
SIC: 2844
    Mfg toilet preparations
Jeffrey S Dame, President

D-U-N-S 80-809-5988   EXP
G V C HOLDINGS INC.
1215 Main St, Port Neches, TX 77651
Phone: (409) 722-8321
Sales: $475,000,000   *Employees:* 1,300
Company Type: Private   *Employees here:* 1
SIC: 2822
    Mfr synthetic rubber carbon black & rubber latex
Mahendra Parekh, President

D-U-N-S 14-423-3541   EXP
GAGE CORPORATION
821 Wanda St, Ferndale, MI 48220
Phone: (248) 691-6737
Sales: $26,700,000   *Employees:* 120
Company Type: Private   *Employees here:* 10
SIC: 2869
    Mfg industrial organic solvents
Michael J Gage, Chairman of the Board

D-U-N-S 00-833-0797   EXP
GANS INK AND SUPPLY CO. INC.
1441 Boyd St, Los Angeles, CA 90033
Phone: (323) 264-2200
Sales: $26,032,000   *Employees:* 220
Company Type: Private   *Employees here:* 95
SIC: 2893
    Mfg printing ink
Jeff Koppelman, President

D-U-N-S 06-106-4713
GARD PRODUCTS INC.
250 Williams St, Carpentersville, IL 60110
Phone: (847) 836-7700
Sales: $25,000,000   *Employees:* 65
Company Type: Private   *Employees here:* 65
SIC: 2879
    Mfg for resale post harvest floral preservatives
Howard Klehm Sr, President

D-U-N-S 78-802-1483   EXP
GARD ROGARD, INC.
250 Williams St, Carpentersville, IL 60110
Phone: (847) 836-7700
Sales: $25,000,000   *Employees:* 65
Company Type: Private   *Employees here:* 65
SIC: 2879
    Mfg agricultural chemicals
Howard Klehm Sr, President

D-U-N-S 96-734-2510
GARST SEED COMPANY
2369 330th St, Slater, IA 50244
Phone: (515) 685-5000
Sales: $97,000,000   *Employees:* 400
Company Type: Private   *Employees here:* 200
SIC: 2899
    Mfg corn/processing plant
Colin Seccombe, President

D-U-N-S 18-635-3157   EXP
GAYLORD CHEMICAL CORPORATION
    (Parent: Gaylord Container Corporation)
106 Galeria Blvd, Slidell, LA 70458
Phone: (504) 649-5464
Sales: $20,000,000   *Employees:* 52
Company Type: Public Family Member   *Employees here:* 41
SIC: 2861
    Mfg chemicals
Louis E Zeillmann, Chairman of the Board

D-U-N-S 01-654-3055
GB BIOSCIENCES CORP.
    (Parent: Zeneca Holdings Inc)
1800 Concord Pike, Wilmington, DE 19803
Phone: (302) 886-3000
Sales: $69,200,000   *Employees:* 340
Company Type: Private   *Employees here:* 340
SIC: 2879
    Manufacture agricultural chemicals
Robert Woods, President

D-U-N-S 96-505-5437
GENCORP PERFORMANCE CHEMICAL
83 Authority Dr, Fitchburg, MA 01420
Phone: (978) 342-5831
Sales: $20,000,000   *Employees:* 30
Company Type: Private   *Employees here:* 30
SIC: 2819
    Mfg chemical materials
John Josub, President

D-U-N-S 61-145-4406   EXP
GENENCOR INTERNATIONAL INC.
1870 Winton Rd S, Rochester, NY 14618
Phone: (716) 256-5200
Sales: $293,643,000   *Employees:* 825
Company Type: Private   *Employees here:* 100
SIC: 2869
    Developers and manufacturers of industrial enzymes &
      chemicals
W T Mitchell, President

D-U-N-S 86-101-0742
GENERAL ALUM & CHEMICAL CORP.
1630 Timber Wolf Dr, Holland, OH 43528
Phone: (419) 865-8000
Sales: $29,000,000   *Employees:* 100
Company Type: Private   *Employees here:* 4
SIC: 2819
    Mfg aluminum & ammonium sulfate chemical broker & whol
      chemical equipment
James A Poure, Chairman of the Board

D-U-N-S 00-626-7616   EXP
GENERAL ALUM NEW ENGLAND CORP.
    (Parent: General Alum & Chemical Corp)
1630 Timber Wolf Dr, Holland, OH 43528
Phone: (419) 865-8000
Sales: $16,000,000   *Employees:* 55
Company Type: Private   *Employees here:* 55
SIC: 2819
    Mfr alum sulfate ammonium sulfate aqua amonia &
      speciality chemical & chemical broker
James A Poure, Chairman of the Board

D-U-N-S 15-427-9434   EXP
GENERAL CHEMICAL CORPORATION
    (Parent: New Hampshire Oak Inc)
90 E Halsey Rd, Fl 3, Parsippany, NJ 07054
Phone: (973) 515-0900

Sales: $519,104,000   *Employees:* 1,869
Company Type: Public Family Member   *Employees here:* 160
SIC: 2819
    Mfg industrial chemicals
Richard R Russell, President

D-U-N-S 19-752-2683   EXP
GENERAL CHEMICAL GROUP INC.
1 Liberty Ln, Hampton, NH 03842
Phone: (603) 929-2606
Sales: $652,977,000   *Employees:* 2,402
Company Type: Public   *Employees here:* 10
SIC: 2812
    Mfr soda ash and calcium chloride
Richard R Russel, President

D-U-N-S 13-588-1076
GENERAL COATINGS TECHNOLOGIES
24 Woodward Ave, Ridgewood, NY 11385
Phone: (718) 821-1232
Sales: $16,500,000   *Employees:* 95
Company Type: Private   *Employees here:* 75
SIC: 2851
    Manufactures paints
Michael Ghitelman, President

D-U-N-S 04-454-6182
GENERAL POLYMERIC CORP.
1136 Morgantown Rd, Reading, PA 19607
Phone: (610) 374-5171
Sales: $15,000,000   *Employees:* 62
Company Type: Private   *Employees here:* 62
SIC: 2821
    Mfg porous plastic materials
Joseph E Ferri, President

D-U-N-S 80-170-6748
GENSET CORPORATION
875 Prospect St, Ste 206, La Jolla, CA 92037
Phone: (619) 551-6551
Sales: $16,396,000   *Employees:* 40
Company Type: Private   *Employees here:* 40
SIC: 2899
    Mfg synthetic dna
Pascal Brandys, President

D-U-N-S 80-131-4378
GEO SPECIALTY CHEMICALS INC.
28601 Chagrin Blvd, Cleveland, OH 44122
Phone: (216) 464-5564
Sales: $16,900,000   *Employees:* 100
Company Type: Private   *Employees here:* 3
SIC: 2819
    Mfg aluminum based chemicals
George Ahearn, President

D-U-N-S 80-096-7705   EXP
THE GEON COMPANY
1 Geon Center Moore Rd, Avon Lake, OH 44012
Phone: (440) 930-1000
Sales: $1,250,000,000   *Employees:* 2,000
Company Type: Public   *Employees here:* 582
SIC: 2821
    Manufactures polyvinyl chloride resins and compounds (pvc)
      vinyl chloride monomer ethylene chlorine and caustic soda
William F Patient, Chairman of the Board

D-U-N-S 61-300-0140
GEORGETOWN HOLDING COMPANY
    (Parent: Foseco Holding Inc)
20200 Sheldon Rd, Cleveland, OH 44142
Phone: (440) 826-4548

Sales: $67,900,000   *Employees:* 480
Company Type: Private   *Employees here:* 2
SIC: 2899
    Mfg exothermic compounds & fluxes
Anthony Money, President

D-U-N-S 12-095-7840   EXP
GEORGIA GULF CORPORATION
400 Perimeter Center Ter, Atlanta, GA 30346
Phone: (770) 395-4500
Sales: $875,018,000   *Employees:* 1,041
Company Type: Public   *Employees here:* 45
SIC: 2812
    Mfg commodity & specialty chemicals
Edward A Schmitt, President

D-U-N-S 00-428-4188   EXP
GFS CHEMICALS, INC.
3041 Home Rd, Powell, OH 43065
Phone: (740) 881-5501
Sales: $15,000,000   *Employees:* 70
Company Type: Private   *Employees here:* 25
SIC: 2819
    Mfg reagent & fine grade chemicals
Darrell A Hutchinson, Chief Executive Officer

D-U-N-S 00-316-2435
GILES CHEMICAL CORP.
102 Commerce St, Waynesville, NC 28786
Phone: (828) 452-4784
Sales: $21,908,000   *Employees:* 39
Company Type: Private   *Employees here:* 39
SIC: 2899
    Mfg epsom salt & magnesium sulfate solutions and whol
        magnesium sulfate solutions
Katherine C Bryson, Secretary

D-U-N-S 00-215-6354   EXP
GIVAUDAN-ROURE CORPORATION
    (*Parent:* Roche Holdings Inc)
1199 Edison Dr, Cincinnati, OH 45216
Phone: (513) 948-8000
Sales: $225,000,000   *Employees:* 1,050
Company Type: Private   *Employees here:* 600
SIC: 2869
    Mfg fragrances & flavors
Geoffrey R Webster, President

D-U-N-S 15-133-4422
THE GLIDDEN COMPANY
    (*Parent:* Ici American Holdings Inc)
925 Euclid Ave, Ste 800, Cleveland, OH 44115
Phone: (216) 344-8000
Sales: $1,000,000,000   *Employees:* 4,600
Company Type: Private   *Employees here:* 500
SIC: 2851
    Mfg paints enamels lacquers and varnishes
Denis Wright, President

D-U-N-S 00-416-2038   EXP
GOJO INDUSTRIES INC.
3783 State Rd, Cuyahoga Falls, OH 44223
Phone: (330) 920-8100
Sales: $100,000,000   *Employees:* 275
Company Type: Private   *Employees here:* 275
SIC: 2842
    Mfg skin care products & dispensing systems
Joseph Kanfer, President

D-U-N-S 18-481-3467
GOLDMAN RESOURCES INC.
    (*Parent:* Goldman Financial Group Inc)
1 Post Office Sq 41, Boston, MA 02109

Phone: (617) 338-1200
Sales: $34,600,000   *Employees:* 200
Company Type: Private   *Employees here:* 10
SIC: 2899
    Mfg chemicals
David Goldman, President

D-U-N-S 09-960-5842   EXP
GOLDSCHMIDT CHEMICAL CORP
914 E Randolph Rd, Hopewell, VA 23860
Phone: (804) 541-8658
Sales: $60,100,000   *Employees:* 260
Company Type: Private   *Employees here:* 135
SIC: 2869
    Mfgs & whol industrial chemicals mfgs exothermic welding
        apparatus and welding and specialty contractor
Eberhard D Koska, President

D-U-N-S 00-104-7786   EXP
GOULSTON TECHNOLOGIES INC.
700 N Johnson St, Monroe, NC 28110
Phone: (704) 289-6464
Sales: $62,000,000   *Employees:* 150
Company Type: Private   *Employees here:* 150
SIC: 2843
    Mfg fiber lubricating oils
Sho Hasegawa, Chief Executive Officer

D-U-N-S 80-309-6676
GRACE CHEMICALS, INC.
    (*Parent:* W R Grace & Co)
1750 Clint Moore Rd, Boca Raton, FL 33487
Phone: (561) 362-2000
Sales: $22,100,000   *Employees:* 140
Company Type: Public Family Member   *Employees here:* 140
SIC: 2819
    Mfg industrial inorganic chemicals
Paul Norris, President

D-U-N-S 00-329-2166
GRACO FERTILIZER COMPANY
Alton Hall Rd, Cairo, GA 31728
Phone: (912) 377-1602
Sales: $18,800,000   *Employees:* 75
Company Type: Private   *Employees here:* 75
SIC: 2873
    Mfg dry nitrogenous fertilizer and potting soil
Thomas K Le Gette Jr, President

D-U-N-S 60-503-1541   EXP
GRAHAM WEBB INTERNATIONAL CORP.
2052 Corte Del Nogal, Carlsbad, CA 92009
Phone: (760) 918-3623
Sales: $75,000,000   *Employees:* 150
Company Type: Private   *Employees here:* 42
SIC: 2844
    Mfg hair care products
Robert R Taylor, Chairman of the Board

D-U-N-S 19-848-4180
GRAIN PROCESSING CORPORATION
    (*Parent:* Varied Investments Inc)
1600 Oregon St, Muscatine, IA 52761
Phone: (319) 264-4211
Sales: $189,600,000   *Employees:* 785
Company Type: Private   *Employees here:* 780
SIC: 2869
    Mfg grain alcohol & corn starch
J T Kautz, Chairman of the Board

D-U-N-S 00-830-2960
GRANITIZE PRODUCTS INC.
11022 Vulcan St, South Gate, CA 90280
Phone: (562) 923-5438

Sales: $17,000,000
Company Type: Private
Employees: 70
Employees here: 70
SIC: 2842
  Mfg auto polish & cleaners
Tony Raymondo Sr, President

D-U-N-S 00-521-2808   EXP
GREAT LAKES CHEMICAL CORP
1 Great Lakes Blvd, West Lafayette, IN 47906
Phone: (765) 497-6100
Sales: $1,311,227,000
Company Type: Public
Employees: 5,100
Employees here: 300
SIC: 2819
  Mfg bromine furfural specialty chemicals & alkyl leads
Mark Bulriss, President

D-U-N-S 00-331-1248
GRIFFIN, LLC
2509 Rocky Ford Rd, Valdosta, GA 31601
Phone: (912) 242-8635
Sales: $237,390,000
Company Type: Private
Employees: 800
Employees here: 250
SIC: 2879
  Mfg agricultural crop protection products
R A Griffin Jr, Chairman of the Board

D-U-N-S 03-720-4617
GUEST SUPPLY INC.
4301 US Highway 1, Monmouth Junction, NJ 08852
Phone: (609) 514-7373
Sales: $236,743,000
Company Type: Public
Employees: 642
Employees here: 65
SIC: 2844
  Mfg & whol guest amenities
Paul T Xenis, Secretary

D-U-N-S 60-408-8849
GULBRANDSEN MANUFACTURING INC.
183 Gulbrandsen Rd, Orangeburg, SC 29115
Phone: (803) 531-2413
Sales: $16,100,000
Company Type: Private
Employees: NA
Employees here: NA
SIC: 2869
  Mfg & processing of chemicals
Donald E Gulbrandsen, President

D-U-N-S 92-690-4186
GULF LITE & WIZARD, INC.
2605 Nonconnah Blvd, Memphis, TN 38132
Phone: (901) 395-0119
Sales: $20,000,000
Company Type: Private
Employees: 75
Employees here: 16
SIC: 2899
  Mfg chemical preparations
Mark Hatgas, President

D-U-N-S 00-807-6424
GULF STATES ASPHALT COMPANY
300 Christi Pl, South Houston, TX 77587
Phone: (713) 941-4410
Sales: $20,168,000
Company Type: Private
Employees: 90
Employees here: 65
SIC: 2891
  Mfg sealants adhesives & asphalt paving mixtures
Luis X Pena, Chairman of the Board

D-U-N-S 03-816-2533
GULF STATES SPECIALTIES INC.
  (Parent: Gulf States Asphalt Company)
300 Christi Pl, South Houston, TX 77587
Phone: (713) 941-4410

Sales: $20,168,000
Company Type: Private
Employees: 90
Employees here: 65
SIC: 2891
  Mfg concrete sealants extruded tapes & adhesives
Luis X Pena, President

D-U-N-S 00-624-7167   EXP
GUSTAFSON, INC.
  (Parent: Uniroyal Chemical Company)
1400 Preston Rd, Ste 400, Plano, TX 75093
Phone: (972) 985-8877
Sales: $93,238,000
Company Type: Public Family Member
Employees: 250
Employees here: 55
SIC: 2879
  Mfg seed treating agricultural chemicals
T G Austin, President

D-U-N-S 00-136-0866   EXP
H & R FLORASYNTH
300 North St, Teterboro, NJ 07608
Phone: (201) 288-3200
Sales: $230,000,000
Company Type: Private
Employees: 600
Employees here: 250
SIC: 2899
  Mfg chemical fragrances flavors & essential oils
R L White, Chairman

D-U-N-S 00-615-9776
H B FULLER COMPANY
1200 Willow Lake Blvd, Saint Paul, MN 55110
Phone: (651) 236-5900
Sales: $1,347,241,000
Company Type: Public
Employees: 6,000
Employees here: 100
SIC: 2891
  Mfg adhesives sealants coatings sanitation preparations and
  waxes
Albert P Stroucken, President

D-U-N-S 80-772-2947
H20 PLUS, LP
845 W Madison St, Chicago, IL 60607
Phone: (312) 850-9283
Sales: $20,000,000
Company Type: Private
Employees: 300
Employees here: 60
SIC: 2844
  Mfg whol & ret cosmetic & beauty products
John H Melk, Chief Executive Officer

D-U-N-S 00-214-0804   EXP
HAARMANN & REIMER CORP
  (Parent: Bayer Corporation)
300 North St, Teterboro, NJ 07608
Phone: (201) 288-3200
Sales: $350,000,000
Company Type: Private
Employees: 690
Employees here: 2
SIC: 2899
  Mfg aroma chemicals flavors fragrances and food ingredients
K Birckenstaedt, President

D-U-N-S 00-227-5782   EXP
HAAS CORPORATION
1646 W Chester Pike, West Chester, PA 19382
Phone: (610) 436-9840
Sales: $23,000,000
Company Type: Private
Employees: 40
Employees here: 9
SIC: 2899
  Mfg specialty chemicals
John Fortin, Chief Executive Officer

D-U-N-S 07-787-4162   EXP
HALDOR TOPSOE INC.
17629 El Camino Real, Houston, TX 77058
Phone: (281) 480-2600

Sales: $18,700,000   *Employees:* 133
Company Type: Private   *Employees here:* 71
SIC: 2819
    Mfg chemical catalysts
Erik Vohtz, Executive Vice-President

D-U-N-S 00-421-5224
THE HALL CHEMICAL CO.
    (Parent: Goldman Resources Inc)
28960 Lakeland Blvd, Wickliffe, OH 44092
Phone: (440) 944-8500
Sales: $25,800,000   *Employees:* 150
Company Type: Private   *Employees here:* 100
SIC: 2819
    Mfg inorganic metallic salt
Albert Charbit, President

D-U-N-S 00-607-0239
HALLMAN PAINTS INC.
1717 N Bristol St, Sun Prairie, WI 53590
Phone: (608) 834-8844
Sales: $20,000,000   *Employees:* 90
Company Type: Private   *Employees here:* 45
SIC: 2851
    Mfg & ret paint varnish & allied products
Timothy A Mielcarek, President

D-U-N-S 00-522-6790
HAMMOND GROUP, INC.
1414 Field St Bldg B, Hammond, IN 46320
Phone: (219) 931-9360
Sales: $125,000,000   *Employees:* 270
Company Type: Private   *Employees here:* 33
SIC: 2819
    Mfg lead oxides lead stabilizers & lead acid batteries
W P Wilke Iv, President

D-U-N-S 79-818-9908
HAMPSHIRE CHEMICAL CORP.
    (Parent: Hampshire Holdings Corp)
45 Hayden Ave, Lexington, MA 02421
Phone: (781) 861-9700
Sales: $260,000,000   *Employees:* 750
Company Type: Public Family Member   *Employees here:* 20
SIC: 2869
    Mfg organic chemicals
Jim Mc Ilvenney, President

D-U-N-S 80-132-0177   EXP
HAMPSHIRE HOLDINGS CORP.
    (Parent: The Dow Chemical Company)
55 Hayden Ave, Lexington, MA 02421
Phone: (781) 861-9700
Sales: $260,000,000   *Employees:* 750
Company Type: Public Family Member   *Employees here:* 100
SIC: 2869
    Mfg organic chemicals
James Mc Ilevenny, President

D-U-N-S 00-510-4443
HANDSCHY INDUSTRIES INC.
    (Parent: Field Container Company L P)
120 25th Ave, Bellwood, IL 60104
Phone: (708) 547-9400
Sales: $40,000,000   *Employees:* 154
Company Type: Private   *Employees here:* 100
SIC: 2893
    Mfg printing inks & chemicals
Field Lawrence I, Chief Executive Officer

D-U-N-S 14-706-1592   EXP
HARBOUR GROUP LTD
7701 Forsyth Blvd, Ste 600, Saint Louis, MO 63105

Phone: (314) 727-5550
Sales: $900,000,000   *Employees:* 1,500
Company Type: Private   *Employees here:* 38
SIC: 2822
    Mfg precision mechanical springs & wire forms motor vehicle
    parts plastics industry machinery hot-water cleaning
    equipment
Sam Fox, Chairman of the Board

D-U-N-S 03-241-8311
HARRELL'S INC.
720 Kraft Rd, Lakeland, FL 33815
Phone: (941) 687-2774
Sales: $25,136,000   *Employees:* 54
Company Type: Private   *Employees here:* 53
SIC: 2875
    Mfg fertilizers-mix only
Jack R Harrell Jr, President

D-U-N-S 80-962-9520
HARRIS CHEMICAL NORTH AMERICA,
    (Parent: Imc Inorganic Chemicals Inc)
8300 College Blvd, Shawnee Mission, KS 66210
Phone: (913) 344-9100
Sales: $494,153,000   *Employees:* 2,235
Company Type: Public Family Member   *Employees here:* 188
SIC: 2819
    Mfg industrial inorganic chemicals mfg chemical preparations
Robert E Fowler Jr, Chairman of the Board

D-U-N-S 82-542-0623
HARRIS SPECIALTY CHEMICALS
10245 Centurion Pkwy N, Jacksonville, FL 32256
Phone: (904) 996-6000
Sales: $174,400,000   *Employees:* 790
Company Type: Private   *Employees here:* 110
SIC: 2869
    Holding company
David Fyfe, President

D-U-N-S 00-446-9896
HARRISON PAINT CORP.
1329 Harrison Ave SW, Canton, OH 44706
Phone: (330) 455-5125
Sales: $15,000,000   *Employees:* 139
Company Type: Private   *Employees here:* 90
SIC: 2851
    Mfg paint varnishes & enamels
Roger A Walters, Chairman of the Board

D-U-N-S 78-373-1060
HAWAII CHEMTECT INTERNATIONAL
3452 E Foothill Blvd, Pasadena, CA 91107
Phone: (626) 568-8606
Sales: $20,000,000   *Employees:* 12
Company Type: Private   *Employees here:* 12
SIC: 2899
    Mfg test kits
Robert Goldsmith, President

D-U-N-S 78-972-7997
HC INVESTMENTS, INC.
    (Parent: Henkel Corporation)
2200 Renaissance Blvd, King Of Prussia, PA 19406
Phone: (610) 270-8100
Sales: $536,800,000   *Employees:* 3,400
Company Type: Private   *Employees here:* 10
SIC: 2891
    Mfr adhesives and sealants
John E Knudson, President

D-U-N-S 87-807-1331
HEARTLAND CORN PRODUCTS
Hwy 19 E, Winthrop, MN 55396

Phone: (507) 647-5000
Sales: $23,771,000   *Employees:* 25
Company Type: Private   *Employees here:* 25
SIC: 2869
   Ethanol production and dry grain distillers
Ben Brown, General Manager

D-U-N-S 79-345-3754
HEARTLAND GRN FUELS, LP
38469 133rd St, Aberdeen, SD 57401
Phone: (605) 225-0520
Sales: $19,368,000   *Employees:* 25
Company Type: Private   *Employees here:* 25
SIC: 2869
   Mfg ethanol and feed for livestock
Frank Moore, General Manager

D-U-N-S 00-111-3463   EXP
HEATBATH CORPORATION
107 Front St, Springfield, MA 01151
Phone: (413) 543-3381
Sales: $19,700,000   *Employees:* 115
Company Type: Private   *Employees here:* 37
SIC: 2819
   Mfg industrial inorganic chemicals
Ernest A Walen, President

D-U-N-S 14-491-7333   EXP
HELENE CURTIS INDUSTRIES INC.
   (Parent: Unilever United States Inc)
325 N Wells St, Chicago, IL 60610
Phone: (312) 661-0222
Sales: $1,265,000,000   *Employees:* 2,500
Company Type: Private   *Employees here:* 500
SIC: 2844
   Mfg personal care pdts
Ronald J Gidwitz, President

D-U-N-S 00-128-3944   EXP
HEMPEL COATINGS USA INC.
6901 Cavalcade St, Houston, TX 77028
Phone: (713) 672-6641
Sales: $25,000,000   *Employees:* 80
Company Type: Private   *Employees here:* 62
SIC: 2851
   Mfg marine & industrial paints & coatings
Joel Benetti, Executive Vice-President

D-U-N-S 05-144-1731
HENKEL CORPORATION
   (Parent: Henkel Of America Inc)
2200 Renaissance Blvd, King Of Prussia, PA 19406
Phone: (610) 270-8100
Sales: $2,256,608,000   *Employees:* 8,270
Company Type: Private   *Employees here:* 60
SIC: 2869
   Manufactures specialty chemicals & adhesives
Robert A Lurcott, President

D-U-N-S 05-474-4784
HENKEL OF AMERICA INC.
2200 Renaissance Blvd, King Of Prussia, PA 19406
Phone: (610) 270-8100
Sales: $1,272,857,000   *Employees:* 8,270
Company Type: Private   *Employees here:* 60
SIC: 2869
   Mfr specialty chemicals & adhesives
Dr Harald P Wulff, Chairman of the Board

D-U-N-S 00-848-9452
HENRY THE W W COMPANY
313 W Liberty St, Lancaster, PA 17603
Phone: (717) 396-2642

Sales: $18,700,000   *Employees:* NA
Company Type: Private   *Employees here:* NA
SIC: 2891
   Mfg adhesives
Rick Born, President

D-U-N-S 06-750-3573
HERAEUS-AMERSIL INC.
3473 Satellite Blvd, Duluth, GA 30096
Phone: (770) 623-6000
Sales: $75,100,000   *Employees:* 470
Company Type: Private   *Employees here:* 63
SIC: 2819
   Fabricates fused silica products
Gerhart Vilsmeier, Chairman of the Board

D-U-N-S 94-911-0415
HERBERT'S AMERICA INC.
9800 Genard Rd, Houston, TX 77041
Phone: (713) 939-4000
Sales: $160,000,000   *Employees:* 500
Company Type: Private   *Employees here:* 10
SIC: 2851
   Mfg powder coatings
John R Brvenik, President

D-U-N-S 78-813-7867   EXP
HERBERT'S-O'BRIEN, INC.
   (Parent: Herberts America Inc)
9800 Genard Rd, Houston, TX 77041
Phone: (713) 939-4000
Sales: $110,000,000   *Employees:* 300
Company Type: Private   *Employees here:* 250
SIC: 2851
   Mfg powder coatings
John R Brvenik, President

D-U-N-S 00-125-2840
HERCULES CHEMICAL CO. INC.
111 South St, Passaic, NJ 07055
Phone: (973) 778-5000
Sales: $25,000,000   *Employees:* 80
Company Type: Private   *Employees here:* 80
SIC: 2899
   Mfr chemical specialties
Jay W Fidler, President

D-U-N-S 00-131-5647   EXP
HERCULES INCORPORATED
1313 N Market St, Fl 2, Wilmington, DE 19801
Phone: (302) 594-5000
Sales: $1,866,000,000   *Employees:* 6,834
Company Type: Public   *Employees here:* 542
SIC: 2899
   Mfr speciality industrial organic chemicals
R K Elliott, Chairman of the Board

D-U-N-S 19-667-6134   EXP
HEUCOTECH PL
99 Newbold Rd, Fairless Hills, PA 19030
Phone: (215) 736-0712
Sales: $45,489,000   *Employees:* 70
Company Type: Private   *Employees here:* 70
SIC: 2865
   Mfg color pigment dispersions
Robert W Mihalyi, Chief Financial Officer

D-U-N-S 00-423-5636
HEWITT SOAP CO.
   (Parent: American Safety Razor Company)
333 Linden Ave, Dayton, OH 45403
Phone: (937) 253-1151

Sales: $25,000,000
Employees: 267
Company Type: Public Family Member
Employees here: 247
SIC: 2841
Mfg bar soap
William C Weathersby, Chief Executive Officer

D-U-N-S 60-741-7441
HICKSON DANCHEM CORPORATION
1975 Richmond Blvd, Danville, VA 24540
Phone: (804) 797-8100
Sales: $25,229,000
Employees: 135
Company Type: Private
Employees here: 135
SIC: 2843
Mfg specialty industrial chemicals including textile softeners
Joseph G Ackers, President

D-U-N-S 94-517-4803
HICKSON (USA) CORP.
1955 Lake Park Dr SE, Smyrna, GA 30080
Phone: (770) 801-6600
Sales: $24,900,000
Employees: 156
Company Type: Private
Employees here: 6
SIC: 2899
Holding company
Steve R Wisnewski, Treasurer

D-U-N-S 02-136-6125 EXP
HIGH PLAINS CORPORATION
200 W Douglas Ave, Ste 820, Wichita, KS 67202
Phone: (316) 269-4310
Sales: $84,864,000
Employees: 130
Company Type: Public
Employees here: 9
SIC: 2869
Mfg fuel ethanol
Gary R Smith, Chief Executive Officer

D-U-N-S 00-323-1065 EXP
HIGH POINT CHEMICAL CORP.
243 Woodbine St, High Point, NC 27260
Phone: (336) 884-2214
Sales: $98,714,000
Employees: 211
Company Type: Private
Employees here: 182
SIC: 2843
Mfg surface active agents and textile auxiliary processing
chemicals
Harvey Lowd, President

D-U-N-S 02-997-9804
HILLYARD ENTERPRISES, INC.
302 N 4th St, Saint Joseph, MO 64501
Phone: (816) 233-1321
Sales: $16,200,000
Employees: 160
Company Type: Private
Employees here: 5
SIC: 2842
Mfg cleaning & polishing chemicals
James Carolus, President

D-U-N-S 00-231-7506
HITACHI CHEMICAL DUPONT MICRO
Lancaster Ave Rr 141, Wilmington, DE 19805
Phone: (302) 892-0598
Sales: $21,100,000
Employees: 100
Company Type: Private
Employees here: 100
SIC: 2821
Mfg plastic materials/resins
William Speri, President

D-U-N-S 00-132-6073 EXP
HNA HOLDINGS, INC.
(*Parent:* Hoechst Corporation)
30 Independence Blvd, Warren, NJ 07059
Phone: (908) 231-2000

Sales: $6,166,000,000
Employees: 22,200
Company Type: Private
Employees here: 200
SIC: 2824
Mfr fibers film organic and inorganic chemicals specialty &
industrial pdts & pharmaceuticals
Knut Zeptner, President

D-U-N-S 01-899-3985
HODGSON PROCESS CHEMICALS
7760 S 6th St, Oak Creek, WI 53154
Phone: (414) 764-3200
Sales: $30,000,000
Employees: 65
Company Type: Private
Employees here: 40
SIC: 2842
Mfg leather finishes & colors mfg industrial organic and
inorganic chemicals
Ian J Mcclelland, President

D-U-N-S 09-741-3462 EXP
HOECHST CORPORATION
30 Independence Blvd, Warren, NJ 07059
Phone: (908) 231-2000
Sales: $6,876,000,000
Employees: 29,200
Company Type: Private
Employees here: 1,200
SIC: 2824
Mfg fibers film organic & inorganic chemicals specialty &
industrial products & pharmaceuticals
K Schmieder, Chairman of the Board

D-U-N-S 05-388-6479
HOFFMAN PLASTIC COMPOUNDS
16616 Garfield Ave, Paramount, CA 90723
Phone: (323) 636-3346
Sales: $26,000,000
Employees: 65
Company Type: Private
Employees here: 51
SIC: 2821
Mfg polyvinyl chloride compounds
Ronald P Hoffman, President

D-U-N-S 15-343-7264 EXP
HOLLAND COLORS AMERICAS INC.
1501 Progress Dr, Richmond, IN 47374
Phone: (765) 935-0329
Sales: $16,000,000
Employees: 70
Company Type: Private
Employees here: 70
SIC: 2865
Mfg color pigments for plastics
Gert-Hein De Herr, President

D-U-N-S 03-356-0640
HOLOX USA BV
PO Box 6100, Norcross, GA 30091
Phone: (770) 925-4640
Sales: $200,000,000
Employees: 1,000
Company Type: Private
Employees here: 50
SIC: 2813
Whol compressed gases and welding equipment and supplies
Brian P Haley, President

D-U-N-S 83-025-1062
HOLTRACHEM MANUFACTURING CO., LLC
5 Strathmore Rd, Natick, MA 01760
Phone: (508) 655-2510
Sales: $42,000,000
Employees: 150
Company Type: Private
Employees here: 4
SIC: 2812
Distributor of chlorine caustic soda & muriatic acid
Mark Conley, Chief Financial Officer

D-U-N-S 01-010-2788 EXP
HOSTMANN-STEINBERG INC.
4825 Jennings Ln, Louisville, KY 40218
Phone: (502) 968-5961

Sales: $25,000,000   *Employees:* 118
Company Type: Private   *Employees here:* 36
SIC: 2893
  Mfg printing ink
Winfred Gleue, Chairman of the Board

D-U-N-S 00-226-1535   EXP
HOUGHTON INTERNATIONAL INC.
Madison & Van Buren Ave, Valley Forge, PA 19481
Phone: (610) 666-4000
Sales: $271,645,000   *Employees:* 1,400
Company Type: Private   *Employees here:* 145
SIC: 2869
  Mfg specialty chemicals
William F Macdonald Jr, Chairman of the Board

D-U-N-S 95-643-5119
HOUSTON KIK INC.
2921 Corder St, Houston, TX 77054
Phone: (713) 747-8710
Sales: $35,000,000   *Employees:* 140
Company Type: Private   *Employees here:* 140
SIC: 2842
  Mfg bleach
David Cynamon, President

D-U-N-S 00-621-0728
HOWARD JOHNSON'S ENTERPRISES
700 W Virginia St, Ste 222, Milwaukee, WI 53204
Phone: (414) 276-4656
Sales: $26,000,000   *Employees:* 70
Company Type: Private   *Employees here:* 20
SIC: 2875
  Mfg fertilizers (mixing only) & ice melting compounds
Mark Johnson, Chief Executive Officer

D-U-N-S 01-736-3917
HPD LABORATORIES INC.
  (*Parent:* Morningside Capital Group)
379 Thornall St, Ste 15, Edison, NJ 08837
Phone: (732) 452-1077
Sales: $75,000,000   *Employees:* 100
Company Type: Private   *Employees here:* 14
SIC: 2842
  Manufacturer of household products
William Mooar, Chief Executive Officer

D-U-N-S 16-092-2753
HSC HOLDINGS INC.
  (*Parent:* Harris Specialty Chemicals)
10245 Centurion Pkwy N, Jacksonville, FL 32256
Phone: (904) 996-6000
Sales: $124,300,000   *Employees:* 790
Company Type: Private   *Employees here:* 110
SIC: 2891
  Holding company
David Fyfe, President

D-U-N-S 78-261-9647
HUDSON TECHNOLOGIES, INC.
275 Middleton Rd, Pearl River, NY 10965
Phone: (914) 735-6000
Sales: $23,005,000   *Employees:* 130
Company Type: Public   *Employees here:* 35
SIC: 2869
  Recovery & reclamation of refrigerants
Kevin J Zugibe, Chief Executive Officer

D-U-N-S 07-093-1480   EXP
HUISH DETERGENTS INC.
3540 W 1987 S, Salt Lake City, UT 84104
Phone: (801) 975-3100

Sales: $300,000,000   *Employees:* 1,300
Company Type: Private   *Employees here:* 614
SIC: 2841
  Mfg detergents
Paul Huish, President

D-U-N-S 78-270-9307   EXP
HUMAN PHEROMONE SCIENCES, INC.
4034 Clipper Ct, Fremont, CA 94538
Phone: (510) 226-6874
Sales: $17,170,000   *Employees:* 15
Company Type: Public   *Employees here:* 15
SIC: 2844
  Mfg fragrances
William P Horgan, Chief Executive Officer

D-U-N-S 07-835-4818
HUNTSMAN CHEMICAL CORPORATION
500 Huntsman Way, Salt Lake City, UT 84108
Phone: (801) 584-5700
Sales: $1,203,548,000   *Employees:* 1,600
Company Type: Private   *Employees here:* 60
SIC: 2821
  Mfg styrene monomer polystyrene resins and compounded
    plastics
Jon M Huntsman, Chairman of the Board

D-U-N-S 83-469-7377
HUNTSMAN CORPORATION
500 Huntsman Way, Salt Lake City, UT 84108
Phone: (801) 584-5700
Sales: $3,568,128,000   *Employees:* 7,486
Company Type: Private   *Employees here:* 80
SIC: 2821
  Holding company
Jon M Huntsman, Chairman of the Board

D-U-N-S 00-739-8357
HUNTSMAN POLYMERS CORPORATION
  (*Parent:* Huntsman Corporation)
500 Huntsman Way, Salt Lake City, UT 84108
Phone: (801) 584-5700
Sales: $419,420,000   *Employees:* 1,320
Company Type: Public   *Employees here:* 119
SIC: 2821
  Mfg polyethylene polypropylene styrene & plastic film
    packaging
Jon M Huntsman, Chief Executive Officer

D-U-N-S 06-267-3454
HURON TECH CORP.
2957 Old Hwy 87 Rd, Delco, NC 28436
Phone: (910) 655-3845
Sales: $80,000,000   *Employees:* 130
Company Type: Private   *Employees here:* 30
SIC: 2812
  Mfg chemicals for pulp bleaching and pulp mill machinery
R E Loftfield, Chairman of the Board

D-U-N-S 09-873-6887
HYDRO/KIRBY AGRI SERVICES
500 Running Pump Rd, Lancaster, PA 17601
Phone: (717) 299-2541
Sales: $25,000,000   *Employees:* 53
Company Type: Private   *Employees here:* 30
SIC: 2875
  Mixing of fertilizer & whol fertilizers & agricultural
    chemicals
Carroll Kirby Jr, President

D-U-N-S 78-797-2835
I C I EXPLOSIVES USA, INC.
3078 Cnty Rd 180 Cedar Rd, Joplin, MO 64801

Phone: (417) 624-0212
Sales: $92,600,000   *Employees:* 800
Company Type: Private   *Employees here:* 200
SIC: 2892
    Mfg commercial explosives
Paul M Wilson, President

D-U-N-S 96-928-5162
I C I PAINTS (PUERTO RICO)
    (Parent: Ici American Holdings Inc)
65th Inf Rd Km 13 Hm 4, Carolina, PR 00987
Phone: (787) 758-9222
Sales: $40,000,000   *Employees:* 100
Company Type: Private   *Employees here:* 100
SIC: 2851
    Mfg paints
Steve Dearborn, President

D-U-N-S 00-839-1815
I P S CORPORATION
17109 S Main St, Gardena, CA 90248
Phone: (310) 366-3300
Sales: $46,900,000   *Employees:* 300
Company Type: Private   *Employees here:* 140
SIC: 2891
    Mfg plastic & cement adhesives and plumbing installation
        boxes
Wat H Tyler, Chairman of the Board

D-U-N-S 78-296-9844   EXP
ICHAUWAY MILLS, INC.
4535 Simonton Rd, Dallas, TX 75244
Phone: (972) 661-5133
Sales: $20,000,000   *Employees:* 14
Company Type: Private   *Employees here:* 14
SIC: 2844
    Mfg home houseware/homefurnishing health care skin care
        cosmetics orthopedic related products
Robert A Inman Jr, President

D-U-N-S 79-867-2218   EXP
ICI AMERICAN HOLDINGS INC.
3411 Silverside Rd, Wilmington, DE 19810
Phone: (302) 887-3000
Sales: $4,004,237,000   *Employees:* 14,800
Company Type: Private   *Employees here:* 500
SIC: 2851
    Mfr paint and related products acrylics starches adhesives
        polyurethanes and other bulk chemicals
John R Danzeisen, Chairman of the Board

D-U-N-S 79-786-5540   EXP
ICI AMERICAS INC.
    (Parent: Ici American Holdings Inc)
3411 Silverside Rd, Wilmington, DE 19810
Phone: (302) 887-3000
Sales: $1,422,900,000   *Employees:* 6,500
Company Type: Private   *Employees here:* 500
SIC: 2821
    Mfg surfactants polyurethanes and chemicals and polymers
John R Danzeisen, Chairman of the Board

D-U-N-S 02-365-5306
ILPEA INC.
3333 Zero St, Fort Smith, AR 72908
Phone: (501) 646-4535
Sales: $40,100,000   *Employees:* 200
Company Type: Private   *Employees here:* 135
SIC: 2821
    Mfg plastic materials/resins
Paolo Cittadini, President

D-U-N-S 13-079-1965   EXP
IMC AGRIBUSINESS INC.
    (Parent: Vigoro Corporation)
6 Executive Dr, Collinsville, IL 62234
Phone: (618) 346-7300
Sales: $873,000,000   *Employees:* 2,000
Company Type: Public Family Member   *Employees here:* 98
SIC: 2873
    Mfg mixes and retails fertilizer
Robert Van Patten, President

D-U-N-S 17-765-7095   EXP
IMC GLOBAL INC.
2100 Sanders Rd, Ste 200, Northbrook, IL 60062
Phone: (847) 272-9200
Sales: $2,988,600,000   *Employees:* 8,950
Company Type: Public   *Employees here:* 38
SIC: 2874
    Produces phosphatic chemicals & mixed fertilizers mines
        potash & phosphatic rock & recovers uranium oxide
Robert E Fowler Jr, Chairman of the Board

D-U-N-S 60-760-5227
IMC GLOBAL OPERATIONS
    (Parent: Imc Global Inc)
2100 Sanders Rd, Ste 200, Northbrook, IL 60062
Phone: (847) 272-9200
Sales: $2,105,700,000   *Employees:* 5,976
Company Type: Public Family Member   *Employees here:* 35
SIC: 2874
    Mfg fertilizer products
Wendell Bueche, Chairman of the Board

D-U-N-S 84-920-7956
IMC INORGANIC CHEMICALS INC.
    (Parent: Imc Global Inc)
8300 College Blvd, Shawnee Mission, KS 66210
Phone: (913) 344-9100
Sales: $700,000,000   *Employees:* 2,235
Company Type: Public Family Member   *Employees here:* 188
SIC: 2819
    Mfg industrial inorganic chemicals & chemical preparations
J B James, Vice-President

D-U-N-S 17-479-4883
IMC NITROGEN COMPANY
    (Parent: Vigoro Corporation)
16675 Hwy 20 W, East Dubuque, IL 61025
Phone: (815) 747-3101
Sales: $33,900,000   *Employees:* 131
Company Type: Public Family Member   *Employees here:* 131
SIC: 2873
    Mfg nitrogenous fertilizer
Robert M Van Patten, President

D-U-N-S 11-894-0279   EXP
IMC SALT INC.
    (Parent: Namsco Inc)
8300 College Blvd, Shawnee Mission, KS 66210
Phone: (913) 344-9100
Sales: $146,211,000   *Employees:* 1,237
Company Type: Public Family Member   *Employees here:* 76
SIC: 2899
    Processes & mines salt
Robert F Clark, President

D-U-N-S 04-161-6806
IMMIX ELASTOMERS, LLC
85 Winter St, Hanover, MA 02339
Phone: (781) 826-5600

Sales: $33,880,000   *Employees:* 80
Company Type: Private   *Employees here:* 50
SIC: 2822
   Mfg specialty rubber and silicone compounds
Mark S Stevens, Finance

D-U-N-S 00-425-1427
IMPERIAL ADHESIVES INC.
   (Parent: Ns Group Inc)
6315 Wiehe Rd, Cincinnati, OH 45237
Phone: (513) 351-1300
Sales: $40,600,000   *Employees:* 210
Company Type: Public Family Member   *Employees here:* 125
SIC: 2891
   Mfr industrial adhesives sealants & caulks
Robert J Johnson, President

D-U-N-S 00-749-2085
IMPERIAL INC.
   (Parent: Cenex/Land Olakes Agronomy Co)
1102 6th Ave, Shenandoah, IA 51601
Phone: (712) 246-2150
Sales: $18,315,000   *Employees:* 90
Company Type: Private   *Employees here:* 12
SIC: 2879
   Mfg of agricultural pesticides herbicides and insecticides
Maury Gulbranson, Vice-President

D-U-N-S 00-135-5395
IMPORTERS SERVICE CORP.
215 Suydam Ave 33, Jersey City, NJ 07304
Phone: (201) 332-6970
Sales: $15,000,000   *Employees:* 40
Company Type: Private   *Employees here:* 40
SIC: 2861
   Mfg water soluble gums
Eric Berliner, President

D-U-N-S 01-136-3913
INCHEM HOLDINGS
800 Celriver Rd, Rock Hill, SC 29730
Phone: (803) 329-8000
Sales: $15,500,000   *Employees:* 78
Company Type: Private   *Employees here:* 3
SIC: 2821
   Holding company
Kenneth Schofield, Chief Executive Officer

D-U-N-S 00-151-9230
INDOPCO INC.
   (Parent: Ici American Holdings Inc)
10 Finderne Ave, Bridgewater, NJ 08807
Phone: (908) 685-5000
Sales: $2,770,000,000   *Employees:* 7,700
Company Type: Private   *Employees here:* 1,000
SIC: 2891
   Mfg adhesives & sealants industrial & food specialty starches
   & synthetic polymers organic chemicals fragrances & flavors
James A Kennedy, Chairman of the Board

D-U-N-S 19-720-4290
INDSPEC CHEMICAL CORPORATION
   (Parent: Indspec Technologies Ltd)
411 7th Ave, Ste 300, Pittsburgh, PA 15219
Phone: (412) 765-1200
Sales: $124,000,000   *Employees:* 378
Company Type: Private   *Employees here:* 25
SIC: 2865
   Mfg chemicals
Frank M Spinola, President

D-U-N-S 82-523-5393
INDSPEC HOLDING CORPORATION
411 7th Ave, Ste 300, Pittsburgh, PA 15219
Phone: (412) 765-1200
Sales: $76,000,000   *Employees:* 378
Company Type: Private   *Employees here:* 25
SIC: 2865
   Mfg
Frank M Spinola, President

D-U-N-S 93-350-7774
INDSPEC TECHNOLOGIES LTD.
   (Parent: Indspec Holding Corporation)
411 7th Ave, Ste 300, Pittsburgh, PA 15219
Phone: (412) 765-1200
Sales: $76,000,000   *Employees:* 378
Company Type: Private   *Employees here:* 1
SIC: 2865
   Holding company
Frank M Spinola, President

D-U-N-S 80-964-2762
INNE DISPENSABLES INC.
   (Parent: Winstar Global Products Inc)
12 Gardner Rd, Fairfield, NJ 07004
Phone: (973) 227-2700
Sales: $30,000,000   *Employees:* 60
Company Type: Public Family Member   *Employees here:* 60
SIC: 2844
   Manufactures bath & body products
Malcolm Julien, President

D-U-N-S 05-976-6675   EXP
INOLEX CHEMICAL COMPANY
   (Parent: Inolex Group Inc)
Jackson & Swanson Sts, Philadelphia, PA 19148
Phone: (215) 271-0800
Sales: $31,600,000   *Employees:* 135
Company Type: Private   *Employees here:* 131
SIC: 2821
   Mfg polyesters proteins synthetic dyes & monoesters
Conrad A Plimpton, Chairman of the Board

D-U-N-S 15-397-4555   EXP
INOLEX GROUP INC.
Jackson & Swanson Sts, Philadelphia, PA 19148
Phone: (215) 271-0800
Sales: $31,600,000   *Employees:* 135
Company Type: Private   *Employees here:* 4
SIC: 2821
   Mfg polyesters & esters
Conrad A Plimpton, Chairman of the Board

D-U-N-S 00-200-1766
INSL-X PRODUCTS CORP.
50 Holt Dr, Stony Point, NY 10980
Phone: (914) 786-5000
Sales: $19,800,000   *Employees:* 125
Company Type: Private   *Employees here:* 100
SIC: 2851
   Mfg paints
James Weil, President

D-U-N-S 00-316-1668   EXP
INSPEC USA, INC.
   (Parent: Inspec Group Inc)
Jay Hawk Plant, Galena, KS 66739
Phone: (316) 783-1321
Sales: $46,796,000   *Employees:* 172
Company Type: Private   *Employees here:* 165
SIC: 2869
   Mfg specialty industrial organic chemicals
Derek Warner, Chairman of the Board

D-U-N-S 83-025-0197

INTERCAT-SAVANNAH INC.
(*Parent:* Intercat Inc)
104 Union Ave, Manasquan, NJ 08736
Phone: (732) 223-4644
Sales: $28,205,000
Company Type: Private
SIC: 2819
   Mfg catalysts
Regis B Lippert, President

Employees: 68
Employees here: 65

D-U-N-S 07-321-5097   EXP

INTERCIT, INC.
(*Parent:* Firmenich Incorporated)
1585 10th St S, Safety Harbor, FL 34695
Phone: (727) 725-1678
Sales: $32,000,000
Company Type: Private
SIC: 2899
   Mfg of citrus oils
Beverly Bateman, General Manager

Employees: 70
Employees here: 70

D-U-N-S 92-608-9855

INTERCONTINENTAL POLYMER INC.
4999 Inca Hwy, Morristown, TN 37813
Phone: (423) 586-1887
Sales: $56,000,000
Company Type: Private
SIC: 2821
   Mfg polyester pbt and pet chips bicomponent staple and 100
     staple
N S Jagannathan, President

Employees: 163
Employees here: 160

D-U-N-S 78-373-5855

INTERNATIONAL ACADEMY
13177 Foothill Blvd, Sylmar, CA 91342
Phone: (818) 361-7724
Sales: $28,800,000
Company Type: Private
SIC: 2869
   Research & development & mfg amusement machines
Sam Cordova, President

Employees: 123
Employees here: 17

D-U-N-S 11-878-4057

INTERNATIONAL CHEMICAL CORP.
55 Woodridge Dr, Amherst, NY 14228
Phone: (716) 689-4600
Sales: $15,000,000
Company Type: Private
SIC: 2819
   Mfg chemical specialties
Gary Robinson, President

Employees: 175
Employees here: 88

D-U-N-S 02-870-9371

INTERNATIONAL FUEL CELLS, LLC
195 Governors Hwy, South Windsor, CT 06074
Phone: (860) 727-2200
Sales: $24,000,000
Company Type: Private
SIC: 2869
   Fuel sell power plant developmentmfg cust support
Robert Suttmiller, President

Employees: 99
Employees here: 99

D-U-N-S 00-638-2253

INTERNATIONAL PAINT INC.
(*Parent:* Akzo Nobel Courtaulds Us Inc)
6001 Antoine Dr, Houston, TX 77091
Phone: (713) 682-1711

Sales: $114,300,000
Company Type: Private
SIC: 2851
   Mfg and sale of paints and coatings distributor of
     wallcoverings and sundry items(100)
Jon Bradley, President

Employees: 750
Employees here: 260

D-U-N-S 96-437-8459   EXP

INTERNATIONAL SPECIALTY PRODUCTS
1361 Alps Rd, Wayne, NJ 07470
Phone: (973) 628-3000
Sales: $749,200,000
Company Type: Private
SIC: 2869
   Manufactures specialty derivative chemicals mines and
     processes roofing granules & manufactures filters
Samuel J Heyman, Chairman of the Board

Employees: 2,500
Employees here: 100

D-U-N-S 00-153-4833   EXP

INTERNTONAL FLAVORS FRAGRANCES
521 W 57th St, New York, NY 10019
Phone: (212) 765-5500
Sales: $1,426,791,000
Company Type: Public
SIC: 2869
   Create & manufacture fragrances & flavors
Eugene P Grisanti, Chairman of the Board

Employees: 4,600
Employees here: 425

D-U-N-S 00-615-1336   EXP

INTERPLASTIC CORPORATION
1225 Willow Lake Blvd, Saint Paul, MN 55110
Phone: (651) 481-6860
Sales: $250,000,000
Company Type: Private
SIC: 2821
   Mfg resins and whol chemicals
James D Wallenfelsz, President

Employees: 330
Employees here: 40

D-U-N-S 04-169-9919

INTERPOLYMER CORP.
200 Dan Rd, Canton, MA 02021
Phone: (781) 828-7120
Sales: $22,000,000
Company Type: Private
SIC: 2821
   Mfg thermoplastic materials
Norwin W Wolff, President

Employees: 50
Employees here: 25

D-U-N-S 10-912-3406   EXP

INTERTECH GROUP INC.
4838 Jenkins Ave, North Charleston, SC 29405
Phone: (843) 744-5174
Sales: $2,564,500,000
Company Type: Private
SIC: 2819
   Holding company (see operation for subsidiary activities)
Jerry Zucker, Chairman of the Board

Employees: 15,832
Employees here: 16

D-U-N-S 18-870-5818   EXP

THE INX GROUP LIMITED
651 Bonnie Ln, Elk Grove Village, IL 60007
Phone: (847) 981-9399
Sales: $306,339,000
Company Type: Private
SIC: 2893
   Mfg printing inks
Toshihiko Tohno, President

Employees: 1,550
Employees here: 3

D-U-N-S 00-510-3528   EXP

INX INTERNATIONAL INK COMPANY
(*Parent:* The Inx Group Limited)
651 Bonnie Ln, Elk Grove Village, IL 60007
Phone: (847) 981-9399

Sales: $264,963,000
Company Type: Private
SIC: 2893
    Mfg printing inks
Frank Moravec, President

Employees: 1,380
Employees here: 53

D-U-N-S 00-528-5317
IOWA PAINT MANUFACTURING CO. INC.
1625 Grand Ave, Des Moines, IA 50309
Phone: (515) 283-1501
Sales: $36,060,000
Company Type: Private
SIC: 2851
    Mfg paint
Thomas Goldman, President

Employees: 250
Employees here: 75

D-U-N-S 03-175-4740
IPI INTERNATIONAL INC.
    (Parent: P M C Inc)
505 Blue Ball Rd Bldg 30, Elkton, MD 21921
Phone: (410) 392-4800
Sales: $36,900,000
Company Type: Private
SIC: 2869
    Manufacturer of organic chemicals
Gary Kamins, President

Employees: 156
Employees here: 36

D-U-N-S 10-151-7290   EXP
ISK AMERICAS INC.
    (Parent: Zeneca Holdings Inc)
7474 Auburn Rd, Mentor, OH 44060
Phone: (440) 357-4620
Sales: $369,066,000
Company Type: Private
SIC: 2879
    Mfg agricultural & specialty chemicals & research &
    development
Frank S Barry, Executive Vice-President

Employees: 800
Employees here: 12

D-U-N-S 60-937-1182
ISOCHEM COLORS INC.
474 Bryant Blvd, Rock Hill, SC 29732
Phone: (803) 325-7640
Sales: $15,000,000
Company Type: Private
SIC: 2865
    Mfg dyes
Rudolf Heer, President

Employees: 45
Employees here: 45

D-U-N-S 00-218-8894   EXP
ISP CHEMICALS INC.
    (Parent: International Specialty Pdts)
455 N Main St, Calvert City, KY 42029
Phone: (502) 395-4165
Sales: $158,700,000
Company Type: Private
SIC: 2869
    Mfg industrial organic chemicals
Samuel J Heyman, Chairman of the Board

Employees: 660
Employees here: 600

D-U-N-S 79-696-1290
ISP GLOBAL TECHNOLOGIES, INC.
    (Parent: International Specialty Pdts)
1361 Alps Rd, Wayne, NJ 07470
Phone: (973) 628-3000
Sales: $27,000,000
Company Type: Private
SIC: 2869
    Holding company
Samuel J Heyman, Chairman of the Board

Employees: 100
Employees here: 1

D-U-N-S 85-848-5519
IT HOLDING INC.
    (Parent: Marsulex Inc)
Highway 68, Copperhill, TN 37317
Phone: (423) 496-3331
Sales: $52,000,000
Company Type: Private
SIC: 2819
    Mfg and whol sulfuric acid and ferric sulfate
William F Mason, President

Employees: 327
Employees here: 20

D-U-N-S 80-500-4462
J B WILLIAMS CO. INC.
    (Parent: J B Williams Holdings Inc)
65 Harristown Rd, Glen Rock, NJ 07452
Phone: (201) 251-8100
Sales: $63,868,000
Company Type: Private
SIC: 2844
    Mfg personal care items oral care products & bar & liquid
    specialty soap products
Dario Margve, President

Employees: 45
Employees here: 45

D-U-N-S 88-493-4456
J B WILLIAMS HOLDINGS INC.
    (Parent: Brynwood Partners I Lp)
65 Harristown Rd, Glen Rock, NJ 07452
Phone: (201) 251-8100
Sales: $63,868,000
Company Type: Private
SIC: 2844
    Mfg men's' personal care items & oral care products
Dario Margve, President

Employees: 45
Employees here: 39

D-U-N-S 03-901-0483
J F DALEY INTERNATIONAL LTD.
5301 S Cicero Ave, Ste 209, Chicago, IL 60632
Phone: (773) 284-9189
Sales: $18,300,000
Company Type: Private
SIC: 2842
    Mfg specialty cleaning & polishing preparations including
    floor waxes
John F Daley, President

Employees: 150
Employees here: 80

D-U-N-S 92-616-0227
J L M CHEMICALS INC.
    (Parent: J L M Industries Inc)
3350 131st St, Blue Island, IL 60406
Phone: (708) 388-9373
Sales: $43,673,000
Company Type: Public Family Member
SIC: 2865
    Mfg chemicals
Wilf Kimball, President

Employees: 52
Employees here: 52

D-U-N-S 88-449-0418
J L S INV GROUP - WP, LLC
4101 County M, Middleton, WI 53562
Phone: (608) 238-2855
Sales: $19,800,000
Company Type: Private
SIC: 2879
    Mfg leisure time & cleaning products
Jay L Smith, Member

Employees: 92
Employees here: 1

D-U-N-S 08-662-5654
J M PRODUCTS INC.
2501 S State St, Ste 400, Little Rock, AR 72206
Phone: (501) 371-0040

Sales: $29,000,000   *Employees:* 110
Company Type: Private   *Employees here:* 15
SIC: 2844
    Mfg hair care products
Ernest P Joshua Sr, Chairman of the Board

D-U-N-S 18-205-4890
J P INDUSTRIAL PRODUCTS INC.
11988 State Route 45, Lisbon, OH 44432
Phone: (330) 424-1110
Sales: $15,000,000   *Employees:* 33
Company Type: Private   *Employees here:* 12
SIC: 2821
    Mfg raw plastics & broker of wood pallets
James Pastore, President

D-U-N-S 55-630-8518
J-VON NA, LLC
25 Litchfield St, Leominster, MA 01453
Phone: (978) 537-4721
Sales: $24,860,000   *Employees:* 55
Company Type: Private   *Employees here:* 55
SIC: 2821
    Mfg plastic materials/resins
Daniel Hunter, Member

D-U-N-S 09-277-8182   EXP
JACOBS INDUSTRIES INCORPORATED
100 S 5th St, Ste 2500, Minneapolis, MN 55402
Phone: (612) 339-9500
Sales: $56,200,000   *Employees:* 440
Company Type: Private   *Employees here:* 1
SIC: 2841
    Mfg household detergents cleansers flavor extracts spices
    health prod whol printing trades mach & franchises print
    units
Gerald A Schwalbach, President

D-U-N-S 04-167-6479   EXP
JAFRA COSMETICS INTERNATIONAL
2451 Townsgate Rd, Thousand Oaks, CA 91361
Phone: (805) 449-2999
Sales: $38,600,000   *Employees:* 330
Company Type: Private   *Employees here:* 300
SIC: 2844
    Mfg cosmetics
Ron Clark, Chairman of the Board

D-U-N-S 00-434-0923
JAMES AUSTIN CO.
115 Downieville Rd, Mars, PA 16046
Phone: (724) 625-1535
Sales: $30,000,000   *Employees:* 175
Company Type: Private   *Employees here:* 150
SIC: 2842
    Mfg household cleaning preparations & soap cleaners
Harry G Austin III, President

D-U-N-S 78-174-6284
JDR & ASSOCIATES INC.
3122 Maple St, Santa Ana, CA 92707
Phone: (714) 751-7086
Sales: $17,100,000   *Employees:* 85
Company Type: Private   *Employees here:* 85
SIC: 2821
    Plastic mold builder
Ernesto Rodriguez, President

D-U-N-S 16-113-5447   IMP EXP
JEAN PHILIPPE FRAGRANCES, INC.
551 5th Ave, Rm 1500, New York, NY 10176
Phone: (212) 983-2640

Sales: $91,462,000   *Employees:* 97
Company Type: Public   *Employees here:* 38
SIC: 2844
    Mfg & distributes fragrances & cosmetics
Jean Madar, Chairman of the Board

D-U-N-S 06-248-5891
JEWEL CHEMICAL CO.
5483 N Northwest Hwy, Chicago, IL 60630
Phone: (773) 465-4737
Sales: $15,500,000   *Employees:* 150
Company Type: Private   *Employees here:* 150
SIC: 2841
    Mfg soap/other detergents
Arnold Janowitz, Owner

D-U-N-S 62-655-9892
JFO, LTD.
3785 E Cedar Ave, Denver, CO 80209
Phone: (303) 980-7377
Sales: $22,400,000   *Employees:* 200
Company Type: Private   *Employees here:* 100
SIC: 2842
    Mfg metal polish buffs polish wheels & chemicals
John Olmstead, President

D-U-N-S 03-924-4694   EXP
JOHANN HALTERMANN LTD.
16717 Jacintoport Blvd, Houston, TX 77015
Phone: (281) 452-5951
Sales: $31,900,000   *Employees:* 130
Company Type: Private   *Employees here:* 130
SIC: 2869
    Processes & distills organic chemicals
Simon Upfill-Brown, President

D-U-N-S 00-215-9507
JOHN C DOLPH COMPANY
320 New Rd, Monmouth Junction, NJ 08852
Phone: (732) 329-2333
Sales: $20,000,000   *Employees:* 50
Company Type: Private   *Employees here:* 50
SIC: 2851
    Mfg insulating varnishes and epoxy resins
John D Mayes, President

D-U-N-S 03-818-5518   EXP
JOHN PAUL MITCHELL SYSTEMS
26455 Golden Valley Rd, Santa Clarita, CA 91350
Phone: (661) 298-0400
Sales: $100,000,000   *Employees:* 90
Company Type: Private   *Employees here:* 50
SIC: 2844
    Mfg & whol hair preparations
John P Dejoria, Chairman of the Board

D-U-N-S 84-936-4195
JOHNSON & JOHNSON CONSUMER CO. PR
    (Parent: Johnson & Johnson)
Km 20 3 Rr 183, Las Piedras, PR 00771
Phone: (787) 733-8220
Sales: $53,000,000   *Employees:* 450
Company Type: Public Family Member   *Employees here:* 450
SIC: 2844
    Mfg dental floss
Collin Goggins, President

D-U-N-S 00-409-7580
JOHNSON PAINTS INC.
2131 Andrea Ln, Fort Myers, FL 33912
Phone: (941) 489-2332

Sales: $18,000,000   *Employees:* 110
Company Type: Private   *Employees here:* 40
SIC: 2851
  Mfg & ret paint
Sam Johnson, President

D-U-N-S 00-520-1082   EXP
JOHNSON PRODUCTS CO. INC.
  (*Parent:* Carson Inc)
8522 S Lafayette Ave, Chicago, IL 60620
Phone: (773) 483-4100
Sales: $50,000,000   *Employees:* 252
Company Type: Public Family Member   *Employees here:* 238
SIC: 2844
  Mfg hair care products and distributes cosmetics
Brian Willhoite, Vice-President

D-U-N-S 96-826-0588
JOHNSON SC COMMERCIAL MARKETS
  (*Parent:* S C Johnson & Son Inc)
8310 16th St, Sturtevant, WI 53177
Phone: (414) 631-4001
Sales: $477,900,000   *Employees:* 4,004
Company Type: Private   *Employees here:* 889
SIC: 2842
  Mfg sanitation products & polymers for the coating industry
S C Johnson, Chairman

D-U-N-S 09-400-6855
JOICO LABORATORIES INC.
345 Baldwin Park Blvd, City Of Industry, CA 91746
Phone: (626) 968-6111
Sales: $51,643,000   *Employees:* 200
Company Type: Private   *Employees here:* 170
SIC: 2844
  Mfg cosmetics
Joyce Cammilleri, Treasurer

D-U-N-S 00-732-7364
JONES-BLAIR COMPANY
2728 Empire Central, Dallas, TX 75235
Phone: (214) 353-1600
Sales: $90,520,000   *Employees:* 575
Company Type: Private   *Employees here:* 175
SIC: 2851
  Mfg paints coatings & waterproofing materials whol
    wallpaper
Tom Wagner, President

D-U-N-S 00-916-6349   EXP
JONES-HAMILTON CO.
8400 Enterprise Dr, Newark, CA 94560
Phone: (510) 797-2471
Sales: $50,000,000   *Employees:* 93
Company Type: Private   *Employees here:* 58
SIC: 2819
  Mfg industrial inorganic chemicals
Robert L James, President

D-U-N-S 06-829-6839
JOS H LOWENSTEIN & SONS INC.
420 Morgan Ave, Brooklyn, NY 11222
Phone: (718) 388-5410
Sales: $30,000,000   *Employees:* 90
Company Type: Private   *Employees here:* 90
SIC: 2865
  Mfg synthetic dyes & industrial chemicals
Stephen J Lowenstein, President

D-U-N-S 62-161-2431
JSR MICROELECTRONICS, INC.
1280 N Mathilda Ave, Sunnyvale, CA 94089
Phone: (408) 543-8800

Sales: $16,800,000   *Employees:* 68
Company Type: Private   *Employees here:* 68
SIC: 2869
  Mfg photoresist chemicals
Jun Hirota, President

D-U-N-S 80-464-3773
JUPITER HOLDINGS, INC.
2801 W Osborn Rd, Phoenix, AZ 85017
Phone: (602) 252-8728
Sales: $51,147,000   *Employees:* 70
Company Type: Private   *Employees here:* 3
SIC: 2873
  Manufactures chemicals
Jordan K Burns, President

D-U-N-S 01-098-1215
K M S RESEARCH INC.
4712 Mountain Lakes Blvd, Redding, CA 96003
Phone: (530) 244-6000
Sales: $21,000,000   *Employees:* 190
Company Type: Private   *Employees here:* 190
SIC: 2844
  Mfg hair preparations
Jamey Mazzotta, President

D-U-N-S 07-625-6494
K O MANUFACTURING INC.
2720 E Division St, Springfield, MO 65803
Phone: (417) 866-8000
Sales: $20,000,000   *Employees:* 75
Company Type: Private   *Employees here:* 38
SIC: 2841
  Mfg detergents
John M Cunninham, President

D-U-N-S 11-291-7349   EXP
KAO CORP.OF AMERICA
902 Market St, Ste 404, Wilmington, DE 19801
Phone: (302) 427-0119
Sales: $179,000,000   *Employees:* 1,500
Company Type: Private   *Employees here:* 3
SIC: 2844
  Holding company which through subsidiaries mfg toiletries &
    floppy discs
Toshio Hoshino, President

D-U-N-S 05-587-1701
KASHA INDUSTRIES INC.
1 Plastic Ln, Grayville, IL 62844
Phone: (618) 375-2511
Sales: $20,000,000   *Employees:* 30
Company Type: Private   *Employees here:* 30
SIC: 2816
  Mfg custom coloring compounds & plastic mold grinding
    service
E E Kasha Jr, President

D-U-N-S 00-828-5009
KASPER INC.
200 Corporate Dr, Mahwah, NJ 07430
Phone: (201) 529-1600
Sales: $26,600,000   *Employees:* 230
Company Type: Private   *Employees here:* 227
SIC: 2844
  Mfg private label cosmetics
Bob Laggan, President

D-U-N-S 00-323-7021   EXP
KAY CHEMICAL COMPANY
  (*Parent:* Ecolab Inc)
8300 Capital Dr, Greensboro, NC 27409
Phone: (336) 668-7290

Sales: $44,400,000   *Employees:* 375
Company Type: Public Family Member   *Employees here:* 275
SIC: 2842
    Mfg custom chemical specialty cleaning items
Randall Kaplan, President

D-U-N-S 07-364-4635
KCA ENGINEERED PLASTICS, INC.
580 California St, San Francisco, CA 94104
Phone: (415) 433-4494
Sales: $35,000,000   *Employees:* 140
Company Type: Private   *Employees here:* 2
SIC: 2821
    Mfg plastic components and plastic injection molding
C S Dienst, Chief Executive Officer

D-U-N-S 94-278-9108   EXP
KCC CORROSION CONTROL CO. LTD.
4010 Trey Dr, Houston, TX 77084
Phone: (281) 550-1199
Sales: $300,500,000   *Employees:* 15
Company Type: Private   *Employees here:* 15
SIC: 2899
    Mfg chemical coatings & linings
Thomas G Priest, General Partner

D-U-N-S 79-783-7721   EXP
KELADON CORPORATION
529 W 4th Ave, Escondido, CA 92025
Phone: (760) 741-5332
Sales: $36,100,000   *Employees:* 200
Company Type: Private   *Employees here:* 75
SIC: 2899
    Mfg ink
Bruce Nichols, President

D-U-N-S 00-912-5303
KELLY-MOORE PAINT COMPANY
987 Commercial St, San Carlos, CA 94070
Phone: (650) 592-8337
Sales: $276,100,000   *Employees:* 2,400
Company Type: Private   *Employees here:* 250
SIC: 2851
    Mfg ret & whol paint property & casualty insurance company
    cattle ranching & mfr drywall taping tools
Joseph P Cristiano, President

D-U-N-S 36-225-1332   EXP
KELMAR INDUSTRIES INC.
310 Spartangreen Blvd, Duncan, SC 29334
Phone: (864) 433-0777
Sales: $18,724,000   *Employees:* 55
Company Type: Private   *Employees here:* 55
SIC: 2819
    Mfg chemical blends
Marvin Anderson, President

D-U-N-S 60-381-3676
KEMIRA HOLDINGS INC.
1 Kemira Rd, Savannah, GA 31404
Phone: (912) 652-1000
Sales: $250,000,000   *Employees:* 720
Company Type: Private   *Employees here:* 4
SIC: 2816
    Holding company
Risto Ojala, President

D-U-N-S 14-443-1913   EXP
KEMIRA PIGMENTS INC.
    (Parent: Kemira Holdings Inc)
1 Kemira Rd, Savannah, GA 31404
Phone: (912) 652-1000

Sales: $250,000,000   *Employees:* 718
Company Type: Private   *Employees here:* 714
SIC: 2816
    Mfg titanium dioxide pigments
Rob Roberts, President

D-U-N-S 04-131-6043
KEMWATER NORTH AMERICA CO
    (Parent: Pioneer Americas Inc)
2185 N California Blvd, Walnut Creek, CA 94596
Phone: (925) 757-8230
Sales: $40,700,000   *Employees:* 200
Company Type: Public Family Member   *Employees here:* 70
SIC: 2819
    Mfg industrial inorganic chemicals
Frank B Belliss, President

D-U-N-S 00-828-6114
KERR-MCGEE CHEMICAL, LLC
    (Parent: Kerr-Mcgee Corporation)
123 Robert S Kerr Ave, Oklahoma City, OK 73102
Phone: (405) 270-1313
Sales: $760,000,000   *Employees:* 2,300
Company Type: Public Family Member   *Employees here:* 125
SIC: 2819
    Mfg industrial inorganic chemicals & synthetic rutile &
        treated railroad cross ties
W P Woodward, Senior Vice-President

D-U-N-S 00-718-8667
KERR-MCGEE CORPORATION
123 Robert S Kerr Ave, Oklahoma City, OK 73102
Phone: (405) 270-1313
Sales: $1,711,000,000   *Employees:* 3,300
Company Type: Public   *Employees here:* 600
SIC: 2816
    Energy & chemicals
Luke R Corbett, Chairman of the Board

D-U-N-S 01-744-9211
KERR-MCGEE OIL & GAS CORP.
    (Parent: Kerr-Mcgee Corporation)
16666 Northchase Dr, Houston, TX 77060
Phone: (281) 618-6000
Sales: $29,400,000   *Employees:* 235
Company Type: Public Family Member   *Employees here:* 235
SIC: 2816
    Oil & gas exploration
Kenneth W Crouch, Chief Executive Officer

D-U-N-S 00-206-4764   EXP
KIND & KNOX GELATIN, INC.
    (Parent: Dgf Stoess Inc)
2445 Port Neal Rd, Sergeant Bluff, IA 51054
Phone: (712) 943-5516
Sales: $36,400,000   *Employees:* 260
Company Type: Private   *Employees here:* 260
SIC: 2899
    Mfg gelatin
Jorg Siebert, President

D-U-N-S 06-464-1798
THE KINGSFORD PRODUCTS CO.
    (Parent: The Clorox Company)
1221 Broadway, Oakland, CA 94612
Phone: (510) 271-7000
Sales: $90,000,000   *Employees:* 1,200
Company Type: Public Family Member   *Employees here:* 75
SIC: 2861
    Mfg charcoal briquets salad dressings & insecticides
Richard T Conti, President

D-U-N-S 62-689-2020   EXP
KISS NAIL PRODUCTS, INC.
2 Harbor Park Dr, Port Washington, NY 11050
Phone: (516) 625-9292
Sales: $31,135,000   *Employees:* 120
Company Type: Private   *Employees here:* 120
SIC: 2844
    Manufactures & imports manicure preparations
Won S Kang, Chairman of the Board

D-U-N-S 00-221-4195
KLEEN BRITE LABORATORIES INC.
200 State St, Brockport, NY 14420
Phone: (716) 637-0630
Sales: $83,300,000   *Employees:* 650
Company Type: Private   *Employees here:* 400
SIC: 2841
    Mfg soap/other detergents
D J Manno, Chairman of the Board

D-U-N-S 18-002-0901
KLEERDEX COMPANY
    (Parent: Sekisui America Corporation)
100 Gaither Dr, Ste B, Mount Laurel, NJ 08054
Phone: (609) 866-1700
Sales: $20,000,000   *Employees:* 95
Company Type: Private   *Employees here:* 10
SIC: 2821
    Mfg plastic sheet

D-U-N-S 07-419-8961
KMCO INC.
16503 Ramsey Rd, Crosby, TX 77532
Phone: (281) 328-3501
Sales: $78,463,000   *Employees:* 140
Company Type: Private   *Employees here:* 102
SIC: 2899
    Mfg specialty chemicals
Artie Mc Ferrin, President

D-U-N-S 78-964-1875
KMG-BERNUTH INC.
    (Parent: Kmg Chemicals Inc)
10611 Harwin Dr, Ste 402, Houston, TX 77036
Phone: (713) 988-9252
Sales: $22,657,000   *Employees:* 14
Company Type: Public Family Member   *Employees here:* 8
SIC: 2869
    Mfg & distributes wood treatment chemicals
David L Hatcher, Chairman of the Board

D-U-N-S 00-974-1745
KMG CHEMICALS INC.
10611 Harwin Dr, Ste 402, Houston, TX 77036
Phone: (713) 988-9252
Sales: $19,485,000   *Employees:* 70
Company Type: Public   *Employees here:* 9
SIC: 2869
    Mfg & whol wood preserving chemicals
Charles M Neff Jr, Treasurer

D-U-N-S 00-536-6679   EXP
KOLENE CORPORATION
12890 Westwood St, Detroit, MI 48223
Phone: (313) 273-9220
Sales: $20,000,000   *Employees:* 49
Company Type: Private   *Employees here:* 49
SIC: 2899
    Mfg metal treating & cleaning compounds
Robert H Shoemaker, Chairman of the Board

D-U-N-S 00-153-5103   EXP
KOLMAR LABORATORIES, INC.
    (Parent: Outsourcing Services Group Inc)
King St, Port Jervis, NY 12771
Phone: (914) 856-5311
Sales: $103,141,000   *Employees:* 1,700
Company Type: Private   *Employees here:* 600
SIC: 2844
    Mfg cosmetics
Chris Denney, President

D-U-N-S 19-333-0446
KOP-COAT INC.
    (Parent: Rpm Inc)
436 7th Ave, Ste 1850, Pittsburgh, PA 15219
Phone: (412) 227-2700
Sales: $61,018,000   *Employees:* 205
Company Type: Public Family Member   *Employees here:* 30
SIC: 2851
    Mfg protective coatings and wood treatments
Charles G Pauli, President

D-U-N-S 19-699-1582   EXP
KOPPERS INDUSTRIES INC.
436 Svnth Av Koppers Bldg, Pittsburgh, PA 15219
Phone: (412) 227-2001
Sales: $593,060,000   *Employees:* 2,000
Company Type: Public   *Employees here:* 125
SIC: 2865
    Mfg coal tar products/ treated wood products
Walter W Turner, President

D-U-N-S 00-539-7021   EXP
KOREX CORPORATION
50000 Pontiac Trl, Wixom, MI 48393
Phone: (248) 624-0000
Sales: $48,000,000   *Employees:* 164
Company Type: Private   *Employees here:* 164
SIC: 2841
    Mfg household powdered laundry detergents dishwasher
        compounds & bleaches
David Kerns, President

D-U-N-S 60-712-1258   EXP
KRONOR INC.
    (Parent: Nl Industries Inc)
16825 Northchase Dr, Houston, TX 77060
Phone: (281) 423-3300
Sales: $852,480,000   *Employees:* 2,500
Company Type: Public Family Member   *Employees here:* 100
SIC: 2816
    Manufactures titanium dioxide pigments
Dr Lawrence A Wigdor, President

D-U-N-S 01-123-9167
KUEHNE CHEMICAL COMPANY INC.
86 N Hackensack Ave, Kearny, NJ 07032
Phone: (973) 589-0700
Sales: $34,200,000   *Employees:* 200
Company Type: Private   *Employees here:* 100
SIC: 2819
    Mfrs sodium hydroxide & hypochlorite packaging &
        warehousing of caustic soda
Peter R Kuehne, President

D-U-N-S 00-423-6139   EXP
KUTOL PRODUCTS COMPANY
7650 Camargo Rd, Cincinnati, OH 45243
Phone: (513) 527-5500

Sales: $15,000,000   *Employees:* 120
Company Type: Private   *Employees here:* 120
SIC: 2841
    Mfg industrial hand cleaners
William C Rhodenbaugh, Chief Executive Officer

D-U-N-S 00-236-5054   EXP
L D DAVIS INDUSTRIES INC.
401 Mason Mill Rd, Huntingdon Valley, PA 19006
Phone: (215) 659-3345
Sales: $15,051,000   *Employees:* 57
Company Type: Private   *Employees here:* 7
SIC: 2891
    Mfg adhesives & glues
Louis D Davis Jr, President

D-U-N-S 00-508-5386   EXP
LA-CO INDUSTRIES, INC.
1201 Pratt Blvd, Elk Grove Village, IL 60007
Phone: (847) 956-7600
Sales: $25,000,000   *Employees:* 129
Company Type: Private   *Employees here:* 129
SIC: 2899
    Mfg industrial markers chemical specialties temperature
        indicator sticks and sealant compounds
Daniel Kleiman, President

D-U-N-S 84-891-4669
LAMAUR CORPORATION
1 Lovell Ave, Mill Valley, CA 94941
Phone: (415) 380-8200
Sales: $118,475,000   *Employees:* 323
Company Type: Public   *Employees here:* 6
SIC: 2844
    Mfg hair care products
Don G Hoff, Chairman of the Board

D-U-N-S 02-003-2470   EXP
LAMBENT TECHNOLOGIES CORP.
    (Parent: Petroferm Inc)
7247 Central Park Ave, Skokie, IL 60076
Phone: (847) 675-3950
Sales: $15,565,000   *Employees:* 50
Company Type: Private   *Employees here:* 50
SIC: 2843
    Mfg surface active agents finishing agents sulfonated oils
        assistants and oleychemicals
Edward Trauh, Vice-President

D-U-N-S 13-135-5554
LANCASTER GROUP US, LLC
    (Parent: Coty Inc)
237 Park Ave, New York, NY 10017
Phone: (212) 850-2460
Sales: $60,000,000   *Employees:* 100
Company Type: Private   *Employees here:* 100
SIC: 2844
    Mfg cosmetics & fragrances
Jean-Andre Rougeot, President

D-U-N-S 09-046-9834
LANCO MANUFACTURING CORP.
5 Urb Aponte, San Lorenzo, PR 00754
Phone: (787) 736-4221
Sales: $40,867,000   *Employees:* 145
Company Type: Private   *Employees here:* 100
SIC: 2891
    Mfg adhesives/sealants mfg paints/allied products
Enrique Blanco, President

D-U-N-S 17-707-0794
LANDEC CORPORATION
3603 Haven Ave, Menlo Park, CA 94025

Phone: (650) 306-1650
Sales: $33,516,000   *Employees:* 162
Company Type: Public   *Employees here:* 50
SIC: 2819
    Mfg polymers
Gary T Steele, Chairman of the Board

D-U-N-S 04-617-7812   EXP
LANDER CO. INC.
    (Parent: Scott Chemical Co Inc)
106 Grand Ave, Englewood, NJ 07631
Phone: (201) 568-9700
Sales: $80,000,000   *Employees:* 300
Company Type: Private   *Employees here:* 40
SIC: 2844
    Mfg health & beauty care products
Norman Auslander, Chairman of the Board

D-U-N-S 00-510-3726   EXP
LAPORTE CNSTR CHEM, NA
    (Parent: Rockwood Industries Inc)
7405 Production Dr, Mentor, OH 44060
Phone: (440) 255-8900
Sales: $24,300,000   *Employees:* 142
Company Type: Private   *Employees here:* 119
SIC: 2891
    Mfg sealing compounds concrete waterproofing curing &
        hardening compounds & mortar & cement colorants
Peter Longo, President

D-U-N-S 93-189-6385   EXP
LAPORTE WATER TECH & BIOCHEM
1400 Bluegrass Lakes Pkwy, Alpharetta, GA 30004
Phone: (770) 521-5999
Sales: $53,000,000   *Employees:* 200
Company Type: Private   *Employees here:* 75
SIC: 2899
    Mfg water purification chemicals and spa and pool
        accessories
Steve D Onfro, President

D-U-N-S 15-099-5942   EXP
LAROCHE INDUSTRIES INC.
1100 Johnson Ferry Rd NE, Atlanta, GA 30342
Phone: (404) 851-0300
Sales: $381,014,000   *Employees:* 1,120
Company Type: Private   *Employees here:* 124
SIC: 2873
    Mfr nitrogen fertilizers & nitrates & whol agri chemicals &
        fertilizer mfg chlorine caustic soda & whol alumina
        chemicals
Harold W Ingalls, President

D-U-N-S 00-902-3524   EXP
LAURENCE-DAVID INC.
    (Parent: Cutler Corporation)
1400 S Bertelsen Rd, Eugene, OR 97402
Phone: (541) 484-1212
Sales: $36,100,000   *Employees:* 200
Company Type: Private   *Employees here:* 17
SIC: 2851
    Mfg wood fillers sealers specialty coatings & plastic wood for
        use in the plywood manufacturing industry
Les Duman, President

D-U-N-S 00-512-1157   EXP
LAWTER INTERNATIONAL INC.
8601 95th St, Pleasant Prairie, WI 53158
Phone: (414) 947-7300

Sales: $206,539,000   *Employees:* 502
Company Type: Public   *Employees here:* 44
SIC: 2893
    Mfg specialty chemicals including inks and additives and
      printing machinery and equipment
John O Mahoney, Chairman of the Board

D-U-N-S 00-132-5661   EXP
LEARONAL INC.
272 Buffalo Ave, Freeport, NY 11520
Phone: (516) 868-8800
Sales: $241,697,000   *Employees:* 1,000
Company Type: Public   *Employees here:* 270
SIC: 2899
    Manufacturer of specialty chemical additives
Ronald Ostrow, President

D-U-N-S 10-138-1879   EXP
LEINER DAVIS GELATIN CORP.
    (Parent: Goodman Fielder Usa Inc)
1010 Northern Blvd, Great Neck, NY 11021
Phone: (516) 829-1370
Sales: $26,800,000   *Employees:* 150
Company Type: Private   *Employees here:* 15
SIC: 2899
    Mfg gelatin
Ian Glasson, President

D-U-N-S 02-893-0238
LENMAR CHEMICAL CORPORATION
2474 Lakeland Rd SE, Dalton, GA 30721
Phone: (706) 277-9505
Sales: $15,000,000   *Employees:* 37
Company Type: Private   *Employees here:* 37
SIC: 2843
    Mfg textile processing assistants
C R Tuck, Chairman of the Board

D-U-N-S 00-306-3278   EXP
LENMAR INC.
    (Parent: Wattyl (us) Limited)
150 S Calverton Rd, Baltimore, MD 21223
Phone: (410) 947-2300
Sales: $16,500,000   *Employees:* 100
Company Type: Private   *Employees here:* 100
SIC: 2851
    Mfg protective & decorative coatings
Christian Bosset, President

D-U-N-S 79-185-5364
LENZING FIBERS CORPORATION
    (Parent: U S A Lenzing Corporation)
Hwy 160, Lowland, TN 37778
Phone: (423) 585-5959
Sales: $105,000,000   *Employees:* 560
Company Type: Private   *Employees here:* 534
SIC: 2823
    Mfg rayon staple fibers
E F Ebner, President

D-U-N-S 00-445-3825
LESCO INC.
20005 Lake Rd, Cleveland, OH 44116
Phone: (440) 333-9250
Sales: $356,841,000   *Employees:* 1,157
Company Type: Public   *Employees here:* 180
SIC: 2875
    Mfg fertilizer turf control products & turf care equipment &
      whol & ret grass seed and lawn care machinery and
      equipment
William A Foley, Chairman of the Board

D-U-N-S 05-709-7818
LIGNOTECH USA INC.
100 Bus Hwy 51 S, Rothschild, WI 54474
Phone: (715) 359-6544
Sales: $34,873,000   *Employees:* 135
Company Type: Private   *Employees here:* 100
SIC: 2861
    Produces lignosulfonate chemicals
Kim J Stone, President

D-U-N-S 00-604-0117   EXP
LILLY INDUSTRIES INC.
733 S West St, Indianapolis, IN 46225
Phone: (317) 687-6700
Sales: $601,296,000   *Employees:* 2,116
Company Type: Public   *Employees here:* 45
SIC: 2851
    Mfg industrial coatings furniture polishes and other
      household products
Robert A Taylor, Chief Operating Officer

D-U-N-S 04-494-2670   EXP
LINDAU CHEMICALS INC.
731 Rosewood Dr, Columbia, SC 29201
Phone: (803) 799-6863
Sales: $16,613,000   *Employees:* 55
Company Type: Private   *Employees here:* 40
SIC: 2869
    Mfg epoxy hardening agents & coating resins
Dr Robert E Robinson, President

D-U-N-S 19-388-1190
LIOCHEM INC.
2145 E Park Dr NE, Conyers, GA 30013
Phone: (770) 922-0800
Sales: $27,000,000   *Employees:* 50
Company Type: Private   *Employees here:* 50
SIC: 2899
    Mfg inks and plastic colorants
Masaaki Ishiyama, President

D-U-N-S 00-168-2251   EXP
LIPO CHEMICALS INC.
207 19th Ave, Paterson, NJ 07504
Phone: (973) 345-8600
Sales: $60,000,000   *Employees:* 87
Company Type: Private   *Employees here:* 87
SIC: 2869
    Manufactures industrial organic chemicals specializing in
      additives for personal care products and food
Louis Frischling, President

D-U-N-S 61-284-0926
LIT TEL SYSTEMS USA INC.
100 Red Schoolhouse Rd, Spring Valley, NY 10977
Phone: (914) 426-7363
Sales: $25,900,000   *Employees:* 120
Company Type: Private   *Employees here:* 120
SIC: 2821
    Mfg furan & phenol based resins crystlography high purity
      specialty chemicals & synthesizing alloys
Hirak Karmaker, President

D-U-N-S 15-034-7268
LIVING EARTH TECHNOLOGY CORP.
    (Parent: Republic Industries Inc)
5625 Crawford Rd, Houston, TX 77041
Phone: (713) 466-7360
Sales: $25,000,000   *Employees:* 200
Company Type: Public Family Member   *Employees here:* 172
SIC: 2875
    Mfg mulch compost soils & recycling
Dana A Egan, Secretary

D-U-N-S 15-421-3128
LOBECO PRODUCTS INC.
23 Venture Rd, Lobeco, SC 29931
Phone: (843) 846-8171
Sales: $18,669,000   *Employees:* 90
Company Type: Private   *Employees here:* 90
SIC: 2865
 Mfg organic dyes & pigments agricultural chemicals cyclic
  organic crudes & intermediates
John M Meeks, President

D-U-N-S 00-896-3589
LOCKHART COMPANY
2873 W Hardies Rd, Gibsonia, PA 15044
Phone: (724) 444-1900
Sales: $20,000,000   *Employees:* 100
Company Type: Private   *Employees here:* 25
SIC: 2819
 Mfg industrial chemicals and mfg paints
Thomas J Gillespie Jr, President

D-U-N-S 00-113-9617
LOCTITE CORPORATION
 (Parent: Hc Investments Inc)
10 Columbus Blvd, Ste 5, Hartford, CT 06106
Phone: (860) 520-5000
Sales: $694,900,000   *Employees:* 4,400
Company Type: Private   *Employees here:* 40
SIC: 2891
 Mfg adhesives & sealants
David Freeman, President

D-U-N-S 09-050-6239
LOCTITE PUERTO RICO INC.
 (Parent: Loctite Corporation)
9 Vicente Quilinchini Ave, Sabana Grande, PR 00637
Phone: (787) 873-6500
Sales: $46,900,000   *Employees:* 300
Company Type: Private   *Employees here:* 300
SIC: 2891
 Mfg industrial adhesives & sealants
James R Polifka, Vice-President

D-U-N-S 15-192-8520   EXP
LOMAC INC.
 (Parent: Pcl Group Inc)
5025 Evanston Ave, Muskegon, MI 49442
Phone: (616) 788-2341
Sales: $34,600,000   *Employees:* 180
Company Type: Private   *Employees here:* 180
SIC: 2865
 Mfg industrial organic chemicals
Marvin Gallisdorfer, President

D-U-N-S 00-164-3170   EXP
LONZA INC.
 (Parent: Alusuisse-Lonza America Inc)
17-17 Route 208, Fair Lawn, NJ 07410
Phone: (201) 794-2400
Sales: $434,900,000   *Employees:* 1,000
Company Type: Private   *Employees here:* 200
SIC: 2899
 Mfg specialty & fine chemicals & imports fine & inorganic
  chemicals
Fredrick Schauder, Chief Financial Officer

D-U-N-S 80-007-7893
LORI DAVIS HAIR, INC.
1230 American Blvd, West Chester, PA 19380
Phone: (610) 430-7800

Sales: $22,090,000   *Employees:* 13
Company Type: Private   *Employees here:* 13
SIC: 2844
 Mfg hair care products
R J Marsh, President

D-U-N-S 80-915-4958
LOUISIANA PIGMENT COMPANY, LP
3300 Bayou Dinde Rd, Westlake, LA 70669
Phone: (318) 882-7000
Sales: $62,500,000   *Employees:* 500
Company Type: Private   *Employees here:* 500
SIC: 2816
 Mfg titanium dioxide pigment
Doug Weaver, General Manager

D-U-N-S 04-780-3051   EXP
LOVELAND INDUSTRIES INC.
 (Parent: United Agri Products Inc)
14520 Weld County Road 64, Greeley, CO 80634
Phone: (970) 356-8920
Sales: $249,000,000   *Employees:* 350
Company Type: Public Family Member   *Employees here:* 75
SIC: 2879
 Mfg agricultural chemicals
Jerry Phillips, President

D-U-N-S 12-258-8510
LSB CHEMICAL CORP.
 (Parent: Lsb Industries Inc)
16 S Pennsylvania Ave, Oklahoma City, OK 73107
Phone: (405) 235-4546
Sales: $132,000,000   *Employees:* 364
Company Type: Public Family Member   *Employees here:* 3
SIC: 2819
 Mfg sulfuric acid & nitric acid & ammonium nitrate &
  industrial explosives
Jack E Golsen, President

D-U-N-S 04-686-0979   EXP
LSB INDUSTRIES, INC.
16 S Pennsylvania Ave, Oklahoma City, OK 73107
Phone: (405) 235-4546
Sales: $313,929,000   *Employees:* 1,685
Company Type: Public   *Employees here:* 29
SIC: 2819
 Mfg chemicals climate control sys & equip automotive and
  industrial products
Jack E Golsen, Chairman of the Board

D-U-N-S 00-417-2565   EXP
LUBRIZOL CORPORATION
29400 Lakeland Blvd, Wickliffe, OH 44092
Phone: (440) 943-4200
Sales: $1,673,782,000   *Employees:* 4,300
Company Type: Public   *Employees here:* 1,300
SIC: 2899
 Mfg oil treating compounds & fuel additives
William G Bares, Chairman of the Board

D-U-N-S 00-521-9290   EXP
LUSTER PRODUCTS INC.
1104 W 43rd St, Chicago, IL 60609
Phone: (773) 579-1800
Sales: $25,000,000   *Employees:* 350
Company Type: Private   *Employees here:* 280
SIC: 2844
 Manufactures hair care products
Jory Luster, President

D-U-N-S 17-409-9531
LYKES AGRI SALES INC.
(Parent: Lykes Bros Inc)
11500 Old Lakeland Hwy, Dade City, FL 33525
Phone: (352) 567-5622
Sales: $22,700,000   *Employees:* 120
Company Type: Private   *Employees here:* 40
SIC: 2875
    Mfg mixed fertilizer & crop protection products
Lenny Pipen, President

D-U-N-S 00-106-0813
LYNWOOD LABORATORIES INC.
945 Great Plain Ave, Needham, MA 02492
Phone: (781) 449-6776
Sales: $19,200,000   *Employees:* 100
Company Type: Private   *Employees here:* 100
SIC: 2879
    Mfg household insecticides & repellents & rodenticides
Dr Irving Kanin, President

D-U-N-S 19-412-3154   EXP
LYONDELL CHEMICAL COMPANY
1221 Mckinney St, Ste 1600, Houston, TX 77010
Phone: (713) 652-7200
Sales: $1,703,000,000   *Employees:* 4,250
Company Type: Public   *Employees here:* 60
SIC: 2869
    Mfr petrochemicals and refined products
Morris Gelb, Chief Operating Officer

D-U-N-S 18-184-3095
LYONDELL CHEMICAL WORLDWIDE
    (Parent: Lyondell Chemical Company)
1221 Mckinney St, Ste 1600, Houston, TX 77010
Phone: (713) 652-7200
Sales: $3,995,000,000   *Employees:* 4,200
Company Type: Public Family Member   *Employees here:* 1,000
SIC: 2869
    Mfr intermediate chemicals and specialty products
Dan F Smith, President

D-U-N-S 00-226-4224
M A BRUDER & SONS INC.
600 Reed Rd, Broomall, PA 19008
Phone: (610) 353-5100
Sales: $100,000,000   *Employees:* 1,000
Company Type: Private   *Employees here:* 80
SIC: 2851
    Mfg paint enamels varnishes stains and other related paint
    products
Thomas A Bruder Jr, Chairman of the Board

D-U-N-S 13-957-7696
M C MARBLE, INC.
316 S 16th St, Lafayette, IN 47905
Phone: (765) 742-2919
Sales: $16,000,000   *Employees:* 6
Company Type: Private   *Employees here:* 6
SIC: 2844
    Mfg cosmetics
Mike Bryan, President

D-U-N-S 10-292-5849   EXP
M P ASSOCIATES INC.
PO Box 546, Ione, CA 95640
Phone: (209) 274-4715
Sales: $18,500,000   *Employees:* 170
Company Type: Private   *Employees here:* 170
SIC: 2892
    Mfg explosives mfg chemical preparations
David Pier, Chief Executive Officer

D-U-N-S 11-291-9956   EXP
MACANDREWS FORBES HOLDINGS INC.
    (Parent: Mafco Holdings Inc (de Corp))
38 E 63rd St, New York, NY 10021
Phone: (212) 688-9000
Sales: $6,196,000,000   *Employees:* 20,075
Company Type: Private   *Employees here:* 40
SIC: 2844
    Manufactures beauty products flavors & cigars film
    processing publishing and television entertainment
Ronald O Perelman, Chairman of the Board

D-U-N-S 00-953-7275
MACKLANBURG-DUNCAN CO.
    (Parent: Macklanburg-Duncan Co)
4041 N Santa Fe Ave, Oklahoma City, OK 73118
Phone: (405) 528-4411
Sales: $250,000,000   *Employees:* 1,200
Company Type: Private   *Employees here:* 900
SIC: 2891
    Mfg adhesives & sealants
David Kilburn, Chief Financial Officer

D-U-N-S 88-443-5900
MACTAC, INC.
    (Parent: Morgan Adhesives Company)
4560 Darrow Rd, Stow, OH 44224
Phone: (330) 688-1111
Sales: $34,400,000   *Employees:* 200
Company Type: Public Family Member   *Employees here:* 5
SIC: 2891
    Mfr adhesive coatings
Robert Mlnarik, Chairman of the Board

D-U-N-S 87-830-4849
MAFCO HOLDINGS INC.
36 E 63rd St, New York, NY 10021
Phone: (212) 688-9000
Sales: $3,460,400,000   *Employees:* 28,843
Company Type: Private   *Employees here:* 40
SIC: 2844
    Holding company
Ronald O Perelman, Chief Executive Officer

D-U-N-S 62-113-4410   EXP
MAGNETICS INTERNATIONAL INC.
    (Parent: Inland Steel Industries Inc)
1111 N State Road 149, Chesterton, IN 46304
Phone: (219) 763-1199
Sales: $15,313,000   *Employees:* 58
Company Type: Public Family Member   *Employees here:* 54
SIC: 2819
    Mfg regenerated acids & iron oxide powders
Bruce Greinke, President

D-U-N-S 09-541-3050   EXP
MAGNI-INDUSTRIES INC.
    (Parent: Magni Group Inc)
2771 Hammond St, Detroit, MI 48209
Phone: (313) 843-7855
Sales: $28,754,000   *Employees:* 58
Company Type: Private   *Employees here:* 20
SIC: 2899
    Mfg rust resisting compounds
Robert Lovell, President

D-U-N-S 15-534-7008   EXP
MAGNOX INCORPORATED
    (Parent: Mitsui Min Smlt Holdings U S A)
1 Magnox Dr, Pulaski, VA 24301
Phone: (540) 980-3500

Sales: $22,800,000   *Employees:* 170
Company Type: Private   *Employees here:* 160
SIC: 2816
    Mfg iron oxide pigments
Tetsuyuki Suzuki, President

D-U-N-S 15-322-6832   EXP
MAGNOX PULASKI INCORPORATED
    (Parent: Magnox Incorporated)
1 Magnox Dr, Pulaski, VA 24301
Phone: (540) 980-3500
Sales: $16,000,000   *Employees:* 135
Company Type: Private   *Employees here:* 135
SIC: 2816
    Mfg iron oxide pigments
Tetsuyuki Suzuki, President

D-U-N-S 01-151-0542   EXP
MAGRUDER COLOR CO. INC.
1029 Newark Ave, Elizabeth, NJ 07208
Phone: (973) 242-1300
Sales: $80,000,000   *Employees:* 350
Company Type: Private   *Employees here:* 200
SIC: 2865
    Mfg dry flush & fluorescent pigments
Allan Weissglass, President

D-U-N-S 82-640-3057
MAJOR CHEM LTD.
2015 Shadowbriar Dr, Houston, TX 77077
Phone: (281) 870-1183
Sales: $25,000,000   *Employees:* 7
Company Type: Private   *Employees here:* 7
SIC: 2842
    Mfg & whol (exports) chemical cleaning products also builds
      & leases commercial buildings
Harold Zeigfinger, President

D-U-N-S 00-121-3487
MALLINCKRODT BAKER, INC.
    (Parent: Mallinckrodt Chemical Inc)
222 Red School Ln, Phillipsburg, NJ 08865
Phone: (908) 859-2151
Sales: $144,800,000   *Employees:* 900
Company Type: Public Family Member   *Employees here:* 133
SIC: 2819
    Mfg industrial inorganic chemicals
Daniel B Mulholland, President

D-U-N-S 04-768-5581   EXP
MANE USA
60 Demarest Dr, Wayne, NJ 07470
Phone: (973) 633-5533
Sales: $40,000,000   *Employees:* 115
Company Type: Private   *Employees here:* 108
SIC: 2869
    Mfg industrial organic chemicals
Michele Mane, President

D-U-N-S 00-130-3015   EXP
MANHATTAN PRODUCTS INC.
333 Starke Rd, Carlstadt, NJ 07072
Phone: (201) 933-3500
Sales: $35,000,000   *Employees:* 180
Company Type: Private   *Employees here:* 180
SIC: 2842
    Mfg cleaning preparations & soap bubbles
Al Nicusanti, Chief Executive Officer

D-U-N-S 79-937-8161
MANTROSE-HAEUSER CO., INC.
    (Parent: William Zinsser & Co Inc)
1175 Post Rd E, Westport, CT 06880

Phone: (203) 454-1800
Sales: $22,000,000   *Employees:* 82
Company Type: Public Family Member   *Employees here:* 14
SIC: 2851
    Mfg industrial coatings
Robert Senior, President

D-U-N-S 83-607-7222
MAPICO, INC.
    (Parent: Laporte Inc)
11116 S Towne Sq, Ste 101, Saint Louis, MO 63123
Phone: (314) 845-2010
Sales: $24,100,000   *Employees:* 110
Company Type: Private   *Employees here:* 11
SIC: 2895
    Mfg inorganic pigments
Thomas Morley, President

D-U-N-S 06-690-9474
MARCHEM SOUTHEAST INC.
    (Parent: Dash Multi-Corp Inc)
400 N Main St, Adairsville, GA 30103
Phone: (770) 773-3300
Sales: $29,652,000   *Employees:* 60
Company Type: Private   *Employees here:* 60
SIC: 2821
    Mfg plastic raw materials
Marvin S Wool, President

D-U-N-S 04-557-0736   EXP
MARIANNA IMPORTS, INC.
11222 I St, Omaha, NE 68137
Phone: (402) 593-0211
Sales: $37,340,000   *Employees:* 220
Company Type: Private   *Employees here:* 190
SIC: 2844
    Mfg & whol beauty products including shampoos hair care
      products & cosmetics
Michael Cosentino, President

D-U-N-S 01-076-5394   EXP
MARIETTA CORPORATION
    (Parent: Bfma Holding Corporation)
37 Huntington St, Cortland, NY 13045
Phone: (607) 753-6746
Sales: $92,400,000   *Employees:* 721
Company Type: Private   *Employees here:* 420
SIC: 2841
    Mfg whol & contract packager guest amenities
Barry W Florescue, President

D-U-N-S 11-331-3969
MARKWINS INTERNATIONAL CORP.
1871 Wright St, La Verne, CA 91750
Phone: (909) 596-8878
Sales: $60,000,000   *Employees:* 50
Company Type: Private   *Employees here:* 50
SIC: 2844
    Mfg cosmetics & beauty supplies
Eric Chen, President

D-U-N-S 08-885-9921
MARPAX
1115 Shore St, West Sacramento, CA 95691
Phone: (916) 372-2452
Sales: $125,000,000   *Employees:* 253
Company Type: Private   *Employees here:* 60
SIC: 2893
    Mfg printing ink
George R Tholke, President

D-U-N-S 19-966-1034
MARTIN COLOR-FI INC.
306 Main St, Edgefield, SC 29824

Phone: (803) 637-7000
Sales: $120,502,000   *Employees:* 881
Company Type: Public   *Employees here:* 12
SIC: 2824
   Mfg polyester fiber and pellets carpets & yarns
James F Martin, Chairman of the Board

D-U-N-S 13-955-7789   EXP
MARY KAY HOLDING CORPORATION
16251 Dallas Pkwy, Dallas, TX 75248
Phone: (972) 687-6300
Sales: $897,102,000   *Employees:* 4,000
Company Type: Private   *Employees here:* 1,700
SIC: 2844
   Mfg cosmetics toiletries & related pdts
Richard R Rogers, Chairman of the Board

D-U-N-S 04-999-4452   EXP
MARY KAY INC.
   (Parent: Mary Kay Holding Corporation)
16251 Dallas Pkwy, Dallas, TX 75248
Phone: (972) 687-6300
Sales: $897,102,000   *Employees:* 4,000
Company Type: Private   *Employees here:* 1,700
SIC: 2844
   Mfg cosmetics toiletries & related pdts
Amy Digeso, President

D-U-N-S 07-228-8681
MAT DEN CORPORATION
2727 Skyway Dr, Santa Maria, CA 93455
Phone: (805) 922-8491
Sales: $95,000,000   *Employees:* 525
Company Type: Private   *Employees here:* 350
SIC: 2844
   Mfg toothpaste and mouth rinse and composite & porcelain
   for cosmetic dentistry
Dr Robert L Ibsen, DDS, President

D-U-N-S 10-623-6144
MATHESON GAS PRODUCTS INC.
959 Route 46, Parsippany, NJ 07054
Phone: (973) 257-1100
Sales: $173,566,000   *Employees:* 850
Company Type: Private   *Employees here:* 60
SIC: 2813
   Manufactures specialty gases and industrial process controls
Donald G Ramlow, President

D-U-N-S 03-728-9170
MATRIX ESSENTIALS INC.
   (Parent: Bristol-Myers Squibb Company)
30601 Carter St, Cleveland, OH 44139
Phone: (440) 248-3700
Sales: $119,000,000   *Employees:* 1,000
Company Type: Public Family Member   *Employees here:* 850
SIC: 2844
   Mfg of hair care & skin care products
Michael A De Gennaro, President

D-U-N-S 00-610-5936
MAUTZ PAINT CO.
925 E Washington Ave, Madison, WI 53703
Phone: (608) 255-1661
Sales: $31,000,000   *Employees:* 260
Company Type: Private   *Employees here:* 110
SIC: 2851
   Mfg & retail paint
Bernhard F Mautz Jr, Chairman of the Board

D-U-N-S 05-103-2399
MAX RITTENBAUM INC.
600 Wharton Cir SW, Atlanta, GA 30336
Phone: (404) 691-7133

Sales: $21,100,000   *Employees:* 185
Company Type: Private   *Employees here:* 175
SIC: 2842
   Mfg specialty cleaning products for automotive marine and
   household use
Jeffrey A Rittenbaum, President

D-U-N-S 36-204-7813
MAY NATIONAL ASSOCIATES
4 Brighton Rd, Ste 300, Clifton, NJ 07012
Phone: (973) 473-3330
Sales: $40,000,000   *Employees:* 55
Company Type: Private   *Employees here:* 12
SIC: 2891
   Mfg adhesives/sealants
Mark Yamout, President

D-U-N-S 00-507-1642   EXP
MAYBELLINE INC.
   (Parent: Cosmair Inc)
575 5th Ave, Fl 15, New York, NY 10017
Phone: (212) 818-1500
Sales: $179,000,000   *Employees:* 1,500
Company Type: Private   *Employees here:* 100
SIC: 2844
   Mfg cosmetics toiletries fragrances & soaps
John R Wendt, President

D-U-N-S 62-144-8323
MAYBELLINE PRODUCTS CO.
   (Parent: Maybelline Sales Inc)
133 Terminal Ave, Clark, NJ 07066
Phone: (732) 499-2838
Sales: $167,000,000   *Employees:* NA
Company Type: Private   *Employees here:* NA
SIC: 2844
   Mfg cosmetics

D-U-N-S 62-624-1913   EXP
MC AULEY'S, INC.
2300 Sitler St, Memphis, TN 38114
Phone: (901) 946-8800
Sales: $30,000,000   *Employees:* 200
Company Type: Private   *Employees here:* 200
SIC: 2844
   Mfg sprays deodorizers potpourri & scents
Bill Mc Auley, Chairman of the Board

D-U-N-S 00-324-8275
MC CORMICK PAINT WORKS CO.
2355 Lewis Ave, Rockville, MD 20851
Phone: (301) 770-3235
Sales: $21,905,000   *Employees:* 160
Company Type: Private   *Employees here:* 75
SIC: 2851
   Mfg & ret paint & related items
Thomas P Mc Cormick Jr, President

D-U-N-S 00-625-0583
MC LAUGHLIN GORMLEY KING CO.
8810 10th Ave N, Minneapolis, MN 55427
Phone: (612) 544-0341
Sales: $43,000,000   *Employees:* 100
Company Type: Private   *Employees here:* 36
SIC: 2879
   Mfg pyrethrum and synthetic pyrethroid chemicals
William D Gullickson Jr, President

D-U-N-S 03-469-3291
MC WHORTER TECHNOLOGIES, INC.
400 E Cottage Ave, Carpentersville, IL 60110
Phone: (847) 428-2657

Sales: $454,930,000   *Employees:* 1,040
Company Type: Public   *Employees here:* 90
SIC: 2821
   Mfg synthetic resins
John R Stevenson, Chairman of the Board

D-U-N-S 09-139-6697
MEDICIA PHARMACEUTICALS CORP.
   (*Parent:* Bli Holdings Inc)
2351 U S Route 130, Dayton, NJ 08810
Phone: (732) 438-3200
Sales: $30,000,000   *Employees:* 400
Company Type: Private   *Employees here:* 399
SIC: 2844
   Manufactures cosmetic creams and lotions
Renato Jose, President

D-U-N-S 05-439-2238
MEGAS BEAUTY CARE INC.
   (*Parent:* American Safety Razor Company)
15501 Industrial Pkwy, Cleveland, OH 44135
Phone: (216) 676-6400
Sales: $31,400,000   *Employees:* 270
Company Type: Public Family Member   *Employees here:* 80
SIC: 2844
   Mfg health & beauty aids
Jack Van Noy, President

D-U-N-S 05-502-3238   EXP
MELAMINE CHEMICALS INC.
   (*Parent:* Borden Chemical Inc)
39041 Hwy 18 W, Donaldsonville, LA 70346
Phone: (225) 473-3121
Sales: $15,200,000   *Employees:* 95
Company Type: Private   *Employees here:* 95
SIC: 2821
   Mfr melamine
Frederic R Huber, President

D-U-N-S 93-848-8913
MEMC PASADENA, INC.
   (*Parent:* Memc Electronic Materials)
3000 N South St, Pasadena, TX 77503
Phone: (713) 740-1414
Sales: $30,000,000   *Employees:* 159
Company Type: Public Family Member   *Employees here:* 159
SIC: 2869
   Mfg granulated polysilicon
Charles W Cooke Jr, Chairman of the Board

D-U-N-S 00-214-6660   EXP
THE MENNEN CO.
   (*Parent:* Colgate-Palmolive Company)
191 E Hanover Ave, Morristown, NJ 07960
Phone: (973) 631-9000
Sales: $500,000,000   *Employees:* 420
Company Type: Public Family Member   *Employees here:* 403
SIC: 2844
   Mfg toiletries & home fragrance products
William S Shanahan, President

D-U-N-S 00-123-6876
MERCURY PAINT CORP.
4808 Farragut Rd, Brooklyn, NY 11203
Phone: (718) 469-8787
Sales: $15,600,000   *Employees:* 100
Company Type: Private   *Employees here:* 75
SIC: 2851
   Manufactures & retails paints
Daniel Berman, President

D-U-N-S 00-810-6999   EXP
MERICHEM COMPANY
4800 Chase Tower, Houston, TX 77002
Phone: (713) 224-3030
Sales: $88,310,000   *Employees:* 321
Company Type: Private   *Employees here:* 49
SIC: 2869
   Mfg industrial organic & inorganic chemicals
John T Files, Chairman of the Board

D-U-N-S 03-134-0495
MERICHEM SALSOL USA, LLC
11821 East Fwy, Ste 600, Houston, TX 77029
Phone: (713) 428-5000
Sales: $33,800,000   *Employees:* 160
Company Type: Private   *Employees here:* 160
SIC: 2869
   Chemical manufacturer
Christophe Lancaster, President

D-U-N-S 00-847-9388   EXP
MERLE NORMAN COSMETICS INC.
9130 Bellanca Ave, Los Angeles, CA 90045
Phone: (310) 641-3000
Sales: $87,485,000   *Employees:* 591
Company Type: Private   *Employees here:* 352
SIC: 2844
   Mfg & retails cosmetics
Arthur O Armstrong, President

D-U-N-S 00-223-3088   EXP
MESSER GRIESHEIM INDUSTRIES
3 Great Valley Pkwy, Malvern, PA 19355
Phone: (610) 695-7400
Sales: $330,000,000   *Employees:* 1,500
Company Type: Private   *Employees here:* 160
SIC: 2813
   Mfg industrial gases
Herbert Rudolf, Chairman of the Board

D-U-N-S 13-046-9406   EXP
METAL COATINGS INTERNATIONAL
275 Industrial Pkwy, Chardon, OH 44024
Phone: (440) 285-2231
Sales: $17,100,000   *Employees:* 130
Company Type: Private   *Employees here:* 46
SIC: 2899
   Mfg corrosion resistant metal coating chemicals
George Palek, President

D-U-N-S 61-898-2516   EXP
METALSAMERICA INC.
135 Old Boiling Springs R, Shelby, NC 28152
Phone: (704) 482-8200
Sales: $55,000,000   *Employees:* 100
Company Type: Private   *Employees here:* 100
SIC: 2899
   Mfg anodes
Peter Schorsch, President

D-U-N-S 10-256-7567   EXP
METREX RESEARCH CORPORATION
   (*Parent:* Kerr Corporation)
1717 W Collins Ave, Orange, CA 92867
Phone: (303) 841-5842
Sales: $15,000,000   *Employees:* 50
Company Type: Public Family Member   *Employees here:* 5
SIC: 2819
   Mfg high purity chemicals refined medical laser systems &
      equipment & commercial medical research
Floyd Pickrell, President

D-U-N-S 18-382-4655
MG INTERNATIONAL INC.
1000 International Pkwy, Dallas, GA 30132
Phone: (770) 505-0004
Sales: $16,835,000
Company Type: Private
SIC: 2821
    Mfg molded precision plastic parts
Takeshi Hoshino, Vice-President

Employees: 230
Employees here: 230

D-U-N-S 11-438-1403
MICRO-FLO CO.
    (Parent: Basf Corporation)
530 Oak Court Dr 100, Memphis, TN 38117
Phone: (901) 432-5000
Sales: $150,000,000
Company Type: Private
SIC: 2879
    Mfg agricultural chemicals
C E Formby, President

Employees: 162
Employees here: 30

D-U-N-S 11-269-3130   EXP
MICRO LITHOGRAPHY, INC.
1257 Elko Dr, Sunnyvale, CA 94089
Phone: (408) 747-1769
Sales: $51,500,000
Company Type: Private
SIC: 2869
    Mfg pellicles
Chris Yen, President

Employees: 225
Employees here: 225

D-U-N-S 61-060-7384   EXP
MICROSI INC.
10028 S 51st St, Phoenix, AZ 85044
Phone: (602) 893-8898
Sales: $18,000,000
Company Type: Private
SIC: 2899
    Mfg high purity organic chemicals
John Sesody, President

Employees: 20
Employees here: 18

D-U-N-S 10-774-0250
MID-ATLNTIC VEGETABLE SHORTENING
193 Christie St, Newark, NJ 07105
Phone: (973) 465-0747
Sales: $18,000,000
Company Type: Private
SIC: 2899
    Packages vegetable oils
Calvin Theobald, President

Employees: 29
Employees here: 22

D-U-N-S 10-332-3689
MIDWEST ZINC CORPORATION
    (Parent: U S Zinc Corporation)
3380 Fite Rd, Millington, TN 38053
Phone: (901) 357-6800
Sales: $18,200,000
Company Type: Public Family Member
SIC: 2816
    Mfg zinc oxide pigments
Barry Hamilton, President

Employees: 131
Employees here: 35

D-U-N-S 12-134-5532
MILFORD FERTILIZER CO.
    (Parent: Agway Inc)
308 NE Front St, Milford, DE 19963
Phone: (302) 422-3001
Sales: $94,158,000
Company Type: Public Family Member
SIC: 2875
    Mfg dry n/k/p blends nitrogen solutions & clear liquid
      fertilizers & whol pesticides & seeds
Robert A Fischer Jr, President

Employees: 150
Employees here: 75

D-U-N-S 95-763-6194
MILLENNIUM CHEMICALS INC.
230 Half Mile Rd, Red Bank, NJ 07701
Phone: (732) 933-5000
Sales: $3,048,000,000
Company Type: Public
SIC: 2816
    Mfg titanium dioxide and related products acetyls and
      specialty chemicals
William M Landuyt, Chairman of the Board

Employees: 4,200
Employees here: 40

D-U-N-S 19-602-2230   EXP
MILLENNIUM INORGANIC CHEMICALS
    (Parent: Millennium Holdings Inc)
200 International Cir, Cockeysville, MD 21030
Phone: (410) 229-4400
Sales: $850,000,000
Company Type: Public Family Member
SIC: 2816
    Mfg titanium dioxide pigment opacifier for paint plastic &
      paper
Robert E Lee, President

Employees: 2,000
Employees here: 300

D-U-N-S 00-133-9415   EXP
MILLENNIUM PETROCHEMICALS INC.
    (Parent: Millennium Holdings Inc)
11500 Northlake Dr, Cincinnati, OH 45249
Phone: (513) 530-6500
Sales: $350,000,000
Company Type: Public Family Member
SIC: 2869
    Mfr of methanol acetic acid and vinyl acetate monomer
Peter P Hanik, President

Employees: 320
Employees here: 40

D-U-N-S 61-738-2817
MILLENNIUM SPECIALTY CHEMICALS
    (Parent: Millennium Holdings Inc)
Foot Of W 61st St, Jacksonville, FL 32201
Phone: (904) 768-5800
Sales: $26,300,000
Company Type: Public Family Member
SIC: 2869
    Mfg industrial organic chemicals
George W Robbins, President

Employees: 108
Employees here: 48

D-U-N-S 00-902-6659
MILLER PAINT CO. INC.
12812 NE Whitaker Way, Portland, OR 97230
Phone: (503) 255-0190
Sales: $31,500,000
Company Type: Private
SIC: 2851
    Mfg paint & ret paint wallpaper & supplies
John Buckinger Jr, President

Employees: 165
Employees here: 20

D-U-N-S 79-692-9313   EXP
MINERALS TECHNOLOGIES INC.
405 Lexington Ave, New York, NY 10174
Phone: (212) 878-1800
Sales: $609,193,000
Company Type: Public
SIC: 2819
    Mfg calcium carbonate & refractory materials mines &
      processes limestone & talc
Jean-Paul Valles, Chairman of the Board

Employees: 2,250
Employees here: 80

D-U-N-S 04-420-1317   EXP
MINI FIBERS INC.
2923 Boones Creek Rd, Johnson City, TN 37615
Phone: (423) 282-4242

Sales: $27,088,000   *Employees:* 85
Company Type: Private   *Employees here:* 30
SIC: 2824
    Processes synthetic fibers
Charles A Keith, President

D-U-N-S 09-776-5788   EXP
MINING SERVICES INTERNATIONAL
8805 Sandy Pkwy, Sandy, UT 84070
Phone: (801) 233-6000
Sales: $26,969,000   *Employees:* 85
Company Type: Public   *Employees here:* 22
SIC: 2892
    Mfg explosives
Dr John T Day, President

D-U-N-S 00-816-1432   EXP
MISSISSIPPI CHEMICAL CORP.
Hwy 49 E, Yazoo City, MS 39194
Phone: (601) 746-4131
Sales: $519,091,000   *Employees:* 1,600
Company Type: Public   *Employees here:* 539
SIC: 2873
    Mfr nitrogen phosphate & potash fertilizers
Charles O Dunn, President

D-U-N-S 62-308-2963
MISSISSIPPI PHOSPHATES CORP.
    (*Parent:* Mississippi Chemical Corp)
601 Industrial Rd, Pascagoula, MS 39581
Phone: (601) 746-5529
Sales: $48,000,000   *Employees:* 240
Company Type: Public Family Member   *Employees here:* 224
SIC: 2874
    Mfr diammonium phosphate fertilizer
Charles O Dunn, President

D-U-N-S 78-760-0360
MITSUI CHEMICALS AMERICA INC.
2500 Westchester Ave, Purchase, NY 10577
Phone: (914) 253-0777
Sales: $40,200,000   *Employees:* 150
Company Type: Private   *Employees here:* 25
SIC: 2869
    Mfg petro chemical products
Tashiro Arimoto, President

D-U-N-S 88-470-0311
MOBIL CHEMICAL COMPANY INC.
    (*Parent:* Mobil Oil Corporation)
3225 Gallows Rd, Fairfax, VA 22037
Phone: (703) 846-3000
Sales: $511,000,000   *Employees:* 3,570
Company Type: Public Family Member   *Employees here:* 20
SIC: 2899
    Mfg chemicals
Robert Swanson, President

D-U-N-S 00-816-3115   EXP
MOBILE PAINT MANUFACTURING CO.
4775 Hamilton Blvd, Theodore, AL 36582
Phone: (334) 443-6110
Sales: $66,520,000   *Employees:* 450
Company Type: Private   *Employees here:* 194
SIC: 2851
    Mfg whol and ret paints varnishes lacquers & enamels &
    whol & ret wallcoverings
Robert A Williams, President

D-U-N-S 00-207-9630
MOHAWK FINISHING PRODUCTS INC.
    (*Parent:* Rpm Inc)
4715 State Highway 30, Amsterdam, NY 12010

Phone: (518) 843-1380
Sales: $48,100,000   *Employees:* 320
Company Type: Public Family Member   *Employees here:* 160
SIC: 2851
    Mfr products for touch-up/repair of wood metal/vinyl
    finishes fillers & extenders as well as whol related hardware
Thomas C Sullivan, Chairman of the Board

D-U-N-S 00-326-6616
MOMAR INC.
1830 Ellsworth Industrial, Atlanta, GA 30318
Phone: (404) 355-4580
Sales: $50,000,000   *Employees:* 500
Company Type: Private   *Employees here:* 200
SIC: 2842
    Mfg specialty cleaning polishing and sanitation preparations
    insecticides and pesticides water treating compounds
Julian B Mohr, President

D-U-N-S 00-214-4392   EXP
MONA INDUSTRIES INC.
    (*Parent:* Ici American Holdings Inc)
76 E 24th St, Paterson, NJ 07514
Phone: (973) 345-8220
Sales: $20,000,000   *Employees:* 146
Company Type: Private   *Employees here:* 139
SIC: 2843
    Manufactures surface active agents and detergent chemicals
J J Mc Andrews, President

D-U-N-S 00-306-4896   EXP
MONARCH RUBBER COMPANY
3500 Pulaski Hwy, Baltimore, MD 21224
Phone: (410) 342-8510
Sales: $17,736,000   *Employees:* 170
Company Type: Private   *Employees here:* 100
SIC: 2822
    Mfg synthetic rubber products
Dr David M Schwaber, Vice-President

D-U-N-S 00-626-6803   EXP
MONSANTO COMPANY
800 N Lindbergh Blvd, Saint Louis, MO 63141
Phone: (314) 694-1000
Sales: $8,648,000,000   *Employees:* 29,000
Company Type: Public   *Employees here:* 3,000
SIC: 2879
    Mfg agricultural products pharmaceuticals and nutrition and
    consumer products
Robert B Shapiro, Chairman of the Board

D-U-N-S 10-374-6855
MONTELL USA INC.
    (*Parent:* Montell North America Inc)
2801 Centerville Rd, Wilmington, DE 19808
Phone: (302) 996-6000
Sales: $1,100,000,000   *Employees:* 2,000
Company Type: Private   *Employees here:* 300
SIC: 2821
    Mfg polypropylene resins
Paolo Morrione, Chairman of the Board

D-U-N-S 06-353-4267
MONTEREY CHEMICAL COMPANY
3654 S Willow Ave, Fresno, CA 93725
Phone: (559) 499-2100
Sales: $40,000,000   *Employees:* 65
Company Type: Private   *Employees here:* 41
SIC: 2879
    Mfg whol & packages agricultural chemicals
John Salmonson, President

D-U-N-S 00-415-5347   EXP
MORGAN ADHESIVES COMPANY
   (*Parent:* Bemis Company Inc)
4560 Darrow Rd, Stow, OH 44224
Phone: (330) 688-1111
Sales: $268,100,000   *Employees:* 1,700
Company Type: Public Family Member   *Employees here:* 600
SIC: 2891
   Mfg adhesive coatings label applicating machines and
    pressure sensitive labels
Robert F Mlnarik, Chairman of the Board

D-U-N-S 04-221-6549   EXP
MORGAN CHEMICAL PRODUCTS INC.
   (*Parent:* Morganite Industries Inc)
4647 Hugh Howell Rd, Tucker, GA 30084
Phone: (770) 934-7800
Sales: $32,500,000   *Employees:* 275
Company Type: Private   *Employees here:* 4
SIC: 2842
   Holding company
Peter Muldowney, Chief Executive Officer

D-U-N-S 03-646-1556   EXP
MORTON INTERNATIONAL, INC.
100 N Riverside Plz, Chicago, IL 60606
Phone: (312) 807-2000
Sales: $2,574,400,000   *Employees:* 10,600
Company Type: Public   *Employees here:* 250
SIC: 2891
   Specialty chemicals and salt
S J Stewart, Chairman of the Board

D-U-N-S 93-822-7634
MULBERRY CORPORATION
State Hwy 60 E, Mulberry, FL 33860
Phone: (941) 425-1176
Sales: $130,000,000   *Employees:* 250
Company Type: Private   *Employees here:* 6
SIC: 2874
   Holding company
Judas Azuelos, Chairman of the Board

D-U-N-S 00-317-6740   EXP
MULBERRY PHOSPHATES INC.
   (*Parent:* Mulberry Corporation)
Rr 60, Mulberry, FL 33860
Phone: (941) 425-1176
Sales: $46,000,000   *Employees:* 230
Company Type: Private   *Employees here:* 230
SIC: 2874
   Mfg phosphatic and nitrogenous fertilizers
Phillip Rinaldi, President

D-U-N-S 60-877-2992
MUSCLE SHOALS MINERALS INC.
510 Mulberry Ln, Cherokee, AL 35616
Phone: (256) 370-7102
Sales: $19,600,000   *Employees:* 124
Company Type: Private   *Employees here:* 74
SIC: 2819
   Processing of fused magnesium oxide
Walter R Johnson, President

D-U-N-S 18-921-6955
MYTEX POLYMERS INCORPORATED
5200 Bayway Dr, Baytown, TX 77520
Phone: (281) 425-5401
Sales: $19,700,000   *Employees:* NA
Company Type: Private   *Employees here:* NA
SIC: 2821
   Mfg plastics
J B Riley, President

D-U-N-S 06-986-9980
N S O RESINS, INC.
211 Joe Bernat Dr, Greenwood, SC 29646
Phone: (864) 229-4377
Sales: $18,400,000   *Employees:* 110
Company Type: Private   *Employees here:* 110
SIC: 2821
   Converter of off grade nylon and polypropylene
Joseph F Flynn, Chairman of the Board

D-U-N-S 04-901-3811
NA-CHURS PLANT FOOD, COMPANY
421 Leader St, Marion, OH 43302
Phone: (740) 382-5701
Sales: $22,142,000   *Employees:* 100
Company Type: Private   *Employees here:* 75
SIC: 2875
   Manufacturer of liquid fertilizer
Debbie Rettig, Exec Asst

D-U-N-S 00-496-2403   EXP
NALCO CHEMICAL COMPANY
1 Nalco Ctr, Naperville, IL 60563
Phone: (630) 305-1000
Sales: $1,433,700,000   *Employees:* 6,502
Company Type: Public   *Employees here:* 1,155
SIC: 2899
   Mfr specialty chemicals equipment and finance leasing and
    mfr adhesives and sealants
Edward J Mooney, Chairman of the Board

D-U-N-S 79-210-8029
NALCO DIVERSIFIED TECHNOLOGIES
   (*Parent:* Nalco Chemical Company)
7145 Pine St, Chagrin Falls, OH 44022
Phone: (440) 247-5000
Sales: $54,000,000   *Employees:* 255
Company Type: Public Family Member   *Employees here:* 100
SIC: 2899
   Mfg water treating compounds
Richard Fruit, Vice-President

D-U-N-S 86-815-9013
NALCO/EXXON ENERGY CHEM, LP
7701 Highway 90a, Sugar Land, TX 77478
Phone: (281) 263-7000
Sales: $471,800,000   *Employees:* 1,500
Company Type: Private   *Employees here:* 450
SIC: 2899
   Mfg specialty chemicals
John R Sutley, President

D-U-N-S 61-812-4507   EXP
NAN YA PLASTICS CORP. AMERICA
9 Peach Tree Hill Rd, Livingston, NJ 07039
Phone: (973) 992-1775
Sales: $612,085,000   *Employees:* 1,130
Company Type: Private   *Employees here:* 17
SIC: 2824
   Mfg polyester fibers ethylene glycol and pvc flexible plastic
    film
Y C Wang, Chairman of the Board

D-U-N-S 00-136-8075
NASSAU METALS CORPORATION
   (*Parent:* Lucent Technologies Inc)
286 Richmond Valley Rd, Staten Island, NY 10309
Phone: (718) 317-4400

Sales: $50,000,000   *Employees:* 100
Company Type: Public Family Member   *Employees here:* 100
SIC: 2819
    Mfg of electroplating chemicals and refinery of precious
    metal scrap
Don Margaritonda, President

D-U-N-S 00-516-9602
NATIONAL CASEIN CO. INC.
601 W 80th St, Chicago, IL 60620
Phone: (773) 846-7300
Sales: $24,247,000   *Employees:* 70
Company Type: Private   *Employees here:* 52
SIC: 2891
    Mfg casein glue & other adhesives
Hope T Cook, President

D-U-N-S 78-942-1757
NATIONAL GENETICS INSTITUTE
2311 Pontius Ave, Los Angeles, CA 90064
Phone: (310) 568-9895
Sales: $30,000,000   *Employees:* 125
Company Type: Private   *Employees here:* 120
SIC: 2869
    Commercial reference lab for infectious diseases and genetic
    testing
Mike Aicher, Chief Executive Officer

D-U-N-S 00-316-2310
NATIONAL WELDERS SUPPLY CO.
810 & 724 Gesco St, Charlotte, NC 28208
Phone: (704) 333-5475
Sales: $130,495,000   *Employees:* 810
Company Type: Private   *Employees here:* 210
SIC: 2813
    Mfg industrial gases & whol welding & cutting equipment &
    robotic equipment & supplies & police supplies
Erroll Sult, Chief Executive Officer

D-U-N-S 13-111-9299   EXP
NATURAL GAS ODORIZING INC.
    (Parent: Oxy Chemical Corporation)
3601 Decker Dr, Baytown, TX 77520
Phone: (281) 424-5568
Sales: $20,000,000   *Employees:* 50
Company Type: Public Family Member   *Employees here:* 50
SIC: 2869
    Mfg gas odorants
L J Story, Chairman of the Board

D-U-N-S 95-918-2577
NATURAL WHITE MANUFACTURING
175 Cooper Ave, Ste 104, Tonawanda, NY 14150
Phone: (716) 874-7190
Sales: $15,500,000   *Employees:* 120
Company Type: Private   *Employees here:* 120
SIC: 2844
    Manufactures toothpaste
Michael Hildick, Vice-President

D-U-N-S 00-896-3910   EXP
NCH CORPORATION
2727 Chemsearch Blvd, Irving, TX 75062
Phone: (972) 438-0211
Sales: $784,095,000   *Employees:* 10,458
Company Type: Public   *Employees here:* 605
SIC: 2842
    Mfg maintenance specialty pdts
Irvin L Levy, President

D-U-N-S 06-367-1234
NELSON BROTHERS INC.
820 Shades Creek Pkwy, Birmingham, AL 35209

Phone: (205) 802-5320
Sales: $26,000,000   *Employees:* 225
Company Type: Private   *Employees here:* 25
SIC: 2892
    Mfg explosives and whol explosive accessories
William H Nelson III, Chief Executive Officer

D-U-N-S 00-201-4595   EXP
NEPERA, INC.
    (Parent: Cambrex Corporation)
Rr 17, Harriman, NY 10926
Phone: (914) 782-1200
Sales: $60,000,000   *Employees:* 130
Company Type: Public Family Member   *Employees here:* 130
SIC: 2869
    Mfg bulk organic chemicals
Thomas Bird, President

D-U-N-S 13-107-5632
NESTE CHEMICALS HOLDING INC.
    (Parent: Neste Corporate Holding Inc)
5 Post Oak Park, Ste 1230, Houston, TX 77027
Phone: (713) 622-7459
Sales: $70,600,000   *Employees:* 450
Company Type: Private   *Employees here:* 1
SIC: 2891
    Holding company whose operating subsidiaries are engaged
    in the mfg of adhesive resins other synthetic resins &
    polysters
Mauri Hattunen, President

D-U-N-S 06-214-5388   EXP
NESTE POLYESTER INC.
    (Parent: Neste Oil Holding (usa))
5106 Wheeler Ave, Fort Smith, AR 72901
Phone: (501) 646-7865
Sales: $22,000,000   *Employees:* 150
Company Type: Private   *Employees here:* 80
SIC: 2851
    Mfg gel coatings for reinforced plastics
Gary Loop, Vice-President

D-U-N-S 00-942-0126
NESTE RESINS CORPORATION
    (Parent: Neste Chemicals Holding Inc)
1600 Valley River Dr, Eugene, OR 97401
Phone: (541) 687-8840
Sales: $180,000,000   *Employees:* 300
Company Type: Private   *Employees here:* 28
SIC: 2821
    Mfg synthetic resins
Ronald W Kroeker, President

D-U-N-S 00-825-4617   EXP
NEUTROGENA CORPORATION
    (Parent: Johnson & Johnson)
5760 W 96th St, Los Angeles, CA 90045
Phone: (310) 642-1150
Sales: $360,000,000   *Employees:* 850
Company Type: Public Family Member   *Employees here:* 662
SIC: 2844
    Mfg skin care & hair care pdts
J M Nugent, President

D-U-N-S 00-433-4157   EXP
NEVILLE CHEMICAL COMPANY
2800 Neville Rd, Pittsburgh, PA 15225
Phone: (412) 331-4200
Sales: $89,500,000   *Employees:* 425
Company Type: Private   *Employees here:* 395
SIC: 2821
    Mfg resins
L V Dauler Jr, Chairman of the Board

D-U-N-S 00-512-5757
NEW ENERGY CORP.
3201 W Calvert St, South Bend, IN 46613
Phone: (219) 233-3116
Sales: $92,421,000 *Employees:* 135
Company Type: Private *Employees here:* 135
SIC: 2869
  Mfg ethanol
Nathan P Kimpel, President

D-U-N-S 10-631-5583
NEW PENDULUM CORPORATION
3411 Silverside Rd, Wilmington, DE 19810
Phone: (302) 478-6160
Sales: $35,500,000 *Employees:* 300
Company Type: Private *Employees here:* 300
SIC: 2842
  Holding company through its subsidiary manufactures
    industrial absorbents
Bernard E Stapelfeld, Chairman of the Board

D-U-N-S 93-380-0377
NEW RIVER ENERGETICS, INC.
  (Parent: Alliant Techsystems Inc)
Radford Ammunition Base, Radford, VA 24141
Phone: (540) 639-7631
Sales: $150,500,000 *Employees:* 1,300
Company Type: Public Family Member *Employees here:* 1,300
SIC: 2892
  Mfg commercial gunpowder
Nicholas G Vlchakis, President

D-U-N-S 83-741-2626
NEW SOUTH CHEMICALS, INC.
2303 Cumberland Pkwy SE, Atlanta, GA 30339
Phone: (770) 436-1542
Sales: $39,500,000 *Employees:* 250
Company Type: Private *Employees here:* 4
SIC: 2819
  Holding company through sub mfg inorganic and organic
    specialty chemicals
Errol J Menke, Chairman of the Board

D-U-N-S 08-968-8360 EXP
NEWPORT ADHESIVES & COMPOSITES
1822 Reynolds Ave, Irvine, CA 92614
Phone: (949) 253-5680
Sales: $33,336,000 *Employees:* 92
Company Type: Private *Employees here:* 92
SIC: 2891
  Mfg adhesives and composite materials
Yuichiro Nogami, President

D-U-N-S 94-226-5927
NFS SERVICE, LLC
3945 Holcomb Bridge Rd, Norcross, GA 30092
Phone: (770) 662-8405
Sales: $45,000,000 *Employees:* 351
Company Type: Private *Employees here:* 1
SIC: 2819
  Holding co & through subsidiary nuclear fuel reclaiming
    reprocessing & fabrication
Paul F Schutt Jr, Chief Executive Officer

D-U-N-S 19-976-8565
NICCA USA INC.
5000 S Nelson Dr, Fountain Inn, SC 29644
Phone: (864) 862-1426
Sales: $16,742,000 *Employees:* 66
Company Type: Private *Employees here:* 66
SIC: 2843
  Mfg textile chemicals
William L Grabowski, President

D-U-N-S 00-516-7242 EXP
NILES CHEMICAL PAINT COMPANY
225 Fort St, Niles, MI 49120
Phone: (616) 683-3377
Sales: $17,831,000 *Employees:* 100
Company Type: Private *Employees here:* 95
SIC: 2851
  Mfg paints
Neil Hannewyk, Chairman of the Board

D-U-N-S 18-554-9730
NINE WEST CORPORATION
  (Parent: Trans-Resources Inc)
9 W 57th St, Ste 3900, New York, NY 10019
Phone: (212) 888-3044
Sales: $122,800,000 *Employees:* 400
Company Type: Private *Employees here:* 3
SIC: 2873
  Mfg nitrate fertilizers organic chemicals & herbicides
Arie Genger, President

D-U-N-S 78-204-7690
NIPPON STEEL CHEMCIAL CORPORATION
6150 Whitmore Lake Rd, Brighton, MI 48116
Phone: (810) 227-3500
Sales: $55,593,000 *Employees:* 153
Company Type: Private *Employees here:* 15
SIC: 2821
  Manufacturer of thermoplastic materials
Shunsuke Sawanda, President

D-U-N-S 00-410-7710
NITRAM INC.
5321 Hartford St, Tampa, FL 33619
Phone: (813) 626-2181
Sales: $19,700,000 *Employees:* 85
Company Type: Private *Employees here:* 85
SIC: 2873
  Mfg nitric acid & ammonia nitrate
John F Harris, Chairman of the Board

D-U-N-S 00-131-7577 EXP
NL INDUSTRIES INC.
  (Parent: Valhi Inc)
16825 Northchase Dr, Houston, TX 77060
Phone: (281) 423-3300
Sales: $837,240,000 *Employees:* 2,600
Company Type: Public *Employees here:* 50
SIC: 2816
  Mfg titanium dioxide pigments
J L Martin, President

D-U-N-S 01-759-1009
NOBEL INDUSTRIES USA, INC.
  (Parent: Akzo Nobel Inc)
300 S Riverside Plz, Chicago, IL 60606
Phone: (312) 906-7500
Sales: $99,500,000 *Employees:* NA
Company Type: Private *Employees here:* NA
SIC: 2899
  Through subsidiaries mfg sodium chlorate whol ink & mfg
    emulsified asphalt equipment
Jan Kihlberg, President

D-U-N-S 87-262-9969 EXP
NOLTEX, LLC
12220 Strang Rd, La Porte, TX 77571
Phone: (281) 842-5000
Sales: $35,000,000 *Employees:* 80
Company Type: Private *Employees here:* 80
SIC: 2821
  Mfg plastic chemical resins
Kenjiro Kuno, President

D-U-N-S 04-987-4555   EXP
NOR-COTE INTERNATIONAL, INC.
506 Lafayette Ave, Crawfordsville, IN 47933
Phone: (765) 362-9180
Sales: $16,895,000   *Employees:* 80
Company Type: Private   *Employees here:* 30
SIC: 2893
   Mfg ultra violet curable inks
Norman G Wolcott Jr, President

D-U-N-S 00-835-2957
NORAC COMPANY INC.
405 S Motor Ave, Azusa, CA 91702
Phone: (626) 334-2908
Sales: $22,100,000   *Employees:* 98
Company Type: Private   *Employees here:* 45
SIC: 2869
   Mfg organic peroxide chemicals metallic stearates & bulk
   pharmaceuticals
Chester M Mc Closkey, Chairman of the Board

D-U-N-S 80-901-2230
NORFLUOR USA, LLC
415 Pablo Ave, Jacksonville Beach, FL 32250
Phone: (904) 241-1200
Sales: $16,000,000   *Employees:* 170
Company Type: Private   *Employees here:* 3
SIC: 2819
   Mfg industrial & heavy chemicals
David Messerlie, Chairman of the Board

D-U-N-S 00-406-2857
NORIT AMERICAS INC.
1050 Crown Pointe Pkwy, Atlanta, GA 30338
Phone: (770) 512-4610
Sales: $60,000,000   *Employees:* 400
Company Type: Private   *Employees here:* 25
SIC: 2819
   Mfg activated carbon
Herman De Groot, President

D-U-N-S 13-041-2182   EXP
NORTH AMERICAN GREEN INC.
14649 Highway 41 N, Evansville, IN 47711
Phone: (812) 867-6632
Sales: $15,400,000   *Employees:* 85
Company Type: Private   *Employees here:* 15
SIC: 2875
   Mfg matting used to prevent erosion
Daniel L Koester, Chief Executive Officer

D-U-N-S 61-140-0854   EXP
NORTH AMERICAN OXIDE, LLC
480 Arcata Blvd, Clarksville, TN 37040
Phone: (931) 552-8080
Sales: $25,000,000   *Employees:* 54
Company Type: Private   *Employees here:* 54
SIC: 2816
   Mfg zinc oxide
Sam R Rechter, Chairman of the Board

D-U-N-S 05-529-6479
NORTHERN LABS INC.
4701 Custer St, Manitowoc, WI 54220
Phone: (920) 684-7137
Sales: $48,020,000   *Employees:* 220
Company Type: Private   *Employees here:* 180
SIC: 2842
   Mfg automotive & household polishes hair & personal care
   products
James D Culea, President

D-U-N-S 61-810-7429
NORTHTEC, INC.
  (Parent: Estee Lauder Inc)
411 Sinclair Rd, Bristol, PA 19007
Phone: (215) 781-1600
Sales: $83,000,000   *Employees:* 700
Company Type: Public Family Member   *Employees here:* 200
SIC: 2844
   Mfg cosmetic components
Leonard A Lauder, Chief Executive Officer

D-U-N-S 04-317-9258
NORTON & SON
5928 Garfield Ave, Los Angeles, CA 90040
Phone: (323) 685-7220
Sales: $28,500,000   *Employees:* 200
Company Type: Private   *Employees here:* 200
SIC: 2851
   Manufactures paints
Edward F Norton Jr, Chairman of the Board

D-U-N-S 00-331-9548
NOTTINGHAM COMPANY
1303 Boyd Ave NW, Atlanta, GA 30318
Phone: (404) 351-3501
Sales: $25,000,000   *Employees:* 35
Company Type: Private   *Employees here:* 25
SIC: 2869
   Mfg chemicals specializing in organic flotation reagents paper
   chemicals and whol organic chemicals
Charles A Little III, Chairman of the Board

D-U-N-S 17-419-0785   EXP
NOVA BOREALIS COMPOUNDS, LLC
176 Thomas Rd, Port Murray, NJ 07865
Phone: (908) 850-6200
Sales: $50,000,000   *Employees:* 50
Company Type: Private   *Employees here:* 50
SIC: 2821
   Mfg plastic materials/resins
Paul Bryant, President

D-U-N-S 10-400-0625
NOVA CHEMICALS INC.
  (Parent: Nova Chemicals Ltd)
400 Frankfort Rd, Monaca, PA 15061
Phone: (724) 774-1000
Sales: $400,000,000   *Employees:* 500
Company Type: Private   *Employees here:* 180
SIC: 2821
   Mfg polyethylene & polystyrene resins
Zoltan J Dorko, President

D-U-N-S 00-132-1595
NOVILLE INC.
3 Empire Blvd, South Hackensack, NJ 07606
Phone: (908) 754-2222
Sales: $38,000,000   *Employees:* 130
Company Type: Private   *Employees here:* 70
SIC: 2899
   Operates as a manufacturer of fragrances and flavors
Daniel Carey, President

D-U-N-S 05-209-0909
NOVO NORDISK BIOCHEM, NA
  (Parent: Novo-Nordisk Of North America)
77 Perry Chapel Church Rd, Franklinton, NC 27525
Phone: (919) 494-3000
Sales: $150,000,000   *Employees:* 350
Company Type: Private   *Employees here:* 350
SIC: 2869
   Mfr industrial and food enzymes
Lee Yarbrough, President

D-U-N-S 00-308-2997
NOXELL CORPORATION
 (*Parent:* The Procter & Gamble Company)
11050 York Rd, Cockeysville, MD 21030
Phone: (410) 785-7300
Sales: $242,600,000   *Employees:* 2,397
Company Type: Public Family Member   *Employees here:* 2
SIC: 2844
 Mfg cosmetics fragrances & toilet preparations
Beth J Kaplan, President

D-U-N-S 78-568-7534   EXP
NPA COATINGS INC.
11110 Berea Rd, Cleveland, OH 44102
Phone: (216) 631-2002
Sales: $48,000,000   *Employees:* 185
Company Type: Private   *Employees here:* 185
SIC: 2851
 Mfg powder paint
Samuel Rhue, President

D-U-N-S 03-872-6444
NS GROUP INC.
9th & Lowell Sts, Newport, KY 41072
Phone: (606) 292-6809
Sales: $409,855,000   *Employees:* 1,803
Company Type: Public   *Employees here:* 10
SIC: 2891
 Steel mini-mills mfr steel tubular pdts pipe hot rolled steel
 bar & semi-fin pdts metal heat treating & mfr indus
 adhesives
John R Parker, Chief Financial Officer

D-U-N-S 06-420-1221   EXP
NU GRO TECHNOLOGIES, INC.
 (*Parent:* Nu-Gro Corporation The)
20 Industrial Pkwy, Gloversville, NY 12078
Phone: (518) 725-2617
Sales: $15,000,000   *Employees:* 26
Company Type: Private   *Employees here:* 22
SIC: 2875
 Mfg fertilizer
John Hill, President

D-U-N-S 16-088-8582
NU-WEST INDUSTRIES, INC.
 (*Parent:* Agrium Us Inc)
3010 Conda Rd, Soda Springs, ID 83230
Phone: (208) 547-4381
Sales: $55,000,000   *Employees:* 275
Company Type: Private   *Employees here:* 275
SIC: 2874
 Mfg agricultural chemicals
John Van Brunt, President

D-U-N-S 62-804-5858   EXP
NU-WORLD CORP.
1100 Milik St, Carteret, NJ 07008
Phone: (732) 632-2911
Sales: $17,268,000   *Employees:* 50
Company Type: Private   *Employees here:* 50
SIC: 2844
 Mfg & fills lipsticks nail polish powders and mascara
Joseph Bogatz, President

D-U-N-S 04-949-8025   EXP
NUCLEAR FUEL SERVICES INC.
 (*Parent:* Nfs Service Llc)
1205 Banner Hill Rd, Erwin, TN 37650
Phone: (423) 743-9141

Sales: $45,000,000   *Employees:* 350
Company Type: Private   *Employees here:* 325
SIC: 2819
 Nuclear fuel reclaiming reprocessing & fabrication
Paul F Schutt Jr, Chief Executive Officer

D-U-N-S 00-725-7355
NUTRA-FLO COMPANY
 (*Parent:* Flo Kay Industries Inc)
1919 Grand Ave, Sioux City, IA 51106
Phone: (712) 277-2011
Sales: $40,000,000   *Employees:* 100
Company Type: Private   *Employees here:* 65
SIC: 2873
 Mfg fertilizer feed supplements & zinc chemicals
Dirk Lohry, President

D-U-N-S 01-812-9254   EXP
NUTRASWEET KELCO COMPANY (INC)
 (*Parent:* Monsanto Company)
200 Merchandise Mart, Chicago, IL 60654
Phone: (312) 840-5000
Sales: $341,200,000   *Employees:* 1,400
Company Type: Public Family Member   *Employees here:* 400
SIC: 2869
 Mfg industrial organic chemicals mfg ice cream/frozen desert
Robert E Flynn, Chief Executive Officer

D-U-N-S 10-573-1673
NYLTECH NORTH AMERICA
333 Sundial Ave, Manchester, NH 03103
Phone: (603) 627-5150
Sales: $28,700,000   *Employees:* 75
Company Type: Private   *Employees here:* 70
SIC: 2821
 Mfg nylon resins
Franco Bertini, President

D-U-N-S 00-154-4717
O'NEIL COLOR AND COMPOUNDING
 (*Parent:* Primex Plastics Corporation)
61 River Dr, Garfield, NJ 07026
Phone: (973) 777-8999
Sales: $38,100,000   *Employees:* 150
Company Type: Private   *Employees here:* 50
SIC: 2865
 Mfg color additive concentrates & compounds
Dr John Farber, Chairman of the Board

D-U-N-S 55-612-1200
OAKITE PRODUCTS, INC.
50 Valley Rd, Berkeley Heights, NJ 07922
Phone: (908) 464-6900
Sales: $70,163,000   *Employees:* 300
Company Type: Private   *Employees here:* 200
SIC: 2842
 Mfg chemical specialty products
Ronald Felber, President

D-U-N-S 06-727-1981   EXP
OCCIDENTAL CHEMICAL CORP.
 (*Parent:* C H Oxy Corporation)
5005 LBJ Fwy, Dallas, TX 75244
Phone: (972) 404-3800
Sales: $2,574,829,000   *Employees:* 7,200
Company Type: Public Family Member   *Employees here:* 700
SIC: 2812
 Mfg industrial & specialty chemicals & plastics
J R Hirl, President

D-U-N-S 14-437-4907
OCCIDENTAL CHEMICAL HOLDING CORP.
   (*Parent:* Occidental Petroleum Inv Co)
5005 LBJ Fwy, Ste 2200, Dallas, TX 75244
Phone: (972) 404-3800
Sales: $4,348,991,000   *Employees:* 10,400
Company Type: Public Family Member   *Employees here:* 800
SIC: 2869
   Mfg organic chemicals plastics fertilizers agricultural
      chemicals & feed products
J R Hirl, President

D-U-N-S 00-690-8354   EXP
OCCIDENTAL PETROLEUM CORP.
10889 Wilshire Blvd, Los Angeles, CA 90024
Phone: (310) 208-8800
Sales: $8,016,000,000   *Employees:* 12,380
Company Type: Public   *Employees here:* 311
SIC: 2812
   Mfg chemicals oil and gas exploration and production
Dr Ray R Irani, Chairman of the Board

D-U-N-S 09-006-8503
OCHOA FERTILIZER CO. INC.
   (*Parent:* Protein Genetics Inc)
Km 1 Hm 9 Rr 333, Guanica, PR 00653
Phone: (787) 821-2200
Sales: $17,146,000   *Employees:* 53
Company Type: Private   *Employees here:* 53
SIC: 2874
   Mfg blend fertilizers fencing & irrigation products &
      wholesales farm insecticides & pesticides
Augusto R Palmer, President

D-U-N-S 62-114-2884
OCI WYOMING, LP
12 Miles N On La Barge Rd, Green River, WY 82935
Phone: (307) 875-2600
Sales: $178,000,000   *Employees:* 490
Company Type: Private   *Employees here:* 490
SIC: 2812
   Mfg soda ash
Christophe T Fraser, Chief Operating Officer

D-U-N-S 00-127-0859
OCTAGON PROCESS INC.
596 River Rd, Edgewater, NJ 07020
Phone: (201) 945-9400
Sales: $40,000,000   *Employees:* 40
Company Type: Private   *Employees here:* 40
SIC: 2899
   Mfg de-icing & anti-icing fluids specialty chemicals & ndt
      products
Steven Kramer, Chief Executive Officer

D-U-N-S 16-007-0363
OHIO SEALANTS INC.
   (*Parent:* Sovereign Specialty Chem Lp)
7405 Production Dr, Mentor, OH 44060
Phone: (440) 255-8900
Sales: $51,600,000   *Employees:* 330
Company Type: Private   *Employees here:* 70
SIC: 2891
   Mfg adhesives/sealants
Pete Longo, General Manager

D-U-N-S 80-178-2590
OHKA AMERICA, INC.
4600 NW Shute Rd, Hillsboro, OR 97124
Phone: (503) 693-7711

Sales: $17,000,000   *Employees:* 47
Company Type: Private   *Employees here:* 35
SIC: 2819
   Mfg liquid chemicals
Akira Yokota, President

D-U-N-S 09-047-5799
OLAY COMPANY INC.
   (*Parent:* The Procter & Gamble Company)
Km 2 Hm 3 Rr 735, Cayey, PR 00736
Phone: (787) 738-2191
Sales: $35,000,000   *Employees:* 300
Company Type: Public Family Member   *Employees here:* 300
SIC: 2844
   Mfg toilet preparations & hair tonics
M P Holland, President

D-U-N-S 62-331-6403
OLD 97 COMPANY
   (*Parent:* Stephan Co Inc)
4829 E Broadway Ave, Tampa, FL 33605
Phone: (813) 248-5761
Sales: $15,000,000   *Employees:* 100
Company Type: Public Family Member   *Employees here:* 15
SIC: 2844
   Manufactures hair care products
Lucille Murphy, President

D-U-N-S 05-220-4864   EXP
OLD BRIDGE CHEMICALS, INC.
Old Water Works Rd, Old Bridge, NJ 08857
Phone: (732) 727-2225
Sales: $20,000,000   *Employees:* 65
Company Type: Private   *Employees here:* 65
SIC: 2819
   Mfg zinc sulfate compounds & copper sulfate
Bruce Bzura, President

D-U-N-S 19-516-6624
OLD WORLD INDUSTRIES, INC.
4065 Commercial Ave, Northbrook, IL 60062
Phone: (847) 559-2000
Sales: $22,900,000   *Employees:* 150
Company Type: Private   *Employees here:* 150
SIC: 2899
   Mfg & dist automotive products & industrial chemicals
Tom Hurvis, Chairman of the Board

D-U-N-S 84-852-0268
OLGA G MARCUS COSMETICS INC.
345 Oser Ave, Hauppauge, NY 11788
Phone: (516) 231-3636
Sales: $22,300,000   *Employees:* 160
Company Type: Private   *Employees here:* 75
SIC: 2844
   Mfg cosmetics
Olga Cohen, President

D-U-N-S 00-133-8086   EXP
OLIN CORPORATION
501 Merritt 7, Norwalk, CT 06851
Phone: (203) 750-3000
Sales: $2,410,000,000   *Employees:* 10,000
Company Type: Public   *Employees here:* 650
SIC: 2812
   Mfg industrial & consumer specialty chemicals sporting
      ammunition and copper & copper alloys
Donald W Griffin, Chairman of the Board

D-U-N-S 55-686-9238   EXP
OM GROUP INC.
50 Public Sq, Ste 3800, Cleveland, OH 44113
Phone: (216) 781-0083

Sales: $487,296,000   *Employees:* 758
Company Type: Public   *Employees here:* 9
SIC: 2819
     Mfg value added metal-based specialty chemicals
James P Mooney, Chairman of the Board

D-U-N-S 00-416-5742   EXP
OMG AMERICA'S INC.
     (Parent: Om Group Inc)
811 Sharon Dr, Cleveland, OH 44145
Phone: (216) 781-8383
Sales: $39,200,000   *Employees:* 160
Company Type: Public Family Member   *Employees here:* 60
SIC: 2869
     Mfg value added metal-based organic & inorganic chemicals
Thomas Fleming, President

D-U-N-S 04-986-5769
OMG FIDELITY INC.
     (Parent: Om Group Inc)
470 Frelinghuysen Ave, Newark, NJ 07114
Phone: (973) 242-4110
Sales: $45,000,000   *Employees:* 135
Company Type: Public Family Member   *Employees here:* 95
SIC: 2899
     Manufactures non precious metal plating solutions &
     specialized electroplating chemicals
Dan Davitt, Chief Financial Officer

D-U-N-S 06-555-1640
OMNI OXIDE, LLC
5901 Lakeside Blvd, Indianapolis, IN 46278
Phone: (317) 290-5000
Sales: $30,000,000   *Employees:* 80
Company Type: Private   *Employees here:* 12
SIC: 2819
     Mfg lead oxide
Greg Stevens, President

D-U-N-S 17-946-2197
OMNIUM, LLC
1417 SW Lower Lake Rd, Saint Joseph, MO 64504
Phone: (816) 238-8111
Sales: $18,050,000   *Employees:* 228
Company Type: Private   *Employees here:* 228
SIC: 2879
     Third party contract manufacturing
Jeffrey Greseph, President

D-U-N-S 07-356-9717
OMYA (CALIFORNIA) INC.
     (Parent: Pluess-Staufer Industries Inc)
7299 Crystal Creek Rd, Lucerne Valley, CA 92356
Phone: (760) 248-7306
Sales: $20,000,000   *Employees:* 82
Company Type: Private   *Employees here:* 82
SIC: 2819
     Processing of calcium carbonate
James Reddy, President

D-U-N-S 00-206-9136   EXP
OMYA, INC.
     (Parent: Pluess-Staufer Industries Inc)
61 Main St, Proctor, VT 05765
Phone: (802) 459-3311
Sales: $29,900,000   *Employees:* 166
Company Type: Private   *Employees here:* 150
SIC: 2819
     Mfg fine ground calcium carbonate generator of hydro-
     electric power & aircraft leasing
Jeremy C Croggon, President

D-U-N-S 02-311-9048
OPAL TECHNOLOGIES INC.
211 E 43rd St, Rm 1102, New York, NY 10017
Phone: (212) 338-0050
Sales: $17,700,000   *Employees:* 61
Company Type: Public   *Employees here:* 61
SIC: 2873
     Mfg & whol organic fertilizers & related products
John Koon, Chairman of the Board

D-U-N-S 10-306-2204   EXP
OPI PRODUCTS INC.
13056 Saticoy St, North Hollywood, CA 91605
Phone: (818) 759-2400
Sales: $30,000,000   *Employees:* 87
Company Type: Private   *Employees here:* 80
SIC: 2844
     Mfg acrylic finger nails
George Schaeffer, President

D-U-N-S 80-605-9275
ORANGE PLASTICS INC.
1860 S Acacia Ave, Compton, CA 90220
Phone: (310) 609-1900
Sales: $20,900,000   *Employees:* 100
Company Type: Private   *Employees here:* 100
SIC: 2821
     Mfg plastic products
Gary Duboff, President

D-U-N-S 10-251-8453   EXP
ORBSEAL, LLC
201 E Highway 10, Richmond, MO 64085
Phone: (816) 776-5024
Sales: $62,700,000   *Employees:* 400
Company Type: Private   *Employees here:* 380
SIC: 2891
     Mfg sealants
Robert J Orscheln, President

D-U-N-S 01-418-6563
OREGON RESEARCH & DEVELOPMENT
     (Parent: Thoro System Products Inc)
10245 Centurion Pkwy N, Jacksonville, FL 32256
Phone: (904) 996-6000
Sales: $15,000,000   *Employees:* 40
Company Type: Private   *Employees here:* 5
SIC: 2899
     Mfg construction products
David Fyfe, President

D-U-N-S 01-850-1999   EXP
ORGANIC DYESTUFFS CORPORATION
74 Valley St 84, East Providence, RI 02914
Phone: (401) 434-3300
Sales: $18,225,000   *Employees:* 134
Company Type: Private   *Employees here:* 45
SIC: 2861
     Mfg dye stuffs & sales promotion agency
Robert Gormley, President

D-U-N-S 02-886-5327
ORIENT CHEMICAL CORP.
65 Springfield Ave, Springfield, NJ 07081
Phone: (973) 258-1600
Sales: $18,633,000   *Employees:* 30
Company Type: Private   *Employees here:* 5
SIC: 2865
     Mfg cyclic crudes/intermediates/dyes
Akihiro Takahashi, President

D-U-N-S 00-120-1045　　　　　　　　　　　　EXP
ORIGINAL BRADFORD SOAP WORKS
200 Providence St, West Warwick, RI 02893
Phone: (401) 821-2141
Sales: $35,000,000　　　　　　　　　　*Employees:* 500
Company Type: Private　　　　　*Employees here:* 425
SIC: 2841
　Mfg soaps & detergents
Frances H Gammell, Treasurer

D-U-N-S 03-739-9623
ORTEC INC.
505 Gentry Memorial Hwy, Easley, SC 29640
Phone: (864) 859-1471
Sales: $15,000,000　　　　　　　　　　*Employees:* 91
Company Type: Private　　　　　*Employees here:* 91
SIC: 2869
　Mfg specialty industrial organic chemicals
Dr David L Brotherton, President

D-U-N-S 84-707-9274
OSI SPECIALTIES HOLDING COMPANY
　(*Parent:* Witco Corporation)
1 American Ln, Greenwich, CT 06831
Phone: (203) 522-2000
Sales: $472,448,000　　　　　　　　*Employees:* 1,200
Company Type: Public Family Member　*Employees here:* 60
SIC: 2821
　Holding company
E G Cook, Chairman of the Board

D-U-N-S 80-666-0775
OSI SPECIALTIES, INC.
　(*Parent:* Osi Specialties Holding Co)
1 American Ln, Greenwich, CT 06831
Phone: (203) 552-2000
Sales: $472,448,000　　　　　　　　*Employees:* 1,200
Company Type: Public Family Member　*Employees here:* 50
SIC: 2821
　Holding company
Dr E G Cook, Chairman of the Board

D-U-N-S 96-884-1494
OUTSOURCING SERVICES GROUP INC.
425 S 9th Ave, City Of Industry, CA 91746
Phone: (626) 968-8531
Sales: $203,000,000　　　　　　　　*Employees:* 1,700
Company Type: Private　　　　　*Employees here:* 200
SIC: 2844
　Mfg cosmetics & packaging service
Walter Lim, President

D-U-N-S 10-705-1823　　　　　　　　　IMP EXP
OWEN OIL TOOLS INC.
　(*Parent:* Core Laboratories Inc)
8900 Forum Way, Fort Worth, TX 76140
Phone: (817) 551-0540
Sales: $50,000,000　　　　　　　　*Employees:* 350
Company Type: Private　　　　　*Employees here:* 100
SIC: 2892
　Mfg oil well field explosives & oil & gas completion tools
Harrold D Owen Sr, Chairman of the Board

D-U-N-S 10-766-7990　　　　　　　　　　　EXP
OXID, LP
4600 Post Oak Place Dr, Houston, TX 77027
Phone: (713) 296-7500
Sales: $17,000,000　　　　　　　　*Employees:* 41
Company Type: Private　　　　　*Employees here:* 4
SIC: 2899
　Mfg chemicals
Mac Medlen, President

D-U-N-S 14-766-7240
OXY CHEMICAL CORPORATION
　(*Parent:* Occidental Chemical Holdg Corp)
5005 LBJ Fwy, Dallas, TX 75244
Phone: (972) 404-3800
Sales: $1,845,000,000　　　　　　*Employees:* 7,500
Company Type: Public Family Member　*Employees here:* 715
SIC: 2869
　Mfg industrial organic chemicals nitrogenous & phosphatic
　fertilizers & metal treating compounds & does plastic
　processing
J R Hirl, Chairman of the Board

D-U-N-S 17-372-7512
OXY PETROCHEMICALS INC.
　(*Parent:* C H Oxy Corporation)
5005 LBJ Fwy, Dallas, TX 75244
Phone: (972) 404-3800
Sales: $321,500,000　　　　　　　*Employees:* 1,320
Company Type: Public Family Member　*Employees here:* 800
SIC: 2869
　Mfg ethylene propylene butadiene benzene and derivatives
Ray R Irani, Chairman of the Board

D-U-N-S 62-154-8908
OXYMAR
Hwy 361, Gregory, TX 78359
Phone: (361) 776-6321
Sales: $31,600,000　　　　　　　　*Employees:* 180
Company Type: Private　　　　　*Employees here:* 180
SIC: 2821
　Mfg vinyl monomer
Roy Yelverton, Business Manager

D-U-N-S 00-712-4357
P B I/GORDON CORPORATION
1217 W 12th St, Kansas City, MO 64101
Phone: (816) 421-4070
Sales: $28,800,000　　　　　　　　*Employees:* 140
Company Type: Private　　　　　*Employees here:* 60
SIC: 2879
　Mfg pesticides & agricultural chemicals
W E Mealman, Chairman of the Board

D-U-N-S 17-507-0242　　　　　　　　　　　EXP
P C R INC.
Airport Industrial Park, Gainesville, FL 32602
Phone: (352) 376-8246
Sales: $50,000,000　　　　　　　　*Employees:* 220
Company Type: Private　　　　　*Employees here:* 210
SIC: 2869
　Mfg organic chemicals
Fredrick M Blum, President

D-U-N-S 00-627-4732　　　　　　　　　　　EXP
THE P D GEORGE COMPANY
5200 N 2nd St, Saint Louis, MO 63147
Phone: (314) 621-5700
Sales: $75,160,000　　　　　　　　*Employees:* 235
Company Type: Private　　　　　*Employees here:* 224
SIC: 2851
　Mfg industrial and electrical coatings
Thomas F George, President

D-U-N-S 10-901-7004
P D GLYCOL LTD.
3510 Gulf States Utilitie, Beaumont, TX 77704
Phone: (409) 838-4521
Sales: $160,000,000　　　　　　　*Employees:* 150
Company Type: Private　　　　　*Employees here:* 150
SIC: 2821
　Mfg ethylene glycol
Jim Balfanz, General Manager

D-U-N-S 04-199-4716
P L C SPECIALTIES INC.
20-10 Maple Ave, Fair Lawn, NJ 07410
Phone: (973) 423-1515
Sales: $53,000,000   *Employees:* 450
Company Type: Private   *Employees here:* 450
SIC: 2844
   Manufactures cosmetics
Michael Assante, President

D-U-N-S 07-619-1519
P M C INC.
12243 Branford St, Sun Valley, CA 91352
Phone: (818) 896-1101
Sales: $649,233,000   *Employees:* 3,600
Company Type: Private   *Employees here:* 58
SIC: 2819
   Mfg chemicals & colors foam & foam systems mfg non-
   metallic packaging plastic sheet & coatings & electronic
   semiconductors
Philip E Kamins, President

D-U-N-S 09-049-2885
P R COLORCON INC.
   (Parent: Berwind Pharmaceutical Svcs)
Km 76 Hm 9 Rr 3, Humacao, PR 00791
Phone: (787) 852-3815
Sales: $31,800,000   *Employees:* 52
Company Type: Private   *Employees here:* 52
SIC: 2816
   Mfg inorganic pigments
Saul Melendez, President

D-U-N-S 16-102-8899
PACE INDUSTRIES INC.
   (Parent: Primex Plastics Corporation)
1400 Industrial St, Reedsburg, WI 53959
Phone: (608) 524-6777
Sales: $25,000,000   *Employees:* 150
Company Type: Private   *Employees here:* 150
SIC: 2821
   Mfg polystyrene sheets & rolls
David Pace, President

D-U-N-S 05-123-9960
PACE INTERNATIONAL, LP
500 7th Ave S, Kirkland, WA 98033
Phone: (425) 827-8711
Sales: $44,500,000   *Employees:* 171
Company Type: Private   *Employees here:* 30
SIC: 2842
   Mfg a broad range of foliar nutrients and other crop
   nutrition/protection products for the agricultural industry
Richard Hunter, President

D-U-N-S 01-092-7762   EXP
PACER TECHNOLOGY
9420 Santa Anita Ave, Rancho Cucamonga, CA 91730
Phone: (909) 987-0550
Sales: $25,678,000   *Employees:* 100
Company Type: Public   *Employees here:* 90
SIC: 2891
   Mfg adhesives & sealants
James T Munn, President

D-U-N-S 10-277-8362
PACIFIC PAC INTERNATIONAL
2340 Bert Dr, Hollister, CA 95023
Phone: (831) 636-5151

Sales: $25,000,000   *Employees:* 60
Company Type: Private   *Employees here:* 56
SIC: 2899
   Processes high purity chemicals
Leif Syrstad, President

D-U-N-S 08-969-3097   EXP
PACIFIC WORLD CORPORATION
25791 Commercentre Dr, Lake Forest, CA 92630
Phone: (949) 598-2400
Sales: $22,500,000   *Employees:* 55
Company Type: Private   *Employees here:* 55
SIC: 2844
   Mfg cosmetics
Robert A Leathers, Chairman of the Board

D-U-N-S 87-898-5928
PACKAGING ADVANTAGE CORP.
4633 S Downey Rd, Los Angeles, CA 90058
Phone: (323) 589-8181
Sales: $15,000,000   *Employees:* 275
Company Type: Private   *Employees here:* 274
SIC: 2841
   Mfg household products
Edward M Zolla III, Chief Executive Officer

D-U-N-S 06-437-1214
PALM COMMODITIES INTERNATIONAL INC.
1289 Bridgestone Pkwy, La Vergne, TN 37086
Phone: (615) 793-1990
Sales: $24,237,000   *Employees:* 55
Company Type: Private   *Employees here:* 45
SIC: 2819
   Mfg liquid nickel sulfate chloride & whol industrial chemicals
William D Fields, President

D-U-N-S 00-234-9249
PALMER INTERNATIONAL INC.
2955 Skippack Pike, Worcester, PA 19490
Phone: (610) 584-4241
Sales: $17,490,000   *Employees:* 45
Company Type: Private   *Employees here:* 25
SIC: 2822
   Mfg friction particles & adhesives
Stephen T Palmer Jr, Chairman of the Board

D-U-N-S 94-567-5098
PAM ACQUISITION CORP.
1 Mornngstar Dr N, Ste 200, Westport, CT 06880
Phone: (203) 226-7664
Sales: $146,000,000   *Employees:* 700
Company Type: Private   *Employees here:* 3
SIC: 2844
   Holding company
Vince Wasik, President

D-U-N-S 05-479-4557
PANCO MEN'S PRODUCTS INC.
45605 Citrus Ave, Indio, CA 92201
Phone: (760) 342-4368
Sales: $16,000,000   *Employees:* 15
Company Type: Private   *Employees here:* 15
SIC: 2844
   Mfg cosmetics & toiletries
Gene Pantuso, President

D-U-N-S 00-260-1656   EXP
PARA-CHEM SOUTHERN INC.
863 SE Main St, Simpsonville, SC 29681
Phone: (864) 967-7691

Sales: $85,000,000   *Employees:* 300
Company Type: Private   *Employees here:* 160
SIC: 2843
  Mfg textile finishing agents & adhesives
John W Jordan III, Chairman of the Board

D-U-N-S 00-129-0667
PARA LABORATORIES INC.
100 Rose Ave, Hempstead, NY 11550
Phone: (516) 538-4600
Sales: $20,000,000   *Employees:* 70
Company Type: Private   *Employees here:* 70
SIC: 2844
  Mfg & sells health & beauty aids
Alan Estrin, President

D-U-N-S 03-751-2746   EXP
PARFUMS DE COEUR LTD.
85 Old Kings Hwy N, Darien, CT 06820
Phone: (203) 655-8807
Sales: $118,000,000   *Employees:* 90
Company Type: Private   *Employees here:* 35
SIC: 2844
  Mfg perfumes & fragranced body sprays
Mark A Laracy, President

D-U-N-S 06-765-3642
PARKER PAINT MANUFACTURING CO.
  (Parent: Williams Paint Holdings Inc)
3003 S Tacoma Way, Tacoma, WA 98409
Phone: (253) 473-1122
Sales: $20,600,000   *Employees:* 130
Company Type: Private   *Employees here:* 100
SIC: 2851
  Mfg paint & ret paint & supplies
Richard La Fond, President

D-U-N-S 14-786-0167   IMP EXP
PARLUX FRAGRANCES INC.
3725 SW 30th Ave, Fort Lauderdale, FL 33312
Phone: (954) 316-9008
Sales: $62,369,000   *Employees:* 136
Company Type: Public   *Employees here:* 76
SIC: 2844
  Mfg fragrances cosmetics & beauty products
Ruben Lisman, Chief Operating Officer

D-U-N-S 10-720-6898
PAULSBORO PACKAGING CO
  (Parent: First Brands Corporation)
301 Mantua Ave, Paulsboro, NJ 08066
Phone: (609) 423-5090
Sales: $15,800,000   *Employees:* 125
Company Type: Public Family Member   *Employees here:* 125
SIC: 2842
  Mfg auto products & polishes
Dale Satterfield, President

D-U-N-S 03-824-2681
PAVION LIMITED
  (Parent: Am Cosmetics Inc)
100 Porete Ave, North Arlington, NJ 07031
Phone: (201) 998-8890
Sales: $70,000,000   *Employees:* 350
Company Type: Private   *Employees here:* 350
SIC: 2844
  Mfg cosmetics & fragrances
Lawrence Bathgate II, President

D-U-N-S 61-870-9760   EXP
PCI, INC.
  (Parent: Pcl Group Inc)
100 Wurts Rd, Wurtland, KY 41144

Phone: (606) 836-3660
Sales: $25,000,000   *Employees:* 62
Company Type: Private   *Employees here:* 62
SIC: 2869
  Mfg special organic chemicals
Marvin Gallisdorfer, President

D-U-N-S 60-857-0362
PCL GROUP, INC.
266 W Mitchell Ave, Cincinnati, OH 45232
Phone: (513) 681-0099
Sales: $60,000,000   *Employees:* 300
Company Type: Private   *Employees here:* 12
SIC: 2865
  Mfg organic color pigments & dye intermediates
Marvin Gallisdorfer, President

D-U-N-S 00-408-8498
PCS JOINT VENTURE LTD.
1801 E Memorial Blvd, Lakeland, FL 33801
Phone: (941) 688-2442
Sales: $65,700,000   *Employees:* 101
Company Type: Private   *Employees here:* 8
SIC: 2875
  Mfg fertilizer & sod farm
Carlos Smith, Chief Operating Officer

D-U-N-S 85-840-4015
PCS NITROGEN FERTILIZER, LP
3175 Lenox Park Blvd, Memphis, TN 38115
Phone: (901) 758-5200
Sales: $1,310,011,000   *Employees:* 1,048
Company Type: Private   *Employees here:* 1
SIC: 2873
  Mfg nitrogenous & phosphatic fertilizers & industrial
    chemical products
Gary E Carlson, Chief Executive Officer

D-U-N-S 60-500-2864
PCS NITROGEN INC.
  (Parent: Potash Corporation Of Saskatc)
3175 Lenox Park Blvd, Memphis, TN 38115
Phone: (901) 758-5200
Sales: $424,100,000   *Employees:* 1,350
Company Type: Private   *Employees here:* 90
SIC: 2873
  Mfg nitrogenous & phosphatic fertilizers & industrial
    chemical products
John F Dietz, N/A

D-U-N-S 00-226-6849   EXP
PECORA CORPORATION
  (Parent: Mellon Ventures Inc)
165 Wambold Rd, Harleysville, PA 19438
Phone: (215) 723-6051
Sales: $30,000,000   *Employees:* 105
Company Type: Private   *Employees here:* 85
SIC: 2891
  Mfg elastomeric industrial sealants for waterproofing
Kevin Cummings, President

D-U-N-S 03-046-4796
PENETONE CORPORATION
  (Parent: West Chemical Products Inc)
74 Hudson Ave, Tenafly, NJ 07670
Phone: (201) 567-3000
Sales: $15,000,000   *Employees:* 64
Company Type: Private   *Employees here:* 22
SIC: 2842
  Mfg cleaning preparations & degreasing solvents & industrial
    lubricants & greases
Elwood W Phares II, Chairman of the Board

D-U-N-S 05-471-1163   EXP
PENN COLOR INC.
400 Old Dublin Pike, Doylestown, PA 18901
Phone: (215) 345-6550
Sales: $100,000,000   *Employees:* 450
Company Type: Private   *Employees here:* 125
SIC: 2865
   Mfg organic & inorganic pigment color dispersions
Edgar Putman, Chairman of the Board

D-U-N-S 00-523-1998   EXP
PENRAY COMPANIES INC.
440 Denniston Ct, Wheeling, IL 60090
Phone: (847) 459-5000
Sales: $31,000,000   *Employees:* 120
Company Type: Private   *Employees here:* 66
SIC: 2899
   Mfg specialty chemicals for automotive and heavy duty
      industry
D D Swick, President

D-U-N-S 18-112-2466   EXP
PERFORMANCE MATERIALS CORP.
1150 Calle Suerte, Camarillo, CA 93012
Phone: (805) 482-1722
Sales: $15,000,000   *Employees:* 100
Company Type: Private   *Employees here:* 50
SIC: 2821
   Mfg high performance footwear
David M Blakeman, President

D-U-N-S 00-793-5257   EXP
PERMIAN MUD SERVICE INC.
3355 W Alabama St, Ste 400, Houston, TX 77098
Phone: (713) 627-1101
Sales: $200,000,000   *Employees:* 824
Company Type: Private   *Employees here:* 75
SIC: 2819
   Mfg industrial inorganic chemicals
John W Johnson, President

D-U-N-S 87-825-2824
PERRIGO COMPANY OF MISSOURI
   (Parent: Perrigo Company)
8515 Page Ave, Saint Louis, MO 63114
Phone: (314) 423-8822
Sales: $16,700,000   *Employees:* 150
Company Type: Public Family Member   *Employees here:* 150
SIC: 2844
   Mfg & dist personal products
Brian Flint, Principal

D-U-N-S 00-403-9053
PERRIGO OF TENNESSEE
   (Parent: Perrigo Company)
1 Swan Dr, Smyrna, TN 37167
Phone: (615) 459-8900
Sales: $119,000,000   *Employees:* 1,000
Company Type: Public Family Member   *Employees here:* 700
SIC: 2844
   Mfg pharmaceutical preparations
Biff Mc Intire, President

D-U-N-S 00-424-6468
PERRY & DERRICK CO
2510 Highland Ave, Cincinnati, OH 45212
Phone: (513) 351-5800
Sales: $17,300,000   *Employees:* 130
Company Type: Private   *Employees here:* 75
SIC: 2851
   Mfg paint varnishes & enamels
Mark E Derrick, President

D-U-N-S 14-433-3010   EXP
PERSTORP POLYOLS INC.
   (Parent: Perstorp Inc)
600 Matzinger Rd, Toledo, OH 43612
Phone: (419) 729-5448
Sales: $18,100,000   *Employees:* 96
Company Type: Private   *Employees here:* 96
SIC: 2869
   Mfg poly alcohols
David Wolf, President

D-U-N-S 00-828-6148
PERVO PAINT COMPANY
6624 Stanford Ave, Los Angeles, CA 90001
Phone: (323) 758-1147
Sales: $18,000,000   *Employees:* 40
Company Type: Private   *Employees here:* 40
SIC: 2851
   Mfg paints
John Haupenthal, President

D-U-N-S 80-957-2365
PETER THOMAS ROTH INC.
630 5th Ave, Ste 811, New York, NY 10111
Phone: (212) 581-5800
Sales: $15,000,000   *Employees:* 20
Company Type: Private   *Employees here:* 20
SIC: 2844
   Mfg clinical skin care products
Peter Roth, Chief Executive Officer

D-U-N-S 05-977-1717
PETROFERM INC.
5415 First Coast Hwy, Fernandina Beach, FL 32034
Phone: (904) 261-8286
Sales: $25,000,000   *Employees:* 125
Company Type: Private   *Employees here:* 50
SIC: 2899
   Mfg specialty chemicals
Michael E Hayes, Chief Executive Officer

D-U-N-S 00-520-3476   EXP
PFANSTIEHL LABORATORIES, INC.
1219 Glen Rock Ave, Waukegan, IL 60085
Phone: (847) 623-0370
Sales: $44,384,000   *Employees:* 100
Company Type: Private   *Employees here:* 100
SIC: 2869
   Mfg organic chemicals and related biochemicals
A G Holstein, President

D-U-N-S 00-129-3216
PFISTER CHEMICAL INC.
1098 State Hwy 46 E, Ridgefield, NJ 07657
Phone: (201) 945-5400
Sales: $20,000,000   *Employees:* 130
Company Type: Private   *Employees here:* 60
SIC: 2865
   Mfg synthetic organic chemical dyestuffs & cyclic
      intermediates
Albert Bendelius, Chairman of the Board

D-U-N-S 78-451-9837   EXP
PHIBRO-TECH, INC.
   (Parent: C P Chemicals Inc)
1 Parker Plz, Fort Lee, NJ 07024
Phone: (201) 944-6020
Sales: $85,000,000   *Employees:* 325
Company Type: Private   *Employees here:* 25
SIC: 2819
   Mfg specialty industrial inorganic chemicals & recycles
      hazardous chemical wastes
Jack C Bendheim, Chief Executive Officer

D-U-N-S 00-698-9008   EXP
PHILIPP BROTHERS CHEMICALS INC.
1 Parker Plz, Fort Lee, NJ 07024
Phone: (201) 944-6020
Sales: $277,983,000   *Employees:* 1,000
Company Type: Private   *Employees here:* 62
SIC: 2819
   Mfg industrial inorganic chemicals & whol fine chemicals
Jack Bendheim, President

D-U-N-S 87-299-1757
PHILLIPS SUMIKA POLYPROPYLENE
2625 Bay Area Blvd, Houston, TX 77058
Phone: (281) 244-3069
Sales: $275,000,000   *Employees:* 100
Company Type: Private   *Employees here:* 100
SIC: 2821
   Mfg plastic materials/resins
John Barrett, General Manager

D-U-N-S 15-525-6233   EXP
PHOSPHATE RESOURCE PARTNERS
   (Parent: Imc Global Inc)
2100 Sanders Rd, Northbrook, IL 60062
Phone: (847) 272-9200
Sales: $842,456,000   *Employees:* 3,871
Company Type: Public   *Employees here:* 10
SIC: 2874
   Mines sulphur & oil production mfg phosphate fertilizer &
     chemicals & mines phosphate rock
Robert E Fowler Jr, General Partner

D-U-N-S 00-812-9202   EXP
PICEU GROUP LIMITED
24671 Telegraph Rd, Southfield, MI 48034
Phone: (248) 353-3035
Sales: $27,000,000   *Employees:* 100
Company Type: Private   *Employees here:* 4
SIC: 2851
   Mfg paints & undercoating & ret paint & painting supplies
John G Piceu Jr, Chief Executive Officer

D-U-N-S 00-321-5779
PIEDMONT CHEMICAL INDUSTRIES
331 Burton Ave, High Point, NC 27262
Phone: (336) 885-5131
Sales: $75,000,000   *Employees:* 265
Company Type: Private   *Employees here:* 37
SIC: 2841
   Mfg textile soaps oils and chemicals
Fred E Wilson Jr, President

D-U-N-S 13-132-7546
PIEDMONT LABORATORIES INC.
   (Parent: Outsourcing Services Group Inc)
2030 Old Candler Rd, Gainesville, GA 30507
Phone: (770) 534-0300
Sales: $44,600,000   *Employees:* 380
Company Type: Private   *Employees here:* 380
SIC: 2844
   Mfg personal care products automotive liquids and
     household cleaning liquids
Christopher Denny, President

D-U-N-S 00-210-8629   EXP
PIERCE & STEVENS CORP.
   (Parent: Sovereign Specialty Chem Lp)
710 Ohio St, Buffalo, NY 14203
Phone: (716) 856-4910

Sales: $60,000,000   *Employees:* 190
Company Type: Private   *Employees here:* 130
SIC: 2891
   Mfg adhesives/coatings
Michael Prude, President

D-U-N-S 02-126-1805   IMP
PIERRE FABRE INC.
1055 W 8th St, Azusa, CA 91702
Phone: (626) 334-3395
Sales: $30,000,000   *Employees:* 200
Company Type: Private   *Employees here:* 70
SIC: 2844
   Mfg & whol cosmetics
Pierre Fabre, Chairman of the Board

D-U-N-S 00-830-2341
PILOT CHEMICAL CO. OF OHIO
   (Parent: Pilot Chemical Corp)
11756 Burke St, Santa Fe Springs, CA 90670
Phone: (562) 698-6778
Sales: $37,615,000   *Employees:* 50
Company Type: Private   *Employees here:* 3
SIC: 2841
   Mfg wetting agents & detergents
Paul Morrisroe, President

D-U-N-S 00-828-7823   EXP
PILOT CHEMICAL CORP.
11756 Burke St, Santa Fe Springs, CA 90670
Phone: (562) 698-6778
Sales: $62,588,000   *Employees:* 150
Company Type: Private   *Employees here:* 30
SIC: 2843
   Mfg wetting agents & detergents
Peter L Morrisroe, Chairman of the Board

D-U-N-S 92-768-8192
PIONEER AMERICAS, INC.
   (Parent: Pioneer Companies Inc)
700 Louisiana St, Ste 4300, Houston, TX 77002
Phone: (713) 225-3831
Sales: $450,000,000   *Employees:* 1,300
Company Type: Public Family Member   *Employees here:* 60
SIC: 2812
   Mfg chlorine and caustic soda
William R Berkley, Chairman of the Board

D-U-N-S 19-519-4147   EXP
PIONEER CHLOR ALKALI COMPANY
   (Parent: Pioneer Americas Inc)
700 Louisiana St, Ste 4300, Houston, TX 77002
Phone: (713) 225-3831
Sales: $250,000,000   *Employees:* 450
Company Type: Public Family Member   *Employees here:* 25
SIC: 2812
   Mfg liquid caustic soda chlorine
Mike Ferris, Chairman of the Board

D-U-N-S 03-925-8413   IMP EXP
PIONEER/ECLIPSE CORPORATION
   (Parent: Amano Partners Usa Inc)
3882 Chestnut Grove Church, Sparta, NC 28675
Phone: (336) 372-8080
Sales: $28,501,000   *Employees:* 139
Company Type: Private   *Employees here:* 135
SIC: 2842
   Mfg janitorial cleaning & polishing preparations & floor
     cleaning equipment
Yoshio Misumi, President

D-U-N-S 00-431-3789
PITT PENN OIL CO. INC.
   (*Parent:* Wesmar Partners)
426 Freeport Rd, Creighton, PA 15030
Phone: (724) 226-2712
Sales: $29,900,000   *Employees:* 200
Company Type: Private   *Employees here:* 200
SIC: 2899
   Blends & packages automotive maintenance preparations
Robert L Ross, Chairman of the Board

D-U-N-S 00-613-0405   EXP
PLASITE PROTECTIVE COATING
   (*Parent:* Rpm Inc)
614 Elizabeth St, Green Bay, WI 54302
Phone: (920) 437-6561
Sales: $23,000,000   *Employees:* 82
Company Type: Public Family Member   *Employees here:* 55
SIC: 2821
   Mfg plastic materials/resins
Richard Murray, Executive Vice-President

D-U-N-S 04-467-1667   EXP
PLAST-O-MERIC INC.
   (*Parent:* The Geon Company)
6225 Sussex Rd, Sussex, WI 53089
Phone: (414) 246-0344
Sales: $75,000,000   *Employees:* 255
Company Type: Public Family Member   *Employees here:* 105
SIC: 2821
   Mfg vinyl & vinyl powders urethane systems & textile
     printing inks
John A Phillips, President

D-U-N-S 09-162-0369   EXP
PLASTI-KOTE CO., INC.
1000 Lake Rd, Medina, OH 44256
Phone: (330) 725-4511
Sales: $95,000,000   *Employees:* 350
Company Type: Private   *Employees here:* 320
SIC: 2851
   Mfg aerosol spray paints & bulk paints
Stephen Briggs, Vice-President

D-U-N-S 05-412-7519   EXP
PLASTICOLORS, INC.
2600 Michigan Ave, Ashtabula, OH 44004
Phone: (440) 997-5137
Sales: $28,000,000   *Employees:* 140
Company Type: Private   *Employees here:* 120
SIC: 2816
   Mfg chemical & pigment dispersions-inorganic & organic &
     compounding of thermoplastics
Steve Walling, President

D-U-N-S 00-607-8240
PLASTICS ENGINEERING COMPANY
3518 Lakeshore Rd, Sheboygan, WI 53083
Phone: (920) 458-2121
Sales: $50,000,000   *Employees:* 425
Company Type: Private   *Employees here:* 45
SIC: 2821
   Mfg synthetic resins & molding compounds
Michael R Brotz, President

D-U-N-S 07-697-5804
PLATTE CHEMICAL CO.
   (*Parent:* United Agri Products Inc)
419 18th St, Greeley, CO 80631
Phone: (970) 356-4400

Sales: $42,600,000   *Employees:* 200
Company Type: Public Family Member   *Employees here:* 30
SIC: 2879
   Mfg agricultural pesticides
Warren Hammerbeck, President

D-U-N-S 94-549-0282
PLEASANT GREEN ENTERPRISES,
1300 E North St, Coal City, IL 60416
Phone: (815) 634-2302
Sales: $20,000,000   *Employees:* 65
Company Type: Private   *Employees here:* 65
SIC: 2844
   Mfg shampoo rinses & conditioners
Yasar Samarah, President

D-U-N-S 08-695-3312   IMP EXP
PLUESS-STAUFER INDUSTRIES INC.
61 Main St, Proctor, VT 05765
Phone: (802) 459-3311
Sales: $58,900,000   *Employees:* 370
Company Type: Private   *Employees here:* 40
SIC: 2819
   Holding company (see operations)
John M Mitchell, President

D-U-N-S 94-278-6666
PMC SPECIALTIES GROUP, INC.
   (*Parent:* P M C Inc)
20525 Center Ridge Rd, Cleveland, OH 44116
Phone: (440) 356-0700
Sales: $192,795,000   *Employees:* 409
Company Type: Private   *Employees here:* 55
SIC: 2819
   Mfg specialty chemicals
Dr Ace Nanda, President

D-U-N-S 05-279-4914
PMP FERMENTATION PRODUCTS
500 Park Blvd, Ste 450, Itasca, IL 60143
Phone: (630) 250-7033
Sales: $24,354,000   *Employees:* 110
Company Type: Private   *Employees here:* 10
SIC: 2869
   Mfg gluconates and industrial enzymes & whol food additives
Keiji Takahashi, President

D-U-N-S 01-219-2241   EXP
POLAROME INTERNATIONAL INC.
200 Theodore Conrad Dr, Jersey City, NJ 07305
Phone: (201) 309-4500
Sales: $100,572,000   *Employees:* 95
Company Type: Private   *Employees here:* 80
SIC: 2869
   Manufactures and distributes essential oils and aromatic
     chemicals and owns nonresidential buildings
Pierre Bruell, Chairman of the Board

D-U-N-S 12-171-8753   EXP
POLYMER DYNAMICS INC.
2200 S 12th St, Allentown, PA 18103
Phone: (610) 798-2200
Sales: $22,000,000   *Employees:* 310
Company Type: Private   *Employees here:* 310
SIC: 2823
   Mfg viscose elastic polymers
William J Peoples, President

D-U-N-S 09-185-8993
POLYMERIC RESOURCES CORP.
55 Haul Rd, Wayne, NJ 07470
Phone: (973) 694-4141

Sales: $42,000,000   *Employees:* 125
Company Type: Private   *Employees here:* 55
SIC: 2821
     Mfg nylon & polymer compounds
Solomon Schlesinger, President

D-U-N-S 87-723-9657
POLYPORE INC.
     (Parent: Intertech Group Inc)
4838 Jenkins Ave, North Charleston, SC 29405
Phone: (843) 744-5174
Sales: $99,400,000   *Employees:* 620
Company Type: Private   *Employees here:* 15
SIC: 2819
     Mfg industrial inorganic chemicals mfg gaskets/packing/
     sealing devices
Jerry Zucker, President

D-U-N-S 04-369-4082
PONDEROSA PAINT MANUFACTURING
4631 W Aeronca St, Boise, ID 83705
Phone: (208) 344-8683
Sales: $18,214,000   *Employees:* 175
Company Type: Private   *Employees here:* 36
SIC: 2851
     Mfg paint ret paint glass and wallpaper
Loren Ellis, Chairman of the Board

D-U-N-S 78-366-4683
PPB TECHNOLOGIES, INC.
135 Old Boiling Springs R, Shelby, NC 28152
Phone: (704) 482-8200
Sales: $15,000,000   *Employees:* 17
Company Type: Private   *Employees here:* 17
SIC: 2819
     Mfg sodium compounds
Peter Schorsch, President

D-U-N-S 00-134-4803
PPG INDUSTRIES INC.
1 Ppg Pl, Pittsburgh, PA 15272
Phone: (412) 434-3131
Sales: $7,510,000,000   *Employees:* 31,900
Company Type: Public   *Employees here:* 1,400
SIC: 2851
     Mfg paints flat glass glass fiber products & chlorine
     chemicals
Raymond W Leboeuf, Chairman of the Board

D-U-N-S 00-228-4933   EXP
PQ CORPORATION
1200 W Swedesford Rd, Berwyn, PA 19312
Phone: (610) 651-4200
Sales: $378,454,000   *Employees:* 1,923
Company Type: Private   *Employees here:* 225
SIC: 2819
     Mfg industrial inorganic chemicals glass beads &
     microspheres
Richard W Kelso, President

D-U-N-S 04-284-5636   EXP
PRAXAIR DISTRIBUTION INC.
     (Parent: Praxair Inc)
7000 High Grove Blvd, Hinsdale, IL 60521
Phone: (630) 320-4000
Sales: $823,900,000   *Employees:* 7,250
Company Type: Public Family Member   *Employees here:* 260
SIC: 2813
     Mfg industrial gases and commercial freezing and
     refrigeration equipment
Edgar G Hotard, President

D-U-N-S 19-715-4586   EXP
PRAXAIR INC.
39 Old Ridgebury Rd, Danbury, CT 06810
Phone: (203) 837-2000
Sales: $4,833,000,000   *Employees:* 25,388
Company Type: Public   *Employees here:* 400
SIC: 2813
     Mfg industrial gases & whol welding supplies & platings &
     coatings of metals
H W Lichtenberger, Chairman of the Board

D-U-N-S 13-143-8335
PRAXAIR PUERTO RICO INC.
     (Parent: Praxair Inc)
Int Rd 931 Rr 189, Gurabo, PR 00778
Phone: (787) 258-7200
Sales: $23,000,000   *Employees:* 98
Company Type: Public Family Member   *Employees here:* 58
SIC: 2813
     Mfg industrial gases
Robert P Sheehan, President

D-U-N-S 00-823-7539   EXP
PRC-DESOTO INTERNATIONAL
     (Parent: Cortex Holding Inc)
5454 San Fernando Rd, Glendale, CA 91203
Phone: (818) 240-2060
Sales: $148,000,000   *Employees:* 731
Company Type: Private   *Employees here:* 400
SIC: 2891
     Mfg sealants adhesives & packaging systems
Ted Clark, Chief Executive Officer

D-U-N-S 00-509-9577   EXP
PREMIER COATINGS, INC.
     (Parent: Coronado Paint Co Inc)
2250 Arthur Ave, Elk Grove Village, IL 60007
Phone: (847) 439-4200
Sales: $18,000,000   *Employees:* 54
Company Type: Private   *Employees here:* 54
SIC: 2851
     Mfg paints
Christian Bosset, President

D-U-N-S 18-069-2899
PREMIERE PACKAGING INC.
6220 Lehman Dr, Flint, MI 48507
Phone: (810) 239-7650
Sales: $34,118,000   *Employees:* 125
Company Type: Private   *Employees here:* 95
SIC: 2842
     Mfg automotive appearance products
Mark Drolet, President

D-U-N-S 00-132-5109
PRENTISS INCORPORATED
21 Vernon St, Floral Park, NY 11001
Phone: (516) 326-1919
Sales: $17,000,000   *Employees:* 40
Company Type: Private   *Employees here:* 14
SIC: 2879
     Manufactures insecticides
Richard A Miller, President

D-U-N-S 05-931-5069
PRESERVATIVE PAINT CO.
     (Parent: Kelly-Moore Paint Company)
5400 Airport Way S, Seattle, WA 98108
Phone: (206) 763-0300

Sales: $16,000,000
Company Type: Private
SIC: 2851
  Mfg & ret paint
Rick Greenhow, President

Employees: 150
Employees here: 50

D-U-N-S 84-915-9744
PRESTONE PRODUCTS CORPORATION
  (Parent: Alliedsignal Inc)
39 Old Ridgebury Rd, Danbury, CT 06810
Phone: (203) 830-7800
Sales: $300,000,000
Company Type: Public Family Member
SIC: 2899
  Manufactures antifreeze and other chemical products
    including deicers and windshield washer fluids
David Lundstedt, President

Employees: 910
Employees here: 80

D-U-N-S 78-265-9197
PRIMEDIA MAGAZINES INC.
  (Parent: Primedia Holdings III Inc)
200 Madison Ave, Fl 8, New York, NY 10016
Phone: (212) 448-4500
Sales: $183,200,000
Company Type: Public Family Member
SIC: 2821
  Magazine publishers
William F Reilly, Chairman of the Board

Employees: 852
Employees here: 132

D-U-N-S 04-341-7414
PRIMESTER
1801 Warrick Dr, Kingsport, TN 37660
Phone: (423) 224-0482
Sales: $18,200,000
Company Type: Private
SIC: 2821

Ernest Davenport, N/A

Employees: 102
Employees here: 102

D-U-N-S 04-513-6884   EXP
PRINCE MANUFACTURING CO. INC.
  (Parent: Philipp Brothers Chemicals Inc)
1 Prince Plz, Quincy, IL 62301
Phone: (217) 222-8854
Sales: $19,500,000
Company Type: Private
SIC: 2879
  Trace minerals
Marvin Sussman, President

Employees: 115
Employees here: 80

D-U-N-S 04-934-5101   EXP
PRO-LINE CORPORATION
2121 Panoramic Cir, Dallas, TX 75212
Phone: (214) 631-4247
Sales: $40,545,000
Company Type: Private
SIC: 2844
  Mfg toiletries
Eric Brown, President

Employees: 300
Employees here: 300

D-U-N-S 00-131-6827   EXP
THE PROCTER & GAMBLE COMPANY
619 Central Ave, Ste 1, Cincinnati, OH 45202
Phone: (513) 983-1100
Sales: $37,154,000,000
Company Type: Public
SIC: 2841
  Laundry & cleaning pdts paper pdts beauty care pdts food &
    beverage pdts & health care pdts
Jager Durk I, President

Employees: 110,000
Employees here: 14,500

D-U-N-S 10-857-6372
PROCTER & GAMBLE FAR EAST
  (Parent: The Procter & Gamble Company)
619 Central Ave, Ste 1, Cincinnati, OH 45202
Phone: (513) 983-1100
Sales: $337,000,000
Company Type: Public Family Member
SIC: 2842
  Mfg laundry cleaning preparations toiletries hair
    preparations & sanitary napkins
W C Berndt, President

Employees: 2,824
Employees here: 10

D-U-N-S 01-806-6519
PROFILE PRODUCTS, LLC
750 W Lake Cook Rd, Buffalo Grove, IL 60089
Phone: (847) 215-1144
Sales: $15,900,000
Company Type: Private
SIC: 2879
  Mfg soil conditioners & cat box filler
Mark Lewry, President

Employees: 75
Employees here: 26

D-U-N-S 11-889-5176
PROGRESSIVE INK COMPANY INC.
  (Parent: Alper Holdings Usa Inc)
710 E Center St, Sheridan, AR 72150
Phone: (870) 942-4700
Sales: $36,300,000
Company Type: Private
SIC: 2893
  Mfg printing ink
Nicolas W Combemale, President

Employees: 297
Employees here: 47

D-U-N-S 05-127-1963
PROTAMEEN CHEMICALS INC.
375 Minnisink Rd, Totowa, NJ 07512
Phone: (973) 256-4374
Sales: $25,000,000
Company Type: Private
SIC: 2819
  Mfg raw materials including chemicals for cosmetics &
    personal care products
Emmanuel Balsamides, President

Employees: 50
Employees here: 40

D-U-N-S 18-050-2684
PROTEIN TECHNOLOGIES INTERNATIONAL
  (Parent: Du Pont E I De Nemours And Co)
1034 Danforth Dr, Saint Louis, MO 63102
Phone: (314) 982-1000
Sales: $160,000,000
Company Type: Public Family Member
SIC: 2824
  Mfg food ingredients and ndustrial protein fibers
C E Coco, Co-President

Employees: 1,600
Employees here: 350

D-U-N-S 78-596-1046   EXP
PURETEK CORPORATION
1145 Arroyo St, Ste D, San Fernando, CA 91340
Phone: (818) 898-2109
Sales: $28,348,000
Company Type: Private
SIC: 2844
  Mfg hair beauty and pharmaceutical preparations
Barry Pressman, President

Employees: 250
Employees here: 190

D-U-N-S 06-452-2196
PURITAN/CHURCHILL CHEMICAL CO.
1341 Capital Cir SE, Ste E, Marietta, GA 30067
Phone: (404) 875-7331

Sales: $26,320,000   *Employees:* 188
Company Type: Private   *Employees here:* 90
SIC: 2842
    Mfg industrial disinfectants and sanitary preparations
Richard P Bruce III, President

D-U-N-S 00-400-5625   EXP
PURSELL INDUSTRIES INC.
201 W 4th St, Sylacauga, AL 35242
Phone: (205) 968-6000
Sales: $60,900,000   *Employees:* 350
Company Type: Private   *Employees here:* 90
SIC: 2875
    Mfg fertilizers
Taylor T Pursell Jr, President

D-U-N-S 78-767-1692
PVC COMPOUNDERS, INC.
6928 N 400 E, Kendallville, IN 46755
Phone: (219) 347-4055
Sales: $25,600,000   *Employees:* 50
Company Type: Private   *Employees here:* 26
SIC: 2821
    Mfg polyvinyl chloride resins
Mike Davidson, President

D-U-N-S 93-883-4736
PVS CHEMICALS INC. (ILLINOIS)
    (Parent: Pressure Vessel Service Inc)
12260 S Carondolet Ave, Chicago, IL 60633
Phone: (773) 933-8800
Sales: $23,678,000   *Employees:* 55
Company Type: Private   *Employees here:* 55
SIC: 2819
    Mfg industrial inorganic chemicals
Jerrold D Panock, President

D-U-N-S 00-254-4922
PVS CHEMICALS INC. (NEW YORK)
    (Parent: Pressure Vessel Service Inc)
55 Lee St, Buffalo, NY 14210
Phone: (716) 825-5762
Sales: $17,032,000   *Employees:* 56
Company Type: Private   *Employees here:* 53
SIC: 2819
    Mfg acids
William E Decker, President

D-U-N-S 15-136-9303
PVS TECHNOLOGIES INC.
    (Parent: Pressure Vessel Service Inc)
10900 Harper Ave, Detroit, MI 48213
Phone: (313) 571-1100
Sales: $18,206,000   *Employees:* 44
Company Type: Private   *Employees here:* 16
SIC: 2819
    Mfg liquid ferric & hydrous ferric chloride
Michael Mc Guirk, President

D-U-N-S 05-067-7772   EXP
QUALITEK INTERNATIONAL, INC.
315 Fairbank St, Addison, IL 60101
Phone: (630) 628-8083
Sales: $25,000,000   *Employees:* 300
Company Type: Private   *Employees here:* 150
SIC: 2899
    Mfg chemical preparations
Phodi Han, President

D-U-N-S 03-006-9140   EXP
QUALITY CHEMICALS INC.
    (Parent: Chemfirst Inc)
Tyrone Industrial Park, Tyrone, PA 16686

Phone: (814) 684-4310
Sales: $70,981,000   *Employees:* 245
Company Type: Public Family Member   *Employees here:* 165
SIC: 2869
    Custom chemical manufacturing
Scott A Martin, President

D-U-N-S 79-761-3155
QUEST INTERNATIONAL FRAGRANCES CO.
400 International Dr, Budd Lake, NJ 07828
Phone: (973) 691-7100
Sales: $390,000,000   *Employees:* 1,000
Company Type: Private   *Employees here:* 1,000
SIC: 2844
    Mfg toilet preparations
Louis Zomer, President

D-U-N-S 16-095-5746
R B H DISPERSIONS INC.
    (Parent: Reichhold Inc)
L-5 Factory Ln, Bound Brook, NJ 08805
Phone: (732) 356-1800
Sales: $25,000,000   *Employees:* 90
Company Type: Private   *Employees here:* 90
SIC: 2865
    Manufactures color dispersions (pigments)
Peter Eckle, Vice-President

D-U-N-S 11-834-9901   EXP
R F S CORPORATION
749 Quequechan St, Fall River, MA 02721
Phone: (508) 676-3481
Sales: $16,000,000   *Employees:* 50
Company Type: Private   *Employees here:* 3
SIC: 2865
    Mfg organic pigments
Stuart E Booth, President

D-U-N-S 10-120-5458
R J S SCIENTIFIC INC.
40 Harbor Park Dr, Port Washington, NY 11050
Phone: (516) 621-5800
Sales: $15,980,000   *Employees:* 87
Company Type: Private   *Employees here:* 87
SIC: 2844
    Manufactures home fragrance products & personal care
      products
Robert Corinaldesi, President

D-U-N-S 60-248-5062   EXP
R P SCHERER CORPORATION
    (Parent: Cardinal Health Inc)
2301 W Big Beaver Rd, Troy, MI 48084
Phone: (248) 649-0900
Sales: $515,300,000   *Employees:* 3,600
Company Type: Public Family Member   *Employees here:* 14
SIC: 2899
    Mfg gelatin capsules
Aleksandar M Erdeljan, Chairman of the Board

D-U-N-S 00-314-9663   EXP
RADIATOR SPECIALTY COMPANY
1900 Wilkinson Blvd, Charlotte, NC 28208
Phone: (704) 377-6555
Sales: $118,204,000   *Employees:* 575
Company Type: Private   *Employees here:* 375
SIC: 2899
    Mfg automotive plumbing & hardware chemicals & rubber
      molded products & whol hand tools
Herman Blumenthal, Chairman of the Board

D-U-N-S 00-218-2228
REAGENT CHEMICAL & RESEARCH
124 River Rd, Middlesex, NJ 08846

Phone: (732) 469-0100
Sales: $70,000,000   Employees: 319
Company Type: Private   Employees here: 45
SIC: 2819
    Mfg sulfur compounds hydrocloric acid clay targets and tube
      filling machinery
John T Skeuse, President

D-U-N-S 09-440-5024   EXP
RECKITT & COLMAN INC.
1655 Valley Rd, Wayne, NJ 07470
Phone: (973) 633-3600
Sales: $1,300,000,000   Employees: 2,000
Company Type: Private   Employees here: 700
SIC: 2842
    Mfg household air fresheners cleaners & disinfectants &
      prepared mustard
Joseph Healy, President

D-U-N-S 00-213-6232   EXP
RED DEVIL INC.
2400 Vauxhall Rd, Union, NJ 07083
Phone: (908) 688-6900
Sales: $33,900,000   Employees: 200
Company Type: Private   Employees here: 120
SIC: 2891
    Manufactures sealants and caulks and home repair hand
      tools
Donald R Mac Pherson, President

D-U-N-S 00-636-9987   EXP
RED SPOT PAINT & VARNISH CO.
1107 E Louisiana St, Evansville, IN 47711
Phone: (812) 428-9100
Sales: $89,281,000   Employees: 525
Company Type: Private   Employees here: 350
SIC: 2851
    Mfg paints & coatings
Charles Storms, President

D-U-N-S 00-836-8334   EXP
REDKEN LABORATORIES INC.
   (Parent: Cosmair Inc)
575 5th Ave, Fl 19, New York, NY 10017
Phone: (212) 818-1500
Sales: $100,000,000   Employees: 200
Company Type: Private   Employees here: 60
SIC: 2844
   Mfg hair preparations including shampoos
Guy Peyrelongue, Chief Executive Officer

D-U-N-S 09-044-5669
REEDCO INC.
   (Parent: Block Drug Company Inc)
Km 76 Hm 9 Rr 3, Humacao, PR 00791
Phone: (787) 852-3400
Sales: $18,367,000   Employees: 300
Company Type: Public Family Member   Employees here: 300
SIC: 2844
    Mfg hair shampoos & pharmaceutical products
Luis R Acevedo, General Manager

D-U-N-S 03-993-5135
REEVE AGRI ENERGY CORP.
S Star Rte, Garden City, KS 67846
Phone: (316) 275-7541
Sales: $20,000,000   Employees: 12
Company Type: Private   Employees here: 12
SIC: 2869
    Mfg ethanol & cattle feed
M P Reeve, President

D-U-N-S 06-921-2843
REGAL CHEMICAL COMPANY
600 Branch Rd, Alpharetta, GA 30004
Phone: (770) 475-4837
Sales: $17,000,000   Employees: 20
Company Type: Private   Employees here: 20
SIC: 2879
    Mfg and distributes agricultural chemicals
James O King, President

D-U-N-S 83-621-5905   EXP
REICHHOLD INC.
   (Parent: Dic Americas Inc)
2400 Ellis Rd, Durham, NC 27703
Phone: (919) 990-7500
Sales: $698,600,000   Employees: 3,200
Company Type: Private   Employees here: 600
SIC: 2821
    Mfg synthetic resins polymers rosin sizes and adhesives
Phillip D Ashkettle, President

D-U-N-S 19-712-5354
REILLY CORP.
   (Parent: Carlyle Partners Leveraged Cap)
1001 Pennsylvania Ave NW, Washington, DC 20004
Phone: (202) 347-2626
Sales: $27,200,000   Employees: 200
Company Type: Private   Employees here: 200
SIC: 2842
    Holding company mfg cleaning chemicals
Gregory S Ledford, Chairman of the Board

D-U-N-S 00-641-8685   EXP
REILLY INDUSTRIES INC.
300 N Meridian St, Indianapolis, IN 46204
Phone: (317) 638-7531
Sales: $103,800,000   Employees: 514
Company Type: Private   Employees here: 50
SIC: 2865
    Mfg speciality chemicals
Thomas E Reilly Jr, Chairman of the Board

D-U-N-S 84-937-9243   EXP
RENAISSANCE COSMETICS, INC.
3 Landmark Sq, Fl 5, Stamford, CT 06901
Phone: (203) 316-9800
Sales: $179,696,000   Employees: 1,189
Company Type: Private   Employees here: 200
SIC: 2844
    Mfg & mkts fragrances cosmetics lipsticks & nail-care
      products
Norbert Becker, President

D-U-N-S 87-973-2600
REPELLO PRODUCTS INC.
319 Willis Ave, Mineola, NY 11501
Phone: (516) 741-2345
Sales: $15,000,000   Employees: 22
Company Type: Private   Employees here: 22
SIC: 2879
    Creates & manufactures non-toxic insect repellents
Dr C J Abraham, Chairman of the Board

D-U-N-S 06-717-4680   EXP
RESINALL CORP.
3065 High Ridge Rd, Stamford, CT 06903
Phone: (203) 329-7100
Sales: $80,000,000   Employees: 135
Company Type: Private   Employees here: 10
SIC: 2821
    Mfg synthetic resins
John M Godina Sr, Chief Executive Officer

D-U-N-S 80-187-0478   EXP
REVLON CONSUMER PRODUCTS CORP.
   (Parent: Revlon Inc)
625 Madison Ave, Fl 8, New York, NY 10022
Phone: (212) 527-4000
Sales: $2,390,900,000   *Employees:* 16,000
Company Type: Private   *Employees here:* 750
SIC: 2844
   Mfg mkts & ret cosmetics skin care pdts fragrances &
      personal care pdts
George Fellows, President

D-U-N-S 00-126-5818   EXP
REVLON HOLDINGS INC.
   (Parent: Rgi Group Incorporated)
625 Madison Ave, Fl 8, New York, NY 10022
Phone: (212) 527-4000
Sales: $2,390,900,000   *Employees:* 16,100
Company Type: Private   *Employees here:* 60
SIC: 2844
   Mfg mkts & ret cosmetics skin care pdts fragrance &
      personal care pdts
George Fellows, President

D-U-N-S 78-882-0165
REVLON INC.
   (Parent: Rev Holdings Inc)
625 Madison Ave, Fl 8, New York, NY 10022
Phone: (212) 527-4000
Sales: $2,390,900,000   *Employees:* 16,000
Company Type: Private   *Employees here:* 40
SIC: 2844
   Mfg mkts & ret cosmetics skin care fragrance & personal
      care pdts
George Fellows, President

D-U-N-S 04-416-1529
REVLON INTERNATIONAL CORP.
   (Parent: Revlon Consumer Products Corp)
625 Madison Ave, Fl 8, New York, NY 10022
Phone: (212) 527-4000
Sales: $719,100,000   *Employees:* 6,000
Company Type: Private   *Employees here:* 5
SIC: 2844
   Mfg mkts & ret cosmetics skin care pdts fragrances &
      personal care pdts
Jerry W Levin, President

D-U-N-S 09-276-3366
REYNOLDS INC.
10 Gates St, Greenville, SC 29611
Phone: (864) 232-6791
Sales: $20,000,000   *Employees:* 75
Company Type: Private   *Employees here:* 75
SIC: 2891
   Mfg adhesives
E H Reynolds, Chairman of the Board

D-U-N-S 17-713-3766   EXP
REYNOLDS POLYMER TECHNOLOGY
607 Hollingsworth St, Grand Junction, CO 81505
Phone: (970) 241-4700
Sales: $15,000,000   *Employees:* 120
Company Type: Private   *Employees here:* 120
SIC: 2821
   Mfg acrylic resins
Roger R Reynolds III, President

D-U-N-S 60-945-4954   EXP
RHEOX INC.
Wycoff Mills Rd, Hightstown, NJ 08520
Phone: (609) 443-2000

Sales: $137,706,000   *Employees:* 361
Company Type: Private   *Employees here:* 131
SIC: 2851
   Mfg rheological additives
Charles Tushel, Chief Executive Officer

D-U-N-S 00-295-9810
RHODIA INC.
259 Prospect Plains Rd, Cranbury, NJ 08512
Phone: (609) 860-4000
Sales: $1,600,000,000   *Employees:* 4,000
Company Type: Private   *Employees here:* 4,000
SIC: 2819
   Mfg chemicals & fibers
Blaise Halluite, President

D-U-N-S 00-801-6495
RICHARDSON SID CARBON & GAS CO.
201 Main St, Fort Worth, TX 76102
Phone: (817) 390-0419
Sales: $118,700,000   *Employees:* 600
Company Type: Private   *Employees here:* 45
SIC: 2895
   Mfg carbon black & natural gas production
Perry R Bass, Chairman of the Board

D-U-N-S 60-734-5238
RICHLAND RESEARCH CORP.
3443 N Central Ave, Phoenix, AZ 85012
Phone: (602) 230-0012
Sales: $20,000,000   *Employees:* 135
Company Type: Private   *Employees here:* 100
SIC: 2869
   Mfg cleaning products for direct sales
David Smilovic, President

D-U-N-S 18-507-1750   EXP
RIMTEC CORPORATION
1702 Beverly Rd, Burlington, NJ 08016
Phone: (609) 387-0011
Sales: $41,666,000   *Employees:* 99
Company Type: Private   *Employees here:* 99
SIC: 2821
   Mfg polyvinyl chloride compounds
Terusha Koeda, President

D-U-N-S 00-524-5717
RIVERDALE CHEMICAL COMPANY
425 W 194th St, Glenwood, IL 60425
Phone: (708) 754-3330
Sales: $30,000,000   *Employees:* 50
Company Type: Private   *Employees here:* 10
SIC: 2879
   Mfg agricultural & industrial chemicals
James K Champion, President

D-U-N-S 03-848-5793
ROBERTET FRAGRANCES INC.
125 Bauer Dr, Oakland, NJ 07436
Phone: (201) 405-1000
Sales: $19,000,000   *Employees:* 65
Company Type: Private   *Employees here:* 45
SIC: 2844
   Mfg fragrance essential oils
Vito G Lenoci, President

D-U-N-S 04-754-7690
ROCKWOOD INDUSTRIES INC.
   (Parent: Laporte Inc)
7101 Muirkirk Rd, Beltsville, MD 20705
Phone: (301) 470-3366

Sales: $48,600,000
Company Type: Private
SIC: 2816

Employees: 389
Employees here: 28

  Mfg inorganic color pigments rust inhibiting & concrete
    hardening compounds metallic yarns & whol concrete
    additives
Ronald L Rapaport, President

D-U-N-S 00-902-0470
RODDA PAINT CO
12000 SW Garden Pl, Portland, OR 97223
Phone: (503) 521-4300
Sales: $66,000,000
Company Type: Private
SIC: 2851

Employees: 420
Employees here: 40

  Mfg paint whol & ret paint & supplies wall & window
    coverings
Thomas J Braden, President

D-U-N-S 04-655-4150   IMP EXP
RODEL INC.
Diamond State Indus Park, Newark, DE 19713
Phone: (302) 366-0500
Sales: $150,000,000
Company Type: Private
SIC: 2842

Employees: 750
Employees here: 690

  Mfg polishing materials including bonded nonwoven pads &
    polishes
William D Budinger, Chairman of the Board

D-U-N-S 00-114-1167   EXP
ROGERS CORPORATION
1 Technology Dr, Rogers, CT 06263
Phone: (860) 774-9605
Sales: $189,652,000
Company Type: Public
SIC: 2821

Employees: 993
Employees here: 450

  Mfg specialty polymer composite materials and components
Walter E Boomer, President

D-U-N-S 00-229-2043   EXP
ROHM AND HAAS COMPANY
100 Independence Mall W, Philadelphia, PA 19105
Phone: (215) 592-3000
Sales: $3,999,000,000
Company Type: Public
SIC: 2821

Employees: 11,592
Employees here: 1,200

  Mfg polymers & resins separations additives biocides
    monomers agricultural & leather chemicals
John P Mulroney, President

D-U-N-S 06-509-6273   EXP
ROHM AND HAAS TEXAS INC.
  (Parent: Rohm And Haas Company)
6600 La Porte Rd, Deer Park, TX 77536
Phone: (281) 228-8100
Sales: $242,600,000
Company Type: Public Family Member
SIC: 2869

Employees: 1,000
Employees here: 990

  Mfg heavy industrial organic chemicals
Robert W Brinly, President

D-U-N-S 02-256-0044   EXP
ROHMAX USA, INC.
723 Electronic Dr, Horsham, PA 19044
Phone: (215) 706-1500
Sales: $20,300,000
Company Type: Private
SIC: 2899

Employees: 115
Employees here: 20

  Chemical manufacturer of oil additives
Greg Bialy, President

D-U-N-S 00-426-3224   EXP
ROMA COLOR INC.
  (Parent: R F S Corporation)
749 Quequechan St, Fall River, MA 02721
Phone: (508) 676-3481
Sales: $16,000,000
Company Type: Private
SIC: 2865

Employees: 50
Employees here: 50

  Mfg organic color pigments
Stuart E Booth, President

D-U-N-S 00-217-7863   EXP
ROMAN ADHESIVES INC.
  (Parent: Roman Holdings Corporation)
824 State St, Calumet City, IL 60409
Phone: (708) 891-0770
Sales: $22,581,000
Company Type: Private
SIC: 2891

Employees: 80
Employees here: 80

  Mfg wallpaper adhesives and wallcovering primers
Richard P Bessette, President

D-U-N-S 78-412-1188   EXP
ROMAN HOLDINGS CORPORATION
824 State St, Calumet City, IL 60409
Phone: (708) 891-0770
Sales: $23,058,000
Company Type: Private
SIC: 2891

Employees: 80
Employees here: 4

  Mfg liquid and dry watercovering adhesives
Richard P Bessette, President

D-U-N-S 06-890-7146
ROSSBOROUGH MANUFACTURING CO., LP
33565 Pin Oak Pkwy, Avon Lake, OH 44012
Phone: (440) 933-9300
Sales: $40,000,000
Company Type: Private
SIC: 2899

Employees: 140
Employees here: 100

  Mfg metallurgical compounds & additives
Gerald Zebrowski, President

D-U-N-S 04-598-2667   EXP
ROUX LABORATORIES INC.
  (Parent: Revlon Consumer Products Corp)
2210 Melson Ave, Jacksonville, FL 32254
Phone: (904) 693-1200
Sales: $100,000,000
Company Type: Private
SIC: 2844

Employees: 500
Employees here: 400

  Mfg hair care products
Carlos Colmer, Chairman of the Board

D-U-N-S 00-129-2499   EXP
ROYCE ASSOCIATES, LP
35 Carlton Ave, East Rutherford, NJ 07073
Phone: (201) 438-5200
Sales: $20,000,000
Company Type: Private
SIC: 2869

Employees: 65
Employees here: 10

  Mfg natural dyestuffs plastic concentrates micronized waxes
    varnishes & other specialty chemicals
Albert J Royce III, General Partner

D-U-N-S 00-415-5651
RPM INC.
2628 Pearl Rd, Medina, OH 44256
Phone: (330) 273-5090
Sales: $1,615,274,000
Company Type: Public
SIC: 2851

Employees: 6,800
Employees here: 40

  Mfg protective coatings
Thomas C Sullivan, Chairman of the Board

D-U-N-S 02-747-2844   EXP
RSA MICROTECH
 (*Parent:* Cenex/Land Olakes Agronomy Co)
101 Elliott Ave W, Ste 110, Seattle, WA 98119
Phone: (206) 282-7878
Sales: $15,560,000   *Employees:* 60
Company Type: Private   *Employees here:* 6
SIC: 2819
   Whol & mfg industrial & agricultural chemicals
Dave Anderson, President

D-U-N-S 00-821-3191
RUBICON INC.
9156 Highway 75, Geismar, LA 70734
Phone: (225) 673-6141
Sales: $374,687,000   *Employees:* 480
Company Type: Private   *Employees here:* 480
SIC: 2865
   Mfg chemicals
Gordon Ross, President

D-U-N-S 01-777-5545
RUCO POLYMER CORPORATION
125 New South Rd, Hicksville, NY 11801
Phone: (516) 931-8104
Sales: $80,789,000   *Employees:* 138
Company Type: Private   *Employees here:* 100
SIC: 2821
   Manufactures polyester polyols & powder resins &
      polyurethane latex & solutions
Anthony Forgione, President

D-U-N-S 00-926-1769   EXP
RUDD COMPANY INC.
1141 NW 50th St, Seattle, WA 98107
Phone: (206) 789-1000
Sales: $20,000,000   *Employees:* 60
Company Type: Private   *Employees here:* 57
SIC: 2851
   Mfg paint finishes
Alan M Park Sr, Chairman of the Board

D-U-N-S 17-496-6473
RUSK INC.
1 Cummings Point Rd, Stamford, CT 06902
Phone: (203) 316-4300
Sales: $36,800,000   *Employees:* 315
Company Type: Private   *Employees here:* 315
SIC: 2844
   Mfg hair care products
Irvine Rusk, President

D-U-N-S 17-323-7959   EXP
RUSSELL JEROME COSMETICS USA
8220 Remmet Ave, Canoga Park, CA 91304
Phone: (818) 999-1222
Sales: $16,000,000   *Employees:* 48
Company Type: Private   *Employees here:* 48
SIC: 2844
   Mfg hair preparations
Garth Beveridge, President

D-U-N-S 00-509-4420   EXP
RUST-OLEUM CORPORATION
 (*Parent:* Rpm Inc)
11 E Hawthorn Pkwy, Vernon Hills, IL 60061
Phone: (847) 367-7700
Sales: $200,000,000   *Employees:* 500
Company Type: Public Family Member   *Employees here:* 150
SIC: 2851
   Mfg consumer and industrial paints and coatings
Michael D Tellor, President

D-U-N-S 00-300-8539   EXP
RUTGERS ORGANICS CORPORATION
201 Struble Rd, State College, PA 16801
Phone: (814) 238-2424
Sales: $70,000,000   *Employees:* 250
Company Type: Private   *Employees here:* 162
SIC: 2865
   Mfg organic chemical intermediates
Dr Thomas W Buttner, Chairman of the Board

D-U-N-S 00-511-1893   EXP
RYCOLINE PRODUCTS INC.
 (*Parent:* Rycoline Incorporated)
5540 N Northwest Hwy, Chicago, IL 60630
Phone: (773) 775-6755
Sales: $15,000,000   *Employees:* 67
Company Type: Private   *Employees here:* 60
SIC: 2842
   Mfg cleaning solvents
Charles L Palmer, Chairman of the Board

D-U-N-S 00-609-1417   EXP
S C JOHNSON & SON INC.
1525 Howe St, Racine, WI 53403
Phone: (414) 631-2000
Sales: $1,600,200,000   *Employees:* 13,400
Company Type: Private   *Employees here:* 1,400
SIC: 2842
   Mfg consumer commercial & specialty chemicals & sanitation
   svcs
William D George Jr, President

D-U-N-S 78-807-8772
S F PHOSPHATES, LLC
515 S Hwy 430, Rock Springs, WY 82901
Phone: (307) 382-1400
Sales: $100,000,000   *Employees:* 317
Company Type: Private   *Employees here:* 190
SIC: 2874
   Mfg phosphate fertilizers
Greg Loughrie, Vice-President

D-U-N-S 87-893-0965
S N F HOLDING COMPANY, INC.
Chemical Plant Rd, Riceboro, GA 31323
Phone: (912) 884-3366
Sales: $18,000,000   *Employees:* NA
Company Type: Private   *Employees here:* NA
SIC: 2899
   Holding company mfg water purification treating compounds
Hubert Issaurat, President

D-U-N-S 00-811-7400
SACHEM, INC.
821 Woodward St, Austin, TX 78704
Phone: (512) 444-3626
Sales: $24,000,000   *Employees:* 75
Company Type: Private   *Employees here:* 35
SIC: 2869
   Mfg industrial organic chemicals
John E Mooney, President

D-U-N-S 62-394-0756
SAINT-GBAIN ADVANCED MTLS CORP.
 (*Parent:* Norton Company)
1600 W Lee St, Louisville, KY 40210
Phone: (502) 778-3311
Sales: $533,700,000   *Employees:* 3,300
Company Type: Private   *Employees here:* 3,300
SIC: 2819
   Holding company-through subsidiary operates as mfg of
      chemicals & electronic crystals & refractors
Robert C Ayotte, President

D-U-N-S 85-872-6011
SAINT-GOBAIN INDUS CERAMICS
    (Parent: Norton Company)
1600 W Lee St, Louisville, KY 40210
Phone: (502) 778-3311
Sales: $242,000,000
Company Type: Private   *Employees here:* 1
SIC: 2819
    Mfg inorganic industrial chemicals & electronic crystals &
        refractories & tools & dies
Robert C Ayotte, President

Employees: 1,500

D-U-N-S 16-002-8114
SALLE' INTERNATIONAL, LLC
3740 Hawthorn Ct, Waukegan, IL 60087
Phone: (847) 662-6600
Sales: $18,000,000   *Employees:* 76
Company Type: Private   *Employees here:* 76
SIC: 2844
    Mfg and distribute consumer products including cologne gel
        candles foot shoe and sneaker spray and haircare products
James Merlo, Member

D-U-N-S 00-131-7395
SALTIRE INDUSTRIAL, INC.
    (Parent: Alper Holdings Usa Inc)
800 3rd Ave, Fl 24, New York, NY 10022
Phone: (212) 750-0200
Sales: $160,000,000   *Employees:* 435
Company Type: Private   *Employees here:* 4
SIC: 2893
    Mfr water-based ink products real estate developers & home
        builders
Jeffery Holdsberg, Executive Vice-President

D-U-N-S 00-102-1732
SAMUEL CABOT INCORPORATED
100 Hale St, Newburyport, MA 01950
Phone: (978) 465-1900
Sales: $40,000,000   *Employees:* 98
Company Type: Private   *Employees here:* 68
SIC: 2851
    Mfg wood stains & architectural coatings
Samuel Cabot III, President

D-U-N-S 07-871-8053
SAN MAR LABORATORIES INC.
4 Warehouse Ln, Elmsford, NY 10523
Phone: (914) 592-3130
Sales: $30,000,000   *Employees:* 100
Company Type: Private   *Employees here:* 100
SIC: 2844
    Mfg cosmetics & pharmaceutical preparations
Marvin Berkrot, President

D-U-N-S 15-453-4556   EXP
SANDOZ AGRO, INC.
    (Parent: Novartis Corporation)
1300 E Touhy Ave, Des Plaines, IL 60018
Phone: (847) 699-1616
Sales: $247,600,000   *Employees:* 1,200
Company Type: Private   *Employees here:* 387
SIC: 2879
    Mfg crop protection chemicals such as pesticides and
        biological insecticides
Mark Hodgson, Operations-Production-Mfg

D-U-N-S 36-155-5725   EXP
SARTOMER COMPANY INC.
    (Parent: Total America Inc)
502 Thomas Jones Way, Exton, PA 19341
Phone: (610) 363-4100

Sales: $175,000,000   *Employees:* 250
Company Type: Private   *Employees here:* 90
SIC: 2819
    Mfg industrial inorganic & organic specialty chemicals
Hugues Woestelandt, Chairman of the Board

D-U-N-S 00-207-0100
SCHENECTADY INTERNATIONAL
1302 Congress St, Schenectady, NY 12303
Phone: (518) 370-4200
Sales: $300,000,000   *Employees:* 600
Company Type: Private   *Employees here:* 100
SIC: 2865
    Mfg alkyphenols synthetic resins & electrical enamels
Wallace A Graham, Chairman of the Board

D-U-N-S 00-733-4659   EXP
SCHNEE-MOREHEAD INC.
111 N Nursery Rd, Irving, TX 75060
Phone: (972) 438-9111
Sales: $22,670,000   *Employees:* 120
Company Type: Private   *Employees here:* 85
SIC: 2891
    Mfg sealants
Robert A Schnee, President

D-U-N-S 00-253-3230   EXP
SCHWARZKOPF & DEP CORPORATION
2101 E Via Arado, Compton, CA 90220
Phone: (310) 604-0777
Sales: $104,409,000   *Employees:* 320
Company Type: Private   *Employees here:* 290
SIC: 2844
    Mfg & mktg personal care pdts
Robert Berglass, Chairman of the Board

D-U-N-S 61-840-0980   EXP
SCIENTIFIC DESIGN COMPANY
    (Parent: Linde Lift Truck Corp)
49 Industrial Ave, Little Ferry, NJ 07643
Phone: (201) 641-0500
Sales: $29,498,000   *Employees:* 87
Company Type: Private   *Employees here:* 87
SIC: 2819
    Mfg chemical catalysts & chemical engineering services
Dr Joseph V Porcelli, President

D-U-N-S 00-200-1980   EXP
SCOTT CHEMICAL CO, INC.
106 Grand Ave, Englewood, NJ 07631
Phone: (201) 568-9700
Sales: $80,000,000   *Employees:* 350
Company Type: Private   *Employees here:* 40
SIC: 2844
    Mfg health and beauty care products
F G Zigler, Chairman of the Board

D-U-N-S 00-442-7852
SCOTT PAINT CORP.
    (Parent: Bruning Paint Company)
7839 Fruitville Rd, Sarasota, FL 34240
Phone: (941) 371-0015
Sales: $20,000,000   *Employees:* 130
Company Type: Private   *Employees here:* 35
SIC: 2851
    Mfg & ret paint
Bernard Wagman, Chairman of the Board

D-U-N-S 05-140-0604   EXP
SCOTT SPECIALTY GASES INC.
6141 Easton Rd, Plumsteadville, PA 18949
Phone: (215) 766-8861

Sales: $75,000,000   *Employees:* 520
Company Type: Private   *Employees here:* 150
SIC: 2813
    Mfg specialty gases
J F Merz Jr, Chairman of the Board

D-U-N-S 00-707-2176   EXP
SCOTT'S LIQUID GOLD, INC.
4880 Havana St, Denver, CO 80239
Phone: (303) 373-4860
Sales: $50,476,000   *Employees:* 350
Company Type: Public   *Employees here:* 160
SIC: 2842
    Mfg household cleaning & polishing compounds
Mark E Goldstein, President

D-U-N-S 14-721-1270
THE SCOTTS COMPANY
14111 Scottslawn Rd, Marysville, OH 43040
Phone: (937) 644-0011
Sales: $1,113,000,000   *Employees:* 2,500
Company Type: Public   *Employees here:* 650
SIC: 2873
    Mfr fertilizers herbicides insecticides grass seeds organic top
        soils mulches lawn spreader lawn mowers and garden tools
Charles M Berger, Chairman of the Board

D-U-N-S 04-184-3434   EXP
SCOTTS-SIERRA HORT PRODUCTS CO.
    (Parent: The Scotts Company)
14111 Scottslawn Rd, Marysville, OH 43040
Phone: (937) 644-0011
Sales: $107,000,000   *Employees:* 350
Company Type: Public Family Member   *Employees here:* 330
SIC: 2873
    Mfg fertilizers potting soil & pesticides
Todd White, Vice-President

D-U-N-S 96-152-9617
SEA & SKI CORP.
8180 NW 36th St, Ste 105, Miami, FL 33166
Phone: (305) 436-5510
Sales: $15,000,000   *Employees:* 30
Company Type: Private   *Employees here:* 10
SIC: 2844
    Mfg sun and skin care products
Robert Bell, President

D-U-N-S 15-058-4118
SEL-LEB MARKETING INC.
495 River St, Paterson, NJ 07524
Phone: (973) 225-9880
Sales: $17,374,000   *Employees:* 60
Company Type: Public   *Employees here:* 49
SIC: 2844
    Mfg & distributes cosmetics
Paul Sharp, President

D-U-N-S 61-324-2213
SENCO INC.
4563 S Westmoreland Rd, Dallas, TX 75237
Phone: (214) 331-8800
Sales: $23,000,000   *Employees:* 50
Company Type: Private   *Employees here:* 50
SIC: 2844
    Mfg hair preparations
Pettis Norman, President

D-U-N-S 07-674-4010   EXP
SENTINEL CONSUMER PRODUCTS
7750 Tyler Blvd, Mentor, OH 44060
Phone: (440) 974-8144

Sales: $33,000,000   *Employees:* 500
Company Type: Private   *Employees here:* 100
SIC: 2844
    Mfg first aid supplies surgical dressings health & beauty aids
        & shoe innersoles
Michael S Klein, President

D-U-N-S 96-678-8739
SEWELL PRODUCTS OF FLORIDA
    (Parent: Sewell Products Inc)
909 Magnolia Ave, Auburndale, FL 33823
Phone: (941) 967-4463
Sales: $15,000,000   *Employees:* 100
Company Type: Private   *Employees here:* 100
SIC: 2842
    Mfg polish/sanitation goods & soap/other detergents
Stephen H Sewell, President

D-U-N-S 00-510-0789   EXP
SEYMOUR OF SYCAMORE, INC.
917 Crosby Ave, Sycamore, IL 60178
Phone: (815) 895-9101
Sales: $38,000,000   *Employees:* 135
Company Type: Private   *Employees here:* 128
SIC: 2851
    Mfg aerosol paints enamels & lacquers
Nancy S Heatley, Chairman of the Board

D-U-N-S 05-368-7356   EXP
SHARE CORPORATION
7821 N Faulkner Rd, Milwaukee, WI 53224
Phone: (414) 355-4000
Sales: $20,610,000   *Employees:* 213
Company Type: Private   *Employees here:* 44
SIC: 2842
    Whol industrial & municipal maintenance & cleaning
        chemicals
Thomas D Jardins, Chairman of the Board

D-U-N-S 00-610-3766
SHEBOYGAN PAINT COMPANY INC.
1439 N 25th St, Sheboygan, WI 53081
Phone: (920) 458-2157
Sales: $20,600,000   *Employees:* 96
Company Type: Private   *Employees here:* 88
SIC: 2851
    Mfg industrial finishes
John Nelesen, President

D-U-N-S 16-167-7778
SHELL CATALYST VENTURES, INC.
    (Parent: Shell Oil Company)
910 Louisiana St, Houston, TX 77002
Phone: (713) 241-6161
Sales: $177,200,000   *Employees:* 1,100
Company Type: Public Family Member   *Employees here:* 1,100
SIC: 2819
    Catalyst manufacturer
Dick Schimbar, President

D-U-N-S 09-562-2072
SHEPARD BROTHERS INC.
503 S Cypress St, La Habra, CA 90631
Phone: (562) 697-1366
Sales: $15,000,000   *Employees:* 55
Company Type: Private   *Employees here:* 55
SIC: 2842
    Mfg specialty cleaning preparations
Duane Shepard, President

D-U-N-S 78-279-9308
SHINCOR SILICONES, INC.
  (*Parent:* Shin-Etsu Silicones Of America)
1030 Evans Ave, Akron, OH 44305
Phone: (330) 630-9460
Sales: $25,000,000   *Employees:* 70
Company Type: Private   *Employees here:* 70
SIC: 2822
  Mfg silicone rubber compounds
Nobuyuki Haseve, President

D-U-N-S 06-509-5390
SHINTECH INCORPORATED
24 E Greenway Plz, Ste 811, Houston, TX 77046
Phone: (713) 965-0713
Sales: $850,000,000   *Employees:* 206
Company Type: Private   *Employees here:* 15
SIC: 2821
  Mfg polyvinyl chloride
Chihiro Kanagawa, Chairman of the Board

D-U-N-S 80-519-7365
SHIONOGI QUALICAPS, INC.
6505 Franz Warner Pkwy, Whitsett, NC 27377
Phone: (336) 449-3900
Sales: $22,000,000   *Employees:* 200
Company Type: Private   *Employees here:* 200
SIC: 2899
  Mfg gelatin capsules
Duane Monk, President

D-U-N-S 03-267-5345
SHIPLEY COMPANY, LLC
  (*Parent:* Rohm And Haas Company)
455 Forest St, Marlborough, MA 01752
Phone: (508) 481-7950
Sales: $63,800,000   *Employees:* 400
Company Type: Public Family Member   *Employees here:* 400
SIC: 2819
  Mfg industrial inorganic and organic chemicals
Richard C Shipley, Member

D-U-N-S 78-267-7132
SHISEDIO AMERICA INC.
  (*Parent:* Shiseido International Corp)
178 Bauer Dr, Oakland, NJ 07436
Phone: (201) 337-3750
Sales: $90,000,000   *Employees:* 188
Company Type: Private   *Employees here:* 188
SIC: 2844
  Manufactures cosmetic and toilet preparations
Y Kawamata, President

D-U-N-S 19-369-1821
SHISEIDO INTERNATIONAL CORP.
178 Bauer Dr, Oakland, NJ 07436
Phone: (201) 337-3750
Sales: $116,000,000   *Employees:* 975
Company Type: Private   *Employees here:* 2
SIC: 2844
  Manufactures and wholesales cosmetics and toilet
  preparations
Nobuo Takahashi, President

D-U-N-S 62-114-6851   EXP
SHRIEVE CHEMICAL PRODUCTS INC.
  (*Parent:* Shrieve Chemical Company)
1717 Woodstead Ct, Ste 205, The Woodlands, TX 77380
Phone: (281) 367-4226

Sales: $30,413,000   *Employees:* 13
Company Type: Private   *Employees here:* 7
SIC: 2899
  Mfg industrial chemicals
Jim Shrieve, Chairman of the Board

D-U-N-S 93-852-6720   EXP
SIA ADHESIVES INC.
  (*Parent:* Sovereign Specialty Chem Lp)
123 W Bartges St, Akron, OH 44311
Phone: (330) 374-2900
Sales: $26,000,000   *Employees:* 110
Company Type: Private   *Employees here:* 110
SIC: 2891
  Manufactures adhesives
Gerard A Loftus, President

D-U-N-S 14-662-5272   IMP
SICPA INDUSTRIES OF AMERICA
8000 Research Way, Springfield, VA 22153
Phone: (703) 455-8050
Sales: $23,500,000   *Employees:* 119
Company Type: Private   *Employees here:* 80
SIC: 2893
  Mfg high grade printing ink
Maurice A Amon, President

D-U-N-S 87-635-3673   EXP
SIGMA COATINGS USA BV
1401 Destrehan Ave, Harvey, LA 70058
Phone: (504) 347-4321
Sales: $60,000,000   *Employees:* 165
Company Type: Private   *Employees here:* 115
SIC: 2851
  Mfg industrial protective coatings
Jef Verborgt, President

D-U-N-S 00-217-9893   EXP
SIKA CORPORATION
201 Polito Ave, Lyndhurst, NJ 07071
Phone: (201) 933-8800
Sales: $148,353,000   *Employees:* 737
Company Type: Private   *Employees here:* 208
SIC: 2891
  Mfg coatings & adhesives concrete repair compounds &
    admixture chemicals epoxy resins & sealants
Enrico Tissi, President

D-U-N-S 00-239-0284   EXP
SILBERLINE MANUFACTURING CO.
Lincoln Dr, Tamaqua, PA 18252
Phone: (570) 668-6050
Sales: $47,800,000   *Employees:* 382
Company Type: Private   *Employees here:* 100
SIC: 2816
  Mfg aluminum pigments
Lisa J Peretz, President

D-U-N-S 00-229-0492   EXP
SKW BIOSYSTEMS INC.
  (*Parent:* Skw Americas Inc)
2021 Cabot Blvd W, Langhorne, PA 19047
Phone: (215) 702-1000
Sales: $210,000,000   *Employees:* 771
Company Type: Private   *Employees here:* 55
SIC: 2869
  Mfg flavors dairy products & gelatins
Paul J Murphy, President

D-U-N-S 15-134-5444
SKW-MBT SERVICES INC.
23700 Chagrin Blvd, Cleveland, OH 44122
Phone: (216) 831-5500

Sales: $131,700,000   *Employees:* 925
Company Type: Private   *Employees here:* 356
SIC: 2899
   Mfg chemical additives to improve protect and repair
   concrete
Mike Shydlowski, President

D-U-N-S 18-961-4670
SLG CHEMICALS, INC.
   (Parent: Scotts Liquid Gold-Inc)
4880 Havana St, Denver, CO 80239
Phone: (303) 373-4860
Sales: $19,400,000   *Employees:* 150
Company Type: Public Family Member   *Employees here:* 150
SIC: 2899
   Mfg chemical preparations
Mark E Goldstein, President

D-U-N-S 00-825-8873   EXP
SMILAND PAINT COMPANY
620 Lamar St, Los Angeles, CA 90031
Phone: (323) 222-7000
Sales: $33,400,000   *Employees:* 225
Company Type: Private   *Employees here:* 60
SIC: 2851
   Mfg paint
Bronko M Smiland, Chairman of the Board

D-U-N-S 62-226-0305
SOFIX CORPORATION
2800 Riverport Rd, Chattanooga, TN 37406
Phone: (423) 624-3500
Sales: $20,000,000   *Employees:* 27
Company Type: Private   *Employees here:* 27
SIC: 2899
   Mfg colorformer
Kazuhide Ohmaye, President

D-U-N-S 04-153-1260
SOFT SHEEN PRODUCTS
   (Parent: Cosmair Inc)
1000 E 87th St, Chicago, IL 60619
Phone: (773) 978-0700
Sales: $33,800,000   *Employees:* 290
Company Type: Private   *Employees here:* 280
SIC: 2844
   Mfg hair care products
Terri L Gardner, President

D-U-N-S 18-273-4566   EXP
SOFTSOAP ENTERPRISES, INC.
   (Parent: Colgate-Palmolive Company)
134 Columbia Ct, Chaska, MN 55318
Phone: (612) 448-4799
Sales: $19,400,000   *Employees:* 172
Company Type: Public Family Member   *Employees here:* 172
SIC: 2841
   Mfg liquid soaps
Ed Fogarty, President

D-U-N-S 00-413-1181   EXP
SOLAR COSMETIC LABS, INC.
4920 NW 165th St, Hialeah, FL 33014
Phone: (305) 621-5551
Sales: $20,810,000   *Employees:* 75
Company Type: Private   *Employees here:* 75
SIC: 2844
   Mfg suntan lotions and oils
Jaime Dornbusch, President

D-U-N-S 96-682-9947   EXP
SOLKATRONIC CHEMICALS INC.
   (Parent: Air Products And Chemicals)
30 Two Bridges Rd, Ste 210, Fairfield, NJ 07004
Phone: (973) 882-7900
Sales: $25,000,000   *Employees:* 94
Company Type: Public Family Member   *Employees here:* 17
SIC: 2819
   Mfg specialty chemicals
J T Johnson, President

D-U-N-S 04-085-3731
SOLUTIA INC.
10300 Olive Blvd, Saint Louis, MO 63141
Phone: (314) 674-1000
Sales: $2,969,000,000   *Employees:* 8,800
Company Type: Public   *Employees here:* 800
SIC: 2824
   Chemical manufacturer
Michael E Miller, Vice-Chairman

D-U-N-S 15-173-4506
SOLVAY AMERICA INC.
3333 Richmond Ave, Houston, TX 77098
Phone: (713) 525-6000
Sales: $2,200,000,000   *Employees:* 4,600
Company Type: Private   *Employees here:* 225
SIC: 2821
   Mfg plastic resins pharmaceuticals specialty chemicals plastic
   products & soda ash
M W Sadler, President

D-U-N-S 09-397-1430   EXP
SOLVAY INTEROX, INC.
   (Parent: Solvay America Inc)
3333 Richmond Ave, Houston, TX 77098
Phone: (713) 525-6500
Sales: $130,000,000   *Employees:* 211
Company Type: Private   *Employees here:* 60
SIC: 2819
   Mfg industrial inorganic chemicals
Foster Brown, President

D-U-N-S 82-508-2506
SOMERVILLE TECHNOLOGY GROUP
15 Big Pond Rd, Huguenot, NY 12746
Phone: (914) 856-5261
Sales: $15,802,000   *Employees:* 55
Company Type: Private   *Employees here:* 55
SIC: 2819
   Mfg aluminum compounds
Piyush J Patel, Chairman of the Board

D-U-N-S 04-910-9440
SOUTHERN IONICS INC.
201 Commerce St, West Point, MS 39773
Phone: (601) 494-3055
Sales: $77,000,000   *Employees:* 250
Company Type: Private   *Employees here:* 35
SIC: 2819
   Mfg industrial inorganic chemicals
Milton O Sundbeck Jr, President

D-U-N-S 15-774-8237
SOUTHERN RESOURCES INC.
   (Parent: Verdant Brands Inc)
310 Highway 341 S, Fort Valley, GA 31030
Phone: (912) 825-3351

Sales: $15,400,000
Company Type: Public Family Member
SIC: 2879
  Holding company mfg specialty chemicals and owns real
    estate
David K Vansant, Chairman of the Board
Employees: 75
Employees here: 58

D-U-N-S 00-329-3198
SOUTHERN STATES PHOSPHATE FERT.
1600 E President St, Savannah, GA 31404
Phone: (912) 232-1101
Sales: $15,187,000
Company Type: Private
SIC: 2874
  Mfg fertilizer and sulphuric acid
F R Dulany Jr, Chairman of the Board
Employees: 70
Employees here: 70

D-U-N-S 88-356-8370
SOUTHWEST INDUSTRIES INC.
5197 NW 15th St, Ste 124, Pompano Beach, FL 33063
Phone: (954) 979-8799
Sales: $74,000,000
Company Type: Private
SIC: 2851
  Mfg paints and other industrial products
William Singer, President
Employees: 32
Employees here: 32

D-U-N-S 94-431-4830
SOVEREIGN SPECIALTY CHEM, LP
225 W Washington St, Chicago, IL 60606
Phone: (312) 419-4048
Sales: $134,771,000
Company Type: Private
SIC: 2891
  Mfg specialty adhesives
Robert B Covalt, President
Employees: 340
Employees here: 3

D-U-N-S 84-740-3151
SP ACQUISITION CO.
  (Parent: Radnor Holdings Corporation)
3607 N Sylvania Ave, Fort Worth, TX 76111
Phone: (817) 831-3541
Sales: $35,100,000
Company Type: Private
SIC: 2821
  Mfy polystyrene & expandable polystyrene resins
Michael T Kennedy, President
Employees: 165
Employees here: 37

D-U-N-S 00-503-6728   EXP
SPARTAN CHEMICAL CO. INC.
110 N Westwood Ave, Toledo, OH 43607
Phone: (419) 531-5551
Sales: $24,700,000
Company Type: Private
SIC: 2842
  Mfg chemical cleaners whol paper chemicals & janitorial
    supplies
Thomas J Swigart, Chairman of the Board
Employees: 210
Employees here: 152

D-U-N-S 01-957-5760
SPARTECH COMPOUND
  (Parent: Spartech Corporation)
4753 Nash Rd, Cape Girardeau, MO 63702
Phone: (573) 334-3434
Sales: $20,000,000
Company Type: Public Family Member
SIC: 2821
  Mfg & whol synthetic resins
Bradley Buechler, President
Employees: 75
Employees here: 75

D-U-N-S 01-093-7373   EXP
SPAWN MATE INC.
260 Westgate Dr, Watsonville, CA 95076

Phone: (831) 763-5300
Sales: $45,198,000
Company Type: Private
SIC: 2873
  Mfg fertilizers & mushroom farm
Ray Selle, Chief Financial Officer
Employees: 800
Employees here: 34

D-U-N-S 00-826-2529
SPECIAL DEVICES INCORPORATED
16830 Placerita Canyon Rd, Santa Clarita, CA 91321
Phone: (661) 259-0753
Sales: $140,502,000
Company Type: Private
SIC: 2899
  Mfg pyrotechnic devices for automotive and aerospace
    applications
Thomas F Treinen, President
Employees: 1,395
Employees here: 575

D-U-N-S 03-894-6091   EXP
SPECIALTY CHEMICAL RESOURCES
9055 Freeway Dr, Macedonia, OH 44056
Phone: (330) 468-1380
Sales: $40,284,000
Company Type: Public
SIC: 2842
  Custom formulator & packager of specialty chemical
    products
Edwin M Roth, Chairman of the Board
Employees: 219
Employees here: 70

D-U-N-S 00-514-0108
SPECIALTY COATINGS COMPANY
2526 Delta Ln, Elk Grove Village, IL 60007
Phone: (847) 766-3555
Sales: $25,000,000
Company Type: Private
SIC: 2851
  Mfg industrial coatings
Seymour Neems, Chief Executive Officer
Employees: 55
Employees here: 40

D-U-N-S 15-421-3839
SPECIALTY INDUSTRIAL PRODUCTS
195 Brooks Blvd, Spartanburg, SC 29307
Phone: (864) 579-4530
Sales: $40,000,000
Company Type: Private
SIC: 2843
  Mfg emulsifiers surface active agents soluble oils softeners
    textile finishing agents & processing assistants
Louis Frishling, Chairman of the Board
Employees: 55
Employees here: 55

D-U-N-S 62-488-0274
SPECIALTY MINERALS INC.
  (Parent: Minerals Technologies Inc)
405 Lexington Ave, New York, NY 10174
Phone: (212) 878-1800
Sales: $363,800,000
Company Type: Public Family Member
SIC: 2819
  Mfg calcium carbonate
Paul R Saueracker, President
Employees: 1,150
Employees here: 40

D-U-N-S 10-663-2425   EXP
SPECIALTYCHEM PRODUCTS CORP.
  (Parent: Chemdesign Corporation)
2 Stanton St, Marinette, WI 54143
Phone: (715) 735-9033
Sales: $35,000,000
Company Type: Private
SIC: 2869
  Mfg industrial organic chemicals
Kirk Bourgeois, President
Employees: 130
Employees here: 130

D-U-N-S 00-968-2261
SPECTRA-TONE PAINT CORPORATION
1595 E San Bernardino Ave, San Bernardino, CA 92408
Phone: (909) 478-3485
Sales: $20,989,000   *Employees:* 120
Company Type: Private   *Employees here:* 60
SIC: 2851
  Mfg paint
James E Dabbs, President

D-U-N-S 88-407-5680
SPI HOLDINGS, INC.
321 Cherry Ln, New Castle, DE 19720
Phone: (302) 576-8500
Sales: $78,600,000   *Employees:* 335
Company Type: Private   *Employees here:* 180
SIC: 2869
  Holding company
John Burrows, President

D-U-N-S 84-864-2351   EXP
SPI POLYOLS, INC.
321 Cherry Ln, New Castle, DE 19720
Phone: (302) 576-8500
Sales: $78,600,000   *Employees:* 335
Company Type: Private   *Employees here:* 180
SIC: 2869
  Mfg polyols
John Burrows, President

D-U-N-S 00-124-8723   EXP
SPRAYLAT CORPORATION
716 S Columbus Ave, Mount Vernon, NY 10550
Phone: (914) 699-3030
Sales: $60,491,000   *Employees:* 322
Company Type: Private   *Employees here:* 82
SIC: 2851
  Mfg water base high solids and solvent based paints
    industrial coatings and powder coatings
James E Borner, President

D-U-N-S 62-272-7642
SPRINGFIELD PRODUCTS, INC.
70 Industry Dr, Springfield, KY 40069
Phone: (606) 336-5116
Sales: $25,000,000   *Employees:* 280
Company Type: Private   *Employees here:* 280
SIC: 2821
  Mfg polyurethane & vinyl products
Hidetsugi Kato, President

D-U-N-S 07-793-6821   EXP
SPURLOCK ADHESIVES INC.
  (Parent: Spurlock Industries Inc)
125 Bank St, Waverly, VA 23890
Phone: (804) 834-8980
Sales: $30,000,000   *Employees:* 72
Company Type: Public Family Member   *Employees here:* 7
SIC: 2869
  Mfg urea & phenol formaldehyde resins and formalin
    solutions
Phillip S Sumpter, Chairman of the Board

D-U-N-S 94-744-1101   EXP
SPURLOCK INDUSTRIES INC.
125 Bank St, Waverly, VA 23890
Phone: (804) 834-8980
Sales: $24,725,000   *Employees:* 80
Company Type: Public   *Employees here:* 7
SIC: 2869
  Holding company
Phillip S Sumpter, Chairman of the Board

D-U-N-S 05-477-3866
ST IVES LABORATORIES INC.
  (Parent: Alberto-Culver Company)
9201 Oakdale Ave, Chatsworth, CA 91311
Phone: (818) 709-5500
Sales: $59,000,000   *Employees:* 500
Company Type: Public Family Member   *Employees here:* 90
SIC: 2844
  Mfg personal care pdts
Ronald P Marconet, Vice-President

D-U-N-S 00-217-5057   EXP
STANDARD CHLORINE CHEMICAL CO.
745 Governor Lea Rd, New Castle, DE 19720
Phone: (302) 834-4536
Sales: $28,400,000   *Employees:* 150
Company Type: Private   *Employees here:* 150
SIC: 2865
  Manufactures chlorinated benzene
Charles Kummel, President

D-U-N-S 00-177-7051
STANDARD CHLORINE OF DEL CO.
745 Governor Lea Rd, New Castle, DE 19720
Phone: (302) 834-4536
Sales: $33,900,000   *Employees:* 150
Company Type: Private   *Employees here:* 150
SIC: 2865
  Manufactures chlorinated benzenes
Bruce Davis, Chairman of the Board

D-U-N-S 00-307-5348
STANDARD FUSEE CORPORATION
28320 Saint Michaels Rd, Easton, MD 21601
Phone: (410) 822-0318
Sales: $20,000,000   *Employees:* 140
Company Type: Private   *Employees here:* 55
SIC: 2899
  Mfg railroad flares highway flares & marine distress signals
David Mclaughlin, Chairman of the Board

D-U-N-S 08-860-2917
STANDRIDGE COLOR CORPORATION
832 E Hightower Trl, Social Circle, GA 30025
Phone: (770) 464-3362
Sales: $125,000,000   *Employees:* 280
Company Type: Private   *Employees here:* 280
SIC: 2865
  Mfg color concentrates both organic and inorganic
Robert E Standridge, President

D-U-N-S 00-139-0202
STANSON CORPORATION
2 N Hackensack Ave, Kearny, NJ 07032
Phone: (973) 344-8666
Sales: $20,000,000   *Employees:* 100
Company Type: Private   *Employees here:* 75
SIC: 2841
  Manufactures washing compounds
Stanley Holuba Jr, Vice-President

D-U-N-S 00-452-0987   EXP
STATE INDUSTRIAL PRODUCTS CORP.
3100 Hamilton Ave, Cleveland, OH 44114
Phone: (216) 861-7114
Sales: $107,662,000   *Employees:* 1,800
Company Type: Private   *Employees here:* 350
SIC: 2841
  Mfg soaps cleaning compounds degreasing solvents &
    disinfectants
Malcolm Zucker, Chairman of the Board

D-U-N-S 00-513-0182   EXP
STEPAN COMPANY
Edens Expwy & Winnetka Rd, Winnetka, IL 60093
Phone: (847) 446-7500
Sales: $581,949,000   *Employees:* 1,292
Company Type: Public   *Employees here:* 363
SIC: 2843
    Mfg surfactants polymers & specialty chemical pdts
F Q Stepan Sr, Chairman of the Board

D-U-N-S 00-413-5539
STEPHAN CO. INC.
1850 W McNab Rd, Fort Lauderdale, FL 33309
Phone: (954) 971-0600
Sales: $27,113,000   *Employees:* 285
Company Type: Public   *Employees here:* 60
SIC: 2844
    Mfg hair preparations including shampoos conditioners hair
      spray & cosmetic preparations
Frank F Ferola, President

D-U-N-S 09-245-6003   EXP
STEPHEN J SCHERER INC.
    (Parent: Thompson Laboratories)
2850 Commerce Dr, Rochester Hills, MI 48309
Phone: (248) 852-8500
Sales: $16,000,000   *Employees:* 107
Company Type: Private   *Employees here:* 87
SIC: 2844
    Mfg cosmetic manicure preparations
John S Scherer, President

D-U-N-S 15-473-9064   EXP
STERLING CHEMICALS HOLDINGS
1200 Smith St, Ste 1900, Houston, TX 77002
Phone: (713) 650-3700
Sales: $822,590,000   *Employees:* 1,500
Company Type: Public   *Employees here:* 35
SIC: 2865
    Mfg styrene acrylonitrile acetic acid plasticizers lactic acid
      tertiary butylamine sodium cyanide & sodium chlorate
Gary M Spitz, Chief Financial Officer

D-U-N-S 00-588-4440
STERLING CHEMICALS INC.
    (Parent: Sterling Chemicals Holdings)
1200 Smith St, Ste 1900, Houston, TX 77002
Phone: (713) 650-3700
Sales: $822,590,000   *Employees:* 1,500
Company Type: Public Family Member   *Employees here:* 35
SIC: 2865
    Mfr styrene acrylonitrile acetic acid methanol plasticizers tba
      sodium cyanide sodium chlorate & sodium chlorite
Peter De Leeuw, President

D-U-N-S 00-290-9120
STERLING FIBERS INC.
    (Parent: Sterling Chemicals Holdings)
5005 Steriling Way, Milton, FL 32571
Phone: (850) 994-5311
Sales: $33,300,000   *Employees:* 333
Company Type: Public Family Member   *Employees here:* 330
SIC: 2824
    Manufacture acyrilic fibers
Frank P Diassi, Chairman of the Board

D-U-N-S 00-633-9196
STERLING PAINT, INC.
1300 E 6th St, Little Rock, AR 72202
Phone: (501) 372-4106

Sales: $17,200,000   *Employees:* 130
Company Type: Private   *Employees here:* 80
SIC: 2851
    Mfg paint and varnishes & retails paint and paint supplies
D E Fortson, President

D-U-N-S 00-138-9261
STEVENS PAINT CORP
50 Holt Dr, Stony Point, NY 10980
Phone: (914) 786-5000
Sales: $19,500,000   *Employees:* 125
Company Type: Private   *Employees here:* 125
SIC: 2851
    Mfg paint varnish & enamel
James Weil, President

D-U-N-S 06-775-9142
STIC-ADHESIVE PRODUCTS COMPANY
3950 Medford St, Los Angeles, CA 90063
Phone: (323) 268-2956
Sales: $88,000,000   *Employees:* 15
Company Type: Private   *Employees here:* 15
SIC: 2891
    Mfg adhesives & paints
Junho Suh, President

D-U-N-S 08-990-6614   EXP
STOCKHAUSEN INC.
2401 Doyle St, Greensboro, NC 27406
Phone: (336) 333-3500
Sales: $195,000,000   *Employees:* 311
Company Type: Private   *Employees here:* 311
SIC: 2869
    Mfg specialty organic chemicals
Peter R Wasmer, President

D-U-N-S 04-845-0683
STOLLER GROUP, INC.
8580 Katy Fwy, Ste 200, Houston, TX 77024
Phone: (713) 461-1493
Sales: $60,000,000   *Employees:* 250
Company Type: Private   *Employees here:* 3
SIC: 2879
    Holding company
Jerry Stoller, Chairman of the Board

D-U-N-S 00-321-8484   EXP
STONHARD INC.
    (Parent: Rpm Inc)
1 Park Ave, Maple Shade, NJ 08052
Phone: (609) 779-7500
Sales: $195,670,000   *Employees:* 750
Company Type: Public Family Member   *Employees here:* 120
SIC: 2851
    Manufactures polymer based floors linings & coatings
Jeffrey M Stork, President

D-U-N-S 00-702-3112   EXP
STRICKLAND J & CO.
1400 Ragan St, Memphis, TN 38106
Phone: (901) 774-9023
Sales: $15,900,000   *Employees:* 150
Company Type: Private   *Employees here:* 125
SIC: 2844
    Mfr cosmetics toiletries hair conditioners face cream & lotion
Mildred B Long, President

D-U-N-S 09-262-2547   EXP
STRUKTOL COMPANY OF AMERICA
201 E Steels Corners Rd, Stow, OH 44224
Phone: (330) 928-5188

Sales: $31,629,000   *Employees:* 77
Company Type: Private   *Employees here:* 77
SIC: 2869
  Mfg industrial organic chemicals
Michael E Wolers, President

D-U-N-S 96-635-2718   IMP EXP
STYLING TECHNOLOGY CORPORATION
7400 E Tierra Buena Ln, Scottsdale, AZ 85260
Phone: (602) 609-6000
Sales: $38,108,000   *Employees:* 225
Company Type: Public   *Employees here:* 20
SIC: 2844
  Mfg & whol beauty supplies
Sam L Leopold, Chairman of the Board

D-U-N-S 09-605-4945   EXP
STYROCHEM US INC.
  (Parent: Sp Acquisition Co)
7980 W Buckeye Rd, Phoenix, AZ 85043
Phone: (602) 936-1791
Sales: $26,800,000   *Employees:* 125
Company Type: Private   *Employees here:* 6
SIC: 2821
  Mfg plastic materials/resins
Michael T Kennedy, President

D-U-N-S 15-452-8913   EXP
SUD-CHEMIE & CO., LP
  (Parent: Sud-Chemie North America De)
1600 W Hill St, Louisville, KY 40210
Phone: (502) 634-7200
Sales: $246,151,000   *Employees:* 1,450
Company Type: Private   *Employees here:* 500
SIC: 2819
  Mfg catalysts
Frank Wathen, Chief Financial Officer

D-U-N-S 15-452-8855   EXP
SUD-CHEMIE INC.
  (Parent: Sud-Chemie & Co Ltd Partnr De)
1600 W Hill St, Louisville, KY 40210
Phone: (502) 634-7200
Sales: $246,000,000   *Employees:* 950
Company Type: Private   *Employees here:* 950
SIC: 2819
  Mfg catalysts
Dr Karl Wamsler, President

D-U-N-S 15-452-8970   EXP
SUD-CHEMIE, NA
1600 W Hill St, Louisville, KY 40210
Phone: (502) 634-7200
Sales: $253,000,000   *Employees:* 1,950
Company Type: Private   *Employees here:* 500
SIC: 2819
  Mfg catalysts
Dr Juergn Kammer, Executive Vice-President

D-U-N-S 11-292-3172
SUGAR FOODS CORPORATION
950 3rd Ave, New York, NY 10022
Phone: (212) 753-6900
Sales: $205,000,000   *Employees:* 500
Company Type: Private   *Employees here:* 25
SIC: 2869
  Mfrs sugar substitutes non-dairy creamers sugar packets salt
    & pepper croutons stuffing & salted snack mixes
Donald G Tober, Chairman of the Board

D-U-N-S 06-744-8977
SUMMIT LABORATORIES INC.
303 State St, Chicago Heights, IL 60411

Phone: (708) 758-7800
Sales: $35,000,000   *Employees:* 90
Company Type: Private   *Employees here:* 60
SIC: 2844
  Mfg hair and skin care products
Clyde Hammond Sr, President

D-U-N-S 14-463-8558   EXP
SUN CHEMICAL CORPORATION
222 Bridge Plz S, Fort Lee, NJ 07024
Phone: (201) 224-4600
Sales: $2,825,015,000   *Employees:* 4,500
Company Type: Private   *Employees here:* 200
SIC: 2893
  Mfg high quality printing inks & organic pigments
Henri Dyner, President

D-U-N-S 06-547-1112   EXP
SUN DRILLING PRODUCTS CORP.
503 Main St, Belle Chasse, LA 70037
Phone: (504) 393-2778
Sales: $20,132,000   *Employees:* 55
Company Type: Private   *Employees here:* 25
SIC: 2899
  Mfg drilling fluid additives & pollution control equipment
Polete J Astugue, President

D-U-N-S 04-241-8988
SUN PHARMACEUTICALS
  (Parent: Playtex Products Inc)
50 N Dupont Hwy, Dover, DE 19901
Phone: (302) 678-6000
Sales: $90,000,000   *Employees:* 115
Company Type: Public Family Member   *Employees here:* 15
SIC: 2844
  Mfg suntan lotion & skin care products
Max Recone, President

D-U-N-S 18-190-0143   EXP
SUNBELT CORPORATION
2120 Burkett Rd, Rock Hill, SC 29730
Phone: (803) 329-9787
Sales: $28,396,000   *Employees:* 46
Company Type: Private   *Employees here:* 43
SIC: 2865
  Mfg dyes & chemicals
Sudhir Trivedi, President

D-U-N-S 06-820-6705
SUNSHINE MAKERS INC.
15922 Pacific Coast Hwy, Huntington Beach, CA 92649
Phone: (562) 795-6000
Sales: $58,000,000   *Employees:* 70
Company Type: Private   *Employees here:* 40
SIC: 2842
  Mfg non-toxic biodegradable cleaner & degreasing solvent
Bruce P Fabrizio, President

D-U-N-S 84-740-7418
SUPERIOR MANUFACTURED FIBERS
117 Cedar St, Plantersville, MS 38862
Phone: (601) 844-8255
Sales: $15,000,000   *Employees:* 20
Company Type: Private   *Employees here:* 9
SIC: 2824
  Garnet pick & blow polyester fiber
James Matthews Sr, President

D-U-N-S 00-136-0494
SUPERIOR PRINTING INK CO. INC.
70 Bethune St, New York, NY 10014
Phone: (212) 741-3600

Sales: $75,000,000   Employees: 525
Company Type: Private   Employees here: 175
SIC: 2893
   Mfg printing inks & varnishes
Nathan Rosen, Managing Director

D-U-N-S 60-855-6809   EXP
SYBRON CHEMICALS INC.
Birmingham Rd, Birmingham, NJ 08011
Phone: (609) 893-1100
Sales: $188,814,000   Employees: 738
Company Type: Public   Employees here: 275
SIC: 2843
   Mfg specialty chemical products
Richard M Klein, President

D-U-N-S 78-559-2627
SYLVACHEM CORP.
   (Parent: Arizona Chemical Company)
1001 E Bus Hwy 98, Panama City, FL 32401
Phone: (850) 785-6700
Sales: $36,800,000   Employees: 154
Company Type: Public Family Member   Employees here: 1
SIC: 2869
   Mfg industrial organic chemicals
Ernest Spinner, Business Manager

D-U-N-S 06-761-9825
SYNAIR CORPORATION
2003 Amnicola Hwy, Chattanooga, TN 37406
Phone: (423) 698-8801
Sales: $19,000,000   Employees: 110
Company Type: Private   Employees here: 50
SIC: 2821
   Mfg urethane systems
Edward N Gomberg, Chairman of the Board

D-U-N-S 00-330-6461   EXP
SYNERGISTICS INDUSTRIES TEXAS
   (Parent: The Geon Company)
9733 Meador Rd, Conroe, TX 77303
Phone: (409) 856-2995
Sales: $17,400,000   Employees: 100
Company Type: Public Family Member   Employees here: 100
SIC: 2821
   Mfg (compounds) polyvinyl chloride
William F Patient, President

D-U-N-S 03-872-1056
SYSTECH ENVIRONMENTAL CORP.
   (Parent: Lafarge Corporation)
245 N Valley Rd, Xenia, OH 45385
Phone: (937) 372-8077
Sales: $26,000,000   Employees: 121
Company Type: Public Family Member   Employees here: 25
SIC: 2869
   Converts liquid waste to fuel combustives
Carl A Evers, President

D-U-N-S 61-095-4455   EXP
SYSTEMS MCH AUTOMTN COMPONENTS
5807 Van Allen Way, Carlsbad, CA 92008
Phone: (760) 929-7575
Sales: $20,000,000   Employees: 140
Company Type: Private   Employees here: 90
SIC: 2822
   Mfg polyurethane tubes/coil actuators/assembly systems
Edward A Neff, President

D-U-N-S 80-466-4746
T-CHEM HOLDINGS, INC.
9028 Dice Rd, Santa Fe Springs, CA 90670
Phone: (562) 946-6427

Sales: $27,200,000   Employees: 80
Company Type: Private   Employees here: 2
SIC: 2842
   Mfg bleaches fabric softener ammonia & cleaning products
Richard Wadley, Chairman of the Board

D-U-N-S 05-148-2784
T-CHEM PRODUCTS
   (Parent: T-Chem Holdings Inc)
9028 Dice Rd, Santa Fe Springs, CA 90670
Phone: (562) 946-6427
Sales: $27,000,000   Employees: 90
Company Type: Private   Employees here: 90
SIC: 2842
   Mfg bleaches fabric softeners ammonia & cleaning products
Richard Wadley, Chairman of the Board

D-U-N-S 15-096-8113
T M V CORPORATION
4401 Ponce De Leon Blvd, Miami, FL 33146
Phone: (305) 446-5666
Sales: $26,000,000   Employees: 225
Company Type: Private   Employees here: 25
SIC: 2844
   Holding company through subsidiaries operates as a
     manufacturer of cosmetics a beauty school and an esthetic
     care institute
Jordi Dalmau, President

D-U-N-S 60-963-3136   EXP
TA MANUFACTURING. CO.
   (Parent: Esterline Technologies Corp)
28065 Franklin Pkwy, Valencia, CA 91355
Phone: (661) 775-1100
Sales: $53,300,000   Employees: 260
Company Type: Public Family Member   Employees here: 230
SIC: 2821
   Mfg elastomers & metal clamps
George Jones, President

D-U-N-S 04-706-2021   IMP
TACC INTERNATIONAL CORPORATION
   (Parent: Illinois Tool Works Inc)
Air Station Industrial Pa, Rockland, MA 02370
Phone: (781) 878-7015
Sales: $51,600,000   Employees: 330
Company Type: Public Family Member   Employees here: 175
SIC: 2891
   Mfg adhesives sealants & coatings
Michael A D Amelio, President

D-U-N-S 04-361-4601   EXP
TAKASAGO INTERNATIONAL CORP., USA
4 Volvo Dr, Northvale, NJ 07647
Phone: (201) 767-9001
Sales: $120,000,000   Employees: 275
Company Type: Private   Employees here: 65
SIC: 2844
   Mfg perfume & flavor compounds & whol aromatic
     chemicals
Anthony Griffiths, President

D-U-N-S 05-207-3715
TANNER CHEMICALS INC.
   (Parent: Sovereign Specialty Chem Lp)
Furman Hall Ct, Greenville, SC 29609
Phone: (864) 232-3893
Sales: $25,000,000   Employees: 67
Company Type: Private   Employees here: 67
SIC: 2843
   Mfg textile finishing agents coatings processing assistants &
     adhesives
Gerard Loftus, President

D-U-N-S 04-514-4532   EXP
TANNING RESEARCH LABORATORIES
1190 N US Highway 1, Ormond Beach, FL 32174
Phone: (904) 677-9559
Sales: $41,000,000   *Employees:* 350
Company Type: Private   *Employees here:* 350
SIC: 2844
   Mfg suncare lotions & oils
Ronald J Rice, President

D-U-N-S 02-990-9145
TATE & LYLE CITRIC ACID INC.
   (Parent: Tate & Lyle Inc)
2200 E Eldorado St, Decatur, IL 62521
Phone: (217) 423-4411
Sales: $30,700,000   *Employees:* 200
Company Type: Private   *Employees here:* 20
SIC: 2899
   Mfg citric acid
Gary Durbin, Manager

D-U-N-S 19-717-6167   EXP
TCI INC.
   (Parent: Rpm Inc)
610 Dixon Dr, Ellaville, GA 31806
Phone: (912) 937-5411
Sales: $30,000,000   *Employees:* 140
Company Type: Public Family Member   *Employees here:* 140
SIC: 2851
   Mfg thermal curing coatings
Tom Slade, President

D-U-N-S 60-258-2504   EXP
TEC SPECIALTY PRODUCTS
   (Parent: H B Fuller Company)
315 S Hicks Rd, Palatine, IL 60067
Phone: (847) 358-9500
Sales: $70,000,000   *Employees:* 180
Company Type: Public Family Member   *Employees here:* 125
SIC: 2891
   Mfg adhesives
Real Bourdage, President

D-U-N-S 14-847-4216   EXP
TECHMER PM, LLC
18420 S Laurel Park Rd, Compton, CA 90220
Phone: (310) 632-9211
Sales: $84,000,000   *Employees:* 400
Company Type: Private   *Employees here:* 125
SIC: 2821
   Mfg color & additive concentrates for plastics industry
John R Manuck, President

D-U-N-S 00-120-0252   EXP
TECHNIC INC.
1 Spectacle St, Cranston, RI 02910
Phone: (401) 781-6100
Sales: $100,000,000   *Employees:* 300
Company Type: Private   *Employees here:* 110
SIC: 2899
   Mfr industrial electroplating chemicals & equipment
Hrant Shoushanian, President

D-U-N-S 04-151-1254   EXP
TECHNICAL COATINGS CO.
   (Parent: Benjamin Moore & Co)
360 Route 206, Flanders, NJ 07836
Phone: (973) 252-2500

Sales: $55,000,000   *Employees:* 170
Company Type: Public Family Member   *Employees here:* 20
SIC: 2851
   Mfg chemical coatings & industrial technical paints &
      varnishes
Robert J Hodgson, President

D-U-N-S 82-504-1007
TEDCO, INC.
1512 Bennie Breece St, West Monroe, LA 71292
Phone: (318) 325-4265
Sales: $64,000,000   *Employees:* 500
Company Type: Private   *Employees here:* 500
SIC: 2841
   Mfg soap/other detergents
Kirk Tedeton, President

D-U-N-S 00-145-7605   EXP
TEKNOR COLOR COMPANY
   (Parent: Teknor Apex Company)
505 Central Ave, Pawtucket, RI 02861
Phone: (401) 725-8000
Sales: $36,300,000   *Employees:* 307
Company Type: Private   *Employees here:* 10
SIC: 2821
   Mfg plastic and thermosetting materials
Bertram M Lederer, President

D-U-N-S 87-499-8263
TENNESSEE ELECTRO MINERALS
   (Parent: C-E Minerals Inc)
625 Snapps Ferry Rd, Greeneville, TN 37743
Phone: (423) 639-6891
Sales: $25,000,000   *Employees:* 132
Company Type: Private   *Employees here:* 132
SIC: 2819
   Mfg industrial inorganic chemicals
T J Mc Carthy, President

D-U-N-S 78-300-0979
TERRA NITROGEN COMPANY LP
5100 E Skelly Dr, Ste 800, Tulsa, OK 74135
Phone: (918) 660-0050
Sales: $335,312,000   *Employees:* 368
Company Type: Private   *Employees here:* 90
SIC: 2873
   Mfg nitrogen fertilizer
Lawrence S Hlobik, General Partner

D-U-N-S 14-994-9547
TERRA NITROGEN COMPANY, LP
600 4th St, Sioux City, IA 51101
Phone: (712) 277-1340
Sales: $335,312,000   *Employees:* 350
Company Type: Private   *Employees here:* 90
SIC: 2873
   Mfg nitrogenous fertilizers
Michael L Bennett, President

D-U-N-S 87-758-2874
TESSENDERLO INVESTMENTS, INC.
   (Parent: Tessenderlo Usa Inc)
2801 W Osborn Rd, Phoenix, AZ 85017
Phone: (602) 528-0600
Sales: $75,300,000   *Employees:* 250
Company Type: Private   *Employees here:* 3
SIC: 2873
   Mfg nitrogen and sulfur based fertilizers
Livio Lederer, President

D-U-N-S 17-417-9119
TESSENDERLO KERLEY, INC.
(Parent: Tessenderlo Investments Inc)
2801 W Osborn Rd, Phoenix, AZ 85017
Phone: (602) 528-0600
Sales: $113,386,000   Employees: 485
Company Type: Private   Employees here: 70
SIC: 2873
   Mfg nitrogen and sulfur based fertilizers
Livio Lederer, Chief Executive Officer

D-U-N-S 93-282-0368
TESSENDERLO USA, INC.
2801 W Osborn Rd, Phoenix, AZ 85017
Phone: (602) 528-0600
Sales: $168,385,000   Employees: 550
Company Type: Private   Employees here: 70
SIC: 2873
   Mfg nitrogen & sulfur based fertilizers& mfg vinyl windows
   and accessories
Christian V Rebosch, President

D-U-N-S 00-512-9366   EXP
TESTOR CORPORATION
(Parent: Rpm Inc)
620 Buckbee St, Rockford, IL 61104
Phone: (815) 962-6654
Sales: $50,000,000   Employees: 260
Company Type: Public Family Member   Employees here: 56
SIC: 2851
   Mfg hobby paints & lacquers adhesives & cements plastic kits
   & artists' air brushes
David J Miller, President

D-U-N-S 00-201-0635   EXP
TEVCO INC.
110 Pomponio Ave, South Plainfield, NJ 07080
Phone: (908) 754-7306
Sales: $21,000,000   Employees: 72
Company Type: Private   Employees here: 72
SIC: 2851
   Mfg enamels lacquers & nail polish removers
Eric Wimmer, President

D-U-N-S 00-512-4495
TEXAS PETROCHEMICAL HOLDINGS
8707 Katy Fwy, Ste 300, Houston, TX 77024
Phone: (713) 461-3322
Sales: $74,700,000   Employees: 319
Company Type: Private   Employees here: 2
SIC: 2869
   Holding company for mfg of organic industrial chemicals
Claude E Manning, Chief Financial Officer

D-U-N-S 10-264-7005
TEXAS PETROCHEMICALS CORP.
(Parent: Texas Petrochemical Holdings)
3 Riverway, Ste 1500, Houston, TX 77056
Phone: (713) 627-7474
Sales: $514,790,000   Employees: 318
Company Type: Private   Employees here: 318
SIC: 2869
   Mfg organic industrial chemicals
Bill Waycaster, President

D-U-N-S 05-188-9731   EXP
TEXAS UNITED CORPORATION
4800 San Felipe St, Houston, TX 77056
Phone: (713) 877-2600

Sales: $62,500,000   Employees: 392
Company Type: Private   Employees here: 60
SIC: 2819
   Prod salt from brine evaporation mines rock salt mfg
   inorganic chemicals industrial ceramics rents equip & gas &
   oil storage
Iris P Webre, Chairman of the Board

D-U-N-S 00-181-9655   EXP
TEXWIPE COMPANY, LLC
650 E Crescent Ave, Saddle River, NJ 07458
Phone: (201) 327-9100
Sales: $72,926,000   Employees: 450
Company Type: Private   Employees here: 90
SIC: 2842
   Mfg contamination control products
Edward Paley, Chairman

D-U-N-S 13-491-0215   EXP
TG SODA ASH, INC.
4300 Six Forks Rd, Ste 850, Raleigh, NC 27609
Phone: (919) 785-2040
Sales: $58,700,000   Employees: 375
Company Type: Private   Employees here: 10
SIC: 2812
   Mfg soda ash
Anthony T Massari, President

D-U-N-S 00-293-5591
THERMOFIL INC.
(Parent: Nippon Steel Chemcial Corpora)
6150 Whitmore Lake Rd, Brighton, MI 48116
Phone: (810) 227-3500
Sales: $59,847,000   Employees: 137
Company Type: Private   Employees here: 87
SIC: 2821
   Mfg thermoplastic materials
Randolph E Rudisill, President

D-U-N-S 08-391-3913
THIBIANT INTERNATIONAL INC.
8601 Wilshire Blvd, Beverly Hills, CA 90211
Phone: (310) 709-1345
Sales: $80,000,000   Employees: 250
Company Type: Private   Employees here: 20
SIC: 2844
   Manufacturers cosmetics
Michel Thibiant, President

D-U-N-S 00-835-4938
THOMAS R PECK MANUFACTURING CO.
13001 Seal Beach Blvd, Seal Beach, CA 90740
Phone: (562) 598-8808
Sales: $29,400,000   Employees: 174
Company Type: Private   Employees here: 4
SIC: 2891
   Mfg quicksetting cement and patching compounds
Mike Bilek Sr, Chairman of the Board

D-U-N-S 82-542-1142
THORO SYSTEM PRODUCTS INC.
(Parent: Hsc Holdings Inc)
10245 Centurion Pkwy N, Jacksonville, FL 32256
Phone: (904) 996-6000
Sales: $105,450,000   Employees: 600
Company Type: Private   Employees here: 100
SIC: 2891
   Mfg contruction products
David Fyfe, President

D-U-N-S 92-687-9685
THORO WORLDWIDE INC.
  (Parent: Hsc Holdings Inc)
10245 Centurion Pkwy N, Jacksonville, FL 32256
Phone: (904) 996-6000
Sales: $50,000,000   *Employees:* 100
Company Type: Private   *Employees here:* 100
SIC: 2891
  Holding company
David Fyfe, President

D-U-N-S 19-667-3412
THREE BOND INTERNATIONAL INC.
6184 Schumacher Park Dr, West Chester, OH 45069
Phone: (513) 779-7300
Sales: $24,374,000   *Employees:* 120
Company Type: Private   *Employees here:* 60
SIC: 2891
  Mfrs adhesives & sealants
Ichiro Ukumoy, Chief Executive Officer

D-U-N-S 00-138-1979   EXP
TINKERBELL INC.
  (Parent: Renaissance Cosmetics Inc)
3 Landmark Sq, Fl 5, Stamford, CT 06901
Phone: (203) 316-9800
Sales: $44,800,000   *Employees:* 340
Company Type: Private   *Employees here:* 15
SIC: 2844
  Mfg & mail order sale of toiletries cosmetics & perfumes
Gay A Mayer, President

D-U-N-S 08-397-7561
TIOXIDE AMERICAS INC.
  (Parent: Ici American Holdings Inc)
2001 Butterfield Rd, Downers Grove, IL 60515
Phone: (630) 663-4900
Sales: $220,000,000   *Employees:* 39
Company Type: Private   *Employees here:* 38
SIC: 2819
  Mfg & whol industrial chemicals
John A Collingwood, President

D-U-N-S 06-653-8067
TIRO INDUSTRIES, INC.
2700 E 28th St, Minneapolis, MN 55406
Phone: (612) 721-6591
Sales: $24,000,000   *Employees:* 325
Company Type: Private   *Employees here:* 260
SIC: 2844
  Mfg cosmetic formulations & specialty cleaning polishing &
    sanitation preparations
Robert O Vaa, President

D-U-N-S 00-712-1841
TNEMEC COMPANY, INC.
6800 Corporate Dr, Kansas City, MO 64120
Phone: (816) 483-3400
Sales: $67,696,000   *Employees:* 255
Company Type: Private   *Employees here:* 60
SIC: 2851
  Mfg high performance industrial coatings
Thomas C Osborne, President

D-U-N-S 88-398-8099
TOLARAM POLYMERS, INC.
9140 Arrow Point Blvd, Charlotte, NC 28273
Phone: (704) 521-9607
Sales: $47,000,000   *Employees:* 75
Company Type: Private   *Employees here:* 6
SIC: 2821
  Mfg pta polyester chips
N S Jagannathan, President

D-U-N-S 01-854-4085
TOMA INDUSTRIES
7306 Coldwater Canyon Ave, North Hollywood, CA 91605
Phone: (818) 788-5697
Sales: $15,000,000   *Employees:* 25
Company Type: Private   *Employees here:* 25
SIC: 2844
  Toilet preparations
Benny Borsakian, Partner

D-U-N-S 84-915-6286
TOMAH PRODUCTS, INC.
1012 Terra Dr, Milton, WI 53563
Phone: (608) 868-6811
Sales: $23,817,000   *Employees:* 53
Company Type: Private   *Employees here:* 53
SIC: 2869
  Mfg chemicals
Stephen B King, President

D-U-N-S 80-983-1308
TORAY COMPOSITES OF AMERICA
  (Parent: Toray Marketing & Sales Amer)
19002 50th Avenue Ct E, Tacoma, WA 98446
Phone: (253) 846-1777
Sales: $50,000,000   *Employees:* 130
Company Type: Private   *Employees here:* 130
SIC: 2821
  Mfg carbon fiber resins
Malcolm Katsumoto, Chairman of the Board

D-U-N-S 18-063-7944   EXP
TOYAL AMERICA, INC.
1717 N Naper Blvd, Ste 201, Naperville, IL 60563
Phone: (630) 505-2160
Sales: $40,411,000   *Employees:* 104
Company Type: Private   *Employees here:* 8
SIC: 2816
  Mfg aluminum pigments & powders
H Kosuge, President

D-U-N-S 19-574-9205   EXP
TPR INVESTMENT ASSOCIATES
9 W 57th St, Ste 3900, New York, NY 10019
Phone: (212) 888-3044
Sales: $219,300,000   *Employees:* 1,400
Company Type: Private   *Employees here:* 400
SIC: 2812
  Holding company through its subsidiary mfg & distribute
    specialty fertilizers & chemicals
Arie Genger, Chairman of the Board

D-U-N-S 17-821-2874   EXP
TRANS-RESOURCES INC.
  (Parent: Tpr Investment Associates)
9 W 57th St, Ste 3900, New York, NY 10019
Phone: (212) 888-3044
Sales: $376,531,000   *Employees:* 840
Company Type: Private   *Employees here:* 17
SIC: 2873
  Mfg specialty plant nutrients organic chemicals & industrial
    chemicals
Arie Genger, Chairman of the Board

D-U-N-S 06-185-5185
TRANSTAR AUTOBODY TECHNOLOGIES
  (Parent: Transtar Industries Inc)
2040 Heiserman Rd, Brighton, MI 48114
Phone: (810) 220-3000

Sales: $16,200,000
Company Type: Private
Employees: 125
Employees here: 125
SIC: 2842
  Mfg cleaning & polishing preparations for automobiles
Monte Ahuja, President

D-U-N-S 00-418-8702
TREMCO INCORPORATED
  (Parent: Rpm Inc)
3735 Green Rd, Cleveland, OH 44122
Phone: (216) 292-5000
Sales: $350,000,000
Company Type: Public Family Member
Employees: 1,785
Employees here: 294
SIC: 2891
  Mfg asphalt roofing coatings sealing compounds specialty
    chemicals for protective coatings & contractor of roofing &
    flooring
Richard E Klar, Chief Financial Officer

D-U-N-S 17-909-2028
TRI-GAS INC.
6225 State Highway 161, Irving, TX 75038
Phone: (972) 870-7000
Sales: $173,196,000
Company Type: Private
Employees: 700
Employees here: 50
SIC: 2813
  Mfg liquid industrial gases & whol welding equipment and
    safety supplies
Jeffrey Ellis, President

D-U-N-S 79-284-4680
TRI-TECH LABORATORIES INC.
1000 Robins Rd, Lynchburg, VA 24504
Phone: (804) 845-7073
Sales: $21,800,000
Company Type: Private
Employees: 200
Employees here: 200
SIC: 2844
  Performs contract manufacturing for others which includes
    perfume and health and beauty aids and wholesales general
    merchandise
Willis Ryckman III, Chairman of the Board

D-U-N-S 96-540-6408
TRIAD NITROGEN, INC.
  (Parent: Mississippi Chemical Corp)
39041 Hwy 18 W A K A, Donaldsonville, LA 70346
Phone: (225) 473-9231
Sales: $49,000,000
Company Type: Public Family Member
Employees: 188
Employees here: 188
SIC: 2873
  Mfr urea & anhydrous ammonia
Charles O Dunn, President

D-U-N-S 02-871-5530
TRICAL INC.
8770 Highway 25, Hollister, CA 95023
Phone: (831) 637-0195
Sales: $17,600,000
Company Type: Private
Employees: NA
Employees here: NA
SIC: 2879
  Formulates agricultural chemicals
Dean Storkan, President

D-U-N-S 00-968-6536
TRICO PLASTIC, INC.
  (Parent: Kca Engineered Plastics Inc)
590 S Vincent Ave, Azusa, CA 91702
Phone: (626) 969-1891
Sales: $20,900,000
Company Type: Private
Employees: 100
Employees here: 100
SIC: 2821
  Mfg plastic components
C S Dienst, Chief Executive Officer

D-U-N-S 09-529-5051
TRICO SOLUTIONS, INC.
4404 Anderson Dr, Eau Claire, WI 54703
Phone: (715) 835-0778
Sales: $60,000,000
Company Type: Private
Employees: 140
Employees here: 125
SIC: 2842
  Manufactures & markets specialty cleaning & sanitation
    preparations detergent & soap
Stephen Le Graw, Chief Executive Officer

D-U-N-S 06-828-2466
TRISTAR CORPORATION
12500 San Pedro Ave, San Antonio, TX 78216
Phone: (210) 402-2200
Sales: $67,683,000
Company Type: Public
Employees: 390
Employees here: 134
SIC: 2844
  Develops manufacturers and markets fragrances cosmetics
    and select toiletry products
Richard R Howard, Chief Executive Officer

D-U-N-S 00-214-4517   EXP
TROY CHEMICAL CORP.
  (Parent: Troy Corporation)
1 Avenue L, Newark, NJ 07105
Phone: (973) 589-2500
Sales: $16,000,000
Company Type: Private
Employees: 98
Employees here: 98
SIC: 2851
  Mfg specialty chemicals
William Rudlof, Vice-President

D-U-N-S 79-120-0959
TROY CORPORATION
8 Vreeland Rd, Florham Park, NJ 07932
Phone: (973) 443-0003
Sales: $52,400,000
Company Type: Private
Employees: 180
Employees here: 40
SIC: 2869
  Mfg specialty chemicals industrial additives & biocides for
    paints wood protection products & printing inks
Daryl D Smith, President

D-U-N-S 61-011-5628
TRUE SPECIALTY CORPORATION
10400 W Higgins Rd, Des Plaines, IL 60018
Phone: (847) 298-9000
Sales: $185,000,000
Company Type: Private
Employees: 636
Employees here: 1
SIC: 2819
  Mfg specialty chemicals
Arthur R Sigel, President

D-U-N-S 15-909-4770
TRUSEAL TECHNOLOGIES, INC.
23150 Commerce Park, Cleveland, OH 44122
Phone: (216) 910-1500
Sales: $65,000,000
Company Type: Private
Employees: 280
Employees here: 35
SIC: 2891
  Mfg adhesives/sealants
August J Coppola, Chief Executive Officer

D-U-N-S 60-823-4092   EXP
TSUMURA ENTERPRISES INC.
300 Lighting Way, Secaucus, NJ 07094
Phone: (201) 223-9000
Sales: $71,000,000
Company Type: Private
Employees: 600
Employees here: 2
SIC: 2844
  Manufacturer and wholesaler of toiletries
Motohiko Tsumura, President

D-U-N-S 17-713-8732
TSUMURA INTERNATIONAL
  (*Parent:* Tsumura Enterprises Inc)
300 Lighting Way, Secaucus, NJ 07094
Phone: (201) 223-9000
Sales: $125,000,000   *Employees:* 465
Company Type: Private   *Employees here:* 235
SIC: 2844
  Mfgs & whols bath products home fragrances & children's
    toiletries
Dennis M Newnham, President

D-U-N-S 00-513-8771   EXP
TURTLE WAX INC.
5655 W 73rd St, Chicago, IL 60638
Phone: (708) 563-3600
Sales: $100,000,000   *Employees:* 700
Company Type: Private   *Employees here:* 275
SIC: 2842
  Mfg automotive appearance cleaners shoe & metal polishes
Sondra H Healy, Chairman of the Board

D-U-N-S 00-527-1150
TWIN STATE ENGRG & CHEM CO.
3541 E Kimberly Rd, Davenport, IA 52807
Phone: (319) 359-3624
Sales: $16,500,000   *Employees:* 90
Company Type: Private   *Employees here:* 18
SIC: 2874
  Mfg liquid fertilizer
R H Tinsman Jr, President

D-U-N-S 09-324-8870
TWINCRAFT INC.
2 Tigan St, Winooski, VT 05404
Phone: (802) 655-2200
Sales: $17,000,000   *Employees:* 160
Company Type: Private   *Employees here:* 160
SIC: 2841
  Mfg private label bar soap
Peter Asch, President

D-U-N-S 15-428-8492   EXP
U S A AUSIMONT INC.
  (*Parent:* Ausimont Financial Corp)
10 Leonard Ln, Thorofare, NJ 08086
Phone: (609) 853-8119
Sales: $161,436,000   *Employees:* 200
Company Type: Private   *Employees here:* 150
SIC: 2821
  Manufactures specialty polymerization plastic specialty
    chemicals & synthetic rubber materials & wholesales
    chemical greases
Michael Coates, President

D-U-N-S 78-067-0527
U S A LENZING CORPORATION
Hwy 160, Lowland, TN 37778
Phone: (423) 585-5959
Sales: $54,200,000   *Employees:* 500
Company Type: Private   *Employees here:* 3
SIC: 2823
  Mfg rayon staple fiber
Heinrich Stepniczka, Chairman of the Board

D-U-N-S 19-970-2051
U S AGRI-CHEMICALS CORP
  (*Parent:* Usac Holdings Inc)
3225 State Hwy 630 W, Fort Meade, FL 33841
Phone: (941) 285-8121

Sales: $201,335,000   *Employees:* 290
Company Type: Private   *Employees here:* 290
SIC: 2874
  Mfg diammonium phosphate fertilizer
Malcolm Scott, President

D-U-N-S 11-817-1628   EXP
U S COTTON LLC
590 Laser Dr NE, Rio Rancho, NM 87124
Phone: (505) 892-2269
Sales: $23,600,000   *Employees:* 205
Company Type: Private   *Employees here:* 85
SIC: 2844
  Mfg cotton products
Anthony Thomas, President

D-U-N-S 18-124-1621
U S L PARALLEL PRODUCTS
  (*Parent:* Us Liquids Inc)
12281 Arrow Hwy, Rancho Cucamonga, CA 91739
Phone: (909) 980-1200
Sales: $30,000,000   *Employees:* 101
Company Type: Public Family Member   *Employees here:* 50
SIC: 2869
  Mfg industrial & fuel-grade alcohol
Gregory W Orr, President

D-U-N-S 07-514-6548   EXP
ULTRA-POLY CORP.
102 Demi Rd, Portland, PA 18351
Phone: (570) 897-7500
Sales: $16,000,000   *Employees:* 45
Company Type: Private   *Employees here:* 45
SIC: 2821
  Mfg polyethylene resin
Alan La Fiura, President

D-U-N-S 15-359-2332   EXP
ULTRAFORM CO.
Theodore Industrial Park, Theodore, AL 36582
Phone: (334) 443-1600
Sales: $16,700,000   *Employees:* 100
Company Type: Private   *Employees here:* 100
SIC: 2821
  Mfr chemicals
Dr Manfred Goettsch, General Manager

D-U-N-S 01-443-4315
UNILEVER HOME & PERSONAL
  (*Parent:* Unilever United States Inc)
390 Park Ave, New York, NY 10022
Phone: (212) 888-1260
Sales: $29,000,000   *Employees:* 250
Company Type: Private   *Employees here:* 5
SIC: 2844
  Mfg home & personal care products
Richard Goldstein, Principal

D-U-N-S 00-128-9008   EXP
UNION CARBIDE CORPORATION
39 Old Ridgebury Rd, Danbury, CT 06810
Phone: (203) 794-2000
Sales: $6,502,000,000   *Employees:* 11,813
Company Type: Public   *Employees here:* 1,500
SIC: 2869
  Mfg specialty chemicals and polymers
William H Joyce, Chairman of the Board

D-U-N-S 10-730-3356   EXP
UNIPLAST INC.
616 111th St, Arlington, TX 76011
Phone: (817) 640-3204

Sales: $15,000,000   *Employees:* 50
Company Type: Private   *Employees here:* 50
SIC: 2891
    Mfg hot melt adhesives glitter & colored glue sticks & whol
      glue guns
George Nazzal, President

D-U-N-S 14-492-4883   EXP
UNIROYAL CHEMICAL COMPANY
    (Parent: Uniroyal Chemical Corporation)
Benson Rd, Middlebury, CT 06762
Phone: (203) 573-2000
Sales: $1,183,289,000   *Employees:* 2,750
Company Type: Public Family Member   *Employees here:* 550
SIC: 2822
    Mfg epdm polymers insecticides and fungicides and rubber
      processing antioxidants
Robert J Mazaika, President

D-U-N-S 60-709-5569   EXP
UNIROYAL CHEMICAL CORPORATION
    (Parent: Crompton & Knowles Corporation)
Benson Rd, Middlebury, CT 06762
Phone: (203) 573-2000
Sales: $1,183,289,000   *Employees:* 2,750
Company Type: Public Family Member   *Employees here:* 3
SIC: 2822
    Mfg epdm polymers rubber processing antioxidants
      antiozonants and accelerators and insecticides and
      fungicides
Charles J Marsden, Chief Financial Officer

D-U-N-S 00-638-3483
UNISEAL INC.
    (Parent: George Koch Sons Inc)
1014 Uhlhorn St, Evansville, IN 47710
Phone: (812) 425-1361
Sales: $26,000,000   *Employees:* 230
Company Type: Private   *Employees here:* 130
SIC: 2891
    Mfg sealants & adhesives
Randy Zahn, President

D-U-N-S 00-637-5414   EXP
UNITED CATALYSTS INC.
    (Parent: Sud-Chemie Inc De)
1600 W Hill St, Louisville, KY 40210
Phone: (502) 634-7200
Sales: $246,000,000   *Employees:* 950
Company Type: Private   *Employees here:* 850
SIC: 2819
    Mfg catalysts & clay products
C B Knight, President

D-U-N-S 04-666-7416   EXP
UNITED ELCHEM INDUSTRIES INC.
    (Parent: Oatey Co)
11535 Reeder Rd 39, Dallas, TX 75229
Phone: (972) 241-6601
Sales: $16,000,000   *Employees:* 35
Company Type: Private   *Employees here:* 35
SIC: 2891
    Mfg adhesives/sealants
Raymond Oswalt, Vice-President

D-U-N-S 00-303-3339   EXP
UNITED GILSONITE LABORATORIES
1396 Jefferson Ave, Scranton, PA 18509
Phone: (570) 344-1202

Sales: $27,300,000   *Employees:* 170
Company Type: Private   *Employees here:* 95
SIC: 2851
    Mfg wood finish varnishes & stains masonry paints &
      products & refractory cement products
Malcolm C Mackinnon, President

D-U-N-S 06-852-7704
UNITED INDUSTRIES CORP.
8825 Page Ave, Saint Louis, MO 63114
Phone: (314) 427-0780
Sales: $164,600,000   *Employees:* 800
Company Type: Private   *Employees here:* 150
SIC: 2879
    Mfg lawn and garden products contract mfg of consumer
      products mfg anchoring and fastening devices and contract
      mfg services
David C Pratt, Chairman of the Board

D-U-N-S 00-175-9737   EXP
UNITED LABORATORIES INC.
320 37th Ave, Saint Charles, IL 60174
Phone: (630) 377-0900
Sales: $21,955,000   *Employees:* 300
Company Type: Private   *Employees here:* 75
SIC: 2842
    Mfg & whol specialty cleaning chemicals & solvents
Nicholas J Savaiano, Chairman of the Board

D-U-N-S 00-532-3910   EXP
UNITED PAINT AND CHEMICAL CORP.
    (Parent: Piceu Group Limited)
24671 Telegraph Rd, Southfield, MI 48034
Phone: (248) 353-3035
Sales: $18,100,000   *Employees:* 50
Company Type: Private   *Employees here:* 5
SIC: 2851
    Mfg paints & undercoating
John G Piceu Jr, Chief Executive Officer

D-U-N-S 84-706-1520
U.S. NONWOVENS CORP.
100 Emjay Blvd, Brentwood, NY 11717
Phone: (516) 952-0100
Sales: $22,000,000   *Employees:* 35
Company Type: Private   *Employees here:* 35
SIC: 2821
    Mfg polyester & rayon carded saturate bonded or resin
      bonded nonwovens
Marvin Kagan, President

D-U-N-S 60-653-0285   EXP
U.S. PAINT CORPORATION
831 S 21st St, Saint Louis, MO 63103
Phone: (314) 621-0525
Sales: $35,000,000   *Employees:* 155
Company Type: Private   *Employees here:* 155
SIC: 2851
    Mfg paints/allied products
Christian V Heyde, President

D-U-N-S 02-984-4755
UNITED WTR SVCS MILWAUKEE, LLC
700 E Jones St, Milwaukee, WI 53207
Phone: (414) 482-2040
Sales: $42,100,000   *Employees:* 300
Company Type: Private   *Employees here:* 150
SIC: 2899
    Waste water treatment
John Cheslik, Manager

D-U-N-S 78-554-5773
UNIVERSAL CHEMICAL & SUPPLY
   (*Parent:* Cottrell Ltd)
7399 S Tucson Way, Englewood, CO 80112
Phone: (303) 799-9401
Sales: $15,100,000   *Employees:* 88
Company Type: Private   *Employees here:* 85
SIC: 2819
   Mfg chemicals
Charles E Cottrell, President

D-U-N-S 80-970-6252   EXP
UNIVERSITY MED PRDUCTS/USA INC.
16912 Von Karman Ave, Irvine, CA 92606
Phone: (949) 851-5353
Sales: $20,000,000   *Employees:* 45
Company Type: Private   *Employees here:* 45
SIC: 2844
   Mfg & whol cosmetics & skin care products
Roy Armstrong, Chairman of the Board

D-U-N-S 00-345-9567
U.N.X. INCORPORATED
707 W Arlington Blvd, Greenville, NC 27834
Phone: (252) 756-8616
Sales: $30,000,000   *Employees:* 236
Company Type: Private   *Employees here:* 66
SIC: 2842
   Mfg laundry products
Robert J Stell, President

D-U-N-S 36-116-9238   EXP
USA DETERGENTS INC.
1735 Jersey Ave, North Brunswick, NJ 08902
Phone: (732) 828-1800
Sales: $227,269,000   *Employees:* 592
Company Type: Public   *Employees here:* 245
SIC: 2841
   Mfg cleaning products and detergents
Uri Evan, Chairman of the Board

D-U-N-S 79-054-9265
USAC HOLDINGS INC.
   (*Parent:* Sinochem American Holdings Co)
3225 State Hwy 630 W, Fort Meade, FL 33841
Phone: (941) 285-8121
Sales: $29,652,000   *Employees:* 275
Company Type: Private   *Employees here:* 3
SIC: 2874
   Mfg diammonium phosphate fertilizer
Du R Liang, President

D-U-N-S 04-932-0880
USR OPTONIX INC.
   (*Parent:* Mitsubishi Chemical Amer Inc)
Kings Hwy, Hackettstown, NJ 07840
Phone: (908) 850-1500
Sales: $50,000,000   *Employees:* 200
Company Type: Private   *Employees here:* 180
SIC: 2819
   Mfr inorganic chemicals and x-ray film
Takayoshi Yuki, President

D-U-N-S 80-776-4691
UYEMURA INTERNATIONAL CORP.
2625 E Cedar St, Ontario, CA 91761
Phone: (909) 923-2294
Sales: $50,000,000   *Employees:* 145
Company Type: Private   *Employees here:* 15
SIC: 2819
   Mfg cheimical coatings
Anthony Revier, President

D-U-N-S 00-696-7822   EXP
VALHI INC.
   (*Parent:* Valhi Group Inc)
5430 LBJ Fwy, Ste 1700, Dallas, TX 75240
Phone: (972) 233-1700
Sales: $1,093,091,000   *Employees:* 4,000
Company Type: Public   *Employees here:* 50
SIC: 2816
   Mfr chemicals locks and other hardware
Harold C Simmons, Chairman of the Board

D-U-N-S 00-701-7858
VALLEY PRODUCTS CO.
384 E Brooks Rd, Memphis, TN 38109
Phone: (901) 396-9646
Sales: $17,600,000   *Employees:* 150
Company Type: Private   *Employees here:* 149
SIC: 2841
   Mfg soap
Randy Baldock, Treasurer

D-U-N-S 05-073-6453
VALSPAR CORPORATION
1101 S 3rd St, Minneapolis, MN 55415
Phone: (612) 332-7371
Sales: $1,155,134,000   *Employees:* 3,800
Company Type: Public   *Employees here:* 300
SIC: 2851
   Mfg paints stains varnishes industrial and packaging coatings
      and resins
Richard M Rompala, President

D-U-N-S 00-700-6455   EXP
VAN RU INC.
   (*Parent:* Tioga International (del))
1175 E Diamond Ave, Evansville, IN 47711
Phone: (812) 464-2488
Sales: $25,000,000   *Employees:* 300
Company Type: Private   *Employees here:* 200
SIC: 2891
   Mfg adhesives sealants caulking compounds and plastic
      specialties
George D Lutz, President

D-U-N-S 00-149-5514
VANDERBILT CHEMICAL CORP.
   (*Parent:* R T Vanderbilt Company Inc)
30 Winfield St, Norwalk, CT 06855
Phone: (203) 853-1400
Sales: $29,900,000   *Employees:* 158
Company Type: Private   *Employees here:* 10
SIC: 2869
   Mfg organic & inorganic industrial chemicals
H B Vanderbilt Jr, President

D-U-N-S 00-526-9923
VARIED INVESTMENTS INC.
1600 Oregon St, Muscatine, IA 52761
Phone: (319) 264-4211
Sales: $469,900,000   *Employees:* 2,097
Company Type: Private   *Employees here:* 54
SIC: 2869
   Holding company
James H Kent, Chairman of the Board

D-U-N-S 62-272-9101   EXP
VARNCO HOLDINGS, INC.
8 Allerman Rd, Oakland, NJ 07436
Phone: (201) 337-3600

Sales: $22,000,000   *Employees:* 83
Company Type: Private   *Employees here:* 40
SIC: 2899
  Mfg & distributes specialty chemicals & operates industrial
    buildings
Joseph Von Zwehl, President

D-U-N-S 00-593-7263   EXP
VELSICOL CHEMICAL CORPORATION
  (Parent: True Specialty Corporation Del)
10400 W Higgins Rd, Des Plaines, IL 60018
Phone: (847) 298-9000
Sales: $185,000,000   *Employees:* 600
Company Type: Private   *Employees here:* 70
SIC: 2819
  Mfg specialty chemicals
Arthur R Sigel, President

D-U-N-S 18-404-2521   EXP
VENTANA MEDICAL SYSTEMS, INC.
3865 N Business Center Dr, Tucson, AZ 85705
Phone: (520) 887-2155
Sales: $32,153,000   *Employees:* 150
Company Type: Public   *Employees here:* 93
SIC: 2819
  Mfg chemistry reagents and medical diagnostic instruments
Henry T Pietraszek, President

D-U-N-S 60-618-4489
VENTURE VI INC.
1013 Rig St, Walled Lake, MI 48390
Phone: (248) 669-6667
Sales: $18,000,000   *Employees:* 10
Company Type: Private   *Employees here:* 10
SIC: 2899
  Mfg water treatment chemicals
Randy J Petiprin, Treasurer

D-U-N-S 00-624-7464
VERDANT BRANDS INC.
9555 James Ave S, Ste 200, Minneapolis, MN 55431
Phone: (612) 703-3300
Sales: $30,000,000   *Employees:* 260
Company Type: Public   *Employees here:* 26
SIC: 2879
  Mfg biological & botanical pest control products and organic
    microbiological fertilizers
Stanley Goldberg, Chairman of the Board

D-U-N-S 04-763-1965
VI-CHEM CORPORATION
  (Parent: Nicholas Plastics Inc)
55 Cottage Grove St SW, Grand Rapids, MI 49507
Phone: (616) 247-8501
Sales: $30,000,000   *Employees:* 60
Company Type: Private   *Employees here:* 60
SIC: 2821
  Mfg polyvinyl chloride compounds & alloyed elastomers
James S Nicholas, President

D-U-N-S 00-626-8353   EXP
VI-JON LABORATORIES INC.
6300 Etzel Ave, Saint Louis, MO 63133
Phone: (314) 721-2991
Sales: $55,000,000   *Employees:* 170
Company Type: Private   *Employees here:* 170
SIC: 2844
  Mfg toilet preparations
John G Brunner, Chief Executive Officer

D-U-N-S 80-266-9572
VICKSBURG CHEMICAL COMPANY
  (Parent: Cedar Chemical Corporation)
5100 Poplar Ave, Ste 2414, Memphis, TN 38137
Phone: (901) 685-5348
Sales: $78,000,000   *Employees:* 125
Company Type: Private   *Employees here:* 10
SIC: 2873
  Mfg nitric acid potassium nitrate fertilizer chlorine nitrogen
    tetroxide
Ami Cohen, President

D-U-N-S 03-387-0585
VININGS INDUSTRIES INC.
  (Parent: New South Chemicals Inc)
2303 Cumberland Pkwy SE, Atlanta, GA 30339
Phone: (770) 436-1542
Sales: $36,200,000   *Employees:* 230
Company Type: Private   *Employees here:* 60
SIC: 2819
  Mfg inorganic and organic specialty chemicals
Errol J Menke, Chairman of the Board

D-U-N-S 00-173-6446   EXP
THE VIRKLER COMPANY
12345 Steele Creek Rd, Charlotte, NC 28273
Phone: (704) 588-8500
Sales: $25,000,000   *Employees:* 100
Company Type: Private   *Employees here:* 100
SIC: 2869
  Mfg organic textile chemicals
Howard E Virkler, President

D-U-N-S 00-838-7474
VISTA PAINT CORPORATION
2020 E Orangethorpe Ave, Fullerton, CA 92831
Phone: (714) 680-3800
Sales: $60,400,000   *Employees:* 400
Company Type: Private   *Employees here:* 125
SIC: 2851
  Mfg & ret paints
Eddie R Fischer, President

D-U-N-S 04-798-9082
VITA-GREEN INC.
  (Parent: Greenleaf Products Inc)
Hwy 27 N At RWS Ranch Rd, Haines City, FL 33844
Phone: (941) 422-8220
Sales: $17,800,000   *Employees:* 100
Company Type: Private   *Employees here:* 100
SIC: 2875
  Mfg of potting soil top soil mulch & pine bark
Donald Mason, President

D-U-N-S 00-727-6728
VOGEL PAINT & WAX COMPANY INC.
1110 Albany Pl SE, Orange City, IA 51041
Phone: (712) 737-4993
Sales: $38,661,000   *Employees:* 146
Company Type: Private   *Employees here:* 140
SIC: 2851
  Mfg paint varnishes & lacquers
Franklin Vogel, Chairman of the Board

D-U-N-S 60-387-8752   EXP
VPI MIRREX CORPORATION
  (Parent: Vinyl Plastics Inc)
1389 School House Rd, Delaware City, DE 19706
Phone: (302) 836-5950

Sales: $97,000,000   *Employees:* 440
Company Type: Private   *Employees here:* 310
SIC: 2821
    Mfg ridged semi-ridged & flexible polyvinyl chloride (pvc)
    film
R B Grover, President

D-U-N-S 00-701-7288
W M BARR & CO. INC.
2105 Channel Ave, Memphis, TN 38114
Phone: (901) 775-0100
Sales: $62,700,000   *Employees:* 415
Company Type: Private   *Employees here:* 403
SIC: 2851
    Blends liquid & aerosol chemical products
A V Richmond, President

D-U-N-S 00-136-7846   EXP
W R GRACE & CO.
1750 Clint Moore Rd, Boca Raton, FL 33487
Phone: (561) 362-2000
Sales: $1,479,700,000   *Employees:* 6,300
Company Type: Public   *Employees here:* 190
SIC: 2819
    Specialty chemicals
Paul J Norris, President

D-U-N-S 94-310-3374   EXP
WACKER CHEMICAL HOLDING CORP.
3301 Sutton Rd, Adrian, MI 49221
Phone: (517) 263-5711
Sales: $123,000,000   *Employees:* 515
Company Type: Private   *Employees here:* 8
SIC: 2869
    Holding company
Guenther Lengnick, President

D-U-N-S 07-540-0671
WACKER SILICONES CORPORATION
    (Parent: Wacker Chemical Holding Corp)
3301 Sutton Rd, Adrian, MI 49221
Phone: (517) 263-5711
Sales: $126,700,000   *Employees:* 530
Company Type: Private   *Employees here:* 487
SIC: 2869
    Mfg silicone products
Craig A Rogerson, President

D-U-N-S 84-975-2308   IMP
WAKO CHEMICALS USA, INC.
1600 Bellwood Rd, Richmond, VA 23237
Phone: (804) 271-7677
Sales: $19,000,000   *Employees:* 44
Company Type: Private   *Employees here:* 44
SIC: 2869
    Mfg and whol industrial organic chemicals
Alex Fukushima, President

D-U-N-S 00-543-0244
WARSAW CHEMICAL COMPANY, INC.
390 Argonne Rd, Warsaw, IN 46580
Phone: (219) 267-3251
Sales: $15,047,000   *Employees:* 95
Company Type: Private   *Employees here:* 95
SIC: 2842
    Mfg & whol industrial cleaning compounds
Donald A Sweatland, President

D-U-N-S 00-431-8374
WASHINGTON PENN PLASTIC CO.
2080 N Main St, Washington, PA 15301
Phone: (724) 228-1260

Sales: $132,000,000   *Employees:* 290
Company Type: Private   *Employees here:* 250
SIC: 2821
    Mfg synthetic resins
Paul P Cusolito, Executive Vice-President

D-U-N-S 36-210-3285   EXP
WASSER HIGH-TECH COATINGS INC.
8041 S 228th St, Kent, WA 98032
Phone: (253) 850-2967
Sales: $24,000,000   *Employees:* 55
Company Type: Private   *Employees here:* 55
SIC: 2851
    Mfg single component moisture-cure urethane coatings
Bill Brinton Sr, President

D-U-N-S 00-116-5695
WATERBURY COMPANIES INC.
32 Mattatuck Heights Rd, Waterbury, CT 06705
Phone: (203) 597-1812
Sales: $40,000,000   *Employees:* 240
Company Type: Private   *Employees here:* 36
SIC: 2813
    Mfg aerosol products bathware products & metal buttons
Carl Contadini, President

D-U-N-S 83-495-0552   EXP
WATSON INDUSTRIES, INC.
616 Hite Rd, Harwick, PA 15049
Phone: (412) 362-8300
Sales: $45,000,000   *Employees:* 300
Company Type: Private   *Employees here:* 200
SIC: 2851
    Mfg paints & varnishes and lessor of commercial property
H K Watson III, President

D-U-N-S 00-326-4256
WATTYL PAINT CORPORATION
    (Parent: Wattyl (us) Limited)
5275 Peachtree Industrial, Atlanta, GA 30341
Phone: (770) 455-7000
Sales: $28,000,000   *Employees:* 190
Company Type: Private   *Employees here:* 65
SIC: 2851
    Mfg paints
Christian Bosset, President

D-U-N-S 18-621-8822
WATTYL (US) LIMITED
308 S Old County Rd, Edgewater, FL 32132
Phone: (904) 428-6461
Sales: $60,400,000   *Employees:* 400
Company Type: Private   *Employees here:* 5
SIC: 2851
    Mfg paint enamels & varnishes and ret paints & wallpaper
Christian Bosset, President

D-U-N-S 05-956-9707   EXP
WEATHERLY CONSUMER PRODUCTS
    (Parent: Easy Gardener Inc)
3022 Franklin Ave, Waco, TX 76710
Phone: (254) 753-5353
Sales: $24,900,000   *Employees:* 85
Company Type: Public Family Member   *Employees here:* 20
SIC: 2873
    Mfg nitrogenous fertilizer & lawn & garden products
Robert Kassel, President

D-U-N-S 96-581-7836   EXP
WELL LONG ECONOMIC & TRADE CO.
1788 Clear Lake Ave, Milpitas, CA 95035
Phone: (408) 935-8321

Sales: $20,000,000 *Employees:* 5
Company Type: Private *Employees here:* 5
SIC: 2821
 Mfg plastic materials/resins
Alice Tam, President

D-U-N-S 00-139-9815 EXP
WELLA CORPORATION
12 Mercedes Dr, Montvale, NJ 07645
Phone: (201) 930-1020
Sales: $125,000,000 *Employees:* 870
Company Type: Private *Employees here:* 99
SIC: 2844
 Mfg toilet preparations & shampoos
Karl-Heinz Pitsch, Chairman of the Board

D-U-N-S 00-710-6958
WELLBORN-DE CORP
 (Parent: Dunn-Edwards Corporation)
215 Rossmoor Ave SW, Albuquerque, NM 87105
Phone: (505) 877-5050
Sales: $19,558,000 *Employees:* 170
Company Type: Private *Employees here:* 75
SIC: 2851
 Mfg paint & ret paint industrial coatings stains varnishes &
  painting supplies
Ed Joyal, Principal

D-U-N-S 00-102-1690 EXP
WELLMAN INC.
1040 Broad St, Ste 302, Shrewsbury, NJ 07702
Phone: (732) 542-7300
Sales: $1,083,188,000 *Employees:* 3,100
Company Type: Public *Employees here:* 12
SIC: 2824
 Mfr polyester staple fibers and yarn and polyethylene
  terephthalate (pet)
Thomas M Duff, President

D-U-N-S 00-195-5483
WESCO GASES INC.
 (Parent: Aga Gas Inc)
1 Plank St, Billerica, MA 01821
Phone: (781) 272-0400
Sales: $16,500,000 *Employees:* 90
Company Type: Private *Employees here:* 80
SIC: 2813
 Mfr industrial gases & whol welding equipment
Patrick Murphy, President

D-U-N-S 15-763-3157
WESMAR PARTNERS
3 Gateway Ctr, Ste 16S, Pittsburgh, PA 15222
Phone: (412) 392-2350
Sales: $135,300,000 *Employees:* 950
Company Type: Private *Employees here:* 3
SIC: 2899
 Blends & packages automotive maintenance preparations &
  mfg golf equipment
Richard M Maurer, Co-Manager

D-U-N-S 06-928-8728 EXP
WEST AGRO INC.
 (Parent: Alfa Laval Agri Inc)
11100 N Congress Ave, Kansas City, MO 64153
Phone: (816) 891-1600
Sales: $44,300,000 *Employees:* 220
Company Type: Private *Employees here:* 35
SIC: 2879
 Mfg agricultural disinfectants & chemicals
William T Papineau, President

D-U-N-S 00-149-5209 EXP
WEST CHEMICAL PRODUCTS INC.
 (Parent: Wechco Inc)
1000 Herrontown Rd, Ste 2, Princeton, NJ 08540
Phone: (609) 921-0501
Sales: $22,266,000 *Employees:* 138
Company Type: Private *Employees here:* 3
SIC: 2842
 Mfg specialty cleaning sanitizing preparations & lubricants
Elwood W Phares II, Chairman of the Board

D-U-N-S 00-603-5380 EXP
WESTERN TAR PRODUCTS CORP.
2525 Prairieton Rd, Terre Haute, IN 47802
Phone: (812) 232-2384
Sales: $49,800,000 *Employees:* 250
Company Type: Private *Employees here:* 50
SIC: 2865
 Mfg of tar coal tars wood preserving mfg electric coils
Joseph B Card, President

D-U-N-S 16-025-3787
WESTLAKE C A & O CORPORATION
 (Parent: Westlake Chemical Corporation)
2801 Post Oak Blvd, Houston, TX 77056
Phone: (713) 960-9111
Sales: $33,900,000 *Employees:* 200
Company Type: Private *Employees here:* 2
SIC: 2812
 Mfg chlor-alkali and olefins
Albert Chao, President

D-U-N-S 61-119-2121
WESTLAKE OLEFINS CORPORATION
 (Parent: Westlake Chemical Corporation)
2801 Post Oak Blvd, Fl 6, Houston, TX 77056
Phone: (713) 960-9111
Sales: $119,300,000 *Employees:* 500
Company Type: Private *Employees here:* 3
SIC: 2869
 Mfg ethylene & polyethylene
Albert Chao, President

D-U-N-S 60-836-6308
WESTLAKE PETROCHEMICALS CORP.
 (Parent: Westlake Olefins Corporation)
2801 Post Oak Blvd, Houston, TX 77056
Phone: (713) 960-9111
Sales: $48,900,000 *Employees:* 200
Company Type: Private *Employees here:* 10
SIC: 2869
 Mfg ethylene
Albert Chao, President

D-U-N-S 15-040-3764
WESTLAKE POLYMERS CORPORATION
 (Parent: Westlake Olefins Corporation)
2801 Post Oak Blvd, Houston, TX 77056
Phone: (713) 960-9111
Sales: $18,900,000 *Employees:* 265
Company Type: Private *Employees here:* 30
SIC: 2822
 Mfg polyethylene
Albert Chao, President

D-U-N-S 07-844-5012 EXP
WESTRADE USA, INC.
10260 Westheimer Rd, Houston, TX 77042
Phone: (713) 785-0053

Sales: $20,000,000   *Employees:* 115
Company Type: Private   *Employees here:* 4
SIC: 2879
    Mfg & distributes chemicals
James K Hines, President

D-U-N-S 02-734-8309
WHATCOM FARMER'S CO-OP
415 Depot Rd, Lynden, WA 98264
Phone: (360) 354-2108
Sales: $17,611,000   *Employees:* 100
Company Type: Private   *Employees here:* 89
SIC: 2875
    Mix fertilizer & whol farm supplies
Tim Bouma, Controller

D-U-N-S 05-900-2667
WHITE CAP INC.
1500 E Lancaster Ave, Paoli, PA 19301
Phone: (610) 644-5111
Sales: $25,000,000   *Employees:* 48
Company Type: Private   *Employees here:* 5
SIC: 2842
    Mfg household disinfectant cleaners
Michael Rhoads, Chairman of the Board

D-U-N-S 61-971-2227   EXP
WHITFORD WORLDWIDE COMPANY
33 Sproul Rd, Malvern, PA 19355
Phone: (610) 296-3200
Sales: $40,400,000   *Employees:* 200
Company Type: Private   *Employees here:* 65
SIC: 2891
    Holding company operates through subsidiaries as mfg non-
       stick fluoropolymer coatings
David P Willis Jr, President

D-U-N-S 00-627-8907   EXP
WHITMIRE MICRO-GEN RES LABS
    (Parent: S C Johnson & Son Inc)
3568 Tree Court Industria, Saint Louis, MO 63122
Phone: (314) 225-5371
Sales: $19,100,000   *Employees:* 100
Company Type: Private   *Employees here:* 100
SIC: 2879
    Mfg aerosol insecticides & pesticides
David Callewart, Secretary

D-U-N-S 00-417-8935   EXP
WHITMORE MANUFACTURING CO. INC.
    (Parent: Capital Southwest Corporation)
930 Whitmore Dr, Rockwall, TX 75087
Phone: (972) 771-1000
Sales: $18,491,000   *Employees:* 115
Company Type: Public Family Member   *Employees here:* 51
SIC: 2851
    Mfg protective coatings & related cleaners
Gary L Martin, President

D-U-N-S 00-315-8938
WIKOFF COLOR CORPORATION
1886 Merritt Rd, Fort Mill, SC 29715
Phone: (803) 548-2210
Sales: $58,600,000   *Employees:* 480
Company Type: Private   *Employees here:* 120
SIC: 2893
    Mfg printing ink varnishes & water coatings
Philip L Lambert, President

D-U-N-S 82-751-7384
WILD FLAVORS, INC.
1261 Pacific Ave, Erlanger, KY 41018
Phone: (606) 342-3600

Sales: $46,000,000   *Employees:* 185
Company Type: Private   *Employees here:* 175
SIC: 2869
    Mfr flavors
Michael Ponder, President

D-U-N-S 00-628-9680   EXP
WILLERT HOME PRODUCTS INC.
4044 Park Ave, Saint Louis, MO 63110
Phone: (314) 772-2822
Sales: $20,000,000   *Employees:* 380
Company Type: Private   *Employees here:* 330
SIC: 2879
    Mfg insecticidal chemicals and industrial chemicals
William D Willert, President

D-U-N-S 78-603-0569
WILLIAM E WOFFORD TEXTILE CO.
13700 Tahiti Way Apt 141, Venice, CA 90292
Phone: (310) 827-2591
Sales: $35,000,000   *Employees:* 3
Company Type: Private   *Employees here:* 3
SIC: 2843
    Textile mfg rep
William Wofford, Owner

D-U-N-S 00-121-2695
WILLIAM ZINSSER & CO. INC.
    (Parent: Rpm Inc)
173 Belmont Dr, Somerset, NJ 08873
Phone: (732) 469-8100
Sales: $36,100,000   *Employees:* 200
Company Type: Public Family Member   *Employees here:* 150
SIC: 2851
    Manufactures shellacs shellac based allied products synthetic
       polymers and confectionery coatings
Robert Senior, President

D-U-N-S 05-730-4511
WILLIAMS ETHANOL SERVICES INC.
    (Parent: Williams Energy Ventures Inc)
1300 S 2nd St, Pekin, IL 61554
Phone: (309) 347-9200
Sales: $275,000,000   *Employees:* 243
Company Type: Public Family Member   *Employees here:* 243
SIC: 2869
    Mfg ethanol
David P Berardi, Controller

D-U-N-S 79-282-9459
WILLIAMS PAINT HOLDINGS, INC.
    (Parent: Williams Us Holdings Inc)
1105 N Market St, Ste 1014, Wilmington, DE 19801
Phone: (302) 427-9352
Sales: $245,300,000   *Employees:* 1,600
Company Type: Private   *Employees here:* 1
SIC: 2851
    Mfg paint & whol & ret paint & paint supplies
Martin O Brien, President

D-U-N-S 79-284-3112
WILLIAMS TRADING INC.
    (Parent: Williams Paint Holdings Inc)
1105 N Market St, Ste 1014, Wilmington, DE 19801
Phone: (302) 427-9352
Sales: $16,500,000   *Employees:* 100
Company Type: Private   *Employees here:* 1
SIC: 2851
    Mfg paint
Julian H Baumann Jr, Senior Vice-President

D-U-N-S 79-282-9327
WILLIAMS US HOLDINGS, INC.
　　(Parent: Wna Inc)
1105 N Market St, Ste 1014, Wilmington, DE 19801
Phone: (302) 427-9259
Sales: $1,077,300,000
Company Type: Private　　　　　　　*Employees here:* 1
SIC: 2851
　　Holding company
Martin O Brien, President

D-U-N-S 19-816-5458
WILSONART INTERNATIONAL, INC.
　　(Parent: Premark International Inc)
2400 Wilson Pl, Temple, TX 76504
Phone: (254) 207-7000
Sales: $753,500,000　　　　　　　*Employees:* 3,450
Company Type: Public Family Member　*Employees here:* 1,400
SIC: 2821
　　Mfg decorative plastics & plastic laminated counter tops
William Reeb, President

D-U-N-S 78-018-6011
WINBRO GROUP LTD
70 Conn St, Woburn, MA 01801
Phone: (781) 933-5300
Sales: $15,600,000　　　　　　　*Employees:* 120
Company Type: Private　　　　　　*Employees here:* 5
SIC: 2842
　　Holding company
Kenneth Perry, President

D-U-N-S 80-087-3986
WISCONSIN PHARMACAL CO. INC.
　　(Parent: J L S Inv Group - Wp Llc)
1 Repel Rd, Jackson, WI 53037
Phone: (414) 677-4121
Sales: $18,292,000　　　　　　　*Employees:* 92
Company Type: Private　　　　　　*Employees here:* 80
SIC: 2879
　　Mfg leisure time & cleaning products
James Burt, Chairman of the Board

D-U-N-S 79-312-1781
WONDER COMPANY (INC)
665 Vernon Ave, Nashville, TN 37209
Phone: (615) 356-1315
Sales: $24,800,000　　　　　　　*Employees:* 114
Company Type: Private　　　　　　*Employees here:* 65
SIC: 2879
　　Mfg organic garden products
Ernie Hansel, President

D-U-N-S 00-105-6795　　　　　　　　　　　EXP
WORTHEN INDUSTRIES INC.
3 E Spit Brook Rd, Nashua, NH 03060
Phone: (603) 888-5443
Sales: $34,200,000　　　　　　　*Employees:* 220
Company Type: Private　　　　　　*Employees here:* 105
SIC: 2891
　　Mfg adhesives & industrial coated fabrics
Robert F Worthen, President

D-U-N-S 79-946-9259
WPT CORPORATION
2801 Post Oak Blvd, Houston, TX 77056
Phone: (713) 960-9111
Sales: $22,500,000　　　　　　　*Employees:* 100
Company Type: Private　　　　　　*Employees here:* NA
SIC: 2869
　　Mfg ethylene
Albert Chao, President

D-U-N-S 02-476-6719　　　　　　　　　　　EXP
WRIGHT CHEMICAL CORPORATION
102 Orange St, Wilmington, NC 28401
Phone: (910) 251-0234
Sales: $35,000,000　　　　　　　*Employees:* 125
Company Type: Private　　　　　　*Employees here:* 15
SIC: 2869
　　Mfg organic chemicals
Thomas H Wright III, Chairman of the Board

D-U-N-S 00-513-0323　　　　　　　　　　　EXP
YATES INVESTMENT CASTING WAX
　　(Parent: Burmah Castrol Holdings Inc)
1615 W 15th St, Chicago, IL 60608
Phone: (312) 666-9850
Sales: $25,050,000　　　　　　　*Employees:* 45
Company Type: Private　　　　　　*Employees here:* 45
SIC: 2891
　　Mfg investment casting sealant waxes
John Paraszczak, President

D-U-N-S 17-756-7245
Z L STAR INC.
9341 Baythorne Dr, Houston, TX 77041
Phone: (713) 690-9055
Sales: $30,000,000　　　　　　　*Employees:* 160
Company Type: Private　　　　　　*Employees here:* 3
SIC: 2824
　　Mfg synthetic fibers and recycles polyproplenc plastics
Isaac Bazbaz, President

D-U-N-S 15-727-6551　　　　　　　　　　　EXP
ZACLON INC.
2981 Independence Rd, Cleveland, OH 44115
Phone: (216) 271-1601
Sales: $15,000,000　　　　　　　*Employees:* 45
Company Type: Private　　　　　　*Employees here:* 45
SIC: 2819
　　Mfg industrial inorganic & organic chemicals
Joseph T Turgeon, Chief Executive Officer

D-U-N-S 78-842-5593
ZEELAND CHEMICALS, INC.
　　(Parent: Cambrex Corporation)
215 N Centennial St, Zeeland, MI 49464
Phone: (616) 772-2193
Sales: $40,000,000　　　　　　　*Employees:* 140
Company Type: Public Family Member　*Employees here:* 140
SIC: 2869
　　Mfg chemical intermediaries
Robert Parlman, Vice-President

D-U-N-S 16-161-4870　　　　　　　　　　　EXP
ZEGARELLI GROUP INTERNATIONAL
859 N Hollywood Way 461, Burbank, CA 91505
Phone: (818) 842-8411
Sales: $15,180,000　　　　　　　*Employees:* 287
Company Type: Private　　　　　　*Employees here:* 287
SIC: 2844
　　Mfg cosmetics and hair care products
Alfred E Booth Jr, President

D-U-N-S 05-714-6011　　　　　　　　　　　EXP
ZENECA HOLDINGS INC.
1800 Concord Pike, Wilmington, DE 19803
Phone: (302) 886-3000
Sales: $1,595,600,000　　　　　　*Employees:* 7,700
Company Type: Private　　　　　　*Employees here:* 2,600
SIC: 2879
　　Agricultural chemicals pharmaceuticals and specialty
　　chemicals
A K Willard, Chairman of the Board

D-U-N-S 05-471-8580   EXP
ZENECA INC.
  (Parent: Zeneca Holdings Inc)
1800 Concord Pike, Wilmington, DE 19803
Phone: (302) 886-3000
Sales: $3,200,000,000   *Employees:* 6,000
Company Type: Private   *Employees here:* 5,000
SIC: 2879
  Mfg agricultural chemicals pharmaceuticals and specialty
    chemicals
A K Willard, Chairman of the Board

D-U-N-S 09-977-4952   EXP
ZEOCHEM
1600 W Hill St, Louisville, KY 40210
Phone: (502) 634-7600
Sales: $24,507,000   *Employees:* 92
Company Type: Private   *Employees here:* 30
SIC: 2819
  Mfg inorganic chemicals
Kenneth Gustafson, General Manager

D-U-N-S 15-994-7647
ZEOLYST INTERNATIONAL
1200 W Swedesford Rd, Valley Forge, PA 19482
Phone: (610) 651-4552
Sales: $47,000,000   *Employees:* 45
Company Type: Private   *Employees here:* 45
SIC: 2819
  Mfg zeolite compounds
Jerry Dover, President

D-U-N-S 60-544-3340   EXP
ZEON CHEMICALS INCORPORATED
4100 Bells Ln, Louisville, KY 40211
Phone: (502) 775-7700
Sales: $170,000,000   *Employees:* 400
Company Type: Private   *Employees here:* 280
SIC: 2822
  Manufactures synthetic rubber
William C Niederst, President

D-U-N-S 96-670-6145
ZOTOS INTERNATIONAL INC.
100 Tokeneke Rd, Darien, CT 06820
Phone: (203) 655-8911
Sales: $17,500,000   *Employees:* NA
Company Type: Private   *Employees here:* 140
SIC: 2844
  Mfg and whol professional hair & cosmetic products
Herb Nieporent, Vice-President

CHAPTER 5 - PART I

RANKINGS AND COMPANIES

The companies presented in Chapter 4 - Company Directory are arranged in this chapter in rank order: by sales and by number of employees. Each company's name, rank, location, type, sales, employment figure, and primary SIC are shown. Only companies with reported sales data are included in the "rankings by sales" table; similarly, only companies that report employment data are ranked in the "rankings by employment" table.

Company type is either Public, Private, or Public Family Member. The last category is used to label corporate entities that belong to a group of companies, the relationship being that of a subsidiary or element of a parent. The parents of Public Family Member companies can be found in the company's directory entry presented in Chapter 4.

This product includes proprietary data of Dun & Bradstreet, Inc.

D&B COMPANY RANKINGS BY SALES

Company	Rank	Location	Type	Sales ($ mil.)	Employ-ment	Primary SIC
The Procter & Gamble Company	1	Cincinnati, OH	Public	37,154.0	110,000	2841
The Dow Chemical Company	2	Midland, MI	Public	18,441.0	40,289	2821
Bayer Corporation	3	Pittsburgh, PA	Private	9,257.0	24,300	2821
Colgate-Palmolive Company	4	New York, NY	Public	9,056.7	37,800	2844
Monsanto Company	5	Saint Louis, MO	Public	8,648.0	29,000	2879
Occidental Petroleum Corp.	6	Los Angeles, CA	Public	8,016.0	12,380	2812
PPG Industries Inc.	7	Pittsburgh, PA	Public	7,510.0	31,900	2851
Ashland Inc.	8	Covington, KY	Public	6,933.0	21,200	2819
Hoechst Corporation	9	Warren, NJ	Private	6,876.0	29,200	2824
Union Carbide Corporation	10	Danbury, CT	Public	6,502.0	11,813	2869
MacAndrews Forbes Holdings Inc.	11	New York, NY	Private	6,196.0	20,075	2844
HNA Holdings, Inc.	12	Warren, NJ	Private	6,166.0	22,200	2824
Avon Products, Inc.	13	New York, NY	Public	5,212.7	34,995	2844
Air Products and Chemicals	14	Allentown, PA	Public	4,933.8	16,400	2813
Praxair Inc.	15	Danbury, CT	Public	4,833.0	25,388	2813
Eastman Chemical Company	16	Kingsport, TN	Public	4,678.0	16,100	2821
Occidental Chemical Holding Corp.	17	Dallas, TX	Public Family Member	4,349.0	10,400	2869
FMC Corporation	18	Chicago, IL	Public	4,259.0	16,805	2812
ICI American Holdings Inc.	19	Wilmington, DE	Private	4,004.2	14,800	2851
Rohm and Haas Company	20	Philadelphia, PA	Public	3,999.0	11,592	2821
Lyondell Chemical Worldwide	21	Houston, TX	Public Family Member	3,995.0	4,200	2869
Engelhard Corporation	22	Iselin, NJ	Public	3,630.7	6,872	2819
Estee Lauder Companies Inc.	23	New York, NY	Public	3,618.0	15,300	2844
Huntsman Corporation	24	Salt Lake City, UT	Private	3,568.1	7,486	2821
Basf Corporation	25	Budd Lake, NJ	Private	3,546.0	14,400	2869
Mafco Holdings Inc.	26	New York, NY	Private	3,460.4	28,843	2844
Estee Lauder International Inc.	27	New York, NY	Public Family Member	3,381.6	620	2844
Amoco Chemical Company	28	Chicago, IL	Private	3,222.8	14,700	2821
Zeneca Inc.	29	Wilmington, DE	Private	3,200.0	6,000	2879
Millennium Chemicals Inc.	30	Red Bank, NJ	Public	3,048.0	4,200	2816
IMC Global Inc.	31	Northbrook, IL	Public	2,988.6	8,950	2874
Solutia Inc.	32	Saint Louis, MO	Public	2,969.0	8,800	2824
Sun Chemical Corporation	33	Fort Lee, NJ	Private	2,825.0	4,500	2893
Indopco Inc.	34	Bridgewater, NJ	Private	2,770.0	7,700	2891
The Clorox Company	35	Oakland, CA	Public	2,741.3	6,600	2842
Dow Corning Corporation	36	Midland, MI	Private	2,643.5	9,100	2869
Occidental Chemical Corp.	37	Dallas, TX	Public Family Member	2,574.8	7,200	2812
Morton International, Inc.	38	Chicago, IL	Public	2,574.4	10,600	2891
Akzo Nobel Inc.	39	Chicago, IL	Private	2,567.6	10,540	2869
Intertech Group Inc.	40	North Charleston, SC	Private	2,564.5	15,832	2819
Arteva Specialities Sarl	41	Charlotte, NC	Private	2,410.7	11,000	2821
Olin Corporation	42	Norwalk, CT	Public	2,410.0	10,000	2812
Revlon Consumer Products Corp.	43	New York, NY	Private	2,390.9	16,000	2844
Revlon Holdings Inc.	44	New York, NY	Private	2,390.9	16,100	2844
Revlon Inc.	45	New York, NY	Private	2,390.9	16,000	2844
Degussa Corporation	46	Ridgefield Park, NJ	Private	2,373.0	2,027	2869
Henkel Corporation	47	King Of Prussia, PA	Private	2,256.6	8,270	2869
Solvay America Inc.	48	Houston, TX	Private	2,200.0	4,600	2821
IMC Global Operations	49	Northbrook, IL	Public Family Member	2,105.7	5,976	2874
American Air Liquide Inc.	50	Houston, TX	Private	2,000.0	4,350	2813
Dow Agrosciences LLC	51	Indianapolis, IN	Public Family Member	2,000.0	3,100	2879
Agrium U.S. Inc.	52	Denver, CO	Private	1,937.9	2,450	2873
Elf Atochem North America Inc.	53	Philadelphia, PA	Private	1,903.6	4,500	2812
Hercules Incorporated	54	Wilmington, DE	Public	1,866.0	6,834	2899
C H Oxy Corporation	55	Dallas, TX	Public Family Member	1,845.0	7,500	2869
Oxy Chemical Corporation	56	Dallas, TX	Public Family Member	1,845.0	7,500	2869
Alberto-Culver Company	57	Melrose Park, IL	Public	1,834.7	12,700	2844
Crompton & Knowles Corporation	58	Stamford, CT	Public	1,796.1	5,519	2865
Borden Holdings, Inc.	59	Columbus, OH	Private	1,769.5	11,200	2891
BW Holdings, LLC	60	Columbus, OH	Private	1,769.5	11,200	2891
Kerr-Mcgee Corporation	61	Oklahoma City, OK	Public	1,711.0	3,300	2816
Lyondell Chemical Company	62	Houston, TX	Public	1,703.0	4,250	2869
Lubrizol Corporation	63	Wickliffe, OH	Public	1,673.8	4,300	2899
Ecolab Inc.	64	Saint Paul, MN	Public	1,640.4	10,210	2841
RPM Inc.	65	Medina, OH	Public	1,615.3	6,800	2851
S C Johnson & Son Inc.	66	Racine, WI	Private	1,600.2	13,400	2842
Rhodia Inc.	67	Cranbury, NJ	Private	1,600.0	4,000	2819
Zeneca Holdings Inc.	68	Wilmington, DE	Private	1,595.6	7,700	2879
Ciba Specialty Chemicals Corp.	69	Tarrytown, NY	Private	1,560.0	4,000	2819
BOC Group Inc.	70	New Providence, NJ	Private	1,549.5	8,000	2813

D&B COMPANY RANKINGS BY SALES

Company	Rank	Location	Type	Sales ($ mil.)	Employ-ment	Primary SIC
Formosa Plastics Corp. USA	71	Livingston, NJ	Private	1,500.0	3,800	2821
Borden Inc.	72	Columbus, OH	Private	1,487.7	8,000	2869
W R Grace & Co.	73	Boca Raton, FL	Public	1,479.7	6,300	2819
Nalco Chemical Company	74	Naperville, IL	Public	1,433.7	6,502	2899
CF Industries, Inc.	75	Lake Zurich, IL	Private	1,431.6	1,652	2873
Interntonal Flavors Fragrances	76	New York, NY	Public	1,426.8	4,600	2869
ICI Americas Inc.	77	Wilmington, DE	Private	1,422.9	6,500	2821
Ferro Corporation	78	Cleveland, OH	Public	1,381.3	6,851	2899
Dial Corporation	79	Scottsdale, AZ	Public	1,362.6	3,716	2841
H B Fuller Company	80	Saint Paul, MN	Public	1,347.2	6,000	2891
Great Lakes Chemical Corp	81	West Lafayette, IN	Public	1,311.2	5,100	2819
PCS Nitrogen Fertilizer, LP	82	Memphis, TN	Private	1,310.0	1,048	2873
Reckitt & Colman Inc.	83	Wayne, NJ	Private	1,300.0	2,000	2842
Betzdearborn Inc.	84	Langhorne, PA	Public Family Member	1,294.8	5,300	2899
Borden Chemical Inc.	85	Columbus, OH	Private	1,290.8	3,000	2869
Cytec Industries Inc.	86	West Paterson, NJ	Public	1,290.6	5,200	2899
Henkel Of America Inc.	87	King Of Prussia, PA	Private	1,272.9	8,270	2869
Helene Curtis Industries Inc.	88	Chicago, IL	Private	1,265.0	2,500	2844
The Geon Company	89	Avon Lake, OH	Public	1,250.0	2,000	2821
Contran Corporation	90	Dallas, TX	Private	1,241.2	12,000	2816
Huntsman Chemical Corporation	91	Salt Lake City, UT	Private	1,203.5	1,600	2821
Estee Lauder Inc.	92	New York, NY	Public Family Member	1,199.1	10,000	2844
Uniroyal Chemical Company	93	Middlebury, CT	Public Family Member	1,183.3	2,750	2822
Uniroyal Chemical Corporation	94	Middlebury, CT	Public Family Member	1,183.3	2,750	2822
Valspar Corporation	95	Minneapolis, MN	Public	1,155.1	3,800	2851
Dexter Corporation	96	Windsor Locks, CT	Public	1,147.1	4,800	2891
The Scotts Company	97	Marysville, OH	Public	1,113.0	2,500	2873
Montell USA Inc.	98	Wilmington, DE	Private	1,100.0	2,000	2821
Amoco Fabrics And Fibers Co	99	Atlanta, GA	Private	1,093.7	5,000	2821
Valhi Inc.	100	Dallas, TX	Public	1,093.1	4,000	2816
BOC Group Inc.	101	New Providence, NJ	Private	1,090.9	9,600	2813
Dupont Dow Elastomers LLC	102	Wilmington, DE	Private	1,086.9	3,300	2822
Wellman Inc.	103	Shrewsbury, NJ	Public	1,083.2	3,100	2824
Williams US Holdings, Inc.	104	Wilmington, DE	Private	1,077.3	7,000	2851
Ethyl Corporation	105	Richmond, VA	Public	1,063.6	1,800	2869
G Industries Corp.	106	Wayne, NJ	Private	1,000.6	4,075	2869
The Glidden Company	107	Cleveland, OH	Private	1,000.0	4,600	2851
A Schulman Inc.	108	Akron, OH	Public	996.5	2,250	2821
Formosa Plastics Corp. Texas	109	Livingston, NJ	Private	960.0	300	2821
Chevron Chemical Company, LLC	110	San Ramon, CA	Private	918.1	4,200	2821
Harbour Group Ltd	111	Saint Louis, MO	Private	900.0	1,500	2822
Mary Kay Holding Corporation	112	Dallas, TX	Private	897.1	4,000	2844
Mary Kay Inc.	113	Dallas, TX	Private	897.1	4,000	2844
Georgia Gulf Corporation	114	Atlanta, GA	Public	875.0	1,041	2812
IMC Agribusiness Inc.	115	Collinsville, IL	Public Family Member	873.0	2,000	2873
Block Drug Company Inc.	116	Jersey City, NJ	Public	863.1	3,380	2844
Arch Chemical Inc.	117	Norwalk, CT	Private	862.8	3,000	2819
Kronor Inc.	118	Houston, TX	Public Family Member	852.5	2,500	2816
G-I Holdings Inc.	119	Wayne, NJ	Private	852.0	4,300	2869
Millennium Inorganic Chemicals	120	Cockeysville, MD	Public Family Member	850.0	2,000	2816
Shintech Incorporated	121	Houston, TX	Private	850.0	206	2821
Condea Vista Company	122	Houston, TX	Private	848.0	1,400	2821
Phosphate Resource Partners	123	Northbrook, IL	Public	842.5	3,871	2874
NL Industries Inc.	124	Houston, TX	Public	837.2	2,600	2816
Albemarle Corporation	125	Baton Rouge, LA	Public	829.9	2,700	2821
Praxair Distribution Inc.	126	Hinsdale, IL	Public Family Member	823.9	7,250	2813
Sterling Chemicals Holdings	127	Houston, TX	Public	822.6	1,500	2865
Sterling Chemicals Inc.	128	Houston, TX	Public Family Member	822.6	1,500	2865
NCH Corporation	129	Irving, TX	Public	784.1	10,458	2842
Akzo Nobel Chemicals Inc.	130	Chicago, IL	Private	783.0	2,100	2869
Kerr-Mcgee Chemical, LLC	131	Oklahoma City, OK	Public Family Member	760.0	2,300	2819
Flint Ink Corporation	132	Ann Arbor, MI	Private	757.1	2,600	2893
Wilsonart International, Inc.	133	Temple, TX	Public Family Member	753.5	3,450	2821
Cargill Fertilizer Inc.	134	Riverview, FL	Private	750.0	1,100	2874
International Specialty Products	135	Wayne, NJ	Private	749.2	2,500	2869
Borden Chemical & Plastic, LP	136	Geismar, LA	Public	737.1	800	2821
Revlon International Corp.	137	New York, NY	Private	719.1	6,000	2844
IMC Inorganic Chemicals Inc.	138	Shawnee Mission, KS	Public Family Member	700.0	2,235	2819
Reichhold Inc.	139	Durham, NC	Private	698.6	3,200	2821
Loctite Corporation	140	Hartford, CT	Private	694.9	4,400	2891

D&B COMPANY RANKINGS BY SALES

Company	Rank	Location	Type	Sales ($ mil.)	Employ-ment	Primary SIC
Benjamin Moore & Co.	141	Montvale, NJ	Public	666.3	1,900	2851
Carter-Wallace Inc.	142	New York, NY	Public	662.2	3,360	2844
General Chemical Group Inc.	143	Hampton, NH	Public	653.0	2,402	2812
P M C Inc.	144	Sun Valley, CA	Private	649.2	3,600	2819
Akzo Nobel Courtaulds US Inc.	145	Purchase, NY	Private	645.9	4,200	2851
BP Chemicals Inc.	146	Cleveland, OH	Private	637.0	2,600	2869
Nan Ya Plastics Corp. America	147	Livingston, NJ	Private	612.1	1,130	2824
Minerals Technologies Inc.	148	New York, NY	Public	609.2	2,250	2819
Lilly Industries Inc.	149	Indianapolis, IN	Public	601.3	2,116	2851
Du Pont Agrichemicals Caribe	150	Manati, PR	Public Family Member	598.2	150	2879
Koppers Industries Inc.	151	Pittsburgh, PA	Public	593.1	2,000	2865
Stepan Company	152	Winnetka, IL	Public	581.9	1,292	2843
Church & Dwight Co. Inc.	153	Princeton, NJ	Public	574.9	1,137	2812
Creanova Inc.	154	Somerset, NJ	Private	551.5	1,000	2869
HC Investments, Inc.	155	King Of Prussia, PA	Private	536.8	3,400	2891
Saint-Gbain Advanced Mtls Corp.	156	Louisville, KY	Private	533.7	3,300	2819
General Chemical Corporation	157	Parsippany, NJ	Public Family Member	519.1	1,869	2819
Mississippi Chemical Corp.	158	Yazoo City, MS	Public	519.1	1,600	2873
R P Scherer Corporation	159	Troy, MI	Public Family Member	515.3	3,600	2899
Texas Petrochemicals Corp.	160	Houston, TX	Private	514.8	318	2869
Mobil Chemical Company Inc.	161	Fairfax, VA	Public Family Member	511.0	3,570	2899
Columbian Chemicals Company	162	Marietta, GA	Public Family Member	500.0	1,400	2895
Cultor Food Science, Inc.	163	Ardsley, NY	Private	500.0	500	2869
Dyno Nobel Inc.	164	Salt Lake City, UT	Private	500.0	2,700	2892
Exxon Chemical Americas	165	Baton Rouge, LA	Private	500.0	450	2821
The Mennen Co.	166	Morristown, NJ	Public Family Member	500.0	420	2844
Harris Chemical North America	167	Shawnee Mission, KS	Public Family Member	494.2	2,235	2819
Bush Boake Allen Inc.	168	Montvale, NJ	Public	490.6	1,964	2869
AL America Holdings, Inc.	169	Houston, TX	Private	488.6	4,300	2813
OM Group Inc.	170	Cleveland, OH	Public	487.3	758	2819
Johnson Sc Commercial Markets	171	Sturtevant, WI	Private	477.9	4,004	2842
Ameripol Synpol Corporation	172	Port Neches, TX	Private	475.0	1,190	2822
G V C Holdings Inc.	173	Port Neches, TX	Private	475.0	1,300	2822
OSI Specialties Holding Company	174	Greenwich, CT	Public Family Member	472.4	1,200	2821
OSI Specialties, Inc.	175	Greenwich, CT	Public Family Member	472.4	1,200	2821
Berwind Industries, Inc.	176	Nashville, TN	Private	472.3	3,300	2899
Nalco/Exxon Energy Chem, LP	177	Sugar Land, TX	Private	471.8	1,500	2899
Varied Investments Inc.	178	Muscatine, IA	Private	469.9	2,097	2869
Mc Whorter Technologies, Inc.	179	Carpentersville, IL	Public	454.9	1,040	2821
Air Products, Incorporated	180	Allentown, PA	Public Family Member	454.5	4,000	2813
Pioneer Americas, Inc.	181	Houston, TX	Public Family Member	450.0	1,300	2812
Chemfirst Inc.	182	Jackson, MS	Public	445.8	1,175	2865
Aqualon Company	183	Wilmington, DE	Private	441.1	2,000	2869
Lonza Inc.	184	Fair Lawn, NJ	Private	434.9	1,000	2899
PCS Nitrogen Inc.	185	Memphis, TN	Private	424.1	1,350	2873
Huntsman Polymers Corporation	186	Salt Lake City, UT	Public	419.4	1,320	2821
Cabot Corporation	187	Boston, MA	Public	410.3	4,800	2895
NS Group Inc.	188	Newport, KY	Public	409.9	1,803	2891
Coty US Inc.	189	New York, NY	Private	405.5	1,573	2844
Bio-Lab Inc.	190	Decatur, GA	Public Family Member	400.0	900	2812
Nova Chemicals Inc.	191	Monaca, PA	Private	400.0	500	2821
The Andrew Jergens Company	192	Cincinnati, OH	Private	400.0	500	2844
Quest International Fragrances Co.	193	Budd Lake, NJ	Private	390.0	1,000	2844
Laroche Industries Inc.	194	Atlanta, GA	Private	381.0	1,120	2873
PQ Corporation	195	Berwyn, PA	Private	378.5	1,923	2819
Trans-Resources Inc.	196	New York, NY	Private	376.5	840	2873
Albright & Wilson Americas	197	Glen Allen, VA	Private	375.0	1,400	2819
Rubicon Inc.	198	Geismar, LA	Private	374.7	480	2865
ISK Americas Inc.	199	Mentor, OH	Private	369.1	800	2879
Equistar Chemicals, LP	200	Houston, TX	Private	365.8	1,500	2869
Specialty Minerals Inc.	201	New York, NY	Public Family Member	363.8	1,150	2819
Catalytica Pharmaceuticals	202	Greenville, NC	Public Family Member	360.0	1,300	2869
Neutrogena Corporation	203	Los Angeles, CA	Public Family Member	360.0	850	2844
Lesco Inc.	204	Cleveland, OH	Public	356.8	1,157	2875
DSM Finance USA Inc.	205	Wilmington, DE	Private	352.4	2,233	2891
Formosa Plastics Corp. Louisiana	206	Livingston, NJ	Private	350.0	321	2821
Haarmann & Reimer Corp	207	Teterboro, NJ	Private	350.0	690	2899
Millennium Petrochemicals Inc.	208	Cincinnati, OH	Public Family Member	350.0	320	2869
Tremco Incorporated	209	Cleveland, OH	Public Family Member	350.0	1,785	2891
Nutrasweet Kelco Company (Inc)	210	Chicago, IL	Public Family Member	341.2	1,400	2869

D&B COMPANY RANKINGS BY SALES

Company	Rank	Location	Type	Sales ($ mil.)	Employ-ment	Primary SIC
Procter & Gamble Far East	211	Cincinnati, OH	Public Family Member	337.0	2,824	2842
Terra Nitrogen Company LP	212	Tulsa, OK	Private	335.3	368	2873
Terra Nitrogen Company, LP	213	Sioux City, IA	Private	335.3	350	2873
DSM Copolymer, Inc.	214	Baton Rouge, LA	Private	333.9	700	2822
Messer Griesheim Industries	215	Malvern, PA	Private	330.0	1,500	2813
Calgon Carbon Corporation	216	Pittsburgh, PA	Public	327.5	1,341	2819
Oxy Petrochemicals Inc.	217	Dallas, TX	Public Family Member	321.5	1,320	2869
Composites Cook & Polymers Co.	218	Kansas City, MO	Private	320.6	1,120	2821
Aristech Chemical Corporation	219	Pittsburgh, PA	Private	314.5	1,450	2821
LSB Industries, Inc.	220	Oklahoma City, OK	Public	313.9	1,685	2819
The INX Group Limited	221	Elk Grove Village, IL	Private	306.3	1,550	2893
KCC Corrosion Control Co. Ltd.	222	Houston, TX	Private	300.5	15	2899
American United Distilling Co. LLC	223	Minneapolis, MN	Private	300.0	8	2869
Arizona Chemical Company	224	Panama City, FL	Public Family Member	300.0	1,030	2861
Atohaas Americas Inc.	225	Philadelphia, PA	Public Family Member	300.0	NA	2821
B F Goodrich Freedom Chemical Co.	226	Cleveland, OH	Public Family Member	300.0	1,200	2865
Farmland Hydro, LP	227	Bartow, FL	Private	300.0	306	2874
Huish Detergents Inc.	228	Salt Lake City, UT	Private	300.0	1,300	2841
Prestone Products Corporation	229	Danbury, CT	Public Family Member	300.0	910	2899
Schenectady International	230	Schenectady, NY	Private	300.0	600	2865
Genencor International Inc.	231	Rochester, NY	Private	293.6	825	2869
Philipp Brothers Chemicals Inc.	232	Fort Lee, NJ	Private	278.0	1,000	2819
Kelly-Moore Paint Company	233	San Carlos, CA	Private	276.1	2,400	2851
Clairol Incorporated	234	New York, NY	Public Family Member	275.0	2,300	2844
Phillips Sumika Polypropylene	235	Houston, TX	Private	275.0	100	2821
Williams Ethanol Services Inc.	236	Pekin, IL	Public Family Member	275.0	243	2869
Houghton International Inc.	237	Valley Forge, PA	Private	271.6	1,400	2869
Morgan Adhesives Company	238	Stow, OH	Public Family Member	268.1	1,700	2891
INX International Ink Company	239	Elk Grove Village, IL	Private	265.0	1,380	2893
Del Laboratories, Inc.	240	Uniondale, NY	Public	263.0	2,300	2844
Advanced Elastomer Systems LP	241	Akron, OH	Private	260.5	660	2822
Hampshire Chemical Corp.	242	Lexington, MA	Public Family Member	260.0	750	2869
Hampshire Holdings Corp.	243	Lexington, MA	Public Family Member	260.0	750	2869
CCL Custom Manufacturing, Inc.	244	Des Plaines, IL	Private	257.3	2,000	2841
Cyanamid Agricultural de PR	245	Manati, PR	Public Family Member	257.0	180	2879
Sud-Chemie, NA	246	Louisville, KY	Private	253.0	1,950	2819
Aldrich Chemical Company Inc.	247	Milwaukee, WI	Public Family Member	250.0	884	2869
Beiersdorf Inc.	248	Wilton, CT	Private	250.0	2,000	2844
Combe Incorporated	249	White Plains, NY	Private	250.0	600	2844
Interplastic Corporation	250	Saint Paul, MN	Private	250.0	330	2821
Kemira Holdings Inc.	251	Savannah, GA	Private	250.0	720	2816
Kemira Pigments Inc.	252	Savannah, GA	Private	250.0	718	2816
Macklanburg-Duncan Co.	253	Oklahoma City, OK	Private	250.0	1,200	2891
Pioneer Chlor Alkali Company	254	Houston, TX	Public Family Member	250.0	450	2812
Loveland Industries Inc.	255	Greeley, CO	Public Family Member	249.0	350	2879
Sandoz Agro, Inc.	256	Des Plaines, IL	Private	247.6	1,200	2879
Sud-Chemie & Co., LP	257	Louisville, KY	Private	246.2	1,450	2819
Sud-Chemie Inc.	258	Louisville, KY	Private	246.0	950	2819
United Catalysts Inc.	259	Louisville, KY	Private	246.0	950	2819
Williams Paint Holdings, Inc.	260	Wilmington, DE	Private	245.3	1,600	2851
Noxell Corporation	261	Cockeysville, MD	Public Family Member	242.6	2,397	2844
Rohm And Haas Texas Inc.	262	Deer Park, TX	Public Family Member	242.6	1,000	2869
Saint-Gobain Indus Ceramics	263	Louisville, KY	Private	242.0	1,500	2819
Learonal Inc.	264	Freeport, NY	Public	241.7	1,000	2899
Dap Products Inc.	265	Baltimore, MD	Private	240.0	550	2891
Griffin, LLC	266	Valdosta, GA	Private	237.4	800	2879
Guest Supply Inc.	267	Monmouth Junction, NJ	Public	236.7	642	2844
Clariant Corporation	268	Charlotte, NC	Private	233.8	1,150	2865
H & R Florasynth	269	Teterboro, NJ	Private	230.0	600	2899
USA Detergents Inc.	270	North Brunswick, NJ	Public	227.3	592	2841
EKA Chemicals Inc.	271	Marietta, GA	Private	225.0	450	2899
Givaudan-Roure Corporation	272	Cincinnati, OH	Private	225.0	1,050	2869
Tioxide Americas Inc.	273	Downers Grove, IL	Private	220.0	39	2819
TPR Investment Associates	274	New York, NY	Private	219.3	1,400	2812
French Fragrances, Inc.	275	Hialeah, FL	Private	215.5	190	2844
Alberto-Culver U S A Inc.	276	Melrose Park, IL	Public Family Member	215.0	1,800	2844
Freeport-Mcmoran Sulphur, Inc.	277	New Orleans, LA	Public	211.9	200	2819
SKW Biosystems Inc.	278	Langhorne, PA	Private	210.0	771	2869
Dunn-Edwards Corporation	279	Los Angeles, CA	Private	209.2	1,257	2851
Lawter International Inc.	280	Pleasant Prairie, WI	Public	206.5	502	2893

D&B COMPANY RANKINGS BY SALES

Company	Rank	Location	Type	Sales ($ mil.)	Employ- ment	Primary SIC
Conagra Fertilizer Company	281	Omaha, NE	Public Family Member	206.1	1,000	2879
Sugar Foods Corporation	282	New York, NY	Private	205.0	500	2869
Outsourcing Services Group Inc.	283	City Of Industry, CA	Private	203.0	1,700	2844
U S Agri-Chemicals Corp	284	Fort Meade, FL	Private	201.3	290	2874
A M Todd Company	285	Kalamazoo, MI	Private	200.0	275	2899
Amoco Polymers Inc.	286	Alpharetta, GA	Private	200.0	2,000	2824
Cyro Industries	287	Rockaway, NJ	Private	200.0	700	2821
Devro-Teepak, Inc.	288	Westchester, IL	Private	200.0	1,500	2823
Dystar LP	289	Charlotte, NC	Private	200.0	164	2865
Holox USA BV	290	Norcross, GA	Private	200.0	1,000	2813
Permian Mud Service Inc.	291	Houston, TX	Private	200.0	824	2819
Rust-Oleum Corporation	292	Vernon Hills, IL	Public Family Member	200.0	500	2851
Stonhard Inc.	293	Maple Shade, NJ	Public Family Member	195.7	750	2851
Stockhausen Inc.	294	Greensboro, NC	Private	195.0	311	2869
PMC Specialties Group, Inc.	295	Cleveland, OH	Private	192.8	409	2819
EM Industries, Inc.	296	Hawthorne, NY	Private	191.7	670	2869
Crompton & Knowles Colors Inc.	297	Charlotte, NC	Public Family Member	190.0	800	2899
Rogers Corporation	298	Rogers, CT	Public	189.7	993	2821
Grain Processing Corporation	299	Muscatine, IA	Private	189.6	785	2869
Sybron Chemicals Inc.	300	Birmingham, NJ	Public	188.8	738	2843
Davis Mining & Manufacturing	301	Coeburn, VA	Private	185.2	1,600	2892
Ensign-Bickford Industries	302	Simsbury, CT	Private	185.2	2,278	2892
D S M Engineering Plastic Products	303	Reading, PA	Private	185.0	650	2824
True Specialty Corporation	304	Des Plaines, IL	Private	185.0	636	2819
Velsicol Chemical Corporation	305	Des Plaines, IL	Private	185.0	600	2819
Primedia Magazines Inc.	306	New York, NY	Public Family Member	183.2	852	2821
Neste Resins Corporation	307	Eugene, OR	Private	180.0	300	2821
Renaissance Cosmetics, Inc.	308	Stamford, CT	Private	179.7	1,189	2844
Kao Corp.Of America	309	Wilmington, DE	Private	179.0	1,500	2844
Maybelline Inc.	310	New York, NY	Private	179.0	1,500	2844
OCI Wyoming, LP	311	Green River, WY	Private	178.0	490	2812
Shell Catalyst Ventures, Inc.	312	Houston, TX	Public Family Member	177.2	1,100	2819
Callaway Chemicals Company	313	Columbus, GA	Public Family Member	175.0	450	2819
Sartomer Company Inc.	314	Exton, PA	Private	175.0	250	2819
FMC Wyoming Corporation	315	Green River, WY	Public Family Member	174.6	1,115	2812
Harris Specialty Chemicals	316	Jacksonville, FL	Private	174.4	790	2869
First Chemical Corporation	317	Jackson, MS	Public Family Member	174.3	235	2865
Matheson Gas Products Inc.	318	Parsippany, NJ	Private	173.6	850	2813
Tri-Gas Inc.	319	Irving, TX	Private	173.2	700	2813
Zeon Chemicals Incorporated	320	Louisville, KY	Private	170.0	400	2822
Tessenderlo USA, Inc.	321	Phoenix, AZ	Private	168.4	550	2873
Maybelline Products Co.	322	Clark, NJ	Private	167.0	NA	2844
Diversey Lever Inc.	323	Plymouth, MI	Private	166.9	1,400	2842
United Industries Corp.	324	Saint Louis, MO	Private	164.6	800	2879
Clorox International Co. Inc.	325	Oakland, CA	Public Family Member	162.1	1,360	2842
U S A Ausimont Inc.	326	Thorofare, NJ	Private	161.4	200	2821
Alcoa Minerals Of Jamaica Inc.	327	Pittsburgh, PA	Public Family Member	161.0	1,000	2819
Bulab Holdings, Inc.	328	Memphis, TN	Private	161.0	1,250	2869
Coastal Chem Inc.	329	Cheyenne, WY	Public Family Member	160.0	244	2873
Herbert's America Inc.	330	Houston, TX	Private	160.0	500	2851
P D Glycol Ltd.	331	Beaumont, TX	Private	160.0	150	2821
Protein Technologies International	332	Saint Louis, MO	Public Family Member	160.0	1,600	2824
Saltire Industrial, Inc.	333	New York, NY	Private	160.0	435	2893
Buckman Laboratories, Inc.	334	Memphis, TN	Private	159.0	442	2869
ISP Chemicals Inc.	335	Calvert City, KY	Private	158.7	660	2869
Coty Inc.	336	New York, NY	Private	158.6	1,330	2844
New River Energetics, Inc.	337	Radford, VA	Public Family Member	150.5	1,300	2892
Champion Technologies, Inc.	338	Houston, TX	Private	150.0	725	2819
Micro-Flo Co.	339	Memphis, TN	Private	150.0	162	2879
Novo Nordisk Biochem, NA	340	Franklinton, NC	Private	150.0	350	2869
Rodel Inc.	341	Newark, DE	Private	150.0	750	2842
Brotech Corp.	342	Bala Cynwyd, PA	Private	149.9	700	2821
Sika Corporation	343	Lyndhurst, NJ	Private	148.4	737	2891
Prc-Desoto International	344	Glendale, CA	Private	148.0	731	2891
Clorox Products Manufacturing Co.	345	Aberdeen, MD	Public Family Member	147.8	1,240	2842
Baker Petrolite Incorporated	346	Sugar Land, TX	Public Family Member	146.9	1,031	2899
IMC Salt Inc.	347	Shawnee Mission, KS	Public Family Member	146.2	1,237	2899
Pam Acquisition Corp.	348	Westport, CT	Private	146.0	700	2844
Mallinckrodt Baker, Inc.	349	Phillipsburg, NJ	Public Family Member	144.8	900	2819
Cosmolab Inc.	350	Lewisburg, TN	Private	143.0	1,200	2844

D&B COMPANY RANKINGS BY SALES

Company	Rank	Location	Type	Sales ($ mil.)	Employ-ment	Primary SIC
Special Devices Incorporated	351	Santa Clarita, CA	Private	140.5	1,395	2899
Cedar Chemical Corporation	352	Memphis, TN	Private	140.0	250	2873
Calgon Corporation	353	Pittsburgh, PA	Private	139.6	980	2899
Austin Powder Company	354	Cleveland, OH	Private	138.9	1,200	2892
Rheox Inc.	355	Hightstown, NJ	Private	137.7	361	2851
AGA Inc.	356	Cleveland, OH	Private	136.6	1,202	2813
AGA Gas Inc.	357	Cleveland, OH	Private	136.4	1,200	2813
Wesmar Partners	358	Pittsburgh, PA	Private	135.3	950	2899
Sovereign Specialty Chem, LP	359	Chicago, IL	Private	134.8	340	2891
LSB Chemical Corp.	360	Oklahoma City, OK	Public Family Member	132.0	364	2819
Washington Penn Plastic Co.	361	Washington, PA	Private	132.0	290	2821
El Dorado Chemical Company	362	Oklahoma City, OK	Public Family Member	131.8	325	2819
SKW-MBT Services Inc.	363	Cleveland, OH	Private	131.7	925	2899
National Welders Supply Co.	364	Charlotte, NC	Private	130.5	810	2813
Epsilon Products Co, JV	365	Marcus Hook, PA	Private	130.0	148	2821
Mulberry Corporation	366	Mulberry, FL	Private	130.0	250	2874
Solvay Interox, Inc.	367	Houston, TX	Private	130.0	211	2819
Frazee Industries Inc.	368	San Diego, CA	Private	129.7	850	2851
ESM II Inc.	369	Amherst, NY	Private	129.2	186	2819
Austin Powder Holdings Co.	370	Cleveland, OH	Private	127.3	1,100	2892
The Ensign-Bickford Company	371	Simsbury, CT	Private	127.3	345	2892
Wacker Silicones Corporation	372	Adrian, MI	Private	126.7	530	2869
Elmers Products Inc.	373	Columbus, OH	Private	125.0	250	2891
Hammond Group, Inc.	374	Hammond, IN	Private	125.0	270	2819
Marpax	375	West Sacramento, CA	Private	125.0	253	2893
Standridge Color Corporation	376	Social Circle, GA	Private	125.0	280	2865
Tsumura International	377	Secaucus, NJ	Private	125.0	465	2844
Wella Corporation	378	Montvale, NJ	Private	125.0	870	2844
HSC Holdings Inc.	379	Jacksonville, FL	Private	124.3	790	2891
Indspec Chemical Corporation	380	Pittsburgh, PA	Private	124.0	378	2865
Atotech USA Inc.	381	Rock Hill, SC	Private	123.3	570	2899
Wacker Chemical Holding Corp.	382	Adrian, MI	Private	123.0	515	2869
Nine West Corporation	383	New York, NY	Private	122.8	400	2873
Martin Color-Fi Inc.	384	Edgefield, SC	Public	120.5	881	2824
Bostik Inc.	385	Middleton, MA	Private	120.0	460	2891
Takasago International Corp., USA	386	Northvale, NJ	Private	120.0	275	2844
Advanced Technical Products	387	Roswell, GA	Public	119.4	1,200	2821
Westlake Olefins Corporation	388	Houston, TX	Private	119.3	500	2869
Alberto-Culver International Inc.	389	Melrose Park, IL	Public Family Member	119.0	1,000	2844
Chanel Inc.	390	New York, NY	Private	119.0	1,000	2844
Matrix Essentials Inc.	391	Cleveland, OH	Public Family Member	119.0	1,000	2844
Perrigo Of Tennessee	392	Smyrna, TN	Public Family Member	119.0	1,000	2844
Richardson Sid Carbon & Gas Co.	393	Fort Worth, TX	Private	118.7	600	2895
Lamaur Corporation	394	Mill Valley, CA	Public	118.5	323	2844
Radiator Specialty Company	395	Charlotte, NC	Private	118.2	575	2899
Parfums De Coeur Ltd.	396	Darien, CT	Private	118.0	90	2844
Shiseido International Corp.	397	Oakland, NJ	Private	116.0	975	2844
International Paint Inc.	398	Houston, TX	Private	114.3	750	2851
Foseco Holding Inc.	399	Cleveland, OH	Private	113.8	800	2899
Tessenderlo Kerley, Inc.	400	Phoenix, AZ	Private	113.4	485	2873
Aloe Vera Of America Inc.	401	Dallas, TX	Private	112.6	250	2844
C B Fleet Company Incorporated	402	Lynchburg, VA	Private	110.3	432	2844
Dash Multi-Corp, Inc.	403	Maryland Heights, MO	Private	110.1	403	2821
Dana Perfumes Corp.	404	Stamford, CT	Private	110.0	200	2844
Herbert's-O'brien, Inc.	405	Houston, TX	Private	110.0	300	2851
Carson Inc.	406	Savannah, GA	Public	109.6	372	2844
State Industrial Products Corp.	407	Cleveland, OH	Private	107.7	1,800	2841
Dx Holding Company, Inc.	408	Houston, TX	Private	107.0	450	2869
Scotts-Sierra Hort Products Co.	409	Marysville, OH	Public Family Member	107.0	350	2873
CPAC Inc.	410	Leicester, NY	Public	106.1	662	2842
Thoro System Products Inc.	411	Jacksonville, FL	Private	105.5	600	2891
Lenzing Fibers Corporation	412	Lowland, TN	Private	105.0	560	2823
Schwarzkopf & Dep Corporation	413	Compton, CA	Private	104.4	320	2844
Reilly Industries Inc.	414	Indianapolis, IN	Private	103.8	514	2865
Behr Holdings Corporation	415	Santa Ana, CA	Private	103.6	680	2851
Behr Process Corporation	416	Santa Ana, CA	Private	103.6	680	2851
Kolmar Laboratories, Inc.	417	Port Jervis, NY	Private	103.1	1,700	2844
Aria, Parviz	418	Pasadena, CA	Private	102.4	500	2879
Agrevo U S A Company	419	Wilmington, DE	Private	101.2	494	2879
Polarome International Inc.	420	Jersey City, NJ	Private	100.6	95	2869

D&B COMPANY RANKINGS BY SALES

Company	Rank	Location	Type	Sales ($ mil.)	Employ-ment	Primary SIC
Belae Brands Inc.	421	Phoenix, AZ	Private	100.0	300	2844
Beverly Giorgio Hills Inc.	422	Santa Monica, CA	Public Family Member	100.0	325	2844
Chemdal Corporation	423	Palatine, IL	Public Family Member	100.0	125	2821
Comilog US, Inc.	424	Baltimore, MD	Private	100.0	400	2819
Continental Carbon Company	425	Houston, TX	Private	100.0	315	2895
Eftec North America LLC	426	Madison Heights, MI	Public Family Member	100.0	343	2891
Gojo Industries Inc.	427	Cuyahoga Falls, OH	Private	100.0	275	2842
John Paul Mitchell Systems	428	Santa Clarita, CA	Private	100.0	90	2844
M A Bruder & Sons Inc.	429	Broomall, PA	Private	100.0	1,000	2851
Penn Color Inc.	430	Doylestown, PA	Private	100.0	450	2865
Redken Laboratories Inc.	431	New York, NY	Private	100.0	200	2844
Roux Laboratories Inc.	432	Jacksonville, FL	Private	100.0	500	2844
S F Phosphates, LLC	433	Rock Springs, WY	Private	100.0	317	2874
Technic Inc.	434	Cranston, RI	Private	100.0	300	2899
Turtle Wax Inc.	435	Chicago, IL	Private	100.0	700	2842
Nobel Industries USA, Inc.	436	Chicago, IL	Private	99.5	NA	2899
Polypore Inc.	437	North Charleston, SC	Private	99.4	620	2819
High Point Chemical Corp.	438	High Point, NC	Private	98.7	211	2843
Garst Seed Company	439	Slater, IA	Private	97.0	400	2899
VPI Mirrex Corporation	440	Delaware City, DE	Private	97.0	440	2821
Detrex Corporation	441	Southfield, MI	Public	95.8	353	2842
Fibervisions, Incorporated	442	Covington, GA	Private	95.0	450	2821
Mat Den Corporation	443	Santa Maria, CA	Private	95.0	525	2844
Plasti-Kote Co., Inc.	444	Medina, OH	Private	95.0	350	2851
C P S Chemical Co. Inc.	445	Woodbridge, NJ	Private	94.7	400	2869
Chesebrough-Ponds Manufacturing	446	Las Piedras, PR	Private	94.3	360	2844
Milford Fertilizer Co.	447	Milford, DE	Public Family Member	94.2	150	2875
Gustafson, Inc.	448	Plano, TX	Public Family Member	93.2	250	2879
I C I Explosives USA, Inc.	449	Joplin, MO	Private	92.6	800	2892
New Energy Corp.	450	South Bend, IN	Private	92.4	135	2869
Marietta Corporation	451	Cortland, NY	Private	92.4	721	2841
Jean Philippe Fragrances, Inc.	452	New York, NY	Public	91.5	97	2844
Jones-Blair Company	453	Dallas, TX	Private	90.5	575	2851
Chem Fleur Inc.	454	Newark, NJ	Private	90.0	140	2899
Chemtreat Inc.	455	Glen Allen, VA	Private	90.0	400	2899
Shisedio America Inc.	456	Oakland, NJ	Private	90.0	188	2844
Sun Pharmaceuticals	457	Dover, DE	Public Family Member	90.0	115	2844
The Kingsford Products Co.	458	Oakland, CA	Public Family Member	90.0	1,200	2861
Neville Chemical Company	459	Pittsburgh, PA	Private	89.5	425	2821
Red Spot Paint & Varnish Co.	460	Evansville, IN	Private	89.3	525	2851
Cultor US Inc.	461	Ardsley, NY	Private	88.5	375	2869
Merichem Company	462	Houston, TX	Private	88.3	321	2869
Amerchol Corporation	463	Edison, NJ	Public Family Member	88.0	150	2841
Stic-Adhesive Products Company	464	Los Angeles, CA	Private	88.0	15	2891
Merle Norman Cosmetics Inc.	465	Los Angeles, CA	Private	87.5	591	2844
Americhem Inc.	466	Cuyahoga Falls, OH	Private	85.6	425	2865
Clearon Corp.	467	New York, NY	Private	85.0	200	2812
Para-Chem Southern Inc.	468	Simpsonville, SC	Private	85.0	300	2843
Phibro-Tech, Inc.	469	Fort Lee, NJ	Private	85.0	325	2819
High Plains Corporation	470	Wichita, KS	Public	84.9	130	2869
Techmer PM, LLC	471	Compton, CA	Private	84.0	400	2821
Kleen Brite Laboratories Inc.	472	Brockport, NY	Private	83.3	650	2841
Northtec, Inc.	473	Bristol, PA	Public Family Member	83.0	700	2844
American Plant Food Corp.	474	Galena Park, TX	Private	81.9	100	2875
Eastman Gelatine Corporation	475	Peabody, MA	Public Family Member	81.6	200	2899
Acordis Cellulose Fiber Inc.	476	Axis, AL	Private	81.2	750	2823
Ruco Polymer Corporation	477	Hicksville, NY	Private	80.8	138	2821
BF Goodrich Hilton Davis Inc.	478	Cincinnati, OH	Public Family Member	80.5	400	2865
Carson Products Company	479	Savannah, GA	Public Family Member	80.0	400	2844
Chemdesign Corporation	480	Fitchburg, MA	Private	80.0	390	2869
Drexel Chemical Company	481	Memphis, TN	Private	80.0	180	2879
Fluor Daniel Hanford Inc.	482	Richland, WA	Public Family Member	80.0	500	2819
Huron Tech Corp.	483	Delco, NC	Private	80.0	130	2812
Lander Co. Inc.	484	Englewood, NJ	Private	80.0	300	2844
Magruder Color Co. Inc.	485	Elizabeth, NJ	Private	80.0	350	2865
Resinall Corp.	486	Stamford, CT	Private	80.0	135	2821
Scott Chemical Co, Inc.	487	Englewood, NJ	Private	80.0	350	2844
Thibiant International Inc.	488	Beverly Hills, CA	Private	80.0	250	2844
SPI Holdings, Inc.	489	New Castle, DE	Private	78.6	335	2869
SPI Polyols, Inc.	490	New Castle, DE	Private	78.6	335	2869

D&B COMPANY RANKINGS BY SALES

Company	Rank	Location	Type	Sales ($ mil.)	Employ-ment	Primary SIC
KMCO Inc.	491	Crosby, TX	Private	78.5	140	2899
Vicksburg Chemical Company	492	Memphis, TN	Private	78.0	125	2873
Alpha Gary Corporation	493	Leominster, MA	Private	77.4	370	2821
Dentco Inc.	494	Humacao, PR	Public Family Member	77.0	180	2844
Flecto Company Inc.	495	Oakland, CA	Public Family Member	77.0	80	2851
Southern Ionics Inc.	496	West Point, MS	Private	77.0	250	2819
Clearon Holdings Inc.	497	New York, NY	Private	76.7	200	2812
E Q Holding Company	498	Wayne, MI	Private	76.7	327	2869
Indspec Holding Corporation	499	Pittsburgh, PA	Private	76.0	378	2865
Indspec Technologies Ltd.	500	Pittsburgh, PA	Private	76.0	378	2865
EMS-Grilon Holding Inc.	501	Sumter, SC	Private	75.7	106	2821
Tessenderlo Investments, Inc.	502	Phoenix, AZ	Private	75.3	250	2873
The P D George Company	503	Saint Louis, MO	Private	75.2	235	2851
Heraeus-Amersil Inc.	504	Duluth, GA	Private	75.1	470	2819
Elementis Chromium Inc.	505	Corpus Christi, TX	Private	75.0	190	2819
Graham Webb International Corp.	506	Carlsbad, CA	Private	75.0	150	2844
HPD Laboratories Inc.	507	Edison, NJ	Private	75.0	100	2842
Piedmont Chemical Industries	508	High Point, NC	Private	75.0	265	2841
Plast-O-Meric Inc.	509	Sussex, WI	Public Family Member	75.0	255	2821
Scott Specialty Gases Inc.	510	Plumsteadville, PA	Private	75.0	520	2813
Superior Printing Ink Co. Inc.	511	New York, NY	Private	75.0	525	2893
Texas Petrochemical Holdings	512	Houston, TX	Private	74.7	319	2869
Chirex Inc.	513	Natick, MA	Public	74.6	504	2899
Chemonics Industries, Inc.	514	Phoenix, AZ	Private	74.5	440	2899
Southwest Industries Inc.	515	Pompano Beach, FL	Private	74.0	32	2851
De La Rue Card Systems Inc.	516	Exton, PA	Private	73.0	350	2821
Texwipe Company, LLC	517	Saddle River, NJ	Private	72.9	450	2842
Essex Specialty Products Inc.	518	Auburn Hills, MI	Public Family Member	72.2	460	2891
Criterion Catalyst Company, LP	519	Houston, TX	Private	71.9	450	2819
Tsumura Enterprises Inc.	520	Secaucus, NJ	Private	71.0	600	2844
Quality Chemicals Inc.	521	Tyrone, PA	Public Family Member	71.0	245	2869
Foseco Inc.	522	Cleveland, OH	Private	70.8	500	2899
Neste Chemicals Holding Inc.	523	Houston, TX	Private	70.6	450	2891
Oakite Products, Inc.	524	Berkeley Heights, NJ	Private	70.2	300	2842
3V Inc.	525	Georgetown, SC	Private	70.0	260	2869
Abell Corporation	526	Monroe, LA	Private	70.0	377	2875
American Polymers Inc.	527	Worcester, MA	Private	70.0	42	2821
Apex Specialty Materials Inc.	528	New Castle, DE	Private	70.0	450	2824
Cerdec Corporation	529	Washington, PA	Private	70.0	340	2865
Pavion Limited	530	North Arlington, NJ	Private	70.0	350	2844
Reagent Chemical & Research	531	Middlesex, NJ	Private	70.0	319	2819
Rutgers Organics Corporation	532	State College, PA	Private	70.0	250	2865
TEC Specialty Products	533	Palatine, IL	Public Family Member	70.0	180	2891
Frit Inc.	534	Ozark, AL	Private	69.9	345	2873
Beauticontrol Cosmetics Inc.	535	Carrollton, TX	Public	69.4	280	2844
Gb Biosciences Corp.	536	Wilmington, DE	Private	69.2	340	2879
Georgetown Holding Company	537	Cleveland, OH	Private	67.9	480	2899
American Vanguard Corp.	538	Newport Beach, CA	Public	67.7	206	2879
Tnemec Company, Inc.	539	Kansas City, MO	Private	67.7	255	2851
Tristar Corporation	540	San Antonio, TX	Public	67.7	390	2844
Mobile Paint Manufacturing Co.	541	Theodore, AL	Private	66.5	450	2851
Fiber Industries Inc.	542	Charlotte, NC	Public Family Member	66.0	660	2824
Rodda Paint Co	543	Portland, OR	Private	66.0	420	2851
PCS Joint Venture Ltd.	544	Lakeland, FL	Private	65.7	101	2875
Chemetals Incorporated	545	Baltimore, MD	Private	65.0	285	2819
Croda Inc.	546	Parsippany, NJ	Private	65.0	278	2869
The Butcher Company Inc.	547	Marlborough, MA	Private	65.0	230	2842
Truseal Technologies, Inc.	548	Cleveland, OH	Private	65.0	280	2891
Diefenthal Investments, LLC	549	New Orleans, LA	Private	64.5	311	2821
Ausimont Industries Inc.	550	Thorofare, NJ	Private	64.3	310	2821
Bonne Bell Inc.	551	Cleveland, OH	Private	64.3	544	2844
Ethyl Petroleum Additives Inc.	552	Richmond, VA	Public Family Member	64.3	455	2899
Tedco, Inc.	553	West Monroe, LA	Private	64.0	500	2841
J B Williams Co. Inc.	554	Glen Rock, NJ	Private	63.9	45	2844
J B Williams Holdings Inc.	555	Glen Rock, NJ	Private	63.9	45	2844
Framatome Cogema Fuels	556	Lynchburg, VA	Private	63.8	400	2819
Shipley Company, LLC	557	Marlborough, MA	Public Family Member	63.8	400	2819
Ashta Chemicals Inc.	558	Ashtabula, OH	Private	63.0	100	2812
Orbseal, LLC	559	Richmond, MO	Private	62.7	400	2891
W M Barr & Co. Inc.	560	Memphis, TN	Private	62.7	415	2851

D&B COMPANY RANKINGS BY SALES

Company	Rank	Location	Type	Sales ($ mil.)	Employ-ment	Primary SIC
Pilot Chemical Corp.	561	Santa Fe Springs, CA	Private	62.6	150	2843
Louisiana Pigment Company, LP	562	Westlake, LA	Private	62.5	500	2816
Texas United Corporation	563	Houston, TX	Private	62.5	392	2819
Parlux Fragrances Inc.	564	Fort Lauderdale, FL	Public	62.4	136	2844
Faultless Starch/Bon Ami Co.	565	Kansas City, MO	Private	62.4	150	2842
CSRC USA Corp.	566	Houston, TX	Private	62.3	315	2895
Colgate-Palmolive (Pr) Inc.	567	Guayama, PR	Public Family Member	62.3	200	2842
Chemdal International Corp.	568	Palatine, IL	Public Family Member	62.1	300	2821
Goulston Technologies Inc.	569	Monroe, NC	Private	62.0	150	2843
Dragoco Inc.	570	Totowa, NJ	Private	61.9	240	2869
Coronado Paint Co. Inc.	571	Edgewater, FL	Private	61.4	275	2851
Kop-Coat Inc.	572	Pittsburgh, PA	Public Family Member	61.0	205	2851
Aristech Acrylics LLC	573	Florence, KY	Private	61.0	300	2821
Pursell Industries Inc.	574	Sylacauga, AL	Private	60.9	350	2875
Bee Chemical Company	575	Lansing, IL	Public Family Member	60.7	402	2851
Spraylat Corporation	576	Mount Vernon, NY	Private	60.5	322	2851
Carboline Company	577	Saint Louis, MO	Public Family Member	60.4	400	2851
Vista Paint Corporation	578	Fullerton, CA	Private	60.4	400	2851
Wattyl (US) Limited	579	Edgewater, FL	Private	60.4	400	2851
Goldschmidt Chemical Corp	580	Hopewell, VA	Private	60.1	260	2869
Adhesives Research, Inc.	581	Glen Rock, PA	Private	60.0	350	2891
Aeropres Corporation	582	Shreveport, LA	Private	60.0	140	2813
Airgas - North Central Inc.	583	Waterloo, IA	Public Family Member	60.0	200	2813
Chicago Specialties Inc.	584	Chicago, IL	Private	60.0	130	2869
Cumberland Packing Corp.	585	Brooklyn, NY	Private	60.0	400	2869
E T Browne Drug Co. Inc.	586	Englewood Cliffs, NJ	Private	60.0	175	2844
Lancaster Group US, LLC	587	New York, NY	Private	60.0	100	2844
Lipo Chemicals Inc.	588	Paterson, NJ	Private	60.0	87	2869
Markwins International Corp.	589	La Verne, CA	Private	60.0	50	2844
Nepera, Inc.	590	Harriman, NY	Public Family Member	60.0	130	2869
Norit Americas Inc.	591	Atlanta, GA	Private	60.0	400	2819
PCL Group, Inc.	592	Cincinnati, OH	Private	60.0	300	2865
Pierce & Stevens Corp.	593	Buffalo, NY	Private	60.0	190	2891
Sigma Coatings USA BV	594	Harvey, LA	Private	60.0	165	2851
Stoller Group, Inc.	595	Houston, TX	Private	60.0	250	2879
Trico Solutions, Inc.	596	Eau Claire, WI	Private	60.0	140	2842
Thermofil Inc.	597	Brighton, MI	Private	59.8	137	2821
The Fuller Brush Company	598	Great Bend, KS	Public Family Member	59.4	500	2842
Avon International Operations	599	New York, NY	Public Family Member	59.0	500	2844
Deltech Holdings Corp.	600	Whippany, NJ	Private	59.0	135	2821
St Ives Laboratories Inc.	601	Chatsworth, CA	Public Family Member	59.0	500	2844
Pluess-Staufer Industries Inc.	602	Proctor, VT	Private	58.9	370	2819
TG Soda Ash, Inc.	603	Raleigh, NC	Private	58.7	375	2812
Wikoff Color Corporation	604	Fort Mill, SC	Private	58.6	480	2893
Fritz Industries Inc.	605	Mesquite, TX	Private	58.3	170	2899
Arr-Maz Products, LP	606	Winter Haven, FL	Private	58.0	102	2869
Citrus and Allied Essences	607	New Hyde Park, NY	Private	58.0	95	2899
Sunshine Makers Inc.	608	Huntington Beach, CA	Private	58.0	70	2842
Benckiser Consumer Products	609	Greenwich, CT	Private	57.6	451	2841
Freeman Cosmetic Corporation	610	Los Angeles, CA	Public Family Member	57.4	250	2844
Formosa Plastics Corp.	611	Livingston, NJ	Private	56.6	117	2821
Crystal Springs Water Company	612	Fort Lauderdale, FL	Private	56.4	400	2899
Engineered Carbons, Inc.	613	Port Neches, TX	Private	56.2	284	2895
Jacobs Industries Incorporated	614	Minneapolis, MN	Private	56.2	440	2841
Apollo Colors Inc.	615	Joliet, IL	Private	56.2	210	2865
Intercontinental Polymer Inc.	616	Morristown, TN	Private	56.0	163	2821
Nippon Steel Chemcial Corporation	617	Brighton, MI	Private	55.6	153	2821
DSM Chemicals North America	618	Augusta, GA	Private	55.4	348	2819
Abco Industries Incorporated	619	Roebuck, SC	Public Family Member	55.0	125	2843
Buffalo Color Corporation	620	Parsippany, NJ	Private	55.0	250	2865
Caschem Inc.	621	Bayonne, NJ	Public Family Member	55.0	135	2869
MetalsAmerica Inc.	622	Shelby, NC	Private	55.0	100	2899
Nu-West Industries, Inc.	623	Soda Springs, ID	Private	55.0	275	2874
Technical Coatings Co.	624	Flanders, NJ	Public Family Member	55.0	170	2851
Vi-Jon Laboratories Inc.	625	Saint Louis, MO	Private	55.0	170	2844
D & K Group, Inc.	626	Elk Grove Village, IL	Private	54.8	350	2891
U S A Lenzing Corporation	627	Lowland, TN	Private	54.2	500	2823
Nalco Diversified Technologies	628	Chagrin Falls, OH	Public Family Member	54.0	255	2899
Celgard, LLC	629	Charlotte, NC	Private	53.3	260	2821
Ta Manufacturing. Co.	630	Valencia, CA	Public Family Member	53.3	260	2821

D&B COMPANY RANKINGS BY SALES

Company	Rank	Location	Type	Sales ($ mil.)	Employ- ment	Primary SIC
Dawn Chemical Company Inc.	631	Marietta, GA	Private	53.0	287	2842
Johnson & Johnson Consumer Co. PR	632	Las Piedras, PR	Public Family Member	53.0	450	2844
Laporte Water Tech & Biochem	633	Alpharetta, GA	Private	53.0	200	2899
P L C Specialties Inc.	634	Fair Lawn, NJ	Private	53.0	450	2844
Troy Corporation	635	Florham Park, NJ	Private	52.4	180	2869
American Pacific Corporation	636	Las Vegas, NV	Public	52.3	218	2819
IT Holding Inc.	637	Copperhill, TN	Private	52.0	327	2819
Joico Laboratories Inc.	638	City Of Industry, CA	Private	51.6	200	2844
Ohio Sealants Inc.	639	Mentor, OH	Private	51.6	330	2891
TACC International Corporation	640	Rockland, MA	Public Family Member	51.6	330	2891
Micro Lithography, Inc.	641	Sunnyvale, CA	Private	51.5	225	2869
Jupiter Holdings, Inc.	642	Phoenix, AZ	Private	51.1	70	2873
Copolymer Holding Company Inc.	643	Baton Rouge, LA	Private	51.1	715	2822
A-Veda Corporation	644	Minneapolis, MN	Public Family Member	50.6	430	2844
Scott's Liquid Gold, Inc.	645	Denver, CO	Public	50.5	350	2842
Cosmetic Essence Inc.	646	Edison, NJ	Private	50.0	500	2844
A M Todd Group, Inc.	647	Kalamazoo, MI	Private	50.0	355	2899
Albaugh Inc.	648	Ankeny, IA	Private	50.0	40	2879
Anderson Development Company	649	Adrian, MI	Private	50.0	130	2821
Anzon Inc.	650	Philadelphia, PA	Public Family Member	50.0	110	2899
Christian Dior Perfumes Inc.	651	New York, NY	Private	50.0	198	2844
Color Converting Industries Co.	652	Des Moines, IA	Private	50.0	225	2893
CPS Corp.	653	Dunkirk, NY	Private	50.0	140	2893
D B J Enterprises Inc.	654	Houston, TX	Private	50.0	150	2879
Dover Chemical Corporation	655	Dover, OH	Private	50.0	153	2819
Ethox Chemicals, LLC	656	Greenville, SC	Private	50.0	120	2843
Fragrance Resources Inc.	657	Clifton, NJ	Private	50.0	100	2899
Johnson Products Co. Inc.	658	Chicago, IL	Public Family Member	50.0	252	2844
Jones-Hamilton Co.	659	Newark, CA	Private	50.0	93	2819
Momar Inc.	660	Atlanta, GA	Private	50.0	500	2842
Nassau Metals Corporation	661	Staten Island, NY	Public Family Member	50.0	100	2819
Nova Borealis Compounds, LLC	662	Port Murray, NJ	Private	50.0	50	2821
Owen Oil Tools Inc.	663	Fort Worth, TX	Private	50.0	350	2892
P C R Inc.	664	Gainesville, FL	Private	50.0	220	2869
Plastics Engineering Company	665	Sheboygan, WI	Private	50.0	425	2821
Testor Corporation	666	Rockford, IL	Public Family Member	50.0	260	2851
The Benjamin Ansehl Co.	667	Saint Louis, MO	Private	50.0	230	2844
Thoro Worldwide Inc.	668	Jacksonville, FL	Private	50.0	100	2891
Toray Composites Of America	669	Tacoma, WA	Private	50.0	130	2821
USR Optonix Inc.	670	Hackettstown, NJ	Private	50.0	200	2819
Uyemura International Corp.	671	Ontario, CA	Private	50.0	145	2819
Western Tar Products Corp.	672	Terre Haute, IN	Private	49.8	250	2865
Diversified Chemical Tech	673	Detroit, MI	Private	49.2	145	2891
Triad Nitrogen, Inc.	674	Donaldsonville, LA	Public Family Member	49.0	188	2873
Westlake Petrochemicals Corp.	675	Houston, TX	Private	48.9	200	2869
Rockwood Industries Inc.	676	Beltsville, MD	Private	48.6	389	2816
Mohawk Finishing Products Inc.	677	Amsterdam, NY	Public Family Member	48.1	320	2851
Northern Labs Inc.	678	Manitowoc, WI	Private	48.0	220	2842
Korex Corporation	679	Wixom, MI	Private	48.0	164	2841
Mississippi Phosphates Corp.	680	Pascagoula, MS	Public Family Member	48.0	240	2874
NPA Coatings Inc.	681	Cleveland, OH	Private	48.0	185	2851
Silberline Manufacturing Co.	682	Tamaqua, PA	Private	47.8	382	2816
Bocchi Laboratories, Inc.	683	Walnut, CA	Private	47.0	400	2844
Day-Glo Color Corp.	684	Cleveland, OH	Public Family Member	47.0	175	2816
Fine Fragrances Distributions	685	New York, NY	Private	47.0	129	2844
Tolaram Polymers, Inc.	686	Charlotte, NC	Private	47.0	75	2821
Zeolyst International	687	Valley Forge, PA	Private	47.0	45	2819
Cutler Corporation	688	Portland, OR	Private	46.9	300	2891
I P S Corporation	689	Gardena, CA	Private	46.9	300	2891
Loctite Puerto Rico Inc.	690	Sabana Grande, PR	Private	46.9	300	2891
Carus Corporation	691	Peru, IL	Private	46.8	214	2819
Inspec USA, Inc.	692	Galena, KS	Private	46.8	172	2869
CPH Holding Corp.	693	Chicago, IL	Private	46.6	205	2869
Mulberry Phosphates Inc.	694	Mulberry, FL	Private	46.0	230	2874
Wild Flavors, Inc.	695	Erlanger, KY	Private	46.0	185	2869
Car-Freshner Corp.	696	Watertown, NY	Private	45.9	387	2842
Heucotech PL	697	Fairless Hills, PA	Private	45.5	70	2865
Spawn Mate Inc.	698	Watsonville, CA	Private	45.2	800	2873
Akzo Nobel Fortafil Fibers	699	Rockwood, TN	Private	45.0	163	2824
Allied Industrial Group Inc.	700	Saint Louis, MO	Private	45.0	62	2819

D&B COMPANY RANKINGS BY SALES

Company	Rank	Location	Type	Sales ($ mil.)	Employ- ment	Primary SIC
Anchor/Lith-Kem-Ko, Inc.	701	Orange Park, FL	Private	45.0	150	2899
Daicolor-Pope Inc.	702	Paterson, NJ	Private	45.0	125	2816
NFS Service, LLC	703	Norcross, GA	Private	45.0	351	2819
Nuclear Fuel Services Inc.	704	Erwin, TN	Private	45.0	350	2819
OMG Fidelity Inc.	705	Newark, NJ	Public Family Member	45.0	135	2899
The Euclid Chemical Company	706	Cleveland, OH	Public Family Member	45.0	20	2899
Watson Industries, Inc.	707	Harwick, PA	Private	45.0	300	2851
Aerosol Companies Holding	708	Gainesville, GA	Private	44.9	382	2844
Tinkerbell Inc.	709	Stamford, CT	Private	44.8	340	2844
Piedmont Laboratories Inc.	710	Gainesville, GA	Private	44.6	380	2844
Pace International, LP	711	Kirkland, WA	Private	44.5	171	2842
Kay Chemical Company	712	Greensboro, NC	Public Family Member	44.4	375	2842
Pfanstiehl Laboratories, Inc.	713	Waukegan, IL	Private	44.4	100	2869
Filtrol Corporation	714	Los Angeles, CA	Private	44.3	280	2819
West Agro Inc.	715	Kansas City, MO	Private	44.3	220	2879
California Products Corp.	716	Cambridge, MA	Private	44.0	162	2851
Flo Kay Industries Inc.	717	Sioux City, IA	Private	44.0	115	2873
J L M Chemicals Inc.	718	Blue Island, IL	Public Family Member	43.7	52	2865
Bontex Inc.	719	Buena Vista, VA	Public	43.5	196	2824
Beckman Naguabo, Inc.	720	Naguabo, PR	Public Family Member	43.0	80	2869
Mc Laughlin Gormley King Co.	721	Minneapolis, MN	Private	43.0	100	2879
Chesebrough-Ponds International	722	Englewood Cliffs, NJ	Private	42.7	364	2844
Platte Chemical Co.	723	Greeley, CO	Public Family Member	42.6	200	2879
B F Goodrich Textile Chemicals	724	Charlotte, NC	Public Family Member	42.1	266	2819
United Wtr Svcs Milwaukee, LLC	725	Milwaukee, WI	Private	42.1	300	2899
Holtrachem Manufacturing Co., LLC	726	Natick, MA	Private	42.0	150	2812
Polymeric Resources Corp.	727	Wayne, NJ	Private	42.0	125	2821
American Chemet Corporation	728	Deerfield, IL	Private	41.9	94	2819
Agsco Inc.	729	Grand Forks, ND	Private	41.9	125	2879
Rimtec Corporation	730	Burlington, NJ	Private	41.7	99	2821
Brandt Consolidated, Inc.	731	Pleasant Plains, IL	Private	41.6	85	2875
CCA Industries, Inc.	732	East Rutherford, NJ	Public	41.4	135	2844
Duncan Enterprises	733	Fresno, CA	Private	41.3	276	2851
Amethyst Investment Group	734	Chicago, IL	Private	41.0	350	2844
Aqua Clear Industries, LLC	735	Watervliet, NY	Private	41.0	90	2899
Tanning Research Laboratories	736	Ormond Beach, FL	Private	41.0	350	2844
Lanco Manufacturing Corp.	737	San Lorenzo, PR	Private	40.9	145	2891
Kemwater North America Co	738	Walnut Creek, CA	Public Family Member	40.7	200	2819
Imperial Adhesives Inc.	739	Cincinnati, OH	Public Family Member	40.6	210	2891
Pro-Line Corporation	740	Dallas, TX	Private	40.5	300	2844
Toyal America, Inc.	741	Naperville, IL	Private	40.4	104	2816
Whitford Worldwide Company	742	Malvern, PA	Private	40.4	200	2891
Apache Nitrogen Products Inc.	743	Benson, AZ	Private	40.3	105	2873
Specialty Chemical Resources	744	Macedonia, OH	Public	40.3	219	2842
Mitsui Chemicals America Inc.	745	Purchase, NY	Private	40.2	150	2869
Ilpea Inc.	746	Fort Smith, AR	Private	40.1	200	2821
Armand Products Company	747	Princeton, NJ	Private	40.0	3	2812
Cardinal Companies, LP	748	Columbia, SC	Private	40.0	125	2869
Chemtech Products, Inc.	749	Saint Louis, MO	Private	40.0	62	2819
Comalloy International Company	750	Nashville, TN	Public Family Member	40.0	117	2821
Delta Technical Coatings, Inc.	751	Whittier, CA	Private	40.0	140	2851
Handschy Industries Inc.	752	Bellwood, IL	Private	40.0	154	2893
I C I Paints (Puerto Rico)	753	Carolina, PR	Private	40.0	100	2851
Mane USA	754	Wayne, NJ	Private	40.0	115	2869
May National Associates	755	Clifton, NJ	Private	40.0	55	2891
Monterey Chemical Company	756	Fresno, CA	Private	40.0	65	2879
Nutra-Flo Company	757	Sioux City, IA	Private	40.0	100	2873
Octagon Process Inc.	758	Edgewater, NJ	Private	40.0	40	2899
Rossborough Manufacturing Co., LP	759	Avon Lake, OH	Private	40.0	140	2899
Samuel Cabot Incorporated	760	Newburyport, MA	Private	40.0	98	2851
Specialty Industrial Products	761	Spartanburg, SC	Private	40.0	55	2843
The Braden-Sutphin Ink Co.	762	Cleveland, OH	Private	40.0	250	2893
Waterbury Companies Inc.	763	Waterbury, CT	Private	40.0	240	2813
Zeeland Chemicals, Inc.	764	Zeeland, MI	Public Family Member	40.0	140	2869
New South Chemicals, Inc.	765	Atlanta, GA	Private	39.5	250	2819
Chemtall Incorporated	766	Riceboro, GA	Private	39.3	175	2869
Consep Inc.	767	Bend, OR	Public	39.2	150	2879
All-Pure Chemical Co.	768	Walnut Creek, CA	Public Family Member	39.2	250	2812
OMG America's Inc.	769	Cleveland, OH	Public Family Member	39.2	160	2869
Vogel Paint & Wax Company Inc.	770	Orange City, IA	Private	38.7	146	2851

D&B COMPANY RANKINGS BY SALES

Company	Rank	Location	Type	Sales ($ mil.)	Employ-ment	Primary SIC
Jafra Cosmetics International	771	Thousand Oaks, CA	Private	38.6	330	2844
Deft Incorporated	772	Irvine, CA	Private	38.5	135	2851
Elasco, Inc.	773	Garden Grove, CA	Private	38.4	180	2821
Styling Technology Corporation	774	Scottsdale, AZ	Public	38.1	225	2844
O'neil Color And Compounding	775	Garfield, NJ	Private	38.1	150	2865
Aware Products Inc.	776	Chatsworth, CA	Private	38.0	325	2844
Betco Corporation	777	Toledo, OH	Private	38.0	160	2841
Noville Inc.	778	South Hackensack, NJ	Private	38.0	130	2899
Seymour Of Sycamore, Inc.	779	Sycamore, IL	Private	38.0	135	2851
Pilot Chemical Co. Of Ohio	780	Santa Fe Springs, CA	Private	37.6	50	2841
Airgas Intermountain Inc.	781	Fort Collins, CO	Public Family Member	37.5	330	2813
Marianna Imports, Inc.	782	Omaha, NE	Private	37.3	220	2844
Franklin-Burlington Plastics	783	Kearny, NJ	Public Family Member	37.0	87	2821
IPI International Inc.	784	Elkton, MD	Private	36.9	156	2869
Rusk Inc.	785	Stamford, CT	Private	36.8	315	2844
Sylvachem Corp.	786	Panama City, FL	Public Family Member	36.8	154	2869
Alper Holdings USA, Inc.	787	New York, NY	Private	36.6	300	2893
Dixie Chemical Company, Inc.	788	Houston, TX	Private	36.4	179	2869
Kind & Knox Gelatin, Inc.	789	Sergeant Bluff, IA	Private	36.4	260	2899
Progressive Ink Company Inc.	790	Sheridan, AR	Private	36.3	297	2893
Teknor Color Company	791	Pawtucket, RI	Private	36.3	307	2821
Vinings Industries Inc.	792	Atlanta, GA	Private	36.2	230	2819
Keladon Corporation	793	Escondido, CA	Private	36.1	200	2899
Laurence-David Inc.	794	Eugene, OR	Private	36.1	200	2851
William Zinsser & Co. Inc.	795	Somerset, NJ	Public Family Member	36.1	200	2851
Iowa Paint Manufacturing Co. Inc.	796	Des Moines, IA	Private	36.1	250	2851
Enzyme Bio Systems Ltd.	797	Beloit, WI	Public Family Member	36.0	84	2869
Ablestik Laboratories	798	Compton, CA	Private	35.8	230	2891
Ausimont Financial Corp.	799	Thorofare, NJ	Private	35.8	230	2891
Central Ink Corporation	800	West Chicago, IL	Private	35.6	97	2893
New Pendulum Corporation	801	Wilmington, DE	Private	35.5	300	2842
Coates Brothers Inc.	802	Houston, TX	Private	35.4	290	2893
SP Acquisition Co.	803	Fort Worth, TX	Private	35.1	165	2821
Amco Plastic Materials Inc.	804	Farmingdale, NY	Private	35.0	50	2821
American Carbide & Carbon Corp	805	Keokuk, IA	Public Family Member	35.0	140	2819
Bayshore Industrial Inc.	806	La Porte, TX	Public Family Member	35.0	120	2821
Cosmetic Mnfctring Rsurces LLC	807	Sun Valley, CA	Private	35.0	300	2844
DSM Resins US Inc.	808	Augusta, GA	Private	35.0	35	2821
Elementis Specialties	809	Jersey City, NJ	Private	35.0	108	2851
Houston Kik Inc.	810	Houston, TX	Private	35.0	140	2842
Kca Engineered Plastics, Inc.	811	San Francisco, CA	Private	35.0	140	2821
Manhattan Products Inc.	812	Carlstadt, NJ	Private	35.0	180	2842
Noltex, LLC	813	La Porte, TX	Private	35.0	80	2821
Olay Company Inc.	814	Cayey, PR	Public Family Member	35.0	300	2844
Original Bradford Soap Works	815	West Warwick, RI	Private	35.0	500	2841
Specialtychem Products Corp.	816	Marinette, WI	Private	35.0	130	2869
Summit Laboratories Inc.	817	Chicago Heights, IL	Private	35.0	90	2844
U.S. Paint Corporation	818	Saint Louis, MO	Private	35.0	155	2851
William E Wofford Textile Co.	819	Venice, CA	Private	35.0	3	2843
Wright Chemical Corporation	820	Wilmington, NC	Private	35.0	125	2869
Lignotech USA Inc.	821	Rothschild, WI	Private	34.9	135	2861
Goldman Resources Inc.	822	Boston, MA	Private	34.6	200	2899
Lomac Inc.	823	Muskegon, MI	Private	34.6	180	2865
Albis Corporation	824	Rosenberg, TX	Private	34.4	190	2821
Mactac, Inc.	825	Stow, OH	Public Family Member	34.4	200	2891
Betz International Inc.	826	Langhorne, PA	Public Family Member	34.2	190	2899
Kuehne Chemical Company Inc.	827	Kearny, NJ	Private	34.2	200	2819
Worthen Industries Inc.	828	Nashua, NH	Private	34.2	220	2891
Premiere Packaging Inc.	829	Flint, MI	Private	34.1	125	2842
IMC Nitrogen Company	830	East Dubuque, IL	Public Family Member	33.9	131	2873
Red Devil Inc.	831	Union, NJ	Private	33.9	200	2891
Standard Chlorine Of Del Co.	832	New Castle, DE	Private	33.9	150	2865
Westlake C A & O Corporation	833	Houston, TX	Private	33.9	200	2812
Immix Elastomers, LLC	834	Hanover, MA	Private	33.9	80	2822
Merichem Salsol USA, LLC	835	Houston, TX	Private	33.8	160	2869
Soft Sheen Products	836	Chicago, IL	Private	33.8	290	2844
Landec Corporation	837	Menlo Park, CA	Public	33.5	162	2819
Equistar Chemicals, LP	838	Bay City, TX	Private	33.5	NA	2869
Smiland Paint Company	839	Los Angeles, CA	Private	33.4	225	2851
Newport Adhesives & Composites	840	Irvine, CA	Private	33.3	92	2891

D&B COMPANY RANKINGS BY SALES

Company	Rank	Location	Type	Sales ($ mil.)	Employ- ment	Primary SIC
Chemical Specialties Inc.	841	Charlotte, NC	Private	33.3	212	2819
Sterling Fibers Inc.	842	Milton, FL	Public Family Member	33.3	333	2824
Bemis Associates, Inc.	843	Shirley, MA	Private	33.0	170	2891
Columbia Paint & Coatings	844	Spokane, WA	Private	33.0	195	2851
Sentinel Consumer Products	845	Mentor, OH	Private	33.0	500	2844
Morgan Chemical Products Inc.	846	Tucker, GA	Private	32.5	275	2842
Ventana Medical Systems, Inc.	847	Tucson, AZ	Public	32.2	150	2819
Abitec Corporation	848	Columbus, OH	Private	32.0	52	2844
Dihoma Chemical & Manufacturing	849	Mullins, SC	Private	32.0	7	2869
Intercit, Inc.	850	Safety Harbor, FL	Private	32.0	70	2899
Johann Haltermann Ltd.	851	Houston, TX	Private	31.9	130	2869
P R Colorcon Inc.	852	Humacao, PR	Private	31.8	52	2816
Struktol Company Of America	853	Stow, OH	Private	31.6	77	2869
Inolex Chemical Company	854	Philadelphia, PA	Private	31.6	135	2821
Inolex Group Inc.	855	Philadelphia, PA	Private	31.6	135	2821
Oxymar	856	Gregory, TX	Private	31.6	180	2821
Evode USA Inc.	857	Leominster, MA	Private	31.5	140	2821
Miller Paint Co. Inc.	858	Portland, OR	Private	31.5	165	2851
Megas Beauty Care Inc.	859	Cleveland, OH	Public Family Member	31.4	270	2844
Airgas Carbonic, Inc.	860	Duluth, GA	Public Family Member	31.2	275	2813
Kiss Nail Products, Inc.	861	Port Washington, NY	Private	31.1	120	2844
Cardinal Industrial Finishes	862	El Monte, CA	Private	31.1	210	2851
Mautz Paint Co.	863	Madison, WI	Private	31.0	260	2851
Penray Companies Inc.	864	Wheeling, IL	Private	31.0	120	2899
D H Compounding Company	865	Clinton, TN	Private	30.9	140	2821
Boehme-Filatex Inc.	866	Reidsville, NC	Private	30.7	140	2869
Tate & Lyle Citric Acid Inc.	867	Decatur, IL	Private	30.7	200	2899
Dryvit Systems Inc.	868	West Warwick, RI	Public Family Member	30.6	159	2899
Arizona Natural Resources Inc.	869	Phoenix, AZ	Private	30.5	275	2844
Cast Products Corp.	870	Elkhart, IN	Private	30.5	140	2891
Shrieve Chemical Products Inc.	871	The Woodlands, TX	Private	30.4	13	2899
Bruning Paint Company	872	Baltimore, MD	Private	30.4	205	2851
Anderson Chemical Company Inc.	873	Macon, GA	Private	30.1	200	2899
Autolign Manufacturing Group Inc.	874	Milan, MI	Private	30.0	150	2821
Buckeye International Inc.	875	Maryland Heights, MO	Private	30.0	180	2842
Central Mn Ethanol Co-Op, Inc.	876	Little Falls, MN	Private	30.0	31	2869
Cincinnati Specialties, Inc.	877	Cincinnati, OH	Private	30.0	200	2819
Hodgson Process Chemicals	878	Oak Creek, WI	Private	30.0	65	2842
Inne Dispensables Inc.	879	Fairfield, NJ	Public Family Member	30.0	60	2844
James Austin Co.	880	Mars, PA	Private	30.0	175	2842
Jos H Lowenstein & Sons Inc.	881	Brooklyn, NY	Private	30.0	90	2865
Mc Auley's, Inc.	882	Memphis, TN	Private	30.0	200	2844
Medicia Pharmaceuticals Corp.	883	Dayton, NJ	Private	30.0	400	2844
MEMC Pasadena, Inc.	884	Pasadena, TX	Public Family Member	30.0	159	2869
National Genetics Institute	885	Los Angeles, CA	Private	30.0	125	2869
Omni Oxide, LLC	886	Indianapolis, IN	Private	30.0	80	2819
OPI Products Inc.	887	North Hollywood, CA	Private	30.0	87	2844
Pecora Corporation	888	Harleysville, PA	Private	30.0	105	2891
Pierre Fabre Inc.	889	Azusa, CA	Private	30.0	200	2844
Riverdale Chemical Company	890	Glenwood, IL	Private	30.0	50	2879
San Mar Laboratories Inc.	891	Elmsford, NY	Private	30.0	100	2844
Spurlock Adhesives Inc.	892	Waverly, VA	Public Family Member	30.0	72	2869
TCI Inc.	893	Ellaville, GA	Public Family Member	30.0	140	2851
U S L Parallel Products	894	Rancho Cucamonga, CA	Public Family Member	30.0	101	2869
U.N.X. Incorporated	895	Greenville, NC	Private	30.0	236	2842
Verdant Brands Inc.	896	Minneapolis, MN	Public	30.0	260	2879
Vi-Chem Corporation	897	Grand Rapids, MI	Private	30.0	60	2821
Z L Star Inc.	898	Houston, TX	Private	30.0	160	2824
Omya, Inc.	899	Proctor, VT	Private	29.9	166	2819
Pitt Penn Oil Co. Inc.	900	Creighton, PA	Private	29.9	200	2899
Vanderbilt Chemical Corp.	901	Norwalk, CT	Private	29.9	158	2869
Marchem Southeast Inc.	902	Adairsville, GA	Private	29.7	60	2821
USAC Holdings Inc.	903	Fort Meade, FL	Private	29.7	275	2874
Scientific Design Company	904	Little Ferry, NJ	Private	29.5	87	2819
Kerr-Mcgee Oil & Gas Corp.	905	Houston, TX	Public Family Member	29.4	235	2816
Thomas R Peck Manufacturing Co.	906	Seal Beach, CA	Private	29.4	174	2891
Fashion Laboratories Inc.	907	Fair Lawn, NJ	Public Family Member	29.1	251	2844
Belmay Company, Inc.	908	Yonkers, NY	Private	29.0	250	2844
Cosmair Caribe Inc.	909	San Juan, PR	Private	29.0	NA	2844
General Alum & Chemical Corp.	910	Holland, OH	Private	29.0	100	2819

D&B COMPANY RANKINGS BY SALES

Company	Rank	Location	Type	Sales ($ mil.)	Employ-ment	Primary SIC
J M Products Inc.	911	Little Rock, AR	Private	29.0	110	2844
Unilever Home & Personal	912	New York, NY	Private	29.0	250	2844
Dupli-Color Products Co.	913	Elk Grove Village, IL	Public Family Member	28.9	200	2851
Eaglebrook International Group	914	Matteson, IL	Private	28.9	200	2899
Amax Metals Recovery Inc.	915	Tempe, AZ	Public Family Member	28.8	163	2819
International Academy	916	Sylmar, CA	Private	28.8	123	2869
P B I/Gordon Corporation	917	Kansas City, MO	Private	28.8	140	2879
Magni-Industries Inc.	918	Detroit, MI	Private	28.8	58	2899
Nyltech North America	919	Manchester, NH	Private	28.7	75	2821
Balchem Corporation	920	Slate Hill, NY	Public	28.6	117	2869
Pioneer/Eclipse Corporation	921	Sparta, NC	Private	28.5	139	2842
Ekc Technology Inc.	922	Hayward, CA	Public Family Member	28.5	159	2899
Norton & Son	923	Los Angeles, CA	Private	28.5	200	2851
Standard Chlorine Chemical Co.	924	New Castle, DE	Private	28.4	150	2865
Sunbelt Corporation	925	Rock Hill, SC	Private	28.4	46	2865
Puretek Corporation	926	San Fernando, CA	Private	28.3	250	2844
Intercat-Savannah Inc.	927	Manasquan, NJ	Private	28.2	68	2819
Alliance Agronomics Inc.	928	Mechanicsville, VA	Private	28.0	90	2875
Burtin Urethane Corporation	929	Santa Ana, CA	Private	28.0	55	2821
Plasticolors, Inc.	930	Ashtabula, OH	Private	28.0	140	2816
Wattyl Paint Corporation	931	Atlanta, GA	Private	28.0	190	2851
American Synthetic Rubber Corp	932	Louisville, KY	Private	27.9	390	2822
Cambridge Isotope Laboratories	933	Andover, MA	Private	27.5	100	2869
Dryvit Holdings, Inc.	934	Providence, RI	Public Family Member	27.5	170	2899
Bulk Molding Compounds, Inc.	935	West Chicago, IL	Private	27.4	130	2821
Alden Leeds Inc.	936	Kearny, NJ	Private	27.3	65	2899
Croda Adhesives Inc.	937	Itasca, IL	Private	27.3	78	2891
United Gilsonite Laboratories	938	Scranton, PA	Private	27.3	170	2851
Reilly Corp.	939	Washington, DC	Private	27.2	200	2842
T-Chem Holdings, Inc.	940	Santa Fe Springs, CA	Private	27.2	80	2842
Stephan Co. Inc.	941	Fort Lauderdale, FL	Public	27.1	285	2844
Amrep, Inc.	942	Marietta, GA	Private	27.1	230	2842
Mini Fibers Inc.	943	Johnson City, TN	Private	27.1	85	2824
Brent America, Inc.	944	La Mirada, CA	Private	27.0	120	2869
Du Pont Ag Caribe Industries	945	Manati, PR	Public Family Member	27.0	150	2879
ISP Global Technologies, Inc.	946	Wayne, NJ	Private	27.0	100	2869
Liochem Inc.	947	Conyers, GA	Private	27.0	50	2899
Piceu Group Limited	948	Southfield, MI	Private	27.0	100	2851
T-Chem Products	949	Santa Fe Springs, CA	Private	27.0	90	2842
Mining Services International	950	Sandy, UT	Public	27.0	85	2892
Diamond R Fertilizer Co. Inc.	951	Fort Pierce, FL	Private	26.9	100	2873
Elementis Pigments Inc.	952	Fairview Heights, IL	Private	26.9	194	2816
Leiner Davis Gelatin Corp.	953	Great Neck, NY	Private	26.8	150	2899
Styrochem US Inc.	954	Phoenix, AZ	Private	26.8	125	2821
Gage Corporation	955	Ferndale, MI	Private	26.7	120	2869
Kasper Inc.	956	Mahwah, NJ	Private	26.6	230	2844
Color Wheel Paint Manufacturing Co.	957	Orlando, FL	Private	26.5	230	2851
Puritan/Churchill Chemical Co.	958	Marietta, GA	Private	26.3	188	2842
Millennium Specialty Chemicals	959	Jacksonville, FL	Public Family Member	26.3	108	2869
Dupont Dow Elastomers LLC	960	Louisville, KY	Private	26.2	NA	2822
Gans Ink And Supply Co. Inc.	961	Los Angeles, CA	Private	26.0	220	2893
Catawba-Charlab Inc.	962	Charlotte, NC	Private	26.0	123	2869
Camco Chemical Company Inc.	963	Florence, KY	Private	26.0	100	2842
Dallas Group Of America Inc.	964	Whitehouse, NJ	Private	26.0	90	2819
Davlyn Industries Inc.	965	Cranbury, NJ	Private	26.0	250	2844
Hoffman Plastic Compounds	966	Paramount, CA	Private	26.0	65	2821
Howard Johnson's Enterprises	967	Milwaukee, WI	Private	26.0	70	2875
Nelson Brothers Inc.	968	Birmingham, AL	Private	26.0	225	2892
SIA Adhesives Inc.	969	Akron, OH	Private	26.0	110	2891
Systech Environmental Corp.	970	Xenia, OH	Public Family Member	26.0	121	2869
T M V Corporation	971	Miami, FL	Private	26.0	225	2844
Uniseal Inc.	972	Evansville, IN	Private	26.0	230	2891
Dri-Kleen Inc.	973	Las Vegas, NV	Private	26.0	100	2842
Lit Tel Systems USA Inc.	974	Spring Valley, NY	Private	25.9	120	2821
The Hall Chemical Co.	975	Wickliffe, OH	Private	25.8	150	2819
Pacer Technology	976	Rancho Cucamonga, CA	Public	25.7	100	2891
Brewer Science, Inc.	977	Rolla, MO	Private	25.6	180	2851
Pvc Compounders, Inc.	978	Kendallville, IN	Private	25.6	50	2821
Blue Coral-Slick 50 Ltd	979	Cleveland, OH	Private	25.3	215	2842
Hickson Danchem Corporation	980	Danville, VA	Private	25.2	135	2843

D&B COMPANY RANKINGS BY SALES

Company	Rank	Location	Type	Sales ($ mil.)	Employ-ment	Primary SIC
Harrell's Inc.	981	Lakeland, FL	Private	25.1	54	2875
Yates Investment Casting Wax	982	Chicago, IL	Private	25.0	45	2891
Aabbitt Adhesives Inc.	983	Chicago, IL	Private	25.0	95	2891
Acetylene Oxygen Co.	984	Harlingen, TX	Private	25.0	200	2813
Aervoe Pacific Company, Inc.	985	Gardnerville, NV	Private	25.0	125	2851
Aluchem Inc.	986	Cincinnati, OH	Private	25.0	94	2899
Alzo Inc.	987	Matawan, NJ	Private	25.0	21	2869
Amspec Chemical Corporation	988	Gloucester City, NJ	Private	25.0	90	2819
Anchor Paint Manufacturing Co.	989	Tulsa, OK	Private	25.0	150	2851
Apollo Chemical Corp.	990	Graham, NC	Private	25.0	72	2819
Baerlocher USA	991	Dover, OH	Private	25.0	30	2819
C B Fleet International Inc.	992	Lynchburg, VA	Private	25.0	140	2844
Canning Gumm, Inc.	993	Kearny, NJ	Private	25.0	102	2899
Capital Resin Corporation	994	Columbus, OH	Private	25.0	70	2821
Clean Control Corporation	995	Bonaire, GA	Private	25.0	500	2842
Coroplast Inc.	996	Dallas, TX	Private	25.0	160	2821
Crucible Chemical Co. Inc.	997	Greenville, SC	Private	25.0	40	2842
Davis-Frost, Inc.	998	Minneapolis, MN	Private	25.0	105	2851
E L C Technology, Inc.	999	Fort Lauderdale, FL	Private	25.0	209	2819
Gard Products Inc.	1000	Carpentersville, IL	Private	25.0	65	2879
Gard Rogard, Inc.	1001	Carpentersville, IL	Private	25.0	65	2879
Hempel Coatings USA Inc.	1002	Houston, TX	Private	25.0	80	2851
Hercules Chemical Co. Inc.	1003	Passaic, NJ	Private	25.0	80	2899
Hewitt Soap Co.	1004	Dayton, OH	Public Family Member	25.0	267	2841
Hostmann-Steinberg Inc.	1005	Louisville, KY	Private	25.0	118	2893
Hydro/Kirby Agri Services	1006	Lancaster, PA	Private	25.0	53	2875
La-Co Industries Inc.	1007	Elk Grove Village, IL	Private	25.0	129	2899
Living Earth Technology Corp.	1008	Houston, TX	Public Family Member	25.0	200	2875
Luster Products Inc.	1009	Chicago, IL	Private	25.0	350	2844
Major Chem Ltd.	1010	Houston, TX	Private	25.0	7	2842
North American Oxide, LLC	1011	Clarksville, TN	Private	25.0	54	2816
Nottingham Company	1012	Atlanta, GA	Private	25.0	35	2869
Pace Industries Inc.	1013	Reedsburg, WI	Private	25.0	150	2821
Pacific Pac International	1014	Hollister, CA	Private	25.0	60	2899
PCI, Inc.	1015	Wurtland, KY	Private	25.0	62	2869
Petroferm Inc.	1016	Fernandina Beach, FL	Private	25.0	125	2899
Protameen Chemicals Inc.	1017	Totowa, NJ	Private	25.0	50	2819
Qualitek International, Inc.	1018	Addison, IL	Private	25.0	300	2899
R B H Dispersions Inc.	1019	Bound Brook, NJ	Private	25.0	90	2865
Shincor Silicones, Inc.	1020	Akron, OH	Private	25.0	70	2822
Solkatronic Chemicals Inc.	1021	Fairfield, NJ	Public Family Member	25.0	94	2819
Specialty Coatings Company	1022	Elk Grove Village, IL	Private	25.0	55	2851
Springfield Products, Inc.	1023	Springfield, KY	Private	25.0	280	2821
Tanner Chemicals Inc.	1024	Greenville, SC	Private	25.0	67	2843
Tennessee Electro Minerals	1025	Greeneville, TN	Private	25.0	132	2819
The B F Goodrich Company	1026	Taylors, SC	Private	25.0	160	2843
The Virkler Company	1027	Charlotte, NC	Private	25.0	100	2869
Van Ru Inc.	1028	Evansville, IN	Private	25.0	300	2891
White Cap Inc.	1029	Paoli, PA	Private	25.0	48	2842
Hickson (USA) Corp.	1030	Smyrna, GA	Private	24.9	156	2899
Weatherly Consumer Products	1031	Waco, TX	Public Family Member	24.9	85	2873
J-Von NA, LLC	1032	Leominster, MA	Private	24.9	55	2821
Wonder Company (Inc)	1033	Nashville, TN	Private	24.8	114	2879
Spurlock Industries Inc.	1034	Waverly, VA	Public	24.7	80	2869
Advanced Chemical Company	1035	Warwick, RI	Private	24.7	41	2899
Spartan Chemical Co. Inc.	1036	Toledo, OH	Private	24.7	210	2842
Zeochem	1037	Louisville, KY	Private	24.5	92	2819
Fertilizer Company Arizona Inc.	1038	Casa Grande, AZ	Private	24.5	132	2875
Three Bond International Inc.	1039	West Chester, OH	Private	24.4	120	2891
PMP Fermentation Products	1040	Itasca, IL	Private	24.4	110	2869
Laporte Cnstr Chem, NA	1041	Mentor, OH	Private	24.3	142	2891
National Casein Co. Inc.	1042	Chicago, IL	Private	24.2	70	2891
Palm Commodities International Inc.	1043	La Vergne, TN	Private	24.2	55	2819
Coates Screen Inc.	1044	East Rutherford, NJ	Private	24.2	152	2893
Mapico, Inc.	1045	Saint Louis, MO	Private	24.1	110	2895
Fairfield Processing Corp.	1046	Danbury, CT	Private	24.0	240	2824
Farouk Systems Inc.	1047	Houston, TX	Private	24.0	150	2844
International Fuel Cells, LLC	1048	South Windsor, CT	Private	24.0	99	2869
Sachem, Inc.	1049	Austin, TX	Private	24.0	75	2869
Tiro Industries, Inc.	1050	Minneapolis, MN	Private	24.0	325	2844

D&B COMPANY RANKINGS BY SALES

Company	Rank	Location	Type	Sales ($ mil.)	Employ- ment	Primary SIC
Wasser High-Tech Coatings Inc.	1051	Kent, WA	Private	24.0	55	2851
Atlas Products, Inc.	1052	Des Moines, IA	Private	24.0	45	2851
Tomah Products, Inc.	1053	Milton, WI	Private	23.8	53	2869
Heartland Corn Products	1054	Winthrop, MN	Private	23.8	25	2869
PVS Chemicals Inc. (Illinois)	1055	Chicago, IL	Private	23.7	55	2819
Elan Chemical Company	1056	Newark, NJ	Private	23.7	85	2869
Eastwind Group, Inc.	1057	West Conshohocken, PA	Public	23.6	505	2821
U S Cotton LLC	1058	Rio Rancho, NM	Private	23.6	205	2844
Sicpa Industries Of America	1059	Springfield, VA	Private	23.5	119	2893
Chemical Specialists & Dev.	1060	Conroe, TX	Private	23.3	55	2851
Cordova Labs	1061	Sylmar, CA	Private	23.1	122	2879
Roman Holdings Corporation	1062	Calumet City, IL	Private	23.1	80	2891
Hudson Technologies, Inc.	1063	Pearl River, NY	Public	23.0	130	2869
Crystal Inc.-Pmc	1064	Lansdale, PA	Private	23.0	57	2899
Electrochemicals, Inc.	1065	Maple Plain, MN	Private	23.0	75	2899
Haas Corporation	1066	West Chester, PA	Private	23.0	40	2899
Plasite Protective Coating	1067	Green Bay, WI	Public Family Member	23.0	82	2821
Praxair Puerto Rico Inc.	1068	Gurabo, PR	Public Family Member	23.0	98	2813
Senco Inc.	1069	Dallas, TX	Private	23.0	50	2844
Old World Industries, Inc.	1070	Northbrook, IL	Private	22.9	150	2899
Magnox Incorporated	1071	Pulaski, VA	Private	22.8	170	2816
Dymon, Inc.	1072	Olathe, KS	Public Family Member	22.8	150	2842
Lykes Agri Sales Inc.	1073	Dade City, FL	Private	22.7	120	2875
Schnee-Morehead Inc.	1074	Irving, TX	Private	22.7	120	2891
KMG-Bernuth Inc.	1075	Houston, TX	Public Family Member	22.7	14	2869
Conap Inc.	1076	Olean, NY	Public Family Member	22.6	122	2821
Cardolite Corporation	1077	Newark, NJ	Private	22.6	91	2869
Roman Adhesives Inc.	1078	Calumet City, IL	Private	22.6	80	2891
Pacific World Corporation	1079	Lake Forest, CA	Private	22.5	55	2844
WPT Corporation	1080	Houston, TX	Private	22.5	100	2869
JFO, Ltd.	1081	Denver, CO	Private	22.4	200	2842
Emerson Cming Composite Metals Inc.	1082	Canton, MA	Private	22.4	160	2819
Ecoscience Corporation	1083	East Brunswick, NJ	Public	22.3	70	2879
Olga G Marcus Cosmetics Inc.	1084	Hauppauge, NY	Private	22.3	160	2844
West Chemical Products Inc.	1085	Princeton, NJ	Private	22.3	138	2842
Cosmar Corporation	1086	Garden Grove, CA	Private	22.2	150	2844
Drake Extrusion Inc.	1087	Ridgeway, VA	Private	22.2	124	2821
Na-Churs Plant Food, Company	1088	Marion, OH	Private	22.1	100	2875
Coronado Laboratories Inc.	1089	New Smyrna Beach, FL	Private	22.1	75	2891
Grace Chemicals, Inc.	1090	Boca Raton, FL	Public Family Member	22.1	140	2819
Norac Company Inc.	1091	Azusa, CA	Private	22.1	98	2869
Lori Davis Hair, Inc.	1092	West Chester, PA	Private	22.1	13	2844
Arnco	1093	South Gate, CA	Private	22.0	45	2822
Caesars World Merchandising	1094	Las Vegas, NV	Public Family Member	22.0	180	2844
Clearwater Holdings Inc.	1095	Pittsburgh, PA	Private	22.0	100	2819
Interpolymer Corp.	1096	Canton, MA	Private	22.0	50	2821
Mantrose-Haeuser Co., Inc.	1097	Westport, CT	Public Family Member	22.0	82	2851
Neste Polyester Inc.	1098	Fort Smith, AR	Private	22.0	150	2851
Polymer Dynamics Inc.	1099	Allentown, PA	Private	22.0	310	2823
Shionogi Qualicaps, Inc.	1100	Whitsett, NC	Private	22.0	200	2899
U.S. Nonwovens Corp.	1101	Brentwood, NY	Private	22.0	35	2821
Varnco Holdings, Inc.	1102	Oakland, NJ	Private	22.0	83	2899
United Laboratories Inc.	1103	Saint Charles, IL	Private	22.0	300	2842
Al-Corn Clean Fuel	1104	Claremont, MN	Private	21.9	28	2869
Giles Chemical Corp.	1105	Waynesville, NC	Private	21.9	39	2899
Mc Cormick Paint Works Co.	1106	Rockville, MD	Private	21.9	160	2851
Ceda International, Inc.	1107	Fort Collins, CO	Private	21.8	150	2819
Tri-Tech Laboratories Inc.	1108	Lynchburg, VA	Private	21.8	200	2844
Enzyme Development Corporation	1109	New York, NY	Private	21.7	25	2869
Advanced Chemical Systems	1110	Milpitas, CA	Private	21.5	94	2819
Chemical Packaging Corp.	1111	Paducah, KY	Private	21.2	150	2899
Hitachi Chemical Dupont Micro	1112	Wilmington, DE	Private	21.1	100	2821
Max Rittenbaum Inc.	1113	Atlanta, GA	Private	21.1	185	2842
Dyno Nobel Midwest, Inc.	1114	Quincy, IL	Private	21.0	95	2892
K M S Research Inc.	1115	Redding, CA	Private	21.0	190	2844
Tevco Inc.	1116	South Plainfield, NJ	Private	21.0	72	2851
Spectra-Tone Paint Corporation	1117	San Bernardino, CA	Private	21.0	120	2851
CBI Laboratories Inc.	1118	Carrollton, TX	Public Family Member	20.9	190	2844
Falcon Manufacturing Of Calif Inc.	1119	Los Angeles, CA	Public Family Member	20.9	100	2821
Orange Plastics Inc.	1120	Compton, CA	Private	20.9	100	2821

D&B COMPANY RANKINGS BY SALES

Company	Rank	Location	Type	Sales ($ mil.)	Employ-ment	Primary SIC
Trico Plastic, Inc.	1121	Azusa, CA	Private	20.9	100	2821
Canberra Corp.	1122	Toledo, OH	Private	20.8	200	2842
Solar Cosmetic Labs, Inc.	1123	Hialeah, FL	Private	20.8	75	2844
Alox Corporation	1124	Niagara Falls, NY	Public Family Member	20.7	55	2899
Douglass Fertilizer & Chemical	1125	Altamonte Springs, FL	Private	20.7	70	2875
Share Corporation	1126	Milwaukee, WI	Private	20.6	213	2842
Parker Paint Manufacturing Co.	1127	Tacoma, WA	Private	20.6	130	2851
Sheboygan Paint Company Inc.	1128	Sheboygan, WI	Private	20.6	96	2851
Rohmax USA, Inc.	1129	Horsham, PA	Private	20.3	115	2899
Brooks Industries Inc.	1130	South Plainfield, NJ	Private	20.2	65	2869
Gulf States Asphalt Company	1131	South Houston, TX	Private	20.2	90	2891
Gulf States Specialties Inc.	1132	South Houston, TX	Private	20.2	90	2891
Farrell-Calhoun Inc.	1133	Memphis, TN	Private	20.1	100	2851
Sun Drilling Products Corp.	1134	Belle Chasse, LA	Private	20.1	55	2899
Advanced Aromatics, LP	1135	Houston, TX	Private	20.0	39	2869
Alden & Ott Printing Inks Co.	1136	Arlington Heights, IL	Private	20.0	150	2893
Ampac Inc.	1137	Cedar City, UT	Public Family Member	20.0	190	2873
Becker Underwood Inc.	1138	Ames, IA	Private	20.0	70	2865
Calabrian Chemical Corporation	1139	Kingwood, TX	Private	20.0	110	2869
Calabrian Corporation	1140	Kingwood, TX	Private	20.0	124	2819
Carroll Scientific Inc.	1141	La Grange, IL	Public Family Member	20.0	65	2899
Cemedine U.S.A., Inc.	1142	Oak Creek, WI	Private	20.0	56	2891
Chattem Chemicals, Inc.	1143	Chattanooga, TN	Private	20.0	60	2869
Chem Polymer Corporation	1144	Fort Myers, FL	Private	20.0	65	2821
Clearwater, Inc.	1145	Pittsburgh, PA	Private	20.0	55	2819
Collaborative Laboratories	1146	East Setauket, NY	Private	20.0	140	2844
Cook & Dunn Enterprises, LLC	1147	Lodi, NJ	Private	20.0	72	2851
Crowley Tar Products Co. Inc.	1148	New York, NY	Private	20.0	45	2865
Decoart Inc.	1149	Stanford, KY	Private	20.0	100	2851
Deltech Polymers Corporation	1150	Troy, OH	Private	20.0	40	2821
Dena Corporation	1151	Elk Grove Village, IL	Private	20.0	70	2844
Dispensing Containers Corp.	1152	Glen Gardner, NJ	Private	20.0	100	2813
Finnaren & Haley Inc.	1153	Conshohocken, PA	Private	20.0	170	2851
G P C Sales Inc.	1154	Deer Park, NY	Private	20.0	12	2844
Gaylord Chemical Corporation	1155	Slidell, LA	Public Family Member	20.0	52	2861
Gencorp Performance Chemical	1156	Fitchburg, MA	Private	20.0	30	2819
Gulf Lite & Wizard, Inc.	1157	Memphis, TN	Private	20.0	75	2899
H20 Plus, LP	1158	Chicago, IL	Private	20.0	300	2844
Hallman Paints Inc.	1159	Sun Prairie, WI	Private	20.0	90	2851
Hawaii Chemtect International	1160	Pasadena, CA	Private	20.0	12	2899
Ichauway Mills, Inc.	1161	Dallas, TX	Private	20.0	14	2844
John C Dolph Company	1162	Monmouth Junction, NJ	Private	20.0	50	2851
K O Manufacturing Inc.	1163	Springfield, MO	Private	20.0	75	2841
Kasha Industries Inc.	1164	Grayville, IL	Private	20.0	30	2816
Kleerdex Company	1165	Mount Laurel, NJ	Private	20.0	95	2821
Kolene Corporation	1166	Detroit, MI	Private	20.0	49	2899
Lockhart Company	1167	Gibsonia, PA	Private	20.0	100	2819
Mona Industries Inc.	1168	Paterson, NJ	Private	20.0	146	2843
Natural Gas Odorizing Inc.	1169	Baytown, TX	Public Family Member	20.0	50	2869
Old Bridge Chemicals, Inc.	1170	Old Bridge, NJ	Private	20.0	65	2819
Omya (California) Inc.	1171	Lucerne Valley, CA	Private	20.0	82	2819
Para Laboratories Inc.	1172	Hempstead, NY	Private	20.0	70	2844
Pfister Chemical Inc.	1173	Ridgefield, NJ	Private	20.0	130	2865
Pleasant Green Enterprises	1174	Coal City, IL	Private	20.0	65	2844
Reeve Agri Energy Corp.	1175	Garden City, KS	Private	20.0	12	2869
Reynolds Inc.	1176	Greenville, SC	Private	20.0	75	2891
Richland Research Corp.	1177	Phoenix, AZ	Private	20.0	135	2869
Royce Associates, LP	1178	East Rutherford, NJ	Private	20.0	65	2869
Rudd Company Inc.	1179	Seattle, WA	Private	20.0	60	2851
Scott Paint Corp.	1180	Sarasota, FL	Private	20.0	130	2851
Sofix Corporation	1181	Chattanooga, TN	Private	20.0	27	2899
Spartech Compound	1182	Cape Girardeau, MO	Public Family Member	20.0	75	2821
Standard Fusee Corporation	1183	Easton, MD	Private	20.0	140	2899
Stanson Corporation	1184	Kearny, NJ	Private	20.0	100	2841
Systems Mch Automtn Components	1185	Carlsbad, CA	Private	20.0	140	2822
The Fanning Corporation	1186	Chicago, IL	Private	20.0	26	2899
University Med Prducts/USA Inc.	1187	Irvine, CA	Private	20.0	45	2844
Well Long Economic & Trade Co.	1188	Milpitas, CA	Private	20.0	5	2821
Westrade USA, Inc.	1189	Houston, TX	Private	20.0	115	2879
Willert Home Products Inc.	1190	Saint Louis, MO	Private	20.0	380	2879

D&B COMPANY RANKINGS BY SALES

Company	Rank	Location	Type	Sales ($ mil.)	Employ- ment	Primary SIC
Insl-X Products Corp.	1191	Stony Point, NY	Private	19.8	125	2851
J L S Inv Group - WP, LLC	1192	Middleton, WI	Private	19.8	92	2879
Dexco Polymers	1193	Houston, TX	Private	19.7	100	2821
Heatbath Corporation	1194	Springfield, MA	Private	19.7	115	2819
Mytex Polymers Incorporated	1195	Baytown, TX	Private	19.7	NA	2821
Nitram Inc.	1196	Tampa, FL	Private	19.7	85	2873
Farmers Plant Food, Inc.	1197	Garretson, SD	Private	19.6	12	2873
Akcros Chemicals America	1198	New Brunswick, NJ	Private	19.6	85	2869
Connoisseurs Products Corp.	1199	Woburn, MA	Private	19.6	150	2842
Muscle Shoals Minerals Inc.	1200	Cherokee, AL	Private	19.6	124	2819
Wellborn-De Corp	1201	Albuquerque, NM	Private	19.6	170	2851
Fermpro Manufacturing, LP	1202	Kingstree, SC	Private	19.5	114	2869
Prince Manufacturing Co. Inc.	1203	Quincy, IL	Private	19.5	115	2879
Stevens Paint Corp	1204	Stony Point, NY	Private	19.5	125	2851
KMG Chemicals Inc.	1205	Houston, TX	Public	19.5	70	2869
SLG Chemicals, Inc.	1206	Denver, CO	Public Family Member	19.4	150	2899
Softsoap Enterprises, Inc.	1207	Chaska, MN	Public Family Member	19.4	172	2841
Heartland Grn Fuels, LP	1208	Aberdeen, SD	Private	19.4	25	2869
Eko Systems Inc.	1209	Lakewood, CO	Private	19.3	88	2879
Lynwood Laboratories Inc.	1210	Needham, MA	Private	19.2	100	2879
A B C Compounding Company Inc.	1211	Morrow, GA	Private	19.1	150	2842
Aztec Peroxides, Inc.	1212	Houston, TX	Private	19.1	115	2819
Epoxylite Corporation	1213	Irvine, CA	Private	19.1	109	2851
Whitmire Micro-Gen Res Labs	1214	Saint Louis, MO	Private	19.1	100	2879
Amfibe Inc.	1215	Ridgeway, VA	Private	19.0	200	2824
Car Brite, Inc.	1216	Indianapolis, IN	Private	19.0	65	2842
Robertet Fragrances Inc.	1217	Oakland, NJ	Private	19.0	65	2844
Synair Corporation	1218	Chattanooga, TN	Private	19.0	110	2821
Wako Chemicals USA, Inc.	1219	Richmond, VA	Private	19.0	44	2869
Crest-Hood Foam Company, Inc.	1220	Newburyport, MA	Public Family Member	18.9	112	2851
Westlake Polymers Corporation	1221	Houston, TX	Private	18.9	265	2822
APT Advanced Polymer Tech Corp.	1222	Harmony, PA	Private	18.8	32	2851
Graco Fertilizer Company	1223	Cairo, GA	Private	18.8	75	2873
Kelmar Industries Inc.	1224	Duncan, SC	Private	18.7	55	2819
Haldor Topsoe Inc.	1225	Houston, TX	Private	18.7	133	2819
Henry The W W Company	1226	Lancaster, PA	Private	18.7	NA	2891
Lobeco Products Inc.	1227	Lobeco, SC	Private	18.7	90	2865
Orient Chemical Corp.	1228	Springfield, NJ	Private	18.6	30	2865
Formulabs, Inc.	1229	Escondido, CA	Public Family Member	18.5	105	2899
M P Associates Inc.	1230	Ione, CA	Private	18.5	170	2892
Whitmore Manufacturing Co. Inc.	1231	Rockwall, TX	Public Family Member	18.5	115	2851
D & K International, Inc.	1232	Elk Grove Village, IL	Private	18.4	130	2891
N S O Resins, Inc.	1233	Greenwood, SC	Private	18.4	110	2821
Reedco Inc.	1234	Humacao, PR	Public Family Member	18.4	300	2844
BPI By-Product Industries	1235	Pittsburgh, PA	Private	18.3	28	2899
Advanced Polymer Systems Inc.	1236	Redwood City, CA	Public	18.3	94	2822
Imperial Inc.	1237	Shenandoah, IA	Private	18.3	90	2879
J F Daley International Ltd.	1238	Chicago, IL	Private	18.3	150	2842
Wisconsin Pharmacal Co. Inc.	1239	Jackson, WI	Private	18.3	92	2879
Organic Dyestuffs Corporation	1240	East Providence, RI	Private	18.2	134	2861
Ponderosa Paint Manufacturing	1241	Boise, ID	Private	18.2	175	2851
PVS Technologies Inc.	1242	Detroit, MI	Private	18.2	44	2819
Cartridge Actuated Devices	1243	Fairfield, NJ	Private	18.2	128	2892
Midwest Zinc Corporation	1244	Millington, TN	Public Family Member	18.2	131	2816
Primester	1245	Kingsport, TN	Private	18.2	102	2821
Perstorp Polyols Inc.	1246	Toledo, OH	Private	18.1	96	2869
United Paint And Chemical Corp.	1247	Southfield, MI	Private	18.1	50	2851
Omnium, LLC	1248	Saint Joseph, MO	Private	18.0	228	2879
Frit Industries Inc.	1249	Ozark, AL	Private	18.0	120	2873
Advanced Polymer Alloys, LLC	1250	Wilmington, DE	Private	18.0	5	2822
Agri-Empresa Inc.	1251	Midland, TX	Private	18.0	45	2899
Chemical Products Technologies	1252	Cartersville, GA	Private	18.0	12	2819
Coating and Adhesives Corp.	1253	Leland, NC	Private	18.0	41	2891
Coatings & Chemicals Corp.	1254	Des Plaines, IL	Private	18.0	40	2851
Embers Charcoal Company Inc.	1255	Conway, SC	Private	18.0	155	2861
Foam Supplies Inc.	1256	Earth City, MO	Private	18.0	48	2821
Johnson Paints Inc.	1257	Fort Myers, FL	Private	18.0	110	2851
Microsi Inc.	1258	Phoenix, AZ	Private	18.0	20	2899
Mid-Atlntic Vegetable Shortening	1259	Newark, NJ	Private	18.0	29	2899
Pervo Paint Company	1260	Los Angeles, CA	Private	18.0	40	2851

D&B COMPANY RANKINGS BY SALES

Company	Rank	Location	Type	Sales ($ mil.)	Employ- ment	Primary SIC
Premier Coatings, Inc.	1261	Elk Grove Village, IL	Private	18.0	54	2851
S N F Holding Company, Inc.	1262	Riceboro, GA	Private	18.0	NA	2899
Salle' International, LLC	1263	Waukegan, IL	Private	18.0	76	2844
Venture VI Inc.	1264	Walled Lake, MI	Private	18.0	10	2899
Niles Chemical Paint Company	1265	Niles, MI	Private	17.8	100	2851
Esco Company, LP	1266	Muskegon, MI	Private	17.8	85	2865
Vita-Green Inc.	1267	Haines City, FL	Private	17.8	100	2875
Monarch Rubber Company	1268	Baltimore, MD	Private	17.7	170	2822
Opal Technologies Inc.	1269	New York, NY	Public	17.7	61	2873
Whatcom Farmer's Co-Op	1270	Lynden, WA	Private	17.6	100	2875
ASI Investment Holding Co.	1271	Akron, OH	Public Family Member	17.6	115	2821
Deltech Corp.	1272	Whippany, NJ	Private	17.6	100	2899
Trical Inc.	1273	Hollister, CA	Private	17.6	NA	2879
Valley Products Co.	1274	Memphis, TN	Private	17.6	150	2841
D K USA Ltd.	1275	Garden City, NY	Private	17.5	135	2844
Fremont Industries, Inc.	1276	Shakopee, MN	Private	17.5	120	2819
Zotos International Inc.	1277	Darien, CT	Private	17.5	NA	2844
Palmer International Inc.	1278	Worcester, PA	Private	17.5	45	2822
Synergistics Industries Texas	1279	Conroe, TX	Public Family Member	17.4	100	2821
Sel-Leb Marketing Inc.	1280	Paterson, NJ	Public	17.4	60	2844
Perry & Derrick Co	1281	Cincinnati, OH	Private	17.3	130	2851
Nu-World Corp.	1282	Carteret, NJ	Private	17.3	50	2844
Sterling Paint, Inc.	1283	Little Rock, AR	Private	17.2	130	2851
Human Pheromone Sciences, Inc.	1284	Fremont, CA	Public	17.2	15	2844
Ochoa Fertilizer Co. Inc.	1285	Guanica, PR	Private	17.1	53	2874
JDR & Associates Inc.	1286	Santa Ana, CA	Private	17.1	85	2821
Metal Coatings International	1287	Chardon, OH	Private	17.1	130	2899
Bronner Brothers Inc.	1288	Marietta, GA	Private	17.1	275	2844
PVS Chemicals Inc. (New York)	1289	Buffalo, NY	Private	17.0	56	2819
Alpine Aromatics International	1290	Piscataway, NJ	Private	17.0	45	2869
Apollo Industries Inc.	1291	Smyrna, GA	Private	17.0	120	2813
Auto Wax Company Inc.	1292	Dallas, TX	Private	17.0	60	2842
Continental Carbonic Products Inc.	1293	Decatur, IL	Private	17.0	130	2813
Evans Adhesive Corporation	1294	Columbus, OH	Private	17.0	80	2891
Granitize Products Inc.	1295	South Gate, CA	Private	17.0	70	2842
Ohka America, Inc.	1296	Hillsboro, OR	Private	17.0	47	2819
Oxid, LP	1297	Houston, TX	Private	17.0	41	2899
Prentiss Incorporated	1298	Floral Park, NY	Private	17.0	40	2879
Regal Chemical Company	1299	Alpharetta, GA	Private	17.0	20	2879
Twincraft Inc.	1300	Winooski, VT	Private	17.0	160	2841
Geo Specialty Chemicals Inc.	1301	Cleveland, OH	Private	16.9	100	2819
Nor-Cote International, Inc.	1302	Crawfordsville, IN	Private	16.9	80	2893
MG International Inc.	1303	Dallas, GA	Private	16.8	230	2821
Du Pont-Kansai Auto Coatings	1304	Troy, MI	Public Family Member	16.8	106	2851
JSR Microelectronics, Inc.	1305	Sunnyvale, CA	Private	16.8	68	2869
Cortec Corporation	1306	Saint Paul, MN	Private	16.8	130	2899
Nicca USA Inc.	1307	Fountain Inn, SC	Private	16.7	66	2843
Perrigo Company Of Missouri	1308	Saint Louis, MO	Public Family Member	16.7	150	2844
Ultraform Co.	1309	Theodore, AL	Private	16.7	100	2821
Forrest Paint Co.	1310	Eugene, OR	Private	16.7	75	2851
Lindau Chemicals Inc.	1311	Columbia, SC	Private	16.6	55	2869
Fabricolor Manufacturing Corp	1312	Paterson, NJ	Private	16.5	80	2865
General Coatings Technologies	1313	Ridgewood, NY	Private	16.5	95	2851
Lenmar Inc.	1314	Baltimore, MD	Private	16.5	100	2851
Twin State Engrg & Chem Co.	1315	Davenport, IA	Private	16.5	90	2874
Wesco Gases Inc.	1316	Billerica, MA	Private	16.5	90	2813
Williams Trading Inc.	1317	Wilmington, DE	Private	16.5	100	2851
Atohaas Mexico Inc.	1318	Brownsville, TX	Private	16.4	NA	2821
Biozyme	1319	Saint Joseph, MO	Private	16.4	93	2879
Ecogen Inc.	1320	Langhorne, PA	Public	16.4	60	2879
Genset Corporation	1321	La Jolla, CA	Private	16.4	40	2899
Brent America Holdings, Inc.	1322	La Mirada, CA	Private	16.2	127	2842
Hillyard Enterprises, Inc.	1323	Saint Joseph, MO	Private	16.2	160	2842
Transtar Autobody Technologies	1324	Brighton, MI	Private	16.2	125	2842
Gulbrandsen Manufacturing Inc.	1325	Orangeburg, SC	Private	16.1	NA	2869
Auro Tech Inc.	1326	Menomonee Falls, WI	Public Family Member	16.0	51	2869
Dodge Company Inc.	1327	Cambridge, MA	Private	16.0	105	2869
Emsco Inc.	1328	Girard, PA	Private	16.0	125	2842
G & W Enterprises, Inc.	1329	Fort Worth, TX	Private	16.0	71	2851
General Alum New England Corp.	1330	Holland, OH	Private	16.0	55	2819

D&B COMPANY RANKINGS BY SALES

Company	Rank	Location	Type	Sales ($ mil.)	Employ-ment	Primary SIC
Holland Colors Americas Inc.	1331	Richmond, IN	Private	16.0	70	2865
M C Marble, Inc.	1332	Lafayette, IN	Private	16.0	6	2844
Magnox Pulaski Incorporated	1333	Pulaski, VA	Private	16.0	135	2816
Norfluor USA, LLC	1334	Jacksonville Beach, FL	Private	16.0	170	2819
Panco Men's Products Inc.	1335	Indio, CA	Private	16.0	15	2844
Preservative Paint Co.	1336	Seattle, WA	Private	16.0	150	2851
R F S Corporation	1337	Fall River, MA	Private	16.0	50	2865
Roma Color Inc.	1338	Fall River, MA	Private	16.0	50	2865
Russell Jerome Cosmetics USA	1339	Canoga Park, CA	Private	16.0	48	2844
Stephen J Scherer Inc.	1340	Rochester Hills, MI	Private	16.0	107	2844
Troy Chemical Corp.	1341	Newark, NJ	Private	16.0	98	2851
Ultra-Poly Corp.	1342	Portland, PA	Private	16.0	45	2821
United Elchem Industries Inc.	1343	Dallas, TX	Private	16.0	35	2891
R J S Scientific Inc.	1344	Port Washington, NY	Private	16.0	87	2844
Finetex Inc.	1345	Elmwood Park, NJ	Private	15.9	75	2869
Profile Products, LLC	1346	Buffalo Grove, IL	Private	15.9	75	2879
Strickland J & Co.	1347	Memphis, TN	Private	15.9	150	2844
Atlas Refinery Inc.	1348	Newark, NJ	Private	15.9	40	2843
Aarbor International Corp	1349	Brighton, MI	Private	15.8	17	2865
Somerville Technology Group	1350	Huguenot, NY	Private	15.8	55	2819
Eval Company Of America	1351	Lisle, IL	Private	15.8	86	2821
Paulsboro Packaging Co	1352	Paulsboro, NJ	Public Family Member	15.8	125	2842
Chemron Corporation	1353	Paso Robles, CA	Private	15.6	80	2843
Mercury Paint Corp.	1354	Brooklyn, NY	Private	15.6	100	2851
Winbro Group Ltd	1355	Woburn, MA	Private	15.6	120	2842
Lambent Technologies Corp.	1356	Skokie, IL	Private	15.6	50	2843
RSA Microtech	1357	Seattle, WA	Private	15.6	60	2819
Inchem Holdings	1358	Rock Hill, SC	Private	15.5	78	2821
Jewel Chemical Co.	1359	Chicago, IL	Private	15.5	150	2841
Natural White Manufacturing	1360	Tonawanda, NY	Private	15.5	120	2844
North American Green Inc.	1361	Evansville, IN	Private	15.4	85	2875
Southern Resources Inc.	1362	Fort Valley, GA	Public Family Member	15.4	75	2879
Magnetics International Inc.	1363	Chesterton, IN	Public Family Member	15.3	58	2819
C P I Packaging Inc.	1364	Marlboro, NJ	Private	15.3	74	2821
CLO White Company Inc.	1365	Hampton, GA	Private	15.3	130	2842
Apple Plastics Inc.	1366	Compton, CA	Private	15.2	70	2821
Melamine Chemicals Inc.	1367	Donaldsonville, LA	Private	15.2	95	2821
Southern States Phosphate Fert.	1368	Savannah, GA	Private	15.2	70	2874
Zegarelli Group International	1369	Burbank, CA	Private	15.2	287	2844
Aaba Plastic Sales Associates	1370	New York, NY	Private	15.1	80	2821
Universal Chemical & Supply	1371	Englewood, CO	Private	15.1	88	2819
L D Davis Industries Inc.	1372	Huntingdon Valley, PA	Private	15.1	57	2891
Warsaw Chemical Company, Inc.	1373	Warsaw, IN	Private	15.0	95	2842
AC Products, Inc.	1374	Placentia, CA	Public Family Member	15.0	32	2891
Airgas Dry Ice	1375	San Antonio, TX	Public Family Member	15.0	125	2813
American Silicones Inc.	1376	Garrett, IN	Private	15.0	60	2822
Arcar Graphics, LLC	1377	West Chicago, IL	Private	15.0	96	2893
Aromatic Technologies, Inc.	1378	Somerville, NJ	Private	15.0	50	2844
Axim Concrete Technologies	1379	Middlebranch, OH	Private	15.0	46	2899
Bencyn Inc.	1380	Lafayette, IN	Private	15.0	51	2899
Blue Water Molded Systems Inc.	1381	Saint Clair, MI	Private	15.0	100	2891
Brulin & Company Inc.	1382	Indianapolis, IN	Private	15.0	160	2842
C & I Holdings, Inc.	1383	Saint Louis, MO	Private	15.0	150	2842
California Sulphur	1384	Wilmington, CA	Private	15.0	15	2819
Charm Sciences Inc.	1385	Malden, MA	Private	15.0	90	2899
Chem Comp Systems Inc.	1386	Cypress, CA	Private	15.0	31	2891
Chemtrusion Inc.	1387	Houston, TX	Private	15.0	119	2821
Clinitex Holdings, Inc.	1388	Huntersville, NC	Private	15.0	47	2842
Corsicana Technologies Inc.	1389	Houston, TX	Private	15.0	20	2869
Edlon, Inc.	1390	Avondale, PA	Public Family Member	15.0	134	2821
Flexible Components Inc.	1391	Bridgewater, NJ	Public Family Member	15.0	48	2821
Flor Quim Inc.	1392	Patillas, PR	Private	15.0	27	2869
Floralife, Inc.	1393	Walterboro, SC	Private	15.0	65	2899
General Polymeric Corp.	1394	Reading, PA	Private	15.0	62	2821
GFS Chemicals, Inc.	1395	Powell, OH	Private	15.0	70	2819
Harrison Paint Corp.	1396	Canton, OH	Private	15.0	139	2851
Importers Service Corp.	1397	Jersey City, NJ	Private	15.0	40	2861
International Chemical Corp.	1398	Amherst, NY	Private	15.0	175	2819
Isochem Colors Inc.	1399	Rock Hill, SC	Private	15.0	45	2865
J P Industrial Products Inc.	1400	Lisbon, OH	Private	15.0	33	2821

D&B COMPANY RANKINGS BY SALES

Company	Rank	Location	Type	Sales ($ mil.)	Employ-ment	Primary SIC
Kutol Products Company	1401	Cincinnati, OH	Private	15.0	120	2841
Lenmar Chemical Corporation	1402	Dalton, GA	Private	15.0	37	2843
Metrex Research Corporation	1403	Orange, CA	Public Family Member	15.0	50	2819
Nu Gro Technologies, Inc.	1404	Gloversville, NY	Private	15.0	26	2875
Old 97 Company	1405	Tampa, FL	Public Family Member	15.0	100	2844
Oregon Research & Development	1406	Jacksonville, FL	Private	15.0	40	2899
Ortec Inc.	1407	Easley, SC	Private	15.0	91	2869
Packaging Advantage Corp.	1408	Los Angeles, CA	Private	15.0	275	2841
Penetone Corporation	1409	Tenafly, NJ	Private	15.0	64	2842
Performance Materials Corp.	1410	Camarillo, CA	Private	15.0	100	2821
Peter Thomas Roth Inc.	1411	New York, NY	Private	15.0	20	2844
PPB Technologies, Inc.	1412	Shelby, NC	Private	15.0	17	2819
Repello Products Inc.	1413	Mineola, NY	Private	15.0	22	2879
Reynolds Polymer Technology	1414	Grand Junction, CO	Private	15.0	120	2821
Rycoline Products Inc.	1415	Chicago, IL	Private	15.0	67	2842
Sea & Ski Corp.	1416	Miami, FL	Private	15.0	30	2844
Sewell Products Of Florida	1417	Auburndale, FL	Private	15.0	100	2842
Shepard Brothers Inc.	1418	La Habra, CA	Private	15.0	55	2842
Superior Manufactured Fibers	1419	Plantersville, MS	Private	15.0	20	2824
Toma Industries	1420	North Hollywood, CA	Private	15.0	25	2844
Uniplast Inc.	1421	Arlington, TX	Private	15.0	50	2891
Zaclon Inc.	1422	Cleveland, OH	Private	15.0	45	2819

D&B COMPANY RANKINGS BY EMPLOYMENT

Company	Rank	Location	Type	Sales ($ mil.)	Employ- ment	Primary SIC
The Procter & Gamble Company	1	Cincinnati, OH	Public	37,154.0	110,000	2841
The Dow Chemical Company	2	Midland, MI	Public	18,441.0	40,289	2821
Colgate-Palmolive Company	3	New York, NY	Public	9,056.7	37,800	2844
Avon Products, Inc.	4	New York, NY	Public	5,212.7	34,995	2844
PPG Industries Inc.	5	Pittsburgh, PA	Public	7,510.0	31,900	2851
Hoechst Corporation	6	Warren, NJ	Private	6,876.0	29,200	2824
Monsanto Company	7	Saint Louis, MO	Public	8,648.0	29,000	2879
Mafco Holdings Inc.	8	New York, NY	Private	3,460.4	28,843	2844
Praxair Inc.	9	Danbury, CT	Public	4,833.0	25,388	2813
Bayer Corporation	10	Pittsburgh, PA	Private	9,257.0	24,300	2821
HNA Holdings, Inc.	11	Warren, NJ	Private	6,166.0	22,200	2824
Ashland Inc.	12	Covington, KY	Public	6,933.0	21,200	2819
MacAndrews Forbes Holdings Inc.	13	New York, NY	Private	6,196.0	20,075	2844
FMC Corporation	14	Chicago, IL	Public	4,259.0	16,805	2812
Air Products and Chemicals	15	Allentown, PA	Public	4,933.8	16,400	2813
Eastman Chemical Company	16	Kingsport, TN	Public	4,678.0	16,100	2821
Revlon Holdings Inc.	17	New York, NY	Private	2,390.9	16,100	2844
Revlon Consumer Products Corp.	18	New York, NY	Private	2,390.9	16,000	2844
Revlon Inc.	19	New York, NY	Private	2,390.9	16,000	2844
Intertech Group Inc.	20	North Charleston, SC	Private	2,564.5	15,832	2819
Estee Lauder Companies Inc.	21	New York, NY	Public	3,618.0	15,300	2844
ICI American Holdings Inc.	22	Wilmington, DE	Private	4,004.2	14,800	2851
Amoco Chemical Company	23	Chicago, IL	Private	3,222.8	14,700	2821
Basf Corporation	24	Budd Lake, NJ	Private	3,546.0	14,400	2869
S C Johnson & Son Inc.	25	Racine, WI	Private	1,600.2	13,400	2842
Alberto-Culver Company	26	Melrose Park, IL	Public	1,834.7	12,700	2844
Occidental Petroleum Corp.	27	Los Angeles, CA	Public	8,016.0	12,380	2812
Contran Corporation	28	Dallas, TX	Private	1,241.2	12,000	2816
Union Carbide Corporation	29	Danbury, CT	Public	6,502.0	11,813	2869
Rohm and Haas Company	30	Philadelphia, PA	Public	3,999.0	11,592	2821
Borden Holdings, Inc.	31	Columbus, OH	Private	1,769.5	11,200	2891
BW Holdings, LLC	32	Columbus, OH	Private	1,769.5	11,200	2891
Arteva Specialities Sarl	33	Charlotte, NC	Private	2,410.7	11,000	2821
Morton International, Inc.	34	Chicago, IL	Public	2,574.4	10,600	2891
Akzo Nobel Inc.	35	Chicago, IL	Private	2,567.6	10,540	2869
NCH Corporation	36	Irving, TX	Public	784.1	10,458	2842
Occidental Chemical Holding Corp.	37	Dallas, TX	Public Family Member	4,349.0	10,400	2869
Ecolab Inc.	38	Saint Paul, MN	Public	1,640.4	10,210	2841
Estee Lauder Inc.	39	New York, NY	Public Family Member	1,199.1	10,000	2844
Olin Corporation	40	Norwalk, CT	Public	2,410.0	10,000	2812
BOC Group Inc.	41	New Providence, NJ	Private	1,090.9	9,600	2813
Dow Corning Corporation	42	Midland, MI	Private	2,643.5	9,100	2869
IMC Global Inc.	43	Northbrook, IL	Public	2,988.6	8,950	2874
Solutia Inc.	44	Saint Louis, MO	Public	2,969.0	8,800	2824
Henkel Corporation	45	King Of Prussia, PA	Private	2,256.6	8,270	2869
Henkel Of America Inc.	46	King Of Prussia, PA	Private	1,272.9	8,270	2869
BOC Group Inc.	47	New Providence, NJ	Private	1,549.5	8,000	2813
Borden Inc.	48	Columbus, OH	Private	1,487.7	8,000	2869
Indopco Inc.	49	Bridgewater, NJ	Private	2,770.0	7,700	2891
Zeneca Holdings Inc.	50	Wilmington, DE	Private	1,595.6	7,700	2879
C H Oxy Corporation	51	Dallas, TX	Public Family Member	1,845.0	7,500	2869
Oxy Chemical Corporation	52	Dallas, TX	Public Family Member	1,845.0	7,500	2869
Huntsman Corporation	53	Salt Lake City, UT	Private	3,568.1	7,486	2821
Praxair Distribution Inc.	54	Hinsdale, IL	Public Family Member	823.9	7,250	2813
Occidental Chemical Corp.	55	Dallas, TX	Public Family Member	2,574.8	7,200	2812
Williams US Holdings, Inc.	56	Wilmington, DE	Private	1,077.3	7,000	2851
Engelhard Corporation	57	Iselin, NJ	Public	3,630.7	6,872	2819
Ferro Corporation	58	Cleveland, OH	Public	1,381.3	6,851	2899
Hercules Incorporated	59	Wilmington, DE	Public	1,866.0	6,834	2899
RPM Inc.	60	Medina, OH	Public	1,615.3	6,800	2851
The Clorox Company	61	Oakland, CA	Public	2,741.3	6,600	2842
Nalco Chemical Company	62	Naperville, IL	Public	1,433.7	6,502	2899
ICI Americas Inc.	63	Wilmington, DE	Private	1,422.9	6,500	2821
W R Grace & Co.	64	Boca Raton, FL	Public	1,479.7	6,300	2819
H B Fuller Company	65	Saint Paul, MN	Public	1,347.2	6,000	2891
Revlon International Corp.	66	New York, NY	Private	719.1	6,000	2844
Zeneca Inc.	67	Wilmington, DE	Private	3,200.0	6,000	2879
IMC Global Operations	68	Northbrook, IL	Public Family Member	2,105.7	5,976	2874
Crompton & Knowles Corporation	69	Stamford, CT	Public	1,796.1	5,519	2865
Betzdearborn Inc.	70	Langhorne, PA	Public Family Member	1,294.8	5,300	2899

D&B COMPANY RANKINGS BY EMPLOYMENT

Company	Rank	Location	Type	Sales ($ mil.)	Employ-ment	Primary SIC
Cytec Industries Inc.	71	West Paterson, NJ	Public	1,290.6	5,200	2899
Great Lakes Chemical Corp	72	West Lafayette, IN	Public	1,311.2	5,100	2819
Amoco Fabrics And Fibers Co	73	Atlanta, GA	Private	1,093.7	5,000	2821
Cabot Corporation	74	Boston, MA	Public	410.3	4,800	2895
Dexter Corporation	75	Windsor Locks, CT	Public	1,147.1	4,800	2891
Interntonal Flavors Fragrances	76	New York, NY	Public	1,426.8	4,600	2869
Solvay America Inc.	77	Houston, TX	Private	2,200.0	4,600	2821
The Glidden Company	78	Cleveland, OH	Private	1,000.0	4,600	2851
Elf Atochem North America Inc.	79	Philadelphia, PA	Private	1,903.6	4,500	2812
Sun Chemical Corporation	80	Fort Lee, NJ	Private	2,825.0	4,500	2893
Loctite Corporation	81	Hartford, CT	Private	694.9	4,400	2891
American Air Liquide Inc.	82	Houston, TX	Private	2,000.0	4,350	2813
AL America Holdings, Inc.	83	Houston, TX	Private	488.6	4,300	2813
G-I Holdings Inc.	84	Wayne, NJ	Private	852.0	4,300	2869
Lubrizol Corporation	85	Wickliffe, OH	Public	1,673.8	4,300	2899
Lyondell Chemical Company	86	Houston, TX	Public	1,703.0	4,250	2869
Akzo Nobel Courtaulds US Inc.	87	Purchase, NY	Private	645.9	4,200	2851
Chevron Chemical Company, LLC	88	San Ramon, CA	Private	918.1	4,200	2821
Lyondell Chemical Worldwide	89	Houston, TX	Public Family Member	3,995.0	4,200	2869
Millennium Chemicals Inc.	90	Red Bank, NJ	Public	3,048.0	4,200	2816
G Industries Corp.	91	Wayne, NJ	Private	1,000.6	4,075	2869
Johnson Sc Commercial Markets	92	Sturtevant, WI	Private	477.9	4,004	2842
Air Products, Incorporated	93	Allentown, PA	Public Family Member	454.5	4,000	2813
Ciba Specialty Chemicals Corp.	94	Tarrytown, NY	Private	1,560.0	4,000	2819
Mary Kay Holding Corporation	95	Dallas, TX	Private	897.1	4,000	2844
Mary Kay Inc.	96	Dallas, TX	Private	897.1	4,000	2844
Rhodia Inc.	97	Cranbury, NJ	Private	1,600.0	4,000	2819
Valhi Inc.	98	Dallas, TX	Public	1,093.1	4,000	2816
Phosphate Resource Partners	99	Northbrook, IL	Public	842.5	3,871	2874
Formosa Plastics Corp. USA	100	Livingston, NJ	Private	1,500.0	3,800	2821
Valspar Corporation	101	Minneapolis, MN	Public	1,155.1	3,800	2851
Dial Corporation	102	Scottsdale, AZ	Public	1,362.6	3,716	2841
P M C Inc.	103	Sun Valley, CA	Private	649.2	3,600	2819
R P Scherer Corporation	104	Troy, MI	Public Family Member	515.3	3,600	2899
Mobil Chemical Company Inc.	105	Fairfax, VA	Public Family Member	511.0	3,570	2899
Wilsonart International, Inc.	106	Temple, TX	Public Family Member	753.5	3,450	2821
HC Investments, Inc.	107	King Of Prussia, PA	Private	536.8	3,400	2891
Block Drug Company Inc.	108	Jersey City, NJ	Public	863.1	3,380	2844
Carter-Wallace Inc.	109	New York, NY	Public	662.2	3,360	2844
Berwind Industries, Inc.	110	Nashville, TN	Private	472.3	3,300	2899
Dupont Dow Elastomers LLC	111	Wilmington, DE	Private	1,086.9	3,300	2822
Kerr-Mcgee Corporation	112	Oklahoma City, OK	Public	1,711.0	3,300	2816
Saint-Gbain Advanced Mtls Corp.	113	Louisville, KY	Private	533.7	3,300	2819
Reichhold Inc.	114	Durham, NC	Private	698.6	3,200	2821
Dow Agrosciences LLC	115	Indianapolis, IN	Public Family Member	2,000.0	3,100	2879
Wellman Inc.	116	Shrewsbury, NJ	Public	1,083.2	3,100	2824
Arch Chemical Inc.	117	Norwalk, CT	Private	862.8	3,000	2819
Borden Chemical Inc.	118	Columbus, OH	Private	1,290.8	3,000	2869
Procter & Gamble Far East	119	Cincinnati, OH	Public Family Member	337.0	2,824	2842
Uniroyal Chemical Company	120	Middlebury, CT	Public Family Member	1,183.3	2,750	2822
Uniroyal Chemical Corporation	121	Middlebury, CT	Public Family Member	1,183.3	2,750	2822
Albemarle Corporation	122	Baton Rouge, LA	Public	829.9	2,700	2821
Dyno Nobel Inc.	123	Salt Lake City, UT	Private	500.0	2,700	2892
BP Chemicals Inc.	124	Cleveland, OH	Private	637.0	2,600	2869
Flint Ink Corporation	125	Ann Arbor, MI	Private	757.1	2,600	2893
NL Industries Inc.	126	Houston, TX	Public	837.2	2,600	2816
Helene Curtis Industries Inc.	127	Chicago, IL	Private	1,265.0	2,500	2844
International Specialty Products	128	Wayne, NJ	Private	749.2	2,500	2869
Kronor Inc.	129	Houston, TX	Public Family Member	852.5	2,500	2816
The Scotts Company	130	Marysville, OH	Public	1,113.0	2,500	2873
Agrium U.S. Inc.	131	Denver, CO	Private	1,937.9	2,450	2873
General Chemical Group Inc.	132	Hampton, NH	Public	653.0	2,402	2812
Kelly-Moore Paint Company	133	San Carlos, CA	Private	276.1	2,400	2851
Noxell Corporation	134	Cockeysville, MD	Public Family Member	242.6	2,397	2844
Clairol Incorporated	135	New York, NY	Public Family Member	275.0	2,300	2844
Del Laboratories, Inc.	136	Uniondale, NY	Public	263.0	2,300	2844
Kerr-Mcgee Chemical, LLC	137	Oklahoma City, OK	Public Family Member	760.0	2,300	2819
Ensign-Bickford Industries	138	Simsbury, CT	Private	185.2	2,278	2892
A Schulman Inc.	139	Akron, OH	Public	996.5	2,250	2821
Minerals Technologies Inc.	140	New York, NY	Public	609.2	2,250	2819

D&B COMPANY RANKINGS BY EMPLOYMENT

Company	Rank	Location	Type	Sales ($ mil.)	Employment	Primary SIC
Harris Chemical North America	141	Shawnee Mission, KS	Public Family Member	494.2	2,235	2819
IMC Inorganic Chemicals Inc.	142	Shawnee Mission, KS	Public Family Member	700.0	2,235	2819
DSM Finance USA Inc.	143	Wilmington, DE	Private	352.4	2,233	2891
Lilly Industries Inc.	144	Indianapolis, IN	Public	601.3	2,116	2851
Akzo Nobel Chemicals Inc.	145	Chicago, IL	Private	783.0	2,100	2869
Varied Investments Inc.	146	Muscatine, IA	Private	469.9	2,097	2869
Degussa Corporation	147	Ridgefield Park, NJ	Private	2,373.0	2,027	2869
Amoco Polymers Inc.	148	Alpharetta, GA	Private	200.0	2,000	2824
Aqualon Company	149	Wilmington, DE	Private	441.1	2,000	2869
Beiersdorf Inc.	150	Wilton, CT	Private	250.0	2,000	2844
CCL Custom Manufacturing, Inc.	151	Des Plaines, IL	Private	257.3	2,000	2841
IMC Agribusiness Inc.	152	Collinsville, IL	Public Family Member	873.0	2,000	2873
Koppers Industries Inc.	153	Pittsburgh, PA	Public	593.1	2,000	2865
Millennium Inorganic Chemicals	154	Cockeysville, MD	Public Family Member	850.0	2,000	2816
Montell USA Inc.	155	Wilmington, DE	Private	1,100.0	2,000	2821
Reckitt & Colman Inc.	156	Wayne, NJ	Private	1,300.0	2,000	2842
The Geon Company	157	Avon Lake, OH	Public	1,250.0	2,000	2821
Bush Boake Allen Inc.	158	Montvale, NJ	Public	490.6	1,964	2869
Sud-Chemie, NA	159	Louisville, KY	Private	253.0	1,950	2819
PQ Corporation	160	Berwyn, PA	Private	378.5	1,923	2819
Benjamin Moore & Co.	161	Montvale, NJ	Public	666.3	1,900	2851
General Chemical Corporation	162	Parsippany, NJ	Public Family Member	519.1	1,869	2819
NS Group Inc.	163	Newport, KY	Public	409.9	1,803	2891
Alberto-Culver U S A Inc.	164	Melrose Park, IL	Public Family Member	215.0	1,800	2844
Ethyl Corporation	165	Richmond, VA	Public	1,063.6	1,800	2869
State Industrial Products Corp.	166	Cleveland, OH	Private	107.7	1,800	2841
Tremco Incorporated	167	Cleveland, OH	Public Family Member	350.0	1,785	2891
Kolmar Laboratories, Inc.	168	Port Jervis, NY	Private	103.1	1,700	2844
Morgan Adhesives Company	169	Stow, OH	Public Family Member	268.1	1,700	2891
Outsourcing Services Group Inc.	170	City Of Industry, CA	Private	203.0	1,700	2844
LSB Industries, Inc.	171	Oklahoma City, OK	Public	313.9	1,685	2819
CF Industries, Inc.	172	Lake Zurich, IL	Private	1,431.6	1,652	2873
Davis Mining & Manufacturing	173	Coeburn, VA	Private	185.2	1,600	2892
Huntsman Chemical Corporation	174	Salt Lake City, UT	Private	1,203.5	1,600	2821
Mississippi Chemical Corp.	175	Yazoo City, MS	Public	519.1	1,600	2873
Protein Technologies International	176	Saint Louis, MO	Public Family Member	160.0	1,600	2824
Williams Paint Holdings, Inc.	177	Wilmington, DE	Private	245.3	1,600	2851
Coty US Inc.	178	New York, NY	Private	405.5	1,573	2844
The INX Group Limited	179	Elk Grove Village, IL	Private	306.3	1,550	2893
Devro-Teepak, Inc.	180	Westchester, IL	Private	200.0	1,500	2823
Equistar Chemicals, LP	181	Houston, TX	Private	365.8	1,500	2869
Harbour Group Ltd	182	Saint Louis, MO	Private	900.0	1,500	2822
Kao Corp.Of America	183	Wilmington, DE	Private	179.0	1,500	2844
Maybelline Inc.	184	New York, NY	Private	179.0	1,500	2844
Messer Griesheim Industries	185	Malvern, PA	Private	330.0	1,500	2813
Nalco/Exxon Energy Chem, LP	186	Sugar Land, TX	Private	471.8	1,500	2899
Saint-Gobain Indus Ceramics	187	Louisville, KY	Private	242.0	1,500	2819
Sterling Chemicals Holdings	188	Houston, TX	Public	822.6	1,500	2865
Sterling Chemicals Inc.	189	Houston, TX	Public Family Member	822.6	1,500	2865
Aristech Chemical Corporation	190	Pittsburgh, PA	Private	314.5	1,450	2821
Sud-Chemie & Co., LP	191	Louisville, KY	Private	246.2	1,450	2819
Albright & Wilson Americas	192	Glen Allen, VA	Private	375.0	1,400	2819
Columbian Chemicals Company	193	Marietta, GA	Public Family Member	500.0	1,400	2895
Condea Vista Company	194	Houston, TX	Private	848.0	1,400	2821
Diversey Lever Inc.	195	Plymouth, MI	Private	166.9	1,400	2842
Houghton International Inc.	196	Valley Forge, PA	Private	271.6	1,400	2869
Nutrasweet Kelco Company (Inc)	197	Chicago, IL	Public Family Member	341.2	1,400	2869
TPR Investment Associates	198	New York, NY	Private	219.3	1,400	2812
Special Devices Incorporated	199	Santa Clarita, CA	Private	140.5	1,395	2899
INX International Ink Company	200	Elk Grove Village, IL	Private	265.0	1,380	2893
Clorox International Co. Inc.	201	Oakland, CA	Public Family Member	162.1	1,360	2842
PCS Nitrogen Inc.	202	Memphis, TN	Private	424.1	1,350	2873
Calgon Carbon Corporation	203	Pittsburgh, PA	Public	327.5	1,341	2819
Coty Inc.	204	New York, NY	Private	158.6	1,330	2844
Huntsman Polymers Corporation	205	Salt Lake City, UT	Public	419.4	1,320	2821
Oxy Petrochemicals Inc.	206	Dallas, TX	Public Family Member	321.5	1,320	2869
Catalytica Pharmaceuticals	207	Greenville, NC	Public Family Member	360.0	1,300	2869
G V C Holdings Inc.	208	Port Neches, TX	Private	475.0	1,300	2822
Huish Detergents Inc.	209	Salt Lake City, UT	Private	300.0	1,300	2841
New River Energetics, Inc.	210	Radford, VA	Public Family Member	150.5	1,300	2892

D&B COMPANY RANKINGS BY EMPLOYMENT

Company	Rank	Location	Type	Sales ($ mil.)	Employ-ment	Primary SIC
Pioneer Americas, Inc.	211	Houston, TX	Public Family Member	450.0	1,300	2812
Stepan Company	212	Winnetka, IL	Public	581.9	1,292	2843
Dunn-Edwards Corporation	213	Los Angeles, CA	Private	209.2	1,257	2851
Bulab Holdings, Inc.	214	Memphis, TN	Private	161.0	1,250	2869
Clorox Products Manufacturing Co.	215	Aberdeen, MD	Public Family Member	147.8	1,240	2842
IMC Salt Inc.	216	Shawnee Mission, KS	Public Family Member	146.2	1,237	2899
AGA Inc.	217	Cleveland, OH	Private	136.6	1,202	2813
Advanced Technical Products	218	Roswell, GA	Public	119.4	1,200	2821
AGA Gas Inc.	219	Cleveland, OH	Private	136.4	1,200	2813
Austin Powder Company	220	Cleveland, OH	Private	138.9	1,200	2892
B F Goodrich Freedom Chemical Co.	221	Cleveland, OH	Public Family Member	300.0	1,200	2865
Cosmolab Inc.	222	Lewisburg, TN	Private	143.0	1,200	2844
Macklanburg-Duncan Co.	223	Oklahoma City, OK	Private	250.0	1,200	2891
OSI Specialties Holding Company	224	Greenwich, CT	Public Family Member	472.4	1,200	2821
OSI Specialties, Inc.	225	Greenwich, CT	Public Family Member	472.4	1,200	2821
Sandoz Agro, Inc.	226	Des Plaines, IL	Private	247.6	1,200	2879
The Kingsford Products Co.	227	Oakland, CA	Public Family Member	90.0	1,200	2861
Ameripol Synpol Corporation	228	Port Neches, TX	Private	475.0	1,190	2822
Renaissance Cosmetics, Inc.	229	Stamford, CT	Private	179.7	1,189	2844
Chemfirst Inc.	230	Jackson, MS	Public	445.8	1,175	2865
Lesco Inc.	231	Cleveland, OH	Public	356.8	1,157	2875
Clariant Corporation	232	Charlotte, NC	Private	233.8	1,150	2865
Specialty Minerals Inc.	233	New York, NY	Public Family Member	363.8	1,150	2819
Church & Dwight Co. Inc.	234	Princeton, NJ	Public	574.9	1,137	2812
Nan Ya Plastics Corp. America	235	Livingston, NJ	Private	612.1	1,130	2824
Composites Cook & Polymers Co.	236	Kansas City, MO	Private	320.6	1,120	2821
Laroche Industries Inc.	237	Atlanta, GA	Private	381.0	1,120	2873
FMC Wyoming Corporation	238	Green River, WY	Public Family Member	174.6	1,115	2812
Austin Powder Holdings Co.	239	Cleveland, OH	Private	127.3	1,100	2892
Cargill Fertilizer Inc.	240	Riverview, FL	Private	750.0	1,100	2874
Shell Catalyst Ventures, Inc.	241	Houston, TX	Public Family Member	177.2	1,100	2819
Givaudan-Roure Corporation	242	Cincinnati, OH	Private	225.0	1,050	2869
PCS Nitrogen Fertilizer, LP	243	Memphis, TN	Private	1,310.0	1,048	2873
Georgia Gulf Corporation	244	Atlanta, GA	Public	875.0	1,041	2812
Mc Whorter Technologies, Inc.	245	Carpentersville, IL	Public	454.9	1,040	2821
Baker Petrolite Incorporated	246	Sugar Land, TX	Public Family Member	146.9	1,031	2899
Arizona Chemical Company	247	Panama City, FL	Public Family Member	300.0	1,030	2861
Alberto-Culver International Inc.	248	Melrose Park, IL	Public Family Member	119.0	1,000	2844
Alcoa Minerals Of Jamaica Inc.	249	Pittsburgh, PA	Public Family Member	161.0	1,000	2819
Chanel Inc.	250	New York, NY	Private	119.0	1,000	2844
Conagra Fertilizer Company	251	Omaha, NE	Public Family Member	206.1	1,000	2879
Creanova Inc.	252	Somerset, NJ	Private	551.5	1,000	2869
Holox USA BV	253	Norcross, GA	Private	200.0	1,000	2813
Learonal Inc.	254	Freeport, NY	Public	241.7	1,000	2899
Lonza Inc.	255	Fair Lawn, NJ	Private	434.9	1,000	2899
M A Bruder & Sons Inc.	256	Broomall, PA	Private	100.0	1,000	2851
Matrix Essentials Inc.	257	Cleveland, OH	Public Family Member	119.0	1,000	2844
Perrigo Of Tennessee	258	Smyrna, TN	Public Family Member	119.0	1,000	2844
Philipp Brothers Chemicals Inc.	259	Fort Lee, NJ	Private	278.0	1,000	2819
Quest International Fragrances Co.	260	Budd Lake, NJ	Private	390.0	1,000	2844
Rohm And Haas Texas Inc.	261	Deer Park, TX	Public Family Member	242.6	1,000	2869
Rogers Corporation	262	Rogers, CT	Public	189.7	993	2821
Calgon Corporation	263	Pittsburgh, PA	Private	139.6	980	2899
Shiseido International Corp.	264	Oakland, NJ	Private	116.0	975	2844
Sud-Chemie Inc.	265	Louisville, KY	Private	246.0	950	2819
United Catalysts Inc.	266	Louisville, KY	Private	246.0	950	2819
Wesmar Partners	267	Pittsburgh, PA	Private	135.3	950	2899
SKW-MBT Services Inc.	268	Cleveland, OH	Private	131.7	925	2899
Prestone Products Corporation	269	Danbury, CT	Public Family Member	300.0	910	2899
Bio-Lab Inc.	270	Decatur, GA	Public Family Member	400.0	900	2812
Mallinckrodt Baker, Inc.	271	Phillipsburg, NJ	Public Family Member	144.8	900	2819
Aldrich Chemical Company Inc.	272	Milwaukee, WI	Public Family Member	250.0	884	2869
Martin Color-Fi Inc.	273	Edgefield, SC	Public	120.5	881	2824
Wella Corporation	274	Montvale, NJ	Private	125.0	870	2844
Primedia Magazines Inc.	275	New York, NY	Public Family Member	183.2	852	2821
Frazee Industries Inc.	276	San Diego, CA	Private	129.7	850	2851
Matheson Gas Products Inc.	277	Parsippany, NJ	Private	173.6	850	2813
Neutrogena Corporation	278	Los Angeles, CA	Public Family Member	360.0	850	2844
Trans-Resources Inc.	279	New York, NY	Private	376.5	840	2873
Genencor International Inc.	280	Rochester, NY	Private	293.6	825	2869

D&B COMPANY RANKINGS BY EMPLOYMENT

Company	Rank	Location	Type	Sales ($ mil.)	Employ-ment	Primary SIC
Permian Mud Service Inc.	281	Houston, TX	Private	200.0	824	2819
National Welders Supply Co.	282	Charlotte, NC	Private	130.5	810	2813
Borden Chemical & Plastic, LP	283	Geismar, LA	Public	737.1	800	2821
Crompton & Knowles Colors Inc.	284	Charlotte, NC	Public Family Member	190.0	800	2899
Foseco Holding Inc.	285	Cleveland, OH	Private	113.8	800	2899
Griffin, LLC	286	Valdosta, GA	Private	237.4	800	2879
I C I Explosives USA, Inc.	287	Joplin, MO	Private	92.6	800	2892
ISK Americas Inc.	288	Mentor, OH	Private	369.1	800	2879
Spawn Mate Inc.	289	Watsonville, CA	Private	45.2	800	2873
United Industries Corp.	290	Saint Louis, MO	Private	164.6	800	2879
Harris Specialty Chemicals	291	Jacksonville, FL	Private	174.4	790	2869
HSC Holdings Inc.	292	Jacksonville, FL	Private	124.3	790	2891
Grain Processing Corporation	293	Muscatine, IA	Private	189.6	785	2869
SKW Biosystems Inc.	294	Langhorne, PA	Private	210.0	771	2869
OM Group Inc.	295	Cleveland, OH	Public	487.3	758	2819
Acordis Cellulose Fiber Inc.	296	Axis, AL	Private	81.2	750	2823
Hampshire Chemical Corp.	297	Lexington, MA	Public Family Member	260.0	750	2869
Hampshire Holdings Corp.	298	Lexington, MA	Public Family Member	260.0	750	2869
International Paint Inc.	299	Houston, TX	Private	114.3	750	2851
Rodel Inc.	300	Newark, DE	Private	150.0	750	2842
Stonhard Inc.	301	Maple Shade, NJ	Public Family Member	195.7	750	2851
Sybron Chemicals Inc.	302	Birmingham, NJ	Public	188.8	738	2843
Sika Corporation	303	Lyndhurst, NJ	Private	148.4	737	2891
Prc-Desoto International	304	Glendale, CA	Private	148.0	731	2891
Champion Technologies, Inc.	305	Houston, TX	Private	150.0	725	2819
Marietta Corporation	306	Cortland, NY	Private	92.4	721	2841
Kemira Holdings Inc.	307	Savannah, GA	Private	250.0	720	2816
Kemira Pigments Inc.	308	Savannah, GA	Private	250.0	718	2816
Copolymer Holding Company Inc.	309	Baton Rouge, LA	Private	51.1	715	2822
Brotech Corp.	310	Bala Cynwyd, PA	Private	149.9	700	2821
Cyro Industries	311	Rockaway, NJ	Private	200.0	700	2821
DSM Copolymer, Inc.	312	Baton Rouge, LA	Private	333.9	700	2822
Northtec, Inc.	313	Bristol, PA	Public Family Member	83.0	700	2844
Pam Acquisition Corp.	314	Westport, CT	Private	146.0	700	2844
Tri-Gas Inc.	315	Irving, TX	Private	173.2	700	2813
Turtle Wax Inc.	316	Chicago, IL	Private	100.0	700	2842
Haarmann & Reimer Corp	317	Teterboro, NJ	Private	350.0	690	2899
Behr Holdings Corporation	318	Santa Ana, CA	Private	103.6	680	2851
Behr Process Corporation	319	Santa Ana, CA	Private	103.6	680	2851
EM Industries, Inc.	320	Hawthorne, NY	Private	191.7	670	2869
CPAC Inc.	321	Leicester, NY	Public	106.1	662	2842
Advanced Elastomer Systems LP	322	Akron, OH	Private	260.5	660	2822
Fiber Industries Inc.	323	Charlotte, NC	Public Family Member	66.0	660	2824
ISP Chemicals Inc.	324	Calvert City, KY	Private	158.7	660	2869
D S M Engineering Plastic Products	325	Reading, PA	Private	185.0	650	2824
Kleen Brite Laboratories Inc.	326	Brockport, NY	Private	83.3	650	2841
Guest Supply Inc.	327	Monmouth Junction, NJ	Public	236.7	642	2844
True Specialty Corporation	328	Des Plaines, IL	Private	185.0	636	2819
Estee Lauder International Inc.	329	New York, NY	Public Family Member	3,381.6	620	2844
Polypore Inc.	330	North Charleston, SC	Private	99.4	620	2819
Combe Incorporated	331	White Plains, NY	Private	250.0	600	2844
H & R Florasynth	332	Teterboro, NJ	Private	230.0	600	2899
Richardson Sid Carbon & Gas Co.	333	Fort Worth, TX	Private	118.7	600	2895
Schenectady International	334	Schenectady, NY	Private	300.0	600	2865
Thoro System Products Inc.	335	Jacksonville, FL	Private	105.5	600	2891
Tsumura Enterprises Inc.	336	Secaucus, NJ	Private	71.0	600	2844
Velsicol Chemical Corporation	337	Des Plaines, IL	Private	185.0	600	2819
USA Detergents Inc.	338	North Brunswick, NJ	Public	227.3	592	2841
Merle Norman Cosmetics Inc.	339	Los Angeles, CA	Private	87.5	591	2844
Jones-Blair Company	340	Dallas, TX	Private	90.5	575	2851
Radiator Specialty Company	341	Charlotte, NC	Private	118.2	575	2899
Atotech USA Inc.	342	Rock Hill, SC	Private	123.3	570	2899
Lenzing Fibers Corporation	343	Lowland, TN	Private	105.0	560	2823
Dap Products Inc.	344	Baltimore, MD	Private	240.0	550	2891
Tessenderlo USA, Inc.	345	Phoenix, AZ	Private	168.4	550	2873
Bonne Bell Inc.	346	Cleveland, OH	Private	64.3	544	2844
Wacker Silicones Corporation	347	Adrian, MI	Private	126.7	530	2869
Mat Den Corporation	348	Santa Maria, CA	Private	95.0	525	2844
Red Spot Paint & Varnish Co.	349	Evansville, IN	Private	89.3	525	2851
Superior Printing Ink Co. Inc.	350	New York, NY	Private	75.0	525	2893

D&B COMPANY RANKINGS BY EMPLOYMENT

Company	Rank	Location	Type	Sales ($ mil.)	Employ-ment	Primary SIC
Scott Specialty Gases Inc.	351	Plumsteadville, PA	Private	75.0	520	2813
Wacker Chemical Holding Corp.	352	Adrian, MI	Private	123.0	515	2869
Reilly Industries Inc.	353	Indianapolis, IN	Private	103.8	514	2865
Eastwind Group, Inc.	354	West Conshohocken, PA	Public	23.6	505	2821
Chirex Inc.	355	Natick, MA	Public	74.6	504	2899
Lawter International Inc.	356	Pleasant Prairie, WI	Public	206.5	502	2893
Aria, Parviz	357	Pasadena, CA	Private	102.4	500	2879
Avon International Operations	358	New York, NY	Public Family Member	59.0	500	2844
Clean Control Corporation	359	Bonaire, GA	Private	25.0	500	2842
Cosmetic Essence Inc.	360	Edison, NJ	Private	50.0	500	2844
Cultor Food Science, Inc.	361	Ardsley, NY	Private	500.0	500	2869
Fluor Daniel Hanford Inc.	362	Richland, WA	Public Family Member	80.0	500	2819
Foseco Inc.	363	Cleveland, OH	Private	70.8	500	2899
Herbert's America Inc.	364	Houston, TX	Private	160.0	500	2851
Louisiana Pigment Company, LP	365	Westlake, LA	Private	62.5	500	2816
Momar Inc.	366	Atlanta, GA	Private	50.0	500	2842
Nova Chemicals Inc.	367	Monaca, PA	Private	400.0	500	2821
Original Bradford Soap Works	368	West Warwick, RI	Private	35.0	500	2841
Roux Laboratories Inc.	369	Jacksonville, FL	Private	100.0	500	2844
Rust-Oleum Corporation	370	Vernon Hills, IL	Public Family Member	200.0	500	2851
Sentinel Consumer Products	371	Mentor, OH	Private	33.0	500	2844
St Ives Laboratories Inc.	372	Chatsworth, CA	Public Family Member	59.0	500	2844
Sugar Foods Corporation	373	New York, NY	Private	205.0	500	2869
Tedco, Inc.	374	West Monroe, LA	Private	64.0	500	2841
The Andrew Jergens Company	375	Cincinnati, OH	Private	400.0	500	2844
The Fuller Brush Company	376	Great Bend, KS	Public Family Member	59.4	500	2842
U S A Lenzing Corporation	377	Lowland, TN	Private	54.2	500	2823
Westlake Olefins Corporation	378	Houston, TX	Private	119.3	500	2869
Agrevo U S A Company	379	Wilmington, DE	Private	101.2	494	2879
OCI Wyoming, LP	380	Green River, WY	Private	178.0	490	2812
Tessenderlo Kerley, Inc.	381	Phoenix, AZ	Private	113.4	485	2873
Georgetown Holding Company	382	Cleveland, OH	Private	67.9	480	2899
Rubicon Inc.	383	Geismar, LA	Private	374.7	480	2865
Wikoff Color Corporation	384	Fort Mill, SC	Private	58.6	480	2893
Heraeus-Amersil Inc.	385	Duluth, GA	Private	75.1	470	2819
Tsumura International	386	Secaucus, NJ	Private	125.0	465	2844
Bostik Inc.	387	Middleton, MA	Private	120.0	460	2891
Essex Specialty Products Inc.	388	Auburn Hills, MI	Public Family Member	72.2	460	2891
Ethyl Petroleum Additives Inc.	389	Richmond, VA	Public Family Member	64.3	455	2899
Benckiser Consumer Products	390	Greenwich, CT	Private	57.6	451	2841
Apex Specialty Materials Inc.	391	New Castle, DE	Private	70.0	450	2824
Callaway Chemicals Company	392	Columbus, GA	Public Family Member	175.0	450	2819
Criterion Catalyst Company, LP	393	Houston, TX	Private	71.9	450	2819
Dx Holding Company, Inc.	394	Houston, TX	Private	107.0	450	2869
EKA Chemicals Inc.	395	Marietta, GA	Private	225.0	450	2899
Exxon Chemical Americas	396	Baton Rouge, LA	Private	500.0	450	2821
Fibervisions, Incorporated	397	Covington, GA	Private	95.0	450	2821
Johnson & Johnson Consumer Co. PR	398	Las Piedras, PR	Public Family Member	53.0	450	2844
Mobile Paint Manufacturing Co.	399	Theodore, AL	Private	66.5	450	2851
Neste Chemicals Holding Inc.	400	Houston, TX	Private	70.6	450	2891
P L C Specialties Inc.	401	Fair Lawn, NJ	Private	53.0	450	2844
Penn Color Inc.	402	Doylestown, PA	Private	100.0	450	2865
Pioneer Chlor Alkali Company	403	Houston, TX	Public Family Member	250.0	450	2812
Texwipe Company, LLC	404	Saddle River, NJ	Private	72.9	450	2842
Buckman Laboratories, Inc.	405	Memphis, TN	Private	159.0	442	2869
Chemonics Industries, Inc.	406	Phoenix, AZ	Private	74.5	440	2899
Jacobs Industries Incorporated	407	Minneapolis, MN	Private	56.2	440	2841
VPI Mirrex Corporation	408	Delaware City, DE	Private	97.0	440	2821
Saltire Industrial, Inc.	409	New York, NY	Private	160.0	435	2893
C B Fleet Company Incorporated	410	Lynchburg, VA	Private	110.3	432	2844
A-Veda Corporation	411	Minneapolis, MN	Public Family Member	50.6	430	2844
Americhem Inc.	412	Cuyahoga Falls, OH	Private	85.6	425	2865
Neville Chemical Company	413	Pittsburgh, PA	Private	89.5	425	2821
Plastics Engineering Company	414	Sheboygan, WI	Private	50.0	425	2821
Rodda Paint Co	415	Portland, OR	Private	66.0	420	2851
The Mennen Co.	416	Morristown, NJ	Public Family Member	500.0	420	2844
W M Barr & Co. Inc.	417	Memphis, TN	Private	62.7	415	2851
PMC Specialties Group, Inc.	418	Cleveland, OH	Private	192.8	409	2819
Dash Multi-Corp, Inc.	419	Maryland Heights, MO	Private	110.1	403	2821
Bee Chemical Company	420	Lansing, IL	Public Family Member	60.7	402	2851

D&B COMPANY RANKINGS BY EMPLOYMENT

Company	Rank	Location	Type	Sales ($ mil.)	Employ- ment	Primary SIC
BF Goodrich Hilton Davis Inc.	421	Cincinnati, OH	Public Family Member	80.5	400	2865
Bocchi Laboratories, Inc.	422	Walnut, CA	Private	47.0	400	2844
C P S Chemical Co. Inc.	423	Woodbridge, NJ	Private	94.7	400	2869
Carboline Company	424	Saint Louis, MO	Public Family Member	60.4	400	2851
Carson Products Company	425	Savannah, GA	Public Family Member	80.0	400	2844
Chemtreat Inc.	426	Glen Allen, VA	Private	90.0	400	2899
Comilog US, Inc.	427	Baltimore, MD	Private	100.0	400	2819
Crystal Springs Water Company	428	Fort Lauderdale, FL	Private	56.4	400	2899
Cumberland Packing Corp.	429	Brooklyn, NY	Private	60.0	400	2869
Framatome Cogema Fuels	430	Lynchburg, VA	Private	63.8	400	2819
Garst Seed Company	431	Slater, IA	Private	97.0	400	2899
Medicia Pharmaceuticals Corp.	432	Dayton, NJ	Private	30.0	400	2844
Nine West Corporation	433	New York, NY	Private	122.8	400	2873
Norit Americas Inc.	434	Atlanta, GA	Private	60.0	400	2819
Orbseal, LLC	435	Richmond, MO	Private	62.7	400	2891
Shipley Company, LLC	436	Marlborough, MA	Public Family Member	63.8	400	2819
Techmer PM, LLC	437	Compton, CA	Private	84.0	400	2821
Vista Paint Corporation	438	Fullerton, CA	Private	60.4	400	2851
Wattyl (US) Limited	439	Edgewater, FL	Private	60.4	400	2851
Zeon Chemicals Incorporated	440	Louisville, KY	Private	170.0	400	2822
Texas United Corporation	441	Houston, TX	Private	62.5	392	2819
American Synthetic Rubber Corp	442	Louisville, KY	Private	27.9	390	2822
Chemdesign Corporation	443	Fitchburg, MA	Private	80.0	390	2869
Tristar Corporation	444	San Antonio, TX	Public	67.7	390	2844
Rockwood Industries Inc.	445	Beltsville, MD	Private	48.6	389	2816
Car-Freshner Corp.	446	Watertown, NY	Private	45.9	387	2842
Aerosol Companies Holding	447	Gainesville, GA	Private	44.9	382	2844
Silberline Manufacturing Co.	448	Tamaqua, PA	Private	47.8	382	2816
Piedmont Laboratories Inc.	449	Gainesville, GA	Private	44.6	380	2844
Willert Home Products Inc.	450	Saint Louis, MO	Private	20.0	380	2879
Indspec Chemical Corporation	451	Pittsburgh, PA	Private	124.0	378	2865
Indspec Holding Corporation	452	Pittsburgh, PA	Private	76.0	378	2865
Indspec Technologies Ltd.	453	Pittsburgh, PA	Private	76.0	378	2865
Abell Corporation	454	Monroe, LA	Private	70.0	377	2875
Cultor US Inc.	455	Ardsley, NY	Private	88.5	375	2869
Kay Chemical Company	456	Greensboro, NC	Public Family Member	44.4	375	2842
TG Soda Ash, Inc.	457	Raleigh, NC	Private	58.7	375	2812
Carson Inc.	458	Savannah, GA	Public	109.6	372	2844
Alpha Gary Corporation	459	Leominster, MA	Private	77.4	370	2821
Pluess-Staufer Industries Inc.	460	Proctor, VT	Private	58.9	370	2819
Terra Nitrogen Company LP	461	Tulsa, OK	Private	335.3	368	2873
Chesebrough-Ponds International	462	Englewood Cliffs, NJ	Private	42.7	364	2844
LSB Chemical Corp.	463	Oklahoma City, OK	Public Family Member	132.0	364	2819
Rheox Inc.	464	Hightstown, NJ	Private	137.7	361	2851
Chesebrough-Ponds Manufacturing	465	Las Piedras, PR	Private	94.3	360	2844
A M Todd Group, Inc.	466	Kalamazoo, MI	Private	50.0	355	2899
Detrex Corporation	467	Southfield, MI	Public	95.8	353	2842
NFS Service, LLC	468	Norcross, GA	Private	45.0	351	2819
Adhesives Research, Inc.	469	Glen Rock, PA	Private	60.0	350	2891
Amethyst Investment Group	470	Chicago, IL	Private	41.0	350	2844
D & K Group, Inc.	471	Elk Grove Village, IL	Private	54.8	350	2891
De La Rue Card Systems Inc.	472	Exton, PA	Private	73.0	350	2821
Loveland Industries Inc.	473	Greeley, CO	Public Family Member	249.0	350	2879
Luster Products Inc.	474	Chicago, IL	Private	25.0	350	2844
Magruder Color Co. Inc.	475	Elizabeth, NJ	Private	80.0	350	2865
Novo Nordisk Biochem, NA	476	Franklinton, NC	Private	150.0	350	2869
Nuclear Fuel Services Inc.	477	Erwin, TN	Private	45.0	350	2819
Owen Oil Tools Inc.	478	Fort Worth, TX	Private	50.0	350	2892
Pavion Limited	479	North Arlington, NJ	Private	70.0	350	2844
Plasti-Kote Co., Inc.	480	Medina, OH	Private	95.0	350	2851
Pursell Industries Inc.	481	Sylacauga, AL	Private	60.9	350	2875
Scott Chemical Co, Inc.	482	Englewood, NJ	Private	80.0	350	2844
Scott's Liquid Gold, Inc.	483	Denver, CO	Public	50.5	350	2842
Scotts-Sierra Hort Products Co.	484	Marysville, OH	Public Family Member	107.0	350	2873
Tanning Research Laboratories	485	Ormond Beach, FL	Private	41.0	350	2844
Terra Nitrogen Company, LP	486	Sioux City, IA	Private	335.3	350	2873
DSM Chemicals North America	487	Augusta, GA	Private	55.4	348	2819
Frit Inc.	488	Ozark, AL	Private	69.9	345	2873
The Ensign-Bickford Company	489	Simsbury, CT	Private	127.3	345	2892
Eftec North America LLC	490	Madison Heights, MI	Public Family Member	100.0	343	2891

D&B COMPANY RANKINGS BY EMPLOYMENT

Company	Rank	Location	Type	Sales ($ mil.)	Employ- ment	Primary SIC
Cerdec Corporation	491	Washington, PA	Private	70.0	340	2865
Gb Biosciences Corp.	492	Wilmington, DE	Private	69.2	340	2879
Sovereign Specialty Chem, LP	493	Chicago, IL	Private	134.8	340	2891
Tinkerbell Inc.	494	Stamford, CT	Private	44.8	340	2844
SPI Holdings, Inc.	495	New Castle, DE	Private	78.6	335	2869
SPI Polyols, Inc.	496	New Castle, DE	Private	78.6	335	2869
Sterling Fibers Inc.	497	Milton, FL	Public Family Member	33.3	333	2824
Airgas Intermountain Inc.	498	Fort Collins, CO	Public Family Member	37.5	330	2813
Interplastic Corporation	499	Saint Paul, MN	Private	250.0	330	2821
Jafra Cosmetics International	500	Thousand Oaks, CA	Private	38.6	330	2844
Ohio Sealants Inc.	501	Mentor, OH	Private	51.6	330	2891
TACC International Corporation	502	Rockland, MA	Public Family Member	51.6	330	2891
E Q Holding Company	503	Wayne, MI	Private	76.7	327	2869
IT Holding Inc.	504	Copperhill, TN	Private	52.0	327	2819
Aware Products Inc.	505	Chatsworth, CA	Private	38.0	325	2844
Beverly Giorgio Hills Inc.	506	Santa Monica, CA	Public Family Member	100.0	325	2844
El Dorado Chemical Company	507	Oklahoma City, OK	Public Family Member	131.8	325	2819
Phibro-Tech, Inc.	508	Fort Lee, NJ	Private	85.0	325	2819
Tiro Industries, Inc.	509	Minneapolis, MN	Private	24.0	325	2844
Lamaur Corporation	510	Mill Valley, CA	Public	118.5	323	2844
Spraylat Corporation	511	Mount Vernon, NY	Private	60.5	322	2851
Formosa Plastics Corp. Louisiana	512	Livingston, NJ	Private	350.0	321	2821
Merichem Company	513	Houston, TX	Private	88.3	321	2869
Millennium Petrochemicals Inc.	514	Cincinnati, OH	Public Family Member	350.0	320	2869
Mohawk Finishing Products Inc.	515	Amsterdam, NY	Public Family Member	48.1	320	2851
Schwarzkopf & Dep Corporation	516	Compton, CA	Private	104.4	320	2844
Reagent Chemical & Research	517	Middlesex, NJ	Private	70.0	319	2819
Texas Petrochemical Holdings	518	Houston, TX	Private	74.7	319	2869
Texas Petrochemicals Corp.	519	Houston, TX	Private	514.8	318	2869
S F Phosphates, LLC	520	Rock Springs, WY	Private	100.0	317	2874
Continental Carbon Company	521	Houston, TX	Private	100.0	315	2895
CSRC USA Corp.	522	Houston, TX	Private	62.3	315	2895
Rusk Inc.	523	Stamford, CT	Private	36.8	315	2844
Diefenthal Investments, LLC	524	New Orleans, LA	Private	64.5	311	2821
Stockhausen Inc.	525	Greensboro, NC	Private	195.0	311	2869
Ausimont Industries Inc.	526	Thorofare, NJ	Private	64.3	310	2821
Polymer Dynamics Inc.	527	Allentown, PA	Private	22.0	310	2823
Teknor Color Company	528	Pawtucket, RI	Private	36.3	307	2821
Farmland Hydro, LP	529	Bartow, FL	Private	300.0	306	2874
Alper Holdings USA, Inc.	530	New York, NY	Private	36.6	300	2893
Aristech Acrylics LLC	531	Florence, KY	Private	61.0	300	2821
Belae Brands Inc.	532	Phoenix, AZ	Private	100.0	300	2844
Chemdal International Corp.	533	Palatine, IL	Public Family Member	62.1	300	2821
Cosmetic Mnfctring Rsurces LLC	534	Sun Valley, CA	Private	35.0	300	2844
Cutler Corporation	535	Portland, OR	Private	46.9	300	2891
Formosa Plastics Corp. Texas	536	Livingston, NJ	Private	960.0	300	2821
H20 Plus, LP	537	Chicago, IL	Private	20.0	300	2844
Herbert's-O'brien, Inc.	538	Houston, TX	Private	110.0	300	2851
I P S Corporation	539	Gardena, CA	Private	46.9	300	2891
Lander Co. Inc.	540	Englewood, NJ	Private	80.0	300	2844
Loctite Puerto Rico Inc.	541	Sabana Grande, PR	Private	46.9	300	2891
Neste Resins Corporation	542	Eugene, OR	Private	180.0	300	2821
New Pendulum Corporation	543	Wilmington, DE	Private	35.5	300	2842
Oakite Products, Inc.	544	Berkeley Heights, NJ	Private	70.2	300	2842
Olay Company Inc.	545	Cayey, PR	Public Family Member	35.0	300	2844
Para-Chem Southern Inc.	546	Simpsonville, SC	Private	85.0	300	2843
PCL Group, Inc.	547	Cincinnati, OH	Private	60.0	300	2865
Pro-Line Corporation	548	Dallas, TX	Private	40.5	300	2844
Qualitek International, Inc.	549	Addison, IL	Private	25.0	300	2899
Reedco Inc.	550	Humacao, PR	Public Family Member	18.4	300	2844
Technic Inc.	551	Cranston, RI	Private	100.0	300	2899
United Laboratories Inc.	552	Saint Charles, IL	Private	22.0	300	2842
United Wtr Svcs Milwaukee, LLC	553	Milwaukee, WI	Private	42.1	300	2899
Van Ru Inc.	554	Evansville, IN	Private	25.0	300	2891
Watson Industries, Inc.	555	Harwick, PA	Private	45.0	300	2851
Progressive Ink Company Inc.	556	Sheridan, AR	Private	36.3	297	2893
Coates Brothers Inc.	557	Houston, TX	Private	35.4	290	2893
Soft Sheen Products	558	Chicago, IL	Private	33.8	290	2844
U S Agri-Chemicals Corp	559	Fort Meade, FL	Private	201.3	290	2874
Washington Penn Plastic Co.	560	Washington, PA	Private	132.0	290	2821

D&B COMPANY RANKINGS BY EMPLOYMENT

Company	Rank	Location	Type	Sales ($ mil.)	Employ-ment	Primary SIC
Dawn Chemical Company Inc.	561	Marietta, GA	Private	53.0	287	2842
Zegarelli Group International	562	Burbank, CA	Private	15.2	287	2844
Chemetals Incorporated	563	Baltimore, MD	Private	65.0	285	2819
Stephan Co. Inc.	564	Fort Lauderdale, FL	Public	27.1	285	2844
Engineered Carbons, Inc.	565	Port Neches, TX	Private	56.2	284	2895
Beauticontrol Cosmetics Inc.	566	Carrollton, TX	Public	69.4	280	2844
Filtrol Corporation	567	Los Angeles, CA	Private	44.3	280	2819
Springfield Products, Inc.	568	Springfield, KY	Private	25.0	280	2821
Standridge Color Corporation	569	Social Circle, GA	Private	125.0	280	2865
Truseal Technologies, Inc.	570	Cleveland, OH	Private	65.0	280	2891
Croda Inc.	571	Parsippany, NJ	Private	65.0	278	2869
Duncan Enterprises	572	Fresno, CA	Private	41.3	276	2851
A M Todd Company	573	Kalamazoo, MI	Private	200.0	275	2899
Airgas Carbonic, Inc.	574	Duluth, GA	Public Family Member	31.2	275	2813
Arizona Natural Resources Inc.	575	Phoenix, AZ	Private	30.5	275	2844
Bronner Brothers Inc.	576	Marietta, GA	Private	17.1	275	2844
Coronado Paint Co. Inc.	577	Edgewater, FL	Private	61.4	275	2851
Gojo Industries Inc.	578	Cuyahoga Falls, OH	Private	100.0	275	2842
Morgan Chemical Products Inc.	579	Tucker, GA	Private	32.5	275	2842
Nu-West Industries, Inc.	580	Soda Springs, ID	Private	55.0	275	2874
Packaging Advantage Corp.	581	Los Angeles, CA	Private	15.0	275	2841
Takasago International Corp., USA	582	Northvale, NJ	Private	120.0	275	2844
USAC Holdings Inc.	583	Fort Meade, FL	Private	29.7	275	2874
Hammond Group, Inc.	584	Hammond, IN	Private	125.0	270	2819
Megas Beauty Care Inc.	585	Cleveland, OH	Public Family Member	31.4	270	2844
Hewitt Soap Co.	586	Dayton, OH	Public Family Member	25.0	267	2841
B F Goodrich Textile Chemicals	587	Charlotte, NC	Public Family Member	42.1	266	2819
Piedmont Chemical Industries	588	High Point, NC	Private	75.0	265	2841
Westlake Polymers Corporation	589	Houston, TX	Private	18.9	265	2822
3V Inc.	590	Georgetown, SC	Private	70.0	260	2869
Celgard, LLC	591	Charlotte, NC	Private	53.3	260	2821
Goldschmidt Chemical Corp	592	Hopewell, VA	Private	60.1	260	2869
Kind & Knox Gelatin, Inc.	593	Sergeant Bluff, IA	Private	36.4	260	2899
Mautz Paint Co.	594	Madison, WI	Private	31.0	260	2851
Ta Manufacturing. Co.	595	Valencia, CA	Public Family Member	53.3	260	2821
Testor Corporation	596	Rockford, IL	Public Family Member	50.0	260	2851
Verdant Brands Inc.	597	Minneapolis, MN	Public	30.0	260	2879
Nalco Diversified Technologies	598	Chagrin Falls, OH	Public Family Member	54.0	255	2899
Plast-O-Meric Inc.	599	Sussex, WI	Public Family Member	75.0	255	2821
Tnemec Company, Inc.	600	Kansas City, MO	Private	67.7	255	2851
Marpax	601	West Sacramento, CA	Private	125.0	253	2893
Johnson Products Co. Inc.	602	Chicago, IL	Public Family Member	50.0	252	2844
Fashion Laboratories Inc.	603	Fair Lawn, NJ	Public Family Member	29.1	251	2844
All-Pure Chemical Co.	604	Walnut Creek, CA	Public Family Member	39.2	250	2812
Aloe Vera Of America Inc.	605	Dallas, TX	Private	112.6	250	2844
Belmay Company, Inc.	606	Yonkers, NY	Private	29.0	250	2844
Buffalo Color Corporation	607	Parsippany, NJ	Private	55.0	250	2865
Cedar Chemical Corporation	608	Memphis, TN	Private	140.0	250	2873
Davlyn Industries Inc.	609	Cranbury, NJ	Private	26.0	250	2844
Elmers Products Inc.	610	Columbus, OH	Private	125.0	250	2891
Freeman Cosmetic Corporation	611	Los Angeles, CA	Public Family Member	57.4	250	2844
Gustafson, Inc.	612	Plano, TX	Public Family Member	93.2	250	2879
Iowa Paint Manufacturing Co. Inc.	613	Des Moines, IA	Private	36.1	250	2851
Mulberry Corporation	614	Mulberry, FL	Private	130.0	250	2874
New South Chemicals, Inc.	615	Atlanta, GA	Private	39.5	250	2819
Puretek Corporation	616	San Fernando, CA	Private	28.3	250	2844
Rutgers Organics Corporation	617	State College, PA	Private	70.0	250	2865
Sartomer Company Inc.	618	Exton, PA	Private	175.0	250	2819
Southern Ionics Inc.	619	West Point, MS	Private	77.0	250	2819
Stoller Group, Inc.	620	Houston, TX	Private	60.0	250	2879
Tessenderlo Investments, Inc.	621	Phoenix, AZ	Private	75.3	250	2873
The Braden-Sutphin Ink Co.	622	Cleveland, OH	Private	40.0	250	2893
Thibiant International Inc.	623	Beverly Hills, CA	Private	80.0	250	2844
Unilever Home & Personal	624	New York, NY	Private	29.0	250	2844
Western Tar Products Corp.	625	Terre Haute, IN	Private	49.8	250	2865
Quality Chemicals Inc.	626	Tyrone, PA	Public Family Member	71.0	245	2869
Coastal Chem Inc.	627	Cheyenne, WY	Public Family Member	160.0	244	2873
Williams Ethanol Services Inc.	628	Pekin, IL	Public Family Member	275.0	243	2869
Dragoco Inc.	629	Totowa, NJ	Private	61.9	240	2869
Fairfield Processing Corp.	630	Danbury, CT	Private	24.0	240	2824

D&B COMPANY RANKINGS BY EMPLOYMENT

Company	Rank	Location	Type	Sales ($ mil.)	Employ-ment	Primary SIC
Mississippi Phosphates Corp.	631	Pascagoula, MS	Public Family Member	48.0	240	2874
Waterbury Companies Inc.	632	Waterbury, CT	Private	40.0	240	2813
U.N.X. Incorporated	633	Greenville, NC	Private	30.0	236	2842
First Chemical Corporation	634	Jackson, MS	Public Family Member	174.3	235	2865
Kerr-Mcgee Oil & Gas Corp.	635	Houston, TX	Public Family Member	29.4	235	2816
The P D George Company	636	Saint Louis, MO	Private	75.2	235	2851
Ablestik Laboratories	637	Compton, CA	Private	35.8	230	2891
Amrep, Inc.	638	Marietta, GA	Private	27.1	230	2842
Ausimont Financial Corp.	639	Thorofare, NJ	Private	35.8	230	2891
Color Wheel Paint Manufacturing Co.	640	Orlando, FL	Private	26.5	230	2851
Kasper Inc.	641	Mahwah, NJ	Private	26.6	230	2844
MG International Inc.	642	Dallas, GA	Private	16.8	230	2821
Mulberry Phosphates Inc.	643	Mulberry, FL	Private	46.0	230	2874
The Benjamin Ansehl Co.	644	Saint Louis, MO	Private	50.0	230	2844
The Butcher Company Inc.	645	Marlborough, MA	Private	65.0	230	2842
Uniseal Inc.	646	Evansville, IN	Private	26.0	230	2891
Vinings Industries Inc.	647	Atlanta, GA	Private	36.2	230	2819
Omnium, LLC	648	Saint Joseph, MO	Private	18.0	228	2879
Color Converting Industries Co.	649	Des Moines, IA	Private	50.0	225	2893
Micro Lithography, Inc.	650	Sunnyvale, CA	Private	51.5	225	2869
Nelson Brothers Inc.	651	Birmingham, AL	Private	26.0	225	2892
Smiland Paint Company	652	Los Angeles, CA	Private	33.4	225	2851
Styling Technology Corporation	653	Scottsdale, AZ	Public	38.1	225	2844
T M V Corporation	654	Miami, FL	Private	26.0	225	2844
Gans Ink And Supply Co. Inc.	655	Los Angeles, CA	Private	26.0	220	2893
Marianna Imports, Inc.	656	Omaha, NE	Private	37.3	220	2844
Northern Labs Inc.	657	Manitowoc, WI	Private	48.0	220	2842
P C R Inc.	658	Gainesville, FL	Private	50.0	220	2869
West Agro Inc.	659	Kansas City, MO	Private	44.3	220	2879
Worthen Industries Inc.	660	Nashua, NH	Private	34.2	220	2891
Specialty Chemical Resources	661	Macedonia, OH	Public	40.3	219	2842
American Pacific Corporation	662	Las Vegas, NV	Public	52.3	218	2819
Blue Coral-Slick 50 Ltd	663	Cleveland, OH	Private	25.3	215	2842
Carus Corporation	664	Peru, IL	Private	46.8	214	2819
Share Corporation	665	Milwaukee, WI	Private	20.6	213	2842
Chemical Specialties Inc.	666	Charlotte, NC	Private	33.3	212	2819
High Point Chemical Corp.	667	High Point, NC	Private	98.7	211	2843
Solvay Interox, Inc.	668	Houston, TX	Private	130.0	211	2819
Apollo Colors Inc.	669	Joliet, IL	Private	56.2	210	2865
Cardinal Industrial Finishes	670	El Monte, CA	Private	31.1	210	2851
Imperial Adhesives Inc.	671	Cincinnati, OH	Public Family Member	40.6	210	2891
Spartan Chemical Co. Inc.	672	Toledo, OH	Private	24.7	210	2842
E L C Technology, Inc.	673	Fort Lauderdale, FL	Private	25.0	209	2819
American Vanguard Corp.	674	Newport Beach, CA	Public	67.7	206	2879
Shintech Incorporated	675	Houston, TX	Private	850.0	206	2821
Bruning Paint Company	676	Baltimore, MD	Private	30.4	205	2851
CPH Holding Corp.	677	Chicago, IL	Private	46.6	205	2869
Kop-Coat Inc.	678	Pittsburgh, PA	Public Family Member	61.0	205	2851
U S Cotton LLC	679	Rio Rancho, NM	Private	23.6	205	2844
Acetylene Oxygen Co.	680	Harlingen, TX	Private	25.0	200	2813
Airgas - North Central Inc.	681	Waterloo, IA	Public Family Member	60.0	200	2813
Amfibe Inc.	682	Ridgeway, VA	Private	19.0	200	2824
Anderson Chemical Company Inc.	683	Macon, GA	Private	30.1	200	2899
Canberra Corp.	684	Toledo, OH	Private	20.8	200	2842
Cincinnati Specialties, Inc.	685	Cincinnati, OH	Private	30.0	200	2819
Clearon Corp.	686	New York, NY	Private	85.0	200	2812
Clearon Holdings Inc.	687	New York, NY	Private	76.7	200	2812
Colgate-Palmolive (Pr) Inc.	688	Guayama, PR	Public Family Member	62.3	200	2842
Dana Perfumes Corp.	689	Stamford, CT	Private	110.0	200	2844
Dupli-Color Products Co.	690	Elk Grove Village, IL	Public Family Member	28.9	200	2851
Eaglebrook International Group	691	Matteson, IL	Private	28.9	200	2899
Eastman Gelatine Corporation	692	Peabody, MA	Public Family Member	81.6	200	2899
Freeport-Mcmoran Sulphur, Inc.	693	New Orleans, LA	Public	211.9	200	2819
Goldman Resources Inc.	694	Boston, MA	Private	34.6	200	2899
Ilpea Inc.	695	Fort Smith, AR	Private	40.1	200	2821
JFO, Ltd.	696	Denver, CO	Private	22.4	200	2842
Joico Laboratories Inc.	697	City Of Industry, CA	Private	51.6	200	2844
Keladon Corporation	698	Escondido, CA	Private	36.1	200	2899
Kemwater North America Co	699	Walnut Creek, CA	Public Family Member	40.7	200	2819
Kuehne Chemical Company Inc.	700	Kearny, NJ	Private	34.2	200	2819

D&B COMPANY RANKINGS BY EMPLOYMENT

Company	Rank	Location	Type	Sales ($ mil.)	Employ-ment	Primary SIC
Laporte Water Tech & Biochem	701	Alpharetta, GA	Private	53.0	200	2899
Laurence-David Inc.	702	Eugene, OR	Private	36.1	200	2851
Living Earth Technology Corp.	703	Houston, TX	Public Family Member	25.0	200	2875
Mactac, Inc.	704	Stow, OH	Public Family Member	34.4	200	2891
Mc Auley's, Inc.	705	Memphis, TN	Private	30.0	200	2844
Norton & Son	706	Los Angeles, CA	Private	28.5	200	2851
Pierre Fabre Inc.	707	Azusa, CA	Private	30.0	200	2844
Pitt Penn Oil Co. Inc.	708	Creighton, PA	Private	29.9	200	2899
Platte Chemical Co.	709	Greeley, CO	Public Family Member	42.6	200	2879
Red Devil Inc.	710	Union, NJ	Private	33.9	200	2891
Redken Laboratories Inc.	711	New York, NY	Private	100.0	200	2844
Reilly Corp.	712	Washington, DC	Private	27.2	200	2842
Shionogi Qualicaps, Inc.	713	Whitsett, NC	Private	22.0	200	2899
Tate & Lyle Citric Acid Inc.	714	Decatur, IL	Private	30.7	200	2899
Tri-Tech Laboratories Inc.	715	Lynchburg, VA	Private	21.8	200	2844
U S A Ausimont Inc.	716	Thorofare, NJ	Private	161.4	200	2821
USR Optonix Inc.	717	Hackettstown, NJ	Private	50.0	200	2819
Westlake C A & O Corporation	718	Houston, TX	Private	33.9	200	2812
Westlake Petrochemicals Corp.	719	Houston, TX	Private	48.9	200	2869
Whitford Worldwide Company	720	Malvern, PA	Private	40.4	200	2891
William Zinsser & Co. Inc.	721	Somerset, NJ	Public Family Member	36.1	200	2851
Christian Dior Perfumes Inc.	722	New York, NY	Private	50.0	198	2844
Bontex Inc.	723	Buena Vista, VA	Public	43.5	196	2824
Columbia Paint & Coatings	724	Spokane, WA	Private	33.0	195	2851
Elementis Pigments Inc.	725	Fairview Heights, IL	Private	26.9	194	2816
Albis Corporation	726	Rosenberg, TX	Private	34.4	190	2821
Ampac Inc.	727	Cedar City, UT	Public Family Member	20.0	190	2873
Betz International Inc.	728	Langhorne, PA	Public Family Member	34.2	190	2899
CBI Laboratories Inc.	729	Carrollton, TX	Public Family Member	20.9	190	2844
Elementis Chromium Inc.	730	Corpus Christi, TX	Private	75.0	190	2819
French Fragrances, Inc.	731	Hialeah, FL	Private	215.5	190	2844
K M S Research Inc.	732	Redding, CA	Private	21.0	190	2844
Pierce & Stevens Corp.	733	Buffalo, NY	Private	60.0	190	2891
Wattyl Paint Corporation	734	Atlanta, GA	Private	28.0	190	2851
Puritan/Churchill Chemical Co.	735	Marietta, GA	Private	26.3	188	2842
Shisedio America Inc.	736	Oakland, NJ	Private	90.0	188	2844
Triad Nitrogen, Inc.	737	Donaldsonville, LA	Public Family Member	49.0	188	2873
ESM II Inc.	738	Amherst, NY	Private	129.2	186	2819
Max Rittenbaum Inc.	739	Atlanta, GA	Private	21.1	185	2842
NPA Coatings Inc.	740	Cleveland, OH	Private	48.0	185	2851
Wild Flavors, Inc.	741	Erlanger, KY	Private	46.0	185	2869
Brewer Science, Inc.	742	Rolla, MO	Private	25.6	180	2851
Buckeye International Inc.	743	Maryland Heights, MO	Private	30.0	180	2842
Caesars World Merchandising	744	Las Vegas, NV	Public Family Member	22.0	180	2844
Cyanamid Agricultural de PR	745	Manati, PR	Public Family Member	257.0	180	2879
Dentco Inc.	746	Humacao, PR	Public Family Member	77.0	180	2844
Drexel Chemical Company	747	Memphis, TN	Private	80.0	180	2879
Elasco, Inc.	748	Garden Grove, CA	Private	38.4	180	2821
Lomac Inc.	749	Muskegon, MI	Private	34.6	180	2865
Manhattan Products Inc.	750	Carlstadt, NJ	Private	35.0	180	2842
Oxymar	751	Gregory, TX	Private	31.6	180	2821
TEC Specialty Products	752	Palatine, IL	Public Family Member	70.0	180	2891
Troy Corporation	753	Florham Park, NJ	Private	52.4	180	2869
Dixie Chemical Company, Inc.	754	Houston, TX	Private	36.4	179	2869
Chemtall Incorporated	755	Riceboro, GA	Private	39.3	175	2869
Day-Glo Color Corp.	756	Cleveland, OH	Public Family Member	47.0	175	2816
E T Browne Drug Co. Inc.	757	Englewood Cliffs, NJ	Private	60.0	175	2844
International Chemical Corp.	758	Amherst, NY	Private	15.0	175	2819
James Austin Co.	759	Mars, PA	Private	30.0	175	2842
Ponderosa Paint Manufacturing	760	Boise, ID	Private	18.2	175	2851
Thomas R Peck Manufacturing Co.	761	Seal Beach, CA	Private	29.4	174	2891
Inspec USA, Inc.	762	Galena, KS	Private	46.8	172	2869
Softsoap Enterprises, Inc.	763	Chaska, MN	Public Family Member	19.4	172	2841
Pace International, LP	764	Kirkland, WA	Private	44.5	171	2842
Bemis Associates, Inc.	765	Shirley, MA	Private	33.0	170	2891
Dryvit Holdings, Inc.	766	Providence, RI	Public Family Member	27.5	170	2899
Finnaren & Haley Inc.	767	Conshohocken, PA	Private	20.0	170	2851
Fritz Industries Inc.	768	Mesquite, TX	Private	58.3	170	2899
M P Associates Inc.	769	Ione, CA	Private	18.5	170	2892
Magnox Incorporated	770	Pulaski, VA	Private	22.8	170	2816

D&B COMPANY RANKINGS BY EMPLOYMENT

Company	Rank	Location	Type	Sales ($ mil.)	Employ-ment	Primary SIC
Monarch Rubber Company	771	Baltimore, MD	Private	17.7	170	2822
Norfluor USA, LLC	772	Jacksonville Beach, FL	Private	16.0	170	2819
Technical Coatings Co.	773	Flanders, NJ	Public Family Member	55.0	170	2851
United Gilsonite Laboratories	774	Scranton, PA	Private	27.3	170	2851
Vi-Jon Laboratories Inc.	775	Saint Louis, MO	Private	55.0	170	2844
Wellborn-De Corp	776	Albuquerque, NM	Private	19.6	170	2851
Omya, Inc.	777	Proctor, VT	Private	29.9	166	2819
Miller Paint Co. Inc.	778	Portland, OR	Private	31.5	165	2851
Sigma Coatings USA BV	779	Harvey, LA	Private	60.0	165	2851
SP Acquisition Co.	780	Fort Worth, TX	Private	35.1	165	2821
Dystar LP	781	Charlotte, NC	Private	200.0	164	2865
Korex Corporation	782	Wixom, MI	Private	48.0	164	2841
Akzo Nobel Fortafil Fibers	783	Rockwood, TN	Private	45.0	163	2824
Amax Metals Recovery Inc.	784	Tempe, AZ	Public Family Member	28.8	163	2819
Intercontinental Polymer Inc.	785	Morristown, TN	Private	56.0	163	2821
California Products Corp.	786	Cambridge, MA	Private	44.0	162	2851
Landec Corporation	787	Menlo Park, CA	Public	33.5	162	2819
Micro-Flo Co.	788	Memphis, TN	Private	150.0	162	2879
Betco Corporation	789	Toledo, OH	Private	38.0	160	2841
Brulin & Company Inc.	790	Indianapolis, IN	Private	15.0	160	2842
Coroplast Inc.	791	Dallas, TX	Private	25.0	160	2821
Emerson Cming Composite Metals Inc.	792	Canton, MA	Private	22.4	160	2819
Hillyard Enterprises, Inc.	793	Saint Joseph, MO	Private	16.2	160	2842
Mc Cormick Paint Works Co.	794	Rockville, MD	Private	21.9	160	2851
Merichem Salsol USA, LLC	795	Houston, TX	Private	33.8	160	2869
Olga G Marcus Cosmetics Inc.	796	Hauppauge, NY	Private	22.3	160	2844
OMG America's Inc.	797	Cleveland, OH	Public Family Member	39.2	160	2869
The B F Goodrich Company	798	Taylors, SC	Private	25.0	160	2843
Twincraft Inc.	799	Winooski, VT	Private	17.0	160	2841
Z L Star Inc.	800	Houston, TX	Private	30.0	160	2824
Dryvit Systems Inc.	801	West Warwick, RI	Public Family Member	30.6	159	2899
Ekc Technology Inc.	802	Hayward, CA	Public Family Member	28.5	159	2899
MEMC Pasadena, Inc.	803	Pasadena, TX	Public Family Member	30.0	159	2869
Vanderbilt Chemical Corp.	804	Norwalk, CT	Private	29.9	158	2869
Hickson (USA) Corp.	805	Smyrna, GA	Private	24.9	156	2899
IPI International Inc.	806	Elkton, MD	Private	36.9	156	2869
Embers Charcoal Company Inc.	807	Conway, SC	Private	18.0	155	2861
U.S. Paint Corporation	808	Saint Louis, MO	Private	35.0	155	2851
Handschy Industries Inc.	809	Bellwood, IL	Private	40.0	154	2893
Sylvachem Corp.	810	Panama City, FL	Public Family Member	36.8	154	2869
Dover Chemical Corporation	811	Dover, OH	Private	50.0	153	2819
Nippon Steel Chemcial Corporation	812	Brighton, MI	Private	55.6	153	2821
Coates Screen Inc.	813	East Rutherford, NJ	Private	24.2	152	2893
A B C Compounding Company Inc.	814	Morrow, GA	Private	19.1	150	2842
Alden & Ott Printing Inks Co.	815	Arlington Heights, IL	Private	20.0	150	2893
Amerchol Corporation	816	Edison, NJ	Public Family Member	88.0	150	2841
Anchor Paint Manufacturing Co.	817	Tulsa, OK	Private	25.0	150	2851
Anchor/Lith-Kem-Ko, Inc.	818	Orange Park, FL	Private	45.0	150	2899
Autolign Manufacturing Group Inc.	819	Milan, MI	Private	30.0	150	2821
C & I Holdings, Inc.	820	Saint Louis, MO	Private	15.0	150	2842
Ceda International, Inc.	821	Fort Collins, CO	Private	21.8	150	2819
Chemical Packaging Corp.	822	Paducah, KY	Private	21.2	150	2899
Connoisseurs Products Corp.	823	Woburn, MA	Private	19.6	150	2842
Consep Inc.	824	Bend, OR	Public	39.2	150	2879
Cosmar Corporation	825	Garden Grove, CA	Private	22.2	150	2844
D B J Enterprises Inc.	826	Houston, TX	Private	50.0	150	2879
Du Pont Ag Caribe Industries	827	Manati, PR	Public Family Member	27.0	150	2879
Du Pont Agrichemicals Caribe	828	Manati, PR	Public Family Member	598.2	150	2879
Dymon, Inc.	829	Olathe, KS	Public Family Member	22.8	150	2842
Farouk Systems Inc.	830	Houston, TX	Private	24.0	150	2844
Faultless Starch/Bon Ami Co.	831	Kansas City, MO	Private	62.4	150	2842
Goulston Technologies Inc.	832	Monroe, NC	Private	62.0	150	2843
Graham Webb International Corp.	833	Carlsbad, CA	Private	75.0	150	2844
Holtrachem Manufacturing Co., LLC	834	Natick, MA	Private	42.0	150	2812
J F Daley International Ltd.	835	Chicago, IL	Private	18.3	150	2842
Jewel Chemical Co.	836	Chicago, IL	Private	15.5	150	2841
Leiner Davis Gelatin Corp.	837	Great Neck, NY	Private	26.8	150	2899
Milford Fertilizer Co.	838	Milford, DE	Public Family Member	94.2	150	2875
Mitsui Chemicals America Inc.	839	Purchase, NY	Private	40.2	150	2869
Neste Polyester Inc.	840	Fort Smith, AR	Private	22.0	150	2851

D&B COMPANY RANKINGS BY EMPLOYMENT

Company	Rank	Location	Type	Sales ($ mil.)	Employ-ment	Primary SIC
O'neil Color And Compounding	841	Garfield, NJ	Private	38.1	150	2865
Old World Industries, Inc.	842	Northbrook, IL	Private	22.9	150	2899
P D Glycol Ltd.	843	Beaumont, TX	Private	160.0	150	2821
Pace Industries Inc.	844	Reedsburg, WI	Private	25.0	150	2821
Perrigo Company Of Missouri	845	Saint Louis, MO	Public Family Member	16.7	150	2844
Pilot Chemical Corp.	846	Santa Fe Springs, CA	Private	62.6	150	2843
Preservative Paint Co.	847	Seattle, WA	Private	16.0	150	2851
SLG Chemicals, Inc.	848	Denver, CO	Public Family Member	19.4	150	2899
Standard Chlorine Chemical Co.	849	New Castle, DE	Private	28.4	150	2865
Standard Chlorine Of Del Co.	850	New Castle, DE	Private	33.9	150	2865
Strickland J & Co.	851	Memphis, TN	Private	15.9	150	2844
The Hall Chemical Co.	852	Wickliffe, OH	Private	25.8	150	2819
Valley Products Co.	853	Memphis, TN	Private	17.6	150	2841
Ventana Medical Systems, Inc.	854	Tucson, AZ	Public	32.2	150	2819
Epsilon Products Co, JV	855	Marcus Hook, PA	Private	130.0	148	2821
Mona Industries Inc.	856	Paterson, NJ	Private	20.0	146	2843
Vogel Paint & Wax Company Inc.	857	Orange City, IA	Private	38.7	146	2851
Diversified Chemical Tech	858	Detroit, MI	Private	49.2	145	2891
Lanco Manufacturing Corp.	859	San Lorenzo, PR	Private	40.9	145	2891
Uyemura International Corp.	860	Ontario, CA	Private	50.0	145	2819
Laporte Cnstr Chem, NA	861	Mentor, OH	Private	24.3	142	2891
Aeropres Corporation	862	Shreveport, LA	Private	60.0	140	2813
American Carbide & Carbon Corp	863	Keokuk, IA	Public Family Member	35.0	140	2819
Boehme-Filatex Inc.	864	Reidsville, NC	Private	30.7	140	2869
C B Fleet International Inc.	865	Lynchburg, VA	Private	25.0	140	2844
Cast Products Corp.	866	Elkhart, IN	Private	30.5	140	2891
Chem Fleur Inc.	867	Newark, NJ	Private	90.0	140	2899
Collaborative Laboratories	868	East Setauket, NY	Private	20.0	140	2844
CPS Corp.	869	Dunkirk, NY	Private	50.0	140	2893
D H Compounding Company	870	Clinton, TN	Private	30.9	140	2821
Delta Technical Coatings, Inc.	871	Whittier, CA	Private	40.0	140	2851
Evode USA Inc.	872	Leominster, MA	Private	31.5	140	2821
Grace Chemicals, Inc.	873	Boca Raton, FL	Public Family Member	22.1	140	2819
Houston Kik Inc.	874	Houston, TX	Private	35.0	140	2842
Kca Engineered Plastics, Inc.	875	San Francisco, CA	Private	35.0	140	2821
KMCO Inc.	876	Crosby, TX	Private	78.5	140	2899
P B I/Gordon Corporation	877	Kansas City, MO	Private	28.8	140	2879
Plasticolors, Inc.	878	Ashtabula, OH	Private	28.0	140	2816
Rossborough Manufacturing Co., LP	879	Avon Lake, OH	Private	40.0	140	2899
Standard Fusee Corporation	880	Easton, MD	Private	20.0	140	2899
Systems Mch Automtn Components	881	Carlsbad, CA	Private	20.0	140	2822
TCI Inc.	882	Ellaville, GA	Public Family Member	30.0	140	2851
Trico Solutions, Inc.	883	Eau Claire, WI	Private	60.0	140	2842
Zeeland Chemicals, Inc.	884	Zeeland, MI	Public Family Member	40.0	140	2869
Harrison Paint Corp.	885	Canton, OH	Private	15.0	139	2851
Pioneer/Eclipse Corporation	886	Sparta, NC	Private	28.5	139	2842
Ruco Polymer Corporation	887	Hicksville, NY	Private	80.8	138	2821
West Chemical Products Inc.	888	Princeton, NJ	Private	22.3	138	2842
Thermofil Inc.	889	Brighton, MI	Private	59.8	137	2821
Parlux Fragrances Inc.	890	Fort Lauderdale, FL	Public	62.4	136	2844
Caschem Inc.	891	Bayonne, NJ	Public Family Member	55.0	135	2869
CCA Industries, Inc.	892	East Rutherford, NJ	Public	41.4	135	2844
D K USA Ltd.	893	Garden City, NY	Private	17.5	135	2844
Deft Incorporated	894	Irvine, CA	Private	38.5	135	2851
Deltech Holdings Corp.	895	Whippany, NJ	Private	59.0	135	2821
Hickson Danchem Corporation	896	Danville, VA	Private	25.2	135	2843
Inolex Chemical Company	897	Philadelphia, PA	Private	31.6	135	2821
Inolex Group Inc.	898	Philadelphia, PA	Private	31.6	135	2821
Lignotech USA Inc.	899	Rothschild, WI	Private	34.9	135	2861
Magnox Pulaski Incorporated	900	Pulaski, VA	Private	16.0	135	2816
New Energy Corp.	901	South Bend, IN	Private	92.4	135	2869
OMG Fidelity Inc.	902	Newark, NJ	Public Family Member	45.0	135	2899
Resinall Corp.	903	Stamford, CT	Private	80.0	135	2821
Richland Research Corp.	904	Phoenix, AZ	Private	20.0	135	2869
Seymour Of Sycamore, Inc.	905	Sycamore, IL	Private	38.0	135	2851
Edlon Inc.	906	Avondale, PA	Public Family Member	15.0	134	2821
Organic Dyestuffs Corporation	907	East Providence, RI	Private	18.2	134	2861
Haldor Topsoe Inc.	908	Houston, TX	Private	18.7	133	2819
Fertilizer Company Arizona Inc.	909	Casa Grande, AZ	Private	24.5	132	2875
Tennessee Electro Minerals	910	Greeneville, TN	Private	25.0	132	2819

D&B COMPANY RANKINGS BY EMPLOYMENT

Company	Rank	Location	Type	Sales ($ mil.)	Employ-ment	Primary SIC
IMC Nitrogen Company	911	East Dubuque, IL	Public Family Member	33.9	131	2873
Midwest Zinc Corporation	912	Millington, TN	Public Family Member	18.2	131	2816
Anderson Development Company	913	Adrian, MI	Private	50.0	130	2821
Bulk Molding Compounds, Inc.	914	West Chicago, IL	Private	27.4	130	2821
Chicago Specialties Inc.	915	Chicago, IL	Private	60.0	130	2869
CLO White Company Inc.	916	Hampton, GA	Private	15.3	130	2842
Continental Carbonic Products Inc.	917	Decatur, IL	Private	17.0	130	2813
Cortec Corporation	918	Saint Paul, MN	Private	16.8	130	2899
D & K International, Inc.	919	Elk Grove Village, IL	Private	18.4	130	2891
High Plains Corporation	920	Wichita, KS	Public	84.9	130	2869
Hudson Technologies, Inc.	921	Pearl River, NY	Public	23.0	130	2869
Huron Tech Corp.	922	Delco, NC	Private	80.0	130	2812
Johann Haltermann Ltd.	923	Houston, TX	Private	31.9	130	2869
Metal Coatings International	924	Chardon, OH	Private	17.1	130	2899
Nepera, Inc.	925	Harriman, NY	Public Family Member	60.0	130	2869
Noville Inc.	926	South Hackensack, NJ	Private	38.0	130	2899
Parker Paint Manufacturing Co.	927	Tacoma, WA	Private	20.6	130	2851
Perry & Derrick Co	928	Cincinnati, OH	Private	17.3	130	2851
Pfister Chemical Inc.	929	Ridgefield, NJ	Private	20.0	130	2865
Scott Paint Corp.	930	Sarasota, FL	Private	20.0	130	2851
Specialtychem Products Corp.	931	Marinette, WI	Private	35.0	130	2869
Sterling Paint, Inc.	932	Little Rock, AR	Private	17.2	130	2851
Toray Composites Of America	933	Tacoma, WA	Private	50.0	130	2821
Fine Fragrances Distributions	934	New York, NY	Private	47.0	129	2844
La-Co Industries, Inc.	935	Elk Grove Village, IL	Private	25.0	129	2899
Cartridge Actuated Devices	936	Fairfield, NJ	Private	18.2	128	2892
Brent America Holdings, Inc.	937	La Mirada, CA	Private	16.2	127	2842
Abco Industries Incorporated	938	Roebuck, SC	Public Family Member	55.0	125	2843
Aervoe Pacific Company, Inc.	939	Gardnerville, NV	Private	25.0	125	2851
Agsco Inc.	940	Grand Forks, ND	Private	41.9	125	2879
Airgas Dry Ice	941	San Antonio, TX	Public Family Member	15.0	125	2813
Cardinal Companies, LP	942	Columbia, SC	Private	40.0	125	2869
Chemdal Corporation	943	Palatine, IL	Public Family Member	100.0	125	2821
Daicolor-Pope Inc.	944	Paterson, NJ	Private	45.0	125	2816
Emsco Inc.	945	Girard, PA	Private	16.0	125	2842
Insl-X Products Corp.	946	Stony Point, NY	Private	19.8	125	2851
National Genetics Institute	947	Los Angeles, CA	Private	30.0	125	2869
Paulsboro Packaging Co	948	Paulsboro, NJ	Public Family Member	15.8	125	2842
Petroferm Inc.	949	Fernandina Beach, FL	Private	25.0	125	2899
Polymeric Resources Corp.	950	Wayne, NJ	Private	42.0	125	2821
Premiere Packaging Inc.	951	Flint, MI	Private	34.1	125	2842
Stevens Paint Corp	952	Stony Point, NY	Private	19.5	125	2851
Styrochem US Inc.	953	Phoenix, AZ	Private	26.8	125	2821
Transtar Autobody Technologies	954	Brighton, MI	Private	16.2	125	2842
Vicksburg Chemical Company	955	Memphis, TN	Private	78.0	125	2873
Wright Chemical Corporation	956	Wilmington, NC	Private	35.0	125	2869
Calabrian Corporation	957	Kingwood, TX	Private	20.0	124	2819
Drake Extrusion Inc.	958	Ridgeway, VA	Private	22.2	124	2821
Muscle Shoals Minerals Inc.	959	Cherokee, AL	Private	19.6	124	2819
Catawba-Charlab Inc.	960	Charlotte, NC	Private	26.0	123	2869
International Academy	961	Sylmar, CA	Private	28.8	123	2869
Conap Inc.	962	Olean, NY	Public Family Member	22.6	122	2821
Cordova Labs	963	Sylmar, CA	Private	23.1	122	2879
Systech Environmental Corp.	964	Xenia, OH	Public Family Member	26.0	121	2869
Apollo Industries Inc.	965	Smyrna, GA	Private	17.0	120	2813
Bayshore Industrial Inc.	966	La Porte, TX	Public Family Member	35.0	120	2821
Brent America, Inc.	967	La Mirada, CA	Private	27.0	120	2869
Ethox Chemicals, LLC	968	Greenville, SC	Private	50.0	120	2843
Fremont Industries, Inc.	969	Shakopee, MN	Private	17.5	120	2819
Frit Industries Inc.	970	Ozark, AL	Private	18.0	120	2873
Gage Corporation	971	Ferndale, MI	Private	26.7	120	2869
Kiss Nail Products, Inc.	972	Port Washington, NY	Private	31.1	120	2844
Kutol Products Company	973	Cincinnati, OH	Private	15.0	120	2841
Lit Tel Systems USA Inc.	974	Spring Valley, NY	Private	25.9	120	2821
Lykes Agri Sales Inc.	975	Dade City, FL	Private	22.7	120	2875
Natural White Manufacturing	976	Tonawanda, NY	Private	15.5	120	2844
Penray Companies Inc.	977	Wheeling, IL	Private	31.0	120	2899
Reynolds Polymer Technology	978	Grand Junction, CO	Private	15.0	120	2821
Schnee-Morehead Inc.	979	Irving, TX	Private	22.7	120	2891
Spectra-Tone Paint Corporation	980	San Bernardino, CA	Private	21.0	120	2851

D&B COMPANY RANKINGS BY EMPLOYMENT

Company	Rank	Location	Type	Sales ($ mil.)	Employ- ment	Primary SIC
Three Bond International Inc.	981	West Chester, OH	Private	24.4	120	2891
Winbro Group Ltd	982	Woburn, MA	Private	15.6	120	2842
Chemtrusion Inc.	983	Houston, TX	Private	15.0	119	2821
Sicpa Industries Of America	984	Springfield, VA	Private	23.5	119	2893
Hostmann-Steinberg Inc.	985	Louisville, KY	Private	25.0	118	2893
Balchem Corporation	986	Slate Hill, NY	Public	28.6	117	2869
Comalloy International Company	987	Nashville, TN	Public Family Member	40.0	117	2821
Formosa Plastics Corp.	988	Livingston, NJ	Private	56.6	117	2821
ASI Investment Holding Co.	989	Akron, OH	Public Family Member	17.6	115	2821
Aztec Peroxides, Inc.	990	Houston, TX	Private	19.1	115	2819
Flo Kay Industries Inc.	991	Sioux City, IA	Private	44.0	115	2873
Heatbath Corporation	992	Springfield, MA	Private	19.7	115	2819
Mane USA	993	Wayne, NJ	Private	40.0	115	2869
Prince Manufacturing Co. Inc.	994	Quincy, IL	Private	19.5	115	2879
Rohmax USA, Inc.	995	Horsham, PA	Private	20.3	115	2899
Sun Pharmaceuticals	996	Dover, DE	Public Family Member	90.0	115	2844
Westrade USA, Inc.	997	Houston, TX	Private	20.0	115	2879
Whitmore Manufacturing Co. Inc.	998	Rockwall, TX	Public Family Member	18.5	115	2851
Fermpro Manufacturing, LP	999	Kingstree, SC	Private	19.5	114	2869
Wonder Company (Inc)	1000	Nashville, TN	Private	24.8	114	2879
Crest-Hood Foam Company, Inc.	1001	Newburyport, MA	Public Family Member	18.9	112	2851
Anzon Inc.	1002	Philadelphia, PA	Public Family Member	50.0	110	2899
Calabrian Chemical Corporation	1003	Kingwood, TX	Private	20.0	110	2869
J M Products Inc.	1004	Little Rock, AR	Private	29.0	110	2844
Johnson Paints Inc.	1005	Fort Myers, FL	Private	18.0	110	2851
Mapico, Inc.	1006	Saint Louis, MO	Private	24.1	110	2895
N S O Resins, Inc.	1007	Greenwood, SC	Private	18.4	110	2821
PMP Fermentation Products	1008	Itasca, IL	Private	24.4	110	2869
SIA Adhesives Inc.	1009	Akron, OH	Private	26.0	110	2891
Synair Corporation	1010	Chattanooga, TN	Private	19.0	110	2821
Epoxylite Corporation	1011	Irvine, CA	Private	19.1	109	2851
Elementis Specialties	1012	Jersey City, NJ	Private	35.0	108	2851
Millennium Specialty Chemicals	1013	Jacksonville, FL	Public Family Member	26.3	108	2869
Stephen J Scherer Inc.	1014	Rochester Hills, MI	Private	16.0	107	2844
Du Pont-Kansai Auto Coatings	1015	Troy, MI	Public Family Member	16.8	106	2851
EMS-Grilon Holding Inc.	1016	Sumter, SC	Private	75.7	106	2821
Apache Nitrogen Products Inc.	1017	Benson, AZ	Private	40.3	105	2873
Davis-Frost, Inc.	1018	Minneapolis, MN	Private	25.0	105	2851
Dodge Company Inc.	1019	Cambridge, MA	Private	16.0	105	2869
Formulabs, Inc.	1020	Escondido, CA	Public Family Member	18.5	105	2899
Pecora Corporation	1021	Harleysville, PA	Private	30.0	105	2891
Toyal America, Inc.	1022	Naperville, IL	Private	40.4	104	2816
Arr-Maz Products, LP	1023	Winter Haven, FL	Private	58.0	102	2869
Canning Gumm, Inc.	1024	Kearny, NJ	Private	25.0	102	2899
Primester	1025	Kingsport, TN	Private	18.2	102	2821
PCS Joint Venture Ltd.	1026	Lakeland, FL	Private	65.7	101	2875
U S L Parallel Products	1027	Rancho Cucamonga, CA	Public Family Member	30.0	101	2869
American Plant Food Corp.	1028	Galena Park, TX	Private	81.9	100	2875
Ashta Chemicals Inc.	1029	Ashtabula, OH	Private	63.0	100	2812
Blue Water Molded Systems Inc.	1030	Saint Clair, MI	Private	15.0	100	2891
Cambridge Isotope Laboratories	1031	Andover, MA	Private	27.5	100	2869
Camco Chemical Company Inc.	1032	Florence, KY	Private	26.0	100	2842
Clearwater Holdings Inc.	1033	Pittsburgh, PA	Private	22.0	100	2819
Decoart Inc.	1034	Stanford, KY	Private	20.0	100	2851
Deltech Corp.	1035	Whippany, NJ	Private	17.6	100	2899
Dexco Polymers	1036	Houston, TX	Private	19.7	100	2821
Diamond R Fertilizer Co. Inc.	1037	Fort Pierce, FL	Private	26.9	100	2873
Dispensing Containers Corp.	1038	Glen Gardner, NJ	Private	20.0	100	2813
Dri-Kleen Inc.	1039	Las Vegas, NV	Private	26.0	100	2842
Falcon Manufacturing Of Calif Inc.	1040	Los Angeles, CA	Public Family Member	20.9	100	2821
Farrell-Calhoun Inc.	1041	Memphis, TN	Private	20.1	100	2851
Fragrance Resources Inc.	1042	Clifton, NJ	Private	50.0	100	2899
General Alum & Chemical Corp.	1043	Holland, OH	Private	29.0	100	2819
Geo Specialty Chemicals Inc.	1044	Cleveland, OH	Private	16.9	100	2819
Hitachi Chemical Dupont Micro	1045	Wilmington, DE	Private	21.1	100	2821
HPD Laboratories Inc.	1046	Edison, NJ	Private	75.0	100	2842
I C I Paints (Puerto Rico)	1047	Carolina, PR	Private	40.0	100	2851
ISP Global Technologies, Inc.	1048	Wayne, NJ	Private	27.0	100	2869
Lancaster Group US, LLC	1049	New York, NY	Private	60.0	100	2844
Lenmar Inc.	1050	Baltimore, MD	Private	16.5	100	2851

D&B COMPANY RANKINGS BY EMPLOYMENT

Company	Rank	Location	Type	Sales ($ mil.)	Employ-ment	Primary SIC
Lockhart Company	1051	Gibsonia, PA	Private	20.0	100	2819
Lynwood Laboratories Inc.	1052	Needham, MA	Private	19.2	100	2879
Mc Laughlin Gormley King Co.	1053	Minneapolis, MN	Private	43.0	100	2879
Mercury Paint Corp.	1054	Brooklyn, NY	Private	15.6	100	2851
MetalsAmerica Inc.	1055	Shelby, NC	Private	55.0	100	2899
Na-Churs Plant Food, Company	1056	Marion, OH	Private	22.1	100	2875
Nassau Metals Corporation	1057	Staten Island, NY	Public Family Member	50.0	100	2819
Niles Chemical Paint Company	1058	Niles, MI	Private	17.8	100	2851
Nutra-Flo Company	1059	Sioux City, IA	Private	40.0	100	2873
Old 97 Company	1060	Tampa, FL	Public Family Member	15.0	100	2844
Orange Plastics Inc.	1061	Compton, CA	Private	20.9	100	2821
Pacer Technology	1062	Rancho Cucamonga, CA	Public	25.7	100	2891
Performance Materials Corp.	1063	Camarillo, CA	Private	15.0	100	2821
Pfanstiehl Laboratories, Inc.	1064	Waukegan, IL	Private	44.4	100	2869
Phillips Sumika Polypropylene	1065	Houston, TX	Private	275.0	100	2821
Piceu Group Limited	1066	Southfield, MI	Private	27.0	100	2851
San Mar Laboratories Inc.	1067	Elmsford, NY	Private	30.0	100	2844
Sewell Products Of Florida	1068	Auburndale, FL	Private	15.0	100	2842
Stanson Corporation	1069	Kearny, NJ	Private	20.0	100	2841
Synergistics Industries Texas	1070	Conroe, TX	Public Family Member	17.4	100	2821
The Virkler Company	1071	Charlotte, NC	Private	25.0	100	2869
Thoro Worldwide Inc.	1072	Jacksonville, FL	Private	50.0	100	2891
Trico Plastic, Inc.	1073	Azusa, CA	Private	20.9	100	2821
Ultraform Co.	1074	Theodore, AL	Private	16.7	100	2821
Vita-Green Inc.	1075	Haines City, FL	Private	17.8	100	2875
Whatcom Farmer's Co-Op	1076	Lynden, WA	Private	17.6	100	2875
Whitmire Micro-Gen Res Labs	1077	Saint Louis, MO	Private	19.1	100	2879
Williams Trading Inc.	1078	Wilmington, DE	Private	16.5	100	2851
WPT Corporation	1079	Houston, TX	Private	22.5	100	2869
International Fuel Cells, LLC	1080	South Windsor, CT	Private	24.0	99	2869
Rimtec Corporation	1081	Burlington, NJ	Private	41.7	99	2821
Norac Company Inc.	1082	Azusa, CA	Private	22.1	98	2869
Praxair Puerto Rico Inc.	1083	Gurabo, PR	Public Family Member	23.0	98	2813
Samuel Cabot Incorporated	1084	Newburyport, MA	Private	40.0	98	2851
Troy Chemical Corp.	1085	Newark, NJ	Private	16.0	98	2851
Central Ink Corporation	1086	West Chicago, IL	Private	35.6	97	2893
Jean Philippe Fragrances, Inc.	1087	New York, NY	Public	91.5	97	2844
Arcar Graphics, LLC	1088	West Chicago, IL	Private	15.0	96	2893
Perstorp Polyols Inc.	1089	Toledo, OH	Private	18.1	96	2869
Sheboygan Paint Company Inc.	1090	Sheboygan, WI	Private	20.6	96	2851
Aabbitt Adhesives Inc.	1091	Chicago, IL	Private	25.0	95	2891
Citrus and Allied Essences	1092	New Hyde Park, NY	Private	58.0	95	2899
Dyno Nobel Midwest, Inc.	1093	Quincy, IL	Private	21.0	95	2892
General Coatings Technologies	1094	Ridgewood, NY	Private	16.5	95	2851
Kleerdex Company	1095	Mount Laurel, NJ	Private	20.0	95	2821
Melamine Chemicals Inc.	1096	Donaldsonville, LA	Private	15.2	95	2821
Polarome International Inc.	1097	Jersey City, NJ	Private	100.6	95	2869
Warsaw Chemical Company, Inc.	1098	Warsaw, IN	Private	15.0	95	2842
Advanced Chemical Systems	1099	Milpitas, CA	Private	21.5	94	2819
Advanced Polymer Systems Inc.	1100	Redwood City, CA	Public	18.3	94	2822
Aluchem Inc.	1101	Cincinnati, OH	Private	25.0	94	2899
American Chemet Corporation	1102	Deerfield, IL	Private	41.9	94	2819
Solkatronic Chemicals Inc.	1103	Fairfield, NJ	Public Family Member	25.0	94	2819
Biozyme	1104	Saint Joseph, MO	Private	16.4	93	2879
Jones-Hamilton Co.	1105	Newark, CA	Private	50.0	93	2819
J L S Inv Group - WP, LLC	1106	Middleton, WI	Private	19.8	92	2879
Newport Adhesives & Composites	1107	Irvine, CA	Private	33.3	92	2891
Wisconsin Pharmacal Co. Inc.	1108	Jackson, WI	Private	18.3	92	2879
Zeochem	1109	Louisville, KY	Private	24.5	92	2819
Cardolite Corporation	1110	Newark, NJ	Private	22.6	91	2869
Ortec Inc.	1111	Easley, SC	Private	15.0	91	2869
Alliance Agronomics Inc.	1112	Mechanicsville, VA	Private	28.0	90	2875
Amspec Chemical Corporation	1113	Gloucester City, NJ	Private	25.0	90	2819
Aqua Clear Industries, LLC	1114	Watervliet, NY	Private	41.0	90	2899
Charm Sciences Inc.	1115	Malden, MA	Private	15.0	90	2899
Dallas Group Of America Inc.	1116	Whitehouse, NJ	Private	26.0	90	2819
Gulf States Asphalt Company	1117	South Houston, TX	Private	20.2	90	2891
Gulf States Specialties Inc.	1118	South Houston, TX	Private	20.2	90	2891
Hallman Paints Inc.	1119	Sun Prairie, WI	Private	20.0	90	2851
Imperial Inc.	1120	Shenandoah, IA	Private	18.3	90	2879

D&B COMPANY RANKINGS BY EMPLOYMENT

Company	Rank	Location	Type	Sales ($ mil.)	Employ-ment	Primary SIC
John Paul Mitchell Systems	1121	Santa Clarita, CA	Private	100.0	90	2844
Jos H Lowenstein & Sons Inc.	1122	Brooklyn, NY	Private	30.0	90	2865
Lobeco Products Inc.	1123	Lobeco, SC	Private	18.7	90	2865
Parfums De Coeur Ltd.	1124	Darien, CT	Private	118.0	90	2844
R B H Dispersions Inc.	1125	Bound Brook, NJ	Private	25.0	90	2865
Summit Laboratories Inc.	1126	Chicago Heights, IL	Private	35.0	90	2844
T-Chem Products	1127	Santa Fe Springs, CA	Private	27.0	90	2842
Twin State Engrg & Chem Co.	1128	Davenport, IA	Private	16.5	90	2874
Wesco Gases Inc.	1129	Billerica, MA	Private	16.5	90	2813
Eko Systems Inc.	1130	Lakewood, CO	Private	19.3	88	2879
Universal Chemical & Supply	1131	Englewood, CO	Private	15.1	88	2819
Franklin-Burlington Plastics	1132	Kearny, NJ	Public Family Member	37.0	87	2821
Lipo Chemicals Inc.	1133	Paterson, NJ	Private	60.0	87	2869
OPI Products Inc.	1134	North Hollywood, CA	Private	30.0	87	2844
R J S Scientific Inc.	1135	Port Washington, NY	Private	16.0	87	2844
Scientific Design Company	1136	Little Ferry, NJ	Private	29.5	87	2819
Eval Company Of America	1137	Lisle, IL	Private	15.8	86	2821
Akcros Chemicals America	1138	New Brunswick, NJ	Private	19.6	85	2869
Brandt Consolidated, Inc.	1139	Pleasant Plains, IL	Private	41.6	85	2875
Elan Chemical Company	1140	Newark, NJ	Private	23.7	85	2869
Esco Company, LP	1141	Muskegon, MI	Private	17.8	85	2865
JDR & Associates Inc.	1142	Santa Ana, CA	Private	17.1	85	2821
Mini Fibers Inc.	1143	Johnson City, TN	Private	27.1	85	2824
Mining Services International	1144	Sandy, UT	Public	27.0	85	2892
Nitram Inc.	1145	Tampa, FL	Private	19.7	85	2873
North American Green Inc.	1146	Evansville, IN	Private	15.4	85	2875
Weatherly Consumer Products	1147	Waco, TX	Public Family Member	24.9	85	2873
Enzyme Bio Systems Ltd.	1148	Beloit, WI	Public Family Member	36.0	84	2869
Varnco Holdings, Inc.	1149	Oakland, NJ	Private	22.0	83	2899
Mantrose-Haeuser Co., Inc.	1150	Westport, CT	Public Family Member	22.0	82	2851
Omya (California) Inc.	1151	Lucerne Valley, CA	Private	20.0	82	2819
Plasite Protective Coating	1152	Green Bay, WI	Public Family Member	23.0	82	2821
Aaba Plastic Sales Associates	1153	New York, NY	Private	15.1	80	2821
Beckman Naguabo, Inc.	1154	Naguabo, PR	Public Family Member	43.0	80	2869
Chemron Corporation	1155	Paso Robles, CA	Private	15.6	80	2843
Evans Adhesive Corporation	1156	Columbus, OH	Private	17.0	80	2891
Fabricolor Manufacturing Corp	1157	Paterson, NJ	Private	16.5	80	2865
Flecto Company Inc.	1158	Oakland, CA	Public Family Member	77.0	80	2851
Hempel Coatings USA Inc.	1159	Houston, TX	Private	25.0	80	2851
Hercules Chemical Co. Inc.	1160	Passaic, NJ	Private	25.0	80	2899
Immix Elastomers, LLC	1161	Hanover, MA	Private	33.9	80	2822
Noltex, LLC	1162	La Porte, TX	Private	35.0	80	2821
Nor-Cote International, Inc.	1163	Crawfordsville, IN	Private	16.9	80	2893
Omni Oxide, LLC	1164	Indianapolis, IN	Private	30.0	80	2819
Roman Adhesives Inc.	1165	Calumet City, IL	Private	22.6	80	2891
Roman Holdings Corporation	1166	Calumet City, IL	Private	23.1	80	2891
Spurlock Industries Inc.	1167	Waverly, VA	Public	24.7	80	2869
T-Chem Holdings, Inc.	1168	Santa Fe Springs, CA	Private	27.2	80	2842
Croda Adhesives Inc.	1169	Itasca, IL	Private	27.3	78	2891
Inchem Holdings	1170	Rock Hill, SC	Private	15.5	78	2821
Struktol Company Of America	1171	Stow, OH	Private	31.6	77	2869
Salle' International, LLC	1172	Waukegan, IL	Private	18.0	76	2844
Coronado Laboratories Inc.	1173	New Smyrna Beach, FL	Private	22.1	75	2891
Electrochemicals, Inc.	1174	Maple Plain, MN	Private	23.0	75	2899
Finetex Inc.	1175	Elmwood Park, NJ	Private	15.9	75	2869
Forrest Paint Co.	1176	Eugene, OR	Private	16.7	75	2851
Graco Fertilizer Company	1177	Cairo, GA	Private	18.8	75	2873
Gulf Lite & Wizard, Inc.	1178	Memphis, TN	Private	20.0	75	2899
K O Manufacturing Inc.	1179	Springfield, MO	Private	20.0	75	2841
Nyltech North America	1180	Manchester, NH	Private	28.7	75	2821
Profile Products, LLC	1181	Buffalo Grove, IL	Private	15.9	75	2879
Reynolds Inc.	1182	Greenville, SC	Private	20.0	75	2891
Sachem, Inc.	1183	Austin, TX	Private	24.0	75	2869
Solar Cosmetic Labs, Inc.	1184	Hialeah, FL	Private	20.8	75	2844
Southern Resources Inc.	1185	Fort Valley, GA	Public Family Member	15.4	75	2879
Spartech Compound	1186	Cape Girardeau, MO	Public Family Member	20.0	75	2821
Tolaram Polymers, Inc.	1187	Charlotte, NC	Private	47.0	75	2821
C P I Packaging Inc.	1188	Marlboro, NJ	Private	15.3	74	2821
Apollo Chemical Corp.	1189	Graham, NC	Private	25.0	72	2819
Cook & Dunn Enterprises, LLC	1190	Lodi, NJ	Private	20.0	72	2851

D&B COMPANY RANKINGS BY EMPLOYMENT

Company	Rank	Location	Type	Sales ($ mil.)	Employ-ment	Primary SIC
Spurlock Adhesives Inc.	1191	Waverly, VA	Public Family Member	30.0	72	2869
Tevco Inc.	1192	South Plainfield, NJ	Private	21.0	72	2851
G & W Enterprises, Inc.	1193	Fort Worth, TX	Private	16.0	71	2851
Apple Plastics Inc.	1194	Compton, CA	Private	15.2	70	2821
Becker Underwood Inc.	1195	Ames, IA	Private	20.0	70	2865
Capital Resin Corporation	1196	Columbus, OH	Private	25.0	70	2821
Dena Corporation	1197	Elk Grove Village, IL	Private	20.0	70	2844
Douglass Fertilizer & Chemical	1198	Altamonte Springs, FL	Private	20.7	70	2875
Ecoscience Corporation	1199	East Brunswick, NJ	Public	22.3	70	2879
GFS Chemicals, Inc.	1200	Powell, OH	Private	15.0	70	2819
Granitize Products Inc.	1201	South Gate, CA	Private	17.0	70	2842
Heucotech PL	1202	Fairless Hills, PA	Private	45.5	70	2865
Holland Colors Americas Inc.	1203	Richmond, IN	Private	16.0	70	2865
Howard Johnson's Enterprises	1204	Milwaukee, WI	Private	26.0	70	2875
Intercit, Inc.	1205	Safety Harbor, FL	Private	32.0	70	2899
Jupiter Holdings, Inc.	1206	Phoenix, AZ	Private	51.1	70	2873
KMG Chemicals Inc.	1207	Houston, TX	Public	19.5	70	2869
National Casein Co. Inc.	1208	Chicago, IL	Private	24.2	70	2891
Para Laboratories Inc.	1209	Hempstead, NY	Private	20.0	70	2844
Shincor Silicones, Inc.	1210	Akron, OH	Private	25.0	70	2822
Southern States Phosphate Fert.	1211	Savannah, GA	Private	15.2	70	2874
Sunshine Makers Inc.	1212	Huntington Beach, CA	Private	58.0	70	2842
Intercat-Savannah Inc.	1213	Manasquan, NJ	Private	28.2	68	2819
JSR Microelectronics, Inc.	1214	Sunnyvale, CA	Private	16.8	68	2869
Rycoline Products Inc.	1215	Chicago, IL	Private	15.0	67	2842
Tanner Chemicals Inc.	1216	Greenville, SC	Private	25.0	67	2843
Nicca USA Inc.	1217	Fountain Inn, SC	Private	16.7	66	2843
Alden Leeds Inc.	1218	Kearny, NJ	Private	27.3	65	2899
Brooks Industries Inc.	1219	South Plainfield, NJ	Private	20.2	65	2869
Car Brite, Inc.	1220	Indianapolis, IN	Private	19.0	65	2842
Carroll Scientific Inc.	1221	La Grange, IL	Public Family Member	20.0	65	2899
Chem Polymer Corporation	1222	Fort Myers, FL	Private	20.0	65	2821
Floralife, Inc.	1223	Walterboro, SC	Private	15.0	65	2899
Gard Products Inc.	1224	Carpentersville, IL	Private	25.0	65	2879
Gard Rogard, Inc.	1225	Carpentersville, IL	Private	25.0	65	2879
Hodgson Process Chemicals	1226	Oak Creek, WI	Private	30.0	65	2842
Hoffman Plastic Compounds	1227	Paramount, CA	Private	26.0	65	2821
Monterey Chemical Company	1228	Fresno, CA	Private	40.0	65	2879
Old Bridge Chemicals, Inc.	1229	Old Bridge, NJ	Private	20.0	65	2819
Pleasant Green Enterprises	1230	Coal City, IL	Private	20.0	65	2844
Robertet Fragrances Inc.	1231	Oakland, NJ	Private	19.0	65	2844
Royce Associates, LP	1232	East Rutherford, NJ	Private	20.0	65	2869
Penetone Corporation	1233	Tenafly, NJ	Private	15.0	64	2842
Allied Industrial Group Inc.	1234	Saint Louis, MO	Private	45.0	62	2819
Chemtech Products, Inc.	1235	Saint Louis, MO	Private	40.0	62	2819
General Polymeric Corp.	1236	Reading, PA	Private	15.0	62	2821
PCI, Inc.	1237	Wurtland, KY	Private	25.0	62	2869
Opal Technologies Inc.	1238	New York, NY	Public	17.7	61	2873
American Silicones Inc.	1239	Garrett, IN	Private	15.0	60	2822
Auto Wax Company Inc.	1240	Dallas, TX	Private	17.0	60	2842
Chattem Chemicals, Inc.	1241	Chattanooga, TN	Private	20.0	60	2869
Ecogen Inc.	1242	Langhorne, PA	Public	16.4	60	2879
Inne Dispensables Inc.	1243	Fairfield, NJ	Public Family Member	30.0	60	2844
Marchem Southeast Inc.	1244	Adairsville, GA	Private	29.7	60	2821
Pacific Pac International	1245	Hollister, CA	Private	25.0	60	2899
RSA Microtech	1246	Seattle, WA	Private	15.6	60	2819
Rudd Company Inc.	1247	Seattle, WA	Private	20.0	60	2851
Sel-Leb Marketing Inc.	1248	Paterson, NJ	Public	17.4	60	2844
Vi-Chem Corporation	1249	Grand Rapids, MI	Private	30.0	60	2821
Magnetics International Inc.	1250	Chesterton, IN	Public Family Member	15.3	58	2819
Magni-Industries Inc.	1251	Detroit, MI	Private	28.8	58	2899
Crystal Inc.-Pmc	1252	Lansdale, PA	Private	23.0	57	2899
L D Davis Industries Inc.	1253	Huntingdon Valley, PA	Private	15.1	57	2891
Cemedine U.S.A., Inc.	1254	Oak Creek, WI	Private	20.0	56	2891
PVS Chemicals Inc. (New York)	1255	Buffalo, NY	Private	17.0	56	2819
Alox Corporation	1256	Niagara Falls, NY	Public Family Member	20.7	55	2899
Burtin Urethane Corporation	1257	Santa Ana, CA	Private	28.0	55	2821
Chemical Specialists & Dev.	1258	Conroe, TX	Private	23.3	55	2851
Clearwater, Inc.	1259	Pittsburgh, PA	Private	20.0	55	2819
General Alum New England Corp.	1260	Holland, OH	Private	16.0	55	2819

D&B COMPANY RANKINGS BY EMPLOYMENT

Company	Rank	Location	Type	Sales ($ mil.)	Employ-ment	Primary SIC
J-Von NA, LLC	1261	Leominster, MA	Private	24.9	55	2821
Kelmar Industries Inc.	1262	Duncan, SC	Private	18.7	55	2819
Lindau Chemicals Inc.	1263	Columbia, SC	Private	16.6	55	2869
May National Associates	1264	Clifton, NJ	Private	40.0	55	2891
Pacific World Corporation	1265	Lake Forest, CA	Private	22.5	55	2844
Palm Commodities International Inc.	1266	La Vergne, TN	Private	24.2	55	2819
PVS Chemicals Inc. (Illinois)	1267	Chicago, IL	Private	23.7	55	2819
Shepard Brothers Inc.	1268	La Habra, CA	Private	15.0	55	2842
Somerville Technology Group	1269	Huguenot, NY	Private	15.8	55	2819
Specialty Coatings Company	1270	Elk Grove Village, IL	Private	25.0	55	2851
Specialty Industrial Products	1271	Spartanburg, SC	Private	40.0	55	2843
Sun Drilling Products Corp.	1272	Belle Chasse, LA	Private	20.1	55	2899
Wasser High-Tech Coatings Inc.	1273	Kent, WA	Private	24.0	55	2851
Harrell's Inc.	1274	Lakeland, FL	Private	25.1	54	2875
North American Oxide, LLC	1275	Clarksville, TN	Private	25.0	54	2816
Premier Coatings, Inc.	1276	Elk Grove Village, IL	Private	18.0	54	2851
Hydro/Kirby Agri Services	1277	Lancaster, PA	Private	25.0	53	2875
Ochoa Fertilizer Co. Inc.	1278	Guanica, PR	Private	17.1	53	2874
Tomah Products, Inc.	1279	Milton, WI	Private	23.8	53	2869
Abitec Corporation	1280	Columbus, OH	Private	32.0	52	2844
Gaylord Chemical Corporation	1281	Slidell, LA	Public Family Member	20.0	52	2861
J L M Chemicals Inc.	1282	Blue Island, IL	Public Family Member	43.7	52	2865
P R Colorcon Inc.	1283	Humacao, PR	Private	31.8	52	2816
Auro Tech Inc.	1284	Menomonee Falls, WI	Public Family Member	16.0	51	2869
Bencyn Inc.	1285	Lafayette, IN	Private	15.0	51	2899
Amco Plastic Materials Inc.	1286	Farmingdale, NY	Private	35.0	50	2821
Aromatic Technologies, Inc.	1287	Somerville, NJ	Private	15.0	50	2844
Interpolymer Corp.	1288	Canton, MA	Private	22.0	50	2821
John C Dolph Company	1289	Monmouth Junction, NJ	Private	20.0	50	2851
Lambent Technologies Corp.	1290	Skokie, IL	Private	15.6	50	2843
Liochem Inc.	1291	Conyers, GA	Private	27.0	50	2899
Markwins International Corp.	1292	La Verne, CA	Private	60.0	50	2844
Metrex Research Corporation	1293	Orange, CA	Public Family Member	15.0	50	2819
Natural Gas Odorizing Inc.	1294	Baytown, TX	Public Family Member	20.0	50	2869
Nova Borealis Compounds, LLC	1295	Port Murray, NJ	Private	50.0	50	2821
Nu-World Corp.	1296	Carteret, NJ	Private	17.3	50	2844
Pilot Chemical Co. Of Ohio	1297	Santa Fe Springs, CA	Private	37.6	50	2841
Protameen Chemicals Inc.	1298	Totowa, NJ	Private	25.0	50	2819
Pvc Compounders, Inc.	1299	Kendallville, IN	Private	25.6	50	2821
R F S Corporation	1300	Fall River, MA	Private	16.0	50	2865
Riverdale Chemical Company	1301	Glenwood, IL	Private	30.0	50	2879
Roma Color Inc.	1302	Fall River, MA	Private	16.0	50	2865
Senco Inc.	1303	Dallas, TX	Private	23.0	50	2844
Uniplast Inc.	1304	Arlington, TX	Private	15.0	50	2891
United Paint And Chemical Corp.	1305	Southfield, MI	Private	18.1	50	2851
Kolene Corporation	1306	Detroit, MI	Private	20.0	49	2899
Flexible Components Inc.	1307	Bridgewater, NJ	Public Family Member	15.0	48	2821
Foam Supplies Inc.	1308	Earth City, MO	Private	18.0	48	2821
Russell Jerome Cosmetics USA	1309	Canoga Park, CA	Private	16.0	48	2844
White Cap Inc.	1310	Paoli, PA	Private	25.0	48	2842
Clinitex Holdings, Inc.	1311	Huntersville, NC	Private	15.0	47	2842
Ohka America, Inc.	1312	Hillsboro, OR	Private	17.0	47	2819
Axim Concrete Technologies	1313	Middlebranch, OH	Private	15.0	46	2899
Sunbelt Corporation	1314	Rock Hill, SC	Private	28.4	46	2865
Agri-Empresa Inc.	1315	Midland, TX	Private	18.0	45	2899
Alpine Aromatics International	1316	Piscataway, NJ	Private	17.0	45	2869
Arnco	1317	South Gate, CA	Private	22.0	45	2822
Atlas Products, Inc.	1318	Des Moines, IA	Private	24.0	45	2851
Crowley Tar Products Co. Inc.	1319	New York, NY	Private	20.0	45	2865
Isochem Colors Inc.	1320	Rock Hill, SC	Private	15.0	45	2865
J B Williams Co. Inc.	1321	Glen Rock, NJ	Private	63.9	45	2844
J B Williams Holdings Inc.	1322	Glen Rock, NJ	Private	63.9	45	2844
Palmer International Inc.	1323	Worcester, PA	Private	17.5	45	2822
Ultra-Poly Corp.	1324	Portland, PA	Private	16.0	45	2821
University Med Prducts/USA Inc.	1325	Irvine, CA	Private	20.0	45	2844
Yates Investment Casting Wax	1326	Chicago, IL	Private	25.0	45	2891
Zaclon Inc.	1327	Cleveland, OH	Private	15.0	45	2819
Zeolyst International	1328	Valley Forge, PA	Private	47.0	45	2819
PVS Technologies Inc.	1329	Detroit, MI	Private	18.2	44	2819
Wako Chemicals USA, Inc.	1330	Richmond, VA	Private	19.0	44	2869

D&B COMPANY RANKINGS BY EMPLOYMENT

Company	Rank	Location	Type	Sales ($ mil.)	Employ-ment	Primary SIC
American Polymers Inc.	1331	Worcester, MA	Private	70.0	42	2821
Advanced Chemical Company	1332	Warwick, RI	Private	24.7	41	2899
Coating and Adhesives Corp.	1333	Leland, NC	Private	18.0	41	2891
Oxid, LP	1334	Houston, TX	Private	17.0	41	2899
Albaugh Inc.	1335	Ankeny, IA	Private	50.0	40	2879
Atlas Refinery Inc.	1336	Newark, NJ	Private	15.9	40	2843
Coatings & Chemicals Corp.	1337	Des Plaines, IL	Private	18.0	40	2851
Crucible Chemical Co. Inc.	1338	Greenville, SC	Private	25.0	40	2842
Deltech Polymers Corporation	1339	Troy, OH	Private	20.0	40	2821
Genset Corporation	1340	La Jolla, CA	Private	16.4	40	2899
Haas Corporation	1341	West Chester, PA	Private	23.0	40	2899
Importers Service Corp.	1342	Jersey City, NJ	Private	15.0	40	2861
Octagon Process Inc.	1343	Edgewater, NJ	Private	40.0	40	2899
Oregon Research & Development	1344	Jacksonville, FL	Private	15.0	40	2899
Pervo Paint Company	1345	Los Angeles, CA	Private	18.0	40	2851
Prentiss Incorporated	1346	Floral Park, NY	Private	17.0	40	2879
Advanced Aromatics, LP	1347	Houston, TX	Private	20.0	39	2869
Giles Chemical Corp.	1348	Waynesville, NC	Private	21.9	39	2899
Tioxide Americas Inc.	1349	Downers Grove, IL	Private	220.0	39	2819
Lenmar Chemical Corporation	1350	Dalton, GA	Private	15.0	37	2843
DSM Resins US Inc.	1351	Augusta, GA	Private	35.0	35	2821
Nottingham Company	1352	Atlanta, GA	Private	25.0	35	2869
U.S. Nonwovens Corp.	1353	Brentwood, NY	Private	22.0	35	2821
United Elchem Industries Inc.	1354	Dallas, TX	Private	16.0	35	2891
J P Industrial Products Inc.	1355	Lisbon, OH	Private	15.0	33	2821
AC Products, Inc.	1356	Placentia, CA	Public Family Member	15.0	32	2891
APT Advanced Polymer Tech Corp.	1357	Harmony, PA	Private	18.8	32	2851
Southwest Industries Inc.	1358	Pompano Beach, FL	Private	74.0	32	2851
Central Mn Ethanol Co-Op, Inc.	1359	Little Falls, MN	Private	30.0	31	2869
Chem Comp Systems Inc.	1360	Cypress, CA	Private	15.0	31	2891
Baerlocher USA	1361	Dover, OH	Private	25.0	30	2819
Gencorp Performance Chemical	1362	Fitchburg, MA	Private	20.0	30	2819
Kasha Industries Inc.	1363	Grayville, IL	Private	20.0	30	2816
Orient Chemical Corp.	1364	Springfield, NJ	Private	18.6	30	2865
Sea & Ski Corp.	1365	Miami, FL	Private	15.0	30	2844
Mid-Atlntic Vegetable Shortening	1366	Newark, NJ	Private	18.0	29	2899
Al-Corn Clean Fuel	1367	Claremont, MN	Private	21.9	28	2869
BPI By-Product Industries	1368	Pittsburgh, PA	Private	18.3	28	2899
Flor Quim Inc.	1369	Patillas, PR	Private	15.0	27	2869
Sofix Corporation	1370	Chattanooga, TN	Private	20.0	27	2899
Nu Gro Technologies, Inc.	1371	Gloversville, NY	Private	15.0	26	2875
The Fanning Corporation	1372	Chicago, IL	Private	20.0	26	2899
Enzyme Development Corporation	1373	New York, NY	Private	21.7	25	2869
Heartland Corn Products	1374	Winthrop, MN	Private	23.8	25	2869
Heartland Grn Fuels, LP	1375	Aberdeen, SD	Private	19.4	25	2869
Toma Industries	1376	North Hollywood, CA	Private	15.0	25	2844
Repello Products Inc.	1377	Mineola, NY	Private	15.0	22	2879
Alzo Inc.	1378	Matawan, NJ	Private	25.0	21	2869
Corsicana Technologies Inc.	1379	Houston, TX	Private	15.0	20	2869
Microsi Inc.	1380	Phoenix, AZ	Private	18.0	20	2899
Peter Thomas Roth Inc.	1381	New York, NY	Private	15.0	20	2844
Regal Chemical Company	1382	Alpharetta, GA	Private	17.0	20	2879
Superior Manufactured Fibers	1383	Plantersville, MS	Private	15.0	20	2824
The Euclid Chemical Company	1384	Cleveland, OH	Public Family Member	45.0	20	2899
Aarbor International Corp	1385	Brighton, MI	Private	15.8	17	2865
PPB Technologies, Inc.	1386	Shelby, NC	Private	15.0	17	2819
California Sulphur	1387	Wilmington, CA	Private	15.0	15	2819
Human Pheromone Sciences, Inc.	1388	Fremont, CA	Public	17.2	15	2844
KCC Corrosion Control Co. Ltd.	1389	Houston, TX	Private	300.5	15	2899
Panco Men's Products Inc.	1390	Indio, CA	Private	16.0	15	2844
Stic-Adhesive Products Company	1391	Los Angeles, CA	Private	88.0	15	2891
Ichauway Mills, Inc.	1392	Dallas, TX	Private	20.0	14	2844
KMG-Bernuth Inc.	1393	Houston, TX	Public Family Member	22.7	14	2869
Lori Davis Hair, Inc.	1394	West Chester, PA	Private	22.1	13	2844
Shrieve Chemical Products Inc.	1395	The Woodlands, TX	Private	30.4	13	2899
Chemical Products Technologies	1396	Cartersville, GA	Private	18.0	12	2819
Farmers Plant Food, Inc.	1397	Garretson, SD	Private	19.6	12	2873
G P C Sales Inc.	1398	Deer Park, NY	Private	20.0	12	2844
Hawaii Chemtect International	1399	Pasadena, CA	Private	20.0	12	2899
Reeve Agri Energy Corp.	1400	Garden City, KS	Private	20.0	12	2869

D&B COMPANY RANKINGS BY EMPLOYMENT

Company	Rank	Location	Type	Sales ($ mil.)	Employ-ment	Primary SIC
Venture VI Inc.	1401	Walled Lake, MI	Private	18.0	10	2899
American United Distilling Co. LLC	1402	Minneapolis, MN	Private	300.0	8	2869
Dihoma Chemical & Manufacturing	1403	Mullins, SC	Private	32.0	7	2869
Major Chem Ltd.	1404	Houston, TX	Private	25.0	7	2842
M C Marble, Inc.	1405	Lafayette, IN	Private	16.0	6	2844
Advanced Polymer Alloys, LLC	1406	Wilmington, DE	Private	18.0	5	2822
Well Long Economic & Trade Co.	1407	Milpitas, CA	Private	20.0	5	2821
Armand Products Company	1408	Princeton, NJ	Private	40.0	3	2812
William E Wofford Textile Co.	1409	Venice, CA	Private	35.0	3	2843

CHAPTER 6 - PART I

MERGERS & ACQUISITIONS

The following essay presents a look at merger and acquisition activity in the Chemicals sector. A general overview of M&A activity is followed by a listing of actual merger and acquisition events. Purchasing companies are listed in alphabetical order, with a paragraph set aside for each acquisition.

This essay discusses recent merger and acquisition activity in the industry and its effect on the industry. The essay is followed by a list of significant acquisitions and mergers.

The late 1990s saw intense levels of merger and acquisition activity within the chemical industry. In 1998, deals involving chemical-related companies hit $350 billion while solely chemical transactions reached $37 billion, an increase of 11 percent from the previous year. Most chemical companies seem to be following one of two trends: boosting existing product lines through mergers and acquisitions or divesting peripheral holdings to focus on core chemical operations. But regardless of the reason for the consolidations, companies need time to make the deals work once the agreements have been struck. Even so, pressure to deliver sustainable earnings are not giving chemical-industry executives the opportunity to focus on the aftermath of so much merger and acquisition activity. In a December 1998 survey by the firm Arthur D. Little, European chemical companies listed post-merger and acquisition integration as their third priority, following behind growth and innovation.

The chemical industry is truly a globalized manufacturing commerce. As a result, the industry felt the effects of the Asian economic crisis of the 1990s. Mergers and acquisitions in that area of the world slowed. Most of the merger and acquisition activity in Asia focused on smaller deals and mainly in Korea. For instance, Shipley Co. acquired the 49 percent of LG Chemical, its Korean joint venture, which it did not already own, in June of 1999. Into the 2000s, Western companies might be looking for mergers with companies in other Asian nations, such as Japan. At a 1999 Chemical Meeting in Singapore, chemical companies pledged to continue investing in Asia.

Traditionally consolidations within the chemicals industry involved smaller players, but the late 1990s saw major players step up their levels of merger and acquisition activity. The merger between Dow Chemical Co. and Union Carbide in August 1999 created the world's second-largest chemical company. Dow, which produces Saran Wrap and Styrofoam, paid $11.6 billion for Union Carbide, a producer of chemicals used by other companies for consumer items such as pharmaceuticals and personal-care products. It is expected that it will take two to three years for the two

companies to totally merge. After that time, the combined company will operate in nearly 170 countries, employ about 50,000 people, and have revenues of $24 billion.

Mergers and acquisitions have been especially heavy in the higher margin and thus more profitable specialty chemical industry. For example, Hercules Inc., a leading U.S. specialty chemicals producer, despite failed attempts to merge with National Starch and Chemical and Allied Colloids Group PLC, completed two acquisitions in October of 1998 and then went on to further acquisitions in 1999. The company first bought Alliance Technical Products Ltd., a resin dispersions maker based in Stonehouse, England. A few weeks later, Hercules finalized its purchase of BetzDearborn Inc., the world's leading supplier of engineered chemical water treatment products, for $2.4 billion in cash and a $700 million debt assumption. In August 1999, Hercules purchased Scripset, as a way to strengthen its position in the paper industry. There were other major transactions throughout 1998 and 1999, including the January 1998 $2.3 billion purchase of Allied Colloids Group PLC, a water treatment adhesives maker, by Ciba Specialty Chemicals; the February 1998 acquisition of Imperial Chemical Industries PLC's polyester film business by E.I. du Pont de Nemours and Co. for approximately $3 billion; and the July 1998 purchase of Arco Chemical Co., an olefins and polyolefins maker, by Lyondell Petrochemical Corp. for $5.6 billion.

One of the largest acquisitions between two specialty chemicals companies was completed in July of 1997 when Imperial Chemical Industries PLC, based in London, England, bought the specialty chemicals units of Unilever Group for $8 billion. The four units purchased were National Starch & Chemical, a manufacturer of adhesives and starch; Quest International, a maker of flavorings and food; Unichemal International, a producer of oleochemicals; and Crosfield, a manufacturer of silicas, silicates, and zeolites. At the same time, the transaction allowed Unilever Group to refocus on its consumer goods operations.

One of the largest mergers in corporate history took place on December 20, 1996, when Ciba-Geigy Ltd. and Sandoz Ltd. merged to form Novartis AG, the largest life sciences company and pesticide manufacturer in the world. The $36 billion transaction was the largest to date in the chemicals and pharmaceuticals industries. Less than a year after its inception, Novartis bought the crop protection business of Merck and Company Inc. for $910 million in July of 1997.

Life science represents a fast-growing segment and for several years, leading agricultural, pesticide, and plant biotechnology companies have pursued acquisitions. At the same time, they have also divested operations that were not in their core business. Some companies, notably Du Pont, Dow Chemical, and BASF AG, are increasing life science operations while still maintaining substantial chemical businesses. Other companies, such as Monsanto, Hoeschst AG, and Novartis AG have taken a more aggressive tact and are selling off all their non-life-sciences operations to fund their seed acquisitions. For example, Monsanto divested its sweetener, biogrum, and algins businesses in 1999. These sales will help to pay for the company's acquisitions, which amounted to over $4 billion in 1988. Monsanto has been buying up seed business and bought its remaining 60 percent share of DEKALB Genetics Corp., a biotechnology seed operation based in DeKalb, Illinois, for $2.5 billion in cash in 1988. Previous acquisitions include: $1.02 billion in January of 1997 for Holden's Foundation Seeds Inc., a seed and plant genetics firm based in Williamsburg, Iowa; $1.8 billion in May of 1998 for Delta and Pine Land Co., a cotton seed and plant genetics firm based in Scott, Mississippi; $66 million in May of 1998 for two Puerto Rican plants, one which manufactures bulk chemicals and one which makes diagnostic imaging agents, from Nycomed Amersham PLC; and $1.4 billion in July of 1998 for the international seed assets of Cargill Inc.

Many other sectors within the chemicals industry have fewer major players due to intense levels of consolidation over the past few years. For example, the adhesives industry has seen an unprecedented amount of merger and acquisition activity as companies strive to increase the range of goods and services they offer clients. Elf Atochem made three noteworthy acquisitions in 1998: the acrylics operations of Hanwha Chemical Corp., based in Jinhae, South Korea; and the Memphis, Tennessee-based hydrogen peroxide plant of E.I. du Pont de Nemours and Co. RPM Inc. has been involved in similar activity. In February of 1997, the company bought Tremco Inc., the Cleveland, Ohio-based sealants and coatings subsidiary of BFGoodrich Co.,

for $230 million in cash. A year and a half later, in July of 1998, RPM bought Nullifire Ltd., an industrial and commercial fireproof coatings manufacturer based in Coventry, England.

The increasing globalization of the adhesives sector has also spurred consolidation. In fact, one of the largest mergers in the adhesives market was finalized in January of 1997 when Henkel KgaA, based in Dusseldorf, Germany, bought Loctite Corp., a large manufacturer of adhesives with annual sales in excess of $800 million, for $1.3 billion. Henkel pursed the acquisition as a means of strengthening its position in the U.S. market. Also hoping to compete on a more global scale, H.B. Fuller Co., based in St. Paul, Minnesota, and EMS-Chemie Holding AG, located in Zurich, Switzerland, merged their automotive adhesives, sealants, and coatings operations into Madison Heights, Michigan-based Eftec, the world's largest automotive industry supplier of adhesives and sealants, in June of 1997.

Water treatment chemicals firms have been pursing mergers and acquisitions at a frenetic pace over the past years in an attempt to boost sagging profit margins and secure additional market share. Nalco Chemical, the largest water treatment chemicals operation in the U.S., completed four acquisitions in 1999 before receiving a tender offer for its shares by Suez Lyonnaise des Eux in September of 1999. During 1997 and 1998, the company completed over 15 acquisitions, including the following companies: the pulp and paper enzyme operations of chemicals giant Ciba Specialty Chemicals Inc., based in Basel, Switzerland; USF Houseman Waterbehandeling B.V., based in Holland; Trident Chemical Company Inc., based in Baton Rouge, Louisiana; Texo Corp., based in Cincinnati, Ohio; UNICO Corp., based in Seoul, South Korea; DiverseyLever Ltd., based in the United Kingdom; Pace International, based in Seattle, Washington; CSC-Kemico Sdn. Bhd., based in Shah Alam, Malaysia; and United Chemasia Sdn. Bhd., based in Penang, Malaysia.

The coatings segment, which has traditionally been rather splintered, has seen many manufacturing companies pursue acquisitions and mergers in an effort to gain access to technical expertise and deeper research and development and international marketing pockets. To remain competitive, coatings companies have sought and continue to seek methods of capitalizing on the globalization taking place across the industry, as well as dealing with tighter governmental regulations. For many firms, finding partners who have the technology in place to meet certain regulations or the marketing resources to target international clients has become a top priority because acquiring these assets is quite often cheaper than developing them in-house.

PPG Industries, one of the world's leading automotive and industrial coatings manufacturers, made several global acquisitions in the late 1990s. The firm bought MaxMeyer Duco S.p.A., an automotive refinishes and fleet finishes manufacturer based in Milan, Italy, in November of 1997; the container coatings unit of BASF AG in December of 1997; Keeler and Long Inc., an industrial high-performance and coil coatings manufacturer based in Watertown, Connecticut, in December of 1997; Sipsy Chimie Fine S.C.A., an Avrille, France-based maker of intermediate chemicals for pharmaceutical production, in January of 1998; and the automotive coatings operations of Helios-Lacke Bollig & Kemper GmbH & Co. KG, a Cologne, Germany-based maker of coatings and resins, in February of 1998. Another major merger took place in the coatings segment in January of 1997 when Sherwin-Williams Co. bought Thompson Miniwax Holding Corp., a maker and marketer of interior stains, varnishes, exterior water sealers, and finishing and enamel coatings, for $830 million.

Fertilizer manufacturers are also engaged in rapid consolidation due in large part to the instability inherent in that segment of the chemicals market. Rather than produce a single fertilizer, many firms are diversifying in an attempt to reduce dependence on a single product. For example, in March of 1997 Potash Corp. paid $1.2 billion for Memphis, Tennessee-based Arcadian Corp., one of the world's largest nitrogen fertilizer manufacturers, and became the world&rsquo's leading consolidated fertilizer manufacturer with annual revenues of roughly $2.5 billion. On March 1, 1996, IMC Global Inc. became the leading potash supplier in the United States with its $1.3 billion stock purchase of Vigoro Corp. In December of 1997, IMC Global diversified its holdings with the $750 million acquisition of Freeport-McMoRan Inc., a phosphate and fertilizer manufacturer. Finally, on December 13, 1996, Agrium Inc. bought Viridian Inc., a fertilizer manufacturer based in Alberta, Canada, and became the largest producer of nitrogen fertilizer in North America with annual sales in excess of $1.9 billion.

Plastics is yet another segment of the chemicals industry that has seen an increased level of merger and acquisition activity during the late 1990s, including the $5.6 billion merger between Arco Chemical and Lyondell Petrochemical in July of 1998. In December of 1997 Millennium Chemicals Inc. and Lyondell Petrochemical merged their petrochemicals and plastics operations into Equistar Chemicals, L.P., worth an estimated $5 billion. Roughly six months after its creation, in June of 1998, Equistar Chemicals bought the petrochemical operations of Occidental Petroleum Corp. to become the largest propylene producer in the United States. An additional noteworthy transaction took place in July of 1997 when DSM bought the polypropylene and polyethylene businesses of Vestolen for $496 million. Finally, in October of 1998, Elenac, a polyethylene joint venture between BASF AG and Shell, agreed to purchase the polyethylene unit of Hoechst AG, which generates roughly $500 million in annual sales.

Many analysts predict that merger and acquisition activity in the chemicals industry will continue its rapid pace, particularly as growth within certain segments slows. Consolidation will be necessary for firms looking to diversify product lines, cut costs, find new sources of research and development funding, and maintain and gain market share.

Mergers and Acquisitions

Air Products & Chemicals Inc. bought **Solkatronic Chemicals,** a chemicals, gases, and gas handling equipment manufacturer based in Fairfield, New Jersey, in early 1998. [*Electronic News,* 11/10/97, p. 25.]

AlliedSignal Inc. bought **Pharmaceutical Fine Chemicals S.A.,** an active and intermediate pharmaceutical fine chemicals producer and distributor based in Lugano, Switzerland, on June 19, 1998. [*Business Wire,* 6/19/98.]

—bought **IroPharm,** a pharmaceuticals and speciality chemicals manufacturer located in Ireland, in August of 1997. [*ECN-European Chemical News,* 8/11/97, p. 40.]

Ashland Specialty Chemical Co. bought the remaining 50 percent ownership of its Austrian joint venture, **Donau Drew,** a supplier of specialty products and services for water treatment, on May 31, 1999. [*PR Newswire,* 6/3/99.

BASF AG agreed to purchase German-based **Ultraform GmbH** and U.S.-based **Ultraform Company**, manufacturers of a plastic used in automotive components, on September 13, 1999. ["BASF to Buy Out Ultraform Partner." Available at http://www. basf-ag.basf.de/BASF/PressReleases/P+370e.sql]

—agreed to purchase **Hydro Coatings Group, UK,,** the international coil coatings business of **Norsk Hydro ASA,** based in Norway, on September 7, 1999. ["BASF to Acquire Norsk Hydro Coil Coatings Business." Available at http://www.basf-ag.basf.de/BASF/PressReleases/P+Coat17.sql]

—bought the Netherlands-based acrylonitrile butadiene styrene unit of **DSM** in October of 1998. [*Chemical Week,* 102/28/98.]

—bought the surfectants and paper chemicals operations of **PPG Industries Inc.,** the largest manufacturer of automotive and industrial coatings in the world with annual sales of $7.2 billion, in December of 1997. [*PR Newswire,* 12/2/97.]

BetzDearborn Inc. bought **Argo Scientific,** a membrane support technology firm located in San Marcos, California, on November 25, 1997. [*PR Newswire,* 11/25/97.]

BFGoodrich Co. bought **C.H. Patrick & Co., Inc.,** a Taylors, South Carolina-based additives and dyes maker serving the textiles industry, in late 1997. [*PR Newswire,* 12/9/97.]

Borden Chemical, Inc. bought **Melamine Chemicals, Inc.,** a melamine crystal producer and marketer located in Donaldsonville, Louisiana, on November 14, 1997. [*Business Wire,* 11/14/97.]

Catalytica Fine Chemicals Inc. bought a chemical and pharmaceutical plant based in Greenville, North Carolina, from **Glaxo Wellcome Inc.** for $247 million in cash in June of 1997. [*Chemical Market Reporter,* 2/10/97, p. 1.]

Ciba Specialty Chemicals bought **Allied Colloids Group PLC,** a water treatment adhesives maker, for $2.3 billion in January of 1998. [*Chemical & Engineering News,* 1/26/98, p. 10.]

Cincinnati Milacron Inc. bought **Manpo Chemicals Co.,** a cutting fluid manufacturer based in Ulsan City, Korea, on August 3, 1998. [*PR Newswire,* 8/3/98.]

Compass Plastics & Technologies Inc. bought **Gumsung Plastics USA,** an injection molded plastic monitor and television components manufacturer based in Mexicali, Mexico, in November of 1998. [*Business Wire,* 10/14/98.]

CRI International Inc. bought **Chemical Research and Licensing Co.,** a Bayport, Texas-based subsidiary of **NOVA Chemicals Inc.** in May of 1997. [*The Oil and Gas Journal,* 5/4/98, p. 128.]

Crompton & Knowles bought **Uniroyal,** a Middlebury, Connecticut-based producer of rubber, rubber chemicals, crop protection chemicals, and prepolymers, for $354 million in stock and a $1.1 billion debt assumption in March of 1997. [*Chemical & Engineering News,* 3/17/97, p. 14.]

Cytec Industries Inc. bought a 50 percent share of **Dyno-Cytec,** its European chemicals joint venture with **Dyno Industries,** in July of 1998. [*Business Wire,* 7/31/98.]

—bought the amino coatings resins unit of **Dyno Industrier ASA,** based in Oslo, Norway, in July of 1998. [*Business Wire,* 7/31/98.]

D.A. Stuart Co. bought the can lubricants unit of **W.R. Grace & Co.,** one of the largest specialty chemical firms in the world, in May of 1998. [*Chemical Market Reporter,* 6/1/98, p. 37.]

Degussa Corp. bought the Gibbons, Alberta, Canada-based hydrogen peroxide plant of **E.I. du Pont de Nemours and Co.** in October of 1998. [*Chemical Market Reporter,* 10/5/98, p. 3.]

Dow Chemical Co. and **Union Carbide** agreed to a merger in August of 1999 that will make them the second-largest chemical company in the world. Dow Chemical will acquire Danbury, Connecticut-based

Union Carbide for $11.6 billion in stock and debt. [*PR Newswire*, 8/4/99.]

—bought **ANGUS Chemical Co.**, a leading specialty chemicals firm, on August 2, 1999. [*PR Newswire*, 8/4/99.]

—bought the shares it didn't already own—for a total of 99.3 percent total of outstanding shares—of **Mycogen Corporation,** an agribusiness and biotechnology company based in San Diego, California, in November of 1998. [*PR Newswire*, 10/5/98 and 11/2/98.]

—bought **Sentrachem Ltd.,** a chemicals manufacturer based in South Africa, in December of 1997. [*Chemical Market Reporter*, 12/8/97, p. 1.]

—bought the 40 percent it didn't already own of **DowElanco,** one of the largest agricultural products companies in the world, from **Eli Lilly and Co.** for $900 million in June of 1997. [*PR Newswire*, 6/30/97.]

DSM bought the polypropylene and polyethylene businesses of **Vestolen** for $496 million in July of 1997. [*ECN-European Chemical News*, 7/28/97, p. 8.]

DuPont bought **Herberts,** the coatings subsidiary of Hoeschst AG for $1.9 million on March 1, 1999. ["DuPont Announces the Completion of Its Acquisition of Herberts." Available from http://www.dupont. com/corp/whats-new/releases/99/herbertscomp.html

E.I. du Pont de Nemours and Co. bought the elastane fibers operations of **Tongkook Synthetic Fiber Co.,** located in South Korea, in a deal valued at roughly $200 million in September of 1998. [*Chemical Market Reporter*, 9/7/98, p. 1.]

—bought the polyester film business of **Imperial Chemical Industries PLC,** based in London, England, for approximately $3 billion in February of 1998. [*PR Newswire*, 2/2/98.]

—bought **Protein Technologies International Holdings Inc.,** the leading manufacturer of soy proteins in the world, in August of 1997. [*Chemical & Engineering News*, 9/1/97, p. 9.]

—bought a 20 percent share of **Pioneer Hi-Bred International Inc.,** the leading manufacturer of seeds and the largest agricultural genetics supplier in the world, in July of 1997. [*Feedstuffs*, 8/18/97, p. 1.]

Eastman Chemical Co. bought **Ernst Jager, Fabrik Chemischer Rohstoffe GmbH & Co.,** a specialty polymers manufacturer located in Germany, in September of 1998. [*Business Wire*, 9/15/98.]

El Dorado Chemical Co. bought the agricultural chemicals distribution unit of **Eubanks Agri, Inc.** in September of 1998. [*PR Newswire*, 9/8/98.]

Elan Corporation PLC bought **NanoSystems L.L.C.,** a drug delivery firm focused on improving delivery of drugs which are not water soluble, for roughly $150 million in cash and warrants on October 1, 1998. [*PR Newswire*, 10/1/98.]

Elf Atochem S.A. bought the acrylics operations of **Hanwha Chemical Corp.,** based in Jinhae, South Korea, in October of 1998. [*Chemical Market Reporter*, 10/19/98, p. 19.]

—bought the Memphis, Tennessee-based hydrogen peroxide plant of **E.I. du Pont de Nemours and Co.** in October of 1998. [*Chemical Market Reporter*, 10/5/98, p. 3.]

Engelhard Corp. bought the catalyst business of **Mallinckrodt Inc.,** a producer of petroleum refining, chemical processing and emission control catalysts, for $210 million in May of 1997. [*Chemical Market Reporter*, 5/11/98, p. 5.]

Equistar Chemicals, L.P. bought the petrochemical operations of **Occidental Petroleum Corp.** in June of 1998. Upon completion of the acquisition, Equistar Chemicals became largest propylene producer in the United States. [*Chemical & Engineering News*, 6/8/98, p. 22.]

Esterline Technologies Corp. bought **Kirkhill Rubber Co.,** a privately owned elastomer components manufacturer based in California, in August of 1998. [*PR Newswire*, 8/10/98.]

H.B. Fuller Co., based in St. Paul, Minnesota, and **EMS-Chemie Holding AG,** located in Zurich,

Switzerland, merged their automotive adhesives, sealants, and coatings operations into Madison Heights, Michigan-based **Eftec,** the world's largest automotive industry supplier of adhesives and sealants, in June of 1997. [*Ward's Auto World,* 6/97, p. 47.]

GEO Specialty Chemicals bought the paper chemicals and construction and process chemicals units of **Henkel Corp.** and **Henkel Canada Ltd.** in March of 1997. [*PR Newswire,* 3/25/97.]

Geon Co. bought **Adchem, Inc.,** a vinyl plastisols and polymer additives maker and seller located in Kennesaw, Georgia, on September 8, 1998. [*PR Newswire,* 9/8/98.]

Gibson-Homans Co. bought the primers and adhesives unit of **Evans Adhesive Corp.** in October of 1998. [*American Paint & Coatings Journal,* 10/7/98, p. 7.]

M.A. Hanna Co. bought the manufacturing operations of **Harwick Chemical Corp.** in September of 1998. [*PR Newswire,* 9/2/98.]

Henkel KgaA, based in Dusseldorf, Germany, bought **DEP Corp.,** a personal care products manufacturer, marketer, and distributor, on August 14, 1998. [*Business Wire,* 8/17/98.]

—bought **Loctite Corp.,** a large manufacturer of adhesives with annual sales in excess of $800 million, for $1.3 billion in January of 1997. [*PR Newswire,* 1/15/97.]

Hercules Inc. bought **Scriptset,** a water-soluble polymer resin business on August 3, 1999. ["Hercules Acquires Scriptset Business from Solutia." Available from http://www. herc.com/abouthercules/news/99/ Scrptset.htm.]

—bought **BetzDearborn Inc.,** a supplier of engineered chemical water treatment products, for $2.4 billion in cash and a $700 million debt assumption on October 15, 1998. [*Business Wire,* 10/15/98.]

—bought **Alliance Technical Products Ltd.,** a resin dispersions maker based in Stonehouse, England, in October of 1998. [*American Paint & Coatings Journal,* 10/7/98, p. 4.]

Hunstman Corp. bought British-based **ICI,** an industrial chemical business, for $2.8 billion in April of 1999. After the purchase, family-owned Hunstman became the third-largest petrochemical company in the United States. [*BBC Online Network,* April 15, 1999.]

—bought **Rexene Corp.,** a styrene and olefins manufacturer, for $600 million in cash and debt assumption in June of 1997. [*Chemcial Week,* 6/18/97, p. 10.]

ICO Inc. bought **Verplast S.p.A.,** a petrochemical processing services supplier based in Italy, on July 22, 1997. [*PR Newswire,* 7/22/97.]

IMC Global Inc. bought **Freeport-McMoRan Inc.,** a phosphate and fertilizer manufacturer, for approximately $750 million in stock in December of 1997. [*Business Wire,* 11/18/97.]

Imperial Chemical Industries PLC (ICI), based in London, England, bought the specialty chemicals units of **Unilever Group** for $8 billion in July of 1997 in one of the largest acquisitions in the specialty chemicals sector. The four units purchased were **National Starch & Chemical,** a manufacturer of adhesives and starch; **Quest International,** a maker of flavorings and food; **Unichemal International,** a producer of oleochemicals; and **Crosfield,** a manufacturer of silicas, silicates, and zeolites. [*ECN-European Chemical News,* 5/19/97, p. 16]

Isonics Corp. bought **Chemotrade GmbH,** a stable and radioactive isotopes supplier based in Dusseldorf, Germany, for $2.5 million in cash, notes, and stock on July 21, 1998. [*PR Newswire,* 7/21/98.]

LaFarge Pentures S.A.S. bought the decorative coatings business of **MaxMeyer Duco S.p.A.,** a coatings manufacturer based in Italy, in August of 1998. [*PR Newswire,* 7/6/98.]

Lubrizol Corp. bought **Adibis,** the lubricant and fuel additives unit of **British Petroleum Company PLC** for roughly $100 million in July of 1998. [*PR Newswire,* 7/31/98]

—bought **Carl Becker Chemie,** a metalworking additives maker based in Hamburg, Germany, in January of 1998. The purchase allowed Lubrizol to increase its market share, as the leading lubricant and fuel additives maker in the world, from 35 percent to 38 percent. [*Chemical Week,* 4/29/98, p. 31.]

Lyondell Petrochemical Corp. bought **Arco Chemical Co.,** an olefins and polyolefins maker, for $5.6 billion in July of 1998. Upon completion of the transaction, Lyondell Petrochemical became the largest corporate consumer of propylene in the world. [*Oil Daily,* 7/24/98.]

MANE Group bought the Milford, Ohio-based seasoning division of **Technology Flavors & Fragrances, Inc.** for $5.5 million in cash in August of 1998. [*Business Wire,* 8/26/98.]

Mellon Ventures Inc. bought **Pecora Corp.,** a specialty chemicals manufacturer located in Harleysville, Pennsylvania, in June of 1998. [*PR Newswire,* 6/19/98.]

Millennium Chemicals Inc. and **Lyondell Petrochemical Corp.** merged their petrochemicals and plastics operations into **Equistar Chemicals, L.P.,** worth an estimated $5 billion, in December of 1997. [*Chemical Market Reporter,* 12/1/97, p. 1.]

Monsanto Co. bought the international seed assets of **Cargill Inc.** for approximately $1.4 billion in July of 1998. [*Feedstuffs,* 7/6/98, p. 1.]

—bought the 60 percent it did not already own of **DEKALB Genetics Corp.,** a biotechnology seed operation based in DeKalb, Illinois, for $2.5 billion in cash in May of 1998. [*Chemical Week,* 5/20/98, p. 10.]

—bought two Puerto Rican plants, one which manufactures bulk chemicals and one which makes medical diagnostic imaging agents, from **Nycomed Amersham PLC,** a global imaging agent manufacturer based in Norway, for $66 million in May of 1998. [*Chemical Market Reporter,* 5/25/98, p. 3.]

—bought **Delta and Pine Land Co.,** a cotton seed and plant genetics firm based in Scott, Mississippi, for $1.8 billion in stock in May of 1998. [*Chemical Week,* 5/20/98, p. 10.]

—bought **Holden's Foundation Seeds Inc.,** a privately owned seed and plant genetics firm based in Wil-

liamsburg, Iowa, that produces 35 percent of the corn crop in the United States, for $1.02 billion in January of 1997. [*Chemical Week,* 1/15/97, p. 7.]

Morgan Grenfell Development Capital Ltd. bought **Vianova Resins GmbH,** the synthetic resins arm of **Hoechst AG** in October of 1998. [*Business Wire,* 10/12/98.]

Nalco Chemical Co. bought the businesses of two Scandinavian companies and one Italian company in March of 1999. The purchased businesses were suppliers and marketers of chemicals used for pulp and paper manufacturing in their respective countries. The businesses were: Finish-based **Voimax Trading Oy** and **HaSne Oy,** Swedish-based **Scanmax Kemi AB,** and Italian-based **Papirkemie Italiana SpA.** [*PR Newswire,* 3/10/99 .]

—bought **Pure Chem Products Company, Inc.,** a manufacturer and marketer of cleaners and water-treatment services for the food and beverage market based in Stanton, California, in August of 1999. [*PR Newswire,* 8/17/99.]

—bought **United Chemasia Sdn. Bhd.,** a water- treatment products supplier based in Penang, Malaysia, in August of 1998. [*PR Newswire,* 8/25/98.]

—bought **CSC-Kemico Sdn. Bhd.,** a water treatment products and services supplier based in Shah Alam, Malaysia, in July of 1998. [*PR Newswire,* 7/9/98.]

—bought **Pace International,** a water treatment division of **Pacific Chemicals,** based in Seattle, Washington, in June of 1998. [*Chemical Week,* 6/17/98, p.13.]

—bought **DiverseyLever Ltd.,** a water treatment products and services supplier based in the United Kingdom, in May of 1998. [*Chemical Market Reporter,* 6/1/98, p. 11.]

—bought **UNICO Corp.,** a wastewater treatment and process chemicals supplier based in Seoul, South Korea, in April of 1998. [*PR Newswire,* 4/20/98.]

—bought **Texo Corp.,** a Cincinnati, Ohio-based specialty and performance chemicals supplier with annual sales of roughly $30 million, in April of 1998. [*PR Newswire,* 7/13/98.]

—bought **Trident Chemical Company Inc.,** a Baton Rouge, Louisiana-based water treatment chemicals supplier and water treatment services marketer with annual sales of approximately $9 million, in January of 1998. [*PR Newswire,* 1/23/98.]

—bought **USF Houseman Waterbehandeling B.V.,** a Dutch water treatment chemicals and services supplier with annual sales of approximately $3 million, in January of 1998. [*PR Newswire,* 1/21/98.]

—bought **Chemco Water Technology Inc.,** a Vancouver, Washington-based boiler and cooling water treatment chemicals and services supplier with annual sales in excess of $7 million, in November of 1997. [*PR Newswire,* 11/21/97.]

—bought **Gamus Quimica, Ltda.,** a Brazilian water treatment chemicals and services supplier and marketer serving textile and food industries, in October of 1997. [*PR Newswire,* 10/7/97.]

—bought **Chemical Technologies, Inc.** a Jackson, Michigan-based synthetic fluids and metal products lubricants maker and marketer with annual revenues of $18 million, on October 1, 1997. [*PR Newswire,* 10/1/97.]

—bought the pulp and paper enzyme operations of chemicals giant **Ciba Specialty Chemicals Inc.,** based in Basel, Switzerland, in July of 1997. [*Pulp & Paper,* 7/97, p. 139.]

—bought **International Water Consultants Beheer B.V.,** a water treatment chemicals and services manufacturer and marketer based in Maarssen, The Netherlands, in February of 1997. [*PR Newswire,* 2/5/97.]

—bought **Nutmeg Technologies Inc.,** a privately owned water treatment chemicals and services firm based in New Haven, Connecticut, in January of 1997. [*PR Newswire,* 1/14/97.]

NEN Life Science Products, Inc. bought **Advanced Bioconcept Ltd.,** a proprietary fluorescent peptide maker based in Montreal, Canada, in September of 1998. [*Business Wire,* 9/25/98.]

Novartis AG bought the crop protection business of **Merck and Company Inc.** for $910 million on July 3, 1997. [*Business Wire,* 7/3/97.]

Potash Corp. bought Memphis, Tennessee-based **Arcadian Corp.,** one of the world's largest nitrogen fertilizer manufacturers, for $1.2 billion in March of 1997. Upon completion of the acquisition, Potash became the world&rsquo's leading consolidated fertilizer manufacturer with annual revenues of roughly $2.5 billion. [*Feedstuffs,* 3/17/97.]

PPG Industries Inc. bought the technical coatings business of **Orica Ltd.,** based in Melbourne, Australia, for $150 million on September 25, 1998. [*PR Newswire,* 9/25/98.]

—bought the pretreatment and process lubricants operations of **Man-Gill Chemical Co.,** located in Ohio, in May of 1998. [*Appliance,* 5/98, p. 21.]

—bought the automotive coatings operations of **Helios-Lacke Bollig & Kemper GmbH & Co. KG,** a Cologne, Germany-based maker of coatings and resins, in February of 1998. [*PR Newswire,* 2/2/98.]

—bought **Sipsy Chimie Fine S.C.A.,** an Avrille, France-based maker of intermediate chemicals for pharmaceutical production, on January 2, 1998. [*PR Newswire,* 1/2/98.]

—bought **Keeler and Long Inc.,** an industrial high-performance and coil coatings manufacturer based in Watertown, Connecticut, in December of 1997. [*PR Newswire,* 12/10/97.]

—bought the container coatings unit of **BASF AG,** which boasted annual revenues of $150 million, in December of 1997. [*PR Newswire,* 12/2/97.]

—bought **MaxMeyer Duco S.p.A.,** an automotive refinishes and fleet finishes manufacturer based in Milan, Italy, on November 24, 1997. [*PR Newswire,* 11/24/97.]

—bought an additional 35 percent stake in **PPG-AN Automotive Coatings,** its South American coatings venture with **Akzo Nobel NV** in February of 1997. [*PR Newswire,* 2/20/97.]

Roche Holdings AG bought **Tastemaker,** a flavorings joint venture owned by **Hercules Inc.** and **Mallinckrodt Inc.,** for $1.1 billion in April of 1997. [*Feedstuffs,* 2/24/97, p. 7.]

Rohm and Hass Co. bought **Morton International,** a manufacturer of chemicals and salt, based in Chicago, Illinois, for $4.9 billion in June of 1998. [*PR Newswire,* 6/21/98.]

RPM, Inc. bought **Nullifire Ltd.,** an industrial and commercial fireproof coatings manufacturer based in Coventry, England, in July of 1998. [*PR Newswire,* 7/8/98.]

—bought **Tremco Inc.,** the Cleveland, Ohio-based sealants and coatings subsidiary of **BFGoodrich Co.,** for $230 million in cash on February 3, 1997. [*PR Newswire,* 2/3/97.]

The Scotts Co. bought **Rhone-Poulenc Jardin,** the leading consumer lawn and garden products firm in Europe, in October of 1998. [*Business Wire,* 10/7/98.]

Sherwin-Williams Co. bought **Thompson Miniwax Holding Corp.,** a maker and marketer of interior stains, varnishes, exterior water sealers, and finishing and enamel coatings, for $830 million on January 7, 1997. [*PR Newswire,* 1/8/97.]

Shin-Etsu bought **Rovin,** the polyvinyl chloride and vinyl chloride monomer joint venture between **Shell** and **Akzo Nobel,** in October of 1998. [*Chemical Market Reporter,* 10/19/98, p. 6.]

Shipley Co. bought the remaining 49 percent shares it didn't already own in **LG Chemical,** a South Korean-based semiconductor manufacturer, in June of 1998. [*PR Newswire,* 6/2/98.]

Specified Fuels & Chemicals L.L.C. bought the reference fuels and chemical custom manufacturing operations of **Howell Corp.,** located in Houston, Texas, for $20 million in August of 1997. [*The Oil and Gas Journal,* 8/18/97, p. 29.]

Sterling Chemicals Holdings, Inc. bought the acrylic fibers unit of **Cytec Industries Inc.** for $100 million in cash and $9 million in debt assumption on January 31, 1997. [*Business Wire,* 2/3/97.]

Suez Lyonnaise des Eaux bought **Nalco Chemical Co.,** a Naperville, Illinois-based waste water treatment business, for $4.1 billion in June of 1999. [*Chicago Tribune,* 6/29/99.]

Tetra Technologies, Inc. bought the Amboy, California-based calcium chloride manufacturing plant of **Cargill, Inc.** in August of 1998. [*Business Wire,* 8/20/98.]

Toagosei Co. Ltd. bought **ACI Japan Ltd.,** an adhesives manufacturer based in Tokyo, in September of 1998. Upon completion of the acquisition, ACI Japan was renamed **Aron Ever-Grip Ltd.** [*Chemical Market Reporter,* 9/21/98, p. 25.]

Tripos UK Holdings bought **Receptor Research Ltd.,** a United Kingdom-based specialty chemicals company focused on molecular informatics, design, and analysis for pharmaceutical, agricultural, and biotechnology industries, on November 18, 1997. [*PR Newswire,* 11/18/97.]

U.S. Home & Garden Inc. bought **Ampro Industries Inc.,** a specialty seed and mulch manufacturer and marketer with annual sales of $20 million, for $23 million in October of 1998. [*Business Wire,* 10/19/98.]

Bibliography

"Acquisitions, Expansions." *Rubber World,* 2/96, p. 6.

"Arthur D. Little: Growth and innovation are top priorities—The 1998 Chemical Industry Survey." *M2 PressWire,* 12/11/98.

Baker, John. "Petchem Producers Focus on M&A Deals." *ECN-European Chemical News,* 9/21/98, p. 17.

Chang, Joseph. "Chem Makers Curb Spending as Profits and Margins Erode." *Chemical Market Reporter,* 9/14/98, p. 1.

"Chemical Performance Boosted by M&A Activity." *ECN-European Chemical News,* 4/27/98, p. 16.

"Chemicals: Basic." *Standard & Poor's Industry Survey,* 7/30/98.

"Chemicals: Specialty." *Standard & Poor's Industry Survey,* 5/7/98.

"Consolidation Drives UK Corporates." *Acquisitions Monthly,* 3/97, p. 12.

"European M&A Activity Set to Boom in 1997." *ECN-European Chemical News,* 3/31/97, p. 4.

"Executive Q&A." *Chemical Market Reporter,* 8/10/98, p. 40.

Hamilton, Martha M. "Chemical Giants Agree to Merger; Dow to Acquire Union Carbide." *The Washington Post,* 8/5/99, p. E01.

"Hercules Completes Acquisition of BetzDearborn." *Business Wire,* 10/15/98.

Holmes, Lawrie. "The Deal of the Century?" *ECN-European Chemical News,* 5/19/97, p. 16.

Howie, Michael. "DuPont/Pioneer Deal May Spur Industry Reorganization." *Feedstuffs,* 8/18/97, p. 1.

Hunter, David. "CW Ranks the Banks." *Chemical Week,* 3/31/1999.

"Monsanto Announces Plan to Fund Seed Company Acquisitions." *PR Newswire,* 11/11/98.

"ICI Takes Over Unilever's Quest." *Cosmetics International,* 5/25/97, p. 1.

Kovski, Alan. "Additives Business Consolidates as Firms Wrestle with Costs." *The Oil Daily,* 7/15/98.

"Monsanto: The Makings of an Agro Monopoly?" *ECN-European Chemical News,* 5/25/98, p. 25.

Morse, Paige. " Equistar Dominates Petrochemicals." *Chemical & Engineering News,* 6/8/98, p. 22.

"New Global Coatings JV." *Ward's Auto World,* 7/97, p. 47.

Reisch, Marc S. "ICI: Less Imperial, More Specialty." *Chemical & Engineering News,* 8/25/97, p. 15.

Reisch, Marc S. "Ciba Ousts Hercules in Battle for Allied Colloids." *Chemical & Engineering News,* 1/26/98, p. 10.

Stevens, Tim. "Sowing Seeds of Success." *Industry Week,* 9/6/99.

Walsh, Kerri. "Nalco: Changing for the Better." *Chemical Week,* 8/25/97, p. 38.

Westervelt, Robert. "PPG's Priorities." *Chemical Week,* 2/25/98, p. 27.

Young, Ian. "Investors Keep the Faith in Asia." *Chemical Week,* 3/3/1999.

—AnnaMarie L. Sheldon, updated by Katherine Wagner.

CHAPTER 7 - PART I

ASSOCIATIONS

This chapter presents a selection of business and professional associations active in the Chemicals sector. The information shown is adapted from Gale's *Encyclopedia of Associations* series and provides detailed and comprehensive information on nonprofit membership organizations.

Entries are arranged in alphabetical order. Categories included are name, address, contact person, telphone, toll-free number, fax number, E-mail address and web site URL (when provided). A text block shows founding date, staff, number of members, budget, and a general description of activities.

ADHESIVE AND SEALANT COUNCIL
7979 Old Georgetown Rd.
Bethesda, MD 20814
Kerry L. Lake, Pres.
PH: (301)986-9700
FX: (301)986-9795
URL: www.ascouncil.org
Founded: 1957. **Staff:** 9. **Members:** 184. **Budget:** 1,300,000. Firms manufacturing and selling adhesives and sealants in either solid or liquid form; raw materials and equipment suppliers; consulting firms. Operates Adhesive and Sealant Council Education Foundation; compiles statistics.

ADHESIVES MANUFACTURERS ASSOCIATION
401 N. Michigan Ave., 24th Fl.
Chicago, IL 60611-4267
Christine Norris, Exec.Dir.
PH: (312)644-6610
FX: (312)321-6869
E-mail: ama@sba.com
URL: www.adhesives.org/ama
Founded: 1933. **Staff:** 4. **Members:** 41. Manufacturers of formulated adhesives or formulated adhesives coatings for industrial use and suppliers of chemicals used in manufacturing adhesives.

AGRICULTURAL RETAILERS ASSOCIATION
11701 Borman Dr., Ste. 110
St. Louis, MO 63146
Paul E. Kindinger, Pres./CEO
PH: (314)567-6655
TF: (800)844-4900
FX: (314)567-6808
E-mail: ara@agretailersassn.org
URL: www.agretailerassn.org
Founded: 1954. **Staff:** 19. **Members:** 1,100. Retailers, manufacturers, and suppliers of fertilizers and agrichemicals; equipment manufacturers; retail affiliations; and state association affiliates.

AMERICAN ASSOCIATION OF RADON SCIENTISTS AND TECHNOLOGISTS
1313 Dolly Madison Blvd. Ste. 402
Mc Lean, VA 22101
Linda Hansen, Exec.Sec.
PH: (703)790-1745
TF: (800)893-9960
FX: (703)790-2672
E-mail: aarst@burkinc.com
Founded: 1986. **Staff:** 2. **Members:** 1,100. **Budget:** 100,000. Scientists and tradespeople engaged in radon gas testing and remediation. Seeks to improve members' skills and effectiveness; conducts educational and research programs; maintains speakers' bureau; compiles statistics.

AMERICAN HEALTH AND BEAUTY AIDS INSTITUTE
401 N. Michigan, Ste. 2200
Chicago, IL 60611-4267
Geri Duncan Jones, Exec. Dir.
PH: (312)644-6610
FX: (312)527-6658
E-mail: ahbai@sba.com
URL: www.proudlady.org
Founded: 1981. **Staff:** 3. **Members:** 18. Minority-owned companies engaged in manufacturing and marketing health and beauty aids for the black consumer. Represents the interests of members and the industry before local, state, and federal governmental agencies. Assists with business development and economic progress within the minority community by providing informational and educational resources. Maintains speakers' bureau. Conducts annual Proud Lady Beauty Show.

AMERICAN SOCIETY OF ELECTROPLATED PLASTICS
112 J Elden Street
Herndon, VA 20170
David W. Barrack, Exec.Dir.

PH: (703)709-1034
FX: (703)709-1036
E-mail: namf@erols.com
URL: www.namf.org
Founded: 1967. **Staff:** 3. **Members:** 40. **Budget:** 130,000. Firms engaged in the manufacture, sale, and/or development of equipment, materials, processes, or provision of services to the electroplating on plastics industry. Has developed quality standards for the manufacture and electroplating of articles handled by metal finishing firms. Represents the industry in legislative and governmental matters. Conducts automotive and consumer products technical conferences and electronics shielding seminar.

ARCHITECTURAL SPRAY COATERS ASSOCIATION
895 Doncaster Dr.
Paulsboro, NJ 08066
Alan J. Carlson, Exec.Dir.
PH: (609)848-6120
FX: (609)251-1243
E-mail: ascassoc@erols.com
URL: www.ascassoc.com
Founded: 1986. **Staff:** 1. **Members:** 25. Companies that apply high-performance and fluorocarbon finishes to metals used in architecture (16); related manufacturers/ suppliers (8). Goals are to: promote excellence in metal spray coating; improve business and industry methods; share technical information and educate the construction industry in the use of architectural spray coatings; establish standards for high-performance specifications of spray coaters for architectural and industrial applications. Conducts sessions on topics such as metallic and architectural finishing, air pollution, and solid waste disposal. Informs members of legislation pertinent to the industry.

ASSOCIATION OF ROTATIONAL MOLDERS
2000 Spring Rd., Ste. 511
Oak Brook, IL 60523
Charles D. Frederick, Exec.Dir.
PH: (630)571-0611
FX: (630)571-0616
E-mail: 104360.204@compuserve.com
URL: www.rotomolding.org
Founded: 1976. **Staff:** 6. **Members:** 460. **Budget:** 1,200,000. Plastic processors who use the rotational molding process; their suppliers; overseas molders. Purposes are to increase awareness of rotomolding, exchange technical information, provide education, and standardize production guidelines. Conducts research; produces seminars and educational video and slide programs. Sponsors product contest.

BEAUTY AND BARBER SUPPLY INSTITUTE
11811 N. Tatum Blvd., Ste. 1085
Phoenix, AZ 85028
Frederic P. Polk, Exec.VP
TF: (800)468-2274
FX: (602)404-1800
E-mail: spano@bbsi.org
URL: www.bbsi.org
Founded: 1904. **Staff:** 9. **Members:** 1,500. Wholesalers and manufacturers of beauty and barber salon equipment and supplies. Offers group life and major medical insurance; furnishes information on sales management. Conducts educational programs; maintains hall of fame.

CHEMICAL FABRICS AND FILM ASSOCIATION
1300 Sumner Ave.
Cleveland, OH 44115-2851
Charles M. Stockinger, Exec.Sec.
PH: (216)241-7333
FX: (216)241-0105
E-mail: cffa@aol.com
URL: www.taol.com/cffa
Founded: 1927. **Staff:** 3. **Members:** 38. Manufacturers of chemically coated materials, supported and unsupported vinyl, and urethane materials. Associate member raw suppliers.

COMPRESSED GAS ASSOCIATION
1725 Jefferson Davis Hwy., Ste. 1004
Arlington, VA 22202-4100
Carl T. Johnson, CEO & Pres.
PH: (703)412-0900
FX: (703)412-0128
E-mail: cga@cganet.com
URL: www.cganet.com
Founded: 1913. **Staff:** 16. **Members:** 230. **Budget:** 3,000,000.
Firms producing and distributing compressed, liquefied, and cryogenic gases; manufacturers of related equipment. Submits recommendations to appropriate government agencies to improve safety standards and methods of handling, transporting, and storing gases; acts as advisor to regulatory authorities and other agencies concerned with safe handling of compressed gases; collaborates with national organizations to develop specifications and standards of safety; compiles information. Maintains 25 technical committees.

COSMETIC EXECUTIVE WOMEN
20 E. 69th St., Ste. 5C
New York, NY 10021
Jean Hoehn Zimmerman, Pres.
PH: (212)717-2415
FX: (212)717-2419
E-mail: cexecutive@aol.com
URL: www.beautyawards.com
Founded: 1954. **Staff:** 2. **Members:** 1,000. Women who have served for more than three years in executive positions in the cosmetic and allied industries. Unites women executives in the cosmetic field for industry awareness and business advancement. Conducts seminars and luncheons.

COSMETIC INDUSTRY BUYERS AND SUPPLIERS
J. Palazzolo Son, Inc.
36 Lakeville Rd.
New Hyde Park, NY 11040
Joseph A. Palazzolo, Exec. Officer
PH: (516)775-0220
FX: (516)328-9789
Founded: 1948. **Members:** 385. Buyers and suppliers of essential oils, chemicals, packaging, and finished goods relative to the cosmetic industry. To enhance growth, stability, prosperity, and protection of the American cosmetic industry through close personal contact and the exchange of ideas and experiences.

COSMETIC INGREDIENT REVIEW
1101 17 St. NW, Ste. 310
Washington, DC 20036
Dr. F. Alan Andersen, Dir./Scientific Coor.
PH: (202)331-0651
FX: (202)331-0088
E-mail: cirinfo@ctfa-cir.org
URL: www.ctfa-cir.org
Founded: 1976. **Staff:** 6. A cosmetic industry self-regulatory organization sponsored by the Cosmetic, Toiletry, and Fragrance Association. Seeks to assure the safety of ingredients used in cosmetics. Reviews scientific data on the safety of ingredients used in cosmetics; documents validity of tests used to study ingredients.

COSMETIC, TOILETRY AND FRAGRANCE ASSOCIATION
1101 17th St. NW, Ste. 300
Washington, DC 20036
E. Edward Kavanaugh, Pres.
PH: (202)331-1770
FX: (202)331-1969
URL: www.ctfa.org/
Founded: 1894. **Staff:** 45. **Members:** 525. **Budget:** 8,000,000.
Manufacturers and distributors of finished cosmetics, fragrances, and personal care products; suppliers of raw materials and services. Provides scientific, legal, regulatory, and legislative services; coordinates public service, educational, and public affairs activities.

FERTILIZER INDUSTRY ROUND TABLE
5234 Glen Arm Rd.
Glen Arm, MD 21057
Paul J. Prosser, Sec.-Treas.
PH: (410)592-6271
FX: (410)592-5796
Founded: 1951. Participants include production, technical, and research personnel in the fertilizer industry. Acts as a forum for discussion of technical and production problems.

THE FERTILIZER INSTITUTE
501 2nd St. NE
Washington, DC 20002
Gary D. Myers, Pres.
PH: (202)675-8250
FX: (202)544-8123
URL: www.tfi.org
Founded: 1970. **Staff:** 22. **Members:** 300. Producers, manufacturers, retailers, trading firms, and equipment manufacturers. Represents members in various legislative, educational, and technical areas. Provides information and public relations programs.

FIBER SOCIETY
161 Sirrine Hall
Clemson Univ.
Fiber and Polymer Science
School of Textiles
Clemson, SC 29634-1307
Dr. Bhuvenesh Goswami, Sec./Treas.
PH: (864)656-5957
FX: (864)656-5973
E-mail: gbhuven@clemson.edu
Founded: 1941. **Members:** 400. **Budget:** 25,000. Chemists, physicists, engineers, biologists, mathematicians, and other scientists conducting research in fibers, fiber products, and fibrous materials. Sponsors lecture program.

FORAGERS OF AMERICA
25 Central Park W., Apt. 121
New York, NY 10023
Adam Finkelstein, Pres.
PH: (718)648-4903
FX: (212)754-2256
Founded: 1897. **Members:** 200. Cosmetic sales executives and cosmetic buyers. Seeks to create a forum for both retailer and manufacturer to discuss their mutual problems. Conducts buyer symposia.

GLOVE SHIPPERS ASSOCIATION
PO Box 1908
San Juan Capistrano, CA 92693-1908
James A. Murphy, Managing Dir.
PH: (714)487-7270
TF: (877)877-8780
FX: (714)487-7271
E-mail: gloveship@earthlink.net
URL: www.gloveshippers.com
Founded: 1989. **Staff:** 9. **Members:** 1,300. **Budget:** 750,000.
Latex, nitrite, synthetic, and plastic glove, medical and allied products manufacturers and distributors. Conducts research programs; compiles statistics. Maintains a worldwide exclusive insurance and shipping program.

INDEPENDENT COSMETIC MANUFACTURERS AND
DISTRIBUTORS
1220 W. Northwest Hwy.
Palatine, IL 60067
Penni Jones, Exec.Dir.
PH: (847)991-4499
TF: (800)33-ICMAD
FX: (847)991-8161
E-mail: info@icmad.org
URL: www.icmad.org
Founded: 1974. **Staff:** 5. **Members:** 650. Represents small cosmetic manufacturers, distributors, and retailers. Presents members'

views and problems to Congress, the FDA, consumers, and the media. Areas of concern include product testing procedures, escalating costs for product liability insurance, and manufacturing practice regulations. Upholds the principle of meaningful consumer protection. Provides a group program for product liability insurance.

INDUSTRIAL COMPRESSOR DISTRIBUTORS ASSOCIATION
412 Harbor View Ln.
Largo, FL 33760-2707
Margot Gillian, Exec.Dir.
PH: (727)586-3693
FX: (727)586-3573
Founded: 1979. **Staff:** 2. **Members:** 83. Represents the interests of companies involved in the sales and distribution of industrial compressors, especially those manufactured by Cooper Industries IMD Division. (Industrial compressors are machines that compress air for industrial use.) Establishes educational standards and sponsors educational programs; conducts manufacturer relations activities.

INSTITUTE OF MAKERS OF EXPLOSIVES
1120 19th St. NW, Ste. 310
Washington, DC 20036
J. Christopher Ronay, Pres.
PH: (202)429-9280
FX: (202)293-2420
E-mail: info@ime.org
URL: www.ime.org
Founded: 1913. **Staff:** 8. **Members:** 33. Manufacturers of commercial explosives and blasting supplies concerned with the safety and protection of their employees, user, the public and the environment. Provides technically accurate information and recommendations concerning explosive material and their uses. Serves as a source of reliable information. Conducts national blasting cap safety education program.

INTERNATIONAL ALOE SCIENCE COUNCIL
1300 E Rochelle Blvd., Ste. A1047
Irving, TX 75062
Gene Hale, Mgr.Dir.
PH: (972)258-8772
FX: (972)258-8777
E-mail: iasc@airmail.net
URL: www.iasc.org
Founded: 1981. **Staff:** 2. **Members:** 206. **Budget:** 175,000. Manufacturers and marketers of foods, drugs, and cosmetics containing gel of the aloe vera plant. Goals are: to provide scientific research for support of product claims; to educate members on the plant and its products and uses; to act as a liaison for government agency regulations on aloe vera business.

INTERNATIONAL ASSOCIATION OF BOMB TECHNICIANS AND INVESTIGATORS
PO Box 8629
Naples, FL 33941
Glenn E. Wilt, Exec.Dir.
PH: (941)353-6843
FX: (941)353-6841
Founded: 1973. **Staff:** 1. **Members:** 3,600. **Budget:** 367,000. Seeks to: increase professionalism and training of bomb technicians and investigators; foster an exchange of ideas and information within the field of explosives, both technical and investigative; encourage friendship and cooperation among technical and investigative personnel; stimulate research and the development of new techniques within the field of explosives.

INTERNATIONAL ASSOCIATION OF PLASTICS DISTRIBUTORS
4707 College Blvd., Ste. 105
Leawood, KS 66211
Deborah M. Hamlin, CAE, Exec.Dir.
PH: (913)345-1005
FX: (913)345-1006
E-mail: iapd@iapd.org
URL: www.iapd.org
Founded: 1955. **Staff:** 6. **Members:** 450. **Budget:** 825,000. Distributors of plastics materials, piping, and resins; firms that both manufacture and distribute these materials; manufacturers who sell their products through plastics distributors. Objectives are to promote education and training of plastics distributors. Maintains liaison with associated organizations. Compiles statistics.

INTERNATIONAL FERTILIZER DEVELOPMENT CENTER
PO Box 2040
Muscle Shoals, AL 35662
Dr. Amit H. Roy, Pres. & CEO
PH: (205)381-6600
FX: (205)381-7408
E-mail: general@ifdc.org
URL: www.ifdc.org
Founded: 1974. **Staff:** 180. **Budget:** 13,500,000. Participants include scientists, engineers, economists, and specialists in market research and development, communications, and personnel development. To alleviate world hunger by increasing agricultural production in the tropics and subtropics through development of improved fertilizer and fertilizer use. Studies ways of processing indigenous resources of phosphate rock into efficient fertilizers; conducts nitrogen efficiency research; examines the agronomic efficiency of sulfur sources such as gypsum, anhydrite, and pyrites; sponsors studies of potassium, magnesium, and calcium use. Conducts in-depth studies of fertilizer markets in order to design plans for the implementation of appropriate working systems. Sponsors human resource development programs in the areas of fertilizer marketing, evaluation and use, and production. Offers production courses on fluid fertilizers, granulation, ammonia/urea plant operations, sustainable crop production, environmental issues, and manufacturing process economics. Compiles and analyzes data in areas including plant investment, worldwide production capacity, price trends, raw materials deposits, and distribution costs. Advises countries on agribusiness policies and technologies with the goal of economic development and increased production. Maintains laboratories and greenhouses, pilot-scale fertilizer manufacturing plants, and training centers.

INTERNATIONAL INSTITUTE OF SYNTHETIC RUBBER PRODUCERS
2077 S. Gessner Rd., Ste. 133
Houston, TX 77063-1123
Richard J. Killian
PH: (713)783-7511
FX: (713)783-7253
E-mail: info@iisrp.com
URL: www.iisrp.com
Founded: 1960. **Staff:** 6. **Members:** 50. **Budget:** 1,000,000. Synthetic rubber manufacturers in 19 countries. Promotes standardization of synthetic rubber polymers; cooperates with governmental departments and agencies in matters affecting the industry; compiles statistics. Has made research grants to universities and institutes in Japan, United States, France, United Kingdom, Germany, and the Netherlands. European office is in London, England; Far Eastern Office is in Tokyo, Japan.

INTERNATIONAL OXYGEN MANUFACTURERS ASSOCIATION
PO Box 16248
Cleveland, OH 44116-0248
Richard S. Croy, Exec.Dir.
PH: (216)228-2166
FX: (216)228-5810
Founded: 1943. **Members:** 190. **Budget:** 500,000. Producers and distributors of compressed and liquefied industrial and medical gases and acetylene; manufacturers of products and equipment used by the industrial gas and cryogenics industries.

INTERNATIONAL OZONE ASSOCIATION
31 Strawberry Hill Ave.
Stamford, CT 06902
Margit Istok, Exec.Dir.
PH: (203)348-3542
FX: (203)967-4845
E-mail: mistok@int-ozone-assoc.org
URL: www.int-ozone-assoc.org
Founded: 1973. **Staff:** 3. **Members:** 800. **Budget:** 150,000. Individuals, companies, consulting engineering firms, service/support organizations that design, sell, service, or use ozone equipment, manufacturers, municipal services, institutions, and cooperating organizations. Works to advance the positive applications of ozone; further ozone technology through scientific and educational means.

INTERNATIONAL SOCIETY OF EXPLOSIVES ENGINEERS
29100 Aurora Rd.
Cleveland, OH 44139-1800
Jeffrey L. Dean, Exec.Dir. and Gen.Counsel
PH: (216)349-4004
FX: (216)349-3788
E-mail: isee@isee.org
URL: www.isee.org
Founded: 1975. **Staff:** 9. **Members:** 4,000. **Budget:** 1,000,000. Persons engaged in, or who have been engaged in, explosives engineering; interested persons and organizations, including those involved in the fields of construction, quarrying, mining, demolition, geophysical prospecting, vibration control, drilling and blasting, and the use and handling of explosives in general. Offers services in matters affecting the manufacture, transportation, storage, and use of explosives and related equipment. Acts as a repository for all information, both inside and outside of the U.S., on explosives engineering. Promotes standardization of terminology in explosives engineering and develops standard methods. Encourages inclusion of explosives engineering instruction in engineering curricula. Maintains speakers' bureau and placement service.

NATIONAL PAINT AND COATINGS ASSOCIATION
1500 Rhode Island Ave. NW
Washington, DC 20005-5597
James A. Doyle, Pres.
PH: (202)462-6272
FX: (202)462-8549
E-mail: npca@paint.org
URL: www.paint.org
Founded: 1933. **Staff:** 40. **Members:** 450. **Budget:** 6,000,000. Manufacturers of paints and chemical coatings; suppliers of raw materials and equipment. Conducts: statistical surveys; research, government, and public relations programs. Provides management information programs and management and technician development programs. Compiles statistics.

NATIONAL SPRAY EQUIPMENT MANUFACTURERS ASSOCIATION
550 Randall Rd.
Elyria, OH 44035
Don R. Scarbrough, Exec.Sec.
PH: (440)366-6808
FX: (440)366-1760
Founded: 1922. **Members:** 16. Manufacturers of spray-painting and related equipment. Provides fire prevention and safety information. Serves as forum within the industry for the sharing of safety and environmental information. **Publications:** none.

NATURAL-SOURCE VITAMIN E ASSOCIATION
c/o William R. Pendergast
1050 Connecticut Ave. NW,
Washington, DC 20036-5339
William R. Pendergast, Exec.Dir.
PH: (202)857-6029
FX: (202)857-6395
Founded: 1984. **Members:** 3. Corporations engaged in the manufacture of natural source vitamin E. Purpose is to promote the sale of natural source vitamin E.

NORTH AMERICAN INDUSTRIAL HEMP COUNCIL
PO Box 259329
Madison, WI 53725-9329
Erwin A. Sholts, Chm.
PH: (608)258-0243
Founded: 1995. Works to re-establish and expand the use of industrial hemp.

PLASTIC AND METAL PRODUCTS MANUFACTURERS ASSOCIATION
145 West 45th St., Ste. 800
New York, NY 10036
Sheldon M. Edelman, Exec.Dir.
PH: (212)398-5400
FX: (212)398-7818
Founded: 1937. **Staff:** 7. **Members:** 120. Manufacturers of housewares, toys, handbag accessories and parts, costume jewelry, and optical frames.

PLASTIC SOFT MATERIALS MANUFACTURERS ASSOCIATION
145 W. 45th St., Ste. 800
New York, NY 10036-4008
Sheldon M. Edelman, Exec.Dir.
Staff: 9. **Members:** 70. No further information was available for this edition.

PLASTICS EDUCATION FOUNDATION
14 Fairfield Dr.
Brookfield, CT 06804-0403
Michael R. Cappelletti, Exec.Dir.
PH: (203)775-0471
FX: (203)775-8490
Founded: 1968. Assists in the planning, organization, and coordination of educational activities in plastics. Develops media-based plastics training and education programs, especially for operators, technicians, and technologists. Plans and coordinates development of instructional materials which are made available to educational institutions and plastics processing plants. Absorbed as division of Society of Plastics Engineers (see separate entry) in 1983. **Convention/ Meeting:** none.

PLASTICS INSTITUTE OF AMERICA
333 Aiken St.
Lowell, MA 01854-3617
Dr. Aldo Crugnola, Exec.Dir.
PH: (978)934-3130
FX: (978)459-9420
E-mail: pia@cae.uml.edu
URL: www.eng.uml.edu/Dept/PIA
Founded: 1961. **Staff:** 6. **Members:** 50. Educational and research organization supported on a cooperative basis by companies in the plastics and allied industries. Established to conduct fundamental research in plastics science and engineering, to carry on educational activities at the graduate school level in these fields, and to provide comprehensive technical information to its members. Conducts a graduate level program of education for plastics scientists and engineers, in cooperation with major U.S. universities and colleges involved in polymer science and engineering.

POLYURETHANE DIVISION, SOCIETY OF THE PLASTICS INDUSTRY
1801 K St. NW, Ste. 600k
Washington, DC 20006-1300
Fran W. Lichtenberg, Exec.Dir.
PH: (202)974-5364
FX: (202)296-7005
URL: www.polyurethane.org
Founded: 1962. **Staff:** 5. **Members:** 60. **Budget:** 1,800,000. Manufacturers of chemicals used in the manufacture of polyurethane foam and foam products such as furniture cushions, bedding, and building insulation; equipment manufacturers.

POLYURETHANE FOAM ASSOCIATION
PO Box 1459
Wayne, NJ 07470
Louis H. Peters, Exec.Dir.
PH: (973)633-9044
FX: (973)628-8986
URL: www.pfa.org
Founded: 1980. **Staff:** 1. **Members:** 61. Manufacturers of flexible polyurethane foam; suppliers of goods and services to the industry. Provides a forum for discussion of industry issues and makes current information available to members. Monitors legal and regulatory issues. Conducts technical research with other organizations on subjects including test procedures and standards. Compiles marketing statistics.

POLYURETHANE MANUFACTURERS ASSOCIATION
800 Roosevelt Rd., Bldg. C, Ste. 20
Glen Ellyn, IL 60137-5833
Richard W. Church, Exec.Dir.
PH: (630)858-2670
FX: (630)790-3095
Founded: 1971. **Staff:** 4. **Members:** 120. Manufacturing companies whose products are primarily of polyurethane raw materials; suppliers to these manufacturers. Purposes are to improve conditions in the industry and exchange information. Maintains speakers' bureau.

PRESSURE SENSITIVE TAPE COUNCIL
401 N. Michigan Ave., No. 2200
Chicago, IL 60611-4267
Glen R. Anderson, Exec.VP
PH: (312)644-6610
FX: (312)527-6640
E-mail: pstc@sba.com
URL: www.pstc.org
Founded: 1953. **Staff:** 3. **Members:** 28. **Budget:** 500,000. Manufacturers of cellophane, cloth, paper, plastic, and rubber pressure sensitive tape products. Maintains research on test methods and standards of nomenclature, and on characteristics of products under all conditions of humidity and temperature. Works with code and specification writing agencies.

RUBBER MANUFACTURERS ASSOCIATION
1400 K St. NW, Ste. 900
Washington, DC 20005
Donald Shea, Pres.
Founded: 1915. **Staff:** 22. **Members:** 97. **Budget:** 4,000,000. Manufacturers of tires, tubes, mechanical and industrial products, roofing, sporting goods, and other rubber products. Compiles monthly, quarterly, and annual statistics on rubber and rubber products.

RUBBER TRADE ASSOCIATION OF NORTH AMERICA
220 Maple Ave.
PO Box 196
Rockville Centre, NY 11571
Fred B. Finley, Sec.
PH: (516)536-2218
FX: (516)536-3771
Founded: 1914. **Staff:** 2. **Members:** 43. **Budget:** 100,000. Dealers' group: importers of crude natural rubber from the Far East and exporters of synthetic rubber. Brokers' and agents' group: representatives of Far Eastern shippers. Associate members' group: suppliers of services to the rubber trade, such as steamship companies and banks. RTA is a local organization; however, members import more than 75% of crude rubber consumed in the U.S.

SEALANT WATERPROOFING AND RESTORATION INSTITUTE
2841 Main
Kansas City, MO 64108
Kenneth R. Bowman, Exec.VP
PH: (816)472-7974
FX: (816)472-7765
URL: www.swrionline.org
Founded: 1976. **Staff:** 9. **Members:** 160. **Budget:** 100,000. Sealant contractors; suppliers of sealants and related products; other interested persons. Works to: promote exchange of ideas for the development of the highest standards and operating efficiency within the industry; develop industry-wide standards and specifications; improve conditions affecting the sealant and waterproofing industry.

SOAP AND DETERGENT ASSOCIATION
475 Park Ave. S., 27th Fl.
New York, NY 10016
Gerald R. Pflug, Ph.D., Pres.
PH: (212)725-1262
FX: (212)213-0685
Founded: 1926. **Staff:** 20. **Members:** 145. Manufacturers of cleaning products, their ingredients and finished packaging. Activities include consumer information, environmental and human safety research, and government liaison.

SOCIETY FOR WOMEN IN PLASTICS
PO Box 325
Sterling Heights, MI 48311-0325
Founded: 1979. **Members:** 102. Women with education or employment experience in the field of plastics or related businesses. Promotes knowledge of the plastics industry. Conducts plant tours; operates speakers' bureau.

SOCIETY OF PLASTICS ENGINEERS
14 Fairfield Dr.
Brookfield, CT 06804-0403
Michael R. Cappelletti, Exec.Dir.
PH: (203)775-0471
FX: (203)775-8490
E-mail: 4spemail@4spe.org
URL: www.4spe.org
Founded: 1942. **Staff:** 41. **Members:** 36,000. **Budget:** 8,000,000. Professional society of plastics scientists, engineers, sales professionals, educators, students, and others interested in the design, development, production, and utilization of plastics materials, products, and equipment. Conducts seminars. Maintains 92 sections.

SOCIETY OF THE PLASTICS INDUSTRY
1801 K St. NW, Ste. 600K
Washington, DC 20006
Larry L. Thomas, Pres.
PH: (202)974-5200
FX: (202)296-7005
E-mail: feedback@socplas.org
URL: www.socplas.org
Founded: 1937. **Staff:** 130. **Members:** 2,000. Manufacturers and processors of molded, extruded, fabricated, laminated, calendered, and reinforced plastics; manufacturers of raw materials, machinery, tools, dies, and molds; testing laboratories; consultants. Supports research; proposes standards for plastics products. Compiles statistics. Sponsors tradeshow. Organizes competitions.

SPI COMPOSITES INSTITUTE
1801 K St. NW, Ste. 600K
Washington, DC 20006-1301
Catherine A. Randazzo, Exec.Dir.
PH: (914)381-3572
FX: (914)381-1253
E-mail: ci@socplas.org
Founded: 1945. **Staff:** 12. **Members:** 415. A division of the Society of the Plastics Industry. Companies and individuals who are molders and fabricators of glass and other fiber reinforced plastics; materials and equipment suppliers; consultants and users of fiberglass/ composite products. Represents members in all matters pertaining to the industry; compiles statistical reports, promotional programs, analyses of governmental relations; makes available legal guidance; assists in the development of testing procedures. Through its committees, seeks to develop technical procedures, promote professional advancement of its members, and supply information to the government and the public. Sponsors exhibits and plant tours. Compiles statistics.

SSPC: THE SOCIETY FOR PROTECTIVE COATINGS
40 24th St., 6th Fl.
Pittsburgh, PA 15222-4656
Dr. Bernard R. Appleman, Exec.Dir.
PH: (412)281-2331
TF: (877)281-7772
FX: (412)281-9992
URL: www.sspc.org
Founded: 1950. **Staff:** 30. **Members:** 8,600. **Budget:** 3,700,000.
Seeks to advance the technology and promote the use of protective
coatings to preserve industrial, marine and commercial structures,
components and substrates.

UNITED STATES SHELLAC IMPORTERS ASSOCIATION
173 Belmont Dr.
Somerset, NJ 08875
Kevin Harrington, Pres.
PH: (732)469-8100
FX: (732)469-4539
Founded: 1910. **Members:** 10. Importers, wholesalers, and manu-
facturers.

**UNITED STEEL WORKERS OF AMERICA, RUBBER/
 PLASTICS INDUSTRY CONFERENCE**
570 White Pond Dr.
Akron, OH 44320-1156
John Sellers, Contact
PH: (330)869-0320
FX: (330)869-5627
Founded: 1935. **Members:** 90,000. AFL-CIO, Canadian Labour
Congress.

CONSULTANTS

Consultants and consulting organizations active in the Chemicals sector are featured in this chapter. Entries are adapted from Gale's *Consultants and Consulting Organizations Directory* (*CCOD*). Each entry represents an expertise which may be of interest to business organizations, government agencies, non-profit institutions, and individuals requiring technical and other support. The listees shown are located in the United States and Canada.

In Canada, the use of the term "consultant" is restricted. The use of the word, in this chapter, does not necessarily imply that the firm has been granted the "consultant" designation in Canada.

Entries are arranged in alphabetical order. Categories include contact information (address, phone, fax, web site, E-mail); names and titles of executive officers; and a descriptive block that begins with founding year and staff.

AGES CORP.
1151 S. Trooper Rd.
Norristown, Pennsylvania 19403
A.A. Fungaroli, Ph.D., P.E.
PH: (610)666-7404
FX: (610)666-1350
Founded: 1975. **Staff:** 35. **Activities:** AGES is the acronym for Applied Geotechnical and Environmental Services Corp.; it signifies a concept for providing comprehensive consulting services that has evolved from first-hand experience in solving complex environmental and geotechnical problems. Integrated professional services include engineering - civil, environmental, geotechnical, chemical, and engineering geology; analytical laboratory including soils testing and evaluation; total waste management including landfill services, industrial wastestream assessment, and energy generation systems; applied earth sciences - geology and hydrogeology for subsurface investigations; resource recovery systems; hazardous waste management, monitoring, analysis and pre-treatment facilities; and environmental assessment and impact statements. Clients include architects, attorneys, contractors, engineers, federal agencies, industrial developers, insurance companies, land use planners, local governments, real estate developers, and state governments.

AGRA EARTH & ENVIRONMENTAL
221-18 St. SE
Calgary, Alberta, Canada T2E 6J5
W. A. Slusarchuk, President
PH: (403)248-4331
FX: (403)248-2188
URL: www.agra.com/aee
Founded: 1951. **Staff:** 1500. **Activities:** AGRA Earth & Environmental is one of North America's largest full service engineering consulting firms, experienced in all aspects of earth and environmental engineering requirements including: environmental management, science and engineering services; geotechnical engineering; materials engineering and testing; mining services; human environmental services; water resources services; and environmental management information systems. The company provides comprehensive services to clients from the private sector, various levels of government, international financial institutions and Fortune 500 companies, and has developed numerous local, national and international client partnerships with major corporations throughout North America. International experience includes oil and gas related work, liability assessments and remediation, water resource projects, environmental impact assessment, cold region work, materials testing, geotechnical engineering and the development of customized environmental management information systems in more than 40 countries from the Soviet Union and Easter Europe to Asia, Africa, South America and the Pacific Rim.

AMBRIC TESTING & ENGINEERING ASSOCIATES, INC.
3502 Scotts Ln.
Philadelphia, Pennsylvania 19129
D.D. Meisel, P.E., CEO/Vice Chairman
PH: (215)438-1800
FX: (215)438-7110
E-mail: ambric@aol.com
URL: www.ambric.com
Founded: 1961. **Staff:** 130. **Activities:** Offers expertise in the following areas: laboratory testing; forensic, engineering, and inspection services; and seismographic, geotechnical, and chemical services. Has experience in environmental testing and assessments. Offers complete consultation on Total Quality System Management and its implementation in compliance with ISO 9000/ISO 14000/QS 9000.

AMERICAN ANALYTICAL LABORATORIES
840 S. Main St.
Akron, Ohio 44311
Richard E. Moore, President
PH: (330)535-1300
TF: (800)837-2251
FX: (330)535-7246
E-mail: aal@raex.com
URL: www.aalinc.com
Founded: 1985. **Staff:** 42. **Activities:** Offers chemical analysis consulting. Performs testing and classification of hazardous materials, and industrial hygiene/environmental chemical analyses.

AMERICAN ENGINEERING TESTING INC.
2102 University Ave., W.
St. Paul, Minnesota 55114
Terrance E. Swor, President
PH: (612)659-9001
TF: (800)97-AM-ENG
FX: (612)659-1379
E-mail: aet@amengtest.com
Founded: 1970. **Staff:** 145. **Activities:** Soil testing, geotechnical engineering, environmental, and construction materials consultancy offering the following: monitoring well installation, environmental site assessments, remedial investigations, slope stability analysis, foundation engineering, field quality control for both geotechnical and construction activities and materials testing and engineering. Serves private industries as well as government agencies.

ANALYTICAL DEVELOPMENT CORP.
4405 N. Chestnut St.
Colorado Springs, Colorado 80907
Robert J. Pollock, President
PH: (719)260-1711
FX: (719)260-0695
E-mail: adclabs@sprynet.com
URL: www.home.sprynet.com/~adclabs
Founded: 1970. **Staff:** 18. **Activities:** Conducts contract analytical studies in support of product development and registration for the pharmaceutical, animal health, and agricultural chemical industries. Specializes in applied studies of biologically active compounds in a variety of matrices. Specific studies include analytical methods development and validation, pharmaceutical stability, analysis of therapeutic drug levels in fluids and tissues, animal and plant metabolism, and pesticide residue analysis. All studies conducted under current FDA and EPA Good Laboratory Practices. Company also provides compliance consulting and monitoring services for GLP studies.

APPLIED TECHNICAL SERVICES, INC. (ATS)
1190 Atlanta Industrial Dr.
Marietta, Georgia 30066
J.J. Hills, President
PH: (770)423-1400
FX: (770)424-6415
E-mail: ats@mindspring.com
URL: www.ats.com
Founded: 1967. **Staff:** 80. **Activities:** Offers independent laboratory and consulting services for mechanical testing, chemical analysis, metallurgy, failure analysis, nondestructive testing, calibration, accelerated environmental testing, and fire investigation. Serves private industries as well as government agencies.

APTECH ENGINEERING SERVICES, INC.
1282 Reamwood Ave.
Sunnyvale, California 94089
Geoffrey R. Egan, President
PH: (408)745-7000
TF: (800)477-2228
FX: (408)734-0445
Founded: 1979. **Staff:** 75. **Activities:** An internationally known consulting firm dedicated to the prediction, prevention, investigation, and analysis of failures. Founded as a multidisciplined engineering firm with experts in the following areas: metallurgy and materials engineering; engineering mechanics and welding technology; mechanical, civil, and marine engineering; risk and economic analysis; petrochemical, power, process, and production engineering; chemical engineering; combustion engineering; thermodynamics; and fluid mechanics. These products include condition assessments;

remaining useful life assessment; probabilistic risk assessments; run versus retire versus replace economic analyses; accident investigations, analyses, and reconstruction; and failure analyses. Industries served: nuclear, fossil, oil and gas, petrochemical, transportation, government, and litigation support.

ASSOCIATED ANALYTICAL LABS., INC.
51 E. 42nd St., Ste. 1210
New York, New York 10017
Stuart C. Lerner
PH: (212)682-2544
FX: (212)682-1940
Founded: 1924. **Staff:** 30. Activities: Analytical chemists with expertise in foods, beverages, liquors, chemicals, drugs and waters. Serves the fields of chemistry, microbiology, sanitation, and toxicology. Industries served: individuals, companies, and state and federal agencies.

ASTB/ANALYTICAL SERVICES INC.
4027 New Castle Ave.
New Castle, Delaware 19720
R.G. Rowe, Director
PH: (302)571-8882
TF: (800)221-5170
FX: (302)571-0582
Founded: 1975. **Staff:** 18. Activities: Consulting chemists and environmental scientists to the chemical, manufacturing, insurance, pharmaceutical, food, agricultural, and petroleum industries. Activities also include forensic sciences, environmental studies, and toxicology. Serves private industries as well as government agencies.

BARR ENGINEERING CO.
4700 W. 77th St.
Minneapolis, Minnesota 55435-4803
Douglas E. Connell, Vice President
PH: (612)832-2600
TF: (800)632-2277
FX: (612)832-2601
E-mail: tkramer@barr.com
URL: www.barr.com
Founded: 1966. **Staff:** 320. Activities: Provides air emission control design, air quality sampling, computer modeling, database design, environmental assessments, environmental audits, environmental management systems, geographic information systems, geotechnical, groundwater quality investigations, groundwater treatment design, hazardous waste sampling, hazardous waste treatment systems design, health and safety plans, industrial hygiene, Internet and Intranet applications, laboratory waste management, landfill design, permitting, pollution prevention, process controls, remedial feasibility studies, remedial investigations, risk assessments, sanitary or storm sewer design, stack testing, toxicological studies, training, underground tank management, waste minimization, wastewater sampling, wastewater treatment plant design and water use reduction.

BC LABORATORIES, INC.
4100 Atlas Ct.
Bakersfield, California 93308
J.J. Eglin, President
PH: (805)327-4911
TF: (800)878-4911
FX: (805)327-1918
Founded: 1949. **Staff:** 87. Activities: Analytical consulting laboratory working in the areas of petroleum testing (oil, water, gas and geochemical analysis), environmental pollutants (purgeable halocarbons, and volatile organics), GC/MS, and ICAP/MS.

B.C. RESEARCH INC.
3650 Wesbrook Mall
Vancouver, British Columbia, Canada V6S 2L2
Hugh Wynne-Edwards, President
PH: (604)224-4331
FX: (604)224-0540
E-mail: bcri@bcr.bc.ca
URL: www.bcr.bc.ca

Founded: 1993. **Staff:** 85. Activities: Corporation solves practical industrial problems for clients in both the private and public sectors by performing contract research on a confidential basis. Expertise is offered in the fields of advanced industrial materials, air quality emissions, aquaculture biotechnology, bulk handling, chemical analysis, chemical products and processes, engine systems, extractive metallurgy, fisheries and food products, forest biotechnology, industrial testing, mechanical engineering, natural gas vehicles, occupational health, ocean engineering, redox chemistry, and waste management. Industries served: performs multidisciplinary industrial research in the broad areas of forestry, fisheries, engineering, mining, environmental, and chemical industries. Also serves government agencies.

BECHDON CO. INC.
300 Commerce Dr.
Upper Marlboro, Maryland 20774-8746
William Turley, President
PH: (301)249-0900
FX: (301)249-0919
Founded: 1967. **Staff:** 85. Activities: Offers engineering and design services for precision machining, CNC Milling and turning, MIG and TIG welding, and MILSPEC and industrial painting needs.

BIOCHEM TECHNOLOGY, INC.
100 Ross Rd., Ste. 201
King of Prussia, Pennsylvania 19406-2100
George J.F. Lee, President
PH: (610)768-9360
FX: (610)768-9363
E-mail: sales@bioguide.com
URL: bioguide.com
Founded: 1977. **Staff:** 12. Activities: Consultants in wastewater treatment processes specializing in evaluation and optimization of biological nutrient removal facilities. On-line process monitoring and control of wastewater treatment processes as well as yeast, bacterial or fungal fermentation. Experience in biochemical process development, wastewater treatment process design, fermentation system design, process and plant design, biochemical engineering research and a variety of engineering specialties. Undertakes a wide variety of projects which range from preliminary feasibility studies to the development and optimization of a biological process.

BLYMYER ENGINEERS, INC.
1829 Clement Ave.
Alameda, California 94501
H.S. Lewis, President
PH: (510)521-3773
TF: (800)753-3773
FX: (510)865-2594
E-mail: blymyer.com
Founded: 1961. **Staff:** 35. Activities: Offers design engineering and construction management consulting for transportation facilities and major material handling equipment. Also advises on terminal/depot spill prevention counter measures and industrial equipment design and installation. Environmental Division consists of three departments: Underground Storage Tank Services, Environmental Planning and Assessment, and Geotechnical and Remediation Services. Services include environmental audit and site assessment services, soil and groundwater sampling, remediation design, and stormwater compliance services. Serves private industries as well as government agencies.

L.J. BROUTMAN & ASSOCIATES LTD.
3424 S. State St.
Chicago, Illinois 60616
Lawrence J. Broutman, Chairman
PH: (312)842-4100
FX: (312)842-3583
E-mail: infor@broutman.com
URL: www.broutman.com
Founded: 1980. **Staff:** 25. Activities: An international materials technology and chemistry consulting firm and laboratory specializing in polymers, composites, adhesives, glass, ceramics, construc-

tion materials and chemicals. Laboratory and field services provided in conduct of failure analysis, materials testing and evaluation, research and development and product and process design. Clients include compounders and producers of polymers and composite materials; manufacturers of industrial, medical, aerospace, automotive and consumer products; water and gas utility companies; electric power transmission companies; petrochemical companies and refineries; materials trade associations; research institutions and agencies; federal, state, and local governmental bodies; radio and television news documentary producers; and legal firms and insurance companies involved in product or materials litigation.

THOMAS G. BROWN ASSOCIATES
209 Fox Ln.
Wallingford, Pennsylvania 19086
Thomas G. Brown
PH: (610)565-4393
FX: (610)891-8771
E-mail: tomo_tgba@compserve.com
Founded: 1985. **Staff:** 12. Activities: Consulting chemist offering services in commercial development, including marketing, technical, and management assistance to paint, plastics, ink, adhesives and related industries. Can provide formulation assistance for evaluation and demonstration of new raw materials. Also provides market assessment, strategic planning, and product development services. Serves private industries as well as government agencies.

BUFFALO TESTING LABS, INC.
902 Kenmore Ave.
Buffalo, New York 14216
Edward J. Kris
PH: (716)873-2302
FX: (716)873-9914
Founded: 1927. **Staff:** 20. Activities: Provides investigation, field sampling, laboratory testing and analytical services. Areas of expertise include chemical, metallurgical, mechanical, electrical and civil engineering. Industries served include ceramics, chemical, construction, government, healthcare, insurance, legal profession, petroleum, pharmaceutical, plastics and rubber.

CARLTECH ASSOCIATES INC.
PO Box 457
Columbia, Maryland 21045-0457
J.C. Uhrmacher
PH: (410)997-5155
Founded: 1980. **Staff:** 24. Activities: Chemical engineering consultants offering chemical, biochemical and biological evaluations as well as technical information management. Related activities include technical report preparation and industrial hygiene.

THE CATALYST GROUP, INC.
PO Box 637
Spring House, Pennsylvania 19477
Clyde F. Payn, CEO
PH: (215)628-4447
FX: (215)628-2267
E-mail: cap@catalystgrp.com
URL: www.catalystgrp.com
Founded: 1984. **Staff:** 80. Activities: Offers technology, management business expertise, and information services for the refining, petrochemical, polymer, chemical, fine chemical, pharmatical and environmental industries. Activities include technology development, technology transfer, mergers and acquisitions/JV's, single and multiclient research and development programs, scientific software development, scientific and industry technical conferences, leading technology multiclient reports and single client confidential projects.

CELSIS LABORATORY GROUP LABORATORY DIVISION
123 Hawthorne St.
Roselle Park, New Jersey 07204-0206
Edwin C. Rothstein, President
PH: (908)245-1933
TF: (800)523-LABS
FX: (908)245-6253
E-mail: leberco@celsis.com
Founded: 1939. **Staff:** 47. Activities: Offers consulting in animal toxicology, in-vitro toxicology, microbiology and chemical analysis to the pharmaceutical, cosmetic, toiletry, medical device, bacteriocide, pesticide, coatings, graphic arts, and specialty chemical industries. Also serves government agencies.

CELSIS LABORATORY GROUP, ST. LOUIS DIVISION
6200 S. Lindbergh Blvd.
St. Louis, Missouri 63123
Richard T. Hollis, President
PH: (314)487-6776
TF: (800)523-5227
FX: (314)487-8991
URL: www.celsic.com
Founded: 1946. **Staff:** 84. Activities: Provides chemical, microbiological, toxicological, and biological laboratory and consulting services to the food, chemical, pharmaceutical and cosmetic industries.

THE CENTER FOR PROFESSIONAL ADVANCEMENT
144 Tices Ln.
East Brunswick, New Jersey 08816
Charles Bendel, Jr., President
PH: (732)238-1600
FX: (732)238-9113
E-mail: info@cfpa.com
URL: www.cfpa.com
Founded: 1967. **Staff:** 85. Activities: Provides training (2-5 day intensive short courses) for scientists, engineers and technical manager in applied industrial technology. Many faculty members are also available for consulting. Industries served: chemical process, ceramics and glass, mechanical design, environmental and safety, pharmaceuticals, analytical chemistry, manufacturing engineering, and government agencies.

CENTRIFUGAL CASTING MACHINE CO., INC.
PO Box 947
Tulsa, Oklahoma 74101
W. Thomas McKee, President
PH: (918)835-7323
FX: (918)835-9643
E-mail: ccmco@world.att.net
Founded: 1940. **Staff:** 50. Activities: Offers consultation on start-up and installation services for foundries; develops casting process, mold design, and machine design for specific customer castings; and operates a research and development foundry for experimental use. Serves private industries as well as government agencies.

CHEM SERVICE, INC.
660 Tower Ln.
West Chester, Pennsylvania 19381-0599
Lyle Phifer, President
PH: (610)692-3026
TF: (800)452-9994
FX: (610)692-8729
E-mail: marketing@chemservice.com
URL: www.chemservice.com
Founded: 1963. **Staff:** 25. Activities: Consulting specialists in preparation of organic chemicals with purities near 100%. Industries served: analytical analysis for the chemical, governmental and scientific communities.

CHEM SYSTEMS INC.
303 S. Broadway
Tarrytown, New York 10591
Peter H. Spitz, Chairman of the Board
PH: (914)631-2828
FX: (914)631-8851
URL: www.chemsystems.com
Founded: 1964. **Staff:** 70. Activities: International chemical and energy consulting firm.

CHEMIC ENGINEERS & CONSTRUCTORS INC.
4820 FM 2004 Rd.
Hitchcock, Texas 77563-1034
Jerry Hartenberger, President
PH: (409)986-6504
FX: (409)986-6900
E-mail: chemic@chemic.com
URL: www.chemic.com
Founded: 1977. **Staff:** 75. Activities: Chemic engineers providing complete engineering and construction management services for the chemical, petrochemical, and refinery industries, including process design, estimating, civil/structural, instrument, electrical, architectural, mechanical, and environmental.

CHEMICAL ENGINEERING RESEARCH CONSULTANTS, LTD.
200 College St.
Toronto, Ontario, Canada M5S 1A4
David G.B. Boocock, President
PH: (416)979-2013
FX: (416)978-8605
E-mail: webmaster@cercl.com
URL: www.cercl.on.ca
Founded: 1962. **Staff:** 30. Activities: Offers consulting services to Canadian industries, businesses, and government. Consultants are professors at the Department of Chemical Engineering and Applied Chemistry at the University of Toronto. Areas of expertise include fluid mechanics, heat transfer, chemical reaction engineering, nuclear processes, optimization, and environmental engineering.

CHEMIR/POLYTECH LABORATORIES, INC.
2672 Metro Blvd.
Maryland Heights, Missouri 63043
Shri Thanedar, Technical Director
PH: (314)291-6620
FX: (314)291-6630
E-mail: info@chemir.com
URL: www.chemir.com
Founded: 1959. **Staff:** 28. Activities: Analytical service facility specializing in the evaluation, testing, identification and quality control of industrial polymers, adhesives, coatings, plastics, and elastomers. Polymer testing services include the following: mechanical - tensile compression, impact and flexural; thermal -melt index, DSC, TGA, and failure - scanning electron microscopy and FT-IR analysis. Special consultants are available in the field of mechanical and engineer testing and infrared spectroscopy. Specialists are qualified to provide data and expert testimony for patent infringement, product liability and related legal proceedings. Industries served: chemical manufacturing, attorneys, government, paint, plastics, ink, and pharmaceutical.

CHEMSULTANTS INTERNATIONAL NETWORK
Heisley Commerce Park
9349 Hamilton Dr.
Mentor, Ohio 44060
Richard P. Muny, President
PH: (440)352-0218
FX: (440)352-8572
URL: chemsultants.com
Founded: 1981. **Staff:** 20. Activities: Specialists in the development, manufacturing, and testing of pressure sensitive adhesives and converting products. Services range from formulating of composition of an article to plant design and operation. Specific areas covered include materials management, process development and control, and product design and development. Related experience in market surveys and competitive evaluations. Industries served: adhesives and converting industries, tapes, labels, converting, as well as government agencies.

CLIMAX RESEARCH SERVICES
29205 Country Club Dr., C-40
Farmington Hills, Michigan 48331-5718
Dr. John M. Tartaglia

PH: (248)489-0720
FX: (248)489-8997
Founded: 1987. **Staff:** 46. Activities: A metallurgical laboratory and engineering consulting firm employing nationally recognized experts in the structure, properties, and failure analysis of a wide spectrum of ferrous metals and nonferrous metals including steels, cast irons, and aluminum alloys. Accredited by A2LA and FQA with facilities for mechanical and fastener testing, chemical analysis, metallography, optical and electron microscopy, machining, fatigue, wear, phase transformation, residual stress, and corrosion testing. Industries served: automotive, metals, manufacturing, mining, and government agencies.

CMAI
11757 Katy Fwy., Ste. 750
Houston, Texas 77079
James R. Crocco, Exec. Vice President
PH: (281)531-4660
FX: (281)531-9966
E-mail: cmai@cmaiglobal.com
URL: www.cmaiglobal.com
Founded: 1979. **Staff:** 40. Activities: Technical consultants working with petrochemicals; chemical intermediates and monomers; plastics, elastomers, and rubbers; and synthetic fibers. Industries served: petrochemical.

CONATECH CONSULTING GROUP, INC.
287 N. Lindbergh Blvd., Ste. 208
Creve Coeur, Missouri 63141-7849
Robert J. Bockserman, President
PH: (314)995-9767
FX: (314)995-9766
Founded: 1985. **Staff:** 42. Activities: Offers consulting services in packaging including: product development, package development, designing engineering systems, package design, material handling, warehousing, cost reduction, and legal testimony for food products, drugs, medical devices, industrial and electronic products, consumer and home-care products. Also assists clients in manufacturing and process systems with planning and design, and manufacturers and distributors in chemicals, agricultural and veterinary products. Also provides literature research for processes and products including market research. Industries served: food, pharmaceutical, medical device, cosmetic, automotive, electronic, and chemical.

COVANCE INC.
210 Carnegie Ctr.
Princeton, New Jersey 08540
Chris Kuebler, CEO
PH: (609)452-8550
FX: (609)514-1986
E-mail: covance@viani.com
URL: www.covance.com
Staff: 6000. Activities: Global consulting firm offering full service research and development services to biotechnology and pharmaceutical manufacturers in North America, Europe, Australia, and Japan.

COX-WALKER & ASSOCIATES, INC.
8922 Jefferson Hwy.
Baton Rouge, Louisiana 70809
Eugene R. Cox, Jr., President
PH: (504)927-0094
FX: (504)927-5324
E-mail: office@coxwalker.com
Founded: 1974. **Staff:** 25. Activities: Provides chemical, civil, mechanical, and environmental engineering services for the process industries and government agencies.

CROSBY & OVERTON
1610 W. 17th St.
Long Beach, California 90813-1295
Marguerite M. Dundee, Vice President
PH: (562)432-5445
FX: (562)436-7540
Founded: 1950. **Staff:** 50. Activities: Provides environmental engi-

neering services to refineries and chemical, plating, and paint companies in California.

CURTIS & TOMPKINS LTD.
2323 5th St.
Berkeley, California 94710
C. Bruce Godfrey, President
PH: (510)486-0900
FX: (510)486-0532
Founded: 1878. **Staff:** 60. Activities: Offers analytical chemistry consulting and testing services to the environmental, agricultural, government agencies, energy, and related industries.

DELTA PROCESS MANAGEMENT, INC.
1985 Nonconnah Blvd.
Memphis, Tennessee 38132
Jim E. Fowler, President
PH: (901)398-5151
FX: (901)398-5172
Founded: 1980. **Staff:** 22. Activities: Industrial process engineering consulting firm specializing in chemical plant expansions and new processes. Experienced in plant process and energy studies, capital cost estimates, and economic evaluations. Industries served: chemical and food processing and government agencies.

DFL LABORATORIES
3401 Crow Canyon Rd., Ste. 110
San Ramon, California 94583
Randy Young, President
PH: (510)830-0350
FX: (510)830-0379
E-mail: blagoyevich@worldnet.att.net
Founded: 1925. **Staff:** 60. Activities: Offers quality control systems and microbiological evaluation of products. Also provides complete microbiological and chemical analyses of food and dairy products, water analysis, in-plant sanitation inspections, consultation, and complete nutritional analyses.

DOAR & ASSOCIATES P A
7504 E. Independence Blvd., Ste. 103
Charlotte, North Carolina 28212-6747
William H. Todd
PH: (704)569-0525
FX: (704)569-9360
E-mail: hed@doar.mhs.compuserve.com
Founded: 1986. **Staff:** 85. Activities: Full-service engineering firm providing a total range of services for pulp and paper, chemical, textile, and other heavy industrial manufacturing, power, and government facilities. Services include conceptual and feasibility studies, detail engineering and design, procurement, estimating, scheduling, and construction management. Capabilities include automated process control, process integration, chemical and mechanical process, electrical instrumentation, mechanical, piping, civil, structural, and architectural engineering and design. Software development, process hazard analysis, check-out and start-up services as well as operator training are also available.

DSET LABORATORIES
45601 N. 47th Ave.
Phoenix, Arizona 85027-7042
Larry Masters, President
PH: (602)465-7356
TF: (800)255-3738
FX: (602)465-9409
E-mail: info@atlaswsg.com
URL: www.atlaswsg.com
Founded: 1948. **Staff:** 75. Activities: Materials science consultants offering the following: weathering test service of paints, plastics, coatings and textiles for automotive, building and other industries; diagnostic measurements including color, optical and mechanical tests worldwide; 22 outdoor exposure facilities worldwide for testing in a variety of end use environments.

DUXBURY CONSULTANTS GROUP
15 Depot St.
Duxbury, Massachusetts 02331
William Campbell
PH: (617)934-5205
FX: (617)934-2001
Founded: 1983. **Staff:** 50. Activities: Multidisciplinary consulting firm provides advisory services in the following disciplines: engineering and construction - with specialized expertise in chemical: adhesives, sealants, printing inks, papers, environment; civil: hydrography, waterfront, deep foundations, survey; mechanical; and structural. Financial - tax planning; estate planning; investment analysis; corporate development; mergers and divestitures; venture capital and financial restructure; loan consulting, packaging and procurement. Productivity and management - direct marketing, sales, distribution; information flow analysis; office productivity and technology selection; project management systems and training; strategic and interorganizational planning; computer systems analysis, design, programming; and manufacturing and production engineering. Healthcare expertise available in clinical laboratory management, diagnostics, technology, and legalities. International expertise available in trade, real estate market analysis, and product development areas. Personnel and human services include salary market surveys, fringe benefit surveys, attitude surveys, and compensation system review. Industries served: as applicable, usually small to medium sized firms, and government agencies.

EARTH TECHNOLOGY CORP. (USA)
100 W. Broadway, Ste. 5000
Long Beach, California 90802
Diane Creel, President/CEO
PH: (562)495-4449
TF: (800)688-9828
FX: (562)495-2825
Founded: 1970. **Staff:** 2000. Activities: International provider of total water management, engineering and construction, transportation, and environmental services and remediation for government and industry. Provides contract operations and design/build/finance/ operate services for public and private water supply and wastewater treatment systems, as well as traditional engineering, design, and planning services for water/wastewater management. Also provides environmental, engineering, and construction services for transportation systems. Provides a full range of engineering, design/build, and construction management services for the rehabilitation, relocation, and new construction of various facility types including manufacturing operations, universities, hospitals, and municipal and federal facilities. Services include chemical/process engineering, and architecture and interior design. The firm's environmental services and remediation division offers the full spectrum of environmental and remediation services, from site assessment/investigation to remedial design and cleanup. Its services include remediation design and construction, facility decontamination and demolition, strategic environmental management, brownfield redevelopment, air quality consulting and engineering, and resource management and planning.

ENGINEERING CONSULTING SERVICES
1940 The Alameda
San Jose, California 95126
D. Olsen, President
PH: (408)247-4937
FX: (408)247-7540
Founded: 1963. **Staff:** 54. Activities: Multidisciplined consulting engineers: civil, electrical power distribution and lighting, mechanical-thermal, structural analysis, and forensic engineering consultation. Serves the legal community regarding product failures and major catastrophes. Industries served: legal, insurance, manufacturing communities for forensic consultation, including the construction industry.

ENGINEERING SERVICES GROUP
29200 Northwestern Highway
Southfield, Michigan 48034-1055
Michael J. Marlo, CEO

PH: (248)945-2000
FX: (248)945-2001
E-mail: engsvcs.com
Founded: 1988. **Staff:** 200. Activities: A consortium of independent design and consulting companies providing engineering services for facilities and manufacturing processes, including productivity assessment, industrial finishing systems design, information systems implementation and contract labor integration, and material handling systems design. ESG serves manufacturers, equipment suppliers, and service companies, worldwide.

ENI LAB INC.
2394 Rte. 130
Dayton, New Jersey 08810-1519
Ralph Shapiro, President
PH: (732)329-2999
TF: (800)841-1110
FX: (732)329-1031
E-mail: enilab@aol.com
Founded: 1969. **Staff:** 30. Activities: Designs and develops tests for evaluating efficacy and safety of products and provides guidance for claims substantiation. Also advises on subjects related to analytical chemistry, microbiology, quality control, toxicology, nutrition, and product labeling.

ENSANIAN PHYSICOCHEMICAL INSTITUTE
PO Box 98
Eldred, Pennsylvania 16731
Minas Ensanian, Chairman/President
PH: (814)225-3296
Founded: 1963. **Staff:** 40. Activities: Industrial engineering consultants active in nondestructive testing of metals, failure analysis of metals, robotics and artificial intelligence. Also works in areas of electronic diagnostic medicine, manufacturing in space (zero gravity), electrochemistry, solid state physics and chemistry, and surface phenomena. Industries served: aerospace, metalworking, marine, automotive, electronics, biomedical, bioengineering, government, sports medicine, healthcare, and cosmetics.

ENVIRONMENTAL RISK LTD.
120 Mountain Ave.
Bloomfield, Connecticut 06002
Richard S. Atkins
PH: (860)242-9933
TF: (800)883-1568
FX: (860)243-9055
E-mail: info@erl.com
URL: erl.com
Founded: 1985. **Staff:** 46. Activities: Environmental consulting firm which specializes in process safety management, risk management planning, waste-to-energy and cogeneration permitting, hazardous waste permitting and management, air quality and air toxic modeling, air pollution emission measurement services, site investigations and remediation, environmental audits and risk assessments, wastewater and stormwater management, and aquatic toxicity testing. Its client base includes private and public corporations, system vendors, engineering firms, municipalities, and public authorities.

ENVIRONMENTAL STRATEGIES CORP.
11911 Freedom Dr., Ste. 900
Reston, Virginia 20190
Lynne Miller, CEO
PH: (703)709-6500
FX: (703)709-8505
Founded: 1986. **Staff:** 120. Activities: Full service consulting firm specializing in remedial action programs and environmental risk management. Areas of expertise include: environmental science, engineering, chemistry, and hydrogeology. Industries served: private sector.

ENVIRONMENTAL TESTING & CONSULTING, INC.
38900 Huron River Dr.
Romulus, Michigan 48174
Jeremy Westcott, General Mgr.

PH: (734)955-6600
TF: (800)864-3236
FX: (734)955-6604
Founded: 1989. **Staff:** 29. Activities: Conducts Phase 1, 2, and 3 environmental audits, geotechnical studies, ISO 14000 EMS Development & Auditing, laboratory services, lead and asbestos inspections and testing, indoor air quality and management specifications, UST (underground storage tank) management, (qualified UST consultant) and other industrial hygiene related services. Industries served: banking, healthcare, chemical, education, and government.

ENVIROSYSTEMS, INC.
9200 Rumsey Rd., Ste. B102
Columbia, Maryland 21045
Mohan Khare, Ph.D., President/CEO
PH: (410)964-0330
FX: (410)740-9306
E-mail: info@envsystems.com
URL: www.envsystems.com/envsys
Founded: 1989. **Staff:** 15. Activities: Offers methods development and research and development in areas of environmental analytical chemistry and laboratory services. Industries served: chemical, pharmaceutical, food/feed, engineering, environmental and government agencies in the United States at Federal and State level.

ERLIN, HIME ASSOCIATES - DIVISION OF WISS, JANNEY, ELSTNER ASSOCIATES, INC.
330 Pfingston Rd.
Northbrook, Illinois 60062
J.D. Connolly
PH: (847)272-7730
FX: (847)291-5189
E-mail: jdc@wje.com
Founded: 1971. **Staff:** 25. Activities: Offers consulting on the failure of materials of construction, primarily through petrographic studies and chemical analyses. Also specialized chemical and instrumental analyses. Serves private industries as well as government agencies.

ESARCO INC.
50 S. Buckhout St.
Irvington, New York 10533
Maureen McGuire, President/Owner
PH: (914)591-9010
FX: (914)591-9011
E-mail: esarco@aol.com
Founded: 1981. **Staff:** 12. Activities: Offers chemical and water analysis consulting specializing in water and wastewater pollution control. Industries served: chemical, petrochemical, pharmaceutical, railroad, food, and metal manufacturing.

EVERGREEN ANALYTICAL INC.
4036 Youngfield St.
Wheat Ridge, Colorado 80033
John H. Barney, President
PH: (303)425-6021
TF: (800)845-7400
FX: (303)425-6854
E-mail: evergreen@mho.net
Founded: 1983. **Staff:** 34. Activities: An independent firm offering analytical laboratory services to environmental, waste management, energy, and chemical industries as well as government agencies. Services include environmental testing. Offers laboratory analyses.

EXPERIMENTAL PATHOLOGY LABORATORIES, INC.
PO Box 474
Herndon, Virginia 20172-0474
John F. Ferrell, Director
PH: (703)471-7060
FX: (703)471-8447
E-mail: eplva@aol.com
URL: www.epl.inc.com
Founded: 1971. **Staff:** 115. Activities: Toxicologic pathology services offered to chemical, agricultural chemical, pharmaceutical and

cosmetic industries as well as to the federal government. Specializes in pathology, histology, electron microscopy and related activities. Provides full advisory consultation in anatomic pathology and study design from original concept to complete plan. Presents results to the required agency. Provides complete toxicology support services including laboratory selection, study monitoring, report review and SOP preparation. Complete GLP services including study audits, laboratory compliance audits and training. Provides onsite management of pathology and toxicology facilities.

FLUORAMICS INC.
18 Industrial Ave.
Mahwah, New Jersey 07430
Franklin G. Reick, President
PH: (201)825-8110
TF: (800)922-0075
FX: (201)825-7035
Founded: 1966. **Staff:** 11. Activities: Specializes in the development and manufacture of lubricants for a variety of industrial purposes. Recent emphasis has been on the development of high levitation superconductors. Industries served: automotive and industrial in the United States and Canada.

FRAZIER-SIMPLEX, INC.
PO Box 493
Washington, Pennsylvania 15301
J.E. Frazier, II, Chairman of the Board
PH: (412)225-1100
FX: (412)225-3114
E-mail: info@frazier-simplex.com
URL: www.frazier-simplex.com
Founded: 1918. **Staff:** 25. Activities: Engineering consultancy specializing in services to the glass and steel industries (suspended refractories), and to the construction industry.

FRIEDMAN & BRUYA INC.
3012 16th Ave. W.
Seattle, Washington 98119-2029
James E. Bruya, President
PH: (206)285-8282
TF: (800)487-8231
FX: (206)283-5044
E-mail: fbi@isomedia.com
URL: www.isomedia.com/homes/fbi
Founded: 1985. **Staff:** 12. Activities: Consulting chemists experienced with industrial and environmental applications. National experts in petroleum forensic testing.

FROEHLING & ROBERTSON INC.
PO Box 27524
Richmond, Virginia 23261
Samuel Kirby, Jr., President
PH: (804)264-2701
FX: (804)264-1202
Founded: 1881. **Staff:** 313. Activities: Consulting engineers and chemists providing the engineering and materials analyses required by the construction industry. Also offer product/process evaluations and failure analyses. As one of the oldest independent engineering laboratories in the nation, F&R offers the services of professional engineers, chemists, construction inspectors, and materials technicians. Specific areas of expertise include: geotechnical, soils, asphalt, concrete, metals N.D.T., chemicals, and environmental. Industries served: construction design, building and supply, and government agencies.

FTI ANAMET
3400 Investment Blvd.
Hayward, California 94545
Ken Pytlewski, Business Manager
PH: (510)887-8811
FX: (510)887-8427
E-mail: anamet@fticonsulting.com
URL: www.ftianamet.com
Founded: 1958. **Staff:** 18. Activities: Consulting firm and testing

laboratory dedicated to solving problems in Applied Mechanics, Metallurgical Failure Analysis, Materials Testing, Accident Reconstruction, Biomechanics and Vehicle Occupant Dynamics. On site laboratory capabilities: inorganic chemical analysis, high-temperature mechanical testing and metallurgical evaluation which include creep, impact, fracture toughness and fatigue testing. Expert witness testimony. Offers computer graphics, simulation, and animation for courtroom exhibits.

GEO-TEST, INC.
3204 Richards Ln.
Santa Fe, New Mexico 87505
PH: (505)857-0933
E-mail: geotest@geo-test.com
URL: www.geo-test.com
Founded: 1985. **Staff:** 38. Activities: Provides geotechnical, materials and environmental engineering investigations, site assessments, and materials testing. Minority owned.

GHESQUIERE PLASTIC TESTING, INC.
20450 Harper
Harper Woods, Michigan 48225
J.D. Ghesquiere, President
PH: (313)885-3535
FX: (313)885-1771
Founded: 1971. **Staff:** 18. Activities: An independent testing laboratory specializing in evaluation and testing of plastic products, components and materials to various government, industrial and commercial standards.

GREAT LAKES CARBON TREATMENT
3300 U.S. 131 N.
PO Box 968
Kalkaska, Michigan 49646
Bill Pierce, President
PH: (616)258-8014
TF: (800)258-8014
FX: (616)258-6993
Founded: 1989. **Staff:** 19. Activities: Firm offers extensive knowledge in environmental equipment, including air strippers, soil vapor extraction, air-sparging activated carbon, and bio filtration. Also specializes in pumps, blowers, organoclays, metal and odor removal, advanced oxidation, and treatability studies. Serves petroleum/ chemical, plating, steel manufacturing, and wastewater treatment industries.

HAN-PADRON ASSOCIATES, LLP
11 Penn Plaza
New York, New York 10001
Dennis V. Padron
PH: (212)736-5466
FX: (212)629-4406
E-mail: hpany@han-padron.com
URL: www.han-padron.com
Founded: 1979. **Staff:** 120. Activities: Consulting services include planning, design and construction supervision for marine terminals, ports and harbors, coastal structures, single point moorings, pipelines, conveyors, offshore structures, tank farms, bulk storage facilities and marinas for the energy, mining, and marine transportation industries and for various federal, state and local government agencies.

HAUSER LABORATORIES
5555 Airport Blvd.
Boulder, Colorado 80301
Dean Stull, CEO
PH: (303)443-4662
TF: (800)241-2322
FX: (303)441-5800
URL: www.Hauser.com/Hauser
Founded: 1961. **Staff:** 48. Activities: Independent laboratory providing consulting services to industry and government. Expertise in engineering and chemistry. Also provides product and process development, materials testing, chemical analysis, failure analysis,

thermal insulations, forensic investigations and expert testimony in the United States.

HOFFMANN & FEIGE, INC.
Croton River Executive Park
3 Fallsview Ln.
Brewster, New York 10509
Richard A. Hoffmann, President
PH: (914)277-4401
FX: (914)277-4701
E-mail: metalmen@hoffman-feige.com
URL: www.hoffmann-feige.com
Founded: 1978. **Staff:** 12. Activities: Offers metallurgical, materials, and mechanical engineering expertise in failure analysis, corrosion evaluations and quality assurance. Specializes in plastics and composites. Industries served: electrical, natural gas utilities, general industry and process industry, real estate, railroads, construction, and government agencies worldwide.

COLIN A. HOUSTON AND ASSOCIATES INC.
PO Box 427
Pound Ridge, New York 10576
Joel H. Houston, President
PH: (914)764-1022
FX: (914)764-1067
E-mail: cahai@colinhouston.com
URL: www.colinhouston.com
Founded: 1971. **Staff:** 16. Activities: A research organization specializing in techno-economic studies, management consulting, and strategic planning for the petrochemical and detergent industries. Conducts multi-client studies on surfactants, oleochemicals and other specialty and commodity chemicals worldwide. Also engaged in seeking out new ventures and advising on acquisitions and mergers in the chemical area.

HUNTINGDON ENGINEERING & ENVIRONMENTAL
1225 N. Loop W, Ste. 1000
Houston, Texas 77008
Edwin A. Maass, Treasurer
PH: (713)869-7913
FX: (713)869-7374
Founded: 1912. **Staff:** 660. Activities: Specialists in materials, environmental, and geotechnical engineering, including non-destructive, metallurgical, and analytical services.

INALAB INC.
3615 Harding Ave., Ste. 304
Honolulu, Hawaii 96816
PH: (808)735-0422
FX: (808)735-0047
E-mail: mark_hagadone@msn.com; inalab@msn.com
Founded: 1978. **Staff:** 20. Activities: Provides professional consultation in analytical chemistry and the application of scientific methodology to clients' needs (arson, forensics, drugs/narcotics). Evaluates workers' occupational environment and provides board-certified industrial hygiene services. Provides expert witness testimony. Industries served: insurance, contractors (general), asbestos and lead abatement contractors, attorneys, other laboratories, environmental agencies, building managers and owners, military, architects and engineers, and government agencies.

THE INDUSTRIAL LABORATORIES CO.
1450 E. 62nd Ave.
Denver, Colorado 80216
Loretta Zapp, President
PH: (303)287-9691
TF: (800)456-5288
FX: (303)287-0964
E-mail: Rhonda@scientificsolutions.com
URL: www.scientificsolutions.com
Founded: 1994. **Staff:** 42. Activities: Provides consultation in the areas of method development and validation for dietary supplements, including botanicals, GMP requirements for foods & dietary supplements, antioxidant capacity, and supplement labeling.

INDUSTRIAL TESTING BODY COTE
2350 S. 7th St.
St. Louis, Missouri 63104-7111
Allan M. Siegel, President & CEO
PH: (314)771-7111
TF: (800)467-5227
FX: (314)771-9573
Founded: 1923. **Staff:** 40. Activities: Firm has special knowledge in asbestos and industrial hygiene chemistry, chemical analysis, metallurgy, failure analysis, and lead.

INDUSTRIAL TESTING LABORATORIES
50 Madison Ave.
New York, New York 10010
Kenneth J. Kohlhof, President
PH: (212)685-8788
FX: (212)689-8742
E-mail: clinres@mail.idt.net
Founded: 1887. **Staff:** 21. Activities: Analytical and consulting chemists to the pharmaceutical, petroleum, food, cosmetic, and chemical industries. Also provides forensic consulting including analysis of biological fluids and fire investigations, as well as courtroom testimony.

INTERNATIONAL TESTING LABORATORIES
580 Market St.
Newark, New Jersey 07105
M.M. Sackoff, Executive Director
PH: (973)589-4772
TF: (800)982-2171
FX: (973)589-8485
Founded: 1934. **Staff:** 25. Activities: Materials testing and consulting engineers offer chemical consulting services to include product evaluations, chemical testing and investigations, water and waste analyses, and asbestos determinations. Other services include metallurgical failure analyses and tire and glass failure analyses, product evaluations, and expert testimony in support of possible litigation. Industries served: aerospace, nuclear, fastener distributors, welding, construction, chemical, environmental, legal community, and government agencies.

INTERTECH SERVICES INC.
14926 Hickorytex
Humble, Texas 77396
Sam Brown
PH: (281)441-8989
FX: (281)441-7896
E-mail: isixpert@aol.com
URL: members.aol.com/lsixpert.index.html
Founded: 1983. **Staff:** 60. Activities: Offers engineering consulting and laboratory services in: (1) civil and mechanical design, analysis, research, development, and forensic needs; (2) architectural engineering design and retrofit; (3) environmental, microbiological and chemical; water treating and oil analysis for failure prevention; (4) metallurgical analysis and testing; (5) fluid controls design and analysis; (6) reliability and risk analysis; (7) computer simulations; and (8) qualification and testing. Additionally provides short courses and workshops for professional development. Industries served: petrochemical, government (national, state, county, city), power industry, manufacturers, large architecture engineering firms, large institutional owner-operator-purchasers of architect, civil, and equipment.

JENIKE AND JOHANSON, INC.
1 Technology Park Dr.
Westford, Massachusetts 01886
John W. Carson, President
PH: (508)392-0300
FX: (508)392-9980
E-mail: mail@jenike.com
URL: www.jenike.com
Founded: 1966. **Staff:** 30. Activities: A consulting engineering firm specializing in the storage and flow of bulk solids. Originated the scientific approach to the measurement of flow properties of bulk solids (ores, coal, chemicals, powders) and to the design of storage

vessels and feeders for controlled flow of material. Maintains a solids flow testing laboratory and modeling facility.

JMS PROCESS CONTRACTING INC.
PO Box 541
Grand Island, New York 14072
Jasprit M. Singh, President
PH: (716)773-4666
FX: (716)773-6420
Founded: 1982. **Staff:** 11. Activities: Provides turnkey contracting of chemical process plants; relocations of used process plants; engineering design; procurement and project management services; assists with technology transfer and licensing. Industries served: chemicals/speciality chemicals/minerals processing worldwide.

KATZEN INTERNATIONAL, INC.
2300 Wall St., Ste. K
Cincinnati, Ohio 45212
Dale A. Monceaux, Sr. Vice President
PH: (513)351-7500
FX: (513)351-0810
E-mail: project@katzen.com
Founded: 1955. **Staff:** 16. Activities: A consulting engineering firm organized to provide engineering and technical management services for the chemical and biochemical process and related industries worldwide. These services include technology transfer, research and development evaluations, process design and development, technical and economic studies, design of new plants, improvement of existing installations, training of staff for clients with new operations, technical problem-solving, and monitoring of project execution and costs for financial organizations. Industries served: petrochemicals, organic chemicals, biochemicals, wood chemicals, pulp chemical recovery and by-products, sugar by-products, cryogenics, air pollution, waste disposal, energy conservation, and synthetic fuels.

KLEINFELDER, INC.
2121 N. California Blvd., Ste. 570
Walnut Creek, California 94596
Michael Mahoney, Chairman
PH: (510)938-5610
FX: (510)938-5419
URL: www.kleinfelder.com
Founded: 1961. **Staff:** 750. Activities: An engineering consulting firm specializing in the earth, air and water sciences and engineering including the environmental, civil, chemical, geotechnical and materials engineering disciplines. As a multidisciplinary organization, firm also provides construction management, engineering management and testing of geotechnical and construction materials. Serves all major industries.

KTA-TATOR, INC.
115 Technology Dr.
Pittsburgh, Pennsylvania 15275
Kenneth B. Tator, President/CEO
PH: (412)788-1300
TF: (800)245-6379
FX: (412)788-1306
E-mail: info@kta.com
URL: www.kta.com
Founded: 1949. **Staff:** 215. Activities: A consulting engineering firm specializing in protective coatings. Areas of specialization are: (1) failure analysis expert witness testimony, legal work, corrective recommendation; (2) analytical laboratory testing and evaluation - physical and chemical environmental testing; microscopic, chemical, infrared and atomic emission/absorption spectroscopy; (3) coating application inspection services; (4) manufacture and sale of coating inspection instruments; (5) paint (coatings) testing and evaluation - field panel exposures; and (6) lead paint management services. Specializes in industrial, marine and nuclear protective coatings and linings.

LANCASTER LABORATORIES - DIVISION OF THERMO ANALYTICAL INC.
2425 New Holland Pike
Lancaster, Pennsylvania 17605-2425
Carol D. Hess, Executive V.P. for HR and Admin.
PH: (717)656-2300
FX: (717)656-2681
URL: www.lancasterlabs.com
Founded: 1961. **Staff:** 640. Activities: An independent analytical laboratory offering technical services in chemistry and biology, including microbiological testing, chemical analyses, contract research and development, and consulting. Product is accurate and timely technical information. Projects include comprehensive services in the environmental sciences, air quality and industrial hygiene, food microbiology animal health sciences, and pharmaceutical sciences. Serves private industry as well as government agencies. Serves clients in the U.S. and selective international markets.

LANDAU ASSOCIATES INC.
PO Box 1029
Edmonds, Washington 98020
J. Daniel Ballbach, CEO
PH: (425)778-0907
TF: (800)522-5957
FX: (425)778-6409
E-mail: info@landauinc.com
URL: www.landauinc.com
Founded: 1982. **Staff:** 70. Activities: Environmental and geotechnical consultants specializing in soil and groundwater contamination assessment, air quality assessment, regulatory evaluation compliance management, risk assessment, permitting, and remediation design assistance. Also offers expertise in soils and foundation engineering. Services provided principally to industry, port, local municipality, and law firms. Specific industries served include: aerospace, aluminum, chemical, construction, lumber, pulp and paper, petroleum, real estate, and utilities.

LEXINGTON GROUP INTERNATIONAL, INC.
10300 North Central Expressway, Ste. 330
Dallas, Texas 75231
Norman A. Ofstad, President
PH: (214)750-9090
FX: (214)750-9393
E-mail: lgi_dallas@nova1.net
Founded: 1991. **Staff:** 20. Activities: Offers Process Safety Management (PSM), environmental and process engineering services, and computer software development and sales. Specializes in sour gas process sector including sulfur recovery units, amine units, and tail gas treating units. Also has expertise in gas plant processing units; environmental planning; permitting; industrial hygiene; with all services including fugitive emissions tied into the LGI proprietary software system Site Manager. Industries served: general industrial, chemical, construction management, refinery, power, hospital, semiconductor, computer software, and gas processing in the U.S.

MABBETT & ASSOCIATES INC. - ENVIRONMENTAL CONSULTANTS AND ENGINEERS
5 Alfred Cir.
Bedford, Massachusetts 01730-2346
Arthur N. Mabbett, President
PH: (781)275-6050
TF: (800)877-6050
FX: (781)275-5651
E-mail: mabbett@shore.net
URL: www.mabbett.com
Founded: 1980. **Staff:** 18. Activities: Offers comprehensive and multidisciplinary consulting and engineering design services in the fields of waste minimization and pollution prevention, industrial wastewater, and groundwater treatment; local exhaust ventilation and air pollution control; hazardous materials and waste management, site assessment and remediation action plans, and risk assessment; underground storage tank removal and management; industrial hygiene, safety, toxicology, and hazard communication; training, environmental management systems and auditing, chemical process;

and mechanical pollution control systems engineering. Industries served: industrial manufacturing, commercial companies, legal profession, institutions, and government agencies.

HOMER MADISON- COMMERCIAL TESTING LABORATORY, INC. (CTL)
514 Main St.
Colfax, Wisconsin 54730
Mike Bean, President
PH: (715)962-3121
TF: (800)962-5227
FX: (715)962-4030
Founded: 1952. **Staff:** 40. Activities: Independent laboratory providing a wide range of chemical (USDA certified) and microbiological analyses for the food industry and agri-businesses. Offers ingredient analyses, nutritional analyses and labeling; the lab also tests additives, feeds, and forages. Also active in environmental testing in areas such as sewage, groundwater, drinking water, sludge, and regulatory compliance. Serves private industry as well as government agencies. SDWA certified for Drinking Water. Certified for testing Stormwater Discharge.

MASTIO & CO., INC.
802 Francis St.
St. Joseph, Missouri 64501-1916
Richard C. Mastio, President/Secretary
PH: (816)364-6200
FX: (816)364-3606
Founded: 1989. **Staff:** 22. Activities: Specializes in materials management consulting for plastics, paper, metal, and glass. Serves clients in the raw materials industries, major equipment suppliers, and plastics fabrications industries worldwide.

MAXXAM ANALYTICS, INC.
9420 Cote De Liesse Rd.
Lachine, Quebec, Canada H8T 1A1
J.D. Fenwick, President
PH: (514)636-6219
FX: (514)631-9814
E-mail: info@qc.maxxam.ca
URL: www.maxxam.ca
Founded: 1975. **Staff:** 65. Activities: Environmental laboratory network whose capabilities include trace organic analysis for environmental studies and for industrial hygiene, quality control, and related research and counseling. Services also include toxicological analysis of blood and urine for drugs of abuse and for drug control programs. Industries served: utilities, government agencies, and consulting engineers.

MEDTRONIC INC.
7000 Central Ave. NE
Minneapolis, Minnesota 55432
PH: (612)574-4000
FX: (612)574-4879
Founded: 1972. **Staff:** 34. Activities: Works with industrial and government agencies to develop procedures to test chemicals and drugs or medical device products to meet federal regulations for Food and Drug Administration, Environmental Protection Agency, Department of Transportation, and other regulatory agencies.

MESCH ENGINEERING P.C.
285 Market St.
Lockport, New York 14094
J.F. Panza, President
PH: (716)434-6276
FX: (716)434-0464
Founded: 1963. **Staff:** 30. Activities: Multidisciplinary consulting firm with skills in the following areas: electrical, civil, structural engineering, chemical process, environmental control design, RECA closures, landfills, mechanical, materials handling, food process design, pipe stress analysis, pressure vessel design, project management, estimating, architectural, planning, and CADD.

METCUT RESEARCH ASSOCIATES, INC.
3980 Rosslyn Dr.
Cincinnati, Ohio 45209
John P. Kahles, President
PH: (513)271-5100
FX: (513)271-9511
URL: www.metcut.usa.com
Founded: 1948. **Staff:** 100. Activities: Active in the field of materials testing and materials engineering. Specialized expertise in the area of coatings evaluation and failure analysis, including fatigue, tensile, and creep. Industries served: commercial industry, and government agencies.

METUCHEN ANALYTICAL, INC. - KENDALL INFRARED LABORATORIES
25 Mack Dr.
Edison, New Jersey 08817
J. Stephen Duerr, President
PH: (732)287-8898
TF: (800)848-4LAB
FX: (732)287-0980
E-mail: chemlab@compuserve.com
Founded: 1953. **Staff:** 13. Activities: Consulting chemists specializing in infrared spectroscopy, chromatography, and scanning electron microscopy. Offers assistance with problem-solving where identification of unknown is a factor. Also provides forensic services (except for blood chemistry). Specific services include: materials failure analysis, analytical chemistry and microbiology research services, identification of materials and residues, formulation development, and product liability investigations. Serves private industries as well as government agencies.

MICHELSON LABORATORIES, INC.
6280 Chalet Dr.
Commerce, California 90040
Jack Michelson, CEO
PH: (562)928-0553
FX: (562)927-6625
E-mail: mlabs@michelsonlab.com
URL: www.michelab.com
Founded: 1970. **Staff:** 70. Activities: Complete independent analytical testing laboratory conducting chemical, microbiological, and microanalytical analyses on foods, cosmetics, wastewaters, pesticides, dairy products and environmental, and seafoods. Industries served: food manufacturers; dairy, meat, produce industries; drinking and wastewater analysis.

MICRON, INC.
3815 Lancaster Pike
Wilmington, Delaware 19805
James F. Ficca, Jr., President
PH: (302)998-1184
FX: (302)998-1836
E-mail: 102225.3716@compuserve.com
URL: www.micronanalysis.com
Founded: 1966. **Staff:** 11. Activities: Analytical and consulting laboratory specializing in microstructural and microchemical analysis, failure analysis, electron probe x-ray microanalysis, scanning electronic microscopy, optical microscopy, quantitative particle size analysis, x-ray diffraction, x-ray fluorescence, and electron spectroscopy quantitative analysis. Industries served: chemical, electronics, minerals, government, and pharmaceuticals.

MIDWEST RESEARCH INSTITUTE
425 Volker Blvd.
Kansas City, Missouri 64110
John McKelvey, President/CEO
PH: (816)753-7600
FX: (816)753-8420
URL: www.mriresearch.org
Founded: 1944. **Staff:** 1000. Activities: An independent, not-for-profit corporation that performs research and development under contract with industry, government, and other private and public groups. Areas of current research and development include: chemis-

try, biological sciences, toxicology, health research, management sciences, environmental sciences, hazardous waste, renewable energy, materials sciences, transportation, and international programs. Has operated and managed the National Renewable Energy Laboratory (NREL) in Golden, Colorado for the U.S. Department of Energy since its inception in 1977.

MONARCH ANALYTICAL LABS, INC.
349 Tomahawk Dr.
Maumee, Ohio 43537-1696
D.A. Brengartner, President
PH: (419)897-9000
FX: (419)897-9111
Founded: 1987. **Staff:** 30. Activities: Industrial scientific laboratory which offers a broad range of chemical analyses, physical property measurements and environmental compliance testing services. Can solve testing problems or provide special facilities and instrumentation to supplement in-house capability. Can also aid in the development of analytical methodology. Industries served: all technical and manufacturing industries as well as government.

MORRISON-KNUDSEN ENGINEERS, INC.
1 Market Steuart, Ste. 400
San Francisco, California 94105
James Ellis, President
PH: (415)442-7300
FX: (415)442-7405
Founded: 1945. **Staff:** 450. Activities: Consulting engineers, domestic and worldwide whose services range from conceptual development, financial planning, and field investigations to engineering, project management, and quality control, including: program management for private sector clients and government agencies; construction management from construction planning through start-up; procurement and complete logistics support, including materials control, expediting and shipping, warehousing and source inspection; comprehensive project control systems for small to mega projects, including planning and scheduling, estimating, cost engineering, materials, and document control; and operations and maintenance including repair, alterations, communications, transportation services, purchasing and contracting in all major public utilities, transportation and military facilities. Specific market segments cover electric utilities; transportation; water resources; oil and gas; hazardous waste design; minerals such as base metals, industrial metals, precious metals, and strategic minerals; and public works.

MULTIFIBRE PROCESS LTD.
18775 - 54th Ave.
Surrey, British Columbia, Canada V3S 8E5
Derek G. Lobley, President
PH: (604)576-1947
FX: (604)576-1229
E-mail: llobley@direct.ca
Founded: 1967. **Staff:** 12. Activities: As technical consultant to the pulp and paper industry, the firm designs, engineers, contracts, installs and commissions chlorine dioxide generating and chemical preparation plants. Methods of chlorine dioxide production include reduction of sodium chlorate using sulphur dioxide, sodium chloride or methanol, and recycling of the separated spent sulphuric acid, back to the reactor using the "L" Process.

THE NATIONAL FOOD LABORATORY, INC.
6363 Clark Ave.
Dublin, California 94568
Kevin Buck
PH: (510)828-1440
FX: (510)833-8795
Founded: 1972. **Staff:** 60. Activities: Food science consultants offering services in process engineering, chemistry, microbiology, sensory evaluation, marketing research, sanitation, product development and technical regulatory interface. Maintains 55,000 square foot laboratory and pilot plant for development of food and beverage products.

NEBRASKA TESTING GROUP, MAXIM TECHNOLOGIES, INC.
5058 South 111th St.
Omaha, Nebraska 68137
Al Rahman, Manager, Omaha Operations
PH: (402)331-4453
FX: (402)331-5961
Founded: 1955. **Staff:** 50. Activities: A commercial and independent testing, engineering and consulting laboratory providing service to government, business, industry and individuals in the fields of soil and material engineering, construction testing, industrial hygiene, chemical, bacteriological and environmental sciences, non-destructive testing and related services. Industries served: engineering, environmental, construction services, and government agencies.

NEC NUCLEAR ENERGY CONSULTANTS, INC.
15713 Crabbs Branch Way
Rockville, Maryland 20855
William R. Mills, President
PH: (301)840-2964
FX: (301)840-1162
E-mail: 680861@mcihail.com
Founded: 1983. **Staff:** 100. Activities: An engineering and consulting firm that provides a broad spectrum of technical services to the nuclear industry. NEC's staff is composed of managers, engineers and technicians specializing in the areas of electrical, mechanical, nuclear and chemical engineering; nuclear power plant construction, design start-up, operation and maintenance; development of procedures for nuclear plant administration, operation instrumentation and control maintenance; and surveillance procedures. Additional assistance with utility prudency reviews, training regulatory affairs and compliance, quality assurance/quality control, planning and scheduling, and systems engineering. served: national and international.

NOFSINGER INC. - A BURNS & MCDONNELL CO.
9400 Ward Pkwy.
Kansas City, Missouri 64114
Donald F. Greenwood, President
PH: (816)361-7999
FX: (816)333-3690
E-mail: rnofsin@burnsmcd.com
URL: www.burnsmcd.com
Founded: 1950. **Staff:** 90. Activities: Provides engineering and consulting services for the process industries. Activities include chemical, mechanical, instrument, electrical and civil engineering for the food, petroleum, chemical, and petrochemical industries, including consulting, process and economic feasibility studies, process engineering and detailed design engineering. Works with various government agencies. The company also provides construction design build capabilities and start-up services.

NORTHVIEW LABORATORIES, INC.
1880 Holste Rd.
Northbrook, Illinois 60062
Martin J. Spalding, CEO
PH: (847)564-8181
FX: (847)564-8269
E-mail: info@northviewlabs.com
URL: www.northviewlabs.com
Founded: 1972. **Staff:** 100. Activities: An independent laboratory offering comprehensive testing capabilities in microbiology, sterility testing services, analytical chemistry and toxicology for the medical device, pharmaceutical, food and feed, cosmetic, specialty chemical, and consumer product industries.

NUCRO-TECHNICS INC.
2000 Ellesmere Rd., Unit 16
Scarborough, Ontario, Canada M1H 2W4
John C. Fanaras, President
PH: (416)438-6727
FX: (416)438-3463
Founded: 1971. **Staff:** 60. Activities: Health and safety consultants to the food, cosmetic, chemical, and pharmaceutical industry, as well as to government agencies. Consulting staff are backed up with ana-

lytical laboratories in the areas of chemistry, microbiology, and animal toxicology.

O'BRIEN & GERE ENGINEERS INC.
5000 Brittonfield Pkwy.
Syracuse, New York 13221
Gary N. Kirsch, P.E., Executive Vice President
PH: (315)437-6100
FX: (315)463-7554
URL: www.obg.com
Founded: 1945. **Staff:** 600. Activities: Multidisciplined engineering firm comprised of civil, sanitary, environmental, structural, chemical, geotechnical, mechanical, and electrical engineers; architects; hydrogeologists; industrial hygienists; toxicologists; chemists; biologists; and construction administrators. Offers consulting services in the following areas: water resources, water pollution control, air quality, hazardous and solid waste management, asbestos management, gas pipeline design, storage tank management, industrial hygiene, facilities engineering and site development. Full spectrum of services includes planning and feasibility studies, engineering design, and construction-phase services. Serves private industry and government agencies, including the Departments of Defense and Energy, worldwide.

OCM TEST LABORATORY INC.
3883 E. Eagle Dr.
Anaheim, California 92807-1722
Gerald Sauer, P.E./President
PH: (714)630-3003
TF: (800)359-8378
FX: (714)630-4443
E-mail: jsauer@ocmtestlabs.com
URL: www.ocmtestlabs.com
Founded: 1976. **Staff:** 18. Activities: Provides testing and consulting services of advanced composites, plastics, elastomers and metallics. Capabilities include mechanical, physical, chemical, metallurgical, fastener, fatigue, vacuum outgassing, thermal, environmental conditioning, machining and specimen preparation. Other services include FAA repair station testing, creep stress and rupture at elevated temperatures, and fastener testing. Industries served: aerospace and commercial industry.

PACKER ENGINEERING, INC.
1950 N. Washington St.
Naperville, Illinois 60566-0353
Kenneth F. Packer, Chairman/CEO
PH: (708)505-5722
TF: (800)323-0114
FX: (708)505-1986
URL: www.packereng.com
Founded: 1962. **Staff:** 100. Activities: A multidisciplinary engineering company offering automotive, aviation, corrosion and materials, electrical and electronic, environmental, biomechanical and biomedical, mechanical, safety, structural, metallurgical and manufacturing engineering expertise to industry. Clients include utilities, manufacturing companies, industrial processing, insurance companies and law firms. Activities include cause and origin investigations, research, problem solving, failure analysis, accident investigation and reconstruction, routine and customized testing, product and process performance assessment, and experimental development.

PALMER ELECTRONICS INC.
156 Belmont Ave.
Garfield, New Jersey 07026-2395
Victor R. Palmeri, President
PH: (201)772-5900
FX: (201)772-6054
E-mail: 103176.614@compuserve.com
Founded: 1965. **Staff:** 16. Activities: Consulting firm offering services regarding the fabrication of ceramic materials and products (porcelain, refractories, ceramic colors, enamels, and glazes) and the machinery, equipment and automation needed to produce ceramics. Industries served: electronics, refractories, ceramics, porcelain, and semiconductors.

PAPER CHEMISTRY CONSULTING LABORATORY, INC.
PO Box 402
Somers, New York 10589
John G. Penniman, Chairman
PH: (914)277-4269
FX: (914)277-8733
E-mail: zetapcl@aol.com
URL: www.papermakingchemistry.com
Founded: 1977. **Staff:** 14. Activities: Provides consulting services on papermaking wet end chemistry. Also manufactures and markets instrumentation for the paper industry. Instruments include: MK III and IV Dynamic Hand Sheet Mold, Dynamic Paper Chemistry Jar(tm), on-line Zeta potential instrument, the on-line Zeta Data(tm), and the laboratory Zeta Data(tm).

PAULI SYSTEMS, INC.
1820 Walter Ct.
Fairfield, California 94533
Robert Pauli, President
PH: (707)429-2434
FX: (707)429-2424
E-mail: info@paulisystems.com
URL: www.paulisystems.com
Founded: 1996. **Staff:** 15. Activities: Provides plastic and starch media dry paint stripping systems.

S.G. PINNEY & ASSOCIATES, INC.
1323 S.W. Bilthore St.
PO Box 9220
Port St. Lucie, Florida 34984
Stephen G. Pinney, CEO
PH: (561)337-3080
FX: (561)337-0294
E-mail: sgpinney@emi.net
URL: www.sgpinney.com
Founded: 1977. **Staff:** 60. Activities: Provides engineering, inspection and laboratory services in the field of industrial protective coatings. Services include failure analysis, training and certification, field inspection, underwater inspection and repair, specification preparation, expert testimony and plant surveys. Serves private industries as well as government agencies.

PLASTICS TECHNOLOGY LABS INC.
50 Pearl St.
Pittsfield, Massachusetts 01201
James Beauregard, President
PH: (413)499-0983
FX: (413)499-2339
E-mail: ptli@ptli.com
URL: www.plasticstechlabs.com
Founded: 1986. **Staff:** 11. Activities: An independent analytical, mechanical, thermal, electrical, and rheological testing laboratory dedicated to plastics, elastomers, composites, and polymers. Areas of specialization include plastic medical products performance; quality programs; specification testing; failure analysis; and ASTM, ISO, and FDA tests. The company is ISO 9002 certified and A2LA (ISO 25) accredited.

POLYMER INSTITUTE/POLYMER TECHNOLOGIES, INC., UNIVERSITY OF DETROIT MERCY
4001 W. McNichols Rd.
Detroit, Michigan 48219-0900
Kurt C. Frisch, Director
PH: (313)993-1270
FX: (313)993-1409
Founded: 1968. **Staff:** 40. Activities: Offers Applied and fundamental R&D in polymers technical support services, involving polymers: plastics, urethanes and polyurethanes, elastomers, paints, sealants, coatings, adhesives, foams, composites, RIM, including testing and analysis, failure analysis, and research and development projects and recycling. Also provides technical data and reports, expert testimony, education and training services. Industries served: aerospace, architecture, automotive, chemical, communications, construction, medical and pharmaceuticals, defense, durable goods, edu-

cation, energy, government, healthcare, oil and gas, packaging, plastics, recreation, rubber, transportation, textile and utilities.

PONDEROSA ASSOCIATES LTD. - CONSULTING ENGINEERS AND SCIENTISTS

130 Miners Dr.
Lafayette, Colorado 80026
Robert J. Caldwell, President
PH: (303)666-8112
FX: (303)666-4169
Founded: 1974. **Staff:** 22. Activities: Firm of high-technology consultants in multiple engineering and scientific disciplines, including chemical, electrical, industrial, mechanical, and civil engineering. Services include accident reconstruction and product liability. Serves industries, engineering colleges, government, insurance companies, research and development groups and the legal profession.

PRESSURE CHEMICAL

3419-25 Smallman St.
Pittsburgh, Pennsylvania 15201
Lawrence J. Rosen, Chairman/CEO
PH: (412)682-5882
TF: (800)722-5247
FX: (412)682-5864
E-mail: service@presschem.com
URL: www.presschem.com
Founded: 1964. **Staff:** 45. Activities: A pilot plant and research laboratory offering synthesis of special materials on a custom basis. Organic and inorganic synthesis; polymerization reactions. Areas of expertise include high pressure reactions, organometallic and organophosphorous compounds and anionic polymerization. Offers product development through semi-works manufacturing. Industries served: chemicals, pharmaceuticals, manufacturing, power, food, and cosmetics.

PROFESSIONAL SERVICE INDUSTRIES, INC.

4820 W. 15th St.
Lawrence, Kansas 66049-3846
Tom Boogher
PH: (785)865-9108
TF: (800)548-7901
FX: (785)865-9170
E-mail: info@psiusa.com
URL: www.psiusa.com
Founded: 1961. **Staff:** 3000. Activities: Provides environmental consulting, geotechnical engineering, and construction testing from offices nationwide. Offers construction testing and quality control, materials testing and certification, nondestructive examination and testing, roof and pavement consulting, geotechnical engineering and drilling services, environmental and asbestos consulting, analytical services, and training programs.

JACQUES PROOT

54, Meloche
Ste. Anne de Bellevue, Quebec, Canada H9X 3L2
Jacques Proot, Metalurgist
PH: (514)457-8008
FX: (514)457-8008
E-mail: jackproot@aol.com
URL: members.aol.com/jackproot/met/index.html
Founded: 1995. **Staff:** 15. Activities: Independent metallurgic (mineral chemistry) consultant.

RAYTHEON ENGINEERS & CONSTRUCTORS INTERNATIONAL INC.

141 Spring St.
Lexington, Massachusetts 02173
Charles Q. Miller, Chairman/CEO
PH: (617)862-6600
FX: (617)860-2845
Founded: 1993. **Staff:** 16000. Activities: Offers consulting services in engineering, design, construction, and maintenance of utility and industrial power plants petroleum and mining facilities, chemical, pharmaceutical and biotechnology, foods, metals, and general manu-

facturing plants, high-technology research laboratories, government facilities, and infrastructure facilities in transportation, highways, and water resources. Also provides special consulting on site planning, environmental assessments and testing, process technologies, control systems integration, environmental engineering, generation planning and licensing, and quality programs.

RECON ENVIRONMENTAL

5 Johnson Dr.
Raritan, New Jersey 08869-0130
Norman J. Weinstein, President
PH: (908)526-1000
FX: (908)526-7886
Founded: 1969. **Staff:** 170. Activities: Offers engineering, consulting, project management, testing and operation/maintenance and certification/monitoring services in pollution control, chemical processing, and energy conservation. Specialties in stack testing; soil sampling; installation of monitoring wells; asbestos management; industrial wastewater treatment; odor measurement, control, and dispersion modeling; waste oil technology; incinerator testing and design; flue gas conditioning; fluidized bed technology; coal conversion technology; industrial hygiene; contaminated site investigations; and soil and groundwater remediation. Fully equipped pollution control laboratory, including hazardous waste determinations and field testing equipment. Workload is primarily industrial with some federal and local government contract work.

REYA ASSOCIATES

6326 E. Livingston Ave., Ste. 322
Reynoldsburg, Ohio 43068-4004
Roger E. Yost, President
PH: (614)927-7897
FX: (614)866-3168
Founded: 1986. **Staff:** 12. Activities: REYA is a technical, engineering, and management consulting service providing services exclusively for the reinforced plastics/composites industry. Services include processing, product development, and production improvement.. Involved with all FRP processes, design, engineering, technical service, process selection, feasibility studies, and management. Educational seminars, opinion reports, expert witness, assessment of cause, technology upgrading, man hours requirements, material selection, and new product concepts as well as cost reduction and equipment utilization are provided. Complete FRP troubleshooting. Industries served: reinforced plastic/composite - marine, construction, industrial, non-corrosion, consumer products, recreational vehicles, aerospace, and government agencies.

SAFETY CONSULTING ENGINEERS, INC.

2131 Hammond Dr.
Schaumburg, Illinois 60173
C. James Dahn, President
PH: (847)925-8100
FX: (847)925-8120
E-mail: sceinc@sceinc.com
URL: www.sceinc.com
Founded: 1977. **Staff:** 11. Activities: Performs safety hazards analyses and testing for dust explosibility, electrostatic buildup, impact, electrostatic discharge, spontaneous heating, volumetric resistivity, thermal conductivity, flammability, and thermal stability. Refrigerant flammability characterization, flammability characterization of liquids, vapors, and solids. Processes safety and OSHA safety audits. Also conducts differential scanning calorimetry and gas chromatography processes. Industries served: chemical processing industry, pharmaceuticals, government, mining, aerospace, petroleum, and plastics.

SANI-PURE FOOD LABORATORIES

178-182 Saddle River Rd.
Saddle Brook, New Jersey 07663-4619
Helene Schnitzer
PH: (201)843-2525
FX: (201)843-4934
E-mail: sanipure@mail.idt.net
URL: www.angelfire.com/nj/sanipure/sanipure.html

Founded: 1946. **Staff:** 17. Activities: An independent testing facility offering the following major analytical services: in food chemistry, nutritional analyses, pesticide residues, trace elements, additives, filth and extraneous matter, and chromatography; in food microbiology, quality control analyses, salmonella, listeria, campylobacter, sanitation inspections, and shelf-life studies; in pharmaceuticals, USP, NF testing, antibiotics, and stability; and in water and wastewater, microbiological and chemical analyses, EPA priority pollutants, and field sampling. Industries served: food, cosmetic, government, and pharmaceutical.

SCHLOWSKY ENGINEERS INC.
45 Eisenhower Dr.
Paramus, New Jersey 07652
George J. Schlowsky, President
PH: (201)368-9299
FX: (201)368-8989
E-mail: sei@intercall.com
Founded: 1978. **Staff:** 11. Activities: Organic chemical consultancy offers a complete design of chemical processing systems. Particular expertise in distillation (fractional, continuous, simple, and batch), heat transfer (reboilers, evaporators, etc.) fluid flow (pumping systems, piping design), instrumentation (advanced control techniques, including computer automation), liquid-liquid extraction, and computer-aided drafting "CAD" (AutoCAD). Construction services include equipment drawing, general arrangement, piping design, structural design, instrument and equipment specification. Also provides supervision, project management and inspection of all equipment. Industries served: chemical, pharmaceutical, printing, petrochemical and any industry requiring removal of chemicals from wastewater.

SD LABORATORIES, INC.
PO Box 230
Convent Station, New Jersey 07961
Scott D. Wohlstein, President
PH: (201)538-5252
FX: (201)538-5252
E-mail: sdli@aol.com
Founded: 1980. **Staff:** 13. Activities: SD Laboratories, Inc. is an independent consulting group specializing in the research, design, development and application of photonics (lasers, electro/acousto/magneto/ and fiber-optics) everything from the source and transmission, to the detection of light. Areas of expertise include: chemistry, specifically, NIR spectroscopy; physics, specifically, high and low energy physics/nuclear physics and related instrumentation; and vacuum and thermal technologies, including environmental controls and instrumentation. Known internationally for practical applications and approach to the most difficult of projects. Industries served: commercial, industrial, scientific, medical fields, as well as military and government agencies.

SEA, INC.
7349 Worthington-Galena Rd.
Columbus, Ohio 43085
PH: (614)888-4160
TF: (800)782-6851
FX: (614)885-8014
Founded: 1970. **Staff:** 110. Activities: Provides consulting services in the areas of mechanical, metallurgical, electrical, structural, fire, and chemical engineering. Specialties include component and system analysis in product liability cases and accident investigation and reconstruction. Serves manufacturing firms, government agencies, insurance companies, and the legal profession.

SHERRY LABORATORIES
2203 S. Madison St.
Muncie, Indiana 47302
Kelly N. Stanley, Chairman
PH: (765)747-9000
TF: (800)874-3563
FX: (765)747-0228
URL: www.industry.net/sherry.laboratories
Founded: 1947. **Staff:** 57. Activities: Offers metallurgical consulting services. Provides failure analysis, welder qualification, metals

application, and chemical and mechanical testing. Offers environmental testing services for assessment of soil, sediment, sludge, hazardous waste, wastewater, and ground water for metals, inorganics, nutrients, pesticides, herbicides, PCBs and priority pollutants. Industries served: government and industrial concerns.

SHERRY LABORATORIES/OKLAHOMA
6825 E. 38th St.
Tulsa, Oklahoma 74145
Dan M. Lawson, President
PH: (918)664-7767
TF: (800)324-8378
FX: (918)627-3062
Founded: 1976. **Staff:** 32. Activities: Industrial/manufacturing consultants in metallurgical and chemical materials and processes, analytical chemistry, mechanical and functional testing, and failure analysis.

SHUSTER LABORATORIES, INC.
5 Hayward St.
Quincy, Massachusetts 02171
Patricia Baressi, Marketing Manager
PH: (617)328-7600
TF: (800)444-8705
FX: (617)770-0957
E-mail: tbaressi@shusterlabs.com
URL: www.shusterlabs.com
Founded: 1955. **Staff:** 120. Activities: Offers technical and management consulting, consumer research, and analytical testing for the food, pharmaceutical, cosmetic, chemical specialty, paper, plastics, and medical device/in vitro diagnostics industries. Services include product development; regulatory advice/interfacing; shelf-life studies, plant engineering, nutrition labeling; and analytical, microbiological and physical testing.

SILLIKER LABORATORIES GROUP, INC.
900 Maple Rd.
Homewood, Illinois 60430
Robert I. Solomon, Vice President Marketing
PH: (708)957-7878
FX: (708)957-8449
E-mail: info@silliker.com
URL: www.silliker.com
Founded: 1967. **Staff:** 950. Activities: Offers consultation in the areas of food chemistry, food microbiology, nutrition analysis, hazard analysis, and testing for extraneous matter, pesticide residues and trace metals. Custom designs client-sponsored research programs. Provides in-house problem solving, quality control programs, food plant sanitation audits, court testimony, food poisoning investigations, continuing education programs, customized video training programs, storage studies, and samplings. Industries served: food industry - all facets, including government agencies.

SKEIST INC.
375 Rte. 10
Whippany, New Jersey 07981
Jerry Miron, President
PH: (201)515-2020
FX: (201)515-0022
Founded: 1955. **Staff:** 12. Activities: Provides techno-economic-marketing studies, consulting services, merger-acquisition studies, and licensing arrangements for more than three hundred organizations on six continents. Industries served: chemical and polymer industries.

SRS INTERNATIONAL, INC.
1625 K St. NW, Ste. 1000
Washington, District of Columbia 20006-1604
John A. Todhunter
PH: (202)223-0157
FX: (202)835-8970
E-mail: mainsrs@srsinternational.com
URL: www.srsinternational.com
Founded: 1983. **Staff:** 11. Activities: Offers new product develop-

ment and compliance expertise to the drug, chemical, pesticide, medical device and biotechnology industries including regulatory strategy for marketing and development of products. Services include design, management, and monitoring of clinical trials including data base management and data analysis, safety evaluation, data/literature review, writing preclinical and clinical protocols, placement of studies, monitoring, good laboratory practice audits, and legal assistance.

SSM/SPOTTS, STEVENS AND MCCOY, INC.

345 N. Wyomissing Blvd.
Reading, Pennsylvania 19610-0307
J. Carlton Godlove, II, PE, CEO & Pres
PH: (610)376-6581
FX: (610)376-6950
Founded: 1932. **Staff:** 160. Activities: Offers consulting engineering, environmental, land development, and laboratory services to industrial, commercial and governmental clients. Engineering services include civil, mechanical, electrical, structural, sanitary, and highway/traffic. Environmental services include air/water pollution control, wetlands, PSAs, USTs/ASTs, hazardous waste management and industrial hygiene. Maintains AIHA - accredited laboratory certified in five states. Also provides land development, planning, and surveying services.

STANDARDS TESTING LABORATORIES, INC.

PO Box 592
Massillon, Ohio 44646
Matt Merritt, Mgr. (TTI/STL)
PH: (330)833-8548
TF: (800)833-8547
FX: (330)833-7902
Founded: 1972. **Staff:** 80. Activities: Industrial testing consultants working in areas of tire and wheel research, design construction, manufacturing technology and performance, and failure analysis and standards; rubber and polymer chemistry; suspension systems; and race car operation. Also offers forensic consulting, including preliminary analysis, discovery process, case preparation and depositions; accident reconstruction; laboratory and fleet testing; and closed circuit testing. Industries served: automotive, aerospace, and government agencies worldwide.

STRASBURGER AND SIEGEL, INC.

7249 National Dr.
Hanover, Maryland 21076
Alan D. Parker
PH: (410)712-7373
TF: (888)726-3753
FX: (410)712-7378
URL: www.sas-labs.com
Founded: 1926. **Staff:** 26. Activities: Consulting chemists, microbiologists and food scientists serving the food industry. Clients include...food processors & manufacturers, foodservice firms, grocery distributors and retailers. Services include food analysis, product development, food safety and quality management programs.

SUPERIOR ENGINEERING CORP.

2345 167th St.
Hammond, Indiana 46323
Martin C. Heidtman, Chairman
PH: (219)844-7030
FX: (219)844-4217
E-mail: superior@netnitco.net
URL: www.superiorengineering.com
Founded: 1962. **Staff:** 130. Activities: Engineering firm with expertise in mechanical, electrical, architectural, structural, chemical and civil work. Services include scoping, facility planning, feasibility studies, engineering, design, construction documents, project scheduling, field engineering and construction/project management. Experienced in air pollution abatement. Serves steel, oil, chemicals, utilities, pharmaceuticals, foods, and manufacturing industries, and government in the U.S. and some of North and South America.

TARGET GROUP, INC.

1000 Harston Ln.
Erdenheim, Pennsylvania 19038-7037
Peter R. Lantos, President
PH: (215)233-4083
FX: (215)836-2518
E-mail: peterrl@aol.com
URL: www.maconsultants.com/target.htm
Founded: 1980. **Staff:** 25. Activities: Provides expertise in plastics industry, in management science and the marketing of technical products. The firm's main goal is to assist manufacturers/marketers of plastics and related products. Also to improve the effectiveness of the research and development organization as regards productivity, creativity and leadership skills. Also active with government agencies, plastics, and chemicals.

TECH MART, INC.

408 Cardinal Dr.
Crown Point, Indiana 46307
Thomas L. Kablach, President
PH: (219)663-8773
FX: (219)663-8714
Founded: 1987. **Staff:** 15. Activities: Offers technical consulting to metals industries: metallurgy, quality control, nondestructive testing, failure analysis, and expert witness services. Industries served: basic steel industry, steel foundries, steel forge shops, machinery builders, and government agencies.

TERRA GROUP OF COMPANIES

1245 E. 7th Ave.
Vancouver, British Columbia, Canada V5T 1R1
Stan Russell, Owner
PH: (604)874-1245
FX: (604)874-2358
E-mail: info@terra.ca
URL: www.terra.ca
Staff: 120. Activities: Geotechnical engineering services include geotechnical land use planning and feasibility assessments, transportation, infrastructure and resource development, forensic engineering, expert witness and document reviews, forest industry consulting, environmental engineering, environmental remediation, asphalt materials engineering and testing, concrete materials engineering and testing, building materials engineering and testing, soils testing, quality systems program management.

TERRONICS DEVELOPMENT CORP.

7565 West 900 North
Elwood, Indiana 46036
William H. Brown, Vice President
PH: (765)552-0808
FX: (765)552-0810
URL: www.terronics.com
Founded: 1984. **Staff:** 18. Activities: Provides electrostatic coating expertise with both liquids or powders. Industries served: glass, steel, rubber, paper, and food.

TEST LAB INC.

4619 W. Curtis St.
Tampa, Florida 33614
Helen Cornwell
PH: (813)872-7821
FX: (813)872-1876
Founded: 1973. **Staff:** 21. Activities: Offers services in materials and foundation testing and engineering. Industries served: owners, architects, engineers, and contractors, as well as government agencies.

TOUCHSTONE RESEARCH LABORATORY, LTD.

The Millennium Centre
Triadelphia, West Virginia 26059
Elizabeth Kraftician, Chief Executive Officer

PH: (304)547-5800
FX: (304)547-5764
E-mail: jkm@gold.trl.com
URL: www.trl.com
Founded: 1980. **Staff:** 26. Activities: A leading industrial problem-solving and applied research company. The firm operates in the fields of materials science, metallurgy, industrial problem solving, technology transfer, failure analysis, environmental sciences and microbiology. Staff includes: metallurgical, mechanical, aerospace, electrical and chemical engineers; materials scientists; chemists; physicists; computer scientists and microbiologists. Services include manufacturing process development, product evaluation, reverse engineering, on-site engineering consultation, non-standards testing development, quality control program development, chemical analysis, qualification and characterization of materials, corrosion testing, composite interfacial property evaluation, custom test equipment development, video production, tensile and compression testing, fatigue and thermomechanical fatigue testing, water testing, computer modeling, software development, and expert testimony.

TOWNSEND TARNELL INC.
12914 I-45 North, Ste. 707
Houston, Texas 77290
Phillip Townsend, President & CEO
PH: (281)873-8733
TF: (888)877-6809
FX: (281)875-1915
E-mail: townsend@ptai.com
URL: www.ptai.com
Founded: 1999. **Staff:** 160. Activities: BENCHMARKING AND OPERATIONS MANAGEMENT CONSULTING: Industry Benchmarking of operations for plastics, intermediates and chemicals; Functional Benchmarking of R&D, and Maintenance practices; Operations improvement consulting based on Benchmarking data; Plastic Market Monthly monitoring reports. MARKET RESEARCH AND STRATEGIC CONSULTING: Volume Plastics concentration on Polyethylene, Polypropylene, Polystyrene and PVC; Specialty Plastics and Chemicals group concentrating on Engineering Thermoplastics, Chemical Additives for Plastics, Speciality chemicals, Fine chemicals; End Use Markets focus on Automotive, Construction, Packaging, Thermoplastic Pipe and other plastics and paper applications and related industries; Mergers and Acquisitions support bringing market insights to the value chain analysis of businesses for sale or purchase; Customer Satisfaction studies. BUSINESS INFORMATION AND DATABASE SERVICES: Plastics converter databases covering all plastics resins, primary and auxiliary processing equipment, all markets; Purchasing Paying Records reports on purchasing habits and buying potential of plastic material buying locations; Resume reports summarizing plastics processors' financial, managerial, and operational assets; Newsletter of action events that effect resin suppliers; Market Share Reports on segment analysis of plastics and processes including film extrusion, sheet extrusion, blow molding, and injection molding.

TOXICON, INC.
6337 Highland Dr., Ste. 2054
Salt Lake City, Utah 84121
Carol B. Done, President
PH: (801)277-2241
FX: (801)277-0867
Founded: 1988. **Staff:** 12. Activities: Safety consulting firm provides toxicologic advice, evaluation, research, publication, and litigation support. Offers additional services in toxic risk assessment, toxic incident investigation, toxicity diagnosis, employee drug abuse or safety programs, case evaluation and trial preparation, drug or toxin causation of disease or birth defects, toxicity or drug data presentation, employee education, and temporary or part-time project or management employment. In addition to its own staff, toxicologic consultants from various parts of the world can be supplied for whatever expertise or credentials are required. Industries served: health services, pharmaceutical/chemical industry, government, legal, and business.

TSL ENVIRONMENTAL LABORATORIES
1301 Fewster Dr.
Mississauga, Ontario, Canada L4W 1A2
Peter Cooper, President
PH: (905)625-1544
FX: (905)625-8368
Founded: 1948. **Staff:** 30. Activities: Offers general environmental and industrial testing of chemical composition, phytotoxicology, industrial quality assurance, and industrial problem solving. Industries served: environmental consultants, food industry, waste generating industry, and manufacturing industries.

VACUUM COATING CONSULTANTS LTD.
5547 Central Ave.
Boulder, Colorado 80301
Ted VanVorous, President
PH: (303)417-0953
FX: (303)444-0104
E-mail: cathodes@ix.netcom.com
Founded: 1976. **Staff:** 32. Activities: Provides technical process and plant engineering consulting for vacuum coating fields and export management consulting to provide worldwide sales/marketing of high technology equipment. Also provides assistance in training technicians who will install equipment overseas. Recent experience in liquid crystal display plant engineering, and polymer concrete plant engineering. Industries served: chemical, hospital, superconductor, and tool coating.

WALTERS FORENSIC ENGINEERING
4166 Dundas St. W
Toronto, Ontario, Canada M8X 1X3
Ken Belbeck, President & CEO
PH: (416)236-2569
TF: (800)387-1950
FX: (416)236-3681
E-mail: engineer@waltersforensic.com
URL: www.waltersforensic.com
Founded: 1969. **Staff:** 22. Activities: Offers a range of services including rehabilitation and inspection of a forensic engineering nature to the private and public sectors, particularly the insurance and construction industries, and the legal and engineering professions. These services are interdisciplinary including the mechanical, electrical, civil, chemical, and metallurgical fields. Provides consulting services worldwide.

WARDROP ENGINEERING INC.
400 386 Broadway
Winnipeg, Manitoba, Canada R3C 4M8
E.C. Card, Vice Chairman and CEO
PH: (204)956-0980
FX: (204)957-5389
E-mail: winnipeg@wardrop.com
URL: www.wardrop.com
Founded: 1955. **Staff:** 150. Activities: Engineering consultants offering services in aerospace, chemical, civil, electrical, instrumentation, environmental, mechanical, and nuclear engineering; land use planning; pollution control; and technology transfer. Specialists in the application of finite element computer codes to provide industry with accurate, cost-effective engineering analysis for design optimization, failure diagnosis, viability of new designs, and prototype development. Industries served: aerospace, nuclear, food processing, pulp and paper, mining, manufacturing, public works, transportation, and defense/military agencies.

WILSON COMPOSITE GROUP, INC.
Folsom, California 95630
Brian A. Wilson, President
PH: (916)989-4812
FX: (916)989-1714
E-mail: norma-anders@wcgi.com
URL: www.wcgi.com
Founded: 1987. **Staff:** 45. Activities: Provides aerospace and civil engineering applications of advanced composite materials including design, laminate analysis for continuous and discontinuous fiber sys-

tems, hybrid structures, and finite element analysis using ANSYS and NASTRAN codes. Additional services include market studies, expert witness, and Total Quality Management services, proposal management services, including "Red Team" leadership, and consortium management.

TRADE INFORMATION SOURCES

Adapted from Gale's *Encyclopedia of Business Information Sources* (*EBIS*), the entries featured in this chapter show trade journals and other published sources, including web sites and databases. Entries list the title of the work, the name of the author (where available), name and address of the publisher, frequency or year of publication, prices or fees, and Internet address (in many cases).

ADHESION SCIENCE
Available from American Chemical Society Publications.
1155 16th St., N. W.
Washington, DC 20036
PH: (800)227-9919
FX: (202)872-6067
E-mail: acsbooks@acs.org
URL: http://www.chemcenter.org
J. Comyn. 1997. $40.00. Published by The Royal Society of Chemistry. Provides basic scientific and technical information on "common adhesives."

ADHESIVES AGE DIRECTORY
Intertec Publishing Corp.
6151 Powers Ferry Rd., NW
Atlanta, GA 30339-2941
PH: (800)621-9907
FX: (800)633-6219
Annual. $59.95. Formerly *Adhesives Red Book.*

ADHESIVES AND SEALANTS
ASM International
6939 Kinsman Rd.
Materials Park, OH 44073-0002
PH: (800)336-5152
FX: (216)338-4634
E-mail: Mem-Serv@po.ASM-Intl.org
URL: http://www.asm.intl.org
1990. $160.00. Volume three. (Engineered Materials Handbook Series).

ADVANCED COATINGS AND SURFACE TECHNOLOGY
Technical Insights, Inc.
32 N. Dean St.
Englewood, NJ 07631-2807
PH: (201)568-4744
FX: (201)568-8247
E-mail: htminfo@insights.com
URL: http://www.insights.com
Monthly. $590.00 per year. Newsletter on technical developments relating to industrial coatings.

ADVANCES IN POLYMER TECHNOLOGY
Polymer Processing Institute
605 Third Ave.
New York, NY 10158-0012
PH: (800)225-5945
FX: (212)850-6088
John Wiley & Sons, Inc., Journals Div. Quarterly. $653.00 per year.

AGRICOLA ON SILVERPLATTER
Available from SilverPlatter Information, Inc.
100 River Ridge Rd.
Norwood, MA 02062-5026
PH: (800)343-0064
FX: (781)769-8763
Quarterly. $825.00 per year. Produced by the National Agricultural Library. Provides about three million citations on CD-ROM to the literature of agriculture, agricultural economics, animal sciences, entomology, fertilizer, food, forestry, nutrition, pesticides, plant science, water resources, and other topics. Each quarterly disc covers the past ten years, with archival discs available from 1970.

A.I.C.H.E.
American Institute of Chemical Engineers
345 E. 47th St.
New York, NY 10017-2396
PH: (800)242-4363
FX: (212)705-8400
URL: http://www.198.6.4.175/docs/publication/journal/index.html
Monthly. $715.00. Devoted to research and technological developments in chemical engineering and allied fields.

AMERICAN OIL CHEMISTS' SOCIETY JOURNAL
AOCS Press
Post Office Box 3489
Champaign, IL 61821-0489
PH: (217)359-2344
FX: (217)351-8091
E-mail: publications@aocs.orgf
URL: http://www.aocs.org
Monthly. Individuals, $145.00 per year; institutions, $195.00 per year. Includes *INFORM: International News on Fats, Oils and Related Materials.*

ANNUAL REVIEW OF THE CHEMICAL INDUSTRY
United Nations Publications
Rm. DC2-853
Two United Nations Plaza
New York, NY 10017
PH: (800)253-9646
FX: (212)963-3489
Annual. $42.00.

ANNUAL SURVEY OF MANUFACTURES
Available from U. S. Government Printing Office.
Washington, DC 20402
PH: (202)512-1800
FX: (202)512-2250
E-mail: gpoaccess@gpo.gov
URL: http://www.access.gpo.gov
Annual. Issued by the U.S. Census Bureau as an interim update to the *Census of Manufactures.* Includes data on number of manufacturing establishments in various industries, employment, labor costs, value of shipments, capital expenditures, inventories, energy costs, and assets. (See also Census Bureau home page, http://www.census.gov/.)

AOAC INTERNATIONAL JOURNAL
AOAC International
481 N. Frederick Ave., Suite 500
Gaithersberg, MD 20877-2917
PH: (301)924-7077
FX: (301)924-7089
Bimonthly. Members $176.00 per year; non-members, $242.00 per year; institutions, $262.00 per year. Formerly *Association of Official Analytical Chemist Journal.*

APPLIED SCIENCE AND TECHNOLOGY INDEX
H. W. Wilson Co.
950 University Ave.
Bronx, NY 10452
PH: (800)367-6770
FX: (718)590-1617
E-mail: hwwmsg@info.hwwilson.com
URL: http://www.hwwilson.com
Published 11 times a year. Quarterly and annual cumulations. Service basis. Indexes a wide variety of English language technical, industrial, and engineering periodicals.

ASLIB BOOK GUIDE: A MONTHLY LIST OF RECOMMENDED SCIENTIFIC AND TECHNICAL BOOKS
Available from Information Today, Inc.
143 Old Marlton Pike
Medford, NJ 08055-8750
PH: (800)300-9868
FX: (609)654-4309
Monthly. $204.00 per year. Published in London by Aslib: The Association for Information Management. Formerly *Aslib Book List.*

ASM ENGINEERED MATERIALS REFERENCE BOOK
ASM International, Materials Information
9639 Kinsman Rd.
Materials Park, OH 44073-0002

PH: (800)336-5152
FX: (216)338-4634
E-mail: Mem-Serv@po.ASM-Intl.org
URL: http://www.asm-intl.org
Michael L. Bauccio. 1994. $121.00. Second edition. Provides information on a wide range of materials, with special sections on ceramics, industrial glass products, and plastics.

ASM HANDBOOK: SURFACE ENGINEERING
ASM International, Materials Information
9639 Kinsman Rd.
Materials Park, OH 44073-0002
PH: (800)336-5152
FX: (216)338-4634
E-mail: Mem-Serv@po.ASM-Intl.org
URL: http://www.asm.intl.org
1994. $160.00. Covers industrial coating, plating, electroplating, and other metal finishing topics. Includes an extensive glossary of terms. (ASM Handbook series, vol. 5.)

ASM MATERIALS ENGINEERING DICTIONARY
ASM International, Materials Information
9639 Kinsman Rd.
Materials Park, OH 44073-0002
PH: (800)336-5152
FX: (216)338-4634
E-mail: Mem-Serv@po.ASM-Intl.org
URL: http://www.asm.intl.org
Joseph R. Davis, editor. 1992. $111.00. Contains 10,000 entries, 700 illustrations, and 150 tables relating to metals, plastics, ceramics, composites, and adhesives. Includes "Technical Briefs" on 64 key material groups.

CA SEARCH
Chemical Abstracts Service.
2540 Olentangy River Rd.
Columbus, OH 43210
PH: (800)753-4227
FX: (614)447-3751
Guide to chemical literature, 1967 to present. Inquire as to online cost and availability.

CEC COMMUNICATIONS (CHEMICAL ENGINEERING COMMUNICATIONS)
Gordon and Breach Publishers, Inc.
Post Office Box 200029
Riverfront Plaza Station
Newark, NJ 07102
PH: (800)545-8398
FX: (973)643-7676
URL: http://www.zic.com
Bimonthly. $50.00 per year. Formerly *Chemical Engineering Communications.*

CHEM-BANK
SilverPlatter Information, Inc.
100 River Ridge Rd.
Norwood, MA 02062
PH: (800)343-0064
FX: (781)769-8763
Quarterly. $1,595.00 per year. Provides CD-ROM information on hazardous substances, including 110,000 chemicals in the *Registry of Toxic Effects of Chemical Substances* and 60,000 materials covered by the *Toxic Substances Control Act Initial Inventory.*

CHEM SOURCES—INTERNATIONAL
Chemical Sources International, Inc.
Post Office Box 1824
Clemson, SC 29633-6190
PH: (800)222-4531
FX: (864)646-9938
URL: http://www.chemssources.com
Biennial. $750.00. List of 2,500 chemical producers and distributors

in 80 countries; lists agents and representatives of 5,000 industry firms.

CHEM SOURCES—USA
Chemical Sources International, Inc.
Post Office Box 1824
Clemson, SC 29633-6190
PH: (800)222-4531
FX: (864)646-9938
URL: http://www.chemssources.com
Annual. $395.00. List of 100 chemical producers and distributors in the U. S.

CHEMICAL ABSTRACTS
Chemical Abstracts Service
Post Office Box 3012
Columbus, OH 43210-0012
PH: (614)447-3600
FX: (614)447-3713
Weekly. $19,800.00 per year.

CHEMICAL ENGINEERING
McGraw-Hill.
1221 Ave of the Americas
New York, NY 10020
PH: (800)722-4726
FX: (212)512-2821
Monthly. $29.50 per year.

CHEMICAL ENGINEERING—BUYER'S GUIDE
McGraw-Hill.
1221 Ave of the Americas
New York, NY 10020
PH: (800)722-4726
FX: (212)512-2821
Annual. $38.00. Over 4,000 firms supplying equipment and machinery to the chemical processing industry. Formerly *Chemical Engineering-Equipment Buyer's Guide.*

CHEMICAL ENGINEERING FOR CHEMISTS
American Chemical Society Publications
1155 16th St., N. W.
Washington, DC 20036
PH: (800)227-9919
FX: (202)872-6067
E-mail: acsbooks@acs.org
URL: http://www.chemcenter.org
Richard G. Griskey. 1997. $124.95. Provides basic knowledge of chemical engineering and engineering economics.

CHEMICAL AND ENGINEERING NEWS
American Chemical Society
1155 16th St., NW
Washington, DC 20036
PH: (800)333-9511
FX: (202)872-6067
E-mail: acsbooks@acs.org
URL: http://www.chemcenter.org
Weekly. Free to members; institutional non-members, $140.00 per year.

CHEMICAL AND ENGINEERING NEWS—FACTS AND FIGURES ISSUE
American Chemical Society, Microforms and Back Issues Office
1155 16th St., N. W.
Washington, DC 20036
PH: (800)333-9511
FX: (202)872-6067
E-mail: acsbooks@acs.org
URL: http://www.chemcenter.org
Annual. $20.00. List of 100 largest chemical producers by total chemical sales.

CHEMICAL ENGINEERING PROGRESS
American Institute of Chemical Engineers
345 E. 47th St.
New York, NY 10017
PH: (800)242-4363
FX: (212)705-8400
URL: http://www.198.6.4.175/docs/cep/index.html
Monthly. Free to members; non-members, $85.00 per year. Covers current advances and trends in the chemical process and related industries. Supplement available *AICh Extra*.

CHEMICAL INDUSTRY EUROPE
State Mutual Book and Periodical Service, Ltd.
521 Fifth Ave., 17th Fl.
New York, NY 10175
PH: (718)261-1704
FX: (516)537-0412
Annual. $228.00. About 11,000 companies within the chemical industry. Formerly *Chemical Industry Directory*.

CHEMICAL INDUSTRY NOTES
Chemical Abstracts Service
Post Office Box 3012
Columbus, OH 43210-0012
PH: (614)447-3600
FX: (614)447-3713
Weekly. $995.00 per year.

CHEMICAL MARKETING REPORTER
Schnell Publishing Co., Inc.
80 Broad St.
New York, NY 10004-2203
PH: (212)248-4177
FX: (212)248-4903
URL: http://www.chemexpo.com
Weekly. $99.00 per year. Quotes current prices for a wide range of chemicals.

CHEMICAL PROCESSING
The Putman Publishing Group
301 E. Erie St.
Chicago, IL 60611
PH: (312)644-2020
FX: (312)644-1131
URL: http://www.putnam.com
Monthly. Free to qualified personnel; others, $105.00 per year.

CHEMICAL REGULATION REPORTER: A WEEKLY REVIEW OF AFFECTING CHEMICAL USERS AND MANUFACTURERS
Bureau of National Affairs, Inc.
1250 23rd St., NW
Washington, DC 20037
PH: (800)372-1033
FX: (202)822-8092
URL: http://www.bna.com
Weekly. $1,740.00 per year. Six volumes. Looseleaf.

CHEMICAL WEEK
Chemical Week Associates
888 Seventh Ave., 26th Fl.
New York, NY 10106-2698
PH: (212)621-4900
FX: (212)621-4949
E-mail: webmaster@chemweek.com
URL: http://www.chemweek.com
49 times a year. $99.00 per year. Includes annual *Buyers' Guide*.

CHEMICAL WEEK—BUYERS GUIDE
Chemical Week Associates
888 Seventh Ave., 26th Fl.
New York, NY 10106-2698

PH: (212)621-4900
FX: (212)621-4949
E-mail: bpunsalan@chemweek.com
URL: http://www.chemweek.com
Annual. $115.00. Included in subscription to *Chemical Week*.

CHEMICAL WEEK: FINANCIAL SURVEY OF THE 300 LARGEST COMPANIES IN THE U. S. CHEMICAL PROCESS INDUSTRIES
Chemical Week Associates
888 Seventh Ave., 26th Fl.
New York, NY 10106-2698
PH: (212)621-4900
FX: (212)621-4949
E-mail: bpunsalan@chemweek.com
URL: http://www.chemweek.com
Annual. $8.00. Supersedes *Chemical Week-Chemical Week 300*.

CHEMICAL WHOLESALERS DIRECTORY
American Business Information, Inc.
5711 S. 86th Circle
Omaha, NE 68127
PH: (800)555-6124
FX: (402)331-5481
E-mail: directory@abii.com
URL: http://www.abii.com
Annual. Price on application. Lists 8,082 United States wholesalers and 1,199 Canadian wholesalers. Compiled from telephone company yellow pages.

THE CHEMISTRY AND PHYSICS OF COATINGS
1155 16th St., N. W.
Washington, DC 20036
PH: (800)227-9919
FX: (202)872-6067
E-mail: acsbooks@acs.org
URL: http://www.chemcenter.org
A. R. Marrion, editor. Available from American Chemical Society Publications. 1996. $30.00. Published by The Royal Society of Chemistry. Provides an overview of paint science and technology, including environmental considerations.

CHEMISTRY TODAY AND TOMORROW: THE CENTRAL, USEFUL, AND CREATIVE SCIENCE
American Chemical Society Publications
1155 16th St., N. W.
Washington, DC 20036
PH: (800)227-9919
FX: (202)872-6067
E-mail: acsbooks@acs.org
URL: http://www.chemcenter.org
Ronald Breslow. 1996. $19.95. Written in nontechnical language for the general reader. Discusses the various disciplines of chemistry, such as medicinal, environmental, and industrial.

COATINGS-PROTECTIVE DIRECTORY
American Business Information, Inc.
5711 S. 86th Circle
Omaha, NE 68127
PH: (800)555-6124
FX: (402)331-5481
E-mail: directory@abii.com
URL: http://www.abii.com
Annual. Price on application. Lists about 2,900 sources of corrosion control protective coatings. Includes number of employees and name of manager or owner.

COMPENDEX PLUS
Engineering Information, Inc.
Castle Point on the Hudson
Hoboken, NJ 07030
PH: (800)221-1044
FX: (201)216-8532
Engineering Information, Inc. Provides online indexing and abstract-

ing of the world's engineering and technical information appearing in journals, reports, books, and proceedings. Time period is 1970 to date, with weekly updates. Inquire as to online cost and availability.

THE COMPOSITES AND ADHESIVES NEWSLETTER
T/C Press.
P.O. Box 36006
Los Angeles, CA 90036-0006
PH: (213)938-6923
FX: (213)938-6923
Bimonthly. $150.00. Presents news of the composite materials and adhesives industries, with particular coverage of new products and applications.

COMPREHENSIVE GUIDE TO THE HAZARDOUS PROPERTIES OF CHEMICAL SUBSTANCES
Van Nostrand Reinhold
115 Fifth Ave.
New York, NY 10003
PH: (800)842-3636
FX: (212)254-9499
E-mail: info@vnr.com
URL: http://www.vnr.com
Pradyot Patnaik. 1998. $130.00. Second edition.

CONSULTING SERVICES
Association of Consulting Chemists and Chemical Engineers
40 W. 45th St.
New York, NY 10036
PH: (212)983-3160
FX: (212)983-3161
E-mail: 104206.1620@compuserve.com
URL: http://www.provider.com
Biennial. $25.00. Directory containing one-page "scope sheet" for each member and an extensive classified directory.

CORROSION ABSTRACTS: ABSTRACTS OF THE WORLD'S LITERATURE ON CORROSION AND CORROSION MITIGATION
National Association of Corrosion Engineers.
P.O. Box 218340
Houston, TX 77218
PH: (713)492-0535
FX: (713)492-8254
E-mail: pubs@mail.nace.org
URL: http://www.nace.org
NACE International. Bimonthly. $250.00 per year. Provides abstracts of the worldwide literature of corrosion and corrosion control. Also available on CD-ROM.

CORROSION CONTROL
Chapman and Hall
115 Fifth Ave., 4th Fl.
New York, NY 10003-1004
PH: (800)842-3636
Samuel A. Bradford. 1992. $72.95. Discusses basic corrosion theory, corrosion causes, coatings, plastics, metals, and many other highly detailed, technical topics.

CORROSION: JOURNAL OF SCIENCE AND ENGINEERING
National Association of Corrosion Engineers
P.O. Box 218340
Houston, TX 77218
PH: (713)492-0535
FX: (713)492-8254
E-mail: pubs@mail.nace.org
URL: http://www.nace.org
NACE International. Monthly. $130.00 per year. Covers corrosion control science, theory, engineering, and practice.

CPI DIGEST (CHEMICAL PROCESS INDUSTRIES): KEY TO WORLD LITERATURE SERVING THE COATINGS, PLASTICS, FIBERS, ADHESIVES, AND RELATED INDUSTRIES
CPI Information Services
2117 Cherokee Parkway
Louisville, KY 40204
PH: (502)456-6288
FX: (502)454-4808
Monthly. $297.00 per year. Abstracts of business and technical articles for polymer-based, chemical process industries. Includes a monthly list of relevant U. S. patents. International coverage.

CROP PROTECTION CHEMICALS REFERENCE
Chemical and Pharmaceutical Press, Inc.
888 Seventh Ave., Suite 2800
New York, NY 10106
PH: (800)544-7377
FX: (212)399-9703
Contains the complete text of product labels. Indexed by manufacturer, product category, pest use, crop use, chemical name, and brand name.

DEALER PROGRESS: FOR FERTILIZER/AG CHEMICAL RETAILERS
Clear Window, Inc.
15444 Clayton Rd., Suite 314
Ballwin, MO 63011
PH: (314)527-4001
FX: (314)527-4010
Bimonthly. $40.00 per year. Published in association with the Fertilizer Institute. Includes information on fertilizers and agricultural chemicals, including farm pesticides. Formerly *Fertilizer Progress*.

DERWENT CROP PROTECTION FILE
Derwent, Inc.
1725 Duke St., Suite 250
Alexandria, VA 22314
PH: (800)451-3551
FX: (703)519-5829
E-mail: info@derwent.com
URL: http://www.derwent.com
Provides citations to the international journal literature of agricultural chemicals and pesticides from 1968 to date, with updating eight times per year. Formerly *PESTDOC*. Inquire as to online cost and availability.

THE DEVELOPMENT OF PLASTICS
Available from American Chemical Society Publications.
1155 16th St., N. W.
Washington, DC 20036
PH: (800)227-9919
FX: (202)872-6067
E-mail: acsbooks@acs.org
URL: http://www.chemcenter.org
S. Mossman and P. Morris, editors. 1996. $83.00. Published by The Royal Society of Chemistry. Covers the history of plastics from the Victorian era to the present. Includes technical, scientific, and cultural perspectives.

DICTIONARY OF CHEMICAL TERMINOLOGY
Elsevier Science
655 Ave. of the Americas
New York, NY 10010
PH: (888)437-4636
FX: (212)633-3680
E-mail: usinfo-f@elsevier.com
URL: http://www.elsevier.com
D. Kryt. 1980. $190.75. Includes French, German, Polish, and Russian.

DICTIONARY OF PLASTICS TECHNOLOGY
John Wiley and Sons, Inc.
605 Third Ave.
New York, NY 10158-0012
PH: (800)225-5945
E-mail: info@atsqm.jwiley.com
URL: http://www.wiley.com/compbooks/
H. D. Junge. 1987. $150.00.

DIRECTORY OF CHEMICAL PRODUCERS - UNITED
STATES
SRI International Process Industries Div.
Chemical Marketing Research Center
Menlo Park, CA 94025
PH: (415)859-3627
FX: (415)859-4623
Annual. $1,600.00. Information on over 1,500 United States basic chemical producers, manufacturing nearly 10,000 chemicals in commercial quantities at 4,500 plant locations.

ENCYCLOPEDIA OF PHYSICAL SCIENCES AND
ENGINEERING INFORMATION SOURCES
Gale Group
27500 Drake Rd.
Farmington Hills, MI 48331
PH: (800)877-GALE
Irregular. $155.00. Includes print, electronic, and other information sources for a wide range of scientific, technical, and engineering topics.

ENCYCLOPEDIA OF POLYMER SCIENCE AND
ENGINEERING
John Wiley and Sons, Inc.
605 Third Ave.
New York, NY 10158-0012
PH: (800)526-5368
FX: (212)850-6088
H.F. Mark and others. 1985. $4,959.00. 19 volumes, volume 22. $290.00 per volume. Second edition.

ENERGY AND FUELS
American Chemical Society Publications
1155 16th St., N. W.
Washington, DC 20036
PH: (800)227-9919
FX: (202)872-6067
E-mail: service@acs.org
URL: http://www.chemcenter.org
Bimonthly. $395.00 per year. An interdisciplinary technical journal covering non-nuclear energy sources: petroleum, coal, natural gas, synthetic fuels, etc.

FARM CHEMICALS HANDBOOK
Meister Publishing Co.
37733 Euclid Ave.
Willoughby, OH 44094
PH: (440)942-2000
FX: (440)942-0662
E-mail: meister.publ.com
Annual. $89.00. Manufacturers and suppliers of fertilizers, pesticides, and related equipment used in agribusiness.

FEDERATION OF SOCIETIES FOR COATINGS
TECHNOLOGY: YEAR BOOK AND MEMBERSHIP
DIRECTORY
Federation of Societies for Coatings Technology
492 Norristown Rd.
Blue Bell, PA 19422
PH: (215)940-0777
FX: (215)940-0292
Annual. $150.00. About 7,500 chemists, technicians, and supervisory production personnel in the decorative and protective coatings industry who are members of the 26 constituent societies of the federation. Formerly Federation of Societies for Paint Technology.

GREEN MARKETS
Pike and Fischer, Inc.
4600 East-West Highway, Suite 200
Bethesda, MD 20814
PH: (301)654-6262
FX: (301)654-6297
Weekly. $890.00 per year. Newsletter including prices for potash and other agricultural chemicals.

GUIDE TO ENGINEERING MATERIALS PRODUCERS
ASM International, Materials Information
9639 Kinsman Rd.
Materials Park, OH 44073-0002
PH: (800)336-5152
FX: (216)338-4634
E-mail: Mem-Serv@po.ASM.Intl.org
URL: http://www.asm.intl.org
J. C. Bittence, editor. 1993. $153.00. Provides information on more than 900 producers of metallic and non-metallic engineered materials, in 75 categories.

HANDBOOK OF CHEMICAL ENGINEERING
CALCULATIONS
McGraw-Hill, Inc.
1221 Ave. of the Americas
New York, NY 10020-1095
PH: (800)722-4726
FX: (212)512-2821
Nicholas P. Chopey and Tyler G. Hicks, editors. 1993. $74.50. Second edition.

HANDBOOK OF PETROCHEMICALS AND PROCESSES
Available from Ashgate Publishing Co.
Old Post Rd.
Brookfield, VT 05036
PH: (800)535-9544
FX: (802)276-3837
G. Margaret Wells. 1991. $120.00. (Published by Gower, UK.)

HOW TO FIND CHEMICAL INFORMATION: A GUIDE
FOR PRACTICING CHEMISTS, EDUCATORS, AND
STUDENTS
605 Third Ave.
New York, NY 10158-0012
PH: (800)526-5368
FX: (212)850-6088
Robert E. Maizell. John Wiley and Sons, Inc. 1987. $87.95. Second edition.

HYDROCARBON PROCESSING
Gulf Publishing Co.
P.O. Box 2608
Houston, TX 77252-2608
PH: (800)231-6275
FX: (281)520-4438
E-mail: ezorder@gulfpub.com
URL: http://www.gulfpub.com
Monthly. Free to qualified personnel; others, $24.00 per year.

INDUSTRIAL AND ENGINEERING CHEMISTRY
RESEARCH
American Chemical Society
1155 16th St., NW
Washington, DC 20036
PH: (800)333-9511
FX: (202)872-6067
E-mail: acsbooks@acs.org
URL: http://www.chemcenter.org
Monthly. Members, $74.00 per year; institutional non-members, $882.00 per year. Formerly *Industrial and Engineering Chemistry Product Research and Development*.

INFORMATION SOURCES IN CHEMISTRY

Bowker-Saur, Reed Reference Publishing
121 Chanlon Rd.
New Providence, NJ 07974
PH: (800)521-8110
FX: (908)665-6688
R. T. Bottle and J. F. B. Rowland, editors. 1993. $75.00. Fourth edition. Evaluates information sources on a wide range of chemical topics. (Guides to Information Sources Series).

INTERNATIONAL JOURNAL OF ADHESION AND ADHESIVES

Available from Elsevier Science.
655 Ave. of the Americas
New York, NY 10010
PH: (888)437-4636
FX: (212)633-3680
E-mail: usinfo-f@elsevier.com
URL: http://www.elsevier.com
Quarterly. $622.00 per year. Published in England.

INTERNATIONAL PLASTICS SELECTOR

Data Business Publishing
Post Office Box 6510
Englewood, CO 80155-6510
PH: (800)447-4666
FX: (303)799-4082
Semiannual. CD-ROM index version (technical data only), $695.00 per year or $495.00 per disc. CD-ROM image version (technical data and specification sheet images), $1,295.00 per year or $995.00 per disc. Provides detailed information on the properties of 20,000 types of plastic, both current and obsolete. Time period is 1977 to date. Includes trade names and supplier names and addresses.

JOURNAL OF APPLIED POLYMER SCIENCE

John Wiley & Sons, Inc., Journals Div.
605 Third Ave.
New York, NY 10158-0012
PH: (800)526-5368
FX: (212)850-6088
Weekly. $8,395.00 per year.

JOURNAL OF CHEMICAL AND ENGINEERING DATA

American Chemical Society
1155 16th St., NW
Washington, DC 20036
PH: (800)333-9511
FX: (202)872-6067
E-mail: acsbooks@acs.org
URL: http://www.chemcenter.org
Quarterly. Members, $43.00 per year; institutional non-members, $496.00 per year.

JOURNAL OF CHEMICAL INFORMATION AND COMPUTER SCIENCES

American Chemical Society
1155 16th St., NW
Washington, DC 20036
PH: (800)333-9511
FX: (202)872-6067
E-mail: acsbooks@acs.org
URL: http://www.chemcenter.org
Bimonthly. Members, $27.00 per year; institutional non-members, $298.00 per year

JOURNAL OF CHEMICAL TECHNOLOGY AND BIOTECHNOLOGY

John Wiley and Sons, Inc. Journals Div.
605 Third Ave.
New York, NY 10158-0012
PH: (212)526-5368
FX: (212)850-6088
Monthly. $1075.00 per year. Formerly *Biotechnology*.

KIRK-OTHMER ENCYCLOPEDIA OF CHEMICAL TECHNOLOGY

John Wiley & Sons, Inc.
605 Third Ave.
New York, NY 10158-0012
PH: (800)526-5368
FX: (212)850-6088
1991-95. $4,550.00, prepaid. 14 volumes. Fourth edition. Four volumes are scheduled to be published each year, with individual volumes available at $325.00.

MAJOR CHEMICAL AND PETROCHEMICAL COMPANIES OF EUROPE

European Business Publications, Inc.
P.O. Box 891
Darien, CT 06820
PH: (203)658-2701
FX: (203)655-8332
E-mail: centralbank@easynet.co.uk
URL: http://www.easyweb.easynet.co.uk/centralbank
Annual. $330.00. Published by Graham & Whiteside Ltd., London. Includes financial, personnel, and product information for chemical companies in Western Europe.

MATERIALS RESEARCH CENTRES: A WORLD DIRECTORY OF ORGANIZATIONS AND PROGRAMMES IN MATERIALS SCIENCE

Available from Stockton Press.
345 Park Ave., S., 10th Fl.
New York, NY 10010-1707
PH: (212)627-5757
FX: (212)687-9256
E-mail: grove@grovestocktn.com
URL: http://www.stocktonpress.com
Irregular. $425.00. Published by Catermill International. Profiles of research centers in 75 countries. Materials include plastics, metals, fibers, etc.

MCCUTCHEON'S: EMULSIFIERS AND DETERGENTS, INTERNATIONAL EDITION

MC Publishing Co., Inc., McCutcheon Division
175 Rock Rd.
Glen Rock, NJ 07452
PH: (201)652-2655
FX: (201)652-3419
Annual. $72.00. Contains detailed information on surface active agents produced in Europe and Asia or in any country outside North America. Company names, addresses and telephone numbers are included.

MCCUTCHEON'S EMULSIFIERS AND DETERGENTS, NORTH AMERICAN EDITION

MC Publishing Co., Inc., McCutcheon Division
175 Rock Rd.
Glen Rock, NJ 07452
PH: (201)652-2655
FX: (201)652-3419
Annual. $72.00. Contains detailed information on surface active agents produced in North America. Company names, addresses and telephone numbers are included.

MCCUTCHEON'S: FUNCTIONAL MATERIALS, NORTH AMERICAN EDITION

MC Publishing Co., Inc., McCutcheon Division
175 Rock Rd.
Glen Rock, NJ 07452
PH: (201)652-2655
FX: (201)652-3419
Annual. $72.00. Contains detailed information on surfactant-related products produced in North America. Examples are enzymes, lubricants, waxes, and corrosion inhibitors. Company names, addresses and telephone numbers are included.

MCCUTCHEON'S VOL. 2: FUNCTIONAL MATERIALS BLISHING CO., INC., MCCUTCHEON DIVISION
Glen Rock, NJ 07452
PH: (201)652-2655
FX: (201)652-3419
Annual. $165.00. Contains detailed information on surfactant-related products produced in Europe and Asia or in any country outside North America. Examples are enzymes, lubricants, waxes, and corrosion inhibitors. Company names, addresses and telephone numbers are included. Formerly *McCutcheon's Functional Materials.*

METADEX COLLECTION: METALS-POLYMERS-CERAMICS
Materials Information, ASM International.
9639 Kinsman Rd.
Materials Park, OH 44073
PH: (216)338-5151
FX: (216)338-4634
Quarterly. $6,950.00 per year. Provides CD-ROM citations to the worldwide literature of materials science and metallurgy. Corresponds to *Metals Abstracts, Alloys Index, Steels Alert, Nonferrous Alert, Polymers/Ceramics/Composites Alert,* and *Engineered Materials Abstracts.*

NTIS ALERTS: ENVIRONMENTAL POLLUTION & CONTROL
U. S. Department of Commerce
5285 Port Royal Rd.
Technology Administration
Springfield, VA 22161
PH: (800)553-6847
FX: (703)321-8547
National Technical Information Service. Semimonthly. $175.00 per year. Formerly *Abstract Newsletter.* Provides descriptions of government-sponsored research reports and software, with ordering information. Covers the following categories of environmental pollution: air, water, solid wastes, radiation, pesticides, and noise.

NTIS ALERTS: MATERIALS SCIENCES
U. S. Department of Commerce
5285 Port Royal Rd.
Technology Administration
Springfield, VA 22161
PH: (800)553-6847
FX: (703)321-8547
National Technical Information Service. Semimonthly. $145.00 per year. Formerly *Abstract Newsletter.* Provides descriptions of government-sponsored research reports and software, with ordering information. Covers ceramics, glass, coatings, composite materials, alloys, plastics, wood, paper, adhesives, fibers, lubricants, and related subjects.

NTIS BIBLIOGRAPHIC DATA BASE
5285 Port Royal Rd.
Springfield, VA 22161
PH: (800)553-6847
FX: (703)487-4134
National Technical Information Service. Contains citations and abstracts to unrestricted reports of government-sponsored research, 1964 to date. Covers a wide range of technical, engineering, business, and social science topics. Monthly updates. Inquire as to online cost and availability.

OPD CHEMICAL BUYERS DIRECTORY
Schnell Publishing Co., Inc.
80 Broad St.
New York, NY 10004-2203
PH: (212)248-4177
FX: (212)248-4901
Annual. $95.00. Included in subscription to *Chemical Marketing Reporter.* About 1,500 suppliers of chemical process materials and more than 300 companies which transport and store chemicals in the U.S.

PAINT RED BOOK
PTN Publishing Co.
445 Broad Hollow Rd.
Melville, NY 11747
PH: (516)845-2700
FX: (515)845-7109
Annual. $53.00. Lists manufacturers of paint, varnish, lacquer, and specialized coatings. Suppliers of raw materials, chemicals, and equipment are included.

PAPERCHEM DATABASE
Institute of Paper Science and Technology
500 Tenth St., NW
Atlanta, GA 30318
PH: (404)853-9500
FX: (404)853-9510
Information Services Div. Worldwide coverage of the scientific and technical paper industry chemical literature, including patents, 1967 to present. Monthly updates. Inquire as to online cost and availability.

PESTICIDE BIOCHEMISTRY AND PHYSIOLOGY: AN INTERNATIONAL JOURNAL
Academic Press, Inc. Journal Division
525 B St., Suite 1900
San Diego, CA 92101-4495
PH: (800)321-5068
FX: (800)235-0256
E-mail: apsubs@acad.com
URL: http://www.apnet.com
Nine times a year. $585.00 per year.

PLASTICS EXTRUSION TECHNOLOGY HANDBOOK
Industrial Press, Inc.
200 Madison Ave.
New York, NY 10016
PH: (212)889-6330
FX: (212)545-8327
E-mail: induspress@aol.com
URL: http://www.industrialpress.com
Sidney Levy and others. 1989. $44.95. Second edition.

PLASTICS WEEK: THE GLOBAL NEWSLETTER
McGraw-Hill Chemical and Plastics Information Service
1221 Ave. of the Americas
New York, NY 10020
PH: (800)722-4726
FX: (212)512-2821
Weekly. $530.00 per year. Newsletter. Covers international trends in plastics production, technology, research, and legislation.

POLYMER ENGINEERING AND SCIENCE
Society of Plastics Engineers, Inc.
P.O. Box 403
Brookfield, CT 06804-0403
PH: (203)775-0471
FX: (203)775-8490
Semimonthly. $190.00 per year. Includes six special issues.

PURCHASING/CPI CHEMICALS YELLOW PAGES
Cahners Publishing Co.
275 Washington St.
Newton, MA 02158-1630
PH: (800)662-7776
FX: (617)558-4327
E-mail: marketaccess@cahners.com
URL: http://www.cahners.com
Annual. $85.00. Manufacturers and distributors of 10,000 chemicals and raw materials, containers and packaging, transportation services and storage facilities; includes environmental servicer companies. Formerly *CPI Purchasing-Chemicals Directory.*

SCIENCE CITATION INDEX
Institute for Scientific Information.
3501 Market St.
Philadelphia, PA 19104
PH: (800)386-4474
FX: (215)386-2991
Bimonthly. $15,020.00 per year. Annual cumulation. (Compact Disc Edition also available. Quarterly. $10,950.00 per year; $5,300.00to hard copy subscribers.)

SCISEARCH
Institute for Scientific Information.
3501 Market St.
Philadelphia, PA 19104
PH: (800)523-1850
FX: (215)386-2911
URL: http://www.isinet.com
Broad, multidisciplinary index to the literature of science and technology, 1974 to present. Inquire as to online cost and availability. Coverage of literature is worldwide, with weekly updates.

SURFACE FINISHING TECHNOLOGY
ASM International, Materials Information
9639 Kinsman Rd.
Materials Park, OH 44073-0002
PH: (800)336-5152
FX: (216)338-4634
E-mail: Mem-Serv@po.ASM-Intl.org
URL: http://www.asm-intl.org
Monthly. Monthly members, $130.00 per year; non-members, $160.00 per year. Provides abstracts of the international literature of metallic and nonmetallic industrial coating and finishing. Formerly *Cleaning-Finishing-Coating Digest*.

SYNTHETIC ORGANIC CHEMICALS: UNITED STATES PRODUCTION AND SALES
Available from U.S. Government Printing Office
Washington, DC 20402
PH: (202)512-1800
FX: (202)512-2250
International Trade Commission Annual. $26.00.

UNITED STATES CENSUS OF MANUFACTURES
U.S. Bureau of the Census
Washington, DC 20233-0800
PH: (301)457-4100
FX: (301)457-3842
URL: http://www.census.gov
Quinquennial. Results presented in reports, tape, CD-ROM, and Diskette files.

URETHANES TECHNOLOGY
Crain Communications, Inc.
Suite 300
1725 Merriman Rd.
Akron, OH 44313
PH: (800)678-9595
FX: (216)836-1005
E-mail: ckosek@crain.com
URL: http://www.urethanecontractorin.co.uk
Bimonthly. $118.00 per year. Covers the international polyurethane industry.

WASTE MANAGEMENT GUIDE: AN ADVISORY BULLETIN ON INDUSTRY PRACTICES, REGULATORY IMPACT, AND CONTROL TECHNIQUES
Bureau of National Affairs, Inc.
1250 23rd St., NW
Washington, DC 20037
PH: (800)372-1033
FX: (202)822-8092
URL: http://www.bna.com
Biweekly. $680.00 per year. Looseleaf. Covers legal aspects of che-

mical substance management. Formerly *Chemical Substances Control*.

WHO'S WHO IN SCIENCE AND ENGINEERING
Marquis Who's Who, Reed Reference Publishing
121 Chanlon Rd.
New Providence, NJ 07974
PH: (800)521-8110
FX: (908)665-6688
E-mail: info@reedref.com
URL: http://www.reedref.com
Biennial. $272.95. Provides concise biographical information on 23,600 prominent engineers and scientists. International coverage, with geographical and professional indexes.

WHO'S WHO IN TECHNOLOGY
Gale Group
27500 Drake Rd.
Farmington Hills, MI 48331
PH: (800)877-GALE
Covers the fields of electronics, computer science, physics, optics, chemistry, biotechnology, mechanics, energy, and earth science. Provides online biographical profiles of over 25,000 American scientists, engineers, and others in technology-related occupations. Inquire as to online cost and availability.

WHO'S WHO IN WORLD PETROCHEMICALS AND PLASTICS
Who's Who Information Services
3730 Kirby Dr.
Houston, TX 77098
PH: (713)623-4627
FX: (713)623-4628
Annual. $150.00. Names, addresses, telephone numbers, and company affiliations of individuals active in the petrochemical business. Formerly *Who's Who in World Petrochemicals*.

TRADE SHOWS

Information presented in this chapter is adapted from Gale's *Trade Shows Worldwide* (*TSW*). Entries present information needed for all those planning to visit or to participate in trade shows for the Construction sector. *TSW* entries include U.S. and Canadian shows and exhibitions.

Entries are arranged in alphabetical order by the name of the event and include the exhibition management company with full contact information, frequency of the event, audience, and principal exhibits.

ADHESION SOCIETY ANNUAL MEETING
2 Davidson Hall
Virginia Tech
Blacksburg, VA 24061-0201
PH: (540)231-7257
FX: (540)231-3971
E-mail: adhesoc@vt.edu
URL: http://www.mse.uc.edu/adsoc.htm
Frequency: Annual. **Audience:** Chemists, engineers, biologists, mathematicians, physicists, physicians, and dentists. **Principal Exhibits:** Exhibits relating to the study of adhesion's role in coatings, composite materials, the function of biological tissues, and the performance of bonded structures. **Dates and Locations:** 1999 Feb 21-24; Panama Beach, FL.

ADHESIVE AND SEALANT COUNCIL CONVENTION
1627 K St. NW, Ste. 1000
Washington, DC 20006-1702
PH: (202)452-1500
FX: (202)452-1501
Frequency: Semiannual, and October. **Audience:** Adhesive and sealant manufacturers with decision making authority. **Principal Exhibits:** Industry related services and supplies. **Dates and Locations:** 1998 Mar 22-25; Orlando, FL • 1998 Oct 25-28.

AMERICAN CHEMICAL SOCIETY SPRING NATIONAL EXPOSITION
1155 16th St. NW, Rm. 214
Washington, DC 20036
PH: (202)872-4485
FX: (202)872-6067
Frequency: Annual. **Principal Exhibits:** Chemicals and related equipment, supplies, and services. **Dates and Locations:** 1998 Mar 03 - Apr 01 • 1999 Mar 22-24; Anaheim, CA • 2000 Mar 27-29.

ANTEC - SOCIETY OF PLASTICS ENGINEERS ANNUAL TECHNICAL CONFERENCE AND EXHIBITION
14 Fairfield Dr.
Brookfield, CT 06804
PH: (203)775-0471
FX: (203)775-8490
URL: http://www.bbsnet.com/SPE
Frequency: Annual. **Audience:** Plastics engineers, sales and marketing personnel, and management. **Principal Exhibits:** Machinery and supplies; chemical and resin supplies; and processing instruments. **Dates and Locations:** 1998 Apr 26 - May 01; Atlanta, GA • 1999 May 02-06; New York, NY • 2000 May 07-11; Orlando, FL.

ARGENPLAS - INTERNATIONAL PLASTICS EXHIBITION
Salguero 1939
1425 Buenos Aires, Argentina
PH: 821 9603
FX: 826 5480
Frequency: Biennial. **Principal Exhibits:** Thermoplastics, resins, transformers, converters, molds and dies.

ASEANPLAS - INTERNATIONAL PLASTICS AND RUBBER TRADE SHOW
128 Sophia Rd., No. 01-01
Singapore 228184, Singapore
PH: 65 337 3476
FX: 65 337 0694
Frequency: Annual. **Principal Exhibits:** Plastics and rubber machinery and equipment; raw and auxiliary materials for modern plastics and rubber products.

ASIA PLAS EXHIBITION
1 Temasek Ave.
17-01 Millenia Tower
Singapore 039192, Singapore
PH: 65 338 2002
FX: 65 338 2112
Frequency: Biennial. **Audience:** Designers and engineers, importers, exporters, and related professionals. **Principal Exhibits:** Processing equipment, components and instrumentation, materials, molds, dies, automation techniques, additives, and ancillary equipment, supplies, and services. **Held in conjunction with:** Asia Pack; Asia Print.

ASIAN-PACIFIC INTERNATIONAL PLASTICS & RUBBER INDUSTRY EXPO
Tung Wai Commercial Bldg., Rm. 1703
109 Gloucester Rd.
Wanchai, Hong Kong
PH: 852 2 511 7427
FX: 852 2 511 9692
E-mail: cpexhbit@hk.super.net
URL: http://www.hk.super.net/~cpexhbit
Principal Exhibits: Equipment, supplies, and services for the plastic and rubber industry.

BRASILPLAST - BRAZILIAN PLASTICS INDUSTRY TRADE FAIR
Rua Brasilio Machado, 60
01230-905 Sao Paulo, SP, Brazil
PH: 55 11 8269111
FX: 55 11 8256043
E-mail: amfp@alcantara.com.br
URL: http://www.alcantara.com.br
Frequency: Biennial. **Audience:** Trade professionals. **Principal Exhibits:** Plastic transformers, thermoplastic resins, thermofixes, elastomers, raw chemical materials, machines, instruments, controls, tools, dyes, technical services, banking services, and publications.

CAN CLEAN
300 Mill Rd., No. G10
Etobicoke, ON, Canada M9C 4W7
PH: (416)620-9320
FX: (416)620-7199
E-mail: cssa@the-wire.com
URL: http://www.cssa.com
Frequency: Annual. **Audience:** Distributors of sanitary maintenance products. **Principal Exhibits:** Sanitary maintenance products. **Dates and Locations:** 1998 May 06-07; Toronto, ON.

CANADIAN CHEMICAL CONFERENCE
130 Slater St., Ste. 550
Ottawa, ON, Canada K1P 6E2
PH: (613)232-6252
FX: (613)232-5862
E-mail: cic_adm@fox.nstn.ca
URL: http://www.fax.nstn.ca/~cic_adm/
Frequency: Annual. **Principal Exhibits:** Exhibits related to chemical research, development, management, and education. **Dates and Locations:** 1998 May 31 - Jun 04; Whistler, ON.

CANADIAN CHEMICAL CONFERENCE
130 Slater St., Ste. 550
Ottawa, ON, Canada K1P 6E2
PH: (613)232-6252
FX: (613)232-5862
E-mail: cic_adm@fox.nstn.ca
URL: http://www.fax.nstn.ca/~cic_adm/
Frequency: Annual. **Principal Exhibits:** Exhibits related to chemical research, development, management, and education. **Dates and Locations:** 1998 May 31 - Jun 04; Whistler, ON.

CANADIAN SOCIETY FOR CHEMISTRY CONFERENCE AND EXHIBITION
130 Slater St., Ste. 550
Ottawa, ON, Canada K1P 6E2
PH: (613)232-6252
FX: (613)232-5862
URL: http://www.chem_inst_can.org
Frequency: Annual. **Audience:** Industrial and academic chemists, engineers, and technicians. **Principal Exhibits:** Chemical products and related apparatus. **Dates and Locations:** 1998 May 31 - Jun 04; Vancouver, BC • 1999 May 30 - Jun 03; Toronto, ON.

**CARTES - FORUM FOR PLASTIC CARD TECHNOLOGIES
AND APPLICATIONS**
1 rue du Parc
F-92593 Levallois Perret, France
PH: 331 49685100
FX: 331 47377438
E-mail: simd@cepexposium.fr
URL: http://www.simd.fr
Frequency: Annual. **Principal Exhibits:** Plastic card technologies
and applications.

CHEM-DISTRIBUTION
1421 S. Sheridan
Tulsa, OK 74101
PH: (918)831-9727
FX: (918)831-9834
Audience: Trade professionals. **Principal Exhibits:** Technology for
the distribution, transfer, and storage of chemicals and petrochemi-
cals. **Dates and Locations:** 1999.

**CHEM - INTERNATIONAL EXHIBITION OF CHEMISTRY,
ENVIRONMENT, AND WATER**
Halepa 1 and Aegealias 21
Marousi
GR-151 25 Athens, Greece
PH: 3 01 6844961
FX: 3 01 6841796
E-mail: kee-expo@otenet.gr
Frequency: Triennial. **Audience:** Chemists, chemical engineers, en-
vironmentalists, technical managers from food, plastic, chemical,
cosmetic, pharmaceutical, and detergents industries. **Principal Exhi-
bits:** Laboratory equipment, chemical processing systems and ma-
chines, raw chemicals, industrial chemicals, specialty chemicals,
medicine, environmental protection equipment, and water treatment
equipment.

CHEM-SAFE
1421 S. Sheridan
Tulsa, OK 74101
PH: (918)831-9727
FX: (918)831-9834
Audience: Trade professionals. **Principal Exhibits:** Environmental,
safety, and health technology for the chemical and process indus-
tries. **Dates and Locations:** 1999.

**THE CHEM SHOW - CHEMICAL PROCESS INDUSTRIES
EXPOSITION**
15 Franklin St.
Westport, CT 06880-5958
PH: (203)221-9232
FX: (203)221-9260
Frequency: Biennial. **Audience:** Professionals directly related to
the chemical process industries, including engineers and managers.
Principal Exhibits: Process equipment (powders, liquids, gases),
fluids handling equipment and systmes, solids handling equipment
and systems, chemicals, engineered materials, instruments, controls,
software, environment and safety equipment, services, and systems,
and distributed process controls. **Dates and Locations:** 1999 Nov
16-18; New York, NY • 2001 Nov; New York, NY • 2003 Nov 18-
20; New York, NY.

**CHEMASIA - ASIAN INTERNATIONAL CHEMICAL AND
PROCESS ENGINEERING AND CONTRACTING
EXHIBITION AND CONFERENCE**
2 Handy Rd.
15-09 Cathay Bldg.
Singapore 229233, Singapore
PH: 65 3384747
FX: 65 3395651
E-mail: info@sesmontnet.com
URL: http://www.sesmontnet.com
Frequency: Biennial. **Audience:** Trade professionals. **Principal
Exhibits:** Chemical and process engineering equipment, supplies,

and services; plant maintenance equipment; pollution control equipment; contracting equipment, supplies, and services.

**CHEMEXPO - INTERNATIONAL TRADE EXHIBITION
FOR CHEMICAL INDUSTRY**
PO Box 44
H-1441 Budapest, Hungary
PH: 36 1 263 6000
FX: 36 1 263 6098
E-mail: hungexpo@hungexpo.hu
URL: http://www.hungexpo.hu
Frequency: Biennial. **Principal Exhibits:** Anaorganic and organic
chemicals and fertilizers; photochemistry; paints and varnishes; pet-
rochemicals; agrochemicals; biotechnology; processing equipment;
and quality assurance. HUNGAROMEDICIN: chemicals for the
pharmaceutical industry; HUNGARORUBBER: chemicals for the
rubber industry; HUNGAROPLAST: chemicals for the plastics industry; HUNGAROKORR: corrosion protection chemicals. **Incorporating:** HUNGAROKORR; HUNGAROMEDICIN;
HUNGAROPLAST; HUNGARORUBBER.

CHEMICAL PROCESSING TABLE TOP SHOW
Putman Publishing Co.
301 E. Erie St.
Chicago, IL 60611
PH: (312)644-2020
FX: (312)644-7402
Frequency: Ten per year. **Audience:** Engineers, plant supervisors,
and related trades. **Principal Exhibits:** Industrial equipment, sup-
plies, and services, including pumps, valves, mixers, pipes, dryers,
and related instruments. **Dates and Locations:** 1998. **Formerly:**
Plant Services Table Top Show.

**CHEMICAL SPECIALITIES EUROPE - EXHIBITION FOR
PERFORMANCE AND FINE CHEMICALS AND ORGANIC
INTERMEDIATES**
Messeplatz 1, Postfach
CH-4021 Basel, Switzerland
PH: 41 61 686 20 20
FX: 41 61 686 21 94
E-mail: swisstech@messebasel.ch
URL: http://www.messebasel.ch
Frequency: Triennial. **Principal Exhibits:** Organic intermediates
for the synthesis of pesticides, medicaments, photochemical pro-
ducts and dyestuffs; chiral synthesis processes; catalysts and fine
chemicals for the elecrical industry.

CHEMICTECH
Herler Strasse 103-109
Postfach 800349
51003 Cologne, Germany
PH: 49 694011
FX: 49 695865
Frequency: Triennial. **Principal Exhibits:** Equipment for chemical
machinery, technology, technical processes, materials and control
systems for technological processes.

**CHEMINDIA - INTERNATIONAL EXHIBITION &
CONFERENCE FOR THE CHEMICAL &
PETROCHEMICAL INDUSTRIES, PLANTS &
EQUIPMENT AND INSTRUMENTATION**
A-35, 1st Fl., Street No. 2
MIDC-Marol, Andheri (East)
Mumbai 400093, India
PH: 9122 835 0570
FX: 9122 835 0575
Frequency: Biennial. **Principal Exhibits:** Chemicals and petroche-
micals for industry.

**CHEMISTRY SPECIALIZED INTERNATIONAL
EXHIBITION**
Krasnaya Presnya Exhibition Complex
1st Krasnogvardeisky Proyezd 12, Hall 2, Tower 1
123100 Moscow, Russia

PH: 7 095 2597229
FX: 7 095 2302505
Frequency: Biennial. **Principal Exhibits:** Machines, equipment and technology for manufacture of chemicals.

CHEMSPEC EUROPE - INTERNATIONAL SPECIALIZED TRADE FAIR FOR CHEMICAL PRODUCTS AND THEIR DEVELOPMENT
Messehaus Norbertstr.
Postfach 100165
45131 Essen, Germany
PH: 201 7244 512
FX: 201 7244 513
URL: http://www.messe-essen.de
Frequency: Annual. **Audience:** Technical and research directors, chemists, laboratory managers, technologists, and buyers from chemical manufacturers. **Principal Exhibits:** Speciality, performance, effect, and fine chemicals, and organic intermediates used in manufacturing. **Formerly:** Swiss Industries Fair.

CHENGDU INTERNATIONAL PLASTICS & PACKAGING EXHIBITION
Room 15, 5/F Wah Shing Centre
1 Kwun Tong
11 Shing Yip Street
Kowloon, Hong Kong
PH: 27639011
FX: 23410379
URL: http://www.machinery.com.hk/machine.html
Frequency: Annual. **Audience:** Trade. **Principal Exhibits:** Packaging machine and automatic production line, food and pharmaceutical packaging, converting machinery, printing machinery, bottling and canning, labeling, ink jet and bar coding, transport packaging, consultancy and testing laboratory services; processing machinery, ancillary equipment and parts, testing equipment and services for the plastics industry. **Held in conjunction with:** Hong Kong International Machine Tool; Quality Management.

CHINAPLAS - INTERNATIONAL EXHIBITION ON PLASTICS AND RUBBER INDUSTRIES
4/F Stanhope House
734 King's Rd.
North Point, Hong Kong
PH: 852 2811 8897
FX: 852 2516 5024
E-mail: aes@adsaleexh.com
URL: http://www.adsaleexh.com
Frequency: Every 18 mos. **Principal Exhibits:** Equipment, supplies, and services related to the plastics and rubber industries.

COMPEX - ADVANCED COMPOSITE AND REINFORCED PLASTICS EXHIBITION
11 Manchester Sq.
London W1M 5AB, England
PH: 44 0 171 886 3000
FX: 44 0 171 886 3001
E-mail: exhibit@montnet.com
URL: http://www.montnet.com
Frequency: Biennial. **Audience:** Trade professionals. **Principal Exhibits:** Plastics industry equipment, supplies, and services.

EMEX
1st Fl. KPMG Bldg.
Newmarket
PO Box 9682
9 Princes St.
Auckland 9682, New Zealand
PH: 09 300 3950
FX: 09 379 3358
Frequency: Biennial. **Audience:** Trade professionals. **Principal Exhibits:** Engineering technology, instrumentation and control systems, and related equipment, supplies, and services for the plastics industry.

EUROPLAST - INTERNATIONAL PLASTICS AND RUBBER EXHIBITION
70 rue Rivay
F-92532 Levallois-Perret, France
PH: 33 1 47 56 50 00
FX: 33 1 47 56 91 86
E-mail: mffrance@unmf.fr
URL: http://www.unmf.fr
Frequency: Biennial. **Audience:** Plastics and rubber industries, engineers, and related professionals. **Principal Exhibits:** Raw materials, machines and equipment, and applications and finished products related to the plastics and rubber industries. **Held in conjunction with:** IRC Exhibition - International Rubber Exhibition.

EUROPLAST MOSCOW
Byron House
112A Shirland Rd.
London W9 EQ, England
PH: 44 171 286 9720
FX: 44 171 266 1126
E-mail: healthcare@ITE-Group.com
Frequency: Annual. **Principal Exhibits:** Every component of the plastics and rubber chain. Raw materials, machinery, moulds, finished and semi-finished products, plastics waste recovery.

EUROPLASTICA - SYNTHETIC AND COMPOSITE MATERIAL FAIR
Parc des Expositions
Place de Belgique
B-1020 Brussels, Belgium
PH: 32 2 474 8447
FX: 32 2 474 8540
URL: http://www.bitf.be
Frequency: Biennial. **Audience:** Trade professionals. **Principal Exhibits:** Industry related equipment, supplies, and services. **Held in conjunction with:** CIMEX; EUROSUPPLY; EUROTECH; HYDROPNEUMA; INTERREGIO.

FAKUMA - INTERNATIONAL TRADE FAIR FOR PLASTICS PROCESSING
Gustav-Werner-Strasse 6
D-72636 Frickenhausen-Linsenhofen, Germany
PH: 70 25 92 06 0
FX: 70 25 92 06 20
E-mail: info@schall-messen.de
URL: http://www.schall-messen.de
Frequency: Annual. **Audience:** Trade professionals. **Principal Exhibits:** Plastics processing equipment, supplies, and services.

FCE LATIN AMERICA - INTERNATIONAL EXHIBITION AND CONFERENCE ON FINE CHEMICALS, CHEMICAL ENGINEERING AND BIOTECHNOLOGY
Rua Traipu 657
01235-000 Sao Paulo, Brazil
PH: 55 11 366 22021
FX: 55 11 826 4458
Frequency: Annual. **Audience:** Trade professionals. **Principal Exhibits:** Raw materials and packaging technology for the pharmaceutical and cosmetic industries.

INCHEBA - INTERNATIONAL CHEMICAL FAIR
Viedenska cesta 7
852 51 Bratislava, Slovakia
PH: 421 7 802024
FX: 421 7 5811665
E-mail: incheba@incheba.sk
URL: http://www.incheba.sk
Frequency: Annual. **Principal Exhibits:** Equipment, services, and supplies for the chemical, crude oil, petrochemical, pulp and paper processing, silicate, pharmaceutical, and biochemical industries.

INDOPLAS
1 Temasek Ave.
17-01 Millenia Tower
Singapore 039192, Singapore
PH: 65 338 2002
FX: 65 338 2112
Frequency: Biennial. **Audience:** Trade and business professionals.
Principal Exhibits: Plastics and rubber technology, and related
equipment, supplies, and services. **Held in conjunction with:**
IndoPack; IndoPrint.

**INTERCHIMIE - RAW MATERIAL TRANSFORMATION
　EQUIPMENT AND TECHNOLOGY**
55, quai Alphonse Le Gallo
BP 317
92107 Boulogne, France
PH: 33 1 49 09 60 00
FX: 33 1 49 09 60 03
E-mail: info@comite-expo-paris.asso.fr
URL: http://www.comite-expo-paris.asso.fr
Frequency: Biennial. **Audience:** Professionals in the chemical industry. **Principal Exhibits:** Equipment, methods, and processes in
the chemical engineering field, including research and development,
documentation and training, complete installations, machinery, hollow ware, piping, valves, pumps, compressors, heating, furnaces,
measurement instruments, monitoring equipment, automated equipment, surface treatments, petroleum products, pollution control
equipment, cryogenics, freeze-drying equipment, and related equipment, supplies, and services. **Held in conjunction with:**
LABORATOIRE Exposition de Physique.

**INTERNATIONAL ASSOCIATION OF PLASTICS
　DISTRIBUTORS CONFERENCE**
4707 College Blvd., Ste. 105
Leawood, KS 66211
PH: (913)345-1005
FX: (913)345-1006
E-mail: iapd@iapd.org
URL: http://www.iapd.org
Frequency: Annual. **Principal Exhibits:** Equipment, supplies, and
services for manufacturers and distributors of plastics materials, pip-
ing, and resins. **Dates and Locations:** 1998 Oct 14-18; San Diego,
CA • 1999 Aug 09-15; Toronto, ON.

**INTERPLAS ENGLAND - INTERNATIONAL PLASTICS
　AND RUBBER EXHIBITION**
Oriel House
26 The Quadrant
Richmond, Surrey TW9 1DL, England
PH: 181 910 7825
FX: 181 910 7926
E-mail: info@reedexpo.co.uk
URL: http://www.reedexpo.com
Frequency: Triennial. **Audience:** Plastics and rubber trades. **Princi-
pal Exhibits:** Equipment, supplies, and services for the plastics,
rubber, and polymer industries, including materials, machinery, and
recycling equipment.

INTERPLAS THAILAND
1611-1613, 16/F BB Bldg.
54 Asoke Rd., Sukhumvit 21
Bangkok 10110, Thailand
PH: 2 2607103
FX: 2 2607109
Frequency: Annual. **Principal Exhibits:** Plastics and rubber technology equipment, supplies, and services. **Held in conjunction
with:** Thai Manufacturing Technology Week.

**INTERPLASTECH - INTERNATIONAL TRADE FAIR FOR
　PLASTICS AND RUBBER INDUSTRIES**
Herler Strasse 103-109
Postfach 800349
51003 Cologne, Germany

PH: 49 694011
FX: 49 695865
Frequency: Biennial. **Principal Exhibits:** Plastic, rubber and rela-
ted products, equipment, supplies, and services.

**INTERPLASTICA - INTERNATIONAL TRADE FAIR FOR
　PLASTICS AND RUBBER**
Stockumer Kirchstrasse 61
PO Box 101006
D-40474 Dusseldorf, Germany
PH: 211 4560 01
FX: 211 4560 668
URL: http://messe.dus.tradefair.de
Frequency: Triennial. **Principal Exhibits:** Plastics and rubber ma-
chinery, molds, and accessories; raw and auxiliary materials; new
materials; and semi-finished and finished products and technical
components. **Held in conjunction with:** Laki I Kraski.

**ISRACHEM - INTERNATIONAL EXHIBITION ON
　PROCESSING EQUIPMENT CHEMICAL ENGINEERING,
　MEASUREMENT CONTROL AND INSTRUMENTATION**
12 Tverski St.
67210 Tel Aviv, Israel
PH: 972 3 5626090
FX: 972 3 5615463
E-mail: expo@stier.co.il
URL: http://www.stier.co.il
Frequency: Biennial. **Audience:** Managers, engineers, scientists
and technicians in the chemical, food processing, pharmaceutical
and biochemical industry. **Principal Exhibits:** Equipment, supplies,
and services for chemical engineering, measurement, control, instru-
mentation, and automation. **Held in conjunction with:** ANALIZA.

**K - INTERNATIONAL TRADE FAIR FOR PLASTICS AND
　RUBBER**
Stockumer Kirchstrasse 61
PO Box 101006
D-40474 Dusseldorf, Germany
PH: 211 4560 01
FX: 211 4560 668
URL: http://messe.dus.tradefair.de
Frequency: Triennial. **Audience:** Trade professionals; raw materi-
als suppliers, suppliers of machinery, processors, product users,
service providers. **Principal Exhibits:** Plastics and rubber technolo-
gy, including raw materials and auxiliaries; semi-finished products,
technical parts, and reinforced plastic products; and machinery,
equipment, and services for the plastics and rubber industry.

**KEMIA - THE FINNISH CHEMICAL CONGRESS AND
　EXHIBITION**
Helsinki Fair Centre
PO Box 21
Messuaukio 1
FIN-00521 Helsinki, Finland
PH: 358 9 150 91
FX: 358 9 142 358
E-mail: info@finnexpo.fi
URL: http://www.finnexpo.fi
Frequency: Annual. **Audience:** Trade professionals. **Principal Ex-
hibits:** Laboratory instruments, accessories, equipment, and furni-
ture; chemicals and other production materials; industrial machinery
and equipment; environmental protection and process automation
methods and equipment; engineering and other services; research
and educational information; and related products and services.

**LATINOPLAST - LATIN AMERICAN PLASTIC AND
　RUBBER FAIR**
Rua Marcelo Gama 218
90540-040 Porto Alegre, Rio Grande do Sul, Brazil
PH: 5551 337 3131
FX: 5551 337 3131
E-mail: efep@nutecnet.com.br
Frequency: Biennial. **Principal Exhibits:** Plastic and rubber equip-
ment, supplies, and services.

**MACHEVO, INCORPORATING FOODTECH AND
   CHEMTECH**
Jaarbeursplein-Utrecht
PO Box 8500
NL-3503 RM Utrecht, Netherlands
PH: 30 295 5911
FX: 30 294 0379
E-mail: info@jaarbeursutrecht.nl
URL: http://www.jaarbeursutrecht.nl
Frequency: Triennial. **Principal Exhibits:** Foodtech features process equipment for the dairy, foodprocessing, and beverage industries, as well as relevant biotechnology and pharmacy. Chemtech profiles process equipment for the chemical industry.

MALAYSIA INTERNATIONAL MACHINERY FAIR (MIMF)
289 Tanjong Katong Rd.
Singapore 1542, Singapore
PH: 65 3455188
FX: 65 3460797
Frequency: Annual. **Audience:** Trade professionals. **Principal Exhibits:** Packaging, printing, rubber, plastics, screen print and machine tools. **Formerly:** Malaysia International Packing, Printing, Rubber, and plastics Exhibition.

**MOULDING TECHASIA - ASIAN INTERNATIONAL
   EXHIBITION OF MACHINERY AND ACCESSORIES FOR
   THE PLASTICS MOULDING INDUSTRY**
2 Handy Rd.
15-09 Cathay Bldg.
Singapore 229233, Singapore
PH: 65 3384747
FX: 65 3395651
E-mail: info@sesmontnet.com
URL: http://www.sesmontnet.com
Frequency: Biennial. **Principal Exhibits:** Dies and moulds equipment, supplies, and services.

NATIONAL AGRICULTURAL PLASTICS CONGRESS
526 Brittany Dr.
State College, PA 16803-1420
PH: (814)238-7045
FX: (814)238-7051
E-mail: peh4@psu.edu
Frequency: Annual. **Principal Exhibits:** Equipment, supplies, and services relating to agriculture, horticulture, vegetable crops, and agricultural engineering. **Dates and Locations:** 1999 May • 2000 Sep.

NATIONAL PLASTICS EXPOSITION
98 E. Naperville Rd., Ste. 200
Westmont, IL 60559
PH: (630)434-7779
TF: (800)752-6312
FX: (708)434-1216
URL: http://www.heiexpo.com
Frequency: Triennial. **Audience:** Plastics industry professionals and plastics end market representatives, buyers and specifiers. **Principal Exhibits:** Molded, extruded, fabricated, laminated, calendered, and reinforced plastics machinery and equipment; raw materials; tools; dies and molds; research and testing laboratory equipment, supplies, and services. **Dates and Locations:** 2000 Jun; Chicago, IL.

**PAPER, PLASTICS, AND ALLIED PRODUCTS
   EXPOSITION**
111 Great Neck Rd.
Great Neck, NY 11021
PH: (516)829-3070
FX: (516)829-3074
Frequency: Annual. **Audience:** Wholesale paper distributors. **Principal Exhibits:** Industrial papers, plastics, and plastic products allied to the paper industry. **Dates and Locations:** 1998 Apr; San Francisco, CA.

**PETROTEK CHINA - INTERNATIONAL REFINERY,
   PETROCHEMICAL & CHEMICAL PROCESSING
   TECHNOLOGY EXHIBITION**
Room A803
No. 318-322 Xian Xia Rd.
Singular Mansion
Shanghai 200335, People's Republic of China
PH: 86 21 62095209
FX: 86 21 62095210
E-mail: tmnchina@uninet.com.cn
Frequency: Biennial. **Principal Exhibits:** Refinery, petrochemical & chemical processing technology.

**PETROTEK CHINA - INTERNATIONAL REFINERY,
   PETROCHEMICAL & CHEMICAL PROCESSING
   TECHNOLOGY EXHIBITION**
Room A803
No. 318-322 Xian Xia Rd.
Singular Mansion
Shanghai 200335, People's Republic of China
PH: 86 21 62095209
FX: 86 21 62095210
E-mail: tmnchina@uninet.com.cn
Frequency: Biennial. **Principal Exhibits:** Refinery, petrochemical & chemical processing technology.

**PHILPLAS - INTERNATIONAL PLASTIC MACHINERY
   AND MATERIALS EXHIBITION**
6/F China Harbour Blvd.
370 King's Rd.
Hong Kong, Hong Kong
PH: 28077633
FX: 25705903
E-mail: owpshk@netvigator.com
Frequency: Biennial. **Principal Exhibits:** Plastic machinery and materials.

PLAST-EX
365 Bloor St. E., Ste. 1900
Toronto, ON, Canada M4W 3L4
PH: (416)323-1883
FX: (416)323-9404
Frequency: Triennial. **Principal Exhibits:** Plastics machinery and equipment, raw material suppliers, and the latest plastics technology. **Dates and Locations:** 1998 May; Mississauga, ON.

**PLAST IMAGEN - INTERNATIONAL EXPOSITION AND
   CONFERENCE OF THE PLASTICS INDUSTRY**
Aviacion Comercial 36
Fracc. Industrial Puerto Aereo
15710 Mexico City, DF, Mexico
PH: 5 785 7553
FX: 5 785 7638
E-mail: oprex@interweb.com.mx
URL: http://www.interweb.com.mx/oprex
Frequency: Annual. **Principal Exhibits:** Equipment, supplies, and services for the plastics industry.

PLASTECH THAILAND
41 Lertpanya Bldg., Ste. 801
Khet Rajathewee
Kwaeng Thanon Phyathai
8th Fl., Soi Lertpanya
Bangkok 10400, Thailand
PH: 662 6426911
FX: 662 6426919
Frequency: Annual. **Principal Exhibits:** Plastic and rubber processing technology and raw materials exhibition.

PLASTEXPO
70 rue Rivay
F-92532 Levallois-Perret, France

PH: 33 1 47 56 50 00
FX: 33 1 47 56 91 86
E-mail: mffrance@unmf.fr
URL: http://www.unmf.fr
Frequency: Triennial. **Audience:** Trade professionals. **Principal Exhibits:** Plastics and rubber for industrial manufacturing.

PLASTIC INDUSTRY/PAKISTAN
Tung Wai Commercial Bldg., Rm. 1703
109 Gloucester Rd.
Wanchai, Hong Kong
PH: 852 2 511 7427
FX: 852 2 511 9692
E-mail: cpexhbit@hk.super.net
URL: http://www.hk.super.net/~cpexhbit
Principal Exhibits: Plastic Industry.

PLASTICA - PLASTICS, RUBBER AND MACHINES EXHIBITION
Halepa 1 and Aegealias 21
Marousi
GR-151 25 Athens, Greece
PH: 3 01 6844961
FX: 3 01 6841796
E-mail: kee-expo@otenet.gr
Frequency: Biennial. **Audience:** Technicians, production managers, and buyers. **Principal Exhibits:** Raw, intermediary, semi-finished, and finished plastics and rubber; and processing machinery.

PLASTICS ASIA - INTERNATIONAL PLASTICS MACHINERY, MATERIALS, PRODUCTION TECHNOLOGY, AND ANCILLARY EQUIPMENT EXHIBITION FOR ASIA
Unit 1223, 12/F, Hong Kong International Trade & Exhibition
1 Trademart Dr.
Kowloon Bay, Hong Kong
PH: 852 2865 2633
FX: 852 2866 1770
Frequency: Annual. **Principal Exhibits:** Processing machinery, production technology, auxiliary equipment, accessories, and materials for the plastics and mould and die industries. **Held in conjunction with:** Pack & Print Asia.

PLASTICS FAIR - ATLANTIC CITY
7500 Old Oak Blvd.
Cleveland, OH 44130
PH: (440)891-2701
TF: (800)225-4569
FX: (440)891-2741
URL: http://www.advanstar-expos.com
Principal Exhibits: Equipment, supplies, and services for the plastic industry. **Dates and Locations:** 1998 Sep 22-24; Atlantic City, NJ.

PLASTICS FAIR - CHARLOTTE
7500 Old Oak Blvd.
Cleveland, OH 44130
PH: (440)891-2701
TF: (800)225-4569
FX: (440)891-2741
URL: http://www.advanstar-expos.com
Principal Exhibits: Equipment, supplies, and services for the plastic industry. **Dates and Locations:** 1999 Nov 09-11; Charlotte, NC.

PLASTICS FAIR - CHICAGO
7500 Old Oak Blvd.
Cleveland, OH 44130
PH: (440)891-2701
TF: (800)225-4569
FX: (440)891-2741
URL: http://www.advanstar-expos.com
Principal Exhibits: Equipment, supplies, and services for the plastic industry. **Dates and Locations:** 1999 Jun 15-17; Rosemont, IL.

PLASTICS FAIR - CLEVELAND
7500 Old Oak Blvd.
Cleveland, OH 44130
PH: (440)891-2701
TF: (800)225-4569
FX: (440)891-2741
URL: http://www.advanstar-expos.com
Frequency: 3/yr. **Audience:** Trade professionals. **Principal Exhibits:** Plastics machinery, equipment, materials, services, and supplies. **Dates and Locations:** 1998 Jun 23-25; Cleveland, OH.

PLASTICS FAIR PROVIDENCE
7500 Old Oak Blvd.
Cleveland, OH 44130
PH: (440)891-2701
TF: (800)225-4569
FX: (440)891-2741
URL: http://www.advanstar-expos.com
Frequency: Triennial. **Principal Exhibits:** Equipment and supplies for plastics industries. **Dates and Locations:** 1999; Providence, RI.

PLASTICS FAIR - SAN ANTONIO
7500 Old Oak Blvd.
Cleveland, OH 44130
PH: (440)891-2701
TF: (800)225-4569
FX: (440)891-2741
URL: http://www.advanstar-expos.com
Principal Exhibits: Equipment, supplies, and services for the plastic industry. **Dates and Locations:** 1999 Feb 16-18; San Antonio, TX.

PLASTICS - ISTANBUL INTERNATIONAL TRADE FAIR FOR PLASTICS
Mim Kemal Oke Cad, No. 10 Nisantasi
TR-80200 Istanbul, Turkey
PH: 212 2250920
FX: 212 2250933
Frequency: Annual. **Audience:** Trade professionals. **Principal Exhibits:** Plastics industry equipment, supplies, and services.

PLASTICS MALAYSIA - THE INTERNATIONAL PLASTICS INDUSTRY EXHIBITION FOR MALAYSIA
Unit 1223, 12/F, Hong Kong International Trade & Exhibition
1 Trademart Dr.
Kowloon Bay, Hong Kong
PH: 852 2865 2633
FX: 852 2866 1770
Frequency: Biennial. **Principal Exhibits:** Equipment, supplies, and services for the plastics industry. **Held in conjunction with:** MOULD & DIE MALAYSIA - The International Mold and Die Exhibition for Malaysia.

PLASTICS & PACKAGING EXPO - INTERNATIONAL TRADE FAIR FOR THE PLASTICS AND PACKAGING INDUSTRY
PO Box 2460
Germantown, MD 20875-2460
PH: (301)515-0012
FX: (301)515-0016
E-mail: glahe@glahe.com
Frequency: Biennial. **Audience:** Trade professionals. **Principal Exhibits:** Equipment, supplies, and services for plastics and packaging industries.

PLASTICS PHILIPPINES - INTERNATIONAL PLASTICS MACHINERY, PROCESSING & MATERIALS EXHIBITION
Room 909, 9th Floor
Sen. Gil Puyat Avenue, corner Urban Ave.
PS Bank Tower
Makati City 1200, Philippines

PH: 632 759 3263
FX: 632 759 3228
E-mail: piecinc@portalink.com
Frequency: Biennial. **Principal Exhibits:** Plastics machinery equipment; supplies, and services.

PLASTICS AND RUBBER INDONESIA - INTERNATIONAL PLASTICS AND RUBBER MACHINERY, PROCESSING AND MATERIALS EXHIBITION
Deutsche Bank Bldg.
Jl. Imam Bonjol 80
13th Fl
10310 Jakarta, Indonesia
PH: 62 0 21 3162001
FX: 62 0 21 3161981
E-mail: pamindo@rad.net.id
Frequency: Annual. **Audience:** Government ministers and employees and buyers and specifiers of plastic and rubber machinery. **Principal Exhibits:** Plastic and rubber processing machinery and materials, injection molding machines, extruding machinery, and blowing machinery. **Incorporating:** Mould & Die Indonesia.

PLASTICS & RUBBER - MALAYSIAN INTERNATIONAL PLASTICS AND RUBBER MACHINERY AND MATERIALS EXHIBITION
Suite 1402, 14th Fl., IGB Plaza
Jalan Kampar off Jalan Tun Razak
50400 Kuala Lumpur, Malaysia
PH: 60 3 4410311
FX: 60 3 4437241
E-mail: exhibit@mes.nasionet.net.my
Frequency: Annual. **Audience:** Regional trade. **Principal Exhibits:** Production machinery for the rubber and plastics industries.

PLASTICS TECHNOLOGY ASIA - INTERNATIONAL PLASTICS & RUBBER PROCESSING MACHINERY & MATERIAL EXHIBITION
20 Harrison Ave.
Waldwick, NJ 07463-1709
PH: (201)652-7070
FX: (201)652-3898
E-mail: 74161.1167@compuserve.com
URL: http://www.kallman.com
Principal Exhibits: Equipment, supplies, and services for the processing of plastic and rubber.

PROPAK AFRICA - PACKAGING, PROCESSING & PLASTICS EXHIBITION
PO Box 82196
Southdale 2135, Republic of South Africa
PH: 27 11 835 1565
FX: 27 11 496 1161
E-mail: specialx@icon.co.za
URL: http://www.specialised.com
Frequency: Biennial. **Principal Exhibits:** Equipment, supplies, and services for packaging, processing & plastics.

RADTECH INTERNATIONAL UV/EB PROCESSING CONFERENCE AND EXHIBITION
60 Revere Dr., Ste. 500
Northbrook, IL 60062
PH: (847)480-9576
FX: (847)480-9282
E-mail: uveb@radtech.org
URL: http://www.radtech.org
Frequency: Biennial. **Audience:** Suppliers and users of UV/EB processing technology. **Principal Exhibits:** Equipment, supplies, and services related to ultraviolet (UV) and electron beam (EB) processing. **Dates and Locations:** 1998 Apr 19-22; Chicago, IL • 2000 Apr 09-12; Baltimore, MD.

RADTECH INTERNATIONAL UV/EB PROCESSING CONFERENCE AND EXHIBITION
60 Revere Dr., Ste. 500
Northbrook, IL 60062
PH: (847)480-9576
FX: (847)480-9282
E-mail: uveb@radtech.org
URL: http://www.radtech.org
Frequency: Biennial. **Audience:** Suppliers and users of UV/EB processing technology. **Principal Exhibits:** Equipment, supplies, and services related to ultraviolet (UV) and electron beam (EB) processing. **Dates and Locations:** 1998 Apr 19-22; Chicago, IL • 2000 Apr 09-12; Baltimore, MD.

RT REINIGUNGS-TECHNIK - INTERNATIONAL TRADE FAIR AND CONGRESS FOR THE CLEANING TRADE
Messedamm 22
D-14055 Berlin, Germany
PH: 49 30 3038 0
FX: 49 30 3038 2325
E-mail: marketing@messe-berlin.de
URL: http://www.messe-berlin.de
Frequency: Biennial. **Principal Exhibits:** Building cleaning chemicals and services.

SAUDIPLAS - PLASTICS TECHNOLOGY SHOW
PO Box 56010
Riyadh 11554, Saudi Arabia
PH: 966 1 454 1448
FX: 966 1 454 4846
E-mail: recsa@midleast.net
Frequency: Biennial. **Principal Exhibits:** Plastic-making machinery, moulds, raw materials, extrusion, plastic products, and rubber machinery.

SCANLAB - TECHNICAL TRADE FAIR AND CONFERENCE FOR LABORATORY EQUIPMENT, MEASURING TECHNOLOGY, AND PROCESS CONTROL
Center Blvd.
DK-2300 Copenhagen S, Denmark
PH: 45 32 52 88 11
FX: 45 32 51 96 36
E-mail: bc@bella.dk
URL: http://www.bellacenter.dk
Frequency: Annual. **Audience:** Chemical engineers, analysts, biotechnologists, pharmacologists, and chemists. **Principal Exhibits:** Equipment for the chemical industry, including biotechnology, food stuffs control, and environmental control. **Formerly:** KEMTEK - International Fair of Plant and Equipment for the Chemical and Process Industries.

SF CHINA/PCB CHINA - INTERNATIONAL EXHIBITION OF SURFACE TECHNOLOGY AND PRINTED BOARD CIRCUITS
1501 Connaught Commercial Bldg.
185 Wanchai Rd.
Wanchai, Hong Kong
PH: 852 28650062
FX: 852 28042250
Frequency: Biennial. **Audience:** Trade professionals. **Principal Exhibits:** Surface technology and printed board circuits equipment, supplies, and services.

SIBCHEMISTRY - INTERNATIONAL CHEMICAL AND PROCESS ENGINEERING, INSTRUMENTATION AND LABORATORY EQUIPMENT EXHIBITION
16 Gorky St.
6300099 Novosibirsk, Russia
PH: 7 3832 102674
FX: 7 3832 236335
E-mail: siberian.fair@sovcust.sprint.com
Frequency: Annual. **Principal Exhibits:** Chemicals, laboratory, mineral oils, and fuel oil refining products.

SIBCOLOUR
16 Gorky St.
6300099 Novosibirsk, Russia
PH: 7 3832 102674
FX: 7 3832 236335
E-mail: siberian.fair@sovcust.sprint.com
Frequency: Annual. **Audience:** Trade professionals, general public.
Principal Exhibits: Chemicals and chemical technology. **Formerly:** Sibbytkhim.

SICHEM - SEOUL INTERNATIONAL CHEMICAL PLANT EXHIBITION
PO Box 2460
Germantown, MD 20875-2460
PH: (301)515-0012
FX: (301)515-0016
E-mail: glahe@glahe.com
Frequency: Biennial. **Principal Exhibits:** Chemicals and related products.

SOUTH CHINA INTERNATIONAL PLASTICS & PACKAGING EXHIBITION
Room 15, 5/F Wah Shing Centre
1 Kwun Tong
11 Shing Yip Street
Kowloon, Hong Kong
PH: 27639011
FX: 23410379
URL: http://www.machinery.com.hk/machine.html
Principal Exhibits: Processing machinery, ancillary equipment and parts, plastics materials, testing equipment, services; equipment, supplies and services for the packaging industry.

SPRING RAW MATERIALS SEMINAR
1627 K St. NW, Ste. 1000
Washington, DC 20006-1702
PH: (202)452-1500
FX: (202)452-1501
Frequency: Annual. **Audience:** Manufacturers and industry suppliers of adhesives and sealants. **Principal Exhibits:** Small equipment product samples of adhesives and sealants. **Dates and Locations:** 1998 Mar.

TAIPEI CHEM
11 Manchester Sq.
London W1M 5AB, England
PH: 44 0 171 862 2000
FX: 44 0 171 862 2098
E-mail: oes@montnet.com
URL: http://www.montnet.com
Frequency: Triennial. **Principal Exhibits:** Oil, petrochemical and chemical process engineering, instrumentation and analytical technology.

TAIPEI PLAS - TAIPEI INTERNATIONAL PLASTICS & RUBBER INDUSTRY SHOW
CETRA Exhibition Dept.
5 Hsinyi Rd., Sec. 5
Taipei World Trade Center Exhibition Hall
Taipei 110, Taiwan
PH: 886 2 2725 1111
FX: 886 2 2725 1314
E-mail: cetra@cetra.org.tw
URL: http://www.taipeitradeshows.org.tw
Frequency: Biennial. **Audience:** Trade professionals. **Principal Exhibits:** Raw materials, molds, machinery, engineering components, and semi-finished and finished products, and auxiliary equipment, supplies, and services.

THAIPLAS - INTERNATIONAL EXHIBITION ON PLASTIC AND RUBBER MACHINERY, MATERIALS, MOULDS, AND DIES
6/F China Harbour Blvd.
370 King's Rd.
Hong Kong, Hong Kong
PH: 28077633
FX: 25705903
E-mail: owpshk@netvigator.com
Frequency: Annual. **Audience:** End users of plastic processing machinery, resins, and raw materials. **Principal Exhibits:** Raw materials, including petrochemicals, polymers and resins, intermediates, alloys, and composites; speciality chemicals, including master batches, additives, colorants, fillers, and reinforcements; and processing machinery and equipment.

UFA.CHEMESTRY
PO Box 318
450080 Ufa, Russia
PH: 3472 525386
FX: 3472 525593
Principal Exhibits: Chemical industry equipment, supplies, and services.

VIETNAM SHOES AND LEATHER INDUSTRY EXPO
Tung Wai Commercial Bldg., Rm. 1703
109 Gloucester Rd.
Wanchai, Hong Kong
PH: 852 2 511 7427
FX: 852 2 511 9692
E-mail: cpexhbit@hk.super.net
URL: http://www.hk.super.net/~cpexhbit
Frequency: Annual. **Principal Exhibits:** Shoemaking machinery, leather processing machinery, skin hides, finished leather, tools and material for shoemaking and leather goods production, plastic machinery, plastic material, rubber machinery, and rubber processing materials.

WESTERN PLASTICS EXPO
7500 Old Oak Blvd.
Cleveland, OH 44130
PH: (440)891-2701
TF: (800)225-4569
FX: (440)891-2741
URL: http://www.advanstar-expos.com
Frequency: Triennial. **Audience:** Trade professionals. **Principal Exhibits:** Plastics machinery, equipment, materials, supplies, and related services. **Dates and Locations:** 2001.

PART II

PHARMACEUTICALS

FOREWORD

THE PHARMACEUTICAL INDUSTRY:
ON THE EDGE OF A NEW MILLENIUM

Perry Cohen
Michael J. Sax

Pharmaceuticals demonstrate the advances in health care technology better than any other sector of the industry. Coupling these results with the advances in information technology, they are changing the delivery of health care and the roles of health care professionals.

Other businesses and technologies often use analogies to describe their environments. They pepper their discussions with phrases like bull pens, war zones, and roller-coaster ride. It is difficult to find a suitable analogy for the pharmaceutical industry. The enormity of our progress and problems over the last ten year sets the stage for tremendous change as we enter the 21st century. Our systems are complex, our customers are divergent, and our goals are lofty and ever-changing.

Discussion about, or provision of, health care can be emotionally charged. Health care affects all of us throughout our lives, and pharmaceuticals are an integral part of intervention. Pharmacists' skills are in demand, and the opportunities are unlimited. Most industries and businesses are moving toward customer-driven policies and processes. The pharmaceutical industry is no exception.

For the purposes of this forward, the pharmaceutical industry includes manufacturers, distributors, insurers, prescription benefits managers, regulatory personnel, educators, and pharmacists. Our ultimate customers, once called patients, now go by an assortment of names. Depending on the setting, they may be referred to as patients, lives, consumers, members, clients, or even residents.

Our tangential customers have expanded from simply the physician to a host of others; we now deal with a variety of prescribers, physician extenders, and care givers who have extensive information needs. Our patients also need more counseling and education, and look to pharmacy practitioners as approachable health care providers. In the broader definition of customer, we are all each others' customers. Now more than ever before, we are relying on customer need to drive our systems and determine future directions.

The development of more potent therapeutic agents increases the demand on health care professionals and the health care system to ensure appropriate use of pharmaceuticals.

The Health Care Milieu

All of our health care processes and institutions are being redefined as our population ages and customer expectation changes. With one American baby boomer turning 50 years old every 7.5 seconds (a phenomena that started in 1996), and Americans living more than twice as long as they did 200 years ago, our customer is more likely to be older and facing the problems of aging.

The entire health care industry is reeling as our work force ages, issues of geriatric care move to the forefront, and customer expectation becomes more sophisticated.

Whereas our turn-of-the-century customer was likely to focus on the product we provided with few questions, today's customer is more likely to ask about food-drug and drug-drug interactions, adverse reactions, natural alternatives, and cost effectiveness. Today's customer knows that there are many places to find health care, and can identify alternatives. From now on, we will have to focus on trust, loyalty, and retaining customers. Outreach and educational activities are important and will gain merit in the coming years. Our customers in the 21st century will be mature, demanding, and complicated.

Health Care Delivery

To respond to demographic changes, the American health care delivery system has been forced to make revolutionary changes. The influence of cost, cost containment, and prevention cannot be minimized. Fifty years ago, our system allowed the physician in private practice to dictate care. As care became more and more expensive, various mechanisms were introduced to address cost.

One program with tremendous impact was the Health Care Financing Administration's Diagnosis Related Group (DRG) regulations. These regulations defined appropriate interventions and lengths of stay for various diagnoses. Government payers, primarily Medicare and Medicaid, would only pay costs identified as allowable. Initially, some adjustments were needed for DRGs that were too restrictive or unduly harsh. During the maturation process, DRGs were revised and adapted, and still undergo review as medical advances appear.

Introduced in the 1970s, these guidelines became the basis for many other insurers. DRGs not only shortened hospital stays and reduced costs, but stimulated research into alternatives to hospitalization, including drugs.

The first Health Maintenance Organization (HMO) began in 1929, but the managed care movement grew with the passage of the HMO Act of 1973 during the Nixon administration. This federal legislation authorized funding to increase the number of HMOs and ensure access to the employer funded health insurance market.

Focusing on prevention and early intervention, managed care organizations adapted many tools from other settings to identify problems early. Formularies, guidelines and economy-of-scale techniques were employed to reduce cost. The concept of disease management—examining the patient's entire disease rather than just looking at his medications—has been a useful preventive tool and a budget control tool.

The Pharmaceutical Industry

Trends in the pharmaceutical industry reflect trends in other industries; mergers, consolidations, and corporate streamlining are common. Various factors have contributed to the development of these trends. Cost and pricing pressures from ultimate customers, third party payers, and the legal system have had serious impact. Tremendous growth in the field of generic substitution (up to 44% of all prescriptions in 1997 were filled with generic drugs) has added a serious element of competition, and decreased profitability for manufacturers. The population's increasing reliance on government health care programs has contributed an added element of scrutiny from tax payers and their elected representatives. Merging with smaller competitors has kept profit reasonable, and improved economy of scale.

Many industries have acquired related (but different) product lines and complimentary service opportunities. This type of corporate growth maintains profitability. It also provides not only a buffer when one product or service line is in recession, but expands the company's

client base, solvency and business possibilities. In the case of pharmaceuticals, many manufacturers have acquired or formed alliances with other companies that manufacturer other health care products, supply a generic line of drugs, provide health care information systems, or create and implement disease management systems. They have integrated product and service in a way that enhances overall efficiency and viability. Their new lines of drugs, diagnostics, and information management tools allow them to manage disease states more effectively.

Pharmaceutical manufacturers have had an additional impetus for research and development. Since the 1980s, our attempts to still the effects of the human immunodeficiency virus (HIV) and stop its devastating effect on the health of the nation has improved our knowledge of human immunology, infectious disease, and neurology. Public outcry for cures and ameliorative treatments has forced the U.S. Food and Drug Administration to hasten the drug approval process. The spillover has been remarkable; advocacy groups wield considerable influence in the drug approval process. Alzheimer's disease, Parkinson's disease, and cancer advocacy groups are some of the most successful.

Pharmaceutical manufacturers also face the daunting challenge of widespread patent expiration. The patents on one-third of the best selling drugs will expire during the next 3 to 5 years. Manufacturers are looking for profitable replacements for these drugs. Their research emphasis is finding medications to meet urgent medical needs; identifying drugs to cure previously untreatable conditions; focusing on new products that improve therapy or reduce costs; developing products in dosing forms that are more palatable or enhance compliance; and creating products that are unique and difficult to copy.

A new strategy has been instituted to review old drugs using new techniques. Excellent treatment options have been revisited; new technology offers a measure of safety and helps the patient deal with undesired side effects. Modern monitoring techniques help identify problems before they become critical. Dapsone, once used to treat leprosy, is now used to prevent infection in HIV+ people. Thalidomide, a drug that shook the very foundation of the drug approval process in other countries when babies were born with limb deformations, is back on the market. Doctors are now prescribing Thalidomide to AIDS and cancer victims, in order to prevent a common symptom—wasting.

In the future, we can expect that the pressures of generic and therapeutic substitution, evolving disease states, and consumer demand will increase competition and innovation in the pharmaceutical manufacturers' arena. Much of our activity may come from abroad, where materials and labor are less expensive and other drugs are used. Marginal product lines will be eliminated as a cost-containment step, and drug distribution systems will become more responsive to customers at every level.

Patient Expectation

The ultimate consumer of pharmaceutical products and services—the patient—is considerably more sophisticated than even ten years ago. Various groups have successfully educated our consumers to ask the right questions. Technology and its success in prolonging life and making health care information accessible has also had significant impact. Consumers want better drugs with fewer side effects, and they want to be informed of any potential effects before they start the drug.

At this time, we are on the brink of a major change. Patients are beginning to understand that drug cost is only one factor in total health care expenditure. Insurers are maturing, and gathering expertise in medical management. Hospitals are seeking new ways to fill empty beds with ingenious, reimbursable programs. Standards of care and treatment algorithms are meeting with less resistance, and being developed using terminology that is appropriate to the client's level of understanding. Consumers throughout the health care system are becoming advocates of prevention. Formularies are being revised to include the precepts of disease management. Throughout these processes, the tendency is to include the patient as a partner.

Quality

The quality movement has evolved over the years, and is now the hue and cry of legislators, lobbyists, and advocacy groups. Most health care organizations look to accrediting and certifying bodies to set standards and provide guidance. At the patient level, quality is measured differently. Patients look for communication, experience, and positive emotional bonds.

The pharmaceutical industry has always been a leader in quality at every level. We boast an impressive record of safety, and are attuned to the potential for adverse consequences of any error or deviation from standard practice. The quality movement has advanced from an emphasis on quality control, to quality assurance, to quality assessment, to performance improvement. At every step, the pharmaceutical industry and pharmacy practitioners have been leaders. Our attention to detail, training, collective experience, and concern with side effects has made us experts in performance improvement.

In its current and developing phase, most organizations look for quality programs that consider every aspect of a problem. Process, product, people, environment and equipment must be examined. Most important, the outcomes (or results) of different processes must be compared. Those that produce the best outcomes must be promoted.

In our industry, noncompliance is considered a major quality problem. Noncompliance costs the U.S. approximately $100 billion annually. It increases hospitalizations, the need for nursing care, and premature death. The National Counsel on Patient Information and Education defines two types of noncompliance: acts of omission and acts of commission. Acts of omission are those that omit or reduce doses. Examples include failure to fill a prescription, missing a dose or doses, or taking less than the prescribed dose. Acts of commission include sharing medication with someone for whom it was not prescribed, or taking any foods or drugs that can interact with a drug concurrently. Improved compliance with health care interventions, including medication, conclusively improves outcome. This is health care's greatest challenge—motivating compliance.

Health maintenance organizations, medical groups and hospitals must establish a record of quality to stay in business. The preponderance of uninsured and indigent patients has placed substantial cost constraints on most health care systems. Government is trying to address health care issues and indigence at every level, but few programs have been successful. Most states are moving toward enrolling Medicaid recipients in managed care organizations. To date, approximately 13% of Medicaid recipients are enrolled in HMOs.

Information Systems

Health care has become a business based on management of information that is very similar to financial systems. Availability of readily retrievable data has made health care more of a science: from drug development, to distribution, to administration, to assessment of outcome.

We have come a long way since slide rules were replaced by calculators in the late 1960s. The early calculators were bulky, costly and slow by today's standard. Their computer counterparts were so large and so expensive that only established businesses could justify the cost. Advances have made computerization the cornerstone of the pharmaceutical industry and pharmaceutical care. For manufacturers, computer assisted drug design has replaced previous processes and helped target and manipulate chemical moieties with the best potential for development.

In the drug distribution system, computerization has created just-in-time delivery systems. They require less staff and reduce inventories and their associated costs. Just-in-time delivery systems have been tailored to meet the needs of special patients as well. Recipients of biotechnological entities can now receive these expensive agents immediately before they are needed. This eliminates storage problems and waste. Technology also assists health care providers with counseling. Automated documentation provides a more comprehensive and individualized profile of each client. Specialized programs remind clinicians to renew prescriptions, call and counsel the clients, or reassess therapy.

At the direct patient care level, information systems have made assessment of outcomes a reality. Governed by the National Council of Prescription Drug Programs standards, prescription drug data processing systems now collect and store large quantities of information. Standards ensure that the data is collected responsibly and interpreted reliably. Advances have made storage of data less expensive, and affordable processing is readily available to all viable business entities; in fact, it is an essential survival tool.

Using accumulated data, we can consolidate, compare, and analyze to determine best practices. Populations can be grouped in various ways to examine drug use patterns, disease distribution, geographic influences, and demographic differences. Most important, findings and information can be distributed quickly to promote compliance with best practices. This is particularly important when simple, cost effective measures—that make significant differences—are identified. Communication is imperative.

Two types of data analysis have been essential to managing pharmaceutical use. The first is a type of electronic link used primarily for claims processing of prescription drugs. This financial system adjudicated drug claims in an on-line, real time mode, generating patient specific claims data on prescription drug use in a timely and accurate fashion. Managed care companies analyze this data to determine clinical implications and determine ways to improve drug use.

The second type of data analysis occurs when prescription drug data is integrated with other medical information to perform pharmacoeconomic evaluations. Allowing the determination of best practices, outcome measurement, and treatment guidelines. This type of integration usually helps identify high risk and problem prone patients that generate a high utilization of healthcare resources.

Data collection is playing a greater role in work force management as well. Managers are now able to look at work volume in an objective manner, and integrate information throughout the process.

Regulatory Issues

Regulatory activity covers every aspect of the pharmaceutical environment. As cost containment measures have increased and the pharmacist's scope of practice has changed, consumers at various levels have sought legal intervention. There are too many issues to debate here, but three of the most important are included because of the intensity of concerns across the nation.

Formularies continue to be the object of review. Three types of formularies exist. The open formulary allows prescribers to use any drug they desire. Closed formularies restrict prescribing to a list of approved drug entities. Partially closed formularies represent a middle ground; prescribers are encouraged to use formulary drugs, but can use a process controlled by the organization to request nonformulary items. Health maintenance organizations are most likely to use formularies because they do control costs. However, recent research indicates that formularies may not be as cost-effective as they once appeared. Funds saved on drugs may be translated into other health care costs such as aggravation of concurrent conditions or hospitalization.

Consumer groups generally oppose use of the most restrictive formularies. Physicians generally oppose them as well, and perceive that formularies limit their practice options. Health care administrators, however, generally recognize the value of formularies and prefer to keep them. Consequently, formularies have been subject to legal and regulatory review in many jurisdictions with mixed results. Most accrediting and certifying bodies oppose closed formularies, and encourage integration of disease management strategies with formulary decisions.

The concept of therapeutic substitution also creates dissension among members of the pharmaceutical industry and the health care team. Some organizations, primarily HMOs and hospitals, allow pharmacists to substitute one medication for another if the products are therapeutically equivalent. Therapeutic equivalence should be established based on controlled studies. There are many examples, and most decisions to implement a therapeutic substitution program are based on the cost of the individual agents, and the holding costs associated with stocking many (as opposed to few) drugs.

Generally, a substitution protocol is established. For example, a facility may decide not to stock ampicillin, but carry amoxicillin instead. Prescriptions written for ampicillin, 500mg four times daily, would be filled with amoxicillin 500mg three times daily for most infections. This is a therapeutically equivalent dose, and the three times daily dosing schedule should improve compliance.

Various institutions handle therapeutic substitution in various ways, and different states have different laws governing its use. Some institutions implement an introductory program, where physicians are called before the substitution is made, for several months. Other

simply notify their medical staffs and proceed. In our example, an institution may determine the conditions—or indications—for which ampicillin is necessary and will not be substituted. They would develop a procedure to handle exceptions.

Therapeutic substitution engenders debate for several reasons. Manufacturers fear loss of market share despite any efforts they make to encourage prescribing. Prescribers often sense a loss of territory and authority, and resent the practice. Pharmacists, in general, consider this a natural exercise of their professional expertise. However, they do have concerns about liability if misadventure occurs, and worry about creating a breach of trust with prescribers. Hence, this is a practice ripe for litigation and regulation.

The concept of "any willing provider" is an offshoot of managed care practices. Many managed care organizations limit member access to participating community pharmacies only in an effort to contain cost. This move from an open to a closed system affected many non-participating pharmacies in terms of business volume. In several states, pharmacists organized. In response, legislation was created indicating that any willing provider—that is any pharmacy that was willing to follow the rules of participation and accept the reimbursement schedule of the HMO—could fill prescriptions for HMO members. The impact of any willing provider legislation will result in higher healthcare costs.

The Food and Drug Administration

In response to consumer demands and pressures from pharmaceutical manufacturers and disease advocacy groups, the Food and Drug Administration (FDA) has revisited their drug approval process and made considerable changes. The FDA Modernization Act of 1997 could be considered a performance improvement initiative. Its intent is already being realized.

The time to secure FDA approval of a new drug is shorter, which has reduced associated (and significant) administrative costs for manufacturers. Hopefully, the savings will be passed on to consumers. It has also made promising drugs available to patients more quickly.

In addition, the FDA has relaxed its regulations concerning off-label use of drugs. In the past, drug sales representatives were not allowed to discuss any indication of a drug unless it was included in the FDA-approved labeling. In reality, once a drug is approved, released, and employed in a large population, new indications may become evident. Their discovery may be by accident, or by plan. Until recently, manufacturers would have to complete a lengthy and costly re-labeling application before they could direct marketing to the indication. Now, these indications can be discussed if peer-reviewed scientific literature is available to support the new indication. There are no restrictions on discussion.

Other changes at the FDA have increased emphasis on development and approval of drugs for women and children in a safe and responsible way, and improved access to investigational drugs in life-threatening situations.

Changes to the rules governing advertising have affected the dynamics of the pharmaceutical industry as well as the provider-patient relationship. Specifically, approval of direct-to-consumer advertising has allowed manufacturers to market their prescription drug products directly to potential patients. Advertisements now appear in all types of lay publications.

The regulations restrict the type of information that can be provided, and require provision of supplementary information via toll-free telephone number, Internet access, or in writing, upon request. They also encourage use of understandable language. Clinicians report that increasing numbers of patients are asking for drug products by name. In the past, the prescriber diagnosed and prescribed after assessment of target symptoms. As sales techniques like this encourage the patient to take a greater role in self-diagnosis, the dynamics of the clinician-patient relationship shift. Different patients respond differently. Sometimes, the information that a drug is available to treat a symptom encourages patients to engage in the health care system. However, sometimes, the patient's predisposition to a certain drug can be an impediment to good care. Prescribers increasingly report patient insistence on a particular drug or brand.

The FDA is also participating in the International Conference on Harmonization, a project that aims to decrease redundancy in the drug development process among nations. For the last eight years, the FDA has worked with other governments to share information on approved drugs, thus improving timely access to drugs everywhere.

Boards of Pharmacy

At the direct care level, the state board of pharmacy is the ultimate sign of authority. They possess the power to bestow or revoke licenses, or curtail practice. Historically, boards have been cautious and slow to change. Two specific changes could, theoretically, have a tremendous impact on the practice of pharmacy.

At the national level, several states are sanctioning certificate programs for pharmacists. This initiative began in Mississippi, and has been approved in four states as this foreword is written. Pharmacists who complete an approved certificate program in these states are allowed to become reimbursable Medicaid providers. Four states of disease are currently included: asthma, diabetes, dyslipidemia, and anticoagulation. Diabetic counseling, lipids clinics are two examples of how A pharmacist can help manage chronic diseases in an ambulatory setting through lipids clinics and diabetic counseling.

This program has forced pharmacy organizations to address the potential practice implications of certification specifically, and expanded practice in general. The National Association of Chain Drugs Stores and the National Community Pharmacists Association are working with the National Association of Boards of Pharmacy. They have convened a certification summit to address certification and other issues of expanded practice.

Pharmacy practice has changed considerably over the last ten years, and major changes are expected over the next ten years. Pharmacists are no longer primarily dispensing drugs. Their role is being redefined to that of care providers. Reflective of these changes, The Pharmacy Practice Acts in most states are being modified to address the new roles for pharmacists.

The Pharmaceutical Market

There is no debate that pharmaceuticals reduce a patient's risk of death from disease. Antibiotics and vaccines have made a large difference in quality of life.

Increasingly, payers look for drugs that can reduce other health care expenses.

As we write, the 20 largest pharmaceutical manufacturers account for 75% of sales. Total annual sales of pharmaceuticals grew from $4.1 billion in 1965 to $75.2 billion in 1992, with sales in the United States accounting for $50.2 billion. The industry is vulnerable because profit margins are at record levels, generic substitution is very high, and many health care organizations are seeking cost-containment tactics that will lower manufacturers profits.

Experts predict five to ten years of turmoil in the pharmaceuticals market. Pharmaceutical manufacturers will use several approaches to remain stable and promote growth. First, they will focus on those diseases and syndromes that are in the public eye. These include AIDS, Alzheimer's disease, arthritis, cancer, mental illness, osteoporosis, and stroke. Extensive research and development efforts will be concentrated in these areas, which cost the American health system $640 million annually. Their specific emphasis will be the search for novel compounds that are less susceptible to competition.

We can expect manufacturers to employ other strategies as well. Look for more mergers as companies acquire minor competitors to eliminate competition. Also look for more programs that provide free medication to the uninsured; these increase goodwill. Just as direct care providers attempt to make the patient a partner in care, manufacturers will try to make their customers—HMOs, hospitals, physician provider organizations, etc.—a partner using cooperative management arrangements. Finally, vertical and horizontal integration will take on new meaning as manufacturers execute integration plans on a worldwide basis.

There is still opportunity. The industry's strengths include the potential to provide alternatives to surgery and hospitalization that are cost effective; exceptional data management experience that translates well into health management modules; and finely tuned marketing strategies that, if adapted to target patients and health care organizations as opposed to physicians, could be highly successful.

Employment Trends

There is conflicting opinion about employment trends in the pharmaceutical industry. Clearly, if manufacturers are able to meet new demands and create products that meet customer needs, employment opportunities will increase throughout the industry. Highly skilled technical employees will always be in demand. In addition to a need for research and development personnel, there will be an increased need for staff to support more complex data operations.

Over the last ten years, public and private funding for disease research has increased. Some of this funding has been provided by the federal government. Academia has also received additional funds, and private corporations have joined in the quest for cures for many pressing problems.

For direct care providers including pharmacists, technicians, and support staff, employment opportunities will only be limited by our adaptive abilities. Although the Pew Commission predicted a surplus of pharmacists within ten years, most other pharmacy pundits predict growth in opportunity.

One predictor of employment opportunity is prescription volume. In 1990, approximately 1.5 billion prescriptions were filled. In the year 2000, that number will rise to more than 2.5 billion. Although automation buffers the need for personnel, it will not negate the growth. Certification of pharmacists in new areas will mandate a new measure of workload that may actually decrease prescription volume. And as our baby boomers age and retire, many practicing pharmacists will leave the work force, creating practice opportunities for new graduates.

Technicians and support personnel will become more essential than they already are. As pharmacists move from the dispensing to the care providing role, technicians will have to assume more of the technical duties of pharmacy. Our reliance on automation and data will create a specialty field for information specialists who have a contiguous knowledge of pharmacy.

Increased reliance on drugs, particularly those that eliminate a surgical procedure or prevent hospitalization, will increase the portion of the health care budget spent on drugs. Pharmacists will be needed to supervise this transition. Twenty years ago, nuclear pharmacists were considered fringe practitioners. Today, nuclear pharmacy is a tenable career choice for pharmacists. In the same way, pharmacy benefits managers are considered fringe practitioners today. In the 2000s, their unique blend of clinical, administrative and financial acumen will make them key pharmacy practitioners.

Most schools of pharmacy have lengthened their programs and changed their focus. The Pharm.D., once considered a professional peccadillo, is now the entry level degree. Practicing pharmacists who have not had the training and experience provided by Pharm.D. programs are enhancing their skills in many ways. Certificate programs are growing. Masters and doctoral pharmacy programs are filled to capacity in most places. Because advanced education opens new doors and creates opportunity, many pharmacists are seeking complimentary degrees in business, finance, epidemiology, health care management, and other subjects.. In this last century, apothecaries and druggists have transformed themselves into true drug experts. The specialty fields they have developed ensure improved and cost effective care for patients.

As a profession, we will have to ensure that competence is maintained among our technical and support members. The press for continuous competency evaluation is strong at this time; constant review of skills is essential to protect public safety. Competency evaluation will have to address not only those skills that relate to the practice of pharmacy or application of scientific skills, but a host of other issues. Key among them are the ability to communicate in a manner acceptable to the customer; cultural sensitivity in a society that is rapidly changing; and the ability to use advanced technology well.

Conclusion

Pharmaceuticals will continue to be a cost-effective part of health care. As more new products are invented to cure and treat disease, the quality of life for all people will be greatly improved. With the right balance of new products and drug use management systems, we can ensure the appropriate utilization of pharmaceuticals and healthcare resources.

—Perry Cohen, Pharm.D. and Michael J. Sax, Pharm.D.

Perry Cohen, Pharm.D. is a co-founder and past president of the Academy of Managed Care Pharmacy and a member of the National Advisory Board University of Arizona School of Pharmacy, Contributing Editor for the Journal of Managed Care Pharmacy, *and* Drug Topics Editorial Advisory Board. *He has over 20 years experience in managed health care and is currently responsible for administration and marketing of The Pharmacy Group LLC, a health care consulting company.*

Michael J. Sax, Pharm.D. is a member of the Academy of Managed Care Pharmacy, American Society of Health Systems Pharmacist, and the American College of Clinical Pharmacology. He is currently responsible for the clinical operations of The Pharmacy Group LLC.

INDUSTRY OVERVIEW

This chapter presents a comprehensive overview of the Pharmaceuticals industry. Major topics covered include an Industry Snapshot, Organization and Structure, Background and Development, Pioneers in the Industry, Current Conditions and Future Projections, Industry Leaders, Work Force, and North America and the World. A suggested list for further reading, including web sites to visit, completes the chapter. Additional company information is presented in Chapter 6 - Mergers & Acquisitions.

Industry Snapshot

According to the U.S. Health Care Financing Administration, Americans spent $878.77 billion on personal health care in 1995. Of that nearly $83 billion was spent on drugs, both prescription and over-the-counter (OTC). The pharmaceutical industry is a strong one. Product shipments in 1995 were valued at $80.88 billion, just over 2 percent of the nation's total output of manufactured goods. In 1998, the average cost of an over-the-counter drug was $5, according to the Non-prescription Drug Manufacturers Association (NDMA), prescription drugs averaged $22. Medical insurance plans are important to the pharmaceutical industry. According to IMS Health, a health care information company, only 24 percent of prescription drugs are paid for entirely out-of-pocket; all the rest are paid for at least in part by third parties.

The U.S. pharmaceutical industry is international; many American companies operate facilities overseas, including factories, sales offices and distribution operations. At the same time, a number of foreign producers have plants and other facilities in the Unites States.

The pharmaceutical industry is intensely competitive. It is also one of the most research-oriented sectors of the American economy. While the average manufacturing company in the U.S. spends only four to five percent of its total sales on R&D, according to *U.S. Industry & Trade Outlook 1998*, pharmaceutical companies churn nearly half of their total sales back into the development of new products. Research is expected to expand sharply. Competitive forces in the drug market, for example the increasing popularity of generic drugs, are expected to keep prices down, and pharmaceutical firms will be challenged to maintain their research spending. Pharmaceutical Research and Manufacturers of America (PhRMA) reported that in 1998 there were about 500 distinct targets for drug interventions; the number is expected to grow to between 3,000 and 10,000 in the next few years.

In 1996, *Fortune* magazine rated pharmaceuticals as the nation's most profitable industry. According to the Congressional Budget Office, however, this ranking did not take into account expensive R&D outlays or the risk involved in the development of new pharmaceutical products.

In recent years, the growth of the pharmaceutical industry in the United States has slowed somewhat; the result of a drive by hospitals and managed care organizations to contain health care costs. Nonetheless, during the twelve months ending in June 1998, the U.S. pharmaceutical market grew at a rate of 10.9 percent. According to IMS Health, the worldwide market for pharmaceutical products should grow at a rate of 7 percent, compared with a rate of 1.7 percent in 1997 in constant U.S. dollars.

According to a Coopers & Lybrand survey, many executives in the industry believe they must deploy their marketing resources earlier, while products are still under development. Pharmaceutical advertising was one of the fastest growing types of advertising during the 1990s. In 1990, only 10 prescription medicines were advertised directly to consumers; by 1997 the number had grown to 79.

One of the greatest challenges to the industry is shortening the time between a product's conception and its introduction on the market. Pre-clinical and clinical tests, plus the necessary Food and Drug Administration (FDA) approval process can extend over fourteen years. The rise of the generic drugs is a motivating factor as well. Drug patents last only 20 years; after that, generic manufacturers can produce and sell them for as much as 90 percent less than name brands. As a result, name brands often find their market shrinking by some 80 percent a year after the patent expires.

In 1996 the FDA approved 139 new drugs and biological preparations, according to the *U.S. Trade and Industry Outlook*. 53 of those were brand new molecular entities. One of the most sensational new products of the 1990s was a pharmaceutical: Viagra, a drug for male impotence.

Organization and Structure

The pharmaceutical industry is divided into four broad categories covered by the Standard Industrial Classification (SIC) code 283: **2833: Medicinals and Botanicals, 2834: Pharmaceutical Preparations, 2835: In Vivo and in Vitro Diagnostic Substances**, and **2836: Biological Products, except diagnostics**. Companies in the Medicinals and Botanicals industry primarily produce bulk organic and inorganic medicinal chemicals and their derivatives, and process bulk botanical drugs and herbs. They manufacture products of natural origin, hormonal products, and basic vitamins, as well as products which isolate active medicinal principals such as alkaloids from botanical drugs and herbs. The Pharmaceutical Preparations industry uses these substances as active ingredients in pharmaceutical preparations for human and veterinary use. Active ingredients are the part of a drug's make-up that are responsible for its therapeutic effect. Finished products are sold in many dosage forms, compressed or coated tablets, capsules, syrups, spirits, lotions, pastes, sprays, and powders. Medicinals and Botanicals and Pharmaceutical Preparations are often produced by one company.

In vivo and in vitro diagnostic substances are chemical, biological, and radioactive substances used in diagnosing and monitoring health by testing body fluids and tissues. In vivo means that the test is conducted inside a living organism, while in vitro tests are run in test tubes. In vivo diagnostic substances enhance images of targeted organs or functions during diagnostic procedures such as magnetic resonance imaging or computer tomography. Biological Products are bacterial and virus vaccines, toxoids, allergenic extracts, serums, plasma, and other blood derivatives for human and veterinary use, other than in vitro and in vivo diagnostic substances.

Pharmaceuticals include preparations intended for use by patients and the general public, and those to be used by professionals only. Some pharmaceutical products can be purchased—like any other product—in various retail stores like drug stores, super markets, and retail chains, or by mail order via telephone or the Internet. This group is called over-the-counter (OTC) drugs. OTC drug manufacturers have to insure that consumers are able to self-diagnose the condition for which the drug is designed, such as a cold or seasonal allergy, and that directions for use are understandable by the consumer. The second group, prescription drugs, are also available to the public, but can only be purchased with a prescription from a licensed health care professional who is allowed to prescribe. Besides receiving prescriptions for drugs from doctors, patients are administered drugs directly in hospitals and practices; they frequently are given samples by their physicians, free of charge. A third group of pharmaceuticals are used within healthcare institutions such as doctors'

practices, clinics and hospitals by dental, medical, or veterinary professionals for diagnosis, analysis, and research. Most diagnostic substances are used in medical laboratories. However, more and more OTC home tests are becoming available.

Government is a major purchaser of pharmaceuticals. For example, Medicaid, Veteran Administration hospitals, the Department of Defense, or senior citizen assistance programs provide beneficiaries with prescription drugs and have negotiated price controls of one kind or another with manufacturers, for example rebates or limiting price increases. Access to prescription drugs is restricted by certain programs as well. Medicare, by and large, does not cover prescription drug costs, but most recipients are enrolled in managed-care programs with their own prescription drug coverage.

Prescription drugs are divided into brand-name prescription drugs, sometimes also called "ethical" or "innovator" drugs, and generic drugs. Brand name drugs contain one or more specific ingredients used for the first time for a particular purpose. After discovering a compound with medical potential, ethical pharmaceutical companies usually apply for a patent, which is normally valid for 20 years from the date of application. After the patent has expired, other manufacturers are allowed to produce drugs containing the same active ingredients. Those products are called "generic" and may include different inactive ingredients than the original formula. Most generic drug companies do not conduct research intended to identify and develop innovator drugs. However, producers of brand name drugs may have subsidiaries that manufacture generic products.

Pharmaceutical products as well as the processes and facilities used to manufacture them are extensively regulated. While pharmaceutical products influence public health and individual well-being, their production has an significant impact on the natural environment. The U.S. Food and Drug Administration (FDA) in the Department of Health and Human Services has the statutory authority to regulate a wide range of pharmaceutical products, based on the Federal Food, Drug and Cosmetic Act, the Public Health Service Act, and several other laws. The FDA regulates the manufacture, safety, efficacy, and labeling of pharmaceutical products. FDA offices throughout the U.S. are the base for testing FDA-regulated articles and for investigators who visit U.S. and foreign facilities to confirm compliance with FDA regulations. The FDA departments most concerned with the pharmaceutical industry are the Center for Drug Evaluation and Research (CDER), the Center for Biologics Evaluation and Research (CBER), and the Center for Veterinary Medicine (CVM).

All prescription drugs for humans must undergo a rigorous approval process that includes pre-clinical research on animal subjects, a three-phase series of clinical studies on humans, followed by a review of the findings by the CDER. With the advent of illness like AIDS, the FDA has developed accelerated approval processes to enable seriously ill patients to receive the drug before the approval process has been completed. Companies wanting to manufacture a generic drug must show evidence that the generic version is "bioequivalent," which means that the rate and extent of drug absorption differs by no more than 25 percent, and no less than 20 percent from the original drug. Prior to FDA marketing approval, production facilities are inspected and labeling is reviewed. OTC drugs are divided into more than 80 regulatory classes. New OTC drugs are reviewed to establish whether their composition and labeling matches that of other drugs in their class. If so, they can be marketed immediately; if not, they must undergo review. Animal drugs, which include drugs used in feed, are tested by the CVM for efficacy and safety in a multi-stage process. Each change in ingredients, manufacturing processes, and test and control methods requires FDA approval either before or after they are made, as specified in the FDA regulations.

CDER regulates manufacturing facilities, methods, and controls used in the production, processing, and packaging of drugs for human use. Each change in ingredients, manufacturing processes, or test and control methods must be reported to CDER, and requires FDA approval either before or after they are made, as specified in the FDA regulations. CDER field investigators verify the information submitted on-site to assure the company has complied with FDA's Good Manufacturing Practices (GMPs).

The pharmaceutical industry is subject to most environmental laws governing the generation, handling, storage and disposal of hazardous waste. Important statutes include the Resource Conservation and Re-

covery Act of 1976 (RCRA), the Comprehensive Environmental Response, Compensation and Liability Act (Superfund), the Clean Water Act (CWA), the Clean Air Act (CAA), and the Toxic Substances Control Act (TSCA). These acts often include provisions specific to the pharmaceutical industry. For example, the CAA sets specific limits on pharmaceutical plant emissions. Water treatment guidelines for the pharmaceutical industry in the CWA are currently being revised. Many byproducts of pharmaceutical production processes are classified as hazardous waste under the RCRA.

Most states have established environmental regulatory programs. Although many of these were meant to implement federal programs state programs can be, and sometimes are, more stringent than federal. States with high concentrations of pharmaceutical manufacturing facilities, for example, New York and New Jersey, have their own regulations pertaining specifically to the industry.

Pharmaceutical manufacturing is sometimes subject to the Controlled Substances Act under which the Drug Enforcement Administration (DEA) enforces regulations on the manufacture, distribution, and dispensing of controlled substances. Pharmaceutical products regulated under this Act include Demerol, Percodan, Ritalin, Valium, and Darvon. To control distribution, DEA may set production quotas. The law regulates how such compounds are handled and stored; when disposed of, controlled substances must be destroyed in the presence of DEA personnel.

Key vendors to pharmaceutical preparations manufacturers are fine chemicals companies which often have their own pharmaceuticals division. Bulk manufacturing processes are used to produce medicinal chemicals and botanical products as well as finished preparations. In some manufacturing processes, relatively small, highly concentrated quantities of active ingredients are extracted from much larger volumes of raw material. The Environmental Protection Agency (EPA) reported in 1997, "the industry's production yield for these operations is correspondingly low." Manufacturing processes for Botanicals involve drying, grinding, grading, and milling of botanical products, and often solvent baths and distillation procedures. Antibiotics are grown in fermentation tanks. Other biological products are made on a comparably small scale using organisms or their cellular, subcellular, or molecular components.

A variety of trade associations represent the interests of different groups within the industry. Pharmaceutical Research and Manufacturers of America (PhRMA) assists research-based ethical pharmaceutical companies in discovering, developing, and marketing new drugs. Member companies are primarily involved in research and development (R&D), and manufacture and market their own brand name drugs. The National Pharmaceutical Alliance (NPA) represents small pharmaceutical companies which develop generic versions of major brand name drugs, create alternative products with varying combinations, strengths and dosage forms, and market products which would not otherwise be available to the public because big pharmaceutical firms do not produce them. The National Association of Pharmaceutical Manufacturers, a national non-profit trade group, represents the political interests of independent generic drug manufacturers and suppliers of bulk pharmaceutical chemicals. The American Pharmaceutical Association (APhA), a professional society, is dedicated to high quality of pharmacy services and their appropriate use. APhA represents a broad variety of professionals including practicing pharmacists, pharmaceutical scientists, pharmacy students, technicians, and others interested in the field. AphA's main periodical is the monthly journal *American Pharmacy*. Other relevant organizations are the Generic Pharmaceutical Industry Association (GPIA), trade association for manufacturers and distributors of generic drugs; the United States Pharmacopeial Convention which publishes legally recognized compendia of drug standards such as the *National Formulary*; and the Biotechnology Industry Organization, representing biotechnology companies, academic institutions, and state biotechnology centers.

One of the major tasks of the industry is to discover new compounds for medicines and to further develop them into medical products which can be used for the diagnosis and treatment of human or animal diseases. The necessary research can last several years. After a new drug or compound which might be useful in diagnosing, treating, or preventing illness has been discovered, pre-clinical toxicology tests and clinical trials for safety and effectiveness are conducted. If they are they successful, a New Drug Application (NDA) is submitted to the FDA for approval, which includes the new compound, and any drug to be made from it. After the FDA has approved a new formula, it can be distributed in the U.S. In the late 1990s, it took 15 years on average from the time a drug was developed in the laboratory until its market introduction. Because of the extremely high competition in the brand name drug market, a significant proportion of the industry's sales are reinvested into research and development.

Background and Development

19th Century

While compounding, buying and selling drugs is as old as human civilization, mass production of drugs in the United States began in the early 19th century. By 1810, patent medicines were one of the largest industries in the U.S. Particularly successful were Lydia Pinkham's Vegetable Compound and Carter's Little Liver Pills. Since drugs were cheap and easy to manufacture, and demand was high, pharmacies began manufacturing their own drugs. New York City was a center of the wholesale trade, and influential Midwestern companies emerged, such as Parke Davis in Detroit, Eli Lilly in Indianapolis, and Upjohn in Kalamazoo. Philadelphia was a pharmaceutical capital. At least six enduring manufacturers were founded there around 1820. Pharmacy schools arose throughout the country: 1821 in Philadelphia, 1823 in Massachusetts, 1829 in New York City, 1840 in Maryland, and 1859 in Chicago. The schools were instrumental in forming the American Pharmaceutical Association. In 1825 the school in Philadelphia introduced the first American pharmaceutical journal, which became the *American Journal of Pharmacy*.

The demand for pharmaceuticals increased exponentially during Civil War. The ability to machine-produce large quantities of quality opium, quinine, and ergot, and supply the Union army with them reliably, established the reputations of companies like Eli Lilly and E.R. Squibb. To save money, the Army eventually opened its own production lab in 1864. According to census records, between 1860 and 1870 the number of manufacturers in Philadelphia rose from 173 to 292, and the level of capital investment rose from $1.97 million to $12.75 million. Since products, even from leading manufacturers, varied in widely from batch to batch in strength and composition, standardization became an important issue in the latter half of the nineteenth century.

Until the first state pharmacy laws in the 1870s, all drugs in the United States were non-prescription. In the 1880s, several states adopted prescription laws similar to the current two-class drug system. In the 1880s and 1890s, the industry took on modern form: The telegraph and railroad improved ordering, distribution, and inventory control, and companies began departmentalizing for greater efficiency. By the 1890s all the large companies produced a full range of standard preparations. In 1885, a physician invented machinery which mass produced pills of uniform dosage and purity. He went on to found the Upjohn company.

Toward century's end, companies began hiring trained scientific and medical staff, especially those who had studied the new field of bacteriology with German pioneers. However, scientific staff concentrated on standardizing drug preparation, they rarely did research. Companies instead sought new pharmaceutical agents on elaborate botanical expeditions to places like Canada, Mexico and South America.

The Early Twentieth Century

In 1900, Bayer brought out its aspirin tablet in America and it became an over-the-counter (OTC) drug in 1915. Other enduring OTC products of the time were Pepto-Bismol (1902), Ex-Lax (1906), and Listerine (1914). The Biologicals Control Act of 1902 restricted production of biologicals to firms with scientifically trained staff. In 1906 the Pure Food and Drugs Act, prohibiting the manufacture and distribution of adulterated drugs, established the first federal government control over drug-making. In 1910, the German bacteriologist Paul Ehrlich, convinced chemicals could kill microorganisms without injuring the patient, developed salvarsan, a drug to treat syphilis. Its success demonstrated the importance of chemotherapeuticals and showed the potential of research and development.

Some drug makers were already selling vaccines to city public health authorities, however World War I significantly increased demand for mass produced medicines. The industry became more concentrated in the 1920s. Companies cut back their product lines and became more specialized partly because of more stringent FDA regulations; smaller companies merged with larger competitors. The number of chain drugstores increased threefold in the 1920s and their organized buying added a new force to the market.

Until the 1930s, the drug industry was based on a few well-known active ingredients. New products were usually new combinations of already known drug compounds. In the 1930s, though, drug prices had stabilized. They were no longer a major factor for competition and in-house scientific research and innovation took on new importance. New medicines began to outsell older brands and combination drugs, which fought two or more symptoms at the same time, came into vogue. Once research started improving, American pharmaceutical companies began challenging German companies in cutting-edge development.

The 1930s through the Second World War

Sulfa drugs were introduced in the 1930s; in 1937, over 100 Americans, treated with the "Elixir of Sulfanilamide" died because of a toxic solvent in the new drug. Manufacturers responded with more sophisticated testing programs, created to lower the health and legal risks of new drugs. In 1938, a new Food, Drug, and Cosmetic Act introduced pre-market screening procedures for new drugs, which gave the FDA greater control over drug safety. Companies were allowed to provide drugs still under research to qualified experts as long as they were labeled as such. If the FDA did not respond within 60 or 180 days, the new drug received automatic approval. However, the clinical research findings, as well as the data made available to the FDA once a drug was approved, were determined mainly by the drug firms themselves. The new law distinguished prescription and nonprescription medicines, but did not call for disclosure of ingredients by nonprescription drug manufacturers.

Drug demand during World War II enabled manufacturers to produce larger quantities, encouraged them to refine technologies and to search for more efficient treatments. Sulfa drugs or sulfonamide, used to protect soldiers from infections, were greatly refined. Fine chemical firms such as Merck and Lederle produced high quantities in bulk form. Upjohn, another producer of Sulfa powders and tablets, developed important sterilization and packaging technology. The war also created a high demand for penicillin, the first antibiotic drug discovered in 1928 by Scottish medical researcher Alexander Fleming; the deep tank fermentation process developed by Pfizer made large scale production of penicillin possible. Penicillin finally became available on the civilian market in 1946 and, according to

Meir Statman, over half of the total penicillin output (in bulk form) was produced by Pfizer. With demand for new drugs rising, more firms such as Sandoz and Ciba entered the market.

The Post-War Era

By 1950, according to *American Druggist,* total drug store sales grew from $1.6 billion in 1939 to $4.1 billion. Ethical pharmaceutical companies increased their R&D activity tremendously. According to Statman, between 1940 and 1949 there were 192 new single chemical entities (NCE), or drugs synthesized from NCE, introduced in the United States. This number more than doubled during the next ten years with 453 new drugs introduced between 1950 and 1959. R&D costs in the ethical pharmaceutical industry rose from $83 million in 1951, to $328 million in 1961; in constant 1972 dollars, an increase of almost 300 percent. Drug sales during this time grew more than twice as fast as the gross national product in real terms. Many manufacturers took advantage of the new medium of television to advertise using novel spokesmen, such as Speedy Alka-Seltzer, who personified the brand names. New FDA laws of the 1940s and 1950s included testing and certification of insulin (1941), certification of antibiotics (1945—1949), the Durham-Humphrey Amendment on prescription drugs (1951) which, according to Wyndham Davies, involved the investigation of 56,000 retail drugs, and the Food Additives Amendments (1958).

Stricter Regulation in the 1960s

In 1959, the Antitrust and Monopoly Subcommittee held hearings on drug companies selling drugs with questionable effects often at high prices. Chairman Senator Estes Kefauver sponsored a bill in 1961 proposing government regulation on drug efficacy, which was modified into the 1962 amendments to the 1938 Food, Drug, and Cosmetics Act. In 1962, after the birth of deformed babies in Europe was linked to their mothers' use of thalidomide, an OTC sleeping pill, the American manufacturer of the drug withdrew its NDA and stopped all distribution. Approximately 8,000 babies with deformations caused by thalidomide were born worldwide.

This episode contributed to strict regulations for clinical drug testing. Under the new law, pharmaceutical companies were required to get FDA approval prior to any tests of new drugs on humans. Approval was also required to distribute new drugs to other states for clinical research, which was only given after comprehensive results of animal tests were furnished. Before pharmaceutical companies were permitted to put a new drug onto the market, they had to prove its efficacy and that manufacturer's claims for it were accurate; information about side effects, contraindications, and effectiveness of the new drug had to be included in advertising materials. FDA had six months to review applications as well as the right to extend its review period indefinitely.

Drug makers were required to demonstrate the effectiveness of OTC drugs for the first time as well. As a result of the 1962 amendments, untested as well as ineffective products were eliminated from the pharmaceuticals market, and manufacturers claims were controlled. At the same time, stricter regulation made fewer drugs available to physicians and their patients in the United States than in other countries, many smaller firms with limited financial resources were forced out of the ethical drug market concentrating the market in the hands of the larger companies.

1962 through 1979

In 1966, a new biological product entered the U.S. market. Factor VIII, a blood protein that controls clotting, helped hemophilia A patients control bleeding episodes. Factor IX for hemophilia B patients followed. In 1967, the APhA first published the *Handbook on Nonprescription Drugs*, which presented all available formulas for OTC drugs. Over time, the resistance of OTC manufacturers to disclose their product formulas shrunk and even nonactive ingredients were published. In 1969 the FDA reported that half of about 500 OTC product samples they examined were not effective. In 1970 the agency modified its OTC review procedures, examining active ingredients rather than individual products.

In the mid-1960s, with more and more drugs on the market, competition increased. New drug revenue growth began to decline, while research outlays increased. According to Statman, ethical drug manufacturers spent $161.5 million on R&D for human-use drugs in 1958, $449.5 million in 1968, and $1.3 billion in 1978. However, the number of new drugs introduced to the United States market dropped significantly during this period. Only 236 NTC drugs or synthesized drugs were introduced between 1960 and 1961, a 90 percent drop from the decade before. This number decreased again by almost one third between 1970 until 1979, with 162 new drugs introduced. R&D expenditures per NTC drug rose from $5 million in 1960 to $69 million in 1978. Time needed for research increased as well. While NTC drugs introduced in the United States in 1960 had been under development 4 years on average, NTC drugs introduced in 1978 required 11 years development time. In 1978, the Department of Commerce reported that pharmaceutical preparations (SIC 2834) accounted for a full 80 percent of all drug and pharmaceutical sales.

Two successful OTC drugs introduced during that time were the two pain relievers Tylenol (acetaminophen), introduced in 1976, and Advil (ibuprofen), introduced in 1984. By 1988, the government reported that about two-thirds of American diagnosed most of their illnesses themselves and treated them with OTC drugs.

The Generic Drug Industry

By the 1980s, although some 160 drug patents had expired, the FDA was very arbitrary in handling new drug applications and was only approving applications for drugs whose patents had expired before 1962. Meanwhile, the brand drug industry was lobbying, in vain, for passage of the Patent Restoration Act, a law which would have extended drug patents. The Drug Price Competition and Patent Term Restoration Act (Waxman-Hatch Act) was a 1984 compromise that clarified the rules for generic drugs. Brand drug companies were permitted to market their drugs for a period without competition and an extension to products' patents were permitted. Generic companies, at the same time, were allowed to develop generic substitutes before the brand drug's patent expired.

The Pfizer Journal stated that, according to the Boston Consulting Group, the FDA received over 800 abbreviated new drug applications in the first seven months after the passage of the Waxman-Hatch Act. But in 1985, spurred by complaints of unfair FDA handling of drug applications, the House began investigating FDA practices and the generic drug industry as a whole. A plethora of corrupt activities were discovered, including payoffs, disregard of agency guidelines, even rigged pre-approval tests of drugs. FDA officials served prison terms after being found guilty of accepting bribes and the half-dozen generic companies found guilty of fraud and deceptive practices closed. The FDA's generic division was reorganized from the ground up and onsite, pre-approval inspections of drug companies were begun.

The confidence of the public in generic drugs was shaken initially. The reorganized FDA, performed a comprehensive survey of the generic drugs on the market and called them safe. The nation's pharmacists also contributed to restoring the public's confidence by removing suspect products from their shelves and educating the public about the efficacy of generics. Once the scandal had passed, the generic market grew rapidly, spurred by the rise of health maintenance organizations, an aggressive marketing campaign by the industry to promote public awareness of generic drugs, and a large number of expired drug patents. In 1987, according the *U.S. Industrial Outlook,* nine out of ten of the most widely used prescription drugs were available in generic substitutes. *The Pfizer Journal* quoted a finding of the Boston Consulting Group, that generics' share of the prescription market doubled from 15 percent in 1983 to over 30 percent in 1989. *The American Druggist* reported that while only 2 percent of all prescriptions in 1980 were for generics, in the mid-1990s they had reached about 45 percent.

Veterinary Pharmaceuticals

The veterinary pharmaceutical industry first surged after the Second World War. At that time, drug companies hired veterinarians to guide animal drug research and development, and drugs already used for humans were adapted for animal use, including antibiotics and anti-inflammatory steroids. The most important developments in veterinary health included parasite control in farm and other domestic animals, effective animal vaccines, and antibiotic food additives that suppressed infections and enabled farmers to confine large numbers of animals together. The 1950s saw a concentrated search for new drugs and a general consolidation of the industry as companies closed or merged with others. Sulfanamide production for animals increased in the 1960s to compensate for hog cholera serums which had been banned. By 1989, sales of animal drugs had reached $1 billion dollars a year according to the Animal Health Institute (AHI), and $350 million was being spent on research on veterinary pharmaceuticals.

Biologicals and Diagnostics

In the early 1980s, producers of blood proteins, struggling with HIV contamination—the *Wall Street Journal* estimated that half of all 20,000 hemophiliacs in the United States were infected primarily by using Factor VIII and IX products—and heat treatment was introduced into production technologies. New biological products were approved in the 1980s and biotechnology began to change the pharmaceuticals market. In 1982, human insulin for the treatment of diabetes was approved by the FDA; HGH, a human growth hormone, received approval in 1985; a genetically engineered vaccine against hepatitis-B, monoclonal antibodies (MABs) (to help prevent kidney rejection in transplant patients), and alpha interferon (for the treatment of hairy cell leukemia) in 1986; as well as Erythropoietin (EPO), a stimulant for red blood cell production.

But while biotech companies like Genentech, Inc. (founded in 1976), Biogen, Inc. (1978), Amgen, Inc. (1980), and Chiron Corp. (1981), were able to introduce new products, other companies struggled to survive while awaiting FDA approvals. EPO was immediately approved under the Medicare program and the number of dialysis patients treated with the drug grew to about 82,000 within a few years.

Chemicalweek quoted a Consulting Resources study that stated products developed using recombinant DNA proteins—the primary biotechnology at the time which combined the genetic components of two or more living cells— were worth $1 billion by the end of the 1980s. According to the U.S. Department of Commerce, biological products shipments (SIC 2836) reached $2.16 billion in 1990, including non-medical biotech products.

One of the main applications of biologicals is the field of diagnostics. At the end of the 1980s, hospitals accounted for 70 percent of diagnostic product sales. Diagnostic test kit sales, both to hospitals and over the counter increased rapidly in the 1980s and 1990s. An inorganic, in vivo diagnostic product was approved in 1989. The new non-ionic contrast media used with X-rays "dispersed more readily" and reduced side effects

such as nausea, pain, and allergic reactions. *U.S. Industry & Trade Outlook '98* estimates the value of industry shipments for diagnostic substances in 1989 at $2,4 million.

Pioneers and Newsmakers in the Industry

Herbert Boyer

Herbert Boyer, a biochemist and genetic engineer, co-developed recombinant DNA technology, the first fundamental biotechnology, and co-founded one of the first and most successful biotechnology companies in the United States. Born in 1936, he went to college in Latrobe, Pennsylvania and studied biology and chemistry. During his junior year in 1954, Boyer gave his first presentation on the structure of DNA in a cell physiology course. Inspired by genetics and evolution courses he had taken, Boyer abandoned his original idea of becoming a physician. He received his B.S. in 1958, went to graduate school at the University of Pittsburgh, and soon became a passionate bacterial geneticist. After receiving both his M.S. in and Ph.D. in bacteriology in 1960 and 1963 respectively, Boyer did post-graduate work in biochemistry, protein chemistry, and enzymology at Yale University.

In 1966, Boyer became an assistant professor at the University of California in San Francisco (UCSF), where he began to do work in enzymology. While on a trip to Cold Spring Harbor, Boyer met two scientists who showed him an electrophoresed agarose gel containing ethydium bromide stained adenoviral DNA generated by the Eco R1 endonuclease. This technology enabled Boyer to make his breakthrough. He was able to recover DNA strands from E coli, a common bacteria in the intestine. The so-called "sticky ends" that remained could be used to paste pieces of DNA together. At a presentation in Hawaii, Boyer met Stanford scientist Stanley Cohen, who had developed a method of removing plasmids, small ringlets of DNA, from one cell and then reinserting them into other cells. Combining their technologies, the two men were able to recombine segments of DNA which they could insert into bacterial cells. Those cells could then be used to manufacture specific proteins. The breakthrough, called recombinant DNA technology or the molecular cloning of DNA, is the foundation of the biotechnology industry.

In 1976, Boyer was a professor of biochemistry and biophysics at UCSF and the director of the graduate program in genetics. Robert Swanson, a 29-year-old venture capitalist, asked him if it would be possible to develop and market useful products using recombinant DNA technology. The combination of three technologies—chemical synthesis of DNA, the technology to sequence DNA, and the technology of recombinant DNA—made Boyer believe in their commercial potential. Using some venture capital, Boyer and his colleague Art Riggs proved that a gene could be synthesized chemically and inserted into E coli, which could synthesize the human hormone somatostatin.

On April 7, 1976 Robert Swanson and Dr. Herbert Boyer founded Genentech, Inc. Genentech went public in 1980, in one of the largest stock run-ups ever, raising $35 million with an offering that jumped from $35 a share to a high of $88 after less than an hour on the market. Genentech's first recombinant DNA drug, human insulin, was licensed to Eli Lilly and Co. in 1982. Genentech was the first biotechnology firm to launch its own biopharmaceutical product in 1985: human growth hormone (HGH). Many other innovations followed. In 1990, Genentech and Roche Holding Ltd. of Basel, Switzerland merged, a deal worth $2.1 billion. In 1992, Genentech opened the Founders Research Center, the largest biotechnology research facility in the world. Boyer remained vice-president of Genentech from its founding until 1990, when he switched to the Board of Directors.

Eli Lilly

Eli Lilly, an inspirational business leader who made important contributions to the development of the pharmaceutical industry, was associated with his family's business, Eli Lilly and Company, for more than 80 years. Born on April 1, 1885 in Indianapolis, Indiana, he was named after his grandfather Colonel Eli Lilly, who had founded the company nine years earlier. Eli Lilly was ten when he began washing bottles, grinding herbs and washing out calves' stomachs at the family firm. Lilly attended the Philadelphia College of Pharmacy, from which his father had graduated. By the time he earned his degree of pharma-

ceutical chemist, he had worked in many of the company's departments in his spare time.

Eli Lilly entered the company on June 1, 1907 as "roving commissioner of efficiency" and joined the Board of Directors the same year. Lilly's rapid advancement in the following years was based on far more than his family ties, however. He and his brother, J. K. Lilly Jr., initiated a thorough study of the company's production practices in order to introduce systematic management. While his brother established progressive standards and practices in company human relations, Eli Lilly organized time-motion studies, wrote standardized job descriptions, and began giving efficient Lilly employees bonuses. In 1909 he became superintendent of the manufacturing division and was named general superintendent in 1915. In 1919, thanks to his initiative, Eli Lilly and Co. pioneered straight-line production methods in pharmaceutical manufacturing processes. By the time it was fully operational in 1928, the company's output increased by 50 percent while labor turnover was cut by nearly 70 percent.

After becoming vice president in 1920, Eli Lilly gave his approval to the company's director of research to approach two Canadian scientists who had just isolated insulin in 1921. Impressed by Lilly's scientists, its large-scale production capabilities, and its offer to use the full research resources for the project, the University of Toronto agreed to cooperate with the company on the development of injectable insulin. In 1923, Eli Lilly and Co. first introduced insulin commercially to the United States. Eli Lilly went on to organize other unique research ventures including the ground-breaking establishment of a clinical research facility at the Indianapolis City Hospital in 1926, and "scientific fellowships"—formalized grant programs for cooperative research with several universities. As a result of these research efforts, the company discovered the first in a series of barbiturate sedatives and hypnotics, and developed the first liver extract for control of pernicious anemia.

Eli Lilly became company president in 1932. Under his leadership, all 1700 Lilly workers were kept on at full pay during the height of the Great Depression, even if they had to paint walls and fences or wash windows. Under Eli Lilly, the company remained essentially healthy despite the difficult economic times. While other companies were folding, Lilly's sales force grew and a new research facility was built. The company continued its growth during the Second World War, thanks to the mass production of penicillin and other antibiotics. In 1943, Eli Lilly International and Eli Lilly Pan-American were founded to market the firm's products abroad.

In 1948 Eli Lilly resigned the presidency to assume Chairmanship of the Board. In his 16 years as president, company sales increased from $13 million to $117 million a year, while its workforce grew from 1700 to 6900. While Eli Lilly was Board Chairman, the company led in the development of the polio vaccine discovered by Jonas Salk, a drug that virtually eradicated the disease in the United States. Eli Lilly resigned as Chairman in 1961, and took control of the company for three more years on the death of his brother in 1966. When he died on January 24, 1977 at the age of 91, his life had spanned the heroic age of pharmaceuticals. Eli Lilly's determination and foresight turned the family business into an international, billion dollar a year enterprise, whose products were sold in more than 140 countries.

John Wyeth

John Wyeth, born in 1834, laid the groundwork for one of the world's leading ethical drug manufacturers. Instead of joining his family's newspaper business, John Wyeth enrolled at the Philadelphia College of Pharmacy at the age of eighteen, where his teachers recognized John's talent for pharmaceutical research. While in school, he worked part-time for his sponsor, pharmacist Henry C. Blair, who later made him a partner in his business. In 1860, John Wyeth opened a drugstore in Philadelphia with his younger brother Frank Wyeth who had also chosen pharmacy as a career. John Wyeth continued experimenting in the back room of their store, and created an assortment of sweetened tinctures which became popular for their pleasant taste.

The Wyeth brothers were respected by local physicians for their pharmaceutical knowledge as well as their professionalism. Eventually, Dr. John Shoemaker, a prominent Philadelphia physician and friend, asked John Wyeth to produce his favorite medicines in larger quantities, to reduce the amount of time his patients spent waiting for their medicine. Wyeth not only fulfilled Shoemaker's request but convinced other Phi-

ladelphia physicians to buy pre-manufactured medical compounds from his firm. The first *John Wyeth & Brother* catalogue, released in 1862, listed all the elixirs, tonics, and other drug preparations available from the company. The company emerged as a major supplier to the Union Army during the Civil War and, in the 1870s, began exporting their products to England and Canada.

In 1872, Henry Bower, a tablet maker working for John Wyeth & Brother, invented the first rotary tablet press. It replaced the hand press and made possible the mass production of uniformly sized and dosed pills. Over the following years, Wyeth employees refined and improved the tableting technology. In 1877, the Wyeth brothers were awarded a trademark for the term "compressed tablets." They also pioneered other important technologies such as sugar coated tablets, effervescent salts, and soluble gelatin capsules. In 1883, Wyeth opened its first foreign facility in Montreal; in the 1920s it became the first commercially operated biological laboratory in Canada, producing biologically tested cod liver oil. By 1891, John Wyeth and Brother were producing approximately 1 million compressed tablets per day and employed over 400 people, 300 of them women.

The Wyeths' company set quality control standards for the mass production of drugs for the emerging industry. Later company achievements include: the pioneering development of an infant formula patterned after mother's milk; the first orally active estrogen which became the pioneer product for estrogen replacement therapy; the first penicillin tablets; the first effective therapeutic agent for preventing and controlling epileptic seizures; the development of a heat-stable, freeze-dried vaccine and the bifurcated needle, (which led to the worldwide eradication of smallpox); and the first diphtheria/tetanus/acellular pertussis (DTaP) vaccine available in the United States. The Wyeth rotary die tablet press was placed on permanent exhibition in the Smithsonian Institution in Washington, DC, and Wyeth Laboratories Inc. is now part of Wyeth-Ayerst Laboratories, a division of American Home Products Corporation.

Current Conditions, Future Projections

The value of pharmaceutical industry shipments in 1996, according to the *U.S. Annual Survey of Manufacturers*, broke down as follows: **SIC 2833: Medicinals and Botanicals** $8.9 billion; **SIC 2834: Pharmaceutical Preparations** $61.5 billion; **SIC 2835: Diagnostic Substances** $9.7 billion; and **SIC 2836: Biological Products** $6.4 billion. Between 1992 and 1996, shipments of medicinals and botanicals grew by 36 percent; pharmaceutical preparations by 22 percent; diagnostic substances by 41 percent; and for biological products by 60 percent.

IMS Health, a health care information company, reported U.S. pharmaceutical industry sales of approximately $94 billion in 1997—an increase of 11.4 percent from 1996. Over 2.5 billion prescriptions were written by doctors in 1997, a 5 percent increase from 1996. IMS found that the main impetus for growth in the late 1990s could be traced to factors not related to price. Increased prescription volumes, record sales of new products, along with other non-price factors, accounted for over 80 percent of industry growth in 1997. In the same year, more than one third of the industry's growth came from products less than two years old.

AC Nielsen findings cited by the Nonprescription Drug Manufacturers Association (NDMA) showed that OTC retail sales amounted $16.6 billion in 1997. PhRMA projected that sales by research-based pharmaceutical companies would reach $124.6 billion in 1998, an increase of 12.4 percent. Of that, $81.3 billion would be attributable to United States sales by both American and foreign-owned research-based companies. Foreign sales by American companies would account for remaining $43.3 billion.

The *U.S. Industry & Trade Outlook 1998* projected the pharmaceuticals market growth of 8 to 10 percent annually in the coming years, based on growing numbers of elderly people, rising living standards in developing countries, and the discovery of new drugs brought about by intensified research and development. Products for treatment of conditions typical of the elderly, such as hypertension, arthritis, Alzheimer's disease, and depression, are expected to be in especially high demand, together with new treatments for cancer,

AIDS, and other viral diseases. U.S. pharmaceutical preparations shipments are projected to grow up to ten percent in 1999, while drug prices for established drugs are expected to remain stable. Profits of leading brand-name drug manufacturers are projected to grow by an average 12 to 14 percent in the coming few years.

Warner-Lambert Co.'s dollar volume increased 87 percent in 1997, thanks to the release of two best-selling new products. Astra Merck's anti-ulcerant, Prilosec, had the highest dollar volume for a single drug, with sales growing 33 percent in 1997 to $2.28 billion. Eli Lilly and Co.'s Prozac was the number two drug in sales with volumes of $1.94 billion. American Home Products Corp.'s estrogen replacement drug, Premarin, continued to be the nation's most prescribed drug in 1997.

In 1997, 61 new prescription drugs were released, IMS reported. Those drugs had sales of $2.4 billion from 20.4 million prescriptions. Parke-Davis' Lipitor, an anti-cholesterol drug, was the best-selling newcomer with sales of $583 million, giving it 15 percent of the market for cholesterol drugs.

PhRMA reported that five major product types of human prescription drugs accounted for the lion's share of U.S. sales in 1996. Drugs for the central nervous system were the best-selling class with 23.9 percent of the U.S. prescription market; cardiovascular drugs followed with 18.8 percent; drugs for the endocrine system, cancers and metabolic diseases were third with 17.9 percent of U.S. sales; anti-infective drugs accounted for 14.9 percent of the U.S. market; drugs for the digestive and genitourinary system had 14.2 percent of U.S. sales. Other types included respiratory drugs with 7.4 percent of the market, dermatological products with 2.0 percent, and vitamins and nutrients with less than 1 percent. Therapeutic classes that showed significant sales growth in 1997, according to IMS, included anti-psychotics (61 percent increase), oral diabetes medications (50 percent), cholesterol reducers (36 percent), and anti-depressants and specific neurotransmitter modulators (21 percent).

Johnson & Johnson's general pain reliever Tylenol was the number one OTC drug in the U.S. in 1997, according to Kline & Company, generating $664 million retail sales. Other top ten bestsellers included American Home Products' Advil, another general pain reliever; SmithKline Beecham Corp.'s Nicorette and Nicoderm CQ, two smoking cessation aids; and two antacids and anti-gas drugs which, according to *American Druggist*, were both introduced with nearly $100 million advertising campaigns: Pepcid AC introduced in 1995 by Johnson & Johnson and Merck and Company Inc., and Zantac 75 introduced in 1996 by Warner-Lambert Co.

The Center for Veterinary Medicine (CVM) approved 102 new animal-related drugs in 1997; 37 of them for generic drugs. Five of the six NCEs approved were for dogs.

Consumption, Distribution, Promotion

The U.S. Department of Commerce reported that consumer spending on prescription drugs, in relation to other items, is relatively low. Per capita expenditures on pharmaceuticals in 1997 averaged 64 cents a day compared to expenditures of $7.94 a day for food, $2.84 for clothing, and $1.07 for telephone services. American outpatient drug expenditures in 1996 totaled approximately $62.2 billion. Of that, about 34 percent were out-of-pocket payments by consumers.

Most of the 2.5 billion prescriptions in 1997, were dispensed in chain pharmacies (51 percent), independent pharmacies (29 percent), and pharmacies in food stores (11 percent), according to IMS Health. Retail stores accounted for more than 60 percent of dollar sales of American prescriptions. Hospital pharmacies comprised 14 percent of the market, mail-order pharmacies 11 percent, and clinics 6 percent. The number of pharmacies has remained steady between 1987 and 1997 according to the National Council on Prescription Drug Programs (NCPDP). NCPDP reports however that chain pharmacies are gradually replacing independent pharmacies in the Unites States.

IMS reported that $4.2 billion were spent for pharmaceutical promotion in the U.S. in 1997, 67 percent of which were spent for sales activities directed toward office-based physicians. About 14.6 percent were spent for sales activities directed to hospital-based physicians. Advertising in medical journals for ethical, ethical OTC, and proprietary products normally prescribed or recommended by physicians accounted for 13.4 percent of the 1997 total. 5 percent, or about $214

million was spent on direct-to-consumer television advertising for prescription products. Following revised FDA TV advertising guidelines, allowing companies to advertise brand name and indication in the same commercial, IMS expects the industry's investment for TV advertising to double.

An invisible effect on the pharmaceutical industry comes from patients who do not comply with doctors' instructions. The National Pharmaceutical Council estimated that patients who do not have prescriptions filled result in losses of about $25 billion to pharmacies and $15 to $20 billion to manufacturers every year.

Managed Health Care

After record annual earnings growth of an average 18 percent between 1987 and 1990, operating profit growth of leading ethical drug companies dropped 8 to 10 percent between 1991 and 1993, according to *U.S. Industry & Trade Outlook 1998*. In addition to worldwide efforts to cut health care costs, this was primarily the result of fundamental changes in the U.S. marketplace caused by political pressure to keep drug prices low and by the appearance of a new force with tremendous buying power: managed health care organizations. Consequently, profit growth was achieved by cost cutting rather than by price increases.

According to PhRMA, nearly 80 percent of all working Americans participate in a managed health care plan, for example a health maintenance organization (HMO)or a preferred provider organization (PPO). Managed-care organizations use a various means of controlling costs, and many are directed specifically at pharmaceutical expenses. About 90 percent of HMOs base their prescription coverage on lists of approved drugs known as formularies. If an HMOs uses an "open" formulary, all drugs, both listed and non-listed, are reimbursed; if coverage is based on a "closed" formulary, only listed drugs are eligible for reimbursement. Closed formularies often limit reimbursement for new, more expensive and experimental drugs. In 1996, around 31 percent of HMOs used closed formularies, 27 percent higher than in 1995, according to a *Hoechst Marion Roussel Managed Care Digest.*

HMOs limit pharmaceutical costs by other means as well. One cost-reducing measure is therapeutic interchange. With therapeutic interchange, a drug with a different chemical composition, though usually of the therapeutic class, is substituted for the drug prescribed. Only about 18 percent of HMOs use therapeutic interchange and its use has declined through the 1990s. Another cost-reducing measure, Step-Care Therapy, requires doctors to work through a prescribed sequence of treatments or drugs, generally starting with cheapest and moving on to more expensive if earlier ones fail. HMOs often require generic substitution for brand-name drugs and regularly review physician prescription patterns.

In attempts to avoid expensive surgical procedures, shorten hospital stays, and reduce the number of doctor office visits and nursing home admissions, managed care organizations encourage the use of prescription drugs that are efficient as well as cost-effective. The market dominated by managed care offers certain other advantages to pharmaceutical companies as well. Since HMOs frequently replace individual physicians as the target group for marketing activities, sales staff can be cut back significantly.

Older Americans will be a primary factor in the growing demand for prescription drugs. *U.S. Industry & Trade Outlook 1998* cited the findings of recent drug utilization studies that Medicare patients in HMO plans use about three times as many prescriptions as patients under age 65. Current demographic trends indicate that the number of persons over age 65 could grow by 17 percent from 1996 through 2010.

Government (through the Medicaid program, veterans' hospitals, the Defense Department, various state-run assistance programs for senior citizens, and AIDS drug assistance programs) is an important purchaser of pharmaceuticals. Government programs usually require price control measures for prescription drugs. These include rebates, discounts, caps on prices, limits on price increases and restricting eligibility. In 1998, Medicaid rebates are projected to be $2 billion in 1998 but they have leveled off as many Medicaid recipients join managed-care programs.

IMS Health reports that 71 percent of all retail outpatient drug sales were paid for by various third-party sources, insurance companies, HMOs Medicaid and the like. That share increased 37 percent from 1990, although most of the rise was accounted for by private

organizations—Medicaid's portion has remained steady since the beginning of the 1990s.

The trend toward more strict management of insurance benefits has also given rise to a new breed of company, pharmacy benefit managers (PBMs). PBMs specialize in pharmaceutical care; their services are used by employers, insurance companies, Medicaid and the like. They manage drug benefits for about 50 percent of insured Americans. Five of the approximately 40 PBMs in the United States account for over 75 percent of the market. More and more, since the early 1990s, the largest PBMs have been absorbed by or formed strategic alliances with major pharmaceutical companies.

Legislation

The FDA Modernization Act of 1997 extended the Prescription Drug User Fee Act of 1992. That law established a schedule of fees paid by the pharmaceutical industry that totaled $327 million between 1993 and 1997. The monies were used by the FDA to hire 600 additional drug review personnel. PhRMA estimates that some $550 million in fees will be paid out over the next five years. The new law was expected to reduce the length of drug approvals by as much as a year. In 1996, the FDA approved 65 percent more new drugs and biological products than in the previous year, according to *U.S. Industry & Trade Outlook 1998*, and general approval times were significantly shorter.

The Animal Drug Availability Act of 1996 permitted the FDA to waive the requirement that every new product be investigated if the new product could be shown to have "substantial equivalence" to an already approved drug. The law created a new class of "veterinary feed directive drugs," drugs which would be used in animal feed, largely without veterinary supervision.

Consolidation

According to the latest U.S. Census of Manufacturers (in 1992), there were 209 companies active in **SIC 2833: Medicinals and Botanicals**, 578 companies in **SIC 2834: Pharmaceutical Preparations**, 207 companies in **SIC 2835: Diagnostic Substances**, and 197 firms in **SIC 2836: Biological Products**.

However, in response to shortened product life, the pressure to lower costs, and greater research opportunities, the pharmaceutical industry is consolidating heavily. Companies whose drug patents are about to expire and who will not be able to launch new products soon, are looking for strong partners. Companies that merge gain competitive advantages in the managed healthcare environment by offering a broader product range, combining R&D and marketing power, and cutting costs through economies of scale. *U.S. Industry & Trade Outlook 1998* estimated that restructuring, downsizing, and consolidation programs resulted in industry-wide cost reductions of more than $8.5 billion, and worldwide elimination of approximately 60,000 jobs between 1995 and 1997. Between 1986 and 1997, strategic alliances increased from 121 to 635. They involved a broad range of organizations, for example domestic and foreign pharmaceutical companies, biotech firms, university research centers, and contract research organizations.

Generic Competition

Pharmaceutical competition is intensifying. The time a first drug in a new therapeutic class goes unchallenged is shrinking. Competitors often appear within a few months of the first drug's release. Generic drug manufacturers also present intense competition to brand-name manufacturers. When new drug approval delays are taken into account, the useful length of a patent shrinks from 20 years to about 12 years. Generic companies are not handicapped by long and expensive research and development processes, nor by lengthy FDA drug approvals. They must merely wait until a patent has expired, then show that their generic copies are bioequivalent to gain immediate market approval. Immediately after patent expiration of brand name drugs, generic drug companies offer drugs at prices 60 percent to 90 percent lower than the brand name's list price, according to the Department of Commerce.

Between 1984 and 1997 generic drugs' share of the prescription market increased from 18.6 to 44.3 percent. Patents for a large number of significant brand drugs are due to expire during the next decade; this should lead to further growth in the generics industry. Grabowski and Vernon found that when an originator drug lost patent protection between 1989 and 1990, within 18 months generics had taken over 47 percent of its market. In 1991-1992, generics won 72 percent

of new markets within 18 months. Low cost is expected to lead to continuous growth of this industry segment and *U.S. Industry & Trade Outlook 1998* estimates that the market share of generics will reach nearly 66 percent by 2000.

In the early 1990s, many brand companies attempted to organize generic divisions. Unable to match the broad product lines offered by generic companies and lacking the generics' market savvy, the brand companies shifted their strategies. They began buying generic companies outright or negotiated agreements with them to market generics and the brand companies' proprietary drugs. Milton Bass of the NAPM predicted in *American Druggist* that brand companies will soon control about 95 percent of the generic drug market and that they have already begun bringing out their own generic versions weeks before their patents expire.

Diagnostic and Biological Pharmaceuticals

More than 500 companies were engaged in developing new diagnostic tests in the United States in 1997. However, the *U.S. Industry & Trade Outlook 1998* reported that only about 15 companies from the United States and Europe, such as Abbott Laboratories (United States), Bayer AG (Germany), Boehringer Mannheim Diagnostics (Germany), Hoffmann-La Roche AG (Switzerland), and Johnson & Johnson (United States), generated 75 percent of worldwide diagnostic substances sales. The domestic diagnostic products market was particularly influenced by mushrooming managed care organizations and accompanying consolidation of health care institutions. Hospitals, clinics, and laboratories requested lower prices for diagnostic products from suppliers. Products capable of handling larger test volumes in a shorter time—thereby cutting down labor cost or patient hospital stays—were also in high demand. Between 1992 and 1995, diagnostics industry shipments had grown from $6.8 billion to $9.5 billion, and were expected to reach $13 billion by 2002.

The OTC home diagnostic test sales grew much faster than the rest of the industry. Sales growth of 10 percent a year is expected, fueled by the aging of the population and increased awareness of personal health. Home test kits are mostly easy to use and guarantee privacy. Johnson & Johnson's One Touch diabetes test kit was the second best selling OTC drug in 1997, generating $341 million in retail sales, according to Kline & Company. IMS reported that blood glucose tests as a therapeutic class generated $992 million in 1997, a 9 percent increase from 1996. Other popular home tests included kits for HIV, pregnancy, ovulation and cholesterol. Another fast growing segment in the diagnostics market were biological tests, using monoclonal antibodies, genetic amplification, and DNA probes, for example.

The U.S. Bureau of Commerce estimated that biological pharmaceuticals, including 16 new drugs, 1 vaccine, several in vivo and hundreds of in vitro diagnostic tests on the market, accounted for $8.9 million in 1996. According to PhRMA, the largest increases are expected in gene therapy and vaccines. National and international pharmaceutical companies have acquired or formed alliances with U.S. biotech firms to get access to state-of-the art technologies and genetic research results, particularly in the new fields of genomics and gene therapy. *Industry Week*'s Tim Stevens pointed out that only 3 biotech companies, Amgen Inc., Genzyme Corp., and Biogen Inc., independently marketed a product under their own label in 1997. Other significant biotech companies offering brand-name products were fully or partially owned by large pharmaceutical companies., such as Genetics Institute Inc. by American Home Products Corp., Genentech Inc. by Hoffmann-La Roche AG, and Chiron Corp. by Novartis AG.

The U.S. Department of Commerce forecasts biological pharmaceutical revenues growing by at least 10 percent annually until the end of the decade. PhRMA stated that the FDA has approved a total of 50 new biological therapeutics and vaccines. Another 350 biotechnology medicines are under development.

Industry Leaders

Bristol-Myers Squibb

Bristol-Myers Squibb Co. is a leading company in both pharmaceuticals and over-the-counter (OTC) drugs. Product of a 1989 merger of Bristol Myers Company and Squibb Corporation, it overtook Glaxo Wellcome, PLC. in the lead in dollar sales for pharmaceuticals in 1997, according to IMS America, holding

more than 6 percent of the U.S. pharmaceuticals market.

Squibb Corporation founded in 1856 in Brooklyn, New York, by Edward Robinson Squibb, committed itself to the manufacture of the purest pharmaceuticals possible. In 1944, Squibb opened the world's largest plant (at that time) for the manufacture of penicillin. In 1946 it began international expansion with the incorporation of Squibb International and the construction of plants in Mexico, South America and Europe.

The Bristol-Myers Company was incorporated in 1899, in Clinton, New York. Its first successes early in the century, were OTC products: mineral water and a disinfectant toothpaste. By the time the company went public in 1929, its products were being sold in 26 countries. Instituting a program of acquiring successful smaller companies, Bristol-Myers entered a period of growth in the mid-1950s.

When Bristol-Myers and Squibb merged in 1989, they created the second largest pharmaceutical company at the time. Bristol-Myers Squibb is comprised of three core business groups: Worldwide Medicines, Nutritionals & Medical Devices, and Worldwide Beauty Care. Worldwide Medicines is responsible for the company's pharmaceutical and OTC products. Bristol-Myers Squibb had operations in over 50 countries in 1998, selling their products throughout the world.

According to the Bristol-Myers Squibb's 1997 annual report, its most important pharmaceuticals are medications for cardiovascular, metabolic and infectious disease, skin and central nervous system disorders, and cancer. The pharmaceutical segment's $9.93 billion in sales represented 59 percent of the company's total $16.7 billion in sales in 1997, up 15 percent from the previous year. In 1997 U.S. sales increased 23 percent, international sales grew 13 percent.

Cardiovascular drugs led the pharmaceutical segment in 1997 sales with $2.9 billion, up 3 percent from the year before. Pravachol, a cholesterol-lowering agent, was Bristol-Myers Squibb's best-selling product in 1997 with $1.4 billion in worldwide sales. Taxol, a cancer drug, generated $941 million and Glucophage, a medication for people with type 2 non-insulin-dependent diabetes, $579 million in 1997.

Worldwide Consumer Medicines, Bristol-Myers Squibb's OTC segment, produced pain management, women's health care, and skin care products, cough and cold remedies, and vitamins. Its leading OTC product, Exedrin, led 3 percent growth in sales of analgesics. In January 1998, the FDA approved Exedrin Migraine, the first and only non-prescription migraine remedy permitted in the U.S. market.

Pfizer Inc.

Founded in 1849 in New York as Charles Pfizer and Company, Pfizer Inc. made its way from a manufacturer of bulk chemicals up the ranks of the ethical pharmaceutical industry, pioneering antibiotics research and mass production in the middle of the 20th century until it dominated the headlines in 1998 with the spectacular market introduction of Viagra, the first impotency drug approved by the FDA.

According to an IMS America ranking, In 1997 Pfizer was number 6 in the U.S. with domestic pharmaceutical sales of $4.92 billion and number 7 worldwide with pharmaceutical sales $8.4 billion. Pfizer consists broadly of its Central Research division, founded in 1950, the Consumer Health Care Group which manufactures OTC products, and Disease Management Division produces anti-infective agents, psychotropic and cardiology drugs.

In the 1980s potential problems were arising. Feldene, Pfizer's best-selling drug for arthritis, was scheduled to go off patent and the company had no replacement ready for approval, wrote David Stipp in *Fortune.* In response to the looming crisis, Pfizer began spending 15 percent of its sales on R&D. The move resulted in a rash of discoveries in the Pfizer labs: Norvasc, the best-selling hypertension drug in 1997, Zoloft, a hypertension drug with expected sales around $2 billion in 1998, and Trovan, an antibiotic that can be used to treat 14 kinds of infections, the most versatile of any new drug.

Pfizer's labs are among the most efficient in the industry. According to *Fortune*'s David Stipp, they require less than a third of the industry average time to bring a compound from its initial conception to clinical trials. Pfizer owes part of its development success to the fact that rather than do all testing in house, it farms out much of the work to smaller companies.

Pfizer's most sensational discovery was Viagra. The drug was originally under development as a heart medication. In 1992 an unexpected side effect was discovered during clinical tests: Viagra caused increased erections. As a result, Pfizer changed the focus of research and began developing Viagra as a treatment for impotence. The drug was first marketed in March 1998. In the first three months it was prescribed 2.9 million times, resulting in $259.5 million in sales, a record for a new prescription drug. IMS forecast record sales of $1 billion for Viagra in its first year.

At the same time it boosted its R&D, Pfizer eliminated non-core businesses, and enlarging its sales department to 14,500 in 1997—the largest in the industry according to Cowen & Co. IMS reports that, in 1996, physicians rated Pfizer number two in the industry for sales performance and reputation. Using its sales strength, Pfizer began forging alliances to promote drugs developed by other companies as well as its own. In 1997 Pfizer and Warner-Lambert launched Liptor, a cholesterol-lowering medication which racked up $865 million its first year on the market, a record for first-year sales. Other joint releases include Aricept, an Alzheimer's drug launched with Eisai, a Japanese company, and Celebra, an arthritis medication developed by G.D. Searle.

Johnson & Johnson

Johnson & Johnson, the world leader in OTC product sales in November 1996, was incorporated in 1887 by Robert Wood Johnson and his two brothers, James Wood Johnson and Edward Mead Johnson. Recognizing the demand for antiseptic surgical supplies early, the company designed and mass-produced soft, absorbent, cotton and gauze dressings and adhesive medical plasters in New Brunswick, New Jersey. By 1910, Johnson & Johnson was an established health care firm. In 1924, the first overseas affiliate, Johnson & Johnson Ltd., was created in Great Britain. In the 1930s, Robert Wood Johnson, the son of the founder, who carried his father's name, began decentralizing the company, creating a number of relatively autonomous divisions and affiliates. The policy was continued over the years, and as sections of the company grew they were made divisions or subsidiaries themselves.

In 1959 McNeil Laboratories, Inc., a producer of prescription pharmaceuticals, was acquired and later split into McNeil Pharmaceutical and McNeil Consumer Products Company, the maker of top selling OTC pain reliever Tylenol. Lifescan, a company that specialized in home blood tests for diabetics, was acquired in 1986. It entered a joint venture with Merck Consumer Pharmaceuticals Co. in 1989 to develop and market non-prescription products. Johnson & Johnson formed their own biotechnology company with Ortho Biotech in 1990 and in 1993 Ortho-McNeil Pharmaceutical was formed.

A Kodak clinical diagnostic division, acquired in 1994 and later named Johnson & Johnson Clinical Diagnostics, joined Johnson & Johnson's other diagnostics businesses, including Ortho Diagnostic Systems, Inc., LifeScan and Advanced Care Products. The company sells diagnostic products to laboratories and for home use; they are used to diagnose diabetes, asthma, liver conditions, and strep A, and other conditions. Johnson & Johnson launched a major OTC product in 1995—Pepcid AC, the first new antacid in more than 100 years.

Expanding internationally since the 1930s, Johnson & Johnson became a worldwide conglomerate of more than 180 companies in 51 countries, marketing health care products in more than 175 countries in 1998. The Company's approximately 91,400 employees—42,900 of them in the United States—were engaged in three business segments, consumer, professional, and pharmaceutical. Pharmaceuticals were, in general, sold under the Janssen Pharmaceutical, McNeil Pharmaceutical, or Ortho Pharmaceutical brands, not Johnson & Johnson.

Amgen

Amgen, in 1998 the largest independent biotechnology company, develops and markets human therapeutic agents based on its work in cellular and molecular biology. The company started out as AMGen (Applied Molecular Genetics Inc.) in California in 1980. Active in therapeutics based on cellular and molecular biology, it began formal operations in 1981 at Thousand Oaks, close to major Southern Californian research centers, with approximately $19 million in capital and seven employees. Public stock offerings on NASDAQ

in 1983, 1986 and 1987 boosted Amgen's capital base and between 1989 and 1992, it established clinical, marketing and sales operations in Europe, Australia, Canada, Hong Kong, and Japan. When sales hit $1 billion in 1992, Amgen joined the *Fortune* 500, ranked at number 427.

In 1987, Amgen patented the DNA used in its first product Epogen, a stimulator for the production of red blood cells, to treat anemia associated with renal failure, which was approved by the FDA in 1989. That same year, Amgen's second product Neupogen, an immune system stimulator, was patented in the United States and received FDA marketing approval in 1991 first for use in cancer chemotherapy, and later for other indications. The company's third product, Infergen, is a bioengineered interferon for chronic hepatitis. The FDA gave it marketing clearance in October 1997.

Amgen continued its strong growth in the mid 1990s. Revenues increased from $2.2 billion in 1996 to $2.4 billion in 1994. Net income in 1997 was $645 million. According to IMS, both Epogen and Neupogen had 1997 sales of approximately $1 billion. Its worldwide staff which numbered 479 in 1988 and 1084 in 1990, had increased to 5400 by late 1997, with 3500 employees at the Thousand Oaks headquarters alone.

Amgen has forged research and marketing alliances throughout the world, with Rockefeller University, the Massachusetts Institute of Technology, Guilford Pharmaceuticals, and Yamanouchi, the pharmaceutical unit of the Japanese Kirin Brewery, and the Swiss giant F. Hoffmann-LaRoche AG, to name a few. These moves enabled Amgen Inc. to stay ahead of its competitors in the biotech market. Amgen also reinvests a sizable portion of its revenues in research. Amgen's research efforts have been focused on blood cell production, inflammation and auto-immunity, neurobiology, and soft tissue repair and its genome division has made important contributions to cancer therapy.

Work Force

Once considered "recession proof," the pharmaceutical industry went into a period of unprecedented downsizing in the 1990s, a trend which had a profound impact upon its workforce. According to Bureau of Labor Statistics cited by PhRMA, employment in the industry grew at a rate of 2.9 percent between 1983 and 1993. The industry workforce peaked in 1993 at 264,400; over the next four years, however, it declined by nearly 2 percent to 260,300 industry workers.

The *Wall Street Journal* estimated industry-wide job losses between 1991 and 1994 at 22 percent. According to PhRMA, as part of mergers and acquisitions, large pharmaceutical companies downsized about one fifth of their workforce, resulting in the elimination of approximately 57,820 jobs between 1991 and 1995. Glaxo Wellcome PLC. alone cut 7,000 jobs during that period, Pharmacia & Upjohn Inc. cut 4,100, and American Home Products Corp. eliminated over 11,000 jobs after acquiring American Cyanamid Co., according to *Wall Street Journal* figures cited in *Pfizer Journal*. On the other hand, the growing biotechnology sector is creating new job opportunities.

In 1996, according to the 1997 *Annual Survey of Manufacturers*, 231,200 employees were on the drug industry's payroll in 1996, about half of them production workers. The majority of those—136,900—were active in Pharmaceutical Preparations (SIC 2834), a sector whose workforce is about 53 percent production workers. The Medicinals and Botanicals segment (SIC 2833) employed about 7.9 percent of the drug industry workforce—16,800 people. The Diagnostic Substances sector (SIC 2835) employed 39,000 people in 1996, 18.7 percent of the drug industry's total. Production workers constituted about 39 percent of this field. Finally, 19,600 people, or 9.2 percent of all drug industry employees, worked in the Biological Products sector (SIC 2836).

Important professions employed by the pharmaceutical industry include chemists, biologists, pharmacists and medical research staff. Depending on the point in the manufacturing cycle and the industry sector, there are numerous areas of specialization. In his book *Innovation in the Pharmaceutical Industry*, David Schwartzman found that Pfizer Inc. distinguished nine different classes of specialists in their research laboratories in the 1970s, which were broken down further into 35 subspecialties. They included for example: medical, analytical, and process chemists; research biologists such as biochemists, immunologists, microbiologists, toxicologists and pathologists; clinical researchers including medical monitors (M.D.'s), statisticians, data processors, and FDA liaisons; and

administrative staff such as research administrators, technical librarians, information research specialists, and data coordinators.

With the rapid growth in the biotechnology sector, demand for molecular biologists should rise; the application of information technology in research processes will create new opportunities for computer specialists. The new field of bioinformatics—the analysis of data from experiments, databases, instrumentation and other sources to generate computer models of biological systems—has created a new profession that may be studied at universities.

Since a pharmaceutical company's success depends to a large degree on the number of potential new products it has in the pipeline, clinical research will also be in high demand. A diverse team is needed to plan, conduct, monitor, analyze, and write about clinical trials; this will provide opportunities for individuals with a solid life science or health care background, detail-orientation, and good interpersonal skills. Positions available on clinical trials include project managers, medical investigators, study coordinators, clinical research associates, data managers, biostatisticians, and medical writers. Because much of the knowledge and skills required are learned on the job, the ability to understand procedures quickly is necessary. Data coordinators skilled in software and systems write computer programs which catalog and manipulate the hundreds or thousands of patient experiences recorded for the trial. Biostatisticians who analyze the data often have an M.S. or Ph.D. degree. Clinical trials are run by traditional pharmaceutical firms as well as by biotech companies. M. E. Watanabe wrote in *The Scientist* that more and more pharmaceutical companies were outsourcing clinical trials to Clinical research organizations (CROs). CROs thus provide most of the new employment opportunities in the clinical trials area.

A salary survey conducted by MedZilla, a recruiter in biotech, pharmaceutical, and medical industries, in 1995, indicated that entry level positions for people without a college degree started at about $20,000 annually and, after ten years in the industry, ranged from $36,000 to $72,000. Entry level positions for B.A.'s, M.A.'s, and M.B.A.'s started at about $24,000, according to the survey, while Ph.D.'s started slightly higher at about $29,000. After 10 years industry experience, annual salaries reached $60,000 to $80,000 on average. Salaries for M.D.'s varied heavily, most likely depending on different work and research experience. They started anywhere from $32,000 to over $100,000, increasing to $70,000 to over $200,000 after 10 years of industry experience. *The Scientist* reported that project managers and clinical research assistants positions often start in the upper $30,000s. Biostatisticians, Ph.D.s or people with the appropriate experience start close to $50,000. According to *U.S. Industry and Trade Outlook 1998*, employees in the Diagnostic Substances sector (SIC 2835) earned $18.31 per hour on average in 1995, compared with an average of $16.03 per hour for the Drug Industry (SIC 283) as a whole.

Compensation also varies depending on company location. A new study of the California biomedical R&D industry, conducted by California Healthcare Institute (CHI) and KPMG Peat Marwick, LLP (KPMG), showed that the 29,000, workers employed by one of the 322 healthcare technology organizations in Silicon Valley earned an average salary of $70,103 in 1997, the highest wage for the industry of all regions in California. The study estimated that 61 percent of those organizations were primarily active in R&D on medical devices and diagnostics, while 33 percent focused on biotechnology and pharmaceutical R&D.

North America and the World

The U.S. Pharmaceutical industry is becoming more and more multinational. Major companies develop, manufacture, and market their products throughout the world. According to Jean-Charles Tschudin in *Pharmaceutical Executive,* the world pharmaceutical market enjoyed steady growth of 5.6 percent in 1993, 6 percent in 1994, and 8 percent in 1995. *U.S. Industry & Trade Outlook 1998* estimated the global pharmaceutical market at over $320 billion in 1996 and forecast growth rates of 8 to 10 percent over the next few years, based on two assumptions: one, that—compared with other measures—relatively low-cost pharmaceuticals will often be the first step in medical therapy throughout the world, and two, that standards of living will further improve in Latin America, the Asia-Pacific Rim region, and Eastern Europe. IMS expected worldwide prescription drug sales to reach $308 billion in 1998, and an 8 percent annual rate of global market growth from 1998 through 2002. For all European markets, IMS forecast growth between 1997 and 1998

to range from low single-digit to low double-digit rates when measured in constant dollars. However, IMS reports of Latin American and Asian markets "growing at high single-digit rates, while Japan remained down slightly" in terms of constant dollars in mid-September 1998 were made when the financial crisis in Japan, Asia, and Latin America had just begun. Its influence on the global pharmaceutical market remained an open question.

Cath Blackledge, in a 1998 story in *The European,* wrote that a quarter of the world's top 20 medicines had been developed in Great Britain, including Pfizer's Viagra. He reported that Pfizer, Inc. was one of the largest investors in the United Kingdom with $1.19 billion investments into Pfizer's R&D facility in Sandwich, Kent, since 1990.

According to IMS data, the United States was the world's largest market for pharmaceuticals accounting for one-third of global pharmaceutical sales in 1996, followed by Europe with over 29 percent, and Japan with almost 18 percent. However, according to OECD health data, per-capita spending for pharmaceuticals, measured in 1997 purchasing power parity, was higher in France at $328 than in the United States at $307.

From 1980 to 1995, innovative U.S. firms were able to globalize—i.e. launch in the U.S., Europe, and Japan—23 percent of their new drug products, according to a report by C. E. Lumley and S. Dorabjee cited by PhRMA, as compared to a rate of 11 percent by European companies and 4 percent of Japanese firms.

In the rapidly growing field of biotechnology, U.S. companies have a commanding lead in patenting their innovations. The 1996 *PhRMA Annual Patent Survey* showed that of the 150 genetic engineering health-care patents issued by the U.S. Patent and Trademark Office in 1995, 122 went to U.S. applicants, 11 to applicants from European countries, and 6 to Japanese applicants.

The United States accounted for about 40 percent of global diagnostics output in 1996, according to *U.S. Industry & Trade Outlook 1998*. U.S. diagnostics manufacturers exported 20 percent of their output in 1996, worth approximately $1.9 billion. They increased exports by more than 8 percent, resulting in a positive trade balance of $1.3 billion. 84 percent of U.S. exports were shipped to Western Europe, Japan, and Canada. Germany, the next largest force in worldwide diagnostics production accounted for a quarter of global output.

According to PhRMA data, U.S.-owned companies conducted 75 percent of their overseas research in Western Europe and 13 percent in Japan in 1994. Smaller but growing R&D centers were found in Latin America, and Australia.

As the world's largest pharmaceutical market and the only market not subject to governmental price controls, the United States is targeted by many foreign drug manufacturers. International companies with major presence in the U.S. pharmaceutical market of the late 1990s were mostly based in Europe and Japan, and had their own operations in the United States or acquired U.S. firms.

According to the NDMA, six of the world's top ten OTC drug manufacturers were based in the U.S. The United States and Germany alone accounted for about 50 percent of the worldwide OTC market. According to Jean-Charles Tschudin writing in *Pharmaceutical Executive,* reasons for this dominance were regulatory restrictions and limitations on mass media access by pharmaceutical companies in other countries.

Tschudin also wrote that the market for generic drugs is becoming a worldwide phenomenon. In Germany generics sales increased more than 50 percent in 1995. Demand has even spread to countries where drugs are low in price, such as Portugal and France. Retail sales of generics throughout the world are expected to undergo significant growth by the end of the millennium. Sales of $21 billion by the year 2000 have been predicted, according to Tschudin. European sales should represent some 14 percent of that market, up from 9 percent in the mid-1990s.

The pharmaceutical industry is confronted with widely varying and complex regulations in the global market. National governments—often the largest purchasers of pharmaceuticals—use their power to control drug prices, directly or indirectly, according to PhRMA. Methods include price freezes, establishment of drug prices by governments, reductions for bulk purchases, or government pre-approval of drug prices. Sometimes national governments force pharmaceutical companies

to make investments in the country. In Europe, delays between drug approval and market introduction, delays caused by price- and cost-control mechanisms, can be up to 12 months, PhRMA reported. Tschudin wrote in *Pharmaceutical Executive* that French and German legislators "are even planning prescription bar-code systems to evaluate and control what doctors prescribe ... gradually replacing the free initiative of individual physicians to prescribe."

An average of 22 percent of drug sales that are reimbursable by national authorities are for drugs still under patent. A problem arises when governments take advantage of regulated differences in drug prices in other nations and promote parallel imports to obtain cheaper pharmaceuticals. This practice interferes with pharmaceutical trade first by subjecting drugs to price controls and second by undercutting sales of drugs by domestic manufacturers. Most patented pharmaceuticals are protected from parallel importation. South Africa, Israel and Singapore are markets where parallel importation poses a threat to free pharmaceutical trade.

As pharmaceutical companies more and more take on a global character, the issue of effective protection of patents throughout the world takes on growing importance. A system that would harmonize the registration and approval process for drugs in Europe, the U.S., and Japan has been proposed by the International Conference on Harmonization. According to PhRMA, however, the issue is even more critical for pharmaceutical companies in developing countries.

Another potential problem, described by Henry I. Miller in the *Los Angeles Times,* involves an agreement between the U.S. and the European Union (EU) to accept each other's product testing and certification. The agreement would require the United States to recognize all standards recognized by the EU, even by EU members whose standards are significantly lower than those in the United States. Miller pointed out that the agreement could lead to a decline in pharmaceutical safety and to a loss of facilities in the U.S. when manufacturers move factories to countries with less stringent regulation.

Research and Technology

Research is extremely important to the pharmaceutical industry. According to the *U.S. Industry & Trade Outlook 1998* the pharmaceutical industry in the United States spends an average of ten times more on research than other American industries. The reasons for this are clear. According to estimates of Congressional Office of Technology Assessment (OTA) and the Boston Consulting Group, in the early 1990s it cost between $359 million and $500 million to develop and get approval for a new drug. What's more, only three out of 10 drug products approved ever recover their R&D costs, according to PhRMA. Research costs have increased significantly over the past twenty years. In 1980 about 11.9 percent of sales revenues were spent on research; by 1990, the figure had nearly doubled, reaching 20 percent. PhRMA's 1998 industry profile indicated that the R&D expenditures of research-based companies more than doubled between 1990 and 1998. PhRMA projected that in 1998 $17.2 billion would be spent in the United States by American and foreign-owned firms, in addition to another $3.8 billion spent abroad by U.S.-owned firms in 1998. those expenditures would represent a 10.8 percent increase over 1997.

The search for new products accounts for nearly 84 percent of all R&D expenses in the U.S.; the rest is aimed at improving or modifying already developed products. Approximately 40 percent of R&D budgets are spent on pre-clinical research. Eleven percent goes toward the extraction or synthesis of potentially useful new compounds. Another 16 percent is spent to screen and evaluate the thousands of new compounds that are developed every year, a small fraction of which will ever be further developed. Toxicology tests, dosage formation and stability tests altogether account for approximately 15 percent of R&D costs

In 1996 about 23 percent of pharmaceutical research dollars were targeted at problems of the central nervous system and sensory organs, including Alzheimer's disease, Parkinson's disease, schizophrenia, depression, and epilepsy. Some 21 percent was spent on products affecting neoplasms, metabolic diseases and the endocrine system. Typical diseases include cancer, osteoporosis, and diabetes. Cardiovascular disease accounted for 15 percent, research on parasitic and infectious disease, including antibiotics and anti-viral com-

pounds 14 percent of R&D expenditures. Seven percent was spent on product for respiratory problems such as asthma. Four percent was spent on biological products, such as vaccines. According to PhRMA estimates, pharmaceutical companies spent $900 million for research on new biologicals, $100 million on new diagnostic agents, and $500 million on new veterinary pharmaceuticals in 1996.

Future R&D funds depend on companies' success in discovering, patenting and bringing a steady stream of new products to market. In 1998, according to PhRMA, there were about 500 distinct targets for drug interventions. The organization expected that number to increase to between 3,000 and 10,000 in the next few years.

Traditional labor-intensive and paper-based research processes—the so-called "pipeline"—are being replaced more and more by a combination of automated research and information technology. Global computer networks transmit data back and forth between research laboratories, clinical trial sites, manufacturing plants, and sales staff, while customized software helps streamline official approval processes.

Technological breakthroughs in new compound development provide countless potential drugs. But, a great deal of money is required to develop that potential into a marketable product. And with new drug discovery accelerating at a breakneck pace, companies must crank out increasing numbers of new drugs to keep pace with their competitors. Even when important new discoveries are made, state-of-the-art techniques enable rivals to duplicate them quickly.

Robochemistry

The most important recent development in pharmaceutical R&D is a process called robochemistry. Still in its infancy as a technique, robochemistry is essentially the mechanization, computerization and miniaturization of chemical research. The application of these techniques to pharmaceutical R&D accelerates development time one thousand-fold. In 1995, according to *Fortune* writer David Stipp, a compound required 190 person-years of work to move from conception to its first clinical trials. A large research staff is lucky to develop 50 promising new compounds in a year. Complicating development even further, Stipp wrote that only one compound in seven million screened by researchers ever reaches marketable product stage.

Robochemistry, as it is being developed by the pharmaceutical industry, involves four elements: genomics, high-throughput screening, combinatorial chemistry, and bioinformatics. Genomics studies the structure and function of the genes that relate to a particular condition. It may be a gene in an intruding virus, like the AIDS virus, a gene that predisposes an individual to a disease, or a gene responsible for production of an essential hormone such as insulin. Function is established by comparing genes using gene sequencing technology and gene databases.

Pharmaceutical companies screen public sources such as the federal government's Human Genome Project and create company-internal gene databases. They may also team up with specialized genomic firms, or license technology from them and pay royalties on any drugs that result. Zina Moukheiber noted in *Forbes,* that laboratories needed two months to sequence the 150 nucleotides that make up a single gene. In the late 1990s it was possible to sequence 11 million nucleotides a day, vastly increasing research efficiency.

High-throughput screening utilizes robots which test the effect of chemical compounds on a target that has been identified by genomics. Traditionally company scientists had to mix compounds themselves under exacting laboratory conditions. By 1998, robot arms injected test compounds into rows and rows of small devices in which reactions where monitored, evaluated, and stored in a computer. Within the next few years it is expected that miniaturized micro-machine technology, in which microscopic amounts of test compound will flow through channels etched in silicon, will replace large robot arms. "It will be like the flow of electrons in a Pentium processor," Moukheiber wrote. Miniaturization will vastly decrease the cost of research, as the number of human scientists drops and the amount of test compound needed for a test decreases.

Combinatorial chemistry makes possible the rapid design of thousands of variations on an original compound, variations that may have more specific effects or different side effects. Combining high-throughput screening and combinatorial chemistry, an extremely broad array of different but related compounds can be tested simultaneously. According to *Information Week* contributor Justin Hibbard, new techniques enable companies to test 75,000 compounds a day, the same amount they used to test in an entire year.

Finally, the science of bioinformatics develops software that enable computers to analyze the vast amounts of data that the assembly line testing generates. Computerization also provides instantaneous access to data as well as to tools that allow researchers to virtually modify sequences and to compare the result with other genes in their database.

According to Zina Moukheiber, robochemistry had cut development time from four years to two by 1998. However, it only cuts time for pre-clinical development. Clinical testing and government approval times are unaffected. The development of worldwide information networks and databases for clinical data should contribute to shorter clinical test periods as well.

Environmental Considerations

Pharmaceuticals are complex chemical compounds which are produced by means of three general processes, alone or in combination: chemical synthesis, fermentation, and isolation from natural sources. The bulk manufacturing processes which the pharmaceutical industry uses results in a large percentage of by-product, hazardous and non-hazardous wastes. Fermentation and natural product extraction, in particular, generate large quantities of waste. The EPA reported that the 117 million pounds of pollutants discharged into the environment or shipped off site for disposal or incineration accounted for about ten percent of the chemical industry's waste, and about three percent of waste produced by all manufacturing companies. Some by-products can be sold or reused in other pharmaceutical manufacturing processes. Solid waste is usually shipped to another site for disposal or incineration.

According to an Environmental Protection Agency (EPA) survey, the pharmaceutical industry in the U.S. as a whole generates 266 million gallons of waste water every day. Half of the facilities polled by the EPA had implemented water conservation measures. The EPA also established that the areas of the production process that resulted in the highest sources of emissions were dryers, reactors, distillation units, and material storage and transfer.

The industry uses a number of means of reducing waste generation and the EPA reports that in general the number of toxic releases by pharmaceutical firms has decreased over the 1990s—reported releases dropped by 46 percent between 1988 and 1995. A number of companies have adopted their own individual environmental practices in addition to the Good Manufacturing Practices (GMP) outlined by the FDA. 34 pharmaceutical companies participated in the EPA's 33/50 Program, a voluntary program aimed at reducing certain high-priority types of pollution by 33 percent by 1992 and by 50 percent by 1995. Both goals were reached ahead of schedule. Both PhRMA and the Chemical Manufacturers Association (CMA) have worked on developing responses to industry specific environmental issues. Individual pharmaceutical companies have implemented their own programs as well.

Besides U.S. statutes and regulations, a number of international laws, regulations, treaties, conventions, and initiatives affect the environmental behavior of the pharmaceutical industry. Among the most important are the Basel Convention, ISO 14000 standards, NAFTA requirements, and environmental directives and regulations being developed by the European Union.

Further Reading

1997 Annual Report Bristol-Myers Squibb Company. Available from: http://www.bms.com/newsfinance/index.html.

"A History of Bristol-Myers Squibb." Available from: http://www.bms.com/aboutbms/index.html

"Amgen Backgrounder." Available from: http://wwwext.amgen.com/cgi-bin/genobject/amgenBackgrounder/tigNHYrmCjQ#history.

"Amgen Fact Sheet." Available from: http://wwwext.amgen.com/cgi-bin/genobject/amgenFactSheet/tigNHYrmCjQ.

"Amgen Inc." *Hoover's Company Capsules.* Hoover's, Inc., Austin, Texas, 1998.

"Amgen Investor Center." Available from: http://wwwext.amgen.com/cgi-bin/genobject/investorCenter.

Amgen Inc. "Product Pipeline." http://wwwext.amgen.com/cgi-bin/genobject/productPipelineAndApproval/tigNHYrmCjQ.

"Amgen Reports Fourth Quarter and Fiscal Year Results." *Business Wire,* January 21 1998.

Barrett, Amy, John Carey Melcher, and Larry Armstrong. "War Against the Microbes." *Business Week,* 6 April 1998.

Barrett, Amy, Heidi Dawley, and Joan Hamilton. "Britain: Powerful Medicine." *Business Week International,* 16 February 1998.

Bellenir, Karen, and Nancy Hatch Woodward. "Biological Products, Except Diagnostic Substances." *Gale Business Resources,* version 2.3, Detroit: Gale Research, 1998.

Bellenir, Karen, and Nancy Hatch Woodward. "In Vitro and In Vivo Diagnostic Substances." *Gale Business Resources,* version 2.3, Detroit: Gale Research, 1998.

Biotechnology Industry Organization. "Chiron Corporation." Available from: http://www.bio.org/memberprofile/welcome.dgw

Blackledge, Cath, "British Drug Firms Take Centre Stage." *The European,* 22 June 1998.

Burton, Thomas M. "Hemophiliacs Sue Firms, Foundation over AIDS in '80s." *Wall Street Journal,* 1 October 1993.

Bristol-Myers Squibb. "About our Company." Available from: http://www.bms.com/aboutbms/index.html

Chetley, Andrew. *A Healthy Business? World Health and the Pharmaceutical Industry.* Atlantic Highlands, New Jersey: Zed Books Ltd., 1990.

"Colonel Lilly's Victory." *Resident Physician.* January 1969.

Congress of the United States, General Accounting Office. *Pharmacy Benefit Managers: Early Results on Ventures with Drug Manufacturers.* Washington, DC, 1995.

Conlan, Michael F. "Generic, Brand Firms Battle across Atlantic on Patents." *Drug Topics,* 3 November 1997.

Davies, Wyndham. *The Pharmaceutical Industry.* Long Island City, New York: Pergamon Press Inc., 1967.

DeBoest, Henry F. "The Train Trip That Was a Turning Point." *Nation's Business*, January 1971.

"Dr. Herbert W. Boyer Named New Allergan Chairman." Available from http://www.allergan.com/news/press/pr100397.htm.

"From Corned Beef to Cloning." Available from: http://www.gene.com/ae/AB/WYW/boyer/boyer_11.html.

Genentech—Chronology. Available from: http://www.gene.com/Company/timeline.html.

Genentech—The Founders. Available from: http://www.gene.com/Company/founders.html.

Grabowski, H., and J. Vernon. "Longer Patents for Increased Generic Competition in the U.S.: The Waxman-Hatch Act after One Decade." *Pharmaco Economics,* 1996;10(suppl 2).

Harrington, Elizabeth, Patricia Pesanello, and Glenn Saldanha. "Building Value through Global Markets." *Pharmaceutical Executive*, 1 December 1997.

Heil, Karl. "Genetic Engineering." *Gale Business Resources*, version 2.3, Detroit: Gale Research, 1998.

Hibbard, Justin. "Research Gains from IT Boom—Top Drug Makers Depend on Technology for More Than Just Speeding Production." *Information Week.*, 14 September 1998.

"HMO-PPO/Medicaid Digest." *Hoechst Marion Roussel Managed Care Digest*, 1997

Holt, Cody. "The Evolution of the OTC Drug Industry." *American Druggist*, April 1996.

"IMS Analysis Describes Major Market Shifts." *Pharmacy Times* Homepage. Available from: http://www.pharmacytimes.com/top200.html.

"IMS Health Forecasts Viagra Sales to Reach $1 Billion in First Year." *IMS America: What's News.* 6 July 1998. Available from: http://www.ims-america.com/communications/pr_Viagra_July6.htm.

"IMS Health Reports U.S. Market Continues to Drive Worldwide Pharmaceutical Sales Growth." Available from: http://www.imshealth.com/html/news_arc/09_17_1998_106.htm.

Johnson & Johnson 1997 Annual Report. Available from: http://www.johnsonandjohnson.com/cgi-bin/news_finance.

Johnson & Johnson-1998 fact book. Available from: http://www.johnsonandjohnson.com/who_is_jnj/factbook/98fb_index.html.

Johnson & Johnson-Company History. Available from http://www.johnsonandjohnson.com/who_is_jnj/hist_index.html

"John Wyeth: A Man with a Vison." Public Relations Material. St. David's, PA: Wyeth-Ayerst Laboratories, 1998.

Jones, Jacob J., and Gertrude Mandeville. "Medical Chemicals and Botanical Products." *Gale Business Resources*, version 2.3. Detroit: Gale Research, 1998.

Katterman, Lee. "Scientists at All Educational Levels Needed to Conduct Clinical Trials." Available from: http://www.the-scientist.library.upenn.edu/yr1996/june/prof_960624.html

King, R. T. "Corporate Focus: Is Job Cutting by Drug Makers Bad Medicine?" *Wall Street Journal.* 23 August 1995.

Levine, David. "Biotechnology." *Gale Business Resources*, version 2.3. Detroit: Gale Research, 1998.

Liebenau, Jonathan. *Medical Science and Medical Industry*. Baltimore, Maryland: The Johns Hopkins University Press, 1987.

Lilly, Ely. "Values for a Second Century." Indianapolis: Eli Lilly and Company, 1976.

Lindsay, Cotton M., ed. *The Pharmaceutical Industry*. New York: John Wiley & Sons, Inc., 1978

Lipin S., S. D. Moore, and T. M. Burton. "Upjohn and Pharmacia Sign $6 Billion Merger." *Wall Street Journal*. 21 August 1995.

Lumley, C. E., and Dorabjee, S., *Trends in Pharmaceutical R&D—1996 CMR Fact Book*. CMR International, 1997.

McCornick, Gene E. "The Making of a Modern Enterprise." Indianapolis: Eli Lilly and Company, 1991.

"Medicinal and Botanical Products." *Gale Business Resources*, version 2.3, Detroit: Gale Research, 1998.

"Merger of American Home Products and SmithKline Beecham Would Move Company to Number One Slot in Prescription Sales." *IMS America: What's News*, 20 January 1997. Available from: http://www.ims-america.com/communications/press.html.

"Merger of Glaxo Wellcome and SmithKline Beecham Could Mean $19 Billion in Worldwide Pharmaceutical Sales, $7.6 Billion More Than the Nearest Competitor". *IMS America: What's News*. Available from: http://www.ims-america.com/communications/press.html.

Milestones in U.S. Food and Drug Law History. Available from: http://www.fda.gov/opacom/backgrounders/miles.html.

Miller, Henry I. "Perspective on Commerce." *Los Angeles Times*, 25 June 1997.

Moukheiber, Zina. "A Hail of Silver Bullets." *Forbes Magazine*, 26 January 1998.

"Mr. Eli Lilly 1885-1977." *Lilly News*, 25 January 1977. Indianapolis: Eli Lilly and Company, 1977.

National Pharmaceutical Council. *Noncompliance with Medication Regimens: An Economic Tragedy*, June 1992.

Office of Management and Budget. *Standard Industrial Classification Manual*. Washington, DC, 1987.

Pharmaceutical Industry Job Cuts. Washington, DC: Pharmaceutical Research and Manufacturers of America (PhRMA), 1995.

Pharmaceutical Industry Waste Minimization Initiatives. Washington, DC: Pharmaceutical Research and Manufacturers of America (PhRMA), 1997.

Pfizer, Inc. 1998 Mid-year Report. Available from: http://www.pfizer.com/pfizerinc/investing/midyear/1998midyear.html.

"Pfizer, Inc." *Corptech Capsule Reports,* 12 September 1998. Available from: http://www.corptech.com/Research Areas/CompanyCapsule.cfm?URI=10EGJQ.

"Pfizer, Inc.—Viagra Receives Approval in Europe." Available from: http://www.pfizer.com/pfizerinc/about/viagraeurope.html.

"Physicians Give 1 Ratings to Merck for Company Reputation and Astra Merck for Sales Force Performance." *IMS America: What's News*. Available from: http://www.ims-america.com/communications/press.html.

Prescription Drug Prices and Profits. Washington, DC: Pharmaceutical Research and Manufacturers of America (PhRMA), 1996.

Salary Survey Results. Available from: http://www.medzilla.com/survey95.html.

Schwartzman, David. *Innovation in the Pharmaceutical Industry*. Baltimore, Maryland: The Johns Hopkins University Press, 1976.

Shortridge, Norm. "The Lilly Legacy: Part II." *Indianapolis Magazine*, September 1974.

Shortridge, Norm. "The Lilly Legacy: Part III." *Indianapolis Magazine*, October 1974.

"Silicon Valley Healthcare Technology Workers Highest-Paid in California." *Business Wire*, 11 September 1998.

Stalheim, Ole H. V. *The Winning of Animal Health*. Ames, Iowa: Iowa State University Press, 1994.

Statman, Meir. *Competition in the Pharmaceutical Industry*. Washington, DC: American Enterprise Institute for Public Policy Research, 1983.

Stipp, David. "Why Pfizer is So Hot." *Fortune*, 11 May 1998.

The Changing Environment for U.S. Pharmaceuticals: The Role of Pharmaceutical Companies in a System Approach to Health Care. Boston, Massachusetts: The Boston Consulting Group, Inc., 1993.

"The Fortune Global 500 Ranked by Performance." *Fortune*, 3 August 1998.

"The Pharmaceutical Industry at the Start of a New Century." *The Pfizer Journal*, Winter 1997.

Tschudin, Jean-Charles. "Industry's New World Order." *Pharmaceutical Executive*, 1 February 1997.

"Update on Drug Approvals in FY 97." *FDA Veterinarian*, January/February 1998.

U.S. Department of Commerce. *1995 Annual Survey of Manufacturers*. Washington, DC: GPO, 1997.

U.S. Department of Commerce. Bureau of the Census. *U.S. 1992 Census of Manufactures*, Industry Series, Washington, DC: GPO 1992.

U.S. Department of Commerce. International Trade Administration. *U.S. Industrial Outlook 1993*. Washington, DC: GPO, 1994.

U.S. Department of Commerce. International Trade Administration. *U.S. Industry & Trade Outlook '98*. DRI/McGraw-Hill, Standard & Poor's, 1998.

U.S. Department of Commerce. International Trade Administration. *1988 U.S. Industrial Outlook*. Washington DC: GPO, 1988.

U.S. Department of Commerce. *1978 U.S. Industrial Outlook*. Washington DC: GPO, 1978.

U.S. Department of Commerce. *1968 U.S. Industrial Outlook*. Washington DC: GPO, 1967.

U.S. Environmental Protection Agency. Office of Compliance. *Profile of the Pharmaceutical Manufacturing Industry*. Washington, DC: GPO, 1997.

Vaczek, David. "The Rise of the Generic Drug Industry." *American Druggist*, April 1996.

Wiegand, Susan. "Herbert Boyer (1936—)." Available from: http://www.gene.com/ae/AB/BC/Herbert_Boyer.html.

Wierenga, W. "Strategic Alliances and the Changing Drug Discovery Process." *Pharmaceutical News*, 1996;3(3).

—Evelyn Hauser.

Evelyn Hauser is a freelance editor and writer based in Arcata, California.

CHAPTER 2 - PART II

INDUSTRY STATISTICS & PERFORMANCE INDICATORS

This chapter presents statistical information on the Pharmaceuticals industry. This view of the industry is through the lens of federal statistics. All the data shown are drawn from government sources, including the 100 percent surveys of the Economic Census and the partial surveys of manufacturing, services, and other industries conducted annually by the U.S. Department of Commerce.

Tables for the Manufacturing sector begin with a graphic charting the value of industry shipments. Thereafter, general statistics, indices of change, and selected ratios are presented.

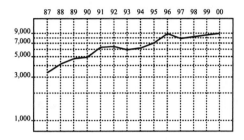

87 88 89 90 91 92 93 94 95 96 97 98 99 00

Revenues ($ millions)

SIC 2833 MEDICINALS AND BOTANICALS: GENERAL STATISTICS

Year	Estab-lish-ments	Employment			Compensation		Production ($ mil.)		
		Total (000)	Production		Payroll ($ mil.)	Wages ($/hr)	Cost of Materials	Value of Shipments	Capital Inves.
			Workers (000)	Hours (mil.)					
1987	225	11.6	6.1	12.0	376.5	15.32	1,613.4	3,350.2	114.5
1988	223	11.3	6.2	11.7	381.4	16.09	2,052.9	4,150.4	150.5
1989	221	11.7	6.6	13.3	420.3	16.29	2,596.0	4,752.5	219.3
1990	226	12.7	6.5	13.1	423.4	17.35	2,579.2	4,919.4	194.5
1991	226	12.5	7.2	14.3	540.2	20.06	3,200.0	6,308.2	487.3
1992	225	13.0	7.4	15.1	587.1	18.91	3,245.9	6,438.5	550.5
1993	248	13.0	7.7	16.3	610.8	19.62	2,757.8	5,925.8	482.4
1994	243	13.9	7.8	15.6	613.7	19.71	2,953.0	6,189.3	504.7
1995	261	14.3	7.7	17.0	689.6	20.09	3,302.9	7,037.9	383.9
1996	244[1]	16.8	8.9	19.9	840.1	20.83	4,238.0	8,883.8	835.3
1997	246[1]	12.6[1]	6.9[1]	15.0[1]	687.9[1]	22.28[1]	3,753.8[1]	7,868.9[1]	594.1[1]
1998	248[1]	12.4[1]	6.8[1]	14.9[1]	707.9[1]	23.00[1]	3,926.6[1]	8,231.1[1]	626.2[1]
1999	249[1]	12.2[1]	6.7[1]	14.8[1]	728.0[1]	23.72[1]	4,099.4[1]	8,593.3[1]	658.3[1]
2000	251[1]	12.0[1]	6.6[1]	14.7[1]	748.0[1]	24.44[1]	4,272.2[1]	8,955.5[1]	690.4[1]

Source: 1987 and 1992 Economic Census; *Annual Survey of Manufactures,* 88-91, 93-96. Establishment counts for non-Census years are from *County Business Patterns.* Extracted from *Manufacturing USA,* 6th Edition, Gale, 1998. Note: 1. Projections by the editors.

SIC 2833 MEDICINALS AND BOTANICALS: INDICES OF CHANGE

Year	Estab-lish-ments	Employment			Compensation		Production ($ mil.)		
		Total (000)	Production		Payroll ($ mil.)	Wages ($/hr)	Cost of Materials	Value of Shipments	Capital Inves.
			Workers (000)	Hours (mil.)					
1987	100	89	82	79	64	81	50	52	21
1988	99	87	84	77	65	85	63	64	27
1989	98	90	89	88	72	86	80	74	40
1990	100	98	88	87	72	92	79	76	35
1991	100	96	97	95	92	106	99	98	89
1992	100	100	100	100	100	100	100	100	100
1993	110	100	104	108	104	104	85	92	88
1994	108	107	105	103	105	104	91	96	92
1995	116	110	104	113	117	106	102	109	70
1996	108[1]	129	120	132	143	110	131	138	152
1997	109[1]	97[1]	94[1]	100[1]	117[1]	118[1]	116[1]	122[1]	108[1]
1998	110[1]	95[1]	92[1]	99[1]	121[1]	122[1]	121[1]	128[1]	114[1]
1999	111[1]	94[1]	90[1]	98[1]	124[1]	125[1]	126[1]	133[1]	120[1]
2000	112[1]	92[1]	89[1]	97[1]	127[1]	129[1]	132[1]	139[1]	125[1]

Source: Same as General Statistics. Values reflect change from the base year, 1992. Values above 100 mean greater than 1992, values below 100 mean less than 1992, and a value of 100 in the 1982-91 or 1993-2000 period means same as 1992. Note: 1. Projections by the editors.

SIC 2833 MEDICINALS AND BOTANICALS: SELECTED RATIOS

For 1996	Average of All Manufacturing	Analyzed Industry	Index
Employees per Establishment	49	69	141
Payroll per Establishment	1,574,035	3,442,413	219
Payroll per Employee	32,350	50,006	155
Production Workers per Establishment	34	36	107
Wages per Establishment	890,687	1,698,534	191
Wages per Production Worker	26,064	46,575	179
Hours per Production Worker	2,055	2,236	109
Wages per Hour	12.68	20.83	164
Value Added per Establishment	4,932,584	19,397,735	393
Value Added per Employee	101,376	281,780	278
Value Added per Production Worker	144,340	531,899	369
Cost per Establishment	5,569,059	17,365,724	312
Cost per Employee	114,457	252,262	220
Cost per Production Worker	162,965	476,180	292
Shipments per Establishment	10,422,474	36,402,459	349
Shipments per Employee	214,207	528,798	247
Shipments per Production Worker	304,989	998,180	327
Investment per Establishment	394,953	3,422,744	867
Investment per Employee	8,117	49,720	613
Investment per Production Worker	11,557	93,854	812

Source: Same as General Statistics. The 'Average of All Manufacturing' column represents the average of all manufacturing industries reported for the most recent complete year available. The Index shows the relationship between the Average and the Analyzed Industry. For example, 100 means that they are equal; 500 that the Analyzed Industry is five times the average; 50 means that the Analyzed Industry is half the national average. The abbreviation 'na' is used to show that data are 'not available'.

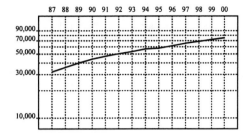

Revenues ($ millions)

SIC 2834 PHARMACEUTICAL PREPARATIONS: GENERAL STATISTICS

| Year | Estab-lish-ments | Employment | | | Compensation | | Production ($ mil.) | | |
| | | Total (000) | Production | | Payroll ($ mil.) | Wages ($/hr) | Cost of Materials | Value of Shipments | Capital Inves. |
			Workers (000)	Hours (mil.)					
1987	732	131.6	59.9	117.5	4,168.1	12.42	8,463.0	32,094.1	1,471.1
1988	718	133.4	60.8	119.0	4,458.3	12.93	9,755.5	35,825.4	1,724.9
1989	699	143.9	62.4	121.5	5,142.6	13.83	10,717.3	40,028.0	1,932.5
1990	680	144.0	61.5	121.5	5,530.9	14.71	11,763.7	44,182.3	1,808.7
1991	703	129.1	59.2	117.0	5,012.3	14.77	12,869.8	47,375.6	1,771.6
1992	691	122.8	62.5	126.9	4,949.4	14.71	13,542.5	50,417.9	2,450.0
1993	765	128.2	62.8	126.5	5,418.9	15.81	14,120.2	53,280.8	2,493.2
1994	706	134.2	68.6	133.3	5,753.8	16.04	14,497.3	56,960.5	2,713.7
1995	711	142.4	78.3	155.7	6,257.2	15.40	16,805.8	57,943.3	3,133.9
1996	723[1]	136.9	72.3	151.3	6,196.7	15.88	18,555.7	61,554.3	2,588.2
1997	726[1]	138.9[1]	70.2[1]	143.1[1]	6,543.0[1]	17.15[1]	19,786.8[1]	65,638.2[1]	3,070.7[1]
1998	728[1]	139.8[1]	71.1[1]	145.5[1]	6,778.8[1]	17.62[1]	20,762.2[1]	68,873.9[1]	3,228.9[1]
1999	731[1]	140.8[1]	71.9[1]	147.8[1]	7,014.5[1]	18.09[1]	21,737.6[1]	72,109.7[1]	3,387.2[1]
2000	734[1]	141.8[1]	72.8[1]	150.2[1]	7,250.2[1]	18.55[1]	22,713.1[1]	75,345.4[1]	3,545.4[1]

Source: 1987 and 1992 Economic Census; *Annual Survey of Manufactures,* 88-91, 93-96. Establishment counts for non-Census years are from *County Business Patterns.* Extracted from *Manufacturing USA,* 6th Edition, Gale, 1998. Note: 1. Projections by the editors.

SIC 2834 PHARMACEUTICAL PREPARATIONS: INDICES OF CHANGE

| Year | Estab-lish-ments | Employment | | | Compensation | | Production ($ mil.) | | |
| | | Total (000) | Production | | Payroll ($ mil.) | Wages ($/hr) | Cost of Materials | Value of Shipments | Capital Inves. |
			Workers (000)	Hours (mil.)					
1987	106	107	96	93	84	84	62	64	60
1988	104	109	97	94	90	88	72	71	70
1989	101	117	100	96	104	94	79	79	79
1990	98	117	98	96	112	100	87	88	74
1991	102	105	95	92	101	100	95	94	72
1992	100	100	100	100	100	100	100	100	100
1993	111	104	100	100	109	107	104	106	102
1994	102	109	110	105	116	109	107	113	111
1995	103	116	125	123	126	105	124	115	128
1996	105[1]	111	116	119	125	108	137	122	106
1997	105[1]	113[1]	112[1]	113[1]	132[1]	117[1]	146[1]	130[1]	125[1]
1998	105[1]	114[1]	114[1]	115[1]	137[1]	120[1]	153[1]	137[1]	132[1]
1999	106[1]	115[1]	115[1]	116[1]	142[1]	123[1]	161[1]	143[1]	138[1]
2000	106[1]	115[1]	116[1]	118[1]	146[1]	126[1]	168[1]	149[1]	145[1]

Source: Same as General Statistics. Values reflect change from the base year, 1992. Values above 100 mean greater than 1992, values below 100 mean less than 1992, and a value of 100 in the 1982-91 or 1993-2000 period means same as 1992. Note: 1. Projections by the editors.

SIC 2834 PHARMACEUTICAL PREPARATIONS: SELECTED RATIOS

For 1996	Average of All Manufacturing	Analyzed Industry	Index
Employees per Establishment	49	189	389
Payroll per Establishment	1,574,035	8,573,683	545
Payroll per Employee	32,350	45,264	140
Production Workers per Establishment	34	100	293
Wages per Establishment	890,687	3,324,271	373
Wages per Production Worker	26,064	33,232	128
Hours per Production Worker	2,055	2,093	102
Wages per Hour	12.68	15.88	125
Value Added per Establishment	4,932,584	60,060,885	1,218
Value Added per Employee	101,376	317,089	313
Value Added per Production Worker	144,340	600,408	416
Cost per Establishment	5,569,059	25,673,453	461
Cost per Employee	114,457	135,542	118
Cost per Production Worker	162,965	256,649	157
Shipments per Establishment	10,422,474	85,165,822	817
Shipments per Employee	214,207	449,630	210
Shipments per Production Worker	304,989	851,373	279
Investment per Establishment	394,953	3,581,004	907
Investment per Employee	8,117	18,906	233
Investment per Production Worker	11,557	35,798	310

Source: Same as General Statistics. The 'Average of All Manufacturing' column represents the average of all manufacturing industries reported for the most recent complete year available. The Index shows the relationship between the Average and the Analyzed Industry. For example, 100 means that they are equal; 500 that the Analyzed Industry is five times the average; 50 means that the Analyzed Industry is half the national average. The abbreviation 'na' is used to show that data are 'not available'.

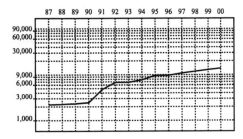

Revenues ($ millions)

SIC 2835 DIAGNOSTIC SUBSTANCES: GENERAL STATISTICS

Year	Estab-lish-ments	Employment Total (000)	Production Workers (000)	Hours (mil.)	Compensation Payroll ($ mil.)	Wages ($/hr)	Production ($ mil.) Cost of Materials	Value of Shipments	Capital Inves.
1987	158	15.4	6.8	13.6	437.1	10.74	657.4	2,205.0	93.5
1988	161	16.2	7.5	15.3	476.4	10.93	752.4	2,261.3	93.3
1989	159	15.8	6.8	13.5	526.8	11.54	754.3	2,325.1	116.8
1990	161	16.4	6.6	13.1	499.0	11.80	686.8	2,462.2	147.1
1991	171	30.5	9.9	19.4	1,253.5	18.17	1,165.9	4,746.1	302.0
1992	234	39.8	14.6	29.5	1,658.3	14.03	1,701.2	6,837.8	587.3
1993	236	39.3	14.9	30.8	1,759.1	15.64	1,623.3	6,864.4	666.5
1994	232	38.4	15.6	30.0	1,778.9	16.90	1,951.9	7,777.7	561.1
1995	251	39.8	15.6	32.6	1,918.8	18.31	2,652.4	9,676.4	555.9
1996	264[1]	39.9	15.5	31.6	1,988.2	19.15	2,680.3	9,692.3	517.6
1997	277[1]	48.4[1]	18.3[1]	37.2[1]	2,379.7[1]	20.11[1]	3,008.7[1]	10,879.9[1]	734.8[1]
1998	291[1]	51.9[1]	19.6[1]	39.8[1]	2,588.8[1]	21.08[1]	3,280.0[1]	11,860.8[1]	802.2[1]
1999	304[1]	55.4[1]	20.9[1]	42.4[1]	2,797.9[1]	22.06[1]	3,551.3[1]	12,841.8[1]	869.6[1]
2000	318[1]	58.9[1]	22.1[1]	45.0[1]	3,007.0[1]	23.04[1]	3,822.5[1]	13,822.7[1]	937.0[1]

Source: 1987 and 1992 Economic Census; *Annual Survey of Manufactures*, 88-91, 93-96. Establishment counts for non-Census years are from *County Business Patterns*. Extracted from *Manufacturing USA*, 6th Edition, Gale, 1998. Note: 1. Projections by the editors.

SIC 2835 DIAGNOSTIC SUBSTANCES: INDICES OF CHANGE

Year	Estab-lish-ments	Employment Total (000)	Production Workers (000)	Hours (mil.)	Compensation Payroll ($ mil.)	Wages ($/hr)	Production ($ mil.) Cost of Materials	Value of Shipments	Capital Inves.
1987	68	39	47	46	26	77	39	32	16
1988	69	41	51	52	29	78	44	33	16
1989	68	40	47	46	32	82	44	34	20
1990	69	41	45	44	30	84	40	36	25
1991	73	77	68	66	76	130	69	69	51
1992	100	100	100	100	100	100	100	100	100
1993	101	99	102	104	106	111	95	100	113
1994	99	96	107	102	107	120	115	114	96
1995	107	100	107	111	116	131	156	142	95
1996	113[1]	100	106	107	120	136	158	142	88
1997	118[1]	122[1]	126[1]	126[1]	144[1]	143[1]	177[1]	159[1]	125[1]
1998	124[1]	130[1]	134[1]	135[1]	156[1]	150[1]	193[1]	173[1]	137[1]
1999	130[1]	139[1]	143[1]	144[1]	169[1]	157[1]	209[1]	188[1]	148[1]
2000	136[1]	148[1]	152[1]	153[1]	181[1]	164[1]	225[1]	202[1]	160[1]

Source: Same as General Statistics. Values reflect change from the base year, 1992. Values above 100 mean greater than 1992, values below 100 mean less than 1992, and a value of 100 in the 1982-91 or 1993-2000 period means same as 1992. Note: 1. Projections by the editors.

SIC 2835 DIAGNOSTIC SUBSTANCES: SELECTED RATIOS

For 1996	Average of All Manufacturing	Analyzed Industry	Index
Employees per Establishment	49	151	311
Payroll per Establishment	1,574,035	7,543,761	479
Payroll per Employee	32,350	49,830	154
Production Workers per Establishment	34	59	172
Wages per Establishment	890,687	2,296,062	258
Wages per Production Worker	26,064	39,041	150
Hours per Production Worker	2,055	2,039	99
Wages per Hour	12.68	19.15	151
Value Added per Establishment	4,932,584	26,589,840	539
Value Added per Employee	101,376	175,637	173
Value Added per Production Worker	144,340	452,123	313
Cost per Establishment	5,569,059	10,169,772	183
Cost per Employee	114,457	67,175	59
Cost per Production Worker	162,965	172,923	106
Shipments per Establishment	10,422,474	36,775,169	353
Shipments per Employee	214,207	242,915	113
Shipments per Production Worker	304,989	625,310	205
Investment per Establishment	394,953	1,963,912	497
Investment per Employee	8,117	12,972	160
Investment per Production Worker	11,557	33,394	289

Source: Same as General Statistics. The 'Average of All Manufacturing' column represents the average of all manufacturing industries reported for the most recent complete year available. The Index shows the relationship between the Average and the Analyzed Industry. For example, 100 means that they are equal; 500 that the Analyzed Industry is five times the average; 50 means that the Analyzed Industry is half the national average. The abbreviation 'na' is used to show that data are 'not available'.

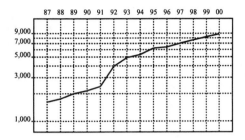

Revenues ($ millions)

SIC 2836 BIOLOGICAL PRODUCTS EXC DIAGNOSTIC: GENERAL STATISTICS

Year	Estab-lish-ments	Employment Total (000)	Production Workers (000)	Production Hours (mil.)	Compensation Payroll ($ mil.)	Compensation Wages ($/hr)	Production ($ mil.) Cost of Materials	Production ($ mil.) Value of Shipments	Production ($ mil.) Capital Inves.
1987	241	13.3	6.8	12.1	322.1	8.87	676.1	1,614.1	69.9
1988	231	13.7	6.5	12.3	340.9	9.13	742.0	1,749.5	89.1
1989	231	15.3	7.0	12.7	384.0	9.30	895.6	2,008.3	123.6
1990	220	14.4	6.8	13.4	397.4	9.15	901.9	2,155.8	129.9
1991	248	12.1	6.4	12.1	391.5	11.00	962.4	2,405.6	108.3
1992	275	18.4	8.0	15.1	627.2	12.48	1,313.5	3,974.0	294.3
1993	296	19.0	9.2	18.1	732.5	12.57	1,483.2	4,914.0	405.1
1994	286	19.8	9.9	18.6	788.3	13.81	1,570.3	5,310.2	360.6
1995	284	21.1	11.0	20.4	854.5	13.74	1,719.2	6,226.6	452.7
1996	300[1]	19.6	9.7	19.1	865.5	14.06	1,713.2	6,402.0	359.5
1997	309[1]	21.7[1]	10.8[1]	20.9[1]	962.0[1]	15.19[1]	1,882.7[1]	7,035.5[1]	484.2[1]
1998	318[1]	22.6[1]	11.3[1]	21.9[1]	1,033.2[1]	15.87[1]	2,046.2[1]	7,646.3[1]	528.8[1]
1999	326[1]	23.5[1]	11.8[1]	22.9[1]	1,104.4[1]	16.56[1]	2,209.6[1]	8,257.1[1]	573.3[1]
2000	335[1]	24.5[1]	12.3[1]	24.0[1]	1,175.6[1]	17.25[1]	2,373.1[1]	8,867.9[1]	617.8[1]

Source: 1987 and 1992 Economic Census; *Annual Survey of Manufactures*, 88-91, 93-96. Establishment counts for non-Census years are from *County Business Patterns*. Extracted from *Manufacturing USA*, 6th Edition, Gale, 1998. Note: 1. Projections by the editors.

SIC 2836 BIOLOGICAL PRODUCTS EXC DIAGNOSTIC: INDICES OF CHANGE

Year	Estab-lish-ments	Employment Total (000)	Production Workers (000)	Production Hours (mil.)	Compensation Payroll ($ mil.)	Compensation Wages ($/hr)	Production ($ mil.) Cost of Materials	Production ($ mil.) Value of Shipments	Production ($ mil.) Capital Inves.
1987	88	72	85	80	51	71	51	41	24
1988	84	74	81	81	54	73	56	44	30
1989	84	83	88	84	61	75	68	51	42
1990	80	78	85	89	63	73	69	54	44
1991	90	66	80	80	62	88	73	61	37
1992	100	100	100	100	100	100	100	100	100
1993	108	103	115	120	117	101	113	124	138
1994	104	108	124	123	126	111	120	134	123
1995	103	115	138	135	136	110	131	157	154
1996	109[1]	107	121	126	138	113	130	161	122
1997	112[1]	118[1]	135[1]	139[1]	153[1]	122[1]	143[1]	177[1]	165[1]
1998	116[1]	123[1]	141[1]	145[1]	165[1]	127[1]	156[1]	192[1]	180[1]
1999	119[1]	128[1]	148[1]	152[1]	176[1]	133[1]	168[1]	208[1]	195[1]
2000	122[1]	133[1]	154[1]	159[1]	187[1]	138[1]	181[1]	223[1]	210[1]

Source: Same as General Statistics. Values reflect change from the base year, 1992. Values above 100 mean greater than 1992, values below 100 mean less than 1992, and a value of 100 in the 1982-91 or 1993-2000 period means same as 1992. Note: 1. Projections by the editors.

SIC 2836 BIOLOGICAL PRODUCTS EXC DIAGNOSTIC: SELECTED RATIOS

For 1996	Average of All Manufacturing	Analyzed Industry	Index
Employees per Establishment	49	65	134
Payroll per Establishment	1,574,035	2,881,265	183
Payroll per Employee	32,350	44,158	137
Production Workers per Establishment	34	32	94
Wages per Establishment	890,687	893,994	100
Wages per Production Worker	26,064	27,685	106
Hours per Production Worker	2,055	1,969	96
Wages per Hour	12.68	14.06	111
Value Added per Establishment	4,932,584	15,518,217	315
Value Added per Employee	101,376	237,832	235
Value Added per Production Worker	144,340	480,567	333
Cost per Establishment	5,569,059	5,703,274	102
Cost per Employee	114,457	87,408	76
Cost per Production Worker	162,965	176,619	108
Shipments per Establishment	10,422,474	21,312,373	204
Shipments per Employee	214,207	326,633	152
Shipments per Production Worker	304,989	660,000	216
Investment per Establishment	394,953	1,196,782	303
Investment per Employee	8,117	18,342	226
Investment per Production Worker	11,557	37,062	321

Source: Same as General Statistics. The 'Average of All Manufacturing' column represents the average of all manufacturing industries reported for the most recent complete year available. The Index shows the relationship between the Average and the Analyzed Industry. For example, 100 means that they are equal; 500 that the Analyzed Industry is five times the average; 50 means that the Analyzed Industry is half the national average. The abbreviation 'na' is used to show that data are 'not available'.

CHAPTER 3 - PART II

FINANCIAL NORMS AND RATIOS

Industry-specific financial norms and ratios are shown in this chapter for four industries in the Pharmaceuticals sector. For each industry, balance sheets are presented for the years 1996 through 1998, with the most recent year shown first. As part of each balance sheet, additional financial averages for net sales, gross profits, net profits after tax, and working capital are shown. The number of establishments used to calculate the averages are shown for each year.

The second table in each display shows D&B Key Business Ratios for the SIC-denominated industry. These data, again, are for the years 1996 through 1998. Ratios measuring solvency (e.g., Quick ratio), efficiency (e.g., Collection period, in days), and profitability (e.g. % return on sales) are shown. A total of 14 ratios are featured. Ratios are shown for the upper quartile, median, and lowest quartile of the D&B sample.

This product includes proprietary data of Dun & Bradstreet Inc.

D&B INDUSTRY NORMS: SIC 2833 - MEDICINALS AND BOTANICALS

	1998 (39) Estab.		1997 (40) Estab.		1996 (41) Estab.	
	$	%	$	%	$	%
Cash	521,255	18.6	312,632	18.0	276,930	17.2
Accounts Receivable	529,662	18.9	404,685	23.3	362,263	22.5
Notes Receivable	8,407	.3	6,947	.4	3,220	.2
Inventory	695,006	24.8	416,843	24.0	394,464	24.5
Other Current Assets	156,937	5.6	34,737	2.0	99,824	6.2
Total Current Assets	1,911,267	68.2	1,175,844	67.7	1,136,701	70.6
Fixed Assets	680,994	24.3	363,001	20.9	367,093	22.8
Other Non-current Assets	210,183	7.5	198,001	11.4	106,264	6.6
Total Assets	2,802,444	100.0	1,736,846	100.0	1,610,058	100.0
Accounts Payable	333,491	11.9	284,843	16.4	251,169	15.6
Bank Loans	-	-	-	-	-	-
Notes Payable	67,259	2.4	26,053	1.5	46,692	2.9
Other Current Liabilities	456,798	16.3	213,632	12.3	215,748	13.4
Total Current Liabilities	857,548	30.6	524,528	30.2	513,609	31.9
Other Long Term	389,540	13.9	213,632	12.3	109,484	6.8
Deferred Credits	5,605	.2	5,211	.3	-	-
Net Worth	1,549,752	55.3	993,476	57.2	986,966	61.3
Total Liabilities & Net Worth	2,802,445	100.0	1,736,847	100.0	1,610,059	100.0
Net Sales	8,767,784	100.0	5,388,587	100.0	4,010,979	100.0
Gross Profits	4,138,394	47.2	2,295,538	42.6	1,885,160	47.0
Net Profit After Tax	350,711	4.0	237,098	4.4	132,362	3.3
Working Capital	1,053,719	-	651,317	-	623,093	-

Source: Dun & Bradstreet. Data in this table are copyright (c) 1999 of Dun & Bradstreet. Reprinted by special arrangement with D&B. *Notes:* Values in parentheses above columns indicate the number of establishments in the sample. Data shown are for all companies.

D&B KEY BUSINESS RATIOS: SIC 2833

	1998			1997			1996		
	UQ	MED	LQ	UQ	MED	LQ	UQ	MED	LQ
Solvency									
Quick ratio	1.5	1.2	.6	2.8	1.4	.9	2.8	1.1	.6
Current ratio	4.0	2.3	1.3	4.5	2.5	1.5	5.0	2.4	1.4
Current liabilities/Net worth (%)	21.8	38.7	102.4	16.2	34.6	52.9	22.3	46.8	79.0
Current liabilities/Inventory (%)	51.9	108.8	194.5	48.2	105.3	147.9	63.3	108.0	168.4
Total liabilities/Net worth (%)	23.6	46.0	157.9	20.1	47.6	90.3	22.3	48.1	114.4
Fixed assets/Net worth (%)	16.8	37.1	75.1	15.2	29.8	77.4	10.8	36.4	66.3
Efficiency									
Collection period (days)	21.8	34.9	47.9	33.6	47.8	59.5	34.0	46.7	51.3
Sales to Inventory	13.2	7.9	4.7	12.6	7.1	5.5	13.5	7.4	5.8
Assets/Sales (%)	30.1	45.1	69.2	32.1	46.9	68.9	28.5	41.5	57.7
Sales/Net Working Capital	13.7	6.0	3.6	14.6	5.6	3.9	13.4	6.1	4.3
Accounts payable/Sales (%)	3.2	4.5	8.7	3.7	7.5	12.2	2.6	5.9	8.1
Profitability									
Return - Sales (%)	7.3	6.2	1.4	6.9	3.7	2.2	8.3	4.0	1.6
Return - Assets (%)	20.5	10.9	3.2	16.3	8.2	3.8	22.4	12.2	3.1
Return - Net Worth (%)	32.3	22.5	13.4	35.2	18.8	7.5	38.7	18.8	4.8

Source: Dun & Bradstreet. Data in this table are copyright (c) 1999 of Dun & Bradstreet. Reprinted by special arrangement with D&B. *Note:* UQ stands for "Upper Quartile" and represents the top 25 percent of sample; MED stands for "Median"; and LQ stands for "Lower Quartile" and represents the lowest 25 percent.

D&B INDUSTRY NORMS: SIC 2834 - PHARMACEUTICAL PREPARATIONS

	1998 (187) Estab.		1997 (203) Estab.		1996 (177) Estab.	
	$	%	$	%	$	%
Cash	4,171,873	16.5	1,558,029	15.3	1,731,305	17.2
Accounts Receivable	4,298,293	17.0	1,995,907	19.6	1,932,620	19.2
Notes Receivable	101,136	.4	61,099	.6	20,131	.2
Inventory	4,399,429	17.4	2,006,090	19.7	1,821,897	18.1
Other Current Assets	3,034,089	12.0	977,587	9.6	996,507	9.9
Total Current Assets	16,004,820	63.3	6,598,712	64.8	6,502,460	64.6
Fixed Assets	5,537,213	21.9	2,281,037	22.4	2,345,314	23.3
Other Non-current Assets	3,742,043	14.8	1,303,449	12.8	1,217,953	12.1
Total Assets	25,284,076	100.0	10,183,198	100.0	10,065,727	100.0
Accounts Payable	2,781,248	11.0	1,303,449	12.8	1,288,413	12.8
Bank Loans	-	-	20,366	.2	20,131	.2
Notes Payable	556,250	2.2	254,580	2.5	291,906	2.9
Other Current Liabilities	2,932,953	11.6	1,333,999	13.1	1,087,099	10.8
Total Current Liabilities	6,270,451	24.8	2,912,394	28.6	2,687,549	26.7
Other Long Term	4,096,020	16.2	1,384,915	13.6	1,348,807	13.4
Deferred Credits	50,568	.2	20,366	.2	30,197	.3
Net Worth	14,867,037	58.8	5,865,523	57.6	5,999,173	59.6
Total Liabilities & Net Worth	25,284,076	100.0	10,183,198	100.0	10,065,726	100.0
Net Sales	13,930,418	100.0	8,078,000	100.0	10,625,170	100.0
Gross Profits	6,143,314	44.1	3,659,334	45.3	5,238,209	49.3
Net Profit After Tax	599,008	4.3	444,290	5.5	510,008	4.8
Working Capital	9,734,369	-	3,686,318	-	3,814,911	-

Source: Dun & Bradstreet. Data in this table are copyright (c) 1999 of Dun & Bradstreet. Reprinted by special arrangement with D&B. *Notes:* Values in parentheses above columns indicate the number of establishments in the sample. Data shown are for all companies.

D&B KEY BUSINESS RATIOS: SIC 2834

	1998			1997			1996		
	UQ	MED	LQ	UQ	MED	LQ	UQ	MED	LQ
Solvency									
Quick ratio	2.0	1.2	.7	2.2	1.2	.7	2.6	1.2	.7
Current ratio	3.8	2.6	1.6	4.0	2.3	1.5	4.5	2.5	1.5
Current liabilities/Net worth (%)	21.3	41.3	74.1	18.7	40.1	77.4	19.0	35.3	82.8
Current liabilities/Inventory (%)	78.0	156.1	254.9	79.2	133.6	252.5	75.0	132.4	239.6
Total liabilities/Net worth (%)	29.7	70.8	129.7	22.8	66.7	123.5	23.0	52.6	130.6
Fixed assets/Net worth (%)	13.1	42.8	74.9	14.7	41.7	66.6	11.8	33.6	63.4
Efficiency									
Collection period (days)	39.9	53.3	73.6	36.5	51.5	77.0	36.3	51.5	70.9
Sales to Inventory	10.6	6.5	4.7	11.4	7.3	5.3	13.3	7.7	5.1
Assets/Sales (%)	55.6	109.0	172.7	47.6	73.8	129.1	46.5	75.8	132.0
Sales/Net Working Capital	7.5	3.8	1.8	8.0	4.5	2.2	8.4	4.4	2.1
Accounts payable/Sales (%)	5.2	8.2	13.3	4.9	7.8	12.1	4.7	7.3	12.2
Profitability									
Return - Sales (%)	16.2	5.7	1.4	15.0	4.8	-.6	12.8	3.5	.3
Return - Assets (%)	19.5	7.7	.8	18.8	7.1	-.4	15.7	5.5	-.4
Return - Net Worth (%)	36.5	14.7	.8	36.1	13.8	-1.4	32.9	12.9	.4

Source: Dun & Bradstreet. Data in this table are copyright (c) 1999 of Dun & Bradstreet. Reprinted by special arrangement with D&B. *Note:* UQ stands for "Upper Quartile" and represents the top 25 percent of sample; MED stands for "Median"; and LQ stands for "Lower Quartile" and represents the lowest 25 percent.

D&B INDUSTRY NORMS: SIC 2835 - DIAGNOSTIC SUBSTANCES

	1998 (43) Estab.		1997 (47) Estab.		1996 (35) Estab.	
	$	%	$	%	$	%
Cash	2,370,909	20.3	1,478,005	16.3	1,838,723	21.9
Accounts Receivable	2,043,887	17.5	1,686,557	18.6	1,578,447	18.8
Notes Receivable	-	-	-	-	-	-
Inventory	1,857,017	15.9	1,586,815	17.5	1,217,419	14.5
Other Current Assets	1,354,805	11.6	1,124,372	12.4	688,472	8.2
Total Current Assets	7,626,618	65.3	5,875,749	64.8	5,323,061	63.4
Fixed Assets	2,464,344	21.1	2,158,068	23.8	2,048,623	24.4
Other Non-current Assets	1,588,392	13.6	1,033,696	11.4	1,024,311	12.2
Total Assets	11,679,354	100.0	9,067,513	100.0	8,395,995	100.0
Accounts Payable	899,310	7.7	761,671	8.4	797,620	9.5
Bank Loans	11,679	.1	-	-	50,376	.6
Notes Payable	128,473	1.1	108,810	1.2	125,940	1.5
Other Current Liabilities	1,378,164	11.8	1,205,979	13.3	797,620	9.5
Total Current Liabilities	2,417,626	20.7	2,076,460	22.9	1,771,556	21.1
Other Long Term	1,459,919	12.5	1,142,507	12.6	1,217,419	14.5
Deferred Credits	58,397	.5	27,203	.3	16,792	.2
Net Worth	7,743,412	66.3	5,821,343	64.2	5,390,229	64.2
Total Liabilities & Net Worth	11,679,354	100.0	9,067,513	100.0	8,395,996	100.0
Net Sales	9,909,744	100.0	14,466,660	100.0	6,622,161	100.0
Gross Profits	4,647,670	46.9	7,811,996	54.0	3,456,768	52.2
Net Profit After Tax	594,585	6.0	665,466	4.6	105,955	1.6
Working Capital	5,208,993	-	3,799,288	-	3,551,506	-

Source: Dun & Bradstreet. Data in this table are copyright (c) 1999 of Dun & Bradstreet. Reprinted by special arrangement with D&B. *Notes:* Values in parentheses above columns indicate the number of establishments in the sample. Data shown are for all companies.

D&B KEY BUSINESS RATIOS: SIC 2835

	1998			1997			1996		
	UQ	MED	LQ	UQ	MED	LQ	UQ	MED	LQ
Solvency									
Quick ratio	3.0	1.8	1.0	3.0	1.7	1.2	3.6	2.0	1.2
Current ratio	6.8	3.7	1.8	6.0	4.1	1.8	6.5	4.1	2.0
Current liabilities/Net worth (%)	10.7	20.9	41.6	11.9	20.1	54.5	12.5	16.0	59.7
Current liabilities/Inventory (%)	63.3	119.1	213.3	71.6	104.3	224.8	64.1	118.2	222.1
Total liabilities/Net worth (%)	13.8	28.4	70.9	16.9	27.4	89.1	18.7	45.2	117.4
Fixed assets/Net worth (%)	8.9	26.5	45.4	14.8	30.4	49.9	18.3	28.9	59.6
Efficiency									
Collection period (days)	52.6	68.6	89.4	51.5	62.8	84.9	49.1	54.8	75.1
Sales to Inventory	12.9	4.8	3.8	12.8	5.9	4.6	17.4	7.6	5.2
Assets/Sales (%)	72.3	107.3	142.1	73.8	101.8	136.8	72.8	99.0	118.9
Sales/Net Working Capital	3.2	2.4	1.5	4.6	2.2	1.4	4.6	2.5	1.7
Accounts payable/Sales (%)	3.6	6.1	8.8	4.2	6.4	8.6	3.9	6.2	10.3
Profitability									
Return - Sales (%)	13.9	5.4	2.2	10.6	6.4	1.3	8.2	3.9	.6
Return - Assets (%)	9.3	4.2	.2	12.5	5.4	2.4	10.6	5.4	.8
Return - Net Worth (%)	20.1	5.8	1.3	18.4	9.1	3.1	22.8	11.7	1.3

Source: Dun & Bradstreet. Data in this table are copyright (c) 1999 of Dun & Bradstreet. Reprinted by special arrangement with D&B. *Note:* UQ stands for "Upper Quartile" and represents the top 25 percent of sample; MED stands for "Median"; and LQ stands for "Lower Quartile" and represents the lowest 25 percent.

D&B INDUSTRY NORMS: SIC 2836 - BIOLOGICAL PRODUCTS, EXCEPT DIAGNOSTIC SUBSTANCES

	1998 (30) Estab.		1997 (37) Estab.		1996 (34) Estab.	
	$	%	$	%	$	%
Cash	8,156,639	24.6	713,920	13.1	1,167,241	15.8
Accounts Receivable	5,470,917	16.5	1,084,504	19.9	1,484,908	20.1
Notes Receivable	33,157	.1	-	-	73,876	1.0
Inventory	4,807,775	14.5	1,198,949	22.0	1,440,583	19.5
Other Current Assets	2,884,665	8.7	550,427	10.1	620,559	8.4
Total Current Assets	21,353,153	64.4	3,547,800	65.1	4,787,167	64.8
Fixed Assets	6,233,529	18.8	1,378,792	25.3	1,824,738	24.7
Other Non-current Assets	5,570,388	16.8	523,178	9.6	775,698	10.5
Total Assets	33,157,070	100.0	5,449,770	100.0	7,387,603	100.0
Accounts Payable	2,088,895	6.3	523,178	9.6	849,574	11.5
Bank Loans	-	-	-	-	-	-
Notes Payable	663,141	2.0	354,235	6.5	258,566	3.5
Other Current Liabilities	4,045,163	12.2	768,418	14.1	1,034,264	14.0
Total Current Liabilities	6,797,199	20.5	1,645,831	30.2	2,142,404	29.0
Other Long Term	4,874,089	14.7	801,116	14.7	1,196,792	16.2
Deferred Credits	132,628	.4	5,450	.1	14,775	.2
Net Worth	21,353,153	64.4	2,997,374	55.0	4,033,631	54.6
Total Liabilities & Net Worth	33,157,069	100.0	5,449,771	100.0	7,387,602	100.0
Net Sales	23,286,000	100.0	9,430,250	100.0	8,608,447	100.0
Gross Profits	12,504,582	53.7	5,054,614	53.6	4,614,128	53.6
Net Profit After Tax	908,154	3.9	348,919	3.7	473,465	5.5
Working Capital	14,555,954	-	1,901,969	-	2,644,762	-

Source: Dun & Bradstreet. Data in this table are copyright (c) 1999 of Dun & Bradstreet. Reprinted by special arrangement with D&B. *Notes:* Values in parentheses above columns indicate the number of establishments in the sample. Data shown are for all companies.

D&B KEY BUSINESS RATIOS: SIC 2836

	1998			1997			1996		
	UQ	MED	LQ	UQ	MED	LQ	UQ	MED	LQ
Solvency									
Quick ratio	5.0	1.5	1.1	2.4	1.0	.7	3.8	1.4	.6
Current ratio	8.0	4.4	2.5	4.1	2.5	1.5	5.0	3.2	1.3
Current liabilities/Net worth (%)	11.8	17.6	45.4	19.3	47.8	104.2	22.3	33.7	69.8
Current liabilities/Inventory (%)	80.1	88.4	246.8	60.3	118.2	192.0	58.0	164.4	230.2
Total liabilities/Net worth (%)	24.4	42.3	103.3	30.6	62.1	204.6	26.0	64.1	179.5
Fixed assets/Net worth (%)	12.8	23.5	58.9	18.6	56.3	105.3	21.7	33.7	88.7
Efficiency									
Collection period (days)	55.9	63.9	71.2	38.9	48.6	56.8	36.4	50.2	60.4
Sales to Inventory	5.6	4.8	2.6	9.6	7.1	3.0	9.7	4.9	3.2
Assets/Sales (%)	67.8	104.9	201.5	45.7	94.5	137.2	53.0	82.6	109.0
Sales/Net Working Capital	3.5	2.1	1.4	5.7	3.6	1.2	5.6	2.7	1.7
Accounts payable/Sales (%)	5.4	6.9	11.6	3.0	6.1	7.6	4.7	7.4	11.1
Profitability									
Return - Sales (%)	9.9	4.9	.3	11.1	5.5	.3	10.9	3.8	-.3
Return - Assets (%)	11.9	3.6	.6	15.8	6.5	.3	14.1	4.4	-1.5
Return - Net Worth (%)	17.5	4.8	1.9	33.7	13.1	1.7	23.2	15.1	-3.3

Source: Dun & Bradstreet. Data in this table are copyright (c) 1999 of Dun & Bradstreet. Reprinted by special arrangement with D&B. *Note:* UQ stands for "Upper Quartile" and represents the top 25 percent of sample; MED stands for "Median"; and LQ stands for "Lower Quartile" and represents the lowest 25 percent.

COMPANY DIRECTORY

This chapter presents brief profiles of 992 companies in the Pharmaceuticals sector. Companies are public, private, and elements of public companies ("public family members").

Each entry features the *D-U-N-S* access number for the company, the company name, its parent (if applicable), address, telephone, sales, employees, the company's primary SIC classification, a brief description of the company's business activity, and the name and title of its chairman, president, or other high-ranking officer. If the company is an exporter, importer, or both, the fact is indicated by the abbreviations EXP, IMP, and IMP EXP shown facing the *D-U-N-S* number.

Rankings of these companies are shown in Chapter 5. Additional financial data—on an aggregated, industry level—are shown in Chapter 3.

This product includes proprietary data of Dun & Bradstreet, Inc.

D-U-N-S 80-853-9274
3-DIMENSIONAL PHARMACEUTICALS
665 Stockton Dr, Ste 104, Exton, PA 19341
Phone: (610) 458-8959
Sales: $4,768,000   *Employees:* 75
Company Type: Private   *Employees here:* 75
SIC: 2834
   Pharmaceutical research & development
Thomas P Stagnaro, President

D-U-N-S 05-531-3712
A & S PHARMACEUTICAL CORP.
480 Barnum Ave, Bridgeport, CT 06608
Phone: (203) 368-2538
Sales: $2,200,000   *Employees:* 25
Company Type: Private   *Employees here:* 25
SIC: 2834
   Mfg pharmaceutical preparations
Arnold Lewis, President

D-U-N-S 06-349-6335   EXP
A & V INCORPORATED
   (Parent: Wilson Group Inc)
N62w22632 Village Dr, Sussex, WI 53089
Phone: (414) 246-6922
Sales: $12,000,000   *Employees:* 50
Company Type: Private   *Employees here:* 50
SIC: 2836
   Mfg microbial/enzyme products specialty cleaners and lake
     algaecides
Edwin J Wilson, Chairman of the Board

D-U-N-S 92-682-0705
A & Z PHARMACEUTICAL INC.
180 Oser Ave, Ste 300, Hauppauge, NY 11788
Phone: (516) 952-3800
Sales: $3,000,000   *Employees:* 35
Company Type: Private   *Employees here:* 34
SIC: 2834
   Manufactures pharmaceutical products
Brian Li, President

D-U-N-S 10-189-6231   EXP
AARON INDUSTRIES INC.
Hwy 72 W, Clinton, SC 29325
Phone: (864) 833-0178
Sales: $10,000,000   *Employees:* 43
Company Type: Private   *Employees here:* 43
SIC: 2834
   Manufactures over-the-counter pharmaceutical preparations
John Pate, President

D-U-N-S 09-013-1251
ABBOTT CHEMICALS INC.
   (Parent: Abbott Laboratories)
P.O. Box 278, Barceloneta, PR 00617
Phone: (787) 846-3500
Sales: $15,400,000   *Employees:* 166
Company Type: Public Family Member   *Employees here:* 166
SIC: 2833
   Mfg antibiotics
Joe Mattingly, Chief Executive Officer

D-U-N-S 11-814-9871
ABBOTT DIAGNOSTICS INC.
   (Parent: Abbott Laboratories)
P.O. Box 278, Barceloneta, PR 00617
Phone: (787) 846-3500
Sales: $56,500,000   *Employees:* NA
Company Type: Public Family Member   *Employees here:* NA
SIC: 2834
   Mfg pharmaceutical preparations
Duane L Burnham, Chairman of the Board

D-U-N-S 09-035-8029
ABBOTT HEALTH PRODUCTS INC.
   (Parent: Abbott Laboratories)
100 Abbott Park Rd, North Chicago, IL 60064
Phone: (847) 937-6100
Sales: $201,400,000   *Employees:* 1,575
Company Type: Public Family Member   *Employees here:* 10
SIC: 2834
   Mfg pharmaceutical products
Gary Coughlan, Chief Financial Officer

D-U-N-S 00-130-7602   EXP
ABBOTT LABORATORIES
100 Abbott Park Rd, North Chicago, IL 60064
Phone: (847) 937-6100
Sales: $12,477,845,000   *Employees:* 54,487
Company Type: Public   *Employees here:* 12,284
SIC: 2834
   Mfg pharmaceutical nutritional hospital & laboratory pdts &
     infant formula
Miles White, Chairman of the Board

D-U-N-S 12-224-5764
ABLE LABORATORIES, INC.
   (Parent: Dynagen Inc)
6 Hollywood Ct, South Plainfield, NJ 07080
Phone: (908) 754-2253
Sales: $3,200,000   *Employees:* 30
Company Type: Public Family Member   *Employees here:* 30
SIC: 2834
   Mfg generic pharmaceutical preparations
Indu Muni, President

D-U-N-S 04-802-2727   EXP
ABS CORPORATION
7031 N 16th St, Omaha, NE 68112
Phone: (402) 453-6970
Sales: $5,300,000   *Employees:* 62
Company Type: Private   *Employees here:* 62
SIC: 2834
   Vitamins & animal care products commercial real estate
     operation whol medical equipment
Richard Wood, President

D-U-N-S 83-546-9768
AC MOLDING COMPOUNDS
S Cherry St, Wallingford, CT 06492
Phone: (203) 269-4481
Sales: $88,700,000   *Employees:* 700
Company Type: Private   *Employees here:* 700
SIC: 2834
   Mfg pharmaceutical preparations
Cytek Industries, Partner

D-U-N-S 80-342-6873
ACCUCORP PACKAGING INC.
10101 Roosevelt Blvd, Philadelphia, PA 19154
Phone: (215) 671-1403
Sales: $16,200,000   *Employees:* 120
Company Type: Private   *Employees here:* 120
SIC: 2834
   Packaging & mfg pharmaceutical preparations
Leslie Leff, President

D-U-N-S 80-888-2815
ACCUMED INC.
2572 Brunswick Ave, Lawrenceville, NJ 08648
Phone: (609) 883-1818
Sales: $3,000,000   *Employees:* 23
Company Type: Private   *Employees here:* 23
SIC: 2834
   Mfg pharmaceuticals & over the counter drugs
Burgise Palkhiwala, President

D-U-N-S 03-825-3845   EXP
ADH HEALTH PRODUCTS, INC.
215 N Route 303, Congers, NY 10920
Phone: (914) 268-0027
Sales: $7,500,000   *Employees:* 65
Company Type: Private   *Employees here:* 65
SIC: 2834
    Mfg pharmaceutical preparations & health food supplements
Balram Advani, President

D-U-N-S 87-768-3672   EXP
ADM LABORATORIES, INC.
    (Parent: Hdi Nutrients Inc)
5536 W Roosevelt St, Ste 1, Phoenix, AZ 85043
Phone: (602) 272-3777
Sales: $3,900,000   *Employees:* 40
Company Type: Private   *Employees here:* 40
SIC: 2833
    Mfg nutritional supplements
Richard Davis, President

D-U-N-S 03-988-5165
ADVANCE DEVELOPMENT CO.
480 Oberlin Ave S, Lakewood, NJ 08701
Phone: (732) 364-8855
Sales: $4,900,000   *Employees:* 50
Company Type: Private   *Employees here:* 50
SIC: 2834
    Mfg pharmaceutical preparations
Stephen Hoffman, General Partner

D-U-N-S 18-782-4339
ADVANCE PHARMACEUTICAL INC.
2201 5th Ave, Ste F, Ronkonkoma, NY 11779
Phone: (516) 981-4600
Sales: $3,792,000   *Employees:* 30
Company Type: Private   *Employees here:* 30
SIC: 2834
    Manufactures pharmaceuticals
Tasrin Hossain, President

D-U-N-S 95-750-1968
ADVANCED BIO INSTITUTE
1530 Baker St, Ste J, Costa Mesa, CA 92626
Phone: (714) 540-0727
Sales: $4,500,000   *Employees:* 5
Company Type: Private   *Employees here:* 5
SIC: 2834
    Mfg nutritional supplements
Armand Wijckmans, Owner

D-U-N-S 04-844-4467
ADVANCED BIOTECHNOLOGIES, INC.
9108 Guilford Rd, Columbia, MD 21046
Phone: (410) 792-9779
Sales: $3,102,000   *Employees:* 34
Company Type: Private   *Employees here:* 34
SIC: 2836
    Mfg & services biological products
Dr James E Whitman Jr, President

D-U-N-S 01-751-1155   EXP
ADVANCED MAGNETICS INC.
61 Mooney St, Cambridge, MA 02138
Phone: (617) 497-2070
Sales: $11,002,000   *Employees:* 68
Company Type: Public   *Employees here:* 50
SIC: 2834
    Mfg contrast agents for use with mri equipment
Leonard M Baum, President

D-U-N-S 93-854-1810
ADVANCED MANUFACTURING SYSTEMS
4450 Arapahoe Ave, Ste 100, Boulder, CO 80303
Phone: (303) 415-2587
Sales: $3,000,000   *Employees:* 18
Company Type: Private   *Employees here:* 18
SIC: 2834
    Mfg vitamins & nutritional supplements
Jonathan Hager, President

D-U-N-S 01-350-4407
ADVANCED NUTRACEUTICALS INC.
500 Metuchen Rd, South Plainfield, NJ 07080
Phone: (908) 668-0088
Sales: $30,800,000   *Employees:* 195
Company Type: Private   *Employees here:* 3
SIC: 2834
    Vitamin preparation
Joseph R Schortz, President

D-U-N-S 96-912-4536
ADVANCED VISION RESEARCH
7 Alfred St, Ste 330, Woburn, MA 01801
Phone: (781) 932-8327
Sales: $2,500,000   *Employees:* 4
Company Type: Private   *Employees here:* 4
SIC: 2834
    Mfg pharmaceutical preparations
Jeffery Gilbard, President

D-U-N-S 96-424-5518   EXP
AESTHETIC TECHNOLOGIES CORP.
    (Parent: Collagen Aesthetics Inc)
1850 Embarcadero Rd, Palo Alto, CA 94303
Phone: (650) 856-0200
Sales: $69,300,000   *Employees:* 200
Company Type: Public Family Member   *Employees here:* 200
SIC: 2836
    Mfg biocompatible surgical products
Gary S Petersmeyer, President

D-U-N-S 80-468-2573
AFFYMETRIX, INC.
3380 Central Expy, Santa Clara, CA 95051
Phone: (408) 731-5000
Sales: $19,765,000   *Employees:* 242
Company Type: Public   *Employees here:* 220
SIC: 2835
    Mfg diagnostic systems
Stephen P Fodor, President

D-U-N-S 18-488-5226
AGGROW OILS LLC
780 N 11th St, Carrington, ND 58421
Phone: (701) 652-1990
Sales: $6,500,000   *Employees:* 17
Company Type: Private   *Employees here:* 17
SIC: 2833
    Mfg vegetable oils & other specialty oils
John Gardner, General Manager

D-U-N-S 14-577-2760
AGOURON PHARMACEUTICALS INC.
10350 N Torrey Pines Rd, La Jolla, CA 92037
Phone: (619) 622-3000
Sales: $466,505,000   *Employees:* 991
Company Type: Public   *Employees here:* 640
SIC: 2834
    Mfg & whol pharmaceutical products
Peter Johnson, President

D-U-N-S 80-912-8226
AGRI-NUTRITION GROUP LIMITED
13801 Riverport Dr, Maryland Heights, MO 63043
Phone: (314) 298-7330
Sales: $32,944,000   *Employees:* 220
Company Type: Public   *Employees here:* 4
SIC: 2834
  Holding company
Bruce G Baker, President

D-U-N-S 78-752-4586   EXP
AIM INTERNATIONAL, INC.
3904 E Flamingo Ave, Nampa, ID 83687
Phone: (208) 465-5116
Sales: $47,759,000   *Employees:* 150
Company Type: Private   *Employees here:* 3
SIC: 2833
  Whol health foods
Dennis J Itami, Chairman of the Board

D-U-N-S 96-661-9769
AJAY CHEMICALS INC.
1400 Industry Rd, Powder Springs, GA 30127
Phone: (770) 943-6202
Sales: $3,800,000   *Employees:* 35
Company Type: Private   *Employees here:* 10
SIC: 2834
  Mfg chemicals for pharmaceuticals and food additives &
    livestock feed additives
Alan Shipp, President

D-U-N-S 06-142-5104   EXP
AJAY NORTH AMERICA LLC
  (Parent: Ajay Chemicals Inc)
1400 Industry Rd, Powder Springs, GA 30127
Phone: (770) 943-6202
Sales: $3,400,000   *Employees:* 32
Company Type: Private   *Employees here:* 32
SIC: 2834
  Mfg pharmaceuticals and food additives and chemicals for
    livestock feed additives
Alan Shipp, President

D-U-N-S 06-264-9876   EXP
AKORN, INC.
2500 Millbrook Dr, Buffalo Grove, IL 60089
Phone: (847) 279-6100
Sales: $42,323,000   *Employees:* 266
Company Type: Public   *Employees here:* 73
SIC: 2834
  Mfg ophthalmic pharmaceuticals & contract mfg of
    pharmaceutical injectables
Floyd Benjamin, President

D-U-N-S 07-359-9342   EXP
ALACER CORP.
19631 Pauling, El Toro, CA 92610
Phone: (949) 951-9660
Sales: $6,017,000   *Employees:* 70
Company Type: Private   *Employees here:* 70
SIC: 2833
  Mfg vitamins and nutritional supplements
Jay Patrick, President

D-U-N-S 78-779-3900
ALBANY MOLECULAR RESEARCH
21 Corporate Cir, Albany, NY 12203
Phone: (518) 464-0279

Sales: $9,000,000   *Employees:* 122
Company Type: Public   *Employees here:* 70
SIC: 2833
  Mfg & whol specialty fine drugs & drug intermediates &
    organic chemical research
Thomas E D Ambra, Chairman of the Board

D-U-N-S 09-105-8560
ALBERTO BARTOLOMEI
Gurabo Indus Park Rr 189, Gurabo, PR 00778
Phone: (787) 737-8445
Sales: $5,323,000   *Employees:* 18
Company Type: Private   *Employees here:* 18
SIC: 2833
  Mfg vitamins & pharmaceutical products
Alberto Bartolomei, Owner

D-U-N-S 09-976-0563   EXP
ALCIDE CORPORATION
8561 154th Ave NE, Redmond, WA 98052
Phone: (425) 882-2555
Sales: $12,999,000   *Employees:* 15
Company Type: Public   *Employees here:* 15
SIC: 2834
  Mfg animal & human health products and disinfectants
Joseph A Sasenick, President

D-U-N-S 00-801-8525   IMP
ALCON LABORATORIES, INC.
6201 South Fwy, Fort Worth, TX 76134
Phone: (817) 293-0450
Sales: $1,253,000,000   *Employees:* 4,500
Company Type: Private   *Employees here:* 2,500
SIC: 2834
  Mfg ophthalmic pharmaceutical solutions & ophthalmic
    surgical products
Timothy R Sear, President

D-U-N-S 01-683-5456
ALCON PUERTO RICO INC.
6201 South Fwy, Fort Worth, TX 76134
Phone: (817) 293-0450
Sales: $157,000,000   *Employees:* 251
Company Type: Private   *Employees here:* 6
SIC: 2834
  Mfg pharmaceutical products
Timothy R Sear, President

D-U-N-S 18-635-1581   EXP
ALEXON-TREND INC.
  (Parent: Erie Scientific Co)
14000 Unity St NW, Anoka, MN 55303
Phone: (612) 323-7800
Sales: $4,400,000   *Employees:* 55
Company Type: Private   *Employees here:* 55
SIC: 2835
  Mfg diagnostic products
David Taus, President

D-U-N-S 11-403-9886
ALFA-FLOUR INC.
25101 County Road 35, Wray, CO 80758
Phone: (970) 332-3124
Sales: $4,300,000   *Employees:* 47
Company Type: Private   *Employees here:* 47
SIC: 2834
  Mfg vitamin & nutritional supplements
Alva Deterding, President

D-U-N-S 80-674-7317
ALFRED KHALILY INC.
98 Kings Point Rd, Great Neck, NY 11024
Phone: (516) 504-0059

Sales: $2,800,000   *Employees:* 5
Company Type: Private   *Employees here:* 4
SIC: 2834
   Manufactures pharmaceutical preparations
Alfred Khalily, President

D-U-N-S 16-185-8329   EXP
ALK LABORATORIES INC.
27 Village Ln, Wallingford, CT 06492
Phone: (203) 949-2727
Sales: $15,000,000   *Employees:* 53
Company Type: Private   *Employees here:* 25
SIC: 2836
   Mfg allergenic extracts and other related products
Brien J De Bari, President

D-U-N-S 83-871-6025
ALK LABORATORIES INC.
1700 Royston Ln, Round Rock, TX 78664
Phone: (512) 251-0037
Sales: $4,500,000   *Employees:* NA
Company Type: Private   *Employees here:* 50
SIC: 2834
   Pharmaceutical preparations
Jerry Friesen, Manager

D-U-N-S 80-003-4472   EXP
ALL AMERICAN PHARMACEUTICALS
1831 Main St, Billings, MT 59105
Phone: (406) 245-5793
Sales: $15,000,000   *Employees:* 55
Company Type: Private   *Employees here:* 55
SIC: 2834
   Mfg nutritional supplements & over-the-counter drugs
Daniel Golini, Chief Executive Officer

D-U-N-S 93-110-3683
ALL NATURAL PRODUCTS CORP.
174 Herricks Rd, Mineola, NY 11501
Phone: (516) 741-3304
Sales: $2,200,000   *Employees:* 20
Company Type: Private   *Employees here:* 20
SIC: 2833
   Mfg medicinal/botanical products
Tom Sethi, President

D-U-N-S 78-950-9759
ALLEN & ASSOCIATES INTL LTD.
3333 K St NW, Ste 210, Washington, DC 20007
Phone: (202) 342-2424
Sales: $5,600,000   *Employees:* 48
Company Type: Private   *Employees here:* 10
SIC: 2834
   Mfg pharmaceutical preparations
Albert J Allen, Chairman of the Board

D-U-N-S 04-647-0852
ALLERDERM INC.
   (Parent: Virbac Inc)
3200 Meacham Blvd, Fort Worth, TX 76137
Phone: (817) 831-5030
Sales: $7,100,000   *Employees:* 68
Company Type: Private   *Employees here:* 68
SIC: 2834
   Mfg veterinary supplies
Roger Brandt, President

D-U-N-S 14-479-6497
ALLERGAN INC.
2525 Dupont Dr, Irvine, CA 92612
Phone: (714) 246-4500

Sales: $1,138,000,000   *Employees:* 6,124
Company Type: Public   *Employees here:* 1,300
SIC: 2834
   Mfg pharmaceutical solutions intraocular lenses &
      ophthalmic surgical pdts
David E I, President

D-U-N-S 12-221-0271
ALLERGY CONTROL PRODUCTS, INC.
96 Danbury Rd Apt D, Ridgefield, CT 06877
Phone: (203) 438-9580
Sales: $2,900,000   *Employees:* 42
Company Type: Private   *Employees here:* 42
SIC: 2836
   Manufactures & develops allergen avoidance products
Annette Miller, President

D-U-N-S 60-645-8024
ALOE LABORATORIES, INC.
   (Parent: Pharmaceutical Laboratories)
6908 W Expressway 83, Harlingen, TX 78552
Phone: (956) 428-8416
Sales: $2,400,000   *Employees:* 25
Company Type: Public Family Member   *Employees here:* 25
SIC: 2834
   Mfg pharmaceutical preparations
R C Benson, President

D-U-N-S 09-269-4538   EXP
ALPHA THERAPEUTIC CORPORATION
   (Parent: Green Cross Corp of America)
5555 Valley Blvd, Los Angeles, CA 90032
Phone: (323) 225-2221
Sales: $384,718,000   *Employees:* 2,800
Company Type: Private   *Employees here:* 1,400
SIC: 2836
   Mfg plasma derivatives
Ralph M Galustian, President

D-U-N-S 07-095-4094   EXP
ALPHARMA INC.
1 Executive Dr, Fort Lee, NJ 07024
Phone: (201) 947-7774
Sales: $500,288,000   *Employees:* 700
Company Type: Public   *Employees here:* 75
SIC: 2834
   Mfg pharmaceuticals animal health micronutrients feed
      additives & bulk antibiotics
Einar W Sissener, Chairman of the Board

D-U-N-S 02-240-2994
ALPHARMA USPD INC.
   (Parent: Alpharma Inc)
7205 Windsor Blvd, Baltimore, MD 21244
Phone: (410) 298-1000
Sales: $88,700,000   *Employees:* 700
Company Type: Public Family Member   *Employees here:* 535
SIC: 2834
   Mfg pharmaceuticals
George S Barrett, President

D-U-N-S 09-727-4328
ALRA LABORATORIES INC.
3850 Clearview Ct, Gurnee, IL 60031
Phone: (847) 244-9440
Sales: $12,000,000   *Employees:* 80
Company Type: Private   *Employees here:* 80
SIC: 2834
   Mfg pharmaceuticals
Dr Raj Bhutani, President

D-U-N-S 04-383-8424
ALTANA INC.
60 Baylis Rd, Melville, NY 11747
Phone: (516) 454-7677
Sales: $213,241,000   *Employees:* 854
Company Type: Private   *Employees here:* 200
SIC: 2834
  Mfg pharmaceuticals varnishes paints chemical additives
    measuring instruments test & inspection equipment
George Cole, President

D-U-N-S 06-749-0607
AM PHARM CORP.
12 Dwight Pl, Fairfield, NJ 07004
Phone: (973) 276-1330
Sales: $2,300,000   *Employees:* 22
Company Type: Private   *Employees here:* 22
SIC: 2834
  Mfr generic pharmaceuticals and vitamins
Al Bagwell, President

D-U-N-S 01-024-6643
AMBICO INC.
  (Parent: Intervet Inc)
902 Sugar Grove Ave, Dallas Center, IA 50063
Phone: (515) 992-3842
Sales: $4,600,000   *Employees:* 85
Company Type: Private   *Employees here:* 85
SIC: 2836
  Mfg animal vaccines

D-U-N-S 19-868-0068   EXP
AMBION INC.
2130 Woodward St, Ste 200, Austin, TX 78744
Phone: (512) 445-6979
Sales: $6,972,000   *Employees:* 78
Company Type: Private   *Employees here:* 78
SIC: 2836
  Mfg kits & reagents for biomedical research
Matt Winkler, Chief Executive Officer

D-U-N-S 83-457-3180
AMERI-KAL, INC.
2360 Wilbur Way, Auburn, CA 95602
Phone: (530) 888-1497
Sales: $2,000,000   *Employees:* 45
Company Type: Private   *Employees here:* 45
SIC: 2833
  Mfg vitamins and nutritional supplements
S Darmohusodo I, President

D-U-N-S 19-550-5177
AMERICAN BIOLOGICAL TECH
940 Crossroads Blvd, Seguin, TX 78155
Phone: (830) 372-1391
Sales: $7,400,000   *Employees:* 100
Company Type: Private   *Employees here:* 100
SIC: 2835
  Mfg serums
Michael Schrage, President

D-U-N-S 09-933-9301
AMERICAN BIORGANICS INC.
  (Parent: Angus Chemical Company)
2236 Liberty Dr, Niagara Falls, NY 14304
Phone: (716) 283-1434
Sales: $2,400,000   *Employees:* 30
Company Type: Private   *Employees here:* 30
SIC: 2836
  Mfg biochemicals including culture media
Fayyaz Hussain, President

D-U-N-S 08-728-5037
AMERICAN CHELATES INC.
227 Union St, Northvale, NJ 07647
Phone: (201) 784-0500
Sales: $2,100,000   *Employees:* 20
Company Type: Private   *Employees here:* 20
SIC: 2833
  Mfg botanical products
Heginio Arriaza, President

D-U-N-S 00-215-0001
AMERICAN CYANAMID COMPANY
  (Parent: American Home Products Corp)
1 Campus Dr, Parsippany, NJ 07054
Phone: (973) 683-2000
Sales: $2,575,000,000   *Employees:* 20,000
Company Type: Public Family Member   *Employees here:* 1,000
SIC: 2834
  Mfg medical & pharmaceutical pdts & agricultural pdts
John R Stafford, Chairman of the Board

D-U-N-S 80-645-3908
AMERICAN ECO-SYSTEMS INC.
125 129 9th Ave, Wellman, IA 52356
Phone: (319) 646-2943
Sales: $5,000,000   *Employees:* 12
Company Type: Private   *Employees here:* 12
SIC: 2836
  Manufacture air filters
J P Laccoarce, Chairman of the Board

D-U-N-S 00-131-7130   EXP
AMERICAN HOME PRODUCTS CORP.
5 Giralda Farms, Madison, NJ 07940
Phone: (973) 660-5000
Sales: $14,196,026,000   *Employees:* 60,523
Company Type: Public   *Employees here:* 850
SIC: 2834
  Mfg pharmaceuticals vaccines veterinary biologicals otc
    medications medical devices & instruments & agricultural
    pdts
John R Stafford, Chairman of the Board

D-U-N-S 60-604-0269   EXP
AMERICAN INGREDIENTS INC.
2929 E White Star Ave, Anaheim, CA 92806
Phone: (714) 630-6000
Sales: $15,000,000   *Employees:* 14
Company Type: Private   *Employees here:* 14
SIC: 2833
  Distributor of nutritional chemicals & botanical products
Arthur Salerno, President

D-U-N-S 03-645-4056
AMERICAN PHRM PARTNERS
  (Parent: Vivorx Inc)
10866 Wilshire Blvd, Los Angeles, CA 90024
Phone: (310) 470-4222
Sales: $3,673,000   *Employees:* 600
Company Type: Private   *Employees here:* 400
SIC: 2834
  Mfg pharmaceutical preparations
Patrick Soon-Shinog, Chairman of the Board

D-U-N-S 36-110-8459
AMERIFIT, INC.
166 Highland Park Dr, Bloomfield, CT 06002
Phone: (860) 242-3476
Sales: $20,000,000   *Employees:* 54
Company Type: Private   *Employees here:* 54
SIC: 2833
  Mfg nutritional food supplements
Martin Herman, President

D-U-N-S 88-436-2070
AMERILAB TECHNOLOGIES, INC.
3101 Louisiana Ave N, Minneapolis, MN 55427
Phone: (612) 525-1262
Sales: $3,000,000   *Employees:* 40
Company Type: Private   *Employees here:* 40
SIC: 2834
   Mfg pharmaceutical preparations
Fred J Wehling, President

D-U-N-S 87-722-1465
AMERSHAM CORPORATION
   (Parent: Amersham Holdings Inc (del))
2636 S Clearbrook Dr, Arlington Heights, IL 60005
Phone: (847) 593-6300
Sales: $100,000,000   *Employees:* 383
Company Type: Private   *Employees here:* 300
SIC: 2835
   Mfg and distributes quality and safety assurance products
      and radiography products and services
C G Marlow, President

D-U-N-S 79-453-7043
AMERSHAM HOLDINGS INC.
2636 S Clearbrook Dr, Arlington Heights, IL 60005
Phone: (847) 593-6300
Sales: $270,000,000   *Employees:* 1,050
Company Type: Private   *Employees here:* 250
SIC: 2835
   Mfg and whol life science and nuclear medicines
C G Marlow, President

D-U-N-S 88-371-4214
AMGEN HOLDING INC.
1 Amgen Way, Thousand Oaks, CA 91320
Phone: (805) 499-5725
Sales: $615,700,000   *Employees:* 4,791
Company Type: Private   *Employees here:* 3,047
SIC: 2834
   Mfg pharmaceutical preparations
Gordon Binder, President

D-U-N-S 03-997-6196
AMGEN INC.
1840 Dehavilland Dr, Thousand Oaks, CA 91320
Phone: (805) 447-1000
Sales: $2,401,000,000   *Employees:* 5,308
Company Type: Public   *Employees here:* 2,577
SIC: 2834
   Mfg pharmaceutical preparations
Gordon M Binder, Chairman of the Board

D-U-N-S 78-580-0020
AMGEN PUERTO RICO INC.
   (Parent: Amgen Inc)
Km 24 Hm 6 Rr 31, Juncos, PR 00777
Phone: (787) 734-2000
Sales: $439,879,000   *Employees:* 240
Company Type: Public Family Member   *Employees here:* 240
SIC: 2836
   Mfg bio-pharmaceutical products
Ed Bjurstrom, General Manager

D-U-N-S 10-123-9622
AMIDE PHARMACEUTICAL INC.
101 E Main St, Ste 1, Little Falls, NJ 07424
Phone: (973) 890-1440
Sales: $26,199,000   *Employees:* 90
Company Type: Private   *Employees here:* 90
SIC: 2834
   Mfg prescription pharmaceutical products
Chandu Patel, President

D-U-N-S 14-997-9650   EXP
AMOCO TECHNOLOGY COMPANY
   (Parent: BP Amoco Corporation)
3100 Woodcreek Dr, Downers Grove, IL 60515
Phone: (630) 271-7000
Sales: $45,000,000   *Employees:* NA
Company Type: Private   *Employees here:* NA
SIC: 2835
   Mfg solar cells panels & related systems laser systems &
      DNA probe based diagnostic tests & develops genetic
      software
Robert C Carr, President

D-U-N-S 02-473-6733
AMPHASTAR PHARMACUTICALS INC.
13760 Magnolia Ave, Chino, CA 91710
Phone: (909) 364-1143
Sales: $51,400,000   *Employees:* 410
Company Type: Private   *Employees here:* 10
SIC: 2834
   Mfg pharmaceutical preparations
Jack Zahang, President

D-U-N-S 18-916-5483   EXP
AMT LABS INC.
536 N 700 W, North Salt Lake, UT 84054
Phone: (801) 299-1661
Sales: $18,775,000   *Employees:* 22
Company Type: Private   *Employees here:* 22
SIC: 2833
   Mfg nutritional products
Bing L Fang, President

D-U-N-S 60-355-4007
AMTL CORPORATION
1 Oakwood Blvd, Ste 130, Hollywood, FL 33020
Phone: (954) 923-2990
Sales: $4,500,000   *Employees:* 33
Company Type: Private   *Employees here:* 23
SIC: 2835
   Mfg diagnostic systems and provides medical testing
Roger Deutsch, President

D-U-N-S 18-984-0259
ANERGEN, INC.
301 Penobscot Dr, Redwood City, CA 94063
Phone: (650) 361-8901
Sales: $6,328,000   *Employees:* NA
Company Type: Public   *Employees here:* NA
SIC: 2834
   Develops proprietary therapies
Barry Sherman, President

D-U-N-S 60-398-2497
ANSYS DIAGNOSTICS INC.
25200 Commercentre Dr, Lake Forest, CA 92630
Phone: (949) 770-9381
Sales: $18,964,000   *Employees:* 241
Company Type: Private   *Employees here:* 241
SIC: 2835
   Mfg medical diagnostic supplies
Stephen Schultheis, Chairman of the Board

D-U-N-S 00-963-6705   EXP
ANTHONY PRODUCTS CO.
5600 Peck Rd, Arcadia, CA 91006
Phone: (626) 357-8711
Sales: $14,390,000   *Employees:* 50
Company Type: Private   *Employees here:* 5
SIC: 2834
   Mfg veterinary pharmaceutical products
James D Viscio, President

D-U-N-S 03-070-5628
ANTIGEN LABORATORIES INC.
30 S Main St 34, Liberty, MO 64068
Phone: (816) 781-5222
Sales: $2,500,000 | *Employees:* 23
Company Type: Private | *Employees here:* 23
SIC: 2834
　Mfr allergenic extracts & diagnostic substances
Tom Willoughby, President

D-U-N-S 82-489-1022
APOTEX USA, INC.
3384 Long Beach Rd, Oceanside, NY 11572
Phone: (516) 594-5700
Sales: $10,000,000 | *Employees:* 70
Company Type: Private | *Employees here:* 3
SIC: 2834
　Mfg & distributor of pharmaceuticals
Jack H Schramm, President

D-U-N-S 09-231-2735
APOTHECARY PRODUCTS INC.
11531 Rupp Dr, Burnsville, MN 55337
Phone: (612) 890-1940
Sales: $25,000,000 | *Employees:* 200
Company Type: Private | *Employees here:* 200
SIC: 2834
　Wholesales pharmaceutical supplies manufactures and
　　distributes pharmaceutical items
Terrance Noble, President

D-U-N-S 93-345-5354
APPLICARE, INC.
　(Parent: Mcbar Medical Industries Inc)
455 S 4th Ave, Ste 825, Louisville, KY 40202
Phone: (502) 581-1708
Sales: $21,300,000 | *Employees:* 160
Company Type: Private | *Employees here:* 2
SIC: 2834
　Mfg of antimicrobial & personal care medical products
Rod Mcnerney, President

D-U-N-S 62-239-8170 　　　　　　　　　EXP
APPLIED BIOTECH, INC.
10237 Flanders Ct, San Diego, CA 92121
Phone: (619) 587-6771
Sales: $15,964,000 | *Employees:* 175
Company Type: Private | *Employees here:* 175
SIC: 2835
　Mfg medical diagnostic reagents and pregnancy test kits
Shung-Ho Chang, President

D-U-N-S 11-733-7220
APPLIED LABORATORIES INC.
3240 N Indianapolis Rd, Columbus, IN 47201
Phone: (812) 372-2607
Sales: $6,000,000 | *Employees:* 65
Company Type: Private | *Employees here:* 65
SIC: 2834
　Mfg liquid & aerosol medical solutions
Anthony Moravec, President

D-U-N-S 83-931-8888 　　　　　　　　　EXP
ARCHON VITAMIN CORP.
209 40th St, Irvington, NJ 07111
Phone: (973) 371-1700
Sales: $6,000,000 | *Employees:* 42
Company Type: Private | *Employees here:* 42
SIC: 2834
　Mfg medicinal/botanical products mfg pharmaceutical
　　preparations
Thomas F Pugsley, President

D-U-N-S 00-134-1601 　　　　　　　　　IMP
ARENOL CORPORATION
189 Meister Ave, Somerville, NJ 08876
Phone: (908) 526-5900
Sales: $6,000,000 | *Employees:* 15
Company Type: Private | *Employees here:* 15
SIC: 2833
　Mfg organic medicinal & fine chemicals
Richard D Vorisek, President

D-U-N-S 04-975-3143
ARGONEX HOLDINGS INC.
2044 India Rd, Ste 202, Charlottesville, VA 22901
Phone: (804) 975-4300
Sales: $9,100,000 | *Employees:* 102
Company Type: Private | *Employees here:* 8
SIC: 2835

Sheridan G Snyder, Chief Executive Officer

D-U-N-S 96-195-3304 　　　　　　　　　EXP
ARIZONA NUTRITIONAL SUPPLEMENT
402 S Perry Ln, Ste 5, Tempe, AZ 85281
Phone: (602) 966-9630
Sales: $6,000,000 | *Employees:* 22
Company Type: Private | *Employees here:* 22
SIC: 2834
　Mfg & packager of nutritional supplements & botanicals
Jonathan P Pinkus, President

D-U-N-S 00-118-5115
ARMSTRONG LABORATORIES INC.
423 Lagrange St, West Roxbury, MA 02132
Phone: (617) 323-7404
Sales: $32,300,000 | *Employees:* 200
Company Type: Private | *Employees here:* 200
SIC: 2834
　Mfg pharmaceuticals
Benjamin Shepard, President

D-U-N-S 61-873-2200
ASCENT PEDIATRICS, INC.
187 Ballardvale St, Wilmington, MA 01887
Phone: (978) 658-2500
Sales: $2,073,000 | *Employees:* 15
Company Type: Public | *Employees here:* 15
SIC: 2834
　Pharmaceutical development
Alan R Fox, President

D-U-N-S 92-946-2034
ASH CORP.
3600 25th Ave, Gulfport, MS 39501
Phone: (228) 863-1702
Sales: $10,800,000 | *Employees:* 98
Company Type: Private | *Employees here:* 98
SIC: 2834
　Mfg pharmaceuticals
Tllan Sirkin, President

D-U-N-S 96-221-3518
ASHFORD PHARMALOGIC CORP.
Ashford Medical Ctr, San Juan, PR 00907
Phone: (787) 721-2128
Sales: $3,000,000 | *Employees:* 11
Company Type: Private | *Employees here:* 6
SIC: 2834
　Mfg pharmaceutical preparations
Angel A Rivera, President

D-U-N-S 07-657-4078
ASSOCIATES OF CAPE COD, INC.
704 Main St, Falmouth, MA 02540

Phone: (508) 540-3444
Sales: $2,300,000   *Employees:* 28
Company Type: Private   *Employees here:* 28
SIC: 2835
   Mfg biological products
Earlene MacDowell, Treasurer

D-U-N-S 87-651-6568
ASTRA PHARMACEUTICALS, LP
725 Chesterbrook Blvd, Wayne, PA 19087
Phone: (610) 695-1000
Sales: $2,700,000,000   *Employees:* 3,800
Company Type: Private   *Employees here:* 1,000
SIC: 2834
   Developer manufacturer & marketer of pharmaceutical
      products
Carl-Gusta Johansson, President

D-U-N-S 88-461-2490
ASTRA RESEARCH CENTER BOSTON
128 Sidney St, Cambridge, MA 02139
Phone: (617) 576-3900
Sales: $6,400,000   *Employees:* 70
Company Type: Private   *Employees here:* 70
SIC: 2835
   Pharmaceutical research
Dr Hans Nilsson, President

D-U-N-S 96-490-7406
ATLANTIC PHARMACEUTICAL SVCS
   (Parent: Niro Inc)
11200 Gundry Ln, Owings Mills, MD 21117
Phone: (410) 413-1000
Sales: $9,500,000   *Employees:* 85
Company Type: Private   *Employees here:* 85
SIC: 2834
   Mfg pharmaceutical bulk powders
Steven M Kaplan, President

D-U-N-S 96-868-4803
AU NATUREL, INC.
   (Parent: Nutraceutical Corporation)
Freeport Ctr Bldg G9, Clearfield, UT 84016
Phone: (801) 775-0800
Sales: $3,300,000   *Employees:* 35
Company Type: Public Family Member   *Employees here:* 35
SIC: 2834
   Mfg vitamins
Frank W Gay II, President

D-U-N-S 04-079-3114
AVANT IMMUNOTHERAPEUTICS INC.
119 4th Ave, Needham, MA 02494
Phone: (781) 433-0771
Sales: $10,000,000   *Employees:* 80
Company Type: Private   *Employees here:* 80
SIC: 2833
   Mfg diagnostics & therapeutic health care products
Una S Ryan, President

D-U-N-S 07-547-3496   EXP
AVANTI POLAR LIPIDS INC.
700 Industrial Park Dr, Alabaster, AL 35007
Phone: (205) 663-2494
Sales: $3,500,000   *Employees:* 45
Company Type: Private   *Employees here:* 45
SIC: 2833
   Mfg phospholipids & pharmaceutical products
Dr Walter A Shaw, President

D-U-N-S 60-838-0622
AXYS PHARMACEUTICALS, INC.
180 Kimball Way, South San Francisco, CA 94080
Phone: (650) 829-1000

Sales: $24,814,000   *Employees:* 256
Company Type: Public   *Employees here:* 160
SIC: 2834
   Mfg pharmaceuticals
John P Walker, President

D-U-N-S 17-325-0903
B & C NUTRITIONAL PRODUCTS
2550 Pioneer Ave, Vista, CA 92083
Phone: (760) 727-0992
Sales: $10,000,000   *Employees:* 43
Company Type: Private   *Employees here:* 38
SIC: 2833
   Mfg nutritional supplements
John A Butler, President

D-U-N-S 62-152-4198
B. BRAUN/MC GAW, INC.
   (Parent: B Braun of America Inc)
2525 Mcgaw Ave, Irvine, CA 92614
Phone: (949) 660-2000
Sales: $350,000,000   *Employees:* 3,000
Company Type: Private   *Employees here:* 1,700
SIC: 2834
   Mfg intravenous solutions other pharmaceutical preparations
      & related infusion supplies & equipment
William J Degoede, President

D-U-N-S 00-385-4403   EXP
B F ASCHER & COMPANY INC.
15501 W 109th St, Shawnee Mission, KS 66219
Phone: (913) 888-1880
Sales: $3,200,000   *Employees:* 42
Company Type: Private   *Employees here:* 42
SIC: 2834
   Mfg pharmaceutical preparations
James J Ascher, Chairman of the Board

D-U-N-S 09-356-1652
B I CHEMICALS INC.
   (Parent: Boehringer Ingelheim Corp)
900 Ridgebury Rd, Ridgefield, CT 06877
Phone: (203) 798-9988
Sales: $22,300,000   *Employees:* 150
Company Type: Private   *Employees here:* 4
SIC: 2834
   Manufactures pharmaceutical chemicals
Michael Zaleski, President

D-U-N-S 17-905-8730
BACHEM BIOSCIENCE INC.
3700 Horizon Dr, King Of Prussia, PA 19406
Phone: (610) 239-0300
Sales: $8,000,000   *Employees:* 22
Company Type: Private   *Employees here:* 22
SIC: 2836
   Develops & manufactures biologicals & pharmaceuticals
Peter Grogg, President

D-U-N-S 07-724-3640   EXP
BACHEM INC.
3132 Kashiwa St, Torrance, CA 90505
Phone: (310) 539-4171
Sales: $6,700,000   *Employees:* 100
Company Type: Private   *Employees here:* 70
SIC: 2836
   Mfg research and biomedical chemicals
Rao Makineni, President

D-U-N-S 94-220-3118
BACTOLAC PHARMACEUTICAL INC.
51 Brooklyn Ave, Westbury, NY 11590
Phone: (516) 333-4483

Sales: $4,172,000   *Employees:* 29
Company Type: Private   *Employees here:* 29
SIC: 2833
    Manufacturer of vitamins
Pailla Shadhnan, President

D-U-N-S 62-098-6182
BAKER CUMMINS DERMATOLOGICALS INC.
    (Parent: Norton Baker Pharmaceuticals)
50 NW 176th St, Miami, FL 33169
Phone: (305) 575-6750
Sales: $3,500,000   *Employees:* 37
Company Type: Public Family Member   *Employees here:* 37
SIC: 2834
    Manufacturer of dermatologicals
Richard Wildnauer, President

D-U-N-S 00-219-3829
BANNER PHARMACAPS INC.
    (Parent: Sobel Usa Inc)
4125 Premier Dr, High Point, NC 27265
Phone: (336) 812-8700
Sales: $200,000,000   *Employees:* 897
Company Type: Private   *Employees here:* 515
SIC: 2834
    Mfg pharmaceutical preparations
James W Warren Jr, Chief Executive Officer

D-U-N-S 14-424-6774
BARD DIAGNOSTIC SCIENCES DIVISION
    (Parent: C R Bard Inc)
12277 134th Ct NE, Ste 100, Redmond, WA 98052
Phone: (425) 821-1010
Sales: $5,300,000   *Employees:* 55
Company Type: Public Family Member   *Employees here:* 55
SIC: 2835
    Mfg invitro diagnostic kits
Max Lyon, President

D-U-N-S 61-870-9687
BARIATRIX INTERNATIONAL INC.
    (Parent: Produits Bariatrix Intl Inc)
40 Allen Rd, South Burlington, VT 05403
Phone: (802) 862-9242
Sales: $23,020,000   *Employees:* 26
Company Type: Private   *Employees here:* 26
SIC: 2834
    Mfg food supplements consisting of vitamin & mineral
    additives
Thomas Egger, President

D-U-N-S 05-630-6780
BARR LABORATORIES INC.
2 Quaker Rd, Pomona, NY 10970
Phone: (914) 362-1100
Sales: $377,304,000   *Employees:* 557
Company Type: Public   *Employees here:* 170
SIC: 2834
    Mfg & whol pharmaceutical pdts
Bruce L Downey, Chairman of the Board

D-U-N-S 93-336-6353
BARTELS INC.
    (Parent: Intracel Corporation)
2005 NW Sammamish Rd, Issaquah, WA 98027
Phone: (425) 392-2992
Sales: $17,000,000   *Employees:* 125
Company Type: Private   *Employees here:* 125
SIC: 2835
    Mfg biological products
Simon Mc Kenzie, President

D-U-N-S 17-404-9759
BASF PHARMACEUTICALS, INC.
    (Parent: Knoll Pharmaceutical Company)
Km 2 Hm 6 Rr 144, Jayuya, PR 00664
Phone: (787) 828-0990
Sales: $9,200,000   *Employees:* 95
Company Type: Private   *Employees here:* 95
SIC: 2834
    Mfg drugs
Carter H Eckert, President

D-U-N-S 80-792-7397
BAUSCH & LOMB PHARMACEUTICALS
    (Parent: Bausch & Lomb Incorporated)
8500 Hidden River Pkwy, Tampa, FL 33637
Phone: (813) 975-7700
Sales: $50,100,000   *Employees:* 400
Company Type: Public Family Member   *Employees here:* 400
SIC: 2834
    Mfg pharmaceuticals
Thomas M Riedhamer PhD, President

D-U-N-S 09-112-7555
BAXTER CARIBE, INC.
    (Parent: Ohmeda Inc)
Km 142 Hm 5 Rr 3, Guayama, PR 00784
Phone: (787) 864-5050
Sales: $57,000,000   *Employees:* 211
Company Type: Private   *Employees here:* 211
SIC: 2833
    Mfg anesthetics
Harry Kraemer, Chairman of the Board

D-U-N-S 00-508-3209
BAXTER HEALTHCARE CORPORATION
    (Parent: Baxter International Inc)
1 Baxter Pkwy, Deerfield, IL 60015
Phone: (847) 948-2000
Sales: $3,763,000,000   *Employees:* 15,000
Company Type: Public Family Member   *Employees here:* 1,200
SIC: 2834
    Mfg & whol health-care pdts systems & svcs
Harry J Kraemer Jr, President

D-U-N-S 00-514-6311   EXP
BAXTER INTERNATIONAL INC.
1 Baxter Pkwy, Deerfield, IL 60015
Phone: (847) 948-2000
Sales: $6,138,000,000   *Employees:* 41,000
Company Type: Public   *Employees here:* 1,500
SIC: 2834
    Mfg & whol healthcare pdts systems & svcs
Vernon R Loucks Jr, Chairman of the Board

D-U-N-S 04-414-1757
BAXTER PHARMACEUTICAL PRODUCTS
    (Parent: Baxter International Inc)
110 Allen Rd, Liberty Corner, NJ 07938
Phone: (908) 604-7678
Sales: $37,200,000   *Employees:* 300
Company Type: Public Family Member   *Employees here:* 300
SIC: 2834
    Mfg pharmaceutical preparations
Ronald Quadrel, Vice-President

D-U-N-S 80-011-7194   EXP
BAYWOOD INTERNATIONAL, INC.
14950 N 83rd Pl, Ste 1, Scottsdale, AZ 85260
Phone: (602) 951-3956

Sales: $3,234,000   *Employees:* 4
Company Type: Public   *Employees here:* 4
SIC: 2834
    Mfg nutrition supplements & beauty products
Neil Reithinger, Chief Financial Officer

D-U-N-S 03-276-3633
BEACH PRODUCTS INC.
5220 S Manhattan Ave, Tampa, FL 33611
Phone: (813) 839-6565
Sales: $9,900,000   *Employees:* 90
Company Type: Private   *Employees here:* 8
SIC: 2834
    Mfg pharmaceutical preparations
Richard B Jenkins, President

D-U-N-S 94-151-2584
BEAUTY & HEALTH INTERNATIONAL
1627 Boyd St, Santa Ana, CA 92705
Phone: (714) 742-8825
Sales: $6,600,000   *Employees:* 50
Company Type: Private   *Employees here:* 25
SIC: 2834
    Mfg import & export beauty & health aids
Charles G Myung, President

D-U-N-S 03-639-1746
BENNETT CHEM LTD.
800 E Northwest Hwy, Palatine, IL 60067
Phone: (847) 963-1014
Sales: $4,000,000   *Employees:* 19
Company Type: Private   *Employees here:* 7
SIC: 2833
    Manufacturers organic chemicals
Bruce W Bennett, President

D-U-N-S 06-966-6733
BENTLEY PHARMACEUTICALS INC.
4830 W Kennedy Blvd, Tampa, FL 33609
Phone: (813) 286-4401
Sales: $14,902,000   *Employees:* 110
Company Type: Public   *Employees here:* 6
SIC: 2834
    Mfg pharmaceuticals
James R Murphy, President

D-U-N-S 10-292-8033
BERKELEY ANTIBODY COMPANY
1223 S 47th St, Richmond, CA 94804
Phone: (510) 222-4940
Sales: $5,285,000   *Employees:* 52
Company Type: Private   *Employees here:* 40
SIC: 2833
    Develops antibodies
Thomas R Anderson, President

D-U-N-S 04-524-1023   EXP
BERKELEY NUTRITIONAL MFG.
2353 Industrial Pkwy W, Hayward, CA 94545
Phone: (510) 887-0101
Sales: $4,000,000   *Employees:* 29
Company Type: Private   *Employees here:* 29
SIC: 2834
    Mfg vitamins
Theodore Aarons, President

D-U-N-S 09-826-2173
BERLEX LABORATORIES INC.
    (Parent: Schering Berlin Inc)
340 Change Bridge Rd, Montville, NJ 07045
Phone: (973) 276-2000

Sales: $576,319,000   *Employees:* 1,440
Company Type: Private   *Employees here:* 195
SIC: 2834
    Manufactures ethical pharmaceutical products
Lutz Lingnau, Chairman of the Board

D-U-N-S 18-413-9772
BERLIN INDUSTRIES INC.
14174 Ellsworth Rd, Berlin Center, OH 44401
Phone: (330) 547-2225
Sales: $4,000,000   *Employees:* 21
Company Type: Private   *Employees here:* 21
SIC: 2834
    Mfg veterinary pharmaceutical products
William J Barnett, President

D-U-N-S 00-807-0484
BERTEK PHARMACEUTICALS, INC.
    (Parent: Mylan Laboratories Inc)
10410 Corporate Dr, Sugar Land, TX 77478
Phone: (281) 240-1000
Sales: $50,000,000   *Employees:* 250
Company Type: Public Family Member   *Employees here:* 40
SIC: 2834
    Mfg pharmaceutical preparations
William Richardson, President

D-U-N-S 14-864-2002
BERWIND PHARMACEUTICAL SVCS
415 Moyer Blvd, West Point, PA 19486
Phone: (215) 699-7733
Sales: $142,020,000   *Employees:* 600
Company Type: Private   *Employees here:* 275
SIC: 2834
    Mfg pharmaceutical tablet coating material
Michael B McLelland, President

D-U-N-S 08-635-2655   EXP
BEST INDUSTRIES INC.
7643 Fullerton Rd, Springfield, VA 22153
Phone: (703) 451-2378
Sales: $3,900,000   *Employees:* 42
Company Type: Private   *Employees here:* 42
SIC: 2834
    Mfg radiological pharmaceuticals
Krishnan Suthanthiran, President

D-U-N-S 93-272-7407
BFG CLINIPAD INVESTORS, LP
1500 Market St, Philadelphia, PA 19102
Phone: (215) 563-2800
Sales: $56,800,000   *Employees:* 452
Company Type: Private   *Employees here:* 2
SIC: 2834
    Mfg iodine solutions surgical appliances and supplies OEM
        and contract flexible packaging paper
Peter G Gould, President

D-U-N-S 94-962-0223   EXP
BIGMAR, INC.
9711 Sportsman Club Rd, Johnstown, OH 43031
Phone: (740) 966-5800
Sales: $6,483,000   *Employees:* 50
Company Type: Public   *Employees here:* 50
SIC: 2834
    Mfg pharmaceutical preparations
John Tramontana, President

D-U-N-S 06-032-0967   EXP
BIO BOTANICA INC.
75 Commerce Dr, Hauppauge, NY 11788
Phone: (516) 231-5522

Sales: $6,400,000   *Employees:* 50
Company Type: Private   *Employees here:* 50
SIC: 2833
     Manufactures herbal extracts & botanical extracts
Frank D Amelio Sr, Chief Executive Officer

D-U-N-S 86-747-9693
BIO-ENERGETICS INC.
11 Kirby Ln N, Rye, NY 10580
Phone: (914) 967-2704
Sales: $2,600,000   *Employees:* 25
Company Type: Private   *Employees here:* 25
SIC: 2834
     Pharmaceutical research and development
Joseph Chira, President

D-U-N-S 06-196-2775
BIO MED PLASTICS INC.
1430 W Blancke St, Linden, NJ 07036
Phone: (908) 862-5550
Sales: $4,900,000   *Employees:* 50
Company Type: Private   *Employees here:* 50
SIC: 2834
     Mfg pharmaceutical products
Jack W Kaufman, President

D-U-N-S 13-130-4081
BIO-TRENDS INTERNATIONAL, INC.
2510 Boatman Ave, West Sacramento, CA 95691
Phone: (916) 371-1795
Sales: $2,700,000   *Employees:* 30
Company Type: Private   *Employees here:* 30
SIC: 2835
     Research develops & mfg veterinary vaccines
Charles J York, President

D-U-N-S 03-801-0310
BIOCHEMICAL SCIENCES INC.
     (Parent: Fisher Scientific Intl)
200 Commodore Dr, Swedesboro, NJ 08085
Phone: (609) 467-1813
Sales: $4,800,000   *Employees:* 50
Company Type: Public Family Member   *Employees here:* 50
SIC: 2835
     Mfg of diagnostic stains & reagents
R Thompson, Vice-President

D-U-N-S 03-032-2395
BIOCOR ANIMAL HEALTH INC.
2720 N 84th St, Omaha, NE 68134
Phone: (402) 393-7440
Sales: $10,000,000   *Employees:* 70
Company Type: Private   *Employees here:* 70
SIC: 2836
     Mfg animal vaccines
Hugh Middleton, President

D-U-N-S 62-343-0006
BIOCORE MEDICAL TECH INC.
1605 SW 41st St, Topeka, KS 66609
Phone: (785) 267-4800
Sales: $5,700,000   *Employees:* 50
Company Type: Private   *Employees here:* 35
SIC: 2833
     Manufacturing and research company
Dr Manoj Jain, President

D-U-N-S 96-176-3992   EXP
BIOCORE MEDICAL TECHNOLOGIES
1605 SW 41st St, Topeka, KS 66609
Phone: (785) 267-4800

Sales: $4,700,000   *Employees:* 47
Company Type: Private   *Employees here:* 47
SIC: 2833
     Mfg medical products
Dr Manoj Jain, President

D-U-N-S 19-709-6209
BIODESIGN INTERNATIONAL
     (Parent: Meridian Diagnostics Inc)
105 York St, Kennebunk, ME 04043
Phone: (207) 985-1944
Sales: $2,700,000   *Employees:* 24
Company Type: Public Family Member   *Employees here:* 24
SIC: 2833
     Mfg antibodies
Holly Scribner, President

D-U-N-S 07-483-5455
BIOFLUIDS INC.
1114 Taft St, Rockville, MD 20850
Phone: (301) 424-4140
Sales: $2,286,000   *Employees:* 13
Company Type: Private   *Employees here:* 13
SIC: 2836
     Mfg sterile biological
Dr Robert R Rafajko, President

D-U-N-S 04-269-7045   EXP
BIOGENEX LABORATORIES
4600 Norris Canyon Rd, San Ramon, CA 94583
Phone: (925) 275-0550
Sales: $12,700,000   *Employees:* 125
Company Type: Private   *Employees here:* 101
SIC: 2835
     Mfg histogy & cytolgy diagnostic kits and reagents &
     instrumentation for automated immunohistochemistry
     procedures
Kris Kalra, President

D-U-N-S 10-872-3891
BIOGLAN INC.
20481 Crescent Bay Dr, Lake Forest, CA 92630
Phone: (949) 951-5150
Sales: $2,200,000   *Employees:* 20
Company Type: Private   *Employees here:* 6
SIC: 2834
     Mfg nutritional products
Edward Alosio, President

D-U-N-S 10-342-0113
BIOLOG INC.
3938 Trust Way, Hayward, CA 94545
Phone: (510) 785-2564
Sales: $3,600,000   *Employees:* 40
Company Type: Private   *Employees here:* 40
SIC: 2835
     Mfg disposable microbiology test kits & software
Donald Barnby, President

D-U-N-S 79-651-8439
BIOLOGICALLY ACTIVE SUBSTANCES
2354 Garden Rd, Monterey, CA 93940
Phone: (831) 656-1600
Sales: $6,000,000   *Employees:* 50
Company Type: Private   *Employees here:* 50
SIC: 2833
     Mfg herbal based nutritional supplements
Vaughn Feather, President

D-U-N-S 01-149-0562   EXP
BIOMATRIX, INC.
65 Railroad Ave, Ste 2, Ridgefield, NJ 07657
Phone: (201) 945-9550

Sales: $32,564,000
Employees: 350
Company Type: Public
Employees here: 200
SIC: 2836
  Mfg biological products
Dr Endre A Balazs MD, Officer

D-U-N-S 78-653-3398
BIOMETRIC IMAGING INC.
1025b Terra Bella Ave, Mountain View, CA 94043
Phone: (650) 903-5870
Sales: $5,000,000
Employees: 60
Company Type: Private
Employees here: 60
SIC: 2835
  Mfg diagnostic equipment
Christophe English, President

D-U-N-S 79-077-5001
BIOMUNE COMPANY
8906 Rosehill Rd, Shawnee Mission, KS 66215
Phone: (913) 894-0230
Sales: $4,400,000
Employees: 65
Company Type: Private
Employees here: 61
SIC: 2836
  Mfg biological products
Ronald Plylar, President

D-U-N-S 10-687-7426 EXP
BIOMUNE SYSTEMS, INC.
2401 Foothill Dr, Salt Lake City, UT 84109
Phone: (801) 466-3441
Sales: $2,807,000
Employees: 20
Company Type: Public
Employees here: 14
SIC: 2833
  Research & development firm
Michael Acton, Chief Executive Officer

D-U-N-S 62-221-1571
BIONIKE LABORATORIES, INC.
1011 Grandview Dr, South San Francisco, CA 94080
Phone: (650) 737-7937
Sales: $2,232,000
Employees: 23
Company Type: Private
Employees here: 23
SIC: 2835
  Mfg diagnostic testing kits
Dr Kai Wang, Chairman of the Board

D-U-N-S 10-118-7037
BIONOSTICS INC.
2 Craig Rd, Acton, MA 01720
Phone: (978) 263-3856
Sales: $4,600,000
Employees: 50
Company Type: Private
Employees here: 50
SIC: 2835
  Mfg standards controls & reagents
Bruce A Blessington, President

D-U-N-S 14-749-0700
BIOPHARMACEUTICS INC.
  (Parent: Biopharmaceutics Inc)
990 Station Rd, Bellport, NY 11713
Phone: (516) 286-5900
Sales: $4,100,000
Employees: 40
Company Type: Public Family Member
Employees here: 40
SIC: 2834
  Manufactures pharmaceuticals
Edward Fine, Chairman of the Board

D-U-N-S 05-202-0005 EXP
BIOSAN LABORATORIES INC.
8 Bowers Rd, Derry, NH 03038
Phone: (603) 432-5022

Sales: $4,000,000
Employees: 32
Company Type: Private
Employees here: 30
SIC: 2833
  Mfg vitamins & minerals
John Bragg, Chairman of the Board

D-U-N-S 19-485-4949
BIOSITE DIAGNOSTICS INC.
11030 Roselle St, San Diego, CA 92121
Phone: (619) 455-4808
Sales: $31,677,000
Employees: 209
Company Type: Public
Employees here: 209
SIC: 2835
  Develop & mfg medical diagnostic products
Kim Blickenstaff, President

D-U-N-S 60-666-6469 EXP
BIOSOURCE INTERNATIONAL INC.
820 Flynn Rd, Camarillo, CA 93012
Phone: (805) 987-0086
Sales: $20,572,000
Employees: 68
Company Type: Public
Employees here: 55
SIC: 2836
  Whol biological/allied products & mfg pharmaceutical
  preparations invitro/invivo diagnostic substances
James H Chamberlain, Chairman of the Board

D-U-N-S 18-170-1178
BIOSOURCE TECHNOLOGIES, INC.
3333 Vaca Valley Pkwy, Vacaville, CA 95688
Phone: (707) 446-5501
Sales: $2,000,000
Employees: 60
Company Type: Private
Employees here: 50
SIC: 2833
  Mfg biochemical products
Robert Erwin, Chairman of the Board

D-U-N-S 19-772-1129 EXP
BIOSPACIFIC INC.
4240 Hollis St, Ste 290, Emeryville, CA 94608
Phone: (510) 652-6155
Sales: $4,000,000
Employees: 10
Company Type: Private
Employees here: 8
SIC: 2835
  Mfg diagnostic components
Sandy Koshkin, President

D-U-N-S 55-635-4769 EXP
BIOSPECIFICS TECHNOLOGIES
35 Wilbur St, Lynbrook, NY 11563
Phone: (516) 593-7000
Sales: $5,825,000
Employees: 41
Company Type: Public
Employees here: 30
SIC: 2836
  Mfg biological products & provides biological research
Edwin Wegman, President

D-U-N-S 93-851-9287
BIOVAIL LABORATORIES INC.
  (Parent: Biovail Corporation Internati)
Res Sabana Abajo, Carolina, PR 00982
Phone: (787) 750-5350
Sales: $16,921,000
Employees: 90
Company Type: Private
Employees here: 90
SIC: 2834
  Mfg pharmaceutical preparations
C Rodriguez, General Manager

D-U-N-S 60-909-5955 EXP
BIOWHITTAKER INC.
  (Parent: Cambrex Corporation)
8830 Biggs Ford Rd, Walkersville, MD 21793
Phone: (301) 898-7025

Sales: $60,000,000   *Employees:* 400
Company Type: Public Family Member   *Employees here:* 390
SIC: 2836
   Mfg biological products
Noel Buterbaugh, President

D-U-N-S 55-556-4293   EXP
BIOZONE LABORATORIES, INC.
580 Garcia Ave, Pittsburg, CA 94565
Phone: (925) 473-1000
Sales: $2,904,000   *Employees:* 35
Company Type: Private   *Employees here:* 35
SIC: 2834
   Mfg pharmaceuticals and cosmetics
Dan Fisher, President

D-U-N-S 55-696-6521
BLACKHAWK BIOSYSTEMS INC.
12945 Alcosta Blvd, San Ramon, CA 94583
Phone: (925) 866-1458
Sales: $2,888,000   *Employees:* 15
Company Type: Private   *Employees here:* 15
SIC: 2835
   Develop computer software & chemical reagents
Carole Polito, President

D-U-N-S 05-373-5346
BLANSETT PHARMACAL COMPANY
3304 Pike Ave, North Little Rock, AR 72118
Phone: (501) 758-8635
Sales: $2,000,000   *Employees:* 24
Company Type: Private   *Employees here:* 24
SIC: 2834
   Mfg & whol pharmaceuticals
Larry Blansett, President

D-U-N-S 00-512-6354   EXP
BLISTEX INC.
1800 Swift Dr, Oak Brook, IL 60523
Phone: (630) 571-2870
Sales: $28,000,000   *Employees:* 126
Company Type: Private   *Employees here:* 115
SIC: 2834
   Mfg pharmaceutical preparations
David C Arch, Chairman

D-U-N-S 80-972-8207
BLUE BONNETT NUTRITION CORP.
12503 Exchange Dr, Ste 530, Stafford, TX 77477
Phone: (281) 240-3332
Sales: $2,382,000   *Employees:* 20
Company Type: Private   *Employees here:* 20
SIC: 2833
   Mfg vitamins
Gary Barrows, President

D-U-N-S 07-270-1865   EXP
BOEHRINGER INGELHEIM CORP.
   (Parent: Pharma-Investment Limited)
900 Ridgebury Rd, Ridgefield, CT 06877
Phone: (203) 798-9988
Sales: $358,000,000   *Employees:* 2,790
Company Type: Private   *Employees here:* 1,514
SIC: 2834
   Mfg human medical & veterinary pharmaceuticals
Werner Gerstenberg, President

D-U-N-S 00-713-4091   EXP
BOEHRINGER INGELHEIM VETMEDICA
   (Parent: Boehringer Ingelheim Corp)
2621 N Belt Hwy, Saint Joseph, MO 64506
Phone: (816) 233-2571

Sales: $120,000,000   *Employees:* 550
Company Type: Private   *Employees here:* 440
SIC: 2836
   Mfg serums vaccines pharmaceuticals & whol insecticides
Fintan Molloy, President

D-U-N-S 60-317-5944
BOEHRNGER INGLHEIM PHARMACEUTICALS
   (Parent: Boehringer Ingelheim Corp)
900 Ridgebury Rd, Ridgefield, CT 06877
Phone: (203) 798-9988
Sales: $230,400,000   *Employees:* 1,800
Company Type: Private   *Employees here:* 1,300
SIC: 2834
   Mfg pharmaceuticals
Werner Gerstenberg, President

D-U-N-S 01-489-2269
BOIRON BORNEMAN INC.
6 Campus Blvd, Newtown Square, PA 19073
Phone: (610) 325-7464
Sales: $11,019,000   *Employees:* 70
Company Type: Private   *Employees here:* 35
SIC: 2833
   Mfg homeopathic drugs
Christian Boiron, Chairman of the Board

D-U-N-S 96-686-5545
BORREGAARD SYNTHESES, INC.
9 Opportunity Way, Newburyport, MA 01950
Phone: (978) 462-5555
Sales: $3,600,000   *Employees:* 33
Company Type: Private   *Employees here:* 33
SIC: 2834
   Mfg pharmaceuticals & polymer chemicals
Dr Hargovind Rathore, President

D-U-N-S 12-535-4308   EXP
BOSTON BIOMEDICA, INC.
375 West St, West Bridgewater, MA 02379
Phone: (508) 580-1900
Sales: $22,299,000   *Employees:* 250
Company Type: Public   *Employees here:* 100
SIC: 2835
   Mfg medical diagnostic apparatus & medical research
    laboratory
Richard Schumacher, President

D-U-N-S 04-048-5187
BOTANICAL LABORATORIES INC.
1441 W Smith Rd, Ferndale, WA 98248
Phone: (360) 384-5656
Sales: $10,800,000   *Employees:* 84
Company Type: Private   *Employees here:* 84
SIC: 2834
   Mfg medicines
Jim Coyne, President

D-U-N-S 84-923-4661
BRACCO DIAGNOSTICS INC.
   (Parent: Bracco Usa Inc)
107 College Rd E, Princeton, NJ 08540
Phone: (609) 514-2200
Sales: $219,470,000   *Employees:* 270
Company Type: Private   *Employees here:* 135
SIC: 2835
   Develops diagnostic contrast imaging agents
John Cornille, President

D-U-N-S 03-635-9917
BRACCO U.S.A. INC.
107 College Rd E, Princeton, NJ 08540
Phone: (609) 514-2200

Sales: $228,289,000 — *Employees:* 290
Company Type: Private — *Employees here:* 2
SIC: 2835
  Holding company
Dr Elio F Bracco, President

D-U-N-S 18-375-4753
BRAMTON COMPANY, (INC)
  (Parent: Nch Corporation)
2727 Chemsearch Blvd, Irving, TX 75062
Phone: (972) 438-0397
Sales: $2,600,000 — *Employees:* 35
Company Type: Public Family Member — *Employees here:* 35
SIC: 2835
  Mfg odor eating & stain removal enzymes
Irvin L Levey, President

D-U-N-S 96-678-7087
BRANEL LABORATORIES INC.
Rural Route 1 Box 6b, Hill City, KS 67642
Phone: (785) 421-6292
Sales: $8,000,000 — *Employees:* 15
Company Type: Private — *Employees here:* 15
SIC: 2834
  Mfr tablets
Nelson Corazza, President

D-U-N-S 94-999-4206
BREATHIES INTERNATIONAL INC.
8460 Higuera St, Culver City, CA 90232
Phone: (310) 204-7888
Sales: $4,000,000 — *Employees:* 9
Company Type: Private — *Employees here:* 2
SIC: 2834
  Mfg pharmaceutical preparations
Sharon Fever, President

D-U-N-S 04-950-6330 — EXP
BRISTOL CARIBBEAN INC.
  (Parent: Bristol-Myers Squibb Company)
Zona Libre 7 Guanajibo, Mayaguez, PR 00680
Phone: (787) 834-0185
Sales: $600,000,000 — *Employees:* 89
Company Type: Public Family Member — *Employees here:* 89
SIC: 2834
  Mfg pharmaceutical products
Richard L Gelb, Chairman of the Board

D-U-N-S 09-003-6021 — EXP
BRISTOL-MYERS BARCELONETA INC.
  (Parent: Bristol-Myers Squibb Company)
Km 56 Hm 4 Rr 2, Barceloneta, PR 00617
Phone: (787) 846-3800
Sales: $426,233,000 — *Employees:* 650
Company Type: Public Family Member — *Employees here:* 650
SIC: 2834
  Mfg pharmaceutical products
Abramo Virgilio, President

D-U-N-S 00-128-8497 — EXP
BRISTOL-MYERS SQUIBB COMPANY
345 Park Ave, New York, NY 10022
Phone: (212) 546-4000
Sales: $16,701,000,000 — *Employees:* 53,600
Company Type: Public — *Employees here:* 600
SIC: 2834
  Mfg pharmaceutical & non-prescription health pdts
    nutritionals medical devices & beauty care pdts
Peter Dolan, President

D-U-N-S 13-144-5967
BRISTOL-MYERS SQUIBB LABORATOIRES
  (Parent: Bristol-Myers Squibb Company)
Zona Libre 7 Guanajibo, Mayaguez, PR 00680
Phone: (787) 834-0185
Sales: $847,444,000 — *Employees:* 527
Company Type: Public Family Member — *Employees here:* 527
SIC: 2834
  Mfg pharmaceutical preparations
Teo Iliapulus, General Manager

D-U-N-S 00-533-8108
C AND M PHARMACAL INC.
1721 Maplelane Ave, Hazel Park, MI 48030
Phone: (248) 548-7846
Sales: $3,105,000 — *Employees:* 30
Company Type: Private — *Employees here:* 30
SIC: 2834
  Mfg dermatological compounds
Jodi Anstandig, Treasurer

D-U-N-S 00-814-4388
C J MARTIN & SON INC.
  (Parent: Texas Farm Products Company)
606 W Main St, Nacogdoches, TX 75964
Phone: (409) 560-8202
Sales: $2,500,000 — *Employees:* 12
Company Type: Private — *Employees here:* 12
SIC: 2834
  Mfg veterinary supplies & pesticides
Thomas Wright, Chairman of the Board

D-U-N-S 18-874-0278
CALBIOCHEM-NOVABIOCHEM CORP.
  (Parent: CN Biosciences Inc)
10394 Pacific Center Ct, San Diego, CA 92121
Phone: (619) 450-9600
Sales: $21,544,000 — *Employees:* 150
Company Type: Public Family Member — *Employees here:* 100
SIC: 2836
  Mfg biological/biochemical products
Stelios B Papadopoulos, Chairman of the Board

D-U-N-S 79-544-7143
CALIX CORPORATION
128 Spring St, Lexington, MA 02421
Phone: (781) 861-9303
Sales: $15,100,000 — *Employees:* 99
Company Type: Private — *Employees here:* 3
SIC: 2834
  Mfg medicinal chemicals and physical research laboratory
Eugene Klim, President

D-U-N-S 15-153-0540
CALTAG INC.
1849 Bayshore Hwy, Ste 200, Burlingame, CA 94010
Phone: (650) 652-0468
Sales: $4,339,000 — *Employees:* 37
Company Type: Private — *Employees here:* 37
SIC: 2836
  Mfg biological products
Robert Johnson, Executive Vice-President

D-U-N-S 15-059-6716 — EXP
CAMBREX CORPORATION
1 Meadowlands Plz, East Rutherford, NJ 07073
Phone: (201) 804-3000
Sales: $457,240,000 — *Employees:* 1,790
Company Type: Public — *Employees here:* 21
SIC: 2834
  Mfg specialty pharmaceutical & fine industrial organic
    chemicals
Cyril C Baldwin Jr, Chairman of the Board

D-U-N-S 60-529-4917
CAPPSEALS INC.
12607 NE 95th St, Ste 100, Vancouver, WA 98682
Phone: (360) 944-9420
Sales: $5,000,000   *Employees:* 32
Company Type: Private   *Employees here:* 32
SIC: 2834
  Mfg capsulate vitamins
Don Webb, President

D-U-N-S 85-856-0477
CARDIOVASCULAR DYNAMICS INC.
13700 Alton Pkwy, Ste 160, Irvine, CA 92618
Phone: (949) 457-9546
Sales: $11,332,000   *Employees:* 170
Company Type: Public   *Employees here:* 170
SIC: 2834
  Development of drug delivery & advanced angioplasty
    catheters
Jeffrey F O'Donnell, President

D-U-N-S 78-641-3617   EXP
CARE TECHNOLOGIES, INC.
10 Corbin Dr, Darien, CT 06820
Phone: (203) 655-9680
Sales: $5,864,000   *Employees:* 10
Company Type: Private   *Employees here:* 10
SIC: 2834
  Mfg over the counter drugs
Thomas Mcguire, Chairman of the Board

D-U-N-S 00-609-0153   EXP
CARMA LABORATORIES, INC.
5801 W Airways Ave, Franklin, WI 53132
Phone: (414) 421-7707
Sales: $15,158,000   *Employees:* 55
Company Type: Private   *Employees here:* 55
SIC: 2834
  Mfg pharmaceutical preparations
Alfred G Woelbing, President

D-U-N-S 00-522-4175
CAROLINA MEDICAL PRODUCTS CO.
8026 Hwy 264 Alt E, Farmville, NC 27828
Phone: (252) 753-7111
Sales: $4,158,000   *Employees:* 24
Company Type: Private   *Employees here:* 24
SIC: 2834
  Mfg pharmaceuticals
James Olsen, President

D-U-N-S 06-898-3857   EXP
CARRINGTON LABORATORIES INC.
2001 W Walnut Hill Ln, Irving, TX 75038
Phone: (972) 518-1300
Sales: $23,559,000   *Employees:* 252
Company Type: Public   *Employees here:* 106
SIC: 2834
  Mfg non prescription pharmaceutical products
Carlton E Turner, President

D-U-N-S 03-077-6314   EXP
CAYMAN CHEMICAL COMPANY INC.
1180 E Ellsworth Rd, Ann Arbor, MI 48108
Phone: (734) 971-3335
Sales: $5,341,000   *Employees:* 52
Company Type: Private   *Employees here:* 52
SIC: 2834
  Mfg biological pharmaceuticals
Kirk Maxey, President

D-U-N-S 00-467-0501
CEDARBURG LABORATORIES INC.
870 Badger Cir, Grafton, WI 53024
Phone: (414) 376-1467
Sales: $3,500,000   *Employees:* 17
Company Type: Private   *Employees here:* 17
SIC: 2834
  Mfg active ingredients for pharmaceuticals
James G Yarger, President

D-U-N-S 60-963-1569
CELL GENESYS, INC.
342 Lakeside Dr, Foster City, CA 94404
Phone: (650) 358-9600
Sales: $23,806,000   *Employees:* 177
Company Type: Public   *Employees here:* 102
SIC: 2836
  Mfg biological products
Stephen A Sherwin, Chairman of the Board

D-U-N-S 06-670-7340
CENTEON BIO-SERVICES INC.
  (Parent: Rhone-Poulenc Rorer Inc)
6016 Brookvale Ln, Ste 152, Knoxville, TN 37919
Phone: (423) 588-0651
Sales: $108,900,000   *Employees:* 1,800
Company Type: Private   *Employees here:* 26
SIC: 2836
  Mfg plasma vaccines
Shannon T Foster, Executive Vice-President

D-U-N-S 93-189-6963
CENTEON LLC
1020 1st Ave, King Of Prussia, PA 19406
Phone: (610) 878-4000
Sales: $904,300,000   *Employees:* 918
Company Type: Private   *Employees here:* 100
SIC: 2836
  Mfg plasma protein derivatives
Ruedi Waeger, Chief Executive Officer

D-U-N-S 94-244-9612
CENTER FOR DIAGNOSTIC PRODUCTS
  (Parent: Intergen Company)
25 Birch St, Milford, MA 01757
Phone: (508) 478-5510
Sales: $2,300,000   *Employees:* 32
Company Type: Private   *Employees here:* 32
SIC: 2836
  Process human & bovine blood products
Robert Beckman, President

D-U-N-S 04-329-0803
CENTER LABORATORIES INC.
  (Parent: Heska Corp)
35 Channel Dr, Port Washington, NY 11050
Phone: (516) 767-1800
Sales: $5,000,000   *Employees:* 75
Company Type: Public Family Member   *Employees here:* 75
SIC: 2834

D-U-N-S 09-909-1753   EXP
CENTOCOR INC.
200 Great Valley Pkwy, Malvern, PA 19355
Phone: (610) 651-6000
Sales: $200,784,000   *Employees:* 640
Company Type: Public   *Employees here:* 400
SIC: 2834
  Develops & mfg pharmaceutical pdts
David P Holveck, Chief Executive Officer

D-U-N-S 78-410-7856
CENTRAL ADMIXTURE PHRM SVCS
(Parent: B Braun/McGaw Inc)
2525 McGaw Ave, Irvine, CA 92614
Phone: (949) 660-2000
Sales: $26,000,000　　　　　　　　*Employees:* 130
Company Type: Private　　　　　　*Employees here:* 10
SIC: 2834
　Mfg pharmaceutical preparations
Robert Kutteh, President

D-U-N-S 92-949-5901
CERES ORGANIC HARVEST INC.
3245 Broad St, Dexter, MI 48130
Phone: (734) 426-1221
Sales: $2,433,000　　　　　　　　*Employees:* 4
Company Type: Private　　　　　　*Employees here:* 3
SIC: 2833
　Mfg organic ingridients
Britten Eustis, President

D-U-N-S 94-159-2925
CHAMPION EXIMPORT ENTERPRISE,
13200 Brooks Dr, Ste J, Baldwin Park, CA 91706
Phone: (626) 337-2387
Sales: $3,000,000　　　　　　　　*Employees:* 8
Company Type: Private　　　　　　*Employees here:* 8
SIC: 2833
　Mfg nutritional supplements and wholesales outerwear
James Chan, President

D-U-N-S 15-463-5312
CHAMPION PERFORMANCE PRODUCTS
2615 Stanwell Dr, Concord, CA 94520
Phone: (925) 689-1790
Sales: $14,164,000　　　　　　　*Employees:* 42
Company Type: Private　　　　　　*Employees here:* 42
SIC: 2834
　Mfg nutritional supplements
Michael Zumpano, Chairman of the Board

D-U-N-S 13-128-8771
CHANTAL PHARMACEUTICAL CORP.
5757 W Century Blvd, Los Angeles, CA 90045
Phone: (310) 207-1950
Sales: $6,663,000　　　　　　　　*Employees:* 47
Company Type: Public　　　　　　*Employees here:* 47
SIC: 2834
　Mfg pharmaceutical preparations
Chantal Burnison, Chairman of the Board

D-U-N-S 01-090-7426
CHART CORP INC.
787 E 27th St, Paterson, NJ 07504
Phone: (973) 345-5554
Sales: $3,600,000　　　　　　　　*Employees:* 35
Company Type: Private　　　　　　*Employees here:* 32
SIC: 2833
　Mfg botanical extracts
Charles Blum, President

D-U-N-S 80-141-3642
CHARTER LABORATORIES INC.
(Parent: Paco Pharmaceutical Services)
1200 Paco Way, Lakewood, NJ 08701
Phone: (732) 367-9000
Sales: $8,000,000　　　　　　　　*Employees:* 150
Company Type: Public Family Member　*Employees here:* 150
SIC: 2834
　Mfg pharmaceuticals
Jerry Dorsey, President

D-U-N-S 00-333-6013
CHATTEM, INC.
1715 W 38th St, Chattanooga, TN 37409
Phone: (423) 821-4571
Sales: $220,064,000　　　　　　　*Employees:* 364
Company Type: Public　　　　　　*Employees here:* 278
SIC: 2834
　Mfg pharmaceuticals cosmetics & toiletries
Zan Guerry, Chairman of the Board

D-U-N-S 01-001-9073
CHELSEA LABORATORIES INC.
(Parent: Watson Pharmaceuticals Inc)
8606 Reading Rd, Cincinnati, OH 45215
Phone: (513) 948-4500
Sales: $4,300,000　　　　　　　　*Employees:* 45
Company Type: Public Family Member　*Employees here:* 45
SIC: 2834
　Research and development for the manufacturing of
　pharmaceuticals
Neal Parikh, Vice-President

D-U-N-S 05-049-0903
CHEM INTERNATIONAL INC.
201 Us Highway 22, Hillside, NJ 07205
Phone: (973) 926-0816
Sales: $11,127,000　　　　　　　*Employees:* 100
Company Type: Public　　　　　　*Employees here:* 21
SIC: 2834
　Mfg pharmaceutical preparations
Gerald Kaye, President

D-U-N-S 16-034-8470
CHEMBIO DIAGNOSTIC SYSTEMS
3661 Horseblock Rd, Medford, NY 11763
Phone: (516) 924-1133
Sales: $4,000,000　　　　　　　　*Employees:* 45
Company Type: Private　　　　　　*Employees here:* 45
SIC: 2835
　Manufactures diagnostic test kits
Tomas Haendler, President

D-U-N-S 36-068-4898　　　　　　　　　　EXP
CHEMDEX, INC.
(Parent: Polydex Pharmaceuticals Limit)
12340 Santa Fe Dr, Shawnee Mission, KS 66215
Phone: (913) 888-7500
Sales: $6,900,000　　　　　　　　*Employees:* 63
Company Type: Private　　　　　　*Employees here:* 1
SIC: 2834
　Manufactures pharmaceuticals
Alec Keith, Chairman of the Board

D-U-N-S 10-866-1737　　　　　　　　　　EXP
CHEMICAL COMPOUNDS INC.
29 Riverside Ave 75, Newark, NJ 07104
Phone: (973) 485-3212
Sales: $3,500,000　　　　　　　　*Employees:* 18
Company Type: Private　　　　　　*Employees here:* 18
SIC: 2834
　Mfg pharmaceutical preparations mfg cyclic crudes/
　intermediates/dyes
Alberto Celleri, President

D-U-N-S 13-755-4606
CHEMICALS INC.
12321 Hatcherville Rd, Baytown, TX 77521
Phone: (281) 383-2569
Sales: $3,911,000　　　　　　　　*Employees:* 58
Company Type: Private　　　　　　*Employees here:* 58
SIC: 2834
　Mfg pharmaceutical & industrial chemicals
Dr Ashok Moza, President

D-U-N-S 01-063-7544
CHEMINS COMPANY INC.
1835 E Cheyenne Rd, Colorado Springs, CO 80906
Phone: (719) 579-9650
Sales: $37,000,000   *Employees:* 155
Company Type: Private   *Employees here:* 155
SIC: 2834
     Mfg pharmaceutical preparations
James R Cameron, President

D-U-N-S 00-235-6900
CHEMOCENTRYX
1539 Industrial Rd, San Carlos, CA 94070
Phone: (650) 632-2900
Sales: $2,500,000   *Employees:* 6
Company Type: Private   *Employees here:* 6
SIC: 2834
     Mfg pharmaceutical preparations
Tom Schall, President

D-U-N-S 06-625-6900
CHEMRICH LABORATORIES INC.
5211 Telegraph Rd, Los Angeles, CA 90022
Phone: (323) 261-3838
Sales: $2,400,000   *Employees:* 13
Company Type: Private   *Employees here:* 13
SIC: 2834
     Mfg pharmaceutical drugs
Arthur Perez, President

D-U-N-S 10-108-5694   EXP
CHEMSOURCE CORPORATION
P.O. Box 10010, Guayama, PR 00785
Phone: (787) 864-4545
Sales: $9,000,000   *Employees:* 50
Company Type: Private   *Employees here:* 50
SIC: 2834
     Mfg pharmaceutical preparations
Braulio Mejia, General Manager

D-U-N-S 05-078-3398   EXP
CHESAPEAKE BIOLOGICAL LABS
1111 S Paca St, Baltimore, MD 21230
Phone: (410) 843-5000
Sales: $7,016,000   *Employees:* 60
Company Type: Public   *Employees here:* 15
SIC: 2834
     Specialty pharmaceutical & medical device manufacturer
Dr William P Tew, Chairman of the Board

D-U-N-S 00-423-7806
CHESTER LABS, INC.
1900 Section Rd A, Cincinnati, OH 45237
Phone: (513) 458-3840
Sales: $11,000,000   *Employees:* 70
Company Type: Private   *Employees here:* 70
SIC: 2834
     Manufactures pharmaceutical & dermatological preparations
     shampoos and mouthwashes
John Armstrong, President

D-U-N-S 01-726-3125
CHIRAGENE INC.
     (Parent: Cambrex Corporation)
7 Powderhorn Dr, Warren, NJ 07059
Phone: (732) 805-3660
Sales: $2,400,000   *Employees:* 23
Company Type: Public Family Member   *Employees here:* 23
SIC: 2834
     Manufacturers pharmaceutical intermediates
John Stanulonis, President

D-U-N-S 01-616-0744
CHIREX, INC.
300 Atlantic St, Ste 402, Stamford, CT 06901
Phone: (203) 356-9054
Sales: $94,100,000   *Employees:* 360
Company Type: Private   *Employees here:* 100
SIC: 2833
     Mfg medicinal chemicals
Michael A Griffith, Chairman of the Board

D-U-N-S 04-686-6463   EXP
CHIRON CORPORATION
4560 Horton St, Emeryville, CA 94608
Phone: (510) 655-8730
Sales: $1,162,058,000   *Employees:* 6,482
Company Type: Public   *Employees here:* 1,500
SIC: 2835
     Mfg diagnostics therapeutics & vaccines commercial
     biotechnology research labs
Sean Lance, President

D-U-N-S 95-693-2719
CHUCK MILLS
371 Oak Pl, Ste J, Brea, CA 92821
Phone: (714) 672-9042
Sales: $16,000,000   *Employees:* 1
Company Type: Private   *Employees here:* 1
SIC: 2833
     Mfg topical anesthetic
Chuck Mills, Owner

D-U-N-S 85-873-0583
CHUGAI PHARMA USA INC.
6275 Nancy Ridge Dr, San Diego, CA 92121
Phone: (619) 535-5900
Sales: $92,137,000   *Employees:* 292
Company Type: Private   *Employees here:* 4
SIC: 2835
     Holding company
Henry L Nordhoff, President

D-U-N-S 17-362-5823   EXP
CIMA LABS INC.
10000 Valley View Rd, Eden Prairie, MN 55344
Phone: (612) 947-8700
Sales: $4,910,000   *Employees:* 49
Company Type: Public   *Employees here:* 36
SIC: 2834
     Mfg pharmaceutical preparations
John M Siebert, President

D-U-N-S 00-147-2257
CIRCA PHARMACEUTICALS INC.
     (Parent: Watson Pharmaceuticals Inc)
33 Ralph Ave, Copiague, NY 11726
Phone: (516) 842-8383
Sales: $8,300,000   *Employees:* 60
Company Type: Public Family Member   *Employees here:* 53
SIC: 2834
     Mfg pharmaceutical preparations
Dr Alan Chao MD, Chairman of the Board

D-U-N-S 62-321-4079
CLARK LABORATORIES INC.
     (Parent: Trinity Biotech Inc)
2823 Girts Rd, Jamestown, NY 14701
Phone: (716) 483-3851
Sales: $6,519,000   *Employees:* 76
Company Type: Private   *Employees here:* 76
SIC: 2835
     Mfg infectious disease and auto immune immunodiagnostic
     reagents to clinical laboratories
Brendan Farrell, President

D-U-N-S 07-884-6912　　　　　　　　　　EXP
CLAY-PARK LABORATORIES INC.
1700 Bathgate Ave, Bronx, NY 10457
Phone: (718) 901-2800
Sales: $20,000,000　　　　　　　　　*Employees:* 720
Company Type: Private　　　　　*Employees here:* 500
SIC: 2834
　　Mfg pharmaceuticals for topical use
Giora Carni, President

D-U-N-S 88-388-1302
CLEARVALUE, INC.
15700 Lexington Blvd, Sugar Land, TX 77478
Phone: (281) 980-4777
Sales: $2,500,000　　　　　　　　　*Employees:* 14
Company Type: Private　　　　　　*Employees here:* 14
SIC: 2836
　　Mfg bacterial & chemicals
Richard A Haase, President

D-U-N-S 80-761-8400　　　　　　　　　　EXP
CLINICAL DIAGNOSTICS, INC.
2606 Eden Ter, Rock Hill, SC 29730
Phone: (803) 980-1020
Sales: $2,200,000　　　　　　　　　*Employees:* 25
Company Type: Private　　　　　　*Employees here:* 25
SIC: 2835
　　Mfg medical diagnostic test kits
Kevin Phillips, President

D-U-N-S 18-469-2044
CLINICAL SPECIALTIES, INC.
3201 E Royalton Rd, Cleveland, OH 44147
Phone: (440) 717-1700
Sales: $4,000,000　　　　　　　　　*Employees:* 32
Company Type: Private　　　　　　*Employees here:* 32
SIC: 2834
　　Mfg pharmaceutical preparations
Edward Rivalsky, President

D-U-N-S 79-308-6935
CN BIOSCIENCES, INC.
10394 Pacific Center Ct, San Diego, CA 92121
Phone: (619) 450-9600
Sales: $39,445,000　　　　　　　　*Employees:* 230
Company Type: Public　　　　　　*Employees here:* 4
SIC: 2836
　　Mfg biological products
Stelios B Papadopoulos, Chairman of the Board

D-U-N-S 08-280-9666　　　　　　　　　　EXP
COATING PLACE INCORPORATED
200 Paoli St, Verona, WI 53593
Phone: (608) 845-9521
Sales: $2,800,000　　　　　　　　　*Employees:* 36
Company Type: Private　　　　　　*Employees here:* 36
SIC: 2834
　　Mfg capsuled medicines chemical & food preparations
Harlan S Hall, President

D-U-N-S 10-805-2663
COCALICO BIOLOGICALS INC.
449 Stevens Rd, Reamstown, PA 17567
Phone: (717) 336-1990
Sales: $2,400,000　　　　　　　　　*Employees:* 36
Company Type: Private　　　　　　*Employees here:* 36
SIC: 2836
　　Mfg biological products
Jeanette Whitesell, President

D-U-N-S 61-006-7746
COCENSYS INC.
201 Technology Dr, Irvine, CA 92618

Phone: (949) 753-6100
Sales: $11,914,000　　　　　　　　*Employees:* 107
Company Type: Public　　　　　　*Employees here:* 65
SIC: 2834
　　Mfg biopharmaceutical preparations
F R Nichol, Chairman of the Board

D-U-N-S 96-880-1118
COLGATE ORAL PHARMACEUTICALS
　　(Parent: Colgate-Palmolive Company)
1 Colgate Way, Canton, MA 02021
Phone: (781) 821-2880
Sales: $26,700,000　　　　　　　　*Employees:* 188
Company Type: Public Family Member　*Employees here:* 188
SIC: 2834
　　Mfg pharmaceutical preparations
Nicholas Vinke, Principal

D-U-N-S 07-716-9803　　　　　　　　　　EXP
COLLAGEN AESTHETICS, INC.
1850 Embarcadero Rd, Palo Alto, CA 94303
Phone: (650) 856-0200
Sales: $82,772,000　　　　　　　　*Employees:* 280
Company Type: Public　　　　　　*Employees here:* 106
SIC: 2836
　　Mfg biocompatible products
Michael A Bates, Chief Financial Officer

D-U-N-S 00-705-6542　　　　　　　　　　EXP
COLORADO SERUM COMPANY
4950 York St, Denver, CO 80216
Phone: (303) 295-7527
Sales: $5,800,000　　　　　　　　　*Employees:* 100
Company Type: Private　　　　　　*Employees here:* 100
SIC: 2836
　　Mfg serums vaccines & veterinary biological products
Joseph N Huff, President

D-U-N-S 61-732-1922
CONCORD LABORATORIES, INC.
140 New Dutch Ln, Fairfield, NJ 07004
Phone: (973) 227-6757
Sales: $2,500,000　　　　　　　　　*Employees:* 20
Company Type: Private　　　　　　*Employees here:* 20
SIC: 2834
　　Mfg pharmaceutical preparations
N K Rao, President

D-U-N-S 08-672-3285　　　　　　　　　　EXP
CONNAUGHT LABORATORIES INC.
　　(Parent: Connaught Laboratories Limited)
Rr 611, Swiftwater, PA 18370
Phone: (570) 839-7187
Sales: $333,535,000　　　　　　　*Employees:* 970
Company Type: Private　　　　　　*Employees here:* 600
SIC: 2836
　　Mfg biological products
David J Williams, President

D-U-N-S 82-615-3629
CONNETICS CORP.
3400 W Bayshore Rd, Palo Alto, CA 94303
Phone: (650) 843-2800
Sales: $6,803,000　　　　　　　　　*Employees:* 50
Company Type: Public　　　　　　*Employees here:* 50
SIC: 2834
　　Mfg pharmaceuticals
Thomas G Wiggans, President

D-U-N-S 00-309-4406　　　　　　　　　　EXP
CONSOLIDATED PHARMACEUTICALS GROUP
6110 Robinwood Rd, Baltimore, MD 21225
Phone: (410) 789-7800

Sales: $5,200,000   *Employees:* 50
Company Type: Private   *Employees here:* 50
SIC: 2834
  Mfg semi-synthetic pencillin
M T Turgut, Chief Executive Officer

D-U-N-S 09-406-4912
CONTINENTAL SERVICES GROUP
1300 NW 36th St, Miami, FL 33142
Phone: (305) 633-7700
Sales: $3,300,000   *Employees:* 40
Company Type: Private   *Employees here:* 30
SIC: 2835
  Mfg biological & diagnostic blood components
Cherry D Wheeler-Capik, Chief Executive Officer

D-U-N-S 06-935-0478   EXP
COPLEY PHARMACEUTICAL, INC.
  (Parent: HCCP Acquisition Corporation)
25 John Rd, Canton, MA 02021
Phone: (781) 821-6111
Sales: $121,483,000   *Employees:* 404
Company Type: Public   *Employees here:* 395
SIC: 2834
  Mfg & whol pharmaceutical pdts
Daniel Korpolinski, President

D-U-N-S 62-529-0382
CORANGE INTERNATIONAL LIMITED
Punto Oro Industrial Park, Ponce, PR 00731
Phone: (787) 843-6195
Sales: $14,400,000   *Employees:* NA
Company Type: Private   *Employees here:* 140
SIC: 2833
  Manufactures medical chemicals
Hector Pecan, N/A

D-U-N-S 87-621-8090   EXP
CORIXA CORPORATION
1124 Columbia St, Ste 200, Seattle, WA 98104
Phone: (206) 754-5711
Sales: $14,367,000   *Employees:* 104
Company Type: Public   *Employees here:* 104
SIC: 2834
  Mfg pharmaceutical preparations
Dr Steven Gillis, President

D-U-N-S 04-719-4139   EXP
CORNWELL CORPORATION
107 Riverdale Rd, Riverdale, NJ 07457
Phone: (973) 831-9800
Sales: $10,000,000   *Employees:* 50
Company Type: Private   *Employees here:* 50
SIC: 2835
  Mfg diagnostic reagents used in hospital & clinical
   laboratories
John Cornwell, President

D-U-N-S 60-777-7778
COROMED INC.
  (Parent: Omnicare Inc)
185 Jordan Rd, Troy, NY 12180
Phone: (518) 283-4000
Sales: $9,000,000   *Employees:* 135
Company Type: Public Family Member   *Employees here:* 105
SIC: 2834
  Pharmaceutical research and development
Dale B Evans, President

D-U-N-S 07-623-0317   EXP
COSMO-PHARM INC.
11751 Vose St 53, North Hollywood, CA 91605
Phone: (818) 983-1432

Sales: $5,000,000   *Employees:* 39
Company Type: Private   *Employees here:* 39
SIC: 2833
  Mfg vitamins
Ashwin Patel, President

D-U-N-S 88-494-5882
COULTER PHARMACEUTICAL, INC.
600 Gateway Blvd, South San Francisco, CA 94080
Phone: (650) 842-7306
Sales: $9,300,000   *Employees:* 66
Company Type: Public   *Employees here:* 60
SIC: 2834
  Mfg pharmaceuticals
Michael F Bigham, President

D-U-N-S 17-345-1063
COUNTRY FARMS INC.
100 Lehigh Dr, Fairfield, NJ 07004
Phone: (973) 575-6591
Sales: $19,300,000   *Employees:* 150
Company Type: Private   *Employees here:* 150
SIC: 2834
  Mfg pharmaceutical preparations
Edward Frankel, President

D-U-N-S 93-393-5587
COVANCE BIOTECHNOLOGY SERVICES
  (Parent: Covance Inc)
6051 George Watts Hill Dr, Research Triangle Pa, NC 27709
Phone: (919) 468-9400
Sales: $25,000,000   *Employees:* 208
Company Type: Public Family Member   *Employees here:* 208
SIC: 2834
  Mfg pharmaceuticals
John Brown, President

D-U-N-S 09-001-0174
CREATIVE MEDICAL CORPORATION
Km 19 Hm 5 Pepsi Park Rr, Toa Baja, PR 00949
Phone: (787) 251-4593
Sales: $2,637,000   *Employees:* 32
Company Type: Private   *Employees here:* 32
SIC: 2834
  Mfg pharmaceutical preparations
Salem M Yassin, President

D-U-N-S 07-280-6847
CTM INDUSTRIES LTD.
  (Parent: Life Resources Inc)
22005 97th Ave, Ste 2, Jamaica, NY 11429
Phone: (718) 479-3300
Sales: $2,200,000   *Employees:* 33
Company Type: Private   *Employees here:* 33
SIC: 2836
  Wholesales & mfrs blood plasma
Perry Ciarletta, President

D-U-N-S 09-144-8258
CUSTOM COATINGS INC.
7 Michael Ave, Farmingdale, NY 11735
Phone: (516) 753-1110
Sales: $6,000,000   *Employees:* 119
Company Type: Private   *Employees here:* 119
SIC: 2834
  Manufactures coating used on pharmaceutical tablets
Joseph Errigo, President

D-U-N-S 80-014-9437
CUSTOM HEALTH PRODUCTS
210 12th St, Waynesboro, VA 22980
Phone: (540) 949-8399

Sales: $3,600,000　　　　　　　　　*Employees:* 40
Company Type: Private　　　　　　*Employees here:* 40
SIC: 2834
　Mfg pharmaceutical preparations
Thomas Thorpe, Owner

D-U-N-S 11-419-2610　　　　　　　　　　　　　EXP
CYANOTECH CORPORATION
73-4460 Queen K Hwy 102, Kailua Kona, HI 96740
Phone: (808) 326-1353
Sales: $7,627,000　　　　　　　　　*Employees:* 68
Company Type: Public　　　　　　*Employees here:* 68
SIC: 2836
　Mfg nutritional biological products and flourescent pigments
Gerald R Cysewski, President

D-U-N-S 15-083-7318
CYGNUS, INC.
400 Penobscot Dr, Redwood City, CA 94063
Phone: (650) 369-4300
Sales: $29,502,000　　　　　　　*Employees:* 157
Company Type: Public　　　　　　*Employees here:* 157
SIC: 2834
　Development of diagnostic and drug delivery systems for the
　pharmaceutical industry
John C Hodgman, President

D-U-N-S 79-024-8942　　　　　　　　　　　　　EXP
CYPRESS PHARMACEUTICAL INC.
135 Industrial Blvd, Madison, MS 39110
Phone: (601) 856-4393
Sales: $3,051,000　　　　　　　　　*Employees:* 10
Company Type: Private　　　　　　*Employees here:* 10
SIC: 2834
　Mfg pharmaceutical preparations
Max Draughn, President

D-U-N-S 06-075-8885
D & F INDUSTRIES INC.
　(*Parent:* Global Health Sciences Corp)
987 N Enterprise St, Orange, CA 92867
Phone: (714) 695-9578
Sales: $26,900,000　　　　　　　*Employees:* 220
Company Type: Private　　　　　　*Employees here:* 40
SIC: 2834
　Mfg vitamins
Richard Marconi, Chairman of the Board

D-U-N-S 09-805-8431
D V M PHARMACEUTICALS INC.
　(*Parent:* IVAX Corporation)
4400 Biscayne Blvd, Miami, FL 33137
Phone: (305) 575-6200
Sales: $19,300,000　　　　　　　*Employees:* 80
Company Type: Public Family Member　*Employees here:* 80
SIC: 2834
　Mfg veterinary pharmaceutical preparation
Jane H Hsiao, Chief Executive Officer

D-U-N-S 93-274-5698
DADE BEHRING HOLDINGS
1717 Deerfield Rd, Deerfield, IL 60015
Phone: (847) 267-5300
Sales: $978,000,000　　　　　　*Employees:* 7,500
Company Type: Private　　　　　　*Employees here:* 250
SIC: 2835
　Mfg & whol clinical diagnostic products
Steven W Barnes, President

D-U-N-S 62-653-2535
DADE BEHRING INC.
　(*Parent:* Dade Behring Holdings (del))
1717 Deerfield Rd, Deerfield, IL 60015

Phone: (847) 267-5300
Sales: $980,500,000　　　　　　*Employees:* 7,400
Company Type: Private　　　　　　*Employees here:* 125
SIC: 2835
　Mfg & svc clinical diagnostic products
John Sullivan, President

D-U-N-S 05-159-7896
DANBURY PHARMACAL INC.
　(*Parent:* Schein Pharmaceutical Inc)
1033 Stoneleigh Ave, Carmel, NY 10512
Phone: (914) 767-2000
Sales: $108,100,000　　　　　　*Employees:* 850
Company Type: Public Family Member　*Employees here:* 500
SIC: 2834
　Mfg generic solid dosage pharmaceuticals
Martin Sperber, President

D-U-N-S 85-848-3779
DANBURY PHARMACAL PUERTO RICO
　(*Parent:* Danbury Pharmacal Inc)
Km 76 Hm 9 Rr 3, Humacao, PR 00791
Phone: (787) 852-5151
Sales: $50,000,000　　　　　　　*Employees:* 130
Company Type: Public Family Member　*Employees here:* 130
SIC: 2834
　Mfg generic capsules and tablets
Blanca Melendez, President

D-U-N-S 05-849-8536　　　　　　　　　　　　　EXP
DATA MEDICAL ASSOCIATES INC.
　(*Parent:* Thermo Bioanalysis Corp)
845 Avenue G, Arlington, TX 76011
Phone: (817) 640-0965
Sales: $5,000,000　　　　　　　　*Employees:* 31
Company Type: Public Family Member　*Employees here:* 31
SIC: 2833
　Mfg diagnostic chemical reagents
Bret Hendzel, President

D-U-N-S 00-121-0558　　　　　　　　　　　　　EXP
DEL PHARMACEUTICALS INC.
　(*Parent:* Del Laboratories Inc)
178 Eab Plz, Uniondale, NY 11553
Phone: (516) 844-2020
Sales: $55,750,000　　　　　　　*Employees:* 100
Company Type: Public Family Member　*Employees here:* 63
SIC: 2834
　Manufacturer & distributor of over-the-counter
　pharmaceuticals
Dan K Wassong, Chairman of the Board

D-U-N-S 00-227-6053　　　　　　　　　　　　　EXP
DELAVAU J W S CO INC.
10101 Roosevelt Blvd, Philadelphia, PA 19154
Phone: (215) 671-1400
Sales: $50,000,000　　　　　　　*Employees:* 300
Company Type: Private　　　　　　*Employees here:* 280
SIC: 2834
　Contract mfg of pharmaceutical & nutritional products
Richard M Leff, Chief Executive Officer

D-U-N-S 00-120-7208
DENISON PHARMACEUTICALS INC.
60 Dunnell Ln, Pawtucket, RI 02860
Phone: (401) 723-5500
Sales: $2,600,000　　　　　　　　*Employees:* 30
Company Type: Private　　　　　　*Employees here:* 30
SIC: 2834
　Mfg pharmaceuticals
Edward S Stone, President

D-U-N-S 00-233-3847
DERCHER ENTERPRISES INC.
6801 Ludlow St, Upper Darby, PA 19082
Phone: (610) 734-2011
Sales: $2,700,000   *Employees:* 27
Company Type: Private   *Employees here:* 27
SIC: 2834
   Mfg pharmaceutical preparations
Sue E Dercher, President

D-U-N-S 14-428-0088   EXP
DERMA SCIENCES, INC.
214 Carnegie Ctr, Princeton, NJ 08540
Phone: (609) 514-4744
Sales: $4,010,000   *Employees:* 35
Company Type: Public   *Employees here:* 14
SIC: 2834
   Mfg ointments
Edward J Quilty, Chairman of the Board

D-U-N-S 88-392-5562
DERMARITE INDUSTRIES LLC
168 E Main St, Paterson, NJ 07508
Phone: (973) 595-5599
Sales: $2,700,000   *Employees:* 20
Company Type: Private   *Employees here:* 20
SIC: 2834
   Mfg pharmaceutical preparations mfg toilet preparations
Norman Braunstein, President

D-U-N-S 06-196-9432
DERMIK LABORATORIES INC.
   (Parent: Rhone-Plenc Rrer Phrmceuticals)
500 Arcola Rd, Collegeville, PA 19426
Phone: (610) 454-8000
Sales: $139,000,000   *Employees:* 230
Company Type: Private   *Employees here:* 106
SIC: 2834
   Mfg dermatological preparations
Robert Bitterman, President

D-U-N-S 78-280-4041   EXP
DESERET LABORATORIES INC.
1414 E 3850 S, St George, UT 84790
Phone: (435) 628-4170
Sales: $8,500,000   *Employees:* 80
Company Type: Private   *Employees here:* 80
SIC: 2833
   Mfg medicinal/botanical products
Scott A Gubler, President

D-U-N-S 84-062-1494   EXP
DESIGNING HEALTH INC.
28310 Avenue Crocker, Valencia, CA 91355
Phone: (661) 257-1705
Sales: $2,770,000   *Employees:* 27
Company Type: Private   *Employees here:* 27
SIC: 2833
   Mfg natural food supplements
Bernard Collett, Chief Executive Officer

D-U-N-S 02-840-7120
DEVLAN INC.
24543 Indoplex Cir, Farmington Hills, MI 48335
Phone: (248) 442-2960
Sales: $4,000,000   *Employees:* 45
Company Type: Private   *Employees here:* 2
SIC: 2834
   Pharmaceutical consulting validation
Francisco De Vecchi, Chairman of the Board

D-U-N-S 19-477-5557
DEY INC.
   (Parent: Lipha Americas Inc)
2751 Napa Valley Corporat, Napa, CA 94558
Phone: (707) 224-3200
Sales: $219,810,000   *Employees:* 670
Company Type: Private   *Employees here:* 560
SIC: 2834
   Mfg pharmaceuticals
Charles A Rice, President

D-U-N-S 96-551-6164
DFB HOLDING INC.
318 Mccullough Ave, San Antonio, TX 78215
Phone: (210) 223-3281
Sales: $50,007,000   *Employees:* 18
Company Type: Private   *Employees here:* 18
SIC: 2834
   Mfg pharmaceutical preparations
H P Dorman, Chairman of the Board

D-U-N-S 80-017-6893
DGA INC.
201 Lafayette Cir, Ste 200, Lafayette, CA 94549
Phone: (925) 299-9000
Sales: $4,100,000   *Employees:* 34
Company Type: Private   *Employees here:* 4
SIC: 2834
   Mfg vitamin supplements & nutritional drink mixes
D G Gillespie, Owner

D-U-N-S 06-460-8573
DIAGNOSTIC PRODUCTS CORP.
5700 W 96th St, Los Angeles, CA 90045
Phone: (323) 776-0180
Sales: $186,264,000   *Employees:* 1,467
Company Type: Public   *Employees here:* 532
SIC: 2835
   Mfg medical immunodiagnostic test kits
Sigi Ziering PhD, Chairman of the Board

D-U-N-S 78-583-3278
DIAGNOSTIC REAGENTS, INC.
601 W California Ave, Sunnyvale, CA 94086
Phone: (408) 738-8788
Sales: $5,192,000   *Employees:* 45
Company Type: Private   *Employees here:* 45
SIC: 2835
   Mfg liquid immunoassay reagents
Dr Yuh-Geng Tsay, President

D-U-N-S 10-291-3878
DIAMOND ANIMAL HEALTH, INC.
   (Parent: Heska Corp)
2538 SE 43rd St, Des Moines, IA 50317
Phone: (515) 263-8600
Sales: $7,100,000   *Employees:* 120
Company Type: Public Family Member   *Employees here:* 120
SIC: 2836
   Mfg biological products
Lyle Hohnke, Chairman of the Board

D-U-N-S 03-342-9783
DIASORIN INC.
   (Parent: American Standard Inc)
1990 Industrial Blvd S, Stillwater, MN 55082
Phone: (651) 439-9710
Sales: $28,100,000   *Employees:* 340
Company Type: Public Family Member   *Employees here:* 330
SIC: 2835
   Mfg in-vitro diagnostic clinical & research test kits
Fred Allardyce, Senior Vice-President

D-U-N-S 00-537-8179
DIFCO LABORATORIES INC.
   (Parent: Becton Dickinson and Company)
17197 N Laurel Park Dr, Livonia, MI 48152
Phone: (313) 442-8800
Sales: $24,200,000   *Employees:* 400
Company Type: Public Family Member   *Employees here:* 120
SIC: 2836
   Mfg biological products & whol chemical reagents
William B Burnett, President

D-U-N-S 13-025-0723
DIGENE CORPORATION
9000 Virginia Manor Rd, Beltsville, MD 20705
Phone: (301) 470-6500
Sales: $12,009,000   *Employees:* 135
Company Type: Public   *Employees here:* 80
SIC: 2835
   Mfg biotechnology diagnostic products
Charles M Fleischman, Chief Operating Officer

D-U-N-S 00-520-4532   EXP
DIOSYNTH INC.
   (Parent: Akzo Nobel Inc)
2745 N Elston Ave, Chicago, IL 60647
Phone: (773) 235-7500
Sales: $48,000,000   *Employees:* 33
Company Type: Private   *Employees here:* 12
SIC: 2836
   Mfg anti-coagulate
P K Kluit, Treasurer

D-U-N-S 80-738-6024
DIRECT THERAPEUTICS, INC.
2 Gannett Dr, Ste 200, White Plains, NY 10604
Phone: (914) 696-7700
Sales: $4,000,000   *Employees:* 37
Company Type: Private   *Employees here:* 37
SIC: 2834
   Developer of pharmaceuticals
Dennis Pietronigro PhD, Chairman of the Board

D-U-N-S 82-619-5083
DOCTORS SGNATURE SLS MKTG INTL
2705 Via Orange Way, Ste B, Spring Valley, CA 91978
Phone: (619) 660-1270
Sales: $10,000,000   *Employees:* 22
Company Type: Private   *Employees here:* 22
SIC: 2833
   Health foods
Robert W Hillman, Chairman of the Board

D-U-N-S 10-685-8681
DOLISOS AMERICA INC.
3014 Rigel Ave, Las Vegas, NV 89102
Phone: (702) 871-7153
Sales: $3,000,000   *Employees:* 33
Company Type: Private   *Employees here:* 33
SIC: 2833
   Mfg homeopathic medicine
Luke Clouatre, President

D-U-N-S 62-178-2218   EXP
DPT LABORATORIES LTD.
318 Mccullough Ave, San Antonio, TX 78215
Phone: (210) 223-3281
Sales: $68,568,000   *Employees:* 550
Company Type: Private   *Employees here:* 105
SIC: 2834
   Mfg pharmaceutical preparations
H P Dorman, Chairman of the Board

D-U-N-S 62-140-7758
DU PONT PHARMACEUTICALS CO.
Km 2 Hm 3 Rr 686, Manati, PR 00674
Phone: (787) 854-1105
Sales: $33,300,000   *Employees:* 270
Company Type: Private   *Employees here:* 270
SIC: 2834
   Mfg pharmaceutical products
Manuel Rivera, Chief Financial Officer

D-U-N-S 03-214-4438
DURA PHARMACEUTICALS INC.
7475 Lusk Blvd, San Diego, CA 92121
Phone: (619) 457-2553
Sales: $181,323,000   *Employees:* 331
Company Type: Public   *Employees here:* 300
SIC: 2834
   Mfg & ret mail order pharmaceuticals
Cam L Garner, Chairman of the Board

D-U-N-S 60-400-5116
DYNAGEN INC.
840 Memorial Dr, Ste 4, Cambridge, MA 02139
Phone: (617) 491-2527
Sales: $14,010,000   *Employees:* 140
Company Type: Public   *Employees here:* 25
SIC: 2834
   Mfg pharmaceutical tablets & engaged in biological and
      medical research
Indu A Muni, President

D-U-N-S 01-413-0053
DYNPORT LLC
   (Parent: Dyncorp)
2000 Edmund Halley Dr, Reston, VA 20191
Phone: (703) 264-0330
Sales: $5,000,000   *Employees:* 20
Company Type: Private   *Employees here:* 20
SIC: 2836
   Mfg biological warfare vaccines
Paul Lombardi, Partner

D-U-N-S 19-866-8170
E EXCEL INTERNATIONAL INC.
1198 Spring Creek Pl, Springville, UT 84663
Phone: (801) 489-4588
Sales: $24,610,000   *Employees:* 100
Company Type: Private   *Employees here:* 100
SIC: 2833
   Mfg herbal vitamins
Jau-Fei Chen, President

D-U-N-S 18-750-5656
E R SQIBB SONS INTR-MRCAN CORP
   (Parent: Bristol-Myers Squibb Company)
Province Line Rd Rr 206, Princeton, NJ 08543
Phone: (609) 252-4000
Sales: $31,600,000   *Employees:* 200
Company Type: Public Family Member   *Employees here:* 1
SIC: 2834
   Mfg of pharmaceuticals
Quintan Oswald, President

D-U-N-S 00-204-1226   EXP
E-Z-EM, INC.
717 Main St, Westbury, NY 11590
Phone: (516) 333-8230
Sales: $102,884,000   *Employees:* 923
Company Type: Public   *Employees here:* 344
SIC: 2835
   Mfg diagnostic products
Howard S Stern, Chairman of the Board

D-U-N-S 03-078-5752   EXP
EAST EARTH HERB INC.
4091 W 11th Ave, Ste C, Eugene, OR 97402
Phone: (541) 687-0155
Sales: $7,084,000   *Employees:* 70
Company Type: Private   *Employees here:* 70
SIC: 2834
   Mfg chinese herbs
William H Brevoort, President

D-U-N-S 79-211-0322
EASY RETURNS WORLDWIDE, INC.
100 Teduke Ct, Saint Charles, MO 63301
Phone: (314) 236-0044
Sales: $10,200,000   *Employees:* 82
Company Type: Private   *Employees here:* 82
SIC: 2834
   Preparation of pharmaceuticals
David Mogil, President

D-U-N-S 62-779-5115   IMP EXP
ECKHART CORPORATION
1620 Grant Ave, Ste 2, Novato, CA 94945
Phone: (415) 892-3880
Sales: $6,000,000   *Employees:* 7
Company Type: Private   *Employees here:* 7
SIC: 2834
   Imports and exports vitamins
Deepak Chopra, President

D-U-N-S 00-407-5250
ECO PAX, INC.
   (Parent: One Family Inc)
8160 Blakeland Dr Ab, Littleton, CO 80125
Phone: (303) 865-1000
Sales: $5,000,000   *Employees:* 10
Company Type: Private   *Employees here:* 10
SIC: 2834
   Vitamin preparations
Steven Cantor, President

D-U-N-S 14-795-7443
ELAN HOLDINGS INC.
   (Parent: Elan Pharmaceutical Res Ga)
2 Thurber Blvd, Smithfield, RI 02917
Phone: (401) 233-3526
Sales: $11,900,000   *Employees:* 80
Company Type: Private   *Employees here:* 80
SIC: 2834
   Mfg & whol medical nutritional products
Peter Mc Henry, Ex Vice Pres

D-U-N-S 05-758-5150
ELAN PHARMACEUTICAL RES
   (Parent: Elan Pharmaceuticals)
1300 Gould Dr, Gainesville, GA 30504
Phone: (770) 534-8239
Sales: $12,528,000   *Employees:* 174
Company Type: Private   *Employees here:* 95
SIC: 2834
   Mfg hypertension drug and does research & development of
     pharmaceutical products
Donald Geaney, President

D-U-N-S 17-834-1020
ELAN PHARMACEUTICALS
800 Gateway Blvd, South San Francisco, CA 94080
Phone: (650) 877-0900
Sales: $63,000,000   *Employees:* 500
Company Type: Private   *Employees here:* 350
SIC: 2834
   Mfg pharmaceutical products
John Groom, President

D-U-N-S 78-398-2093
ELAN TRANSDERMAL TECHNOLOGIES
3250 Commerce Pkwy, Pembroke Pines, FL 33025
Phone: (954) 430-3340
Sales: $15,000,000   *Employees:* 100
Company Type: Private   *Employees here:* 100
SIC: 2834
   Research development and manufacturing of pharmaceutical
     preparations
Reginald Hardy, President

D-U-N-S 62-249-7659
ELANCO ANIMAL HOUSE INC.
   (Parent: Eli Lilly and Company)
Lilly Corporate Center, Indianapolis, IN 46285
Phone: (317) 276-2000
Sales: $27,000,000   *Employees:* 200
Company Type: Public Family Member   *Employees here:* 50
SIC: 2834
   Mfg pharmaceuticals medical instruments & animal health
     products
Randall Tobias, President

D-U-N-S 95-788-1972
ELEMENTIS CATALYSTS INC.
   (Parent: Elementise America Inc)
1 W Allen St, Allentown, PA 18102
Phone: (610) 432-9054
Sales: $5,000,000   *Employees:* 15
Company Type: Private   *Employees here:* 15
SIC: 2833
   Mfg chemicals
Ken Free, Vice-President

D-U-N-S 61-065-5136
ELGE INC.
1000 Cole Ave, Rosenberg, TX 77471
Phone: (281) 342-8228
Sales: $2,500,000   *Employees:* 25
Company Type: Private   *Employees here:* 25
SIC: 2834
   Contract manufacturer & packager of pharmaceuticals
Larry Gremminger, President

D-U-N-S 00-642-1325   EXP
ELI LILLY AND COMPANY
Lilly Corporate Center, Indianapolis, IN 46285
Phone: (317) 276-2000
Sales: $8,517,600,000   *Employees:* 31,100
Company Type: Public   *Employees here:* 8,600
SIC: 2834
   Mfg pharmaceutical products
Sidney Taurel, Chairman of the Board

D-U-N-S 17-807-4951
ENDO PHARMACEUTICALS INC.
223 Wilmington W Chester, Chadds Ford, PA 19317
Phone: (610) 558-9800
Sales: $9,100,000   *Employees:* 65
Company Type: Private   *Employees here:* 35
SIC: 2834
   Mfg pharmaceutical preparations
Carol A Ammon, Chief Executive Officer

D-U-N-S 16-115-7540
ENDOGEN INC.
30 Commerce Way, Ste 2, Woburn, MA 01801
Phone: (781) 937-0890
Sales: $10,033,000   *Employees:* 72
Company Type: Public   *Employees here:* 30
SIC: 2835
   Mfg diagnostic substances
Owen A Dempsey, President

D-U-N-S 79-620-7645
ENTERIC PRODUCTS INC.
(Parent: E-Z-Em Inc (delaware))
25 E Loop Rd, Stony Brook, NY 11790
Phone: (516) 444-8872
Sales: $2,100,000   *Employees:* 20
Company Type: Public Family Member   *Employees here:* 20
SIC: 2834
    Manufactures pharmaceuticals
Howard Stern, Principal

D-U-N-S 78-630-3867
ENZO DIAGNOSTICS INC.
(Parent: Enzo Biochem Inc)
60 Executive Blvd, Farmingdale, NY 11735
Phone: (516) 694-7070
Sales: $14,500,000   *Employees:* 30
Company Type: Public Family Member   *Employees here:* 30
SIC: 2835
    Manufacturer marketer and researcher of diagnostic and
      research products
Elazar Rabbani, Chairman of the Board

D-U-N-S 10-168-6731
ENZON INC.
20 Kingsbridge Rd, Piscataway, NJ 08854
Phone: (732) 980-4500
Sales: $12,727,000   *Employees:* 85
Company Type: Public   *Employees here:* 30
SIC: 2834
    Manufactures pharmaceuticals and medical research and
      development
Abraham Abuchowski PhD, Chairman of the Board

D-U-N-S 05-654-4166
ENZYMATIC THERAPY INC.
825 Challenger Dr, Green Bay, WI 54311
Phone: (920) 469-1313
Sales: $35,600,000   *Employees:* 285
Company Type: Private   *Employees here:* 285
SIC: 2833
    Mfg vitamins & health additives
Terrence Lemerond, President

D-U-N-S 80-101-2444
EON LABS MANUFACTURING, INC.
22715 N Conduit Ave, Springfield Gardens, NY 11413
Phone: (718) 276-8600
Sales: $40,000,000   *Employees:* 200
Company Type: Private   *Employees here:* 200
SIC: 2834
    Mfg generic pharmaceutical drugs
Bernard Hampl PhD, President

D-U-N-S 11-415-2184
EPITOPE INC.
8505 SW Creekside Pl, Beaverton, OR 97008
Phone: (503) 641-6115
Sales: $9,792,000   *Employees:* 90
Company Type: Public   *Employees here:* 90
SIC: 2835
    Mfg diagnostic agents
John W Morgan, President

D-U-N-S 05-329-6778
ESS GROUP, INC.
78 Carranza Rd, Vincentown, NJ 08088
Phone: (609) 268-1200
Sales: $15,000,000   *Employees:* 40
Company Type: Private   *Employees here:* 40
SIC: 2835
    Mfg diagnostic substances
James T Egan, Chief Executive Officer

D-U-N-S 09-791-6506
EURAND AMERICA INCORPORATED
(Parent: American Home Products Corp)
845 Center Dr, Vandalia, OH 45377
Phone: (937) 898-9669
Sales: $12,000,000   *Employees:* 67
Company Type: Public Family Member   *Employees here:* 67
SIC: 2834
    Mfg of products for drug delivery
Gearoid Faherty, General Manager

D-U-N-S 07-117-0534
EVERETT LABORATORIES INC.
29 Spring St, West Orange, NJ 07052
Phone: (973) 324-0200
Sales: $2,400,000   *Employees:* 27
Company Type: Private   *Employees here:* 27
SIC: 2834
    Mfr & whol pharmaceutical preparations
Everett Felper, President

D-U-N-S 06-472-3588   EXP
EVERGOOD PRODUCTS CORPORATION
140 Lauman Ln, Hicksville, NY 11801
Phone: (516) 822-1230
Sales: $31,000,000   *Employees:* 95
Company Type: Private   *Employees here:* 95
SIC: 2833
    Manufactures & distributes vitamins
Melvin Rich, President

D-U-N-S 09-047-8330   EXP
EX-LAX INC.
Km 1 Hm 3 Rr 909, Humacao, PR 00791
Phone: (787) 852-3190
Sales: $40,000,000   *Employees:* 100
Company Type: Private   *Employees here:* 100
SIC: 2834
    Mfg pharmaceutical preparations
Santos Troche, Treasurer

D-U-N-S 09-049-3917
F P SYNTEX INC.
Km 1 Hm 1 Rr 909, Humacao, PR 00791
Phone: (787) 852-0909
Sales: $44,900,000   *Employees:* 360
Company Type: Private   *Employees here:* 360
SIC: 2834
    Mfg pharmaceutical preparations
Geoffrey Murgatoyd, President

D-U-N-S 03-087-0083   EXP
F.A.M.G. INC.
27655b Avenue Hopkins, Santa Clarita, CA 91355
Phone: (661) 294-9999
Sales: $56,000,000   *Employees:* 85
Company Type: Private   *Employees here:* 85
SIC: 2833
    Mfg vitamins & supplements
Solomon Levy, Chief Executive Officer

D-U-N-S 10-894-0198
FAR RESEARCH INC.
307 Amherst Rd, Morganton, NC 28655
Phone: (828) 438-0101
Sales: $4,200,000   *Employees:* 25
Company Type: Private   *Employees here:* 1
SIC: 2834
    Mfg specialty chemicals for the pharmaceutical industry
Raymond A Pinard, President

D-U-N-S 15-994-1434
FARMANATURAL INC.
2525 Davie Rd, Ste 330, Fort Lauderdale, FL 33317
Phone: (954) 236-9053
Sales: $2,800,000   *Employees:* 30
Company Type: Private   *Employees here:* 30
SIC: 2834
    Manufacture of vitamins and dietary supplements
Theodore J Klein, Agent

D-U-N-S 10-886-0917
FAULDING INC.
200 Elmora Ave, Elizabeth, NJ 07202
Phone: (908) 527-9100
Sales: $102,127,000   *Employees:* 479
Company Type: Private   *Employees here:* 4
SIC: 2834
    Manufactures generic pharmaceuticals & drugs
Richard F Moldin, President

D-U-N-S 83-607-4971
FAULDING, INC.
Pararel Rd Bldg 1071, Aguadilla, PR 00603
Phone: (787) 890-3000
Sales: $11,500,000   *Employees:* NA
Company Type: Private   *Employees here:* 116
SIC: 2834
    Mfg pharmacuetical products
Michael Ashton, President

D-U-N-S 00-532-0536   EXP
FERNDALE LABORATORIES INC.
780 W 8 Mile Rd, Ferndale, MI 48220
Phone: (248) 548-0900
Sales: $23,777,000   *Employees:* 210
Company Type: Private   *Employees here:* 185
SIC: 2834
    Mfg pharmaceuticals
James T McMillan II, President

D-U-N-S 10-372-2955
FERRING PHARMACEUTICALS INC.
120 White Plains Rd, Tarrytown, NY 10591
Phone: (914) 333-8900
Sales: $16,000,000   *Employees:* 35
Company Type: Private   *Employees here:* 35
SIC: 2834
    Manufacturer & distributor of pharmaceuticals
Frederik Paulsen, Chairman of the Board

D-U-N-S 83-557-3239
FIBROGEN, INC.
225 Gateway Blvd, South San Francisco, CA 94080
Phone: (650) 866-7200
Sales: $10,800,000   *Employees:* 75
Company Type: Private   *Employees here:* 60
SIC: 2834
    Biotechnology research
Thomas B Neff, President

D-U-N-S 17-992-5722   EXP
FIRST PRIORITY INC.
1585 Todd Farm Dr, Elgin, IL 60123
Phone: (847) 289-1600
Sales: $3,318,000   *Employees:* 11
Company Type: Private   *Employees here:* 11
SIC: 2834
    Whol & mfg veterinary pharmaceutical preparations and
        products
Lawrence F Schneider, President

D-U-N-S 61-452-9642
FISONS US INVESTMENT HOLDINGS
3711 Kennett Pike, Ste 200, Wilmington, DE 19807
Phone: (302) 777-7222
Sales: $127,400,000   *Employees:* 1,000
Company Type: Private   *Employees here:* 4
SIC: 2834
    Mfg pharmaceuticals
Phil Ridolfi, President

D-U-N-S 00-649-1351
FLEMING & COMPANY INC.
1600 Fenpark Dr, Fenton, MO 63026
Phone: (314) 343-8200
Sales: $11,900,000   *Employees:* 110
Company Type: Private   *Employees here:* 110
SIC: 2834
    Mfg pharmaceutical preparations
Thomas E Fleming, President

D-U-N-S 80-914-7440
FONTAROME CHEMICAL INC.
    (Parent: Wixon Industries Inc)
4170 S Nevada St, Milwaukee, WI 53235
Phone: (414) 744-3993
Sales: $5,000,000   *Employees:* 21
Company Type: Private   *Employees here:* 21
SIC: 2833
    Manufactures organic chemicals
Michel Combe, President

D-U-N-S 10-518-6506   EXP
FOOD SCIENCE CORP.
20 New England Dr, Essex Junction, VT 05452
Phone: (802) 878-5508
Sales: $11,302,000   *Employees:* 54
Company Type: Private   *Employees here:* 54
SIC: 2833
    Mfg nutritional supplements
Lou R Drudi, President

D-U-N-S 07-058-0477
FOOD SCIENCES CORPORATION
821 E Gate Dr, Mount Laurel, NJ 08054
Phone: (609) 778-9200
Sales: $8,000,000   *Employees:* 65
Company Type: Private   *Employees here:* 65
SIC: 2833
    Mfg nutritional food supplements
Robert Schwartz, President

D-U-N-S 00-128-8281   EXP
FOREST LABORATORIES INC.
909 3rd Ave, New York, NY 10022
Phone: (212) 421-7850
Sales: $427,086,000   *Employees:* 1,854
Company Type: Public   *Employees here:* 175
SIC: 2834
    Mfg pharmaceutical preparations
Kenneth E Goodman, President

D-U-N-S 13-941-9675
FOREST PHARMACEUTICALS INC.
    (Parent: Forest Laboratories Inc)
13622 Lakefront Dr, Earth City, MO 63045
Phone: (314) 344-8870
Sales: $350,000,000   *Employees:* 1,150
Company Type: Public Family Member   *Employees here:* 200
SIC: 2834
    Mfg pharmaceutical preparations
Howard Solomon, Principal

D-U-N-S 06-252-5910
FORMULATION TECHNOLOGY INC.
571 Armstrong Way, Oakdale, CA 95361
Phone: (209) 847-0331
Sales: $8,149,000   *Employees:* 49
Company Type: Private   *Employees here:* 49
SIC: 2834
   Mfg vitamins
Keith Hensley, President

D-U-N-S 16-134-6762   EXP
FORTITECH INC.
2105 Technology Dr, Schenectady, NY 12308
Phone: (518) 372-5155
Sales: $35,000,000   *Employees:* 59
Company Type: Private   *Employees here:* 59
SIC: 2834
   Manufactures nutrient systems
Walter S Borisenok, President

D-U-N-S 96-302-8154
FORTTA GROUP LLC
25 Fairview Ave, Plainville, CT 06062
Phone: (860) 747-5674
Sales: $2,500,000   *Employees:* 1
Company Type: Private   *Employees here:* 1
SIC: 2834
   Mfg nutritional supplements
Michael Smith, Member

D-U-N-S 00-136-8174
THE FREDERICK PURDUE COMPANY
   (*Parent:* Pharmaceutical Research Assoc)
100 Connecticut Ave, Norwalk, CT 06850
Phone: (203) 853-0123
Sales: $100,000,000   *Employees:* 207
Company Type: Private   *Employees here:* 200
SIC: 2834
   Mfg & distributor of pharmaceuticals
Dr Mortimer D Sackler, Secretary

D-U-N-S 00-155-1308   EXP
FRUTAROM MEER CORPORATION
   (*Parent:* International Frutarom Corp)
9500 Railroad Ave, North Bergen, NJ 07047
Phone: (201) 861-9500
Sales: $33,328,000   *Employees:* 160
Company Type: Private   *Employees here:* 151
SIC: 2833
   Mfg medicinal/botanical products mfg flavor extracts/syrup
     mfg food preparations
Anthony Cicitta, President

D-U-N-S 04-852-4263
FUJIREBIO DIAGNOSTIC INC.
244 Great Valley Pkwy, Malvern, PA 19355
Phone: (610) 651-6144
Sales: $27,000,000   *Employees:* 60
Company Type: Private   *Employees here:* 60
SIC: 2835
   Diagnostic substances, nsk
Aris Petropoulos, Chief Financial Officer

D-U-N-S 60-576-4828   EXP
FUJISAWA HEALTHCARE, INC.
3 Parkway N, Deerfield, IL 60015
Phone: (847) 317-8800
Sales: $240,000,000   *Employees:* 1,000
Company Type: Private   *Employees here:* 500
SIC: 2834
   Mfg critical care injectable pharmaceutical products
Noboru Maeda, President

D-U-N-S 05-613-9553
G & S ENTERPRISES INCORPORATED
10863 Rockley Rd, Houston, TX 77099
Phone: (281) 530-3077
Sales: $3,000,000   *Employees:* 21
Company Type: Private   *Employees here:* 21
SIC: 2834
   Mfg pharmaceuticals
John W Shadle, President

D-U-N-S 00-127-1188   EXP
G & W LABORATORIES INC.
111 Coolidge St, South Plainfield, NJ 07080
Phone: (908) 753-2000
Sales: $26,600,000   *Employees:* 200
Company Type: Private   *Employees here:* 150
SIC: 2834
   Mfg pharmaceuticals
Burton Greenblatt, President

D-U-N-S 00-223-8863
G C HANFORD MFG CO INC.
304 Oneida St, Syracuse, NY 13202
Phone: (315) 476-7418
Sales: $20,000,000   *Employees:* 240
Company Type: Private   *Employees here:* 130
SIC: 2834
   Mfg penicillin & cephalosporin preparations
George R Hanford, Chairman of the Board

D-U-N-S 11-530-0493   EXP
G D S TECHNOLOGY INC.
25235 Leer Dr, Elkhart, IN 46514
Phone: (219) 264-7384
Sales: $2,100,000   *Employees:* 27
Company Type: Private   *Employees here:* 27
SIC: 2835
   Mfg diagnostic test kits & enzymes
Surendra K Gupta PhD, President

D-U-N-S 00-509-3570   EXP
G D SEARLE & CO.
   (*Parent:* Monsanto Company)
5200 Old Orchard Rd, Skokie, IL 60077
Phone: (847) 982-7000
Sales: $1,999,000,000   *Employees:* 8,700
Company Type: Public Family Member   *Employees here:* 1,700
SIC: 2834
   Mfg pharmaceutical preparations
Richard U DeSchutter, Chairman of the Board

D-U-N-S 04-735-0186   IMP EXP
GALDERMA LABORATORIES INC.
3000 Altamesa Blvd, Fort Worth, TX 76133
Phone: (817) 263-2600
Sales: $156,787,000   *Employees:* 179
Company Type: Private   *Employees here:* 80
SIC: 2834
   Mfg dermatological products
Stephen W Clark, President

D-U-N-S 96-335-4253
GALEN INC.
2661 Audubon Rd, Audubon, PA 19403
Phone: (610) 666-9500
Sales: $8,798,000   *Employees:* 165
Company Type: Private   *Employees here:* 155
SIC: 2834
   Mfg clinical trial supplies
Timothy Brewer, President

D-U-N-S 12-118-3016   EXP
GALLIPOT INC.
2020 Silver Bell Rd, Saint Paul, MN 55122
Phone: (612) 681-9517
Sales: $2,087,000   *Employees:* 16
Company Type: Private   *Employees here:* 16
SIC: 2834
  Mfg pharmaceuticals & cosmetics
Michael Jones, President

D-U-N-S 05-110-1715   EXP
GAMMA BIOLOGICALS INC.
  (Parent: Immucor Inc)
3700 Mangum Rd, Houston, TX 77092
Phone: (713) 681-8481
Sales: $18,254,000   *Employees:* 113
Company Type: Public Family Member   *Employees here:* 110
SIC: 2835
  Mfg diagnostic reagents
Edward L Gallup, President

D-U-N-S 00-121-3784
GANES CHEMICALS, INC.
630 Broad St, Carlstadt, NJ 07072
Phone: (201) 507-4300
Sales: $77,275,000   *Employees:* 275
Company Type: Private   *Employees here:* 90
SIC: 2833
  Mfg medicinal chemicals
Dr Rolf H Reinfried, President

D-U-N-S 19-450-5517
GARRISON INDUSTRIES, INC.
200 N Jefferson Ave, El Dorado, AR 71730
Phone: (870) 862-5692
Sales: $7,700,000   *Employees:* 30
Company Type: Private   *Employees here:* 4
SIC: 2833
  Mfg specialty chemicals
Rodney Landes, Chairman of the Board

D-U-N-S 00-416-6021   EXP
GEBAUER COMPANY
9410 Saint Catherine Ave, Cleveland, OH 44104
Phone: (216) 271-5252
Sales: $4,000,000   *Employees:* 25
Company Type: Private   *Employees here:* 25
SIC: 2834
  Mfg pharmaceuticals
Ernest Rose Jr, Chairman of the Board

D-U-N-S 05-594-2270
GEMINI PHARMACEUTICALS INC.
81 Keyland Ct, Bohemia, NY 11716
Phone: (516) 563-8700
Sales: $5,000,000   *Employees:* 30
Company Type: Private   *Employees here:* 30
SIC: 2833
  Manufactures vitamins and food supplements
Andrew Finamore, President

D-U-N-S 78-949-7310
GENAISSANCE PHARMACEUTICAL
5 Science Park, New Haven, CT 06511
Phone: (203) 773-1450
Sales: $2,000,000   *Employees:* 22
Company Type: Private   *Employees here:* 22
SIC: 2834
  Customized pharmaceutical research and preparation
Richard Kouri, Chairman of the Board

D-U-N-S 18-069-5348
GENELABS TECHNOLOGIES, INC.
505 Penobscot Dr, Redwood City, CA 94063
Phone: (650) 369-9500
Sales: $12,790,000   *Employees:* 147
Company Type: Public   *Employees here:* 70
SIC: 2834
  Mfg pharmaceutical products
Irene A Chow PhD, President

D-U-N-S 08-012-9000   EXP
GENENTECH INC.
  (Parent: Roche Holdings Inc)
1 Dna Way, South San Francisco, CA 94080
Phone: (650) 225-1000
Sales: $1,150,943,000   *Employees:* 3,242
Company Type: Public   *Employees here:* 1,900
SIC: 2834
  Mfg human pharmaceuticals
Arthur D Levinson, President

D-U-N-S 15-763-1821   EXP
GENERAL NUTRITION PRODUCTS INC.
  (Parent: General Nutrition Incorporated)
300 6th Ave, Pittsburgh, PA 15222
Phone: (412) 288-4600
Sales: $120,000,000   *Employees:* 800
Company Type: Public Family Member   *Employees here:* 5
SIC: 2834
  Mfg vitamins
William E Watts, President

D-U-N-S 06-382-4601
GENERAL RESEARCH LABORATORIES
8900 Winnetka Ave, Northridge, CA 91324
Phone: (818) 349-9911
Sales: $7,246,000   *Employees:* 27
Company Type: Private   *Employees here:* 27
SIC: 2834
  Mfg vitamin supplements
Alex S Geczy, President

D-U-N-S 96-634-7072   EXP
GENESIS TECHNOLOGIES INC.
3000 Langford Rd, Ste 2600, Norcross, GA 30071
Phone: (770) 825-0186
Sales: $5,300,000   *Employees:* 3
Company Type: Private   *Employees here:* 3
SIC: 2836
  Mfg bacterial concentrates
John Kubiak, President

D-U-N-S 06-271-4225   EXP
GENETICS INSTITUTE INC.
  (Parent: American Home Products Corp)
87 Cambridge Park Dr, Cambridge, MA 02140
Phone: (617) 876-1170
Sales: $172,055,000   *Employees:* 980
Company Type: Public Family Member   *Employees here:* 450
SIC: 2834
  Devl & mfg bio-pharmaceutical pdts
Patrick Gage PhD, President

D-U-N-S 00-538-7188
GENEVA PHARMACEUTICALS, INC.
2555 W Midway Blvd, Broomfield, CO 80020
Phone: (303) 466-2400
Sales: $93,900,000   *Employees:* 740
Company Type: Private   *Employees here:* 620
SIC: 2834
  Mfg oral pharmaceutical products & whol pharmaceuticals
David M Hurley, President

D-U-N-S 17-534-2625
GENOSYS BIOTECHNOLOGIES, INC.
1442 Lake Front Cir, The Woodlands, TX 77380
Phone: (281) 363-3693
Sales: $11,685,000   *Employees:* 130
Company Type: Private   *Employees here:* 90
SIC: 2833
   Mfg synthetic polynucleotides (dna)
Dr Kenneth Beattie, Chairman of the Board

D-U-N-S 17-323-4162
GENSIA SICOR INC.
19 Hughes, Irvine, CA 92618
Phone: (949) 455-4700
Sales: $149,681,000   *Employees:* 1,124
Company Type: Public   *Employees here:* 260
SIC: 2834
   Mfg pharmaceutical pdts
Carlo Salvi, Chief Executive Officer

D-U-N-S 79-436-2533
GENSIA SICOR PHARMACEUTICALS
   (Parent: Gensia Sicor Inc)
19 Hughes, Irvine, CA 92618
Phone: (949) 455-4700
Sales: $32,000,000   *Employees:* 260
Company Type: Public Family Member   *Employees here:* 260
SIC: 2834
   Mfg pharmaceutical products
Michael Cannon, President

D-U-N-S 01-487-0273   EXP
GENTRAC, INC.
   (Parent: Jones Pharma Inc)
2232 Evergreen Rd, Middleton, WI 53562
Phone: (608) 836-3500
Sales: $5,600,000   *Employees:* 93
Company Type: Public Family Member   *Employees here:* 93
SIC: 2836
   Mfg coagulation products
Dennis M Jones, President

D-U-N-S 02-532-2157   EXP
GENZYME CORPORATION
1 Kendall Sq, Ste 1400, Cambridge, MA 02139
Phone: (617) 252-7500
Sales: $608,841,000   *Employees:* 2,500
Company Type: Public   *Employees here:* 600
SIC: 2835
   Mfg biological human health care products
Henri A Termeer, Chairman of the Board

D-U-N-S 11-293-2306   EXP
GENZYME DIAGNOSTICS MEDIX BIOT
   (Parent: Genzyme Corporation)
1531 Industrial Rd, San Carlos, CA 94070
Phone: (650) 594-0513
Sales: $3,500,000   *Employees:* 49
Company Type: Public Family Member   *Employees here:* 49
SIC: 2836
   Mfg biochemical products
Bill Leiva, President

D-U-N-S 04-585-9923
GERIATRIC PHARMACEUTICAL CORP.
   (Parent: Roberts Pharmaceutical Corp)
16820 Ridgeview Dr, Brookfield, WI 53005
Phone: (414) 272-2552
Sales: $2,000,000   *Employees:* 23
Company Type: Public Family Member   *Employees here:* 1
SIC: 2834
   Mfg of pharmaceuticals
James Hinz, Chairman of the Board

D-U-N-S 85-885-4490
GERON CORPORATION
230 Constitution Dr, Menlo Park, CA 94025
Phone: (650) 473-7700
Sales: $7,253,000   *Employees:* 96
Company Type: Public   *Employees here:* 96
SIC: 2834
   Mfg novel pharmaceuticals
Ronald W Eastman, President

D-U-N-S 18-504-9848
GILEAD SCIENCES, INC.
333 Lakeside Dr, Foster City, CA 94404
Phone: (650) 574-3000
Sales: $40,037,000   *Employees:* 289
Company Type: Public   *Employees here:* 289
SIC: 2834
   Mfg pharmaceuticals
John C Martin PhD, President

D-U-N-S 19-871-5773
GLAXO WELCOME AMERICAS INC.
499 Park Ave Fl 21, New York, NY 10022
Phone: (212) 308-1210
Sales: $964,700,000   *Employees:* 7,500
Company Type: Private   *Employees here:* 5
SIC: 2834
   Mfrs prescription pharmaceutical preparations
Richard Sykes, President

D-U-N-S 92-949-9168
GLEN COPEL PHARMACEUTICALS INC.
249 Hope St, Providence, RI 02906
Phone: (401) 454-1217
Sales: $3,544,000   *Employees:* 6
Company Type: Private   *Employees here:* 4
SIC: 2834
   Mfg pharmaceutical & health care products
Dr Ricky Mccullough MD, President

D-U-N-S 15-984-2384
GLENWOOD LLC
82 N Summit St, Tenafly, NJ 07670
Phone: (201) 569-0050
Sales: $28,300,000   *Employees:* 180
Company Type: Private   *Employees here:* 25
SIC: 2834
   Mfg pharmaceuticals
Christophe Fuhrmann, Member

D-U-N-S 19-681-1640
GLIATECH INC.
23420 Commerce Park, Cleveland, OH 44122
Phone: (216) 831-3200
Sales: $13,150,000   *Employees:* 55
Company Type: Public   *Employees here:* 55
SIC: 2834
   Mfg medical devices specializing in surgical gel used to inhibit
      surgical scarring & adhesions
Thomas O Oesterling PhD, President

D-U-N-S 02-905-8232
GLOBAL HEALTH SCIENCES CORP.
987 N Enterprise St, Orange, CA 92867
Phone: (714) 633-2320
Sales: $52,700,000   *Employees:* 224
Company Type: Private   *Employees here:* 4
SIC: 2834
   Holding company
Richard Marconi, Chairman of the Board

D-U-N-S 78-131-8985
GLOBAL SOURCE MGT & CONSULTING
3001 N 29th Ave, Hollywood, FL 33020
Phone: (954) 921-0006
Sales: $25,000,000   *Employees:* 17
Company Type: Private   *Employees here:* 8
SIC: 2834
  Mfg and whol pharmaceuticals and through subsidiary retail
    kiosks of nutritionals
Gary R Dubin, President

D-U-N-S 62-362-2685
GLOBAL VITALITY, INC.
2035 E Cedar St, Tempe, AZ 85281
Phone: (602) 731-9605
Sales: $3,000,000   *Employees:* 27
Company Type: Private   *Employees here:* 27
SIC: 2834
  Manufactures vitamins & herbs
Dave Roderick, President

D-U-N-S 87-675-4375
GMP LABORATORIES AMERICA INC.
3880 E Eagle Dr, Anaheim, CA 92807
Phone: (714) 630-2467
Sales: $3,800,000   *Employees:* 35
Company Type: Private   *Employees here:* 35
SIC: 2833
  Mfg medicinal products
Mohammad Ishaq, President

D-U-N-S 80-937-4291
GOLDCAPS, INC.
(Parent: IVAX Corporation)
50 NW 176th St, Miami, FL 33169
Phone: (305) 575-6865
Sales: $15,800,000   *Employees:* 2
Company Type: Public Family Member   *Employees here:* 2
SIC: 2834
  Wholesales pharmaceutical preparations
Rafik Heinen, President

D-U-N-S 07-341-6737   EXP
GOLDEN PHARMACEUTICALS INC.
3000 W Warner Ave, Santa Ana, CA 92704
Phone: (714) 754-5800
Sales: $6,444,000   *Employees:* 90
Company Type: Public   *Employees here:* 8
SIC: 2834
  Repackager of pharmaceuticals
Charles R Drummond, Chairman of the Board

D-U-N-S 06-513-0353   EXP
GRAND LABORATORIES INC.
44130 279th St, Freeman, SD 57029
Phone: (605) 925-7611
Sales: $17,511,000   *Employees:* 160
Company Type: Private   *Employees here:* 20
SIC: 2836
  Mfg biological products
Dr Duane Pankratz, President

D-U-N-S 08-550-5196
GRANT INDUSTRIES, INC.
125 Main Ave, Elmwood Park, NJ 07407
Phone: (201) 791-6700
Sales: $6,900,000   *Employees:* 60
Company Type: Private   *Employees here:* 52
SIC: 2834
  Mfg textile chemical specialties & cosmetic specialties
Charles Granatell, President

D-U-N-S 15-394-2792   EXP
GRANUTEC INC.
(Parent: Novopharm Limited)
4409 Airport Dr NW, Wilson, NC 27896
Phone: (252) 291-9100
Sales: $70,000,000   *Employees:* 400
Company Type: Private   *Employees here:* 200
SIC: 2834
  Mfr over-the-counter cough and cold solid pharmaceuticals
David Howard, President

D-U-N-S 87-811-9007   EXP
GREEN CROSS CORP. OF AMERICA
5555 Valley Blvd, Los Angeles, CA 90032
Phone: (323) 225-2221
Sales: $384,718,000   *Employees:* 2,900
Company Type: Private   *Employees here:* 3
SIC: 2836
  Mfg plasma derivatives
Kazunari Doi, President

D-U-N-S 02-467-1414
GREER LABORATORIES INC.
639 Nuway Cir NE, Lenoir, NC 28645
Phone: (828) 754-5327
Sales: $14,264,000   *Employees:* 205
Company Type: Private   *Employees here:* 195
SIC: 2836
  Mfg pharmaceutical vaccines
William White Jr, Chairman of the Board

D-U-N-S 11-921-0276   EXP
GUARDIAN DRUG COMPANY INC.
72 Prince St, Trenton, NJ 08638
Phone: (609) 394-5300
Sales: $12,000,000   *Employees:* 90
Company Type: Private   *Employees here:* 90
SIC: 2834
  Mfg pharmaceuticals for the stomach
Dr Arvind B Dhruv, President

D-U-N-S 03-783-8844
GUY & O'NEILL, INC.
617 Tower Dr, Fredonia, WI 53021
Phone: (414) 692-2469
Sales: $14,000,000   *Employees:* 150
Company Type: Private   *Employees here:* 120
SIC: 2834
  Mfg wet-wipe products pharmaceutical preparations business
    services
Michael G Guy, President

D-U-N-S 83-675-4341
GYNETICS INC.
105 Raider Blvd, Ste 203, Belle Mead, NJ 08502
Phone: (908) 359-2429
Sales: $13,000,000   *Employees:* 10
Company Type: Private   *Employees here:* 10
SIC: 2834
  Mfg pharmaceuticals & medical devices
Roderick Mackenzie, Chairman of the Board

D-U-N-S 00-202-7514
HALOCARBON PRODUCTS CORP.
887 Kinderkamack Rd, River Edge, NJ 07661
Phone: (201) 262-8899
Sales: $15,800,000   *Employees:* 123
Company Type: Private   *Employees here:* 15
SIC: 2834
  Mfg pharmaceutical preparations
Robert L Ehrenfeld, President

D-U-N-S 00-131-5530
HALSEY DRUG CO INC.
695 N Perryville Rd, Rockford, IL 61107
Phone: (815) 399-2060
Sales: $9,088,000   *Employees:* 200
Company Type: Public   *Employees here:* 6
SIC: 2834
  Mfg generic pharmaceuticals
Michael Reicher, President

D-U-N-S 03-998-1550
HARDY MEDIA INC.
1430 W Mccoy Ln, Santa Maria, CA 93455
Phone: (805) 346-2766
Sales: $9,000,000   *Employees:* 55
Company Type: Private   *Employees here:* 55
SIC: 2836
  Mfg agar culture media and whol medical supplies medical
    laboratory equipment and diagnostic kits
Jay R Hardy, President

D-U-N-S 11-626-6230   EXP
HAUSER INC.
5555 Airport Blvd, Boulder, CO 80301
Phone: (303) 443-4662
Sales: $32,038,000   *Employees:* 354
Company Type: Public   *Employees here:* 264
SIC: 2833
  Develop manufacture and market special products
Dean P Stull, Chairman of the Board

D-U-N-S 94-724-4539
HCCP ACQUISITION CORPORATION
  (Parent: Hoechst Corporation)
1041 Us Route 202 206 N, Somerville, NJ 08876
Phone: (908) 231-2000
Sales: $64,300,000   *Employees:* 510
Company Type: Private   *Employees here:* 1
SIC: 2834
  Mfg & whol pharmaceuticals
Dr G Metz, President

D-U-N-S 17-197-0106
HDI NUTRIENTS INC.
5536 W Roosevelt St, Ste 1, Phoenix, AZ 85043
Phone: (602) 272-3777
Sales: $4,500,000   *Employees:* 40
Company Type: Private   *Employees here:* 1
SIC: 2833
  Mfg nutritional supplements
Richard Davis, President

D-U-N-S 01-753-0226
HEALTH FACTORS INTERNATIONAL
  (Parent: Twin Laboratories Inc)
429 S Siesta Ln, Tempe, AZ 85281
Phone: (602) 921-1991
Sales: $15,000,000   *Employees:* 100
Company Type: Public Family Member   *Employees here:* 100
SIC: 2833
  Mfg medicinal/botanical products
Ross Blechman, President

D-U-N-S 13-127-9275
HEALTH PLUS INC.
13837 Magnolia Ave, Chino, CA 91710
Phone: (909) 627-9393
Sales: $9,000,000   *Employees:* 28
Company Type: Private   *Employees here:* 28
SIC: 2834
  Mfg nutritional supplements and contract manufacturing and
    packaging of same
Rita Mediratta, President

D-U-N-S 09-311-8354
HEALTH PRODUCTS INTL CORP.
  (Parent: MMS Holding Company)
10 Mountain Springs Pkwy, Springville, UT 84663
Phone: (801) 489-1520
Sales: $2,100,000   *Employees:* 26
Company Type: Private   *Employees here:* 26
SIC: 2833
  Mfg botanical dietary supplements over the counter
    pharmaceutical preparations
Kenneth Murdock, Chairman of the Board

D-U-N-S 96-563-4504   EXP
HEALTHPOINT LTD.
2600 Airport Fwy, Fort Worth, TX 76111
Phone: (817) 900-4000
Sales: $16,086,000   *Employees:* 115
Company Type: Private   *Employees here:* 115
SIC: 2834
  Mfg pharmaceutical preparations
H P Dorman, Chairman of the Board

D-U-N-S 02-590-0114
HEALTHSPAN, INC.
2615 Pacific Coast Hwy, Hermosa Beach, CA 90254
Phone: (310) 379-2852
Sales: $3,000,000   *Employees:* 6
Company Type: Private   *Employees here:* 6
SIC: 2834
  Mfg pharmaceutical preparations
Steven S Cady, Chief Executive Officer

D-U-N-S 10-278-3016   EXP
HEEL INC.
11600 Cochiti Rd SE, Albuquerque, NM 87123
Phone: (505) 293-3843
Sales: $5,800,000   *Employees:* 53
Company Type: Private   *Employees here:* 53
SIC: 2833
  Mfg homeopathic medicine
Fredrick Doerper, President

D-U-N-S 78-813-7255
HEICO CHEMICALS, INC.
  (Parent: Cambrex Corporation)
Rr 611, Delaware Water Gap, PA 18327
Phone: (570) 476-0353
Sales: $12,000,000   *Employees:* 48
Company Type: Public Family Member   *Employees here:* 48
SIC: 2833
  Mfg chemicals
Cyril C Baldwin Jr, Chairman of the Board

D-U-N-S 14-782-7216   EXP
HEMAGEN DIAGNOSTICS INC.
40 Bear Hill Rd, Waltham, MA 02451
Phone: (781) 890-3766
Sales: $12,327,000   *Employees:* 109
Company Type: Public   *Employees here:* 39
SIC: 2835
  Mfg diagnostic agents
Carl Franzblau PhD, President

D-U-N-S 00-700-1662   EXP
HEMATRONIX, INC.
1505 Capital Ave, Plano, TX 75074
Phone: (972) 596-6165
Sales: $8,500,000   *Employees:* 100
Company Type: Private   *Employees here:* 60
SIC: 2835
  Mfg hematology products & develops computer software
William C Buxbaum, President

D-U-N-S 00-226-1220
HERB PENN CO. LTD.
10601 Decatur Rd, Ste 2, Philadelphia, PA 19154
Phone: (215) 632-6336
Sales: $3,500,000					*Employees:* 36
Company Type: Private				*Employees here:* 30
SIC: 2833
   Mfg & mail order of herbal medicines & products
William P Betz Sr, President

D-U-N-S 03-964-4526
HERB SOURCE ENTERPRISE INC.
13840 Magnolia Ave, Chino, CA 91710
Phone: (909) 590-8816
Sales: $2,500,000					*Employees:* 25
Company Type: Private				*Employees here:* 25
SIC: 2834

Jie J Wen, President

D-U-N-S 96-285-6308
HERBA AROMATICA INC.
23785 Cabot Blvd, Ste 318, Hayward, CA 94545
Phone: (510) 266-0850
Sales: $5,000,000					*Employees:* 50
Company Type: Private				*Employees here:* 50
SIC: 2833
   Mfg botanical products
Galina Lisin, President

D-U-N-S 15-271-0315
HERCON LABORATORIES CORP.
   (Parent: Health-Chem Corporation)
1212 Avenue Of The Americ, New York, NY 10036
Phone: (212) 398-0700
Sales: $12,500,000					*Employees:* 90
Company Type: Public Family Member		*Employees here:* 4
SIC: 2834
   Mfg transdermal nitroglycerin patches & controlled release
   chemicals
Marvin M Speiser, Chairman of the Board

D-U-N-S 03-728-4445						EXP
HESS & CLARK, INC.
   (Parent: United Agri Products Inc)
7th & Orange Sts, Ashland, OH 44805
Phone: (419) 289-9129
Sales: $11,700,000					*Employees:* 105
Company Type: Public Family Member		*Employees here:* 105
SIC: 2834
   Mfg animal health care products
Bruce L Bookmyer, President

D-U-N-S 10-119-6749
HI-TECH PHARMACAL CO, INC.
369 Bayview Ave, Amityville, NY 11701
Phone: (516) 789-8228
Sales: $22,366,000					*Employees:* 135
Company Type: Public					*Employees here:* 135
SIC: 2834
   Manufactures generic pharmaceuticals
David S Seltzer, President

D-U-N-S 07-180-7358
HIGHLAND LABORATORIES, INC.
110 S Garfield St, Mount Angel, OR 97362
Phone: (503) 845-9223
Sales: $4,100,000					*Employees:* 41
Company Type: Private				*Employees here:* 41
SIC: 2833
   Mfg natural vitamin supplements & skin care items
Kenneth Scott, President

D-U-N-S 09-836-6990
HILL DERMACEUTICALS INC.
2650 S Mellonville Ave, Sanford, FL 32773
Phone: (407) 323-1887
Sales: $3,600,000					*Employees:* 35
Company Type: Private				*Employees here:* 20
SIC: 2834
   Mfg drugs
Jerry S Roth, President

D-U-N-S 84-749-9423
HILL LABS, INC.
2650 S Mellonville Ave, Sanford, FL 32773
Phone: (407) 323-1887
Sales: $3,300,000					*Employees:* 35
Company Type: Private				*Employees here:* 35
SIC: 2834
   Mfg pharmaceutical preparations
Jerry Roth, President

D-U-N-S 92-897-4351
HILLESTAD PHARMACEUTICALS,
178 Us Highway 51 N, Woodruff, WI 54568
Phone: (715) 358-2113
Sales: $2,000,000					*Employees:* 25
Company Type: Private				*Employees here:* 25
SIC: 2834
   Mfg vitamins
Don Hillestad, President

D-U-N-S 94-669-7323
HOECHST MARION ROUSSEL
   (Parent: Hoechst Marion Roussel Inc)
Amelia Ind Park A, Guaynabo, PR 00968
Phone: (787) 782-1900
Sales: $17,000,000					*Employees:* 25
Company Type: Private				*Employees here:* 25
SIC: 2834
   Mfg pharmaceuticals
Francisco Nordelo, President

D-U-N-S 00-711-9555						EXP
HOECHST MARION ROUSSEL INC.
10236 Marion Park Dr, Kansas City, MO 64137
Phone: (816) 966-4000
Sales: $610,500,000					*Employees:* 4,750
Company Type: Private				*Employees here:* 750
SIC: 2834
   Mfg pharmaceuticals
Richard J Markham, Chief Executive Officer

D-U-N-S 00-219-1211
HOFFMANN-LA ROCHE INC.
   (Parent: Roche Holdings Inc)
340 Kingsland St, Nutley, NJ 07110
Phone: (973) 235-5000
Sales: $2,500,000,000				*Employees:* 5,000
Company Type: Private				*Employees here:* 3,000
SIC: 2834
   Mfg pharmaceuticals
Patrick J Zenner, President

D-U-N-S 83-776-9546
HOLOPACK INTERNATIONAL, LP
1 Technology Cir, Columbia, SC 29203
Phone: (803) 806-3300
Sales: $6,500,000					*Employees:* 60
Company Type: Private				*Employees here:* 60
SIC: 2834
   Mfg pharmaceuticals
Walter Zahn, General Partner

D-U-N-S 15-972-6637   EXP
HORIZON PHARMACEUTICALS INC.
11800 28th St N, Saint Petersburg, FL 33716
Phone: (727) 573-2404
Sales: $2,277,000   *Employees:* 25
Company Type: Private   *Employees here:* 25
SIC: 2834
   Mfg vitamin mineral & herbal preparations
Michael Creamer, President

D-U-N-S 07-892-2762
HOUBA INC.
   (*Parent:* Halsey Drug Co Inc)
16235 State Road 17, Culver, IN 46511
Phone: (219) 842-3305
Sales: $2,500,000   *Employees:* 30
Company Type: Public Family Member   *Employees here:* 30
SIC: 2834
   Mfg pharmaceutical raw materials and products and specialty
     chemicals
Micheal K Reicher, N/A

D-U-N-S 84-733-7961
H.T.I. BIO-PRODUCTS INC.
26578 Old Julian Hwy, Santa Ysabel, CA 92070
Phone: (760) 788-9691
Sales: $7,700,000   *Employees:* 80
Company Type: Private   *Employees here:* 80
SIC: 2835
   Mfg in vitro and in vivo diagnostis substances
Robert J Harman, Chairman of the Board

D-U-N-S 82-567-2884
HUMCO HOLDING GROUP, INC.
   (*Parent:* PLP Ltd)
7400 Alumax Rd, Texarkana, TX 75501
Phone: (903) 831-7808
Sales: $29,500,000   *Employees:* 240
Company Type: Private   *Employees here:* 110
SIC: 2834
   Mfg pharmaceutical preparations
Gregory C Pulido, President

D-U-N-S 03-007-6988
HVL INC.
600 Boyce Rd, Pittsburgh, PA 15205
Phone: (412) 494-0100
Sales: $50,000,000   *Employees:* 200
Company Type: Private   *Employees here:* 200
SIC: 2833
   Mfr vitamins
L D Lioon, President

D-U-N-S 01-055-8476
HYCOR BIOMEDICAL INC.
7272 Chapman Ave, Garden Grove, CA 92841
Phone: (714) 933-3000
Sales: $20,084,000   *Employees:* 220
Company Type: Public   *Employees here:* 130
SIC: 2835
   Mfg medical diagnostic products
J D Tholen, President

D-U-N-S 84-931-7615
HYSEQ, INC.
670 Almanor Ave, Sunnyvale, CA 94086
Phone: (408) 524-8100
Sales: $6,199,000   *Employees:* 169
Company Type: Public   *Employees here:* 169
SIC: 2835
   Medical related research and development of invitro and in
     vivo diagnostic substances
Robert D Weist, Chairman of the Board

D-U-N-S 11-628-8226   EXP
ICN BIOMEDICALS, INC.
   (*Parent:* ICN Pharmaceuticals Inc)
3300 Hyland Ave, Costa Mesa, CA 92626
Phone: (714) 545-0100
Sales: $38,000,000   *Employees:* 460
Company Type: Public Family Member   *Employees here:* 305
SIC: 2835
   Mfg research chemical products & cell biology products whol
     research chemicals & biomedical products
Milan Panic, Chairman of the Board

D-U-N-S 60-723-9605
ICN EAST, INC.
   (*Parent:* ICN Pharmaceuticals Inc)
750 Lexington Ave Fl 14, New York, NY 10022
Phone: (212) 754-4422
Sales: $13,000,000   *Employees:* 88
Company Type: Public Family Member   *Employees here:* 88
SIC: 2834
   Mfg pharmaceutical products
Cliff Saffron, Manager

D-U-N-S 04-223-0623   EXP
ICN PHARMACEUTICALS, INC.
3300 Hyland Ave, Costa Mesa, CA 92626
Phone: (714) 545-0100
Sales: $752,202,000   *Employees:* 17,000
Company Type: Public   *Employees here:* 330
SIC: 2834
   Mfg pharmaceutical products research chemicals &
     diagnostic products
Milan Panic, Chairman of the Board

D-U-N-S 01-809-9247
ICONIX PHARMACEUTICALS INC.
850 Maude Ave, Mountain View, CA 94043
Phone: (650) 526-3030
Sales: $2,800,000   *Employees:* 27
Company Type: Private   *Employees here:* 27
SIC: 2834
   Pharmaceutical research
Keith A Bostian, President

D-U-N-S 61-332-6719
ICOS CORPORATION
22021 20th Ave SE, Bothell, WA 98021
Phone: (425) 485-1900
Sales: $31,576,000   *Employees:* 275
Company Type: Public   *Employees here:* 275
SIC: 2834
   Mfg bio-pharmaceuticals
Dr George B Rathmann, Chairman of the Board

D-U-N-S 01-103-6910   EXP
IGI INC.
Lincoln Ave & Wheat Rd, Buena, NJ 08310
Phone: (609) 697-1441
Sales: $34,193,000   *Employees:* 209
Company Type: Public   *Employees here:* 30
SIC: 2836
   Mfg animal health cosmetic & consumer products
Dr Edward B Hager MD, Chairman of the Board

D-U-N-S 01-724-0230
IGX CORP.
1 Springfield Ave, Summit, NJ 07901
Phone: (908) 598-4675

Sales: $2,500,000   *Employees:* 31
Company Type: Private   *Employees here:* 5
SIC: 2836
   Mfg pharmaceutical preparations commercial physical
   research
Albert J Henry, Chairman of the Board

D-U-N-S 78-299-6045
IMARX PHARMACEUTICAL CORP.
1635 E 18th St, Tucson, AZ 85719
Phone: (520) 770-1259
Sales: $6,004,000   *Employees:* 30
Company Type: Private   *Employees here:* 30
SIC: 2835
   Dev of pharmaceuticals for diagnostic imaging
Dr Evan Unger MD, President

D-U-N-S 00-250-7622   EXP
IMMUCELL CORPORATION
56 Evergreen Dr, Portland, ME 04103
Phone: (207) 878-2770
Sales: $4,557,000   *Employees:* 23
Company Type: Public   *Employees here:* 21
SIC: 2835
   Mfg therapeutic medical products
Michael F Brigham, Chief Financial Officer

D-U-N-S 06-144-6282
IMMUCOR INC.
3130 Gateway Dr, Norcross, GA 30071
Phone: (770) 441-2051
Sales: $39,790,000   *Employees:* 229
Company Type: Public   *Employees here:* 141
SIC: 2835
   Mfg blood diagnostic reagents
Edward L Gallup, Chairman of the Board

D-U-N-S 17-434-7732
IMMUNETICS INC.
63 Rogers St, Cambridge, MA 02142
Phone: (617) 492-5416
Sales: $2,500,000   *Employees:* 25
Company Type: Private   *Employees here:* 25
SIC: 2835
   Mfg diagnostic tests & biological products
Nancy J Levy, President

D-U-N-S 02-813-4799   EXP
IMMUNEX CORPORATION
   (Parent: American Cyanamid Company)
51 University St, Seattle, WA 98101
Phone: (206) 587-0430
Sales: $185,297,000   *Employees:* 886
Company Type: Public   *Employees here:* 700
SIC: 2834
   Mfg & mktg therapeutic pdts & biotherapeutic research
Edward V Fritzky, Chairman of the Board

D-U-N-S 02-776-0552   EXP
IMMUNO - U S INC.
1200 Parkdale Rd, Rochester, MI 48307
Phone: (248) 652-7872
Sales: $93,888,000   *Employees:* 660
Company Type: Private   *Employees here:* 175
SIC: 2836
   Mfg blood plasma products
John Bacich, Chief Executive Officer

D-U-N-S 03-827-1904
IMMUNO CONCEPTS INC.
9779 Business Park Dr, Sacramento, CA 95827
Phone: (916) 363-2649

Sales: $2,600,000   *Employees:* 25
Company Type: Private   *Employees here:* 22
SIC: 2835
   Mfg diagnostic substances
Bert R Williams III, President

D-U-N-S 79-344-6428
IMMUNOGENETICS INC.
   (Parent: IGI Inc)
Lincoln Ave & Wheat Rd, Buena, NJ 08310
Phone: (609) 697-1441
Sales: $20,600,000   *Employees:* 150
Company Type: Public Family Member   *Employees here:* 150
SIC: 2834
   Mfg veterinary vaccines & pharmaceuticals
John P Gallo, President

D-U-N-S 18-362-4907
IMMVAC INC.
6080 E Bass Ln, Columbia, MO 65201
Phone: (573) 443-5363
Sales: $3,000,000   *Employees:* 16
Company Type: Private   *Employees here:* 16
SIC: 2836
   Mfg animal serumn & vaccines
Ronald F Sprouse, President

D-U-N-S 60-613-1381
IMPACT NUTRITION, INC.
4320 Anthony Ct, Ste 1, Rocklin, CA 95677
Phone: (916) 652-0716
Sales: $3,200,000   *Employees:* 30
Company Type: Private   *Employees here:* 30
SIC: 2834
   Mfg vitamins pet vitamins & pet supplies
Patrick Frazier, President

D-U-N-S 92-622-5608
IMPAX PHARMACEUTICALS INC.
30831 Huntwood Ave, Hayward, CA 94544
Phone: (510) 471-3600
Sales: $3,200,000   *Employees:* 30
Company Type: Private   *Employees here:* 30
SIC: 2834
   Mfg pharmaceutical preparations
Charles Shaio, President

D-U-N-S 01-814-9612
INFUSION ORLANDO REGIONAL
379 W Michigan St, Ste 204, Orlando, FL 32806
Phone: (407) 425-7114
Sales: $3,000,000   *Employees:* 20
Company Type: Private   *Employees here:* 20
SIC: 2834
   Mfg pharmaceutical preparations
Judy Allen, General Manager

D-U-N-S 87-792-7954
INNOMINATA
15222 Avenue Of Science, San Diego, CA 92128
Phone: (619) 592-9300
Sales: $2,400,000   *Employees:* 25
Company Type: Private   *Employees here:* 25
SIC: 2835
   Mfg diagnostic substances
Fred Adler, President

D-U-N-S 96-429-0522
INNOVATIVE NATURAL PRODUCTS
2140 Enterprise St, Escondido, CA 92029
Phone: (760) 738-7890

Sales: $2,000,000   *Employees:* 30
Company Type: Private   *Employees here:* 30
SIC: 2834
   Mfg pharmaceutical preparations
Edward J Ayala, President

D-U-N-S 18-835-4831
INOVA DIAGNOSTICS, INC.
10810 Scripps Ranch Blvd, San Diego, CA 92131
Phone: (619) 586-9900
Sales: $10,711,000   *Employees:* 86
Company Type: Private   *Employees here:* 86
SIC: 2835
   Mfg medical diagnostic re-agents
Walter Binder, President

D-U-N-S 04-882-2253
INOVISION HOLDINGS LP
22699 Old Canal Rd, Yorba Linda, CA 92887
Phone: (714) 998-9600
Sales: $60,000,000   *Employees:* 400
Company Type: Private   *Employees here:* 12
SIC: 2835
   Mfg barium diagnostic agents & nuclear instruments &
      monitoring systems
Herbert Hoebel, Partner

D-U-N-S 01-208-9038
INTEGRATED HEALTH NUTRITIONALS
4022 S 20th St, Phoenix, AZ 85040
Phone: (602) 921-1188
Sales: $9,600,000   *Employees:* 75
Company Type: Private   *Employees here:* 28
SIC: 2833
   Mfg vitamins and supplements
Ryuji Hirooka, President

D-U-N-S 09-929-0389
INTERFERON SCIENCES INC.
783 Jersey Ave, New Brunswick, NJ 08901
Phone: (732) 249-3250
Sales: $2,956,000   *Employees:* 100
Company Type: Public   *Employees here:* 100
SIC: 2835
   Manufacturer of human leukocyte alpha interferon
Lawrence M Gordon, Chief Executive Officer

D-U-N-S 18-303-5047
INTERGEN COMPANY
2 Manhattanville Rd, Purchase, NY 10577
Phone: (914) 694-1700
Sales: $30,000,000   *Employees:* 100
Company Type: Private   *Employees here:* 27
SIC: 2836
   Mfg biochemicals & biochemical reagents
Robert Beckman, President

D-U-N-S 96-681-3396
INTERGLOW NUTRITIONAL SYSTEMS
   (Parent: Nittany Pharmaceuticals Inc)
5135 Us Hwy 322, Milroy, PA 17063
Phone: (717) 667-2141
Sales: $7,000,000   *Employees:* 75
Company Type: Private   *Employees here:* 75
SIC: 2834
   Mfg herbal & dietary supplements vitamins face creams
      analgesics
Beth Kerstetter, President

D-U-N-S 18-378-4347   EXP
INTERHEALTH NUTRITIONALS, INC.
1320 Galaxy Way, Concord, CA 94520
Phone: (925) 827-4400

Sales: $15,000,000   *Employees:* 30
Company Type: Private   *Employees here:* 25
SIC: 2833
   Mfg nutritional supplements
William A Seroy, President

D-U-N-S 05-575-0020
INTERNATIONA MEDICATION SYSTEM
1886 Santa Anita Ave, El Monte, CA 91733
Phone: (909) 612-7400
Sales: $50,000,000   *Employees:* 380
Company Type: Private   *Employees here:* 380
SIC: 2834
   Manufactures generic drugs
Gayle M Deflin, President

D-U-N-S 07-874-2335   EXP
INTERNATIONAL ENZYME INC.
1432b S Mission Rd, Fallbrook, CA 92028
Phone: (760) 728-5205
Sales: $7,200,000   *Employees:* 42
Company Type: Private   *Employees here:* 10
SIC: 2836
   Mfg & whol biologicals
Charles G Haugh, President

D-U-N-S 82-723-8890
INTERNATIONAL FRUTAROM CORP.
9500 Railroad Ave, North Bergen, NJ 07047
Phone: (201) 861-7600
Sales: $40,000,000   *Employees:* 130
Company Type: Private   *Employees here:* 65
SIC: 2833
   Mfg of botanical products flavor extracts and food
      preparations
Israel Ben-Yehuda, President

D-U-N-S 07-496-9007   EXP
INTERNATIONAL IMMUNOLOGY CORP.
25549 Adams Ave, Murrieta, CA 92562
Phone: (909) 677-5629
Sales: $4,500,000   *Employees:* 36
Company Type: Private   *Employees here:* 36
SIC: 2835
   Mfg medical diagnostic substances
Katsyhiro Katiyama, President

D-U-N-S 79-704-7834
INTERNATIONAL PROCESSING CORP.
1100 Enterprise Dr, Winchester, KY 40391
Phone: (606) 745-2200
Sales: $25,000,000   *Employees:* 180
Company Type: Private   *Employees here:* 180
SIC: 2834
   Powder processing service for the pharmaceutical industry
Kenneth W Olsen, President

D-U-N-S 19-732-3959
INTERNATIONAL TOLLERS INC.
1711 Tiles Ct, Grand Haven, MI 49417
Phone: (616) 846-0377
Sales: $4,500,000   *Employees:* 54
Company Type: Private   *Employees here:* 54
SIC: 2834
   Pharmaceutical preparations
Joel G Bouwens, President

D-U-N-S 18-468-7226
INTERNTNAL BCHMICALS GROUP INC.
2204 Tmberlock Pl, Ste 260, The Woodlands, TX 77380
Phone: (281) 298-9410

Sales: $12,000,000   *Employees:* 120
Company Type: Private   *Employees here:* 20
SIC: 2836
    Mfr biological products for wastewater treatment &
    remediation of hazardous & non-hazardous waste
J P Perez, President

D-U-N-S 93-299-9410
INTERNTNAL FRMLTION MNFCTURING
5660 Eastgate Dr, San Diego, CA 92121
Phone: (619) 546-8933
Sales: $3,000,000   *Employees:* 30
Company Type: Private   *Employees here:* 30
SIC: 2834
    Mfg vitamins
Jack Watkins, President

D-U-N-S 13-089-1401
INTERPHARM INC.
3 Fairchild Ave, Plainview, NY 11803
Phone: (516) 349-1730
Sales: $8,105,000   *Employees:* 55
Company Type: Private   *Employees here:* 55
SIC: 2834
    Manufactures generic pharmaceuticals
Bob Sutaria, President

D-U-N-S 03-767-8216
INTERVET INC.
    (Parent: Akzo Nobel Inc)
405 State St, Millsboro, DE 19966
Phone: (302) 934-8051
Sales: $19,100,000   *Employees:* 315
Company Type: Private   *Employees here:* 230
SIC: 2836
    Mfg veterinary products
Dr Klaus Olbers, President

D-U-N-S 10-123-5554
INVAMED INCORPORATED
2400 Rte 130 N, Dayton, NJ 08810
Phone: (732) 274-2400
Sales: $37,000,000   *Employees:* 160
Company Type: Private   *Employees here:* 160
SIC: 2834
    Manufactures pharmaceuticals
Ashok Patel, President

D-U-N-S 18-215-8873
INVITROGEN CORPORATION
1600 Faraday Ave, Carlsbad, CA 92008
Phone: (760) 603-7200
Sales: $32,000,000   *Employees:* 165
Company Type: Public   *Employees here:* 140
SIC: 2836
    Mfg med devices & research & development
Lyle Turner, Chairman of the Board

D-U-N-S 15-693-1248
IPR PHARMACEUTICAL, INC.
Sabana Gardens Ind, Carolina, PR 00983
Phone: (787) 750-5353
Sales: $900,000,000   *Employees:* 530
Company Type: Private   *Employees here:* 250
SIC: 2834
    Mfg pharmaceutical preparations
Ruben Freyre, President

D-U-N-S 05-747-5246
IRVINE SCIENTIFIC SALES CO.
2511 Daimler St, Santa Ana, CA 92705
Phone: (949) 261-7800

Sales: $16,866,000   *Employees:* 100
Company Type: Private   *Employees here:* 100
SIC: 2836
    Mfg biological chemicals blood derivatives and culture media
    and whol medical laboratory equipment
Dr Michael J Kelly, President

D-U-N-S 88-401-8946
ISP CO INC.
RR 1 Box 130c, Wolf Summit, WV 26426
Phone: (304) 624-4725
Sales: $4,375,000   *Employees:* 3
Company Type: Private   *Employees here:* 3
SIC: 2836
    Mfg vet products/ret horseshoes/boarding services
Steven J Garvin, President

D-U-N-S 00-430-4861
ISP FINE CHEMICALS INC.
    (Parent: International Specialty Pdts)
1979 Atlas St, Columbus, OH 43228
Phone: (614) 529-3300
Sales: $8,500,000   *Employees:* 78
Company Type: Private   *Employees here:* 78
SIC: 2834
    Mfg pharmaceutical preparations
Dr Paul Taylor, Vice-President

D-U-N-S 18-415-0258   EXP
IVAX CORPORATION
4400 Biscayne Blvd, Miami, FL 33137
Phone: (305) 575-6000
Sales: $602,110,000   *Employees:* 4,500
Company Type: Public   *Employees here:* 175
SIC: 2834
    Mfg pharmaceuticals cosmetics vacuum pump fluids &
    medical diagnostic pdts
Dr Phillip Frost MD, Chairman of the Board

D-U-N-S 05-811-7482
IVC INDUSTRIES, INC.
500 Halls Mill Rd, Freehold, NJ 07728
Phone: (732) 308-3000
Sales: $119,775,000   *Employees:* 691
Company Type: Public   *Employees here:* 250
SIC: 2834
    Mfg retail & mail-order sales of vitamins & nutritional
    supplements
E J Edell, Chairman of the Board

D-U-N-S 05-015-6392   EXP
IVY ANIMAL HEALTH, INC.
8857 Bond St, Shawnee Mission, KS 66214
Phone: (913) 888-2192
Sales: $4,900,000   *Employees:* 50
Company Type: Private   *Employees here:* 50
SIC: 2834

James Sollins, Chief Executive Officer

D-U-N-S 60-206-5443
J & D LABORATORIES, INC.
2640 Progress St, Vista, CA 92083
Phone: (760) 734-6800
Sales: $3,200,000   *Employees:* 30
Company Type: Private   *Employees here:* 30
SIC: 2833
    Mfg vitamins
Kiran Majmudar, President

D-U-N-S 07-369-5777
JACKSON IMMUNORESEARCH LABS
872 W Baltimore Pike, West Grove, PA 19390

Phone: (610) 869-4024
Sales: $8,500,000   *Employees:* 40
Company Type: Private   *Employees here:* 40
SIC: 2834
    Mfg purified serium protein & purified antibodies
Dr William Stegeman, President

D-U-N-S 05-412-0571   EXP
JAME FINE CHEMICALS
100 W Main St, Bound Brook, NJ 08805
Phone: (732) 469-7760
Sales: $8,768,000   *Employees:* 34
Company Type: Private   *Employees here:* 34
SIC: 2833
    Mfg medicinal chemicals and specialty chemical products
        including chemical luminescents
James Schleck, President

D-U-N-S 06-313-7772
JANSSEN PHARMACEUTICA INC.
    (*Parent:* Johnson & Johnson)
1125 Trenton Harbourton R, Titusville, NJ 08560
Phone: (609) 730-2000
Sales: $206,200,000   *Employees:* 1,600
Company Type: Public Family Member   *Employees here:* 1,100
SIC: 2833
    Pharmaceutical manufacturer
Bruce Gable, VP Human Resources

D-U-N-S 04-335-2855   EXP
JASON PHARMACEUTICALS INC.
    (*Parent:* Healthrite Inc)
11445 Cron Hill Dr, Owings Mills, MD 21117
Phone: (410) 581-8042
Sales: $5,213,000   *Employees:* 35
Company Type: Public Family Member   *Employees here:* 35
SIC: 2834
    Mfg & whol medical food
David Illingworth, President

D-U-N-S 08-589-3071
JB LABORATORIES INC.
13295 Reflections Dr, Holland, MI 49424
Phone: (616) 738-8500
Sales: $24,919,000   *Employees:* 175
Company Type: Private   *Employees here:* 165
SIC: 2833
    Mfg medicinal chemicals & nutritional supplements
William J Baker Jr, President

D-U-N-S 07-225-6019   EXP
JBL SCIENTIFIC INC.
    (*Parent:* Genta Incorporated)
277 Granada Dr, San Luis Obispo, CA 93401
Phone: (805) 544-8524
Sales: $5,500,000   *Employees:* 53
Company Type: Public Family Member   *Employees here:* 53
SIC: 2833
    Mfg medicinal chemicals
Lauren R Brown, President

D-U-N-S 00-285-4370   IMP EXP
JEUNIQUE INTERNATIONAL INC.
19501 E Walnut Dr S, City Of Industry, CA 91748
Phone: (909) 598-8598
Sales: $27,900,000   *Employees:* 225
Company Type: Private   *Employees here:* 150
SIC: 2833
    Mfg vitamins & cosmetics & mfg foundation garments
Mulford J Nobbs, President

D-U-N-S 11-904-4956
JMI-CANTON PHARMACEUTICALS
    (*Parent:* Jones Pharma Inc)
1945 Craig Rd, Saint Louis, MO 63146
Phone: (314) 576-6100
Sales: $2,837,000   *Employees:* 40
Company Type: Public Family Member   *Employees here:* 3
SIC: 2834
    Mfg pharmaceuticals
Dennis M Jones, President

D-U-N-S 01-732-8837
JMI-DANIELS PHARMACEUTICAL
    (*Parent:* Jones Pharma Inc)
2527 25th Ave N, Saint Petersburg, FL 33713
Phone: (727) 323-8141
Sales: $7,200,000   *Employees:* 65
Company Type: Public Family Member   *Employees here:* 65
SIC: 2834
    Mfr prescription pharmaceutical products
Dennis M Jones, President

D-U-N-S 09-115-7792
JOHNSON JOHNSON PHRM PARTNERS
Gurabo, PR 00778
Phone: (787) 789-5000
Sales: $82,300,000   *Employees:* 650
Company Type: Private   *Employees here:* 650
SIC: 2834
    Mfg pharmaceutical preparations
Tomas Ramirez, General Manager

D-U-N-S 02-767-0702
JONES PHARMA INC.
1945 Craig Rd, Saint Louis, MO 63146
Phone: (314) 576-6100
Sales: $88,781,000   *Employees:* 235
Company Type: Public   *Employees here:* 165
SIC: 2834
    Mfg pharmaceutical preparations
Dennis M Jones, President

D-U-N-S 09-690-6185   EXP
JRH BIOSCIENCES, INC.
13804 W 107th St, Shawnee Mission, KS 66215
Phone: (913) 469-5580
Sales: $35,000,000   *Employees:* 140
Company Type: Private   *Employees here:* 70
SIC: 2836
    Mfg cell culture products
Paul Bordonaro, President

D-U-N-S 09-634-4916
JUNEAU PACKAGING CORPORATION
    (*Parent:* Difco Laboratories Inc)
1 Ensch St, Mauston, WI 53948
Phone: (608) 847-7334
Sales: $5,100,000   *Employees:* 72
Company Type: Public Family Member   *Employees here:* 72
SIC: 2835
    Mfg medical devices
Jon Stevens, Finance

D-U-N-S 08-757-1980
K & K LABORATORIES INC.
3305 Tyler St, Carlsbad, CA 92008
Phone: (760) 434-6044
Sales: $3,500,000   *Employees:* 35
Company Type: Private   *Employees here:* 35
SIC: 2834
    Mfg vitamins & food supplements
Alex Kononchuk, President

D-U-N-S 16-161-5505
KABCO PHARMACEUTICALS, INC.
2000 New Horizons Blvd, Amityville, NY 11701
Phone: (516) 842-3600
Sales: $21,000,000   *Employees:* 98
Company Type: Private   *Employees here:* 98
SIC: 2834
    Manufactures vitamins & dietary supplements
Abu M Kabir, Chairman of the Board

D-U-N-S 96-977-3902
KAIZEN INC.
12760 W Washington Blvd, Los Angeles, CA 90066
Phone: (310) 574-0682
Sales: $2,200,000   *Employees:* 4
Company Type: Private   *Employees here:* 4
SIC: 2834
    Mfg & whol nutritional supplements
Lewis Routbard, President

D-U-N-S 88-408-8618   EXP
KANEC (USA), INC.
3399 NW 151st Ter, Opa Locka, FL 33054
Phone: (305) 688-3999
Sales: $3,000,000   *Employees:* 3
Company Type: Private   *Employees here:* 3
SIC: 2834
    Mfg pharmaceutical preparations and cosmetics
Ebere Ikejiani, President

D-U-N-S 17-445-0460
KC PHARMACEUTICAL INC.
3201 Producer Way, Pomona, CA 91768
Phone: (909) 598-9499
Sales: $7,510,000   *Employees:* 60
Company Type: Private   *Employees here:* 11
SIC: 2834
    Mfg pharmaceuticals
L T Khouw, Chairman of the Board

D-U-N-S 14-845-2873
KELATRON INC.
1675 W 2750 S, Ogden, UT 84401
Phone: (801) 394-4558
Sales: $5,400,000   *Employees:* 50
Company Type: Private   *Employees here:* 22
SIC: 2834
    Pharmaceutical lab
William C Romney, President

D-U-N-S 80-958-7413   EXP
KING PHARMACEUTICALS, INC.
501 5th St, Bristol, TN 37620
Phone: (423) 989-8000
Sales: $163,463,000   *Employees:* 1,000
Company Type: Public   *Employees here:* 290
SIC: 2834
    Mfg pharmaceutical preparations
Jeff Gregory, President

D-U-N-S 04-493-9833   EXP
KING'S LABORATORY INCORPORATED
424 Blythewood Rd, Blythewood, SC 29016
Phone: (803) 754-5152
Sales: $2,936,000   *Employees:* 25
Company Type: Private   *Employees here:* 25
SIC: 2833
    Manufacture of specialty organic chemicals for the
        pharmaceutical industry
John A Montgomery Jr, President

D-U-N-S 09-758-4916   EXP
KIRKEGAARD & PERRY LABS INC.
2 Cessna Ct, Gaithersburg, MD 20879
Phone: (301) 948-7755
Sales: $4,700,000   *Employees:* 71
Company Type: Private   *Employees here:* 25
SIC: 2836
    Manufactures biological
Albert Perry, President

D-U-N-S 10-246-3866
KONSYL PHARMACEUTICALS INC.
4200 S Hulen St, Ste 513, Fort Worth, TX 76109
Phone: (817) 763-8011
Sales: $7,600,000   *Employees:* 65
Company Type: Private   *Employees here:* 20
SIC: 2834
    Mfg pharmaceuticals
Frank X Buhler, President

D-U-N-S 36-192-2446
KOS PHARMACEUTICALS INC.
1001 Brickell Bay Dr, Miami, FL 33131
Phone: (305) 577-3464
Sales: $2,892,000   *Employees:* 361
Company Type: Public   *Employees here:* 40
SIC: 2834
    Manufactures pharmaceuticals
Daniel Bell, President

D-U-N-S 03-235-9171
KULTIVAR, INC.
3171 Brook Rd, Plainfield, VT 05667
Phone: (802) 454-0182
Sales: $2,100,000   *Employees:* 20
Company Type: Private   *Employees here:* 20
SIC: 2833
    Develop/produce culinary & medicinal herbal products
Suzanne Johnson, President

D-U-N-S 00-629-1405   EXP
KV PHARMACEUTICAL COMPANY
2503 S Hanley Rd, Saint Louis, MO 63144
Phone: (314) 645-6600
Sales: $98,486,000   *Employees:* 358
Company Type: Public   *Employees here:* 25
SIC: 2834
    Research mfg pharmaceutical products
Marc S Hermelin, Vice-Chairman

D-U-N-S 00-601-3346
L PERRIGO COMPANY
    (Parent: Perrigo Company)
117 Water St, Allegan, MI 49010
Phone: (616) 673-8451
Sales: $903,000   *Employees:* 2,200
Company Type: Public Family Member   *Employees here:* 1,800
SIC: 2834
    Mfg pharmaceutical preparations
Mark Olesnavage, President

D-U-N-S 17-771-0852   EXP
LAFAYETTE PHARMACEUTICALS INC.
    (Parent: Inovision Holdings Lp)
22699 Old Canal Rd, Yorba Linda, CA 92887
Phone: (714) 998-9600
Sales: $10,800,000   *Employees:* 100
Company Type: Private   *Employees here:* 12
SIC: 2835
    Mfg barium diagnostic agents
Herbert Hoebel, President

D-U-N-S 00-227-7481
LANNETT COMPANY INC.
9000 State Rd, Philadelphia, PA 19136
Phone: (215) 333-9000
Sales: $9,465,000   *Employees:* 98
Company Type: Public   *Employees here:* 98
SIC: 2834
    Mfg pharmaceuticals
Jeffrey M Moshal, Treasurer

D-U-N-S 09-119-7301   EXP
LEDERLE PARENTERALS INC.
    (Parent: American Home Products Corp)
65th Inf Ave Km 9 Hm 7, Carolina, PR 00987
Phone: (787) 752-7474
Sales: $56,500,000   *Employees:* 450
Company Type: Public Family Member   *Employees here:* 450
SIC: 2834
    Mfg pharmaceutical products
Alfredo Nadal, Manager

D-U-N-S 09-116-5993   EXP
LEDERLE PIPERACILLIN INC.
    (Parent: American Home Products Corp)
65th Inf Ave Km 9 Hm 7, Carolina, PR 00985
Phone: (787) 752-7474
Sales: $12,100,000   *Employees:* 114
Company Type: Public Family Member   *Employees here:* 114
SIC: 2834
    Mfg pharmaceutical preparations
Alfredo Nadal, General Manager

D-U-N-S 04-297-3891
LEE LABORATORIES INC.
    (Parent: Difco Laboratories Inc)
1475 Athens Hwy, Grayson, GA 30017
Phone: (770) 972-4450
Sales: $2,800,000   *Employees:* 35
Company Type: Public Family Member   *Employees here:* 35
SIC: 2833
    Mfg biological reagents
Jack D Guthrie Jr, Director

D-U-N-S 79-339-6433
LEINER HEALTH PRODUCTS GROUP
901 E 233rd St, Carson, CA 90745
Phone: (310) 835-8400
Sales: $178,900,000   *Employees:* 1,400
Company Type: Private   *Employees here:* 400
SIC: 2834
    Manufactures vitamins food supplements and over-the-
      counter drug products
Robert Kaminski, Chief Executive Officer

D-U-N-S 03-947-9332
LEINER HEALTH PRODUCTS INC.
    (Parent: Leiner Hlth Pdts Group De Corp)
901 E 233rd St, Carson, CA 90745
Phone: (310) 835-8400
Sales: $502,110,000   *Employees:* 1,683
Company Type: Private   *Employees here:* 300
SIC: 2834
    Manufactures and distributes vitamins minerals and
      nutritional supplements
Robert M Kaminski, Chief Executive Officer

D-U-N-S 80-817-1730
LEUKOSITE, INC.
215 1st St 1c, Cambridge, MA 02142
Phone: (617) 621-9350

Sales: $5,726,000   *Employees:* 51
Company Type: Public   *Employees here:* 51
SIC: 2834
    Research and development of pharmaceuticals
Christophe K Mirabelli, Chairman of the Board

D-U-N-S 83-828-2705
LIFE ENHANCEMENT PRODUCTS
1340 Industrial Ave, Ste B, Petaluma, CA 94952
Phone: (707) 762-6144
Sales: $3,863,000   *Employees:* 22
Company Type: Private   *Employees here:* 22
SIC: 2834
    Mfg & ret nutritional supplements by mail order
Will Block, President

D-U-N-S 62-098-0151   EXP
LIFE SERVICES SUPPLEMENTS
3535 Hwy 66, Neptune, NJ 07753
Phone: (732) 922-0009
Sales: $6,100,000   *Employees:* 52
Company Type: Private   *Employees here:* 52
SIC: 2834
    Mfg & markets nutrient vitamin supplements & private label
      vitamins
Arne Bey, President

D-U-N-S 10-153-0103   EXP
LIFE TECHNOLOGIES INC.
    (Parent: Dexter Corporation)
9800 Medical Center Dr, Rockville, MD 20850
Phone: (301) 610-8000
Sales: $330,967,000   *Employees:* 1,586
Company Type: Public   *Employees here:* 575
SIC: 2836
    Mfg biological pdts biochemical agents & enzymes
J S Thompson, President

D-U-N-S 15-340-9313   EXP
LIFESCAN INC.
    (Parent: Johnson & Johnson)
1000 Gibraltar Dr, Milpitas, CA 95035
Phone: (408) 263-9789
Sales: $165,200,000   *Employees:* 2,000
Company Type: Public Family Member   *Employees here:* 1,000
SIC: 2835
    Mfg plastic reagent strips & blood glucose monitoring
      equipment
Richard J Wiesner, President

D-U-N-S 09-000-9457
LILLY DEL CARIBE INC.
    (Parent: Eli Lilly and Company)
65th Inf Ave Km 12 Hm 6, Carolina, PR 00987
Phone: (787) 257-5555
Sales: $130,600,000   *Employees:* 1,025
Company Type: Public Family Member   *Employees here:* 850
SIC: 2834
    Mfg pharmaceutical products
Vaughn D Bryson, Chairman of the Board

D-U-N-S 61-180-3503   EXP
LIPHA AMERICAS INC.
2751 Napa Valley Corporat, Napa, CA 94558
Phone: (707) 224-3200
Sales: $300,000,000   *Employees:* 750
Company Type: Private   *Employees here:* 2
SIC: 2834
    Mfg pharmaceutical products & research & development
      laboratory
Charles Rice, President

D-U-N-S 80-442-7128
THE LIPOSOME MFG CO. INC.
  (Parent: Liposome Company Inc)
6925 Guion Rd, Indianapolis, IN 46268
Phone: (317) 290-8108
Sales: $7,700,000   *Employees:* 70
Company Type: Public Family Member   *Employees here:* 70
SIC: 2833
  Mfg liposomes
Charles A Baker, Chairman of the Board

D-U-N-S 78-430-6318
LITTLE SILVER CORP.
1400 N Weber Ave, Sioux Falls, SD 57103
Phone: (605) 335-7449
Sales: $4,000,000   *Employees:* 80
Company Type: Private   *Employees here:* 80
SIC: 2833
  Mfg animal based products
Gerald C Marshall, President

D-U-N-S 09-495-3197
LIVRON INC.
3 Pearl Ct, Allendale, NJ 07401
Phone: (201) 868-6610
Sales: $6,000,000   *Employees:* 18
Company Type: Private   *Employees here:* 3
SIC: 2833
  Mfg medicinal/botanical products
Gary Viole, President

D-U-N-S 00-728-1942   EXP
LLOYD INC. OF IOWA
604 W Thomas Ave, Shenandoah, IA 51601
Phone: (712) 246-4000
Sales: $4,300,000   *Employees:* 55
Company Type: Private   *Employees here:* 55
SIC: 2834
  Mfg veterinarian pharmaceuticals
Dr W E Lloyd, Chairman of the Board

D-U-N-S 05-564-0916
LOBOB LABORATORIES INC.
1440 Atteberry Ln, San Jose, CA 95131
Phone: (408) 432-0580
Sales: $4,310,000   *Employees:* 35
Company Type: Private   *Employees here:* 35
SIC: 2834
  Mfg contact lens solutions
Robert M Lohr, President

D-U-N-S 78-766-0513
LOHMANN THERAPY SYSTEMS CORP.
21 Henderson Dr, Caldwell, NJ 07006
Phone: (973) 575-5170
Sales: $9,135,000   *Employees:* 55
Company Type: Private   *Employees here:* 55
SIC: 2834
  Mfg nicotine patches
Cornelia Bockhorn, President

D-U-N-S 16-094-4971
LONDON INTERNATIONAL GROUP INC.
  (Parent: LRC North America Inc)
3585 Engrg Dr, Ste 200, Norcross, GA 30092
Phone: (770) 582-2222
Sales: $200,000,000   *Employees:* 900
Company Type: Private   *Employees here:* 96
SIC: 2834
  Manufactures proprietary pharmaceutical products sundry
    rubber products industrial rubber gloves and nail care
    implements
Garth Clarke, President

D-U-N-S 96-524-3082
LONDON INTERNATIONAL GROUP INC.
3585 Engrg Dr, Ste 200, Norcross, GA 30092
Phone: (770) 582-2222
Sales: $11,700,000   *Employees:* NA
Company Type: Private   *Employees here:* 105
SIC: 2834
  Sales for consumer products including latex gloves &
    condoms
Tom Grant, VP Sales

D-U-N-S 80-909-4402
LONZA BIOLOGICS INC.
101 International Dr, Portsmouth, NH 03801
Phone: (603) 334-6100
Sales: $11,500,000   *Employees:* NA
Company Type: Private   *Employees here:* 92
SIC: 2834
  Mfg pharmaceutical preparations
David Jackson, Manager

D-U-N-S 00-203-3710
LUITPOLD PHARMACEUTICALS, INC.
  (Parent: Sankyo Pharma Inc)
1 Luitpold Dr, Shirley, NY 11967
Phone: (516) 924-4000
Sales: $45,700,000   *Employees:* 366
Company Type: Private   *Employees here:* 122
SIC: 2834
  Manufactures pharmaceuticals
Ralf Lange, President

D-U-N-S 08-682-4430
LUYTIES PHARMACAL COMPANY
  (Parent: Middle States Management Corp)
4200 Laclede Ave, Saint Louis, MO 63108
Phone: (314) 533-9600
Sales: $5,200,000   *Employees:* 60
Company Type: Private   *Employees here:* 60
SIC: 2834
  Mfg pharmaceuticals
Forrest J Murphy, President

D-U-N-S 05-351-0459
LYNE LABORATORIES INC.
10 Burke Dr, Brockton, MA 02301
Phone: (508) 583-8700
Sales: $8,163,000   *Employees:* 130
Company Type: Private   *Employees here:* 50
SIC: 2834
  Mfg pharmaceutical preparations
Dr Robert Crisafi, Chief Executive Officer

D-U-N-S 79-717-9611
LYNX THERAPEUTICS INC.
25861 Industrial Blvd, Hayward, CA 94545
Phone: (510) 670-9300
Sales: $4,582,000   *Employees:* 73
Company Type: Public   *Employees here:* 73
SIC: 2834
  Mfg dna based drugs for therapeutics
Sam Eletr, Chairman of the Board

D-U-N-S 05-821-0568   EXP
M V P LABORATORIES INC.
5404 Miller Ave, Omaha, NE 68127
Phone: (402) 331-5106
Sales: $3,000,000   *Employees:* 35
Company Type: Private   *Employees here:* 35
SIC: 2834
  Mfg veterinary biological products
Mary L Chapek, President

D-U-N-S 00-201-2599   EXP
MADIS BOTANICALS, INC.
  (Parent: Pure World Inc)
375 Huyler St, South Hackensack, NJ 07606
Phone: (201) 440-5000
Sales: $9,702,000   *Employees:* 70
Company Type: Public Family Member   *Employees here:* 50
SIC: 2833
  Mfg botanical extracts
Paul Koether, Chief Executive Officer

D-U-N-S 04-022-8389
MAINE BIOLOGICAL LABORATORIES
China Rd, Waterville, ME 04901
Phone: (207) 873-3989
Sales: $7,273,000   *Employees:* 63
Company Type: Private   *Employees here:* 63
SIC: 2836
  Manufactures vaccines
John Donahoe, President

D-U-N-S 62-194-0980
MALLINCKRODT CHEMICAL, INC.
  (Parent: MSCH Company)
675 Mcdonnell Blvd, Hazelwood, MO 63042
Phone: (314) 654-2000
Sales: $258,100,000   *Employees:* 2,000
Company Type: Public Family Member   *Employees here:* 248
SIC: 2833
  Manufactures medical chemicals
Michael Collins, Vice-President

D-U-N-S 05-127-6434
MANHATTAN DRUG CO. INC.
  (Parent: Chem International Inc)
201 Us Highway 22, Hillside, NJ 07205
Phone: (973) 926-0816
Sales: $12,000,000   *Employees:* 75
Company Type: Public Family Member   *Employees here:* 45
SIC: 2834
  Mfg vitamin & nutritional supplements
Gerald Kay, President

D-U-N-S 07-591-0356
MARCUS RESEARCH LABORATORY
1820 Delmar Blvd, Saint Louis, MO 63103
Phone: (314) 241-8772
Sales: $2,300,000   *Employees:* 25
Company Type: Private   *Employees here:* 25
SIC: 2833
  Manufacture medicinal chemicals & biologicals
Norman C Gilbert, President

D-U-N-S 05-942-1099   EXP
MARDEL LABORATORIES INC.
  (Parent: Agri-Nutrition Group Limited)
1958 Brandon Ct, Glendale Heights, IL 60139
Phone: (630) 351-0606
Sales: $5,000,000   *Employees:* 50
Company Type: Public Family Member   *Employees here:* 50
SIC: 2833
  Mfg & whol medicinal chemicals for pets
Ramon A Mulholland, Chairman of the Board

D-U-N-S 62-282-3227
MARION & COMPANY
Km 2 Hm 7 Rr 670, Manati, PR 00674
Phone: (787) 854-3005
Sales: $294,535,000   *Employees:* 250
Company Type: Private   *Employees here:* 250
SIC: 2834
  Mfg pharmaceutical products
Roland Ely, President

D-U-N-S 02-122-7376   EXP
MARLYN NUTRACEUTICALS, INC.
14851 N Scottsdale Rd, Scottsdale, AZ 85254
Phone: (602) 991-0200
Sales: $18,000,000   *Employees:* 80
Company Type: Private   *Employees here:* 80
SIC: 2833
  Mfg vitamins and food supplements
Joachim Lehmann, President

D-U-N-S 13-109-9335
MARSAM PHARMACEUTICALS, INC.
  (Parent: Schein Pharmaceutical Inc)
24 Olney Ave, Cherry Hill, NJ 08003
Phone: (609) 424-5600
Sales: $40,000,000   *Employees:* 260
Company Type: Public Family Member   *Employees here:* 260
SIC: 2834
  Mfg prescription drugs
Marvin S Samson, President

D-U-N-S 10-211-3867   EXP
MAST IMMUNOSYSTEMS, INC.
630 Clyde Ct, Mountain View, CA 94043
Phone: (650) 961-5501
Sales: $21,279,000   *Employees:* 190
Company Type: Private   *Employees here:* 95
SIC: 2835
  Mfg in-vitro diagnostic substances & precision liquid
    handling equipment
Tetsuo Odashiro, Chief Executive Officer

D-U-N-S 09-698-1386
MATERIALS PROCESSING TECH
95 Prince St, Paterson, NJ 07501
Phone: (973) 279-4133
Sales: $7,000,000   *Employees:* 75
Company Type: Private   *Employees here:* 75
SIC: 2834
  Mfg pharmaceutical preparations specialty chemicals and
    food ingredients
Norman D Alworth, President

D-U-N-S 19-181-4599
MATRIX PHARMACEUTICAL INC.
34700 Campus Dr, Fremont, CA 94555
Phone: (510) 742-9900
Sales: $12,100,000   *Employees:* 162
Company Type: Public   *Employees here:* 100
SIC: 2836
  Mfg biological products
Michael D Casey, Chairman of the Board

D-U-N-S 00-234-7102   EXP
MCNEIL CONSUMER HEALTHCARE CO.
  (Parent: Johnson & Johnson)
7050 Camp Hill Rd, Fort Washington, PA 19034
Phone: (215) 233-7000
Sales: $256,200,000   *Employees:* 2,000
Company Type: Public Family Member   *Employees here:* 900
SIC: 2834
  Mfg pharmaceuticals
Larry Pickering, President

D-U-N-S 15-147-5449
MCNEIL CONSUMER PRODUCTS PR
  (Parent: McNeil Consumer Healthcare Co)
Km 19 Hm 3 Rr 183, Las Piedras, PR 00771
Phone: (787) 733-1000

Sales: $700,000,000
Company Type: Public Family Member
SIC: 2834
  Mfg pharmaceutical products
Bryan Perkings, President

     Employees: 500
     Employees here: 500

D-U-N-S 07-360-2757
MD PHARMACEUTICAL INC.
3501 W Garry Ave, Santa Ana, CA 92704
Phone: (714) 556-3941
Sales: $9,400,000
Company Type: Private
SIC: 2833
  Mfg drugs
Gayle Deflin, President

     Employees: 73
     Employees here: 73

D-U-N-S 80-948-2961
MEDEVA MA, INC.
423 Lagrange St, Boston, MA 02132
Phone: (617) 323-7404
Sales: $27,700,000
Company Type: Private
SIC: 2834
  Mfr pharmaceuticals
Ben Shepherd, President

     Employees: 173
     Employees here: 170

D-U-N-S 78-277-4459
MEDEVA PHARMACEUTICALS, INC.
3950 Sheldon Cir, Bethlehem, PA 18017
Phone: (610) 974-9760
Sales: $3,500,000
Company Type: Private
SIC: 2834
  Mfg pharmaceuticals
Carl Rohmann, Secretary

     Employees: 36
     Employees here: 36

D-U-N-S 05-972-1944
MEDEVA PHARMACUETICALS MFG.
755 Jefferson Rd, Rochester, NY 14623
Phone: (716) 475-9000
Sales: $34,200,000
Company Type: Private
SIC: 2834
  Mfg pharmaceuticals
Dr William Bogie, President

     Employees: 277
     Employees here: 277

D-U-N-S 05-304-6579
MEDI-PHYSICS, INC.
  (Parent: Amersham Holdings Inc (del))
2636 S Clearbrook Dr, Arlington Heights, IL 60005
Phone: (847) 593-6300
Sales: $150,000,000
Company Type: Private
SIC: 2833
  Mfg and distributes radiopharmaceuticals medical sources
    and nuclear medical products and services
C G Marlow, President

     Employees: 500
     Employees here: 100

D-U-N-S 18-130-2050
MEDIATECH INC.
13884 Park Center Rd, Herndon, VA 20171
Phone: (703) 471-5955
Sales: $4,100,000
Company Type: Private
SIC: 2836
  Mfg biological products
James Deolden, President

     Employees: 70
     Employees here: 70

D-U-N-S 07-225-6134
MEDICAL ANALYSIS SYSTEMS INC.
542 Flynn Rd, Camarillo, CA 93012
Phone: (805) 987-7891

Sales: $10,900,000
Company Type: Private
SIC: 2835
  Mfg blood testing reagents
Ivan Modrovich, Chairman of the Board

     Employees: 120
     Employees here: 75

D-U-N-S 00-229-0302   EXP
MEDICAL PRODUCTS LABORATORIES
9990 Global Rd, Philadelphia, PA 19115
Phone: (215) 677-2700
Sales: $4,900,000
Company Type: Private
SIC: 2834
  Mfg pharmaceutical preparations specializing in dental
    pharmaceuticals
Elliot Stone, President

     Employees: 50
     Employees here: 50

D-U-N-S 94-276-7575
MEDICAL RESEARCH INDUSTRIES
3101 SW 10th St, Pompano Beach, FL 33069
Phone: (954) 972-9898
Sales: $8,000,000
Company Type: Private
SIC: 2834
  Mfg & distributes homeopathic medical remedies specializing
    in diet and nutrition products conducting research in similar
    areas
William J Tishman, Chief Executive Officer

     Employees: 100
     Employees here: 100

D-U-N-S 18-283-7492
MEDICIS PHARMACEUTICAL CORP.
4343 E Camelback Rd, Phoenix, AZ 85018
Phone: (602) 808-8800
Sales: $41,159,000
Company Type: Public
SIC: 2834
  Develops markets and distributes products and technologies
    in the area of dermatology
Mark A Prygocki Sr, Chief Financial Officer

     Employees: 90
     Employees here: 35

D-U-N-S 19-063-9906
MEDIMMUNE, INC.
35 W Watkins Mill Rd, Gaithersburg, MD 20878
Phone: (301) 417-0770
Sales: $27,436,000
Company Type: Public
SIC: 2836
  Mfg vaccines & research & development
Wayne T Hockmeyer PhD, Chairman of the Board

     Employees: 350
     Employees here: 230

D-U-N-S 01-795-8195
MEDPHARM INC.
1776 K St NW, Ste 800, Washington, DC 20006
Phone: (202) 452-7996
Sales: $12,000,000
Company Type: Private
SIC: 2834
  Mfg pharmaceuticals and medical products
Joseph Tretin, Chief Financial Officer

     Employees: 12
     Employees here: 12

D-U-N-S 13-976-0102   EXP
MELALEUCA INC.
3910 S Yellowstone Hwy, Idaho Falls, ID 83402
Phone: (208) 522-0700
Sales: $154,300,000
Company Type: Private
SIC: 2833
  Mfg & whol nutritional health care personal care & home
    hygiene products
Frank Vandersloot, President

     Employees: 1,200
     Employees here: 816

D-U-N-S 00-210-5757
MENTHOLATUM COMPANY INC.
707 Sterling Dr, Orchard Park, NY 14127
Phone: (716) 677-2500
Sales: $95,000,000   *Employees:* 150
Company Type: Private   *Employees here:* 150
SIC: 2834
   Mfg pharmaceutical preparations to include analgesics & lip
   balms
Masashi Yoshida, President

D-U-N-S 00-223-2122
MERCER MILLING CO.
4 Syracuse St, Baldwinsville, NY 13027
Phone: (315) 635-3001
Sales: $3,163,000   *Employees:* 11
Company Type: Private   *Employees here:* 11
SIC: 2834
   Mfg animal vitamins minerals & feed & ret feed & pet food
William J Colten, President

D-U-N-S 00-131-7064   IMP EXP
MERCK & CO INC.
1 Merck Dr, Whitehouse Station, NJ 08889
Phone: (908) 423-1000
Sales: $23,636,900,000   *Employees:* 53,800
Company Type: Public   *Employees here:* 1,600
SIC: 2834
   Mfg human & animal health pdts mail order pharmacies
   processing prescription claims
Judy C Lewent, Chief Financial Officer

D-U-N-S 78-319-2800
MERCK HOLDINGS, INC.
   (Parent: Merck & Co Inc)
1 Merck Dr, Whitehouse Station, NJ 08889
Phone: (908) 423-1000
Sales: $101,600,000   *Employees:* 800
Company Type: Public Family Member   *Employees here:* 10
SIC: 2834
   Mfg drugs
Peter Nugent, President

D-U-N-S 09-847-7540   EXP
MERIAL AH INC.
115 Trans Tech Dr, Athens, GA 30601
Phone: (706) 548-9292
Sales: $17,600,000   *Employees:* 138
Company Type: Private   *Employees here:* 138
SIC: 2834
   Mfg veterinary pharmaceutical preparations
Don Hildebrand, President

D-U-N-S 60-892-9212
MERIAL LIMITED
2116 8th Ave S, Fort Dodge, IA 50501
Phone: (515) 576-4225
Sales: $11,800,000   *Employees:* NA
Company Type: Private   *Employees here:* 120
SIC: 2834
   Mfg veterinary pharmaceuticals
Tom Strohl, Branch Manager

D-U-N-S 06-150-6796
MERIAL LTD.
115 Trans Tech Dr, Athens, GA 30601
Phone: (706) 548-9292
Sales: $575,000,000   *Employees:* 1,800
Company Type: Private   *Employees here:* 250
SIC: 2836
   Mfg vaccines pharmaceuticals and diagnostic products
Louis Champel, Chief Executive Officer

D-U-N-S 05-421-9928
MERIAL SELECT, INC.
1168 Airport Pkwy, Gainesville, GA 30501
Phone: (770) 536-8787
Sales: $22,900,000   *Employees:* 378
Company Type: Private   *Employees here:* 265
SIC: 2836
   Mfg& sales of poultry vaccine
Benoit Adelus, President

D-U-N-S 03-872-6550
MERRELL PHARMACEUTICALS INC.
   (Parent: Hoechst Marion Roussel Inc)
2110 E Galbraith Rd, Cincinnati, OH 45237
Phone: (513) 948-9111
Sales: $75,800,000   *Employees:* 600
Company Type: Private   *Employees here:* 600
SIC: 2834
   Mfg pharmaceuticals
Gerald P Belle, Chief Executive Officer

D-U-N-S 94-437-4974
MERZ, INCORPORATED
4215 Tudor Ln, Greensboro, NC 27410
Phone: (336) 856-2003
Sales: $20,000,000   *Employees:* 70
Company Type: Private   *Employees here:* 35
SIC: 2834
   Mfg & distribute pharmaceutical and over the counter
   products
Deepak Massand, President

D-U-N-S 13-124-8809
METABOLIC MAINTENANCE PDTS INC.
68994 N Pine St, Sisters, OR 97759
Phone: (541) 549-7800
Sales: $4,000,000   *Employees:* 29
Company Type: Private   *Employees here:* 29
SIC: 2834
   Mfg vitamins
Ed Fitzjarrell, President

D-U-N-S 19-634-9393   EXP
METABOLIC NUTRITION INC.
2299 NE 164th St, Miami, FL 33160
Phone: (305) 940-0962
Sales: $2,900,000   *Employees:* 6
Company Type: Private   *Employees here:* 6
SIC: 2834
   Mfg vitamin preparation specializing in nutritional
   supplements
Dr Murray Cohen, President

D-U-N-S 61-644-3024
METRA BIOSYSTEMS, INC.
265 N Whisman Rd, Mountain View, CA 94043
Phone: (650) 903-9100
Sales: $6,725,000   *Employees:* 60
Company Type: Public   *Employees here:* 45
SIC: 2835
   Mfg diagnostic products
Debby R Dean, Vice-President

D-U-N-S 02-157-4355   EXP
MGI PHARMA, INC.
9900 Bren Rd E, Ste 300e, Hopkins, MN 55343
Phone: (612) 935-7335
Sales: $12,435,000   *Employees:* 65
Company Type: Public   *Employees here:* 65
SIC: 2834
   Specialty pharmaceutical and medical products
Charles N Blitzer, President

D-U-N-S 83-879-1325
MGP HOLDING CORP
6451 Main St, Morton Grove, IL 60053
Phone: (847) 967-5600
Sales: $47,000,000
Company Type: Private   *Employees here:* 1
SIC: 2834   *Employees:* 170
  Mfg liquid generic pharmaceuticals
Brian Tambi, Chairman of the Board

D-U-N-S 82-468-6703
MICELLE LABORATORIES INC.
20481 Crescent Bay Dr, Lake Forest, CA 92630
Phone: (949) 951-5150
Sales: $8,000,000   *Employees:* 65
Company Type: Private   *Employees here:* 65
SIC: 2834
  Mfg nutritional supplements
Edward Alosio, President

D-U-N-S 06-046-7826   EXP
MICRO BIO LOGICS
217 Osseo Ave N, Saint Cloud, MN 56303
Phone: (320) 253-1640
Sales: $2,100,000   *Employees:* 27
Company Type: Private   *Employees here:* 19
SIC: 2835
  Mfg diagnostic substances testing laboratory
Robert Coborn Jr, President

D-U-N-S 80-006-4909
MICROCIDE PHARMACEUTICALS
850 Maude Ave, Mountain View, CA 94043
Phone: (650) 428-1550
Sales: $14,894,000   *Employees:* 150
Company Type: Public   *Employees here:* 150
SIC: 2834
  Mfg pharmaceuticals
James E Rurka, President

D-U-N-S 07-977-4212
MIDDLE STATES MANAGEMENT CORP.
4200 Laclede Ave, Saint Louis, MO 63108
Phone: (314) 533-9600
Sales: $10,700,000   *Employees:* 100
Company Type: Private   *Employees here:* 75
SIC: 2834
  Mfg drugs publishes & whol books owns/operates commc
    prpty & apts oper adv agency does timber & farming & gen
    investing
Forrest J Murphy, President

D-U-N-S 03-003-4847
MIKART INC.
1750 Chattahoochee Ave NW, Atlanta, GA 30318
Phone: (404) 351-4510
Sales: $29,599,000   *Employees:* 170
Company Type: Private   *Employees here:* 80
SIC: 2834
  Contract mfg facility to the pharmaceutical industry
Miguel Arteche, President

D-U-N-S 00-509-5120
MILEX PRODUCTS, INC.
4311 N Normandy Ave, Chicago, IL 60634
Phone: (773) 736-5500
Sales: $20,000,000   *Employees:* NA
Company Type: Private   *Employees here:* NA
SIC: 2834
  Mfg pharmaceuticals surgical instruments and medical
    devices
Hymen T Milgrom, President

D-U-N-S 07-298-5468   EXP
MINERAL RESOURCES INT'L
1990 W 3300 S, Ogden, UT 84401
Phone: (801) 731-6051
Sales: $5,000,000   *Employees:* 70
Company Type: Private   *Employees here:* 70
SIC: 2834
  Mfg vitamin and herbal supplements
Bruce Anderson, President

D-U-N-S 60-694-1227   EXP
MIRAVANT MEDICAL TECHNOLOGIES
7408 Hollister Ave, Goleta, CA 93117
Phone: (805) 685-9880
Sales: $2,278,000   *Employees:* 145
Company Type: Public   *Employees here:* 29
SIC: 2834
  Mfg pharmaceutical preparations and surgical instruments
Gary S Kledzik, Chairman of the Board

D-U-N-S 55-547-9831
MIRAVANT PHARMACEUTICALS INC.
  (Parent: Miravant Medical Technologies)
7408 Hollister Ave, Goleta, CA 93117
Phone: (805) 685-9880
Sales: $11,700,000   *Employees:* 90
Company Type: Public Family Member   *Employees here:* 90
SIC: 2834
  Mfg pharmaceutical preparations
Gary S Kledzik, Chief Executive Officer

D-U-N-S 00-811-7095   EXP
MISSION PHARMACAL COMPANY
10999 Ih 10 W, Ste 1000, San Antonio, TX 78230
Phone: (210) 696-8400
Sales: $51,299,000   *Employees:* 225
Company Type: Private   *Employees here:* 45
SIC: 2834
  Mfg pharmaceutical products
Neill B Walsdorf Sr, Chairman of the Board

D-U-N-S 79-881-2376
MITOTIX, INC.
1 Kendall Sq, Ste 600, Cambridge, MA 02139
Phone: (617) 225-0001
Sales: $5,800,000   *Employees:* 64
Company Type: Private   *Employees here:* 64
SIC: 2834
  Pharmaceutical development
William Helman, Chairman of the Board

D-U-N-S 80-361-8008
MIZUHO USA, INC.
6730 Mesa Ridge Rd, Ste D, San Diego, CA 92121
Phone: (619) 457-9734
Sales: $4,000,000   *Employees:* 29
Company Type: Private   *Employees here:* 29
SIC: 2835
  Mfg diagnostic kits
Fuminari Karakawa, Chairman of the Board

D-U-N-S 04-626-2341
MML DIAGNOSTICS PACKAGING INC.
1625 NW Sundial Rd, Troutdale, OR 97060
Phone: (503) 666-8398
Sales: $4,100,000   *Employees:* 70
Company Type: Private   *Employees here:* 70
SIC: 2836
  Mfg bacteriological media products
Dale Pestes, President

D-U-N-S 09-755-8506   EXP
MOLECULAR PROBES INC.
4849 Pitchford Ave, Eugene, OR 97402
Phone: (541) 465-8300
Sales: $11,800,000   *Employees:* 148
Company Type: Private   *Employees here:* 148
SIC: 2835
   Mfg chemical for scientific research
Dr Richard P Haugland, President

D-U-N-S 79-785-4221
MOLECUMETICS, LTD.
   (Parent: Tredegar Industries Inc)
2023 120th Ave NE, Ste 400, Bellevue, WA 98005
Phone: (425) 646-8865
Sales: $4,000,000   *Employees:* 50
Company Type: Public Family Member   *Employees here:* 50
SIC: 2836
   Mfg biological products mfg pharmaceutical preparations
Edward L Field, N/A

D-U-N-S 15-526-9541
MOLOROKALIN INC.
397 Churchill Hubbard Rd, Youngstown, OH 44505
Phone: (330) 759-1332
Sales: $4,600,000   *Employees:* 45
Company Type: Private   *Employees here:* 40
SIC: 2834
   Compound & prepare intravenous solutions
Leonard Holman, President

D-U-N-S 78-705-9153   EXP
MONOMER-POLYMER & DAJAC LABS
1675 Bustleton Pike, Feasterville Trevose, PA 19053
Phone: (215) 364-1155
Sales: $2,188,000   *Employees:* 9
Company Type: Private   *Employees here:* 9
SIC: 2835
   Mfg monomer & polymer reagents & diagnostic chemicals
Jack Dickstein PhD, President

D-U-N-S 14-417-4711   EXP
MONTANA NATURALS INT'L INC.
   (Parent: Healthrite Inc)
19994 Us Highway 93, Arlee, MT 59821
Phone: (406) 726-3214
Sales: $10,000,000   *Employees:* 72
Company Type: Public Family Member   *Employees here:* 72
SIC: 2833
   Mfg bee pollen propolis royal jelly products & related natural
     health food products vitamins & herbs
Sterling Gabbitas, President

D-U-N-S 00-406-0240
MONTICELLO COMPANIES INC.
1604 Stockton St, Jacksonville, FL 32204
Phone: (904) 384-3666
Sales: $3,800,000   *Employees:* 115
Company Type: Private   *Employees here:* 9
SIC: 2834
   Mfg cold preparations & cough medicine whol drug &
     toiletries
Henry E Dean III, President

D-U-N-S 00-710-2155
MORNINGSTAR DIAGNOSTICS, INC.
1376 Lead Hill Blvd 130, Roseville, CA 95661
Phone: (916) 772-0526
Sales: $4,000,000   *Employees:* 12
Company Type: Private   *Employees here:* 8
SIC: 2835
   Mfg diagnostic substances tests
Michael A Cuhna, President

D-U-N-S 80-189-7505
MORTON GROVE PHARMACEUTICALS
   (Parent: Mgp Holding Corp (del))
6451 Main St, Morton Grove, IL 60053
Phone: (847) 967-5600
Sales: $23,000,000   *Employees:* 170
Company Type: Private   *Employees here:* 170
SIC: 2834
   Mfg liquid generic pharmaceuticals
Brian Tambi, Chairman of the Board

D-U-N-S 00-702-4359
MORTON PHARMACEUTICALS INC.
1625 N Highland St, Memphis, TN 38108
Phone: (901) 386-8840
Sales: $5,900,000   *Employees:* 60
Company Type: Private   *Employees here:* 50
SIC: 2834
   Mfg pharmaceuticals
William J Morton, President

D-U-N-S 17-405-0377   EXP
MOVA PHARMACEUTICAL CORP.
Km 34 Rr 1, Caguas, PR 00725
Phone: (787) 746-8500
Sales: $55,815,000   *Employees:* 744
Company Type: Private   *Employees here:* 724
SIC: 2834
   Mfg pharmaceutical preparations
Joaquin B Viso, President

D-U-N-S 00-642-6316
MUELLER SPORTS MEDICINE INC.
1 Quench Dr, Prairie Du Sac, WI 53578
Phone: (608) 643-8530
Sales: $5,800,000   *Employees:* 70
Company Type: Private   *Employees here:* 70
SIC: 2834
   Mfg athletic pharmaceuticals & training supplies
Curt Mueller, President

D-U-N-S 00-104-6523
MURO PHARMACEUTICAL INC.
890 East St, Tewksbury, MA 01876
Phone: (978) 851-5981
Sales: $85,000,000   *Employees:* 320
Company Type: Private   *Employees here:* 320
SIC: 2834
   Mfg pharmaceuticals
Colin Stewart, President

D-U-N-S 12-173-5955
MUTUAL PHARMACEUTICAL COMPANY
   (Parent: Pharmaceutical Holdings Corp)
1100 Orthodox St, Philadelphia, PA 19124
Phone: (215) 288-6500
Sales: $30,800,000   *Employees:* NA
Company Type: Private   *Employees here:* NA
SIC: 2834
   Mfg pharmaceuticals
Dr Richard Roberts MD, President

D-U-N-S 15-692-7717
MYLAN INC.
   (Parent: Mylan Laboratories Inc)
Caguas W Rr 156, Caguas, PR 00725
Phone: (787) 746-0003
Sales: $45,000,000   *Employees:* 123
Company Type: Public Family Member   *Employees here:* 108
SIC: 2834
   Mfg pharmaceutical preparations
Carlos Machin, President

D-U-N-S 05-929-8141
MYLAN LABORATORIES INC.
1030 Century Bldg, Pittsburgh, PA 15222
Phone: (412) 232-0100
Sales: $555,423,000   *Employees:* 1,946
Company Type: Public   *Employees here:* 7
SIC: 2834
   Mfg generic & proprietary pharmaceutical pdts
Robert W Smiley, Secretary

D-U-N-S 05-929-5980
MYLAN PHARMACEUTICALS INC.
   (Parent: Mylan Laboratories Inc)
781 Chestnut Ridge Rd, Morgantown, WV 26505
Phone: (304) 599-2595
Sales: $123,500,000   *Employees:* 970
Company Type: Public Family Member   *Employees here:* 919
SIC: 2834
   Mfg pharmaceutical preparations
Clarence B Todd, President

D-U-N-S 04-886-2726   EXP
NABI
5800 Park Of Commerce Blv, Boca Raton, FL 33487
Phone: (561) 989-5800
Sales: $238,744,000   *Employees:* 2,122
Company Type: Public   *Employees here:* 229
SIC: 2836
   Mfg biological products/substances
David J Gury, Chairman of the Board

D-U-N-S 96-024-5207
NAIAD TECHNOLOGIES INC.
2611 SW 3rd Ave, Ste 200, Portland, OR 97201
Phone: (503) 274-4407
Sales: $3,000,000   *Employees:* 14
Company Type: Private   *Employees here:* 14
SIC: 2835
   Mfg diagnostic substances
Nanette Newell, President

D-U-N-S 00-131-5282
NAPP TECHNOLOGIES INC.
299 Market St, Saddle Brook, NJ 07663
Phone: (201) 843-4664
Sales: $15,000,000   *Employees:* 36
Company Type: Private   *Employees here:* 36
SIC: 2834
   Mfg bulk pharmaceuticals
Hans P Kirchgaessner, President

D-U-N-S 94-431-2685   EXP
NASSMITH PHARMACEUTICALS, INC.
2515 Industry St, Oceanside, CA 92054
Phone: (760) 433-4700
Sales: $4,100,000   *Employees:* 38
Company Type: Private   *Employees here:* 38
SIC: 2834
   Mfg nutitional supplements
Scott Smith, President

D-U-N-S 11-413-1113   EXP
NASTECH PHARMACEUTICAL COMPANY
45 Davids Dr, Hauppauge, NY 11788
Phone: (516) 273-0101
Sales: $5,522,000   *Employees:* 43
Company Type: Public   *Employees here:* 43
SIC: 2834
   Research & development of pharmaceutical products
      specifically for the nasal drug delivery system
Dr Vincent D Romeo, Chief Executive Officer

D-U-N-S 92-608-9723
NATCO PHARMA USA LLC
37 Veronica Ave 39, Somerset, NJ 08873
Phone: (732) 249-0009
Sales: $3,000,000   *Employees:* 19
Company Type: Private   *Employees here:* 19
SIC: 2834
   Mfr nutritional products
Dr Nehru Gaddipati, President

D-U-N-S 18-286-4181
NATIONAL MEDICAL INDUSTRIES,
1444 W Bannock St, Boise, ID 83702
Phone: (208) 343-3639
Sales: $4,700,000   *Employees:* 45
Company Type: Private   *Employees here:* 7
SIC: 2834
   Mfg pharmaceuticl lotions and wheelchair conveyance
      equipment
Anthony A Maher, President

D-U-N-S 07-727-9206
NATIONAL NUTRITIONAL LABS
548 Route 110, Melville, NY 11747
Phone: (516) 293-0030
Sales: $4,800,000   *Employees:* 40
Company Type: Private   *Employees here:* 40
SIC: 2833
   Manufactures vitamins
Gerald Kessler, Chief Executive Officer

D-U-N-S 10-209-8324
NATIONAL VITAMIN CO INC.
2075 W Scranton Ave, Porterville, CA 93257
Phone: (559) 781-8871
Sales: $18,000,000   *Employees:* 120
Company Type: Private   *Employees here:* 100
SIC: 2834
   Mfg vitamins & cosmetics
Earl Courtney, President

D-U-N-S 04-767-0380
NATIONAL VITAMIN COMPANY LLC
   (Parent: National Vitamin Co Inc)
7440 Industrial Rd, Las Vegas, NV 89139
Phone: (702) 269-9600
Sales: $9,000,000   *Employees:* 4
Company Type: Private   *Employees here:* 4
SIC: 2834
   Mfg vitamins
Earl Courtney, General Manager

D-U-N-S 05-588-8903   EXP
NATROL INC.
21411 Prairie St, Chatsworth, CA 91311
Phone: (818) 739-6000
Sales: $42,875,000   *Employees:* 185
Company Type: Public   *Employees here:* 115
SIC: 2834
   Mfg vitamin food supplements
Elliott Balbert, President

D-U-N-S 05-479-3658   EXP
NATURAL ALTERNATIVES INTL
1185 Linda Vista Dr, Ste D, San Marcos, CA 92069
Phone: (760) 744-7340
Sales: $67,894,000   *Employees:* 130
Company Type: Public   *Employees here:* 130
SIC: 2833
   Mfg vitamins and nutritional supplements
Mark A LeDoux, President

D-U-N-S 12-139-9869   EXP
NATURAL BALANCE INC.
3155 Commerce Ct Bldg A, Castle Rock, CO 80104
Phone: (303) 688-6633
Sales: $16,400,000   *Employees:* 140
Company Type: Private   *Employees here:* 130
SIC: 2834
  Mfg natural herb food supplements
A M Owens, President

D-U-N-S 94-380-5564
NATURAL BIOLOGICS, LLC
  (Parent: Alex Pharmaceutical Co L L C)
1215 Hershey St, Albert Lea, MN 56007
Phone: (507) 373-1542
Sales: $2,500,000   *Employees:* 30
Company Type: Private   *Employees here:* 30
SIC: 2834
  Mfg pharmaceutical preparations
David Saveraid, Chief Executive Officer

D-U-N-S 06-473-1987   IMP EXP
NATURAL ORGANICS INC.
548 Broadhollow Rd, Melville, NY 11747
Phone: (516) 293-0030
Sales: $37,600,000   *Employees:* 300
Company Type: Private   *Employees here:* 230
SIC: 2833
  Manufactures vitamins
Gerald Kessler, Chief Executive Officer

D-U-N-S 08-183-2388
NATURE'S SUNSHINE PRODUCTS
75 E 1700 S, Provo, UT 84606
Phone: (801) 342-4300
Sales: $280,902,000   *Employees:* 966
Company Type: Public   *Employees here:* 394
SIC: 2833
  Mfg nutritional & personal care pdts
Kristine F Hughes, Chairman of the Board

D-U-N-S 79-031-8406
NATURES VALUE INC.
48 Drexel Dr, Bay Shore, NY 11706
Phone: (516) 273-3137
Sales: $5,100,000   *Employees:* 40
Company Type: Private   *Employees here:* 40
SIC: 2833
  Manufacturer of vitamins
Oscar Ramjeet, President

D-U-N-S 02-233-1685
NATURES WORLD
920 Armorlite Dr, San Marcos, CA 92069
Phone: (760) 510-9787
Sales: $3,000,000   *Employees:* 20
Company Type: Private   *Employees here:* 20
SIC: 2833
  Mfg vitamins
Adrian Costilla, Owner

D-U-N-S 04-487-0673   EXP
NATUROPATHIC FORMULATIONS
9775 SW Commerce Cir, Wilsonville, OR 97070
Phone: (503) 682-9755
Sales: $7,000,000   *Employees:* 52
Company Type: Private   *Employees here:* 52
SIC: 2833
  Mfg natural vitamins
Bruce L Canvasser, President

D-U-N-S 13-055-3431
NATUROPATHIC LABORATORIES INT'L
60 Madison Ave, New York, NY 10010
Phone: (212) 532-9700
Sales: $2,200,000   *Employees:* 20
Company Type: Private   *Employees here:* 8
SIC: 2834
  Manufactures topical analgesic
David Popofsky, Chairman of the Board

D-U-N-S 05-279-0318
NBTY, INC.
90 Orville Dr, Bohemia, NY 11716
Phone: (516) 567-9500
Sales: $572,124,000   *Employees:* 5,300
Company Type: Public   *Employees here:* 870
SIC: 2834
  Mfg ret & direct mail vitamins food supplements & personal
    care pdts
Harvey Kamil, Chief Financial Officer

D-U-N-S 96-507-0428
NCB TECHNOLOGY CORP.
4102 Valley Blvd, Walnut, CA 91789
Phone: (909) 869-0666
Sales: $10,000,000   *Employees:* 25
Company Type: Private   *Employees here:* 25
SIC: 2833
  Whol general groceries
Lynn Leung, President

D-U-N-S 02-932-5032
NEO-LIFE COMPANY OF AMERICA
3500 Gateway Blvd, Fremont, CA 94538
Phone: (510) 651-0405
Sales: $9,100,000   *Employees:* 65
Company Type: Private   *Employees here:* 45
SIC: 2834
  Mfg vitamins & protein supplements
Robert E Brassfield, President

D-U-N-S 06-955-0929   EXP
NEOGEN CORPORATION
620 Lesher Pl, Lansing, MI 48912
Phone: (517) 372-9200
Sales: $15,259,000   *Employees:* 200
Company Type: Public   *Employees here:* 60
SIC: 2835
  Mfg predictive & diagnostic products & veterinary
    instruments
James L Herbert, President

D-U-N-S 12-117-2209
NEORX CORPORATION
410 W Harrison St, Seattle, WA 98119
Phone: (206) 281-7001
Sales: $7,548,000   *Employees:* 57
Company Type: Public   *Employees here:* 57
SIC: 2835
  Cancer research
Dr Paul G Abrams MD, Chief Executive Officer

D-U-N-S 15-510-0969
NEUREX CORPORATION
3760 Haven Ave, Menlo Park, CA 94025
Phone: (650) 853-1500
Sales: $2,392,000   *Employees:* 56
Company Type: Public   *Employees here:* 56
SIC: 2836
  Develops biopharmaceutical products
Paul Goddard, Chairman of the Board

D-U-N-S 80-098-1276
NEUROCRINE BIOSCIENCES INC.
3050 Science Park Rd, San Diego, CA 92121
Phone: (619) 658-7600
Sales: $26,144,000   *Employees:* 126
Company Type: Public   *Employees here:* 120
SIC: 2835
   Pharmaceutical research and development
Gary Lyons, President

D-U-N-S 17-359-1595
NEW CHAPTER INC.
22 High St, Brattleboro, VT 05301
Phone: (802) 257-9345
Sales: $5,000,000   *Employees:* 24
Company Type: Private   *Employees here:* 21
SIC: 2833
   Mfg vitamins food supplements & natural cosmetics
Paul Schulick, President

D-U-N-S 00-827-3802
NEW LIFE HEALTH PRODUCTS INC.
4191 N Bulldog Rd, Cedar City, UT 84720
Phone: (435) 865-0664
Sales: $10,000,000   *Employees:* 5
Company Type: Private   *Employees here:* 5
SIC: 2834
   Mfg pharmaceutical preparations
Benjamin Loewy, President

D-U-N-S 16-182-0212   EXP
NEWAYS INC.
150 E 400 N, Salem, UT 84653
Phone: (801) 423-2800
Sales: $70,000,000   *Employees:* 300
Company Type: Private   *Employees here:* 91
SIC: 2833
   Mfg herbal healthcare and skin care products
Thomas Mower Sr, President

D-U-N-S 55-629-8115   EXP
NEXSTAR PHARMACEUTICALS INC.
2860 Wilderness Pl, Boulder, CO 80301
Phone: (303) 444-5893
Sales: $89,152,000   *Employees:* 580
Company Type: Public   *Employees here:* 260
SIC: 2834
   Mfg & mkts pharmaceutical products
Lawrence M Gold, Chairman of the Board

D-U-N-S 01-678-7207   EXP
NICODROP
P.O. Box 2177, La Mesa, CA 91941
Phone: (619) 461-5788
Sales: $10,000,000   *Employees:* 4
Company Type: Private   *Employees here:* 4
SIC: 2834
   Whol drugs/sundries
Lawrence Christopher, Owner

D-U-N-S 02-579-1815
NITTANY PHARMACEUTICALS INC.
Rr 322, Milroy, PA 17063
Phone: (717) 667-3510
Sales: $25,500,000   *Employees:* 175
Company Type: Private   *Employees here:* 100
SIC: 2834
   Mfg non-prescription drugs
Beth Kerstetter, President

D-U-N-S 05-723-4486
NORAMCO, (DELAWARE) INC.
   (Parent: Johnson & Johnson)
One Johnson/Johnson Plaza, New Brunswick, NJ 08933
Phone: (732) 524-0400
Sales: $14,300,000   *Employees:* 100
Company Type: Public Family Member   *Employees here:* 100
SIC: 2833
   Mfg intermediate pharmaceuticals
Edward Graham, President

D-U-N-S 18-929-3624
NORIAN CORPORATION
10260 Bubb Rd, Cupertino, CA 95014
Phone: (408) 252-6800
Sales: $3,074,000   *Employees:* 73
Company Type: Private   *Employees here:* 65
SIC: 2836
   Mfg biomaterials
Brent Constantz, President

D-U-N-S 08-309-1991   EXP
NORTHRIDGE LABORATORIES INC.
20832 Dearborn St, Chatsworth, CA 91311
Phone: (818) 882-5622
Sales: $6,400,000   *Employees:* 50
Company Type: Private   *Employees here:* 35
SIC: 2833
   Mfg vitamins
Jane D Richman, Chief Executive Officer

D-U-N-S 10-888-4289   EXP
NORTHWEST MARKETING CORP.
320 E Crowther Ave, Placentia, CA 92870
Phone: (714) 577-0980
Sales: $2,600,000   *Employees:* 25
Company Type: Private   *Employees here:* 25
SIC: 2833
   Mfg vitamins & dietary supplements
Jack Brown, President

D-U-N-S 61-715-3093
NORWICH OVERSEAS, INC.
   (Parent: Procter Gamble Pharmaceuticals)
619 Central Ave, Ste 1, Cincinnati, OH 45202
Phone: (513) 983-1100
Sales: $10,700,000   *Employees:* 100
Company Type: Public Family Member   *Employees here:* 10
SIC: 2834
   Mfg pharmaceuticals
Mark Collar, President

D-U-N-S 60-967-1433   EXP
NOVAGEN INC.
   (Parent: CN Biosciences Inc)
601 Science Dr, Madison, WI 53711
Phone: (608) 238-6110
Sales: $5,000,000   *Employees:* 45
Company Type: Public Family Member   *Employees here:* 45
SIC: 2835
   Mfg molecular biological products
Robert Mierendorf, President

D-U-N-S 00-122-1845
NOVARTIS CORPORATION
564 Morris Ave, Summit, NJ 07901
Phone: (908) 522-6700
Sales: $8,400,000,000   *Employees:* 20,000
Company Type: Private   *Employees here:* 2,500
SIC: 2834
   Mfg pharmaceuticals vision care pdts agribusiness pdts &
      nutrition pdts
Douglas G Watson, Chief Executive Officer

D-U-N-S 96-661-6633   EXP
NOVARTIS CROP PROTECTION INC.
(Parent: Novartis Corporation)
410 S Swing Rd, Greensboro, NC 27409
Phone: (336) 632-6000
Sales: $230,400,000   *Employees:* 1,800
Company Type: Private   *Employees here:* 700
SIC: 2834
  Mfg agricultural products
Emilio J Bontempo, President

D-U-N-S 00-214-7023
NOVARTIS PHARMACEUTICALS CORP.
(Parent: Novartis Corporation)
59 Route 10, East Hanover, NJ 07936
Phone: (973) 503-7500
Sales: $900,300,000   *Employees:* 7,000
Company Type: Private   *Employees here:* 4,600
SIC: 2834
  Mfg pharmaceuticals
Wayne P Yetter, President

D-U-N-S 14-858-5441
NOVEN PHARMACEUTICALS INC.
11960 SW 144th St, Miami, FL 33186
Phone: (305) 253-5099
Sales: $15,191,000   *Employees:* 160
Company Type: Public   *Employees here:* 150
SIC: 2834
  Mfg transdermal drug delivery systems & does commercial
    research for the same
Robert Strauss, President

D-U-N-S 82-640-4089
NOVO HOLDINGS INC.
(Parent: Novopharm Limited)
165 Commerce Dr, Schaumburg, IL 60173
Phone: (847) 882-4200
Sales: $6,300,000   *Employees:* 55
Company Type: Private   *Employees here:* 1
SIC: 2834
  Holding company
Leslie Dan, President

D-U-N-S 62-292-0320   EXP
NOVO NORDISK PHRM INDS INC.
(Parent: Novo-Nordisk of North America)
3612 Powhatan Rd, Clayton, NC 27520
Phone: (919) 550-2200
Sales: $23,865,000   *Employees:* 145
Company Type: Private   *Employees here:* 145
SIC: 2833
  Mfg pharmaceuticals specifically insulin
John Pratt, General Manager

D-U-N-S 60-360-9454
NOVOPHARM, USA INC.
(Parent: Novo Holdings Inc (de))
165 Commerce Dr, Schaumburg, IL 60173
Phone: (847) 882-4200
Sales: $300,000,000   *Employees:* 65
Company Type: Private   *Employees here:* 65
SIC: 2834
  Mfg & distributes pharmaceuticals
Robert J Gunter, President

D-U-N-S 01-697-1629
NUHEALTH MANUFACTURING, LLC
9627 44th Ave NW, Gig Harbor, WA 98332
Phone: (253) 851-3943

Sales: $10,000,000   *Employees:* 25
Company Type: Private   *Employees here:* 25
SIC: 2834
  Mfg food supplements and medical foods
Jeffrey Bland, Chief Executive Officer

D-U-N-S 88-349-2720   EXP
NUTRACEUTICAL CORPORATION
(Parent: Nutraceutical International)
1104 Country Hills Dr, Ogden, UT 84403
Phone: (801) 626-4900
Sales: $25,300,000   *Employees:* 208
Company Type: Public Family Member   *Employees here:* 140
SIC: 2834
  Mfg vitamins
Bruce Hough, President

D-U-N-S 00-512-7654
NUTRACEUTICAL INTERNATIONAL
1400 Kearns Blvd Fl 2, Park City, UT 84060
Phone: (435) 655-6000
Sales: $104,688,000   *Employees:* 450
Company Type: Public   *Employees here:* 450
SIC: 2834
  Mfg nutritional supplements
Bruce R Hough, President

D-U-N-S 10-288-2719   EXP
NUTRACEUTIX, INC.
8340 154th Ave NE, Redmond, WA 98052
Phone: (425) 883-9518
Sales: $4,307,000   *Employees:* 42
Company Type: Private   *Employees here:* 18
SIC: 2834
  Mfg health & nutritional supplements mfg biotechnology
    products & product research/development
William D St John, President

D-U-N-S 61-861-3590
NUTRAMAX PRODUCTS, INC.
51 Blackburn Dr, Gloucester, MA 01930
Phone: (978) 282-1800
Sales: $128,434,000   *Employees:* 1,200
Company Type: Public   *Employees here:* 300
SIC: 2834
  Mfg health & personal care products
Donald E Lepone, President

D-U-N-S 62-544-3130
NUTRI-WELL INTERNATIONAL INC.
1627 Boyd St, Santa Ana, CA 92705
Phone: (714) 903-6878
Sales: $5,100,000   *Employees:* 45
Company Type: Private   *Employees here:* 45
SIC: 2834
  Mfg natural vitamins and cosmetics
Charles G Myung, President

D-U-N-S 10-907-3049
NUTRITION CENTER, INCORPORATED
2132 Richards St, Douglas, WY 82633
Phone: (307) 358-5066
Sales: $4,804,000   *Employees:* 40
Company Type: Private   *Employees here:* 40
SIC: 2833
  Mfg medicinal chemicals
Dr Paul White, President

D-U-N-S 82-476-6935
NUTRITION MEDICAL, INC.
9850 51st Ave N 100, Minneapolis, MN 55442
Phone: (612) 551-9595

Sales: $4,105,000   *Employees:* 25
Company Type: Public   *Employees here:* 25
SIC: 2834
  Mfg vitamin & nutrient preparations
Richard Hegstrand, Acting COO

D-U-N-S 18-077-2683   EXP
NUTRITION NOW INC.
6350 NE Campus Dr, Vancouver, WA 98661
Phone: (360) 737-6800
Sales: $5,357,000   *Employees:* 42
Company Type: Private   *Employees here:* 42
SIC: 2834
  Mfg nutritional supplements
Martin Rifkin, President

D-U-N-S 19-766-3586   EXP
NUTRITION RESOURCE
865 Parallel Dr, Lakeport, CA 95453
Phone: (707) 263-0411
Sales: $6,219,000   *Employees:* 24
Company Type: Private   *Employees here:* 21
SIC: 2834
  Mfg nutritional supplements ointments dental gel & bubble
   bath
Richard Perry, President

D-U-N-S 00-730-6970
NUTRITIONAL LABORATORIES INT'L
11300 Hwy 93 S, Lolo, MT 59847
Phone: (406) 273-5493
Sales: $9,000,000   *Employees:* 50
Company Type: Private   *Employees here:* 50
SIC: 2833
  Mfg nutritional dietary supplements
Terry Benishek, President

D-U-N-S 03-115-2127
NUTRO LABORATORIES INC.
650 Hadley Rd, South Plainfield, NJ 07080
Phone: (908) 754-9300
Sales: $32,000,000   *Employees:* 140
Company Type: Private   *Employees here:* 140
SIC: 2834
  Mfg pharmaceuticals
Michael Slade, President

D-U-N-S 07-664-1299
NW ALPHARMA INC.
  (Parent: Alpharma Inc)
1720 130th Ave NE, Bellevue, WA 98005
Phone: (425) 882-0448
Sales: $9,000,000   *Employees:* 30
Company Type: Public Family Member   *Employees here:* 30
SIC: 2834
  Mfg fish vaccines
Knut Moksnes, President

D-U-N-S 87-717-8574
NYCOMED AMERSHAM, INC.
101 Carnegie Ctr, Princeton, NJ 08540
Phone: (609) 514-6000
Sales: $62,800,000   *Employees:* 760
Company Type: Private   *Employees here:* 190
SIC: 2835
  Pharmaceutical research and development
Daniel L Peters, President

D-U-N-S 11-628-3714   EXP
O E M CONCEPTS
1889 Lakewood Rd, Ste 96, Toms River, NJ 08755
Phone: (732) 341-3570

Sales: $2,011,000   *Employees:* 12
Company Type: Private   *Employees here:* 4
SIC: 2835
  Mfg & distributes bulk biological materials for diagnostic use
Robert Minarchi, President

D-U-N-S 16-086-2330   EXP
OCLASSEN PHARMACEUTICALS INC.
  (Parent: Watson Pharmaceuticals Inc)
2171 Francisco Blvd E, San Rafael, CA 94901
Phone: (415) 258-4500
Sales: $16,000,000   *Employees:* 106
Company Type: Public Family Member   *Employees here:* 96
SIC: 2834
  Develops and markets pharmaceuticals
Glenn A Oclassen, Vice-Chairman of the Board

D-U-N-S 82-505-6179
OCULEX PHARMACEUTICALS INC.
639 N Pastoria Ave, Sunnyvale, CA 94086
Phone: (408) 481-0424
Sales: $4,300,000   *Employees:* 40
Company Type: Private   *Employees here:* 40
SIC: 2834
  Mfg pharmaceuticals
Dr Jerry Gin, President

D-U-N-S 07-627-1709
OCUMED INC.
119 Harrison Ave, Roseland, NJ 07068
Phone: (973) 226-2330
Sales: $2,800,000   *Employees:* 25
Company Type: Private   *Employees here:* 25
SIC: 2834
  Mfr ophthalmic pharmaceuticals
Alfred R Caggia, President

D-U-N-S 05-156-5745   EXP
OHM LABORATORIES INC.
  (Parent: Ranlab Inc)
1385 Livingston Ave, North Brunswick, NJ 08902
Phone: (732) 297-3030
Sales: $15,497,000   *Employees:* 100
Company Type: Private   *Employees here:* 80
SIC: 2834
  Mfg pharmaceuticals
Arun Heble, President

D-U-N-S 11-828-9289
ONE LAMBDA INC.
21001 Kittridge St, Canoga Park, CA 91303
Phone: (818) 702-0042
Sales: $17,500,000   *Employees:* 120
Company Type: Private   *Employees here:* 119
SIC: 2833
  Mfg medical reagents
Dr Terasaki Paul I, Chairman of the Board

D-U-N-S 61-249-2678
OPTIMAL RESEARCH, INC.
251 Hilton Dr, St George, UT 84770
Phone: (435) 673-1076
Sales: $2,100,000   *Employees:* 20
Company Type: Private   *Employees here:* 20
SIC: 2833
  Mfg vitamins and whol sportswear
Dave Smith, President

D-U-N-S 87-757-2503
OPTIMUM NUTRITION, INC.
12424 NW 39th St, Coral Springs, FL 33065
Phone: (954) 755-9822

Sales: $3,200,000   *Employees:* 30
Company Type: Private   *Employees here:* NA
SIC: 2834
    Manufactures and wholesales sports nutritional items
Mike Costello, President

D-U-N-S 00-512-3690
ORGANICS/LAGRANGE, INC.
1935 Techny Rd, Ste 14, Northbrook, IL 60062
Phone: (847) 480-1800
Sales: $3,100,000   *Employees:* 50
Company Type: Private   *Employees here:* 50
SIC: 2834
    Mfg bulk pharmaceuticals
Lawrence A Hicks, Chairman of the Board

D-U-N-S 00-215-2858
ORGANON INC.
    (Parent: Akzo Nobel Inc)
375 Mount Pleasant Ave, West Orange, NJ 07052
Phone: (973) 325-4500
Sales: $300,000,000   *Employees:* 1,100
Company Type: Private   *Employees here:* 1,000
SIC: 2834
    Mfg pharmaceutical preparations
Hans Vemer, President

D-U-N-S 84-741-2871
ORPHAN MEDICAL, INC.
13911 Ridgedale Dr, Hopkins, MN 55305
Phone: (612) 513-6900
Sales: $3,100,000   *Employees:* 35
Company Type: Public   *Employees here:* 35
SIC: 2834
    Mfg medical products
William B Adams, Chairman of the Board

D-U-N-S 06-871-5424
ORTHO DIAGNOSTIC SYSTEMS INC.
    (Parent: Johnson & Johnson)
1001 Us Highway 202, Raritan, NJ 08869
Phone: (908) 218-8000
Sales: $132,100,000   *Employees:* 1,600
Company Type: Public Family Member   *Employees here:* 1,000
SIC: 2835
    Mfg pharmaceutical products
Jack Goldstein, President

D-U-N-S 00-104-4767
OTIS CLAPP & SON INC.
115 Shawmut Rd, Canton, MA 02021
Phone: (781) 821-5400
Sales: $4,300,000   *Employees:* 45
Company Type: Private   *Employees here:* 45
SIC: 2834
    Mfg pharmaceuticals & first aid kits & whol surgical supplies
        & equipment
Donald J Breen, President

D-U-N-S 10-360-0375   EXP
OXYCAL LABORATORIES INC.
    (Parent: Zila Inc)
533 Madison Ave, Prescott, AZ 86301
Phone: (520) 778-0732
Sales: $5,000,000   *Employees:* 46
Company Type: Public Family Member   *Employees here:* 43
SIC: 2833
    Mfg vitamin products
Joseph Hines, Chairman of the Board

D-U-N-S 80-001-4821
P & L DEVELOPMENT NY CORP.
240 Smith St, Farmingdale, NY 11735

Phone: (516) 249-0867
Sales: $6,590,000   *Employees:* 30
Company Type: Private   *Employees here:* 30
SIC: 2834
    Manufactures over-the-counter pharmaceuticals
Morton Rezak, President

D-U-N-S 01-892-7392
P J NOYES CO INC.
Bridge St, Lancaster, NH 03584
Phone: (603) 788-4952
Sales: $4,500,000   *Employees:* 45
Company Type: Private   *Employees here:* 45
SIC: 2834
    Mfg over the counter pharmaceuticals
David C Hill, President

D-U-N-S 06-913-2066
PACIFIC BIOTECH, INC.
    (Parent: Quidel Corporation)
10165 Mckellar Ct, San Diego, CA 92121
Phone: (619) 552-1100
Sales: $7,500,000   *Employees:* 78
Company Type: Public Family Member   *Employees here:* 78
SIC: 2835
    Mfg diagnostic test kits
Steven T Frankel, President

D-U-N-S 94-977-8013
PACIFIC INTERNATIONAL
18310 Clemson Ave, Saratoga, CA 95070
Phone: (408) 370-6669
Sales: $15,000,000   *Employees:* 45
Company Type: Private   *Employees here:* 45
SIC: 2835
    Mfg medical tests & aircraft parts
Mohsen Arayesh, Owner

D-U-N-S 07-774-4035
PACO PHARMACEUTICAL SERVICES
    (Parent: West Pharmaceutical Services)
1200 Paco Way, Lakewood, NJ 08701
Phone: (732) 367-9000
Sales: $238,700,000   *Employees:* 1,864
Company Type: Public Family Member   *Employees here:* 900
SIC: 2834
    Pharmaceutical and toiletries contract manufacturing and
        packaging
J E Dorsey, Chairman of the Board

D-U-N-S 08-611-6803   EXP
PADDOCK LABORATORIES INC.
3940 Quebec Ave N, Minneapolis, MN 55427
Phone: (612) 546-4676
Sales: $20,433,000   *Employees:* 110
Company Type: Private   *Employees here:* 110
SIC: 2834
    Mfg pharmaceuticals
Bruce G Paddock, President

D-U-N-S 96-631-7117   EXP
PAN AM PHARMACEUTICALS, INC.
130 William St Rm 501, New York, NY 10038
Phone: (212) 962-1877
Sales: $3,636,000   *Employees:* 10
Company Type: Private   *Employees here:* 10
SIC: 2834
    Mfg & whol pharmaceuticals
Lev Lievinov, President

D-U-N-S 80-010-6361
PANVERA CORPORATION
545 Science Dr, Madison, WI 53711
Phone: (608) 233-9450

Sales: $6,000,000   *Employees:* 30
Company Type: Private   *Employees here:* 30
SIC: 2835
　　Mfg molecular biological reagents
Terry Sivesind, President

D-U-N-S 09-273-3690
PAR PHARMACEUTICAL, INC.
　　(Parent: Pharmaceutical Resources Inc)
1 Ram Ridge Rd, Spring Valley, NY 10977
Phone: (914) 425-7100
Sales: $53,100,000   *Employees:* 340
Company Type: Public Family Member   *Employees here:* 320
SIC: 2834
　　Mfg generic pharmaceuticals
Sawyer Kenneth I, President

D-U-N-S 01-660-7629
PARKE DAVIS PHARMACEUTICALS LTD.
Km 1/9 Rr 689, Vega Baja, PR 00693
Phone: (787) 858-2323
Sales: $63,000,000   *Employees:* 500
Company Type: Private   *Employees here:* 500
SIC: 2834
　　Mfg pharmaceutical preparations
Luis Albors, President

D-U-N-S 00-949-8101
PARKEDALE PHARMACEUTICAL INC.
　　(Parent: King Pharmaceuticals Inc)
870 Parkdale Rd, Rochester, MI 48307
Phone: (248) 651-9081
Sales: $11,300,000   *Employees:* 100
Company Type: Public Family Member   *Employees here:* 100
SIC: 2834
　　Pharmaceutical preparations
Steve Samet, Vice-President

D-U-N-S 01-198-2337   EXP
PARTICLE DYNAMICS INC.
　　(Parent: KV Pharmaceutical Company)
2601 S Hanley Rd, Saint Louis, MO 63144
Phone: (314) 645-6600
Sales: $11,000,000   *Employees:* 26
Company Type: Public Family Member   *Employees here:* 26
SIC: 2834
　　Mfg vitamin preparations
Marc S Hermelin, Chairman of the Board

D-U-N-S 04-689-4064
PASTEUR MERIEUX CONNAUGHT
Discovery Dr, Swiftwater, PA 18370
Phone: (570) 839-4282
Sales: $153,100,000   *Employees:* 1,200
Company Type: Private   *Employees here:* 1,200
SIC: 2834
　　Mfg pharmaceuticals
Dave Williams, President

D-U-N-S 01-207-7228
PCR PUERTO RICO INC.
　　(Parent: PCR Inc)
Km 76 Hm 9 Rr 3, Humacao, PR 00791
Phone: (787) 852-4520
Sales: $3,500,000   *Employees:* 11
Company Type: Private   *Employees here:* 11
SIC: 2834
　　Mfg pharmaceutical preparations
Fred Blum, Vice-President

D-U-N-S 01-728-5776
PDK LABS INC.
145 Ricefield Ln, Hauppauge, NY 11788

Phone: (516) 273-2630
Sales: $51,352,000   *Employees:* 162
Company Type: Public   *Employees here:* 162
SIC: 2834
　　Manufactures pharmaceutical preparations
Reginald Spinello, Chairman of the Board

D-U-N-S 10-845-4760
PEGASUS LABORATORIES INC.
8809 Ely St, Pensacola, FL 32514
Phone: (850) 478-2770
Sales: $2,600,000   *Employees:* 28
Company Type: Private   *Employees here:* 28
SIC: 2834
　　Mfg veterinary pharmaceuticals
Jack Antis, President

D-U-N-S 08-258-0754   EXP
PEL-FREEZ, INC.
205 S Arkansas St, Rogers, AR 72756
Phone: (501) 636-4361
Sales: $11,100,000   *Employees:* 142
Company Type: Private   *Employees here:* 64
SIC: 2835
　　Mfg medical research & diagnostic products process rabbit
　　　meat
David W Dubbell, President

D-U-N-S 00-634-5292   EXP
PEL-FREEZ RABBIT MEAT, INC.
　　(Parent: Pel-Freez Inc)
205 S Arkansas St, Rogers, AR 72756
Phone: (501) 636-4361
Sales: $2,000,000   *Employees:* 34
Company Type: Private   *Employees here:* 34
SIC: 2836
　　Mfg medical research biological products & diagnostic
　　　products process rabbit meat
David W Dubbell, President

D-U-N-S 00-519-1044   EXP
PELRON CORPORATION
7847 47th St, Lyons, IL 60534
Phone: (708) 442-9100
Sales: $3,212,000   *Employees:* 40
Company Type: Private   *Employees here:* 40
SIC: 2833
　　Mfg specialty organic chemicals
Floy Pelletier, President

D-U-N-S 19-160-0790
PENEDERM INCORPORATED
　　(Parent: Mylan Laboratories Inc)
320 Lakeside Dr, Foster City, CA 94404
Phone: (650) 358-0100
Sales: $12,500,000   *Employees:* 95
Company Type: Public Family Member   *Employees here:* 95
SIC: 2834
　　Mfg dermatological preparations
Lloyd H Malchow, President

D-U-N-S 09-821-5619
PENICK CORPORATION
　　(Parent: Penick Pharmaceutical Inc)
158 Mount Olivet Ave, Newark, NJ 07114
Phone: (973) 242-6655
Sales: $5,900,000   *Employees:* 49
Company Type: Private   *Employees here:* 49
SIC: 2833
　　Mfg medicinal chemicals & pharmaceutical preparations
John Mcroberts, General Manager

D-U-N-S 02-001-8479   EXP
PENINSULA LABORATORIES INC.
  (Parent: Itoham Usa Inc)
611 Taylor Way, Belmont, CA 94002
Phone: (650) 592-5392
Sales: $10,400,000   *Employees:* 71
Company Type: Private   *Employees here:* 60
SIC: 2833
    Mfg bulk peptides immunology test kits & biological
    laboratory
Hiroshi Morihara, Chairman of the Board

D-U-N-S 03-861-6769   EXP
PERRIGO COMPANY
515 Eastern Ave, Allegan, MI 49010
Phone: (616) 673-8451
Sales: $902,637,000   *Employees:* 4,868
Company Type: Public   *Employees here:* 300
SIC: 2834
    Mfg pharmaceuticals vitamins & personal care products
Richard G Hansen, President

D-U-N-S 05-755-5484
PERRIGO COMPANY
  (Parent: Perrigo Company)
4615 Dairy Dr, Greenville, SC 29607
Phone: (864) 288-5521
Sales: $75,000,000   *Employees:* 285
Company Type: Public Family Member   *Employees here:* 275
SIC: 2834
    Mfg vitamin supplements
Michael J Jandernoa, Chairman of the Board

D-U-N-S 00-848-2473
PERSON & COVEY INC.
616 Allen Ave, Glendale, CA 91201
Phone: (818) 240-1030
Sales: $6,000,000   *Employees:* 67
Company Type: Private   *Employees here:* 67
SIC: 2834
    Mfg pharmaceuticals
Lorne Person Sr, Chairman of the Board

D-U-N-S 01-522-3951
PETNET PHARMACEUTICAL SVCS LLC
650 Engineering Dr, Norcross, GA 30092
Phone: (770) 239-1945
Sales: $4,300,000   *Employees:* 44
Company Type: Private   *Employees here:* 8
SIC: 2835
    Mfg radioactive pharmaceuticals
Jim Monaco, President

D-U-N-S 09-825-8726
PF LABORATORIES, INC.
  (Parent: Pharmaceutical Research Assoc)
700 Union Blvd, Totowa, NJ 07512
Phone: (973) 256-3103
Sales: $30,800,000   *Employees:* 250
Company Type: Private   *Employees here:* 250
SIC: 2834
    Manufactures pharmaceutical preparations
Dr Raymond R Sackler, President

D-U-N-S 00-132-5919   EXP
PFIZER CORPORATION
235 E 42nd St, New York, NY 10017
Phone: (212) 573-2323
Sales: $30,800,000   *Employees:* 250
Company Type: Private   *Employees here:* 50
SIC: 2834
    Mfg pharmaceuticals & other health care products
Patrick J Cooney, Treasurer

D-U-N-S 00-132-6495   EXP
PFIZER INC.
235 E 42nd St, New York, NY 10017
Phone: (212) 573-2323
Sales: $12,504,000,000   *Employees:* 49,200
Company Type: Public   *Employees here:* 2,500
SIC: 2834
    Mfg pharmaceuticals medical devices otc health care pdts
    animal health pdts & personal care pdts
William C Steere Jr, Chairman of the Board

D-U-N-S 09-034-6909
PFIZER PHARMACEUTICALS INC.
  (Parent: Pfizer Inc)
Km 58 Hm 2 Rr 2, Barceloneta, PR 00617
Phone: (787) 846-4300
Sales: $1,336,483,000   *Employees:* 1,000
Company Type: Public Family Member   *Employees here:* 1,000
SIC: 2834
    Mfg pharmaceutical preparations
Eduard C Bessey, President

D-U-N-S 01-701-5517
PHARBCO MARKETING GROUP INC.
3554 Round Barn Blvd, Santa Rosa, CA 95403
Phone: (707) 521-3630
Sales: $10,000,000   *Employees:* 6
Company Type: Private   *Employees here:* 6
SIC: 2834
    Mfg pharmaceutical preparations
Mark De Matti, President

D-U-N-S 05-577-4186
PHARM-ECO LABORATORIES INC.
  (Parent: Calix Corporation)
128 Spring St, Lexington, MA 02421
Phone: (781) 861-9303
Sales: $15,100,000   *Employees:* 99
Company Type: Private   *Employees here:* 79
SIC: 2834
    Mfg medicinal/botanical products commercial physical
    research
David Wade, President

D-U-N-S 78-694-6376   EXP
PHARMA LABS LLC
  (Parent: Golden Pharmaceuticals Inc)
2931 E La Jolla St, Anaheim, CA 92806
Phone: (714) 632-1184
Sales: $3,200,000   *Employees:* 30
Company Type: Public Family Member   *Employees here:* 30
SIC: 2833
    Mfg vitamins
Bruce Goldberg, President

D-U-N-S 60-339-9205
PHARMA TECH INDUSTRIES, INC.
1310 Stylemaster Ln, Union, MO 63084
Phone: (314) 583-8664
Sales: $6,000,000   *Employees:* 100
Company Type: Private   *Employees here:* 100
SIC: 2834
    Mfg pharmaceutical preparations
Edward T Noland, President

D-U-N-S 07-982-2375
PHARMA-TEK INC.
1000 Fort Salonga Rd, Northport, NY 11768
Phone: (516) 757-5522

Sales: $8,000,000   *Employees:* 15
Company Type: Private   *Employees here:* 4
SIC: 2834
    Mfg and whol pharmaceuticals
Dan J Badia, President

D-U-N-S 04-494-0096
PHARMACEUTICAL ASSOCIATES INC.
    (Parent: Beach Products Inc)
5220 S Manhattan Ave, Tampa, FL 33611
Phone: (813) 839-6565
Sales: $9,900,000   *Employees:* 90
Company Type: Private   *Employees here:* 8
SIC: 2834
    Mfg pharmaceutical preparations
Richard B Jenkins, Chairman of the Board

D-U-N-S 04-550-3000
PHARMACEUTICAL FORMULATIONS
    (Parent: Icc Industries Inc)
460 Plainfield Ave, Edison, NJ 08817
Phone: (732) 985-7100
Sales: $80,829,000   *Employees:* 378
Company Type: Public   *Employees here:* 378
SIC: 2834
    Mfg pharmaceutical preparations
John Oram, Chairman of the Board

D-U-N-S 17-851-6183
PHARMACEUTICAL HOLDINGS CORP.
1100 Orthodox St, Philadelphia, PA 19124
Phone: (215) 288-6500
Sales: $130,000,000   *Employees:* 350
Company Type: Private   *Employees here:* 3
SIC: 2834
    Holding company
Dr Richard Roberts MD, President

D-U-N-S 06-748-6548
PHARMACEUTICAL INNOVATIONS
897 Frelinghuysen Ave, Newark, NJ 07114
Phone: (973) 242-2900
Sales: $4,900,000   *Employees:* 50
Company Type: Private   *Employees here:* 50
SIC: 2834
    Mfg medical devices
Gilbert Buchalter, President

D-U-N-S 15-119-8074
PHARMACEUTICAL LABORATORIES
3117 Cabaniss Rd, Corpus Christi, TX 78415
Phone: (361) 855-7500
Sales: $5,259,000   *Employees:* 50
Company Type: Public   *Employees here:* 20
SIC: 2833
    Mfg vitamins minerals & herbal products
Jerry Mcclure, President

D-U-N-S 93-291-8642
PHARMACEUTICAL RECOVERY SVCS
5422 Carrier Dr, Orlando, FL 32819
Phone: (407) 679-9040
Sales: $2,700,000   *Employees:* 29
Company Type: Private   *Employees here:* 29
SIC: 2834
    Pharmaceutical preparations
Keith Griffin, President

D-U-N-S 06-339-7731
PHARMACEUTICAL RESEARCH ASSOC.
    (Parent: PRA Holdings Inc)
100 Connecticut Ave, Norwalk, CT 06850
Phone: (203) 853-0123

Sales: $100,000,000   *Employees:* 650
Company Type: Private   *Employees here:* 3
SIC: 2834
    Holding company
Dr Mortimer Sackler, President

D-U-N-S 78-200-0269
PHARMACEUTICAL RESOURCES, INC.
1 Ram Ridge Rd, Spring Valley, NY 10977
Phone: (914) 425-7100
Sales: $53,172,000   *Employees:* 340
Company Type: Public   *Employees here:* 320
SIC: 2834
    Mfg generic pharmaceuticals
Dennis O'Connor, VP Finance

D-U-N-S 09-039-8074   EXP
PHARMACIA & UPJOHN CARIBE
    (Parent: Pharmacia & Upjohn Inc)
P.O. Box 11307, Arecibo, PR 00617
Phone: (787) 782-3578
Sales: $400,000,000   *Employees:* 685
Company Type: Public Family Member   *Employees here:* 685
SIC: 2834
    Mfg pharmaceutical preparations
Manuel Hormaza, Vice-President

D-U-N-S 00-532-0742
PHARMACIA & UPJOHN COMPANY
    (Parent: Pharmacia & Upjohn Inc)
95 Corporate Dr, Bridgewater, NJ 08807
Phone: (908) 306-4400
Sales: $7,286,000,000   *Employees:* 16,900
Company Type: Public Family Member   *Employees here:* 6,700
SIC: 2834
    Mfg human pharmaceutical & animal health products
Jan Ekberg, Chief Executive Officer

D-U-N-S 92-949-7972
PHARMACIA & UPJOHN, INC.
95 Corporate Dr, Bridgewater, NJ 08807
Phone: (908) 306-4400
Sales: $6,586,000,000   *Employees:* 30,000
Company Type: Public   *Employees here:* 400
SIC: 2834
    Mfg pharmaceutical and healthcare products
Fred Hassan, President

D-U-N-S 03-094-5307
PHARMACIA HEPAR INC.
    (Parent: Pharmacia & Upjohn Company)
160 Industrial Dr, Franklin, OH 45005
Phone: (513) 746-3603
Sales: $18,000,000   *Employees:* 60
Company Type: Public Family Member   *Employees here:* 60
SIC: 2833
    Mfg medical chemicals specifically bulk heparin & heparin-
    like substances
Ola Andersson, President

D-U-N-S 79-117-9526
PHARMACYCLICS INC.
995 E Arques Ave, Sunnyvale, CA 94086
Phone: (408) 774-0330
Sales: $3,531,000   *Employees:* 80
Company Type: Public   *Employees here:* 80
SIC: 2834
    Pharmaceuticals development
Richard A Miller, President

D-U-N-S 94-494-6144
PHARMANEX INC.
625 Cochran St, Simi Valley, CA 93065

Phone: (805) 582-9300
Sales: $15,000,000   *Employees:* 44
Company Type: Private   *Employees here:* 44
SIC: 2834
   Health supplements
Henry Burdick, Chairman of the Board

D-U-N-S 87-646-9438
PHARMASCIENCES INC.
1 Tower Brg, Ste 814, West Conshohocken, PA 19428
Phone: (610) 941-2747
Sales: $6,986,000   *Employees:* 45
Company Type: Private   *Employees here:* 2
SIC: 2834
   Mfg controlled release pharmaceutical products
Richard Storm, President

D-U-N-S 79-063-1725
PHARMATECH LABORATORIES INC.
   (Parent: Enrich Corporation)
380 N 880 W, Lindon, UT 84042
Phone: (801) 225-8848
Sales: $7,800,000   *Employees:* 64
Company Type: Private   *Employees here:* 60
SIC: 2834
   Mfg pharmaceutical preparations
Kenneth Brailsford, President

D-U-N-S 05-389-0000
PHARMAVITE CORPORATION
   (Parent: Otsuka America Inc)
15451 San Fernando Missi, Mission Hills, CA 91345
Phone: (818) 837-3633
Sales: $82,000,000   *Employees:* 642
Company Type: Private   *Employees here:* 172
SIC: 2833
   Mfg vitamins
Henry E Burdick, President

D-U-N-S 19-498-7426   EXP
PHARMINGEN
   (Parent: Becton Dickinson and Company)
10975 Torreyana Rd, San Diego, CA 92121
Phone: (619) 812-8800
Sales: $44,000,000   *Employees:* 300
Company Type: Public Family Member   *Employees here:* 300
SIC: 2835
   Mfg biotechnical products
Ernest C Huang, President

D-U-N-S 83-495-1576
PHILLIPS PHARMATECH LABS INC.
8767 115th Ave, Largo, FL 33773
Phone: (727) 397-7881
Sales: $9,600,000   *Employees:* 75
Company Type: Private   *Employees here:* 60
SIC: 2834
   Mfg vitamins creams & lotions
Brett J Phillips, President

D-U-N-S 00-399-8259
PHOENIX LABORATORIES INC.
   (Parent: Evergood Products Corporation)
140 Lauman Ln, Hicksville, NY 11801
Phone: (516) 822-1230
Sales: $17,950,000   *Employees:* 4
Company Type: Private   *Employees here:* 4
SIC: 2833
   Manufactures vitamins
Melvin Rich, President

D-U-N-S 62-525-4461   EXP
PHOENIX SCIENTIFIC INC.
3915 S 48th Ter, Saint Joseph, MO 64503

Phone: (816) 364-3777
Sales: $30,400,000   *Employees:* 125
Company Type: Private   *Employees here:* 125
SIC: 2834
   Mfg veterinary pharmaceuticals
C W Remington, Board of Directors

D-U-N-S 02-764-8083
PLANET EMU INC.
1521 Alton Rd 187, Miami, FL 33139
Phone: (305) 538-5758
Sales: $6,000,000   *Employees:* 8
Company Type: Private   *Employees here:* 8
SIC: 2834

Julie Brumlik, President

D-U-N-S 19-147-3214
PLANTATION BOTANICALS, INC.
1401 County Rd 830, Felda, FL 33930
Phone: (941) 675-2984
Sales: $59,600,000   *Employees:* 500
Company Type: Private   *Employees here:* 500
SIC: 2833
   Mfg botanical products
Marlin D Huffman, President

D-U-N-S 93-358-7826
PLP, LTD.
7400 Alumax Rd, Texarkana, TX 75501
Phone: (903) 831-7808
Sales: $29,500,000   *Employees:* 240
Company Type: Private   *Employees here:* 1
SIC: 2834
   Mfg pharmaceutical preparations
Gregory C Pulido, General Partner

D-U-N-S 04-979-2153   EXP
PML MICROBIOLOGICALS INC.
   (Parent: Pml Inc)
27120 SW 95th Ave, Wilsonville, OR 97070
Phone: (503) 570-2500
Sales: $13,936,000   *Employees:* 184
Company Type: Public Family Member   *Employees here:* 110
SIC: 2836
   Mfg bacteriological media
Ken Minton, President

D-U-N-S 80-003-4399   EXP
PMLL INC.
27120 SW 95th Ave, Wilsonville, OR 97070
Phone: (503) 570-2500
Sales: $13,936,000   *Employees:* 185
Company Type: Public   *Employees here:* 1
SIC: 2836
   Mfg bacteriological media
Kenneth L Minton, President

D-U-N-S 93-337-8903
POWER ENGINEERING & MFG INC.
368 W County D, Saint Paul, MN 55112
Phone: (651) 633-3935
Sales: $3,000,000   *Employees:* 3
Company Type: Private   *Employees here:* 3
SIC: 2836
   Mfg biological products engineering services
Andrew Amighi, President

D-U-N-S 18-840-0337
PRA HOLDINGS, INC.
100 Connecticut Ave, Norwalk, CT 06850
Phone: (203) 853-0123

Sales: $100,000,000   *Employees:* 650
Company Type: Private   *Employees here:* 3
SIC: 2834
  Holding company
Dr Mortimer D Sackler, Secretary

D-U-N-S 09-034-5463
PRALEX CORPORATION
  (Parent: Zenith Laboratories Inc)
5127 Mount Welcome, Christiansted, VI 00820
Phone: (340) 773-2470
Sales: $2,700,000   *Employees:* 38
Company Type: Public Family Member   *Employees here:* 38
SIC: 2834
  Mfg pharmaceutical preparations
Hatcher Brown, General Manager

D-U-N-S 01-945-6362
PREMIUM PROCESSING, INC.
65 Mall Dr, Commack, NY 11725
Phone: (516) 864-3756
Sales: $5,000,000   *Employees:* 7
Company Type: Private   *Employees here:* 7
SIC: 2834
  Manufactures vitamins
Keith Schmidt, President

D-U-N-S 36-291-7692
PRINCETON BIOMEDITECH CORP.
4242 Us Highway 1, Monmouth Junction, NJ 08852
Phone: (732) 274-1000
Sales: $10,000,000   *Employees:* 140
Company Type: Private   *Employees here:* 140
SIC: 2835
  Mfg medical diagnostic test kits
Jemo Kang, President

D-U-N-S 03-920-6933
PRO PAC LABS INC.
3804 Airport Rd, Ogden, UT 84405
Phone: (801) 621-0900
Sales: $10,902,000   *Employees:* 80
Company Type: Private   *Employees here:* 80
SIC: 2834
  Mfg vitamins
Kim Wheelwright, Secretary

D-U-N-S 82-484-5457
PROCLINICAL INC.
300 Kimberton Rd, Phoenixville, PA 19460
Phone: (610) 935-4300
Sales: $15,800,000   *Employees:* 105
Company Type: Private   *Employees here:* 93
SIC: 2834
  Pharmaceutical services
Gary Casey, President

D-U-N-S 01-697-2051
PROCTER GAMBLE PHARMACEUTICALS
  (Parent: Richardson-Vicks Inc)
619 Central Ave, Ste 1, Cincinnati, OH 45202
Phone: (513) 983-1100
Sales: $164,700,000   *Employees:* 1,290
Company Type: Public Family Member   *Employees here:* 11
SIC: 2834
  Mfg pharmaceuticals
G G Cloyd, President

D-U-N-S 09-047-7134
PROCTER GAMBLE PHARMACEUTICALS
  (Parent: Procter Gamble Pharmaceuticals)
Rr 2, Manati, PR 00674
Phone: (787) 854-1520

Sales: $12,500,000   *Employees:* 125
Company Type: Public Family Member   *Employees here:* 125
SIC: 2834
  Mfg pharmaceuticals
Ramon Sepulveda, President

D-U-N-S 04-995-1668   EXP
PROCTOR & GAMBLE HEALTH PDTS
  (Parent: The Procter & Gamble Company)
7000 St Km 2 Hm 3 Rr 735, Cayey, PR 00736
Phone: (787) 738-2191
Sales: $37,200,000   *Employees:* 300
Company Type: Public Family Member   *Employees here:* 300
SIC: 2834
  Mfg pharmaceuticals
T A Moore, President

D-U-N-S 19-555-1247
PROGENICS PHARMACEUTICALS INC.
777 Old Saw Mill River Rd, Tarrytown, NY 10591
Phone: (914) 789-2800
Sales: $15,614,000   *Employees:* 30
Company Type: Public   *Employees here:* 30
SIC: 2834
  Developer of pharmaceuticals
Paul J Maddon, Chairman of the Board

D-U-N-S 79-347-1723
PROLAB NUTRITION INC.
11 Britton Dr, Bloomfield, CT 06002
Phone: (860) 769-5550
Sales: $18,000,000   *Employees:* 14
Company Type: Private   *Employees here:* 14
SIC: 2834
  Mfg nutritional sports supplements
John Morin, Chief Executive Officer

D-U-N-S 08-985-5696   EXP
PROMEGA CORPORATION
2800 Woods Hollow Rd, Madison, WI 53711
Phone: (608) 274-4330
Sales: $76,000,000   *Employees:* 510
Company Type: Private   *Employees here:* 400
SIC: 2836
  Mfg biological research products
William A Linton, President

D-U-N-S 15-508-4460
PROTEIN DESIGN LABS INC.
34801 Campus Dr, Fremont, CA 94555
Phone: (510) 574-1400
Sales: $20,255,000   *Employees:* 217
Company Type: Public   *Employees here:* 135
SIC: 2834
  Mfg pharmaceutical products
Laurence J Korn PhD, Chairman of the Board

D-U-N-S 01-518-2181
PURDUE PHARMA COMPANY
100 Connecticut Ave, Norwalk, CT 06850
Phone: (203) 853-0123
Sales: $100,000,000   *Employees:* 2
Company Type: Private   *Employees here:* 2
SIC: 2834
  Mfg & distributor of pharmaceuticals
Dr Mortimer D Sackler, Secretary

D-U-N-S 93-232-3652
PURDUE PHARMA LP
100 Connecticut Ave, Norwalk, CT 06850
Phone: (203) 853-0123

Sales: $100,000,000   *Employees:* 550
Company Type: Private   *Employees here:* 275
SIC: 2834
    Mfg & distributor of pharmaceuticals
Dr Mortimer D Sackler, Secretary

D-U-N-S 03-755-6511
PURE WORLD INC.
376 Main St, Bedminster, NJ 07921
Phone: (908) 234-9220
Sales: $12,721,000   *Employees:* 70
Company Type: Public   *Employees here:* 13
SIC: 2833
    Manufacturer of botanical extracts
Voldemar Madis, Vice-Chairman

D-U-N-S 09-926-2404
PUREPAC PHARMACEUTICAL CO.
    (Parent: Faulding Inc)
200 Elmora Ave, Ste 2, Elizabeth, NJ 07202
Phone: (908) 527-9100
Sales: $75,000,000   *Employees:* 301
Company Type: Private   *Employees here:* 296
SIC: 2834
    Mfg generic prescription drugs
Richard F Moldin, President

D-U-N-S 96-948-5432
PURITAN QUARTZ, INC.
27665b Avenue Hopkins, Santa Clarita, CA 91355
Phone: (661) 294-9999
Sales: $11,200,000   *Employees:* 85
Company Type: Private   *Employees here:* 85
SIC: 2833
    Mfg vitamins & supplements
Solomon Levy, Chief Executive Officer

D-U-N-S 08-537-6846   EXP
QUALIS INC.
4600 Park Ave, Des Moines, IA 50321
Phone: (515) 243-3000
Sales: $19,900,000   *Employees:* 180
Company Type: Private   *Employees here:* 150
SIC: 2834
    Mfg pharmaceuticals & personal care products & chemical
        specialties
Roxi Downing, Chairman of the Board

D-U-N-S 10-392-6911
QUALITY BIOLOGICAL INC.
7581 Lindbergh Dr, Gaithersburg, MD 20879
Phone: (301) 840-9331
Sales: $3,200,000   *Employees:* 48
Company Type: Private   *Employees here:* 48
SIC: 2836
    Manufactures tissue culture media & reagents for molecular
        biology research
Sol Graham, President

D-U-N-S 82-495-2584
QUALITY CARE PHRMCEUTICALS INC.
    (Parent: Golden Pharmaceuticals Inc)
3000 W Warner Ave, Santa Ana, CA 92704
Phone: (714) 754-5800
Sales: $5,502,000   *Employees:* 70
Company Type: Public Family Member   *Employees here:* 70
SIC: 2834
    Repackager of pharmaceuticals
John Grant, Chief Operating Officer

D-U-N-S 01-071-7890   EXP
QUANTIMETRIX
2005 Manhattan Beach Blvd, Redondo Beach, CA 90278

Phone: (310) 536-0006
Sales: $4,000,000   *Employees:* 50
Company Type: Private   *Employees here:* 50
SIC: 2835
    Mfg clinical diagnostic reagents & controls
Dr Robert Ban, President

D-U-N-S 09-702-0739   EXP
QUIDEL CORPORATION
10165 Mckellar Ct, San Diego, CA 92121
Phone: (619) 552-1100
Sales: $49,479,000   *Employees:* 300
Company Type: Public   *Employees here:* 275
SIC: 2835
    Mfg medical diagnostic products
Andre De Bruin, Vice-Chairman

D-U-N-S 62-055-7298   IMP EXP
QUIGLEY CORP.
10 S Clinton St, Doylestown, PA 18901
Phone: (215) 345-0919
Sales: $71,000,000   *Employees:* 16
Company Type: Public   *Employees here:* 16
SIC: 2834
    Mfg & whol homeopatic cold remedies
Guy J Quigley, President

D-U-N-S 79-008-6458
QXL CORPORATION
18 E University Dr, Mesa, AZ 85201
Phone: (602) 898-1661
Sales: $2,900,000   *Employees:* 2
Company Type: Private   *Employees here:* 2
SIC: 2834
    Manufacture skin care preparations
Martin K Zachreson, Chief Executive Officer

D-U-N-S 10-276-1673
RAINBOW LGHT NTRTIONAL SYSTEMS
207 Mcpherson St, Santa Cruz, CA 95060
Phone: (831) 429-9089
Sales: $10,500,000   *Employees:* 80
Company Type: Private   *Employees here:* 80
SIC: 2833
    Mfg nutritional supplements
Linda Kahler, President

D-U-N-S 93-789-0044
RANBAXY PHARMACEUTICALS INC.
600 College Rd E, Ste 2, Princeton, NJ 08540
Phone: (609) 720-5613
Sales: $15,327,000   *Employees:* 20
Company Type: Private   *Employees here:* 12
SIC: 2834
    Mfg & whol pharmaceuticals
Dipak Chattaraj, President

D-U-N-S 00-914-3223
RANDAL NUTRITIONAL PRODUCTS
1595 Hampton Way, Santa Rosa, CA 95407
Phone: (707) 528-1800
Sales: $5,000,000   *Employees:* 32
Company Type: Private   *Employees here:* 32
SIC: 2834
    Mfg vitamins
Louis L Frey, President

D-U-N-S 96-439-1320   EXP
RANLAB INC.
    (Parent: Ranbaxy Pharmaceuticals Inc)
600 College Rd E, Ste 2, Princeton, NJ 08540
Phone: (609) 720-5613

Sales: $15,497,000   *Employees:* 80
Company Type: Private   *Employees here:* 1
SIC: 2834
  Holding company
Dipak Chattaraj, President

D-U-N-S 13-166-0755
RASI LABORATORIES INC.
62 Veronica Ave, Somerset, NJ 08873
Phone: (732) 828-9466
Sales: $6,250,000   *Employees:* 16
Company Type: Private   *Employees here:* 16
SIC: 2834
  Mfg pharmaceutical preparations
Rao Vallabhaneni, President

D-U-N-S 04-801-6281
RAVEN BIOLOGICAL LABORATORIES,
8607 Park Dr, Omaha, NE 68127
Phone: (402) 593-0781
Sales: $2,400,000   *Employees:* 25
Company Type: Private   *Employees here:* 25
SIC: 2835
  Mfg sterilization test strips
Robert Dwyer Jr, President

D-U-N-S 09-911-2369   EXP
REAGENTS APPLICATIONS INC.
  (Parent: Hemagen Diagnostics Inc)
8225 Mercury Ct, San Diego, CA 92111
Phone: (619) 569-8009
Sales: $3,100,000   *Employees:* 32
Company Type: Public Family Member   *Employees here:* 32
SIC: 2835
  Mfg biological chemicals
Carl Franzblau, President

D-U-N-S 00-506-5594   EXP
REGIS TECHNOLOGIES, INC.
8210 Austin Ave, Morton Grove, IL 60053
Phone: (847) 967-6000
Sales: $5,000,000   *Employees:* 48
Company Type: Private   *Employees here:* 48
SIC: 2835
  Mfg pharmaceutical chemicals
Dr Louis J Glunz, President

D-U-N-S 09-618-9998
RELIANCE VITAMIN CO INC.
185 Industrial Pkwy, Ste C, Somerville, NJ 08876
Phone: (908) 218-1221
Sales: $3,200,000   *Employees:* 50
Company Type: Private   *Employees here:* 50
SIC: 2834
  Manufactures and wholesales vitamins
Terrell Vigeant, President

D-U-N-S 15-209-9479   EXP
RELIV' INTERNATIONAL INC.
136 Chesterfield Mall, Chesterfield, MO 63017
Phone: (314) 537-9715
Sales: $46,836,000   *Employees:* 170
Company Type: Public   *Employees here:* 150
SIC: 2834
  Mfg & whol of nutritional & dietary supplements
Robert L Montgomery, President

D-U-N-S 06-576-9564
REMEL INC.
  (Parent: Erie Scientific Co)
12076 Santa Fe Dr, Shawnee Mission, KS 66215
Phone: (913) 888-0939

Sales: $27,800,000   *Employees:* NA
Company Type: Private   *Employees here:* NA
SIC: 2836
  Mfg culture media
Frank H Jellinek Jr, President

D-U-N-S 03-696-9426
REMINGTON HEALTH PRODUCTS LLC
932 Blue Mound Rd, Fort Worth, TX 76131
Phone: (817) 847-0606
Sales: $18,000,000   *Employees:* 8
Company Type: Private   *Employees here:* 7
SIC: 2834
  Business service
William E Steele, Member

D-U-N-S 93-298-7449   EXP
RENAISSANCE PHARMACEUTICAL
1248 Hidden Woods Dr, Zephyr Cove, NV 89448
Phone: (775) 586-8177
Sales: $2,435,000   *Employees:* 10
Company Type: Private   *Employees here:* 10
SIC: 2834
  Mfg pharmaceutical preparations
Darlene Mccord, President

D-U-N-S 08-724-8183   EXP
RESEARCH AND DIAGNSTC SYSTEMS
  (Parent: Techne Corporation)
614 Mckinley Pl NE, Minneapolis, MN 55413
Phone: (612) 379-2956
Sales: $57,286,000   *Employees:* 390
Company Type: Public Family Member   *Employees here:* 390
SIC: 2833
  Mfg antibodies & hematology diagnostic kits
Thomas E Oland, Chairman of the Board

D-U-N-S 10-115-7964
RESEARCH BIOCHEMICALS INC.
  (Parent: Sigma-Aldrich Corporation)
1 Strathmore Rd, Natick, MA 01760
Phone: (508) 651-8151
Sales: $10,000,000   *Employees:* 47
Company Type: Public Family Member   *Employees here:* 25
SIC: 2836
  Mfg biological products
Evelyn Friedman, President

D-U-N-S 88-390-1019
RESPA PHARMACEUTICALS, INC.
P.O. Box 88222, Carol Stream, IL 60188
Phone: (630) 462-9986
Sales: $9,000,000   *Employees:* 35
Company Type: Private   *Employees here:* 35
SIC: 2834
  Mfg pharmaceutical preparations
Ansar Ahmed, President

D-U-N-S 78-375-2116
REXALL SHOWCASE INTERNATIONAL
  (Parent: Rexall Sundown Inc)
851 Broken Sound Pkwy NW, Boca Raton, FL 33487
Phone: (561) 241-9400
Sales: $159,000,000   *Employees:* 200
Company Type: Public Family Member   *Employees here:* 200
SIC: 2834
  Whol diet foods health foods & wellness products
Damon Desantis, Chief Executive Officer

D-U-N-S 07-182-5897
RHONE-POULENC RORER
  (Parent: Rhone-Poulenc Rorer Inc)
Cotto Norte Ind Pk Rd 604, Manati, PR 00674

Phone: (787) 854-1058
Sales: $118,354,000   *Employees:* 275
Company Type: Private   *Employees here:* 275
SIC: 2834
   Mfg pharmaceuticals
Carlos Santiago, General Manager

D-U-N-S 15-729-6518   EXP
RHONE-POULENC RORER PHARMACEUTICALS
   (Parent: Rhone-Poulenc Rorer Inc)
500 Arcola Rd, Collegeville, PA 19426
Phone: (610) 454-8000
Sales: $1,200,000,000   *Employees:* 2,800
Company Type: Private   *Employees here:* 1,800
SIC: 2834
   Mfg pharmaceuticals
Michel De Rosen, President

D-U-N-S 03-523-7940   EXP
RIBI IMMUNOCHEM RESEARCH INC.
553 Old Corvallis Rd, Hamilton, MT 59840
Phone: (406) 363-6214
Sales: $6,123,000   *Employees:* 107
Company Type: Public   *Employees here:* 107
SIC: 2834
   Mfg research & develop biological products
Robert E Ivy, Chairman of the Board

D-U-N-S 01-741-1737
RICHARDSON-VICKS INC.
   (Parent: The Procter & Gamble Company)
619 Central Ave, Ste 1, Cincinnati, OH 45202
Phone: (513) 983-1100
Sales: $40,400,000   *Employees:* 325
Company Type: Public Family Member   *Employees here:* 112
SIC: 2834
   Mfg pharmaceutical preps toiletries hare care products skin
     cream & sun care products
Wolfgang C Berndt, President

D-U-N-S 14-467-9156
RIJ PHARMACEUTICAL CORP.
40 Commercial Ave, Middletown, NY 10941
Phone: (914) 692-5799
Sales: $6,000,000   *Employees:* 27
Company Type: Private   *Employees here:* 3
SIC: 2834
   Mfg pharmaceuticals
Brij Gupta, President

D-U-N-S 04-284-3086   EXP
R.I.T.A. CORPORATION
1725 Kilkenny Ct, Woodstock, IL 60098
Phone: (815) 337-2500
Sales: $45,000,000   *Employees:* 118
Company Type: Private   *Employees here:* 35
SIC: 2833
   Mfg bulk medicinal chemicals
Stephen T Goode Jr, Chairman of the Board

D-U-N-S 12-224-7265   EXP
ROBERTS LABORATORIES INC.
   (Parent: Roberts Pharmaceutical Corp)
4 Industrial Way W, Eatontown, NJ 07724
Phone: (732) 389-1182
Sales: $150,000,000   *Employees:* 250
Company Type: Public Family Member   *Employees here:* 250
SIC: 2834
   Prescription drug development
Dr Robert A Vukovich, Chairman of the Board

D-U-N-S 12-224-7240
ROBERTS PHARMACEUTICAL CORP.
4 Industrial Way W, Eatontown, NJ 07724

Phone: (732) 676-1200
Sales: $122,508,000   *Employees:* 448
Company Type: Public   *Employees here:* 300
SIC: 2834
   Mfg & whol pharmaceuticals
John T Spitznagel, President

D-U-N-S 83-156-0578   EXP
ROBINSON PHARMA, INC.
2638 S Croddy Way, Santa Ana, CA 92704
Phone: (714) 241-0235
Sales: $17,785,000   *Employees:* 150
Company Type: Private   *Employees here:* 145
SIC: 2834
   Mfg pharmaceutical preparations
Tam H Nguyen, President

D-U-N-S 80-993-3534
ROCHE CAROLINA INC.
   (Parent: Hoffmann-La Roche Inc)
6173 E Old Marion Hwy, Florence, SC 29506
Phone: (843) 629-4300
Sales: $18,300,000   *Employees:* 150
Company Type: Private   *Employees here:* 150
SIC: 2834
   Pharmaceutical development & bulk manufacturing
Don Herriott, President

D-U-N-S 07-647-0525
ROCHE COLORADO CORP.
   (Parent: Syntex (usa) Inc)
2075 55th St, Boulder, CO 80301
Phone: (303) 442-1926
Sales: $80,000,000   *Employees:* 290
Company Type: Private   *Employees here:* 290
SIC: 2833
   Mfg bulk organic pharmaceutical compounds
Erik Lodewijk, President

D-U-N-S 18-907-5674
ROCHE HOLDINGS, INC.
1 Commerce Ctr, Ste 1050, Wilmington, DE 19801
Phone: (302) 425-4701
Sales: $1,735,100,000   *Employees:* 13,480
Company Type: Private   *Employees here:* 3
SIC: 2834
   Mfg pharmaceutical preparations vitamins chemicals &
     medicinal products diagnostic substances & perfumes &
     cosmetics
Fritz Gerber, President

D-U-N-S 09-058-4152   IMP EXP
ROCHE PRODUCTS INC.
Km 1 Hm 1 Rr 909, Humacao, PR 00791
Phone: (787) 852-0909
Sales: $20,700,000   *Employees:* 200
Company Type: Private   *Employees here:* 200
SIC: 2834
   Mfg pharmaceutical products
Lorence Mascera, President

D-U-N-S 16-014-7252
ROCHE VITAMINS INC.
   (Parent: Roche Holdings Inc)
45 Waterview Blvd, Parsippany, NJ 07054
Phone: (973) 257-1063
Sales: $153,100,000   *Employees:* 1,200
Company Type: Private   *Employees here:* 1,200
SIC: 2834
   Mfg pharmaceutical preparations
Paul Gilgen, President

D-U-N-S 05-883-9929
ROXANE LABORATORIES INC.
 (Parent: Boehringer Ingelheim Corp)
1809 Wilson Rd, Columbus, OH 43228
Phone: (614) 276-4000
Sales: $350,000,000
Company Type: Private
SIC: 2834
 Mfg pharmaceutical preparations
Werner Gerstenberg, President
Employees: 900
Employees here: 800

D-U-N-S 87-300-5094
ROYAL SOURCE, INC.
918 Sherwood Dr, Lake Bluff, IL 60044
Phone: (847) 234-1999
Sales: $2,800,000
Company Type: Private
SIC: 2833
 Mfg vitamin supplements
Mark A Nottoli, President
Employees: 30
Employees here: 30

D-U-N-S 60-623-0993
RX FOR FLEAS INC.
6555 NW 9th Ave, Ste 412, Fort Lauderdale, FL 33309
Phone: (954) 351-9244
Sales: $28,200,000
Company Type: Private
SIC: 2834
 Manufacturer and distributor of pest control products
Melvin Yarmouth, President
Employees: 200
Employees here: 185

D-U-N-S 87-496-5262
SAFETEC OF AMERICA INC.
1055 E Delavan Ave, Buffalo, NY 14215
Phone: (716) 895-1822
Sales: $3,800,000
Company Type: Private
SIC: 2834
 Manufacture of infection devices and control products
Scott B Weinstein, Chief Executive Officer
Employees: 35
Employees here: 35

D-U-N-S 62-612-0919 EXP
SAGE PHARMACEUTICALS, INC.
5408 Interstate Dr, Shreveport, LA 71109
Phone: (318) 635-1594
Sales: $2,168,000
Company Type: Private
SIC: 2834
 Pharmaceutical manufacturer & research & development
Jivn-Ren Chen, President
Employees: 30
Employees here: 30

D-U-N-S 96-743-1552
ST MARY'S CHEMICALS INC.
201 S 3rd St, Ste C, Saint Peter, MN 56082
Phone: (507) 931-8977
Sales: $2,300,000
Company Type: Private
SIC: 2834
 Mfg pharmaceutical preparations
Pat Soderland, President
Employees: 4
Employees here: 3

D-U-N-S 78-297-4257 EXP
SALSBURY CHEMICALS, INC.
 (Parent: Cambrex Corporation)
1205 11th St, Charles City, IA 50616
Phone: (515) 257-1000
Sales: $19,700,000
Company Type: Public Family Member
SIC: 2833
 Mfg chemicals pharmaceuticals & intermediate
  pharmaceuticals
Rudi Moerck, President
Employees: 180
Employees here: 180

D-U-N-S 60-552-4719
SANGSTAT MEDICAL CORPORATION
1505 Adams Dr, Menlo Park, CA 94025
Phone: (650) 328-0300
Sales: $4,527,000
Company Type: Public
SIC: 2834
 Mfg monitoring test products & therapeutic products for use
  in transplantation
Jean J Bienaime, Chief Executive Officer
Employees: 112
Employees here: 95

D-U-N-S 04-179-7775
SANKYO PHARMA INC.
1 Luitpold Dr, Shirley, NY 11967
Phone: (516) 924-4000
Sales: $50,100,000
Company Type: Private
SIC: 2834
 Mfg pharmaceuticals
Ralf Lange, President
Employees: 400
Employees here: 5

D-U-N-S 78-265-5427
SANTA CRUZ BIOTECHNOLOGY INC.
2161 Delaware Ave, Santa Cruz, CA 95060
Phone: (831) 457-3800
Sales: $8,100,000
Company Type: Private
SIC: 2836
 Mfg antibodies
Dr John R Stephenson, President
Employees: 115
Employees here: 115

D-U-N-S 08-757-7680 EXP
SCANTIBODIES LABORATORY INC.
9336 Abraham Way, Santee, CA 92071
Phone: (619) 258-9300
Sales: $18,860,000
Company Type: Private
SIC: 2835
 Mfg bulk reagents pregnancy test kits and chemical
  diagnostic test kits
Thomas Cantor, President
Employees: 280
Employees here: 240

D-U-N-S 17-725-3754
SCHEIN PHARMACEUTICAL INC.
100 Campus Dr, Florham Park, NJ 07932
Phone: (973) 593-5500
Sales: $490,170,000
Company Type: Public
SIC: 2834
 Mfg & distributor of solid dosage and parenteral (injectable)
  pharmaceuticals
Martin Sperber, Chairman of the Board
Employees: 2,000
Employees here: 150

D-U-N-S 00-413-5307
SCHERER HEALTHCARE INC.
120 Interstate North Pkwy, Atlanta, GA 30339
Phone: (770) 933-1800
Sales: $13,853,000
Company Type: Public
SIC: 2834
 Manage/dispose of medical waste & mkt med products
Robert P Scherer Jr, Chairman of the Board
Employees: 130
Employees here: 10

D-U-N-S 09-317-0199 EXP
SCHERING BERLIN INC.
340 Changebridge Rd, Montville, NJ 07045
Phone: (973) 276-2200
Sales: $718,538,000
Company Type: Private
SIC: 2834
 Manufactures ethical pharmaceutical preparations and
  vascular injection systems
Lutz Lingnau, President
Employees: 2,100
Employees here: 250

D-U-N-S 00-131-7601
SCHERING CORPORATION
(*Parent:* Schering-Plough Corporation)
2000 Galloping Hill Rd, Kenilworth, NJ 07033
Phone: (908) 298-4000
Sales: $6,778,000,000 — *Employees:* 18,400
Company Type: Public Family Member — *Employees here:* 3,200
SIC: 2834
   Mfg pharmaceutical pdts
Raul E Cesan, Chairman of the Board

D-U-N-S 05-455-4290 — EXP
SCHERING-PLOUGH CORPORATION
1 Giralda Farms, Madison, NJ 07940
Phone: (973) 822-7000
Sales: $8,077,000,000 — *Employees:* 20,600
Company Type: Public — *Employees here:* 275
SIC: 2834
   Mfg pharmaceutical & healthcare pdts
Raul E Cesan, President

D-U-N-S 15-148-7410 — EXP
SCHERING PLOUGH PRODUCTS INC.
(*Parent:* Schering-Plough Corporation)
P.O. Box 486, Manati, PR 00674
Phone: (787) 854-2700
Sales: $153,100,000 — *Employees:* 1,200
Company Type: Public Family Member — *Employees here:* 800
SIC: 2834
   Mfg pharmaceutical products
Richard J Kogan, President

D-U-N-S 00-821-1401
SCHERING-PLOUGH VETERINARY
(*Parent:* Schering-Plough Corporation)
2667 W Dual Dr, Baton Rouge, LA 70814
Phone: (225) 275-1356
Sales: $12,000,000 — *Employees:* 60
Company Type: Public Family Member — *Employees here:* 60
SIC: 2834
   Mfg animal health products
Richard J Kogan, President

D-U-N-S 00-701-7452
SCHERNG-PLOUGH HEALTHCARE PDTS
(*Parent:* Schering-Plough Corporation)
110 Allen Rd, Liberty Corner, NJ 07938
Phone: (908) 604-1640
Sales: $700,000,000 — *Employees:* 1,235
Company Type: Public Family Member — *Employees here:* 250
SIC: 2834
   Mfg drug products foot care and sun care products
Rodolfo C Bryce, Chairman of the Board

D-U-N-S 00-609-1672 — EXP
SCHWARZ PHARMA INC.
(*Parent:* Schwarz Pharma Usa Holdings)
6140 W Executive Dr, Thiensville, WI 53092
Phone: (414) 354-4300
Sales: $179,386,000 — *Employees:* 475
Company Type: Private — *Employees here:* 100
SIC: 2834
   Mfg pharmaceutical products
Klaus Veitinger, President

D-U-N-S 00-642-2406 — EXP
SCHWARZ PHARMA MANUFACTURING
(*Parent:* Schwarz Pharma Usa Holdings)
120 E 3rd St, Seymour, IN 47274
Phone: (812) 522-3915

Sales: $41,265,000 — *Employees:* 225
Company Type: Private — *Employees here:* 50
SIC: 2834
   Mfg pharmaceuticals
John R Lee, VP Operations

D-U-N-S 78-593-9141
SCICLONE PHARMACEUTICALS, INC.
901 Mariners Island Blvd, San Mateo, CA 94404
Phone: (650) 358-3456
Sales: $2,223,000 — *Employees:* 40
Company Type: Public — *Employees here:* 29
SIC: 2834
   Mfg pharmaceuticals
Donald R Sellers, President

D-U-N-S 93-291-9772 — EXP
SCIENCE INTERNATIONAL INC.
6251 Monroe St, Ste 200, Daphne, AL 36526
Phone: (334) 626-2040
Sales: $20,000,000 — *Employees:* 42
Company Type: Private — *Employees here:* 12
SIC: 2834
   Pharmaceutical preparations
Jack W Boykin, President

D-U-N-S 88-349-0450
SCIENTIA BIOLOGICAL
Commercial Ave Bldg 140, Wolsey, SD 57384
Phone: (605) 883-4532
Sales: $2,005,000 — *Employees:* 3
Company Type: Private — *Employees here:* 3
SIC: 2836
   Raw fetal blood processing & meat trading
Raynie Pullman, Partner

D-U-N-S 06-524-0319 — EXP
SCIENTIFIC PROTEIN LABS
(*Parent:* American Home Products Corp)
700 E Main St, Waunakee, WI 53597
Phone: (608) 849-5944
Sales: $15,600,000 — *Employees:* 120
Company Type: Public Family Member — *Employees here:* 120
SIC: 2834
   Mfg pharmaceutical & biochemical products
David Strunce, President

D-U-N-S 06-476-9292
SCIOS INC.
2450 Bayshore Pkwy, Mountain View, CA 94043
Phone: (650) 966-1550
Sales: $47,429,000 — *Employees:* 350
Company Type: Public — *Employees here:* 200
SIC: 2834
   Mfg pharmaceuticals
Richard B Brewer, President

D-U-N-S 00-120-3918 — EXP
SCOT-TUSSIN PHARMACAL CO INC.
50 Clemence St, Cranston, RI 02920
Phone: (401) 942-8555
Sales: $3,700,000 — *Employees:* 40
Company Type: Private — *Employees here:* 40
SIC: 2834
   Mfg pharmaceuticals
Salvatore G Scotti, President

D-U-N-S 06-913-2629 — EXP
SCRIPPS LABORATORIES, INC.
6838 Flanders Dr, San Diego, CA 92121
Phone: (619) 546-5800

Sales: $2,400,000   *Employees:* 25
Company Type: Private   *Employees here:* 25
SIC: 2835
    Mfg bulk diagnostic biochemicals
Simon C Khoury, President

D-U-N-S 94-837-0911
SEABELLA INC.
44 Rajon Rd, Bayport, NY 11705
Phone: (516) 243-5426
Sales: $4,000,000   *Employees:* 9
Company Type: Private   *Employees here:* 3
SIC: 2834
    Vitamin granulation
Harvey Kovitz, Chairman of the Board

D-U-N-S 09-037-8225
SEARLE & CO.
    (Parent: G D Searle & Co Del)
P.O. Box 363826, Caguas, PR 00936
Phone: (787) 746-6201
Sales: $256,082,000   *Employees:* 650
Company Type: Public Family Member   *Employees here:* 650
SIC: 2834
    Mfg pharmaceutical preparations
Daniel Lebron, President

D-U-N-S 86-903-2763   EXP
SEARLE, LTD.
    (Parent: Monsanto Company)
Km 64 4 Rr 140, Barceloneta, PR 00617
Phone: (787) 846-5000
Sales: $600,000,000   *Employees:* 492
Company Type: Public Family Member   *Employees here:* 492
SIC: 2834
    Mfg pharmaceutical products
Hector Jove, Vice-President

D-U-N-S 16-110-7156
SENTRY SUPPLEMENT CO. INC.
13001 NW 38th Ave, Opa Locka, FL 33054
Phone: (305) 681-1996
Sales: $5,000,000   *Employees:* 31
Company Type: Private   *Employees here:* 31
SIC: 2834
    Mfg vitamin preparations and food supplements
Leonard S Wayne, President

D-U-N-S 02-923-1842
SEQUUS PHARMACEUTICALS INC.
960 Hamilton Ave, Menlo Park, CA 94025
Phone: (650) 323-9011
Sales: $39,952,000   *Employees:* 260
Company Type: Public   *Employees here:* 250
SIC: 2834
    Mfg pharmaceutical products
Craig Henderson I, Chairman of the Board

D-U-N-S 61-139-8033   EXP
SERACARE TECHNOLOGY INC.
    (Parent: Seracare Inc)
2170 Woodward St, Ste 100, Austin, TX 78744
Phone: (512) 445-5100
Sales: $5,500,000   *Employees:* 40
Company Type: Public Family Member   *Employees here:* 32
SIC: 2835
    Mfg diagnostic equipment
William Cone, President

D-U-N-S 06-511-9034   EXP
SERGEANT'S PET PRODUCTS, INC.
    (Parent: Conagra Inc)
1 Central Park Plz, Omaha, NE 68102

Phone: (402) 595-7000
Sales: $15,200,000   *Employees:* 140
Company Type: Public Family Member   *Employees here:* 40
SIC: 2834
    Mfg pet supplies
Rick Vocik, General Manager

D-U-N-S 61-237-8166   EXP
SGM BIOTECH, INC.
10 Evergreen Dr, Ste E, Bozeman, MT 59715
Phone: (406) 585-9535
Sales: $3,000,000   *Employees:* 34
Company Type: Private   *Employees here:* 34
SIC: 2836
    Mfg biological indicators
John Gillis, President

D-U-N-S 00-921-0378   EXP
SHAKLEE CORPORATION
    (Parent: Yamanouchi Group Holding Inc)
444 Market St, Ste 3600, San Francisco, CA 94111
Phone: (415) 954-3000
Sales: $666,075,000   *Employees:* 3,000
Company Type: Private   *Employees here:* 180
SIC: 2834
    Mfg nutritional household personal care & water purification
      pdts & mail orders fine fruits & gourmet foods & roses
Charles L Orr, President

D-U-N-S 61-210-5841
SHAMAN PHARMACEUTICALS INC.
213 E Grand Ave, South San Francisco, CA 94080
Phone: (650) 952-7070
Sales: $3,500,000   *Employees:* 120
Company Type: Public   *Employees here:* 120
SIC: 2833
    Mfg ethnobotanical-based pharmaceuticals
Lisa A Conte, President

D-U-N-S 61-851-0226
SHAPERITE CONCEPTS, LTD.
9850 S 300 W, Sandy, UT 84070
Phone: (801) 562-3600
Sales: $12,400,000   *Employees:* 105
Company Type: Private   *Employees here:* 105
SIC: 2833
    Mfg natural food supplements
Greg Martin, Chief Executive Officer

D-U-N-S 62-487-0812
SHIRE LABORATORIES INC.
1550 E Gude Dr, Rockville, MD 20850
Phone: (301) 838-2500
Sales: $10,800,000   *Employees:* 93
Company Type: Private   *Employees here:* 93
SIC: 2834
    Pharmaceuticals development
Robert S Cohen, President

D-U-N-S 09-496-5662
SIDMAK LABORATORIES INC.
17 West St, East Hanover, NJ 07936
Phone: (973) 386-5566
Sales: $84,160,000   *Employees:* 470
Company Type: Private   *Employees here:* 400
SIC: 2834
    Mfg generic pharmaceutical drugs
Dr Satishchan Patel, President

D-U-N-S 93-265-1516
SIGA PHARMACEUTICALS INC.
420 Lexington Ave Rm 620, New York, NY 10170
Phone: (212) 672-9100

Sales: $2,100,000　　　　　　　　　*Employees:* 18
Company Type: Public　　　　　　　*Employees here:* 6
SIC: 2834
　　Pharmaceutical development
Joshua D Schein, Chief Executive Officer

　　D-U-N-S 00-627-3726　　　　　　　　　EXP
SIGMA CHEMICAL COMPANY
　　(*Parent:* Sigma-Aldrich Corporation)
3050 Spruce St, Saint Louis, MO 63103
Phone: (314) 771-5765
Sales: $108,900,000　　　　　　　*Employees:* 1,800
Company Type: Public Family Member　　*Employees here:* 500
SIC: 2836
　　Mfg biochemical products
David Julien, President

　　D-U-N-S 80-569-4569
SIGNAL PHARMACEUTICALS, INC.
5555 Oberlin Dr, Ste 100, San Diego, CA 92121
Phone: (619) 558-7500
Sales: $7,580,000　　　　　　　　*Employees:* 109
Company Type: Private　　　　　　*Employees here:* 109
SIC: 2834
　　Develop pharmaceuticals
Alan J Lewis PhD, President

　　D-U-N-S 80-541-4596
SLIM SCIENCE CORPORATION
17401 Ventura Blvd, Ste B7, Encino, CA 91316
Phone: (818) 783-9993
Sales: $3,000,000　　　　　　　　*Employees:* 7
Company Type: Private　　　　　　*Employees here:* 7
SIC: 2833
　　Mfg and wholesaler of health products
Steven Hendrix, President

　　D-U-N-S 09-060-7375　　　　　　　　　EXP
SMITHKLINE BEECHAM
　　(*Parent:* Smithkline Beecham Puerto Rico)
Km 9 1 Rr 172, Cidra, PR 00739
Phone: (787) 739-8401
Sales: $800,000,000　　　　　　　*Employees:* 650
Company Type: Private　　　　　　*Employees here:* 650
SIC: 2834
　　Mfg pharmaceutical products
Jose L Rosado, President

　　D-U-N-S 00-138-1342
SMITHKLINE BEECHAM CORPORATION
1 Franklin Plz, Ste 1800, Philadelphia, PA 19102
Phone: (215) 751-4000
Sales: $6,661,900,000　　　　　　*Employees:* 21,600
Company Type: Private　　　　　　*Employees here:* 250
SIC: 2834
　　Mfg ethical pharmaceuticals cough & cold pdts clinical
　　laboratory svcs & benefits management svcs
Jan Leschly, President

　　D-U-N-S 79-099-8132
SMITHKLINE BEECHAM PUERTO RICO
　　(*Parent:* Smithkline Beecham Corporation)
1 Franklin Plz, Ste 1800, Philadelphia, PA 19102
Phone: (215) 751-4000
Sales: $101,700,000　　　　　　　*Employees:* 801
Company Type: Private　　　　　　*Employees here:* 1
SIC: 2834
　　Holding company for pharmceutical products
Donald F Parman, Vice-President

　　D-U-N-S 60-937-7783　　　　　　　　　EXP
SOBEL USA INC.
300 Executive Dr, Ste 225, West Orange, NJ 07052

Phone: (973) 731-9222
Sales: $127,400,000　　　　　　　*Employees:* 1,000
Company Type: Private　　　　　　*Employees here:* 10
SIC: 2834
　　Manufactures pharmaceutical preparations specializing in
　　vitamins and gelatin capsules
Daniel Van Doorn, Chairman of the Board

　　D-U-N-S 83-610-1956
SOFT GEL TECHNOLOGIES, INC.
6982 Bandini Blvd, Los Angeles, CA 90040
Phone: (323) 726-0700
Sales: $14,000,000　　　　　　　　*Employees:* 38
Company Type: Private　　　　　　*Employees here:* 38
SIC: 2834
　　Mfg gel capsules
Satomi Tseuchibe, President

　　D-U-N-S 07-309-1860　　　　　　　　　EXP
SOLARAY INC.
　　(*Parent:* Nutraceutical International)
1400 Kearns Blvd Fl 2, Park City, UT 84060
Phone: (435) 655-6000
Sales: $16,700,000　　　　　　　　*Employees:* NA
Company Type: Public Family Member　　*Employees here:* NA
SIC: 2834
　　Mfg vitamins
F W Gay II, President

　　D-U-N-S 84-208-3123
SOLGAR LABORATORIES, INC.
500 Willow Tree Rd, Leonia, NJ 07605
Phone: (201) 944-2311
Sales: $3,600,000　　　　　　　　*Employees:* 40
Company Type: Private　　　　　　*Employees here:* 40
SIC: 2834
　　Manufactures food supplements
Allen Skolnick, President

　　D-U-N-S 93-151-5209
SOLOPAK LABORATORIES INC.
1845 Tonne Rd, Elk Grove Village, IL 60007
Phone: (847) 806-0080
Sales: $30,800,000　　　　　　　　*Employees:* 250
Company Type: Private　　　　　　*Employees here:* 250
SIC: 2834
　　Mfg pharmaceuticals
Otto T Nonnenmann, President

　　D-U-N-S 00-330-9358
SOLVAY PHARMACEUTICALS INC.
　　(*Parent:* Solvay America Inc)
901 Sawyer Rd, Marietta, GA 30062
Phone: (770) 578-9000
Sales: $400,000,000　　　　　　　*Employees:* 1,100
Company Type: Private　　　　　　*Employees here:* 900
SIC: 2834
　　Mfg pharmaceuticals
David A Dodd, President

　　D-U-N-S 62-316-8267
SOVEREIGN PHARMACEUTICALS
　　(*Parent:* Anda Development Corp)
7590 Sand St, Fort Worth, TX 76118
Phone: (817) 284-0429
Sales: $7,722,000　　　　　　　　*Employees:* 84
Company Type: Private　　　　　　*Employees here:* 80
SIC: 2834
　　Mfg pharmaceutical preparations
Larry Boos, President

　　D-U-N-S 11-995-0020
SP PHARMACEUTICALS, LLC
4272 Balloon Park Rd NE, Albuquerque, NM 87109

Phone: (505) 345-0500
Sales: $18,000,000   Employees: 180
Company Type: Private   Employees here: 84
SIC: 2834
   Mfg pharmaceutical preparations
H J Larsen, President

D-U-N-S 01-878-7325
SPAFAS, INCORPORATED
   (Parent: Charles River Laboratories)
190 Route 165, Preston, CT 06365
Phone: (860) 889-1389
Sales: $14,000,000   Employees: 141
Company Type: Public Family Member   Employees here: 25
SIC: 2836
   Mfg specific pathogen free chicken eggs for vaccines
Joseph Glennon, President

D-U-N-S 60-101-2305
SPORTPHARMA USA INC.
1915 Mark Ct, Ste 150, Concord, CA 94520
Phone: (925) 686-1451
Sales: $25,000,000   Employees: 22
Company Type: Private   Employees here: 22
SIC: 2833
   Mfg sports supplements
Robert M Walls, President

D-U-N-S 05-077-9487
SPRAY-TEK INC.
344 Cedar Ave, Middlesex, NJ 08846
Phone: (732) 469-0050
Sales: $6,860,000   Employees: 28
Company Type: Private   Employees here: 28
SIC: 2834
   Custom dehydration of pharmaceutical products
Mark Epstein, Chairman of the Board

D-U-N-S 09-002-1668
SQUIBB MANUFACTURING INC.
   (Parent: Bristol-Myers Squibb Company)
Km 77 Hm 5 Rr 3, Humacao, PR 00791
Phone: (787) 852-1255
Sales: $501,169,000   Employees: 700
Company Type: Public Family Member   Employees here: 650
SIC: 2834
   Mfg pharmaceutical preparations
Hector Totti, Vice-President

D-U-N-S 00-328-8321
SSS COMPANY
71 University Ave SW, Atlanta, GA 30315
Phone: (404) 521-0857
Sales: $5,200,000   Employees: 52
Company Type: Private   Employees here: 50
SIC: 2834
   Mfg non-prescription pharmaceuticals
Chas M Bentley, President

D-U-N-S 00-831-6655   EXP
STANDARD HOMEOPATHIC COMPANY
154 W 131st St, Los Angeles, CA 90061
Phone: (323) 321-4284
Sales: $9,225,000   Employees: 70
Company Type: Private   Employees here: 64
SIC: 2834
   Mfg homeopathic pharmaceuticals and drugs
Jack Craig, President

D-U-N-S 80-743-7553
STASON INDUSTRIAL CORPORATION
11 Morgan, Irvine, CA 92618
Phone: (949) 380-4327

Sales: $3,600,000   Employees: 30
Company Type: Private   Employees here: 15
SIC: 2834
   Mfg pharmaceuticals and prescription drugs
Harry Fan, Chief Operating Officer

D-U-N-S 93-261-1049
STASON PHARMACEUTICAL INC.
   (Parent: Stason Industrial Corporation)
11 Morgan, Irvine, CA 92618
Phone: (949) 380-0752
Sales: $2,300,000   Employees: 22
Company Type: Private   Employees here: 22
SIC: 2834
   Mfr pharmaceuticals
Harry Fan, Chief Operating Officer

D-U-N-S 94-290-9862
STELLA LABS LLC
4801 Florida Ave, Ste 201, New Orleans, LA 70117
Phone: (504) 947-4787
Sales: $3,000,000   Employees: 9
Company Type: Private   Employees here: 9
SIC: 2833
   Mfg chemicals medicinal organic and inorganic bulk
     uncompounded
Allen Mcpherson, President

D-U-N-S 15-365-8356
STERIS LABORATORIES, INC.
   (Parent: Schein Pharmaceutical Inc)
620 N 51st Ave, Phoenix, AZ 85043
Phone: (602) 278-1400
Sales: $43,600,000   Employees: 350
Company Type: Public Family Member   Employees here: 300
SIC: 2834
   Mfg sterile multi-source injectable pharmaceutical products
     & otic & ophthalmic products
Martin Sperber, Chairman of the Board

D-U-N-S 07-932-9330
STERITEK, INC.
121 Moonachie Ave, Moonachie, NJ 07074
Phone: (201) 460-0500
Sales: $8,675,000   Employees: 150
Company Type: Public   Employees here: 150
SIC: 2834
   Contract manufacturer & packaging of pharmaceutical &
     health care products & mfg biomedical devices
Albert J Wozniak, President

D-U-N-S 04-926-5333
STEVENS ASH INC.
5861 John C Lodge Fwy, Detroit, MI 48202
Phone: (313) 872-6400
Sales: $6,850,000   Employees: 43
Company Type: Private   Employees here: 15
SIC: 2834
   Pharmaceutical research & development
Dr Calvin L Stevens, Chairman of the Board

D-U-N-S 00-206-3378   EXP
STIEFEL LABORATORIES INC.
255 Alhambra Cir, Ste 1000, Coral Gables, FL 33134
Phone: (305) 443-3807
Sales: $214,135,000   Employees: 1,470
Company Type: Private   Employees here: 40
SIC: 2834
   Mfg and whol pharmaceutical preparations
Werner Stiefel, Chief Executive Officer

D-U-N-S 06-158-0593   EXP
STRAIGHT ARROW PRODUCTS INC.
2020 Highland Ave, Bethlehem, PA 18020
Phone: (610) 882-9606
Sales: $8,000,000
Company Type: Private   *Employees:* 34
SIC: 2834   *Employees here:* 29
   Mfg of health & beauty aids for animals & humans
Devon Katzev, President

D-U-N-S 13-193-4184
STRATAGENE
   (Parent: Stratagene Holding Corp)
11011 N Torrey Pines Rd, La Jolla, CA 92037
Phone: (619) 535-5400
Sales: $14,900,000   *Employees:* 200
Company Type: Private   *Employees here:* 190
SIC: 2836
   Manufactures biology reagents
Dr Joseph A Sorge MD, Chief Executive Officer

D-U-N-S 17-186-9332
STRATAGENE HOLDING CORP.
11011 N Torrey Pines Rd, La Jolla, CA 92037
Phone: (619) 535-5400
Sales: $12,200,000   *Employees:* 201
Company Type: Private   *Employees here:* 1
SIC: 2836
   Mfg biological products
Joseph A Sorge, President

D-U-N-S 07-291-5986   EXP
STRECK LABORATORIES INC.
14306 Industrial Rd, Omaha, NE 68144
Phone: (402) 333-1982
Sales: $21,505,000   *Employees:* 220
Company Type: Private   *Employees here:* 212
SIC: 2835
   Mfg hematology chemistry & histology products
Dr Wayne L Ryan, Chairman of the Board

D-U-N-S 78-548-1672
SUGEN INC.
230 E Grand Ave, South San Francisco, CA 94080
Phone: (650) 553-8300
Sales: $6,031,000   *Employees:* 216
Company Type: Public   *Employees here:* 216
SIC: 2834
   Mfg pharmaceuticals
Stephen Evans-Freke, Chairman of the Board

D-U-N-S 06-835-9710
SUMMA RX LABORATORIES INC.
2940 Fm 3028, Mineral Wells, TX 76067
Phone: (940) 325-0771
Sales: $3,315,000   *Employees:* 31
Company Type: Private   *Employees here:* 30
SIC: 2834
   Mfg pharmaceutical preparations
Jerry A Nelson, President

D-U-N-S 00-919-9618
SUNSET NUTRITIONAL PRODUCTS
5859 Kanan Rd, Ste 365, Agoura Hills, CA 91301
Phone: (818) 706-9845
Sales: $2,500,000   *Employees:* 10
Company Type: Private   *Employees here:* 10
SIC: 2834
   Mfg nutritional products
Jim Kaplan, President

D-U-N-S 11-416-8131
SUNSTAR PHARMACEUTICALS, INC.
   (Parent: John O Butler Company Del)
1300 Abbott Dr, Elgin, IL 60123
Phone: (847) 888-1141
Sales: $8,000,000   *Employees:* 100
Company Type: Private   *Employees here:* 100
SIC: 2834
   Mfg & packaging of health care products
Michael Bava, Chairman of the Board

D-U-N-S 61-192-1669   EXP
SWISS-AMERICAN PRODUCTS INC.
4315 Alpha Rd, Dallas, TX 75244
Phone: (972) 385-2900
Sales: $2,200,000   *Employees:* 25
Company Type: Private   *Employees here:* 25
SIC: 2834
   Mfg skin care wound care and incontinence products
Bill Kling, Chairman of the Board

D-U-N-S 04-128-3219
SYNBIOTICS CORPORATION
11011 Via Frontera, San Diego, CA 92127
Phone: (619) 451-3771
Sales: $23,286,000   *Employees:* 63
Company Type: Public   *Employees here:* 53
SIC: 2836
   Dev and mfg monoclonal antibodies and whol biological
      products
Robert Widerkehr, President

D-U-N-S 00-712-1387
SYNTEX AGRIBUSINESS INC.
2460 W Bennett St, Springfield, MO 65807
Phone: (417) 868-3373
Sales: $16,300,000   *Employees:* 125
Company Type: Private   *Employees here:* 6
SIC: 2834
   Mfg veterinary pharmaceuticals
Eric Lodewijk, President

D-U-N-S 17-451-7060
SYNTRON BIORESEARCH, INC.
2774 Loker Ave W, Carlsbad, CA 92008
Phone: (760) 930-2200
Sales: $20,000,000   *Employees:* 278
Company Type: Private   *Employees here:* 278
SIC: 2835
   Mfg medical diagnostic substances
Jin P Lee, President

D-U-N-S 12-124-2713   EXP
SYSTEMIC FORMULA INC.
1877 W 2800 S, Ogden, UT 84401
Phone: (801) 621-8840
Sales: $2,500,000   *Employees:* 20
Company Type: Private   *Employees here:* 20
SIC: 2834
   Mfg food supplements
Stuart Wheelwright, President

D-U-N-S 19-725-0350
SYSTEMIX INC.
3155 Porter Dr, Palo Alto, CA 94304
Phone: (650) 856-4901
Sales: $29,500,000   *Employees:* 240
Company Type: Private   *Employees here:* 225
SIC: 2834
   Biopharmaceutical company
Michael Perry, President

D-U-N-S 15-092-1450
TAG PHARMACEUTICALS INC.
1510 Delp Dr, Kulpsville, PA 19443
Phone: (215) 256-8400
Sales: $500,000,000
Company Type: Private   *Employees:* 1,000
SIC: 2834   *Employees here:* 1,000
    Mfg pharmaceuticals
William A Fletcher, President

D-U-N-S 85-858-4642
TATRAS INC.
19 Sullivan St, Claremont, NH 03743
Phone: (603) 542-6536
Sales: $4,000,000
Company Type: Private   *Employees:* 35
SIC: 2836   *Employees here:* 35
    Mfg plasma consumable products
Jiri Zapletal, President

D-U-N-S 00-514-3086
TAYLOR PHARMACEUTICALS INC.
    (Parent: Akorn Inc)
150 S Wyckles Rd, Decatur, IL 62522
Phone: (217) 428-1100
Sales: $26,900,000
Company Type: Public Family Member   *Employees:* 220
SIC: 2834   *Employees here:* 100
    Mfg pharmaceutical compounds
Floyd Benjamin, President

D-U-N-S 19-668-7362   EXP
TECHNE CORPORATION
614 Mckinley Pl NE, Minneapolis, MN 55413
Phone: (612) 379-8854
Sales: $67,291,000
Company Type: Public   *Employees:* 450
SIC: 2835   *Employees here:* 2
    Mfg antibodies & hemotology diagnostic kits
Roger C Lucas PhD, Secretary

D-U-N-S 78-754-3818   EXP
TECHNICAL CHEMICALS & PRODUCTS
3341 SW 15th St, Pompano Beach, FL 33069
Phone: (954) 979-0400
Sales: $6,194,000
Company Type: Public   *Employees:* 55
SIC: 2835   *Employees here:* 40
    Mfg medical diagnostic products
Jack L Aronowitz, Chairman of the Board

D-U-N-S 18-506-7774   EXP
TECO DIAGNOSTICS
4925 E Hunter Ave, Anaheim, CA 92807
Phone: (714) 693-7788
Sales: $6,000,000
Company Type: Private   *Employees:* 50
SIC: 2835   *Employees here:* 50
    Mfg diagnostic reagents
Dr K C Chen, President

D-U-N-S 15-464-5063
TELIK INC.
750 Gateway Blvd, South San Francisco, CA 94080
Phone: (650) 244-9303
Sales: $3,710,000
Company Type: Private   *Employees:* 47
SIC: 2834   *Employees here:* 47
    Mfg pharmaceuticals
Michael M Wick, President

D-U-N-S 06-443-7304   EXP
TENDER CORPORATION
Littleton Industrial Park, Littleton, NH 03561
Phone: (603) 444-5464
Sales: $6,000,000
Company Type: Private   *Employees:* 55
SIC: 2834   *Employees here:* 30
    Manufactures & packages pharmaceutical products
    specializing in ointments for insect bites insect repellent &
    first aid
C B Bush, President

D-U-N-S 04-660-4583
TERA PHARMACEUTICALS INC.
    (Parent: Research Medical Inc)
6864 S 300 W, Midvale, UT 84047
Phone: (801) 562-0200
Sales: $4,000,000
Company Type: Public Family Member   *Employees:* 28
SIC: 2834   *Employees here:* 3
    Mfg pharmaceuticals and sterile solutions
Michael N Kelly, President

D-U-N-S 00-162-7975
TEVA PHARMACEUTICALS USA INC.
650 Cathill Rd, Sellersville, PA 18960
Phone: (215) 256-8400
Sales: $487,869,000
Company Type: Private   *Employees:* 1,200
SIC: 2834   *Employees here:* 350
    Mfg generic pharmaceuticals
William A Fletcher, President

D-U-N-S 06-032-0777
THAMES PHARMACAL CO INC.
2100 5th Ave, Ronkonkoma, NY 11779
Phone: (516) 737-1155
Sales: $14,300,000
Company Type: Private   *Employees:* 96
SIC: 2834   *Employees here:* 96
    Manufactures pharmaceutical preparations
Harry Schlakman, Chief Executive Officer

D-U-N-S 87-626-9168
THERACOM INC.
6931 Arlington Rd, Ste 501, Bethesda, MD 20814
Phone: (301) 215-7400
Sales: $4,500,000
Company Type: Private   *Employees:* 45
SIC: 2834   *Employees here:* 45
    Pharmaceutical
Robert J Dresing, Chief Executive Officer

D-U-N-S 18-618-2739
THERAPEUTICS INC.
256 E Grand Ave, Ste 80, South San Francisco, CA 94080
Phone: (650) 244-6800
Sales: $22,190,000
Company Type: Public   *Employees:* 152
SIC: 2834   *Employees here:* 152
    Mfg biopharmaceutical products
Vaughn M Kailian, President

D-U-N-S 15-487-1511   EXP
THERATECH INC.
417 Wakara Way, Salt Lake City, UT 84108
Phone: (801) 583-6028
Sales: $39,750,000
Company Type: Public   *Employees:* 243
SIC: 2834   *Employees here:* 170
    Mfg pharmaceutical delivery systems
Dinesh C Patel PhD, Chairman of the Board

D-U-N-S 78-894-3918   EXP
THIRD WAVE TECHNOLOGIES, INC.
502 S Rosa Rd, Madison, WI 53719
Phone: (608) 273-8933
Sales: $4,000,000   *Employees:* 49
Company Type: Private   *Employees here:* 49
SIC: 2835
    Mfg research kits
Lance Fors PhD, President

D-U-N-S 00-147-7496   IMP EXP
THOMPSON MEDICAL COMPANY INC.
777 S Flagler Dr, West Palm Beach, FL 33401
Phone: (561) 820-9900
Sales: $3,900,000   *Employees:* 42
Company Type: Private   *Employees here:* 29
SIC: 2834
    Mfg and distributors of non-prescription drugs & health care
    products
Daniel H Horwitz, President

D-U-N-S 02-119-2216
THRESHOLD ENTERPRISES LTD.
23 Janis Way, Scotts Valley, CA 95066
Phone: (831) 438-6851
Sales: $37,600,000   *Employees:* 300
Company Type: Private   *Employees here:* 300
SIC: 2833
    Whol & mfg nutritional supplements
Ira Goldberg, President

D-U-N-S 03-705-2099   EXP
TIME-CAP LABORATORIES INC.
7 Michael Ave, Farmingdale, NY 11735
Phone: (516) 753-9090
Sales: $15,000,000   *Employees:* 55
Company Type: Private   *Employees here:* 55
SIC: 2834
    Wholesales pharmaceuticals
Joseph Errigo, President

D-U-N-S 06-034-5949
TISHCON CORP.
30 New York Ave, Westbury, NY 11590
Phone: (516) 333-3050
Sales: $45,000,000   *Employees:* 280
Company Type: Private   *Employees here:* 125
SIC: 2834
    Manufactures vitamins minerals & over-the-counter
    pharmaceuticals
Raj Chopra, President

D-U-N-S 03-812-6736
TISSUE CULTURE BIOLOGICALS
1515 E Tulare Ave, Tulare, CA 93274
Phone: (559) 688-9391
Sales: $2,500,000   *Employees:* 6
Company Type: Private   *Employees here:* 6
SIC: 2836
    Mfg serums
Ross Hodges, President

D-U-N-S 36-292-5489   EXP
TME ENTERPRISES
11100 Greenstone Ave, Santa Fe Springs, CA 90670
Phone: (562) 944-8323
Sales: $4,500,000   *Employees:* 40
Company Type: Private   *Employees here:* 15
SIC: 2834
    Mfg and whol vitamins and commodity trading
James Mcdaniel Jr, Agent

D-U-N-S 83-469-5454
TOA MEDICAL ELECTRONICS (USA)
    (Parent: Sysmex Corporation of America)
10716 Reagan St, Los Alamitos, CA 90720
Phone: (562) 799-4001
Sales: $4,500,000   *Employees:* 17
Company Type: Private   *Employees here:* 17
SIC: 2835
    Mfg chemical preparations
Tak Kanamari, President

D-U-N-S 09-740-5302
TOLL COMPACTION SERVICE INC.
14 Memorial Dr, Neptune, NJ 07753
Phone: (732) 776-8225
Sales: $2,600,000   *Employees:* 38
Company Type: Private   *Employees here:* 38
SIC: 2833
    Processor of pharmaceuticals and chemicals
Paul B Pritchard, Chief Executive Officer

D-U-N-S 83-493-1909
TOTAL WELLNESS, INC.
19501 E Parker Sq Dr, Parker, CO 80134
Phone: (303) 841-6203
Sales: $5,000,000   *Employees:* 30
Company Type: Private   *Employees here:* 30
SIC: 2833
    Mfg vitamin supplements
Christy Logan, President

D-U-N-S 00-158-7203
TOWER LABORATORIES, LTD.
8 Essex Industrial Pk Rd, Essex, CT 06426
Phone: (860) 767-2127
Sales: $4,432,000   *Employees:* 45
Company Type: Private   *Employees here:* 37
SIC: 2834
    Mfg effervescent products
Norman Needleman, President

D-U-N-S 14-838-9158
TRACO LABS INC.
3102 W Clark Rd, Champaign, IL 61822
Phone: (217) 352-5800
Sales: $20,000,000   *Employees:* 30
Company Type: Private   *Employees here:* 30
SIC: 2833
    Mfg nutritional health food supplements
Sidney Tracy, President

D-U-N-S 86-741-8089   EXP
TREND PHARMACEUTICALS INC.
745 Hollywood Blvd NW, Fort Walton Beach, FL 32548
Phone: (850) 244-4104
Sales: $2,000,000   *Employees:* 40
Company Type: Private   *Employees here:* 40
SIC: 2834
    Mfg pharmaceutical preparations
Robert P Osborne, President

D-U-N-S 83-740-8657
TRIANGLE PHARMACEUTICALS, INC.
4 University Pl, Durham, NC 27707
Phone: (919) 493-5980
Sales: $9,800,000   *Employees:* 85
Company Type: Public   *Employees here:* 85
SIC: 2834
    Pharmaceutical development company
Dr David W Barry, Chairman of the Board

D-U-N-S 12-776-7754   EXP
TRIMAR HOLLYWOOD INC.
19265 Vanowen St, Reseda, CA 91335
Phone: (818) 342-0100
Sales: $2,500,000   *Employees:* 18
Company Type: Private   *Employees here:* 18
SIC: 2835
   Mfg blood derivative diagnostic products
Anna Kane, President

D-U-N-S 12-066-6219
TTS ALZA RESEARCH PARTNERS
   (Parent: Alza Corporation)
950 Page Mill Rd, Palo Alto, CA 94304
Phone: (650) 494-5300
Sales: $10,354,000   *Employees:* 7
Company Type: Public Family Member   *Employees here:* 7
SIC: 2836
   Mfg biological products
Patti Eisenhaur, Principal

D-U-N-S 87-663-8826
TWENTY-FIRST CENTURY LABS
2445 W 12th St, Ste 2, Tempe, AZ 85281
Phone: (602) 966-8201
Sales: $3,036,000   *Employees:* 30
Company Type: Private   *Employees here:* 30
SIC: 2834
   Mfg & whol nutritional products & vitamins
Steve Snyder, President

D-U-N-S 07-002-9764   EXP
TWIN LABORATORIES INC.
   (Parent: Twinlab Corporation)
150 Motor Pkwy, Hauppauge, NY 11788
Phone: (516) 467-3140
Sales: $213,229,000   *Employees:* 701
Company Type: Public Family Member   *Employees here:* 485
SIC: 2833
   Mfg nutritional & herbal supplements & herb teas magazine
    & book publisher
Ross Blechman, Chairman of the Board

D-U-N-S 05-498-2384   EXP
TWINLAB CORPORATION
150 Motor Pkwy, Hauppauge, NY 11788
Phone: (516) 467-3140
Sales: $213,229,000   *Employees:* 734
Company Type: Public   *Employees here:* 50
SIC: 2833
   Mfg nutritional & herbal supplements & herbal teas
    magazine & book publisher
Ross Blechman, Chairman of the Board

D-U-N-S 06-322-9348
TYLER DISTRIBUTION INC.
2204 NW Birdsdale Ave, Gresham, OR 97030
Phone: (503) 661-5401
Sales: $6,400,000   *Employees:* 50
Company Type: Private   *Employees here:* 40
SIC: 2833
   Mfg health food supplements
Jack Simms, President

D-U-N-S 79-041-1599
U S DIRECT INC.
1113 Stanley Ave, North Las Vegas, NV 89030
Phone: (702) 399-6896
Sales: $2,100,000   *Employees:* 22
Company Type: Private   *Employees here:* 22
SIC: 2834
   Mfg/exportor over-the-counter products
Alcinda Miller, President

D-U-N-S 55-646-5557
U S DIVERSIFIED TECHNOLOGIES
6950 Bryan Dairy Rd, Largo, FL 33777
Phone: (727) 544-8866
Sales: $5,743,000   *Employees:* 80
Company Type: Private   *Employees here:* 3
SIC: 2834
   Through subsidiary mfg vitamins
Paul Santostasi, Chairman

D-U-N-S 04-730-8911
UCKELE ANIMAL HEALTH DISTRG CO.
5600 Silberhorn Hwy, Blissfield, MI 49228
Phone: (517) 486-4341
Sales: $2,129,000   *Employees:* 16
Company Type: Private   *Employees here:* 16
SIC: 2834
   Mfg animal pharmaceuticals
William E Uckele Jr, President

D-U-N-S 14-455-4680
UDL LABORATORIES INC.
   (Parent: UDL Laboratories Inc)
7265 Ulmerton Rd, Largo, FL 33771
Phone: (727) 530-1633
Sales: $18,100,000   *Employees:* 130
Company Type: Public Family Member   *Employees here:* 90
SIC: 2833
   Mfg pharmaceutical drugs
Michael Reicher, President

D-U-N-S 82-743-1180
ULMER PHARMACAL COMPANY
   (Parent: Minnesota Quarries Inc)
2440 Fernbrook Ln N, Minneapolis, MN 55447
Phone: (612) 559-0601
Sales: $10,000,000   *Employees:* 8
Company Type: Private   *Employees here:* 8
SIC: 2834
   Mfg pharmaceutical preparations
Robert Coughlan, President

D-U-N-S 79-694-8834
UNI-HEALTH INC.
1 Carol St, Clifton, NJ 07014
Phone: (973) 779-3898
Sales: $4,000,000   *Employees:* 15
Company Type: Private   *Employees here:* 15
SIC: 2834
   Mfg pharmaceutical preparations
Marlon Durham, Vice-President

D-U-N-S 00-215-6669
UNIMED PHARMACEUTICALS, INC.
2150 E Lake Cook Rd, Buffalo Grove, IL 60089
Phone: (847) 541-2525
Sales: $8,918,000   *Employees:* 20
Company Type: Public   *Employees here:* 20
SIC: 2834
   Mfg ethical pharmaceutical compounds
Dr John N Kapoor, Chairman of the Board

D-U-N-S 11-601-5769   EXP
UNIPACK, INC.
3253 Old Frankstown Rd, Pittsburgh, PA 15239
Phone: (724) 733-7381
Sales: $2,512,000   *Employees:* 15
Company Type: Private   *Employees here:* 9
SIC: 2834
   Mfr pharmaceuticals cosmetics & private label mfg
Harilal Patel, President

D-U-N-S 06-606-3439
UNITED STATES BIOCHEMICAL CORP.
(Parent: Amersham Life Science Inc Del)
26101 Miles Rd, Cleveland, OH 44128
Phone: (216) 464-9277
Sales: $6,800,000   *Employees:* 100
Company Type: Private   *Employees here:* 100
SIC: 2835
   Mfg and distributes biochemical products and molecular
      biological products
C G Marlow, President

D-U-N-S 96-632-1200
UNIVERA PHARMACEUTICALS, INC.
100 Technology Dr, Ste 160, Broomfield, CO 80021
Phone: (303) 438-8666
Sales: $2,300,000   *Employees:* 25
Company Type: Private   *Employees here:* 25
SIC: 2834
   Mfg pharmaceutical preparations
B W Lee, Chief Executive Officer

D-U-N-S 09-926-8245
UNIVERSAL PROTEIN SUPPLEMENTS
3 Terminal Rd, New Brunswick, NJ 08901
Phone: (732) 545-3130
Sales: $29,700,000   *Employees:* 200
Company Type: Private   *Employees here:* 200
SIC: 2834
   Manufactures vitamin preparations
Clyde Rockoff, President

D-U-N-S 61-344-0684
UNIVERSAL PROTEINS INC.
9500 New Horizons Blvd, Amityville, NY 11701
Phone: (516) 957-5600
Sales: $2,100,000   *Employees:* 20
Company Type: Private   *Employees here:* 20
SIC: 2834
   Manufactures protein drinks
Gerald Kessler, President

D-U-N-S 18-844-0614
UNIVERSITY PHARMACEUTICALS
20 N Pine St Rm 775, Baltimore, MD 21201
Phone: (410) 706-2470
Sales: $2,300,000   *Employees:* 25
Company Type: Private   *Employees here:* 25
SIC: 2834
   Drug development
Harold Chappelear, President

D-U-N-S 04-426-1170
UPJOHN INTERNATIONAL INC.
(Parent: Pharmacia & Upjohn Company)
7000 Portage Rd, Kalamazoo, MI 49001
Phone: (616) 323-4000
Sales: $900,300,000   *Employees:* 7,000
Company Type: Public Family Member   *Employees here:* 7,000
SIC: 2834
   Mfg of pharmaceuticals & agricultural chemicals
Don Schmitz, Secretary

D-U-N-S 80-441-3250   EXP
USANA INC.
3838 Parkway Blvd, Salt Lake City, UT 84120
Phone: (801) 954-7910
Sales: $85,200,000   *Employees:* 359
Company Type: Public   *Employees here:* 330
SIC: 2833
   Mfg natural or synthetic bulk vitamins
Myron Wentz PhD, President

D-U-N-S 04-323-4264
USB CORPORATION
26111 Miles Rd, Cleveland, OH 44128
Phone: (216) 765-5000
Sales: $2,900,000   *Employees:* 35
Company Type: Private   *Employees here:* 35
SIC: 2835
   Mfg biochemical enzymes
Mike Lachman, President

D-U-N-S 87-918-4489
V I TECHNOLOGIES, INC.
155 Duryea Rd, Melville, NY 11747
Phone: (516) 752-7314
Sales: $44,000,000   *Employees:* 275
Company Type: Public   *Employees here:* 10
SIC: 2834
   Supplier of virally inactivated and fractionated blood
      products
John Barr, President

D-U-N-S 07-542-3491
VALENTINE ENTERPRISES INC.
940 Collins Hill Rd, Lawrenceville, GA 30043
Phone: (770) 995-0661
Sales: $25,000,000   *Employees:* 35
Company Type: Private   *Employees here:* 35
SIC: 2834
   Mfg food supplements product development engineering
      consulting
Donald Mcdaniel, President

D-U-N-S 93-185-6926
VECTECH PHARMACEUTICAL CONS
(Parent: Devlan Inc)
24543 Indoplex Cir, Farmington Hills, MI 48335
Phone: (248) 442-7620
Sales: $4,185,000   *Employees:* 40
Company Type: Private   *Employees here:* 40
SIC: 2834
   Pharmaceutical consulting validation
Francisco De Vecchi, Chairman of the Board

D-U-N-S 09-832-0922
VECTOR LABORATORIES INC.
30 Ingold Rd, Burlingame, CA 94010
Phone: (650) 697-3600
Sales: $5,400,000   *Employees:* 48
Company Type: Private   *Employees here:* 43
SIC: 2833
   Mfg biochemicals
Dr James Whitehead, President

D-U-N-S 14-797-9082   EXP
VETERINARY LABORATORIES, INC.
(Parent: Chemdex Inc)
12340 Santa Fe Dr, Shawnee Mission, KS 66215
Phone: (913) 888-7500
Sales: $6,100,000   *Employees:* 60
Company Type: Private   *Employees here:* 60
SIC: 2834
   Mfg veterinarian pharmaceuticals
Natu Patel, Chief Executive Officer

D-U-N-S 06-613-2549
VIRAL ANTIGENS INC.
5171 Wilfong Ln, Memphis, TN 38134
Phone: (901) 382-8716
Sales: $3,800,000   *Employees:* 49
Company Type: Private   *Employees here:* 49
SIC: 2835
   Mfg antigens & veterinary diagnostic tests
Preston H Dorsett PhD, President

D-U-N-S 06-646-7275
VITA ELIXIR COMPANY INC.
845 Mlk Jr Dr NW, Atlanta, GA 30314
Phone: (404) 505-9799
Sales: $12,000,000   *Employees:* 3
Company Type: Private   *Employees here:* 3
SIC: 2834
    Mfg pharmacetical preparations
J W Tibbs Jr, President

D-U-N-S 15-078-5020
VITA-KEY PACKAGING
1021 Business Dr, Fontana, CA 92337
Phone: (909) 355-1023
Sales: $3,500,000   *Employees:* 35
Company Type: Private   *Employees here:* 35
SIC: 2834
    Vitamin packaging service
Douglas Delia Jr, President

D-U-N-S 18-721-1792
VITA PURE INC.
410 W 1st Ave, Roselle, NJ 07203
Phone: (908) 245-1212
Sales: $8,000,000   *Employees:* 25
Company Type: Private   *Employees here:* 25
SIC: 2833
    Manufacture vitamins
Achyut Sahasra, President

D-U-N-S 96-055-8609
VITA QUEST INTERNATIONAL INC.
8 Henderson Dr, Caldwell, NJ 07006
Phone: (973) 575-9200
Sales: $100,000,000   *Employees:* 425
Company Type: Private   *Employees here:* 375
SIC: 2834
    Mfr & distributes health foods & specialty products mainly
      vitamins
Keith Frankel, Chief Operating Officer

D-U-N-S 08-151-9134   EXP
VITAMIN POWER INC.
39 Saint Marys Pl, Freeport, NY 11520
Phone: (516) 378-0900
Sales: $4,011,000   *Employees:* 31
Company Type: Private   *Employees here:* 31
SIC: 2834
    Mfg vitamins & health food supplements
Edward Friedlander, Chairman of the Board

D-U-N-S 00-834-9722
VITAMINERALS INC.
1815 Flower St, Glendale, CA 91201
Phone: (818) 500-8718
Sales: $8,200,000   *Employees:* 75
Company Type: Private   *Employees here:* 75
SIC: 2833
    Mfg vitamins & pharmaceutical preparations
John F Gorman Jr, President

D-U-N-S 00-506-3805
VITAMINS, INC.
200 E Randolph St, Chicago, IL 60601
Phone: (312) 861-0700
Sales: $10,000,000   *Employees:* 45
Company Type: Private   *Employees here:* 12
SIC: 2834
    Mfg vitamins minerals and related items
Louis E Kovacs, Chairman

D-U-N-S 80-822-6252
VITARICH LABORATORIES, INC.
2241 Trade Center Way A, Naples, FL 34109
Phone: (941) 591-2100
Sales: $2,135,000   *Employees:* 21
Company Type: Private   *Employees here:* 21
SIC: 2834
    Mfg and dist of supplements & whol food concentrates
Kevin Thomas, President

D-U-N-S 00-835-9994   EXP
VITATECH INTERNATIONAL INC.
2832 Dow Ave, Tustin, CA 92780
Phone: (714) 832-9700
Sales: $19,300,000   *Employees:* 150
Company Type: Private   *Employees here:* 150
SIC: 2834
    Mfg vitamins & food supplements
Thomas T Tierney, President

D-U-N-S 78-277-2263
VIVUS INC.
605 Fairchild Dr, Mountain View, CA 94043
Phone: (650) 934-5200
Sales: $138,337,000   *Employees:* 100
Company Type: Public   *Employees here:* 25
SIC: 2834
    Mfg pharmaceutical products
Leland F Wilson, President

D-U-N-S 10-365-4794   EXP
VM NUTRI
    (*Parent:* Life Plus)
570 Stadium Dr, Batesville, AR 72501
Phone: (870) 698-2344
Sales: $2,800,000   *Employees:* 30
Company Type: Private   *Employees here:* 2
SIC: 2834
    Mfg nutritional supplements
Timothy A Nolan, President

D-U-N-S 87-826-3359
VYSIS, INC.
    (*Parent:* Amoco Technology Company Del)
3100 Woodcreek Dr, Downers Grove, IL 60515
Phone: (630) 271-7000
Sales: $18,233,000   *Employees:* 153
Company Type: Public   *Employees here:* 100
SIC: 2835
    Mfg diagnostic products & analytical instruments
John L Bishop, President

D-U-N-S 00-111-4669
W F YOUNG INCORPORATED
111 Lyman St, Springfield, MA 01103
Phone: (413) 737-0201
Sales: $20,000,000   *Employees:* 28
Company Type: Private   *Employees here:* 25
SIC: 2834
    Mfg patented liniments & pharmaceutical preparations
Tyler F Young, President

D-U-N-S 95-720-3177
WARNER CHILCOTT, INC.
100 Enterprise Dr, Ste 280, Rockaway, NJ 07866
Phone: (973) 442-3200
Sales: $75,827,000   *Employees:* 50
Company Type: Private   *Employees here:* 50
SIC: 2834
    Mfg pharmaceutical preparations
James Anders, Chief Executive Officer

D-U-N-S 00-134-4506   EXP
WARNER-LAMBERT COMPANY
201 Tabor Rd, Morris Plains, NJ 07950
Phone: (973) 540-2000
Sales: $8,179,800,000   *Employees:* 40,000
Company Type: Public   *Employees here:* 2,800
SIC: 2834
   Mfg ethical & OTC pharmaceuticals biologicals capsules
      razor & blades chewing gums mints & pet care products
Melvin R Goodes, Chairman of the Board

D-U-N-S 84-005-4118
WATSON LABORATORIES, INC.
   (Parent: Watson Pharmaceuticals Inc)
311 Bonnie Cir, Corona, CA 91720
Phone: (909) 270-1400
Sales: $96,500,000   *Employees:* 760
Company Type: Public Family Member   *Employees here:* 760
SIC: 2834
   Manufactures pharmaceutical preparations mfg
Allan Chao PhD, Chief Executive Officer

D-U-N-S 10-693-1488   EXP
WATSON PHARMACEUTICALS, INC.
311 Bonnie Cir, Corona, CA 91720
Phone: (909) 270-1400
Sales: $324,015,000   *Employees:* 2,554
Company Type: Public   *Employees here:* 380
SIC: 2834
   Mfg pharmaceuticals
Allen Y Chao PhD, Chairman of the Board

D-U-N-S 06-456-6771
WEIDER HEALTH AND FITNESS
   (Parent: MLE Holding Co Ltd)
21100 Erwin St, Woodland Hills, CA 91367
Phone: (818) 884-6800
Sales: $101,600,000   *Employees:* 800
Company Type: Private   *Employees here:* 200
SIC: 2834
   Mfg and distributes nutritional products and publishes
      magazines
Richard J Renaud, Chairman of the Board

D-U-N-S 96-160-5649
WELLNESS WAY INC.
4016 82nd St Fl 2, Elmhurst, NY 11373
Phone: (718) 651-4724
Sales: $5,000,000   *Employees:* 6
Company Type: Private   *Employees here:* 6
SIC: 2834

Chao Yang, President

D-U-N-S 15-972-9318
WELLQUEST INTERNATIONAL INC.
230 5th Ave, New York, NY 10001
Phone: (212) 689-9094
Sales: $6,000,000   *Employees:* 6
Company Type: Private   *Employees here:* 6
SIC: 2833
   Mfg & whol natural vitamins & health products
Eddie Mishan, Owner

D-U-N-S 83-488-1195
WENDT PROFESSIONAL LABS
100 Nancy Dr, Belle Plaine, MN 56011
Phone: (612) 873-2288
Sales: $2,000,000   *Employees:* 25
Company Type: Private   *Employees here:* 25
SIC: 2834
   Mfg veterinary pharmaceuticals
Harley Blattner, President

D-U-N-S 04-222-4824
WEST COAST LABORATORIES INC.
116 E Alondra Blvd, Gardena, CA 90248
Phone: (310) 532-6720
Sales: $7,000,000   *Employees:* 50
Company Type: Private   *Employees here:* 15
SIC: 2834
   Mfg vitamins
Maurice Ovadia, President

D-U-N-S 05-525-9279   EXP
WEST LABORATORIES INC.
1305 Harvard Dr, Kankakee, IL 60901
Phone: (815) 935-2266
Sales: $2,914,000   *Employees:* 16
Company Type: Private   *Employees here:* 6
SIC: 2836
   Mfg animal blood plasmas and serums
Gary West, President

D-U-N-S 00-123-0762   EXP
WEST-WARD PHARMACEUTICAL CORP.
465 Industrial Way W, Eatontown, NJ 07724
Phone: (732) 542-1191
Sales: $15,784,000   *Employees:* 120
Company Type: Private   *Employees here:* 120
SIC: 2834
   Mfg generic pharmaceuticals
Nabil Rizk, President

D-U-N-S 05-312-4434   EXP
WESTAR NUTRITION CORP.
1239 Victoria St, Costa Mesa, CA 92627
Phone: (949) 645-6100
Sales: $21,000,000   *Employees:* 200
Company Type: Private   *Employees here:* 140
SIC: 2833
   Mfg vitamins over-the-counter drugs nutritional & skin care
      products & provides packaging & labeling services
David Fan, President

D-U-N-S 04-839-1080   EXP
WESTWOD-SQUIBB PHARMACEUTICALS
   (Parent: Bristol-Myers Squibb Company)
100 Forest Ave, Buffalo, NY 14213
Phone: (716) 887-3400
Sales: $200,000,000   *Employees:* 730
Company Type: Public Family Member   *Employees here:* 550
SIC: 2834
   Mfg pharmaceutical preparations
Jeffrey B Marsh, President

D-U-N-S 00-315-8011   EXP
WILCOX DRUG COMPANY INC.
   (Parent: Zuellig Group Na Inc)
755 George Wilson Rd, Boone, NC 28607
Phone: (828) 264-3615
Sales: $3,100,000   *Employees:* 33
Company Type: Private   *Employees here:* 30
SIC: 2833
   Procures crude medicinal drugs & botanicals
Charles H Wanzer, Vice-President

D-U-N-S 15-084-8125
WILSON GROUP INC.
N62w22632 Village Dr, Sussex, WI 53089
Phone: (414) 246-6922
Sales: $4,500,000   *Employees:* 70
Company Type: Private   *Employees here:* 15
SIC: 2836
   Mfg microbial/enzyme products investors & management
      services
Carol W Wilson, President

D-U-N-S 14-487-2652
WINNING COMBINATION INC.
430 Parkson Rd, Henderson, NV 89015
Phone: (702) 564-9000
Sales: $6,100,000
Company Type: Private
SIC: 2834
  Mfg vitamins
Andrew Lessman, Chief Executive Officer

Employees: 55
Employees here: 55

D-U-N-S 62-150-2475
WORLDWIDE GROUP OF CO. LTD. INC.
1425 Bedford St Fl 14, Stamford, CT 06905
Phone: (203) 323-6444
Sales: $16,800,000
Company Type: Private
SIC: 2833
  Medicinal products manufacturing and marketing services
Andrew Quinton, Chairman of the Board

Employees: 120
Employees here: 120

D-U-N-S 92-979-1275
WORLDWIDE SPORT NUTRITIONAL
10540 72nd St, Largo, FL 33777
Phone: (727) 547-5222
Sales: $3,400,000
Company Type: Private
SIC: 2834
  Mfg whol & ret sport nutritional supplements
Dave McCabe, President

Employees: 32
Employees here: 26

D-U-N-S 18-175-9101   EXP
WORTHINGTON BIOCHEMICAL CORP.
730 Vassar Ave, Lakewood, NJ 08701
Phone: (732) 942-1660
Sales: $3,700,000
Company Type: Private
SIC: 2835
  Mfg high purity enzymes for medical research
Von Worthington, President

Employees: 38
Employees here: 38

D-U-N-S 04-077-2527   EXP
WRIGHT ENRICHMENT INC.
6428 Airport Rd, Crowley, LA 70526
Phone: (318) 783-3096
Sales: $8,600,000
Company Type: Private
SIC: 2834
  Mfg vitamin enrichment mixture
Salmon L Wright III, President

Employees: 100
Employees here: 100

D-U-N-S 08-036-1454   EXP
WYCKOFF CHEMICAL COMPANY INC.
1421 Kalamazoo St, South Haven, MI 49090
Phone: (616) 637-8474
Sales: $31,429,000
Company Type: Private
SIC: 2833
  Mfg organic medicinal chemicals
Ronald Hartgerink, President

Employees: 150
Employees here: 150

D-U-N-S 00-232-3533
WYETH LABORATORIES INC.
  (*Parent:* American Home Products Corp)
555 E Lancaster Ave, Wayne, PA 19087
Phone: (610) 971-5400
Sales: $4,000,000,000
Company Type: Public Family Member
SIC: 2834
  Mfg pharmaceutical biological & medical products
Bernard Poussot, President

Employees: 4,000
Employees here: 675

D-U-N-S 00-300-3381
XF ENTERPRISES INC.
5626 W 19th St, Ste B, Greeley, CO 80634
Phone: (970) 339-4593
Sales: $18,882,000
Company Type: Private
SIC: 2834
  Mfg animal vitamin preparations
R H Klett, President

Employees: 75
Employees here: 12

D-U-N-S 05-134-0339
XOMA CORPORATION
2910 7th St, Ste 100, Berkeley, CA 94710
Phone: (510) 644-1170
Sales: $18,383,000
Company Type: Public
SIC: 2836
  Development production & marketing of biological products
John L Castello, Chairman of the Board

Employees: 160
Employees here: 140

D-U-N-S 36-117-6746
XYLUM CORPORATION
670 White Plains Rd, Scarsdale, NY 10583
Phone: (914) 725-0606
Sales: $3,000,000
Company Type: Private
SIC: 2835
  Mfg clot signature analyzer
Frank Burgel, President

Employees: 39
Employees here: 39

D-U-N-S 60-262-8075
YAMANOUCHI GROUP HOLDING INC.
444 Market St, San Francisco, CA 94111
Phone: (415) 954-3000
Sales: $655,600,000
Company Type: Private
SIC: 2834
  Holding company
Hisakazu Iizuka, President

Employees: 5,100
Employees here: 280

D-U-N-S 05-303-9186   EXP
YERBA PRIMA INC.
740 Jefferson Ave, Ashland, OR 97520
Phone: (541) 488-2228
Sales: $3,600,000
Company Type: Private
SIC: 2834
  Mfg dietary fiber laxatives & supplements
Richard Eatherly, President

Employees: 16
Employees here: 16

D-U-N-S 17-679-6548
YORK PHARMACEUTICALS INC.
1201 Douglas Ave, Kansas City, KS 66103
Phone: (913) 321-1070
Sales: $5,000,000
Company Type: Private
SIC: 2834
  Mfg pharmaceutical preparations
Patrick Lais, President

Employees: 40
Employees here: 5

D-U-N-S 61-298-2504   EXP
YS HEALTH CORPORATION
1117 N Main St, Lombard, IL 60148
Phone: (630) 620-2438
Sales: $7,405,000
Company Type: Private
SIC: 2833
  Mfg vitamins & honey
David Choi, President

Employees: 14
Employees here: 14

D-U-N-S 19-574-9791
ZAMBON CORPORATION
1 Meadowlands Plz Fl 14, East Rutherford, NJ 07073

Phone: (201) 896-2200
Sales: $5,379,000   *Employees:* 22
Company Type: Private   *Employees here:* 22
SIC: 2834
   Research and development of pharmaceutical preparations &
   products
Dr Daniel Sher MD, President

         D-U-N-S 88-407-5235
ZENITH GLDLINE PHARMACEUTICALS
   (Parent: IVAX Corporation)
4400 Biscayne Blvd, Miami, FL 33137
Phone: (305) 575-4100
Sales: $166,000,000   *Employees:* 1,300
Company Type: Public Family Member   *Employees here:* 4
SIC: 2834
   Mfg & market generic pharmaceuticals
Rafick G Henein, President

         D-U-N-S 10-409-6623
ZENITH LABORATORIES CARIBE
   (Parent: Zenith Laboratories Inc)
C St Lot 17 & 18, Cidra, PR 00739
Phone: (787) 739-8421
Sales: $60,000,000   *Employees:* 400
Company Type: Public Family Member   *Employees here:* 400
SIC: 2834
   Mfg pharmaceutical products
William Schreck, President

         D-U-N-S 00-147-9302
ZENITH LABORATORIES INC.
   (Parent: Zenith Gldline Pharmaceuticals)
140 Legrand Ave, Northvale, NJ 07647
Phone: (201) 767-1700
Sales: $73,300,000   *Employees:* 580
Company Type: Public Family Member   *Employees here:* 245
SIC: 2834
   Mfg pharmaceutical pdts
William Schreck, President

         D-U-N-S 01-422-4182   EXP
ZILA, INC.
5227 N 7th St, Ste 100, Phoenix, AZ 85014
Phone: (602) 266-6700
Sales: $62,107,000   *Employees:* 235
Company Type: Public   *Employees here:* 35
SIC: 2834
   Mfg pharmaceuticals
Joseph Hines, Chairman of the Board

         D-U-N-S 12-608-6024
ZUELLIG BOTANICALS INC.
   (Parent: Zuellig Group Na Inc)
2550 E El Presidio St, Long Beach, CA 90810
Phone: (310) 637-9566
Sales: $55,030,000   *Employees:* 130
Company Type: Private   *Employees here:* 96
SIC: 2833
   Mfg herbs spices and botanical products
Ralph Heimann, President

RANKINGS AND COMPANIES

The companies presented in Chapter 4 - Company Directory are arranged in this chapter in rank order based first on sales and next on employment. Each company's name, rank, location, type, sales, employment, and primary SIC are shown. Only companies with reported sales data are included in the "rankings by sales" table; similarly, only companies that report employment are ranked in the "rankings by employment" table.

Company type is either Public, Private, or Public Family Member. The last category is used to label corporate entities that belong to a group of companies, the relationship being that of a subsidiary or element of a parent. The parents of Public Family Member companies can be reviewed in the directory presented in Chapter 4.

This product includes proprietary data of Dun & Bradstreet, Inc.

D&B COMPANY RANKINGS BY SALES

Company	Rank	Location	Type	Sales ($ mil.)	Employ-ment	Primary SIC
Merck & Co Inc.	1	Whitehouse Station, NJ	Public	23,636.9	53,800	2834
Bristol-Myers Squibb Company	2	New York, NY	Public	16,701.0	53,600	2834
American Home Products Corp.	3	Madison, NJ	Public	14,196.0	60,523	2834
Pfizer Inc.	4	New York, NY	Public	12,504.0	49,200	2834
Abbott Laboratories	5	North Chicago, IL	Public	12,477.8	54,487	2834
Eli Lilly And Company	6	Indianapolis, IN	Public	8,517.6	31,100	2834
Novartis Corporation	7	Summit, NJ	Private	8,400.0	20,000	2834
Warner-Lambert Company	8	Morris Plains, NJ	Public	8,179.8	40,000	2834
Schering-Plough Corporation	9	Madison, NJ	Public	8,077.0	20,600	2834
Pharmacia & Upjohn Company	10	Bridgewater, NJ	Public Family Member	7,286.0	16,900	2834
Schering Corporation	11	Kenilworth, NJ	Public Family Member	6,778.0	18,400	2834
Smithkline Beecham Corporation	12	Philadelphia, PA	Private	6,661.9	21,600	2834
Pharmacia & Upjohn, Inc.	13	Bridgewater, NJ	Public	6,586.0	30,000	2834
Baxter International Inc.	14	Deerfield, IL	Public	6,138.0	41,000	2834
Wyeth Laboratories Inc.	15	Wayne, PA	Public Family Member	4,000.0	4,000	2834
Baxter Healthcare Corporation	16	Deerfield, IL	Public Family Member	3,763.0	15,000	2834
Astra Pharmaceuticals, LP	17	Wayne, PA	Private	2,700.0	3,800	2834
American Cyanamid Company	18	Parsippany, NJ	Public Family Member	2,575.0	20,000	2834
Hoffmann-La Roche Inc.	19	Nutley, NJ	Private	2,500.0	5,000	2834
Amgen Inc.	20	Thousand Oaks, CA	Public	2,401.0	5,308	2834
G D Searle & Co.	21	Skokie, IL	Public Family Member	1,999.0	8,700	2834
Roche Holdings, Inc.	22	Wilmington, DE	Private	1,735.1	13,480	2834
Pfizer Pharmaceuticals Inc.	23	Barceloneta, PR	Public Family Member	1,336.5	1,000	2834
Alcon Laboratories, Inc.	24	Fort Worth, TX	Private	1,253.0	4,500	2834
Rhone-Poulenc Rorer Pharmaceuticals	25	Collegeville, PA	Private	1,200.0	2,800	2834
Chiron Corporation	26	Emeryville, CA	Public	1,162.1	6,482	2835
Genentech Inc.	27	South San Francisco, CA	Public	1,150.9	3,242	2834
Allergan Inc.	28	Irvine, CA	Public	1,138.0	6,124	2834
Dade Behring Inc.	29	Deerfield, IL	Private	980.5	7,400	2835
Dade Behring Holdings	30	Deerfield, IL	Private	978.0	7,500	2835
Glaxo Welcome Americas Inc.	31	New York, NY	Private	964.7	7,500	2834
Centeon LLC	32	King Of Prussia, PA	Private	904.3	918	2836
Perrigo Company	33	Allegan, MI	Public	902.6	4,868	2834
Novartis Pharmaceuticals Corp.	34	East Hanover, NJ	Private	900.3	7,000	2834
Upjohn International Inc.	35	Kalamazoo, MI	Public Family Member	900.3	7,000	2834
IPR Pharmaceutical, Inc.	36	Carolina, PR	Private	900.0	530	2834
Bristol-Myers Squibb Laboratoires	37	Mayaguez, PR	Public Family Member	847.4	527	2834
Smithkline Beecham	38	Cidra, PR	Private	800.0	650	2834
ICN Pharmaceuticals, Inc.	39	Costa Mesa, CA	Public	752.2	17,000	2834
Schering Berlin Inc.	40	Montville, NJ	Private	718.5	2,100	2834
McNeil Consumer Products Pr	41	Las Piedras, PR	Public Family Member	700.0	500	2834
Scherng-Plough Healthcare Pdts	42	Liberty Corner, NJ	Public Family Member	700.0	1,235	2834
Shaklee Corporation	43	San Francisco, CA	Private	666.1	3,000	2834
Yamanouchi Group Holding Inc.	44	San Francisco, CA	Private	655.6	5,100	2834
Amgen Holding Inc.	45	Thousand Oaks, CA	Private	615.7	4,791	2834
Hoechst Marion Roussel Inc.	46	Kansas City, MO	Private	610.5	4,750	2834
Genzyme Corporation	47	Cambridge, MA	Public	608.8	2,500	2835
Ivax Corporation	48	Miami, FL	Public	602.1	4,500	2834
Bristol Caribbean Inc.	49	Mayaguez, PR	Public Family Member	600.0	89	2834
Searle, Ltd.	50	Barceloneta, PR	Public Family Member	600.0	492	2834
Berlex Laboratories Inc.	51	Montville, NJ	Private	576.3	1,440	2834
Merial Ltd.	52	Athens, GA	Private	575.0	1,800	2836
NBTY, Inc.	53	Bohemia, NY	Public	572.1	5,300	2834
Mylan Laboratories Inc.	54	Pittsburgh, PA	Public	555.4	1,946	2834
Leiner Health Products Inc.	55	Carson, CA	Private	502.1	1,683	2834
Squibb Manufacturing Inc.	56	Humacao, PR	Public Family Member	501.2	700	2834
Alpharma Inc.	57	Fort Lee, NJ	Public	500.3	700	2834
Tag Pharmaceuticals Inc.	58	Kulpsville, PA	Private	500.0	1,000	2834
Schein Pharmaceutical Inc.	59	Florham Park, NJ	Public	490.2	2,000	2834
Teva Pharmaceuticals USA Inc.	60	Sellersville, PA	Private	487.9	1,200	2834
Agouron Pharmaceuticals Inc.	61	La Jolla, CA	Public	466.5	991	2834
Cambrex Corporation	62	East Rutherford, NJ	Public	457.2	1,790	2834
Amgen Puerto Rico Inc.	63	Juncos, PR	Public Family Member	439.9	240	2836
Forest Laboratories Inc.	64	New York, NY	Public	427.1	1,854	2834
Bristol-Myers Barceloneta Inc.	65	Barceloneta, PR	Public Family Member	426.2	650	2834
Pharmacia & Upjohn Caribe	66	Arecibo, PR	Public Family Member	400.0	685	2834
Solvay Pharmaceuticals Inc.	67	Marietta, GA	Private	400.0	1,100	2834
Alpha Therapeutic Corporation	68	Los Angeles, CA	Private	384.7	2,800	2836
Green Cross Corp. Of America	69	Los Angeles, CA	Private	384.7	2,900	2836
Barr Laboratories Inc.	70	Pomona, NY	Public	377.3	557	2834

D&B COMPANY RANKINGS BY SALES

Company	Rank	Location	Type	Sales ($ mil.)	Employ-ment	Primary SIC
Boehringer Ingelheim Corp.	71	Ridgefield, CT	Private	358.0	2,790	2834
B. Braun/Mc Gaw, Inc.	72	Irvine, CA	Private	350.0	3,000	2834
Forest Pharmaceuticals Inc.	73	Earth City, MO	Public Family Member	350.0	1,150	2834
Roxane Laboratories Inc.	74	Columbus, OH	Private	350.0	900	2834
Connaught Laboratories Inc.	75	Swiftwater, PA	Private	333.5	970	2836
Life Technologies Inc.	76	Rockville, MD	Public	331.0	1,586	2836
Watson Pharmaceuticals, Inc.	77	Corona, CA	Public	324.0	2,554	2834
Lipha Americas Inc.	78	Napa, CA	Private	300.0	750	2834
Novopharm, USA Inc.	79	Schaumburg, IL	Private	300.0	65	2834
Organon Inc.	80	West Orange, NJ	Private	300.0	1,100	2834
Marion & Company	81	Manati, PR	Private	294.5	250	2834
Nature's Sunshine Products	82	Provo, UT	Public	280.9	966	2833
Amersham Holdings Inc.	83	Arlington Heights, IL	Private	270.0	1,050	2835
Mallinckrodt Chemical, Inc.	84	Hazelwood, MO	Public Family Member	258.1	2,000	2833
Mcneil Consumer Healthcare Co.	85	Fort Washington, PA	Public Family Member	256.2	2,000	2834
Searle & Co.	86	Caguas, PR	Public Family Member	256.1	650	2834
Fujisawa Healthcare, Inc.	87	Deerfield, IL	Private	240.0	1,000	2834
Nabi	88	Boca Raton, FL	Public	238.7	2,122	2836
Paco Pharmaceutical Services	89	Lakewood, NJ	Public Family Member	238.7	1,864	2834
Boehrnger Inglheim Pharmaceuticals	90	Ridgefield, CT	Private	230.4	1,800	2834
Novartis Crop Protection Inc.	91	Greensboro, NC	Private	230.4	1,800	2834
Bracco U.S.A. Inc.	92	Princeton, NJ	Private	228.3	290	2835
Chattem, Inc.	93	Chattanooga, TN	Public	220.1	364	2834
Dey Inc.	94	Napa, CA	Private	219.8	670	2834
Bracco Diagnostics Inc.	95	Princeton, NJ	Private	219.5	270	2835
Stiefel Laboratories Inc.	96	Coral Gables, FL	Private	214.1	1,470	2834
Altana Inc.	97	Melville, NY	Private	213.2	854	2834
Twin Laboratories Inc.	98	Hauppauge, NY	Public Family Member	213.2	701	2833
Twinlab Corporation	99	Hauppauge, NY	Public	213.2	734	2833
Janssen Pharmaceutica Inc.	100	Titusville, NJ	Public Family Member	206.2	1,600	2833
Abbott Health Products Inc.	101	North Chicago, IL	Public Family Member	201.4	1,575	2834
Centocor Inc.	102	Malvern, PA	Public	200.8	640	2834
Banner Pharmacaps Inc.	103	High Point, NC	Private	200.0	897	2834
London International Group Inc.	104	Norcross, GA	Private	200.0	900	2834
Westwod-Squibb Pharmaceuticals	105	Buffalo, NY	Public Family Member	200.0	730	2834
Diagnostic Products Corp.	106	Los Angeles, CA	Public	186.3	1,467	2835
Immunex Corporation	107	Seattle, WA	Public	185.3	886	2834
Dura Pharmaceuticals Inc.	108	San Diego, CA	Public	181.3	331	2834
Schwarz Pharma Inc.	109	Thiensville, WI	Private	179.4	475	2834
Leiner Health Products Group	110	Carson, CA	Private	178.9	1,400	2834
Genetics Institute Inc.	111	Cambridge, MA	Public Family Member	172.1	980	2834
Zenith Gldline Pharmaceuticals	112	Miami, FL	Public Family Member	166.0	1,300	2834
Lifescan Inc.	113	Milpitas, CA	Public Family Member	165.2	2,000	2835
Procter Gamble Pharmaceuticals	114	Cincinnati, OH	Public Family Member	164.7	1,290	2834
King Pharmaceuticals, Inc.	115	Bristol, TN	Public	163.5	1,000	2834
Rexall Showcase International	116	Boca Raton, FL	Public Family Member	159.0	200	2834
Alcon Puerto Rico Inc.	117	Fort Worth, TX	Private	157.0	251	2834
Galderma Laboratories Inc.	118	Fort Worth, TX	Private	156.8	179	2834
Melaleuca Inc.	119	Idaho Falls, ID	Private	154.3	1,200	2833
Pasteur Merieux Connaught	120	Swiftwater, PA	Private	153.1	1,200	2834
Roche Vitamins Inc.	121	Parsippany, NJ	Private	153.1	1,200	2834
Schering Plough Products Inc.	122	Manati, PR	Public Family Member	153.1	1,200	2834
Medi-Physics, Inc.	123	Arlington Heights, IL	Private	150.0	500	2833
Roberts Laboratories Inc.	124	Eatontown, NJ	Public Family Member	150.0	250	2834
Gensia Sicor Inc.	125	Irvine, CA	Public	149.7	1,124	2834
Berwind Pharmaceutical Svcs	126	West Point, PA	Private	142.0	600	2834
Dermik Laboratories Inc.	127	Collegeville, PA	Private	139.0	230	2834
Vivus Inc.	128	Mountain View, CA	Public	138.3	100	2834
Ortho Diagnostic Systems Inc.	129	Raritan, NJ	Public Family Member	132.1	1,600	2835
Lilly Del Caribe Inc.	130	Carolina, PR	Public Family Member	130.6	1,025	2834
Pharmaceutical Holdings Corp.	131	Philadelphia, PA	Private	130.0	350	2834
Nutramax Products, Inc.	132	Gloucester, MA	Public	128.4	1,200	2834
Fisons US Investment Holdings	133	Wilmington, DE	Private	127.4	1,000	2834
Sobel Usa Inc.	134	West Orange, NJ	Private	127.4	1,000	2834
Mylan Pharmaceuticals Inc.	135	Morgantown, WV	Public Family Member	123.5	970	2834
Roberts Pharmaceutical Corp.	136	Eatontown, NJ	Public	122.5	448	2834
Copley Pharmaceutical, Inc.	137	Canton, MA	Public	121.5	404	2834
Boehringer Ingelheim Vetmedica	138	Saint Joseph, MO	Private	120.0	550	2836
General Nutrition Products Inc.	139	Pittsburgh, PA	Public Family Member	120.0	800	2834
IVC Industries, Inc.	140	Freehold, NJ	Public	119.8	691	2834

D&B COMPANY RANKINGS BY SALES

Company	Rank	Location	Type	Sales ($ mil.)	Employ-ment	Primary SIC
Rhone-Poulenc Rorer	141	Manati, PR	Private	118.4	275	2834
Centeon Bio-Services Inc.	142	Knoxville, TN	Private	108.9	1,800	2836
Sigma Chemical Company	143	Saint Louis, MO	Public Family Member	108.9	1,800	2836
Danbury Pharmacal Inc.	144	Carmel, NY	Public Family Member	108.1	850	2834
Nutraceutical International	145	Park City, UT	Public	104.7	450	2834
E-Z-Em, Inc.	146	Westbury, NY	Public	102.9	923	2835
Faulding Inc.	147	Elizabeth, NJ	Private	102.1	479	2834
Smithkline Beecham Puerto Rico	148	Philadelphia, PA	Private	101.7	801	2834
Merck Holdings, Inc.	149	Whitehouse Station, NJ	Public Family Member	101.6	800	2834
Weider Health and Fitness	150	Woodland Hills, CA	Private	101.6	800	2834
Amersham Corporation	151	Arlington Heights, IL	Private	100.0	383	2835
Pharmaceutical Research Assoc.	152	Norwalk, CT	Private	100.0	650	2834
PRA Holdings, Inc.	153	Norwalk, CT	Private	100.0	650	2834
Purdue Pharma Company	154	Norwalk, CT	Private	100.0	2	2834
Purdue Pharma LP	155	Norwalk, CT	Private	100.0	550	2834
The Frederick Purdue Company	156	Norwalk, CT	Private	100.0	207	2834
Vita Quest International Inc.	157	Caldwell, NJ	Private	100.0	425	2834
KV Pharmaceutical Company	158	Saint Louis, MO	Public	98.5	358	2834
Watson Laboratories, Inc.	159	Corona, CA	Public Family Member	96.5	760	2834
Mentholatum Company Inc.	160	Orchard Park, NY	Private	95.0	150	2834
Chirex, Inc.	161	Stamford, CT	Private	94.1	360	2833
Geneva Pharmaceuticals, Inc.	162	Broomfield, CO	Private	93.9	740	2834
Immuno - U S Inc.	163	Rochester, MI	Private	93.9	660	2836
Chugai Pharma USA Inc.	164	San Diego, CA	Private	92.1	292	2835
Nexstar Pharmaceuticals Inc.	165	Boulder, CO	Public	89.2	580	2834
Jones Pharma Inc.	166	Saint Louis, MO	Public	88.8	235	2834
AC Molding Compounds	167	Wallingford, CT	Private	88.7	700	2834
Alpharma USPD Inc.	168	Baltimore, MD	Public Family Member	88.7	700	2834
Usana Inc.	169	Salt Lake City, UT	Public	85.2	359	2833
Muro Pharmaceutical Inc.	170	Tewksbury, MA	Private	85.0	320	2834
Sidmak Laboratories Inc.	171	East Hanover, NJ	Private	84.2	470	2834
Collagen Aesthetics, Inc.	172	Palo Alto, CA	Public	82.8	280	2836
Johnson Johnson Phrm Partners	173	Gurabo, PR	Private	82.3	650	2834
Pharmavite Corporation	174	Mission Hills, CA	Private	82.0	642	2833
Pharmaceutical Formulations	175	Edison, NJ	Public	80.8	378	2834
Roche Colorado Corp.	176	Boulder, CO	Private	80.0	290	2833
Ganes Chemicals, Inc.	177	Carlstadt, NJ	Private	77.3	275	2833
Promega Corporation	178	Madison, WI	Private	76.0	510	2836
Warner Chilcott, Inc.	179	Rockaway, NJ	Private	75.8	50	2834
Merrell Pharmaceuticals Inc.	180	Cincinnati, OH	Private	75.8	600	2834
Perrigo Company	181	Greenville, SC	Public Family Member	75.0	285	2834
Purepac Pharmaceutical Co.	182	Elizabeth, NJ	Private	75.0	301	2834
Zenith Laboratories Inc.	183	Northvale, NJ	Public Family Member	73.3	580	2834
Quigley Corp.	184	Doylestown, PA	Public	71.0	16	2834
Granutec Inc.	185	Wilson, NC	Private	70.0	400	2834
Neways Inc.	186	Salem, UT	Private	70.0	300	2833
Aesthetic Technologies Corp.	187	Palo Alto, CA	Public Family Member	69.3	200	2836
DPT Laboratories Ltd.	188	San Antonio, TX	Private	68.6	550	2834
Natural Alternatives Intl	189	San Marcos, CA	Public	67.9	130	2833
Techne Corporation	190	Minneapolis, MN	Public	67.3	450	2835
HCCP Acquisition Corporation	191	Somerville, NJ	Private	64.3	510	2834
Elan Pharmaceuticals	192	South San Francisco, CA	Private	63.0	500	2834
Parke Davis Pharmaceuticals Ltd.	193	Vega Baja, PR	Private	63.0	500	2834
Nycomed Amersham, Inc.	194	Princeton, NJ	Private	62.8	760	2835
Zila, Inc.	195	Phoenix, AZ	Public	62.1	235	2834
Biowhittaker Inc.	196	Walkersville, MD	Public Family Member	60.0	400	2836
Inovision Holdings LP	197	Yorba Linda, CA	Private	60.0	400	2835
Zenith Laboratories Caribe	198	Cidra, PR	Public Family Member	60.0	400	2834
Plantation Botanicals, Inc.	199	Felda, FL	Private	59.6	500	2833
Research And Diagnstc Systems	200	Minneapolis, MN	Public Family Member	57.3	390	2833
Baxter Caribe, Inc.	201	Guayama, PR	Private	57.0	211	2833
BFG Clinipad Investors, LP	202	Philadelphia, PA	Private	56.8	452	2834
Abbott Diagnostics Inc.	203	Barceloneta, PR	Public Family Member	56.5	NA	2834
Lederle Parenterals Inc.	204	Carolina, PR	Public Family Member	56.5	450	2834
F.A.M.G. Inc.	205	Santa Clarita, CA	Private	56.0	85	2833
Mova Pharmaceutical Corp.	206	Caguas, PR	Private	55.8	744	2834
Del Pharmaceuticals Inc.	207	Uniondale, NY	Public Family Member	55.7	100	2834
Zuellig Botanicals Inc.	208	Long Beach, CA	Private	55.0	130	2833
Pharmaceutical Resources, Inc.	209	Spring Valley, NY	Public	53.2	340	2834
Par Pharmaceutical, Inc.	210	Spring Valley, NY	Public Family Member	53.1	340	2834

D&B COMPANY RANKINGS BY SALES

Company	Rank	Location	Type	Sales ($ mil.)	Employ-ment	Primary SIC
Global Health Sciences Corp.	211	Orange, CA	Private	52.7	224	2834
Amphastar Pharmaceuticals Inc.	212	Chino, CA	Private	51.4	410	2834
PDK Labs Inc.	213	Hauppauge, NY	Public	51.4	162	2834
Mission Pharmacal Company	214	San Antonio, TX	Private	51.3	225	2834
Bausch & Lomb Pharmaceuticals	215	Tampa, FL	Public Family Member	50.1	400	2834
Sankyo Pharma Inc.	216	Shirley, NY	Private	50.1	400	2834
DFB Holding Inc.	217	San Antonio, TX	Private	50.0	18	2834
Bertek Pharmaceuticals, Inc.	218	Sugar Land, TX	Public Family Member	50.0	250	2834
Danbury Pharmacal Puerto Rico	219	Humacao, PR	Public Family Member	50.0	130	2834
Delavau J W S Co Inc.	220	Philadelphia, PA	Private	50.0	300	2834
HVL Inc.	221	Pittsburgh, PA	Private	50.0	200	2833
Internationa Medication System	222	El Monte, CA	Private	50.0	380	2834
Quidel Corporation	223	San Diego, CA	Public	49.5	300	2835
Diosynth Inc.	224	Chicago, IL	Private	48.0	33	2836
Aim International, Inc.	225	Nampa, ID	Private	47.8	150	2833
Scios Inc.	226	Mountain View, CA	Public	47.4	350	2834
Mgp Holding Corp	227	Morton Grove, IL	Private	47.0	170	2834
Reliv' International Inc.	228	Chesterfield, MO	Public	46.8	170	2834
Luitpold Pharmaceuticals, Inc.	229	Shirley, NY	Private	45.7	366	2834
Amoco Technology Company	230	Downers Grove, IL	Private	45.0	NA	2835
Mylan Inc.	231	Caguas, PR	Public Family Member	45.0	123	2834
R.I.T.A. Corporation	232	Woodstock, IL	Private	45.0	118	2833
Tishcon Corp.	233	Westbury, NY	Private	45.0	280	2834
F P Syntex Inc.	234	Humacao, PR	Private	44.9	360	2834
Pharmingen	235	San Diego, CA	Public Family Member	44.0	300	2835
V I Technologies, Inc.	236	Melville, NY	Public	44.0	275	2834
Steris Laboratories, Inc.	237	Phoenix, AZ	Public Family Member	43.6	350	2834
Natrol Inc.	238	Chatsworth, CA	Public	42.9	185	2834
Akorn, Inc.	239	Buffalo Grove, IL	Public	42.3	266	2834
Schwarz Pharma Manufacturing	240	Seymour, IN	Private	41.3	225	2834
Medicis Pharmaceutical Corp.	241	Phoenix, AZ	Public	41.2	90	2834
Richardson-Vicks Inc.	242	Cincinnati, OH	Public Family Member	40.4	325	2834
Gilead Sciences, Inc.	243	Foster City, CA	Public	40.0	289	2834
Eon Labs Manufacturing, Inc.	244	Springfield Gardens, NY	Private	40.0	200	2834
Ex-Lax Inc.	245	Humacao, PR	Private	40.0	100	2834
International Frutarom Corp.	246	North Bergen, NJ	Private	40.0	130	2833
Marsam Pharmaceuticals, Inc.	247	Cherry Hill, NJ	Public Family Member	40.0	260	2834
Sequus Pharmaceuticals Inc.	248	Menlo Park, CA	Public	40.0	260	2834
Immucor Inc.	249	Norcross, GA	Public	39.8	229	2835
Theratech Inc.	250	Salt Lake City, UT	Public	39.7	243	2834
CN Biosciences, Inc.	251	San Diego, CA	Public	39.4	230	2836
ICN Biomedicals, Inc.	252	Costa Mesa, CA	Public Family Member	38.0	460	2835
Natural Organics Inc.	253	Melville, NY	Private	37.6	300	2833
Threshold Enterprises Ltd.	254	Scotts Valley, CA	Private	37.6	300	2833
Baxter Pharmaceutical Products	255	Liberty Corner, NJ	Public Family Member	37.2	300	2834
Proctor & Gamble Health Pdts	256	Cayey, PR	Public Family Member	37.2	300	2834
Chemins Company Inc.	257	Colorado Springs, CO	Private	37.0	155	2834
Invamed Incorporated	258	Dayton, NJ	Private	37.0	160	2834
Enzymatic Therapy Inc.	259	Green Bay, WI	Private	35.6	285	2833
Fortitech Inc.	260	Schenectady, NY	Private	35.0	59	2834
JRH Biosciences, Inc.	261	Shawnee Mission, KS	Private	35.0	140	2836
Medeva Pharmacueticals Mfg.	262	Rochester, NY	Private	34.2	277	2834
Igi Inc.	263	Buena, NJ	Public	34.2	209	2836
Frutarom Meer Corporation	264	North Bergen, NJ	Private	33.3	160	2833
Du Pont Pharmaceuticals Co.	265	Manati, PR	Private	33.3	270	2834
Agri-Nutrition Group Limited	266	Maryland Heights, MO	Public	32.9	220	2834
Biomatrix, Inc.	267	Ridgefield, NJ	Public	32.6	350	2836
Armstrong Laboratories Inc.	268	West Roxbury, MA	Private	32.3	200	2834
Hauser Inc.	269	Boulder, CO	Public	32.0	354	2833
Gensia Sicor Pharmaceuticals	270	Irvine, CA	Public Family Member	32.0	260	2834
Invitrogen Corporation	271	Carlsbad, CA	Public	32.0	165	2836
Nutro Laboratories Inc.	272	South Plainfield, NJ	Private	32.0	140	2834
Biosite Diagnostics Inc.	273	San Diego, CA	Public	31.7	209	2835
E R Sqibb Sons Intr-Mrcan Corp	274	Princeton, NJ	Public Family Member	31.6	200	2834
Icos Corporation	275	Bothell, WA	Public	31.6	275	2834
Wyckoff Chemical Company Inc.	276	South Haven, MI	Private	31.4	150	2833
Evergood Products Corporation	277	Hicksville, NY	Private	31.0	95	2833
Advanced Nutraceuticals Inc.	278	South Plainfield, NJ	Private	30.8	195	2834
Mutual Pharmaceutical Company	279	Philadelphia, PA	Private	30.8	NA	2834
PF Laboratories, Inc.	280	Totowa, NJ	Private	30.8	250	2834

D&B COMPANY RANKINGS BY SALES

Company	Rank	Location	Type	Sales ($ mil.)	Employ- ment	Primary SIC
Pfizer Corporation	281	New York, NY	Private	30.8	250	2834
Solopak Laboratories Inc.	282	Elk Grove Village, IL	Private	30.8	250	2834
Phoenix Scientific Inc.	283	Saint Joseph, MO	Private	30.4	125	2834
Intergen Company	284	Purchase, NY	Private	30.0	100	2836
Universal Protein Supplements	285	New Brunswick, NJ	Private	29.7	200	2834
Mikart Inc.	286	Atlanta, GA	Private	29.6	170	2834
Cygnus, Inc.	287	Redwood City, CA	Public	29.5	157	2834
Humco Holding Group, Inc.	288	Texarkana, TX	Private	29.5	240	2834
PLP, Ltd.	289	Texarkana, TX	Private	29.5	240	2834
Systemix Inc.	290	Palo Alto, CA	Private	29.5	240	2834
Glenwood LLC	291	Tenafly, NJ	Private	28.3	180	2834
Rx For Fleas Inc.	292	Fort Lauderdale, FL	Private	28.2	200	2834
Diasorin Inc.	293	Stillwater, MN	Public Family Member	28.1	340	2835
Blistex Inc.	294	Oak Brook, IL	Private	28.0	126	2834
Jeunique International Inc.	295	City Of Industry, CA	Private	27.9	225	2833
Remel Inc.	296	Shawnee Mission, KS	Private	27.8	NA	2836
Medeva MA, Inc.	297	Boston, MA	Private	27.7	173	2834
Medimmune, Inc.	298	Gaithersburg, MD	Public	27.4	350	2836
Elanco Animal House Inc.	299	Indianapolis, IN	Public Family Member	27.0	200	2834
Fujirebio Diagnostic Inc.	300	Malvern, PA	Private	27.0	60	2835
D & F Industries Inc.	301	Orange, CA	Private	26.9	220	2834
Taylor Pharmaceuticals Inc.	302	Decatur, IL	Public Family Member	26.9	220	2834
Colgate Oral Pharmaceuticals	303	Canton, MA	Public Family Member	26.7	188	2834
G & W Laboratories Inc.	304	South Plainfield, NJ	Private	26.6	200	2834
Amide Pharmaceutical Inc.	305	Little Falls, NJ	Private	26.2	90	2834
Neurocrine Biosciences Inc.	306	San Diego, CA	Public	26.1	126	2835
Central Admixture Phrm Svcs	307	Irvine, CA	Private	26.0	130	2834
Nittany Pharmaceuticals Inc.	308	Milroy, PA	Private	25.5	175	2834
Nutraceutical Corporation	309	Ogden, UT	Public Family Member	25.3	208	2834
Apothecary Products Inc.	310	Burnsville, MN	Private	25.0	200	2834
Covance Biotechnology Services	311	Research Triangle Pa, NC	Public Family Member	25.0	208	2834
Global Source Mgt & Consulting	312	Hollywood, FL	Private	25.0	17	2834
International Processing Corp.	313	Winchester, KY	Private	25.0	180	2834
Sportpharma USA Inc.	314	Concord, CA	Private	25.0	22	2833
Valentine Enterprises Inc.	315	Lawrenceville, GA	Private	25.0	35	2834
JB Laboratories Inc.	316	Holland, MI	Private	24.9	175	2833
Axys Pharmaceuticals, Inc.	317	South San Francisco, CA	Public	24.8	256	2834
E Excel International Inc.	318	Springville, UT	Private	24.6	100	2833
Difco Laboratories Inc.	319	Livonia, MI	Public Family Member	24.2	400	2836
Novo Nordisk Phrm Inds Inc.	320	Clayton, NC	Private	23.9	145	2833
Cell Genesys, Inc.	321	Foster City, CA	Public	23.8	177	2836
Ferndale Laboratories Inc.	322	Ferndale, MI	Private	23.8	210	2834
Carrington Laboratories Inc.	323	Irving, TX	Public	23.6	252	2834
Synbiotics Corporation	324	San Diego, CA	Public	23.3	63	2836
Bariatrix International Inc.	325	South Burlington, VT	Private	23.0	26	2834
Morton Grove Pharmaceuticals	326	Morton Grove, IL	Private	23.0	170	2834
Merial Select, Inc.	327	Gainesville, GA	Private	22.9	378	2836
Hi-Tech Pharmacal Co, Inc.	328	Amityville, NY	Public	22.4	135	2834
B I Chemicals Inc.	329	Ridgefield, CT	Private	22.3	150	2834
Boston Biomedica, Inc.	330	West Bridgewater, MA	Public	22.3	250	2835
Therapeutics Inc.	331	South San Francisco, CA	Public	22.2	152	2834
Calbiochem-Novabiochem Corp.	332	San Diego, CA	Public Family Member	21.5	150	2836
Streck Laboratories Inc.	333	Omaha, NE	Private	21.5	220	2835
Applicare, Inc.	334	Louisville, KY	Private	21.3	160	2834
Mast Immunosystems, Inc.	335	Mountain View, CA	Private	21.3	190	2835
Kabco Pharmaceuticals, Inc.	336	Amityville, NY	Private	21.0	98	2834
Westar Nutrition Corp.	337	Costa Mesa, CA	Private	21.0	200	2833
Roche Products Inc.	338	Humacao, PR	Private	20.7	200	2834
Immunogenetics Inc.	339	Buena, NJ	Public Family Member	20.6	150	2834
Biosource International Inc.	340	Camarillo, CA	Public	20.6	68	2836
Paddock Laboratories Inc.	341	Minneapolis, MN	Private	20.4	110	2834
Protein Design Labs Inc.	342	Fremont, CA	Public	20.3	217	2834
Hycor Biomedical Inc.	343	Garden Grove, CA	Public	20.1	220	2835
Amerifit, Inc.	344	Bloomfield, CT	Private	20.0	54	2833
Clay-Park Laboratories Inc.	345	Bronx, NY	Private	20.0	720	2834
G C Hanford Mfg Co Inc.	346	Syracuse, NY	Private	20.0	240	2834
Merz, Incorporated	347	Greensboro, NC	Private	20.0	70	2834
Milex Products, Inc.	348	Chicago, IL	Private	20.0	NA	2834
Science International Inc.	349	Daphne, AL	Private	20.0	42	2834
Syntron Bioresearch, Inc.	350	Carlsbad, CA	Private	20.0	278	2835

D&B COMPANY RANKINGS BY SALES

Company	Rank	Location	Type	Sales ($ mil.)	Employ-ment	Primary SIC
Traco Labs Inc.	351	Champaign, IL	Private	20.0	30	2833
W F Young Incorporated	352	Springfield, MA	Private	20.0	28	2834
Qualis Inc.	353	Des Moines, IA	Private	19.9	180	2834
Affymetrix, Inc.	354	Santa Clara, CA	Public	19.8	242	2835
Salsbury Chemicals, Inc.	355	Charles City, IA	Public Family Member	19.7	180	2833
Country Farms Inc.	356	Fairfield, NJ	Private	19.3	150	2834
D V M Pharmaceuticals Inc.	357	Miami, FL	Public Family Member	19.3	80	2834
Vitatech International Inc.	358	Tustin, CA	Private	19.3	150	2834
Intervet Inc.	359	Millsboro, DE	Private	19.1	315	2836
Ansys Diagnostics Inc.	360	Lake Forest, CA	Private	19.0	241	2835
XF Enterprises Inc.	361	Greeley, CO	Private	18.9	75	2834
Scantibodies Laboratory Inc.	362	Santee, CA	Private	18.9	280	2835
AMT Labs Inc.	363	North Salt Lake, UT	Private	18.8	22	2833
Xoma Corporation	364	Berkeley, CA	Public	18.4	160	2836
Roche Carolina Inc.	365	Florence, SC	Private	18.3	150	2834
Gamma Biologicals Inc.	366	Houston, TX	Public Family Member	18.3	113	2835
Vysis, Inc.	367	Downers Grove, IL	Public	18.2	153	2835
UDL Laboratories Inc.	368	Largo, FL	Public Family Member	18.1	130	2833
Marlyn Nutraceuticals, Inc.	369	Scottsdale, AZ	Private	18.0	80	2833
National Vitamin Co Inc.	370	Porterville, CA	Private	18.0	120	2834
Pharmacia Hepar Inc.	371	Franklin, OH	Public Family Member	18.0	60	2833
Prolab Nutrition Inc.	372	Bloomfield, CT	Private	18.0	14	2834
Remington Health Products LLC	373	Fort Worth, TX	Private	18.0	8	2834
SP Pharmaceuticals, LLC	374	Albuquerque, NM	Private	18.0	180	2834
Phoenix Laboratories Inc.	375	Hicksville, NY	Private	18.0	4	2833
Robinson Pharma, Inc.	376	Santa Ana, CA	Private	17.8	150	2834
Merial Ah Inc.	377	Athens, GA	Private	17.6	138	2834
Grand Laboratories Inc.	378	Freeman, SD	Private	17.5	160	2836
One Lambda Inc.	379	Canoga Park, CA	Private	17.5	120	2833
Bartels Inc.	380	Issaquah, WA	Private	17.0	125	2835
Hoechst Marion Roussel	381	Guaynabo, PR	Private	17.0	25	2834
Biovail Laboratories Inc.	382	Carolina, PR	Private	16.9	90	2834
Irvine Scientific Sales Co.	383	Santa Ana, CA	Private	16.9	100	2836
Worldwide Group Of Co. Ltd. Inc.	384	Stamford, CT	Private	16.8	120	2833
Solaray Inc.	385	Park City, UT	Public Family Member	16.7	NA	2834
Natural Balance Inc.	386	Castle Rock, CO	Private	16.4	140	2834
Syntex Agribusiness Inc.	387	Springfield, MO	Private	16.3	125	2834
Accucorp Packaging Inc.	388	Philadelphia, PA	Private	16.2	120	2834
Healthpoint Ltd.	389	Fort Worth, TX	Private	16.1	115	2834
Chuck Mills	390	Brea, CA	Private	16.0	1	2833
Ferring Pharmaceuticals Inc.	391	Tarrytown, NY	Private	16.0	35	2834
Oclassen Pharmaceuticals Inc.	392	San Rafael, CA	Public Family Member	16.0	106	2834
Applied Biotech, Inc.	393	San Diego, CA	Private	16.0	175	2835
Goldcaps, Inc.	394	Miami, FL	Public Family Member	15.8	2	2834
Halocarbon Products Corp.	395	River Edge, NJ	Private	15.8	123	2834
Proclinical Inc.	396	Phoenixville, PA	Private	15.8	105	2834
West-Ward Pharmaceutical Corp.	397	Eatontown, NJ	Private	15.8	120	2834
Progenics Pharmaceuticals Inc.	398	Tarrytown, NY	Public	15.6	30	2834
Scientific Protein Labs	399	Waunakee, WI	Public Family Member	15.6	120	2834
OHM Laboratories Inc.	400	North Brunswick, NJ	Private	15.5	100	2834
Ranlab Inc.	401	Princeton, NJ	Private	15.5	80	2834
Abbott Chemicals Inc.	402	Barceloneta, PR	Public Family Member	15.4	166	2833
Ranbaxy Pharmaceuticals Inc.	403	Princeton, NJ	Private	15.3	20	2834
Neogen Corporation	404	Lansing, MI	Public	15.3	200	2835
Sergeant's Pet Products, Inc.	405	Omaha, NE	Public Family Member	15.2	140	2834
Noven Pharmaceuticals Inc.	406	Miami, FL	Public	15.2	160	2834
Carma Laboratories, Inc.	407	Franklin, WI	Private	15.2	55	2834
Calix Corporation	408	Lexington, MA	Private	15.1	99	2834
Pharm-Eco Laboratories Inc.	409	Lexington, MA	Private	15.1	99	2834
ALK Laboratories Inc.	410	Wallingford, CT	Private	15.0	53	2836
All American Pharmaceuticals	411	Billings, MT	Private	15.0	55	2834
American Ingredients Inc.	412	Anaheim, CA	Private	15.0	14	2833
Elan Transdermal Technologies	413	Pembroke Pines, FL	Private	15.0	100	2834
Ess Group, Inc.	414	Vincentown, NJ	Private	15.0	40	2835
Health Factors International	415	Tempe, AZ	Public Family Member	15.0	100	2833
Interhealth Nutritionals, Inc.	416	Concord, CA	Private	15.0	30	2833
Napp Technologies Inc.	417	Saddle Brook, NJ	Private	15.0	36	2834
Pacific International	418	Saratoga, CA	Private	15.0	45	2835
Pharmanex Inc.	419	Simi Valley, CA	Private	15.0	44	2834
Time-Cap Laboratories Inc.	420	Farmingdale, NY	Private	15.0	55	2834

D&B COMPANY RANKINGS BY SALES

Company	Rank	Location	Type	Sales ($ mil.)	Employ-ment	Primary SIC
Bentley Pharmaceuticals Inc.	421	Tampa, FL	Public	14.9	110	2834
Stratagene	422	La Jolla, CA	Private	14.9	200	2836
Microcide Pharmaceuticals	423	Mountain View, CA	Public	14.9	150	2834
Enzo Diagnostics Inc.	424	Farmingdale, NY	Public Family Member	14.5	30	2835
Corange International Limited	425	Ponce, PR	Private	14.4	NA	2833
Anthony Products Co.	426	Arcadia, CA	Private	14.4	50	2834
Corixa Corporation	427	Seattle, WA	Public	14.4	104	2834
Noramco, (Delaware) Inc.	428	New Brunswick, NJ	Public Family Member	14.3	100	2833
Thames Pharmacal Co Inc.	429	Ronkonkoma, NY	Private	14.3	96	2834
Greer Laboratories Inc.	430	Lenoir, NC	Private	14.3	205	2836
Champion Performance Products	431	Concord, CA	Private	14.2	42	2834
Dynagen Inc.	432	Cambridge, MA	Public	14.0	140	2834
Guy & O'Neill, Inc.	433	Fredonia, WI	Private	14.0	150	2834
Soft Gel Technologies, Inc.	434	Los Angeles, CA	Private	14.0	38	2834
Spafas, Incorporated	435	Preston, CT	Public Family Member	14.0	141	2836
PML Microbiologicals Inc.	436	Wilsonville, OR	Public Family Member	13.9	184	2836
PMLl Inc.	437	Wilsonville, OR	Public	13.9	185	2836
Scherer Healthcare Inc.	438	Atlanta, GA	Public	13.9	130	2834
Gliatech Inc.	439	Cleveland, OH	Public	13.1	55	2834
Gynetics Inc.	440	Belle Mead, NJ	Private	13.0	10	2834
ICN East, Inc.	441	New York, NY	Public Family Member	13.0	88	2834
Alcide Corporation	442	Redmond, WA	Public	13.0	15	2834
Genelabs Technologies, Inc.	443	Redwood City, CA	Public	12.8	147	2834
Enzon Inc.	444	Piscataway, NJ	Public	12.7	85	2834
Pure World Inc.	445	Bedminster, NJ	Public	12.7	70	2833
Biogenex Laboratories	446	San Ramon, CA	Private	12.7	125	2835
Elan Pharmaceutical Res	447	Gainesville, GA	Private	12.5	174	2834
Hercon Laboratories Corp.	448	New York, NY	Public Family Member	12.5	90	2834
Penederm Incorporated	449	Foster City, CA	Public Family Member	12.5	95	2834
Procter Gamble Pharmaceuticals	450	Manati, PR	Public Family Member	12.5	125	2834
MGI Pharma, Inc.	451	Hopkins, MN	Public	12.4	65	2834
Shaperite Concepts, Ltd.	452	Sandy, UT	Private	12.4	105	2833
Hemagen Diagnostics Inc.	453	Waltham, MA	Public	12.3	109	2835
Stratagene Holding Corp.	454	La Jolla, CA	Private	12.2	201	2836
Lederle Piperacillin Inc.	455	Carolina, PR	Public Family Member	12.1	114	2834
Matrix Pharmaceutical Inc.	456	Fremont, CA	Public	12.1	162	2836
Digene Corporation	457	Beltsville, MD	Public	12.0	135	2835
A & V Incorporated	458	Sussex, WI	Private	12.0	50	2836
Alra Laboratories Inc.	459	Gurnee, IL	Private	12.0	80	2834
Eurand America Incorporated	460	Vandalia, OH	Public Family Member	12.0	67	2834
Guardian Drug Company Inc.	461	Trenton, NJ	Private	12.0	90	2834
Heico Chemicals, Inc.	462	Delaware Water Gap, PA	Public Family Member	12.0	48	2833
Interntnal Bchmicals Group Inc.	463	The Woodlands, TX	Private	12.0	120	2836
Manhattan Drug Co. Inc.	464	Hillside, NJ	Public Family Member	12.0	75	2834
Medpharm Inc.	465	Washington, DC	Private	12.0	12	2834
Schering-Plough Veterinary	466	Baton Rouge, LA	Public Family Member	12.0	60	2834
Vita Elixir Company Inc.	467	Atlanta, GA	Private	12.0	3	2834
Cocensys Inc.	468	Irvine, CA	Public	11.9	107	2834
Elan Holdings Inc.	469	Smithfield, RI	Private	11.9	80	2834
Fleming & Company Inc.	470	Fenton, MO	Private	11.9	110	2834
Merial Limited	471	Fort Dodge, IA	Private	11.8	NA	2834
Molecular Probes Inc.	472	Eugene, OR	Private	11.8	148	2835
Hess & Clark, Inc.	473	Ashland, OH	Public Family Member	11.7	105	2834
London International Group Inc.	474	Norcross, GA	Private	11.7	NA	2834
Miravant Pharmaceuticals Inc.	475	Goleta, CA	Public Family Member	11.7	90	2834
Genosys Biotechnologies, Inc.	476	The Woodlands, TX	Private	11.7	130	2833
Faulding, Inc.	477	Aguadilla, PR	Private	11.5	NA	2834
Lonza Biologics Inc.	478	Portsmouth, NH	Private	11.5	NA	2834
Cardiovascular Dynamics Inc.	479	Irvine, CA	Public	11.3	170	2834
Food Science Corp.	480	Essex Junction, VT	Private	11.3	54	2833
Parkedale Pharmaceutical Inc.	481	Rochester, MI	Public Family Member	11.3	100	2834
Puritan Quartz, Inc.	482	Santa Clarita, CA	Private	11.2	85	2833
Chem International Inc.	483	Hillside, NJ	Public	11.1	100	2834
Pel-Freez, Inc.	484	Rogers, AR	Private	11.1	142	2835
Boiron Borneman Inc.	485	Newtown Square, PA	Private	11.0	70	2833
Advanced Magnetics Inc.	486	Cambridge, MA	Public	11.0	68	2834
Chester Labs, Inc.	487	Cincinnati, OH	Private	11.0	70	2834
Particle Dynamics Inc.	488	Saint Louis, MO	Public Family Member	11.0	26	2834
Pro Pac Labs Inc.	489	Ogden, UT	Private	10.9	80	2834
Medical Analysis Systems Inc.	490	Camarillo, CA	Private	10.9	120	2835

D&B COMPANY RANKINGS BY SALES

Company	Rank	Location	Type	Sales ($ mil.)	Employment	Primary SIC
Ash Corp.	491	Gulfport, MS	Private	10.8	98	2834
Botanical Laboratories Inc.	492	Ferndale, WA	Private	10.8	84	2834
Fibrogen, Inc.	493	South San Francisco, CA	Private	10.8	75	2834
Lafayette Pharmaceuticals Inc.	494	Yorba Linda, CA	Private	10.8	100	2835
Shire Laboratories Inc.	495	Rockville, MD	Private	10.8	93	2834
Inova Diagnostics, Inc.	496	San Diego, CA	Private	10.7	86	2835
Middle States Management Corp.	497	Saint Louis, MO	Private	10.7	100	2834
Norwich Overseas, Inc.	498	Cincinnati, OH	Public Family Member	10.7	100	2834
Rainbow Lght Ntrtional Systems	499	Santa Cruz, CA	Private	10.5	80	2833
Peninsula Laboratories Inc.	500	Belmont, CA	Private	10.4	71	2833
Tts Alza Research Partners	501	Palo Alto, CA	Public Family Member	10.4	7	2836
Easy Returns Worldwide, Inc.	502	Saint Charles, MO	Private	10.2	82	2834
Endogen Inc.	503	Woburn, MA	Public	10.0	72	2835
Aaron Industries Inc.	504	Clinton, SC	Private	10.0	43	2834
Apotex Usa, Inc.	505	Oceanside, NY	Private	10.0	70	2834
Avant Immunotherapeutics Inc.	506	Needham, MA	Private	10.0	80	2833
B & C Nutritional Products	507	Vista, CA	Private	10.0	43	2833
Biocor Animal Health Inc.	508	Omaha, NE	Private	10.0	70	2836
Cornwell Corporation	509	Riverdale, NJ	Private	10.0	50	2835
Doctors Sgnature Sls Mktg Intl	510	Spring Valley, CA	Private	10.0	22	2833
Montana Naturals Int'l Inc.	511	Arlee, MT	Public Family Member	10.0	72	2833
NCB Technology Corp.	512	Walnut, CA	Private	10.0	25	2833
New Life Health Products Inc.	513	Cedar City, UT	Private	10.0	5	2834
Nicodrop	514	La Mesa, CA	Private	10.0	4	2834
Nuhealth Manufacturing, LLC	515	Gig Harbor, WA	Private	10.0	25	2834
Pharbco Marketing Group Inc.	516	Santa Rosa, CA	Private	10.0	6	2834
Princeton Biomeditech Corp.	517	Monmouth Junction, NJ	Private	10.0	140	2835
Research Biochemicals Inc.	518	Natick, MA	Public Family Member	10.0	47	2836
Ulmer Pharmacal Company	519	Minneapolis, MN	Private	10.0	8	2834
Vitamins, Inc.	520	Chicago, IL	Private	10.0	45	2834
Beach Products Inc.	521	Tampa, FL	Private	9.9	90	2834
Pharmaceutical Associates Inc.	522	Tampa, FL	Private	9.9	90	2834
Triangle Pharmaceuticals, Inc.	523	Durham, NC	Public	9.8	85	2834
Epitope Inc.	524	Beaverton, OR	Public	9.8	90	2835
Madis Botanicals, Inc.	525	South Hackensack, NJ	Public Family Member	9.7	70	2833
Integrated Health Nutritionals	526	Phoenix, AZ	Private	9.6	75	2833
Phillips Pharmatech Labs Inc.	527	Largo, FL	Private	9.6	75	2834
Atlantic Pharmaceutical Svcs	528	Owings Mills, MD	Private	9.5	85	2834
Lannett Company Inc.	529	Philadelphia, PA	Public	9.5	98	2834
Md Pharmaceutical Inc.	530	Santa Ana, CA	Private	9.4	73	2833
Coulter Pharmaceutical, Inc.	531	South San Francisco, CA	Public	9.3	66	2834
Standard Homeopathic Company	532	Los Angeles, CA	Private	9.2	70	2834
BASF Pharmaceuticals, Inc.	533	Jayuya, PR	Private	9.2	95	2834
Lohmann Therapy Systems Corp.	534	Caldwell, NJ	Private	9.1	55	2834
Argonex Holdings Inc.	535	Charlottesville, VA	Private	9.1	102	2835
Endo Pharmaceuticals Inc.	536	Chadds Ford, PA	Private	9.1	65	2834
Neo-Life Company Of America	537	Fremont, CA	Private	9.1	65	2834
Halsey Drug Co Inc.	538	Rockford, IL	Public	9.1	200	2834
Albany Molecular Research	539	Albany, NY	Public	9.0	122	2833
Chemsource Corporation	540	Guayama, PR	Private	9.0	50	2834
Coromed Inc.	541	Troy, NY	Public Family Member	9.0	135	2834
Hardy Media Inc.	542	Santa Maria, CA	Private	9.0	55	2836
Health Plus Inc.	543	Chino, CA	Private	9.0	28	2834
National Vitamin Company LLC	544	Las Vegas, NV	Private	9.0	4	2834
Nutritional Laboratories Int'l	545	Lolo, MT	Private	9.0	50	2833
NW Alpharma Inc.	546	Bellevue, WA	Public Family Member	9.0	30	2834
Respa Pharmaceuticals, Inc.	547	Carol Stream, IL	Private	9.0	35	2834
Unimed Pharmaceuticals, Inc.	548	Buffalo Grove, IL	Public	8.9	20	2834
Galen Inc.	549	Audubon, PA	Private	8.8	165	2834
Jame Fine Chemicals	550	Bound Brook, NJ	Private	8.8	34	2833
Steritek, Inc.	551	Moonachie, NJ	Public	8.7	150	2834
Wright Enrichment Inc.	552	Crowley, LA	Private	8.6	100	2834
Deseret Laboratories Inc.	553	St George, UT	Private	8.5	80	2833
Hematronix, Inc.	554	Plano, TX	Private	8.5	100	2835
ISP Fine Chemicals Inc.	555	Columbus, OH	Private	8.5	78	2834
Jackson Immunoresearch Labs	556	West Grove, PA	Private	8.5	40	2834
Circa Pharmaceuticals Inc.	557	Copiague, NY	Public Family Member	8.3	60	2834
Vitaminerals Inc.	558	Glendale, CA	Private	8.2	75	2833
Lyne Laboratories Inc.	559	Brockton, MA	Private	8.2	130	2834
Formulation Technology Inc.	560	Oakdale, CA	Private	8.1	49	2834

D&B COMPANY RANKINGS BY SALES

Company	Rank	Location	Type	Sales ($ mil.)	Employ-ment	Primary SIC
Interpharm Inc.	561	Plainview, NY	Private	8.1	55	2834
Santa Cruz Biotechnology Inc.	562	Santa Cruz, CA	Private	8.1	115	2836
Bachem Bioscience Inc.	563	King Of Prussia, PA	Private	8.0	22	2836
Branel Laboratories Inc.	564	Hill City, KS	Private	8.0	15	2834
Charter Laboratories Inc.	565	Lakewood, NJ	Public Family Member	8.0	150	2834
Food Sciences Corporation	566	Mount Laurel, NJ	Private	8.0	65	2833
Medical Research Industries	567	Pompano Beach, FL	Private	8.0	100	2834
Micelle Laboratories Inc.	568	Lake Forest, CA	Private	8.0	65	2834
Pharma-Tek Inc.	569	Northport, NY	Private	8.0	15	2834
Straight Arrow Products Inc.	570	Bethlehem, PA	Private	8.0	34	2834
Sunstar Pharmaceuticals, Inc.	571	Elgin, IL	Private	8.0	100	2834
Vita Pure Inc.	572	Roselle, NJ	Private	8.0	25	2833
Pharmatech Laboratories Inc.	573	Lindon, UT	Private	7.8	64	2834
Sovereign Pharmaceuticals	574	Fort Worth, TX	Private	7.7	84	2834
Garrison Industries, Inc.	575	El Dorado, AR	Private	7.7	30	2833
H.T.I. Bio-Products Inc.	576	Santa Ysabel, CA	Private	7.7	80	2835
The Liposome Mfg Co. Inc.	577	Indianapolis, IN	Public Family Member	7.7	70	2833
Cyanotech Corporation	578	Kailua Kona, HI	Public	7.6	68	2836
Konsyl Pharmaceuticals Inc.	579	Fort Worth, TX	Private	7.6	65	2834
Signal Pharmaceuticals, Inc.	580	San Diego, CA	Private	7.6	109	2834
Neorx Corporation	581	Seattle, WA	Public	7.5	57	2835
KC Pharmaceutical Inc.	582	Pomona, CA	Private	7.5	60	2834
ADH Health Products, Inc.	583	Congers, NY	Private	7.5	65	2834
Pacific Biotech, Inc.	584	San Diego, CA	Public Family Member	7.5	78	2835
YS Health Corporation	585	Lombard, IL	Private	7.4	14	2833
American Biological Tech	586	Seguin, TX	Private	7.4	100	2835
Maine Biological Laboratories	587	Waterville, ME	Private	7.3	63	2836
Geron Corporation	588	Menlo Park, CA	Public	7.3	96	2834
General Research Laboratories	589	Northridge, CA	Private	7.2	27	2834
International Enzyme Inc.	590	Fallbrook, CA	Private	7.2	42	2836
JMI-Daniels Pharmaceutical	591	Saint Petersburg, FL	Public Family Member	7.2	65	2834
Allerderm Inc.	592	Fort Worth, TX	Private	7.1	68	2834
Diamond Animal Health, Inc.	593	Des Moines, IA	Public Family Member	7.1	120	2836
East Earth Herb Inc.	594	Eugene, OR	Private	7.1	70	2834
Chesapeake Biological Labs	595	Baltimore, MD	Public	7.0	60	2834
Interglow Nutritional Systems	596	Milroy, PA	Private	7.0	75	2834
Materials Processing Tech	597	Paterson, NJ	Private	7.0	75	2834
Naturopathic Formulations	598	Wilsonville, OR	Private	7.0	52	2833
West Coast Laboratories Inc.	599	Gardena, CA	Private	7.0	50	2834
Pharmsciences Inc.	600	West Conshohocken, PA	Private	7.0	45	2834
Ambion Inc.	601	Austin, TX	Private	7.0	78	2836
Chemdex, Inc.	602	Shawnee Mission, KS	Private	6.9	63	2834
Grant Industries, Inc.	603	Elmwood Park, NJ	Private	6.9	60	2834
Spray-Tek Inc.	604	Middlesex, NJ	Private	6.9	28	2834
Stevens Ash Inc.	605	Detroit, MI	Private	6.8	43	2834
Connetics Corp.	606	Palo Alto, CA	Public	6.8	50	2834
United States Biochemical Corp.	607	Cleveland, OH	Private	6.8	100	2835
Metra Biosystems, Inc.	608	Mountain View, CA	Public	6.7	60	2835
Bachem Inc.	609	Torrance, CA	Private	6.7	100	2836
Chantal Pharmaceutical Corp.	610	Los Angeles, CA	Public	6.7	47	2834
Beauty & Health International	611	Santa Ana, CA	Private	6.6	50	2834
P & L Development Ny Corp.	612	Farmingdale, NY	Private	6.6	30	2834
Clark Laboratories Inc.	613	Jamestown, NY	Private	6.5	76	2835
Aggrow Oils LLC	614	Carrington, ND	Private	6.5	17	2833
Holopack International, LP	615	Columbia, SC	Private	6.5	60	2834
Bigmar, Inc.	616	Johnstown, OH	Public	6.5	50	2834
Golden Pharmaceuticals Inc.	617	Santa Ana, CA	Public	6.4	90	2834
Astra Research Center Boston	618	Cambridge, MA	Private	6.4	70	2835
Bio Botanica Inc.	619	Hauppauge, NY	Private	6.4	50	2833
Northridge Laboratories Inc.	620	Chatsworth, CA	Private	6.4	50	2833
Tyler Distribution Inc.	621	Gresham, OR	Private	6.4	50	2833
Anergen, Inc.	622	Redwood City, CA	Public	6.3	NA	2834
Novo Holdings Inc.	623	Schaumburg, IL	Private	6.3	55	2834
Rasi Laboratories Inc.	624	Somerset, NJ	Private	6.3	16	2834
Nutrition Resource	625	Lakeport, CA	Private	6.2	24	2834
Hyseq, Inc.	626	Sunnyvale, CA	Public	6.2	169	2835
Technical Chemicals & Products	627	Pompano Beach, FL	Public	6.2	55	2835
Ribi Immunochem Research Inc.	628	Hamilton, MT	Public	6.1	107	2834
Life Services Supplements	629	Neptune, NJ	Private	6.1	52	2834
Veterinary Laboratories, Inc.	630	Shawnee Mission, KS	Private	6.1	60	2834

D&B COMPANY RANKINGS BY SALES

Company	Rank	Location	Type	Sales ($ mil.)	Employ-ment	Primary SIC
Winning Combination Inc.	631	Henderson, NV	Private	6.1	55	2834
Sugen Inc.	632	South San Francisco, CA	Public	6.0	216	2834
Alacer Corp.	633	El Toro, CA	Private	6.0	70	2833
Imarx Pharmaceutical Corp.	634	Tucson, AZ	Private	6.0	30	2835
Applied Laboratories Inc.	635	Columbus, IN	Private	6.0	65	2834
Archon Vitamin Corp.	636	Irvington, NJ	Private	6.0	42	2834
Arenol Corporation	637	Somerville, NJ	Private	6.0	15	2833
Arizona Nutritional Supplement	638	Tempe, AZ	Private	6.0	22	2834
Biologically Active Substances	639	Monterey, CA	Private	6.0	50	2833
Custom Coatings Inc.	640	Farmingdale, NY	Private	6.0	119	2834
Eckhart Corporation	641	Novato, CA	Private	6.0	7	2834
Livron Inc.	642	Allendale, NJ	Private	6.0	18	2833
Panvera Corporation	643	Madison, WI	Private	6.0	30	2835
Person & Covey Inc.	644	Glendale, CA	Private	6.0	67	2834
Pharma Tech Industries, Inc.	645	Union, MO	Private	6.0	100	2834
Planet Emu Inc.	646	Miami, FL	Private	6.0	8	2834
RIJ Pharmaceutical Corp.	647	Middletown, NY	Private	6.0	27	2834
Teco Diagnostics	648	Anaheim, CA	Private	6.0	50	2835
Tender Corporation	649	Littleton, NH	Private	6.0	55	2834
Wellquest International Inc.	650	New York, NY	Private	6.0	6	2833
Morton Pharmaceuticals Inc.	651	Memphis, TN	Private	5.9	60	2834
Penick Corporation	652	Newark, NJ	Private	5.9	49	2833
Care Technologies, Inc.	653	Darien, CT	Private	5.9	10	2834
Biospecifics Technologies	654	Lynbrook, NY	Public	5.8	41	2836
Colorado Serum Company	655	Denver, CO	Private	5.8	100	2836
Heel Inc.	656	Albuquerque, NM	Private	5.8	53	2833
Mitotix, Inc.	657	Cambridge, MA	Private	5.8	64	2834
Mueller Sports Medicine Inc.	658	Prairie Du Sac, WI	Private	5.8	70	2834
U S Diversified Technologies	659	Largo, FL	Private	5.7	80	2834
Leukosite, Inc.	660	Cambridge, MA	Public	5.7	51	2834
Biocore Medical Tech Inc.	661	Topeka, KS	Private	5.7	50	2833
Allen & Associates Intl Ltd.	662	Washington, DC	Private	5.6	48	2834
Gentrac, Inc.	663	Middleton, WI	Public Family Member	5.6	93	2836
Nastech Pharmaceutical Company	664	Hauppauge, NY	Public	5.5	43	2834
Quality Care Phrmceuticals Inc.	665	Santa Ana, CA	Public Family Member	5.5	70	2834
JBL Scientific Inc.	666	San Luis Obispo, CA	Public Family Member	5.5	53	2833
Seracare Technology Inc.	667	Austin, TX	Public Family Member	5.5	40	2835
Kelatron Inc.	668	Ogden, UT	Private	5.4	50	2834
Vector Laboratories Inc.	669	Burlingame, CA	Private	5.4	48	2833
Zambon Corporation	670	East Rutherford, NJ	Private	5.4	22	2834
Nutrition Now Inc.	671	Vancouver, WA	Private	5.4	42	2834
Cayman Chemical Company Inc.	672	Ann Arbor, MI	Private	5.3	52	2834
Alberto Bartolomei	673	Gurabo, PR	Private	5.3	18	2833
ABS Corporation	674	Omaha, NE	Private	5.3	62	2834
Bard Diagnostic Sciences Division	675	Redmond, WA	Public Family Member	5.3	55	2835
Genesis Technologies Inc.	676	Norcross, GA	Private	5.3	3	2836
Berkeley Antibody Company	677	Richmond, CA	Private	5.3	52	2833
Pharmaceutical Laboratories	678	Corpus Christi, TX	Public	5.3	50	2833
Jason Pharmaceuticals Inc.	679	Owings Mills, MD	Public Family Member	5.2	35	2834
Consolidated Pharmaceuticals Group	680	Baltimore, MD	Private	5.2	50	2834
Luyties Pharmacal Company	681	Saint Louis, MO	Private	5.2	60	2834
SSS Company	682	Atlanta, GA	Private	5.2	52	2834
Diagnostic Reagents, Inc.	683	Sunnyvale, CA	Private	5.2	45	2835
Juneau Packaging Corporation	684	Mauston, WI	Public Family Member	5.1	72	2835
Natures Value Inc.	685	Bay Shore, NY	Private	5.1	40	2833
Nutri-Well International Inc.	686	Santa Ana, CA	Private	5.1	45	2834
American Eco-Systems Inc.	687	Wellman, IA	Private	5.0	12	2836
Biometric Imaging Inc.	688	Mountain View, CA	Private	5.0	60	2835
Cappseals Inc.	689	Vancouver, WA	Private	5.0	32	2834
Center Laboratories Inc.	690	Port Washington, NY	Public Family Member	5.0	75	2834
Cosmo-Pharm Inc.	691	North Hollywood, CA	Private	5.0	39	2833
Data Medical Associates Inc.	692	Arlington, TX	Public Family Member	5.0	31	2833
Dynport LLC	693	Reston, VA	Private	5.0	20	2836
Eco Pax, Inc.	694	Littleton, CO	Private	5.0	10	2834
Elementis Catalysts Inc.	695	Allentown, PA	Private	5.0	15	2833
Fontarome Chemical Inc.	696	Milwaukee, WI	Private	5.0	21	2833
Gemini Pharmaceuticals Inc.	697	Bohemia, NY	Private	5.0	30	2833
Herba Aromatica Inc.	698	Hayward, CA	Private	5.0	50	2833
Mardel Laboratories Inc.	699	Glendale Heights, IL	Public Family Member	5.0	50	2833
Mineral Resources Int'l	700	Ogden, UT	Private	5.0	70	2834

D&B COMPANY RANKINGS BY SALES

Company	Rank	Location	Type	Sales ($ mil.)	Employ-ment	Primary SIC
New Chapter Inc.	701	Brattleboro, VT	Private	5.0	24	2833
Novagen Inc.	702	Madison, WI	Public Family Member	5.0	45	2835
Oxycal Laboratories Inc.	703	Prescott, AZ	Public Family Member	5.0	46	2833
Premium Processing, Inc.	704	Commack, NY	Private	5.0	7	2834
Randal Nutritional Products	705	Santa Rosa, CA	Private	5.0	32	2834
Regis Technologies, Inc.	706	Morton Grove, IL	Private	5.0	48	2835
Sentry Supplement Co. Inc.	707	Opa Locka, FL	Private	5.0	31	2834
Total Wellness, Inc.	708	Parker, CO	Private	5.0	30	2833
Wellness Way Inc.	709	Elmhurst, NY	Private	5.0	6	2834
York Pharmaceuticals Inc.	710	Kansas City, KS	Private	5.0	40	2834
Cima Labs Inc.	711	Eden Prairie, MN	Public	4.9	49	2834
Advance Development Co.	712	Lakewood, NJ	Private	4.9	50	2834
Bio Med Plastics Inc.	713	Linden, NJ	Private	4.9	50	2834
Ivy Animal Health, Inc.	714	Shawnee Mission, KS	Private	4.9	50	2834
Medical Products Laboratories	715	Philadelphia, PA	Private	4.9	50	2834
Pharmaceutical Innovations	716	Newark, NJ	Private	4.9	50	2834
Nutrition Center, Incorporated	717	Douglas, WY	Private	4.8	40	2833
Biochemical Sciences Inc.	718	Swedesboro, NJ	Public Family Member	4.8	50	2835
National Nutritional Labs	719	Melville, NY	Private	4.8	40	2833
Biocore Medical Technologies	720	Topeka, KS	Private	4.7	47	2833
Kirkegaard & Perry Labs Inc.	721	Gaithersburg, MD	Private	4.7	71	2836
National Medical Industries	722	Boise, ID	Private	4.7	45	2834
Ambico Inc.	723	Dallas Center, IA	Private	4.6	85	2836
Bionostics Inc.	724	Acton, MA	Private	4.6	50	2835
Molorokalin Inc.	725	Youngstown, OH	Private	4.6	45	2834
Lynx Therapeutics Inc.	726	Hayward, CA	Public	4.6	73	2834
Immucell Corporation	727	Portland, ME	Public	4.6	23	2835
Sangstat Medical Corporation	728	Menlo Park, CA	Public	4.5	112	2834
Advanced Bio Institute	729	Costa Mesa, CA	Private	4.5	5	2834
ALK Laboratories Inc.	730	Round Rock, TX	Private	4.5	NA	2834
AMTL Corporation	731	Hollywood, FL	Private	4.5	33	2835
HDI Nutrients Inc.	732	Phoenix, AZ	Private	4.5	40	2833
International Immunology Corp.	733	Murrieta, CA	Private	4.5	36	2835
International Tollers Inc.	734	Grand Haven, MI	Private	4.5	54	2834
P J Noyes Co Inc.	735	Lancaster, NH	Private	4.5	45	2834
Theracom Inc.	736	Bethesda, MD	Private	4.5	45	2834
TME Enterprises	737	Santa Fe Springs, CA	Private	4.5	40	2834
TOA Medical Electronics (USA)	738	Los Alamitos, CA	Private	4.5	17	2835
Wilson Group Inc.	739	Sussex, WI	Private	4.5	70	2836
Tower Laboratories, Ltd.	740	Essex, CT	Private	4.4	45	2834
Alexon-Trend Inc.	741	Anoka, MN	Private	4.4	55	2835
Biomune Company	742	Shawnee Mission, KS	Private	4.4	65	2836
ISP Co Inc.	743	Wolf Summit, WV	Private	4.4	3	2836
Caltag Inc.	744	Burlingame, CA	Private	4.3	37	2836
Lobob Laboratories Inc.	745	San Jose, CA	Private	4.3	35	2834
Nutraceutix, Inc.	746	Redmond, WA	Private	4.3	42	2834
Alfa-Flour Inc.	747	Wray, CO	Private	4.3	47	2834
Chelsea Laboratories Inc.	748	Cincinnati, OH	Public Family Member	4.3	45	2834
Lloyd Inc. of Iowa	749	Shenandoah, IA	Private	4.3	55	2834
Oculex Pharmaceuticals Inc.	750	Sunnyvale, CA	Private	4.3	40	2834
Otis Clapp & Son Inc.	751	Canton, MA	Private	4.3	45	2834
Petnet Pharmaceutical Svcs LLC	752	Norcross, GA	Private	4.3	44	2835
Far Research Inc.	753	Morganton, NC	Private	4.2	25	2834
Vectech Pharmaceutical Cons	754	Farmington Hills, MI	Private	4.2	40	2834
Bactolac Pharmaceutical Inc.	755	Westbury, NY	Private	4.2	29	2833
Carolina Medical Products Co.	756	Farmville, NC	Private	4.2	24	2834
Nutrition Medical, Inc.	757	Minneapolis, MN	Public	4.1	25	2834
Biopharmaceutics Inc.	758	Bellport, NY	Public Family Member	4.1	40	2834
DGA Inc.	759	Lafayette, CA	Private	4.1	34	2834
Highland Laboratories, Inc.	760	Mount Angel, OR	Private	4.1	41	2833
Mediatech Inc.	761	Herndon, VA	Private	4.1	70	2836
MML Diagnostics Packaging Inc.	762	Troutdale, OR	Private	4.1	70	2836
Nassmith Pharmaceuticals, Inc.	763	Oceanside, CA	Private	4.1	38	2834
Vitamin Power Inc.	764	Freeport, NY	Private	4.0	31	2834
Derma Sciences, Inc.	765	Princeton, NJ	Public	4.0	35	2834
Bennett Chem Ltd.	766	Palatine, IL	Private	4.0	19	2833
Berkeley Nutritional Mfg.	767	Hayward, CA	Private	4.0	29	2834
Berlin Industries Inc.	768	Berlin Center, OH	Private	4.0	21	2834
Biosan Laboratories Inc.	769	Derry, NH	Private	4.0	32	2833
Biospacific Inc.	770	Emeryville, CA	Private	4.0	10	2835

D&B COMPANY RANKINGS BY SALES

Company	Rank	Location	Type	Sales ($ mil.)	Employ-ment	Primary SIC
Breathies International Inc.	771	Culver City, CA	Private	4.0	9	2834
Chembio Diagnostic Systems	772	Medford, NY	Private	4.0	45	2835
Clinical Specialties, Inc.	773	Cleveland, OH	Private	4.0	32	2834
Devlan Inc.	774	Farmington Hills, MI	Private	4.0	45	2834
Direct Therapeutics, Inc.	775	White Plains, NY	Private	4.0	37	2834
Gebauer Company	776	Cleveland, OH	Private	4.0	25	2834
Little Silver Corp.	777	Sioux Falls, SD	Private	4.0	80	2833
Metabolic Maintenance Pdts Inc.	778	Sisters, OR	Private	4.0	29	2834
Mizuho USA, Inc.	779	San Diego, CA	Private	4.0	29	2835
Molecumetics, Ltd.	780	Bellevue, WA	Public Family Member	4.0	50	2836
Morningstar Diagnostics, Inc.	781	Roseville, CA	Private	4.0	12	2835
Quantimetrix	782	Redondo Beach, CA	Private	4.0	50	2835
Seabella Inc.	783	Bayport, NY	Private	4.0	9	2834
Tatras Inc.	784	Claremont, NH	Private	4.0	35	2836
Tera Pharmaceuticals Inc.	785	Midvale, UT	Public Family Member	4.0	28	2834
Third Wave Technologies, Inc.	786	Madison, WI	Private	4.0	49	2835
Uni-Health Inc.	787	Clifton, NJ	Private	4.0	15	2834
Chemicals Inc.	788	Baytown, TX	Private	3.9	58	2834
ADM Laboratories, Inc.	789	Phoenix, AZ	Private	3.9	40	2833
Best Industries Inc.	790	Springfield, VA	Private	3.9	42	2834
Thompson Medical Company Inc.	791	West Palm Beach, FL	Private	3.9	42	2834
Life Enhancement Products	792	Petaluma, CA	Private	3.9	22	2834
Ajay Chemicals Inc.	793	Powder Springs, GA	Private	3.8	35	2834
Gmp Laboratories America Inc.	794	Anaheim, CA	Private	3.8	35	2833
Monticello Companies Inc.	795	Jacksonville, FL	Private	3.8	115	2834
Safetec Of America Inc.	796	Buffalo, NY	Private	3.8	35	2834
Viral Antigens Inc.	797	Memphis, TN	Private	3.8	49	2835
Advance Pharmaceutical Inc.	798	Ronkonkoma, NY	Private	3.8	30	2834
Telik Inc.	799	South San Francisco, CA	Private	3.7	47	2834
Scot-Tussin Pharmacal Co Inc.	800	Cranston, RI	Private	3.7	40	2834
Worthington Biochemical Corp.	801	Lakewood, NJ	Private	3.7	38	2835
American Phrm Partners	802	Los Angeles, CA	Private	3.7	600	2834
Pan Am Pharmaceuticals, Inc.	803	New York, NY	Private	3.6	10	2834
Biolog Inc.	804	Hayward, CA	Private	3.6	40	2835
Borregaard Syntheses, Inc.	805	Newburyport, MA	Private	3.6	33	2834
Chart Corp Inc.	806	Paterson, NJ	Private	3.6	35	2833
Custom Health Products	807	Waynesboro, VA	Private	3.6	40	2834
Hill Dermaceuticals Inc.	808	Sanford, FL	Private	3.6	35	2834
Solgar Laboratories, Inc.	809	Leonia, NJ	Private	3.6	40	2834
Stason Industrial Corporation	810	Irvine, CA	Private	3.6	30	2834
Yerba Prima Inc.	811	Ashland, OR	Private	3.6	16	2834
Glen Copel Pharmaceuticals Inc.	812	Providence, RI	Private	3.5	6	2834
Pharmacyclics Inc.	813	Sunnyvale, CA	Public	3.5	80	2834
Avanti Polar Lipids Inc.	814	Alabaster, AL	Private	3.5	45	2833
Baker Cummins Dermatologicals Inc.	815	Miami, FL	Public Family Member	3.5	37	2834
Cedarburg Laboratories Inc.	816	Grafton, WI	Private	3.5	17	2834
Chemical Compounds Inc.	817	Newark, NJ	Private	3.5	18	2834
Genzyme Diagnostics Medix Biot	818	San Carlos, CA	Public Family Member	3.5	49	2836
Herb Penn Co. Ltd.	819	Philadelphia, PA	Private	3.5	36	2833
K & K Laboratories Inc.	820	Carlsbad, CA	Private	3.5	35	2834
Medeva Pharmaceuticals, Inc.	821	Bethlehem, PA	Private	3.5	36	2834
PCR Puerto Rico Inc.	822	Humacao, PR	Private	3.5	11	2834
Shaman Pharmaceuticals Inc.	823	South San Francisco, CA	Public	3.5	120	2833
Vita-Key Packaging	824	Fontana, CA	Private	3.5	35	2834
Ajay North America LLC	825	Powder Springs, GA	Private	3.4	32	2834
Worldwide Sport Nutritional	826	Largo, FL	Private	3.4	32	2834
First Priority Inc.	827	Elgin, IL	Private	3.3	11	2834
Summa Rx Laboratories Inc.	828	Mineral Wells, TX	Private	3.3	31	2834
Au Naturel, Inc.	829	Clearfield, UT	Public Family Member	3.3	35	2834
Continental Services Group	830	Miami, FL	Private	3.3	40	2835
Hill Labs, Inc.	831	Sanford, FL	Private	3.3	35	2834
Baywood International, Inc.	832	Scottsdale, AZ	Public	3.2	4	2834
Pelron Corporation	833	Lyons, IL	Private	3.2	40	2833
Able Laboratories, Inc.	834	South Plainfield, NJ	Public Family Member	3.2	30	2834
B F Ascher & Company Inc.	835	Shawnee Mission, KS	Private	3.2	42	2834
Impact Nutrition, Inc.	836	Rocklin, CA	Private	3.2	30	2834
Impax Pharmaceuticals Inc.	837	Hayward, CA	Private	3.2	30	2834
J & D Laboratories, Inc.	838	Vista, CA	Private	3.2	30	2833
Optimum Nutrition, Inc.	839	Coral Springs, FL	Private	3.2	30	2834
Pharma Labs LLC	840	Anaheim, CA	Public Family Member	3.2	30	2833

D&B COMPANY RANKINGS BY SALES

Company	Rank	Location	Type	Sales ($ mil.)	Employ-ment	Primary SIC
Quality Biological Inc.	841	Gaithersburg, MD	Private	3.2	48	2836
Reliance Vitamin Co Inc.	842	Somerville, NJ	Private	3.2	50	2834
Mercer Milling Co.	843	Baldwinsville, NY	Private	3.2	11	2834
C and M Pharmacal Inc.	844	Hazel Park, MI	Private	3.1	30	2834
Advanced Biotechnologies, Inc.	845	Columbia, MD	Private	3.1	34	2836
Organics/Lagrange, Inc.	846	Northbrook, IL	Private	3.1	50	2834
Orphan Medical, Inc.	847	Hopkins, MN	Public	3.1	35	2834
Reagents Applications Inc.	848	San Diego, CA	Public Family Member	3.1	32	2835
Wilcox Drug Company Inc.	849	Boone, NC	Private	3.1	33	2833
Norian Corporation	850	Cupertino, CA	Private	3.1	73	2836
Cypress Pharmaceutical Inc.	851	Madison, MS	Private	3.1	10	2834
Twenty-First Century Labs	852	Tempe, AZ	Private	3.0	30	2834
A & Z Pharmaceutical Inc.	853	Hauppauge, NY	Private	3.0	35	2834
Accumed Inc.	854	Lawrenceville, NJ	Private	3.0	23	2834
Advanced Manufacturing Systems	855	Boulder, CO	Private	3.0	18	2834
Amerilab Technologies, Inc.	856	Minneapolis, MN	Private	3.0	40	2834
Ashford Pharmalogic Corp.	857	San Juan, PR	Private	3.0	11	2834
Champion Eximport Enterprise	858	Baldwin Park, CA	Private	3.0	8	2833
Dolisos America Inc.	859	Las Vegas, NV	Private	3.0	33	2833
G & S Enterprises Incorporated	860	Houston, TX	Private	3.0	21	2834
Global Vitality, Inc.	861	Tempe, AZ	Private	3.0	27	2834
Healthspan, Inc.	862	Hermosa Beach, CA	Private	3.0	6	2834
Immvac Inc.	863	Columbia, MO	Private	3.0	16	2836
Infusion Orlando Regional	864	Orlando, FL	Private	3.0	20	2834
Interntnal Frmltion Mnfcturing	865	San Diego, CA	Private	3.0	30	2834
Kanec (USA), Inc.	866	Opa Locka, FL	Private	3.0	3	2834
M V P Laboratories Inc.	867	Omaha, NE	Private	3.0	35	2834
Naiad Technologies Inc.	868	Portland, OR	Private	3.0	14	2835
Natco Pharma USA LLC	869	Somerset, NJ	Private	3.0	19	2834
Natures World	870	San Marcos, CA	Private	3.0	20	2833
Power Engineering & Mfg Inc.	871	Saint Paul, MN	Private	3.0	3	2836
SGM Biotech, Inc.	872	Bozeman, MT	Private	3.0	34	2836
Slim Science Corporation	873	Encino, CA	Private	3.0	7	2833
Stella Labs LLC	874	New Orleans, LA	Private	3.0	9	2833
Xylum Corporation	875	Scarsdale, NY	Private	3.0	39	2835
Interferon Sciences Inc.	876	New Brunswick, NJ	Public	3.0	100	2835
King's Laboratory Incorporated	877	Blythewood, SC	Private	2.9	25	2833
West Laboratories Inc.	878	Kankakee, IL	Private	2.9	16	2836
Biozone Laboratories, Inc.	879	Pittsburg, CA	Private	2.9	35	2834
Allergy Control Products, Inc.	880	Ridgefield, CT	Private	2.9	42	2836
Metabolic Nutrition Inc.	881	Miami, FL	Private	2.9	6	2834
QXL Corporation	882	Mesa, AZ	Private	2.9	2	2834
USB Corporation	883	Cleveland, OH	Private	2.9	35	2835
KOS Pharmaceuticals Inc.	884	Miami, FL	Public	2.9	361	2834
Blackhawk Biosystems Inc.	885	San Ramon, CA	Private	2.9	15	2835
JMI-Canton Pharmaceuticals	886	Saint Louis, MO	Public Family Member	2.8	40	2834
Biomune Systems, Inc.	887	Salt Lake City, UT	Public	2.8	20	2833
Alfred Khalily Inc.	888	Great Neck, NY	Private	2.8	5	2834
Coating Place Incorporated	889	Verona, WI	Private	2.8	36	2834
Farmanatural Inc.	890	Fort Lauderdale, FL	Private	2.8	30	2834
Iconix Pharmaceuticals Inc.	891	Mountain View, CA	Private	2.8	27	2834
Lee Laboratories Inc.	892	Grayson, GA	Public Family Member	2.8	35	2833
Ocumed Inc.	893	Roseland, NJ	Private	2.8	25	2834
Royal Source, Inc.	894	Lake Bluff, IL	Private	2.8	30	2833
VM Nutri	895	Batesville, AR	Private	2.8	30	2834
Designing Health Inc.	896	Valencia, CA	Private	2.8	27	2833
Bio-Trends International, Inc.	897	West Sacramento, CA	Private	2.7	30	2835
Biodesign International	898	Kennebunk, ME	Public Family Member	2.7	24	2833
Dercher Enterprises Inc.	899	Upper Darby, PA	Private	2.7	27	2834
Dermarite Industries LLC	900	Paterson, NJ	Private	2.7	20	2834
Pharmaceutical Recovery Svcs	901	Orlando, FL	Private	2.7	29	2834
Pralex Corporation	902	Christiansted, VI	Public Family Member	2.7	38	2834
Creative Medical Corporation	903	Toa Baja, PR	Private	2.6	32	2834
Bio-Energetics Inc.	904	Rye, NY	Private	2.6	25	2834
Bramton Company, (Inc)	905	Irving, TX	Public Family Member	2.6	35	2835
Denison Pharmaceuticals Inc.	906	Pawtucket, RI	Private	2.6	30	2834
Immuno Concepts Inc.	907	Sacramento, CA	Private	2.6	25	2835
Northwest Marketing Corp.	908	Placentia, CA	Private	2.6	25	2833
Pegasus Laboratories Inc.	909	Pensacola, FL	Private	2.6	28	2834
Toll Compaction Service Inc.	910	Neptune, NJ	Private	2.6	38	2833

D&B COMPANY RANKINGS BY SALES

Company	Rank	Location	Type	Sales ($ mil.)	Employ-ment	Primary SIC
Unipack, Inc.	911	Pittsburgh, PA	Private	2.5	15	2834
Advanced Vision Research	912	Woburn, MA	Private	2.5	4	2834
Antigen Laboratories Inc.	913	Liberty, MO	Private	2.5	23	2834
C J Martin & Son Inc.	914	Nacogdoches, TX	Private	2.5	12	2834
Chemocentryx	915	San Carlos, CA	Private	2.5	6	2834
Clearvalue, Inc.	916	Sugar Land, TX	Private	2.5	14	2836
Concord Laboratories, Inc.	917	Fairfield, NJ	Private	2.5	20	2834
Elge Inc.	918	Rosenberg, TX	Private	2.5	25	2834
Fortta Group LLC	919	Plainville, CT	Private	2.5	1	2834
Herb Source Enterprise Inc.	920	Chino, CA	Private	2.5	25	2834
Houba Inc.	921	Culver, IN	Public Family Member	2.5	30	2834
IGX Corp.	922	Summit, NJ	Private	2.5	31	2836
Immunetics Inc.	923	Cambridge, MA	Private	2.5	25	2835
Natural Biologics, LLC	924	Albert Lea, MN	Private	2.5	30	2834
Sunset Nutritional Products	925	Agoura Hills, CA	Private	2.5	10	2834
Systemic Formula Inc.	926	Ogden, UT	Private	2.5	20	2834
Tissue Culture Biologicals	927	Tulare, CA	Private	2.5	6	2836
Trimar Hollywood Inc.	928	Reseda, CA	Private	2.5	18	2835
Renaissance Pharmaceutical	929	Zephyr Cove, NV	Private	2.4	10	2834
Ceres Organic Harvest Inc.	930	Dexter, MI	Private	2.4	4	2833
Aloe Laboratories, Inc.	931	Harlingen, TX	Public Family Member	2.4	25	2834
American Biorganics Inc.	932	Niagara Falls, NY	Private	2.4	30	2836
Chemrich Laboratories Inc.	933	Los Angeles, CA	Private	2.4	13	2834
Chiragene Inc.	934	Warren, NJ	Public Family Member	2.4	23	2834
Cocalico Biologicals Inc.	935	Reamstown, PA	Private	2.4	36	2836
Everett Laboratories Inc.	936	West Orange, NJ	Private	2.4	27	2834
Innominata	937	San Diego, CA	Private	2.4	25	2835
Raven Biological Laboratories	938	Omaha, NE	Private	2.4	25	2835
Scripps Laboratories, Inc.	939	San Diego, CA	Private	2.4	25	2835
Neurex Corporation	940	Menlo Park, CA	Public	2.4	56	2836
Blue Bonnett Nutrition Corp.	941	Stafford, TX	Private	2.4	20	2833
Am Pharm Corp.	942	Fairfield, NJ	Private	2.3	22	2834
Associates Of Cape Cod, Inc.	943	Falmouth, MA	Private	2.3	28	2835
Center For Diagnostic Products	944	Milford, MA	Private	2.3	32	2836
Marcus Research Laboratory	945	Saint Louis, MO	Private	2.3	25	2833
St Mary's Chemicals Inc.	946	Saint Peter, MN	Private	2.3	4	2834
Stason Pharmaceutical Inc.	947	Irvine, CA	Private	2.3	22	2834
Univera Pharmaceuticals, Inc.	948	Broomfield, CO	Private	2.3	25	2834
University Pharmaceuticals	949	Baltimore, MD	Private	2.3	25	2834
Biofluids Inc.	950	Rockville, MD	Private	2.3	13	2836
Miravant Medical Technologies	951	Goleta, CA	Public	2.3	145	2834
Horizon Pharmaceuticals Inc.	952	Saint Petersburg, FL	Private	2.3	25	2834
Bionike Laboratories, Inc.	953	South San Francisco, CA	Private	2.2	23	2835
Sciclone Pharmaceuticals, Inc.	954	San Mateo, CA	Public	2.2	40	2834
A & S Pharmaceutical Corp.	955	Bridgeport, CT	Private	2.2	25	2834
All Natural Products Corp.	956	Mineola, NY	Private	2.2	20	2833
Bioglan Inc.	957	Lake Forest, CA	Private	2.2	20	2834
Clinical Diagnostics, Inc.	958	Rock Hill, SC	Private	2.2	25	2835
CTM Industries Ltd.	959	Jamaica, NY	Private	2.2	33	2836
Kaizen Inc.	960	Los Angeles, CA	Private	2.2	4	2834
Naturopathic Laboratories Int'l	961	New York, NY	Private	2.2	20	2834
Swiss-American Products Inc.	962	Dallas, TX	Private	2.2	25	2834
Monomer-Polymer & Dajac Labs	963	Feasterville Trevose, PA	Private	2.2	9	2835
Sage Pharmaceuticals, Inc.	964	Shreveport, LA	Private	2.2	30	2834
Vitarich Laboratories, Inc.	965	Naples, FL	Private	2.1	21	2834
Uckele Animal Health Distrg Co.	966	Blissfield, MI	Private	2.1	16	2834
American Chelates Inc.	967	Northvale, NJ	Private	2.1	20	2833
Enteric Products Inc.	968	Stony Brook, NY	Public Family Member	2.1	20	2834
G D S Technology Inc.	969	Elkhart, IN	Private	2.1	27	2835
Health Products Intl Corp.	970	Springville, UT	Private	2.1	26	2833
Kultivar, Inc.	971	Plainfield, VT	Private	2.1	20	2833
Micro Bio Logics	972	Saint Cloud, MN	Private	2.1	27	2835
Optimal Research, Inc.	973	St George, UT	Private	2.1	20	2833
Siga Pharmaceuticals Inc.	974	New York, NY	Public	2.1	18	2834
U S Direct Inc.	975	North Las Vegas, NV	Private	2.1	22	2834
Universal Proteins Inc.	976	Amityville, NY	Private	2.1	20	2834
Gallipot Inc.	977	Saint Paul, MN	Private	2.1	16	2834
Ascent Pediatrics, Inc.	978	Wilmington, MA	Public	2.1	15	2834
O E M Concepts	979	Toms River, NJ	Private	2.0	12	2835
Scientia Biological	980	Wolsey, SD	Private	2.0	3	2836

D&B COMPANY RANKINGS BY SALES

Company	Rank	Location	Type	Sales ($ mil.)	Employ- ment	Primary SIC
Ameri-Kal, Inc.	981	Auburn, CA	Private	2.0	45	2833
Biosource Technologies, Inc.	982	Vacaville, CA	Private	2.0	60	2833
Blansett Pharmacal Company	983	North Little Rock, AR	Private	2.0	24	2834
Genaissance Pharmaceutical	984	New Haven, CT	Private	2.0	22	2834
Geriatric Pharmaceutical Corp.	985	Brookfield, WI	Public Family Member	2.0	23	2834
Hillestad Pharmaceuticals	986	Woodruff, WI	Private	2.0	25	2834
Innovative Natural Products	987	Escondido, CA	Private	2.0	30	2834
Pel-Freez Rabbit Meat, Inc.	988	Rogers, AR	Private	2.0	34	2836
Trend Pharmaceuticals Inc.	989	Fort Walton Beach, FL	Private	2.0	40	2834
Wendt Professional Labs	990	Belle Plaine, MN	Private	2.0	25	2834
L Perrigo Company	991	Allegan, MI	Public Family Member	0.9	2,200	2834

D&B COMPANY RANKINGS BY EMPLOYMENT

Company	Rank	Location	Type	Sales ($ mil.)	Employ- ment	Primary SIC
American Home Products Corp.	1	Madison, NJ	Public	14,196.0	60,523	2834
Abbott Laboratories	2	North Chicago, IL	Public	12,477.8	54,487	2834
Merck & Co Inc.	3	Whitehouse Station, NJ	Public	23,636.9	53,800	2834
Bristol-Myers Squibb Company	4	New York, NY	Public	16,701.0	53,600	2834
Pfizer Inc.	5	New York, NY	Public	12,504.0	49,200	2834
Baxter International Inc.	6	Deerfield, IL	Public	6,138.0	41,000	2834
Warner-Lambert Company	7	Morris Plains, NJ	Public	8,179.8	40,000	2834
Eli Lilly And Company	8	Indianapolis, IN	Public	8,517.6	31,100	2834
Pharmacia & Upjohn, Inc.	9	Bridgewater, NJ	Public	6,586.0	30,000	2834
Smithkline Beecham Corporation	10	Philadelphia, PA	Private	6,661.9	21,600	2834
Schering-Plough Corporation	11	Madison, NJ	Public	8,077.0	20,600	2834
American Cyanamid Company	12	Parsippany, NJ	Public Family Member	2,575.0	20,000	2834
Novartis Corporation	13	Summit, NJ	Private	8,400.0	20,000	2834
Schering Corporation	14	Kenilworth, NJ	Public Family Member	6,778.0	18,400	2834
ICN Pharmaceuticals, Inc.	15	Costa Mesa, CA	Public	752.2	17,000	2834
Pharmacia & Upjohn Company	16	Bridgewater, NJ	Public Family Member	7,286.0	16,900	2834
Baxter Healthcare Corporation	17	Deerfield, IL	Public Family Member	3,763.0	15,000	2834
Roche Holdings, Inc.	18	Wilmington, DE	Private	1,735.1	13,480	2834
G D Searle & Co.	19	Skokie, IL	Public Family Member	1,999.0	8,700	2834
Dade Behring Holdings	20	Deerfield, IL	Private	978.0	7,500	2835
Glaxo Welcome Americas Inc.	21	New York, NY	Private	964.7	7,500	2834
Dade Behring Inc.	22	Deerfield, IL	Private	980.5	7,400	2835
Novartis Pharmaceuticals Corp.	23	East Hanover, NJ	Private	900.3	7,000	2834
Upjohn International Inc.	24	Kalamazoo, MI	Public Family Member	900.3	7,000	2834
Chiron Corporation	25	Emeryville, CA	Public	1,162.1	6,482	2835
Allergan Inc.	26	Irvine, CA	Public	1,138.0	6,124	2834
Amgen Inc.	27	Thousand Oaks, CA	Public	2,401.0	5,308	2834
NBTY, Inc.	28	Bohemia, NY	Public	572.1	5,300	2834
Yamanouchi Group Holding Inc.	29	San Francisco, CA	Private	655.6	5,100	2834
Hoffmann-La Roche Inc.	30	Nutley, NJ	Private	2,500.0	5,000	2834
Perrigo Company	31	Allegan, MI	Public	902.6	4,868	2834
Amgen Holding Inc.	32	Thousand Oaks, CA	Private	615.7	4,791	2834
Hoechst Marion Roussel Inc.	33	Kansas City, MO	Private	610.5	4,750	2834
Alcon Laboratories, Inc.	34	Fort Worth, TX	Private	1,253.0	4,500	2834
Ivax Corporation	35	Miami, FL	Public	602.1	4,500	2834
Wyeth Laboratories Inc.	36	Wayne, PA	Public Family Member	4,000.0	4,000	2834
Astra Pharmaceuticals, LP	37	Wayne, PA	Private	2,700.0	3,800	2834
Genentech Inc.	38	South San Francisco, CA	Public	1,150.9	3,242	2834
B. Braun/Mc Gaw, Inc.	39	Irvine, CA	Private	350.0	3,000	2834
Shaklee Corporation	40	San Francisco, CA	Private	666.1	3,000	2834
Green Cross Corp. Of America	41	Los Angeles, CA	Private	384.7	2,900	2836
Alpha Therapeutic Corporation	42	Los Angeles, CA	Private	384.7	2,800	2836
Rhone-Poulenc Rorer Pharmaceuticals	43	Collegeville, PA	Private	1,200.0	2,800	2834
Boehringer Ingelheim Corp.	44	Ridgefield, CT	Private	358.0	2,790	2834
Watson Pharmaceuticals, Inc.	45	Corona, CA	Public	324.0	2,554	2834
Genzyme Corporation	46	Cambridge, MA	Public	608.8	2,500	2835
L Perrigo Company	47	Allegan, MI	Public Family Member	0.9	2,200	2834
Nabi	48	Boca Raton, FL	Public	238.7	2,122	2836
Schering Berlin Inc.	49	Montville, NJ	Private	718.5	2,100	2834
Lifescan Inc.	50	Milpitas, CA	Public Family Member	165.2	2,000	2835
Mallinckrodt Chemical, Inc.	51	Hazelwood, MO	Public Family Member	258.1	2,000	2833
Mcneil Consumer Healthcare Co.	52	Fort Washington, PA	Public Family Member	256.2	2,000	2834
Schein Pharmaceutical Inc.	53	Florham Park, NJ	Public	490.2	2,000	2834
Mylan Laboratories Inc.	54	Pittsburgh, PA	Public	555.4	1,946	2834
Paco Pharmaceutical Services	55	Lakewood, NJ	Public Family Member	238.7	1,864	2834
Forest Laboratories Inc.	56	New York, NY	Public	427.1	1,854	2834
Boehrnger Inglheim Pharmaceuticals	57	Ridgefield, CT	Private	230.4	1,800	2834
Centeon Bio-Services Inc.	58	Knoxville, TN	Private	108.9	1,800	2836
Merial Ltd.	59	Athens, GA	Private	575.0	1,800	2836
Novartis Crop Protection Inc.	60	Greensboro, NC	Private	230.4	1,800	2834
Sigma Chemical Company	61	Saint Louis, MO	Public Family Member	108.9	1,800	2836
Cambrex Corporation	62	East Rutherford, NJ	Public	457.2	1,790	2834
Leiner Health Products Inc.	63	Carson, CA	Private	502.1	1,683	2834
Janssen Pharmaceutica Inc.	64	Titusville, NJ	Public Family Member	206.2	1,600	2833
Ortho Diagnostic Systems Inc.	65	Raritan, NJ	Public Family Member	132.1	1,600	2835
Life Technologies Inc.	66	Rockville, MD	Public	331.0	1,586	2836
Abbott Health Products Inc.	67	North Chicago, IL	Public Family Member	201.4	1,575	2834
Stiefel Laboratories Inc.	68	Coral Gables, FL	Private	214.1	1,470	2834
Diagnostic Products Corp.	69	Los Angeles, CA	Public	186.3	1,467	2835
Berlex Laboratories Inc.	70	Montville, NJ	Private	576.3	1,440	2834

D&B COMPANY RANKINGS BY EMPLOYMENT

Company	Rank	Location	Type	Sales ($ mil.)	Employment	Primary SIC
Leiner Health Products Group	71	Carson, CA	Private	178.9	1,400	2834
Zenith Gldline Pharmaceuticals	72	Miami, FL	Public Family Member	166.0	1,300	2834
Procter Gamble Pharmaceuticals	73	Cincinnati, OH	Public Family Member	164.7	1,290	2834
Scherng-Plough Healthcare Pdts	74	Liberty Corner, NJ	Public Family Member	700.0	1,235	2834
Melaleuca Inc.	75	Idaho Falls, ID	Private	154.3	1,200	2833
Nutramax Products, Inc.	76	Gloucester, MA	Public	128.4	1,200	2834
Pasteur Merieux Connaught	77	Swiftwater, PA	Private	153.1	1,200	2834
Roche Vitamins Inc.	78	Parsippany, NJ	Private	153.1	1,200	2834
Schering Plough Products Inc.	79	Manati, PR	Public Family Member	153.1	1,200	2834
Teva Pharmaceuticals USA Inc.	80	Sellersville, PA	Private	487.9	1,200	2834
Forest Pharmaceuticals Inc.	81	Earth City, MO	Public Family Member	350.0	1,150	2834
Gensia Sicor Inc.	82	Irvine, CA	Public	149.7	1,124	2834
Organon Inc.	83	West Orange, NJ	Private	300.0	1,100	2834
Solvay Pharmaceuticals Inc.	84	Marietta, GA	Private	400.0	1,100	2834
Amersham Holdings Inc.	85	Arlington Heights, IL	Private	270.0	1,050	2835
Lilly Del Caribe Inc.	86	Carolina, PR	Public Family Member	130.6	1,025	2834
Fisons US Investment Holdings	87	Wilmington, DE	Private	127.4	1,000	2834
Fujisawa Healthcare, Inc.	88	Deerfield, IL	Private	240.0	1,000	2834
King Pharmaceuticals, Inc.	89	Bristol, TN	Public	163.5	1,000	2834
Pfizer Pharmaceuticals Inc.	90	Barceloneta, PR	Public Family Member	1,336.5	1,000	2834
Sobel Usa Inc.	91	West Orange, NJ	Private	127.4	1,000	2834
Tag Pharmaceuticals Inc.	92	Kulpsville, PA	Private	500.0	1,000	2834
Agouron Pharmaceuticals Inc.	93	La Jolla, CA	Public	466.5	991	2834
Genetics Institute Inc.	94	Cambridge, MA	Public Family Member	172.1	980	2834
Connaught Laboratories Inc.	95	Swiftwater, PA	Private	333.5	970	2836
Mylan Pharmaceuticals Inc.	96	Morgantown, WV	Public Family Member	123.5	970	2834
Nature's Sunshine Products	97	Provo, UT	Public	280.9	966	2833
E-Z-Em, Inc.	98	Westbury, NY	Public	102.9	923	2835
Centeon LLC	99	King Of Prussia, PA	Private	904.3	918	2836
London International Group Inc.	100	Norcross, GA	Private	200.0	900	2834
Roxane Laboratories Inc.	101	Columbus, OH	Private	350.0	900	2834
Banner Pharmacaps Inc.	102	High Point, NC	Private	200.0	897	2834
Immunex Corporation	103	Seattle, WA	Public	185.3	886	2834
Altana Inc.	104	Melville, NY	Private	213.2	854	2834
Danbury Pharmacal Inc.	105	Carmel, NY	Public Family Member	108.1	850	2834
Smithkline Beecham Puerto Rico	106	Philadelphia, PA	Private	101.7	801	2834
General Nutrition Products Inc.	107	Pittsburgh, PA	Public Family Member	120.0	800	2834
Merck Holdings, Inc.	108	Whitehouse Station, NJ	Public Family Member	101.6	800	2834
Weider Health and Fitness	109	Woodland Hills, CA	Private	101.6	800	2834
Nycomed Amersham, Inc.	110	Princeton, NJ	Private	62.8	760	2835
Watson Laboratories, Inc.	111	Corona, CA	Public Family Member	96.5	760	2834
Lipha Americas Inc.	112	Napa, CA	Private	300.0	750	2834
Mova Pharmaceutical Corp.	113	Caguas, PR	Private	55.8	744	2834
Geneva Pharmaceuticals, Inc.	114	Broomfield, CO	Private	93.9	740	2834
Twinlab Corporation	115	Hauppauge, NY	Public	213.2	734	2833
Westwod-Squibb Pharmaceuticals	116	Buffalo, NY	Public Family Member	200.0	730	2834
Clay-Park Laboratories Inc.	117	Bronx, NY	Private	20.0	720	2834
Twin Laboratories Inc.	118	Hauppauge, NY	Public Family Member	213.2	701	2833
AC Molding Compounds	119	Wallingford, CT	Private	88.7	700	2834
Alpharma Inc.	120	Fort Lee, NJ	Public	500.3	700	2834
Alpharma USPD Inc.	121	Baltimore, MD	Public Family Member	88.7	700	2834
Squibb Manufacturing Inc.	122	Humacao, PR	Public Family Member	501.2	700	2834
IVC Industries, Inc.	123	Freehold, NJ	Public	119.8	691	2834
Pharmacia & Upjohn Caribe	124	Arecibo, PR	Public Family Member	400.0	685	2834
Dey Inc.	125	Napa, CA	Private	219.8	670	2834
Immuno - U S Inc.	126	Rochester, MI	Private	93.9	660	2836
Bristol-Myers Barceloneta Inc.	127	Barceloneta, PR	Public Family Member	426.2	650	2834
Johnson Johnson Phrm Partners	128	Gurabo, PR	Private	82.3	650	2834
Pharmaceutical Research Assoc.	129	Norwalk, CT	Private	100.0	650	2834
PRA Holdings, Inc.	130	Norwalk, CT	Private	100.0	650	2834
Searle & Co.	131	Caguas, PR	Public Family Member	256.1	650	2834
Smithkline Beecham	132	Cidra, PR	Private	800.0	650	2834
Pharmavite Corporation	133	Mission Hills, CA	Private	82.0	642	2833
Centocor Inc.	134	Malvern, PA	Public	200.8	640	2834
American Phrm Partners	135	Los Angeles, CA	Private	3.7	600	2834
Berwind Pharmaceutical Svcs	136	West Point, PA	Private	142.0	600	2834
Merrell Pharmaceuticals Inc.	137	Cincinnati, OH	Private	75.8	600	2834
Nexstar Pharmaceuticals Inc.	138	Boulder, CO	Public	89.2	580	2834
Zenith Laboratories Inc.	139	Northvale, NJ	Public Family Member	73.3	580	2834
Barr Laboratories Inc.	140	Pomona, NY	Public	377.3	557	2834

D&B COMPANY RANKINGS BY EMPLOYMENT

Company	Rank	Location	Type	Sales ($ mil.)	Employ-ment	Primary SIC
Boehringer Ingelheim Vetmedica	141	Saint Joseph, MO	Private	120.0	550	2836
DPT Laboratories Ltd.	142	San Antonio, TX	Private	68.6	550	2834
Purdue Pharma LP	143	Norwalk, CT	Private	100.0	550	2834
IPR Pharmaceutical, Inc.	144	Carolina, PR	Private	900.0	530	2834
Bristol-Myers Squibb Laboratoires	145	Mayaguez, PR	Public Family Member	847.4	527	2834
HCCP Acquisition Corporation	146	Somerville, NJ	Private	64.3	510	2834
Promega Corporation	147	Madison, WI	Private	76.0	510	2836
Elan Pharmaceuticals	148	South San Francisco, CA	Private	63.0	500	2834
McNeil Consumer Products Pr	149	Las Piedras, PR	Public Family Member	700.0	500	2834
Medi-Physics, Inc.	150	Arlington Heights, IL	Private	150.0	500	2833
Parke Davis Pharmaceuticals Ltd.	151	Vega Baja, PR	Private	63.0	500	2834
Plantation Botanicals, Inc.	152	Felda, FL	Private	59.6	500	2833
Searle, Ltd.	153	Barceloneta, PR	Public Family Member	600.0	492	2834
Faulding Inc.	154	Elizabeth, NJ	Private	102.1	479	2834
Schwarz Pharma Inc.	155	Thiensville, WI	Private	179.4	475	2834
Sidmak Laboratories Inc.	156	East Hanover, NJ	Private	84.2	470	2834
ICN Biomedicals, Inc.	157	Costa Mesa, CA	Public Family Member	38.0	460	2835
BFG Clinipad Investors, LP	158	Philadelphia, PA	Private	56.8	452	2834
Lederle Parenterals Inc.	159	Carolina, PR	Public Family Member	56.5	450	2834
Nutraceutical International	160	Park City, UT	Public	104.7	450	2834
Techne Corporation	161	Minneapolis, MN	Public	67.3	450	2835
Roberts Pharmaceutical Corp.	162	Eatontown, NJ	Public	122.5	448	2834
Vita Quest International Inc.	163	Caldwell, NJ	Private	100.0	425	2834
Amphastar Pharmacuticals Inc.	164	Chino, CA	Private	51.4	410	2834
Copley Pharmaceutical, Inc.	165	Canton, MA	Public	121.5	404	2834
Bausch & Lomb Pharmaceuticals	166	Tampa, FL	Public Family Member	50.1	400	2834
Biowhittaker Inc.	167	Walkersville, MD	Public Family Member	60.0	400	2836
Difco Laboratories Inc.	168	Livonia, MI	Public Family Member	24.2	400	2836
Granutec Inc.	169	Wilson, NC	Private	70.0	400	2834
Inovision Holdings LP	170	Yorba Linda, CA	Private	60.0	400	2835
Sankyo Pharma Inc.	171	Shirley, NY	Private	50.1	400	2834
Zenith Laboratories Caribe	172	Cidra, PR	Public Family Member	60.0	400	2834
Research And Diagnstc Systems	173	Minneapolis, MN	Public Family Member	57.3	390	2833
Amersham Corporation	174	Arlington Heights, IL	Private	100.0	383	2835
Internationa Medication System	175	El Monte, CA	Private	50.0	380	2834
Merial Select, Inc.	176	Gainesville, GA	Private	22.9	378	2836
Pharmaceutical Formulations	177	Edison, NJ	Public	80.8	378	2834
Luitpold Pharmaceuticals, Inc.	178	Shirley, NY	Private	45.7	366	2834
Chattem, Inc.	179	Chattanooga, TN	Public	220.1	364	2834
KOS Pharmaceuticals Inc.	180	Miami, FL	Public	2.9	361	2834
Chirex, Inc.	181	Stamford, CT	Private	94.1	360	2833
F P Syntex Inc.	182	Humacao, PR	Private	44.9	360	2834
Usana Inc.	183	Salt Lake City, UT	Public	85.2	359	2833
KV Pharmaceutical Company	184	Saint Louis, MO	Public	98.5	358	2834
Hauser Inc.	185	Boulder, CO	Public	32.0	354	2833
Biomatrix, Inc.	186	Ridgefield, NJ	Public	32.6	350	2836
Medimmune, Inc.	187	Gaithersburg, MD	Public	27.4	350	2836
Pharmaceutical Holdings Corp.	188	Philadelphia, PA	Private	130.0	350	2834
Scios Inc.	189	Mountain View, CA	Public	47.4	350	2834
Steris Laboratories, Inc.	190	Phoenix, AZ	Public Family Member	43.6	350	2834
Diasorin Inc.	191	Stillwater, MN	Public Family Member	28.1	340	2835
Par Pharmaceutical, Inc.	192	Spring Valley, NY	Public Family Member	53.1	340	2834
Pharmaceutical Resources, Inc.	193	Spring Valley, NY	Public	53.2	340	2834
Dura Pharmaceuticals Inc.	194	San Diego, CA	Public	181.3	331	2834
Richardson-Vicks Inc.	195	Cincinnati, OH	Public Family Member	40.4	325	2834
Muro Pharmaceutical Inc.	196	Tewksbury, MA	Private	85.0	320	2834
Intervet Inc.	197	Millsboro, DE	Private	19.1	315	2836
Purepac Pharmaceutical Co.	198	Elizabeth, NJ	Private	75.0	301	2834
Baxter Pharmaceutical Products	199	Liberty Corner, NJ	Public Family Member	37.2	300	2834
Delavau J W S Co Inc.	200	Philadelphia, PA	Private	50.0	300	2834
Natural Organics Inc.	201	Melville, NY	Private	37.6	300	2833
Neways Inc.	202	Salem, UT	Private	70.0	300	2833
Pharmingen	203	San Diego, CA	Public Family Member	44.0	300	2835
Proctor & Gamble Health Pdts	204	Cayey, PR	Public Family Member	37.2	300	2834
Quidel Corporation	205	San Diego, CA	Public	49.5	300	2835
Threshold Enterprises Ltd.	206	Scotts Valley, CA	Private	37.6	300	2833
Chugai Pharma USA Inc.	207	San Diego, CA	Private	92.1	292	2835
Bracco U.S.A. Inc.	208	Princeton, NJ	Private	228.3	290	2835
Roche Colorado Corp.	209	Boulder, CO	Private	80.0	290	2833
Gilead Sciences, Inc.	210	Foster City, CA	Public	40.0	289	2834

D&B COMPANY RANKINGS BY EMPLOYMENT

Company	Rank	Location	Type	Sales ($ mil.)	Employ-ment	Primary SIC
Enzymatic Therapy Inc.	211	Green Bay, WI	Private	35.6	285	2833
Perrigo Company	212	Greenville, SC	Public Family Member	75.0	285	2834
Collagen Aesthetics, Inc.	213	Palo Alto, CA	Public	82.8	280	2836
Scantibodies Laboratory Inc.	214	Santee, CA	Private	18.9	280	2835
Tishcon Corp.	215	Westbury, NY	Private	45.0	280	2834
Syntron Bioresearch, Inc.	216	Carlsbad, CA	Private	20.0	278	2835
Medeva Pharmacueticals Mfg.	217	Rochester, NY	Private	34.2	277	2834
Ganes Chemicals, Inc.	218	Carlstadt, NJ	Private	77.3	275	2833
Icos Corporation	219	Bothell, WA	Public	31.6	275	2834
Rhone-Poulenc Rorer	220	Manati, PR	Private	118.4	275	2834
V I Technologies, Inc.	221	Melville, NY	Public	44.0	275	2834
Bracco Diagnostics Inc.	222	Princeton, NJ	Private	219.5	270	2835
Du Pont Pharmaceuticals Co.	223	Manati, PR	Private	33.3	270	2834
Akorn, Inc.	224	Buffalo Grove, IL	Public	42.3	266	2834
Gensia Sicor Pharmaceuticals	225	Irvine, CA	Public Family Member	32.0	260	2834
Marsam Pharmaceuticals, Inc.	226	Cherry Hill, NJ	Public Family Member	40.0	260	2834
Sequus Pharmaceuticals Inc.	227	Menlo Park, CA	Public	40.0	260	2834
Axys Pharmaceuticals, Inc.	228	South San Francisco, CA	Public	24.8	256	2834
Carrington Laboratories Inc.	229	Irving, TX	Public	23.6	252	2834
Alcon Puerto Rico Inc.	230	Fort Worth, TX	Private	157.0	251	2834
Bertek Pharmaceuticals, Inc.	231	Sugar Land, TX	Public Family Member	50.0	250	2834
Boston Biomedica, Inc.	232	West Bridgewater, MA	Public	22.3	250	2835
Marion & Company	233	Manati, PR	Private	294.5	250	2834
PF Laboratories, Inc.	234	Totowa, NJ	Private	30.8	250	2834
Pfizer Corporation	235	New York, NY	Private	30.8	250	2834
Roberts Laboratories Inc.	236	Eatontown, NJ	Public Family Member	150.0	250	2834
Solopak Laboratories Inc.	237	Elk Grove Village, IL	Private	30.8	250	2834
Theratech Inc.	238	Salt Lake City, UT	Public	39.7	243	2834
Affymetrix, Inc.	239	Santa Clara, CA	Public	19.8	242	2835
Ansys Diagnostics Inc.	240	Lake Forest, CA	Private	19.0	241	2835
Amgen Puerto Rico Inc.	241	Juncos, PR	Public Family Member	439.9	240	2836
G C Hanford Mfg Co Inc.	242	Syracuse, NY	Private	20.0	240	2834
Humco Holding Group, Inc.	243	Texarkana, TX	Private	29.5	240	2834
PLP, Ltd.	244	Texarkana, TX	Private	29.5	240	2834
Systemix Inc.	245	Palo Alto, CA	Private	29.5	240	2834
Jones Pharma Inc.	246	Saint Louis, MO	Public	88.8	235	2834
Zila, Inc.	247	Phoenix, AZ	Public	62.1	235	2834
CN Biosciences, Inc.	248	San Diego, CA	Public	39.4	230	2836
Dermik Laboratories Inc.	249	Collegeville, PA	Private	139.0	230	2834
Immucor Inc.	250	Norcross, GA	Public	39.8	229	2835
Jeunique International Inc.	251	City Of Industry, CA	Private	27.9	225	2833
Mission Pharmacal Company	252	San Antonio, TX	Private	51.3	225	2834
Schwarz Pharma Manufacturing	253	Seymour, IN	Private	41.3	225	2834
Global Health Sciences Corp.	254	Orange, CA	Private	52.7	224	2834
Agri-Nutrition Group Limited	255	Maryland Heights, MO	Public	32.9	220	2834
D & F Industries Inc.	256	Orange, CA	Private	26.9	220	2834
Hycor Biomedical Inc.	257	Garden Grove, CA	Public	20.1	220	2835
Streck Laboratories Inc.	258	Omaha, NE	Private	21.5	220	2835
Taylor Pharmaceuticals Inc.	259	Decatur, IL	Public Family Member	26.9	220	2834
Protein Design Labs Inc.	260	Fremont, CA	Public	20.3	217	2834
Sugen Inc.	261	South San Francisco, CA	Public	6.0	216	2834
Baxter Caribe, Inc.	262	Guayama, PR	Private	57.0	211	2833
Ferndale Laboratories Inc.	263	Ferndale, MI	Private	23.8	210	2834
Biosite Diagnostics Inc.	264	San Diego, CA	Public	31.7	209	2835
Igi Inc.	265	Buena, NJ	Public	34.2	209	2836
Covance Biotechnology Services	266	Research Triangle Pa, NC	Public Family Member	25.0	208	2834
Nutraceutical Corporation	267	Ogden, UT	Public Family Member	25.3	208	2834
The Frederick Purdue Company	268	Norwalk, CT	Private	100.0	207	2834
Greer Laboratories Inc.	269	Lenoir, NC	Private	14.3	205	2836
Stratagene Holding Corp.	270	La Jolla, CA	Private	12.2	201	2836
Aesthetic Technologies Corp.	271	Palo Alto, CA	Public Family Member	69.3	200	2836
Apothecary Products Inc.	272	Burnsville, MN	Private	25.0	200	2834
Armstrong Laboratories Inc.	273	West Roxbury, MA	Private	32.3	200	2834
E R Sqibb Sons Intr-Mrcan Corp	274	Princeton, NJ	Public Family Member	31.6	200	2834
Elanco Animal House Inc.	275	Indianapolis, IN	Public Family Member	27.0	200	2834
Eon Labs Manufacturing, Inc.	276	Springfield Gardens, NY	Private	40.0	200	2834
G & W Laboratories Inc.	277	South Plainfield, NJ	Private	26.6	200	2834
Halsey Drug Co Inc.	278	Rockford, IL	Public	9.1	200	2834
HVL Inc.	279	Pittsburgh, PA	Private	50.0	200	2833
Neogen Corporation	280	Lansing, MI	Public	15.3	200	2835

D&B COMPANY RANKINGS BY EMPLOYMENT

Company	Rank	Location	Type	Sales ($ mil.)	Employ- ment	Primary SIC
Rexall Showcase International	281	Boca Raton, FL	Public Family Member	159.0	200	2834
Roche Products Inc.	282	Humacao, PR	Private	20.7	200	2834
Rx For Fleas Inc.	283	Fort Lauderdale, FL	Private	28.2	200	2834
Stratagene	284	La Jolla, CA	Private	14.9	200	2836
Universal Protein Supplements	285	New Brunswick, NJ	Private	29.7	200	2834
Westar Nutrition Corp.	286	Costa Mesa, CA	Private	21.0	200	2833
Advanced Nutraceuticals Inc.	287	South Plainfield, NJ	Private	30.8	195	2834
Mast Immunosystems, Inc.	288	Mountain View, CA	Private	21.3	190	2835
Colgate Oral Pharmaceuticals	289	Canton, MA	Public Family Member	26.7	188	2834
Natrol Inc.	290	Chatsworth, CA	Public	42.9	185	2834
PMLl Inc.	291	Wilsonville, OR	Public	13.9	185	2836
PML Microbiologicals Inc.	292	Wilsonville, OR	Public Family Member	13.9	184	2836
Glenwood LLC	293	Tenafly, NJ	Private	28.3	180	2834
International Processing Corp.	294	Winchester, KY	Private	25.0	180	2834
Qualis Inc.	295	Des Moines, IA	Private	19.9	180	2834
Salsbury Chemicals, Inc.	296	Charles City, IA	Public Family Member	19.7	180	2833
SP Pharmaceuticals, LLC	297	Albuquerque, NM	Private	18.0	180	2834
Galderma Laboratories Inc.	298	Fort Worth, TX	Private	156.8	179	2834
Cell Genesys, Inc.	299	Foster City, CA	Public	23.8	177	2836
Applied Biotech, Inc.	300	San Diego, CA	Private	16.0	175	2835
JB Laboratories Inc.	301	Holland, MI	Private	24.9	175	2833
Nittany Pharmaceuticals Inc.	302	Milroy, PA	Private	25.5	175	2834
Elan Pharmaceutical Res	303	Gainesville, GA	Private	12.5	174	2834
Medeva MA, Inc.	304	Boston, MA	Private	27.7	173	2834
Cardiovascular Dynamics Inc.	305	Irvine, CA	Public	11.3	170	2834
Mgp Holding Corp	306	Morton Grove, IL	Private	47.0	170	2834
Mikart Inc.	307	Atlanta, GA	Private	29.6	170	2834
Morton Grove Pharmaceuticals	308	Morton Grove, IL	Private	23.0	170	2834
Reliv' International Inc.	309	Chesterfield, MO	Public	46.8	170	2834
Hyseq, Inc.	310	Sunnyvale, CA	Public	6.2	169	2835
Abbott Chemicals Inc.	311	Barceloneta, PR	Public Family Member	15.4	166	2833
Galen Inc.	312	Audubon, PA	Private	8.8	165	2834
Invitrogen Corporation	313	Carlsbad, CA	Public	32.0	165	2836
Matrix Pharmaceutical Inc.	314	Fremont, CA	Public	12.1	162	2836
PDK Labs Inc.	315	Hauppauge, NY	Public	51.4	162	2834
Applicare, Inc.	316	Louisville, KY	Private	21.3	160	2834
Frutarom Meer Corporation	317	North Bergen, NJ	Private	33.3	160	2833
Grand Laboratories Inc.	318	Freeman, SD	Private	17.5	160	2836
Invamed Incorporated	319	Dayton, NJ	Private	37.0	160	2834
Noven Pharmaceuticals Inc.	320	Miami, FL	Public	15.2	160	2834
Xoma Corporation	321	Berkeley, CA	Public	18.4	160	2836
Cygnus, Inc.	322	Redwood City, CA	Public	29.5	157	2834
Chemins Company Inc.	323	Colorado Springs, CO	Private	37.0	155	2834
Vysis, Inc.	324	Downers Grove, IL	Public	18.2	153	2835
Therapeutics Inc.	325	South San Francisco, CA	Public	22.2	152	2834
Aim International, Inc.	326	Nampa, ID	Private	47.8	150	2833
B I Chemicals Inc.	327	Ridgefield, CT	Private	22.3	150	2834
Calbiochem-Novabiochem Corp.	328	San Diego, CA	Public Family Member	21.5	150	2836
Charter Laboratories Inc.	329	Lakewood, NJ	Public Family Member	8.0	150	2834
Country Farms Inc.	330	Fairfield, NJ	Private	19.3	150	2834
Guy & O'Neill, Inc.	331	Fredonia, WI	Private	14.0	150	2834
Immunogenetics Inc.	332	Buena, NJ	Public Family Member	20.6	150	2834
Mentholatum Company Inc.	333	Orchard Park, NY	Private	95.0	150	2834
Microcide Pharmaceuticals	334	Mountain View, CA	Public	14.9	150	2834
Robinson Pharma, Inc.	335	Santa Ana, CA	Private	17.8	150	2834
Roche Carolina Inc.	336	Florence, SC	Private	18.3	150	2834
Steritek, Inc.	337	Moonachie, NJ	Public	8.7	150	2834
Vitatech International Inc.	338	Tustin, CA	Private	19.3	150	2834
Wyckoff Chemical Company Inc.	339	South Haven, MI	Private	31.4	150	2833
Molecular Probes Inc.	340	Eugene, OR	Private	11.8	148	2835
Genelabs Technologies, Inc.	341	Redwood City, CA	Public	12.8	147	2834
Miravant Medical Technologies	342	Goleta, CA	Public	2.3	145	2834
Novo Nordisk Phrm Inds Inc.	343	Clayton, NC	Private	23.9	145	2833
Pel-Freez, Inc.	344	Rogers, AR	Private	11.1	142	2835
Spafas, Incorporated	345	Preston, CT	Public Family Member	14.0	141	2836
Dynagen Inc.	346	Cambridge, MA	Public	14.0	140	2834
JRH Biosciences, Inc.	347	Shawnee Mission, KS	Private	35.0	140	2836
Natural Balance Inc.	348	Castle Rock, CO	Private	16.4	140	2834
Nutro Laboratories Inc.	349	South Plainfield, NJ	Private	32.0	140	2834
Princeton Biomeditech Corp.	350	Monmouth Junction, NJ	Private	10.0	140	2835

D&B COMPANY RANKINGS BY EMPLOYMENT

Company	Rank	Location	Type	Sales ($ mil.)	Employ-ment	Primary SIC
Sergeant's Pet Products, Inc.	351	Omaha, NE	Public Family Member	15.2	140	2834
Merial Ah Inc.	352	Athens, GA	Private	17.6	138	2834
Coromed Inc.	353	Troy, NY	Public Family Member	9.0	135	2834
Digene Corporation	354	Beltsville, MD	Public	12.0	135	2835
Hi-Tech Pharmacal Co, Inc.	355	Amityville, NY	Public	22.4	135	2834
Central Admixture Phrm Svcs	356	Irvine, CA	Private	26.0	130	2834
Danbury Pharmacal Puerto Rico	357	Humacao, PR	Public Family Member	50.0	130	2834
Genosys Biotechnologies, Inc.	358	The Woodlands, TX	Private	11.7	130	2833
International Frutarom Corp.	359	North Bergen, NJ	Private	40.0	130	2833
Lyne Laboratories Inc.	360	Brockton, MA	Private	8.2	130	2834
Natural Alternatives Intl	361	San Marcos, CA	Public	67.9	130	2833
Scherer Healthcare Inc.	362	Atlanta, GA	Public	13.9	130	2834
UDL Laboratories Inc.	363	Largo, FL	Public Family Member	18.1	130	2833
Zuellig Botanicals Inc.	364	Long Beach, CA	Private	55.0	130	2833
Blistex Inc.	365	Oak Brook, IL	Private	28.0	126	2834
Neurocrine Biosciences Inc.	366	San Diego, CA	Public	26.1	126	2835
Bartels Inc.	367	Issaquah, WA	Private	17.0	125	2835
Biogenex Laboratories	368	San Ramon, CA	Private	12.7	125	2835
Phoenix Scientific Inc.	369	Saint Joseph, MO	Private	30.4	125	2834
Procter Gamble Pharmaceuticals	370	Manati, PR	Public Family Member	12.5	125	2834
Syntex Agribusiness Inc.	371	Springfield, MO	Private	16.3	125	2834
Halocarbon Products Corp.	372	River Edge, NJ	Private	15.8	123	2834
Mylan Inc.	373	Caguas, PR	Public Family Member	45.0	123	2834
Albany Molecular Research	374	Albany, NY	Public	9.0	122	2833
Accucorp Packaging Inc.	375	Philadelphia, PA	Private	16.2	120	2834
Diamond Animal Health, Inc.	376	Des Moines, IA	Public Family Member	7.1	120	2836
Interntnal Bchmicals Group Inc.	377	The Woodlands, TX	Private	12.0	120	2836
Medical Analysis Systems Inc.	378	Camarillo, CA	Private	10.9	120	2835
National Vitamin Co Inc.	379	Porterville, CA	Private	18.0	120	2834
One Lambda Inc.	380	Canoga Park, CA	Private	17.5	120	2833
Scientific Protein Labs	381	Waunakee, WI	Public Family Member	15.6	120	2834
Shaman Pharmaceuticals Inc.	382	South San Francisco, CA	Public	3.5	120	2833
West-Ward Pharmaceutical Corp.	383	Eatontown, NJ	Private	15.8	120	2834
Worldwide Group Of Co. Ltd. Inc.	384	Stamford, CT	Private	16.8	120	2833
Custom Coatings Inc.	385	Farmingdale, NY	Private	6.0	119	2834
R.I.T.A. Corporation	386	Woodstock, IL	Private	45.0	118	2833
Healthpoint Ltd.	387	Fort Worth, TX	Private	16.1	115	2834
Monticello Companies Inc.	388	Jacksonville, FL	Private	3.8	115	2834
Santa Cruz Biotechnology Inc.	389	Santa Cruz, CA	Private	8.1	115	2836
Lederle Piperacillin Inc.	390	Carolina, PR	Public Family Member	12.1	114	2834
Gamma Biologicals Inc.	391	Houston, TX	Public Family Member	18.3	113	2835
Sangstat Medical Corporation	392	Menlo Park, CA	Public	4.5	112	2834
Bentley Pharmaceuticals Inc.	393	Tampa, FL	Public	14.9	110	2834
Fleming & Company Inc.	394	Fenton, MO	Private	11.9	110	2834
Paddock Laboratories Inc.	395	Minneapolis, MN	Private	20.4	110	2834
Hemagen Diagnostics Inc.	396	Waltham, MA	Public	12.3	109	2835
Signal Pharmaceuticals, Inc.	397	San Diego, CA	Private	7.6	109	2834
Cocensys Inc.	398	Irvine, CA	Public	11.9	107	2834
Ribi Immunochem Research Inc.	399	Hamilton, MT	Public	6.1	107	2834
Oclassen Pharmaceuticals Inc.	400	San Rafael, CA	Public Family Member	16.0	106	2834
Hess & Clark, Inc.	401	Ashland, OH	Public Family Member	11.7	105	2834
Proclinical Inc.	402	Phoenixville, PA	Private	15.8	105	2834
Shaperite Concepts, Ltd.	403	Sandy, UT	Private	12.4	105	2833
Corixa Corporation	404	Seattle, WA	Public	14.4	104	2834
Argonex Holdings Inc.	405	Charlottesville, VA	Private	9.1	102	2835
American Biological Tech	406	Seguin, TX	Private	7.4	100	2835
Bachem Inc.	407	Torrance, CA	Private	6.7	100	2836
Chem International Inc.	408	Hillside, NJ	Public	11.1	100	2834
Colorado Serum Company	409	Denver, CO	Private	5.8	100	2836
Del Pharmaceuticals Inc.	410	Uniondale, NY	Public Family Member	55.7	100	2834
E Excel International Inc.	411	Springville, UT	Private	24.6	100	2833
Elan Transdermal Technologies	412	Pembroke Pines, FL	Private	15.0	100	2834
Ex-Lax Inc.	413	Humacao, PR	Private	40.0	100	2834
Health Factors International	414	Tempe, AZ	Public Family Member	15.0	100	2833
Hematronix, Inc.	415	Plano, TX	Private	8.5	100	2835
Interferon Sciences Inc.	416	New Brunswick, NJ	Public	3.0	100	2835
Intergen Company	417	Purchase, NY	Private	30.0	100	2836
Irvine Scientific Sales Co.	418	Santa Ana, CA	Private	16.9	100	2836
Lafayette Pharmaceuticals Inc.	419	Yorba Linda, CA	Private	10.8	100	2835
Medical Research Industries	420	Pompano Beach, FL	Private	8.0	100	2834

D&B COMPANY RANKINGS BY EMPLOYMENT

Company	Rank	Location	Type	Sales ($ mil.)	Employ-ment	Primary SIC
Middle States Management Corp.	421	Saint Louis, MO	Private	10.7	100	2834
Noramco, (Delaware) Inc.	422	New Brunswick, NJ	Public Family Member	14.3	100	2833
Norwich Overseas, Inc.	423	Cincinnati, OH	Public Family Member	10.7	100	2834
OHM Laboratories Inc.	424	North Brunswick, NJ	Private	15.5	100	2834
Parkedale Pharmaceutical Inc.	425	Rochester, MI	Public Family Member	11.3	100	2834
Pharma Tech Industries, Inc.	426	Union, MO	Private	6.0	100	2834
Sunstar Pharmaceuticals, Inc.	427	Elgin, IL	Private	8.0	100	2834
United States Biochemical Corp.	428	Cleveland, OH	Private	6.8	100	2835
Vivus Inc.	429	Mountain View, CA	Public	138.3	100	2834
Wright Enrichment Inc.	430	Crowley, LA	Private	8.6	100	2834
Calix Corporation	431	Lexington, MA	Private	15.1	99	2834
Pharm-Eco Laboratories Inc.	432	Lexington, MA	Private	15.1	99	2834
Ash Corp.	433	Gulfport, MS	Private	10.8	98	2834
Kabco Pharmaceuticals, Inc.	434	Amityville, NY	Private	21.0	98	2834
Lannett Company Inc.	435	Philadelphia, PA	Public	9.5	98	2834
Geron Corporation	436	Menlo Park, CA	Public	7.3	96	2834
Thames Pharmacal Co Inc.	437	Ronkonkoma, NY	Private	14.3	96	2834
BASF Pharmaceuticals, Inc.	438	Jayuya, PR	Private	9.2	95	2834
Evergood Products Corporation	439	Hicksville, NY	Private	31.0	95	2833
Penederm Incorporated	440	Foster City, CA	Public Family Member	12.5	95	2834
Gentrac, Inc.	441	Middleton, WI	Public Family Member	5.6	93	2836
Shire Laboratories Inc.	442	Rockville, MD	Private	10.8	93	2834
Amide Pharmaceutical Inc.	443	Little Falls, NJ	Private	26.2	90	2834
Beach Products Inc.	444	Tampa, FL	Private	9.9	90	2834
Biovail Laboratories Inc.	445	Carolina, PR	Private	16.9	90	2834
Epitope Inc.	446	Beaverton, OR	Public	9.8	90	2835
Golden Pharmaceuticals Inc.	447	Santa Ana, CA	Public	6.4	90	2834
Guardian Drug Company Inc.	448	Trenton, NJ	Private	12.0	90	2834
Hercon Laboratories Corp.	449	New York, NY	Public Family Member	12.5	90	2834
Medicis Pharmaceutical Corp.	450	Phoenix, AZ	Public	41.2	90	2834
Miravant Pharmaceuticals Inc.	451	Goleta, CA	Public Family Member	11.7	90	2834
Pharmaceutical Associates Inc.	452	Tampa, FL	Private	9.9	90	2834
Bristol Caribbean Inc.	453	Mayaguez, PR	Public Family Member	600.0	89	2834
ICN East, Inc.	454	New York, NY	Public Family Member	13.0	88	2834
Inova Diagnostics, Inc.	455	San Diego, CA	Private	10.7	86	2835
Ambico Inc.	456	Dallas Center, IA	Private	4.6	85	2836
Atlantic Pharmaceutical Svcs	457	Owings Mills, MD	Private	9.5	85	2834
Enzon Inc.	458	Piscataway, NJ	Public	12.7	85	2834
F.A.M.G. Inc.	459	Santa Clarita, CA	Private	56.0	85	2833
Puritan Quartz, Inc.	460	Santa Clarita, CA	Private	11.2	85	2833
Triangle Pharmaceuticals, Inc.	461	Durham, NC	Public	9.8	85	2834
Botanical Laboratories Inc.	462	Ferndale, WA	Private	10.8	84	2834
Sovereign Pharmaceuticals	463	Fort Worth, TX	Private	7.7	84	2834
Easy Returns Worldwide, Inc.	464	Saint Charles, MO	Private	10.2	82	2834
Alra Laboratories Inc.	465	Gurnee, IL	Private	12.0	80	2834
Avant Immunotherapeutics Inc.	466	Needham, MA	Private	10.0	80	2833
D V M Pharmaceuticals Inc.	467	Miami, FL	Public Family Member	19.3	80	2834
Deseret Laboratories Inc.	468	St George, UT	Private	8.5	80	2833
Elan Holdings Inc.	469	Smithfield, RI	Private	11.9	80	2834
H.T.I. Bio-Products Inc.	470	Santa Ysabel, CA	Private	7.7	80	2835
Little Silver Corp.	471	Sioux Falls, SD	Private	4.0	80	2833
Marlyn Nutraceuticals, Inc.	472	Scottsdale, AZ	Private	18.0	80	2833
Pharmacyclics Inc.	473	Sunnyvale, CA	Public	3.5	80	2834
Pro Pac Labs Inc.	474	Ogden, UT	Private	10.9	80	2834
Rainbow Lght Ntrtional Systems	475	Santa Cruz, CA	Private	10.5	80	2833
Ranlab Inc.	476	Princeton, NJ	Private	15.5	80	2834
U S Diversified Technologies	477	Largo, FL	Private	5.7	80	2834
Ambion Inc.	478	Austin, TX	Private	7.0	78	2836
ISP Fine Chemicals Inc.	479	Columbus, OH	Private	8.5	78	2834
Pacific Biotech, Inc.	480	San Diego, CA	Public Family Member	7.5	78	2835
Clark Laboratories Inc.	481	Jamestown, NY	Private	6.5	76	2835
Center Laboratories Inc.	482	Port Washington, NY	Public Family Member	5.0	75	2834
Fibrogen, Inc.	483	South San Francisco, CA	Private	10.8	75	2834
Integrated Health Nutritionals	484	Phoenix, AZ	Private	9.6	75	2833
Interglow Nutritional Systems	485	Milroy, PA	Private	7.0	75	2834
Manhattan Drug Co. Inc.	486	Hillside, NJ	Public Family Member	12.0	75	2834
Materials Processing Tech	487	Paterson, NJ	Private	7.0	75	2834
Phillips Pharmatech Labs Inc.	488	Largo, FL	Private	9.6	75	2834
Vitaminerals Inc.	489	Glendale, CA	Private	8.2	75	2833
XF Enterprises Inc.	490	Greeley, CO	Private	18.9	75	2834

D&B COMPANY RANKINGS BY EMPLOYMENT

Company	Rank	Location	Type	Sales ($ mil.)	Employ- ment	Primary SIC
Lynx Therapeutics Inc.	491	Hayward, CA	Public	4.6	73	2834
Md Pharmaceutical Inc.	492	Santa Ana, CA	Private	9.4	73	2833
Norian Corporation	493	Cupertino, CA	Private	3.1	73	2836
Endogen Inc.	494	Woburn, MA	Public	10.0	72	2835
Juneau Packaging Corporation	495	Mauston, WI	Public Family Member	5.1	72	2835
Montana Naturals Int'l Inc.	496	Arlee, MT	Public Family Member	10.0	72	2833
Kirkegaard & Perry Labs Inc.	497	Gaithersburg, MD	Private	4.7	71	2836
Peninsula Laboratories Inc.	498	Belmont, CA	Private	10.4	71	2833
Alacer Corp.	499	El Toro, CA	Private	6.0	70	2833
Apotex Usa, Inc.	500	Oceanside, NY	Private	10.0	70	2834
Astra Research Center Boston	501	Cambridge, MA	Private	6.4	70	2835
Biocor Animal Health Inc.	502	Omaha, NE	Private	10.0	70	2836
Boiron Borneman Inc.	503	Newtown Square, PA	Private	11.0	70	2833
Chester Labs, Inc.	504	Cincinnati, OH	Private	11.0	70	2834
East Earth Herb Inc.	505	Eugene, OR	Private	7.1	70	2834
Madis Botanicals, Inc.	506	South Hackensack, NJ	Public Family Member	9.7	70	2833
Mediatech Inc.	507	Herndon, VA	Private	4.1	70	2836
Merz, Incorporated	508	Greensboro, NC	Private	20.0	70	2834
Mineral Resources Int'l	509	Ogden, UT	Private	5.0	70	2834
MML Diagnostics Packaging Inc.	510	Troutdale, OR	Private	4.1	70	2836
Mueller Sports Medicine Inc.	511	Prairie Du Sac, WI	Private	5.8	70	2834
Pure World Inc.	512	Bedminster, NJ	Public	12.7	70	2833
Quality Care Phrmceuticals Inc.	513	Santa Ana, CA	Public Family Member	5.5	70	2834
Standard Homeopathic Company	514	Los Angeles, CA	Private	9.2	70	2834
The Liposome Mfg Co. Inc.	515	Indianapolis, IN	Public Family Member	7.7	70	2833
Wilson Group Inc.	516	Sussex, WI	Private	4.5	70	2836
Advanced Magnetics Inc.	517	Cambridge, MA	Public	11.0	68	2834
Allerderm Inc.	518	Fort Worth, TX	Private	7.1	68	2834
Biosource International Inc.	519	Camarillo, CA	Public	20.6	68	2836
Cyanotech Corporation	520	Kailua Kona, HI	Public	7.6	68	2836
Eurand America Incorporated	521	Vandalia, OH	Public Family Member	12.0	67	2834
Person & Covey Inc.	522	Glendale, CA	Private	6.0	67	2834
Coulter Pharmaceutical, Inc.	523	South San Francisco, CA	Public	9.3	66	2834
ADH Health Products, Inc.	524	Congers, NY	Private	7.5	65	2834
Applied Laboratories Inc.	525	Columbus, IN	Private	6.0	65	2834
Biomune Company	526	Shawnee Mission, KS	Private	4.4	65	2836
Endo Pharmaceuticals Inc.	527	Chadds Ford, PA	Private	9.1	65	2834
Food Sciences Corporation	528	Mount Laurel, NJ	Private	8.0	65	2833
JMI-Daniels Pharmaceutical	529	Saint Petersburg, FL	Public Family Member	7.2	65	2834
Konsyl Pharmaceuticals Inc.	530	Fort Worth, TX	Private	7.6	65	2834
MGI Pharma, Inc.	531	Hopkins, MN	Public	12.4	65	2834
Micelle Laboratories Inc.	532	Lake Forest, CA	Private	8.0	65	2834
Neo-Life Company Of America	533	Fremont, CA	Private	9.1	65	2834
Novopharm, USA Inc.	534	Schaumburg, IL	Private	300.0	65	2834
Mitotix, Inc.	535	Cambridge, MA	Private	5.8	64	2834
Pharmatech Laboratories Inc.	536	Lindon, UT	Private	7.8	64	2834
Chemdex, Inc.	537	Shawnee Mission, KS	Private	6.9	63	2834
Maine Biological Laboratories	538	Waterville, ME	Private	7.3	63	2836
Synbiotics Corporation	539	San Diego, CA	Public	23.3	63	2836
ABS Corporation	540	Omaha, NE	Private	5.3	62	2834
Biometric Imaging Inc.	541	Mountain View, CA	Private	5.0	60	2835
Biosource Technologies, Inc.	542	Vacaville, CA	Private	2.0	60	2833
Chesapeake Biological Labs	543	Baltimore, MD	Public	7.0	60	2834
Circa Pharmaceuticals Inc.	544	Copiague, NY	Public Family Member	8.3	60	2834
Fujirebio Diagnostic Inc.	545	Malvern, PA	Private	27.0	60	2835
Grant Industries, Inc.	546	Elmwood Park, NJ	Private	6.9	60	2834
Holopack International, LP	547	Columbia, SC	Private	6.5	60	2834
KC Pharmaceutical Inc.	548	Pomona, CA	Private	7.5	60	2834
Luyties Pharmacal Company	549	Saint Louis, MO	Private	5.2	60	2834
Metra Biosystems, Inc.	550	Mountain View, CA	Public	6.7	60	2835
Morton Pharmaceuticals Inc.	551	Memphis, TN	Private	5.9	60	2834
Pharmacia Hepar Inc.	552	Franklin, OH	Public Family Member	18.0	60	2833
Schering-Plough Veterinary	553	Baton Rouge, LA	Public Family Member	12.0	60	2834
Veterinary Laboratories, Inc.	554	Shawnee Mission, KS	Private	6.1	60	2834
Fortitech Inc.	555	Schenectady, NY	Private	35.0	59	2834
Chemicals Inc.	556	Baytown, TX	Private	3.9	58	2834
Neorx Corporation	557	Seattle, WA	Public	7.5	57	2835
Neurex Corporation	558	Menlo Park, CA	Public	2.4	56	2836
Alexon-Trend Inc.	559	Anoka, MN	Private	4.4	55	2835
All American Pharmaceuticals	560	Billings, MT	Private	15.0	55	2834

D&B COMPANY RANKINGS BY EMPLOYMENT

Company	Rank	Location	Type	Sales ($ mil.)	Employ-ment	Primary SIC
Bard Diagnostic Sciences Division	561	Redmond, WA	Public Family Member	5.3	55	2835
Carma Laboratories, Inc.	562	Franklin, WI	Private	15.2	55	2834
Gliatech Inc.	563	Cleveland, OH	Public	13.1	55	2834
Hardy Media Inc.	564	Santa Maria, CA	Private	9.0	55	2836
Interpharm Inc.	565	Plainview, NY	Private	8.1	55	2834
Lloyd Inc. of Iowa	566	Shenandoah, IA	Private	4.3	55	2834
Lohmann Therapy Systems Corp.	567	Caldwell, NJ	Private	9.1	55	2834
Novo Holdings Inc.	568	Schaumburg, IL	Private	6.3	55	2834
Technical Chemicals & Products	569	Pompano Beach, FL	Public	6.2	55	2835
Tender Corporation	570	Littleton, NH	Private	6.0	55	2834
Time-Cap Laboratories Inc.	571	Farmingdale, NY	Private	15.0	55	2834
Winning Combination Inc.	572	Henderson, NV	Private	6.1	55	2834
Amerifit, Inc.	573	Bloomfield, CT	Private	20.0	54	2833
Food Science Corp.	574	Essex Junction, VT	Private	11.3	54	2833
International Tollers Inc.	575	Grand Haven, MI	Private	4.5	54	2834
ALK Laboratories Inc.	576	Wallingford, CT	Private	15.0	53	2836
Heel Inc.	577	Albuquerque, NM	Private	5.8	53	2833
JBL Scientific Inc.	578	San Luis Obispo, CA	Public Family Member	5.5	53	2833
Berkeley Antibody Company	579	Richmond, CA	Private	5.3	52	2833
Cayman Chemical Company Inc.	580	Ann Arbor, MI	Private	5.3	52	2834
Life Services Supplements	581	Neptune, NJ	Private	6.1	52	2834
Naturopathic Formulations	582	Wilsonville, OR	Private	7.0	52	2833
SSS Company	583	Atlanta, GA	Private	5.2	52	2834
Leukosite, Inc.	584	Cambridge, MA	Public	5.7	51	2834
A & V Incorporated	585	Sussex, WI	Private	12.0	50	2836
Advance Development Co.	586	Lakewood, NJ	Private	4.9	50	2834
Anthony Products Co.	587	Arcadia, CA	Private	14.4	50	2834
Beauty & Health International	588	Santa Ana, CA	Private	6.6	50	2834
Bigmar, Inc.	589	Johnstown, OH	Public	6.5	50	2834
Bio Botanica Inc.	590	Hauppauge, NY	Private	6.4	50	2833
Bio Med Plastics Inc.	591	Linden, NJ	Private	4.9	50	2834
Biochemical Sciences Inc.	592	Swedesboro, NJ	Public Family Member	4.8	50	2835
Biocore Medical Tech Inc.	593	Topeka, KS	Private	5.7	50	2833
Biologically Active Substances	594	Monterey, CA	Private	6.0	50	2833
Bionostics Inc.	595	Acton, MA	Private	4.6	50	2835
Chemsource Corporation	596	Guayama, PR	Private	9.0	50	2834
Connetics Corp.	597	Palo Alto, CA	Public	6.8	50	2834
Consolidated Pharmaceuticals Group	598	Baltimore, MD	Private	5.2	50	2834
Cornwell Corporation	599	Riverdale, NJ	Private	10.0	50	2835
Herba Aromatica Inc.	600	Hayward, CA	Private	5.0	50	2833
Ivy Animal Health, Inc.	601	Shawnee Mission, KS	Private	4.9	50	2834
Kelatron Inc.	602	Ogden, UT	Private	5.4	50	2834
Mardel Laboratories Inc.	603	Glendale Heights, IL	Public Family Member	5.0	50	2833
Medical Products Laboratories	604	Philadelphia, PA	Private	4.9	50	2834
Molecumetics, Ltd.	605	Bellevue, WA	Public Family Member	4.0	50	2836
Northridge Laboratories Inc.	606	Chatsworth, CA	Private	6.4	50	2833
Nutritional Laboratories Int'l	607	Lolo, MT	Private	9.0	50	2833
Organics/Lagrange, Inc.	608	Northbrook, IL	Private	3.1	50	2834
Pharmaceutical Innovations	609	Newark, NJ	Private	4.9	50	2834
Pharmaceutical Laboratories	610	Corpus Christi, TX	Public	5.3	50	2833
Quantimetrix	611	Redondo Beach, CA	Private	4.0	50	2835
Reliance Vitamin Co Inc.	612	Somerville, NJ	Private	3.2	50	2834
Teco Diagnostics	613	Anaheim, CA	Private	6.0	50	2835
Tyler Distribution Inc.	614	Gresham, OR	Private	6.4	50	2833
Warner Chilcott, Inc.	615	Rockaway, NJ	Private	75.8	50	2834
West Coast Laboratories Inc.	616	Gardena, CA	Private	7.0	50	2834
Cima Labs Inc.	617	Eden Prairie, MN	Public	4.9	49	2834
Formulation Technology Inc.	618	Oakdale, CA	Private	8.1	49	2834
Genzyme Diagnostics Medix Biot	619	San Carlos, CA	Public Family Member	3.5	49	2836
Penick Corporation	620	Newark, NJ	Private	5.9	49	2833
Third Wave Technologies, Inc.	621	Madison, WI	Private	4.0	49	2835
Viral Antigens Inc.	622	Memphis, TN	Private	3.8	49	2835
Allen & Associates Intl Ltd.	623	Washington, DC	Private	5.6	48	2834
Heico Chemicals, Inc.	624	Delaware Water Gap, PA	Public Family Member	12.0	48	2833
Quality Biological Inc.	625	Gaithersburg, MD	Private	3.2	48	2836
Regis Technologies, Inc.	626	Morton Grove, IL	Private	5.0	48	2835
Vector Laboratories Inc.	627	Burlingame, CA	Private	5.4	48	2833
Alfa-Flour Inc.	628	Wray, CO	Private	4.3	47	2834
Biocore Medical Technologies	629	Topeka, KS	Private	4.7	47	2833
Chantal Pharmaceutical Corp.	630	Los Angeles, CA	Public	6.7	47	2834

D&B COMPANY RANKINGS BY EMPLOYMENT

Company	Rank	Location	Type	Sales ($ mil.)	Employ- ment	Primary SIC
Research Biochemicals Inc.	631	Natick, MA	Public Family Member	10.0	47	2836
Telik Inc.	632	South San Francisco, CA	Private	3.7	47	2834
Oxycal Laboratories Inc.	633	Prescott, AZ	Public Family Member	5.0	46	2833
Ameri-Kal, Inc.	634	Auburn, CA	Private	2.0	45	2833
Avanti Polar Lipids Inc.	635	Alabaster, AL	Private	3.5	45	2833
Chelsea Laboratories Inc.	636	Cincinnati, OH	Public Family Member	4.3	45	2834
Chembio Diagnostic Systems	637	Medford, NY	Private	4.0	45	2835
Devlan Inc.	638	Farmington Hills, MI	Private	4.0	45	2834
Diagnostic Reagents, Inc.	639	Sunnyvale, CA	Private	5.2	45	2835
Molorokalin Inc.	640	Youngstown, OH	Private	4.6	45	2834
National Medical Industries	641	Boise, ID	Private	4.7	45	2834
Novagen Inc.	642	Madison, WI	Public Family Member	5.0	45	2835
Nutri-Well International Inc.	643	Santa Ana, CA	Private	5.1	45	2834
Otis Clapp & Son Inc.	644	Canton, MA	Private	4.3	45	2834
P J Noyes Co Inc.	645	Lancaster, NH	Private	4.5	45	2834
Pacific International	646	Saratoga, CA	Private	15.0	45	2835
Pharmasciences Inc.	647	West Conshohocken, PA	Private	7.0	45	2834
Theracom Inc.	648	Bethesda, MD	Private	4.5	45	2834
Tower Laboratories, Ltd.	649	Essex, CT	Private	4.4	45	2834
Vitamins, Inc.	650	Chicago, IL	Private	10.0	45	2834
Petnet Pharmaceutical Svcs LLC	651	Norcross, GA	Private	4.3	44	2835
Pharmanex Inc.	652	Simi Valley, CA	Private	15.0	44	2834
Aaron Industries Inc.	653	Clinton, SC	Private	10.0	43	2834
B & C Nutritional Products	654	Vista, CA	Private	10.0	43	2833
Nastech Pharmaceutical Company	655	Hauppauge, NY	Public	5.5	43	2834
Stevens Ash Inc.	656	Detroit, MI	Private	6.8	43	2834
Allergy Control Products, Inc.	657	Ridgefield, CT	Private	2.9	42	2836
Archon Vitamin Corp.	658	Irvington, NJ	Private	6.0	42	2834
B F Ascher & Company Inc.	659	Shawnee Mission, KS	Private	3.2	42	2834
Best Industries Inc.	660	Springfield, VA	Private	3.9	42	2834
Champion Performance Products	661	Concord, CA	Private	14.2	42	2834
International Enzyme Inc.	662	Fallbrook, CA	Private	7.2	42	2836
Nutraceutix, Inc.	663	Redmond, WA	Private	4.3	42	2834
Nutrition Now Inc.	664	Vancouver, WA	Private	5.4	42	2834
Science International Inc.	665	Daphne, AL	Private	20.0	42	2834
Thompson Medical Company Inc.	666	West Palm Beach, FL	Private	3.9	42	2834
Biospecifics Technologies	667	Lynbrook, NY	Public	5.8	41	2836
Highland Laboratories, Inc.	668	Mount Angel, OR	Private	4.1	41	2833
ADM Laboratories, Inc.	669	Phoenix, AZ	Private	3.9	40	2833
Amerilab Technologies, Inc.	670	Minneapolis, MN	Private	3.0	40	2834
Biolog Inc.	671	Hayward, CA	Private	3.6	40	2835
Biopharmaceutics Inc.	672	Bellport, NY	Public Family Member	4.1	40	2834
Continental Services Group	673	Miami, FL	Private	3.3	40	2835
Custom Health Products	674	Waynesboro, VA	Private	3.6	40	2834
Ess Group, Inc.	675	Vincentown, NJ	Private	15.0	40	2835
HDI Nutrients Inc.	676	Phoenix, AZ	Private	4.5	40	2833
Jackson Immunoresearch Labs	677	West Grove, PA	Private	8.5	40	2834
JMI-Canton Pharmaceuticals	678	Saint Louis, MO	Public Family Member	2.8	40	2834
National Nutritional Labs	679	Melville, NY	Private	4.8	40	2833
Natures Value Inc.	680	Bay Shore, NY	Private	5.1	40	2833
Nutrition Center, Incorporated	681	Douglas, WY	Private	4.8	40	2833
Oculex Pharmaceuticals Inc.	682	Sunnyvale, CA	Private	4.3	40	2834
Pelron Corporation	683	Lyons, IL	Private	3.2	40	2833
Sciclone Pharmaceuticals, Inc.	684	San Mateo, CA	Public	2.2	40	2834
Scot-Tussin Pharmacal Co Inc.	685	Cranston, RI	Private	3.7	40	2834
Seracare Technology Inc.	686	Austin, TX	Public Family Member	5.5	40	2835
Solgar Laboratories, Inc.	687	Leonia, NJ	Private	3.6	40	2834
TME Enterprises	688	Santa Fe Springs, CA	Private	4.5	40	2834
Trend Pharmaceuticals Inc.	689	Fort Walton Beach, FL	Private	2.0	40	2834
Vectech Pharmaceutical Cons	690	Farmington Hills, MI	Private	4.2	40	2834
York Pharmaceuticals Inc.	691	Kansas City, KS	Private	5.0	40	2834
Cosmo-Pharm Inc.	692	North Hollywood, CA	Private	5.0	39	2833
Xylum Corporation	693	Scarsdale, NY	Private	3.0	39	2835
Nassmith Pharmaceuticals, Inc.	694	Oceanside, CA	Private	4.1	38	2834
Pralex Corporation	695	Christiansted, VI	Public Family Member	2.7	38	2834
Soft Gel Technologies, Inc.	696	Los Angeles, CA	Private	14.0	38	2834
Toll Compaction Service Inc.	697	Neptune, NJ	Private	2.6	38	2833
Worthington Biochemical Corp.	698	Lakewood, NJ	Private	3.7	38	2835
Baker Cummins Dermatologicals Inc.	699	Miami, FL	Public Family Member	3.5	37	2834
Caltag Inc.	700	Burlingame, CA	Private	4.3	37	2836

D&B COMPANY RANKINGS BY EMPLOYMENT

Company	Rank	Location	Type	Sales ($ mil.)	Employ- ment	Primary SIC
Direct Therapeutics, Inc.	701	White Plains, NY	Private	4.0	37	2834
Coating Place Incorporated	702	Verona, WI	Private	2.8	36	2834
Cocalico Biologicals Inc.	703	Reamstown, PA	Private	2.4	36	2836
Herb Penn Co. Ltd.	704	Philadelphia, PA	Private	3.5	36	2833
International Immunology Corp.	705	Murrieta, CA	Private	4.5	36	2835
Medeva Pharmaceuticals, Inc.	706	Bethlehem, PA	Private	3.5	36	2834
Napp Technologies Inc.	707	Saddle Brook, NJ	Private	15.0	36	2834
A & Z Pharmaceutical Inc.	708	Hauppauge, NY	Private	3.0	35	2834
Ajay Chemicals Inc.	709	Powder Springs, GA	Private	3.8	35	2834
Au Naturel, Inc.	710	Clearfield, UT	Public Family Member	3.3	35	2834
Biozone Laboratories, Inc.	711	Pittsburg, CA	Private	2.9	35	2834
Bramton Company, (Inc)	712	Irving, TX	Public Family Member	2.6	35	2835
Chart Corp Inc.	713	Paterson, NJ	Private	3.6	35	2833
Derma Sciences, Inc.	714	Princeton, NJ	Public	4.0	35	2834
Ferring Pharmaceuticals Inc.	715	Tarrytown, NY	Private	16.0	35	2834
Gmp Laboratories America Inc.	716	Anaheim, CA	Private	3.8	35	2833
Hill Dermaceuticals Inc.	717	Sanford, FL	Private	3.6	35	2834
Hill Labs, Inc.	718	Sanford, FL	Private	3.3	35	2834
Jason Pharmaceuticals Inc.	719	Owings Mills, MD	Public Family Member	5.2	35	2834
K & K Laboratories Inc.	720	Carlsbad, CA	Private	3.5	35	2834
Lee Laboratories Inc.	721	Grayson, GA	Public Family Member	2.8	35	2833
Lobob Laboratories Inc.	722	San Jose, CA	Private	4.3	35	2834
M V P Laboratories Inc.	723	Omaha, NE	Private	3.0	35	2834
Orphan Medical, Inc.	724	Hopkins, MN	Public	3.1	35	2834
Respa Pharmaceuticals, Inc.	725	Carol Stream, IL	Private	9.0	35	2834
Safetec Of America Inc.	726	Buffalo, NY	Private	3.8	35	2834
Tatras Inc.	727	Claremont, NH	Private	4.0	35	2836
USB Corporation	728	Cleveland, OH	Private	2.9	35	2835
Valentine Enterprises Inc.	729	Lawrenceville, GA	Private	25.0	35	2834
Vita-Key Packaging	730	Fontana, CA	Private	3.5	35	2834
Advanced Biotechnologies, Inc.	731	Columbia, MD	Private	3.1	34	2836
DGA Inc.	732	Lafayette, CA	Private	4.1	34	2834
Jame Fine Chemicals	733	Bound Brook, NJ	Private	8.8	34	2833
Pel-Freez Rabbit Meat, Inc.	734	Rogers, AR	Private	2.0	34	2836
SGM Biotech, Inc.	735	Bozeman, MT	Private	3.0	34	2836
Straight Arrow Products Inc.	736	Bethlehem, PA	Private	8.0	34	2834
AMTL Corporation	737	Hollywood, FL	Private	4.5	33	2835
Borregaard Syntheses, Inc.	738	Newburyport, MA	Private	3.6	33	2834
CTM Industries Ltd.	739	Jamaica, NY	Private	2.2	33	2836
Diosynth Inc.	740	Chicago, IL	Private	48.0	33	2836
Dolisos America Inc.	741	Las Vegas, NV	Private	3.0	33	2833
Wilcox Drug Company Inc.	742	Boone, NC	Private	3.1	33	2833
Ajay North America LLC	743	Powder Springs, GA	Private	3.4	32	2834
Biosan Laboratories Inc.	744	Derry, NH	Private	4.0	32	2833
Cappseals Inc.	745	Vancouver, WA	Private	5.0	32	2834
Center For Diagnostic Products	746	Milford, MA	Private	2.3	32	2836
Clinical Specialties, Inc.	747	Cleveland, OH	Private	4.0	32	2834
Creative Medical Corporation	748	Toa Baja, PR	Private	2.6	32	2834
Randal Nutritional Products	749	Santa Rosa, CA	Private	5.0	32	2834
Reagents Applications Inc.	750	San Diego, CA	Public Family Member	3.1	32	2835
Worldwide Sport Nutritional	751	Largo, FL	Private	3.4	32	2834
Data Medical Associates Inc.	752	Arlington, TX	Public Family Member	5.0	31	2833
IGX Corp.	753	Summit, NJ	Private	2.5	31	2836
Sentry Supplement Co. Inc.	754	Opa Locka, FL	Private	5.0	31	2834
Summa Rx Laboratories Inc.	755	Mineral Wells, TX	Private	3.3	31	2834
Vitamin Power Inc.	756	Freeport, NY	Private	4.0	31	2834
Able Laboratories, Inc.	757	South Plainfield, NJ	Public Family Member	3.2	30	2834
Advance Pharmaceutical Inc.	758	Ronkonkoma, NY	Private	3.8	30	2834
American Biorganics Inc.	759	Niagara Falls, NY	Private	2.4	30	2836
Bio-Trends International, Inc.	760	West Sacramento, CA	Private	2.7	30	2835
C and M Pharmacal Inc.	761	Hazel Park, MI	Private	3.1	30	2834
Denison Pharmaceuticals Inc.	762	Pawtucket, RI	Private	2.6	30	2834
Enzo Diagnostics Inc.	763	Farmingdale, NY	Public Family Member	14.5	30	2835
Farmanatural Inc.	764	Fort Lauderdale, FL	Private	2.8	30	2834
Garrison Industries, Inc.	765	El Dorado, AR	Private	7.7	30	2833
Gemini Pharmaceuticals Inc.	766	Bohemia, NY	Private	5.0	30	2833
Houba Inc.	767	Culver, IN	Public Family Member	2.5	30	2834
Imarx Pharmaceutical Corp.	768	Tucson, AZ	Private	6.0	30	2835
Impact Nutrition, Inc.	769	Rocklin, CA	Private	3.2	30	2834
Impax Pharmaceuticals Inc.	770	Hayward, CA	Private	3.2	30	2834

D&B COMPANY RANKINGS BY EMPLOYMENT

Company	Rank	Location	Type	Sales ($ mil.)	Employ-ment	Primary SIC
Innovative Natural Products	771	Escondido, CA	Private	2.0	30	2834
Interhealth Nutritionals, Inc.	772	Concord, CA	Private	15.0	30	2833
Interntnal Frmltion Mnfcturing	773	San Diego, CA	Private	3.0	30	2834
J & D Laboratories, Inc.	774	Vista, CA	Private	3.2	30	2833
Natural Biologics, LLC	775	Albert Lea, MN	Private	2.5	30	2834
NW Alpharma Inc.	776	Bellevue, WA	Public Family Member	9.0	30	2834
Optimum Nutrition, Inc.	777	Coral Springs, FL	Private	3.2	30	2834
P & L Development Ny Corp.	778	Farmingdale, NY	Private	6.6	30	2834
Panvera Corporation	779	Madison, WI	Private	6.0	30	2835
Pharma Labs LLC	780	Anaheim, CA	Public Family Member	3.2	30	2833
Progenics Pharmaceuticals Inc.	781	Tarrytown, NY	Public	15.6	30	2834
Royal Source, Inc.	782	Lake Bluff, IL	Private	2.8	30	2833
Sage Pharmaceuticals, Inc.	783	Shreveport, LA	Private	2.2	30	2834
Stason Industrial Corporation	784	Irvine, CA	Private	3.6	30	2834
Total Wellness, Inc.	785	Parker, CO	Private	5.0	30	2833
Traco Labs Inc.	786	Champaign, IL	Private	20.0	30	2833
Twenty-First Century Labs	787	Tempe, AZ	Private	3.0	30	2834
VM Nutri	788	Batesville, AR	Private	2.8	30	2834
Bactolac Pharmaceutical Inc.	789	Westbury, NY	Private	4.2	29	2833
Berkeley Nutritional Mfg.	790	Hayward, CA	Private	4.0	29	2834
Metabolic Maintenance Pdts Inc.	791	Sisters, OR	Private	4.0	29	2834
Mizuho USA, Inc.	792	San Diego, CA	Private	4.0	29	2835
Pharmaceutical Recovery Svcs	793	Orlando, FL	Private	2.7	29	2834
Associates Of Cape Cod, Inc.	794	Falmouth, MA	Private	2.3	28	2835
Health Plus Inc.	795	Chino, CA	Private	9.0	28	2834
Pegasus Laboratories Inc.	796	Pensacola, FL	Private	2.6	28	2834
Spray-Tek Inc.	797	Middlesex, NJ	Private	6.9	28	2834
Tera Pharmaceuticals Inc.	798	Midvale, UT	Public Family Member	4.0	28	2834
W F Young Incorporated	799	Springfield, MA	Private	20.0	28	2834
Dercher Enterprises Inc.	800	Upper Darby, PA	Private	2.7	27	2834
Designing Health Inc.	801	Valencia, CA	Private	2.8	27	2833
Everett Laboratories Inc.	802	West Orange, NJ	Private	2.4	27	2834
G D S Technology Inc.	803	Elkhart, IN	Private	2.1	27	2835
General Research Laboratories	804	Northridge, CA	Private	7.2	27	2834
Global Vitality, Inc.	805	Tempe, AZ	Private	3.0	27	2834
Iconix Pharmaceuticals Inc.	806	Mountain View, CA	Private	2.8	27	2834
Micro Bio Logics	807	Saint Cloud, MN	Private	2.1	27	2835
RIJ Pharmaceutical Corp.	808	Middletown, NY	Private	6.0	27	2834
Bariatrix International Inc.	809	South Burlington, VT	Private	23.0	26	2834
Health Products Intl Corp.	810	Springville, UT	Private	2.1	26	2833
Particle Dynamics Inc.	811	Saint Louis, MO	Public Family Member	11.0	26	2834
A & S Pharmaceutical Corp.	812	Bridgeport, CT	Private	2.2	25	2834
Aloe Laboratories, Inc.	813	Harlingen, TX	Public Family Member	2.4	25	2834
Bio-Energetics Inc.	814	Rye, NY	Private	2.6	25	2834
Clinical Diagnostics, Inc.	815	Rock Hill, SC	Private	2.2	25	2835
Elge Inc.	816	Rosenberg, TX	Private	2.5	25	2834
Far Research Inc.	817	Morganton, NC	Private	4.2	25	2834
Gebauer Company	818	Cleveland, OH	Private	4.0	25	2834
Herb Source Enterprise Inc.	819	Chino, CA	Private	2.5	25	2834
Hillestad Pharmaceuticals	820	Woodruff, WI	Private	2.0	25	2834
Hoechst Marion Roussel	821	Guaynabo, PR	Private	17.0	25	2834
Horizon Pharmaceuticals Inc.	822	Saint Petersburg, FL	Private	2.3	25	2834
Immunetics Inc.	823	Cambridge, MA	Private	2.5	25	2835
Immuno Concepts Inc.	824	Sacramento, CA	Private	2.6	25	2835
Innominata	825	San Diego, CA	Private	2.4	25	2835
King's Laboratory Incorporated	826	Blythewood, SC	Private	2.9	25	2833
Marcus Research Laboratory	827	Saint Louis, MO	Private	2.3	25	2833
NCB Technology Corp.	828	Walnut, CA	Private	10.0	25	2833
Northwest Marketing Corp.	829	Placentia, CA	Private	2.6	25	2833
Nuhealth Manufacturing, LLC	830	Gig Harbor, WA	Private	10.0	25	2834
Nutrition Medical, Inc.	831	Minneapolis, MN	Public	4.1	25	2834
Ocumed Inc.	832	Roseland, NJ	Private	2.8	25	2834
Raven Biological Laboratories	833	Omaha, NE	Private	2.4	25	2835
Scripps Laboratories, Inc.	834	San Diego, CA	Private	2.4	25	2835
Swiss-American Products Inc.	835	Dallas, TX	Private	2.2	25	2834
Univera Pharmaceuticals, Inc.	836	Broomfield, CO	Private	2.3	25	2834
University Pharmaceuticals	837	Baltimore, MD	Private	2.3	25	2834
Vita Pure Inc.	838	Roselle, NJ	Private	8.0	25	2833
Wendt Professional Labs	839	Belle Plaine, MN	Private	2.0	25	2834
Biodesign International	840	Kennebunk, ME	Public Family Member	2.7	24	2833

D&B COMPANY RANKINGS BY EMPLOYMENT

Company	Rank	Location	Type	Sales ($ mil.)	Employ-ment	Primary SIC
Blansett Pharmacal Company	841	North Little Rock, AR	Private	2.0	24	2834
Carolina Medical Products Co.	842	Farmville, NC	Private	4.2	24	2834
New Chapter Inc.	843	Brattleboro, VT	Private	5.0	24	2833
Nutrition Resource	844	Lakeport, CA	Private	6.2	24	2834
Accumed Inc.	845	Lawrenceville, NJ	Private	3.0	23	2834
Antigen Laboratories Inc.	846	Liberty, MO	Private	2.5	23	2834
Bionike Laboratories, Inc.	847	South San Francisco, CA	Private	2.2	23	2835
Chiragene Inc.	848	Warren, NJ	Public Family Member	2.4	23	2834
Geriatric Pharmaceutical Corp.	849	Brookfield, WI	Public Family Member	2.0	23	2834
Immucell Corporation	850	Portland, ME	Public	4.6	23	2835
Am Pharm Corp.	851	Fairfield, NJ	Private	2.3	22	2834
AMT Labs Inc.	852	North Salt Lake, UT	Private	18.8	22	2833
Arizona Nutritional Supplement	853	Tempe, AZ	Private	6.0	22	2834
Bachem Bioscience Inc.	854	King Of Prussia, PA	Private	8.0	22	2836
Doctors Sgnature Sls Mktg Intl	855	Spring Valley, CA	Private	10.0	22	2833
Genaissance Pharmaceutical	856	New Haven, CT	Private	2.0	22	2834
Life Enhancement Products	857	Petaluma, CA	Private	3.9	22	2834
Sportpharma USA Inc.	858	Concord, CA	Private	25.0	22	2833
Stason Pharmaceutical Inc.	859	Irvine, CA	Private	2.3	22	2834
U S Direct Inc.	860	North Las Vegas, NV	Private	2.1	22	2834
Zambon Corporation	861	East Rutherford, NJ	Private	5.4	22	2834
Berlin Industries Inc.	862	Berlin Center, OH	Private	4.0	21	2834
Fontarome Chemical Inc.	863	Milwaukee, WI	Private	5.0	21	2833
G & S Enterprises Incorporated	864	Houston, TX	Private	3.0	21	2834
Vitarich Laboratories, Inc.	865	Naples, FL	Private	2.1	21	2834
All Natural Products Corp.	866	Mineola, NY	Private	2.2	20	2833
American Chelates Inc.	867	Northvale, NJ	Private	2.1	20	2833
Bioglan Inc.	868	Lake Forest, CA	Private	2.2	20	2834
Biomune Systems, Inc.	869	Salt Lake City, UT	Public	2.8	20	2833
Blue Bonnett Nutrition Corp.	870	Stafford, TX	Private	2.4	20	2833
Concord Laboratories, Inc.	871	Fairfield, NJ	Private	2.5	20	2834
Dermarite Industries LLC	872	Paterson, NJ	Private	2.7	20	2834
Dynport LLC	873	Reston, VA	Private	5.0	20	2836
Enteric Products Inc.	874	Stony Brook, NY	Public Family Member	2.1	20	2834
Infusion Orlando Regional	875	Orlando, FL	Private	3.0	20	2834
Kultivar, Inc.	876	Plainfield, VT	Private	2.1	20	2833
Natures World	877	San Marcos, CA	Private	3.0	20	2833
Naturopathic Laboratories Int'l	878	New York, NY	Private	2.2	20	2834
Optimal Research, Inc.	879	St George, UT	Private	2.1	20	2833
Ranbaxy Pharmaceuticals Inc.	880	Princeton, NJ	Private	15.3	20	2834
Systemic Formula Inc.	881	Ogden, UT	Private	2.5	20	2834
Unimed Pharmaceuticals, Inc.	882	Buffalo Grove, IL	Public	8.9	20	2834
Universal Proteins Inc.	883	Amityville, NY	Private	2.1	20	2834
Bennett Chem Ltd.	884	Palatine, IL	Private	4.0	19	2833
Natco Pharma USA LLC	885	Somerset, NJ	Private	3.0	19	2834
Advanced Manufacturing Systems	886	Boulder, CO	Private	3.0	18	2834
Alberto Bartolomei	887	Gurabo, PR	Private	5.3	18	2833
Chemical Compounds Inc.	888	Newark, NJ	Private	3.5	18	2834
DFB Holding Inc.	889	San Antonio, TX	Private	50.0	18	2834
Livron Inc.	890	Allendale, NJ	Private	6.0	18	2833
Siga Pharmaceuticals Inc.	891	New York, NY	Public	2.1	18	2834
Trimar Hollywood Inc.	892	Reseda, CA	Private	2.5	18	2835
Aggrow Oils LLC	893	Carrington, ND	Private	6.5	17	2833
Cedarburg Laboratories Inc.	894	Grafton, WI	Private	3.5	17	2834
Global Source Mgt & Consulting	895	Hollywood, FL	Private	25.0	17	2834
TOA Medical Electronics (USA)	896	Los Alamitos, CA	Private	4.5	17	2835
Gallipot Inc.	897	Saint Paul, MN	Private	2.1	16	2834
Immvac Inc.	898	Columbia, MO	Private	3.0	16	2836
Quigley Corp.	899	Doylestown, PA	Public	71.0	16	2834
Rasi Laboratories Inc.	900	Somerset, NJ	Private	6.3	16	2834
Uckele Animal Health Distrg Co.	901	Blissfield, MI	Private	2.1	16	2834
West Laboratories Inc.	902	Kankakee, IL	Private	2.9	16	2836
Yerba Prima Inc.	903	Ashland, OR	Private	3.6	16	2834
Alcide Corporation	904	Redmond, WA	Public	13.0	15	2834
Arenol Corporation	905	Somerville, NJ	Private	6.0	15	2833
Ascent Pediatrics, Inc.	906	Wilmington, MA	Public	2.1	15	2834
Blackhawk Biosystems Inc.	907	San Ramon, CA	Private	2.9	15	2835
Branel Laboratories Inc.	908	Hill City, KS	Private	8.0	15	2834
Elementis Catalysts Inc.	909	Allentown, PA	Private	5.0	15	2833
Pharma-Tek Inc.	910	Northport, NY	Private	8.0	15	2834

D&B COMPANY RANKINGS BY EMPLOYMENT

Company	Rank	Location	Type	Sales ($ mil.)	Employ-ment	Primary SIC
Uni-Health Inc.	911	Clifton, NJ	Private	4.0	15	2834
Unipack, Inc.	912	Pittsburgh, PA	Private	2.5	15	2834
American Ingredients Inc.	913	Anaheim, CA	Private	15.0	14	2833
Clearvalue, Inc.	914	Sugar Land, TX	Private	2.5	14	2836
Naiad Technologies Inc.	915	Portland, OR	Private	3.0	14	2835
Prolab Nutrition Inc.	916	Bloomfield, CT	Private	18.0	14	2834
YS Health Corporation	917	Lombard, IL	Private	7.4	14	2833
Biofluids Inc.	918	Rockville, MD	Private	2.3	13	2836
Chemrich Laboratories Inc.	919	Los Angeles, CA	Private	2.4	13	2834
American Eco-Systems Inc.	920	Wellman, IA	Private	5.0	12	2836
C J Martin & Son Inc.	921	Nacogdoches, TX	Private	2.5	12	2834
Medpharm Inc.	922	Washington, DC	Private	12.0	12	2834
Morningstar Diagnostics, Inc.	923	Roseville, CA	Private	4.0	12	2835
O E M Concepts	924	Toms River, NJ	Private	2.0	12	2835
Ashford Pharmalogic Corp.	925	San Juan, PR	Private	3.0	11	2834
First Priority Inc.	926	Elgin, IL	Private	3.3	11	2834
Mercer Milling Co.	927	Baldwinsville, NY	Private	3.2	11	2834
PCR Puerto Rico Inc.	928	Humacao, PR	Private	3.5	11	2834
Biospacific Inc.	929	Emeryville, CA	Private	4.0	10	2835
Care Technologies, Inc.	930	Darien, CT	Private	5.9	10	2834
Cypress Pharmaceutical Inc.	931	Madison, MS	Private	3.1	10	2834
Eco Pax, Inc.	932	Littleton, CO	Private	5.0	10	2834
Gynetics Inc.	933	Belle Mead, NJ	Private	13.0	10	2834
Pan Am Pharmaceuticals, Inc.	934	New York, NY	Private	3.6	10	2834
Renaissance Pharmaceutical	935	Zephyr Cove, NV	Private	2.4	10	2834
Sunset Nutritional Products	936	Agoura Hills, CA	Private	2.5	10	2834
Breathies International Inc.	937	Culver City, CA	Private	4.0	9	2834
Monomer-Polymer & Dajac Labs	938	Feasterville Trevose, PA	Private	2.2	9	2835
Seabella Inc.	939	Bayport, NY	Private	4.0	9	2834
Stella Labs LLC	940	New Orleans, LA	Private	3.0	9	2833
Champion Eximport Enterprise	941	Baldwin Park, CA	Private	3.0	8	2833
Planet Emu Inc.	942	Miami, FL	Private	6.0	8	2834
Remington Health Products LLC	943	Fort Worth, TX	Private	18.0	8	2834
Ulmer Pharmacal Company	944	Minneapolis, MN	Private	10.0	8	2834
Eckhart Corporation	945	Novato, CA	Private	6.0	7	2834
Premium Processing, Inc.	946	Commack, NY	Private	5.0	7	2834
Slim Science Corporation	947	Encino, CA	Private	3.0	7	2833
Tts Alza Research Partners	948	Palo Alto, CA	Public Family Member	10.4	7	2836
Chemocentryx	949	San Carlos, CA	Private	2.5	6	2834
Glen Copel Pharmaceuticals Inc.	950	Providence, RI	Private	3.5	6	2834
Healthspan, Inc.	951	Hermosa Beach, CA	Private	3.0	6	2834
Metabolic Nutrition Inc.	952	Miami, FL	Private	2.9	6	2834
Pharbco Marketing Group Inc.	953	Santa Rosa, CA	Private	10.0	6	2834
Tissue Culture Biologicals	954	Tulare, CA	Private	2.5	6	2836
Wellness Way Inc.	955	Elmhurst, NY	Private	5.0	6	2834
Wellquest International Inc.	956	New York, NY	Private	6.0	6	2833
Advanced Bio Institute	957	Costa Mesa, CA	Private	4.5	5	2834
Alfred Khalily Inc.	958	Great Neck, NY	Private	2.8	5	2834
New Life Health Products Inc.	959	Cedar City, UT	Private	10.0	5	2834
Advanced Vision Research	960	Woburn, MA	Private	2.5	4	2834
Baywood International, Inc.	961	Scottsdale, AZ	Public	3.2	4	2834
Ceres Organic Harvest Inc.	962	Dexter, MI	Private	2.4	4	2833
Kaizen Inc.	963	Los Angeles, CA	Private	2.2	4	2834
National Vitamin Company LLC	964	Las Vegas, NV	Private	9.0	4	2834
Nicodrop	965	La Mesa, CA	Private	10.0	4	2834
Phoenix Laboratories Inc.	966	Hicksville, NY	Private	18.0	4	2833
St Mary's Chemicals Inc.	967	Saint Peter, MN	Private	2.3	4	2834
Genesis Technologies Inc.	968	Norcross, GA	Private	5.3	3	2836
ISP Co Inc.	969	Wolf Summit, WV	Private	4.4	3	2836
Kanec (USA), Inc.	970	Opa Locka, FL	Private	3.0	3	2834
Power Engineering & Mfg Inc.	971	Saint Paul, MN	Private	3.0	3	2836
Scientia Biological	972	Wolsey, SD	Private	2.0	3	2836
Vita Elixir Company Inc.	973	Atlanta, GA	Private	12.0	3	2834
Goldcaps, Inc.	974	Miami, FL	Public Family Member	15.8	2	2834
Purdue Pharma Company	975	Norwalk, CT	Private	100.0	2	2834
QXL Corporation	976	Mesa, AZ	Private	2.9	2	2834
Chuck Mills	977	Brea, CA	Private	16.0	1	2833
Fortta Group LLC	978	Plainville, CT	Private	2.5	1	2834

MERGERS & ACQUISITIONS

The following essay presents a look at merger and acquisition activity in the Pharmaceuticals sector. A general overview of M&A activity is followed by a listing of actual merger and acquisition events. Purchasing companies are listed in alphabetical order, with a paragraph set aside for each acquisition.

Mergers and Acquisitions

This essay discusses recent merger and acquisition activity in the industry and its effect on the industry. The essay is followed by a list of significant acquisitions and mergers.

While the pharmaceutical industry has not seen the frenetic merger and acquisition pace of industries such as telecommunications, financial services, and computers and software over the past few years, certain industry segments, such as analgesics and vaccines, have seen higher levels of consolidation as companies vie for increased market share. Analysts also predict that as a wave of patent expiry among the largest pharmaceutical players begins to break, many of the firms involved in the merger mania of the early nineties will be seeking new merger and acquisition partners. One response to the constant need for new drug development has been the rise of pharmaceutical-biotechnology consolidations. The late 1990s saw pharmaceutical companies showing a willingness to pay millions to acquire biotechnology firms. For often cash-strapped biotech concerns, consolidations offered an infusion of much-needed funds to develop and market drugs.

Even with the merger and acquisition fever, there were several noteworthy failed mergers in 1998. The first of these attempts was the highly touted $70 billion joining of pharmaceutical behemoths Glaxo Wellcome PLC and SmithKline Beecham Corp. What would have been the largest merger in corporate history fell apart in February of 1998, apparently due to disagreements over who would head up the world's largest pharmaceutical concern. Many investors cited a power struggle between the chief executive officers of both companies as the true reason the merger was called off and expressed disappointment that the deal fell through; however, analysts point out that both firms would still benefit from a union this size. In this case, according to a recent article in *Fortune*, Glaxo Wellcome could use the genetic technology of a firm like SmithKline Beecham, and SmithKline Beecham requires the "combinatorial chemistry" of a company like Glaxo Wellcome to cultivate its diverse drug targets.

Even before talks with Glaxo ceased, SmithKline Beecham and American Home Products Corp. announced a mind boggling $130 billion potential merger agreement which would create the not only the world's largest drug company, but also the leading over-the-counter operation as well, with annual sales close to $27 billion. When that deal fell through, AHP and Monsanto Co. announced that they were discussing a more modest $34.4 billion merger, which would also create a new drug industry leader, with roughly $23 billion in annual revenues. Critics of the deal pointed out that the conservative chief executive of AHP and the more fiscally liberal leader of Monsanto might find it difficult to agree on how to best run the newly merged giant. Another concern was the 300 or so lawsuits pending against AHP over serious complications experienced by patients taking the controversial diet drug fen-phen. Accordingly, the third major pharmaceutical industry merger announced in 1998 fell apart in October of that year.

Failed mergers or not, mergers and acquisitions are one way for pharmaceutical companies want to stay competitive. According to Dr. Wang Chong of the consulting firm Arthur D. Little, mergers will be necessary for the firms who want to remain in the top ten industry tier, because to do so will require pharmaceutical companies to introduce at least three new drugs annually. Currently, only three pharmaceutical businesses are capable of doing this: Johnson & Johnson, Merck & Co., and Pfizer Inc. As an example of what it takes to get into that league, Johnson & Johnson acquired 30 firms during the 1990s. But even smaller pharmaceutical companies have used acquisitions to their favor. For these firms, acquisitions and strategic alliances offer a way to grow and possibly reach the top in their industry. For example, Dublin-based Elan Corp. turned its company into a $5 billion business through acquisitions, with activity especially high in 1998. In that year, Elan acquired the following companies: Neurex, a late-stage biopharmaceutical company focusing on pain-management products; Ligand Pharmaceuticals, a company that specializes in gene transcription technology; GWC Health, Inc., the parent company of private pharmaceutical concern Carnrick Laboratories; and NanoSystems, a drug-delivery company. Evidently all those acquisitions weren't enough for the upstart company as Elan also bought the exclusive rights to an antimigraine therapy from Vanguard Medica in 1998.

Consolidations are fueled by the need for intense growth and increasingly global competition. This means that speed-to-market is becoming essential to the success of pharmaceutical firms. To move this quickly, research and development funds, as well as marketing dollars, must be available. Consolidation, which allows for a pooling of financial and research and development assets, allows pharmaceutical companies to commercialize new products with enhanced speed. The $11 billion takeover of Boehringer Mannheim Corp. by Roche Holding AG in June of 1997—which made Roche Holding the sixth largest pharmaceutical company in the world—is an example of an attempt at this kind of synergy. Planning to release five new pharmaceutical products by the end of 1998, Roche Holding pursued the merger to gain access to the marketing might of Boehringer Mannheim, especially in France, Spain, and the United Kingdom.

Another reason for the industry's slower consolidation pace over the past two years, and a major cause of the sporadic nature of merger and acquisition activity in the pharmaceutical industry, is how closely tied merger and acquisition activity is to patent expiry. When patent protection expires on a drug, generic competitors are launched by rival firms, and profits and market share for the firm who held the original patent drop. The bigger the drug, the harder the fall is usually the case, and many key pharmaceutical players are currently facing the impending expiration of patents on major drugs. Consulting firm AT Kearney estimates that between the years 1998 and 2003 expired patents on 42 key drugs will take a $32 billion toll on earnings in the pharmaceutical industry.

One way that larger pharmacuetical companies have responded to this situation is to buy small biotechnology firms, which have the technology and capability to develop much- needed new drugs. For instance, in the summer of 1999, pharmaceutical giant Merck & Co. merged with La Jolla, California-based Sibia Neurosciences, Inc. Sibia focuses on creating treatments for neurological diseases, such as Alzheimer's and Parkinson's. This transaction, valued at $87 million, was the first time that industry-leader Merck had acquired a biotech company. While New Jersey-based Merck is a research-driven pharmaceutical company that researches and develops new products. Even so, in this case, it made more sense to Merck to buy a firm that already had extensive expertise in creating treatments for disorders of the central nervous system rather than pursuing that type of research on its own. The bulk

analgesics market saw a fairly steady pace of merger and acquisition activity in the late 1990s, and the segment is now realizing the benefits from those consolidations. Rhone-Poulenc Chimie S.A. bought the acetaminophen operations of England-based ChiRex, Inc., for $6.3 million in November of 1997. Similarly, BASF Corp. bought the 50 percent of Dallas, Texas-based ibuprofen operation BHC Laboratories it did not already own, from Celanese Corp. in December of 1997. The consolidation has helped to improve excess supply problems within the industry and allowed larger analgesics firms to increase prices for the first time in several years. For example, Mallinckrodt Chemical, one of the largest producers of acetaminophen in the United States, raised its per-kilo prices by three and a half percent at the beginning of 1998. The price hike was the first in five years for the firm.

The vaccines segment, which is currently considered one of the fastest growing sectors in the pharmaceutical industry, has also seen more merger and acquisition activity over the past two years than many other pharmaceutical markets. This is partly because analysts predict that the $4 billion industry will grow fivefold to roughly $20 billion by the year 2010. As an example, in April of 1998 Chiron bought the 51 percent of Chiron Behring it did not already own, for $115.5 million. Smaller players are also gearing up for the predicted growth as evidenced by the early 1998 acquisition of VacTex, Inc., a privately owned vaccine technology developer, by Aquila Pharmaceuticals Inc.

The intense growth in the pharmaceutical industry as a whole over the past few years has also caught the attention of many major chemical firms who have dabbled in pharmaceuticals for years. Many companies who were expected to spin-off pharmaceutical arms are instead hanging on to them, and many firms are increasing their stakes in the pharmaceutical industry. For example, in July of 1998 E.I. du Pont de Nemours & Co. bought the remaining 50 percent of DuPont Pharmaceuticals Co., its joint venture with Merck & Co., for $2.6 billion. Japanese chemical groups Mitsubishi Kagaku and Sumitomo Chemical have also announced plans to increase pharmaceutical holdings through acquisitions. Mitsubishi Kagaku unveiled in 1997 a goal of increasing pharmaceutical sales from three and a half percent to 13 percent of total sales between the years 2000 and 2010, mainly through domestic and global acquisitions. Sumitomo Chemical, who already relies on pharmaceutical sales for roughly 18 percent of annual revenues, is also planning to enter both the domestic and the global pharmaceutical merger and acquisition arena.

The race for pharmaceutical market share is on, and the first place status of Glaxo Wellcome, who holds five percent, may soon be threatened if any of a number of potential mega-mergers actually take place. Bayer recently threw its hat into the ring by announcing plans to increase its two and a third percent share to four percent via a merger, joint venture, or acquisition, preferably in pharmaceuticals. While most other firms have not stated their intentions this explicitly yet, it seems reasonable to expect that the completion of one colossal merger will spawn at least a few more of comparable size.

Mergers and Acquisitions

Abbott Laboratories bought **Perclose, Inc.,** an arterial-closure device manufacturer located in Redwood City, California, for a stock transaction valued at $680 million in July of 1999. [*PR Newswire,* 7/8/1999.

—bought **ALZA Corp.,** a research-based pharmaceutical company, for a stock transaction valued at $7.3 billion in June of 1999. [*PR Newswire,* 6/21/1999.]

—bought **International Murex Technologies Corp.,** a developer, manufacturer, and marketer of infectious disease detection, screening, and monitoring products, on July 10, 1998. [*PR Newswire,* 7/10/98.]

Agouron Pharmaceuticals, Inc. bought **Alanex Corp.,** a privately owned pharmaceutical discovery company based in San Diego, California, for one million shares on April 29, 1997. [*PR Newswire,* 4/29/97.]

Alliance Sante, a European healthcare group, and **Unichem Inc.,** a pharmaceutical company, merged to create **Alliance Unichem,** the largest pharmaceutical wholesale company in Europe, in November of 1997. [*Chemist & Druggist,* 11/29/97, p. 34.]

AlliedSignal Inc. bought **Pharmaceutical Fine Chemicals S.A.,** an active and intermediate pharmaceutical fine chemicals producer and distributor based

in Lugano, Switzerland, on June 19, 1998. [*Business Wire,* 6/19/98.]

Alpha-Beta Technology, Inc. bought **MycoTox Inc.,** an anti-fungal research, development, and marketing company located in Denver, Colorado, for roughly 170,000 shares and $500,000 in cash on June 10, 1997. [*PR Newswire,* 6/10/97.]

American Home Products Corp. bought a pharmaceutical plant in West Greenwich, Rhode Island, owned by **Glaxo Wellcome PLC,** for $60 million in August of 1999. [*Chemical Market Reporter,* 8/30/99.]

Aquila Biopharmaceuticals Inc. bought **VacTex, Inc.,** a privately owned vaccine technology developer, for 1.15 million shares on April 14, 1998. [*PR Newswire,* 4/14/98.]

Ares-Serono Group bought **Geneva Biomedical Research Institute,** a research center owned by Glaxo Wellcome PLC and located in Geneva, Switzerland, in early 1998. [*PR Newswire,* 12/2/97.]

Arris Pharmaceutical Corp. bought **Sequana Therapeutics Inc.,** based in La Jolla, California, on January 9, 1998. Upon completion of the transaction, Arris Pharmaceutical Corp. changed its name to AXYS Pharmaceuticals. [*Business Wire,* 1/9/98.]

AVI BioPharma Inc. bought **ImmunoTherapy Corp.,** an advanced cancer therapeutics firm based in Seattle, Washington, for $24 million in stocks and warrants on September 15, 1998. [*Business Wire,* 9/16/98.]

BASF Corp. bought the remaining 50 percent of Dallas, Texas-based ibuprofen operation **BHC Laboratories** it did not already own from **Celanese Corp.** in December of 1997. [*Chemical Market Reporter,* 1/12/98 p. 6.]

Baxter International Inc. bought **Somatogen, Inc.,** a biopharmaceutical developer of recombinant hemoglobin technology, on May 4, 1998. [*Business Wire,* 5/4/98.]

—bought the Pharmaceutical Products Division of **Ohmeda Inc.,** for $104 million in April of 1998. [*PR Newswire,* 4/3/98.]

Bayer Diagnostics bought **Chiron Diagnostics,** located in Emeryville, California, for $1.1 billion in cash and licensing and royalty fees, in November of 1998. [Bayer news release. Available from http://www.bayerus.com.]

Beckman Instruments, Inc. bought **Coulter Corp.,** a clinical diagnostics and life sciences company based in Miami, Florida, for $875 million in cash and $275 million in debt assumption on October 31, 1997. Upon completion of the purchase, Beckman Instruments changed its name to **Beckman Coulter.** [*Business Wire,* 11/3/97.]

Bioanalytical Systems, Inc. bought Warwickshire, United Kingdom-based**Clinical Innovations, Ltd.,** an analyzer of biological samples for the pharmaceutical industry, in May of 1998. [*Business Wire,* 5/27/98.]

BioMarin Pharmaceutical, Inc. bought **Glyko, Inc.,** a diagnostic and analytical pharmaceutical products manufacturer, on October 8, 1998. [*PR Newswire,* 10/8/98.]

Biomune Systems, Inc. bought **Rockwood Investments, Inc.,** a health and beauty care distributor and marketer, for $5.96 million, plus warrants, in November of 1997. [*PR Newswire,* 11/3/97.]

Biopharmaceutics Inc. bought the San Juan, Puerto Rico-based **Carribean Medical Testing Center**, a specialty medical testing center and research laboratory serving Puerto Rico and the U.S. Virgin Islands, for $7.5 million in cash and notes in June of 1997. [*Business Wire,* 6/5/97.]

BioProgress Technology International, Inc. bought **DHA Nutrition Ltd.,** a pharmaceutical and nutritional supplement sales, marketing, and distribution firm based in Cambridgeshire, England, on August 11, 1998. [*Business Wire,* 8/11/98.]

Bio-Rad Laboratories Inc. bought the Irvine, California-based Quality Controls unit of **Chiron Diagnostics Corp.** on December 22, 1997. [*PR Newswire,* 12/22/97.]

Boehringer Ingelheim Corp. bought **Ben Venue Laboratories,** a sterile pharmaceuticals developer and

manufacturer based in Bedford, Ohio, in December of 1997. [*PR Newswire,* 12/2/97.]

Catalytica Fine Chemicals Inc. bought a pharmaceutical plant based in Greenville, North Carolina, from **Glaxo Wellcome Inc.** for $247 million in cash in June of 1997. [*Chemical Market Reporter,* 2/10/97 p. 1.]

Cell Genesys, Inc. bought **Somatix Therapy Corp.,** a gene therapy company, in a stock transaction on May 30, 1997. [*PR Newswire,* 6/2/97.]

ChiRex bought a pharmaceutical plant based in Annan, Scotland, from **Glaxo Wellcome Inc.** for $66 million in July of 1997. [*Chemical Market Reporter,* 7/14/97, p. 1.]

Chiron Corp. bought the remaining 51 percent stake of **Chiron Behring GmbH,** a human vaccines joint venture with **Hoechst AG** based in Marburg, Germany, for $115.5 million on April 1, 1998. [*Business Wire,* 4/1/98.]

ClinTrials Research Inc. bought **Ovation Healthcare Research Inc.,** a privately owned pharmacoeconomic research and consulting operation based in Highland Park, Illinois, on June 3, 1997. [*PR Newswire,* 6/3/97.]

Cognizant Corp. bought **Walsh International Inc.,** a pharmaceutical sales technology firm, in June of 1998. [*PR Newswire,* 6/247/98.]

Columbia/HCA Healthcare Corp. bought **Value Health Inc.,** a healthcare, pharmaceutical benefits, and disease management company based in Avon, Connecticut, for $1.3 billion on August 6, 1998. [*PR Newswire,* 8/6/97.]

Corixa Corp. bought **GenQuest, Inc.,** a biotechnology development firm, for $11.8 million in cash and stock in June of 1998. [*PR Newswire,* 6/23/98.]

Counsel Corp. bought **Faro Pharmaceuticals, Inc.,** a developer and promoter of below threshold drugs, on August 17, 1998. [*Business Wire,* 8/17/98.]

Draxis Health Inc. bought a pharmaceutical manufacturing facility located in Kirkland, Quebec, from **IVX**

BioScience Inc. for C$12.3 million on May 1, 1998. [*Business Wire, 6/19/98.*]

E.I. du Pont de Nemours & Co. bought the remaining 50 percent of DuPont Pharmaceuticals Co., its Wilmington, Delaware-based joint venture with Merck & Co. for $2.6 billion in July 1998. [*Chemical Market Reporter, 7/13/98, p. 5.*]

Elan Corporation PLC bought NanoSystems L.L.C., a drug delivery firm focused on improving delivery of drugs which are not water soluble, for roughly $150 million in cash and warrants on October 1, 1998. [*PR Newswire, 10/1/98.*]

—bought Neurex Corp., a biopharmaceutical pain management and acute care products developer on August 14, 1998. [*PR Newswire, 8/14/98.*]

—bought GWC Health, Inc., the parent company of private pharmaceutical concern Carnrick Laboratories for $150 million in cash and notes on June 1, 1998. [*PR Newswire, 6/1/98.*]

Erie Scientific Co. bought Diagnostic Reagents, Inc., an immunoassay reagent manufacturer and distributor based in Sunnyvale, California, on January 5, 1998. [*PR Newswire, 1/5/98.*]

Express Scripts, Inc. bought Diversified Pharmaceutical Services, for $700 million in April 1999. [*PR Newswire, 8/16/99.*]

—bought ValueRx, the pharmacy benefit management subsidiary of Columbia/HCA Healthcare Corp., for $445 million in cash on April 1, 1998. [*PR Newswire, 4/1/98.*]

FHC Health Systems, Inc. bought Value Behavioral Health, a subsidiary of Columbia/HCA Healthcare Corp., for $206.5 million on June 18, 1998. Upon completion of the transaction, FHC Health Systems became the second largest behavioral health company in the United States. [*PR Newswire, 6/18/98.*]

Fresenius AG bought the nutrition business of Pharmacia & Upjohn Inc., including a line of intravenous nutrition products for patients unable to digest adequate nutrients, in the second quarter of 1998. [*PR Newswire, 6/8/98.*]

Fuisz Technologies Ltd. bought Pangea Ltd., a privately owned nutritional supplements and skin care products network marketer based in Roswell, Georgia, on May 21, 1997. [*PR Newswire, 5/21/97.*]

—bought Laboratoires Murat, a pharmaceutical distributor located in Paris, France, on April 9, 1997. [*PR Newswire, 4/10/97.*]

Gene Logic Inc. bought OncorMed Inc., a biopharmaceutical firm specializing in tissue biorepository products and services, for 4.85 million shares in July of 1998. [*Business Wire, 7/7/98.*]

Genesis Health Ventures Inc. bought Vitalink Pharmacy Services Inc. for $680 million in cash, stock, and assumed debt in August of 1998. [*Business Wire, 8/31/98.*]

Gensia Sicor Inc. bought the remaining 50 percent stake of Diaspa S.p.A., a privately held bulk fermentation pharmaceutical products company based in Italy, for $5.7 million in cash on July 1, 1998. [*PR Newswire, 7/1/98.*]

—bought a 50 percent interest in Diaspa S.p.A., a privately held bulk fermentation pharmaceutical products company based in Italy, for $2.8 million in cash in December of 1997. [*PR Newswire, 7/1/98.*]

Genstar LLC bought NEN Life Science Products, Inc., a fluorescent, chemiluminescent, and radioactive labeling life science and drug detection products developer based in Boston, Massachusetts, in July of 1997. [*Business Wire, 10/1/98.*]

Hoechst AG and Rhone-Poulenc S.A. agreed to merge their drug and agrochemical businesses in a 50-50 joint venture in December of 1998. The combined company will be known as Aventis S.A. and will be headquartered in Strasbourg, France. The new company will be the world's largest life-sciences group with estimated annual sales of $20 billion. [*Reuters, 12/1/98.*]

Hoechst Roussel Vet bought Tri Bio Laboratory, a poultry vaccines producer based in State College, Pennsylvania, in December of 1998. [*Feedstuffs, 12/8/97, p. 1.*]

ICN Pharmaceuticals, Inc. bought **Vyzkumny Ustav Antibiotik a Biotransformacii (VUAB),** an antibiotics and biotransformation manufacturing and research operation based in the Czech Republic, on June 1, 1998. [*PR Newswire, 6/15/98.*]

Incyte Pharmaceuticals Inc. bought **Hexagen Ltd.,** a privately owned pharmaceuticals company based in Cambridge, England, for $5 million in cash and 976,130 shares on September 22, 1998. [*PR Newswire, 9/22/98.*]

—bought **Synteni, Inc.,** a privately owned gene expression microarray operations located in Fremont, California, for 2.2 million shares in January of 1998. [*PR Newswire, 12/23/97.*]

Initial Acquisition Corp. and **Hollis-Eden Inc.** merged to form **Hollis-Eden Pharmaceuticals, Inc.** on April 1, 1997. [*PR Newswire, 4/1/97.*]

Integra LifeSciences Corp. bought **Rystan Co.,** a pharmaceuticals maker located in Little Falls, New Jersey, for a total of 1.1 million shares on September 28, 1998. [*PR Newswire, 9/28/98.*]

IVAX Corp. bought a pharmaceutical plant located in Kirkland, Canada, from **Glaxo Wellcome Inc.** in February of 1997. [*PR Newswire, 2/4/97.*]

Johnson & Johnson bought **Centocor, Inc.,** a manufacturer of health care products, in stock-for-stock transaction valued at $4.9 million, on September 7, 1999. [Johnson & Johnson news release. Available from http://www.jnj.com.]

—bought the dermatological skin-care business of Racine, Wisconsin-based <S.C. Johnson & Son, Inc., on February 26, 1999. [Johnson & Johnson news release. Available from http://www.jnj.com.]

Kaire International Inc. bought **Interactive Medical Technologies Ltd.,** a network marketer of pharmaceutical preparations, in December of 1997. [*Business Wire, 12/16/97.*]

King Pharmaceuticals, Inc. bought the U.S. rights to the antibiotic Lorabid from **Eli Lilly** for a deal that is valued at $158 million in August of 1999. [*PR Newswire, 8/19/1999.*]

—bought three branded-prescription pharmaceuticals products from **Hoechst Marion Roussel** for $362.5 million in December of 1999. The products acquired include certain rights to Altace, an angiotensin-converting enzyme inhibitor; AVC, a vaginal anti-infective cream; and Silvadene, a burn cream. [*PR Newswire, 12/22/98.*]

La Jolla Diagnostics Inc. bought **ATS Inc.,** a privately owned diagnostics company, on September 17, 1998. [*Business Wire, 9/17/98.*]

Lafayette Pharmaceuticals, Inc. bought **Victoreen, Inc.,** an ionizing radiation detection and measurement instrument supplier and manufacturer based in Cleveland, Ohio, in June of 1998. Following the purchase, Lafayette Pharmaceuticals changed its name to **Inovision, L.P.** [*PR Newswire, 6/25/98.*]

—bought **Nuclear Associates,** a quality control and radiation protection products developer and supplier based in Carle Place, New York, in June of 1998. [*PR Newswire, 6/25/98.*]

Ligand Pharmaceuticals Inc. bought **Allergan Ligand Retinoid Therapeutics, Inc.,** a pharmaceutical preparations manufacturer, on November 24, 1997. [*PR Newswire, 11/24/97.*]

Matrigen, Inc. and **Prizm Pharmaceuticals, Inc.** merged to form **Selective Genetics, Inc.,** a gene therapy company focused on tissue repair and regeneration, in May of 1998. [*PR Newswire, 5/7/98.*]

McKesson Corp. bought **Automated Prescription Systems Inc.,** an automated pharmaceutical preparations counting and dispensing technology firm based in Pineville, Louisiana, for 1.3 million shares and $48 million in debt assumption in September of 1998. [*Drug Store News, 9/21/98, p. 13.*]

McKesson Health Systems Group bought **MedManagement L.L.C.,** a pharmacy management, purchasing, consulting, and information services firm located in Plymouth, Minnesota, on September 14, 1998. [*Business Wire, 9/14/98.*]

MDS Associates Inc. bought **Theratronics International Ltd.,** an isotope radiation therapy firm located in Kanata, Ontario, Canada, for $15.45 million on May 25, 1998. [*PR Newswire,* 5/25/98.]

Medarex, Inc. bought **GenPharm International, Inc.,** a pharmaceuticals firm, for 3.8 million shares worth an estimated total of $19.3 million on September 1, 1998. [*PR Newswire,* 9/1/98.]

MedCath Inc. bought **Ultimed, Inc.,** a cardiovascular disease management services firm based in Los Angeles, California, on May 16, 1997. [*Business Wire,* 5/16/97.]

Medical Industries of America bought **Pharmacy Care Specialists Inc.,** a privately owned pharmaceutical delivery company based in Florida, for 680,000 shares, $90,000 in cash, and additional shares based upon the earnings of Pharmacy Care Specialists, in April of 1998. [*Business Wire,* 4/22/98.]

Medicis Pharmaceutical Corp. bought **GenDerm Corp.,** a privately owned dermatology products manufacturer, for $60 million in cash on December 4, 1997. [*Business Wire,* 12/4/97.]

Medisys Technologies, Inc. bought **Phillips Pharmatech Labs, Inc.,** a privately owned Florida-based pharmaceutical and nutritional products, in December of 1998. [bibcit*Business Wire,* 12/17/98.]

Merck & Co., Inc. bought **Sibia Neurosciences, Inc.,** a biotechnology firm specializing in treatments for neurological diseases located in La Jolla, California, for $87 million in cash in August of 1999.[*San Diego Business Journal,* 8/1999.]

—bought **Istituto Gentili,** a pharmaceutical preparations manufacturer and developer based in Italy, in May of 1997. [*Business Wire,* 5/27/97.]

Meridian Diagnostics, Inc. bought **Gull Laboratories, Inc.,** a medical products manufacturer located in Salt Lake City, Utah, in October of 1998. [*PR Newswire,* 5/25/98.]

MIM Corp. bought **Continental Managed Pharmacy Services,** a pharmacy benefit management services operation located in Cleveland, Ohio, for 3.9 million shares on August 25, 1998. *Business Wire,* 8/25/98.]

Monsanto Co. bought two Puerto Rican pharmaceutical plants, one which manufactures bulk chemicals and one which makes medical diagnostic imaging agents, from **Nycomed Amersham PLC,** a global imaging agent manufacturer based in Norway, for $66 million in May of 1998. [*Chemical Market Reporter,* 5/25/98, p. 3.]

Mylan Laboratories Inc. bought **Penederm Inc.,** a topical drug manufacturer based in Foster City, California, for approximately $205 million, on October 2, 1998. [*Business Wire,* 6/24/98.]

NEN Life Science Products, Inc. bought **Advanced Bioconcept Ltd.,** a proprietary fluorescent peptide maker based in Montreal, Canada, in September of 1998. [*Business Wire,* 9/25/98.]

Neogen Corp. bought **Vetoquinol U.S.A.,** an animal health company based in Tampa, Florida, for $2.2 million in cash on January 5, 1998. [*PR Newswire,* 1/5/98.]

NuOncology Labs Inc., based in Florida, bought **NuOncology Labs Inc.,** a privately owned cancer treatment research and marketing company located in Virginia, in July of 1998. [*Business Wire,* 7/9/98.]

Nycomed A/S, a diagnostic imaging chemicals manufacturer based in Norway, and **Amersham International PLC,** a healthcare and life sciences conglomerate based in the United Kingdom, merged to form **Nycomed Amersham PLC,** in July of 1997. Estimated annual revenues for the newly formed company were roughly $2 billion. [*Pharmaceutical Business News,* 7/16/97, p. 3.]

Panax Pharmaceutical Co. Ltd. bought **CorBec Pharmaceuticals Inc.,** an immune system pharmaceuticals developer based in West Conschohocken, Pennsylvania in May of 1997. [*Business Wire,* 5/8/97.]

Perkin-Elmer Corp. bought **PerSeptive Biosystems Inc.,** a pharmaceutical research firm specializing in genomics, on January 22, 1998. [*PR Newswire,* 1/22/98.]

PPG Industries Inc. bought **Sipsy Chimie Fine S.C.A.,** an Avrille, France-based maker of intermediate chemicals for pharmaceutical production, on December 31, 1997. [*PR Newswire, 1/2/98.*]

RiboGene bought **Cypros Pharmaceutical Corp.**, a developer and marketer of drug products for hospitals located in Carlsbad, California, in August of 1999. [*San Diego Business Journal, 8/1999.*]

Quest Diagnostics bought **SmithKline Beecham Clinical Laboratories,** a clinical laboratory, for $1.025 billion in cash and equity on August 16, 1999. [*Chemical Market Reporter, 8/30/1999.*]

Quintiles Transnational Corp. bought **Q.E.D. International Inc.,** a pharmaceutical marketing and communication services company based in New York, on October 14, 1998. [*PR Newswire, 10/14/98.*]

—bought **The Royce Consultancy plc,** a privately owned pharmaceutical sales firm based in Edinburgh, Scotland, on August 24, 1998. [*PR Newswire, 8/24/98.*]

—bought **CerebroVascular Advances, Inc.,** a clinical research company focusing on stroke clinical trials, for 251,000 shares in late 1997. [*PR Newswire, 5/8/97.*]

Rexall Sundown, Inc. bought **Richardson Labs, Inc.,** a Boise, Idaho-based manufacturer of diet and weight management supplements, for 2.88 million shares, valued at a total of $85 million, in January of 1998. [*PR Newswire, 12/24/98.*]

Rhone-Poulenc Chimie S.A. bought the acetaminophen operations of **ChiRex, Inc.,** based in England, for $6.3 million on November 25, 1997. [*PR Newswire, 4/9/97.*]

—bought its pharmaceuticals arm, **Rhone-Poulenc Rorer,** on November 25, 1997. [*PR Newswire, 11/26/97.*]

Roche Holding AG bought **Boehringer Mannheim Corp.,** a pharmaceutical company, for $11 billion in June of 1997. The purchase made Roche Holding the sixth largest pharmaceutical company in the world. [*Pharmaceutical Business News, 6/4/97, p. 4.*]

Harry Schein, Inc. bought **Columbia Medical, Inc.** a medical and surgical supply company based in Maryland, on September 24, 1998. [*PR Newswire, 9/24/98.*]

Searle, the pharmaceuticals arm of **Monsanto Co.,** bought the pharmaceutical operations of **Poli Industria Chemica,** based in Italy, in June of 1998. [*Chemical Market Reporter, 6/1/98, p. 3.*]

Seton Healthcare Group PLC, a health products specialist, and **Scholl PLC,** a footcare specialist, merged to form **SetonScholl Group** in the beginning of 1998. [*Chemist & Druggist, 8/22/98, p. 24.*]

Sheffield Medical Technologies Inc. bought **Camelot Pharmacal, L.L.C.,** a privately owned pharmaceuticals company based in St. Louis, Missouri, for 600,000 shares on April 28, 1997. [*PR Newswire, 4/28/97.*]

Solvay Group bought **Unimed Pharmaceuticals, Inc.,** a Illinois-based company, for $123 million in June of 1999. [*HealthWire, 6/11/99.*]

Stryker Corp. bought **Howmedica Inc.,** the surgical products division of **Pfizer Inc.,** for $1.9 billion in cash in August of 1998. [*Knight-Ridder/Tribune Business News, 8/15/98.*]

Synbiotics Corp. bought the veterinary diagnostics operations of **Rhone Merieux** for $12 million in cash and 821,000 shares in the second quarter of 1997. [*Business Wire, 5/22/97.*]

Techne Corp. bought the Research Products division of **Genzyme Corp.** for $24.8 million in cash, $17 million in stock and $23.7 million in royalties on June 23, 1998. [*PR Newswire, 6/23/98.*]

Techniclone Corp. bought **Peregrine Pharmaceuticals, Inc.,** a Princeton, New Jersey-based cancer treatment pharmaceuticals company focused on developing molecules that attach to the cells lining a tumor's blood vessels, in a stock transaction on June 4, 1997. [*Business Wire, 6/4/97.*]

Technilab Pharma Inc. bought **Charton Laboratories,** a division of Montreal, Canada-based **Herdt & Charton Inc.,** in December of 1997. [*Business Wire, 12/16/97.*]

Teva Pharmaceutical Industries Ltd. bought **Pharmachemie B.V.,** a generic drug developer in located in Holland, for $87 million in cash in June of 1998. [*Israel Business Today,* 6/30/98.]

Transcell Technologies Inc.and **Intercardia Inc.,** both majority owned subsidiaries of biopharmaceutical firm Interneuron Pharmaceuticals, Inc., merged on May 8, 1998. [*PR Newswire,* 5/6/98.]

Tripos UK Holdings bought **Receptor Research Ltd.,** a United Kingdom-based specialty chemicals company focused on molecular informatics, design, and analysis for pharmaceutical, agricultural, and biotechnology industries, on November 18, 1997. [*PR Newswire,* 11/18/97.]

Tseng Labs Inc. bought **Cell Pathways, Inc.,** a privately owned pharmaceuticals company based in Horsham, Pennsylvania, in October of 1998. [*Business Wire,* 6/24/98.]

Twinlab Corp. bought **Changes International,** a privately owned nutritional supplements network marketer based in Destin, Florida, on November 13, 1997. [*Business Wire,* 11/13/97.]

Warner-Lambert Co. bought the remaining 66 percent of **Jouveinal Group,** a privately owned pharmaceutical company located in France, on May 21, 1997. [*PR Newswire,* 5/21/97.]

Watson Pharmaceuticals Inc. bought **The Rugby Group, Inc.,** the U.S. generic drug subsidiary of **Hoechst Marion Roussel Inc.,** in August of 1997. [*PR Newswire,* 8/26/97.]

Zeneca Group PLC, the largest cancer drug manufacturer in the world, bought the remaining 50 percent of cancer care provider **Salick Health Care Inc.** that it did not already own for $234 million in April of 1997. The transaction marked the first purchase of a healthcare provider by a drug manufacturer in the pharmaceutical and healthcare industries. [*American Medical News,* 5/5/97, p. 1.]

Zila Inc. bought **Oxycal Laboratories, Inc.,** a Prescott, Arizona-based, privately owned manufacturer and marketer of a patented form of vitamin C, on November 10, 1997. [*PR Newswire,* 11/10/97.]

Bibliography

Blackledge, Cath. "The Pressure to Find a Partner." *The European,* 1/26/98, p. 40.

Brown, Julie. "BiotechMergers Latest in Trend." *San Diego Business Journal,* 8/1999, p. 1.

Casagrande, Sabina. "Bayer Ponders the Merger Game." *Pharmaceutical Business News,* 8/12/98, p. 6.

Chang, Joseph. "AHP and Monsanto Merge to Form Colossal Life Science Firm." *Chemical Market Reporter,* 6/8/98, p. 1.

Gillis, Justin. "Wall Street Makes It Official: Biotech Has Arrived." *Washington Post,* 8/22/99, p. H01.

Gopal, Kevin. "Sprited Acquisitions." *Pharmaceutical Executive,* 11/1/1998, p. 36.

Green, Daniel. "Drug Makers Need New Prescription for Success." *The Financial Times,* 1/5/98, p. 27.

Green, Daniel. "Merger Fever Returns to the Drug Industry." *The Financial Times,* 1/21/98, p. 23.

Green, Daniel. "Takeover Fever." *The Financial Times,* 8/22/95, p. 12.

Guyon, Janet. "A Mangled Merger: How Glaxo and SmithKline Overdoses on Ego." *Fortune,* 3/30/98, p. 32.

Hensley, Scott. "Drug Giants Talk Marriage; No Provider Perks in American Home-SmithKline Deal." *Modern Healthcare,* 1/26/98, p. 24.

Lerner, Matthew. "Bulk Analgesics Moving to a Handful of Big Players." *Chemical Market Reporter,* 1/12/98, p. 6.

Moukheiber, Zina. "Party Poopers: Monsanto and American Home Products Plan to Merge, but Trial Lawyers are Threatening the Honeymoon." *Forbes,* 7/6/98, p. 176.

Murray, Barbra. "Hoping 1 Plus 1 Equals 3." *U.S News & World Report,* 6/15/98, p. 47.

Mirasol, Feliza. "DuPont Targets Pharma in Life Sciences Strategy." *Chemical Market Reporter,* 7/13/98, p. 5.

Parry, John. "Takeover is a Shot in the Arm for Roche." *The European,* 5/29/97, p. 16.

Scott, Alex. "Chemicals vs. Drugs." *Chemical Week,* 4/16/97, p. 24.

—AnnaMarie L. Sheldon, updated by Katherine Wagner.

This chapter presents a selection of business and professional associations active in the Pharmaceuticals sector. The information shown is adapted from Gale's *Encyclopedia of Associations* series and provides detailed and comprehensive information on nonprofit membership organizations.

Entries are arranged in alphabetical order. Categories included are e-mail address (when provided), description, founding date, number of memberships, staff; regional, state, and local group counts; national groups; budget, publications, and other information.

ACADEMY OF MANAGED CARE PHARMACY

100 N Pih St., Ste. 400
Alexandria, VA 22314-2747
Judith A. Cahill, Exec.Dir.
PH: (703)683-8416
FX: (703)683-8417
URL: www.amcp.org
Founded: 1989. **Staff:** 14. **Members:** 4,700. Professional society for pharmacists working for managed care health services. Promotes the "development and application of pharmaceutical care in order to ensure appropriate outcomes for all individuals." Represents the views and interests of managed care pharmacy. Conducts educational courses and continuing professional development programs for members.

ACADEMY OF PHARMACEUTICAL RESEARCH AND SCIENCE

American Pharmaceutical Association
2215 Constitution Ave. NW
Washington, DC 20037
Scott S. Antall, Scientific Affairs Program Coor.
PH: (800)237-2742
FX: (202)628-0443
URL: www.aphanet.org
Founded: 1965. **Staff:** 3. **Members:** 3,000. A part of American Pharmaceutical Association (see separate entry). Pharmaceutical scientists from industry and academia. Objective is to serve the profession of pharmacy by developing knowledge and integrating the process of science into the profession. Sponsors national meetings to provide a forum for presentation and discussion of original research, controversial topics, and continuing communication. Provides consultation and advice to: pharmacists on scientific matters as they relate to policy; congressional committees on bills of interest to pharmaceutical scientists; governmental agencies.

ACADEMY OF STUDENTS OF PHARMACY

2215 Constitution Ave., NW
Washington, DC 20037
Eloise D. Thibault, Asso. Dir., Student Dev.
PH: (202)628-4410
TF: (800)237-APHA
FX: (202)783-2351
E-mail: apha-asp@mail.aphanet.org
URL: www.aphanet.org
Founded: 1954. **Staff:** 3. **Members:** 16,000. A program of the American Pharmaceutical Association. Professional society of pharmacy students. Keeps members informed of the affairs of the APhA and the profession. Provides a forum for the expression of student opinion on activities and policies. Seeks to strengthen the program whereby student members, upon graduation, become active members of the APhA. Encourages participation by pharmacy students in interdisciplinary projects that attempt to find solutions to social problems; works in community-oriented drug education programs; supports interdisciplinary clinical training for pharmacists.

ALLIANCE FOR THE PRUDENT USE OF ANTIBIOTICS

PO Box 1372
Boston, MA 02117
Stuart B. Levy, M.D., Pres.
PH: (617)636-0966
FX: (617)636-3999
E-mail: apua@opal.tufts.edu
URL: www.healthsci.tufts.edu/apua/apua.html
Founded: 1981. **Staff:** 3. **Members:** 1,000. International membership of physicians, scientists, and medical and public health personnel; other individuals supporting prudent use of antibiotics. (Believes that extensive use of antibiotics leads to development of resistant strains of pathogenic and common, nonpathogenic bacteria with resistance traits transferable from one bacterium to others. These resistant strains are no longer susceptible to antibiotics and therefore can undermine treatment of infectious bacterial diseases.) Advocates and defines "good usage" of antibiotics; informs and educates the public about the dangers of misusing and overusing antibiotics and other antimicrobial agents; provides data to individuals and organizations interested in preventing antibiotic misuse and overuse. Informs and educates medical and paramedical personnel worldwide about the defined and specific action of antibiotics and the necessity of controlling their dispensation and prescription. Supports research projects. Maintains speakers' bureau; plans to offer computerized services.

AMERICAN ASSOCIATION OF COLLEGES OF PHARMACY

1426 Prince St.
Alexandria, VA 22314
Richard P. Penna, Exec.VP
PH: (703)739-2330
FX: (703)836-8982
E-mail: lalsop@aacp.org
URL: www.aacp.org
Founded: 1900. **Staff:** 15. **Members:** 2,500. **Budget:** 2,900,000. College of pharmacy programs accredited by American Council on Pharmaceutical Education; corporations and individuals. Compiles statistics.

AMERICAN ASSOCIATION OF PHARMACEUTICAL SCIENTISTS

1650 King St., Ste. 200
Alexandria, VA 22314-2747
John B. Cox, CAE, Exec.Dir.
PH: (703)548-3000
FX: (703)684-7349
E-mail: aaps@aaps.org
URL: www.aaps.org
Founded: 1986. **Staff:** 20. **Members:** 7,000. **Budget:** 3,600,000. Pharmaceutical scientists. Provides a forum for exchange of scientific information; serves as a resource in forming public policies to regulate pharmaceutical sciences and related issues of public concern. Promotes pharmaceutical sciences and provides for recognition of individual achievement; works to foster career growth and the development of members. Offers placement service.

AMERICAN COLLEGE OF APOTHECARIES

PO Box 341266
Memphis, TN 38184-1266
Dr. D. C. Huffman, Jr., Exec.VP
PH: (901)383-8119
FX: (901)383-8882
Founded: 1940. **Staff:** 7. **Members:** 1,000. **Budget:** 250,000. Professional society of pharmacists owning and operating ethical prescription pharmacies, including hospital pharmacists, pharmacy students, and faculty of colleges of pharmacy. Primary objective is the translation, transformation, and dissemination of knowledge, research data, and recent developments in the pharmaceutical industry and public health. Sponsors Community Pharmacy Residency Program; offers continuing education courses. Conducts research programs; sponsors charitable program; compiles statistics; operates speakers' bureau.

AMERICAN COLLEGE OF CLINICAL PHARMACOLOGY

3 Ellinwood Court
New Hartford, NY 13413-1105
Susan Ulrich, Exec.Dir.
PH: (315)768-6117
FX: (315)768-6119
E-mail: accp1ssu@aol.com
URL: www.accp1.org
Founded: 1969. **Staff:** 1. **Members:** 1,000. **Budget:** 400,000. Strives to be the premier professional society with the size, influence, and diversity of membership consistent with the breadth of the discipline of clinical pharmacology. Provides educational programs and forum for membership, health professionals, students, and the public. Assists in the development and dissemination of basic and clinical knowledge to improve rational drug use and patient outcomes. Serves as a forum for active public debate to influence scientific, regulatory, and public health policy issues. Provides opportunities to influence future directions of the College. Supports and en-

courages the discovery and development efforts designed to provide improved therapeutic modalities.

AMERICAN COLLEGE OF CLINICAL PHARMACY
3101 Broadway, Ste. 380
Kansas City, MO 64111
Robert M. Elenbaas, Exec.Dir.
PH: (816)531-2177
FX: (816)531-4990
URL: www.accp.com
Founded: 1979. **Members:** 1,600. **Budget:** 600,000. Clinical pharmacists dedicated to: promoting rational use of drugs in society; advancing the practice of clinical pharmacy and interdisciplinary health care; assuring high quality clinical pharmacy by establishing and maintaining standards in education and training at advanced levels. Encourages research and recognizes excellence in clinical pharmacy. Offers educational programs, symposia, research forums, fellowship training, and college-funded grants through competitions. Maintains placement service.

AMERICAN COLLEGE OF NEUROPSYCHOPHARMACOLOGY
320 Centre Bldg.
2014 Broadway
Nashville, TN 37203
Oakley Ray, Ph.D., Exec.Sec.
PH: (615)322-2075
FX: (615)343-0662
E-mail: acnp@acnp.org
URL: www.acnp.org
Founded: 1961. **Staff:** 8. **Members:** 757. Experienced investigators whose work is related to neuropsychopharmacology. Promotes and encourages the scientific study and application of neuropsychopharmacology. Conducts study groups and plenary sessions.

AMERICAN COUNCIL ON PHARMACEUTICAL EDUCATION
311 W. Superior St., Ste. 512
Chicago, IL 60610
Daniel A. Nona, Exec.Dir.
PH: (312)664-3575
FX: (312)664-4652
Founded: 1932. **Staff:** 7. **Members:** 10. Accrediting agency for the professional programs of colleges and schools of pharmacy and approval of providers of continuing pharmaceutical education.

AMERICAN FOUNDATION FOR PHARMACEUTICAL EDUCATION
1 Church St., Ste. 202
Rockville, MD 20850-4158
Robert M. Bachman, Pres.
PH: (301)738-2160
FX: (301)738-2161
Founded: 1942. **Staff:** 2. **Members:** 40. **Budget:** 1,200,000. Established by pharmaceutical and drug trade associations to improve pharmaceutical education, colleges of pharmacy, and pharmacy student performance. Accepts and administers gifts, legacies, bequests, and funds and makes disbursements for fellowships and the promotion of pharmaceutical education.

AMERICAN INSTITUTE OF THE HISTORY OF PHARMACY
Pharmacy Bldg.
425 N. Chater St.
Madison, WI 53706
Gregory J. Higby, Dir.
PH: (608)262-5378
Founded: 1941. **Staff:** 4. **Members:** 1,000. **Budget:** 200,000. Pharmacists, firms, and organizations interested in historical and social aspects of the pharmaceutical field. Maintains pharmaceutical Americana collection; conducts research programs.

AMERICAN PHARMACEUTICAL ASSOCIATION—ACADEMY OF PHARMACY PRACTICE AND MANAGEMENT
2215 Constitution Ave. NW
Washington, DC 20037-2985
Janet N. Edwards, Assoc.Dir., Practice Development
PH: (202)628-4410
TF: (800)237-APHA
FX: (202)783-2351
E-mail: apha-appm@mail.aphanet.org
URL: www.aphanet.org
Founded: 1965. **Staff:** 2. **Members:** 21,000. Pharmacists concerned with rendering professional services directly to the public, without regard for status of employment or environment of practice. Purposes are to provide a forum and mechanism whereby pharmacists may meet to discuss and implement programs and activities relevant and helpful to the practitioner of pharmacy; to recommend programs and courses of action which should be undertaken or implemented by the profession; to coordinate academy efforts so as to be an asset to the progress of the profession. Provides and cosponsors continuing education meetings, seminars, and workshops; produces audiovisual materials.

AMERICAN SOCIETY FOR AUTOMATION IN PHARMACY
492 Norristown Rd., Ste. 160
Blue Bell, PA 19422
William A. Lockwood, Jr., Exec.Dir.
PH: (610)825-7783
FX: (610)825-7641
E-mail: wal@computertalk.com
URL: www.asapnet.com
Founded: 1989. **Staff:** 3. **Members:** 500. Pharmaceutical software developers; pharmaceutical and insurance companies; related organizations. Addresses issues related to computer use in the pharmaceutical industry.

AMERICAN SOCIETY FOR CLINICAL PHARMACOLOGY AND THERAPEUTICS
117 W. Ridge Pike
Conshohocken, PA 19428-1216
Denise Gavetti, Asst.Exec.Dir.
PH: (610)825-3838
FX: (610)834-8652
E-mail: ASCPT@aol.com
URL: www.ascpt.org
Founded: 1900. **Staff:** 4. **Members:** 2,150. Works to "promote and advance the science of human pharmacology and therapeutics and in so doing to maintain the highest standards of research, education, and exchange of scientific information." Provides a Medical Education Program of Continuing Education for practicing physicians.

AMERICAN SOCIETY FOR PHARMACOLOGY AND EXPERIMENTAL THERAPEUTICS
9650 Rockville Pike
Bethesda, MD 20814-3995
Christine K. Carrico, Ph.D., Exec. Officer
PH: (301)530-7060
FX: (301)530-7061
E-mail: aspetinfo@faseb.org
URL: www.faseb.org/aspet
Founded: 1908. **Staff:** 8. **Members:** 4,400. Scientific society of investigators in pharmacology and toxicology interested in research and promotion of pharmacological knowledge and its use among scientists and the public.

AMERICAN SOCIETY OF CLINICAL PSYCHOPHARMACOLOGY
PO Box 2257
New York, NY 10116
Paul H. Wender, M.D., Pres.
PH: (212)268-4260
FX: (212)268-4434
URL: www.ascpp.org
Founded: 1992. **Staff:** 2. **Members:** 1,200. Works to encourage cli-

nical research in psychopharmacology and provide continuing education for members. Sponsors research; facilitates exchange of information; conducts professional educational programs and; provides educational programs on the treatment of psychiatric disorders for patients and families; develops relationships with mental health advocacy groups; advocates public policies which promote research and the delivery of high quality care.

AMERICAN SOCIETY OF CONSULTANT PHARMACISTS
1321 Duke St.
Alexandria, VA 22314-3563
R. Timothy Webster, Exec.Dir.
PH: (703)739-1300
FX: (703)739-1321
E-mail: info@ascp.com
URL: www.ascp.com
Founded: 1969. **Staff:** 45. **Members:** 6,800. **Budget:** 7,500,000. Registered pharmacists and educators who are largely concerned with pharmaceutical procedures within nursing homes and related health facilities. Works to: improve consultant pharmacist services to nursing homes and other long-term care facilities; define professional standards and to promote the certification of the profession; exchange information; sponsor and encourage the development of educational facilities and courses for the advancement of the profession; promote wider public information efforts; represent the interests of the profession before legislative and administrative branches of government; sponsor group service programs; promote public health and welfare. Conducts surveys of long-term care pharmacy operations. Sponsors educational and research programs. Maintains information center, hall of fame, and speakers' bureau; operates placement service; compiles statistics.

AMERICAN SOCIETY OF HEALTH SYSTEM PHARMACISTS
7272 Wisconsin Ave.
Bethesda, MD 20814
Kate Gibbons
PH: (301)657-3000
FX: (301)657-1251
Founded: 1942. **Staff:** 170. **Members:** 30,000. **Budget:** 26,000,000. Professional society of pharmacists employed by hospitals, HMOs, clinics, and other health systems. Provides personnel placement service for members; sponsors professional and personal liability program. Conducts educational and exhibit programs. Has 30 practice interest areas, special sections for home care practitioners and clinical specialists, and research and education foundation.

AMERICAN SOCIETY OF PHARMACOGNOSY
School of Pharmacy
Northeast Louisiana University
Monroe, LA 71209
Katherine McVay, Contact
PH: (318)342-1600
FX: (318)342-1606
E-mail: pybourn@alpha.nlu.edu
Founded: 1959. **Members:** 1,000. **Budget:** 100,000. Professional society of pharmacognosists (persons engaged in the study of drugs from a natural origin) and others interested in the plant sciences and natural products.

ANIMAL HEALTH INSTITUTE
501 Wythe St.
PO Box 1417-D50
Alexandria, VA 22313-1480
Alexander S. Mathews, Pres. CEO
PH: (703)684-0011
FX: (703)684-0125
E-mail: webmaster@ahi.org
URL: www.ahi.org
Founded: 1941. **Staff:** 17. **Members:** 22. **Budget:** 2,500,000. Represents manufacturers of animal health products (vaccines, pharmaceuticals, and feed additives used in modern food production; and medicines for household pets). Works with government agencies and

legislators; prepares position papers; compiles and disseminates information. Sponsors AHI Foundation.

ASHP FOUNDATION
7272 Wisconsin Ave.
Bethesda, MD 20814
Dr. Henry Manasse, Exec.VP
PH: (301)657-3000
FX: (301)657-1251
Founded: 1968. Established for pharmaceutical care and research purposes. Offers fellowships, grants, awards, and anticoagulation and renal dialysis traineeships.

ASPIRIN FOUNDATION OF AMERICA
1555 Connecticut Ave. NW, Ste. 200
Washington, DC 20036
Thomas Bryant, Contact
PH: (202)234-3154
Founded: 1981. **Staff:** 3. **Members:** 8. **Budget:** 1,250,000. Manufacturers, producers, distributors, and processors of aspirin and aspirin products. Works to facilitate and encourage an understanding of the potential health benefits of aspirin and to collect and disseminate that information.

ASSOCIATION OF CLINICAL RESEARCH PROFESSIONALS
1012 14th St. NW, Ste. 807
Washington, DC 20005
Denise F. Olson, Exec.Dir.
PH: (202)737-8100
FX: (202)737-8101
E-mail: office@acrpnet.org
Founded: 1977. **Staff:** 4. **Members:** 4,100. **Budget:** 1,000,000. Individuals engaged in clinical pharmacology and other related research professions, including clinical monitors and research associates, nurses, pharmacists, pharmacologists, physicians, and regulatory professionals. Promotes professional growth in the field through the dissemination of information, the exchange of ideas, and the development of educational programs. Provides continuing education credits to pharmacy and nursing professionals through the American Council on Pharmaceutical Education and the American Nurses Association (see separate entries).

AUXILIARY TO THE AMERICAN PHARMACEUTICAL ASSOCIATION
6051 North Bay Rd.
Miami Beach, FL 34624
Blanche Prine, Pres.
PH: (305)865-3746
Founded: 1936. **Members:** 400. Individuals related to members in the American Pharmaceutical Association; others interested in pharmacy. Grants low-interest loans to pharmacy students annually.

BEHAVIORAL PHARMACOLOGY SOCIETY
c/o Larry D. Byrd, Ph.D.
Yerkes Regional Primate Res. Center
Div. of Behavioral Biology
Emory University
Atlanta, GA 30322
Tam Insel, Ph.D., Dir.
PH: (404)727-7709
E-mail: byrd@rmy.emory.edu
Founded: 1957. **Staff:** 2. **Members:** 200. **Budget:** 15,000. Professional psychologists and pharmacologists interested in behavioral pharmacology and psychopharmacology or the connection between drugs and behavior. Publications: none.

CHAIN DRUG MARKETING ASSOCIATION
43157 W Nine Mile Rd.
Novi, MI 48376
James Devine, Pres.

PH: (248)449-9300
TF: (800)935-2362
FX: (248)449-9396
E-mail: cdma1@aol.com
URL: www.chaindrug.com
Founded: 1926. **Staff:** 13. **Members:** 100. **Budget:** 2,000,000. Drug store chains located throughout the world. Represents members in the market for merchandise; keeps them abreast of trends in relevant fields.

CHRISTIAN PHARMACISTS FELLOWSHIP INTERNATIONAL
PO Box 1717
501 5th St.
Bristol, TN 37621-1717
Allan Sharp, P.D., Admin.Dir.
PH: (423)764-6000
FX: (423)764-4490
E-mail: cpfi@tricon.net
URL: www.cpfi.org
Founded: 1984. **Staff:** 2. **Members:** 1,200. **Budget:** 90,500. To promote and maintain fellowship among Christian pharmacists. Establishes clubs and chapters at universities, colleges, schools, hospitals, and in communities; sponsors activities and retreats for Christian pharmacists and their families. Encourages active Christian witness and evangelism; teaches pharmacists how to share and present the Gospel of Jesus Christ in their practice; disseminates information among Christian pharmacists; identifies areas of service for pharmacists in missions worldwide and sponsors missionaries in the field. Provides and promotes Christian pharmacist-speakers. Conducts gatherings, such as prayer groups, with speakers at state and national pharmacy meetings.

COLLEGIUM INTERNATIONALE NEURO-PSYCHOPHARMACOLOGICUM
2014 Broadway, Ste. 320
Nashville, TN 37203
Oakley Ray, Ph.D., Sec., Presidents Committee
PH: (615)322-2075
FX: (615)343-0662
E-mail: cinp@ctrvax.vanderbilt.edu
Founded: 1957. **Members:** 1,000. Individuals engaged in experimental and clinical neuropsychopharmacological research and teachers in this field. Purposes are to advance the experimental and clinical aspects of the neuropsychopharmacological sciences; facilitate international relations between branches of the neuropsychopharmacological disciplines; further the international exchange of information and promote personal relations; consider the medico-social problems of psychopharmacology.

CONSUMER HEALTH PRODUCT ASSOCIATION
1150 Connecticut Ave. NW
Washington, DC 20036
James D. Cope, Pres.
PH: (202)429-9260
FX: (202)233-6835
Founded: 1881. **Staff:** 40. **Members:** 225. **Budget:** 7,000,000. Marketers (70) of nonprescription drugs, which are packaged, over-the-counter medicines; associate members (150) include suppliers, advertising agencies, and advertising media. Obtains and disseminates business, legislative, regulatory, and scientific information; conducts voluntary labeling review service to assist members in complying with laws and regulations.

COUNCIL ON FAMILY HEALTH
1155 Connecticut Ave., Ste. 400
Washington, DC 20036
William I. Bergman, Pres.
PH: (202)429-6600
URL: www.cfhinfo.org
Founded: 1966. **Members:** 32. **Budget:** 300,000. Manufacturers of prescription and over-the-counter medications. Provides the public and interested organizations with information on proper usage of medications and other family health concerns, such as safety in the home.

DRUG, CHEMICAL AND ALLIED TRADES ASSOCIATION
510 Route 130 Ste B1
East Windsor, NJ 08520
William Cleary, Exec.Dir.
PH: (609)448-1000
FX: (606)448-1944
Founded: 1890. **Staff:** 6. **Members:** 500. **Budget:** 800,000. Manufacturers of drugs, chemicals, and related products (packaging, cosmetics, essential oils); publications, advertising agencies, agents, brokers, and importers.

DRUG INFORMATION ASSOCIATION
501 Office Center Dr., Ste. 450
Fort Washington, PA 19034-3211
Joseph R. Assenzo, PhD, Exec.Dir.
PH: (215)628-2288
FX: (215)641-1229
E-mail: dia@diahome.org
URL: www.diahome.org
Founded: 1965. **Members:** 13,000. Persons who handle drug information in government, industry, the medical and pharmaceutical professions, and allied fields. Seeks to provide mutual instruction on the technology of drug information processing in all areas, including collecting, selecting, abstracting, indexing, coding, vocabulary building, terminology standardizing, computerizing data storage and retrieval, tabulating, correlating, computing, evaluating, writing, editing, reporting, and publishing. Conducts workshops, symposia, and seminars.

FOREIGN PHARMACY GRADUATE EXAMINATION COMMITTEE
c/o Carmen A. Catizone
700 Busse Hwy.
National Association of Boards of Pharmacy
Park Ridge, IL 60068
Carmen A. Catizone, Exec.Dir.
PH: (847)698-6227
FX: (847)698-0124
Founded: 1982. **Staff:** 6. A committee of the National Association of Boards of Pharmacy. Provides information to foreign pharmacy graduates regarding entry into the U.S. pharmacy profession and health care systems. Evaluates qualifications of foreign pharmacy graduates. Gathers and disseminates data on foreign graduates; maintains information on foreign pharmacy schools in order to produce an examination that measures academic competence with regard to U.S. pharmacy school standards.

GENERIC PHARMACEUTICAL INDUSTRY ASSOCIATION
1620 Eye St. NW, Ste. 800
Washington, DC 20006-4005
Dr. Alice Till, Pres.
PH: (202)833-9070
FX: (202)833-9612
E-mail: info@gpia.org
URL: www.gpia.org
Founded: 1981. **Staff:** 6. **Members:** 43. **Budget:** 2,000,000. Manufacturers and distributors of generic medicines and providers of technical services and goods. Members are dedicated to providing quality pharmaceuticals to consumers at affordable prices.

HEALTHCARE COMPLIANCE PACKAGING COUNCIL
1101 Connecticut Ave., Ste. 1000
Washington, DC 20036
Peter G. Mayberry, Staff Dir.
PH: (202)828-2328
FX: (202)828-2400
E-mail: pgmayberry@aol.com
URL: www.unitdose.org
Founded: 1991. **Staff:** 3. **Members:** 65. **Budget:** 200,000. Promotes the use of "unit-dose blister packaging" as a way of insuring compliance with pharmaceutical regimens and other benefits. Con-

ducts speakers' bureau. Compiles statistics. Sponsors research and educational programs.

INTERNATIONAL PHARMACEUTICAL EXCIPIENTS COUNCIL

1361 Alps Rd., Bldg. 3
Wayne, NJ 07470
Louis Blecher, Chm.
PH: (973)628-3231
FX: (973)628-3794
E-mail: ipec@iscorp.com
Founded: 1991. **Members:** 25. **Budget:** 300,000. Pharmaceutical and excipient manufacturing companies. Promotes the use of inactive ingredients (excipients) in pharmaceuticals that do not affect the safety or effectiveness of the final product. Encourages harmonization of worldwide standards to facilitate uniformity of product. Seeks to ensure the safety and quality of excipients and represent the interests of members. Develops safety guidelines and good manufacturing practices guidelines. Provides expertise and information to the U.S. Food and Drug Administration, U.S. Pharmacopoeia and equivalents in Europe and Japan.

INTERNATIONAL SOCIETY FOR PHARMACEUTICAL ENGINEERING

3816 W. Linebaugh Ave., No. 412
Tampa, FL 33624
Robert P. Best, Pres./CEO
PH: (813)960-2105
FX: (813)264-2816
Founded: 1980. **Staff:** 24. **Members:** 11,500. **Budget:** 3,000,000. Pharmaceutical, biotechnological, medical device, diagnostic, and cosmetic engineers and technicians in 60 countries who are responsible for designing, supervising, and maintaining process equipment, systems, and instrumentation in health care materials manufacturing facilities. Promotes information exchange between members and regulatory agencies; enhances productivity. Gathers and disseminates information; sponsors continuing education programs and seminars. Maintains speakers' bureau.

INTERNATIONAL SOCIETY FOR PHARMACOECONOMICS AND OUTCOMES RESEARCH

20 Nassau St., Ste. 307
Princeton, NJ 08542
Marilyn Dix-Smith, Exec.Dir.
PH: (609)252-1305
FX: (609)252-1306
E-mail: info@ispor.org
Founded: 1995. **Staff:** 4. **Members:** 2,000. **Budget:** 1,000,000. Researchers who study the effectiveness of treatments. Researches and users of cost-effectiveness information, health care decision makers.

MEDICAL LETTER

1000 Main St.
New Rochelle, NY 10801
Mark Abramowicz, M.D., Editor
PH: (914)235-0500
FX: (914)576-3377
URL: www.medletter.com
Founded: 1959. **Staff:** 30. Gathers and publishes information on the therapeutic and side effects of drugs for the benefit of physicians and other members of the health professions. Emphasis is on new drugs.

MULTIDISCIPLINARY ASSOCIATION FOR PSYCHEDELIC STUDIES

2105 Robinson Ave.
Sarasota, FL 34232
Sylvia Thyssen, Dir. of Communications
PH: (941)924-6277
FX: (941)924-6265
E-mail: info@maps.org
URL: www.maps.org
Founded: 1986. **Staff:** 3. **Members:** 1,800. **Budget:** 250,000. Promotes the development of beneficial, socially sanctioned uses of psychedelic drugs and marijuana. Helps researchers design, obtain government approval for, fund, conduct and report on psychedelic research in human volunteers; funds MDMA psychotherapy studies; facilitates research and FDA approval for marijuana to be prescribed for medical uses.

NATIONAL ASSOCIATION OF BOARDS OF PHARMACY

700 Busse Hwy.
Park Ridge, IL 60068
Carmen A. Catizone, Exec.Dir.
PH: (847)698-6227
FX: (847)698-0124
URL: www.nabp.net
Founded: 1904. **Staff:** 36. **Members:** 67. **Budget:** 4,000,000. Pharmacy boards of several states, District of Columbia, Puerto Rico, Virgin Islands, several Canadian provinces, and the states of Victoria, Australia, and New South Wales. Provides for inter-state reciprocity in pharmaceutic licensure based upon a uniform minimum standard of pharmaceutic education and uniform legislation; improves the standards of pharmaceutical education licensure and practice. Provides legislative information; sponsors uniform licensure examination; also provides information on accredited school and college requirements. Maintains pharmacy and drug law statistics.

NATIONAL ASSOCIATION OF CHAIN DRUG STORES

413 N. Lee St.
PO Box 1417-D49
Alexandria, VA 22313
Ronald L. Ziegler, Pres. & CEO
PH: (703)549-3001
FX: (703)836-4869
URL: www.nacds.org
Founded: 1933. **Staff:** 90. **Members:** 1,610. **Budget:** 30,000,000. Chain drug members (130); associate members (1400) and (80) international members include manufacturers, suppliers, manufacturer's representatives, publishers, and advertising agencies. Interprets actions by government agencies in such areas as drugs, public health, federal trade, labor, and excise taxes. Sponsors meetings and pharmacy student recruitment program. Maintains library. Offers insurance and discount services to members.

NATIONAL ASSOCIATION OF PHARMACEUTICAL MANUFACTURERS

320 Old Country Rd., Ste. 205
Garden City, NY 11530-1752
Robert S. Milanese, Pres.
PH: (516)741-3699
FX: (516)741-3696
E-mail: napmgenrx@aol.com
URL: www.napmnet.org
Founded: 1954. **Staff:** 3. **Members:** 53. **Budget:** 500,000. Pharmaceutical manufacturers and repackagers. Associate members are distributors of raw material, component, and service suppliers. Purpose is to consider problems arising from laws and regulations, and to establish rapport with federal and state agencies. Organized the Foundation for Pharmaceutical Research. Conducts technical and regulatory symposia and seminars.

NATIONAL CATHOLIC PHARMACISTS GUILD OF THE UNITED STATES

1012 Surrey Hills Dr.
St. Louis, MO 63117-1438
John Paul Winkelmann, Exec.Dir.& Co-Pres.
PH: (314)645-0085
Founded: 1962. **Staff:** 1. **Members:** 400. Catholic pharmacists, pharmacy graduates, students, and pharmacy technicians. Upholds the principles of the Catholic faith and all laws of church and country, especially those pertaining to the practice of pharmacy; assists ecclesiastical authorities in the diffusion of Catholic pharmacy ethics; promotes donations of funds and supplies to the needy; opposes the sale of pornographic literature, especially that which is being sold in pharmacies; fosters solidarity and goodwill among all pharmacists. Provides pharmaceuticals and funds for people worldwide.

NATIONAL COMMUNITY PHARMACISTS ASSOCIATION
205 Daingerfield Rd.
Alexandria, VA 22314-2885
Calvin J. Anthony, Exec.VP
PH: (703)683-8200
TF: (800)544-7447
FX: (703)683-3619
E-mail: calvin.anthony@ncpanet.org
URL: www.ncpanet.org
Founded: 1898. **Staff:** 41. **Members:** 30,000. Owners and managers of independent drugstores and pharmacists employed in retail drugstores offering pharmacy service. Provides support for undergraduate pharmacy education through National Association of Retail Druggists Foundation.

NATIONAL COUNCIL FOR PRESCRIPTION DRUG PROGRAMS
4201 N. 24th St., Ste. 365
Phoenix, AZ 85016
Lee Ann C. Stember, Pres.
PH: (602)957-9105
FX: (602)955-0749
E-mail: ncpdp@ncpdp.org
URL: www.ncpdp.org
Founded: 1977. **Staff:** 17. **Members:** 1,300. **Budget:** 1,500,000. Works to create and promote data interchange and processing standards to the pharmacy services sector of the health care industry; and to provide a continuing source of accurate and reliable information that supports the diverse needs of its membership.

NATIONAL COUNCIL OF STATE PHARMACY ASSOCIATION EXECUTIVES
c/o Al Mellbane
PO Box 151
Chapel Hill, NC 27514-0151
Al Mellbane, Sec.-Treas.
PH: (919)967-2237
TF: (800)852-7343
FX: (919)968-9430
Founded: 1927. **Staff:** 1. **Members:** 52. **Budget:** 20,000. Professional society of the executive officers of state pharmacy associations.

NATIONAL COUNCIL ON PATIENT INFORMATION AND EDUCATION
666 11th St. NW, Ste. 810
Washington, DC 20001-4542
William Ray Bullman, Exec.V.Pres.
PH: (202)347-6711
FX: (202)638-0773
E-mail: ncpie@erols.com
Founded: 1982. **Staff:** 4. **Members:** 260. **Budget:** 500,000. Health care professional organizations, pharmaceutical manufacturing organizations, federal agencies, voluntary health agencies, and consumer groups. Increases the availability of information and improves the dialogue between consumers and health care providers about prescription medicines; increases professional awareness of the need to give adequate information on prescription therapy; expands consumers' participation with health professionals on matters of drug therapy. Communicates with health care providers on the importance of giving consumers oral and written information on prescription medicines and encourages consumers to ask questions about medicines and explain factors that may affect their ability to follow prescriptions.

NATIONAL DRUG TRADE CONFERENCE
c/o Gerald J. Mossinghoff
1100 15th St. NW
Washington, DC 20005
Gerald J. Mossinghoff, Pres.
Founded: 1913. **Members:** 10. Federation of associations of manufacturers, wholesalers, and boards and colleges of pharmacy.

NATIONAL PHARMACEUTICAL ASSOCIATION
13763 Brookgreen Cir.
Dallas, TX 75240-5812
Dr. Billie McMiller, Pres.
PH: (972)235-4211
Founded: 1947. **Members:** 325. State and local associations of professional minority pharmacists. To provide a means whereby members may "contribute to their common improvement, share their experiences, and contribute to the public good."

NATIONAL PHARMACEUTICAL COUNCIL
1894 Preston White Dr.
Reston, VA 20191
Karren Williams, Pres./CEO
PH: (703)620-6390
FX: (703)476-0904
Founded: 1953. **Staff:** 14. **Members:** 29. **Budget:** 3,500,000. Pharmaceutical manufacturers producing high quality prescription medication and other pharmaceutical products. Generates research; conducts specialized educational programs, and forums.

NATIONAL WHOLESALE DRUGGISTS' ASSOCIATION
1821 Michael Faraday Dr., Ste. 400
Reston, VA 20190
Ronald J. Streck, Pres. and CEO
PH: (703)787-0000
FX: (703)787-6930
URL: www.nwda.org
Founded: 1876. **Staff:** 41. **Members:** 456. **Budget:** 9,350,000. Wholesalers and manufacturers of drug and health care products and industry service providers. Compiles statistics; sponsors research and specialized education programs. Has on-line e-mail bulletin service.

PARENTERAL DRUG ASSOCIATION
7500 Old Georgetown Rd., Ste. 620
Bethesda, MD 20814
Edmund M. Fry, Pres.
PH: (301)986-0293
FX: (301)986-0296
E-mail: info@pda.org
URL: www.pda.org
Founded: 1946. **Staff:** 21. **Members:** 8,500. **Budget:** 4,000,000. Individuals working in the research, development, or manufacture of parenteral (injectable) drugs and sterile products. Promotes the advance of parenteral science and technology in the interest of public health. Encourages the exchange of information and technical expertise. Conducts open forums for manufacturers, suppliers, users, regulatory agencies, and academia; sponsors research and educational programs; operates placement service and speakers' bureau.

PHARMACEUTICAL CARE MANAGEMENT ASSOCIATION
2300 9th St. S., Ste. 210
Arlington, VA 22204-2320
Delbert D. Konnor, Pres. & CEO
PH: (703)920-8480
TF: (888)SAY-PCMA
FX: (703)920-8491
E-mail: pcma@pcmanet.org
URL: www.pcmanet.org
Founded: 1975. **Staff:** 14. **Members:** 147. **Budget:** 1,800,000. Represents managed care pharmacy and its healthcare partners in pharmaceutical care: managed healthcare organizations, PBMs, HMOs, PPOs, third party administrators, healthcare insurance companies, drug wholesalers, pharmaceutical manufacturers, and community pharmacy networks. Serves its members and America's healthcare system by promoting education, legislation, practice standards, and research that foster quality, affordable pharmaceutical care. PCMA members serve more than 150 million enrolled lives.

PHARMACEUTICAL RESEARCH AND MANUFACTURERS OF AMERICA

1100 15th St. NW, Ste. 900
Washington, DC 20005
Gerald J. Mossinghoff, Pres.
PH: (202)835-3400
FX: (202)835-3429
URL: www.phrma.org
Founded: 1958. **Staff:** 80. **Members:** 63. Research based manufacturers of ethical pharmaceutical and biological products that are distributed under their own labels. Encourages high standards for quality control and good manufacturing practices; research toward development of new and better medical products; enactment of uniform and reasonable drug legislation for the protection of public health. Disseminates information on governmental regulations and policies, but does not maintain or supply information on specific products, prices, distribution, promotion, or sales policies of its individual members. Has established the Pharmaceutical Manufacturers Association Foundation to promote public health through scientific and medical research.

PHARMACISTS IN OPHTHALMIC PRACTICE

Wills Eye Hospital
900 Walnut St.
Philadelphia, PA 19107
Clement A. Weisbecker, Bd.Chm.
Founded: 1984. **Members:** 26. Pharmacists who serve as directors or chief pharmacists of institutions that specialize in ophthalmology or otolaryngology. Exchanges information and determines standards relating to ophthalmological pharmacy, pharmacology, and formulations. Conducts research and compiles statistics on ophthalmic pharmacy, products, and medication.

RETIRED PERSONS SERVICES

500 Montgomery St.
Alexandria, VA 22314-1563
Brian Frid, Pres.
PH: (703)684-0244
FX: (703)684-0246
Founded: 1959. Mail service pharmacy for members of the American Association of Retired Persons (see separate entry). Provides prescription and nonprescription drugs, vitamins, and other health care items through mail service and walk-in facilities in California, Texas, Missouri, Oregon, Indiana, Connecticut, Florida, Pennsylvania, Nevada, Virginia, and Washington, DC. Encourages consumer awareness, comparison shopping, and use of generic drugs.

SOCIETY OF INFECTIOUS DISEASES PHARMACISTS

PO Box 891154
Houston, TX 77289-1154
E-mail: esmith@solar.cini.utk.edu
Pharmacists with a primary interest and practice in infectious diseases pharmacotherapy, and who have spent at least two years performing pharmacotherpeutic research are active members; pharmacists and other individuals not meeting the requirements for active membership, but who share an interest in infectious diseases pharmacotherapy, are associate members. Seeks to advance the study and practice of infectious diseases pharmacotherapy, and to enhance the professional status of members. Serves as a forum for discussion and exchange of information among members. Encourages pharmacotherpeutic research.

UNITED STATES PHARMACOPEIA

12601 Twinbrook Pky.
Rockville, MD 20852
Jerome A. Halperin, Exec.VP & CEO
PH: (301)881-0666
TF: (800)822-8772
FX: (301)816-8299
E-mail: webmaster@usp.org
URL: www.usp.org
Founded: 1820. **Staff:** 230. **Members:** 395. **Budget:** 20,000,000. Dedicated to promoting the public health by establishing and disseminating officially recognized standards of quality and authoritative information for the use of medicines and other health care technologies by health professionals, patients and consumers.

WOMAN'S ORGANIZATION OF THE NATIONAL ASSOCIATION OF RETAIL DRUGGISTS

205 Daingerfield Rd.
Alexandria, VA 22314
Vivian Przondo, Contact
PH: (703)683-8200
FX: (703)683-3619
Founded: 1905. **Members:** 600. Women and female relatives of men in the pharmaceutical business. Objective is to unite the families of persons interested in all aspects of the pharmaceutical profession. Promotes legislation for the betterment of the retail drug and pharmacy business. Conducts charitable program.

Consultants and consulting organizations active in the Pharmaceuticals sector are featured in this chapter. Entries are adapted from Gale's *Consultants and Consulting Organizations Directory* (*CCOD*). Each entry represents an expertise which may be of interest to business organizations, government agencies, nonprofit institutions, and individuals requiring technical and other support. The listees shown are located in the United States and Canada.

In Canada, the use of the term "consultant" is restricted. The use of the word, in this chapter, does not necessarily imply that the firm has been granted the "consultant" designation in Canada.

Entries are arranged in alphabetical order. Categories include contact information (address, phone, fax, web site, e-mail); names and titles of executive officers; description; special services offered; geographical areas served; and other information (e.g., seminars, workshops).

ADVANCED DERMACEUTICALS INTERNATIONAL

PO Box 209
Scarsdale, NY 10583
Morris Herstein, President
PH: (914)723-5536
FX: (914)725-3774
E-mail: mh.adi@worldnet.att.net
Founded: 1988. **Staff:** 8. Activities: A consumer-oriented technical/ marketing consulting firm with experience in research and development management and problem solving. Areas of special expertise include: developing creative new ideas and concepts including product development; technical marketing; efficacy and safety testing for cosmetics, toiletries and drugs, OTC and prescription. Has worked in the international technical/marketing areas for cosmetic and toiletries; and does competitive technical/marketing analysis and technology forecasting/transfer. Industries served: cosmetics, toiletries, and over-the-counter drug manufacturers.

APPLIED LOGIC ASSOCIATES, INC.

5615 Kirby Dr., Ste. 710
Houston, TX 77005
Kris Gustafson
PH: (713)529-4747
FX: (713)529-4904
E-mail: info@alogic.com
URL: www.alogic.com/
Founded: 1987. Activities: Consulting firm for pharmaceutical, medical device, and biotechnology companies in the areas of clinical/regulatory affairs, clinical study management, information management, and biostatistical analysis and health care economics. Provides services from the conceptual stage to product approval. Provides assistance in clinical data management, statistical analysis, and regulatory affairs.

JACK L. ARONOWITZ

6591 Skyline Dr.
Delray Beach, FL 33446-2201
Jack L. Aronowitz, President
PH: (561)498-3954
FX: (561)498-3954
Founded: 1971. Activities: An association of individual scientists, engineers, technicians, managers, and several specialty consulting companies. Offer clients access to the following areas of expertise and services: biomedical chemistry, pharmaceutical veterinary, analytical and diagnostic instrumentation, reagent development and production, management, quality control, regulatory affairs, toxicological studies, clinical trials and marketing.

INA K. BENDIS, MD

851 Fremont Ave., Ste. 114
Los Altos, CA 94024
PH: (415)941-4100
FX: (415)948-2161
Activities: Specializes in internal medicine, pulmonary diseases, geriatrics, psychosomatics, HMO benefits denials, and claims fraud. Performs Record reviews, examinations, reports, detailed case analyses, and testimony.

DAVID M. BENJAMIN, PH.D.

2 Hammond Pond Pky., Ste. 605
Chestnut Hill, MA 02167
David M. Benjamin, Ph.D.
PH: (617)969-1393
TF: (800)355-9915
FX: (617)969-4285
E-mail: medlaw@channel1.com
URL: www.channel1.com/users/medlaw
Founded: 1986. **Staff:** 1. Activities: Develops educational and risk management programs for physicians, hospitals, healthcare professionals and the pharmaceutical industry. Areas of expertise include drug information, root cause analysis, preparation of IND and New Drug Applications (NDAs), development of clinical research studies, medical-legal case review, and alternative dispute resolution. In-

dustries served: healthcare professionals, pharmaceutical industry, insurance companies, and legal professionals.

BIOBEHAVIORAL RESEARCH FOUNDATION, INC.

218 Beech View Ct.
Baltimore, MD 21286
Faith K. Jaffe, President
PH: (410)337-7319
FX: (410)337-0205
Founded: 1974. **Staff:** 3. Activities: Offers consultation to pharmaceutical corporations, law firms, government agencies, and not-for-profit organizations in areas of problems in pharmacology, substance abuse, toxicology, and forensic medicine.

BIOCHEM TECHNOLOGY, INC.

100 Ross Rd., Ste. 201
King of Prussia, PA 19406-2100
George J.F. Lee, President
PH: (610)768-9360
FX: (610)768-9363
E-mail: sales@bioguide.com
URL: bioguide.com
Founded: 1977. **Staff:** 12. Activities: Consultants in wastewater treatment processes specializing in evaluation and optimization of biological nutrient removal facilities. On-line process monitoring and control of wastewater treatment processes as well as yeast, bacterial or fungal fermentation. Experience in biochemical process development, wastewater treatment process design, fermentation system design, process and plant design, biochemical engineering research and a variety of engineering specialities. Undertakes a wide variety of projects which range from preliminary feasibility studies to the development and optimization of a biological process.

BIOLABS, INC.

15 Sheffield Ct.
Lincolnshire, IL 60069
Clyde R. Goodheart, President
PH: (847)945-2767
Founded: 1969. **Staff:** 1. Activities: Assists with start-up of new companies in the biotechnology/biopharmaceutical/medical area. Performs services in planning, writing business plan, raising capital, and serving as CEO during initial phases. Primarily active with pharmaceutical companies, biopharmaceuticals, medicine; and sales managers in pharmaceutical companies.

BIOMEDICAL ENGINEERING CONSULTANTS

1111 Hermann Dr., Ste. 12B
Houston, TX 77004
David Yadin, President
PH: (713)838-0083
FX: (713)728-8888
E-mail: ybdavid@texaschildrenshospital.org
Founded: 1982. Activities: Tests, evaluates, services, and repairs of medical devices and accessories. Devices range from infusion pumps to anesthesia machines and from lasers to telemedicine. Directs large biomedical engineering program within hospital and home-care environments. Failure analysis and regulatory compliance, Y2K, and EMI testing.

BIOMEDICAL INFORMATION CENTER, INC.

PO Box 1298
Ridgewood, NJ 07451
Karen M. Miner, President
PH: (201)670-7446
FX: (201)670-8836
E-mail: kminer1@idt.net
Founded: 1987. **Staff:** 3. Activities: Medical writing, including scientific papers for publication, clinical reports for regulatory submissions (NDA, INDs), abstracting and indexing. Therapeutic areas of expertise include: cardiovascular disease, cancer, infectious disease, CNS disorders, inflammation and immunology.

BIOPHARMACEUTICAL RESEARCH CONSULTANTS
PO Box 2506
Ann Arbor, MI 48106
JP Hsu
PH: (313)426-2820
FX: (313)426-2849
E-mail: brci@compuserve.com
Activities: Firm provides pharmaceutical research services including clinical trial monitoring, data management, statistical analysis and report writing.

BIOPOLYMER TECHNOLOGIES INTERNATIONAL, INC.
PO Box 84
Westborough, MA 01581
Manssur Yalpani, President
TF: (800)246-7668
FX: (508)366-4089
E-mail: biopolti@aol.com
Founded: 1995. **Staff:** 8. Activities: Offers a range of expertise in the area of analysis, chemistry, biochemistry, biotechnology, pharmakinetics, and preclinical studies for commercial uses. Also provides market studies and multiclient surveys. Industries served: foods, biotechnology, pharmaceuticals, and specialty chemicals worldwide.

JOHN D. BOGDEN, PH.D.
UMDNJ—New Jersey Medical School
185 South Orange Ave.
Department of Preventive Medicine
Newark, NJ 07103-2714
John D. Bogden, Ph.D., Professor
PH: (973)972-5432
FX: (973)972-7625
E-mail: bogden@umdnj.edu
Activities: An environmental toxicology and nutrition consultant, specializing in mineral and trace element nutrition and toxicology, including lead poisoning, chromium toxicity, overdoses of minerals and trace elements, air, soil and water pollutants, and environmental toxins. Analyzes body tissues and fluids. Provides expert reports, deposition and court testimony experience.

NACHMAN BRAUTBAR, MD
6200 Wilshire Blvd., Ste. 1000
Los Angeles, CA 90048
Nachman Brautbar, MD, Principal
PH: (213)634-6500
FX: (213)634-6501
Activities: Medical doctor specializing in internal medicine, nephrology, pharmacology, occupational medicine, toxicology, internal medicine, and nephrology. Offers consultations, assessments, review records, and expert opinion testimony.

DR. GERALD BRENNER
3007 Oakwood Dr.
Norristown, PA 19401
PH: (610)279-3944
FX: (610)279-3944
Activities: Consultant to pharmaceutical, chemical, biotechnology, medical device and allied industries. Development and validation of processes for bulk pharmaceuticals. Physical/Chemical characterization of drug substances and raw materials. Drug development troubleshooting: stability, solubility, bioavailability. Analytical methods development and validation. Stability protocols and data review. Specification development. Formulation development: composition and process, CMC preparation and review. SOP preparation and review. Regulatory compliance, DAI preparation, 483 responses. Patent preparation and review. Expert witness.

BRIGHT + ASSOCIATES INC.
5701 Camelot Dr.
Charlotte, NC 28270-0498
David E. Bright, President
PH: (704)844-6226
FX: (704)844-6226
E-mail: dbright@worldnet.att.net
URL: www.mcs.net/~dbright/
Founded: 1990. **Staff:** 1. Activities: A professional consulting firm dedicated to serving the pharmaceutical, medical device and related industries in specialized areas of regulatory affairs and quality assurance.

PAUL K. BRONSTON, MD
1 Jib St., Ste. 202
Marina del Rey, CA 90292
Paul K. Bronston, MD, Principal
PH: (310)301-9426
FX: (310)823-2433
Activities: Acts as plaintiff or defense expert consultant or witness in medical insurance bad faith evaluations; medical quality assurance evaluations; utilization review; liability evaluations; medical malpractice evaluations; emergency medicine and quality assurance and utilization review; hospital liability; and HMO/managed care liability evaluation.

JOHN D. BULLOCK, MD
Department of Ophthalmology
500 Lincoln Park Blvd., Ste. 104
Wright State University
Dayton, OH 45429-3487
John D. Bullock, MD, Principal
PH: (937)643-2301
FX: (937)297-7690
E-mail: john.bullock@wright.edu
URL: www.forop.com
Activities: Ophthalmologist and forensic examiner experienced in medical-legal investigations, depositions, and court appearances. Specializes in medical malpractice, accident reconstruction and analysis, product liability (including contact lenses and pharmaceuticals), malingering, biophysics of ocular and orbital trauma, postoperative blindness, optometric liability, forensic ocular and orbital microbiology, and insurance/Medicare billing, coding, and fraud.

HAROLD J. BURSZTAJN, MD
96 Larchwood Dr.
Cambridge, MA 02138
Harold J. Bursztajn, MD, Principal
PH: (617)492-8366
FX: (617)441-3195
E-mail: harold-bursztajn@hmsharvard.edu
URL: www.forensic-psych.com
Activities: An expert consultant and witness resource specializing in forensic psychiatry and medicine; managed medical care, medical and psychiatric malpractice; and informed consent; emotional injury (PTSD, loss of consortium); true vs. false memories of trauma; sexual abuse in professional relationships; supervisory responsibility psychiatric and medical disability evaluation; ADA workers' compensation; premises liability; and competence assessment a testamentary capacity.

CALLIDUS CONSULTING, PC
1094 Quince Ave.
Boulder, CO 80304
Franklin D. Aldrich, MD, Ph.D., President
PH: (303)443-2316
FX: (303)938-9420
E-mail: frank.aldrich@atsuchsc.edu
Activities: Offers expert witness testimony and litigation support in the areas of toxicology; environmental, industrial and medical toxicology; environmental health; indoor air quality; internal medicine; occupational/environmental medicine; poisoning; process hazard review; and pesticides.

CARDIOVASCULAR THORACIC SURGERY MEDICAL LEGAL CONSULTATIONS
11828 Rancho Bernardo Rd., Ste. 123-173
San Diego, CA 92128
Michael J. O'Sullivan, MD, Principal
PH: (619)451-1270
FX: (619)451-1270
Activities: Provides medical-legal consultation and expert testimony in the area of cardio-vascular surgery.

CEBRAL
PO Box 3376
Sarasota, FL 34230-3376
PH: (941)923-3268
FX: (941)923-5579
E-mail: CEBRAL@aol.com
Activities: Senior pharmaceutical executives providing consulting services to the Pharmaceutical, Biotech and Chemical Industries.

CELSIS LABORATORY GROUP LABORATORY DIVISION
123 Hawthorne St.
Roselle Park, NJ 07204-0206
Edwin C. Rothstein, President
PH: (908)245-1933
TF: (800)523-LABS
FX: (908)245-6253
E-mail: leberco@celsis.com
Founded: 1939. **Staff:** 47. Activities: Offers consulting in animal toxicology, in-vitro toxicology, microbiology and chemical analysis to the pharmaceutical, cosmetic, toiletry, medical device, bacteriocide, pesticide, coatings, graphic arts, and specialty chemical industries. Also serves government agencies.

BERNHARD CINADER, B.SC., PH.D, D.SC.
73 Langley Ave.
University of Toronto
Medical Sciences Bldg.
Toronto, Canada M4K 1B4
Bernhard Cinader
PH: (416)463-3013
Founded: 1991. **Staff:** 5. Activities: Scientific researcher provides extensive research and training, lecturing and writing in the many areas of immunology and gerontology. Also offers advice on biotechnology network transfer, birth control policies, and immunopharmacology. Industries served: biotechnology and pharmaceuticals.

CLIN/REGS ASSOCIATES
12707 High Bluff Dr., Ste. 200
San Diego, CA 92130
Bruce Merchant, MD, Ph.D., President
PH: (619)350-4324
FX: (619)350-4325
Activities: Specializes in all aspects of biotech/biopharmaceuticals new product development, including research, pre-clinical, clinical, regulatory, quality control, manufacturing practices, FDA interactions, immunology, pathology, cancer, viral diseases, monoclonal antibodies, cytokines, recombinant proteins, and gene therapy.

CLINIMETRICS RESEARCH ASSOC., INC.
1732 N. First St., Ste. 470
San Jose, CA 95112
Brad A. Zaro, President
PH: (408)452-8215
TF: (800)365-9610
FX: (408)452-0912
E-mail: cra@clinimetrics.com
URL: www.clinimetrics.com
Founded: 1988. **Staff:** 138. Activities: Clinical research consultants specialize in the development and management of clinical research trials (phase II through IV) on drugs, biologics and medical devices. Consulting services are offered in the following specific areas: clinical research management, clinical trial monitoring, clinical trial design/development, data management, and regulatory compliance

monitoring. Industries served: pharmaceutical, biotechnology, and medical device.

CLINTRIALS RESEARCH INC.
20 Burton Hills Blvd., Ste. 500
Nashville, TN 37215
Jerry R. Mitchell, MD, Ph.D.
PH: (615)665-9665
TF: (800)346-7931
FX: (615)665-0971
Founded: 1989. **Staff:** 1400. Activities: A contract research services company, designs and performs high quality preclinical and clinical trials. From IND/IDE preparation and Phase I trials, through Phases II, III, IIIB, IV, V, and specialized post-marketing surveillance. Maintains the resources and experiences to handle clinical trials of any size and complexity. Industries served: pharmaceutical, biotechnology, government, and medical devices.

COMPREHENSIVE REIMBURSEMENT CONSULTANTS
8990 Springbrook Dr. NW, Ste. 200
Minneapolis, MN 55433-5880
Julie Zapp, President
PH: (612)785-4400
FX: (612)785-2709
URL: www.crc-online.com

COMPUTERTALK ASSOCIATES, INC.
492 Norristown Rd., Ste. 160
Blue Bell, PA 19422-2355
William A. Lockwood, Jr., President
PH: (610)825-7686
FX: (610)825-7641
URL: www.computertalk.com
Founded: 1980. **Staff:** 3. Activities: Data processing consultants serving the healthcare market: end users such as pharmacists and physicians as well as companies considering these vertical markets.

CONSUMER HEALTH INFORMATION CORP.
8300 Greensboro Dr., Ste. 1220
McLean, VA 22102-3604
Dr. Dorothy Smith, President
PH: (703)734-0650
FX: (703)734-1459
Founded: 1983. Activities: Full-service patient education programs on medications and disease. Industries served: pharmaceutical companies, general public, and managed care industry.

CUSTOM HEALTHCARE ANALYSIS & RESEARCH, INC.
7 Stonewood Pky.
Verona, NJ 07044
Charlotte Schmidt, President
PH: (201)857-9177
FX: (201)857-8654
Founded: 1986. **Staff:** 2. Activities: Provides marketing research consulting services, particularly customized data collection and analysis, for pharmaceutical/diagnostic products industry. Also conducts focus groups and in-depth interviews among healthcare professionals. Industries served: healthcare industry.

ROBERT H. DAILEY, MD
29 Charles Hill Cir.
Orinda, CA 94563
PH: (925)253-8275
FX: (925)253-8373
E-mail: yeliad@aol.com
Activities: Expert in emergency medicine and medicolegal experience, including court appearances.

DESIGN TECHNOLOGY CORP.
5 Suburban Park Dr.
Billerica, MA 01821

PH: (978)663-7000
FX: (978)663-6841
E-mail: sales@design-technology.com
URL: www.designtechnology.com
Founded: 1968. **Staff:** 70. Activities: Design and build automated equipment for processing, assembly, inspection and packaging of medical devices and disposables. Product design and package design, process development for medical and drug-delivery devices. Also develop robotic systems for processing, assembly, packaging, inspection, and testing of biologicals, medical devices, pharmaceuticals, drug-delivery devices and disposables.

DICKSON GABBAY CORP.
1205 Westlakes Dr., Ste. 150
Berwyn, PA 19312
Brian Dickson, Chairman
PH: (610)640-2035
FX: (610)640-2036
Founded: 1989. **Staff:** 26. Activities: Offers expertise in the design and conduct of clinical development programs for pharmaceuticals. Also provides strategic advice on pharmaceutical research and development management and drug compound portfolio management. Performs executive search function for pharmaceutical and healthcare industry. Industries served: pharmaceuticals, healthcare including hospitals and universities, and government agencies.

DOW PHARMACEUTICAL SCIENCES
1330A Redwood Way
Petaluma, CA 94954
Gordon J. Dow, President
PH: (707)793-2600
TF: (877)369-7476
FX: (707)793-0145
E-mail: info@dowpharmsci.com
URL: dowpharmsci.org
Founded: 1973. **Staff:** 45. Activities: Goal is to provide seamless product development services of uncompromised quality and flexibility to meet any project need by offering a wide range of customized pharmaceutical product development services which can be utilized individually or as part of a complete program. Business units include Dow Dermatologics—dermatologic formulation development and GMP pilot manufacturing; Dow Analytical Services—method development, validation and testing; and Dow Clinical Labeling—clinical supplies, labeling and packaging. Industries served: dermatological, pharmaceutical, and biotechnology. international clients.

DRUG RESEARCH AND ANALYSIS CORPORATION
PO Box 240308
Montgomery, AL 36124-0308
Henry A. Frazer, President
PH: (334)265-2700
TF: (800)372-2669
FX: (334)265-2704
E-mail: ind2nda@aol.com
Founded: 1978. **Staff:** 12. Activities: Offers pharmaceutical/device product development service which provides support to pharmaceutical and healthcare industries in areas of clinical research, new product development, and regulatory affairs. Clinical safety/efficacy studies and clinical pharmacology studies can be conducted using in-house facilities or management/monitoring on a multi-center basis. Consultation services available on product research and development issues and on regulatory affairs.

ESTRIN CONSULTING GROUP, INC.
9109 Copenhaver Dr.
Potomac, MD 20854
Norman F. Estrin, Ph.D., President
PH: (301)279-2899
FX: (301)294-0126
E-mail: estrin@cpcug.org
Founded: 1990. **Staff:** 1. Activities: Current areas of consulting include: regulatory submissions (510(k), PDP, PMA, IDE), Food and Drug Administration (FDA) liaison, interpreting FDA requirements,

preparing for and participating in FDA meetings, regulatory strategy development, labeling compliance, litigation support and special projects. Industries served: medical device, drug, and cosmetic.

MARVIN FIRESTONE
225 South Cabillo Hwy., Ste. 105D
Half Moon Bay, CA 94019
PH: (415)712-0880
FX: (415)712-0882
E-mail: firestone@pol.net
Activities: A brain injury rehabilitation specialist. Serves as a consultant in cases involving head injuries, brain dysfunction, and mental distress. Also specializes in clinical psychiatry, psychopharmacology, forensic psychiatry, legal medicine, and neuropsychiatry.

FIRST CONSULTING GROUP
111 W. Ocean Blvd., Ste. 1000
Long Beach, CA 90802
Luther Nussbaum, Chairman/CEO
PH: (562)432-8332
FX: (562)435-8664
URL: www.fcg.com
Founded: 1980. **Staff:** 1500. Activities: A leading provider of consulting, integration and management services to healthcare, pharmaceutical, and other life sciences organizations.

HYMAN W. FISHER, INC.
121 E. Northfield Rd.
Livingston, NJ 07039-0655
Hyman W. Fisher, M.D., President
PH: (201)994-9480
FX: (201)535-8741
E-mail: hwfisher@pol.net
Founded: 1980. Activities: Performs market research, organizes and moderates panels and symposia, recruits expert panels, prepares sales training programs, and advises on pharmaceuticals and medical products development. Other areas of expertise include advertising and promotion, continuing education, and professional service programs. Serves pharmaceutical, medical products, healthcare advertising, public relations, and other industries.

LEONARD FLYNN CONSULTING
254 Tennent Rd.
Morganville, NJ 07751
Dr. Leonard T. Flynn
PH: (732)591-1328
E-mail: lynnflynn@compuserve.com
Founded: 1985. **Staff:** 2. Activities: Provides scientific and regulatory consultation for the pharmaceutical, personal products, and other manufacturing industries. Services include document preparation of scientific reports and submissions to regulatory agencies and review of compliance with federal and state regulatory requirements. Industries served: manufacturers and importers of pharmaceutical, medical device and related health and personal/consumer products plus their raw material suppliers.

FOOD, DRUG, CHEMICAL SERVICES
3771 Center Wy.
Fairfax, VA 22033
Bob West, Ph.D., President
PH: (703)352-5913
FX: (703)255-6434
Founded: 1976. **Staff:** 10. Activities: Provides scientific, regulatory, and management consulting services for a wide variety of product lines and industries including pharmaceutical, industrial and agricultural chemicals, biotechnology, toiletries and cosmetics, food additives, diagnostics, and devices. Areas of expertise include product integrity, scientific affairs, management, medical communications, environmental science, pharmacology and toxicology, clinical studies, FDA liaison, and product licensing.

RICHARD HAMER ASSOCIATES INC.

Wedgwood Sta.
PO Box 16598
Fort Worth, TX 76162
Richard A. Hamer, President
PH: (817)294-3644
FX: (817)294-3761
E-mail: regconsult@aol.com
URL: www.hamerassoc.com
Founded: 1983. **Staff:** 3. Activities: Active in the development of premarket approval strategies for new drug and medical device products; preparation, and submission and approval monitoring of investigational and/or premarketing approval applications (IND, IDE, NDA, ANDA, PMA, 510(k), etc.); monitoring of preclinical and clinical studies for compliance with GLP and GCP compliance; and review of labeling, advertising and promotional materials. Conducts comprehensive facility audits to evaluate GMP compliance, develops practical standard operation procedures and documentation systems to facilitate GMP compliance, and provides effective representation of clients' interests during FDA site inspections or meetings with regulatory agencies. Offers continuous monitoring of regulatory developments and provides recommendations for dealing with issues of specific interest. Industries served: pharmaceuticals, medical devices, cosmetics, and food.

HEALTH COMMUNICATIONS, INC.

20 Highland Ave., Ste. 6
Metuchen, NJ 08840-1949
Joel L. Shapiro
PH: (732)548-9130
FX: (732)548-8555
E-mail: info@hcomm.com
URL: www.hcomm.com
Founded: 1984. **Staff:** 20. Activities: The company's activities focuses on medical writing for pharmaceuticals, producing principally clinical manuscripts, scientific exhibits, regulatory support documents, product monographs, and related projects. The firm offers a complete range of pre-marketing and post-marketing services, including symposium development as well as audiovisual and other specialized programs. Industries served: healthcare, pharmaceutical, and medical device manufacturers.

HEALTHCARE FORECASTING INC.

110 National Dr.
Glastonbury, CT 06033
PH: (860)659-4077
FX: (860)633-6480
Founded: 1984. **Staff:** 12. Activities: Pharmaceutical industry consultants. Industries served: pharmaceuticals, medical supply, and biotechnology.

THE HILL TOP COMPANIES

PO Box 429501
Cincinnati, OH 45242
J. James Pearce, Jr., President/CEO
PH: (513)831-3114
TF: (800)669-1947
FX: (513)831-1217
Founded: 1947. **Staff:** 235. Activities: Specialists in the design, evaluation, and conduct of testing programs for safety, efficacy, and registration of cosmetics, prescription and over-the-counter pharmaceuticals, personal care and household products, specialty chemicals, paper products, nonwovens, and medical devices. Recent activities include consumer and descriptive studies (sensory analysis), as well as research in dermal conditions and dermal products. Services include toxicology and microbiology. Toxicology offers acute testing and delayed contact hypersensitivity (the Buehler Method), as well as photobiology, sunscreen, and intratracheal procedures. The Microbiology Division tests for disinfectant efficacy, preservatives, and topical antimicrobials.

RONALD D. HOOD & ASSOCIATES—CONSULTING TOXICOLOGISTS

University of Alabama
PO Box 870344
Tuscaloosa, AL 35487-0344
Dr. Ronald D. Hood
PH: (205)348-1817
FX: (205)348-1786
E-mail: rhood@biology.as.ua.edu
Founded: 1978. **Staff:** 4. Activities: Specializes in toxicology, especially developmental toxicology (teratology), reproductive toxicology, and environmental toxicology. Provides data interpretation, hazard assessment, literature review, and litigation support. Also conducts laboratory research on a wide range of chemicals, including industrial and agricultural chemicals, pesticides, pharmaceuticals, and environmental pollutants. Special expertise offered in the toxicology and pharmacology of arsenicals. Clients served include: state and federal agencies, especially the Environmental Protection Agency, law firms, and a wide variety of industrial clients.

JOHN E. HOOVER—CONSULTANT

363 Riverview Rd.
Swarthmore, PA 19081
John E. Hoover
PH: (610)328-9786
Founded: 1978. **Staff:** 1. Activities: Consultant in bio-medical communications; offers editorial and writing services for wide variety of clients in pharmaceutical, medical, and other healthcare fields.

INDUSTRIAL TESTING LABORATORIES

50 Madison Ave.
New York, NY 10010
Kenneth J. Kohlhof, President
PH: (212)685-8788
FX: (212)689-8742
E-mail: clinres@mail.idt.net
Founded: 1887. **Staff:** 21. Activities: Analytical and consulting chemists to the pharmaceutical, petroleum, food, cosmetic, and chemical industries. Also provides forensic consulting including analysis of biological fluids and fire investigations, as well as courtroom testimony.

INVERESK RESEARCH (NORTH AMERICA), INC.

4470 Redwood Hwy., Ste. 101
San Rafael, CA 94903
Richard J. D'Agostino, President
PH: (415)491-6460
FX: (415)491-6464
E-mail: inveresk@aol.com
Founded: 1974. **Staff:** 7. Activities: Project management, strategic development, clinical trial monitoring, regulatory affairs are tailored to the sponsors needs for manufacturers of medical devices, diagnostics, pharmaceuticals, and cosmetics.

KAREN JAMES, PH.D.

1584 Hattie Hill Rd.
Vilas, NC 28692
Karen James
PH: (704)297-4084
FX: (704)297-4084
E-mail: karenjames@appstate.campus.mci.net
Founded: 1986. **Staff:** 1. Activities: Offers consulting in clinical immunology including enzyme immunoassays, complement, and immunofluorescence. Provides additional consulting in laboratory management, particularly hospital laboratories for JCAHO preparedness, CAP preparedness, quality assurance, financial management and assessments. Also maintains expertise in physician office laboratories in areas of needs assessment, quality assurance, quality control, staff assessments and CLIA 88, as well as consulting in bedside laboratory test systems such as glucose monitoring, coagulation, and others. Industries served: hospitals, laboratory reagent/kit manufacturers, reference laboratories, physician groups, and government agencies.

HERMAN E. JASS
29 Platz Dr.
Skillman, NJ 08558
Herman E. Jass, Owner
PH: (908)874-4356
FX: (609)683-0079
Founded: 1976. **Staff:** 2. Activities: Active in the development, monitoring, and conduct of preclinical and clinical studies. Offers expertise with investigational new drug and new drug application development, label review, and regulatory services (FDA and FTC). Also provides expert witness testimony in area of skin treatment products, liability, new product development programs, and acquisition aid. Particularly accommodating to foreign firms attempting to market drugs and cosmetics in the U.S. Industries served: pharmaceutical and cosmetic.

JERSEY ANALYTICAL SERVICES, INC.
3 Maple Ave.
Andover, NJ 07821
J. Barandy, President
PH: (201)786-6191
FX: (201)786-6190
Founded: 1970. **Staff:** 4. Activities: Offers analytical services and consulting in the analytical chemical field: pharmaceuticals, food products, plastics, petroleum products, textile, water, effluents, fats and oils, and pesticides. Serves private industries as well as government agencies.

ADA P. KAHN
2562 Wellington Ct.
Evanston, IL 60201-4975
Ada P. Kahn
PH: (847)328-4512
Founded: 1980. **Staff:** 1. Activities: Offers writing services for health related fields and public relations for pharmaceutical and medical products.

BURDE L. KAMATH, PH.D.
Xavier University College of Pharmacy
7325 Palmetto St.
New Orleans, LA 70125
Burde L. Kamath, Ph.D., CC, APC
PH: (504)483-7440
FX: (504)485-7930
Activities: Consultant has expertise in biopharmaceutics and provides the following services: pharmaceutical quality assurance, drug analysis, bio-analysis of drugs, bio-availability and bio-equivalence studies, pharmacokinetics, and drug regulatory compliance.

KEMPER-MASTERSON, INC.
375 Concord Ave.
Belmont, MA 02178
Dr. Clarence Kemper, Chairman of the Board
PH: (617)484-9920
TF: (800)458-9920
FX: (617)484-9068
E-mail: lester@KMInc.com
Founded: 1989. **Staff:** 100. Activities: Firm of engineering professionals and former FDA investigators provide validation and compliance services to pharmaceuticals, biotech, and medical device clients worldwide. Has expertise in process, process control, and IS/IT. Services include training, consulting, and full validation implementation for projects ranging from unit operations and expansion projects to complete new facilities.

KEY AUTOMATION
1301 Corporate Center Dr., Ste. 113
Eagan, MN 55121
Colleen Stanton, President
PH: (612)686-5254
FX: (612)686-5232
E-mail: keyauto.com
URL: www.keyauto.com
Founded: 1988. **Staff:** 8. Activities: Provides engineering knowl-

edge to consumer goods manufacturers, food producers, and pharmaceutical companies in the U.S.

KLEIN CONSULTANT SERVICES
12726 Overbrook
Leawood, KS 66209
Ann Kettering Klein, President
PH: (913)338-3001
FX: (913)338-3039
E-mail: ROCKSTATE3@aol.com
Founded: 1977. **Staff:** 1. Activities: Full service market research company specializes in package goods, medical services, pharmaceuticals and small city research. Serves private industries as well as government agencies.

LACASSE INC.
6727 Quartzite Canyon Pl.
Tucson, AZ 85718
Lorne A. Campbell
PH: (520)299-6171
FX: (520)299-4362
Founded: 1983. **Staff:** 1. Activities: Involved in regulatory matters concerning the food and drug industry, both domestic and foreign, including food additive petitions, NADAs, NDAs, ANDAs, INDs, and pesticide and fungicide regulation. Consults in the development of drugs and their approval by the FDA. Develops protocols on all aspects of pre-clinical and clinical studies, both animal and human. Advises on establishing a pharmaceutical presence in the U.S. for foreign pharmaceutical companies. Expert in generic drug industry.

T. JOSEPH LIN
628 Enchanted Way
Pacific Palisades, CA 90272
PH: (310)454-4355
FX: (310)454-5246
Founded: 1974. Activities: Specialist in emulsion technology and surface chemistry. Serves manufacturers of cosmetics, personal care products, and pharmaceutical products.

LUCENKO CONSULTING ASSOCIATES
7 Clearview Terr.
West Orange, NJ 07052
Leonard K. Lucenko, Ph.D., President
PH: (201)655-7094
FX: (201)731-8290
E-mail: lucenko@saturn.montclair.edu
Activities: Forensic examiners specializing in sports and recreation safety, playground safety inspection, amusements, waterparks, school injuries, health clubs, sports medicine, and facility design and maintenance.

LYCOMING ANALYTICAL LABORATORIES
2687 Euclid Ave.
Duboistown, PA 17702
Clifford Nilsen, President
PH: (570)323-5001
FX: (570)323-0009
Founded: 1989. **Staff:** 6. Activities: Provides technical consultation to chemical and pharmaceutical industries. Services include problem-solving, management plan development and compliance advice for the analytical chemical laboratory, and analytical testing services, including pharmaceutical raw material and finished dosage form testing: assays, monograph testing, stability, methods development and validation, analytical R&D and process and cleaning validation support. Also offered is laboratory-management computer software, custom written for clients.

GIANPAOLO MAESTRONE
4 Sophia Ln.
Staten Island, NY 10304
Gianpaolo Maestrone
PH: (718)987-5010
Founded: 1987. **Staff:** 2. Activities: Professional veterinarian with Board Certification in Veterinary Microbiology, plus twenty-five

years experience in human and veterinary pharmaceutical industry. Conducts feasibility studies, development and clearance of animal health products for systemic, topical, anti-mastitic and growth promotion uses. Specializes in selection, evaluation and registration of fish health products. Serves the aquaculture, agriculture, and pharmaceutical industries.

MALLOY & ASSOCIATES, INC.
354 Whites Landing
Long Beach, CA 90803-6823
John J. Malloy, President
PH: (562)494-1632
FX: (562)494-2842
Founded: 1986. **Staff:** 3. **Activities:** Provides guidance to medical device manufacturers in the area of U.S. Food and Drug Administration and International Standards Organization requirements. Areas of expertise include good manufacturing practices (GMP), International Standards (ISO 9001), and operation audits: 510(k), IDE, PMA, and other submissions to the U.S. Food and Drug Administration. The firm also presents GMP, ISO, and software development seminars. Clients include start-ups, large corporations, international firms, and government agencies worldwide.

MATTSON JACK GROUP INC.
11960 Westline Industrial Dr., Ste. 180
St. Louis, MO 63146
William R. Mattson, Jr., Pres.
PH: (314)469-7600
FX: (314)469-6794
E-mail: vickim@mattsonjack.com
URL: www.mattsonjack.com
Founded: 1986. **Staff:** 45. **Activities:** Advises pharmaceutical companies on strategic issues or opportunities, and corporate development activities.

J.R.D. MCCORMICK
19 Pomona Ln.
Spring Valley, NY 10977-1112
J.R.D. McCormick
PH: (914)354-9149
FX: (914)354-9640
E-mail: jandcmccormick@worlnet.att.net
Founded: 1983. **Staff:** 2. **Activities:** Provides research planning and problem solving by the application of chemical and biochemical principles to the fields of industrial microbiology, fermentation, and the fermentation-like industries, including constructive reviews of existing research programs. Specialist in tetracycline antibiotics and in methodology of screening soil microorganisms. Industries served: Pharmaceuticals and fine chemicals, the fermentation industry, and government agencies.

MEDEDIT ASSOCIATES
5429 SW 80th St.
Gainesville, FL 32608
Barbara G. Cox
PH: (352)376-3071
FX: (352)336-8377
E-mail: BarbCox@aol.com
Founded: 1985. **Staff:** 2. **Activities:** Consultant and editor/writer in biomedical communications. Activities include editing/writing of biomedical research publications for physicians and other health professionals who publish in medical journals; and preparation of patient education materials for pharmaceutical companies. Consultant also teaches seminars and workshops in biomedical writing and publishing to physicians and other health professionals. Industries served: pharmaceutical companies, academic departments of medical schools, physicians in private practice, hospitals, medical publishers, and government agencies.

MEDICAL COMMUNICATIONS CENTER, INC.
5825 Glenridge Dr., Bldg. 2, Ste. 211
Atlanta, GA 30328
Michael Kessler, M.D., President

PH: (404)257-1251
FX: (404)252-8328
E-mail: medcomctr@pol.net
URL: www.medcomctr.com
Founded: 1975. **Activities:** Sales Rep. training and value added marketing programs for the pharmaceutical, medical product and service companies.

MEDICAL MARKETING GROUP, INC.
512 Township Line Rd. 2-800
Blue Bell, PA 19422-2701
PH: (215)641-2900
Activities: Pharmaceutical marketing and consulting company.

MEDICAL RESEARCH CONSORTIUM INC.
6220 Lawrence Dr.
Indianapolis, IN 46226
Jack H. Hall, President
PH: (317)549-3131
FX: (317)549-3670
Founded: 1993. **Staff:** 4. **Activities:** Conduct and consult on research studies and clinical trials.

MEDTRONIC INC.
7000 Central Ave. NE
Minneapolis, MN 55432
PH: (612)574-4000
FX: (612)574-4879
Founded: 1972. **Staff:** 34. **Activities:** Works with industrial and government agencies to develop procedures to test chemicals and drugs or medical device products to meet federal regulations for Food and Drug Administration, Environmental Protection Agency, Department of Transportation, and other regulatory agencies.

MILLIPORE CORP.
80 Ashly Rd.
Bedford, MA 01730
FX: (617)275-5724
Activities: Product and market development firm as well as worldwide leader in the separation of liquids, combining chromatographic and electrophoretic instrumentation, column and membrane chemistries, and information processing. Firm solves applications ranging from the synthesis and sequencing of peptides, and the assurance of product formulations in the chemical industry, to the search for new pharmaceuticals.

RALPH M. MYERSON
310 Maplewood Ave.
Merion Station, PA 19066
Ralph M. Myerson
PH: (215)664-0406
FX: (215)896-2750
Founded: 1985. **Staff:** 2. **Activities:** Provides consultation services to pharmaceutical industries and healthcare establishments by supplying data such as patient information and manuscripts for use in health journals for promotional and educational purposes. Industries served: publishing and pharmaceutical.

NATIONAL BOARD OF FORENSIC CHIROPRACTORS
601 S. Mill St.
PO Box 356
Manning, SC 29102
Preston B. Fitzgerald, Sr., D.C., Executive Director (SC)
PH: (803)435-5078
FX: (803)435-8096
E-mail: omyback@ix.netcom.com
Founded: 1996. **Staff:** 6. **Activities:** Administers exams and designates qualifying chiropractic physicians as having the credential of Certified Independent Forensic Chiropractic Medical Examiner (TM), or CIFCME (TM). After receiving this credential, a doctor is qualified to assist insurance companies, workers' compensation commissions, social security boards, employers, police departments, and attorneys by providing independent assessments of challenging bodily injury cases. The purpose of the NBOFC is to advance the

profession of forensic examination and consultation throughout the chiropractic profession by elevating standards through education, and advanced training, and certification. The Board serves as a national center for this purpose and disseminates information and knowledge by coordinating lectures, seminars, conferences, workshops, Internet, continuing education courses and publications.

NORTHEAST PAIN CONSULTANTS
255 Route 108
Somersworth, NH 03878
M.J. O'Connell, MD
PH: (603)692-3166
TF: (800)660-4004
FX: (603)692-3168
E-mail: info@painmd.com
URL: www.painmd.com
Founded: 1992. **Activities:** Patient care services include spinal catheters and pump implants; medication management; home care pain supervision; diagnostic work-up to determine the exact cause of the pain; nerve blocks and trigger point injections; assistance in restoring functional status; pain coping strategies such as hypnosis, biofeedback, music; and emotional support. Professional consulting services covers the full spectrum of professional pain practice management, including all aspects of financial and medical practice, development.

NORTHVIEW LABORATORIES, INC.
1880 Holste Rd.
Northbrook, IL 60062
Martin J. Spalding, CEO
PH: (847)564-8181
FX: (847)564-8269
E-mail: info@northviewlabs.com
URL: www.northviewlabs.com
Founded: 1972. **Staff:** 100. **Activities:** An independent laboratory offering comprehensive testing capabilities in microbiology, sterility testing services, analytical chemistry and toxicology for the medical device, pharmaceutical, food and feed, cosmetic, specialty chemical, and consumer product industries.

OXFORD RESEARCH INTERNATIONAL CORP.
1425 Broad St.
Clifton, NJ 07013-4221
Richard A. Guarino, M.D., Pres.
PH: (201)777-2800
FX: (201)777-9847
E-mail: emalid@oric.com
URL: www.oric.com
Founded: 1979. **Staff:** 43. **Activities:** Provides medical, legal, and statistical services to pharmaceutical and healthcare industry worldwide.

P R S INC.—PHARMACY SERVICES
PO Box 852
Latrobe, PA 15650
Harry A. Lattanzio, RPH, President
PH: (412)539-7820
TF: (800)338-3688
FX: (412)539-1388
Founded: 1983. **Staff:** 70. **Activities:** Pharmacy consultants. Industries served: grocery and retail pharmacy.

NORBERT P. PAGE
17601 Stoneridge Ct.
Gaithersburg, MD 20878
Norbert P. Page, President
PH: (301)948-9408
FX: (301)948-9408
Founded: 1984. **Staff:** 2. **Activities:** Provides consultation on toxicology; risk assessment of chemicals and radiation; literature compilation and evaluation; design of toxicology studies; compliance with TSCA, FIFRA, international law; new drug applications; toxicology data and experiment evaluation; and report preparation.

PAREXEL INTERNATIONAL CORP.
195 West St.
Waltham, MA 02154
Josef von Rickenbach, Chairman, CEO
PH: (617)487-9900
TF: (800)PAR-EXEL
FX: (617)487-0525
URL: www.PARAEXEL.com
Founded: 1982. **Staff:** 700. **Activities:** An independent pharmaceutical research organization offering clinical trials management, global regulatory affairs, data management, biostatistics, medical writing, strategy development consultation and performance improvement services to the pharmaceutical, biotechnology, medical device and diagnostics industries in North America, the United Kingdom, Asia, and Europe.

PHARM RX CONSULTANTS INC.
1238 Stuivesant
Union, NJ 07083
I. Barton Frenchman, President
PH: (908)686-2063
FX: (908)686-2473
E-mail: bartonk@msn.com
Founded: 1986. **Staff:** 8. **Activities:** Pharmacy consultants for nursing homes and pharmacy and nursing educational programs.

PHARMA-TECH INDUSTRIES, INC.
PO Box 638
Union, MO 63084
PH: (314)583-8664
FX: (314)583-5373
Activities: Offers counsel on packaging of over-the-counter drugs, cosmetics, food and veterinary products.

PHARMACEUTICAL CONSULTANTS INC.
5033 W. 117th
Leawood, KS 66211
Dr. Beth Maggio, CEO
PH: (888)491-9825
TF: (888)491-9825
FX: (888)491-9829
URL: www.pharmconsult.com
Founded: 1985. **Staff:** 10. **Activities:** Pharmaceutical consultants specializing in the F.D.A. drug approval process. Offers full-service research services in Rx to OTC switch, multicenter trials management, statistical analysis, protocol development, and toxicology studies. Industries served: pharmaceutical.

PHARMACEUTICAL INFORMATION ASSOCIATES, LTD.
2761 Trenton Rd.
Levittown, PA 19056
PH: (215)949-0490
FX: (215)949-2594
E-mail: pialtd@ix.netcom.com
URL: www.info.com
Activities: Company communicates scientific information to regulatory and healthcare professionals.

PHARMACEUTICAL RECRUITERS, INC.
271 Madison Ave., Ste. 1200
New York, NY 10016
Linda S. Weiss, President
PH: (212)557-5627
FX: (212)557-5866
Activities: Firm recruits medical professionals for clinical research positions.

PHARMACEUTICAL SYSTEMS INC.
102 Terrace Dr.
Mundelein, IL 60060-3826
Robert Reich, President

PH: (847)566-9229
FX: (847)566-4960
E-mail: rreich@pharmssystems.com
URL: www.pharmsystems.com
Founded: 1988. Staff: 30. Activities: Offers legal, contract auditing, regulatory compliance, lab research, business planning, technology, sterility assurance and quality assurance services to U.S. healthcare medical device and pharmaceutical industries.

PHARMACY CONSULTANTS INC.
348 E. Blackstock Rd., Ste. A
Spartanburg, SC 29301
PH: (864)574-5220
FX: (800)842-2238
Founded: 1976. Activities: Medication consultation services to long-term care facilities, nursing homes, residential-care facilities, group homes for the mentally retarded, prison systems, and trauma recovery centers.

PHARMAMEDICAL CONSULTANTS INTERNATIONAL LLC
5725 Eastwood Ln.
Missoula, MT 59803-3015
David J. Rechtman, M.D., President
PH: (406)251-5098
TF: (800)248-5101
FX: (406)251-5099
E-mail: rechtman@bigsky.net
URL: www.bigsky.net/pmci
Activities: Company provides medical consulting services to pharmaceutical/biotech companies, CROs and managed care groups. Also provides full CRO services through Clinical Consulting Alliance LLC, a joint venture with International Quantitative Consultants Inc.

PLACEMENT ASSOCIATES, LTD.
14222 Blarney Cir.
Cement City, MI 49233
Raymond P. Mooney, Physician Assistant
PH: (517)688-4637
FX: (517)688-4235
E-mail: placementa@ibm.net
URL: expertpages.com/cv/mooney.htm
Activities: Physician's assistant experienced in family medicine, emergency medicine and urgent care medicine. Provides pre- and post-litigation analysis, written opinion, deposition and trial testimony concerning medical malpractice cases involving physician assistant practice. Experienced in recruitment of physician assistants. Knowledge of laws concerning the scope of practice and rules and regulations concerning physician assistant practice. For additional physician assistants and nurse practitioners on a nationwide basis see http://www.panp.com.

LEHECKA PRATT ASSOCIATES, INC.
380 North Ave.
Fanwood, NJ 07023
Elaine Lehecka Pratt, President
PH: (908)889-8162
FX: (908)889-8162
E-mail: lpassociates@worldnet.att.net
URL: www.inc.com/users/LeheckaPratt.html
Founded: 1986. Staff: 2. Activities: Firm specializes in innovative technical training and documentation consulting for the pharmaceutical industry. Services include design, production and presentation of training programs, design of training aids and manuals, SOP writing, in-house seminars, packaged training programs and aids, and custom training projects. Industries served: pharmaceutical, medical device, and chemical industries, including government agencies.

PSYCHIATRIC CONSULTATION—LIAISON PROGRAM
University of California, San Francisco
401 Parnassus
School of Medicine
San Francisco, CA 94143-0984
Stuart J. Eisendrath, MD, Director
PH: (415)476-7868
FX: (415)476-7371
E-mail: eisen@itsa.ucsf.edu
Activities: Provides psychiatric consultation. Specializes in psychosomatic medicine, psychiatric aspects of medical illness, factitious disorders, hysterical conversion, post-traumatic stress disorder, and Munchausen syndrome. Provides claim analysis, depositions, and trial testimony.

PURDUE ASSOCIATES
Four Canoe Brook Dr.
Princeton Junction, NJ 08550
Robert Marchisotto, Executive Director
PH: (609)799-0330
FX: (609)275-3810
E-mail: robertoi@aol.com
Founded: 1971. Staff: 2. Activities: Offers pharmaceutical research and product development expertise in oral and topical dosage forms, applied nutrition and emulsion technology. Also provides expertise in biotechnology, patents, licensing, technology assessment and transfer. Additional assistance in human resources management and training. Industries served: pharmaceutical, biotechnology, technology-transfer and venture capital, as well as government agencies.

QUINTILES BRI
1300 N. 17th St., Ste. 300
Arlington, VA 22209
PH: (703)276-0400
FX: (703)243-9746
Founded: 1971. Activities: Consults on pharmaceuticals and medical devices.

MARVIN RAFAL ASSOCIATES, INC.
33 Turner Dr.
New Rochelle, NY 10804
Marvin Rafal, President
PH: (914)636-5454
FX: (914)387-9038
Founded: 1956. Staff: 4. Activities: Human resources development consultants active primarily with pharmaceutical manufacturers and healthcare industry.

MARK M. RASENICK
Department of Physiology & Biophysics
901 S. Wolcott
Univ. of Illinois, College of Medicine
Chicago, IL 60612-7342
Mark M. Rasenick
PH: (312)996-6641
FX: (312)996-1414
E-mail: raz@uic.edu
Activities: Offers consultation on various aspects of neuropharmacology and psychopharmacology, especially those relating to GTP-binding proteins and neuronal signal transduction. Serves as expert witness for all drug effects upon the central nervous system, especially antidepressant drugs and treatments. Also provides consultation for the preparation of research grant applications. Industries served: biomedical, scientific, legal applications, and government agencies.

RBH ASSOCIATES, INC.
62-44 99th St.
Rego Park, NY 11374
Ruben Robert Ben-Harari, Ph.D.
TF: (800)461-9227
FX: (718)592-6573
E-mail: rbh@interramp.com
Founded: 1993. Staff: 2. Activities: Provides customized resources

drawing together talents of independent specialists to address specific client needs. Services include strategic thinking and creative development; successful new products and product repositioning; client presentations; scientific review and analysis of medical communications ideas and materials; effective publication development for products; advisory and editorial board development from medical opinion leaders; writing expanded into new clinical areas; electronic, video, and slides applied to educational, promotional, and sales training programs; and cost effectiveness studies.

RESEARCH ASSOCIATES
4949 Battery Ln., Ste. 112
Bethesda, MD 20814
Martin McHale Newhouse, President
PH: (301)652-1924
FX: (301)652-1637
E-mail: researchassociates@msn.com
URL: www.researchassociates.com
Founded: 1985. **Staff:** 10. Activities: Information broker for major pharmaceutical companies. Provides various information services for companies, law firms or individuals. Industries served: pharmaceutical companies and law firms.

ROCKY MOUNTAIN INSTRUMENTAL LABORATORIES, INC.
108 Corondo Ct.
Fort Collins, CO 80525
Robert K. Lantz, Ph.D.
PH: (970)266-8108
E-mail: rklantz@rockylab.com
URL: www.rockylab.com
Founded: 1978. **Staff:** 7. Activities: Provides the following consulting services: pharmacologic and pharmacokinetic drug and toxin studies, forensic analysis in toxicology and serology, and product and method development in analytical chemistry and toxicology. Also provides expert witness testimony in state and federal courts. Serves pharmaceutical, forensic, chemical, as well as government agencies.

ROUNDTABLE OF TOXICOLOGY CONSULTANTS
31308 Via Colinas, Ste. 107
Westlake Village, CA 91362
Dr. Patricia Frank, President
PH: (818)706-2410
FX: (818)706-2413
URL: lawinfo.com/biz/toxicology/index.html
Founded: 1980. **Staff:** 50. Activities: Provides general toxicology consulting by experienced doctoral-level scientists. Specialty areas include: legal support in product liability cases, new drug applications, FDA approvals, OSHA and EPA standards, pesticides, food additives, workplace safety, animal testing for regulatory approval, expert testimony, EPA compliance, and many related areas. Offers expert reviews in toxicology, medical, chemical, and other scientific databases. Industries served: attorneys, pharmaceutical, chemical, government, general manufacturing, as well as government agencies.

ROWIN GROUP, INC.
25 E. Spring Valley Ave.
Maywood, NJ 07607
Dilip Phadnis, President
PH: (201)843-9400
FX: (201)909-8707
E-mail: rowin25@aol.com
Founded: 1976. **Staff:** 5. Activities: Independent consulting company exclusively serving the health industry. Conducts multi- and single-client studies in the following areas: new product introduction; new market development, including confidential representation, company analysis, technology transfer, and diversification. Also actively involved in harnessing web technology for dissemination of healthcare information. Targeted segments are international, industry executives, sales training, consumer education and medical professional education.

SAN FRANCISCO SPORTS MEDICINE
Davies Medical Center
45 Castro, Ste. 117
San Francisco, CA 94114
Scott F. Dye, MD, Principal
PH: (415)861-9966
FX: (415)861-0174
Activities: Orthopedic surgeons and board certified medical-legal evaluators. Provide medical record reviews, expert witness testimony, and Spanish and German translation.

EDITH SCHWAGER
4404 Sherwood Rd.
Philadelphia, PA 19131-1526
Edith Schwager
PH: (215)877-1137
FX: (215)877-1137
E-mail: dearedie@compuserve.com
Founded: 1981. **Staff:** 1. Activities: Editorial consultant specializing in English usage, medicine, and pharmaceuticals. Conducts workshops and seminars on medical editing and on English usage and abusage for physicians and nurses, publishing houses, pharmaceutical corporations, universities and colleges, government agencies and other organizations.

SCIENCE, TOXICOLOGY & TECHNOLOGY AND AIL LABORATORIES
PO Box 470116
San Francisco, CA 94147
Michael Scott, President
TF: (800)869-4636
FX: (415)441-3204
E-mail: toxinfo@aol.com
URL: www.toxinfo.com
Founded: 1983. Activities: Provides consultant and expert services in medical toxicology (adverse reactions to chemicals or drugs), veterinary toxicology (food chain contamination), and pharmacology (efficacy and safety). Areas covered include industrial, occupational and environmental toxicology (including "sick building" syndrome); drug/chemical risk assessment and management; veterinary, dietary and environmental chemical exposures; drug regulation and promotion; hospital and pharmacy risk management; terato and carcinogenesis research; and medicolegal evaluation. Industries served: insurance, corporate (industrial and manufacturing), pharmaceutical, pharmacies, legal, public utilities, and state governments.

SCOTT-LEVIN ASSOCIATES INC.
60 Blacksmith Rd.
Newtown, PA 18940
Joy Scott, President
PH: (215)860-0440
FX: (215)860-5477
Founded: 1982. **Staff:** 80. Activities: Firm offers expertise in healthcare and pharmaceutical consulting.

DR. MARK SHAPIRO
27 Redwood Dr.
Richboro, PA 18954
Mark Shapiro
PH: (215)968-9224
FX: (215)443-8587
Founded: 1976. **Staff:** 3. Activities: Provides real-time software services for mini and micro computers including scientific applications and operating system internals. Active primarily with medical and pharmaceutical industries.

SHOTWELL & CARR, INC.
3535 Fire Wheel Dr., Ste. A
Flower Mound, TX 75028
Thomas K. Shotwell, President

PH: (972)243-1634
TF: (800)929-3003
FX: (972)243-3567
E-mail: shotcar@earthlink.com
URL: www.shotcarr.com
Founded: 1974. **Staff:** 7. Activities: Specializes in maximizing cost effectiveness in development, approval, production, and distribution of animal and human drugs, medical devices, and in vitro diagnostics worldwide.

STEVEN M. SIMONS, MD
Cedars—Sinai Medical Center
435 N. Roxbury, Ste. 311
Beverly Hills, CA 90210
PH: (310)274-7303
FX: (310)274-8572
E-mail: simons@csmc.edu
Activities: Offers expert witness testimony in the medical matters, including pulmonary, internal medicine, critical care, asthma, pulmonary embolism, ventilator management, pneumonia, pleural effusion, and bronchoscopy.

BRUCE J. SOBOL
275 Ridgebury Rd.
Ridgefield, CT 06877
Bruce J. Sobol, M.D.
PH: (203)438-3650
Founded: 1983. **Staff:** 2. Activities: Offers medical writing expertise including clinical summaries for submission to the FDA, clinical trial reports for scientific journals, critiquing and writing research protocols, and medical articles for lay publications. Industries served: pharmaceutical and marketing.

SPIEHLER & ASSOCIATES
422 Tustin Ave.
Newport Beach, CA 92663
Vina R. Spiehler, Ph.D., President
PH: (714)642-0574
FX: (714)642-2852
E-mail: spiehleraa@aol.com
Activities: Specializes in pharmacology, pharmacokinetics and toxicology of cocaine, morphine and heroin, amphetamines, phencyclidine, alcohol, pharmaceuticals, poisons and drugs of abuse, immunoassay development and FDA submissions. Reviews employee drug testing, QA/QC, postmortem toxicology and drug testing in hair, saliva or sweat. Also specializes in drugs and DUI, memory, drug concentrations, combinations, time and cause of death.

STEINMAN ASSOCIATES
1033 N. Fairfax St., Ste. 304
Alexandria, VA 22314
Steve Steinman, President
PH: (703)836-2686
FX: (703)836-4084
E-mail: stevsai@aol.com
Founded: 1982. **Staff:** 17. Activities: Provides consulting services to drug development companies, biotechnology companies, and fully integrated pharmaceutical firms regulated under the Federal Food, Drug, and Cosmetic Act. The firm possess expertise in quality assurance, government affairs, drug manufacturing, data management, biostatistics, clinical trials management. Steinman Associates will draft and produce IND applications, New Drug Applications, and Biological Product Licenses.

THOMAS STERN, MD
2636 Telegraph Ave.
Berkeley, CA 94704
PH: (510)841-1647
FX: (510)848-4924
E-mail: drtkstern@aol.com
URL: www.medical-legal-experts.com
Founded: 1974. **Staff:** 20. Activities: Provides medical-legal evaluations and expert testimony for personal injury, workers' compensation, and medical malpractice.

SUTTON ASSOCIATES
300 E. 51st St., Ste. 4C
New York, NY 10022
Yvonne Buchanan Manley, President
PH: (212)753-7068
Founded: 1983. **Staff:** 10. Activities: Communications consultant on pharmaceutical, medical device, and healthcare management for problem solving, promotion, marketing strategy, industrial psychology, and FDA matters. Offers additional focus as literary agent consultant.

ROBERT SWOTINSKY, MD
Boston University Medical Center
88 E. Newton St.
Boston, MA 02118-2393
PH: (617)638-8410
FX: (617)638-8406
E-mail: swotinsky@aol.com
Activities: A medical review officer specializing in workplace drug and alcohol testing, toxicology, occupational medicine, environmental medicine, biological monitoring, and medical surveillance.

THERADEX SYSTEMS INC.
14 Washington Rd.
Princeton Junction, NJ 08550-1028
Dr. Robert Royds
PH: (609)799-7580
FX: (609)799-4148
E-mail: 10200.1507@compuserve.com
URL: www.theradex.com
Founded: 1982. **Staff:** 200. Activities: Pharmaceutical consultants.

JOHN F. TOMERA
354 South St.
Medfield, MA 02052-3127
John F. Tomera
PH: (508)359-4072
FX: (508)359-4072
E-mail: johntomera@prodigy.net
Founded: 1986. **Staff:** 1. Activities: Consulting pharmacologist with experience in the following client markets: pharmaceutical, nutraceutical, chemical, agricultural, cosmetic, medical diagnostic, and environmental toxicology. Significant expertise in medical applications in vivo and in vitro, with therapeutic experience in cardiovascular, breast cancer, biochemical, immusuppression, pharmacorconomics, and trauma research.

TOXCOR ASSOCIATES, INC.
PO Box 454
Flanders, NJ 07836
Marvin Kaminsky, Ph.D., DABT
PH: (973)252-0204
FX: (973)252-0204
E-mail: kaminsky@toxcor-associates.com
URL: toxcor-associates.com
Founded: 1995. **Staff:** 1. Activities: Provides consulting in regulatory toxicology and product safety assessment. Also products liability and toxic tort litigation support/expert witness. Industries served: Pharmaceutical, consumer product, chemical, and cosmetic.

TOXDATA SYSTEMS, INC.
380 Sutton Rd.
Barrington, IL 60010-9378
Carol A. Benkendorf, Ph.D., President
PH: (847)382-5291
FX: (847)382-9406
E-mail: cbenk@flash.net
Founded: 1981. Activities: Offers consultation or expert testimony in lawsuits in the area of industrial and regulatory toxicology. Also specializes in MSDSS; product labels; product safety; industrial chemicals and pharmaceuticals; and cancer causation. Provides: case analysis; alternative causation; online computer searches (medical and business databases); document retrieval; database management; and data summaries.

TOXICOLOGY PATHOLOGY SERVICES, INC.
10424 Middle Mt. Vernon Rd.
Mount Vernon, IN 47620
J.B. Botta, President
PH: (812)985-5900
TF: (800)837-8771
FX: (812)985-3403
E-mail: tps@toxpath.com
URL: www.toxpath.com
Founded: 1975. **Staff:** 34. Activities: Evaluates animal safety data including toxicology, body weight, clinical pathology, gross and microscopic pathology, organ weights, clinical signs and statistics for the pharmaceutical, chemical, petrochemical, and agricultural industries. Emphasis is on product safety through animal research.

UNICA TECHNOLOGIES INC.
55 OLD Bedford Rd.
Lincoln, MA 01773-1125
Indulis Pommers, President
PH: (781)259-5900
TF: (877)864-2261
FX: (781)259-5901
E-mail: unica@unica-usa.com
URL: www.unica-usa.com
Founded: 1992. **Staff:** 35. Activities: Offers data mining and database marketing consulting. Services include: problem analysis, data preparation, modeling, model deployment, market campaign planning and design, development of campaign testing and measurement metrics, campaign optimization, campaign management process development.

V-LABS, INC.
423 N. Theard St.
Covington, LA 70433
Sharon V. Vercellotti
PH: (504)893-0533
FX: (504)893-0517
E-mail: v-labs@wild.net
URL: www.v-labs.com
Founded: 1979. Activities: Offers analytical service for carbohydrates and polysaccharides. Performs contract research and consulting for pharmaceutical, chemical, and food companies. Services include analysis of sugar processing products, dietary fiber determination, custom synthesis and polysaccharide modification, and computerized data acquisition and reporting.

NAOMI VOLAIN, MS, RD
34 Virginia St.
Springfield, MA 01108-2623
Naomi Volain
PH: (413)785-1792
Founded: 1986. **Staff:** 1. Activities: Registered dietitian offering advertising copywriting, specializing in pharmaceuticals, medical instrumentation, and nutrition. Also writes advertising copy, promotional materials, feature articles, direct mail and public relations material. Serves the consumer and healthcare industries in addition to those mentioned above.

W-F PROFESSIONAL ASSOCIATES INC.
400 Lake Cook Rd., Ste. 207
Deerfield, IL 60015
PH: (847)945-8050
FX: (847)945-8050
Founded: 1977. Activities: Consulting firm conducts pharmacy continuing education programs.

HUGH H. WEST, MD, FAAEM, FACEP
10 Morning Sun
Mill Valley, CA 94941
PH: (415)383-2301
FX: (415)383-2388
E-mail: hwestmd@aol.com
Activities: Specialties include: Emergency Medicine; Emergency Department performance of Physicians, Consultants, and Ancillary staff (Nursing, Respiratory, Social Services, etc.); Pre-hospital Care performance of Paramedics and first responders (Police, Fire Department, etc.); Transfers and stabilization (COBRA/EMTALA issues); Trauma (Verified Level II Trauma Center experience); Ultrasound (Emergency Medicine performed/interpreted); Additional formal background training in Neurology and Neurosurgery; Administration (former Medical Director, Associate Medical Director, credentials, etc.).

WHOLE SYSTEMS INTERNATIONAL
255 Washington St., No. 190
Newton, MA 02158
Darrell Griffin, President
PH: (617)928-1555
FX: (617)928-1585
Founded: 1980. **Staff:** 33. Activities: Specializes in serving the training and education needs of the healthcare industry, so that these companies may maximize their marketing and sales strategies. Has served most major pharmaceutical firms worldwide with effective multimedia training systems for a wide spectrum of human resource development applications. Multimedia development capability includes self-instructional text, audio tape, videotape, computer-based tutorials and assessments, computer-based interactive video, and applied workshop programs. Offers standard (off-the-shelf) and customized learning systems for new hire training, continuing education, product launches, management training, and sales training. Each program integrates the development of desired knowledge, skills, and performance in a competency-based structure.

WILMA J. WINTER—MEDICAL COMMUNICATIONS
2111 Jefferson Davis Hwy., Apt. 513 N
Arlington, VA 22202
Wilma J. Winter
PH: (703)415-0610
Founded: 1984. **Staff:** 1. Activities: Provides research and writing expertise on medical affairs. Attends and summarizes science seminars. Writes and researches clinical papers, drug brochures, audiovisuals on drugs, and salesperson's mail pieces. Summarizes pharmacologic and clinical data for government application and review. Industries served: pharmaceutical firms, federal government, medical journals, and local TV (cable).

A.M. WOLVEN, INC.
175 W. Wieuca Rd., Ste. 118
Atlanta, GA 30342
Anne M. Wolven, M.S., President
PH: (404)252-6377
FX: (404)303-0052
Founded: 1978. **Staff:** 4. Activities: Involved in regulatory compliance: EPA, FDA, FHSA (CPSC), OSHA, product development, GLP's, GMP's, quality assurance audits, claim substantiation, planning and contract proposals, PRG-clinical and clinical studies, in vitro technology, and risk assessment. Industries served: chemical, cosmetic, toiletries, food, household products, medical device, and pharmaceuticals.

WORLD BOTANICAL ASSOCIATES
PO Box 2829
Laurel, MD 20709-0829
Richard Spjut, Director
PH: (301)605-5234
TF: (800)772-7216
FX: (301)605-5234
E-mail: rwspjut@erols.com
Founded: 1983. Activities: Consulting biological scientists who: provide botanical/chemical guidance for discovery of potential compounds for medicinal therapies; provide plant samples of indigenous plants for medicinal research; provide resources to conduct floristic inventories; and conduct research on taxonomy of various terrestrial plants. Industries served: government agencies, universities, and pharmaceutical companies.

WORLDWIDE PROMEDICA INC.
577 Airport Blvd., Ste. 130
Burlingame, CA 94010
Joan R. Day, President
PH: (650)344-6242
FX: (650)344-3217
Founded: 1984. Activities: Consulting firm offers marketing research expertise for medical products and services. Industries served: healthcare (pharmaceuticals, diagnostics, biotech). Woman owned firm.

XENOPORE CORP.
299 Wagaraw Rd.
Hawthorne, NJ 07506
Allan Douglas, Principal
PH: (973)423-2400
FX: (973)423-2401
E-mail: xenopore.com
URL: www.xenopore.com
Founded: 1988. Activities: Firm provides consulting services to the pharmaceutical and biotechnological industries.

TRADE INFORMATION SOURCES

Adapted from Gale's *Encyclopedia of Business Information Sources* (*EBIS*), the entries featured in this chapter show trade journals and other information sources, including web sites and databases.

Entries for publications and electronic databases list the title of the work, the name of the author (where available), name of the publisher, frequency or year of publication, prices or fees, and Internet address (in many cases).

Entries for trade associations and research centers provide the organization name, address, telephone numbers, e-mail address, and web site URL. Many of these entries include brief descriptions of the organization.

ABI/INFORM
300 North Zeeb Rd.
Ann Arbor, MI 48103
PH: (800)521-0600
FX: (800)864-0019
URL: http://www.umi.com
UMI. Provides online indexing to business-related material occurring in over 1,000 periodicals from 1971 to the present. Inquire as to online cost and availability.

ABI/INFORM GLOBAL
300 N. Zeeb Rd.
Ann Arbor, MI 48103 ·
PH: (313)761-4700
FX: (800)864-0019
URL: http://www.umi.com
UMI. Monthly. $6,500.00 per year. Provides CD-ROM indexing and abstracting of worldwide business literature appearing in over 1,200 periodicals for the most recent five years. Archival discs are available from 1971. Formerly *ABI/INFORM OnDisc*.

ABSTRACTS IN BIOCOMMERCE
Prudential Bldg.
95 High St.
Slough, Berks SL1 1DH, England
PH: (175)3 511777
FX: (4-1)53 51223
E-mail: biocom@dial.pipex.com
URL: http://www.biospace.com/biocommerce
Biocommerce Data, Ltd. Semimonthly. $878.00 per year. Quarterly cumulation. Emphasis is on commercial biotechnology.

**AGRICULTURAL AND ENVIRONMENTAL
  BIOTECHNOLOGY ABSTRACTS**
7200 Wisconsin Ave., 6th Fl.
Bethesda, MD 20814
PH: (800)843-7751
FX: (301)961-6720
E-mail: market@csa.com
URL: http:///www.csa.com
Cambridge Scientific Abstracts. Bimonthly. $345.00 per year. Formerly *Biotechnology Research Abstracts*.

AHFS DRUG INFORMATION HEALTH-SYSTEM
7272 Wisconsin Ave.
Bethesda, MD 20814
PH: (301)657-3000
FX: (301)657-1641
American Hospital Formulary Service. American Society of Health-System Pharmacists. $125.00 per year. Looseleaf service. Detailed information about drugs and groups of drugs. Formerly American Society of Hospital Pharmacists. Formerly *American Hospital Formulary Service*.

**ALCOHOL AND DRUGS IN THE WORKPLACE: COSTS,
  CONTROLS AND CONTROVERSIES**
1250 23rd St., N.W.
Washington, DC 20037
PH: (800)372-1033
FX: (202)452-4062
URL: http://www.bna.com
Bureau of National Affairs, Inc. 1986. $30.00. (Special Report Series.)

**ALMANAC OF BUSINESS AND INDUSTRIAL FINANCIAL
  RATIOS**
One Lake St.
Upper Saddle River, NJ 07458
PH: (800)223-1360
FX: (800)445-6991
URL: http://www.prenhall.com
Leo Troy. Prentice Hall. Annual. $99.95. Contains financial ratios derived from federal tax returns. Ratios for each of about 200 industries are arranged according to company asset size.

**ALTERED FATES: THE GENETIC RE-ENGINEERING OF
  HUMAN LIFE**
500 Fifth Ave.
New York, NY 10110
PH: (800)223-2584
FX: (212)869-0856
URL: http://www.norton.com
Jeff Lyon and Peter Gorner. W. W. Norton & Co., Inc. 1995. $27.50. A discussion of recent progress in genetic engineering.

AMERICAN COLLEGE OF APOTHECARIES
P.O. Box 341266
Memphis, TN 38184-1266
PH: (901)383-8119
FX: (901)383-8882
A professional society of pharmacists.

**AMERICAN COLLEGE OF OCCUPATIONAL AND
  ENVIRONMENTAL MEDICINE-MEMBERSHIP
  DIRECTORY**
55 W. Seegers Rd.
Arlington Heights, IL 60005
PH: (847)228-6850
FX: (847)228-1856
Annual. $155.00. Lists 6,500 medical directories and plant physicians specializing in occupational medicine and surgery; coverage includes Canada and other foreign countries. Geographically arranged.

AMERICAN DRUG INDEX
111 West Port Plaza, Suite 400
St. Louis, MO 63146
PH: (800)223-0554
FX: (314)878-5563
Facts and Comparison. Annual. $49.50. Lists over 20,000 drug entries in dictionary style.

AMERICAN DRUGGIST
444 Park Ave., S., Room 402
New York, NY 10016-7312
PH: (800)833-7138
FX: (212)686-9098
E-mail: AmDruggist@aol.com
Press Corp. Monthly. $44.00 per year. Provides news and analysis of major trends affecting pharmacists. Includes an annual "Generic Survey" (September).

AMERICAN GENETIC ASSOCIATION
P.O. Box 257
Buckeystown, MD 21717-0257
PH: (301)695-9292
FX: (301)695-9292
Members are scientists engaged in genetics research.

AMERICAN INDUSTRIAL HEALTH COUNCIL
2001 Pennsylvania Ave., N.W., Suite 760
Washington, DC 20006
PH: (202)833-2131
FX: (202)833-2201
E-mail: membershipservices@ainc.org

AMERICAN INDUSTRIAL HYGIENE ASSOCIATION
2700 Prosperity Ave., Suite 250
Fairfax, VA 22031
PH: (703)849-8888
FX: (703)207-3561
E-mail: infonet@aiha.org

**AMERICAN INDUSTRIAL HYGIENE ASSOCIATION
  JOURNAL: A PUBLICATION FOR THE SCIENCE OF
  OCCUPATIONAL AND ENVIRONMENTAL HEALTH**
2700 Prosperity Ave., Suite 250
Fairfax, VA 22031-4307

PH: (703)849-8888
FX: (703)207-3561
E-mail: infonet@aiha.org
URL: http://www.aiha.org
American Industrial Hygiene Association. Monthly. $120.00 per year.

AMERICAN INSTITUTE OF BIOLOGICAL SCIENCES
730 11th St., N.W.
Washington, DC 20001-4521
PH: (202)628-1500
FX: (202)628-1509

AMERICAN INSTITUTE FOR MEDICAL AND BIOLOGICAL ENGINEERING
1901 Pennsylvania Ave., NW, Ste. 401
Washington, DC 200065
PH: (202)496-9660
FX: (202)466-8489

AMERICAN JOURNAL OF HEALTH SYSTEMS PHARMACY
7272 Wisconsin Ave.
Bethesda, MD 20814
PH: (301)657-3000
FX: (301)657-1258
American Society of Health-System Pharmacists. Semimonthly. $141.00 per year. Formerly American Society of Hospital Pharmacists. Formerly *American Journal of Hospital Pharmacy.*

AMERICAN JOURNAL OF INDUSTRIAL MEDICINE
605 Third Ave.
New York, NY 10158-0012
PH: (800)225-5945
FX: (212)850-6088
John Wiley & Sons, Inc., Journals Div. Monthly. $999.00 per year.

AMERICAN PHARMACEUTICAL ASSOCIATION/ ACADEMY OF PHARMACY PRACTICE AND MANAGEMENT
2215 Constitution Ave., N.W.
Washington, DC 20037-2895
PH: (800)237-2742
FX: (202)783-2351
URL: http://www.aphanet.org

AMERICAN SOCIETY OF HEALTH-SYSTEM
7272 Wisconsin Ave.
Bethesda, MD 20814-1439
PH: (301)657-3000
FX: (301)652-8278
URL: http://www.ashp.com

AMERICA'S PHARMACIST
205 Daingerfield Rd.
Alexandria, VA 22314
PH: (800)423-7158
FX: (703)683-3619
National Community Pharmacists Association. Monthly. $50.00 per year. Formerly *N A R D Journal.* Formerly National Association of Retail Druggist.

ANNUAL REPORTS: CORPORATE
201 Plaza Three
Jersey City, NJ 07311-3881
PH: (201)938-3248
FX: (201)938-3780
American Institute of Certified Public Accountants. Financial statements and authoritative accounting literature, most current five years online, 1972 to present offline. Inquire as to online cost and availability.

ANNUAL REVIEW OF BIOPHYSICS AND BIOENGINEERING
Post Office Box 10139
Palo Alto, CA 94303-0139
PH: (800)523-8635
FX: (650)855-9815
E-mail: service @annurev.org
URL: http://www.annurev.org
Annual Reviews, Inc. Annual. $59.00.

ANNUAL REVIEW OF PHARMACOLOGY AND TOXICOLOGY
Post Office Box 10139
Palo Alto, CA 94303-0139
PH: (800)523-8635
FX: (650)424-0910
E-mail: service@annurev.org
URL: http:// http://www.annurev.org
Annual Reviews, Inc. Annual. Individuals, $60.00; institutions, $120.00

ANNUAL SURVEY OF MANUFACTURES
Washington, DC 20402
PH: (202)512-1800
FX: (202)512-2250
E-mail: gpoaccess@gpo.gov
URL: http://www.access.gpo.gov
Available from U. S. Government Printing Office. Annual. Issued by the U. S. Census Bureau as an interim update to the *Census of Manufactures*. Includes data on number of manufacturing establishments in various industries, employment, labor costs, value of shipments, capital expenditures, inventories, energy costs, and assets. (See also Census Bureau home page, http://www.census.gov/.)

APPLIED GENETICS NEWS
25 Van Zant St., Suite 13
Norwalk, CT 06855
PH: (203)853-4266
FX: (203)853-0348
Business Communications Co., Inc. Monthly. $395.00 per year. Newsletter on research developments.

APPLIED SCIENCE AND TECHNOLOGY INDEX
950 University Ave.
Bronx, NY 10452
PH: (800)367-6770
FX: (718)590-1617
E-mail: hwwmsg@info.hwwilson.com
URL: http://www.hwwilson.com
H. W. Wilson Co. 11 times a year. Quarterly and annual cumulations. Service basis. Indexes a wide variety of English language technical, industrial, and engineering periodicals.

APPROVED DRUG PRODUCTS, WITH THERAPEUTIC EQUIVALENCE EVALUATIONS
Washington, DC 20402
PH: (202)512-1800
FX: (202)512-2250
Available from U. S. Government Printing Office. $77.00 for basic manual and supplemental material for an indeterminate period. Issued by the Food and Drug Administration, U. S. Department of Health and Human Services. Lists prescription drugs that have been approved by the FDA. Includes therapeutic equivalents to aid in containment of health costs and to serve State drug selection laws.

ARCHIVES OF ENVIRONMENTAL HEALTH
1319 18th St., N.W.
Washington, DC 20036-1802
PH: (202)296-6267
FX: (202)296-5149
URL: http://www/helderf.org
Helen Dwight Reid Educational Foundation. Heldref Publications. Bimonthly. $123.00 per year. Objective documentation of the effects of environmental agents on human health.

ASLIB BOOK GUIDE: A MONTHLY LIST OF RECOMMENDED SCIENTIFIC AND TECHNICAL BOOKS
143 Old Marlton Pike
Medford, NJ 08055-8750
PH: (800)300-9868
FX: (609)654-4309
Available from Information Today, Inc. Monthly. $204.00 per year. Published in London by Aslib: The Association for Information Management. Formerly *Aslib Book List*.

ATTORNEYS' DICTIONARY OF MEDICINE
Two Park Ave.
New York, NY 10016
PH: (800)223-1940
FX: (212)244-3188
J. E. Schmidt. Matthew Bender & Co., Inc. Five looseleaf volumes. Price on application. Periodic supplementation. Includes common lay words that lead to correct medical terms.

ATTORNEYS' TEXTBOOK OF MEDICINE
Two Park Ave.
New York, NY 10016
PH: (800)223-1940
FX: (212)244-3188
Matthew Bender & Co., Inc. 17 looseleaf volumes. Price on application. Periodic supplementation. Medico-legal material.

BIOBUSINESS
2100 Arch St.
Philadelphia, PA 19103
PH: (800)523-4806
FX: (215)587-2016
BIOSIS. Provides abstracts of international periodical literature relating to business applications of biological and medical research, 1985 to date. Inquire as to online cost and availability.

BIOMEDICAL ENGINEERING SOCIETY
P.O. Box 2399
Culver City, CA 90231
PH: (310)618-9322
E-mail: bmes@netcom.com

BIOMEDICAL INSTRUMENTATION AND TECHNOLOGY
210 South 13th St.
Philadelphia, PA 19107
PH: (215)546-7293
FX: (215)790-9330
Association for the Advancement of Medical Instrumentation. Hanley and Belfus, Inc. Bimonthly. Individuals, $100.00 per year; institutions, $120.00 per year.

BIOMEDICAL PRODUCTS
P.O. Box 650
Morris Plains, NJ 07950-0650
PH: (973)292-5100
FX: (973)605-1220
URL: http://www.bioprodmag
Gordon Publications, Inc. Monthly. $36.00 per year. Features new products and services.

BIOSCAN: THE WORLDWIDE BIOTECH INDUSTRY REPORTING SERVICE
4041 North Central Ave.
Phoenix, AZ 85012-3397
PH: (800)279-6799
FX: (800)279-4663
E-mail: info@oryxpress.com
URL: http://www.oryxpress.com
Oryx Press. Bimonthly. $975.00 per year. Looseleaf. Provides detailed information on over 900 U. S. and foreign companies broadly classified as biotechnological. In addition to medical technology and advanced pharmaceutical firms, includes firms doing research in food processing, waste management, agriculture, and veterinary sci-

ence. Formerly *BioScan: The Biotechnology Corporate Directory Service*.

BIOSCIENCE
1444 Eye St. N. W.
Suite 200
Washington, DC 20005
PH: (202)628-1500
FX: (202)628-1509
E-mail: bioscience@aibs.org
URL: http://www.aibs.org/bioscience.,html
American Institute of Biological Sciences. Monthly. Members, $60.00 per year; institutions, $165.00 per year.

BIOTECH DAILY
1117 N. 19th St., Suite 200
Arlington, VA 22269-1798
PH: (703)247-3434
Washington Business Information, Inc. c/o Karen Harrington. Daily. $897.00 per year. Newsletter on legislative and regulatory concerns. Formerly *Genetic Engineering Letter*.

BIOTECHNIQUES: THE JOURNAL OF LABORATORY TECHNOLOGY FOR BIORESEARCH
154 E. Central St.
Natick, MA 01760
PH: (508)655-8282
FX: (508)655-9910
Eaton Publishing. 12 times a year. $105.00 per year.

BIOTECHNOLOGY
40 West 20th St.
New York, NY 10011
PH: (800)221-4512
FX: (212)691-3239
E-mail: info@cup.org
URL: http://www.cup.org
John E. Smith. Cambridge University Press. 1996. $49.95. Third edition. Provides discussions of biotechnology in relation to medicine, agriculture, food, the environment, biological fuel generation, genetics, ethics, safety, etc. Includes a glossary and bibliography.

BIOTECHNOLOGY FROM A TO Z
198 Madison Ave.
New York, NY 10016-4314
PH: (800)451-7556
FX: (212)726-6446
URL: http://www.oup-usa.org
William Bains. Oxford University Press. 1998. $27.95. Second edition. Covers the terminology of biotechnology for non-specialists.

BIOTECHNOLOGY ABSTRACTS ON CD-ROM
1725 Duke St., Suite 250
Alexandria, VA 22314
PH: (800)451-3551
FX: (703)519-5829
E-mail: info@derwent.com
URL: http://www.derwent.com
Derwent, Inc. Quarterly. Price on application. Provides CD-ROM indexing and abstracting of the world's biotechnology journal literature since 1982, including genetic engineering topics.

BIOTECHNOLOGY DIRECTORY
345 Park Ave. South, 10th Floor
New York, NY 10010-1707
PH: (800)221-2123
FX: (212)689-9711
E-mail: grove@grovestocktn.com
URL: http://www.stocktonpress.com
Stockton Press. Annual. $310.00. Provides information on more than 10,000 biotechnology-related companies and organizations. Geographical arrangement, with name and product indexes.

BIOTECHNOLOGY INDUSTRY ORGANIZATION
1625 K St., N.W., Suite 1100
Washington, DC 20006
PH: (800)255-3304
FX: (202)857-0237

BIOTECHNOLOGY AND THE LAW
155 Pfingsten Rd.
Deerfield, IL 60015
PH: (800)328-4880
FX: (847)948-8955
URL: http://www.westgroup.com
Iver P. Cooper. Clark Boardman Callaghan. Looseleaf. $260.00. per year. Periodic supplementation.

BIOTECHNOLOGY PROCESS ENGINEERING CENTER
Massachusetts Institute of Technology
Room 20A-207
77 Mass Ave.
Cambridge, MA 02139-4307
PH: (617)253-0805
FX: (617)253-2400
E-mail: childs@mit.edu
URL: http://www.web.mit.edu/bpcc/www/
Includes an Industrial Advisory Board and a Biotechnology Industrial Consortium.

BIOWORLD TODAY: THE DAILY BIOTECHNOLOGY NEWSPAPER
Post Office Box 740021
Atlanta, GA 30374
PH: (404)262-7436
FX: (404)814-0759
URL: http://www.ahcpub
American Health Consultants, Inc. BioWorld Publishing Group. Daily. $1350.00 per year. Covers news of the biotechnology and genetic engineering industries, with emphasis on finance, investments, and marketing.

BIOWORLD WEEK: THE WEEKLY BIOTECHNOLOGY REPORT
Post Office Box 740056
Atlanta, GA 30374
PH: (404)262-7436
FX: (404)814-0759
URL: http://www.achpub.com
American Health Consultants, Inc. BioWorld Publishing Group. Weekly. $495.00 per year. Provides a weekly summary of business and financial news relating to the biotechnology and genetic engineering industries.

THE BLUE SHEET: HEALTH POLICY AND BIOMEDICAL RESEARCH
5550 Friendship Blvd., Suite One
Chevy Chase, MD 20815-7278
PH: (800)332-2181
FX: (301)664-7248
E-mail: fdcr@fdcr.com
URL: http://www.fdcr.com
F-D-C Reports, Inc. Weekly. $480.00 per year. Newsletter. Health policy topics include Medicare, the education and supply of health professionals, and public health. Biomedical topics are related to research, regulations, and the role of the National Science Foundation.

BNA'S SAFETY NET
1250 23rd St., N.W.
Washington, DC 20037
PH: (800)372-1033
FX: (202)822-8092
URL: http://www.bna.com
Bureau of National Affairs, Inc. Biweekly. $680.00 per year. Looseleaf. Formerly *Job Safety and Health.*

BULLETIN ON NARCOTICS
Two United Nations Plaza
Rm. DC2-853
New York, NY 10017
PH: (800)253-9646
FX: (212)963-3489
United Nations Publications. Semiannual. $10.00 per issue.

BUSINESS INDEX
362 Lakeside Drive
Foster City, CA 94404
PH: (800)227-8431
FX: (650)378-5369
Information Access Co. Monthly. $3,500.00 per year. Provides comprehensive CD-ROM indexing of more than 800 business and trade journals and selective indexing of 3,000 other magazines and newspapers. Covers the current four years.

BUSINESS PERIODICALS INDEX
950 University Ave.
Bronx, NY 10452
PH: (800)367-6770
FX: (718)590-1617
E-mail: hwwmsg@info.hwwilson.com
URL: http://www.hwwilson.com
H. W. Wilson Co. Monthly, except August, with quarterly and annual cumulations. Price on application.

BUSINESS STATISTICS OF THE UNITED STATES
4611-F Assembly Dr.
Lanham, MD 20706-4391
PH: (800)274-4447
FX: (800)865-3450
E-mail: info@bernan.com
URL: http://www.bernan.com
Courtenay M. Slater, editor. Bernan Associates. 1997. $59.00. Based on *Business Statistics,* formerly issued by the Bureau of Economic Analysis, U. S. Department of Commerce. Provides basic data for a wide variety of U. S. industries, services, and economic indicators. Most statistics are shown annually for 29 years and monthly for the most recent four years.

CARNEGIE MELLON RESEARCH INSTITUTE
Carnegie Mellon University
700 Technology Dr.
Pittsburgh, PA 15219
PH: (412)268-3190
FX: (412)268-3101
E-mail: wk0e@andrew.cmu.edu
URL: http://infoserver.andrew.cmu.edu/cmufront/research.html
Multidisciplinary research activities include expert systems applications, minicomputer and microcomputer systems design, genetic engineering, and transportation systems analysis.

CENTER FOR RETAILING STUDIES
Texas A & M University
Dept. of Marketing
College Station, TX 77843-4112
PH: (409)845-0325
FX: (409)845-5230
E-mail: berryle@tamu.edu
URL: http://www.wehner.tamu.edu/crs
Research areas include retailing issues and consumer economics.

CHAIN DRUG REVIEW: THE REPORTER FOR THE CHAIN DRUG STORE INDUSTRY
220 Fifth Ave.
New York, NY 10001
PH: (212)213-6000
FX: (212)213-6106
Racher Press, Inc. Biweekly. $119.00 per year. Covers news and trends of concern to the chain drug store industry. Includes special articles on OTC (over-the-counter) drugs.

CHAIN STORE AGE: THE NEWSMAGAZINE FOR RETAIL EXECUTIVES
425 Park Ave.
New York, NY 10022
PH: (212)756-5000
FX: (212)756-5250
E-mail: isender@lf.com
URL: http://www.chaindtoreage.com
Lebhar-Friedman, Inc. Monthly. $99.00 per year. Formerly *Chain Store Age Executive with Shopping Center Age.*

CHANGING MEDICAL MARKETS: THE MONTHLY NEWSLETTER FOR EXECUTIVES IN THE HEALTHCARE AND BIOTECHNOLOGY INDUSTRIES
2433 Main St., Suite One
Rocky Hill, CT 06067-2539
PH: (800)995-1550
FX: (860)257-0014
URL: http://www.thetareports.co.uk
Theta Corp. Monthly. $295.00 per year. Newsletter on medical marketing, new products, new technology, company mergers, etc.

THE CHEMISTRY OF MIND-ALTERING DRUGS: HISTORY, PHARMACOLOGY, AND CULTURAL CONTEXT
1155 16th St., N. W.
Washington, DC 20036
PH: (800)227-9919
FX: (202)872-6067
E-mail: acsbooks@acs.org
URL: http://www.chemcenter.org
Daniel M. Perrine. American Chemical Society Publications. 1996. $39.95. Contains detailed descriptions of the pharmacological and psychological effects of a wide variety of drugs, "from alcohol to zopiclone."

CIES: THE FOOD BUSINESS FORUM
5549 Lee Highway
Arlington, VA 22207-1613
PH: (703)534-9080
FX: (703)549-0406

CLIN-ALERT
143 Old Marlton Pike
Medford, NJ 08055-8750
PH: (800)300-9868
FX: (609)654-4309
Information Today, Inc. Biweekly. $99.95 per year. Newsletter. Contains current abstracts of drug adverse reactions and interactions reported in over 600 medical journals. Includes quarterly cumulative indexes.

COMPLETE GUIDE TO PRESCRIPTION AND NON-PRESCRIPTION DRUGS: SIDE EFFECTS, WARNINGS, AND VITAL DATA FOR SAFE USE
200 Madison Ave.
New York, NY 10016
PH: (800)223-0510
FX: (212)213-6706
H. Winter Griffith. Berkley Publishing Group. Annual. $15.95. A guide for consumers.

CONSUMER CANADA
122 S. Michigan Ave., Suite 1200
Chicago, IL 60603
PH: (800)577-3876
FX: (312)922-1157
E-mail: info@euromonitor.com
URL: http://www.euromonitor.com
Euromonitor International. 1997. $750.00. Provides consumer market, socioeconomic, and demographic data for Canada. Includes consumer market size (volume and value) for many specific kinds of products.

THE CONSUMER HEALTH INFORMATION SOURCE BOOK
4041 N. Central Ave.
Phoenix, AZ 85012-3397
PH: (800)279-6799
FX: (800)279-4663
E-mail: info@oryxpress.com
URL: http://www.oryxpress.com
Alan Rees, editor. Oryx Press. 1997. $59.50. Fifth edition. Bibliography of current literature and guide to organizations.

CONSUMER INTERNATIONAL
835 Penobscot Bldg.
Detroit, MI 48226-4094
PH: (800)877-GALE
FX: (800)414-5043
E-mail: galeord@gale.com
URL: http://www.gale.com
Available from Gale Research. 1997. $1,050.00. Fourth edition. Published by Euromonitor. Contains extensive consumer market, economic, and demographic data for 27 major, non-European countries, including the U. S. and Canada. Includes consumer market size (volume and value) for 150 product types in 14 categories (food, clothing, automobiles, cosmetics, appliances, etc.).

CORPORATE TECHNOLOGY DIRECTORY
12 Alfred St.
Suite 200
Woburn, MA 01801-1915
PH: (800)333-8036
FX: (617)932-6335
E-mail: sales@corptech.com
URL: http://www.corptech.com
Corporate Technology Information Services, Inc. Annual. $595.00. Four volumes. Profiles of more than 45,000 manufacturers and developers of high technology products. Includes private companies, publicly-held corporations, and subsidiaries.

COUNCIL ON FAMILY HEALTH
225 Park Ave., S., 17th Fl.
New York, NY 10003
PH: (212)598-3617
FX: (212)598-3665
Members are drug manufacturers. Concerned with proper use of medications.

COUNCIL FOR RESPONSIBLE GENETICS
Five Upland Rd., Suite 3
Cambridge, MA 02140
PH: (617)868-0870
FX: (617)491-5344
Concerned with the social implications of genetic engineering.

CREDIT CONSIDERATIONS: FINANCIAL AND CREDIT CHARACTERISTICS OF SELECTED INDUSTRIES, VOLUME THREE
One Liberty Place, Suite 2300
1650 Market St.
Philadelphia, PA 19103
PH: (800)677-7621
FX: (215)446-4100
URL: http://www.rmahq.org
Robert Morris Associates. Looseleaf. $130.00. Provides financial characteristics, credit risk appraisal, and general description of 27 industries, professions or businesses. An appendix outlines three methods of financing.

CSA LIFE SCIENCES COLLECTION
7200 Wisconsin Ave., Suite 601
Bethesda, MD 20814
PH: (800)843-7751
FX: (301)961-6720
Cambridge Scientific Abstracts. Includes online versions of *Biotechnology Research Abstracts, Entomology Abstracts, Genetics Ab-*

stracts, and about 20 other abstract collections. Time period is 1978 to date, with monthly updates. Inquire as to online cost and availability.

CSA LIFE SCIENCES COLLECTION [CD-ROM]
7200 Wisconsin Ave., Suite 601
Bethesda, MD 20814
PH: (800)843-7751
FX: (301)961-6720
Cambridge Scientific Abstracts. Quarterly. $1,595.00 per year. Includes CD-ROM versions of *Biotechnology Research Abstracts, Entomology Abstracts, Genetics Abstracts*, and about 20 other abstract collections.

CURRENT BIOTECHNOLOGY
Science Park
Milton Rd.
Cambridge CB4 4WF, England
PH: (122) 342 0066
FX: (4 1)2 342 34
The Royal Society of Chemistry. Thomas Graham House. Monthly. $940.00 per year. Reports on the latest scientific, technical and commercial advances in the field of technology. Formerly *Current Biotechnology Abstracts*.

CURRENT CONTENTS: ENGINEERING, COMPUTING AND TECHNOLOGY
3501 Market St.
Philadelphia, PA 19104
PH: (800)336-4474
FX: (215)386-2991
Institute for Scientific Information. Weekly. $730.00 per year. Reproductions of contents pages of technical journals. Formerly *Current Contents: Engineering, Technology and Applied Sciences*.

DEFENSE OF NARCOTICS CASES
Two Park Ave.
New York, NY 10016
PH: (800)223-1940
FX: (212)244-3188
David Bernheim. Matthew Bender & Co., Inc. Three looseleaf volumes. Price on application. Periodic supplementation. Up-to-date coverage of all aspects of narcotics cases and related matters.

DEPARTMENT OF MOLECULAR AND HUMAN GENETICS
Baylor College of Medicine
One Baylor Plaza, Room 904E
Houston, TX 77030
PH: (713)798-6522
FX: (713)798-6521
E-mail: abeaudet@bem.tmc.edu
URL: http://ginger.bcm.tmc.edu:80881
Formerly Institute for Molecular Genetics.

DEPRECIATION HANDBOOK
Two Park Ave.
New York, NY 10016
PH: (800)223-1940
FX: (212)244-3188
Bruce K. Benesh and M. Kevin Bryant. Matthew Bender & Co., Inc. Looseleaf volumes. Periodic supplementation. Price on application. Treatment of depreciation in one volume.

DEPRECIATION AND INVESTMENT CREDIT MANUAL
One Lake St.
Upper Saddle River, NJ 07458
PH: (800)223-1360
FX: (800)445-6991
URL: http://www.prenhall.com
Prentice Hall. Annual. Price on application.

DERWENT BIOTECHNOLOGY ABSTRACTS
1725 Duke St., Suite 250
Alexandria, VA 22314

PH: (800)451-3551
FX: (703)519-5829
E-mail: info@derwent.com
URL: http://www.derwent.com
Derwent, Inc. Provides indexing and abstracting of the world's biotechnology journal literature since 1982, including genetic engineering topics. Monthly updates. Inquire as to online cost and availability.

DERWENT DRUG FILE
1725 Duke St., Suite 250
Alexandria, VA 22314
PH: (800)451-3551
FX: (703)519-5829
E-mail: info@derwent.com
URL: http://www.derwent.com
Derwent, Inc. Provides indexing and abstracting of the world's pharmaceutical journal literature since 1964, with weekly updates. Formerly *RINGDOC*. Inquire as to online cost and availability.

DICTIONARY OF AMERICAN MEDICAL BIOGRAPHY
88 Post Rd. W.
Westport, CT 06881
PH: (800)225-5800
FX: (203)222-1502
Martin Kaufman and others. Greenwood Publishing Group Inc. 1984. $195.00. Two volumes. Vol. one, $100.00; vol. two, $100.00.

DIRECTORY OF AUTOMOTIVE AFTERMARKET SUPPLIERS
3922 Coconut Palm Drive
Tampa, FL 33619
PH: (800)927-9292
FX: (813)664-6682
E-mail: valkelly@sprynet.com
URL: http://www.d-net.com/csgis
Chain Store Guide Information Services. Biennial. $260.00. Covers auto supply store chains. Includes distributors.

DIRECTORY OF CHAIN RESTAURANT OPERATORS
3922 Coconut Palm Drive
Tampa, FL 33619
PH: (800)927-9292
FX: (813)664-6682
E-mail: valkelly@sprynet.com
URL: http://www.d-net.com/csgis
Chain Store Guide Information Services. Annual. $290.00. Includes fast food establishments.

DIRECTORY OF DISCOUNT AND GENERAL MERCHANDISE, VARIETY, AND SPECIALTY STORES
3922 Coconut Palm Drive
Tampa, FL 33619
PH: (800)927-9292
FX: (813)664-6882
E-mail: valkelly@sprynet.com
URL: http://www.d-net.com/csgis
Chain Store Guide Information Services. Annual. $325.00. Includes retailers and wholesalers of housewares, giftwares, novelties, toys, hobby materials, crafts, and stationery. Formerly *Directory of Discount Stores/Catalog Showrooms*.

DIRECTORY OF DRUG STORE AND HBC CHAINS (HEALTH AND BEAUTY CARE)
3922 Coconut Palm Drive
Tampa, FL 33619
PH: (800)927-9292
FX: (813)664-6882
E-mail: valkelly@sprynet.com
URL: http://www.d-net.com/csgis
Chain Store Guide Information Services. Annual. $290.00. HBC stores sell health and beauty care products. Includes distributors. Formerly *Directory of Drug Store and HBA Chains*.

DIRECTORY OF HOME CENTER OPERATORS AND HARDWARE CHAINS
3922 Coconut Palm Drive
Tampa, FL 33619
PH: (800)927-9292
FX: (813)664-6882
E-mail: valkelly@sprynet.com
URL: http://www.d-net.com/csgis
Chain Store Guide Information Services. Annual. $290.00. Nearly 5,800 home center operators, paint and home decorating chains, and lumber and building materials companies.

DIRECTORY OF RETAIL CHAINS IN CANADA
777 Bay St.
Toronto, ON, Canada M5W 1A7
PH: (416)596-5000
FX: (416)596-5553
URL: http://www.mhbizlink.com
Maclean Hunter Business Publications. Annual. $340.00. Provides detailed information on approximately 1,600 retail chains of all sizes in Canada.

DIRECTORY OF SUPERMARKET, GROCERY, AND CONVENIENCE STORE CHAINS
3922 Coconut Palm Drive
Tampa, FL 33619
PH: (800)927-9292
FX: (813)664-6882
E-mail: valkelly@sprynet.com
URL: http://www.d-net.com/csgis
Chain Store Guide Information Services. Annual. $300.00. Provides information on about 4,000 food store chains operating 107,000 individual stores. Store locations are given.

DISCOUNT MERCHANDISER
233 Park Ave., South
New York, NY 10003
PH: (212)979-4860
FX: (212)474-7431
Schwartz Publications. Monthly. $55.00 per year. Mass merchandising retail industry.

DISCOUNT STORE NEWS
425 Park Ave.
New York, NY 10022
PH: (212)756-5000
FX: (212)756-5250
Lebhar-Friedman, Inc. Biweekly. $100.00 per year. Includes *Apparel Merchandising*.

DISCOUNT STORE NEWS - TOP CHAINS
425 Park Ave.
New York, NY 10022
PH: (212)756-5000
FX: (212)756-5250
Lebhar-Friedman, Inc. Annual. $79.00. Formerly *Discount Store News-Top 200 Chains*.

DRI U.S. CENTRAL DATABASE
24 Hartwell Ave.
Lexington, MA 02173-3154
PH: (800)933-3374
FX: (781)860-6332
URL: http://www.dri.mcgraw-hill.com
DRI/McGraw-Hill. Provides more than 23,000 business, financial, demographic, economic, foreign trade, and industry-related time series for the U.S. Includes national income, population, retail-wholesale trade, price indexes, labor data, housing, industrial production, banking, interest rates, money supply, etc. Time period is generally 1947 to date (some data back to 1929). Updating varies. Inquire as to online cost and availability.

DRUG ABUSE AND THE LAW SOURCEBOOK
155 Pfingsten Rd.
Deerfield, IL 60015
PH: (800)328-4880
FX: (847)948-8955
URL: http://www.westgroup.com
Gerald F. Uelmen and Victor G. Haddox. Clark Boardman Callaghan. Two looseleaf volumes. $240.00. Revised annually. Covers drugs of abuse, criminal responsibility, possessory offenses, trafficking offenses, and related topics.

DRUG, CHEMICAL AND ALLIED TRADES ASSOCIATION
Two Roosevelt Ave., Suite 301
Syosset, NY 11791
PH: (516)496-3317
FX: (516)496-2231

DRUG AND COSMETIC INDUSTRY (DCI)
7500 Old Oak Blvd.
Cleveland, OH 44130
PH: (800)346-0085
FX: (216)891-2726
URL: http://www.advanstar.com
Advanstar Communications, Inc. Monthly. $40.00 per year.

DRUG DEVELOPMENT RESEARCH
Journals Div.
605 Third Ave.
New York, NY 10158-0012
PH: (800)225-5945
FX: (212)850-6088
John Wiley and Sons, Inc. Monthly. $2,595.00 per year.

DRUG INFORMATION ASSOCIATION
321 Norristown Rd., Suite 225
Ambler, PA 19002
PH: (215)628-2288
FX: (215)641-1229
E-mail: http://www.diahome.org
Concerned with the technology of drug information processing.

DRUG INFORMATION FULLTEXT
7272 Wisconsin Ave.
Bethesda, MD 20814
PH: (301)657-3000
FX: (301)657-1641
American Society of Health-System Pharmacists. Provides full text monographs from the *American Hospital Formulary Service* and the *Handbook On Injectable Drugs*. Inquire as to online cost and availability.

DRUG LAW REPORT
155 Pfingsten Rd.
Deerfield, IL 60015
PH: (800)328-4880
FX: (847)948-8955
URL: http://www.westgroup.com
National Organization for Reform of Marijuana Laws. Clark Boardman Callaghan. Bimonthly. $175.00 per year. Newsletter on laws and issues relating to illegal drug use.

DRUG PRODUCT LIABILITY
Two Park Ave.
New York, NY 10016
PH: (800)223-1940
FX: (212)244-3188
Marden G. Dixon and others. Matthew Bender & Co., Inc. Three looseleaf volumes. Price on application. Periodic supplementation. All aspects of drugs: manufacturing, marketing, distribution, quality control, multiple prescription problems, drug identification, FDA coverage, etc.

DRUG STORE NEWS
425 Park Ave.
New York, NY 10022
PH: (212)756-5000
FX: (212)756-5250
Lebhar-Friedman Inc. Biweekly. $95.00 per year.

DRUG STORE NEWS FOR THE PHARMACIST
425 Park Ave.
New York, NY 10022
PH: (212)756-5000
FX: (212)756-5250
Lebhar-Friedman, Inc. Monthly. $36.00 per year. Includes an annual "Generic Study" (June).

DRUG TOPICS
Five Paragon Dr.
Montvale, NJ 07645-1742
PH: (800)232-7379
FX: (201)573-4956
Medical Economics Co., Inc. Semimonthly. $58.00 per year. Edited for retail pharmacists, hospital pharmacists, pharmacy chain store executives, buyers, and others concerned with drug dispensing and drug store management. Provides information on new products, including personal care items and cosmetics.

DRUGS OF ABUSE
Washington, DC 20402
PH: (202)512-1800
FX: (202)512-2250
E-mail: gpoaccess@gpo.gov
URL: http://www.access.gpo.gov
Available from U. S. Government Printing Office. 1997. $7.00. Issued by the Drug Enforcement Administration, U. S. Department of Justice (http://www.usdoj.gov). Provides detailed information on various kinds of narcotics, depressants, stimulants, hallucinogens, cannabis, steroids, and inhalants. Contains many color illustrations and a detailed summary of the Controlled Substances Act.

EMBASE
655 Ave. of the Americas
New York, NY 10010
PH: (212)989-5800
FX: (212)633-3975
Elsevier Science, Inc. Worldwide medical literature, 1974 to present. Weekly updates. Inquire as to online cost and availability.

ENCYCLOPEDIA OF EMERGING INDUSTRIES
27500 Drake Rd.
Farmington Hills, MI 48331-3535
PH: (800)877-GALE
FX: (248)699-8070
E-mail: galeord@galegroup.com
URL: http://www.galegroup.com
Gale Group. 1998. $350.00. Provides detailed information on 88 "newly flourishing" industries. Includes historical background, organizational structure, significant individuals, current conditions, major companies, work force, technology trends, research developments, and other industry facts.

ENCYCLOPEDIA OF MEDICAL ORGANIZATIONS AND
  AGENCIES
27500 Drake Rd.
Farmington Hills, MI 48331-3535
PH: (800)877-GALE
FX: (248)699-8070
Gale Group. 1997. $239.00. Seventh edition. Information on over 14,000 public and private organizations in medicine and related medical fields.

ENCYCLOPEDIA OF OCCUPATIONAL HEALTH AND
  SAFETY 1983
1828 L St., N.W., Suite 801
Washington, DC 20036

PH: (202)653-7652
FX: (202)653-7687
E-mail: webinfo@ilo.org
URL: http://www.ilo.org
International Labor Office. 1991. $270.00. Third revised edition. Two volumes.

ENVIRONMENTAL TOXICOLOGY AND WATER
  QUALITY: AN INTERNATIONAL JOURNAL
605 Third Ave.
New York, NY 10158-0012
PH: (800)225-5945
FX: (212)850-6088
John Wiley and Sons, Inc. Journals Div. Quarterly. $395.00 per year. Formerly *Toxicity Assessment.*

EUROMONITOR MARKET RESEARCH
122 S. Michigan Ave., Suite 1200
Chicago, IL 60603
PH: (800)577-3876
FX: (312)922-1157
E-mail: info@euromonitor.com
URL: http://www.euromonitor.com
Euromonitor International. Provides the complete text online of Euromonitor market analysis reports. Covers consumer goods market research data for all major countries, with emphasis on specific product categories. Time period is current. Continuous updating. Inquire as to online cost and availability.

EUROPEAN DIRECTORY OF RETAILERS AND
  WHOLESALERS
27500 Drake Rd.
Farmington Hills, MI 48331-3535
PH: (800)877-GALE
FX: (248)699-8070
E-mail: galeord@galegroup.com
URL: http://www.galegroup.com
Available from Gale Group. 1997. $790.00. Second edition. Published by Euromonitor. Provides detailed information on more than 5,000 major retail and wholesale businesses in 17 countries of Western Europe. Contains 26 categories, such as supermarkets, superstores, department stores, discount stores, franchise operators, mail order, etc. Includes company, product, and geographic indexes.

EUROPEAN MARKETING FORECASTS
27500 Drake Rd.
Farmington Hills, MI 48331-3535
PH: (800)877-GALE
FX: (248)699-8070
E-mail: galeord@galegroup.com
URL: http://www.galegroup.com
Available from Gale Group. 1997. $795.00. Published by Euromonitor. Contains demographic, economic, and market forecasts for the countries of Europe to the year 2010. Forecasts include market-size data for 15 consumer product sectors (food, clothing, automobiles, consumer electronics, etc.).

EUROPEAN PRIVATE LABEL DIRECTORY
27500 Drake Rd.
Farmington Hills, MI 48331-3535
PH: (800)877-GALE
FX: (248)699-8070
E-mail: galeord@galegroup.com
URL: http://www.galegroup.com
Available from Gale Group. 1996. $450.00. Published by Euromonitor. Provides detailed information on 1,000 private label enterprises (500 retailers and 500 manufacturers) in 17 countries of Western Europe. Includes analysis of the private label market.

EXCERPTA MEDICA: BIOPHYSICS, BIOENGINEERING,
  AND MEDICAL INSTRUMENTATION
655 Ave. of the Americas
New York, NY 10010

PH: (888)437-4636
FX: (212)633-3680
E-mail: usinfo-f@elsevier.com
URL: http://www.elsevier.com
Elsevier Science. 16 times a year. $1,876.00 per year. Section 27 of *Excerpta Medica*.

EXCERPTA MEDICA: HUMAN GENETICS
655 Ave. of the Americas
New York, NY 10010
PH: (888)437-4636
FX: (212)633-3680
E-mail: usinfo-f@elsevier.com
URL: http://www.elsevier.com
Elsevier Science. Semimonthly. $2,718.00 per year. Section 22 of *Excerpta Medica*.

EXCERPTA MEDICA: OCCUPATIONAL HEALTH AND INDUSTRIAL MEDICINE
655 Ave. of the Americas
New York, NY 10010
PH: (888)437-4636
FX: (212)633-3680
E-mail: usinfo-f@elsevier.com
URL: http://www.elsevier.com
Elsevier Science. Monthly. $1,557.00 per year. Section 35 of *Excerpta Medica*.

F-D-C REPORTS
5550 Friendship Blvd., Suite One
Chevy Chase, MD 20815
PH: (301)657-9830
FX: (301)656-3094
FDC Reports, Inc. An online version of "The Gray Sheet" (medical devices), "The Pink Sheet" (pharmaceuticals), and "The Rose Sheet" (cosmetics). Contains full-text information on legal, technical, corporate, financial, and marketing developments from 1987 to date, with weekly updates. Inquire as to online cost and availability.

F & S INDEX
27500 Drake Rd.
Farmington Hills, MI 48331-3535
PH: (800)877-GALE
FX: (248)699-8070
E-mail: galeord@galegroup.com
URL: http://www.galegroup.com
Gale Group. Contains about four million citations to worldwide business, financial, and industrial or consumer product literature appearing from 1972 to date. Weekly updates. Inquire as to online cost and availability.

F & S INDEX PLUS TEXT
362 Lakeside Dr.
Foster City, CA 94404
PH: (800)321-6388
FX: (650)358-4759
Information Access Co. Monthly. $7,575.00 per year. Provides CD-ROM citations to worldwide business, marketing, and industrial material appearing in a large assortment of trade journals, newspapers, and other publications. Time period is four years.

FAIRCHILD'S RETAIL STORES FINANCIAL DIRECTORY
Seven West 34th St.
New York, NY 10001
PH: (800)932-4724
FX: (212)630-3868
Fairchild Books, Fairchild Publications, Inc. Annual. $95.00. About 260 publicly held retail companies in the United States and Canada. Formerly *Fairchild's Financial Manual of Retail Stores*.

FAMILY ALMANAC
1608 South Dakota
Sioux Falls, SD 57105
PH: (800)423-7158

National Asociation of Retail Druggists. Creative Comics Syndicates. Annual. $41.00. Formerly *NARD Almanac and Health Guide*.

FDA CONSUMER
Washington, DC 20402
PH: (202)512-1800
FX: (202)512-2250
E-mail: gpoaccess@gpo.gov
URL: http://www.access.gpo.gov
Available from U. S. Government Printing Office. Monthly. $10.00 per year. Issued by the U. S. Food and Drug Administration. Provides consumer information about FDA regulations and product safety.

FDC REPORTS, "THE BLUE SHEET": HEALTH POLICY AND BIOMEDICAL RESEARCH
5550 Friendship Blvd., Suite One
Chevy Chase, MD 20815-7278
PH: (800)332-2181
FX: (301)986-4495
FDC Reports, Inc. Weekly. $390.00 per year. Newsletter. Emphasis is on news of medical research agencies and institutions, especially the National Institutes of Health (NIH).

FDC REPORTS, "THE GREEN SHEET": WEEKLY PHARMACY REPORTS
5550 Friendship Blvd., Suite One
Chevy Chase, MD 20815-7278
PH: (800)332-2181
FX: (301)986-4495
FDC Reports, Inc. Weekly. $60.00 per year. Newsletter for retailers and wholesalers of pharmaceutical products. Includes pricing developments and new drug announcements.

FDC REPORTS, "THE PINK SHEET": PRESCRIPTION PHARMACEUTICALS AND BIOTECHNOLOGY
5550 Friendship Blvd., Suite One
Chevy Chase, MD 20815-7278
PH: (800)332-2181
FX: (301)986-4495
FDC Reports, Inc. Weekly. $750.00 per year. Newsletter covering business and regulatory developments affecting the pharmaceutical and biotechnology industries. Provides information on generic drug approvals and includes a drug sector stock index.

FDC REPORTS, "THE TAN SHEET": NONPRESCRIPTION PHARMACEUTICALS AND NUTRITIONALS
5550 Friendship Blvd., Suite One
Chevy Chase, MD 20815-7278
PH: (800)332-2181
FX: (301)986-4495
FDC Reports, Inc. Weekly. $650.00 per year. Newsletter covering over-the-counter drugs and vitamin supplements. Emphasis is on regulatory activities of the U. S. Food and Drug Administration (FDA).

FEDSTATS
PH: (202)395-7254
E-mail: feedback@www.whitehouse.gov
URL: http://www.fedstats.gov
Federal Interagency Council on Statistical Policy. Web site features an efficient search facility for full-text statistics produced by more than 70 federal agencies, including the Census Bureau, the Bureau of Economic Analysis, and the Bureau of Labor Statistics. Boolean searches can be made within one agency or for all agencies combined. Links are offered to international statistical bureaus, including the UN, IMF, OECD, UNESCO, Eurostat, and 20 individual countries. Fees: Free.

FINANCIAL MANAGEMENT FOR PHARMACISTS: A DECISION-MAKING APPROACH
351 Camden St.
Baltimore, MD 21202-2436

PH: (800)527-5597
FX: (410)528-4422
E-mail: custserv@wilkins.com
URL: http://www.wwilkins.com
Norman V. Carroll. Williams & Wilkins. 1997. Price on application.

FIRST DATABANK BLUE BOOK
645 Stewart Ave.
Garden City, NY 11530-4709
PH: (800)833-7138
FX: (516)227-1405
URL: http://www.hearstcorp.com
Hearst. Annual. $69.00. List of manufacturers of prescription and over-the-counter drugs, sold in retail drug stores. Formerly *American Druggist Blue Book*.

FOOD, DRUG, COSMETIC LAW REPORTS
4025 W. Peterson Ave.
Chicago, IL 60646-6085
PH: (800)248-3248
FX: (800)224-8299
Commerce Clearing House, Inc. $1,985.00 per year. Six looseleaf volumes. Weekly updates. Covers regulation of adulteration, packaging, labeling, and additives.

FRANCHISING WORLD
1350 New York Ave., N.W., Suite 900
Washington, DC 20005-4709
PH: (202)628-8000
FX: (202)628-0812
International Franchise Association. Bimonthly. $12.00 per year. Formerly *Franchising Opportunities*.

GENERIC LINE
5324 Sinclair Rd.
Columbus, OH 43229
PH: (614)433-0648
FX: (614)433-0432
Scitec Services, Inc. Weekly. $280.00 per year. Newsletter. Covers regulation, legislation, technology, marketing, and other issues affecting companies providing generic pharmaceuticals.

GENERIC PHARMACEUTICAL INDUSTRY ASSOCIATION
1620 Eye St., N.W., Suite 800
Washington, DC 20006-4005
PH: (202)833-9070
FX: (202)833-9612
Members are manufacturers, wholesalers, and retailers of generic prescription drugs.

GENERIC PRESCRIPTION DRUGS
Theta Bldg.
Eight Old Indian Trail
Middlefield, CT 06455
PH: (800)995-1550
FX: (203)349-1227
Theta Corp. 1995. $995.00. Contains market data and forecasts. (Theta Market Research Report No. 540.)

GENETIC ENGINEERING FOR ALMOST EVERYBODY
375 Hudson St.
New York, NY 10014-3657
PH: (800)331-4624
FX: (212)366-2666
URL: http://www.gopher://gopherserver.cwis.uci.edu
William Bains. Viking Penguin. 1988. $6.95.

GENETIC ENGINEERING AND BIOTECHNOLOGY FIRMS WORLDWIDE DIRECTORY
217 Nassau St.
Princeton Junction, NJ 08542-4602
PH: (800)962-7004
FX: (609)275-8011
Mega-Type Publishing. Annual. $299.00. About 6,000 firms, inclu-

ding major firms with biotechnology divisions as well as small independent firms.

GENETIC ENGINEERING: CATASTROPHE OR UTOPIA?
175 Fifth Ave.
New York, NY 10010
PH: (800)221-7945
FX: (212)420-9314
P. R. Wheale and Ruth McNally. St. Martin's Press, Inc. 1988. $35.00.

GENETIC ENGINEERING NEWS: THE INFORMATION SOURCE OF THE BIOTECHNOLOGY INDUSTRY
Two Madison Ave.
Larchmont, NY 10538
PH: (914)834-3100
FX: (914)834-3688
E-mail: liebert@pipeline.com
Mary Ann Liebert, Inc. Semimonthly. $276.00 per year. Newsletter. Business and financial coverage.

GENETIC TECHNOLOGY NEWS
32 Dean St.
Englewood, NJ 07631-2807
PH: (201)568-4744
FX: (201)568-8247
E-mail: htminfo@insights.com
URL: http://www.insights.com
Al Hestor, editor. Technical Insights, Inc. Monthly. $650.00 per year. Reports on genetic engineering and its uses in the chemical, pharmaceutical, food processing and energy industries as well as in agriculture, animal breeding and medicine. Includes three supplements: *Patent Update*, *Strategic Partners*, and *Market Forecasts*.

GENETICS ABSTRACTS
7200 Wisconsin Ave., 6th Fl.
Bethesda, MD 20814
PH: (800)843-7751
FX: (301)961-6720
E-mail: market@csa.com
URL: http://www.csa.com
Cambridge Scientific Abstracts. Monthly. $1,035.00 per year.

GENETICS SOCIETY OF AMERICA
9650 Rockville Pike
Bethesda, MD 20814-3998
PH: (301)571-1825
FX: (301)530-7079
E-mail: society@genetics.faseb.org
Members are individuals and organizations with an interest in genetics.

GLOBALBASE
27500 Drake Rd.
Farmington Hills, MI 48331-3535
PH: (800)877-GALE
FX: (248)699-8070
E-mail: galeord@galegroup.com
URL: http://www.galegroup.com
Formerly by IAC. Provides more than one million online summaries of business, industrial, and economic news reports from more than 1,000 publications worldwide. Covers a wide range of material appearing in international trade journals, professional magazines, and newspapers. Time period is 1984 to date, with weekly updates. Inquire as to online cost and availability.

THE GOLD SHEET: QUALITY CONTROL REPORTS
5550 Friendship Blvd., Suite One
Chevy Chase, MD 20815-7278
PH: (800)332-2181
FX: (301)664-7248
E-mail: fdcr@fdcr.com
URL: http://www.fdcr.com
F-D-C Reports, Inc. Monthly. $350.00 per year. Newsletter. Covers

quality control and production techniques for pharmaceutical companies. Emphasis is on Food and Drug Administration (FDA) regulations.

THE GREEN SHEET: WEEKLY PHARMACY REPORTS
5550 Friendship Blvd., Suite One
Chevy Chase, MD 20815-7278
PH: (800)332-2181
FX: (301)664-7248
E-mail: fdcr@fdcr.com
URL: http://www.fdcr.com
F-D-C Reports, Inc. Weekly. $75.00 per year. Newsletter. Edited for pharmacists, drugstore managers, and drug wholesalers. Provides information on new drugs, prices, and regulatory activities.

HANDBOOK OF INDUSTRIAL TOXICOLOGY
192 Lexington Ave, Suite 603
New York, NY 10016
PH: (800)786-3659
FX: (212)889-1537
E. R. Plunkett, editor. Chemical Publishing Co., Inc. 1987. $100.00.

HANDBOOK OF NONPRESCRIPTION DRUGS
2215 Constitution Ave., N. W.
Washington, DC 20037
PH: (800)237-2742
FX: (202)783-2351
American Pharmaceutical Association. 1996. $130.00. 11th revised edition. Contains comprehensive, technical information on over-the-counter drugs.

HANDBOOK OF OVER-THE-COUNTER DRUGS
P.O. Box 7123
Berkeley, CA 94707
PH: (800)841-2665
FX: (510)524-1052
Max Leber and others. Celestial Arts Publishing Co. 1992. $14.95. Provides detailed, consumer information on the ingredients of nonprescription drugs and popular cosmetics.

HANDBOOK OF TOXIC AND HAZARDOUS CHEMICALS AND CARCINOGENS
369 Fairview Ave.
Westwood, NJ 07675
PH: (201)666-2121
FX: (201)666-5111
Marshall Sittig. Noyes Data Corp,. 1992. $197.00. Third edition. Two volumes.

HAYES DRUGGIST DIRECTORY
4229 Birch St.
Newport Beach, CA 92660
PH: (714)756-9063
FX: (714)756-0921
Edward N. Hayes. Annual. $395.00. Lists the financial strength, and credit ratings, and telephone number for 53,000 retail and about 700 wholesale drug comapnies in the U.S.

HAZARDOUS AND TOXIC MATERIALS: SAFE HANDLING AND DISPOSAL
605 Third Ave.
New York, NY 10158-0012
PH: (800)526-5368
FX: (212)850-6088
Howard H. Fawcett. John Wiley and Sons, Inc. 1988. $110.00. Second edition.

HEALTH CARE PRODUCTS AND REMEDIES
625 Ave. of the Americas
New York, NY 10011-2002
PH: (800)346-3787
FX: (212)807-2716
E-mail: catalog@findsvp.com
URL: http://www.findsvp.com

Available from FIND/SVP, Inc. 1997. $600.00 each. Consists of market reports published by Simmons Market Research Bureau on each of about 25 health care product categories. Examples are cold remedies, contraceptives, hearing aids, bandages, headache remedies, eyeglasses, contact lenses, and vitamins. Each report covers buying patterns and demographics.

THE HEALTH CONNECTION
55 W. Oak Ridge Dr.
Hagerstown, MD 21740
PH: (800)548-8700
FX: (301)790-9733

HEALTH NEWS DAILY
5550 Friendship Blvd., Suite 1
Chevy Chase, MD 20815-7278
PH: (800)332-2181
FX: (301)664-7238
FDC Reports, Inc. Daily. $1,350.00 per year. Newsletter providing broad coverage of the healthcare business, including government policy, regulation, research, finance, and insurance. Contains news of pharmaceuticals, medical devices, biotechnology, and healthcare delivery in general.

HEALTH REFERENCE CENTER
27500 Drake Rd.
Farmington Hills, MI 48331-3535
PH: (800)877-GALE
FX: (248)699-8070
Gale Group. Monthly. $5,000.00 per year. Provides CD-ROM citations, abstracts, and selected full-text articles on many health-related subjects. Includes references to medical journals, general periodicals, newsletters, newspapers, pamphlets, and medical reference books.

HEALTHCARE DISTRIBUTOR
5285 W. Louisiana Ave., Suite 112
Lakewood, CO 80232-5976
PH: (303)975-0075
FX: (303)975-0132
Wholesale Drugs Magazine. Monthly. $30.00 per year. Formerly Wholesale Drugs Magazine.

HOSPITAL PHARMACIST REPORT
Five Paragon Drive
Montvale, NJ 07645-1742
PH: (800)232-7379
FX: (201)573-4956
Medical Economics Co., Inc. Monthly. $39.00 per year. Covers both business and clinical topics for hospital pharmacists.

HOUSEHOLD AND PERSONAL PRODUCTS INDUSTRY - BUYERS GUIDE
P.O. Box 555
Ramsey, NJ 07446
PH: (201)825-2552
FX: (201)825-0553
E-mail: editor@happi.com
URL: http://www.happi.com
Rodman Publishing Corp. Annual. $12.00. Lists of suppliers to manufacturers of cosmetics, toiletries, soaps, detergents, and related household and personal products.

HOUSEHOLD AND PERSONAL PRODUCTS INDUSTRY CONTRACT PACKAGING AND PRIVATE LABEL DIRECTORY
P.O. Box 555
Ramsey, NJ 07446
PH: (201)825-2552
FX: (201)825-0553
E-mail: editor@happi.com
URL: http://www.happi.com
Rodman Publishing Corp. Annual. $12.00. Provides information on about 450 companies offering private label or contract packaged

household and personal care products, such as detergents, cosmetics, polishes, insecticides, and various aerosol items.

HOUSEHOLD AND PERSONAL PRODUCTS INDUSTRY: THE MAGAZINE FOR THE DETERGENT, SOAP, COSMETICS AND TOILETRY, WAX, POLISH AND AEROSOL INDUSTRIES
P.O. 555
Ramsey, NJ 07446
PH: (201)825-2552
FX: (201)825-0553
E-mail: editor@happi.com
URL: http://www.happi.com
Rodman Publishing Corp. Monthly. $48.00 per year. Covers marketing, packaging, production, technical innovations, private label developments, and aerosol packaging for soap, detergents, cosmetics, insecticides, and a variety of other household products.

IAC INDUSTRY EXPRESS
27500 Drake Rd.
Farmington Hills, MI 48331-3535
PH: (800)877-GALE
FX: (248)699-8070
E-mail: galeord@galegroup.com
URL: http://www.galegroup.com
Formerly by IAC. Industry Express is an industry-focused database providing current, full-text material appearing in trade journals, newsletters, and other business publications. A wide range of business, industrial, and technical topics are covered. Time period is the most current 30 days, with comprehensive indexing. Inquire as to online cost and availability.

IEEE ENGINEERING IN MEDICINE AND BIOLOGY MAGAZINE
345 E. 47th St.
New York, NY 10017-2394
PH: (800)678-4333
FX: (212)752-4929
Institute of Electrical and Electronics Engineers, Inc. Quarterly. Free to members; non-members, $125.00 per year. Published for biomedical engineers.

INDEX TO HEALTH INFORMATION
4520 East-West Highway, Suite 800
Bethesda, MD 20814-3389
PH: (800)638-8380
FX: (301)654-4033
E-mail: info@cispubs.com
URL: http://www.cispubs
Congressional Information Service, Inc. Quarterly. $945.00 per year, including two-volume annual cumulation. Provides index and abstracts covering the medical and health field in general, with emphasis on statistical sources and government documents. Service with microfiche source documents, $4,995.00 per year.

INDEX MEDICUS
Washington, DC 20402
PH: (202)512-1800
FX: (202)512-2250
National Library of Medicine. Available from U. S. Government Printing Office. Monthly. $509.00 per year. Bibliographic listing of references to current articles from approximately 3,000 of the world's biomedical journals.

INDUSTRIAL HYGIENE NEWS
8650 Babcock Blvd.
Pittsburgh, PA 15237
PH: (800)245-3182
FX: (412)369-9720
E-mail: rimbach@sgi.net
Rimbach Publishing, Inc. Seven times a year. Free to qualified personnel; others, $25.00 per year.

INDUSTRIAL HYGIENE NEWS BUYER'S GUIDE
8650 Babcock Blvd.
Pittsburgh, PA 15237
PH: (800)245-3182
FX: (412)369-9720
E-mail: rimbach@sgi.net
Rimbach Publishing, Inc. Annual. $50.00. List of about 1,000 manufacturers and suppliers of products, equipment, and services to the occupational health, industrial hygiene, and high-tech safety industry.

INDUSTRIAL SAFETY AND HEALTH MANAGEMENT
One Lake St.
Upper Saddle River, NJ 07458
PH: (800)223-1360
FX: (800)445-6991
URL: http://www.prenhall.com
C. Ray Asfahl. Prentice Hall. 1995. $82.00. Third edition.

INFORMATION SOURCES IN THE LIFE SCIENCES
121 Chanlon Rd.
New Providence, NJ 07974
PH: (800)521-8110
FX: (908)665-6688
H. V. Wyatt, editor. Bowker-Saur, Reed Reference Publishing. 1997. $95.00. Fourth edition. Includes an evaluation of biotechnology information sources. (Guides to Information Sources Series).

INSTITUTE OF ELECTRICAL AND ELECTRONICS ENGINEERS; ENGINEERING IN MEDICINE AND BIOLOGY SOCIETY
345 E. 47th St.
New York, NY 10017
PH: (212)705-7900
FX: (212)705-4929

INSTITUTE FOR ENVIRONMENTAL HEALTH SCIENCES
School of Public Health
1420 Washington Heights
University of Michigan
Ann Arbor, MI 48109-2029
PH: (313)764-3188
FX: (313)936-7283

INSTITUTE FOR MOLECULAR AND AGRICULTURAL GENETIC ENGINEERING
University of Idaho
Food Research Center 103
Moscow, ID 83844-1052
PH: (208)885-6580
FX: (208)885-5741
E-mail: crawford@uidaho.edu
URL: http://www.image.fs.uidaho.edu

INTERNATIONAL ACCOUNTING CENTER
320 Commerce W., Box 109
1206 S. Sixth St.
Champaign, IL 61820-6271
PH: (217)333-4545
FX: (217)244-0902
E-mail: bsmith2@commerce.cba.uiuc.edu

INTERNATIONAL INSTRUMENTATION AND CONTROLS: BUYERS GUIDE
150 Great Neck Rd.
Great Neck, NY 11021-3309
PH: (516)829-9210
FX: (516)829-5414
Keller International Publishing Corp. Annual. Controlled circulation. Lists over 310 suppliers of precision instrument products and services.

INTERNATIONAL JOURNAL OF OCCUPATIONAL MEDICINE, IMMUNOLOGY AND TOXICOLOGY
PO Box 2155
428 E. Preston St.
Princeton, NJ 08543
PH: (609)683-4750
FX: (609)683-0838
International Society of Occupational Medicine and Toxicology. Princeton Scientific Publishing Co., Inc. Quarterly. $160.00 per year. Formerly *Journal of Occupational Medicine and Toxicology.*

INTERNATIONAL MARKETING FORECASTS
27500 Drake Rd.
Farmington Hills, MI 48331-3535
PH: (800)877-GALE
FX: (248)699-8070
E-mail: galeord@galegroup.com
URL: http://www.galegroup.com
Available from Gale Group. 1997. $795.00. Published by Euromonitor. Contains demographic, economic, and market forecasts to the year 2010 for major, non-European countries, including the U. S. and Canada. Forecasts include market-size data for 15 consumer product sectors, such as food, clothing, and automobiles.

INTERNATIONAL MASS RETAIL ASSOCIATION
1700 N. Moore St., Suite 2250
Arlington, VA 22209
PH: (703)841-2300
FX: (703)841-1184
URL: http://www.imra.org

INTERNATIONAL PHARMACEUTICAL ABSTRACTS [ONLINE]
7272 Wisconsin Ave.
Bethesda, MD 20814
PH: (301)657-3000
FX: (301)657-1257
American Society of Health-System Pharmacists. Provides online indexing and abstracting of the world's pharmaceutical literature from 1970 to date. Monthly updates. Inquire as to online cost and availability.

INTERNATIONAL PHARMACEUTICAL ABSTRACTS [CD-ROM]
7272 Wisconsin Ave.
Bethesda, MD 20814
PH: (301)657-3000
FX: (301)657-1251
American Society of Health-System Pharmacists. Quarterly. $1,795.00 per year. Contains CD-ROM indexing and abstracting of international pharmaceutical literature from 1970 to date.

INTERNATIONAL PHARMACEUTICAL ABSTRACTS: KEY TO THE WORLD'S LITERATURE OF PHARMACY
7272 Wisconsin Ave.
Bethesda, MD 20814
PH: (301)657-3000
FX: (301)657-1641
American Society of Health-System Pharmacists. Semimonthly. Members, $125.00 per year; non-members, $425.00 per year. Formerly American Society of Hospital Pharmacists.

INTERNATIONAL PRIVATE LABEL DIRECTORY
2125 Center Ave., Suite 305
Fort Lee, NJ 07024-5859
PH: (201)592-7007
FX: (201)592-7171
E. W. Williams Publications Co. Annual. $75.00. Provides information on over 2,000 suppliers of a wide variety of private label and generic products: food, over-the-counter health products, personal care items, and general merchandise. Formerly *Private Label Directory.*

INTERNATIONAL SOCIETY FOR PHARMACEUTICAL ENGINEERING
3816 W. Linebaugh Ave., No. 412
Tampa, FL 33624
PH: (813)960-2105
FX: (813)264-2816

INTERNET TOOLS OF THE PROFESSION
PH: (202)234-4700
FX: (202)265-9317
E-mail: hope@tiac.net
URL: http://www.sla.org/pubs/itotp
Special Libraries Association. Web site is designed to update the printed *Internet Tools of the Profession*. Provides links to a wide range of useful databases in business, finance, industry, information technology, insurance, law, library management, telecommunications, and other subject areas. Fees: Free.

INTERNET TOOLS OF THE PROFESSION: A GUIDE FOR INFORMATION PROFESSIONALS
1700 18th St., N. W.
Washington, DC 20009-2514
PH: (202)234-4700
FX: (202)265-9317
URL: http://www.sla.org
Hope N. Tillman, editor. Special Libraries Association. 1997. $49.00. Second edition. Consists of 14 sections by various authors or compilers. After two introductory articles on searching the Internet, there are 12 annotated lists of useful Web sites, covering the SLA, business and finance, chemistry, education, food and agriculture, information technology, insurance and employee benefits, law, library management, metals and materials, pharmaceuticals, and telecommunications. An index is provided.

INTRODUCTION TO BIOTECHNOLOGY
10 Davis Drive
Belmont, CA 94002
PH: (800)354-9706
FX: (650)637-9955
URL: http://www.thomson.com/wadsworth
Carol M. Barnum. Wadsworth Publishing Co. 1998. $41.95.

ISA: FOOD AND PHARMACEUTICAL DIVISION
67 Alexander Dr.
Research Triangle Park, NC 27709
PH: (919)549-8411
FX: (919)549-8288
E-mail: info@isa.org

JOURNAL OF BIOTECHNOLOGY
655 Ave. of the Americas
New York, NY 10010
PH: (888)437-4636
FX: (212)633-3680
E-mail: usinfo-f@elsevier.com
URL: http://www.elsevier.com
Elsevier Science. 21 times a year. $2,269.00 per year. Text and summaries in English.

JOURNAL OF CHEMICAL TECHNOLOGY AND BIOTECHNOLOGY
605 Third Ave.
New York, NY 10158-0012
PH: (212)526-5368
FX: (212)850-6088
John Wiley and Sons, Inc. Journals Div. Monthly. $1075.00 per year. Formerly *Biotechnology.*

JOURNAL OF PHARMACEUTICAL MARKETING AND MANAGEMENT
10 Alice St.
Binghamton, NY 13904-1580
PH: (800)429-6784
FX: (800)895-0582

Haworth Press, Inc. Quarterly. Individuals, $48.00 per year; institutions, $90.00 per year; libraries, $225.00 per year.

JOURNAL OF RESEARCH IN PHARMACEUTICAL ECONOMICS
10 Alice St.
Binghamton, NY 13904-1580
PH: (800)429-6784
FX: (800)895-0582
Haworth Press, Inc. Quarterly. Individuals, $40.00 per year; institutions, $80.00 per year; libraries, $200.00 per year.

LABORATORY OF ELECTRONICS
Rockefeller University
1230 York Ave.
New York, NY 10021
PH: (212)327-8613
FX: (212)327-7974
E-mail: ros@rockvax.rockefeller.edu
Studies the application of computer engineering and electronics to biomedicine.

LASER BIOMEDICAL RESEARCH CENTER
Massachusetts Institute of Technology
77 Massachusetts Ave.
Cambridge, MA 02139
PH: (617)253-7700
FX: (617)253-4513
Concerned with the medical use of lasers.

LILLY DIGEST
Lilly Corporate Center
Indianapolis, IN 46285
PH: (317)276-3641
FX: (317)276-5985
Eli Lilly and Co. Annual. $30.00. Includes drug store financial data.

LILLY HOSPITAL PHARMACY SURVEY
Lilly Corporate Center
Indianapolis, IN 46285
PH: (317)276-3641
FX: (317)276-5985
Eli Lilly and Co. Annual. $30.00. Includes financial data for drug stores located in hospitals.

MAIL SERVICE PHARMACY MARKET
625 Ave. of the Americas
New York, NY 10011-2002
PH: (800)346-3787
FX: (212)645-7681
FIND/SVP, Inc. 1996. $2,950.00. Provides detailed market data, with forecasts to the year 2000.

MANUFACTURING PROFILES
Washington, DC 20402
PH: (202)512-1800
FX: (202)512-2250
E-mail: gpoaccess@gpo.gov
URL: http://www.access.gpo.gov
Available from U. S. Government Printing Office. Annual. $35.00. Issued by the U. S. Census Bureau. A printed consolidation of the entire *Current Industrial Report* series, presenting "all the data compiled." Contains statistics on production, shipments, inventories, consumption, exports, imports, and orders for a wide variety of manufactured products. (See also Census Bureau home page, http://www.census.gov/.)

THE MARKET FOR GENERIC DRUGS
625 Ave. of the Americas
New York, NY 10011
PH: (800)346-3787
FX: (212)645-7681
FIND/SVP. 1995. $995.00. Market research data. Includes a discus-

sion of current trends in the use of generic prescription drugs to reduce healthcare costs, with forecasts to 1999.

THE MARKET FOR OPHTHALMIC PHARMACEUTICALS
625 Ave. of the Americas
New York, NY 10011-2002
PH: (800)346-3787
FX: (212)807-2716
E-mail: catalog@findsvp.com
URL: http://www.findsvp.com
FIND/SVP, Inc. 1997. $2,500.00. Market research report. Covers topical and internal drugs for eye disorders, with market estimates to the year 2000. Includes pharmaceutical company profiles.

THE MARKET FOR RX-TO-OTC SWITCHED DRUGS
625 Ave. of the Americas
New York, NY 10011-2002
PH: (800)346-3787
FX: (212)807-2716
E-mail: catalog@findsvp.com
URL: http://www.findsvp.com
FIND/SVP, Inc. 1997. $2,500.00. Market research report. Covers the market for over-the-counter drugs that were formerly available only by prescription. Market revenues are estimated to 1999. Includes profiles of relevant pharmaceutical companies.

THE MARKET FOR STRESS MANAGEMENT PRODUCTS AND SERVICES
625 Ave. of the Americas
New York, NY 10011-2002
PH: (800)346-3787
FX: (212)807-2716
E-mail: catalog@findsvp.com
URL: http://www.findsvp.com
Available from FIND/SVP, Inc. 1996. $1,495.00. Market research report published by Marketdata Enterprises. Covers anti-anxiety drugs, stress management clinics, biofeedback centers, devices, seminars, workshops, spas, institutes, etc. Includes market size projections to the year 2000.

MAYO BIOTECHNOLOGY RESEARCH COMPUTER FACILITY
Mayo Clinic
200 First St., S. W.
Rochester, MN 55901
PH: (507)284-4937
FX: (507)284-1632
E-mail: rar@mayo.edu
URL: http://www.mayo.edu/bir-root/home.html
Develops three-dimensional medical imaging systems and software.

MCGRAW-HILL'S BIOTECHNOLOGY NEWSWATCH
1221 Ave. of the Americas
New York, NY 10020
PH: (800)722-4726
FX: (212)512-2821
McGraw-Hill Energy & Business Newsletters. Semimonthly. $825.00 per year. Newsletter.

MEDICAL AND HEALTH CARE BOOKS AND SERIALS IN PRINT: AN INDEX TO LITERATURE IN HEALTH SCIENCES
121 Chanlon Rd.
New Providence, NJ 07974
PH: (800)521-8110
FX: (908)665-6688
R. R. Bowker. Annual. $249.95. Two volumes.

MEDICAL AND HEALTH INFORMATION DIRECTORY
27500 Drake Rd.
Farmington Hills, MI 48331-3535
PH: (800)877-GALE
FX: (248)699-8070
Gale Group. 1997. $569.00. Three volumes. Ninth edition. Volume

one covers medical organizations, agencies, and institutions ($235.00). Volume two includes bibliographic, library, and database information ($235.00). Volume three is a guide to services available for various medical and health problems ($235.00).

MEDICAL RESEARCH CENTRES: A WORLD DIRECTORY OF ORGANIZATIONS AND PROGRAMMES
27500 Drake Rd.
Farmington Hills, MI 48331-3535
PH: (800)877-GALE
FX: (248)699-8070
E-mail: galeord@galegroup.com
URL: http://www.galegroup.com
Gale Group. Irregular. $595.00. Two volumes. Published by The Longman Group. Contains profiles of about 9,000 medical research facilities around the world. Includes medical, dental, nursing, pharmaceutical, psychiatric, and surgical research centers.

MEDICAL SCIENCES INTERNATIONAL WHO'S WHO
345 Park Ave., S., 10th Fl.
New York, NY 10010
PH: (800)221-2123
FX: (212)689-9711
Groves Dictionaries. 1996. $595.00. Sixth edition. Volume seven. Provides biographical data for over 8,000 international figures active in medical research. Published in England by Longman.

MEDLINE
National Library of Medicine
8600 Rockville Pike
Bethesda, MD 20894
PH: (800)638-8480
FX: (301)480-3537
Medlars Management Section. Provides indexing and abstracting of worldwide medical literature, 1966 to date. Inquire as to online cost and availability.

MILESTONES IN BIOTECHNOLOGY
225 Wildwood Ave.
Worburn, MA 01081
PH: (800)366-2665
FX: (617)933-6333
Julian Davies and William Reznikoff, editors. Butterworth-Heinemann. 1992. $42.95. A collection of papers providing historical perspective on the development of biotechnology and genetic engineering.

MOLECULAR BIOLOGY INSTITUTE
University of California, Los Angeles
405 Hilgard Ave.
Los Angeles, CA 90024-1570
PH: (310)206-6298
FX: (310)206-7286
E-mail: berk@ewald.mbi.ucla.edu

MOSBY'S GENRX: ELECTRONIC EDITION
11830 Westline Industrial Drive
St. Louis, MO 63143
PH: (800)426-4545
FX: (800)535-9935
URL: http://www.mosby.com
Mosby Year Book, Inc. Annual. $165.00. The CD-ROM version of *Mosby's GenRx: The Complete Reference for Generic and Brand Drugs*. Contains detailed descriptions of generic and brand name prescription drugs, with additonal information on drug interactions.

MOSBY'S GENRX: THE COMPLETE REFERENCE FOR GENERIC AND BRAND DRUGS
11830 Westline Industrial Drive
St. Louis, MO 63143
PH: (800)426-4545
FX: (800)535-9935
URL: http://www.mosby.com
Mosby Year Book, Inc. Annual. $64.95. Provides detailed informa-

tion on a wide variety of generic and brand name prescription drugs. Includes color identification pictures, prescribing data, and price comparisons. Formerly *Physicians GenRx*.

NARCOTIC DRUGS: ESTIMATED WORLD REQUIREMENTS
Two United Nations Plaza
Rm. DC2-853
New York, NY 10017
PH: (800)253-9646
FX: (212)963-3489
International Narcotics Control Board. United Nations Publications. Annual. Price varies. Includes production and utilization data relating to legal narcotics. Text in French, English and Spanish.

NARCOTICS AND DRUG ABUSE A TO Z
10951 Sorrento Valley Rd., Suite 1-D
San Diego, CA 92121-1613
PH: (800)441-4033
FX: (800)809-0334
Croner Publications, Inc. Three volumes. Price on application. Lists treatment centers.

NATIONAL ASSOCIATION OF BOARDS OF PHARMACY
700 Busse Highway
Park Ridge, IL 60068
PH: (847)698-6227
FX: (847)698-0124

NATIONAL ASSOCIATION OF CHAIN DRUG STORES
c/o Ronald L. Ziegler
P.O. Box 1417-D49
Alexandria, VA 22313-1417
PH: (703)549-3001
FX: (703)836-4869

NATIONAL ASSOCIATION OF CHAIN DRUG STORES - MEMBERSHIP DIRECTORY
413 Lee St.
Alexandria, VA 22313
PH: (703)549-3001
National Association of Chain Drug Stores. Annual. $500.00. About 150 chain drug retailers and their 27,000 individual pharmacies; 900 supplier companies; state boards of pharmacy, pharmaceutical and retail associations, colleges of pharmacy; drug trade associations.

NATIONAL ASSOCIATION OF PHARMACEUTICAL MANUFACTURERS
320 Old Country Rd., Suite 205
Garden City, NY 11530-1752
PH: (516)741-3699
FX: (516)741-3696

NATIONAL ASSOCIATION OF WHOLESALER-DISTRIBUTORS
1725 K St., N.W.
Washington, DC 20006
PH: (202)872-0885
FX: (202)785-0586

NATIONAL BUREAU OF ECONOMIC RESEARCH, INC.
1050 Massachusetts Ave.
Cambridge, MA 02138-5398
PH: (617)868-3900
FX: (617)868-7194
E-mail: lcary@atsnber.org
URL: http://www.nber.org

NATIONAL COUNCIL FOR PRESCRIPTION DRUG PROGRAMS
4201 N. 24th St., Suite 365
Phoenix, AZ 85016
PH: (602)957-9105
FX: (602)955-0749

Concerned with standardization of third party prescription drug programs.

NATIONAL DRUG TRADE CONFERENCE
c/o Gerald J. Mossinghoff
1110 15th St., N.W.
Washington, DC 20005
PH: (202)835-3420
FX: (202)855-3429

NATIONAL LIBRARY OF MEDICINE (NLM)
PH: (888)346-3656
FX: (301)480-3537
E-mail: access@nlm.nih.gov
URL: http://www.nlm.nih.gov
National Institutes of Health (NIH). NLM Web site offers free access through MEDLINE ("PubMed") to about nine million references to articles appearing in some 3,800 biomedical journals, with abstracts. Search interfaces range from "simple keywords to advanced Boolean expressions." The NLM site offers many links to other sources of biomedical and technical information (the National Center for Biotechnology Information, for example). Fees: Free.

NATIONAL PHARMACEUTICAL ASSOCIATION
The Courtyard Office Complex
107 Kilmayne Dr., Suite C
Cary, NC 27511
PH: (800)944-6742
FX: (919)469-5870
A professional society of African-American pharmacists and pharmacy students.

NATIONAL PHARMACEUTICAL COUNCIL
1894 Preston White Dr.
Reston, VA 22091
PH: (703)620-6390
FX: (703)476-0904
Members are drug manufacturers producing prescription medication.

NATIONAL WHOLESALE DRUGGISTS' ASSOCIATION
1821 Michael Faraday Dr., Suite 400
Reston, VA 20190
PH: (703)787-0000
FX: (703)787-6930
URL: http://www.nwda.org

NDA PIPELINE
5550 Friendship Blvd., Suite One
Chevy Chase, MD 20815-7278
PH: (800)332-2181
FX: (301)664-7248
E-mail: fdcr@fdcr.com
URL: http://www.fdcr.com
F-D-C Reports, Inc. Annual. $750.00. Provides information on U. S. drugs in the development stage and products receiving new drug approval (NDA) from the Food and Drug Administration. Listings are company-by-company and by generic name, with orphan drug designations. Includes an industry directory.

NONPRESCRIPTION DRUG MANUFACTURERS ASSOCIATION
1150 Connecticut Ave., N. W.
Washington, DC 20036
PH: (202)429-9260
FX: (202)223-6835
Members are over-the-counter drug manufacturers and suppliers.

NTIS ALERTS: BIOMEDICAL TECHNOLOGY & HUMAN FACTORS ENGINEERING
U. S. Department of Commerce
5285 Port Royal Rd.
Technology Administration
Springfield, VA 22161

PH: (800)553-6847
FX: (703)321-8547
National Technical Information Service. Semimonthly. 145.00 per year. Formerly *Abstract Newsletter*. Provides descriptions of government-sponsored research reports and software, with ordering information. Covers biotechnology, ergonomics, bionics, artificial intelligence, prosthetics, and related subjects.

NWDA OPERATING SURVEY
Reston, VA 22090-5348
PH: (703)787-0000
FX: (703)787-6930
National Wholesale Druggists' Association. Annual. Members, $30.00; non-members, $295.00. A 48-page report of financial and operating ratios for the wholesale drug industry.

OCCUPATIONAL HEALTH AND SAFETY
3700 J.H. Kultgen Freeway
Waco, TX 76706
PH: (817)776-9000
FX: (817)776-9018
Stevens Publishing Corp. Monthly. $69.00 per year. Includes news, interviews, feature articles, legal developments, and reviews of literature. Contains *Buyer's Guide.*

OCCUPATIONAL HEALTH AND SAFETY LETTER...TOWARDS PRODUCTIVITY AND PEACE OF MIND
951 Pershing Dr.
Silver Spring, MD 20910-4464
PH: (800)274-0122
FX: (301)585-9075
E-mail: bpinews@bpinews.com
URL: http://www.bpinews.com
Business Publishers, Inc. Biweekly. $273.00 per year.

OCCUPATIONAL HEALTH AND SAFETY PURCHASING SOURCEBOOK
3700 J.H. Kultgen Freeway
Waco, TX 76706
PH: (817)776-9000
FX: (817)776-9018
Stevens Publishing Corp. Annual. $69.00. Over 1,500 manufacturers, distributors and consultants of poducts and services in the field of safety, health and environmental protection.

PATTY'S INDUSTRIAL HYGIENE AND TOXICOLOGY
605 Third Ave.
New York, NY 10158-0012
PH: (800)225-5945
FX: (212)850-6088
George D. Clayton and Florence E. Clayton, editors. John Wiley and Sons, Inc. 1996. $2,195.00. Three volumes in 10 parts. Provides broad coverage of environmental factors and stresses affecting the health of workers. Contains detailed information on the effects of specific substances.

PDR GENERICS: THE INFORMATION STANDARD FOR PRESCRIPTION DRUGS
Five Paragon Drive
Montvale, NJ 07645-1742
PH: (800)232-7379
FX: (201)573-4956
Medical Economics Publishing Co., Inc. Annual. $79.95. Contains brand names, average wholesale prices, therapeutic/pharmacologic/prescribing information, indications index, and other data for 24,000 prescription drugs. Both brand name and generic products are included. Provides 1,000 color photographs for drug identification.

PDR GUIDE TO DRUG INTERACTIONS, SIDE EFFECTS, INDICATIONS
Five Paragon Drive
Montvale, NJ 07645-1742

PH: (800)232-7379
FX: (201)573-4956
American Medical Association. Medical Economics Co., Inc. Annual. $48.95. Includes a list of prescription drugs by "precise clinical situation."

PHARMA MARKETLETTER
54-55 Wilton Rd.
London SW1V 1DE, England
PH: (171) 8287272
FX: (4 1)1 828041
Marketletter Publications Ltd. Weekly. $1,000.00 per year. Newsletter. Formerly *Marketletter*.

PHARMACEUTICAL ENGINEERING
3816 W. Linebaugh Ave., Suite 412
Tampa, FL 33624-4702
PH: (813)960-2105
FX: (813)264-2816
E-mail: ispehq@ispe.org
URL: http://www.ispe.org
International Society for Pharmaceutical Engineering, Inc. Bimonthly. $30.00 per year. Feature articles provide practical application and specification information on the design, construction, supervision and maintenance of process equipment, plant systems, instrumentation and pharmaceutical facilities.

PHARMACEUTICAL EXECUTIVE: A GLOBAL BUSINESS AND MARKETING PUBLICATION
7500 Old Oak Blvd.
Cleveland, OH 44130
PH: (800)346-0085
FX: (216)891-2726
URL: http://www.advanstar.com
Advanstar Communications, Inc. Monthly. $64.00 per year.

PHARMACEUTICAL LITIGATION REPORTER: THE NATIONAL JOURNAL OF RECORD OF PHARMACEUTICAL LITIGATION
175 Strafford Ave., Bldg. 4, Suite 140
Wayne, PA 19087
PH: (800)345-1101
FX: (610)622-0501
Andrews Publications. Monthly. $750.00 per year. Reports on a wide variety of legal cases involving the pharmaceutical and medical device industries. Includes product liability lawsuits.

PHARMACEUTICAL MARKETERS DIRECTORY
7200 W. Camino Real, Suite 215
Boca Raton, FL 33433
PH: (407)368-9301
FX: (407)368-7870
E-mail: pmd@cpsnet.com
URL: http://www.cpsnet.com
CPS Communications, Inc. Annual. $155.00. About 15,000 personnel of pharmaceutical, medical products and equipment, and biotechnology companies; advertising agencies with clients in the medical field; health care publications; alternative media and medical industry suppliers.

PHARMACEUTICAL MARKETING IN THE 21ST CENTURY
10 Alice St.
Binghamton, NY 13904-1580
PH: (800)429-6784
FX: (800)895-0582
E-mail: getinfo@haworth.com
URL: http://www.haworth.com
Mickey C. Smith, editor. Haworth Press, Inc. 1996. $49.95. Various authors discuss the marketing, pricing, distribution, and retailing of prescription drugs. (Also published in the *Journal of Pharmaceutical Marketing and Management*, vol. 10.)

PHARMACEUTICAL MARKETING AND MANAGEMENT RESEARCH DIVISION
University of Mississippi
Rm. 101
Waller Lab Complex
University, MS 38677
PH: (601)232-5948
FX: (601)232-5262
E-mail: ribfb@atsolemiss.edu
URL: http://www.olemiss.edu/depts/rips/pmmrp/

PHARMACEUTICAL NEWS INDEX
300 N. Zeeb Rd.
Ann Arbor, MI 48103
PH: (800)521-0600
FX: (800)864-0019
URL: http://www.umi.com
UMI. Indexes major pharmaceutical industry newsletters, 1974 to present. Weekly updates. Inquire as to online cost and availability.

PHARMACEUTICAL PROCESSING
P.O. Box 650
Morris Plains, NJ 07950-0650
PH: (973)292-5100
FX: (973)898-9281
Gordon Publications. Monthly. $40.00 per year. Formerly *Pharmaceutical and Cosmetic Equipment*.

PHARMACEUTICAL RESEARCH AND MANUFACTURERS ASSOCIATION
1100 15th St., N.W.
Washington, DC 20005
PH: (202)835-3400
FX: (202)835-3429

PHARMACEUTICAL RESEARCH MANUFACTURERS ASSOCIATION ANNUAL FACT BOOK
1100 15th St. NW, Suite 900
Washington, DC 20005
PH: (202)835-3400
FX: (202)835-3429
Pharmaceutical Rearch and Manufacturers Association. Annual.

PHARMACEUTICAL TECHNOLOGY
7500 Old Oak Blvd.
Cleveland, OH 44130
PH: (800)346-0085
FX: (216)891-2726
URL: http://www.advanstar.com
Advanstar Communications, Inc. Monthly. $64.00 per year. Practical hands on information about the manufacture of pharmaceutical products, focusing on applied technology.

PHARMACOLOGICAL AND CHEMICAL SYNONYMS: A COLLECTION OF NAMES OF DRUGS, PESTICIDES, AND OTHER COMPOUNDS DRAWN FROM THE MEDICAL LITERATURE OF THE WORLD
655 Ave. of the Americas
New York, NY 100010
PH: (888)437-4636
FX: (212)633-3680
E-mail: usinfo-f@elsevier.com
URL: http://www.elsevier.com
E. E. Marler. Elsevier Science. 1994. $292.00. Tenth edition.

PHARMACOLOGY RESEARCH LABORATORY
Indiana University-Purdue University at Indianapolis
635 Barnhill Dr.
School of Medicine
Indianapolis, IN 46202-5120
PH: (317)274-7844
FX: (317)274-7714
E-mail: besch@indiana.edu

PHARMACOPEIAL FORUM
12601 Twinbrook Parkway
Rockville, MD 20852
PH: (800)227 8772
FX: (310)816-8247
URL: http://www.usp.org
United States Pharmacopeial Convention. Bimonthly. $310.00 per year.

PHELON'S DISCOUNT/JOBBING TRADE
330 Main St.
Ridgefield Park, NJ 07022-1228
PH: (800)234-8804
FX: (201)440-8568
Kenneth W. Phelon, Jr., editor. Phelon, Sheldon and Marsar, Inc. Biennial. $175.00. Up-to-date information on the discount and mass merchandising chains, clubs, outlets, stores and warehouses throughout the United States. Also wholesalers, jobbers and distributors of all kinds of goods. Formerly *Phelon's Discount Stores.*

PHYSICIANS' DESK REFERENCE
Five Paragon Drive
Montvale, NJ 07645-1742
PH: (800)232-7379
FX: (201)573-4956
Medical Economics Co., Inc. Annual. $74.95. Generally known as "PDR". Provides detailed descriptions, effects, and adverse reactions for about 3,000 prescription drugs. Includes data on more than 250 drug manufacturers, with brand name and generic name indexes and drug identification photographs. Discontinued drugs are also listed.

PHYSICIANS' DESK REFERENCE LIBRARY ON CD-ROM
Five Paragon Drive
Montvale, NJ 07645
PH: (800)232-7379
FX: (201)573-4956
Medical Economics. Three times a year. $595.00 per year. Contains the CD-ROM equivalent of *Physicians' Desk Reference (PDR), Physicians' Desk Reference for Nonprescription Drugs, Physicians' Desk Reference for Opthalmology,* and other PDR publications.

PHYSICIANS' DESK REFERENCE FOR
NONPRESCRIPTION DRUGS
Five Paragon Drive
Montvale, NJ 07645-1742
PH: (800)222-3045
FX: (201)573-4956
Medical Economics Co., Inc. Annual. $43.95. Contains detailed descriptions of "commonly used" over-the-counter drug products. Includes drug identification photographs. Indexing is by product category, product name, manufacturer, and active ingredient.

PHYSICIANS' DESK REFERENCE FOR
OPHTHALMOLOGY
Five Paragon Drive
Montvale, NJ 07645-1742
PH: (800)232-7379
FX: (201)573-4956
Medical Economics Publishing Co., Inc. Irregular. $39.95. Provides detailed descriptions of ophthalmological instrumentation, equipment, supplies, lenses, and prescription drugs. Indexed by manufacturer, product name, product category, active drug ingredient, and instrumentation. Editorial discussion is included.

THE PINK SHEET: PRESCRIPTION PHARMACEUTICALS
AND BIOTECHNOLOGY
5550 Friendship Blvd., Suite One
Chevy Chase, MD 20815-7278
PH: (800)332-2181
FX: (301)664-7248
E-mail: fdcr@fdcr.com
URL: http://www.fdcr.com
F-D-C Reports, Inc. Weekly. $850.00 per year. Newsletter on the pharmaceutical industry, including biotechnology. Covers regula-

tions, new products, research, generic drugs, mergers, and pharmaceutical company news, with financial information (F-D-C Stock Index).

PLUNKETT'S RETAIL INDUSTRY ALMANAC:
COMPLETE PROFILES ON THE RETAIL 500--THE
LEADING FIRMS IN RETAIL STORES, SERVICES,
CATALOGS, AND ON-LINE SALES
1033 La Posada Drive, Suite 250
Austin, TX 78752
PH: (800)486-8666
FX: (512)374-4501
E-mail: orders@hoovers.com
URL: http://www.hoovers.com
Available from Hoover's, Inc. Annual. $136.49. Published by Plunkett Research. Provides detailed profiles of 500 major U. S. retailers. Industry trends are discussed.

PREDICASTS F & S INDEX UNITED STATES
362 Lakeside Dr.
Foster City, CA 94404
PH: (800)321-6388
FX: (650)358-4759
E-mail: cemarketing@iacnet.com
URL: http://w.iacnet.com
Information Access Co. Monthly, with quarterly and annual cumulations. $975.00 per year. Provides citations to U. S. business, marketing, and industrial material appearing in a large assortment of trade journals, newspapers, and other publications. Arranged by expanded Standard Industrial Classification (SIC) number and by company name. Originally known as *Funk & Scott Index.*

PRIVATE LABEL FOODS AND BEVERAGES
625 Ave. of the Americas
New York, NY 10011-2002
PH: (800)346-3787
FX: (212)807-2716
E-mail: catalog@findsvp.com
URL: http://www.findsvp.com
Available from FIND/SVP, Inc. 1996. $2,150.00. Market research report published by Packaged Facts. Covers the private label market relative to food stores, drug stores, and mass merchandise stores.

PRIVATE LABEL INTERNATIONAL: THE MAGAZINE
FOR STORE LABELS (OWN BRANDS) AND GENERICS
2125 Center Ave., Suite 305
Fort Lee, NJ 07024-5859
PH: (201)592-7007
FX: (201)592-7171
E. W. Williams Publications Co. Quarterly. $20.00 per year. Edited for large chain store buyers and for manufacturers of private label products.

PRIVATE LABEL MANUFACTURERS ASSOCIATION
369 Lexington Ave.
New York, NY 10017
PH: (212)972-3131
FX: (212)983-1382
Members are manufacturers, wholesalers, and retailers of private brand products. Seeks to promote the private label industry.

PRIVATE LABEL NEWS
252 W. Swamp Rd., Suite 13
Doylestown, PA 18901
PH: (215)230-4400
FX: (215)230-4401
Certified Publishers, Inc. Eight times a year. $40.00 per year. Covers new private label product developments for chain stores. Formerly *Private Label Product News.*

PRIVATE LABEL: THE MAGAZINE FOR HOUSE BRANDS
AND GENERICS
2125 Center Ave., Suite 305
Fort Lee, NJ 07024-5859

PH: (201)592-7007
FX: (201)592-7171
E. W. Williams Publications Co. Bimonthly. $33.00 per year. Edited for buyers of private label, controlled packer, and generic-labeled products. Concentrates on food, health and beauty aids, and general merchandise.

PROMT: PREDICASTS OVERVIEW OF MARKETS AND TECHNOLOGY
27500 Drake Rd.
Farmington Hills, MI 48331-3535
PH: (800)877-GALE
FX: (248)699-8070
E-mail: galeord@galegroup.com
URL: http://www.galegroup.com
Gale Group. Companies, products, applied technologies and markets. U.S. and international literature coverage, 1972 to date. Daily updates. Inquire as to online cost and availability. Provides abstracts from more than 1,500 publications.

PSYCHOTROPIC SUBSTANCES
Two United Nations Plaza
Rm. DC2-853
New York, NY 10017
PH: (800)253-9646
FX: (212)963-3489
United Nations Publications. Annual. $42.00.

QUARTERLY FINANCIAL REPORT FOR MANUFACTURING, MINING, AND TRADE CORPORATIONS
Washington, DC 20402
PH: (202)512-1800
FX: (202)512-2250
U.S. Federal Trade Commission and U.S. Securities and Exchange Commission. Available from U.S. Government Printing Office. Quarterly. $33.00 per year.

R M A ANNUAL STATEMENT STUDIES, INCLUDING COMPARATIVE HISTORICAL DATA AND OTHER SOURCES OF COMPOSITE FINANCIAL DATA
One Liberty Place, Suite 2300
1650 Market St.
Philadelphia, PA 19103
PH: (800)677-7621
FX: (215)446-4100
URL: http://www.rmahq.org
Robert Morris Associates: The Association of Lending and Credit Risk Professionals. Annual. $125.00. Median and quartile financial ratios are given for over 400 kinds of manufacturing, wholesale, retail, construction, and consumer finance establishments. Data is sorted by both asset size and sales volume. Includes a clearly written "Definition of Ratios," a bibliography of financial ratio sources, and an alphabetical industry index.

THE RED BOOK
Five Paragon Dr.
Montvale, NJ 07645-1742
PH: (800)222-3045
FX: (201)573-4956
URL: http://www.medec.com
Medical Economics Co., Inc. Annual. $54.95 for basic volume or $99.00 per year with monthly updates. Provides product information and prices for more than 100,000 prescription and nonprescription drugs and other items sold by pharmacies. Also known as *Drug Topics Red Book*.

REPORT OF THE INTERNATIONAL NARCOTICS CONTROL BOARD ON ITS WORK
Two United Nations Plaza
Rm. DC2-853
New York, NY 10017
PH: (800)253-9646
FX: (212)963-3489

United Nations Publications. Annual. $20.00.

RETAIL INSTITUTE
Purdue University
1262 Matthews Hall
West Lafayette, IN 47907-1262
PH: (317)494-8301
FX: (317)494-0869
E-mail: xdj1@vm.cc.purdue.edu
URL: http://www.purdue.edu
An integral unit of the Department of Consumer Sciences and Retailing in the School of Consumer and Family Sciences. Does custom research in retailing and predicts trends in consumer behavior and the retail industry.

RETAIL MONITOR INTERNATIONAL
122 South Michigan Ave., Suite 1200
Chicago, IL 60603
PH: (800)577-3876
FX: (312)922-1157
E-mail: info@euromonitor.com
URL: http://www.euromonitor.com
Euromonitor International. Monthly. $1,090.00 per year. Covers many aspects of international retailing, with emphasis on market research data. Includes profiles of leading retail groups, country profiles, retail news, trends, consumer credit information, and "Retail Factfile" (statistics).

RXLIST: THE INTERNET DRUG INDEX
PH: (707)746-8754
E-mail: info@rxlist.com
URL: http://www.rxlist.com
Neil Sandow. Web site features detailed information (cost, usage, dosage, side effects, etc.) from Mosby, Inc. for about 300 major pharmaceutical products, representing two thirds of prescriptions filled in the U. S. (3,700 other products are listed). The "Top 200" drugs are ranked by number of prescriptions filled. Keyword searching is provided. Fees: Free.

SAFETY AND HEALTH AT WORK
1828 L St., N.W., Suite 801
Washington, DC 20036
PH: (202)653-7652
FX: (202)653-7687
E-mail: webinfo@ilo.org
URL: http://www.ilo.org
International Labor Office. Bimonthly. $240.00 per year. Formerly *Occupational Safety and Health Abstracts*.

SALK INSTITUTE FOR BIOLOGICAL STUDIES
P.O. Box 85800
San Diego, CA 92186-5800
PH: (619)453-4100
FX: (619)552-8285

SCIENCE CITATION INDEX
3501 Market St.
Philadelphia, PA 19104
PH: (800)386-4474
FX: (215)386-2991
Institute for Scientific Information. Bimonthly. $15,020.00 per year. Annual cumulation.

SCIENCE CITATION INDEX: COMPACT DISC EDITION
3501 Market St.
Philadelphia, PA 19104
PH: (800)523-1850
FX: (215)386-2911
Institute for Scientific Information. Quarterly. $10,950.00 per year. ($5,300.00 to hard copy subscribers.) Provides CD-ROM indexing of the world's scientific and technical literature from 1986 to date. Corresponds to online *Scisearch* and printed *Science Citation Index*.

SCISEARCH
3501 Market St.
Philadelphia, PA 19104
PH: (800)523-1850
FX: (215)386-2911
URL: http://www.isinet.com
Institute for Scientific Information. Broad, multidisciplinary index to the literature of science and technology, 1974 to present. Inquire as to online cost and availability. Coverage of literature is worldwide, with weekly updates.

STANDARD & POOR'S INDUSTRY SURVEYS
25 Broadway
New York, NY 10004-1010
PH: (800)221-5277
FX: (212)208-0040
E-mail: speqwebmaster@mcgraw-hill.com
URL: http://www.stockinfo.standardpoor.com
Standard & Poor's. Semiannual. $2,250.00 per year. Two looseleaf volumes. Provides detailed, individual surveys of 52 major industry groups. Each survey is revised on a semiannual basis. Also includes "Monthly Investment Review" (industry group investment analysis) and monthly "Trends & Projections" (economic analysis).

STANDARD & POOR'S STATISTICAL SERVICE.
CURRENT STATISTICS
25 Broadway
New York, NY 10004
PH: (800)221-5277
FX: (212)412-0040
Standard & Poor's. Monthly. $655.00 per year. Includes 10 Basic Statistics sections, Current Statistics Supplements and Annual Security Price Index Record.

STATISTICS ON ALCOHOL, DRUG, AND TOBACCO USE
27500 Drake Rd.
Farmington Hills, MI 48331-3535
PH: (800)877-GALE
FX: (248)699-8070
Gale Group. 1996. $55.00. Includes graphs, charts, and tables arranged within subject chapters. Citations to data sources are provided.

STATISTICS OF INCOME: CORPORATION INCOME TAX
RETURNS
Washington, DC 20402
PH: (202)512-1800
FX: (202)512-2250
U.S. Internal Revenue Service. Available from U.S. Government Printing Office. Annual. $20.00.

STORES
Financial Executives Div.
325 Seventh St., N.W., Suite 1000
Washington, DC 20004-2802
PH: (800)673-4692
FX: (202)626-8191
National Retail Federation. N R F Enterprises, Inc. Monthly. $49.00 per year.

SUBSTANCE ABUSE: A COMPREHENSIVE TEXTBOOK
351 W. Camden St.
Baltimore, MD 21202
PH: (800)527-5597
FX: (410)528-4422
E-mail: custserv@wilkins.com
URL: http://www.wwilkins.com
Joyce H. Lowinson and others. Williams & Wilkins. 1997. Third edition. Price on application. Covers the medical, psychological, socioeconomic, and public health aspects of drug and alcohol abuse.

SURVEY OF CURRENT BUSINESS
Washington, DC 20402

PH: (202)512-1800
FX: (202)512-2250
E-mail: gpoaccess@gpo.gov
URL: http://www.access.gpo.gov
Available from U. S. Government Printing Office. Monthly. $35.00 per year. Issued by Bureau of Economic Analysis, U. S. Department of Commerce. Presents a wide variety of business and economic data.

THE TAN SHEET: NONPRESCRIPTION
PHARMACEUTICALS AND NUTRITIONALS
5550 Friendship Blvd., Suite One
Chevy Chase, MD 20815-7278
PH: (800)332-2181
FX: (301)664-7248
E-mail: fdcr@fdcr.com
URL: http://www.fdcr.com
F-D-C Reports, Inc. Weekly. $740.00 per year. Newsletter. Covers prescription to nonprescription (Rx-to-OTC) changes in drug status and other news, trends, and regulations affecting over-the-counter drugs and dietary supplements.

TOXLINE
8600 Rockville Pike
Bethesda, MD 20894
PH: (800)638-8480
FX: (301)480-3537
National Library of Medicine. Abstracting service covering human and animal toxicity studies, 1981 to present (older studies available in *Toxback* file). Monthly updates. Inquire as to online cost and availability.

TRADE & INDUSTRY INDEX
27500 Drake Rd.
Farmington Hills, MI 48331-3535
PH: (800)877-GALE
FX: (248)699-8070
E-mail: galeord@galegroup.com
URL: http://www.galegroup.com
Gale Group. Provides indexing of business periodicals, January 1981 to date. Daily updates. (Full text articles from some periodicals are available online, 1983 to date, in the companion database, *Trade & Industry ASAP*.) Please inquire about online cost and availability.

THE TREATMENT OF MENTAL ILLNESS IN AN
EVOLVING HEALTH CARE SYSTEM
625 Ave. of the Americas
New York, NY 10011-2002
PH: (800)346-3787
FX: (212)807-2716
E-mail: catalog@findsvp.com
URL: http://www.findsvp.com
Available from FIND/SVP, Inc. 1997. $995.00. Market research report published by Theta Corporation. Provides market data on drugs and therapy used for treatment of mood, anxiety, and psychotic disorders. Includes pharmaceutical company profiles and forecasts to the year 2001.

U. S. INDUSTRY AND TRADE OUTLOOK
1221 Ave. of the Americas
New York, NY 10020
PH: (800)722-4726
FX: (212)512-2821
E-mail: customer.service@mcgraw-hill.com
URL: http://www.mcgraw-hill.com
McGraw-Hill. Annual. $69.95. Produced by the International Trade Administration, U. S. Department of Commerce, in a "public-private" partnership with DRI/McGraw-Hill and Standard & Poor's. Provides basic data, outlook for the current year, and "Long-Term Prospects" (five-year projections) for a wide variety of products and services. Includes high technology industries. Formerly *U. S. Industrial Outlook*.

UNITED STATES PHARMACOPEIA NATIONAL FORMULARY
12601 Twinbrook Parkway
Rockville, MD 20852
PH: (800)227-8772
FX: (301)816-8247
URL: http://www.usp.org
United States Pharmacopeial Convention. Continuously revised. Price on application.

UNITED STATES PHARMACOPEIAL
12601 Twinbrook Parkway
Rockville, MD 20852-1790
PH: (800)227-8772
FX: (301)816-8247
E-mail: external/affairs@usp.org
URL: http://www.usp.org

UPJOHN CENTER FOR CLINICAL PHARMACOLOGY
3709 Upjohn Center
University Medical Center
Ann Arbor, MI 48109-0504
PH: (313)764-9121
FX: (313)763-3438

USAN AND THE USP DICTIONARY OF DRUG NAMES
12601 Twinbrook Parkway
Rockville, MD 20852
PH: (800)227-8772
FX: (301)816-8247
URL: http://www.usp.org
United States Pharmacopeial Convention. Annual. $105.00. Adopted names, brand names, compendial and other generic names, CAS Registry Numbers, molecular weights, and other information.

VALUE RETAIL NEWS: THE JOURNAL OF OUTLET AND OFF-PRICE RETAIL AND DEVELOPMENT
P.O. Box 17209
Clearwater, FL 34622
PH: (800)344-6397
FX: (813)536-4389
Off-Price Specialists, Inc. Monthly. $144.00 per year. Provides news of the off-price and outlet store industry. Emphasis is on real estate for outlet store centers.

WEFA INDUSTRIAL MONITOR
605 Third Ave.
New York, NY 10158-0012
PH: (800)225-5945
FX: (212)850-6088
E-mail: business@jwiley.
URL: http://www.wiley.com
John Wiley and Sons, Inc. Annual. $59.95. Prepared by industry analysts at WEFA, an economic forecasting and consulting firm (originally Wharton Econometric Forecasting Associates). Contains discussions of the outlook for major U. S. industries, with many 10-year forecasts (WEFA Web site is http://www.wefa.com).

WHO'S WHO IN SCIENCE AND ENGINEERING
121 Chanlon Rd.
New Providence, NJ 07974
PH: (800)521-8110
FX: (908)665-6688
E-mail: info@reedref.com
URL: http://www.reedref.com
Marquis Who's Who, Reed Reference Publishing. Biennial. $272.95. Provides concise biographical information on 23,600 prominent engineers and scientists. International coverage, with geographical and professional indexes.

WHO'S WHO IN TECHNOLOGY
27500 Drake Rd.
Farmington Hills, MI 48331-3535

PH: (800)877-GALE
FX: (248)699-8070
Gale Group. 1995. $195.00. Seventh edition. Covers the fields of electronics, computer science, physics, optics, chemistry, biotechnology, mechanics, energy, and earth science.

WILSONDISC: BIOLOGICAL AND AGRICULTURAL INDEX
950 University Ave.
Bronx, NY 10452
PH: (800)367-6770
FX: (718)590-1617
H. W. Wilson Co. Monthly. $1,495.00 per year, including unlimited online access to *Biological and Agricultural Index* through WILSONLINE. Provides CD-ROM indexing of over 200 periodicals covering agriculture, agricultural chemicals, biochemistry, biotechnology, entomology, horticulture, and related topics.

WILSONDISC: WILSON BUSINESS ABSTRACTS
950 University Ave.
Bronx, NY 10452
PH: (800)367-6770
FX: (718)590-1617
E-mail: hwwmsg@info.hwwilson.com
URL: http://www.hwwilson.com
H. W. Wilson Co. Monthly. $2,495.00 per year, including unlimited online access to *Wilson Business Abstracts* through WILSONLINE. Provides CD-ROM "cover-to-cover" abstracting and indexing of over 400 prominent business periodicals. Indexing is from 1982, abstracting from 1990. (*Business Periodicals Index* without abstracts is available on CD-ROM at $1,495 per year.)

WILSONLINE: APPLIED SCIENCE AND TECHNOLOGY ABSTRACTS
950 University Ave.
Bronx, NY 10452
PH: (800)367-6770
FX: (718)590-1617
E-mail: hwwmsg@info.hwwilson.com
URL: http://www.hwwilson.com
H. W. Wilson Co. Provides online indexing and abstracting of 400 major scientific, technical, industrial, and engineering periodicals. Time period is 1983 to date for indexing and 1993 to date for abstracting, with updating twice a week. Inquire as to online cost and availability.

WILSONLINE: WILSON BUSINESS ABSTRACTS
950 University Ave.
Bronx, NY 10452
PH: (800)367-6770
FX: (718)590-1617
E-mail: hwwmsg@info.hwwilson.com
URL: http://ww.hwwilson.com
H. W. Wilson Co. Indexes and abstracts 400 major business periodicals, plus the *Wall Street Journal* and the business section of the *New York Times*. Indexing is from 1982, abstracting from 1990, with the two newspapers included from 1993. Updated daily. Inquire as to online cost and availability. (*Business Periodicals Index* without abstracts is also available online.)

WORLD MARKETING FORECASTS ON CD-ROM
27500 Drake Rd.
Farmington Hills, MI 48331-3535
PH: (800)877-GALE
FX: (248)699-8070
E-mail: galeord@galegroup.com
URL: http://www.galegroup.com
Available from Gale Group. Annual. $1,990.00. Produced by Euromonitor. Provides detailed forecast data for the years to 2010 on CD-ROM for 54 countries in all parts of the world. Covers a wide range of social, demographic, economic, and market factors. Includes specific forecasts for many kinds of consumer products.

WORST PILLS BEST PILLS NEWS
1600 20th St., N. W.
Washington, DC 20009
PH: (202)833-2000
FX: (202)296-1727
Public Citizen. Monthly. $16.00 per year. Newsletter. Provides pharmaceutical news and information for consumers, with an emphasis on harmful drug interactions.

Information presented in this chapter is adapted from Gale's *Trade Shows Worldwide* (*TSW*) or, where appropriate, from Gale's *Encyclopedia of Associations* (industry conferences). Entries present information needed for all those planning to visit or to participate in trade shows for the Pharmaceuticals sector. *TSW* entries include U.S. and international shows and exhibitions as well as companies, organizations, and information sources relating to the trade industry. Events, such as conferences and conventions, are included only if they feature exhibitions.

Entries are arranged in alphabetical order by the name of the event and include the exhibition management company with full contact information, frequency of the event, audience, principal exhibits, dates and locations, and former name of the show (if applicable).

ACADEMY OF PHARMACEUTICAL RESEARCH AND SCIENCE CONVENTION

c/o Naomi U. Kaminsky
2215 Constitution Ave. NW
American Pharmaceutical Association
Washington, DC 20037
PH: (202)628-4410
TF: (800)237-2742
FX: (202)628-0443
Frequency: Annual. **Principal Exhibits:** Pharmaceutical equipment, supplies, and services.

ALIMAQ - INTERNATIONAL EXHIBITION OF MACHINERY FOR THE FOOD, PHARMACEUTICAL, PACKAGING, AND REFRIGERATION EQUIPMENT INDUSTRIES

Rua Brasilio Machado, 60
01230-905 Sao Paulo, SP, Brazil
PH: 55 11 8269111
FX: 55 11 8256043
E-mail: amfp@alcantara.com.br
URL: http://www.alcantara.com.br
Frequency: Biennial. **Principal Exhibits:** Machines and equipment for the food, packing, plastics, pharmaceutical, chemical, and cosmetic industries; devices and systems for marking, identification, weighing, and transport; process controls and instruments; chemical products, inks, and varnishes.

AMERICAN ASSOCIATION OF PHARMACEUTICAL SCIENTISTS CONVENTION

1650 King St., Ste. 200
Alexandria, VA 22314-2747
PH: (703)548-3000
FX: (703)684-7349
E-mail: aaps@aaps.org
URL: http://www.aaps.org
Frequency: Annual. **Audience:** Pharmaceutical scientists involved in R&D, QA, QC, biotechnology, purchasing, regulatory affairs, production & planning. **Principal Exhibits:** Raw materials, supplies, equipment, contract research & contract service labs, computers, packaging, and other suppliers to pharmaceutical scientists. **Dates and Locations:** 2000 Oct 27 - Nov 01; Indianapolis, IN.

AMERICAN COLLEGE OF MEDICAL QUALITY

PO Box 34493
Bethesda, MD 20827-0493
PH: (301)365-3570
TF: (800)924-2149
FX: (301)365-3202
E-mail: acma@aol.com
URL: http://www.acmq.org
Frequency: Annual. **Audience:** Physicians, nurses, and other healthcare professionals interested in medical quality assurance and utilization review and risk management. **Principal Exhibits:** Computer hardware and software, pharmaceuticals, medical publications, and related equipment, supplies, and services. **Formerly:** Managed Care and Care Managers Focusing on Clinical Quality.

AMERICAN PHARMACEUTICAL ASSOCIATION ANNUAL MEETING AND EXHIBIT

2215 Constitution Ave. NW
Washington, DC 20037
PH: (202)429-7547
FX: (202)783-2351
Frequency: Annual. **Principal Exhibits:** Pharmaceutical equipment, supplies, and services.

AMERICAN PSYCHIATRIC ASSOCIATION ANNUAL MEETING

1400 K St., NW
Washington, DC 20005
PH: (202)682-6100
FX: (202)682-6132
URL: http://www.psych.org
Frequency: Annual. **Audience:** Psychiatrists, mental health professionals, and general public. **Principal Exhibits:** Pharmaceuticals, data processing hardware & software, biofeedback instrumentation; furnishings; information from private psychiatric hospitals and state mental health agencies; and related publications.

AMERICAN SOCIETY OF CONSULTANT PHARMACISTS ANNUAL MEETING AND EXHIBITION

1321 Duke St.
Alexandria, VA 22314-3563
PH: (703)739-1300
TF: (800)355-2727
FX: (703)739-1500
E-mail: info@ascp.com
URL: http://www.ascp.com
Frequency: Annual. **Audience:** Pharmacists in the long-term care field, allied professionals, and general public. **Principal Exhibits:** Pharmaceuticals, drug distribution systems, packaging equipment, computers, durable medical equipment, and medical supplies. **Dates and Locations:** 2000 Nov 01-05; Boston, MA.

APA MEETING & CONVENTION

1845 E. Southern Ave.
Tempe, AZ 85282-5831
PH: (602)838-3385
FX: (602)838-3557
E-mail: azpa@juno.com
Frequency: Annual. **Audience:** Trade professionals. **Principal Exhibits:** Pharmaceuticals and other medication, computers, sundries, and related supplies. **Formerly:** Arizona Pharmacy Association Convention.

ARAB HEALTH CAIRO - THE INTERNATIONAL EXHIBITION FOR HOSPITAL & MEDICAL EQUIPMENT AND SERVICES

PO Box 28943
Dubai, United Arab Emirates
PH: 9714 365161
FX: 9714 360137
E-mail: iirx@emirates.net.ae
Frequency: Biennial. **Principal Exhibits:** Medical, dental, and pharmaceutical equipment, supplies, and services. **Incorporating:** Arab Dentistry; Arab Eyecare & Optical.

BALTFARMA

5 Laisves Ave.
2600 Vilnius, Lithuania
PH: 3702 454500
FX: 3702 454511
E-mail: info@litexpo.lt
Frequency: Annual. **Principal Exhibits:** Equipment and supplies for medical engineering, laboratory technology, diagnostics and therapeutics, hospital equipment, pharmaceutical industries, dentistry, stomatology, optics and lasers. **Held in conjunction with:** Baltdent ; Baltmedica ; Baltoptik.

BIOPHARM CONFERENCE

859 Willamette St.
Eugene, OR 97401
PH: (541)343-1200
FX: (541)343-7024
URL: http://www.advanstar-expos.com
Frequency: Annual. **Audience:** Trade professionals.

BRITISH ASSOCIATION FOR PSYCHOPHARMACOLOGY INTERNATIONAL SYMPOSIUM

c/o Susan Chandler
6 Regent Terrace
Cambridge CB2 1AA, England
PH: 44 1223 358395
FX: 44 1223 321268
URL: http://www.bap.org.uk
Frequency: Annual. **Audience:** Psychopharmacologists, psychiat-

rists, neuropharmacologists, psychologists, and neurochemists. **Principal Exhibits:** Exhibits related to psychopharmacology.

**CANADIAN SOCIETY OF HOSPITAL PHARMACISTS
CONFERENCE**
1145 Hunt Club Rd., Ste. 350
Ottawa, ON, Canada K1V 0Y3
PH: (613)736-9733
FX: (613)736-5660
E-mail: bleslie@cshp.cq
Frequency: Annual. **Audience:** Hospital pharmacists, graduate pharmacists; and students. **Principal Exhibits:** Hospital pharmacy equipment, supplies, and services.

CDMA FALL SHOW
104 Wilmot Rd., Ste. 550
Deerfield, IL 60015-5130
PH: (708)267-8800
TF: (800)935-2362
FX: (708)237-9900
Frequency: Semiannual. **Principal Exhibits:** Equipment, supplies, and services for drug store operations. **Dates and Locations:** 1998.

CHEMEX - PHARMACY EXHIBITION
630 Chiswick High Rd.
London W4 5BG, England
PH: 44 181 742 2828
FX: 44 181 747 3856
URL: http://www.mf-exhibitions.co.uk
Frequency: Annual. **Audience:** Pharmacists, wholesalers, manufacturers, grocery chain buyers. **Principal Exhibits:** Medicines, toiletries, cosmetics, perfumes, and babycare, paper and household products. **Held in conjunction with:** Pulse - Doctors Show.

CPHI - PHARMACEUTICAL INGREDIENTS WORLDWIDE
Industrieweg 54
PO Box 200
NL-3600 AE Maarssen, Netherlands
PH: 346573777
FX: 346563811
E-mail: exponl@ibm.net
URL: http://www.mfbv.com
Frequency: Annual. **Audience:** Scientists, technologists, engineers, purchasers, production managers, marketing and sales managers, legal advisors, and consultants. **Principal Exhibits:** Active ingredients, excipients, intermediates, and services of the pharmaceutical industry.

**DEUTSCHER APOTHEKERTAG - PHARMACEUTICAL
EXHIBITION EXPOHARM**
Stockumer Kirchstrasse 61
PO Box 101006
D-40474 Dusseldorf, Germany
PH: 211 4560 01
FX: 211 4560 668
URL: http://messe.dus.tradefair.de
Frequency: Biennial. **Audience:** Trade professionals. **Principal Exhibits:** Pharmaceuticals and related equipment, supplies, and services.

**DEUTSCHER ARZTEKONGRESS BERLIN -
PHARMACEUTICAL AND MEDICO-TECHNICAL
EXHIBITION**
Klingsorstr 21
12167 Berlin, Germany
PH: 30 7913091
FX: 30 7913094
Frequency: Annual. **Audience:** Doctors, nurses, and related specialists. **Principal Exhibits:** Pharmaceutical and medical equipment, supplies, and services.

**DROGISTEN KONTAKT - COSMETICS AND PERFUMERY
TRADE EXHIBITION**
Jaarbeursplein-Utrecht
PO Box 8500
NL-3503 RM Utrecht, Netherlands
PH: 30 295 5911
FX: 30 294 0379
E-mail: info@jaarbeursutrecht.nl
URL: http://www.jaarbeursutrecht.nl
Frequency: Annual. **Principal Exhibits:** Pharmaceuticals and chemist's supplies, perfumery, cosmetics, toiletries, costume jewelry, hair dressers' supplies, herbs, diet-products, health foods. **Formerly:** Drophar.

**EUROPEAN SYMPOSIUM ON RADIOPHARMACY &
RADIOPHARMACEUTICALS**
P.O. Box 1558
6501 BN Nijmegen, Netherlands
PH: 080 234471
Principal Exhibits: Pharmaceuticals.

**EXPOFARMACIA - INTERNATIONAL
PHARMACEUTICAL SPECIALITIES CONGRESS &
EXHIBITION**
Avda. de las Ferias s/n
PO Box 476
E-46080 Valencia, Spain
PH: 34 9 6 386 11 00
FX: 34 9 6 363 61 11
E-mail: feriavalencia@feriavalencia.com
URL: http://www.feriavalencia.com
Frequency: Annual. **Audience:** Trade professionals. **Principal Exhibits:** Pharmaceutical products.

**EXPOPHARM - INTERNATIONAL PHARMACEUTICAL
TRADE FAIR**
Carl-Mannich Str. 26
Postfach 6144
D-65735 Eschborn, Germany
PH: 06196 928410
FX: 06196 928404
URL: http://www.abda.de/wv/expoharm.html
Frequency: Annual. **Principal Exhibits:** Pharmaceuticals, cosmetics, surgery equipment, shop fittings, laboratory apparatus, nursing equipment, nourishment, hygienics and plant protection.

**FARMA - NATIONAL TRADE FAIR OF
PHARMACEUTICAL AND PARAPHARMACEUTICAL
PRODUCTS AND EQUIPMENT**
Consciencestraat 41
2018 Antwerp, Belgium
PH: 03 280 1511
FX: 03 218 5740
Frequency: Biennial.

**FLORIDA PHARMACY ASSOCIATION ANNUAL MEETING
AND CONVENTION**
610 N. Adams St.
Tallahassee, FL 32301
PH: (904)222-2400
FX: (904)561-6758
Frequency: Annual. **Audience:** Trade professionals and general public. **Principal Exhibits:** Pharmaceuticals and other product lines and services provided for and by pharmacists. **Dates and Locations:** 1998; Marco Island, FL.

**GEORGIA PHARMACEUTICAL ASSOCIATION
CONVENTION**
20 Lenox Pointe, NE
PO Box 95527
Atlanta, GA 30347
PH: (404)231-5074
FX: (404)237-8435

Frequency: Annual. **Principal Exhibits:** Pharmaceutical equipment, supplies, and services.

IFFS WORLD CONGRESS ON FERTILITY AND STERILITY
10, rue Charles Amans
3400 Montpellier, France
PH: 33 67 58 59 03
FX: 33 67 58 31 60
Frequency: Triennial. **Principal Exhibits:** Pharmaceutical products.

ILLINOIS PHARMACISTS ASSOCIATION ANNUAL MEETING
223 W. Jackson Blvd., Ste. 1000
Chicago, IL 60606-6906
PH: (312)939-7300
FX: (312)939-7220
Frequency: Annual. **Audience:** Retail and institutional pharmacists. **Principal Exhibits:** Products and services for pharmacists, including drugs and computers.

INDOMED - INDONESIA INTERNATIONAL MEDICAL, PHARMACEUTICAL AND HEALTH CARE EXHIBITION
21/F Tung Wai Commercial Bldg.
109-111 Gloucester Rd.
Wanchai, Hong Kong
PH: 5110511
FX: 5075014
Frequency: Biennial. **Audience:** Trade professionals. **Principal Exhibits:** Medical equipment, computer management systems, pharmaceuticals, supplies and materials, health products, tools, medical aids.

INFARMA - INTERNATIONAL CONGRESS & EXHIBITION FOR THE PHARMACEUTICAL INDUSTRY
Av. Reina Maria Cristina, s/n
E-08004 Barcelona, Spain
PH: 93 804 0102
FX: 93 805 4802
Frequency: Biennial. **Audience:** Trade only. **Principal Exhibits:** Equipment, supplies, and services for the pharmaceutical industry.

INTERNATIONAL CONFERENCE ON PHARMACEUTICAL MEDICINE ICPM
43 Galgenstraat
B-3078 Everberg, Belgium
PH: 32 2 7594531
FX: 32 2 7599980
Frequency: Biennial. **Principal Exhibits:** Exhibits concerning pharmaceutical medicine.

INTERNATIONAL UNION OF PHARMACOLOGY INTERNATIONAL CONGRESS
c/o Prof. W.C. Bowman
Dept. of Physiology & Pharmacology
University of Strathclyde
Glasgow G1 1XW, Scotland
PH: 44 141 5524400
FX: 44 141 5522562
E-mail: w.c.bowman@strath.ac.uk
Frequency: Quadrennial. **Principal Exhibits:** Pharmacology equipment, supplies, and services.

INTERPHEX JAPAN - INTERNATIONAL EXHIBITION FOR THE PHARMACEUTICAL, COSMETICS, TOILETRY, AND ALLIED INDUSTRIES
2F Ginza-Eiwa Bldg.
8-18-7 Ginza Chuo-Ku
Tokyo 104, Japan
PH: 81 3 5565 0861
FX: 81 3 5565 0860
Frequency: Annual. **Audience:** Trade professionals, including buyers, executives, mid-level purchasing managers, and marketing managers. **Principal Exhibits:** Pharmaceutical detergent, cosmetic

industries equipment, supplies, and services, including raw materials, processing equipment, packaging machinery, and computer systems and services.

INTERPHEX UK - INTERNATIONAL PHARMACEUTICAL AND COSMETICS MANUFACTURING EXHIBITION
Oriel House
26 The Quadrant
Richmond, Surrey TW9 1DL, England
PH: 181 910 7825
FX: 181 910 7926
E-mail: info@reedexpo.co.uk
URL: http://www.reedexpo.com
Frequency: Biennial. **Principal Exhibits:** Equipment and services involved in the manufacture of pharmaceuticals and cosmetics, including processing and production equipment, packaging equipment, finished packs, clean rooms, clean room services, laboratory equipment, contract services, and raw materials.

INTERPHEX USA - THE WORLD'S FORUM FOR THE PHARMACEUTICAL INDUSTRY
383 Main Ave.
PO Box 6059
Norwalk, CT 06851
PH: (203)840-5358
FX: (203)840-4804
E-mail: inquiry@nepcon.reedexpo.com
Frequency: Annual. **Audience:** Pharmaceutical manufacturers. **Principal Exhibits:** Plant and laboratory equipment; services for the pharmaceutical industry. **Dates and Locations:** 1998 Apr; Philadelphia, PA.

INTERPHEX WEST
383 Main Ave.
PO Box 6059
Norwalk, CT 06851
PH: (203)840-5358
FX: (203)840-4804
E-mail: inquiry@nepcon.reedexpo.com
Frequency: Annual. **Audience:** Engineers. **Principal Exhibits:** Equipment, materials and supplies. **Dates and Locations:** 1998 Sep; Santa Clara, CA.

IPHARMEX - INTERNATIONAL PHARMACEUTICAL EXHIBITION
Eurexpo - Parc des Expositions de Lyon
BP 87
Ave. Louis Bleriot
F-69683 Chassieu, France
PH: 33 72 22 34 44
FX: 33 72 22 32 70
E-mail: foire@sepelcom.com
URL: http://www.sepelcom.com
Frequency: Biennial. **Audience:** General practitioners, pharmacists, and nurses. **Principal Exhibits:** Biological and industrial equipment, products and services for hospitals and laboratories.

IPSP ANNUAL CONGRESS
c/o IPSF Secretariat
Andries Bickerweg 5
NL-2517 JP The Hague, Netherlands
PH: 31 70 302 1992
FX: 31 70 3633914
E-mail: ipsf@fip.nl
URL: http://www.pharmweb.net/pharmweb/ipsf.html
Frequency: Annual. **Principal Exhibits:** Exhibits related to development funds and student issues.

KENTUCKY NURSES ASSOCIATION ANNUAL CONVENTION
1400 S. 1st
PO Box 2616
Louisville, KY 40201

PH: (502)637-2546
FX: (502)637-8236
E-mail: kentucky.nurses@internet.mci.com
Frequency: Annual. **Audience:** Registered Nurses and students.
Principal Exhibits: Health industry related services and equipment, including pharmaceuticals and recruitment services.

**MANITOBA HEALTH ORGANIZATIONS ANNUAL
    HEALTH CONFERENCE AND EXHIBITION**
PO Box 116
Winnipeg, MB, Canada R3C 2G1
PH: (204)958-7540
FX: (204)958-7547
Frequency: Annual. **Audience:** Health care administrators, board members, purchasing managers, nursing directors, dieticians, pharmacists, lawyers, and related professionals. **Principal Exhibits:** Pharmaceuticals, medical equipment, facility information, and related supplies and services.

**MEDICAL, DENTAL, AND PHARMACEUTICAL FAIR/HO
    CHI MINH CITY**
1384 Giang Vo St.
Hanoi, Vietnam
PH: 4264823
FX: 4264051
Frequency: Annual. **Audience:** Trade professionals. **Principal Exhibits:** Medical, dental, and pharmaceutical supplies and equipment.

**MEDICAL PHARMACY - INTERNATIONAL MEDICAL/
    PHARMACEUTICAL EQUIPMENT AND TECHNOLOGY
    EXHIBITION**
27 Hillier St., Rm. 2403
Fu Fai Commercial Centre
Hong Kong, Hong Kong
PH: 2 8518603
FX: 2 8518637
E-mail: topreput@hkabc.net
Frequency: Annual. **Audience:** Trade professionals. **Principal Exhibits:** Pharmaceuticals and medical equipment, supplies, and services.

**MEDICINA/TEHNIKA - INTERNATIONAL EXHIBITION
    OF MEDICAL EQUIPMENT, PHARMACEUTICALS, AND
    LABORATORY EQUIPMENT**
Avenija Dubrovnik 15
10020 Zagreb, Croatia
PH: 385 1 6503 111
FX: 385 1 6520 643
URL: http://www.zv.hr
Frequency: Annual. **Principal Exhibits:** Medical, pharmaceutical, and laboratory equipment, supplies, and services.

**MEDICINE - INTERNATIONAL TRADE FAIR AND
    GENERAL MEETING OF THE SWEDISH SOCIETY OF
    MEDICINE**
Massvagen 1, Alvsjo
S-125 80 Stockholm, Sweden
PH: 46 8 7494100
FX: 46 8 992044
E-mail: staff@stofair.se
URL: http://www.stofair.se
Frequency: Annual. **Audience:** Doctors, nurses, lab staff, buyers, medical administrative personnel, pharmacy staff, and technicians. **Principal Exhibits:** Laboratory material, testing, and analysis equipment; operation equipment for intensive care, observation, functional support, anaesthetics, maternity care, and surgery; surgical instruments; sutures; implants; injection material; gas; first-aid equipment; X-ray equipment; radiology; laser equipment; pharmaceuticals; literature.

NACDS MARKETPLACE CONFERENCE
c/o Ronald L. Ziegler
PO Box 1417-D49
413 N. Lee St.
Alexandria, VA 22313
PH: (703)549-3001
FX: (703)684-3969
Frequency: Annual. **Principal Exhibits:** Chain drug store equipment, supplies, and services.

**NATIONAL COMMUNITY PHARMACISTS ASSOCIATION
    CONVENTION AND EXHIBITION**
205 Daingerfield Rd.
Alexandria, VA 22314
PH: (703)683-8200
FX: (703)683-3619
Frequency: Annual. **Audience:** Pharmacy owners and managers. **Principal Exhibits:** Pharmaceutical and related equipment, supplies, and services. **Dates and Locations:** Oct 15-19; San Antonio, TX. **Formerly:** National Association of Retail Druggists Convention.

**NEW JERSEY PHARMACISTS ASSOCIATION
    CONVENTION**
3 Marlen Dr., Ste. B
Robbinsville, NJ 08691-1604
PH: (609)584-9063
FX: (609)586-8186
E-mail: njpharm@aol.com
Frequency: Annual. **Audience:** Pharmacists and pharmacy owners. **Principal Exhibits:** Pharmaceuticals and local pharmacy and drug store related products. **Formerly:** New Jersey Pharmaceutical Association Convention.

**NFAS - NATIONAL FACTORY AUTOMATION SHOW,
    MONTREAL**
383 Main Ave.
PO Box 6059
Norwalk, CT 06851
PH: (203)840-5358
FX: (203)840-4804
E-mail: inquiry@nepcon.reedexpo.com
Frequency: Biennial. **Audience:** Production managers and design engineers. **Principal Exhibits:** Plant floor automation and control products. **Dates and Locations:** 2000 May; Montreal, PQ.

OHIO PHARMACISTS ASSOCIATION ANNUAL MEETING
6037 Frantz Rd., Ste. 106
Dublin, OH 43017
PH: (614)798-0037
FX: (614)798-0978
E-mail: opa@ohiopharmacists.org
URL: http://www.ohiopharmacists.org/
Frequency: Annual. **Audience:** Pharmacists, including owners and employers of community, hospital, LTC, and other pharmacy settings. **Principal Exhibits:** Pharmaceutical companies (Brand name & Generic), and pharmaceutical; wholesalers, computer vendors, insurance carriers, and temporary services.

**OMAHA MIDWEST CLINICAL SOCIETY ANNUAL
    POSTGRADUATE ASSEMBLY**
7910 Davenport St.
Omaha, NE 68114
PH: (402)397-1443
Frequency: Annual. **Audience:** Physicians and general public. **Principal Exhibits:** Pharmaceuticals. **Dates and Locations:** 1998 May.

PDA ANNUAL MEETING
7500 Old Georgetown Rd., Ste. 620
Bethesda, MD 20814
PH: (301)986-0293
FX: (301)986-0296
E-mail: info@pda.org

Frequency: Annual. **Audience:** Pharmaceutical manufacturers. **Principal Exhibits:** Supplies and services related to pharmaceuticals.

PHARMACEUTICAL SOCIETY OF THE STATE OF NEW YORK ANNUAL MEETING

210 Washington Ave. Ext.
Albany, NY 12203
PH: (518)869-6595
FX: (518)464-0618
Frequency: Annual. **Audience:** Licensed pharmacists. **Principal Exhibits:** Pharmaceuticals. **Dates and Locations:** 1998 Jun.

PHARMACY

1st Fl. KPMG Bldg.
Newmarket
PO Box 9682
9 Princes St.
Auckland 9682, New Zealand
PH: 09 300 3950
FX: 09 379 3358
Frequency: Annual. **Audience:** Trade professionals. **Principal Exhibits:** Pharmaceutical equipment, supplies, and services.

PHARMAPAK - ASIAN INTERNATIONAL PHARMACEUTICAL & COSMETICS PACKAGING & PROCESSING EXHIBITION

62 Soi 30 Rama V1 Road
Phyathai
Kwang Samsennai
Bangkok 10400, Thailand
PH: 66 2 617 1475
FX: 66 2 271 3223
E-mail: besshows@samart.co.th
URL: http://www.montnet.com
Frequency: Biennial. **Principal Exhibits:** Equipment, supplies, and services for pharmaceutical & cosmetics packaging & processing.

PHARMEXPO - ANNUAL SWEDISH PHARMACEUTICAL CONGRESS AND EXHIBITION

Massvagen 1, Alvsjo
S-125 80 Stockholm, Sweden
PH: 46 8 7494100
FX: 46 8 992044
E-mail: staff@stofair.se
URL: http://www.stofair.se
Frequency: Annual. **Audience:** Trade only. **Principal Exhibits:** Pharmaceuticals and related equipment, supplies, and services.

PHARMTECH CONFERENCE & EXHIBITION

859 Willamette St.
Eugene, OR 97401
PH: (541)343-1200
FX: (541)343-7024
URL: http://www.advanstar-expos.com
Frequency: Annual. **Principal Exhibits:** Pharmacy equipment, supplies, and services.

PHARMTECH PUERTO RICO

859 Willamette St.
Eugene, OR 97401
PH: (541)343-1200
FX: (541)343-7024
URL: http://www.advanstar-expos.com
Frequency: Annual. **Principal Exhibits:** Pharmacy equipment, supplies, and services.

PHIA - PHARMACEUTICAL INGREDIENTS ASIA - INTERNATIONAL EXHIBITION AND CONFERENCE ON PHARMACEUTICAL INGREDIENTS AND INTERMEDIATES FOR THE ASIAN MARKET

100 Beach Rd.
26-00 Shaw Towers
Singapore 189702, Singapore

PH: 65 294 3366
FX: 65 299 9782
E-mail: exnet@singnet.com.sg
Frequency: Annual. **Audience:** Scientists, technologists, engineers, purchasers, production managers, marketing and sales managers, legal advisors and consultants. **Principal Exhibits:** Active ingredients, excipients, intermediates, and services related to the pharmaceutical industry.

PHIUS - PHARMACEUTICAL INGREDIENTS USA

630 Chiswick High Rd.
London W4 5BG, England
PH: 44 181 742 2828
FX: 44 181 747 3856
URL: http://www.mf-exhibitions.co.uk
Frequency: Annual. **Audience:** Executives from R&D purchasing, engineering, production, quality control and general management. **Principal Exhibits:** Active ingredients, excipients and intermediates and services related to the pharmaceutical industry.

PRAGOFARMA - INTERNATIONAL PHARMACEUTICAL, BIOLOGICAL MEDICAMENTS AND BIOTECHNOLOGY EXHIBITION

28, Rijna 13
PO Box 555
CR-111 21 Prague, Czech Republic
PH: 420 2 24 19 51 11
FX: 420 2 24 19 52 86
E-mail: inchmar@mbox.bts.sk
URL: http://www.incheba.sk
Frequency: Annual. **Audience:** Trade Professionals. **Principal Exhibits:** Pharmaceutical products.

PRO-TECH CONFERENCE

1821 Michael Faraday Dr.
Reston, VA 22090-0219
PH: (703)787-0000
FX: (703)548-2184
Frequency: Annual. **Audience:** Pharmacists and related professionals. **Principal Exhibits:** Pharmaceutical equipment, supplies, and services.

ROMMEDICA - ROMPHARMA - ROMCONTROLA

65-67 Marasti Blvd.
PO Box 32-3
R-71331 Bucharest, Romania
PH: 40 1 223 11 60
FX: 40 1 222 61 69
E-mail: romexpo@ccir.ro
URL: http://www.ccir.ro/romexpo/exhb.htm
Frequency: Annual. **Principal Exhibits:** Medical equipment, supplies, and services; pharmaceuticals; measurement and testing/ control equipment, supplies, and services.

RX EXPO - AN EDUCATIONAL FORUM AND BUYING SHOW

205 Daingerfield Rd.
Alexandria, VA 22314
PH: (703)683-8200
FX: (703)683-3619
Frequency: Annual. **Audience:** Independent retail pharmacists, owners, managers, employees, and home infusion nurses. **Principal Exhibits:** General gifts, sundries, and seasonal items; over the counter products; health and beauty aids; electronic products; prescription drug products, personal care products, home health care products, IV products, and related products.

SASKATCHEWAN ASSOCIATION OF HEALTH ORGANIZATIONS ANNUAL CONVENTION AND EXHIBITION

PO Box 116
Winnipeg, MB, Canada R3C 2G1
PH: (204)958-7540
FX: (204)958-7547

Frequency: Annual. **Audience:** Conference delegates and trade professionals. **Principal Exhibits:** Pharmaceuticals, medical equipment, related supplies, and facility information. **Dates and Locations:** 1999 Mar; Regina, SK.

SCHIZOPHRENIA - INTERNATIONAL CONGRESS
375 Water St., Ste. 645
Vancouver, BC, Canada V6B 5C6
PH: (604)681-5226
FX: (604)681-2503
E-mail: congress@venuewest.com
Frequency: Biennial. **Principal Exhibits:** Pharmaceutical equipment, supplies, and services.

SIB - INTERNATIONAL TRADE FAIR FOR IMPORTS AND EXPORTS
ul. Lenina 21/room 713
630081 Novosibirsk, Siberia, Russia
PH: 3832 205785
FX: 3832 205387
Frequency: Annual. **Principal Exhibits:** Construction, food processing, timber and paper, electrical engineering, electronics, coal preparation and processing, environmental technology, clothing and leather industry, pharmaceuticals, raw materials, semi-finished products, finished products, accessories, tools, supplies, waste products.

SIBPHARMA - INTERNATIONAL PHARMACEUTICAL INDUSTRY EXHIBITION
16 Gorky St.
6300099 Novosibirsk, Russia
PH: 7 3832 102674
FX: 7 3832 236335
E-mail: siberian.fair@sovcust.sprint.com
Frequency: Annual. **Principal Exhibits:** Health Care, medical equipment and social welfare, and pharmaceutical.

SLOVFARMA - INTERNATIONAL EXHIBITION OF PHARMACEUTICAL PRODUCTS
28, Rijna 13
PO Box 555
CR-111 21 Prague, Czech Republic
PH: 420 2 24 19 51 11
FX: 420 2 24 19 52 86
E-mail: inchmar@mbox.bts.sk
URL: http://www.incheba.sk
Frequency: Annual. **Principal Exhibits:** Pharmaceutical products.

SOUTHWESTERN CHAPTER, SOCIETY OF NUCLEAR MEDICINE EXHIBITION
PO Box 411106
San Francisco, CA 94141-1106
PH: (415)487-9802
FX: (415)487-9803
E-mail: society@hooked.net
Frequency: Annual. **Audience:** Nuclear medicine physicians, scientists, and technologists also nuclear medicine pharmacists. **Principal Exhibits:** Industry related technology and pharmaceuticals.

SWEDENTAL - FAIR AND ODONTOLOGICAL CONGRESS OF THE SWEDISH DENTAL SOCIETY
Massvagen 1, Alvsjo
S-125 80 Stockholm, Sweden
PH: 46 8 7494100
FX: 46 8 992044
E-mail: staff@stofair.se
URL: http://www.stofair.se
Frequency: Annual. **Audience:** Dental care professionals. **Principal Exhibits:** Dental hygiene articles; pharmaceutical products; expendable articles; implants/systems; fixtures and fittings for clinics, laboratories, waiting rooms; clinical and laboratory equipment; office furnishings and equipment; computer equipment; protective clothing; dental technology; technical information; specialized literature; consulting services.

TENNESSEE SOCIETY OF HOSPITAL PHARMACISTS ANNUAL MEETING
226 Capitol Blvd., Ste. 810
Nashville, TN 37219
PH: (615)256-3023
FX: (615)255-3528
Frequency: Annual. **Audience:** Licensed hospital pharmacists. **Principal Exhibits:** Pharmaceuticals and sundries.

TEXAS PHARMACY ASSOCIATION ANNUAL MEETING AND EXHIBIT
1624 E. Anderson Ln.
PO Box 14709
Austin, TX 78761-4079
PH: (512)836-8350
TF: (800)505-5463
FX: (512)836-0308
Frequency: Annual. **Audience:** Pharmacists. **Principal Exhibits:** Pharmaceuticals. **Dates and Locations:** 2000; Austin, TX.

TRADE FAIR OF PHARMACEUTICAL & PARAPHARMACEUTICAL PRODUCTS & EQUIPMENT
Consciencestraat 41
2018 Antwerp, Belgium
PH: 03 280 1511
FX: 03 218 5740
Frequency: Biennial. **Principal Exhibits:** Pharmaceutical and parapharmaceutical products.

WESTERN PHARMACY EDUCATION FAIR
1112 I St., Ste. 300
Sacramento, CA 95814
PH: (916)444-7811
FX: (916)444-7929
Frequency: Annual. **Audience:** Exhibitors and trade professionals. **Principal Exhibits:** Pharmaceutical equipment, supplies, and services.

WORLD CONGRESS OF PHARMACY AND PHARMACEUTICAL SCIENCES
1785 Alta Vista Dr.
Ottawa, ON, Canada K1G 3Y6
PH: (613)523-7877
FX: (613)523-0445
E-mail: cpha@cdnpharm.ca
URL: http://www.cdnpharm.ca
Frequency: Annual. **Principal Exhibits:** Pharmacy equipment, supplies, and services.

ZDRAVOOKHRANENIYE - INTERNATIONAL EXHIBITION ON HEALTHCARE, MEDICAL ENGINEERING, AND PHARMACEUTICALS
Krasnopresnenskaya nab. 14
123100 Moscow, Russia
PH: 095 268 1340
FX: 095 205 60 55
Frequency: Biennial. **Principal Exhibits:** Diagnostic instrument, including: bomographs, centrifuges, analytical and laboratory equipment; hospital equipment; drugs; and medical tools.

MASTER INDEX

The Master Index presents company and organization names, names of individuals, SIC industry names, and terms. Each entry in the index is followed by one or more page numbers.

Pharmaceutical Formulations, pp. 422, 446, 461
Pharmaceutical Holdings Corp., pp. 422, 445, 461
Pharmaceutical Information Associates, Ltd., p. 501
Pharmaceutical Innovations, pp. 422, 454, 467
Pharmaceutical Laboratories, pp. 422, 453, 467
Pharmaceutical Litigation Reporter, p. 524
Pharmaceutical Marketers Directory, p. 524
*Pharmaceutical Marketing and Management
  Research Division*, p. 524
Pharmaceutical Marketing in the 21st Century, p.
  524
Pharmaceutical News Index, p. 524
Pharmaceutical Preparations (SIC 2834), pp. 326-
  327, 336, 338, 343, 356-357, 365
Pharmaceutical Processing, p. 524
Pharmaceutical Recovery Svcs, pp. 422, 456, 470
Pharmaceutical Recruiters, Inc., p. 501
*Pharmaceutical Research and Manufacturers
  Association*, p. 524
Pharmaceutical Research and Manufacturers of
  America, p. 492
Pharmaceutical Research Assoc., pp. 422, 446, 460
*Pharmaceutical Research Manufacturers
  Association Annual Fact Book*, p. 524
Pharmaceutical Resources, Inc., pp. 422, 446, 461
Pharmaceutical Society of the State of New York
  Annual Meeting, p. 536
Pharmaceutical Systems Inc., p. 501
Pharmaceutical Technology, p. 524
Pharmachemie B.V., p. 482
Pharmacia & Upjohn Caribe, pp. 422, 444, 460
Pharmacia & Upjohn Company, pp. 422, 444, 459
Pharmacia & Upjohn, Inc., pp. 343, 444, 459, 478
Pharmacia Hepar Inc., pp. 422, 449, 466
Pharmacists in Ophthalmic Practice, p. 492
Pharmacological and Chemical Synonyms, p. 524
Pharmacology Research Laboratory, p. 524
Pharmacopeial Forum, p. 525
Pharmacy, p. 536
Pharmacy Care Specialists Inc., p. 480
Pharmacy Consultants Inc., p. 502
Pharmacyclics Inc., pp. 422, 455, 465
PharmaMedical Consultants International LLC, p.
  502
Pharmanex Inc., pp. 422-423, 449, 468
PharmaPak—Asian International Pharmaceutical &
Cosmetics Packaging & Processing Exhibition, p.
  536
Pharmasciences Inc., pp. 423, 452, 468
Pharmatech Laboratories Inc., pp. 423, 452, 466
Pharmavite Corporation, pp. 423, 446, 460
PharmExpo—Annual Swedish Pharmaceutical
  Congress and Exhibition, p. 536
Pharmingen, pp. 423, 447, 461
PharmTech Conference & Exhibition, p. 536
PharmTech Puerto Rico, p. 536
Phelon's Discount/Jobbing Trade, p. 525
PhIA—Pharmaceutical Ingredients Asia—
International Exhibition and Conference on
Pharmaceutical Ingredients and Intermediates for
  the Asian Market, p. 536
Phibro-Tech, Inc., pp. 178, 218, 240
Philipp Brothers Chemicals Inc., pp. 179, 215, 236
Phillips Pharmatech Labs Inc., pp. 423, 451, 465, 480
Phillips Sumika Polypropylene, pp. 179, 215, 248

PHILPLAS, p. 308
PhIUS—Pharmaceutical Ingredients USA, p. 536
phlogiston theory, pp. 18, 21
Phoenix Laboratories Inc., pp. 423, 449, 472
Phoenix Scientific Inc., pp. 423, 448, 464
Phosphate Resource Partners, pp. 179, 213, 234
Phosphatic Fertilizers (SIC 2874), pp. 14, 29, 68-69
*Physicians' Desk Reference for Nonprescription
  Drugs*, p. 525
Physicians' Desk Reference for Ophthalmology,
  p. 525
*Physicians' Desk Reference Library on CD-
  ROM*, p. 525
Physicians' Desk Reference, p. 525
Piceu Group Limited, pp. 179, 225, 248
Piedmont Chemical Industries, pp. 179, 219, 241
Piedmont Laboratories Inc., pp. 179, 222, 239
Pierce & Stevens Corp., pp. 179, 220, 243
Pierre Fabre Inc., pp. 179, 224, 243
Pilot Chemical Co. of Ohio, pp. 223, 251
Pilot Chemical Corp., pp. 179, 220, 245
Pink Sheet, The, p. 525
Pinkham, Lydia, p. 329
Pinney & Associates, Inc., S.G., p. 287
Pioneer Americas, Inc., pp. 179, 214, 236
Pioneer Chlor Alkali Company, pp. 179, 215, 238
Pioneer/Eclipse Corporation, pp. 179, 225, 245
Pioneer Hi-Bred International Inc., p. 260
Pitt Penn Oil Co. Inc., pp. 180, 224, 243
Placement Associates, Ltd., p. 502
Planet Emu Inc., pp. 423, 453, 472
Plantation Botanicals, Inc., pp. 423, 446, 461
Plasite Protective Coating, pp. 180, 227, 249
Plast-Ex, p. 308
Plast Imagen, p. 308
Plast-O-Meric Inc., pp. 180, 219, 241
Plastech Thailand, p. 308
Plastexpo, p. 308
Plasti-Kote Co., Inc., pp. 180, 218, 239
Plastic and Metal Products Manufacturers
  Association, p. 271
Plastic Industry/Pakistan, p. 309
Plastic Soft Materials Manufacturers Association, p.
  271
PLASTICA - Plastics, Rubber and Machines
  Exhibition, p. 309
Plasticolors, Inc., pp. 180, 225, 245
Plastics - Istanbul International Trade Fair for
  Plastics, p. 309
Plastics & Packaging Expo, p. 309
Plastics & Rubber, p. 310
Plastics and Rubber Indonesia, p. 310
Plastics Asia, p. 309
Plastics Education Foundation, p. 271
Plastics Engineering Company, pp. 180, 221, 238
Plastics Extrusion Technology Handbook, p. 300
Plastics Fair - Atlantic City, p. 309
Plastics Fair - Charlotte, p. 309
Plastics Fair - Chicago, p. 309
Plastics Fair - Cleveland, p. 309
Plastics Fair - San Antonio, p. 309
Plastics Fair Providence, p. 309
Plastics Institute of America, p. 271
Plastics Malaysia, p. 309

GEOGRAPHICAL COMPANY INDEX

The Geographical Company Index presents company names by state. Page references are to the company's listing in Chapter 4, Company Directory, in both Part I and Part II.

Geographical Index

Geographical Index

Geographical Index

Geographical Index

COMPANY INDEX BY SIC

The Company Index by SIC presents company names arranged by Standard Industrial Classification codes. Page references are to the company's listing in Chapter 4, Company Directory, in both Part I and Part II.

SIC Index

2835 - continued
Micro Bio Logics, p. 412
Mizuho USA, Inc., p. 412
Molecular Probes Inc., p. 413
Monomer-Polymer & Dajac Labs, p. 413
Morningstar Diagnostics, Inc., p. 413
Naiad Technologies Inc., p. 414
Neogen Corporation, p. 415
Neorx Corporation, p. 415
Neurocrine Biosciences Inc., p. 416
Novagen Inc., p. 416
Nycomed Amersham, Inc., p. 418
O E M Concepts, p. 418
Ortho Diagnostic Systems Inc., p. 419
Pacific Biotech, Inc., p. 419
Pacific International, p. 419
Panvera Corporation, pp. 419-420
Pel-Freez, Inc., p. 420
Petnet Pharmaceutical Svcs LLC, p. 421
Pharmingen, p. 423
Princeton Biomeditech Corp., p. 424
Quantimetrix, p. 425
Quidel Corporation, p. 425
Raven Biological Laboratories,, p. 426
Reagents Applications Inc., p. 426
Regis Technologies, Inc., p. 426
Scantibodies Laboratory Inc., p. 428
Scripps Laboratories, Inc., pp. 429-430
Seracare Technology Inc., p. 430
Streck Laboratories Inc., p. 433
Syntron Bioresearch, Inc., p. 433
Techne Corporation, p. 434
Technical Chemicals & Products, p. 434
Teco Diagnostics, p. 434
Third Wave Technologies, Inc., p. 435
TOA Medical Electronics (USA), p. 435
Trimar Hollywood Inc., p. 436
United States Biochemical Corp., p. 437
USB Corporation, p. 437
Viral Antigens Inc., p. 437
Vysis, Inc., p. 438
Worthington Biochemical Corp., p. 440
Xylum Corporation, p. 440

2836 - Biological Products Except Diagnostic

A & V Incorporated, p. 370
Advanced Biotechnologies, Inc., p. 371
Aesthetic Technologies Corp., p. 371
ALK Laboratories Inc., p. 373
Allergy Control Products, Inc., p. 373
Alpha Therapeutic Corporation, p. 373
Ambico Inc., p. 374
Ambion Inc., p. 374
American Biorganics Inc., p. 374
American Eco-Systems Inc., p. 374
Amgen Puerto Rico Inc., p. 375
Bachem Bioscience Inc., p. 377
Bachem Inc., p. 377
Biocor Animal Health Inc., p. 380
Biofluids Inc., p. 380
Biomatrix, Inc., pp. 380-381
Biomune Company, p. 381
Biosource International Inc., p. 381
Biospecifics Technologies, p. 381

Biowhittaker Inc., pp. 381-382
Boehringer Ingelheim Vetmedica, p. 382
Calbiochem-Novabiochem Corp., p. 383
Caltag Inc., p. 383
Cell Genesys, Inc., p. 384
Centeon Bio-Services Inc., p. 384
Centeon LLC, p. 384
Center for Diagnostic Products, p. 384
Clearvalue, Inc., p. 387
CN Biosciences, Inc., p. 387
Cocalico Biologicals Inc., p. 387
Collagen Aesthetics, Inc., p. 387
Colorado Serum Company, p. 387
Connaught Laboratories Inc., p. 387
CTM Industries Ltd., p. 388
Cyanotech Corporation, p. 389
Diamond Animal Health, Inc., p. 390
Difco Laboratories Inc., p. 391
Diosynth Inc., p. 391
Dynport LLC, p. 391
Genesis Technologies Inc., p. 396
Gentrac, Inc., p. 397
Genzyme Diagnostics Medix Biot, p. 397
Grand Laboratories Inc., p. 398
Green Cross Corp. of America, p. 398
Greer Laboratories Inc., p. 398
Hardy Media Inc., p. 399
Igi Inc., p. 401
IGX Corp., pp. 401-402
Immuno - U S Inc., p. 402
Immvac Inc., p. 402
Intergen Company, p. 403
International Enzyme Inc., p. 403
Interntnal Bchmicals Group Inc., pp. 403-404
Intervet Inc., p. 404
Invitrogen Corporation, p. 404
Irvine Scientific Sales Co., p. 404
ISP Co Inc., p. 404
JRH Biosciences, Inc., p. 405
Kirkegaard & Perry Labs Inc., p. 406
Life Technologies Inc., p. 407
Maine Biological Laboratories, p. 409
Matrix Pharmaceutical Inc., p. 409
Mediatech Inc., p. 410
Medimmune, Inc., p. 410
Merial Ltd., p. 411
Merial Select, Inc., p. 411
MML Diagnostics Packaging Inc., p. 412
Molecumetics, Ltd., p. 413
Nabi, p. 414
Neurex Corporation, p. 415
Norian Corporation, p. 416
Pel-Freez Rabbit Meat, Inc., p. 420
PML Microbiologicals Inc., p. 423
PMLl Inc., p. 423
Power Engineering & Mfg Inc., p. 423
Promega Corporation, p. 424
Quality Biological Inc., p. 425
Remel Inc., p. 426
Research Biochemicals Inc., p. 426
Santa Cruz Biotechnology Inc., p. 428
Scientia Biological, p. 429
SGM Biotech, Inc., p. 430
Sigma Chemical Company, p. 431
Spafas, Incorporated, p. 432

SIC Index

SIC Index

SIC TO NAICS AND NAICS TO SIC CONVERSION GUIDE

This appendix presents complete conversion tables from SIC codes to NAICS codes. SIC stands for *Standard Industrial Classification*, the "old" system of classifying economic activities. NAICS stands for *North American Industry Classification System*, the new classification for classifying economic activities in the United States, Canada, and Mexico.

The first part of the appendix presents the SIC to NAICS Conversion Guide. Four-digit SIC codes and names are shown in bold type. NAICS codes and names are shown beneath, indented, each item labelled "NAICS". An SIC industry may convert to one or more NAICS industries.

The second part, starting on page 647, shows the same information but in the reverse format: the NAICS to SIC Conversion Guide. NAICS codes and names are shown in bold type; the equivalent SIC codes, beneath, are shown indented. A NAICS-coded industry may have one, more than one, or no SIC equivalent (two instances).

SIC TO NAICS CONVERSION GUIDE

AGRICULTURE, FORESTRY, & FISHING

0111 Wheat
NAICS 11114   Wheat Farming
0112 Rice
NAICS 11116   Rice Farming
0115 Corn
NAICS 11115   Corn Farming
0116 Soybeans
NAICS 11111   Soybean Farming
0119 Cash Grains, nec
NAICS 11113   Dry Pea & Bean Farming
NAICS 11112   Oilseed Farming
NAICS 11115   Corn Farming
NAICS 111191 Oilseed & Grain Combination Farming
NAICS 111199 All Other Grain Farming
0131 Cotton
NAICS 11192   Cotton Farming
0132 Tobacco
NAICS 11191   Tobacco Farming
0133 Sugarcane & Sugar Beets
NAICS 111991 Sugar Beet Farming
NAICS 11193   Sugarcane Farming
0134 Irish Potatoes
NAICS 111211 Potato Farming
0139 Field Crops, Except Cash Grains, nec
NAICS 11194   Hay Farming
NAICS 111992 Peanut Farming
NAICS 111219 Other Vegetable & Melon Farming
NAICS 111998 All Other Miscellaneous Crop Farming
0161 Vegetables & Melons
NAICS 111219 Other Vegetable & Melon Farming
0171 Berry Crops
NAICS 111333 Strawberry Farming
NAICS 111334 Berry Farming
0172 Grapes
NAICS 111332 Grape Vineyards
0173 Tree Nuts
NAICS 111335 Tree Nut Farming
0174 Citrus Fruits
NAICS 11131   Orange Groves
NAICS 11132   Citrus Groves
0175 Deciduous Tree Fruits
NAICS 111331 Apple Orchards
NAICS 111339 Other Noncitrus Fruit Farming
0179 Fruits & Tree Nuts, nec
NAICS 111336 Fruit & Tree Nut Combination Farming
NAICS 111339 Other Noncitrus Fruit Farming
0181 Ornamental Floriculture & Nursery Products
NAICS 111422 Floriculture Production
NAICS 111421 Nursery & Tree Production
0182 Food Crops Grown under Cover
NAICS 111411 Mushroom Production
NAICS 111419 Other Food Crops Grown under Cover
0191 General Farms, Primarily Crop
NAICS 111998 All Other Miscellaneous Crop Farming
0211 Beef Cattle Feedlots
NAICS 112112 Cattle Feedlots
0212 Beef Cattle, Except Feedlots
NAICS 112111 Beef Cattle Ranching & Farming

0213 Hogs
NAICS 11221   Hog & Pig Farming
0214 Sheep & Goats
NAICS 11241   Sheep Farming
NAICS 11242   Goat Farming
0219 General Livestock, Except Dairy & Poultry
NAICS 11299   All Other Animal Production
0241 Dairy Farms
NAICS 112111 Beef Cattle Ranching & Farming
NAICS 11212   Dairy Cattle & Milk Production
0251 Broiler, Fryers, & Roaster Chickens
NAICS 11232   Broilers & Other Meat-type Chicken
              Production
0252 Chicken Eggs
NAICS 11231   Chicken Egg Production
0253 Turkey & Turkey Eggs
NAICS 11233   Turkey Production
0254 Poultry Hatcheries
NAICS 11234   Poultry Hatcheries
0259 Poultry & Eggs, nec
NAICS 11239   Other Poultry Production
0271 Fur-bearing Animals & Rabbits
NAICS 11293   Fur-bearing Animal & Rabbit Production
0272 Horses & Other Equines
NAICS 11292   Horse & Other Equine Production
0273 Animal Aquaculture
NAICS 112511 Finfish Farming & Fish Hatcheries
NAICS 112512 Shellfish Farming
NAICS 112519 Other Animal Aquaculture
0279 Animal Specialities, nec
NAICS 11291   Apiculture
NAICS 11299   All Other Animal Production
0291 General Farms, Primarily Livestock & Animal Specialties
NAICS 11299   All Other Animal Production
0711 Soil Preparation Services
NAICS 115112 Soil Preparation, Planting & Cultivating
0721 Crop Planting, Cultivating & Protecting
NAICS 48122   Nonscheduled Speciality Air Transportation
NAICS 115112 Soil Preparation, Planting & Cultivating
0722 Crop Harvesting, Primarily by Machine
NAICS 115113 Crop Harvesting, Primarily by Machine
0723 Crop Preparation Services for Market, Except Cotton Ginning
NAICS 115114 Postharvest Crop Activities
0724 Cotton Ginning
NAICS 115111 Cotton Ginning
0741 Veterinary Service for Livestock
NAICS 54194   Veterinary Services
0742 Veterinary Services for Animal Specialties
NAICS 54194   Veterinary Services
0751 Livestock Services, Except Veterinary
NAICS 311611 Animal Slaughtering
NAICS 11521   Support Activities for Animal Production
0752 Animal Specialty Services, Except Veterinary
NAICS 11521   Support Activities for Animal Production
NAICS 81291   Pet Care Services
0761 Farm Labor Contractors & Crew Leaders
NAICS 115115 Farm Labor Contractors & Crew Leaders
0762 Farm Management Services
NAICS 115116 Farm Management Services
0781 Landscape Counseling & Planning
NAICS 54169   Other Scientific & Technical Consulting
              Services
NAICS 54132   Landscape Architectural Services

0782 Lawn & Garden Services
NAICS 56173   Landscaping Services
0783 Ornamental Shrub & Tree Services
NAICS 56173   Landscaping Services
0811 Timber Tracts
NAICS 111421 Nursery & Tree Production
NAICS 11311   Timber Tract Operations
0831 Forest Nurseries & Gathering of Forest Products
NAICS 111998 All Other Miscellaneous Crop
NAICS 11321   Forest Nurseries & Gathering of Forest
           Products
0851 Forestry Services
NAICS 11531   Support Activities for Forestry
0912 Finfish
NAICS 114111 Finfish Fishing
0913 Shellfish
NAICS 114112 Shellfish Fishing
0919 Miscellaneous Marine Products
NAICS 114119 Other Marine Fishing
NAICS 111998 All Other Miscellaneous Crop Farming
0921 Fish Hatcheries & Preserves
NAICS 112511 Finfish Farming & Fish Hatcheries
NAICS 112512 Shellfish Farming
0971 Hunting, Trapping, & Game Propagation
NAICS 11421   Hunting & Trapping

MINING INDUSTRIES

1011 Iron Ores
NAICS 21221   Iron Ore Mining
1021 Copper Ores
NAICS 212234 Copper Ore & Nickel Ore Mining
1031 Lead & Zinc Ores
NAICS 212231 Lead Ore & Zinc Ore Mining
1041 Gold Ores
NAICS 212221 Gold Ore Mining
1044 Silver Ores
NAICS 212222 Silver Ore Mining
1061 Ferroalloy Ores, Except Vanadium
NAICS 212234 Copper Ore & Nickel Ore Mining
NAICS 212299 Other Metal Ore Mining
1081 Metal Mining Services
NAICS 213115 Support Activities for Metal Mining
NAICS 54136   Geophysical Surveying & Mapping Services
1094 Uranium-radium-vanadium Ores
NAICS 212291 Uranium-radium-vanadium Ore Mining
1099 Miscellaneous Metal Ores, nec
NAICS 212299 Other Metal Ore Mining
1221 Bituminous Coal & Lignite Surface Mining
NAICS 212111 Bituminous Coal & Lignite Surface Mining
1222 Bituminous Coal Underground Mining
NAICS 212112 Bituminous Coal Underground Mining
1231 Anthracite Mining
NAICS 212113 Anthracite Mining
1241 Coal Mining Services
NAICS 213114 Support Activities for Coal Mining
1311 Crude Petroleum & Natural Gas
NAICS 211111 Crude Petroleum & Natural Gas Extraction
1321 Natural Gas Liquids
NAICS 211112 Natural Gas Liquid Extraction
1381 Drilling Oil & Gas Wells
NAICS 213111 Drilling Oil & Gas Wells

1382 Oil & Gas Field Exploration Services
NAICS 48122   Nonscheduled Speciality Air Transportation
NAICS 54136   Geophysical Surveying & Mapping Services
NAICS 213112 Support Activities for Oil & Gas Field
           Operations
1389 Oil & Gas Field Services, nec
NAICS 213113 Other Oil & Gas Field Support Activities
1411 Dimension Stone
NAICS 212311 Dimension Stone Mining & Quarry
1422 Crushed & Broken Limestone
NAICS 212312 Crushed & Broken Limestone Mining &
           Quarrying
1423 Crushed & Broken Granite
NAICS 212313 Crushed & Broken Granite Mining &
           Quarrying
1429 Crushed & Broken Stone, nec
NAICS 212319 Other Crushed & Broken Stone Mining &
           Quarrying
1442 Construction Sand & Gravel
NAICS 212321 Construction Sand & Gravel Mining
1446 Industrial Sand
NAICS 212322 Industrial Sand Mining
1455 Kaolin & Ball Clay
NAICS 212324 Kaolin & Ball Clay Mining
1459 Clay, Ceramic, & Refractory Minerals, nec
NAICS 212325 Clay & Ceramic & Refractory Minerals Mining
1474 Potash, Soda, & Borate Minerals
NAICS 212391 Potash, Soda, & Borate Mineral Mining
1475 Phosphate Rock
NAICS 212392 Phosphate Rock Mining
1479 Chemical & Fertilizer Mineral Mining, nec
NAICS 212393 Other Chemical & Fertilizer Mineral Mining
1481 Nonmetallic Minerals Services Except Fuels
NAICS 213116 Support Activities for Non-metallic Minerals
NAICS 54136   Geophysical Surveying & Mapping Services
1499 Miscellaneous Nonmetallic Minerals, Except Fuels
NAICS 212319 Other Crushed & Broken Stone Mining or
           Quarrying
NAICS 212399 All Other Non-metallic Mineral Mining

CONSTRUCTION INDUSTRIES

1521 General Contractors-single-family Houses
NAICS 23321   Single Family Housing Construction
**1522 General Contractors-residential Buildings, Other than
    Single-family**
NAICS 23332   Commercial & Institutional Building
           Construction
NAICS 23322   Multifamily Housing Construction
1531 Operative Builders
NAICS 23321   Single Family Housing Construction
NAICS 23322   Multifamily Housing Construction
NAICS 23331   Manufacturing & Industrial Building
           Construction
NAICS 23332   Commercial & Institutional Building
           Construction
1541 General Contractors-industrial Buildings & Warehouses
NAICS 23332   Commercial & Institutional Building
           Construction
NAICS 23331   Manufacturing & Industrial Building
           Construction

1542 General Contractors-nonresidential Buildings, Other than Industrial Buildings & Warehouses
NAICS 23332 Commercial & Institutional Building Construction
1611 Highway & Street Construction, Except Elevated Highways
NAICS 23411 Highway & Street Construction
1622 Bridge, Tunnel, & Elevated Highway Construction
NAICS 23412 Bridge & Tunnel Construction
1623 Water, Sewer, Pipeline, & Communications & Power Line Construction
NAICS 23491 Water, Sewer & Pipeline Construction
NAICS 23492 Power & Communication Transmission Line Construction
1629 Heavy Construction, nec
NAICS 23493 Industrial Nonbuilding Structure Construction
NAICS 23499 All Other Heavy Construction
1711 Plumbing, Heating, & Air-conditioning
NAICS 23511 Plumbing, Heating & Air-conditioning Contractors
1721 Painting & Paper Hanging
NAICS 23521 Painting & Wall Covering Contractors
1731 Electrical Work
NAICS 561621 Security Systems Services
NAICS 23531 Electrical Contractors
1741 Masonry, Stone Setting & Other Stone Work
NAICS 23541 Masonry & Stone Contractors
1742 Plastering, Drywall, Acoustical & Insulation Work
NAICS 23542 Drywall, Plastering, Acoustical & Insulation Contractors
1743 Terrazzo, Tile, Marble, & Mosaic Work
NAICS 23542 Drywall, Plastering, Acoustical & Insulation Contractors
NAICS 23543 Tile, Marble, Terrazzo & Mosaic Contractors
1751 Carpentry Work
NAICS 23551 Carpentry Contractors
1752 Floor Laying & Other Floor Work, nec
NAICS 23552 Floor Laying & Other Floor Contractors
1761 Roofing, Siding, & Sheet Metal Work
NAICS 23561 Roofing, Siding, & Sheet Metal Contractors
1771 Concrete Work
NAICS 23542 Drywall, Plastering, Acoustical & Insulation Contractors
NAICS 23571 Concrete Contractors
1781 Water Well Drilling
NAICS 23581 Water Well Drilling Contractors
1791 Structural Steel Erection
NAICS 23591 Structural Steel Erection Contractors
1793 Glass & Glazing Work
NAICS 23592 Glass & Glazing Contractors
1794 Excavation Work
NAICS 23593 Excavation Contractors
1795 Wrecking & Demolition Work
NAICS 23594 Wrecking & Demolition Contractors
1796 Installation or Erection of Building Equipment, nec
NAICS 23595 Building Equipment & Other Machinery Installation Contractors
1799 Special Trade Contractors, nec
NAICS 23521 Painting & Wall Covering Contractors
NAICS 23592 Glass & Glazing Contractors
NAICS 56291 Remediation Services
NAICS 23599 All Other Special Trade Contractors

FOOD & KINDRED PRODUCTS

2011 Meat Packing Plants
NAICS 311611 Animal Slaughtering
2013 Sausages & Other Prepared Meats
NAICS 311612 Meat Processed from Carcasses
2015 Poultry Slaughtering & Processing
NAICS 311615 Poultry Processing
NAICS 311999 All Other Miscellaneous Food Manufacturing
2021 Creamery Butter
NAICS 311512 Creamery Butter Manufacturing
2022 Natural, Processed, & Imitation Cheese
NAICS 311513 Cheese Manufacturing
2023 Dry, Condensed, & Evaporated Dairy Products
NAICS 311514 Dry, Condensed, & Evaporated Milk Manufacturing
2024 Ice Cream & Frozen Desserts
NAICS 31152 Ice Cream & Frozen Dessert Manufacturing
2026 Fluid Milk
NAICS 311511 Fluid Milk Manufacturing
2032 Canned Specialties
NAICS 311422 Specialty Canning
NAICS 311999 All Other Miscellaneous Food Manufacturing
2033 Canned Fruits, Vegetables, Preserves, Jams, & Jellies
NAICS 311421 Fruit & Vegetable Canning
2034 Dried & Dehydrated Fruits, Vegetables, & Soup Mixes
NAICS 311423 Dried & Dehydrated Food Manufacturing
NAICS 311211 Flour Milling
2035 Pickled Fruits & Vegetables, Vegetables Sauces & Seasonings, & Salad Dressings
NAICS 311421 Fruit & Vegetable Canning
NAICS 311941 Mayonnaise, Dressing, & Other Prepared Sauce Manufacturing
2037 Frozen Fruits, Fruit Juices, & Vegetables
NAICS 311411 Frozen Fruit, Juice, & Vegetable Processing
2038 Frozen Specialties, nec
NAICS 311412 Frozen Specialty Food Manufacturing
2041 Flour & Other Grain Mill Products
NAICS 311211 Flour Milling
2043 Cereal Breakfast Foods
NAICS 31192 Coffee & Tea Manufacturing
NAICS 31123 Breakfast Cereal Manufacturing
2044 Rice Milling
NAICS 311212 Rice Milling
2045 Prepared Flour Mixes & Doughs
NAICS 311822 Flour Mixes & Dough Manufacturing from Purchased Flour
2046 Wet Corn Milling
NAICS 311221 Wet Corn Milling
2047 Dog & Cat Food
NAICS 311111 Dog & Cat Food Manufacturing
2048 Prepared Feed & Feed Ingredients for Animals & Fowls, Except Dogs & Cats
NAICS 311611 Animal Slaughtering
NAICS 311119 Other Animal Food Manufacturing
2051 Bread & Other Bakery Products, Except Cookies & Crackers
NAICS 311812 Commercial Bakeries
2052 Cookies & Crackers
NAICS 311821 Cookie & Cracker Manufacturing
NAICS 311919 Other Snack Food Manufacturing
NAICS 311812 Commercial Bakeries

2053 Frozen Bakery Products, Except Bread
NAICS 311813 Frozen Bakery Product Manufacturing
2061 Cane Sugar, Except Refining
NAICS 311311 Sugarcane Mills
2062 Cane Sugar Refining
NAICS 311312 Cane Sugar Refining
2063 Beet Sugar
NAICS 311313 Beet Sugar Manufacturing
2064 Candy & Other Confectionery Products
NAICS 31133　Confectionery Manufacturing from Purchased
　　　　　　　Chocolate
NAICS 31134　Non-chocolate Confectionery Manufacturing
2066 Chocolate & Cocoa Products
NAICS 31132　Chocolate & Confectionery Manufacturing from
　　　　　　　Cacao Beans
2067 Chewing Gum
NAICS 31134　Non-chocolate Confectionery Manufacturing
2068 Salted & Roasted Nuts & Seeds
NAICS 311911 Roasted Nuts & Peanut Butter Manufacturing
2074 Cottonseed Oil Mills
NAICS 311223 Other Oilseed Processing
NAICS 311225 Fats & Oils Refining & Blending
2075 Soybean Oil Mills
NAICS 311222 Soybean Processing
NAICS 311225 Fats & Oils Refining & Blending
2076 Vegetable Oil Mills, Except Corn, Cottonseed, & Soybeans
NAICS 311223 Other Oilseed Processing
NAICS 311225 Fats & Oils Refining & Blending
2077 Animal & Marine Fats & Oils
NAICS 311613 Rendering & Meat By-product Processing
NAICS 311711 Seafood Canning
NAICS 311712 Fresh & Frozen Seafood Processing
NAICS 311225 Edible Fats & Oils Manufacturing
2079 Shortening, Table Oils, Margarine, & Other Edible Fats &
Oils, nec
NAICS 311225 Edible Fats & Oils Manufacturing
NAICS 311222 Soybean Processing
NAICS 311223 Other Oilseed Processing
2082 Malt Beverages
NAICS 31212　Breweries
2083 Malt
NAICS 311213 Malt Manufacturing
2084 Wines, Brandy, & Brandy Spirits
NAICS 31213　Wineries
2085 Distilled & Blended Liquors
NAICS 31214　Distilleries
2086 Bottled & Canned Soft Drinks & Carbonated Waters
NAICS 312111 Soft Drink Manufacturing
NAICS 312112 Bottled Water Manufacturing
2087 Flavoring Extracts & Flavoring Syrups nec
NAICS 31193　Flavoring Syrup & Concentrate Manufacturing
NAICS 311942 Spice & Extract Manufacturing
NAICS 311999 All Other Miscellaneous Food Manufacturing
2091 Canned & Cured Fish & Seafood
NAICS 311711 Seafood Canning
2092 Prepared Fresh or Frozen Fish & Seafoods
NAICS 311712 Fresh & Frozen Seafood Processing
2095 Roasted Coffee
NAICS 31192　Coffee & Tea Manufacturing
NAICS 311942 Spice & Extract Manufacturing
2096 Potato Chips, Corn Chips, & Similar Snacks
NAICS 311919 Other Snack Food Manufacturing

2097 Manufactured Ice
NAICS 312113 Ice Manufacturing
2098 Macaroni, Spaghetti, Vermicelli, & Noodles
NAICS 311823 Pasta Manufacturing
2099 Food Preparations, nec
NAICS 311423 Dried & Dehydrated Food Manufacturing
NAICS 111998 All Other Miscellaneous Crop Farming
NAICS 31134　Non-chocolate Confectionery Manufacturing
NAICS 311911 Roasted Nuts & Peanut Butter Manufacturing
NAICS 311991 Perishable Prepared Food Manufacturing
NAICS 31183　Tortilla Manufacturing
NAICS 31192　Coffee & Tea Manufacturing
NAICS 311941 Mayonnaise, Dressing, & Other Prepared Sauce
　　　　　　　Manufacturing
NAICS 311942 Spice & Extract Manufacturing
NAICS 311999 All Other Miscellaneous Food Manufacturing

TOBACCO PRODUCTS

2111 Cigarettes
NAICS 312221 Cigarette Manufacturing
2121 Cigars
NAICS 312229 Other Tobacco Product Manufacturing
2131 Chewing & Smoking Tobacco & Snuff
NAICS 312229 Other Tobacco Product Manufacturing
2141 Tobacco Stemming & Redrying
NAICS 312229 Other Tobacco Product Manufacturing
NAICS 31221　Tobacco Stemming & Redrying

TEXTILE MILL PRODUCTS

2211 Broadwoven Fabric Mills, Cotton
NAICS 31321　Broadwoven Fabric Mills
2221 Broadwoven Fabric Mills, Manmade Fiber & Silk
NAICS 31321　Broadwoven Fabric Mills
2231 Broadwoven Fabric Mills, Wool
NAICS 31321　Broadwoven Fabric Mills
NAICS 313311 Broadwoven Fabric Finishing Mills
NAICS 313312 Textile & Fabric Finishing Mills
2241 Narrow Fabric & Other Smallware Mills: Cotton, Wool,
Silk, & Manmade Fiber
NAICS 313221 Narrow Fabric Mills
2251 Women's Full-length & Knee-length Hosiery, Except Socks
NAICS 315111 Sheer Hosiery Mills
2252 Hosiery, nec
NAICS 315111 Sheer Hosiery Mills
NAICS 315119 Other Hosiery & Sock Mills
2253 Knit Outerwear Mills
NAICS 315191 Outerwear Knitting Mills
2254 Knit Underwear & Nightwear Mills
NAICS 315192 Underwear & Nightwear Knitting Mills
2257 Weft Knit Fabric Mills
NAICS 313241 Weft Knit Fabric Mills
NAICS 313312 Textile & Fabric Finishing Mills
2258 Lace & Warp Knit Fabric Mills
NAICS 313249 Other Knit Fabric & Lace Mills
NAICS 313312 Textile & Fabric Finishing Mills
2259 Knitting Mills, nec
NAICS 315191 Outerwear Knitting Mills
NAICS 315192 Underwear & Nightwear Knitting Mills
NAICS 313241 Weft Knit Fabric Mills
NAICS 313249 Other Knit Fabric & Lace Mills

2261 Finishers of Broadwoven Fabrics of Cotton
NAICS 313311 Broadwoven Fabric Finishing Mills
2262 Finishers of Broadwoven Fabrics of Manmade Fiber & Silk
NAICS 313311 Broadwoven Fabric Finishing Mills
2269 Finishers of Textiles, nec
NAICS 313311 Broadwoven Fabric Finishing Mills
NAICS 313312 Textile & Fabric Finishing Mills
2273 Carpets & Rugs
NAICS 31411 Carpet & Rug Mills
2281 Yarn Spinning Mills
NAICS 313111 Yarn Spinning Mills
2282 Yarn Texturizing, Throwing, Twisting, & Winding Mills
NAICS 313112 Yarn Texturing, Throwing & Twisting Mills
NAICS 313312 Textile & Fabric Finishing Mills
2284 Thread Mills
NAICS 313113 Thread Mills
NAICS 313312 Textile & Fabric Finishing Mills
2295 Coated Fabrics, Not Rubberized
NAICS 31332 Fabric Coating Mills
2296 Tire Cord & Fabrics
NAICS 314992 Tire Cord & Tire Fabric Mills
2297 Nonwoven Fabrics
NAICS 31323 Nonwoven Fabric Mills
2298 Cordage & Twine
NAICS 314991 Rope, Cordage & Twine Mills
2299 Textile Goods, nec
NAICS 31321 Broadwoven Fabric Mills
NAICS 31323 Nonwoven Fabric Mills
NAICS 313312 Textile & Fabric Finishing Mills
NAICS 313221 Narrow Fabric Mills
NAICS 313113 Thread Mills
NAICS 313111 Yarn Spinning Mills
NAICS 314999 All Other Miscellaneous Textile Product Mills

APPAREL & OTHER FINISHED PRODUCTS MADE FROM FABRICS & SIMILAR MATERIALS

2311 Men's & Boys' Suits, Coats & Overcoats
NAICS 315211 Men's & Boys' Cut & Sew Apparel Contractors
NAICS 315222 Men's & Boys' Cut & Sew Suit, Coat, & Overcoat Manufacturing
2321 Men's & Boys' Shirts, Except Work Shirts
NAICS 315211 Men's & Boys' Cut & Sew Apparel Contractors
NAICS 315223 Men's & Boys' Cut & Sew Shirt, Manufacturing
2322 Men's & Boys' Underwear & Nightwear
NAICS 315211 Men's & Boys' Cut & Sew Apparel Contractors
NAICS 315221 Men's & Boys' Cut & Sew Underwear & Nightwear Manufacturing
2323 Men's & Boys' Neckwear
NAICS 315993 Men's & Boys' Neckwear Manufacturing
2325 Men's & Boys' Trousers & Slacks
NAICS 315211 Men's & Boys' Cut & Sew Apparel Contractors
NAICS 315224 Men's & Boys' Cut & Sew Trouser, Slack, & Jean Manufacturing
2326 Men's & Boys' Work Clothing
NAICS 315211 Men's & Boys' Cut & Sew Apparel Contractors
NAICS 315225 Men's & Boys' Cut & Sew Work Clothing Manufacturing
2329 Men's & Boys' Clothing, nec
NAICS 315211 Men's & Boys' Cut & Sew Apparel Contractors

NAICS 315228 Men's & Boys' Cut & Sew Other Outerwear Manufacturing
NAICS 315299 All Other Cut & Sew Apparel Manufacturing
2331 Women's, Misses', & Juniors' Blouses & Shirts
NAICS 315212 Women's & Girls' Cut & Sew Apparel Contractors
NAICS 315232 Women's & Girls' Cut & Sew Blouse & Shirt Manufacturing
2335 Women's, Misses' & Junior's Dresses
NAICS 315212 Women's & Girls' Cut & Sew Apparel Contractors
NAICS 315233 Women's & Girls' Cut & Sew Dress Manufacturing
2337 Women's, Misses' & Juniors' Suits, Skirts & Coats
NAICS 315212 Women's & Girls' Cut & Sew Apparel Contractors
NAICS 315234 Women's & Girls' Cut & Sew Suit, Coat, Tailored Jacket, & Skirt Manufacturing
2339 Women's, Misses' & Juniors' Outerwear, nec
NAICS 315999 Other Apparel Accessories & Other Apparel Manufacturing
NAICS 315212 Women's & Girls' Cut & Sew Apparel Contractors
NAICS 315299 All Other Cut & Sew Apparel Manufacturing
NAICS 315238 Women's & Girls' Cut & Sew Other Outerwear Manufacturing
2341 Women's, Misses, Children's, & Infants' Underwear & Nightwear
NAICS 315212 Women's & Girls' Cut & Sew Apparel Contractors
NAICS 315211 Men's & Boys' Cut & Sew Apparel Contractors
NAICS 315231 Women's & Girls' Cut & Sew Lingerie, Loungewear, & Nightwear Manufacturing
NAICS 315221 Men's & Boys' Cut & Sew Underwear & Nightwear Manufacturing
NAICS 315291 Infants' Cut & Sew Apparel Manufacturing
2342 Brassieres, Girdles, & Allied Garments
NAICS 315212 Women's & Girls' Cut & Sew Apparel Contractors
NAICS 315231 Women's & Girls' Cut & Sew Lingerie, Loungewear, & Nightwear Manufacturing
2353 Hats, Caps, & Millinery
NAICS 315991 Hat, Cap, & Millinery Manufacturing
2361 Girls', Children's & Infants' Dresses, Blouses & Shirts
NAICS 315291 Infants' Cut & Sew Apparel Manufacturing
NAICS 315223 Men's & Boys' Cut & Sew Shirt, Manufacturing
NAICS 315211 Men's & Boys' Cut & Sew Apparel Contractors
NAICS 315232 Women's & Girls' Cut & Sew Blouse & Shirt Manufacturing
NAICS 315233 Women's & Girls' Cut & Sew Dress Manufacturing
NAICS 315212 Women's & Girls' Cut & Sew Apparel Contractors
2369 Girls', Children's & Infants' Outerwear, nec
NAICS 315291 Infants' Cut & Sew Apparel Manufacturing
NAICS 315222 Men's & Boys' Cut & Sew Suit, Coat, & Overcoat Manufacturing
NAICS 315224 Men's & Boys' Cut & Sew Trouser, Slack, & Jean Manufacturing
NAICS 315228 Men's & Boys' Cut & Sew Other Outerwear Manufacturing
NAICS 315221 Men's & Boys' Cut & Sew Underwear & Nightwear Manufacturing
NAICS 315211 Men's & Boys' Cut & Sew Apparel Contractors

NAICS 315234 Women's & Girls' Cut & Sew Suit, Coat, Tailored Jacket, & Skirt Manufacturing

NAICS 315238 Women's & Girls' Cut & Sew Other Outerwear Manufacturing

NAICS 315231 Women's & Girls' Cut & Sew Lingerie, Loungewear, & Nightwear Manufacturing

NAICS 315212 Women's & Girls' Cut & Sew Apparel Contractors

2371 Fur Goods

NAICS 315292 Fur & Leather Apparel Manufacturing

2381 Dress & Work Gloves, Except Knit & All-leather

NAICS 315992 Glove & Mitten Manufacturing

2384 Robes & Dressing Gowns

NAICS 315231 Women's & Girls' Cut & Sew Lingerie, Loungewear, & Nightwear Manufacturing

NAICS 315221 Men's & Boys' Cut & Sew Underwear & Nightwear Manufacturing

NAICS 315211 Men's & Boys' Cut & Sew Apparel Contractors

NAICS 315212 Women's & Girls' Cut & Sew Apparel Contractors

2385 Waterproof Outerwear

NAICS 315222 Men's & Boys' Cut & Sew Suit, Coat, & Overcoat Manufacturing

NAICS 315234 Women's & Girls' Cut & Sew Suit, Coat, Tailored Jacket, & Skirt Manufacturing

NAICS 315228 Men's & Boys' Cut & Sew Other Outerwear Manufacturing

NAICS 315238 Women's & Girls' Cut & Sew Other Outerwear Manufacturing

NAICS 315291 Infants' Cut & Sew Apparel Manufacturing

NAICS 315999 Other Apparel Accessories & Other Apparel Manufacturing

NAICS 315211 Men's & Boys' Cut & Sew Apparel Contractors

NAICS 315212 Women's & Girls' Cut & Sew Apparel Contractors

2386 Leather & Sheep-lined Clothing

NAICS 315292 Fur & Leather Apparel Manufacturing

2387 Apparel Belts

NAICS 315999 Other Apparel Accessories & Other Apparel Manufacturing

2389 Apparel & Accessories, nec

NAICS 315999 Other Apparel Accessories & Other Apparel Manufacturing

NAICS 315299 All Other Cut & Sew Apparel Manufacturing

NAICS 315231 Women's & Girls' Cut & Sew Lingerie, Loungewear, & Nightwear Manufacturing

NAICS 315212 Women's & Girls' Cut & Sew Apparel Contractors

NAICS 315211 Mens' & Boys' Cut & Sew Apparel Contractors

2391 Curtains & Draperies

NAICS 314121 Curtain & Drapery Mills

2392 Housefurnishings, Except Curtains & Draperies

NAICS 314911 Textile Bag Mills

NAICS 339994 Broom, Brush & Mop Manufacturing

NAICS 314129 Other Household Textile Product Mills

2393 Textile Bags

NAICS 314911 Textile Bag Mills

2394 Canvas & Related Products

NAICS 314912 Canvas & Related Product Mills

2395 Pleating, Decorative & Novelty Stitching, & Tucking for the Trade

NAICS 314999 All Other Miscellaneous Textile Product Mills

NAICS 315211 Mens' & Boys' Cut & Sew Apparel Contractors

NAICS 315212 Women's & Girls' Cut & Sew Apparel Contractors

2396 Automotive Trimmings, Apparel Findings, & Related Products

NAICS 33636 Motor Vehicle Fabric Accessories & Seat Manufacturing

NAICS 315999 Other Apparel Accessories, & Other Apparel Manufacturing

NAICS 323113 Commercial Screen Printing

NAICS 314999 All Other Miscellaneous Textile Product Mills

2397 Schiffli Machine Embroideries

NAICS 313222 Schiffli Machine Embroidery

2399 Fabricated Textile Products, nec

NAICS 33636 Motor Vehicle Fabric Accessories & Seat Manufacturing

NAICS 315999 Other Apparel Accessories & Other Apparel Manufacturing

NAICS 314999 All Other Miscellaneous Textile Product Mills

LUMBER & WOOD PRODUCTS, EXCEPT FURNITURE

2411 Logging

NAICS 11331 Logging

2421 Sawmills & Planing Mills, General

NAICS 321913 Softwood Cut Stock, Resawing Lumber, & Planing

NAICS 321113 Sawmills

NAICS 321914 Other Millwork

NAICS 321999 All Other Miscellaneous Wood Product Manufacturing

2426 Hardwood Dimension & Flooring Mills

NAICS 321914 Other Millwork

NAICS 321999 All Other Miscellaneous Wood Product Manufacturing

NAICS 337139 Other Wood Furniture Manufacturing

NAICS 321912 Hardwood Dimension Mills

2429 Special Product Sawmills, nec

NAICS 321113 Sawmills

NAICS 321913 Softwood Cut Stock, Resawing Lumber, & Planing

NAICS 321999 All Other Miscellaneous Wood Product Manufacturing

2431 Millwork

NAICS 321911 Wood Window & Door Manufacturing

NAICS 321914 Other Millwork

2434 Wood Kitchen Cabinets

NAICS 337131 Wood Kitchen Cabinet & Counter Top Manufacturing

2435 Hardwood Veneer & Plywood

NAICS 321211 Hardwood Veneer & Plywood Manufacturing

2436 Softwood Veneer & Plywood

NAICS 321212 Softwood Veneer & Plywood Manufacturing

2439 Structural Wood Members, nec

NAICS 321913 Softwood Cut Stock, Resawing Lumber, & Planing

NAICS 321214 Truss Manufacturing

NAICS 321213 Engineered Wood Member Manufacturing

2441 Nailed & Lock Corner Wood Boxes & Shook

NAICS 32192 Wood Container & Pallet Manufacturing

2448 Wood Pallets & Skids

NAICS 32192 Wood Container & Pallet Manufacturing

2449 Wood Containers, nec
NAICS 32192   Wood Container & Pallet Manufacturing
2451 Mobile Homes
NAICS 321991 Manufactured Home Manufacturing
2452 Prefabricated Wood Buildings & Components
NAICS 321992 Prefabricated Wood Building Manufacturing
2491 Wood Preserving
NAICS 321114 Wood Preservation
2493 Reconstituted Wood Products
NAICS 321219 Reconstituted Wood Product Manufacturing
2499 Wood Products, nec
NAICS 339999 All Other Miscellaneous Manufacturing
NAICS 337139 Other Wood Furniture Manufacturing
NAICS 337148 Other Nonwood Furniture Manufacturing
NAICS 32192   Wood Container & Pallet Manufacturing
NAICS 321999 All Other Miscellaneous Wood Product
      Manufacturing

FURNITURE & FIXTURES

2511 Wood Household Furniture, Except Upholstered
NAICS 337122 Wood Household Furniture Manufacturing
2512 Wood Household Furniture, Upholstered
NAICS 337121 Upholstered Household Furniture
      Manufacturing
2514 Metal Household Furniture
NAICS 337124 Metal Household Furniture Manufacturing
2515 Mattresses, Foundations, & Convertible Beds
NAICS 33791   Mattress Manufacturing
NAICS 337132 Upholstered Wood Household Furniture
      Manufacturing
**2517 Wood Television, Radio, Phonograph & Sewing Machine
      Cabinets**
NAICS 337139 Other Wood Furniture Manufacturing
2519 Household Furniture, nec
NAICS 337143 Household Furniture (except Wood & Metal)
      Manufacturing
2521 Wood Office Furniture
NAICS 337134 Wood Office Furniture Manufacturing
2522 Office Furniture, Except Wood
NAICS 337141 Nonwood Office Furniture Manufacturing
2531 Public Building & Related Furniture
NAICS 33636   Motor Vehicle Fabric Accessories & Seat
      Manufacturing
NAICS 337139 Other Wood Furniture Manufacturing
NAICS 337148 Other Nonwood Furniture Manufacturing
NAICS 339942 Lead Pencil & Art Good Manufacturing
**2541 Wood Office & Store Fixtures, Partitions, Shelving, &
      Lockers**
NAICS 337131 Wood Kitchen Cabinet & Counter Top
      Manufacturing
NAICS 337135 Custom Architectural Woodwork, Millwork, &
      Fixtures
NAICS 337139 Other Wood Furniture Manufacturing
**2542 Office & Store Fixtures, Partitions Shelving, & Lockers,
      Except Wood**
NAICS 337145 Nonwood Showcase, Partition, Shelving, &
      Locker Manufacturing
2591 Drapery Hardware & Window Blinds & Shades
NAICS 33792   Blind & Shade Manufacturing
2599 Furniture & Fixtures, nec
NAICS 339113 Surgical Appliance & Supplies Manufacturing
NAICS 337139 Other Wood Furniture Manufacturing

NAICS 337148 Other Nonwood Furniture Manufacturing

PAPER & ALLIED PRODUCTS

2611 Pulp Mills
NAICS 32211   Pulp Mills
NAICS 322121 Paper Mills
NAICS 32213   Paperboard Mills
2621 Paper Mills
NAICS 322121 Paper Mills
NAICS 322122 Newsprint Mills
2631 Paperboard Mills
NAICS 32213   Paperboard Mills
2652 Setup Paperboard Boxes
NAICS 322213 Setup Paperboard Box Manufacturing
2653 Corrugated & Solid Fiber Boxes
NAICS 322211 Corrugated & Solid Fiber Box Manufacturing
2655 Fiber Cans, Tubes, Drums, & Similar Products
NAICS 322214 Fiber Can, Tube, Drum, & Similar Products
      Manufacturing
2656 Sanitary Food Containers, Except Folding
NAICS 322215 Non-folding Sanitary Food Container
      Manufacturing
2657 Folding Paperboard Boxes, Including Sanitary
NAICS 322212 Folding Paperboard Box Manufacturing
2671 Packaging Paper & Plastics Film, Coated & Laminated
NAICS 322221 Coated & Laminated Packaging Paper &
      Plastics Film Manufacturing
NAICS 326112 Unsupported Plastics Packaging Film & Sheet
      Manufacturing
2672 Coated & Laminated Paper, nec
NAICS 322222 Coated & Laminated Paper Manufacturing
2673 Plastics, Foil, & Coated Paper Bags
NAICS 322223 Plastics, Foil, & Coated Paper Bag
      Manufacturing
NAICS 326111 Unsupported Plastics Bag Manufacturing
2674 Uncoated Paper & Multiwall Bags
NAICS 322224 Uncoated Paper & Multiwall Bag
      Manufacturing
2675 Die-cut Paper & Paperboard & Cardboard
NAICS 322231 Die-cut Paper & Paperboard Office Supplies
      Manufacturing
NAICS 322292 Surface-coated Paperboard Manufacturing
NAICS 322298 All Other Converted Paper Product
      Manufacturing
2676 Sanitary Paper Products
NAICS 322291 Sanitary Paper Product Manufacturing
2677 Envelopes
NAICS 322232 Envelope Manufacturing
2678 Stationery, Tablets, & Related Products
NAICS 322233 Stationery, Tablet, & Related Product
      Manufacturing
2679 Converted Paper & Paperboard Products, nec
NAICS 322215 Non-folding Sanitary Food Container
      Manufacturing
NAICS 322222 Coated & Laminated Paper Manufacturing
NAICS 322231 Die-cut Paper & Paperboard Office Supplies
      Manufacturing
NAICS 322298 All Other Converted Paper Product
      Manufacturing

PRINTING, PUBLISHING, & ALLIED INDUSTRIES

2711 Newspapers: Publishing, or Publishing & Printing
NAICS 51111　Newspaper Publishers
2721 Periodicals: Publishing, or Publishing & Printing
NAICS 51112　Periodical Publishers
2731 Books: Publishing, or Publishing & Printing
NAICS 51223　Music Publishers
NAICS 51113　Book Publishers
2732 Book Printing
NAICS 323117　Book Printing
2741 Miscellaneous Publishing
NAICS 51114　Database & Directory Publishers
NAICS 51223　Music Publishers
NAICS 511199　All Other Publishers
2752 Commercial Printing, Lithographic
NAICS 323114　Quick Printing
NAICS 323110　Commercial Lithographic Printing
2754 Commercial Printing, Gravure
NAICS 323111　Commercial Gravure Printing
2759 Commercial Printing, nec
NAICS 323113　Commercial Screen Printing
NAICS 323112　Commercial Flexographic Printing
NAICS 323114　Quick Printing
NAICS 323115　Digital Printing
NAICS 323119　Other Commercial Printing
2761 Manifold Business Forms
NAICS 323116　Manifold Business Form Printing
2771 Greeting Cards
NAICS 323110　Commercial Lithographic Printing
NAICS 323111　Commercial Gravure Printing
NAICS 323112　Commercial Flexographic Printing
NAICS 323113　Commercial Screen Printing
NAICS 323119　Other Commercial Printing
NAICS 511191　Greeting Card Publishers
2782 Blankbooks, Loose-leaf Binders & Devices
NAICS 323110　Commercial Lithographic Printing
NAICS 323111　Commercial Gravure Printing
NAICS 323112　Commercial Flexographic Printing
NAICS 323113　Commercial Screen Printing
NAICS 323119　Other Commercial Printing
NAICS 323118　Blankbook, Loose-leaf Binder & Device Manufacturing
2789 Bookbinding & Related Work
NAICS 323121　Tradebinding & Related Work
2791 Typesetting
NAICS 323122　Prepress Services
2796 Platemaking & Related Services
NAICS 323122　Prepress Services

CHEMICALS & ALLIED PRODUCTS

2812 Alkalies & Chlorine
NAICS 325181　Alkalies & Chlorine Manufacturing
2813 Industrial Gases
NAICS 32512　Industrial Gas Manufacturing
2816 Inorganic Pigments
NAICS 325131　Inorganic Dye & Pigment Manufacturing
NAICS 325182　Carbon Black Manufacturing
2819 Industrial Inorganic Chemicals, nec
NAICS 325998　All Other Miscellaneous Chemical Product Manufacturing

NAICS 331311　Alumina Refining
NAICS 325131　Inorganic Dye & Pigment Manufacturing
NAICS 325188　All Other Basic Inorganic Chemical Manufacturing
2821 Plastics Material Synthetic Resins, & Nonvulcanizable Elastomers
NAICS 325211　Plastics Material & Resin Manufacturing
2822 Synthetic Rubber
NAICS 325212　Synthetic Rubber Manufacturing
2823 Cellulosic Manmade Fibers
NAICS 325221　Cellulosic Manmade Fiber Manufacturing
2824 Manmade Organic Fibers, Except Cellulosic
NAICS 325222　Noncellulosic Organic Fiber Manufacturing
2833 Medicinal Chemicals & Botanical Products
NAICS 325411　Medicinal & Botanical Manufacturing
2834 Pharmaceutical Preparations
NAICS 325412　Pharmaceutical Preparation Manufacturing
2835 In Vitro & in Vivo Diagnostic Substances
NAICS 325412　Pharmaceutical Preparation Manufacturing
NAICS 325413　In-vitro Diagnostic Substance Manufacturing
2836 Biological Products, Except Diagnostic Substances
NAICS 325414　Biological Product Manufacturing
2841 Soaps & Other Detergents, Except Speciality Cleaners
NAICS 325611　Soap & Other Detergent Manufacturing
2842 Speciality Cleaning, Polishing, & Sanitary Preparations
NAICS 325612　Polish & Other Sanitation Good Manufacturing
2843 Surface Active Agents, Finishing Agents, Sulfonated Oils, & Assistants
NAICS 325613　Surface Active Agent Manufacturing
2844 Perfumes, Cosmetics, & Other Toilet Preparations
NAICS 32562　Toilet Preparation Manufacturing
NAICS 325611　Soap & Other Detergent Manufacturing
2851 Paints, Varnishes, Lacquers, Enamels, & Allied Products
NAICS 32551　Paint & Coating Manufacturing
2861 Gum & Wood Chemicals
NAICS 325191　Gum & Wood Chemical Manufacturing
2865 Cyclic Organic Crudes & Intermediates, & Organic Dyes & Pigments
NAICS 32511　Petrochemical Manufacturing
NAICS 325132　Organic Dye & Pigment Manufacturing
NAICS 325192　Cyclic Crude & Intermediate Manufacturing
2869 Industrial Organic Chemicals, nec
NAICS 32511　Petrochemical Manufacturing
NAICS 325188　All Other Inorganic Chemical Manufacturing
NAICS 325193　Ethyl Alcohol Manufacturing
NAICS 32512　Industrial Gas Manufacturing
NAICS 325199　All Other Basic Organic Chemical Manufacturing
2873 Nitrogenous Fertilizers
NAICS 325311　Nitrogenous Fertilizer Manufacturing
2874 Phosphatic Fertilizers
NAICS 325312　Phosphatic Fertilizer Manufacturing
2875 Fertilizers, Mixing Only
NAICS 325314　Fertilizer Manufacturing
2879 Pesticides & Agricultural Chemicals, nec
NAICS 32532　Pesticide & Other Agricultural Chemical Manufacturing
2891 Adhesives & Sealants
NAICS 32552　Adhesive & Sealant Manufacturing
2892 Explosives
NAICS 32592　Explosives Manufacturing
2893 Printing Ink
NAICS 32591　Printing Ink Manufacturing

2895 Carbon Black
NAICS 325182 Carbon Black Manufacturing
2899 Chemicals & Chemical Preparations, nec
NAICS 32551 Paint & Coating Manufacturing
NAICS 311942 Spice & Extract Manufacturing
NAICS 325199 All Other Basic Organic Chemical
Manufacturing
NAICS 325998 All Other Miscellaneous Chemical Product
Manufacturing

PETROLEUM REFINING & RELATED INDUSTRIES

2911 Petroleum Refining
NAICS 32411 Petroleum Refineries
2951 Asphalt Paving Mixtures & Blocks
NAICS 324121 Asphalt Paving Mixture & Block Manufacturing
2952 Asphalt Felts & Coatings
NAICS 324122 Asphalt Shingle & Coating Materials
Manufacturing
2992 Lubricating Oils & Greases
NAICS 324191 Petroleum Lubricating Oil & Grease
Manufacturing 2999

RUBBER & MISCELLANEOUS PLASTICS PRODUCTS

3011 Tires & Inner Tubes
NAICS 326211 Tire Manufacturing
3021 Rubber & Plastics Footwear
NAICS 316211 Rubber & Plastics Footwear Manufacturing
3052 Rubber & Plastics Hose & Belting
NAICS 32622 Rubber & Plastics Hoses & Belting
Manufacturing
3053 Gaskets, Packing, & Sealing Devices
NAICS 339991 Gasket, Packing, & Sealing Device
Manufacturing
3061 Molded, Extruded, & Lathe-cut Mechanical Rubber Products
NAICS 326291 Rubber Product Manufacturing for Mechanical
Use
3069 Fabricated Rubber Products, nec
NAICS 31332 Fabric Coating Mills
NAICS 326192 Resilient Floor Covering Manufacturing
NAICS 326299 All Other Rubber Product Manufacturing
3081 Unsupported Plastics Film & Sheet
NAICS 326113 Unsupported Plastics Film & Sheet
Manufacturing
3082 Unsupported Plastics Profile Shapes
NAICS 326121 Unsupported Plastics Profile Shape
Manufacturing
3083 Laminated Plastics Plate, Sheet, & Profile Shapes
NAICS 32613 Laminated Plastics Plate, Sheet, & Shape
Manufacturing
3084 Plastic Pipe
NAICS 326122 Plastic Pipe & Pipe Fitting Manufacturing
3085 Plastics Bottles
NAICS 32616 Plastics Bottle Manufacturing
3086 Plastics Foam Products
NAICS 32615 Urethane & Other Foam Product
Manufacturing
NAICS 32614 Polystyrene Foam Product Manufacturing

3087 Custom Compounding of Purchased Plastics Resins
NAICS 325991 Custom Compounding of Purchased Resin
3088 Plastics Plumbing Fixtures
NAICS 326191 Plastics Plumbing Fixtures Manufacturing
3089 Plastics Products, nec
NAICS 326122 Plastics Pipe & Pipe Fitting Manufacturing
NAICS 326121 Unsupported Plastics Profile Shape
Manufacturing
NAICS 326199 All Other Plastics Product Manufacturing

LEATHER & LEATHER PRODUCTS

3111 Leather Tanning & Finishing
NAICS 31611 Leather & Hide Tanning & Finishing
3131 Boot & Shoe Cut Stock & Findings
NAICS 321999 All Other Miscellaneous Wood Product
Manufacturing
NAICS 339993 Fastener, Button, Needle, & Pin Manufacturing
NAICS 316999 All Other Leather Good Manufacturing
3142 House Slippers
NAICS 316212 House Slipper Manufacturing
3143 Men's Footwear, Except Athletic
NAICS 316213 Men's Footwear Manufacturing
3144 Women's Footwear, Except Athletic
NAICS 316214 Women's Footwear Manufacturing
3149 Footwear, Except Rubber, nec
NAICS 316219 Other Footwear Manufacturing
3151 Leather Gloves & Mittens
NAICS 315992 Glove & Mitten Manufacturing
3161 Luggage
NAICS 316991 Luggage Manufacturing
3171 Women's Handbags & Purses
NAICS 316992 Women's Handbag & Purse Manufacturing
3172 Personal Leather Goods, Except Women's Handbags & Purses
NAICS 316993 Personal Leather Good Manufacturing
3199 Leather Goods, nec
NAICS 316999 All Other Leather Good Manufacturing

STONE, CLAY, GLASS, & CONCRETE PRODUCTS

3211 Flat Glass
NAICS 327211 Flat Glass Manufacturing
3221 Glass Containers
NAICS 327213 Glass Container Manufacturing
3229 Pressed & Blown Glass & Glassware, nec
NAICS 327212 Other Pressed & Blown Glass & Glassware
Manufacturing
3231 Glass Products, Made of Purchased Glass
NAICS 327215 Glass Product Manufacturing Made of
Purchased Glass
3241 Cement, Hydraulic
NAICS 32731 Hydraulic Cement Manufacturing
3251 Brick & Structural Clay Tile
NAICS 327121 Brick & Structural Clay Tile Manufacturing
3253 Ceramic Wall & Floor Tile
NAICS 327122 Ceramic Wall & Floor Tile Manufacturing
3255 Clay Refractories
NAICS 327124 Clay Refractory Manufacturing

3259 Structural Clay Products, nec
NAICS 327123 Other Structural Clay Product Manufacturing

3261 Vitreous China Plumbing Fixtures & China & Earthenware Fittings & Bathroom Accessories
NAICS 327111 Vitreous China Plumbing Fixture & China & Earthenware Fittings & Bathroom Accessories Manufacturing

3262 Vitreous China Table & Kitchen Articles
NAICS 327112 Vitreous China, Fine Earthenware & Other Pottery Product Manufacturing

3263 Fine Earthenware Table & Kitchen Articles
NAICS 327112 Vitreous China, Fine Earthenware & Other Pottery Product Manufacturing

3264 Porcelain Electrical Supplies
NAICS 327113 Porcelain Electrical Supply Manufacturing

3269 Pottery Products, nec
NAICS 327112 Vitreous China, Fine Earthenware, & Other Pottery Product Manufacturing

3271 Concrete Block & Brick
NAICS 327331 Concrete Block & Brick Manufacturing

3272 Concrete Products, Except Block & Brick
NAICS 327999 All Other Miscellaneous Nonmetallic Mineral Product Manufacturing
NAICS 327332 Concrete Pipe Manufacturing
NAICS 32739 Other Concrete Product Manufacturing

3273 Ready-mixed Concrete
NAICS 32732 Ready-mix Concrete Manufacturing

3274 Lime
NAICS 32741 Lime Manufacturing

3275 Gypsum Products
NAICS 32742 Gypsum & Gypsum Product Manufacturing

3281 Cut Stone & Stone Products
NAICS 327991 Cut Stone & Stone Product Manufacturing

3291 Abrasive Products
NAICS 332999 All Other Miscellaneous Fabricated Metal Product Manufacturing
NAICS 32791 Abrasive Product Manufacturing

3292 Asbestos Products
NAICS 33634 Motor Vehicle Brake System Manufacturing
NAICS 327999 All Other Miscellaneous Nonmetallic Mineral Product Manufacturing

3295 Minerals & Earths, Ground or Otherwise Treated
NAICS 327992 Ground or Treated Mineral & Earth Manufacturing

3296 Mineral Wool
NAICS 327993 Mineral Wool Manufacturing

3297 Nonclay Refractories
NAICS 327125 Nonclay Refractory Manufacturing

3299 Nonmetallic Mineral Products, nec
NAICS 32742 Gypsum & Gypsum Product Manufacturing
NAICS 327999 All Other Miscellaneous Nonmetallic Mineral Product Manufacturing

PRIMARY METALS INDUSTRIES

3312 Steel Works, Blast Furnaces , & Rolling Mills
NAICS 324199 All Other Petroleum & Coal Products Manufacturing
NAICS 331111 Iron & Steel Mills

3313 Electrometallurgical Products, Except Steel
NAICS 331112 Electrometallurgical Ferroalloy Product Manufacturing

NAICS 331492 Secondary Smelting, Refining, & Alloying of Nonferrous Metals

3315 Steel Wiredrawing & Steel Nails & Spikes
NAICS 331222 Steel Wire Drawing
NAICS 332618 Other Fabricated Wire Product Manufacturing

3316 Cold-rolled Steel Sheet, Strip, & Bars
NAICS 331221 Cold-rolled Steel Shape Manufacturing

3317 Steel Pipe & Tubes
NAICS 33121 Iron & Steel Pipes & Tubes Manufacturing from Purchased Steel

3321 Gray & Ductile Iron Foundries
NAICS 331511 Iron Foundries

3322 Malleable Iron Foundries
NAICS 331511 Iron Foundries

3324 Steel Investment Foundries
NAICS 331512 Steel Investment Foundries

3325 Steel Foundries, nec
NAICS 331513 Steel Foundries

3331 Primary Smelting & Refining of Copper
NAICS 331411 Primary Smelting & Refining of Copper

3334 Primary Production of Aluminum
NAICS 331312 Primary Aluminum Production

3339 Primary Smelting & Refining of Nonferrous Metals, Except Copper & Aluminum
NAICS 331419 Primary Smelting & Refining of Nonferrous Metals

3341 Secondary Smelting & Refining of Nonferrous Metals
NAICS 331314 Secondary Smelting & Alloying of Aluminum
NAICS 331423 Secondary Smelting, Refining, & Alloying of Copper
NAICS 331492 Secondary Smelting, Refining, & Alloying of Nonferrous Metals

3351 Rolling, Drawing, & Extruding of Copper
NAICS 331421 Copper Rolling, Drawing, & Extruding

3353 Aluminum Sheet, Plate, & Foil
NAICS 331315 Aluminum Sheet, Plate, & Foil Manufacturing

3354 Aluminum Extruded Products
NAICS 331316 Aluminum Extruded Product Manufacturing

3355 Aluminum Rolling & Drawing, nec
NAICS 331319 Other Aluminum Rolling & Drawing,

3356 Rolling, Drawing, & Extruding of Nonferrous Metals, Except Copper & Aluminum
NAICS 331491 Nonferrous Metal Rolling. Drawing, & Extruding

3357 Drawing & Insulating of Nonferrous Wire
NAICS 331319 Other Aluminum Rolling & Drawing
NAICS 331422 Copper Wire Drawing
NAICS 331491 Nonferrous Metal Rolling, Drawing, & Extruding
NAICS 335921 Fiber Optic Cable Manufacturing
NAICS 335929 Other Communication & Energy Wire Manufacturing

3363 Aluminum Die-castings
NAICS 331521 Aluminum Die-castings

3364 Nonferrous Die-castings, Except Aluminum
NAICS 331522 Nonferrous Die-castings

3365 Aluminum Foundries
NAICS 331524 Aluminum Foundries

3366 Copper Foundries
NAICS 331525 Copper Foundries

3369 Nonferrous Foundries, Except Aluminum & Copper
NAICS 331528 Other Nonferrous Foundries

3398 Metal Heat Treating
NAICS 332811 Metal Heat Treating
3399 Primary Metal Products, nec
NAICS 331111 Iron & Steel Mills
NAICS 331314 Secondary Smelting & Alloying of Aluminum
NAICS 331423 Secondary Smelting, Refining, & Alloying of
Copper
NAICS 331492 Secondary Smelting, Refining, & Alloying of
Nonferrous Metals
NAICS 332618 Other Fabricated Wire Product Manufacturing
NAICS 332813 Electroplating, Plating, Polishing, Anodizing, &
Coloring

FABRICATED METAL PRODUCTS, EXCEPT MACHINERY & TRANSPORTATION EQUIPMENT

3411 Metal Cans
NAICS 332431 Metal Can Manufacturing
3412 Metal Shipping Barrels, Drums, Kegs & Pails
NAICS 332439 Other Metal Container Manufacturing
3421 Cutlery
NAICS 332211 Cutlery & Flatware Manufacturing
3423 Hand & Edge Tools, Except Machine Tools & Handsaws
NAICS 332212 Hand & Edge Tool Manufacturing
3425 Saw Blades & Handsaws
NAICS 332213 Saw Blade & Handsaw Manufacturing
3429 Hardware, nec
NAICS 332439 Other Metal Container Manufacturing
NAICS 332919 Other Metal Valve & Pipe Fitting
Manufacturing
NAICS 33251 Hardware Manufacturing
3431 Enameled Iron & Metal Sanitary Ware
NAICS 332998 Enameled Iron & Metal Sanitary Ware
Manufacturing
3432 Plumbing Fixture Fittings & Trim
NAICS 332913 Plumbing Fixture Fitting & Trim Manufacturing
NAICS 332999 All Other Miscellaneous Fabricated Metal
Product Manufacturing
3433 Heating Equipment, Except Electric & Warm Air Furnaces
NAICS 333414 Heating Equipment Manufacturing
3441 Fabricated Structural Metal
NAICS 332312 Fabricated Structural Metal Manufacturing
3442 Metal Doors, Sash, Frames, Molding, & Trim Manufacturing
NAICS 332321 Metal Window & Door Manufacturing
3443 Fabricated Plate Work
NAICS 332313 Plate Work Manufacturing
NAICS 33241 Power Boiler & Heat Exchanger Manufacturing
NAICS 33242 Metal Tank Manufacturing
NAICS 333415 Air-conditioning & Warm Air Heating
Equipment & Commercial & Industrial
Refrigeration Equipment Manufacturing
3444 Sheet Metal Work
NAICS 332322 Sheet Metal Work Manufacturing
NAICS 332439 Other Metal Container Manufacturing
3446 Architectural & Ornamental Metal Work
NAICS 332323 Ornamental & Architectural Metal Work
Manufacturing
3448 Prefabricated Metal Buildings & Components
NAICS 332311 Prefabricated Metal Building & Component
Manufacturing

3449 Miscellaneous Structural Metal Work
NAICS 332114 Custom Roll Forming
NAICS 332312 Fabricated Structural Metal Manufacturing
NAICS 332321 Metal Window & Door Manufacturing
NAICS 332323 Ornamental & Architectural Metal Work
Manufacturing
3451 Screw Machine Products
NAICS 332721 Precision Turned Product Manufacturing
3452 Bolts, Nuts, Screws, Rivets, & Washers
NAICS 332722 Bolt, Nut, Screw, Rivet, & Washer
Manufacturing
3462 Iron & Steel Forgings
NAICS 332111 Iron & Steel Forging
3463 Nonferrous Forgings
NAICS 332112 Nonferrous Forging
3465 Automotive Stamping
NAICS 33637 Motor Vehicle Metal Stamping
3466 Crowns & Closures
NAICS 332115 Crown & Closure Manufacturing
3469 Metal Stamping, nec
NAICS 339911 Jewelry Manufacturing
NAICS 332116 Metal Stamping
NAICS 332214 Kitchen Utensil, Pot & Pan Manufacturing
3471 Electroplating, Plating, Polishing, Anodizing, & Coloring
NAICS 332813 Electroplating, Plating, Polishing, Anodizing, &
Coloring
3479 Coating, Engraving, & Allied Services, nec
NAICS 339914 Costume Jewelry & Novelty Manufacturing
NAICS 339911 Jewelry Manufacturing
NAICS 339912 Silverware & Plated Ware Manufacturing
NAICS 332812 Metal Coating, Engraving , & Allied Services to
Manufacturers
3482 Small Arms Ammunition
NAICS 332992 Small Arms Ammunition Manufacturing
3483 Ammunition, Except for Small Arms
NAICS 332993 Ammunition Manufacturing
3484 Small Arms
NAICS 332994 Small Arms Manufacturing
3489 Ordnance & Accessories, nec
NAICS 332995 Other Ordnance & Accessories Manufacturing
3491
3492 Fluid Power Valves & Hose Fittings
NAICS 332912 Fluid Power Valve & Hose Fitting
Manufacturing
3493 Steel Springs, Except Wire
NAICS 332611 Steel Spring Manufacturing
3494 Valves & Pipe Fittings, nec
NAICS 332919 Other Metal Valve & Pipe Fitting
Manufacturing
NAICS 332999 All Other Miscellaneous Fabricated Metal
Product Manufacturing
3495 Wire Springs
NAICS 332612 Wire Spring Manufacturing
NAICS 334518 Watch, Clock, & Part Manufacturing
3496 Miscellaneous Fabricated Wire Products
NAICS 332618 Other Fabricated Wire Product Manufacturing
3497 Metal Foil & Leaf
NAICS 322225 Laminated Aluminum Foil Manufacturing for
Flexible Packaging Uses
NAICS 332999 All Other Miscellaneous Fabricated Metal
Product Manufacturing
3498 Fabricated Pipe & Pipe Fittings
NAICS 332996 Fabricated Pipe & Pipe Fitting Manufacturing

3499 Fabricated Metal Products, nec
NAICS 337148 Other Nonwood Furniture Manufacturing
NAICS 332117 Powder Metallurgy Part Manufacturing
NAICS 332439 Other Metal Container Manufacturing
NAICS 33251   Hardware Manufacturing
NAICS 332919 Other Metal Valve & Pipe Fitting
          Manufacturing
NAICS 339914 Costume Jewelry & Novelty Manufacturing
NAICS 332999 All Other Miscellaneous Fabricated Metal
          Product Manufacturing

INDUSTRIAL & COMMERCIAL MACHINERY & COMPUTER EQUIPMENT

3511 Steam, Gas, & Hydraulic Turbines, & Turbine Generator Set Units
NAICS 333611 Turbine & Turbine Generator Set Unit
          Manufacturing
3519 Internal Combustion Engines, nec
NAICS 336399 All Other Motor Vehicle Parts Manufacturing
NAICS 333618 Other Engine Equipment Manufacturing
3523 Farm Machinery & Equipment
NAICS 333111 Farm Machinery & Equipment Manufacturing
NAICS 332323 Ornamental & Architectural Metal Work
          Manufacturing
NAICS 332212 Hand & Edge Tool Manufacturing
NAICS 333922 Conveyor & Conveying Equipment
          Manufacturing
3524 Lawn & Garden Tractors & Home Lawn & Garden Equipment
NAICS 333112 Lawn & Garden Tractor & Home Lawn &
          Garden Equipment Manufacturing
NAICS 332212 Hand & Edge Tool Manufacturing
3531 Construction Machinery & Equipment
NAICS 33651   Railroad Rolling Stock Manufacturing
NAICS 333923 Overhead Traveling Crane, Hoist, & Monorail
          System Manufacturing
NAICS 33312   Construction Machinery Manufacturing
3532 Mining Machinery & Equipment, Except Oil & Gas Field Machinery & Equipment
NAICS 333131 Mining Machinery & Equipment Manufacturing
3533 Oil & Gas Field Machinery & Equipment
NAICS 333132 Oil & Gas Field Machinery & Equipment
          Manufacturing
3534 Elevators & Moving Stairways
NAICS 333921 Elevator & Moving Stairway Manufacturing
3535 Conveyors & Conveying Equipment
NAICS 333922 Conveyor & Conveying Equipment
          Manufacturing
3536 Overhead Traveling Cranes, Hoists & Monorail Systems
NAICS 333923 Overhead Traveling Crane, Hoist & Monorail
          System Manufacturing
3537 Industrial Trucks, Tractors, Trailers, & Stackers
NAICS 333924 Industrial Truck, Tractor, Trailer, & Stacker
          Machinery Manufacturing
NAICS 332999 All Other Miscellaneous Fabricated Metal
          Product Manufacturing
NAICS 332439 Other Metal Container Manufacturing
3541 Machine Tools, Metal Cutting Type
NAICS 333512 Machine Tool Manufacturing
3542 Machine Tools, Metal Forming Type
NAICS 333513 Machine Tool Manufacturing

3543 Industrial Patterns
NAICS 332997 Industrial Pattern Manufacturing
3544 Special Dies & Tools, Die Sets, Jigs & Fixtures, & Industrial Molds
NAICS 333514 Special Die & Tool, Die Set, Jig, & Fixture
          Manufacturing
NAICS 333511 Industrial Mold Manufacturing
3545 Cutting Tools, Machine Tool Accessories, & Machinists' Precision Measuring Devices
NAICS 333515 Cutting Tool & Machine Tool Accessory
          Manufacturing
NAICS 332212 Hand & Edge Tool Manufacturing
3546 Power-driven Handtools
NAICS 333991 Power-driven Hand Tool Manufacturing
3547 Rolling Mill Machinery & Equipment
NAICS 333516 Rolling Mill Machinery & Equipment
          Manufacturing
3548 Electric & Gas Welding & Soldering Equipment
NAICS 333992 Welding & Soldering Equipment Manufacturing
NAICS 335311 Power, Distribution, & Specialty Transformer
          Manufacturing
3549 Metalworking Machinery, nec
NAICS 333518 Other Metalworking Machinery Manufacturing
3552
3553 Woodworking Machinery
NAICS 33321   Sawmill & Woodworking Machinery
          Manufacturing
3554 Paper Industries Machinery
NAICS 333291 Paper Industry Machinery Manufacturing
3555 Printing Trades Machinery & Equipment
NAICS 333293 Printing Machinery & Equipment
          Manufacturing
3556 Food Products Machinery
NAICS 333294 Food Product Machinery Manufacturing
3559 Special Industry Machinery, nec
NAICS 33322   Rubber & Plastics Industry Machinery
          Manufacturing
NAICS 333319 Other Commercial & Service Industry
          Machinery Manufacturing
NAICS 333295 Semiconductor Manufacturing Machinery
NAICS 333298 All Other Industrial Machinery Manufacturing
3561 Pumps & Pumping Equipment
NAICS 333911 Pump & Pumping Equipment Manufacturing
3562 Ball & Roller Bearings
NAICS 332991 Ball & Roller Bearing Manufacturing
3563 Air & Gas Compressors
NAICS 333912 Air & Gas Compressor Manufacturing
3564 Industrial & Commercial Fans & Blowers & Air Purification Equipment
NAICS 333411 Air Purification Equipment Manufacturing
NAICS 333412 Industrial & Commercial Fan & Blower
          Manufacturing
3565 Packaging Machinery
NAICS 333993 Packaging Machinery Manufacturing
3566 Speed Changers, Industrial High-speed Drives, & Gears
NAICS 333612 Speed Changer, Industrial High-speed Drive, &
          Gear Manufacturing
3567 Industrial Process Furnaces & Ovens
NAICS 333994 Industrial Process Furnace & Oven
          Manufacturing
3568 Mechanical Power Transmission Equipment, nec
NAICS 333613 Mechanical Power Transmission Equipment
          Manufacturing

3569 General Industrial Machinery & Equipment, nec
NAICS 333999 All Other General Purpose Machinery Manufacturing

3571 Electronic Computers
NAICS 334111 Electronic Computer Manufacturing

3572 Computer Storage Devices
NAICS 334112 Computer Storage Device Manufacturing

3575 Computer Terminals
NAICS 334113 Computer Terminal Manufacturing

3577 Computer Peripheral Equipment, nec
NAICS 334119 Other Computer Peripheral Equipment Manufacturing

3578 Calculating & Accounting Machines, Except Electronic Computers
NAICS 334119 Other Computer Peripheral Equipment Manufacturing
NAICS 333313 Office Machinery Manufacturing

3579 Office Machines, nec
NAICS 339942 Lead Pencil & Art Good Manufacturing
NAICS 334518 Watch, Clock, & Part Manufacturing
NAICS 333313 Office Machinery Manufacturing

3581 Automatic Vending Machines
NAICS 333311 Automatic Vending Machine Manufacturing

3582 Commercial Laundry, Drycleaning, & Pressing Machines
NAICS 333312 Commercial Laundry, Drycleaning, & Pressing Machine Manufacturing

3585 Air-conditioning & Warm Air Heating Equipment & Commercial & Industrial Refrigeration Equipment
NAICS 336391 Motor Vehicle Air Conditioning Manufacturing
NAICS 333415 Air Conditioning & Warm Air Heating Equipment & Commercial & Industrial Refrigeration Equipment Manufacturing

3586 Measuring & Dispensing Pumps
NAICS 333913 Measuring & Dispensing Pump Manufacturing

3589 Service Industry Machinery, nec
NAICS 333319 Other Commercial and Service Industry Machinery Manufacturing

3592 Carburetors, Pistons, Piston Rings & Valves
NAICS 336311 Carburetor, Piston, Piston Ring & Valve Manufacturing

3593 Fluid Power Cylinders & Actuators
NAICS 333995 Fluid Power Cylinder & Actuator Manufacturing

3594 Fluid Power Pumps & Motors
NAICS 333996 Fluid Power Pump & Motor Manufacturing

3596 Scales & Balances, Except Laboratory
NAICS 333997 Scale & Balance Manufacturing

3599 Industrial & Commercial Machinery & Equipment, nec
NAICS 336399 All Other Motor Vehicle Part Manufacturing
NAICS 332999 All Other Miscellaneous Fabricated Metal Product Manufacturing
NAICS 333319 Other Commercial & Service Industry Machinery Manufacturing
NAICS 33271 Machine Shops
NAICS 333999 All Other General Purpose Machinery Manufacturing

ELECTRONIC & OTHER ELECTRICAL EQUIPMENT & COMPONENTS, EXCEPT COMPUTER EQUIPMENT

3612 Power, Distribution, & Specialty Transformers
NAICS 335311 Power, Distribution, & Specialty Transformer Manufacturing

3613 Switchgear & Switchboard Apparatus
NAICS 335313 Switchgear & Switchboard Apparatus Manufacturing

3621 Motors & Generators
NAICS 335312 Motor & Generator Manufacturing

3624 Carbon & Graphite Products
NAICS 335991 Carbon & Graphite Product Manufacturing

3625 Relays & Industrial Controls
NAICS 335314 Relay & Industrial Control Manufacturing

3629 Electrical Industrial Apparatus, nec
NAICS 335999 All Other Miscellaneous Electrical Equipment & Component Manufacturing

3631 Household Cooking Equipment
NAICS 335221 Household Cooking Appliance Manufacturing

3632 Household Refrigerators & Home & Farm Freezers
NAICS 335222 Household Refrigerator & Home Freezer Manufacturing

3633 Household Laundry Equipment
NAICS 335224 Household Laundry Equipment Manufacturing

3634 Electric Housewares & Fans
NAICS 335211 Electric Housewares & Fan Manufacturing

3635 Household Vacuum Cleaners
NAICS 335212 Household Vacuum Cleaner Manufacturing

3639 Household Appliances, nec
NAICS 335212 Household Vacuum Cleaner Manufacturing
NAICS 333298 All Other Industrial Machinery Manufacturing
NAICS 335228 Other Household Appliance Manufacturing

3641 Electric Lamp Bulbs & Tubes
NAICS 33511 Electric Lamp Bulb & Part Manufacturing

3643 Current-carrying Wiring Devices
NAICS 335931 Current-carrying Wiring Device Manufacturing

3644 Noncurrent-carrying Wiring Devices
NAICS 335932 Noncurrent-carrying Wiring Device Manufacturing

3645 Residential Electric Lighting Fixtures
NAICS 335121 Residential Electric Lighting Fixture Manufacturing

3646 Commercial, Industrial, & Institutional Electric Lighting Fixtures
NAICS 335122 Commercial, Industrial, & Institutional Electric Lighting Fixture Manufacturing

3647 Vehicular Lighting Equipment
NAICS 336321 Vehicular Lighting Equipment Manufacturing

3648 Lighting Equipment, nec
NAICS 335129 Other Lighting Equipment Manufacturing

3651 Household Audio & Video Equipment
NAICS 33431 Audio & Video Equipment Manufacturing 3652
NAICS 51222 Integrated Record Production/distribution

3661 Telephone & Telegraph Apparatus
NAICS 33421 Telephone Apparatus Manufacturing
NAICS 334416 Electronic Coil, Transformer, & Other Inductor Manufacturing
NAICS 334418 Printed Circuit/electronics Assembly Manufacturing

3663 Radio & Television Broadcasting & Communication Equipment
NAICS 33422 Radio & Television Broadcasting & Wireless Communications Equipment Manufacturing
3669 Communications Equipment, nec
NAICS 33429 Other Communication Equipment Manufacturing
3671 Electron Tubes
NAICS 334411 Electron Tube Manufacturing
3672 Printed Circuit Boards
NAICS 334412 Printed Circuit Board Manufacturing
3674 Semiconductors & Related Devices
NAICS 334413 Semiconductor & Related Device Manufacturing
3675 Electronic Capacitors
NAICS 334414 Electronic Capacitor Manufacturing
3676 Electronic Resistors
NAICS 334415 Electronic Resistor Manufacturing
3677 Electronic Coils, Transformers, & Other Inductors
NAICS 334416 Electronic Coil, Transformer, & Other Inductor Manufacturing
3678 Electronic ConNECtors
NAICS 334417 Electronic ConNECtor Manufacturing
3679 Electronic Components, nec
NAICS 33422 Radio & Television Broadcasting & Wireless Communications Equipment Manufacturing
NAICS 334418 Printed Circuit/electronics Assembly Manufacturing
NAICS 336322 Other Motor Vehicle Electrical & Electronic Equipment Manufacturing
NAICS 334419 Other Electronic Component Manufacturing
3691 Storage Batteries
NAICS 335911 Storage Battery Manufacturing
3692 Primary Batteries, Dry & Wet
NAICS 335912 Dry & Wet Primary Battery Manufacturing
3694 Electrical Equipment for Internal Combustion Engines
NAICS 336322 Other Motor Vehicle Electrical & Electronic Equipment Manufacturing
3695 Magnetic & Optical Recording Media
NAICS 334613 Magnetic & Optical Recording Media Manufacturing
3699 Electrical Machinery, Equipment, & Supplies, nec
NAICS 333319 Other Commercial & Service Industry Machinery Manufacturing
NAICS 333618 Other Engine Equipment Manufacturing
NAICS 334119 Other Computer Peripheral Equipment Manufacturing Classify According to Function
NAICS 335129 Other Lighting Equipment Manufacturing
NAICS 335999 All Other Miscellaneous Electrical Equipment & Component Manufacturing

TRANSPORTATION EQUIPMENT

3711 Motor Vehicles & Passenger Car Bodies
NAICS 336111 Automobile Manufacturing
NAICS 336112 Light Truck & Utility Vehicle Manufacturing
NAICS 33612 Heavy Duty Truck Manufacturing
NAICS 336211 Motor Vehicle Body Manufacturing
NAICS 336992 Military Armored Vehicle, Tank, & Tank Component Manufacturing
3713 Truck & Bus Bodies
NAICS 336211 Motor Vehicle Body Manufacturing

3714 Motor Vehicle Parts & Accessories
NAICS 336211 Motor Vehicle Body Manufacturing
NAICS 336312 Gasoline Engine & Engine Parts Manufacturing
NAICS 336322 Other Motor Vehicle Electrical & Electronic Equipment Manufacturing
NAICS 33633 Motor Vehicle Steering & Suspension Components Manufacturing
NAICS 33634 Motor Vehicle Brake System Manufacturing
NAICS 33635 Motor Vehicle Transmission & Power Train Parts Manufacturing
NAICS 336399 All Other Motor Vehicle Parts Manufacturing
3715 Truck Trailers
NAICS 336212 Truck Trailer Manufacturing
3716 Motor Homes
NAICS 336213 Motor Home Manufacturing
3721 Aircraft
NAICS 336411 Aircraft Manufacturing
3724 Aircraft Engines & Engine Parts
NAICS 336412 Aircraft Engine & Engine Parts Manufacturing 3728
NAICS 336413 Other Aircraft Part & Auxiliary Equipment Manufacturing
3731 Ship Building & Repairing
NAICS 336611 Ship Building & Repairing
3732 Boat Building & Repairing
NAICS 81149 Other Personal & Household Goods Repair & Maintenance
NAICS 336612 Boat Building
3743 Railroad Equipment
NAICS 333911 Pump & Pumping Equipment Manufacturing
NAICS 33651 Railroad Rolling Stock Manufacturing
3751 Motorcycles, Bicycles, & Parts
NAICS 336991 Motorcycle, Bicycle, & Parts Manufacturing
3761 Guided Missiles & Space Vehicles
NAICS 336414 Guided Missile & Space Vehicle Manufacturing 3764
3769 Guided Missile Space Vehicle Parts & Auxiliary Equipment, nec
NAICS 336419 Other Guided Missile & Space Vehicle Parts & Auxiliary Equipment Manufacturing
3792 Travel Trailers & Campers
NAICS 336214 Travel Trailer & Camper Manufacturing
3795 Tanks & Tank Components
NAICS 336992 Military Armored Vehicle, Tank, & Tank Component Manufacturing
3799 Transportation Equipment, nec
NAICS 336214 Travel Trailer & Camper Manufacturing
NAICS 332212 Hand & Edge Tool Manufacturing
NAICS 336999 All Other Transportation Equipment Manufacturing

MEASURING, ANALYZING, & CONTROLLING INSTRUMENTS

3812 Search, Detection, Navigation, Guidance, Aeronautical, & Nautical Systems & Instruments
NAICS 334511 Search, Detection, Navigation, Guidance, Aeronautical, & Nautical System & Instrument Manufacturing
3821 Laboratory Apparatus & Furniture
NAICS 339111 Laboratory Apparatus & Furniture Manufacturing

3822 Automatic Controls for Regulating Residential & Commercial Environments & Appliances
NAICS 334512 Automatic Environmental Control Manufacturing for Regulating Residential, Commercial, & Appliance Use
3823 Industrial Instruments for Measurement, Display, & Control of Process Variables & Related Products
NAICS 334513 Instruments & Related Product Manufacturing for Measuring Displaying, & Controlling Industrial Process Variables
3824 Totalizing Fluid Meters & Counting Devices
NAICS 334514 Totalizing Fluid Meter & Counting Device Manufacturing
3825 Instruments for Measuring & Testing of Electricity & Electrical Signals
NAICS 334416 Electronic Coil, Transformer, & Other Inductor Manufacturing
NAICS 334515 Instrument Manufacturing for Measuring & Testing Electricity & Electrical Signals
3826 Laboratory Analytical Instruments
NAICS 334516 Analytical Laboratory Instrument Manufacturing
3827 Optical Instruments & Lenses
NAICS 333314 Optical Instrument & Lens Manufacturing
3829 Measuring & Controlling Devices, nec
NAICS 339112 Surgical & Medical Instrument Manufacturing
NAICS 334519 Other Measuring & Controlling Device Manufacturing
3841 Surgical & Medical Instruments & Apparatus
NAICS 339112 Surgical & Medical Instrument Manufacturing
3842 Orthopedic, Prosthetic, & Surgical Appliances & Supplies
NAICS 339113 Surgical Appliance & Supplies Manufacturing
NAICS 334510 Electromedical & Electrotherapeutic Apparatus Manufacturing
3843 Dental Equipment & Supplies
NAICS 339114 Dental Equipment & Supplies Manufacturing
3844 X-ray Apparatus & Tubes & Related Irradiation Apparatus
NAICS 334517 Irradiation Apparatus Manufacturing
3845 Electromedical & Electrotherapeutic Apparatus
NAICS 334517 Irradiation Apparatus Manufacturing
NAICS 334510 Electromedical & Electrotherapeutic Apparatus Manufacturing
3851 Ophthalmic Goods
NAICS 339115 Ophthalmic Goods Manufacturing
3861 Photographic Equipment & Supplies
NAICS 333315 Photographic & Photocopying Equipment Manufacturing
NAICS 325992 Photographic Film, Paper, Plate & Chemical Manufacturing
3873 Watches, Clocks, Clockwork Operated Devices & Parts
NAICS 334518 Watch, Clock, & Part Manufacturing

MISCELLANEOUS MANUFACTURING INDUSTRIES

3911 Jewelry, Precious Metal
NAICS 339911 Jewelry Manufacturing
3914 Silverware, Plated Ware, & Stainless Steel Ware
NAICS 332211 Cutlery & Flatware Manufacturing
NAICS 339912 Silverware & Plated Ware Manufacturing
3915 Jewelers' Findings & Materials, & Lapidary Work
NAICS 339913 Jewelers' Material & Lapidary Work Manufacturing

3931 Musical Instruments
NAICS 339992 Musical Instrument Manufacturing
3942 Dolls & Stuffed Toys
NAICS 339931 Doll & Stuffed Toy Manufacturing
3944 Games, Toys, & Children's Vehicles, Except Dolls & Bicycles
NAICS 336991 Motorcycle, Bicycle & Parts Manufacturing
NAICS 339932 Game, Toy, & Children's Vehicle Manufacturing
3949 Sporting & Athletic Goods, nec
NAICS 33992 Sporting & Athletic Good Manufacturing
3951 Pens, Mechanical Pencils & Parts
NAICS 339941 Pen & Mechanical Pencil Manufacturing
3952 Lead Pencils, Crayons, & Artist's Materials
NAICS 337139 Other Wood Furniture Manufacturing
NAICS 337139 Other Wood Furniture Manufacturing
NAICS 325998 All Other Miscellaneous Chemical Manufacturing
NAICS 339942 Lead Pencil & Art Good Manufacturing
3953 Marking Devices
NAICS 339943 Marking Device Manufacturing
3955 Carbon Paper & Inked Ribbons
NAICS 339944 Carbon Paper & Inked Ribbon Manufacturing
3961 Costume Jewelry & Costume Novelties, Except Precious Metals
NAICS 339914 Costume Jewelry & Novelty Manufacturing
3965 Fasteners, Buttons, Needles, & Pins
NAICS 339993 Fastener, Button, Needle & Pin Manufacturing
3991 Brooms & Brushes
NAICS 339994 Broom, Brush & Mop Manufacturing
3993 Signs & Advertising Specialties
NAICS 33995 Sign Manufacturing
3995 Burial Caskets
NAICS 339995 Burial Casket Manufacturing
3996 Linoleum, Asphalted-felt-base, & Other Hard Surface Floor Coverings, nec
NAICS 326192 Resilient Floor Covering Manufacturing
3999 Manufacturing Industries, nec
NAICS 337148 Other Nonwood Furniture Manufacturing
NAICS 321999 All Other Miscellaneous Wood Product Manufacturing
NAICS 31611 Leather & Hide Tanning & Finishing
NAICS 335121 Residential Electric Lighting Fixture Manufacturing
NAICS 325998 All Other Miscellaneous Chemical Product Manufacturing
NAICS 332999 All Other Miscellaneous Fabricated Metal Product Manufacturing
NAICS 326199 All Other Plastics Product Manufacturing
NAICS 323112 Commercial Flexographic Printing
NAICS 323111 Commercial Gravure Printing
NAICS 323110 Commercial Lithographic Printing
NAICS 323113 Commercial Screen Printing
NAICS 323119 Other Commercial Printing
NAICS 332212 Hand & Edge Tool Manufacturing
NAICS 339999 All Other Miscellaneous Manufacturing

TRANSPORTATION, COMMUNICATIONS, ELECTRIC, GAS, & SANITARY SERVICES

4011 Railroads, Line-haul Operating
NAICS 482111 Line-haul Railroads
4013 Railroad Switching & Terminal Establishments
NAICS 482112 Short Line Railroads
NAICS 48821　Support Activities for Rail Transportation
4111 Local & Suburban Transit
NAICS 485111 Mixed Mode Transit Systems
NAICS 485112 Commuter Rail Systems
NAICS 485113 Bus & Motor Vehicle Transit Systems
NAICS 485119 Other Urban Transit Systems
NAICS 485999 All Other Transit & Ground Passenger Transportation
4119 Local Passenger Transportation, nec
NAICS 62191　Ambulance Service
NAICS 48541　School & Employee Bus Transportation
NAICS 48711　Scenic & Sightseeing Transportation , Land
NAICS 485991 Special Needs Transportation
NAICS 485999 All Other Transit & Ground Passenger Transportation
NAICS 48532　Limousine Service
4121 Taxicabs
NAICS 48531　Taxi Service
4131 Intercity & Rural Bus Transportation
NAICS 48521　Interurban & Rural Bus Transportation
4141 Local Bus Charter Service
NAICS 48551　Charter Bus Industry
4142 Bus Charter Service, Except Local
NAICS 48551　Charter Bus Industry
4151 School Buses
NAICS 48541　School & Employee Bus Transportation
4173 Terminal & Service Facilities for Motor Vehicle Passenger Transportation
NAICS 48849　Other Support Activities for Road Transportation
4212 Local Trucking Without Storage
NAICS 562111 Solid Waste Collection
NAICS 562112 Hazardous Waste Collection
NAICS 562119 Other Waste Collection
NAICS 48411　General Freight Trucking, Local
NAICS 48421　Used Household & Office Goods Moving
NAICS 48422　Specialized Freight Trucking, Local
4213 Trucking, Except Local
NAICS 484121 General Freight Trucking, Long-distance, Truckload
NAICS 484122 General Freight Trucking, Long-distance, less than Truckload
NAICS 48421　Used Household & Office Goods Moving
NAICS 48423　Specialized Freight Trucking, Long-distance
4214 Local Trucking with Storage
NAICS 48411　General Freight Trucking, Local
NAICS 48421　Used Household & Office Goods Moving
NAICS 48422　Specialized Freight Trucking, Local
4215 Couriers Services Except by Air
NAICS 49211　Couriers
NAICS 49221　Local Messengers & Local Delivery
4221 Farm Product Warehousing & Storage
NAICS 49313　Farm Product Storage Facilities
4222 Refrigerated Warehousing & Storage
NAICS 49312　Refrigerated Storage Facilities

4225 General Warehousing & Storage
NAICS 49311　General Warehousing & Storage Facilities
NAICS 53113　Lessors of Miniwarehouses & Self Storage Units
4226 Special Warehousing & Storage, nec
NAICS 49312　Refrigerated Warehousing & Storage Facilities
NAICS 49311　General Warehousing & Storage Facilities
NAICS 49319　Other Warehousing & Storage Facilities
4231 Terminal & Joint Terminal Maintenance Facilities for Motor Freight Transportation
NAICS 48849　Other Support Activities for Road Transportation
4311 United States Postal Service
NAICS 49111　Postal Service
4412 Deep Sea Foreign Transportation of Freight
NAICS 483111 Deep Sea Freight Transportation
4424 Deep Sea Domestic Transportation of Freight
NAICS 483113 Coastal & Great Lakes Freight Transportation
4432 Freight Transportation on the Great Lakes - St. Lawrence Seaway
NAICS 483113 Coastal & Great Lakes Freight Transportation
4449 Water Transportation of Freight, nec
NAICS 483211 Inland Water Freight Transportation
4481 Deep Sea Transportation of Passengers, Except by Ferry
NAICS 483112 Deep Sea Passenger Transportation
NAICS 483114 Coastal & Great Lakes Passenger Transportation
4482 Ferries
NAICS 483114 Coastal & Great Lakes Passenger Transportation
NAICS 483212 Inland Water Passenger Transportation
4489 Water Transportation of Passengers, nec
NAICS 483212 Inland Water Passenger Transportation
NAICS 48721　Scenic & Sightseeing Transportation, Water
4491 Marine Cargo Handling
NAICS 48831　Port & Harbor Operations
NAICS 48832　Marine Cargo Handling
4492 Towing & Tugboat Services
NAICS 483113 Coastal & Great Lakes Freight Transportation
NAICS 483211 Inland Water Freight Transportation
NAICS 48833　Navigational Services to Shipping
4493 Marinas
NAICS 71393　Marinas
4499 Water Transportation Services, nec
NAICS 532411 Commercial Air, Rail, & Water Transportation Equipment Rental & Leasing
NAICS 48831　Port & Harbor Operations
NAICS 48833　Navigational Services to Shipping
NAICS 48839　Other Support Activities for Water Transportation
4512 Air Transportation, Scheduled
NAICS 481111 Scheduled Passenger Air Transportation
NAICS 481112 Scheduled Freight Air Transportation
4513 Air Courier Services
NAICS 49211　Couriers
4522 Air Transportation, Nonscheduled
NAICS 62191　Ambulance Services
NAICS 481212 Nonscheduled Chartered Freight Air Transportation
NAICS 481211 Nonscheduled Chartered Passenger Air Transportation
NAICS 48122　Nonscheduled Speciality Air Transportation
NAICS 48799　Scenic & Sightseeing Transportation , Other

4581 Airports, Flying Fields, & Airport Terminal Services
NAICS 488111 Air Traffic Control
NAICS 488112 Airport Operations, Except Air Traffic Control
NAICS 56172 Janitorial Services
NAICS 48819 Other Support Activities for Air Transportation
4612 Crude Petroleum Pipelines
NAICS 48611 Pipeline Transportation of Crude Oil
4613 Refined Petroleum Pipelines
NAICS 48691 Pipeline Transportation of Refined Petroleum Products
4619 Pipelines, nec
NAICS 48699 All Other Pipeline Transportation
4724 Travel Agencies
NAICS 56151 Travel Agencies
4725 Tour Operators
NAICS 56152 Tour Operators
4729 Arrangement of Passenger Transportation, nec
NAICS 488999 All Other Support Activities for Transportation
NAICS 561599 All Other Travel Arrangement & Reservation Services
4731 Arrangement of Transportation of Freight & Cargo
NAICS 541618 Other Management Consulting Services
NAICS 48851 Freight Transportation Arrangement
4741 Rental of Railroad Cars
NAICS 532411 Commercial Air, Rail, & Water Transportation Equipment Rental & Leasing
NAICS 48821 Support Activities for Rail Transportation
4783 Packing & Crating
NAICS 488991 Packing & Crating
4785 Fixed Facilities & Inspection & Weighing Services for Motor Vehicle Transportation
NAICS 48839 Other Support Activities for Water Transportation
NAICS 48849 Other Support Activities for Road Transportation
4789 Transportation Services, nec
NAICS 488999 All Other Support Activities for Transportation
NAICS 48711 Scenic & Sightseeing Transportation, Land
NAICS 48821 Support Activities for Rail Transportation
4812 Radiotelephone Communications
NAICS 513321 Paging
NAICS 513322 Cellular & Other Wireless Telecommunications
NAICS 51333 Telecommunications Resellers
4813 Telephone Communications, Except Radiotelephone
NAICS 51331 Wired Telecommunications Carriers
NAICS 51333 Telecommunications Resellers
4822 Telegraph & Other Message Communications
NAICS 51331 Wired Telecommunications Carriers
4832 Radio Broadcasting Stations
NAICS 513111 Radio Networks
NAICS 513112 Radio Stations
4833 Television Broadcasting Stations
NAICS 51312 Television Broadcasting
4841 Cable & Other Pay Television Services
NAICS 51321 Cable Networks
NAICS 51322 Cable & Other Program Distribution
4899 Communications Services, nec
NAICS 513322 Cellular & Other Wireless Telecommunications
NAICS 51334 Satellite Telecommunications
NAICS 51339 Other Telecommunications
4911 Electric Services
NAICS 221111 Hydroelectric Power Generation
NAICS 221112 Fossil Fuel Electric Power Generation
NAICS 221113 Nuclear Electric Power Generation

NAICS 221119 Other Electric Power Generation
NAICS 221121 Electric Bulk Power Transmission & Control
NAICS 221122 Electric Power Distribution
4922 Natural Gas Transmission
NAICS 48621 Pipeline Transportation of Natural Gas
4923 Natural Gas Transmission & Distribution
NAICS 22121 Natural Gas Distribution
NAICS 48621 Pipeline Transportation of Natural Gas
4924 Natural Gas Distribution
NAICS 22121 Natural Gas Distribution
4925 Mixed, Manufactured, or Liquefied Petroleum Gas Production And/or Distribution
NAICS 22121 Natural Gas Distribution
4931 Electric & Other Services Combined
NAICS 221111 Hydroelectric Power Generation
NAICS 221112 Fossil Fuel Electric Power Generation
NAICS 221113 Nuclear Electric Power Generation
NAICS 221119 Other Electric Power Generation
NAICS 221121 Electric Bulk Power Transmission & Control
NAICS 221122 Electric Power Distribution
NAICS 22121 Natural Gas Distribution
4932 Gas & Other Services Combined
NAICS 22121 Natural Gas Distribution
4939 Combination Utilities, nec
NAICS 221111 Hydroelectric Power Generation
NAICS 221112 Fossil Fuel Electric Power Generation
NAICS 221113 Nuclear Electric Power Generation
NAICS 221119 Other Electric Power Generation
NAICS 221121 Electric Bulk Power Transmission & Control
NAICS 221122 Electric Power Distribution
NAICS 22121 Natural Gas Distribution
4941 Water Supply
NAICS 22131 Water Supply & Irrigation Systems
4952 Sewerage Systems
NAICS 22132 Sewage Treatment Facilities
4953 Refuse Systems
NAICS 562111 Solid Waste Collection
NAICS 562112 Hazardous Waste Collection
NAICS 56292 Materials Recovery Facilities
NAICS 562119 Other Waste Collection
NAICS 562211 Hazardous Waste Treatment & Disposal
NAICS 562212 Solid Waste Landfills
NAICS 562213 Solid Waste Combustors & Incinerators
NAICS 562219 Other Nonhazardous Waste Treatment & Disposal
4959 Sanitary Services, nec
NAICS 488112 Airport Operations, Except Air Traffic Control
NAICS 56291 Remediation Services
NAICS 56171 Exterminating & Pest Control Services
NAICS 562998 All Other Miscellaneous Waste Management Services
4961 Steam & Air-conditioning Supply
NAICS 22133 Steam & Air-conditioning Supply
4971 Irrigation Systems
NAICS 22131 Water Supply & Irrigation Systems

WHOLESALE TRADE

5012 Automobiles & Other Motor Vehicles
NAICS 42111 Automobile & Other Motor Vehicle Wholesalers

5013 Motor Vehicle Supplies & New Parts
NAICS 44131   Automotive Parts & Accessories Stores - Retail
NAICS 42112   Motor Vehicle Supplies & New Part Wholesalers

5014 Tires & Tubes
NAICS 44132   Tire Dealers - Retail
NAICS 42113   Tire & Tube Wholesalers

5015 Motor Vehicle Parts, Used
NAICS 42114   Motor Vehicle Part Wholesalers

5021 Furniture
NAICS 44211   Furniture Stores
NAICS 42121   Furniture Wholesalers

5023 Home Furnishings
NAICS 44221   Floor Covering Stores
NAICS 42122   Home Furnishing Wholesalers

5031 Lumber, Plywood, Millwork, & Wood Panels
NAICS 44419   Other Building Material Dealers
NAICS 42131   Lumber, Plywood, Millwork, & Wood Panel Wholesalers

5032 Brick, Stone & Related Construction Materials
NAICS 44419   Other Building Material Dealers
NAICS 42132   Brick, Stone & Related Construction Material Wholesalers

5033 Roofing, Siding, & Insulation Materials
NAICS 42133   Roofing, Siding, & Insulation Material Wholesalers

5039 Construction Materials, nec
NAICS 44419   Other Building Material Dealers
NAICS 42139   Other Construction Material Wholesalers

5043 Photographic Equipment & Supplies
NAICS 42141   Photographic Equipment & Supplies Wholesalers

5044 Office Equipment
NAICS 42142   Office Equipment Wholesalers

5045 Computers & Computer Peripheral Equipment & Software
NAICS 42143   Computer & Computer Peripheral Equipment & Software Wholesalers
NAICS 44312   Computer & Software Stores - Retail

5046 Commercial Equipment, nec
NAICS 42144   Other Commercial Equipment Wholesalers

5047 Medical, Dental, & Hospital Equipment & Supplies
NAICS 42145   Medical, Dental & Hospital Equipment & Supplies Wholesalers
NAICS 446199 All Other Health & Personal Care Stores - Retail

5048 Ophthalmic Goods
NAICS 42146   Ophthalmic Goods Wholesalers

5049 Professional Equipment & Supplies, nec
NAICS 42149   Other Professional Equipment & Supplies Wholesalers
NAICS 45321   Office Supplies & Stationery Stores - Retail

5051 Metals Service Centers & Offices
NAICS 42151   Metals Service Centers & Offices

5052 Coal & Other Minerals & Ores
NAICS 42152   Coal & Other Mineral & Ore Wholesalers

5063 Electrical Apparatus & Equipment Wiring Supplies, & Construction Materials
NAICS 44419   Other Building Material Dealers
NAICS 42161   Electrical Apparatus & Equipment, Wiring Supplies & Construction Material Wholesalers

5064 Electrical Appliances, Television & Radio Sets
NAICS 42162   Electrical Appliance, Television & Radio Set Wholesalers

5065 Electronic Parts & Equipment, Not Elsewhere Classified
NAICS 42169   Other Electronic Parts & Equipment Wholesalers

5072 Hardware
NAICS 42171   Hardware Wholesalers

5074 Plumbing & Heating Equipment & Supplies
NAICS 44419   Other Building Material Dealers
NAICS 42172   Plumbing & Heating Equipment & Supplies Wholesalers

5075 Warm Air Heating & Air-conditioning Equipment & Supplies
NAICS 42173   Warm Air Heating & Air-conditioning Equipment & Supplies Wholesalers

5078 Refrigeration Equipment & Supplies
NAICS 42174   Refrigeration Equipment & Supplies Wholesalers

5082 Construction & Mining Machinery & Equipment
NAICS 42181   Construction & Mining Machinery & Equipment Wholesalers

5083 Farm & Garden Machinery & Equipment
NAICS 42182   Farm & Garden Machinery & Equipment Wholesalers
NAICS 44421   Outdoor Power Equipment Stores - Retail

5084 Industrial Machinery & Equipment
NAICS 42183   Industrial Machinery & Equipment Wholesalers

5085 Industrial Supplies
NAICS 42183   Industrial Machinery & Equipment Wholesalers
NAICS 42184   Industrial Supplies Wholesalers
NAICS 81131   Commercial & Industrial Machinery & Equipment Repair & Maintenence

5087 Service Establishment Equipment & Supplies
NAICS 42185   Service Establishment Equipment & Supplies Wholesalers
NAICS 44612   Cosmetics, Beauty Supplies, & Perfume Stores

5088 Transportation Equipment & Supplies, Except Motor Vehicles
NAICS 42186   Transportation Equipment & Supplies Wholesalers

5091 Sporting & Recreational Goods & Supplies
NAICS 42191   Sporting & Recreational Goods & Supplies Wholesalers

5092 Toys & Hobby Goods & Supplies
NAICS 42192   Toy & Hobby Goods & Supplies Wholesalers

5093 Scrap & Waste Materials
NAICS 42193   Recyclable Material Wholesalers

5094 Jewelry, Watches, Precious Stones, & Precious Metals
NAICS 42194   Jewelry, Watch , Precious Stone, & Precious Metal Wholesalers

5099 Durable Goods, nec
NAICS 42199   Other Miscellaneous Durable Goods Wholesalers

5111 Printing & Writing Paper
NAICS 42211   Printing & Writing Paper Wholesalers

5112 Stationery & Office Supplies
NAICS 45321   Office Supplies & Stationery Stores
NAICS 42212   Stationery & Office Supplies Wholesalers

5113 Industrial & Personal Service Paper
NAICS 42213   Industrial & Personal Service Paper Wholesalers

5122 Drugs, Drug Proprietaries, & Druggists' Sundries
NAICS 42221   Drugs, Drug Proprietaries, & Druggists' Sundries Wholesalers

5131 Piece Goods, Notions, & Other Dry Goods
NAICS 313311 Broadwoven Fabric Finishing Mills
NAICS 313312 Textile & Fabric Finishing Mills
NAICS 42231 Piece Goods, Notions, & Other Dry Goods Wholesalers

5136 Men's & Boys' Clothing & Furnishings
NAICS 42232 Men's & Boys' Clothing & Furnishings Wholesalers

5137 Women's Children's & Infants' Clothing & Accessories
NAICS 42233 Women's, Children's, & Infants' Clothing & Accessories Wholesalers

5139 Footwear
NAICS 42234 Footwear Wholesalers

5141 Groceries, General Line
NAICS 42241 General Line Grocery Wholesalers

5142 Packaged Frozen Foods
NAICS 42242 Packaged Frozen Food Wholesalers

5143 Dairy Products, Except Dried or Canned
NAICS 42243 Dairy Products Wholesalers

5144 Poultry & Poultry Products
NAICS 42244 Poultry & Poultry Product Wholesalers

5145 Confectionery
NAICS 42245 Confectionery Wholesalers

5146 Fish & Seafoods
NAICS 42246 Fish & Seafood Wholesalers

5147 Meats & Meat Products
NAICS 311612 Meat Processed from Carcasses
NAICS 42247 Meat & Meat Product Wholesalers

5148 Fresh Fruits & Vegetables
NAICS 42248 Fresh Fruit & Vegetable Wholesalers

5149 Groceries & Related Products, nec
NAICS 42249 Other Grocery & Related Product Wholesalers

5153 Grain & Field Beans
NAICS 42251 Grain & Field Bean Wholesalers

5154 Livestock
NAICS 42252 Livestock Wholesalers

5159 Farm-product Raw Materials, nec
NAICS 42259 Other Farm Product Raw Material Wholesalers

5162 Plastics Materials & Basic Forms & Shapes
NAICS 42261 Plastics Materials & Basic Forms & Shapes Wholesalers

5169 Chemicals & Allied Products, nec
NAICS 42269 Other Chemical & Allied Products Wholesalers

5171 Petroleum Bulk Stations & Terminals
NAICS 454311 Heating Oil Dealers
NAICS 454312 Liquefied Petroleum Gas Dealers
NAICS 42271 Petroleum Bulk Stations & Terminals

5172 Petroleum & Petroleum Products Wholesalers, Except Bulk Stations & Terminals
NAICS 42272 Petroleum & Petroleum Products Wholesalers

5181 Beer & Ale
NAICS 42281 Beer & Ale Wholesalers

5182 Wine & Distilled Alcoholic Beverages
NAICS 42282 Wine & Distilled Alcoholic Beverage Wholesalers

5191 Farm Supplies
NAICS 44422 Nursery & Garden Centers - Retail
NAICS 42291 Farm Supplies Wholesalers

5192 Books, Periodicals, & Newspapers
NAICS 42292 Book, Periodical & Newspaper Wholesalers

5193 Flowers, Nursery Stock, & Florists' Supplies
NAICS 42293 Flower, Nursery Stock & Florists' Supplies Wholesalers
NAICS 44422 Nursery & Garden Centers - Retail

5194 Tobacco & Tobacco Products
NAICS 42294 Tobacco & Tobacco Product Wholesalers

5198 Paint, Varnishes, & Supplies
NAICS 42295 Paint, Varnish & Supplies Wholesalers
NAICS 44412 Paint & Wallpaper Stores

5199 Nondurable Goods, nec
NAICS 54189 Other Services Related to Advertising
NAICS 42299 Other Miscellaneous Nondurable Goods Wholesalers

RETAIL TRADE

5211 Lumber & Other Building Materials Dealers
NAICS 44411 Home Centers
NAICS 42131 Lumber, Plywood, Millwork & Wood Panel Wholesalers
NAICS 44419 Other Building Material Dealers

5231 Paint, Glass, & Wallpaper Stores
NAICS 42295 Paint, Varnish & Supplies Wholesalers
NAICS 44419 Other Building Material Dealers
NAICS 44412 Paint & Wallpaper Stores

5251 Hardware Stores
NAICS 44413 Hardware Stores

5261 Retail Nurseries, Lawn & Garden Supply Stores
NAICS 44422 Nursery & Garden Centers
NAICS 453998 All Other Miscellaneous Store Retailers
NAICS 44421 Outdoor Power Equipment Stores

5271 Mobile Home Dealers
NAICS 45393 Manufactured Home Dealers

5311 Department Stores
NAICS 45211 Department Stores

5331 Variety Stores
NAICS 45299 All Other General Merchandise Stores

5399 Miscellaneous General Merchandise Stores
NAICS 45291 Warehouse Clubs & Superstores
NAICS 45299 All Other General Merchandise Stores

5411 Grocery Stores
NAICS 44711 Gasoline Stations with Convenience Stores
NAICS 44511 Supermarkets & Other Grocery Stores
NAICS 45291 Warehouse Clubs & Superstores
NAICS 44512 Convenience Stores

5421 Meat & Fish Markets, Including Freezer Provisioners
NAICS 45439 Other Direct Selling Establishments
NAICS 44521 Meat Markets
NAICS 44522 Fish & Seafood Markets

5431 Fruit & Vegetable Markets
NAICS 44523 Fruit & Vegetable Markets

5441 Candy, Nut, & Confectionery Stores
NAICS 445292 Confectionary & Nut Stores

5451 Dairy Products Stores
NAICS 445299 All Other Specialty Food Stores

5461 Retail Bakeries
NAICS 722213 Snack & Nonalcoholic Beverage Bars
NAICS 311811 Retail Bakeries
NAICS 445291 Baked Goods Stores

5499 Miscellaneous Food Stores
NAICS 44521 Meat Markets
NAICS 722211 Limited-service Restaurants
NAICS 446191 Food Supplement Stores
NAICS 445299 All Other Specialty Food Stores

5511 Motor Vehicle Dealers
NAICS 44111 New Car Dealers

5521 Motor Vehicle Dealers
NAICS 44112   Used Car Dealers
5531 Auto & Home Supply Stores
NAICS 44132   Tire Dealers
NAICS 44131   Automotive Parts & Accessories Stores
5541 Gasoline Service Stations
NAICS 44711   Gasoline Stations with Convenience Store
NAICS 44719   Other Gasoline Stations
5551 Boat Dealers
NAICS 441222 Boat Dealers
5561 Recreational Vehicle Dealers
NAICS 44121   Recreational Vehicle Dealers
5571 Motorcycle Dealers
NAICS 441221 Motorcycle Dealers
5599 Automotive Dealers, nec
NAICS 441229 All Other Motor Vehicle Dealers
5611 Men's & Boys' Clothing & Accessory Stores
NAICS 44811   Men's Clothing Stores
NAICS 44815   Clothing Accessories Stores
5621 Women's Clothing Stores
NAICS 44812   Women's Clothing Stores
5632 Women's Accessory & Specialty Stores
NAICS 44819   Other Clothing Stores
NAICS 44815   Clothing Accessories Stores
5641 Children's & Infants' Wear Stores
NAICS 44813   Children's & Infants' Clothing Stores
5651 Family Clothing Stores
NAICS 44814   Family Clothing Stores
5661 Shoe Stores
NAICS 44821   Shoe Stores
5699 Miscellaneous Apparel & Accessory Stores
NAICS 315   Included in Apparel Manufacturing Subsector
                Based on Type of Garment Produced
NAICS 44819   Other Clothing Stores
NAICS 44815   Clothing Accessories Stores
5712 Furniture Stores
NAICS 337133 Wood Household Furniture, Except
                Upholstered, Manufacturing
NAICS 337131 Wood Kitchen Cabinet & Counter Top
                Manufacturing
NAICS 337132 Upholstered Household Furniture
                Manufacturing
NAICS 44211   Furniture Stores
5713 Floor Covering Stores
NAICS 44221   Floor Covering Stores
5714 Drapery, Curtain, & Upholstery Stores
NAICS 442291 Window Treatment Stores
NAICS 45113   Sewing, Needlework & Piece Goods Stores
NAICS 314121 Curtain & Drapery Mills
5719 Miscellaneous Homefurnishings Stores
NAICS 442291 Window Treatment Stores
NAICS 442299 All Other Home Furnishings Stores
5722 Household Appliance Stores
NAICS 443111 Household Appliance Stores
5731 Radio, Television, & Consumer Electronics Stores
NAICS 443112 Radio, Television, & Other Electronics Stores
NAICS 44131   Automotive Parts & Accessories Stores
5734 Computer & Computer Software Stores
NAICS 44312   Computer & Software Stores
5735 Record & Prerecorded Tape Stores
NAICS 45122   Prerecorded Tape, Compact Disc & Record
                Stores

5736 Musical Instrument Stores
NAICS 45114   Musical Instrument & Supplies Stores
5812 Eating & Drinking Places
NAICS 72211   Full-service Restaurants
NAICS 722211 Limited-service Restaurants
NAICS 722212 Cafeterias
NAICS 722213 Snack & Nonalcoholic Beverage Bars
NAICS 72231   Foodservice Contractors
NAICS 72232   Caterers
NAICS 71111   Theater Companies & Dinner Theaters
5813 Drinking Places
NAICS 72241   Drinking Places
5912 Drug Stores & Proprietary Stores
NAICS 44611   Pharmacies & Drug Stores
5921 Liquor Stores
NAICS 44531   Beer, Wine & Liquor Stores
5932 Used Merchandise Stores
NAICS 522298 All Other Non-depository Credit
                Intermediation
NAICS 45331   Used Merchandise Stores
5941 Sporting Goods Stores & Bicycle Shops
NAICS 45111   Sporting Goods Stores
5942 Book Stores
NAICS 451211 Book Stores
5943 Stationery Stores
NAICS 45321   Office Supplies & Stationery Stores
5944 Jewelry Stores
NAICS 44831   Jewelry Stores
5945 Hobby, Toy, & Game Shops
NAICS 45112   Hobby, Toy & Game Stores
5946 Camera & Photographic Supply Stores
NAICS 44313   Camera & Photographic Supplies Stores
5947 Gift, Novelty, & Souvenir Shops
NAICS 45322   Gift, Novelty & Souvenir Stores
5948 Luggage & Leather Goods Stores
NAICS 44832   Luggage & Leather Goods Stores
5949 Sewing, Needlework, & Piece Goods Stores
NAICS 45113   Sewing, Needlework & Piece Goods Stores
5961 Catalog & Mail-order Houses
NAICS 45411   Electronic Shopping & Mail-order Houses
5962 Automatic Merchandising Machine Operator
NAICS 45421   Vending Machine Operators
5963 Direct Selling Establishments
NAICS 72233   Mobile Caterers
NAICS 45439   Other Direct Selling Establishments
5983 Fuel Oil Dealers
NAICS 454311 Heating Oil Dealers
5984 Liquefied Petroleum Gas Dealers
NAICS 454312 Liquefied Petroleum Gas Dealers
5989 Fuel Dealers, nec
NAICS 454319 Other Fuel Dealers
5992 Florists
NAICS 45311   Florists
5993 Tobacco Stores & Stands
NAICS 453991 Tobacco Stores
5994 News Dealers & Newsstands
NAICS 451212 News Dealers & Newsstands
5995 Optical Goods Stores
NAICS 339117 Eyeglass & Contact Lens Manufacturing
NAICS 44613   Optical Goods Stores
5999 Miscellaneous Retail Stores, nec
NAICS 44612   Cosmetics, Beauty Supplies & Perfume Stores
NAICS 446199 All Other Health & Personal Care Stores
NAICS 45391   Pet & Pet Supplies Stores

NAICS 45392 Art Dealers
NAICS 443111 Household Appliance Stores
NAICS 443112 Radio, Television & Other Electronics Stores
NAICS 44831 Jewelry Stores
NAICS 453999 All Other Miscellaneous Store Retailers

FINANCE, INSURANCE, & REAL ESTATE

6011 Federal Reserve Banks
NAICS 52111 Monetary Authorities-central Banks
6019 Central Reserve Depository Institutions, nec
NAICS 52232 Financial Transactions Processing, Reserve, &
      Clearing House Activities
6021 National Commercial Banks
NAICS 52211 Commercial Banking
NAICS 52221 Credit Card Issuing
NAICS 523991 Trust, Fiduciary & Custody Activities
6022 State Commercial Banks
NAICS 52211 Commercial Banking
NAICS 52221 Credit Card Issuing
NAICS 52219 Other Depository Intermediation
NAICS 523991 Trust, Fiduciary & Custody Activities
6029 Commercial Banks, nec
NAICS 52211 Commercial Banking
6035 Savings Institutions, Federally Chartered
NAICS 52212 Savings Institutions
6036 Savings Institutions, Not Federally Chartered
NAICS 52212 Savings Institutions
6061 Credit Unions, Federally Chartered
NAICS 52213 Credit Unions
6062 Credit Unions, Not Federally Chartered
NAICS 52213 Credit Unions
6081 Branches & Agencies of Foreign Banks
NAICS 522293 International Trade Financing
NAICS 52211 Commercial Banking
NAICS 522298 All Other Non-depository Credit
      Intermediation
6082 Foreign Trade & International Banking Institutions
NAICS 522293 International Trade Financing
6091 Nondeposit Trust Facilities
NAICS 523991 Trust, Fiduciary, & Custody Activities
6099 Functions Related to Deposit Banking, nec
NAICS 52232 Financial Transactions Processing, Reserve, &
      Clearing House Activities
NAICS 52313 Commodity Contracts Dealing
NAICS 523991 Trust, Fiduciary, & Custody Activities
NAICS 523999 Miscellaneous Financial Investment Activities
NAICS 52239 Other Activities Related to Credit
      Intermediation
6111 Federal & Federally Sponsored Credit Agencies
NAICS 522293 International Trade Financing
NAICS 522294 Secondary Market Financing
NAICS 522298 All Other Non-depository Credit
      Intermediation
6141 Personal Credit Institutions
NAICS 52221 Credit Card Issuing
NAICS 52222 Sales Financing
NAICS 522291 Consumer Lending
**6153 Short-term Business Credit Institutions, Except
  Agricultural**
NAICS 52222 Sales Financing
NAICS 52232 Financial Transactions Processing, Reserve, &
      Clearing House Activities

NAICS 522298 All Other Non-depository Credit
      Intermediation
6159 Miscellaneous Business Credit Institutions
NAICS 52222 Sales Financing
NAICS 532   Included in Rental & Leasing Services
      Subsector by Type of Equipment & Method of
      Operation
NAICS 522293 International Trade Financing
NAICS 522298 All Other Non-depository Credit
      Intermediation
6162 Mortgage Bankers & Loan Correspondents
NAICS 522292 Real Estate Credit
NAICS 52239 Other Activities Related to Credit
      Intermediation
6163 Loan Brokers
NAICS 52231 Mortgage & Other Loan Brokers
6211 Security Brokers, Dealers, & Flotation Companies
NAICS 52311 Investment Banking & Securities Dealing
NAICS 52312 Securities Brokerage
NAICS 52391 Miscellaneous Intermediation
NAICS 523999 Miscellaneous Financial Investment Activities
6221 Commodity Contracts Brokers & Dealers
NAICS 52313 Commodity Contracts Dealing
NAICS 52314 Commodity Brokerage
6231 Security & Commodity Exchanges
NAICS 52321 Securities & Commodity Exchanges
6282 Investment Advice
NAICS 52392 Portfolio Management
NAICS 52393 Investment Advice
**6289 Services Allied with the Exchange of Securities or
  Commodities, nec**
NAICS 523991 Trust, Fiduciary, & Custody Activities
NAICS 523999 Miscellaneous Financial Investment Activities
6311 Life Insurance
NAICS 524113 Direct Life Insurance Carriers
NAICS 52413 Reinsurance Carriers
6321 Accident & Health Insurance
NAICS 524114 Direct Health & Medical Insurance Carriers
NAICS 52519 Other Insurance Funds
NAICS 52413 Reinsurance Carriers
6324 Hospital & Medical Service Plans
NAICS 524114 Direct Health & Medical Insurance Carriers
NAICS 52519 Other Insurance Funds
NAICS 52413 Reinsurance Carriers
6331 Fire, Marine, & Casualty Insurance
NAICS 524126 Direct Property & Casualty Insurance Carriers
NAICS 52519 Other Insurance Funds
NAICS 52413 Reinsurance Carriers
6351 Surety Insurance
NAICS 524126 Direct Property & Casualty Insurance Carriers
NAICS 52413 Reinsurance Carriers
6361 Title Insurance
NAICS 524127 Direct Title Insurance Carriers
NAICS 52413 Reinsurance Carriers
6371 Pension, Health, & Welfare Funds
NAICS 52392 Portfolio Management
NAICS 524292 Third Party Administration for Insurance &
      Pension Funds
NAICS 52511 Pension Funds
NAICS 52512 Health & Welfare Funds
6399 Insurance Carriers, nec
NAICS 524128 Other Direct Insurance Carriers

6411 Insurance Agents, Brokers, & Service
NAICS 52421   Insurance Agencies & Brokerages
NAICS 524291 Claims Adjusters
NAICS 524292 Third Party Administrators for Insurance &
               Pension Funds
NAICS 524298 All Other Insurance Related Activities
6512 Operators of Nonresidential Buildings
NAICS 71131   Promoters of Performing Arts, Sports & Similar
               Events with Facilities
NAICS 53112   Lessors of Nonresidential Buildings
6513 Operators of Apartment Buildings
NAICS 53111   Lessors of Residential Buildings & Dwellings
6514 Operators of Dwellings Other than Apartment Buildings
NAICS 53111   Lessors of Residential Buildings & Dwellings
6515 Operators of Residential Mobile Home Sites
NAICS 53119   Lessors of Other Real Estate Property
6517 Lessors of Railroad Property
NAICS 53119   Lessors of Other Real Estate Property
6519 Lessors of Real Property, nec
NAICS 53119   Lessors of Other Real Estate Property
6531 Real Estate Agents & Managers
NAICS 53121   Offices of Real Estate Agents & Brokers
NAICS 81399   Other Similar Organizations
NAICS 531311 Residential Property Managers
NAICS 531312 Nonresidential Property Managers
NAICS 53132   Offices of Real Estate Appraisers
NAICS 81222   Cemeteries & Crematories
NAICS 531399 All Other Activities Related to Real Estate
6541 Title Abstract Offices
NAICS 541191 Title Abstract & Settlement Offices
6552 Land Subdividers & Developers, Except Cemeteries
NAICS 23311   Land Subdivision & Land Development
6553 Cemetery Subdividers & Developers
NAICS 81222   Cemeteries & Crematories
6712 Offices of Bank Holding Companies
NAICS 551111 Offices of Bank Holding Companies
6719 Offices of Holding Companies, nec
NAICS 551112 Offices of Other Holding Companies
6722 Management Investment Offices, Open-end
NAICS 52591   Open-end Investment Funds
6726 Unit Investment Trusts, Face-amount Certificate Offices, &
       Closed-end Management Investment Offices
NAICS 52599   Other Financial Vehicles
6732 Education, Religious, & Charitable Trusts
NAICS 813211 Grantmaking Foundations
6733 Trusts, Except Educational, Religious, & Charitable
NAICS 52392   Portfolio Management
NAICS 523991 Trust, Fiduciary, & Custody Services
NAICS 52519   Other Insurance Funds
NAICS 52592   Trusts, Estates, & Agency Accounts
6792 Oil Royalty Traders
NAICS 523999 Miscellaneous Financial Investment Activities
NAICS 53311   Owners & Lessors of Other Non-financial
               Assets
6794 Patent Owners & Lessors
NAICS 53311   Owners & Lessors of Other Non-financial
               Assets
6798 Real Estate Investment Trusts
NAICS 52593   Real Estate Investment Trusts
6799 Investors, nec
NAICS 52391   Miscellaneous Intermediation
NAICS 52392   Portfolio Management
NAICS 52313   Commodity Contracts Dealing
NAICS 523999 Miscellaneous Financial Investment Activities

SERVICE INDUSTRIES

7011 Hotels & Motels
NAICS 72111   Hotels & Motels
NAICS 72112   Casino Hotels
NAICS 721191 Bed & Breakfast Inns
NAICS 721199 All Other Traveler Accommodation
7021 Rooming & Boarding Houses
NAICS 72131   Rooming & Boarding Houses
7032 Sporting & Recreational Camps
NAICS 721214 Recreational & Vacation Camps
7033 Recreational Vehicle Parks & Campsites
NAICS 721211 Rv & Campgrounds
7041 Organization Hotels & Lodging Houses, on Membership
     Basis
NAICS 72111   Hotels & Motels
NAICS 72131   Rooming & Boarding Houses
7211 Power Laundries, Family & Commercial
NAICS 812321 Laundries, Family & Commercial
7212 Garment Pressing, & Agents for Laundries
NAICS 812391 Garment Pressing & Agents for Laundries
7213 Linen Supply
NAICS 812331 Linen Supply
7215 Coin-operated Laundry & Drycleaning
NAICS 81231   Coin-operated Laundries & Drycleaners
7216 Drycleaning Plants, Except Rug Cleaning
NAICS 812322 Drycleaning Plants
7217 Carpet & Upholstery Cleaning
NAICS 56174   Carpet & Upholstery Cleaning Services
7218 Industrial Launderers
NAICS 812332 Industrial Launderers
7219 Laundry & Garment Services, nec
NAICS 812331 Linen Supply
NAICS 81149   Other Personal & Household Goods Repair &
               Maintenance
NAICS 812399 All Other Laundry Services
7221 Photographic Studios, Portrait
NAICS 541921 Photographic Studios, Portrait
7231 Beauty Shops
NAICS 812112 Beauty Salons
NAICS 812113 Nail Salons
NAICS 611511 Cosmetology & Barber Schools
7241 Barber Shops
NAICS 812111 Barber Shops
NAICS 611511 Cosmetology & Barber Schools
7251 Shoe Repair Shops & Shoeshine Parlors
NAICS 81143   Footwear & Leather Goods Repair
7261 Funeral Services & Crematories
NAICS 81221   Funeral Homes
NAICS 81222   Cemeteries & Crematories
7291 Tax Return Preparation Services
NAICS 541213 Tax Preparation Services
7299 Miscellaneous Personal Services, nec
NAICS 62441   Child Day Care Services
NAICS 812191 Diet & Weight Reducing Centers
NAICS 53222   Formal Wear & Costume Rental
NAICS 812199 Other Personal Care Services
NAICS 81299   All Other Personal Services
7311 Advertising Agencies
NAICS 54181   Advertising Agencies
7312 Outdoor Advertising Services
NAICS 54185   Display Advertising

7313 Radio, Television, & Publishers' Advertising Representatives
NAICS 54184   Media Representatives
7319 Advertising, nec
NAICS 481219 Other Nonscheduled Air Transportation
NAICS 54183   Media Buying Agencies
NAICS 54185   Display Advertising
NAICS 54187   Advertising Material Distribution Services
NAICS 54189   Other Services Related to Advertising
7322 Adjustment & Collection Services
NAICS 56144   Collection Agencies
NAICS 561491 Repossession Services
7323 Credit Reporting Services
NAICS 56145   Credit Bureaus
7331 Direct Mail Advertising Services
NAICS 54186   Direct Mail Advertising
7334 Photocopying & Duplicating Services
NAICS 561431 Photocopying & Duplicating Services
7335 Commercial Photography
NAICS 48122   Nonscheduled Speciality Air Transportation
NAICS 541922 Commercial Photography
7336 Commercial Art & Graphic Design
NAICS 54143   Commercial Art & Graphic Design Services
7338 Secretarial & Court Reporting Services
NAICS 56141   Document Preparation Services
NAICS 561492 Court Reporting & Stenotype Services
7342 Disinfecting & Pest Control Services
NAICS 56172   Janitorial Services
NAICS 56171   Exterminating & Pest Control Services
7349 Building Cleaning & Maintenance Services, nec
NAICS 56172   Janitorial Services
7352 Medical Equipment Rental & Leasing
NAICS 532291 Home Health Equipment Rental
NAICS 53249   Other Commercial & Industrial Machinery & Equipment Rental & Leasing
7353 Heavy Construction Equipment Rental & Leasing
NAICS 23499   All Other Heavy Construction
NAICS 532412 Construction, Mining & Forestry Machinery & Equipment Rental & Leasing
7359 Equipment Rental & Leasing, nec
NAICS 53221   Consumer Electronics & Appliances Rental
NAICS 53231   General Rental Centers
NAICS 532299 All Other Consumer Goods Rental
NAICS 532412 Construction, Mining & Forestry Machinery & Equipment Rental & Leasing
NAICS 532411 Commercial Air, Rail, & Water Transportation Equipment Rental & Leasing
NAICS 562991 Septic Tank & Related Services
NAICS 53242   Office Machinery & Equipment Rental & Leasing
NAICS 53249   Other Commercial & Industrial Machinery & Equipment Rental & Leasing
7361 Employment Agencies
NAICS 541612 Human Resources & Executive Search Consulting Services
NAICS 56131   Employment Placement Agencies
7363 Help Supply Services
NAICS 56132   Temporary Help Services
NAICS 56133   Employee Leasing Services
7371 Computer Programming Services
NAICS 541511 Custom Computer Programming Services
7372 Prepackaged Software
NAICS 51121   Software Publishers
NAICS 334611 Software Reproducing

7373 Computer Integrated Systems Design
NAICS 541512 Computer Systems Design Services
7374 Computer Processing & Data Preparation & Processing Services
NAICS 51421   Data Processing Services
7375 Information Retrieval Services
NAICS 514191 On-line Information Services
7376 Computer Facilities Management Services
NAICS 541513 Computer Facilities Management Services
7377 Computer Rental & Leasing
NAICS 53242   Office Machinery & Equipment Rental & Leasing
7378 Computer Maintenance & Repair
NAICS 44312   Computer & Software Stores
NAICS 811212 Computer & Office Machine Repair & Maintenance
7379 Computer Related Services, nec
NAICS 541512 Computer Systems Design Services
NAICS 541519 Other Computer Related Services
7381 Detective, Guard, & Armored Car Services
NAICS 561611 Investigation Services
NAICS 561612 Security Guards & Patrol Services
NAICS 561613 Armored Car Services
7382 Security Systems Services
NAICS 561621 Security Systems Services
7383 News Syndicates
NAICS 51411   New Syndicates
7384 Photofinishing Laboratories
NAICS 812921 Photo Finishing Laboratories
NAICS 812922 One-hour Photo Finishing
7389 Business Services, nec
NAICS 51224   Sound Recording Studios
NAICS 51229   Other Sound Recording Industries
NAICS 541199 All Other Legal Services
NAICS 81299   All Other Personal Services
NAICS 54137   Surveying & Mapping Services
NAICS 54141   Interior Design Services
NAICS 54142   Industrial Design Services
NAICS 54134   Drafting Services
NAICS 54149   Other Specialized Design Services
NAICS 54189   Other Services Related to Advertising
NAICS 54193   Translation & Interpretation Services
NAICS 54135   Building Inspection Services
NAICS 54199   All Other Professional, Scientific & Technical Services
NAICS 71141   Agents & Managers for Artists, Athletes, Entertainers & Other Public Figures
NAICS 561422 Telemarketing Bureaus
NAICS 561432 Private Mail Centers
NAICS 561439 Other Business Service Centers
NAICS 561491 Repossession Services
NAICS 56191   Packaging & Labeling Services
NAICS 56179   Other Services to Buildings & Dwellings
NAICS 561599 All Other Travel Arrangement & Reservation Services
NAICS 56192   Convention & Trade Show Organizers
NAICS 561591 Convention & Visitors Bureaus
NAICS 52232   Financial Transactions, Processing, Reserve & Clearing House Activities
NAICS 561499 All Other Business Support Services
NAICS 56199   All Other Support Services
7513 Truck Rental & Leasing, Without Drivers
NAICS 53212   Truck, Utility Trailer & Rv Rental & Leasing

7514 Passenger Car Rental
  NAICS 532111 Passenger Cars Rental
7515 Passenger Car Leasing
  NAICS 532112 Passenger Cars Leasing
7519 Utility Trailer & Recreational Vehicle Rental
  NAICS 53212 Truck, Utility Trailer & Rv Rental & Leasing
7521 Automobile Parking
  NAICS 81293 Parking Lots & Garages
7532 Top, Body, & Upholstery Repair Shops & Paint Shops
  NAICS 811121 Automotive Body, Paint, & Upholstery Repair
         & Maintenance
7533 Automotive Exhaust System Repair Shops
  NAICS 811112 Automotive Exhaust System Repair
7534 Tire Retreading & Repair Shops
  NAICS 326212 Tire Retreading
  NAICS 811198 All Other Automotive Repair & Maintenance
7536 Automotive Glass Replacement Shops
  NAICS 811122 Automotive Glass Replacement Shops
7537 Automotive Transmission Repair Shops
  NAICS 811113 Automotive Transmission Repair
7538 General Automotive Repair Shops
  NAICS 811111 General Automotive Repair
7539 Automotive Repair Shops, nec
  NAICS 811118 Other Automotive Mechanical & Electrical
         Repair & Maintenance
7542 Carwashes
  NAICS 811192 Car Washes
7549 Automotive Services, Except Repair & Carwashes
  NAICS 811191 Automotive Oil Change & Lubrication Shops
  NAICS 48841 Motor Vehicle Towing
  NAICS 811198 All Other Automotive Repair & Maintenance
7622 Radio & Television Repair Shops
  NAICS 811211 Consumer Electronics Repair & Maintenance
  NAICS 443112 Radio, Television & Other Electronics Stores
7623 Refrigeration & Air-conditioning Services & Repair Shops
  NAICS 443111 Household Appliance Stores
  NAICS 81131 Commercial & Industrial Machinery &
         Equipment Repair & Maintenance
  NAICS 811412 Appliance Repair & Maintenance
7629 Electrical & Electronic Repair Shops, nec
  NAICS 443111 Household Appliance Stores
  NAICS 811212 Computer & Office Machine Repair &
         Maintenance
  NAICS 811213 Communication Equipment Repair &
         Maintenance
  NAICS 811219 Other Electronic & Precision Equipment
         Repair & Maintenance
  NAICS 811412 Appliance Repair & Maintenance
  NAICS 811211 Consumer Electronics Repair & Maintenance
7631 Watch, Clock, & Jewelry Repair
  NAICS 81149 Other Personal & Household Goods Repair &
         Maintenance
7641 Reupholster & Furniture Repair
  NAICS 81142 Reupholstery & Furniture Repair
7692 Welding Repair
  NAICS 81149 Other Personal & Household Goods Repair &
         Maintenance
7694 Armature Rewinding Shops
  NAICS 81131 Commercial & Industrial Machinery &
         Equipment Repair & Maintenance
  NAICS 335312 Motor & Generator Manufacturing
7699 Repair Shops & Related Services, nec
  NAICS 561622 Locksmiths
  NAICS 562991 Septic Tank & Related Services

NAICS 56179 Other Services to Buildings & Dwellings
NAICS 48839 Other Supporting Activities for Water
        Transportation
NAICS 45111 Sporting Goods Stores
NAICS 81131 Commercial & Industrial Machinery &
        Equipment Repair & Maintenance
NAICS 11521 Support Activities for Animal Production
NAICS 811212 Computer & Office Machine Repair &
        Maintenance
NAICS 811219 Other Electronic & Precision Equipment
        Repair & Maintenance
NAICS 811411 Home & Garden Equipment Repair &
        Maintenance
NAICS 811412 Appliance Repair & Maintenance
NAICS 81143 Footwear & Leather Goods Repair
NAICS 81149 Other Personal & Household Goods Repair &
        Maintenance
7812 Motion Picture & Video Tape Production
  NAICS 51211 Motion Picture & Video Production
7819 Services Allied to Motion Picture Production
  NAICS 512191 Teleproduction & Other Post-production
         Services
  NAICS 56131 Employment Placement Agencies
  NAICS 53222 Formal Wear & Costumes Rental
  NAICS 53249 Other Commercial & Industrial Machinery &
         Equipment Rental & Leasing
  NAICS 541214 Payroll Services
  NAICS 71151 Independent Artists, Writers, & Performers
  NAICS 334612 Prerecorded Compact Disc , Tape, & Record
         Manufacturing
  NAICS 512199 Other Motion Picture & Video Industries
7822 Motion Picture & Video Tape Distribution
  NAICS 42199 Other Miscellaneous Durable Goods
         Wholesalers
  NAICS 51212 Motion Picture & Video Distribution
7829 Services Allied to Motion Picture Distribution
  NAICS 512199 Other Motion Picture & Video Industries
  NAICS 51212 Motion Picture & Video Distribution
7832 Motion Picture Theaters, Except Drive-ins.
  NAICS 512131 Motion Picture Theaters, Except Drive-in
7833 Drive-in Motion Picture Theaters
  NAICS 512132 Drive-in Motion Picture Theaters
7841 Video Tape Rental
  NAICS 53223 Video Tapes & Disc Rental
7911 Dance Studios, Schools, & Halls
  NAICS 71399 All Other Amusement & Recreation Industries
  NAICS 61161 Fine Arts Schools
7922 Theatrical Producers & Miscellaneous Theatrical Services
  NAICS 56131 Employment Placement Agencies
  NAICS 71111 Theater Companies & Dinner Theaters
  NAICS 71141 Agents & Managers for Artists, Athletes,
         Entertainers & Other Public Figures
  NAICS 71112 Dance Companies
  NAICS 71131 Promoters of Performing Arts, Sports, &
         Similar Events with Facilities
  NAICS 71132 Promoters of Performing Arts, Sports, &
         Similar Events Without Facilities
  NAICS 51229 Other Sound Recording Industries
  NAICS 53249 Other Commercial & Industrial Machinery &
         Equipment Rental & Leasing
7929 Bands, Orchestras, Actors, & Other Entertainers & Entertainment Groups
  NAICS 71113 Musical Groups & Artists
  NAICS 71151 Independent Artists, Writers, & Performers

NAICS 71119 Other Performing Arts Companies

7933 Bowling Centers
NAICS 71395 Bowling Centers

7941 Professional Sports Clubs & Promoters
NAICS 711211 Sports Teams & Clubs
NAICS 71141 Agents & Managers for Artists, Athletes, Entertainers , & Other Public Figures
NAICS 71132 Promoters of Arts, Sports & Similar Events Without Facilities
NAICS 71131 Promoters of Arts, Sports, & Similar Events with Facilities
NAICS 711219 Other Spectator Sports

7948 Racing, Including Track Operations
NAICS 711212 Race Tracks
NAICS 711219 Other Spectator Sports

7991 Physical Fitness Facilities
NAICS 71394 Fitness & Recreational Sports Centers

7992 Public Golf Courses
NAICS 71391 Golf Courses & Country Clubs

7993 Coin Operated Amusement Devices
NAICS 71312 Amusement Arcades
NAICS 71329 Other Gambling Industries
NAICS 71399 All Other Amusement & Recreation Industries

7996 Amusement Parks
NAICS 71311 Amusement & Theme Parks

7997 Membership Sports & Recreation Clubs
NAICS 48122 Nonscheduled Speciality Air Transportation
NAICS 71391 Golf Courses & Country Clubs
NAICS 71394 Fitness & Recreational Sports Centers
NAICS 71399 All Other Amusement & Recreation Industries

7999 Amusement & Recreation Services, nec
NAICS 561599 All Other Travel Arrangement & Reservation Services
NAICS 48799 Scenic & Sightseeing Transportation, Other
NAICS 711119 Other Performing Arts Companies
NAICS 711219 Other Spectator Sports
NAICS 71392 Skiing Facilities
NAICS 71394 Fitness & Recreational Sports Centers
NAICS 71321 Casinos
NAICS 71329 Other Gambling Industries
NAICS 71219 Nature Parks & Other Similar Institutions
NAICS 61162 Sports & Recreation Instruction
NAICS 532292 Recreational Goods Rental
NAICS 48711 Scenic & Sightseeing Transportation, Land
NAICS 48721 Scenic & Sightseeing Transportation, Water
NAICS 71399 All Other Amusement & Recreation Industries

8011 Offices & Clinics of Doctors of Medicine
NAICS 621493 Freestanding Ambulatory Surgical & Emergency Centers
NAICS 621491 Hmo Medical Centers
NAICS 621112 Offices of Physicians, Mental Health Specialists
NAICS 621111 Offices of Physicians

8021 Offices & Clinics of Dentists
NAICS 62121 Offices of Dentists

8031 Offices & Clinics of Doctors of Osteopathy
NAICS 621111 Offices of Physicians
NAICS 621112 Offices of Physicians, Mental Health Specialists

8041 Offices & Clinics of Chiropractors
NAICS 62131 Offices of Chiropractors

8042 Offices & Clinics of Optometrists
NAICS 62132 Offices of Optometrists

8043 Offices & Clinics of Podiatrists
NAICS 621391 Offices of Podiatrists

8049 Offices & Clinics of Health Practitioners, nec
NAICS 62133 Offices of Mental Health Practitioners
NAICS 62134 Offices of Physical, Occupational, & Speech Therapists & Audiologists
NAICS 621399 Offices of All Other Miscellaneous Health Practitioners

8051 Skilled Nursing Care Facilities
NAICS 623311 Continuing Care Retirement Communities
NAICS 62311 Nursing Care Facilities

8052 Intermediate Care Facilities
NAICS 623311 Continuing Care Retirement Communities
NAICS 62321 Residential Mental Retardation Facilities
NAICS 62311 Nursing Care Facilities

8059 Nursing & Personal Care Facilities, nec
NAICS 623311 Continuing Care Retirement Communities
NAICS 62311 Nursing Care Facilities

8062 General Medical & Surgical Hospitals
NAICS 62211 General Medical & Surgical Hospitals

8063 Psychiatric Hospitals
NAICS 62221 Psychiatric & Substance Abuse Hospitals

8069 Specialty Hospitals, Except Psychiatric
NAICS 62211 General Medical & Surgical Hospitals
NAICS 62221 Psychiatric & Substance Abuse Hospitals
NAICS 62231 Specialty Hospitals

8071 Medical Laboratories
NAICS 621512 Diagnostic Imaging Centers
NAICS 621511 Medical Laboratories

8072 Dental Laboratories
NAICS 339116 Dental Laboratories

8082 Home Health Care Services
NAICS 62161 Home Health Care Services

8092 Kidney Dialysis Centers
NAICS 621492 Kidney Dialysis Centers

8093 Specialty Outpatient Facilities, nec
NAICS 62141 Family Planning Centers
NAICS 62142 Outpatient Mental Health & Substance Abuse Centers
NAICS 621498 All Other Outpatient Care Facilities

8099 Health & Allied Services, nec
NAICS 621991 Blood & Organ Banks
NAICS 54143 Graphic Design Services
NAICS 541922 Commercial Photography
NAICS 62141 Family Planning Centers
NAICS 621999 All Other Miscellaneous Ambulatory Health Care Services

8111 Legal Services
NAICS 54111 Offices of Lawyers

8211 Elementary & Secondary Schools
NAICS 61111 Elementary & Secondary Schools

8221 Colleges, Universities, & Professional Schools
NAICS 61131 Colleges, Universities & Professional Schools

8222 Junior Colleges & Technical Institutes
NAICS 61121 Junior Colleges

8231 Libraries
NAICS 51412 Libraries & Archives

8243 Data Processing Schools
NAICS 611519 Other Technical & Trade Schools
NAICS 61142 Computer Training

8244 Business & Secretarial Schools
NAICS 61141 Business & Secretarial Schools

8249 Vocational Schools, nec
NAICS 611513 Apprenticeship Training
NAICS 611512 Flight Training
NAICS 611519 Other Technical & Trade Schools

8299 Schools & Educational Services, nec
NAICS 48122　Nonscheduled speciality Air Transportation
NAICS 611512 Flight Training
NAICS 611692 Automobile Driving Schools
NAICS 61171　Educational Support Services
NAICS 611691 Exam Preparation & Tutoring
NAICS 61161　Fine Arts Schools
NAICS 61163　Language Schools
NAICS 61143　Professional & Management Development
　　　　　　　Training Schools
NAICS 611699 All Other Miscellaneous Schools & Instruction

8322 Individual & Family Social Services
NAICS 62411　Child & Youth Services
NAICS 62421　Community Food Services
NAICS 624229 Other Community Housing Services
NAICS 62423　Emergency & Other Relief Services
NAICS 62412　Services for the Elderly & Persons with
　　　　　　　Disabilities
NAICS 624221 Temporary Shelters
NAICS 92215　Parole Offices & Probation Offices
NAICS 62419　Other Individual & Family Services

8331 Job Training & Vocational Rehabilitation Services
NAICS 62431　Vocational Rehabilitation Services

8351 Child Day Care Services
NAICS 62441　Child Day Care Services

8361 Residential Care
NAICS 623312 Homes for the Elderly
NAICS 62322　Residential Mental Health & Substance Abuse
　　　　　　　Facilities
NAICS 62399　Other Residential Care Facilities

8399 Social Services, nec
NAICS 813212 Voluntary Health Organizations
NAICS 813219 Other Grantmaking & Giving Services
NAICS 813311 Human Rights Organizations
NAICS 813312 Environment, Conservation & Wildlife
　　　　　　　Organizations
NAICS 813319 Other Social Advocacy Organizations

8412 Museums & Art Galleries
NAICS 71211　Museums
NAICS 71212　Historical Sites

8422 Arboreta & Botanical or Zoological Gardens
NAICS 71213　Zoos & Botanical Gardens
NAICS 71219　Nature Parks & Other Similar Institutions

8611 Business Associations
NAICS 81391　Business Associations

8621 Professional Membership Organizations
NAICS 81392　Professional Organizations

8631 Labor Unions & Similar Labor Organizations
NAICS 81393　Labor Unions & Similar Labor Organizations

8641 Civic, Social, & Fraternal Associations
NAICS 81341　Civic & Social Organizations
NAICS 81399　Other Similar Organizations
NAICS 92115　American Indian & Alaska Native Tribal
　　　　　　　Governments
NAICS 62411　Child & Youth Services

8651 Political Organizations
NAICS 81394　Political Organizations

8661 Religious Organizations
NAICS 81311　Religious Organizations

8699 Membership Organizations, nec
NAICS 81341　Civic & Social Organizations
NAICS 81391　Business Associations
NAICS 813312 Environment, Conservation, & Wildlife
　　　　　　　Organizations

NAICS 561599 All Other Travel Arrangement & Reservation
　　　　　　　Services
NAICS 81399　Other Similar Organizations

8711 Engineering Services
NAICS 54133　Engineering Services

8712 Architectural Services
NAICS 54131　Architectural Services

8713 Surveying Services
NAICS 48122　Nonscheduled Air Speciality Transportation
NAICS 54136　Geophysical Surveying & Mapping Services
NAICS 54137　Surveying & Mapping Services

8721 Accounting, Auditing, & Bookkeeping Services
NAICS 541211 Offices of Certified Public Accountants
NAICS 541214 Payroll Services
NAICS 541219 Other Accounting Services

8731 Commercial Physical & Biological Research
NAICS 54171　Research & Development in the Physical
　　　　　　　Sciences & Engineering Sciences
NAICS 54172　Research & Development in the Life Sciences

**8732 Commercial Economic, Sociological, & Educational
Research**
NAICS 54173　Research & Development in the Social Sciences
　　　　　　　& Humanities
NAICS 54191　Marketing Research & Public Opinion Polling

8733 Noncommercial Research Organizations
NAICS 54171　Research & Development in the Physical
　　　　　　　Sciences & Engineering Sciences
NAICS 54172　Research & Development in the Life Sciences
NAICS 54173　Research & Development in the Social Sciences
　　　　　　　& Humanities

8734 Testing Laboratories
NAICS 54194　Veterinary Services
NAICS 54138　Testing Laboratories

8741 Management Services
NAICS 56111　Office Administrative Services
NAICS 23　　　Included in Construction Sector by Type of
　　　　　　　Construction

8742 Management Consulting Services
NAICS 541611 Administrative Management & General
　　　　　　　Management Consulting Services
NAICS 541612 Human Resources & Executive Search Services
NAICS 541613 Marketing Consulting Services
NAICS 541614 Process, Physical, Distribution & Logistics
　　　　　　　Consulting Services

8743 Public Relations Services
NAICS 54182　Public Relations Agencies

8744 Facilities Support Management Services
NAICS 56121　Facilities Support Services

8748 Business Consulting Services, nec
NAICS 61171　Educational Support Services
NAICS 541618 Other Management Consulting Services
NAICS 54169　Other Scientific & Technical Consulting
　　　　　　　Services

8811 Private Households
NAICS 81411　Private Households

8999 Services, nec
NAICS 71151　Independent Artists, Writers, & Performers
NAICS 51221　Record Production
NAICS 54169　Other Scientific & Technical Consulting
　　　　　　　Services
NAICS 51223　Music Publishers
NAICS 541612 Human Resources & Executive Search
　　　　　　　Consulting Services
NAICS 514199 All Other Information Services

NAICS 54162   Environmental Consulting Services

PUBLIC ADMINISTRATION

9111 Executive Offices
NAICS 92111   Executive Offices
9121 Legislative Bodies
NAICS 92112   Legis' tive Bodies
9131 Executive & Legislative Offices, Combined
NAICS 92114   Executive & Legislative Offices, Combined
9199 General Government, nec
NAICS 92119   All Other General Government
9211 Courts
NAICS 92211   Courts
9221 Police Protection
NAICS 92212   Police Protection
9222 Legal Counsel & Prosecution
NAICS 92213   Legal Counsel & Prosecution
9223 Correctional Institutions
NAICS 92214   Correctional Institutions
9224 Fire Protection
NAICS 92216   Fire Protection
9229 Public Order & Safety, nec
NAICS 92219   All Other Justice, Public Order, & Safety
9311 Public Finance, Taxation, & Monetary Policy
NAICS 92113   Public Finance
9411 Administration of Educational Programs
NAICS 92311   Administration of Education Programs
9431 Administration of Public Health Programs
NAICS 92312   Administration of Public Health Programs
9441 Administration of Social, Human Resource & Income Maintenance Programs
NAICS 92313   Administration of Social, Human Resource & Income Maintenance Programs
9451 Administration of Veteran's Affairs, Except Health Insurance
NAICS 92314   Administration of Veteran's Affairs
9511 Air & Water Resource & Solid Waste Management
NAICS 92411   Air & Water Resource & Solid Waste Management
9512 Land, Mineral, Wildlife, & Forest Conservation
NAICS 92412   Land, Mineral, Wildlife, & Forest Conservation
9531 Administration of Housing Programs
NAICS 92511   Administration of Housing Programs
9532 Administration of Urban Planning & Community & Rural Development
NAICS 92512   Administration of Urban Planning & Community & Rural Development
9611 Administration of General Economic Programs
NAICS 92611   Administration of General Economic Programs
9621 Regulations & Administration of Transportation Programs
NAICS 488111 Air Traffic Control
NAICS 92612   Regulation & Administration of Transportation Programs
9631 Regulation & Administration of Communications, Electric, Gas, & Other Utilities
NAICS 92613   Regulation & Administration of Communications, Electric, Gas, & Other Utilities
9641 Regulation of Agricultural Marketing & Commodity
NAICS 92614   Regulation of Agricultural Marketing & Commodity

9651 Regulation, Licensing, & Inspection of Miscellaneous Commercial Sectors
NAICS 92615   Regulation, Licensing, & Inspection of Miscellaneous Commercial Sectors
9661 Space Research & Technology
NAICS 92711   Space Research & Technology
9711 National Security
NAICS 92811   National Security
9721 International Affairs
NAICS 92812   International Affairs
9999 Nonclassifiable Establishments
NAICS 99999   Unclassified Establishments

NAICS TO SIC CONVERSION GUIDE

AGRICULTURE, FORESTRY, FISHING, & HUNTING

11111 Soybean Farming
SIC 0116 Soybeans
11112 Oilseed Farming
SIC 0119 Cash Grains, nec
11113 Dry Pea & Bean Farming
SIC 0119 Cash Grains, nec
11114 Wheat Farming
SIC 0111 Wheat
11115 Corn Farming
SIC 0115 Corn
SIC 0119 Cash Grains, nec
11116 Rice Farming
SIC 0112 Rice
111191 Oilseed & Grain Combination Farming
SIC 0119 Cash Grains, nec
111199 All Other Grain Farming
SIC 0119 Cash Grains, nec
111211 Potato Farming
SIC 0134 Irish Potatoes
111219 Other Vegetable & Melon Farming
SIC 0161 Vegetables & Melons
SIC 0139 Field Crops Except Cash Grains
11131 Orange Groves
SIC 0174 Citrus Fruits
11132 Citrus Groves
SIC 0174 Citrus Fruits
111331 Apple Orchards
SIC 0175 Deciduous Tree Fruits
111332 Grape Vineyards
SIC 0172 Grapes
111333 Strawberry Farming
SIC 0171 Berry Crops
111334 Berry Farming
SIC 0171 Berry Crops
111335 Tree Nut Farming
SIC 0173 Tree Nuts
111336 Fruit & Tree Nut Combination Farming
SIC 0179 Fruits & Tree Nuts, nec
111339 Other Noncitrus Fruit Farming
SIC 0175 Deciduous Tree Fruits
SIC 0179 Fruit & Tree Nuts, nec
111411 Mushroom Production
SIC 0182 Food Crops Grown Under Cover
111419 Other Food Crops Grown Under Cover
SIC 0182 Food Crops Grown Under Cover
111421 Nursery & Tree Production
SIC 0181 Ornamental Floriculture & Nursery Products
SIC 0811 Timber Tracts
111422 Floriculture Production
SIC 0181 Ornamental Floriculture & Nursery Products
11191 Tobacco Farming
SIC 0132 Tobacco
11192 Cotton Farming
SIC 0131 Cotton
11193 Sugarcane Farming
SIC 0133 Sugarcane & Sugar Beets

11194 Hay Farming
SIC 0139 Field Crops, Except Cash Grains, nec
111991 Sugar Beet Farming
SIC 0133 Sugarcane & Sugar Beets
111992 Peanut Farming
SIC 0139 Field Crops, Except Cash Grains, nec
111998 All Other Miscellaneous Crop Farming
SIC 0139 Field Crops, Except Cash Grains, nec
SIC 0191 General Farms, Primarily Crop
SIC 0831 Forest Products
SIC 0919 Miscellaneous Marine Products
SIC 2099 Food Preparations, nec
112111 Beef Cattle Ranching & Farming
SIC 0212 Beef Cattle, Except Feedlots
SIC 0241 Dairy Farms
112112 Cattle Feedlots
SIC 0211 Beef Cattle Feedlots
11212 Dairy Cattle & Milk Production
SIC 0241 Dairy Farms
11213 Dual Purpose Cattle Ranching & Farming
No SIC equivalent
11221 Hog & Pig Farming
SIC 0213 Hogs
11231 Chicken Egg Production
SIC 0252 Chicken Eggs
11232 Broilers & Other Meat Type Chicken Production
SIC 0251 Broiler, Fryers, & Roaster Chickens
11233 Turkey Production
SIC 0253 Turkey & Turkey Eggs
11234 Poultry Hatcheries
SIC 0254 Poultry Hatcheries
11239 Other Poultry Production
SIC 0259 Poultry & Eggs, nec
11241 Sheep Farming
SIC 0214 Sheep & Goats
11242 Goat Farming
SIC 0214 Sheep & Goats
112511 Finfish Farming & Fish Hatcheries
SIC 0273 Animal Aquaculture
SIC 0921 Fish Hatcheries & Preserves
112512 Shellfish Farming
SIC 0273 Animal Aquaculture
SIC 0921 Fish Hatcheries & Preserves
112519 Other Animal Aquaculture
SIC 0273 Animal Aquaculture
11291 Apiculture
SIC 0279 Animal Specialties, nec
11292 Horse & Other Equine Production
SIC 0272 Horses & Other Equines
11293 Fur-Bearing Animal & Rabbit Production
SIC 0271 Fur-Bearing Animals & Rabbits
11299 All Other Animal Production
SIC 0219 General Livestock, Except Dairy & Poultry
SIC 0279 Animal Specialties, nec
SIC 0291 General Farms, Primarily Livestock & Animal
    Specialties;
11311 Timber Tract Operations
SIC 0811 Timber Tracts
11321 Forest Nurseries & Gathering of Forest Products
SIC 0831 Forest Nurseries & Gathering of Forest Products
11331 Logging
SIC 2411 Logging

114111 Finfish Fishing
SIC 0912 Finfish
114112 Shellfish Fishing
SIC 0913 Shellfish
114119 Other Marine Fishing
SIC 0919 Miscellaneous Marine Products
11421 Hunting & Trapping
SIC 0971 Hunting & Trapping, & Game Propagation;
115111 Cotton Ginning
SIC 0724 Cotton Ginning
115112 Soil Preparation, Planting, & Cultivating
SIC 0711 Soil Preparation Services
SIC 0721 Crop Planting, Cultivating, & Protecting
115113 Crop Harvesting, Primarily by Machine
SIC 0722 Crop Harvesting, Primarily by Machine
115114 Other Postharvest Crop Activities
SIC 0723 Crop Preparation Services For Market, Except Cotton
Ginning
115115 Farm Labor Contractors & Crew Leaders
SIC 0761 Farm Labor Contractors & Crew Leaders
115116 Farm Management Services
SIC 0762 Farm Management Services
11521 Support Activities for Animal Production
SIC 0751 Livestock Services, Except Veterinary
SIC 0752 Animal Specialty Services, Except Veterinary
SIC 7699 Repair Services, nec
11531 Support Activities for Forestry
SIC 0851 Forestry Services

MINING

211111 Crude Petroleum & Natural Gas Extraction
SIC 1311 Crude Petroleum & Natural Gas
211112 Natural Gas Liquid Extraction
SIC 1321 Natural Gas Liquids
212111 Bituminous Coal & Lignite Surface Mining
SIC 1221 Bituminous Coal & Lignite Surface Mining
212112 Bituminous Coal Underground Mining
SIC 1222 Bituminous Coal Underground Mining
212113 Anthracite Mining
SIC 1231 Anthracite Mining
21221 Iron Ore Mining
SIC 1011 Iron Ores
212221 Gold Ore Mining
SIC 1041 Gold Ores
212222 Silver Ore Mining
SIC 1044 Silver Ores
212231 Lead Ore & Zinc Ore Mining
SIC 1031 Lead & Zinc Ores
212234 Copper Ore & Nickel Ore Mining
SIC 1021 Copper Ores
212291 Uranium-Radium-Vanadium Ore Mining
SIC 1094 Uranium-Radium-Vanadium Ores
212299 All Other Metal Ore Mining
SIC 1061 Ferroalloy Ores, Except Vanadium
SIC 1099 Miscellaneous Metal Ores, nec
212311 Dimension Stone Mining & Quarrying
SIC 1411 Dimension Stone
212312 Crushed & Broken Limestone Mining & Quarrying
SIC 1422 Crushed & Broken Limestone
212313 Crushed & Broken Granite Mining & Quarrying
SIC 1423 Crushed & Broken Granite

212319 Other Crushed & Broken Stone Mining & Quarrying
SIC 1429 Crushed & Broken Stone, nec
SIC 1499 Miscellaneous Nonmetallic Minerals, Except Fuels
212321 Construction Sand & Gravel Mining
SIC 1442 Construction Sand & Gravel
212322 Industrial Sand Mining
SIC 1446 Industrial Sand
212324 Kaolin & Ball Clay Mining
SIC 1455 Kaolin & Ball Clay
212325 Clay & Ceramic & Refractory Minerals Mining
SIC 1459 Clay, Ceramic, & Refractory Minerals, nec
212391 Potash, Soda, & Borate Mineral Mining
SIC 1474 Potash, Soda, & Borate Minerals
212392 Phosphate Rock Mining
SIC 1475 Phosphate Rock
212393 Other Chemical & Fertilizer Mineral Mining
SIC 1479 Chemical & Fertilizer Mineral Mining, nec
212399 All Other Nonmetallic Mineral Mining
SIC 1499 Miscellaneous Nonmetallic Minerals, Except Fuels
213111 Drilling Oil & Gas Wells
SIC 1381 Drilling Oil & Gas Wells
213112 Support Activities for Oil & Gas Operations
SIC 1382 Oil & Gas Field Exploration Services
SIC 1389 Oil & Gas Field Services, nec
213113 Other Gas & Field Support Activities
SIC 1389 Oil & Gas Field Services, nec
213114 Support Activities for Coal Mining
SIC 1241 Coal Mining Services
213115 Support Activities for Metal Mining
SIC 1081 Metal Mining Services
**213116 Support Activities for Nonmetallic Minerals, Except
Fuels**
SIC 1481 Nonmetallic Minerals Services, Except Fuels

UTILITIES

221111 Hydroelectric Power Generation
SIC 4911 Electric Services
SIC 4931 Electric & Other Services Combined
SIC 4939 Combination Utilities, nec
221112 Fossil Fuel Electric Power Generation
SIC 4911 Electric Services
SIC 4931 Electric & Other Services Combined
SIC 4939 Combination Utilities, nec
221113 Nuclear Electric Power Generation
SIC 4911 Electric Services
SIC 4931 Electric & Other Services Combined
SIC 4939 Combination Utilities, nec
221119 Other Electric Power Generation
SIC 4911 Electric Services
SIC 4931 Electric & Other Services Combined
SIC 4939 Combination Utilities, nec
221121 Electric Bulk Power Transmission & Control
SIC 4911 Electric Services
SIC 4931 Electric & Other Services Combined
SIC 4939 Combination Utilities, NEC
221122 Electric Power Distribution
SIC 4911 Electric Services
SIC 4931 Electric & Other Services Combined
SIC 4939 Combination Utilities, nec
22121 Natural Gas Distribution
SIC 4923 Natural Gas Transmission & Distribution
SIC 4924 Natural Gas Distribution

SIC 4925 Mixed, Manufactured, or Liquefied Petroleum Gas
    Production and/or Distribution
SIC 4931 Electronic & Other Services Combined
SIC 4932 Gas & Other Services Combined
SIC 4939 Combination Utilities, nec

22131 Water Supply & Irrigation Systems
SIC 4941 Water Supply
SIC 4971 Irrigation Systems

22132 Sewage Treatment Facilities
SIC 4952 Sewerage Systems

22133 Steam & Air-Conditioning Supply
SIC 4961 Steam & Air-Conditioning Supply

CONSTRUCTION

23311 Land Subdivision & Land Development
SIC 6552 Land Subdividers & Developers, Except Cemeteries

23321 Single Family Housing Construction
SIC 1521 General contractors-Single-Family Houses
SIC 1531 Operative Builders

23322 Multifamily Housing Construction
SIC 1522 General Contractors-Residential Building, Other
    Than Single-Family
SIC 1531 Operative Builders

23331 Manufacturing & Industrial Building Construction
SIC 1531 Operative Builders
SIC 1541 General Contractors-Industrial Buildings &
    Warehouses

23332 Commercial & Institutional Building Construction
SIC 1522 General Contractors-Residential Building Other than
    Single-Family
SIC 1531 Operative Builders
SIC 1541 General Contractors-Industrial Buildings &
    Warehouses
SIC 1542 General Contractor-Nonresidential Buildings, Other
    than Industrial Buildings & Warehouses

23411 Highway & Street Construction
SIC 1611 Highway & Street Construction, Except Elevated
    Highways

23412 Bridge & Tunnel Construction
SIC 1622 Bridge, Tunnel, & Elevated Highway Construction

2349 Other Heavy Construction

23491 Water, Sewer, & Pipeline Construction
SIC 1623 Water, Sewer, Pipeline, & Communications & Power
    Line Construction

**23492 Power & Communication Transmission Line
Construction**
SIC 1623 Water, Sewer, Pipelines, & Communications & Power
    Line Construction

23493 Industrial Nonbuilding Structure Construction
SIC 1629 Heavy Construction, nec

23499 All Other Heavy Construction
SIC 1629 Heavy Construction, nec
SIC 7353 Construction Equipment Rental & Leasing

23511 Plumbing, Heating & Air-Conditioning Contractors
SIC 1711 Plumbing, Heating & Air-Conditioning

23521 Painting & Wall Covering Contractors
SIC 1721 Painting & Paper Hanging
SIC 1799 Special Trade Contractors, nec

23531 Electrical Contractors
SIC 1731 Electrical Work

23541 Masonry & Stone Contractors
SIC 1741 Masonry, Stone Setting & Other Stone Work

23542 Drywall, Plastering, Acoustical & Insulation Contractors
SIC 1742 Plastering, Drywall, Acoustical, & Insulation Work
SIC 1743 Terrazzo, Tile, Marble & Mosaic work
SIC 1771 Concrete Work

23543 Tile, Marble, Terrazzo & Mosaic Contractors
SIC 1743 Terrazzo, Tile, Marble, & Mosaic Work

23551 Carpentry Contractors
SIC 1751 Carpentry Work

23552 Floor Laying & Other Floor Contractors
SIC 1752 Floor Laying & Other Floor Work, nec

23561 Roofing, Siding & Sheet Metal Contractors
SIC 1761 Roofing, Siding, & Sheet Metal Work

23571 Concrete Contractors
SIC 1771 Concrete Work

23581 Water Well Drilling Contractors
SIC 1781 Water Well Drilling

23591 Structural Steel Erection Contractors
SIC 1791 Structural Steel Erection

23592 Glass & Glazing Contractors
SIC 1793 Glass & Glazing Work
SIC 1799 Specialty Trade Contractors, nec

23593 Excavation Contractors
SIC 1794 Excavation Work

23594 Wrecking & Demolition Contractors
SIC 1795 Wrecking & Demolition Work

**23595 Building Equipment & Other Machinery Installation
Contractors**
SIC 1796 Installation of Erection of Building Equipment, nec

23599 All Other Special Trade Contractors
SIC 1799 Special Trade Contractors, nec

FOOD MANUFACTURING

311111 Dog & Cat Food Manufacturing
SIC 2047 Dog & Cat Food

311119 Other Animal Food Manufacturing
SIC 2048 Prepared Feeds & Feed Ingredients for Animals &
    Fowls, Except Dogs & Cats

311211 Flour Milling
SIC 2034 Dehydrated Fruits, Vegetables & Soup Mixes
SIC 2041 Flour & Other Grain Mill Products

311212 Rice Milling
SIC 2044 Rice Milling

311213 Malt Manufacturing
SIC 2083 Malt

311221 Wet Corn Milling
SIC 2046 Wet Corn Milling

311222 Soybean Processing
SIC 2075 Soybean Oil Mills
SIC 2079 Shortening, Table Oils, Margarine, & Other Edible
    Fats & Oils, nec

311223 Other Oilseed Processing
SIC 2074 Cottonseed Oil Mills
SIC 2079 Shortening, Table Oils, Margarine & Other Edible
    Fats & Oils, nec
SIC 2076 Vegetable Oil Mills, Except Corn, Cottonseed, &
    Soybean

311225 Edible Fats & Oils Manufacturing
SIC 2077 Animal & Marine Fats & Oil, nec
SIC 2074 Cottonseed Oil Mills
SIC 2075 Soybean Oil Mills

SIC 2076 Vegetable Oil Mills, Except Corn, Cottonseed, & Soybean
SIC 2079 Shortening, Table Oils, Margarine, & Other Edible Fats & Oils, nec

31123 Breakfast Cereal Manufacturing
SIC 2043 Cereal Breakfast Foods

311311 Sugarcane Mills
SIC 2061 Cane Sugar, Except Refining

311312 Cane Sugar Refining
SIC 2062 Cane Sugar Refining

311313 Beet Sugar Manufacturing
SIC 2063 Beet Sugar

31132 Chocolate & Confectionery Manufacturing from Cacao Beans
SIC 2066 Chocolate & Cocoa Products

31133 Confectionery Manufacturing from Purchased Chocolate
SIC 2064 Candy & Other Confectionery Products

31134 Non-Chocolate Confectionery Manufacturing
SIC 2064 Candy & Other Confectionery Products
SIC 2067 Chewing Gum
SIC 2099 Food Preparations, nec

311411 Frozen Fruit, Juice & Vegetable Processing
SIC 2037 Frozen Fruits, Fruit Juices, & Vegetables

311412 Frozen Specialty Food Manufacturing
SIC 2038 Frozen Specialties, NEC

311421 Fruit & Vegetable Canning
SIC 2033 Canned Fruits, Vegetables, Preserves, Jams, & Jellies
SIC 2035 Pickled Fruits & Vegetables, Vegetable Sauces, & Seasonings & Salad Dressings

311422 Specialty Canning
SIC 2032 Canned Specialties

311423 Dried & Dehydrated Food Manufacturing
SIC 2034 Dried & Dehydrated Fruits, Vegetables & Soup Mixes
SIC 2099 Food Preparation, nec

311511 Fluid Milk Manufacturing
SIC 2026 Fluid Milk

311512 Creamery Butter Manufacturing
SIC 2021 Creamery Butter

311513 Cheese Manufacturing
SIC 2022 Natural, Processed, & Imitation Cheese

311514 Dry, Condensed, & Evaporated Milk Manufacturing
SIC 2023 Dry, Condensed & Evaporated Dairy Products

31152 Ice Cream & Frozen Dessert Manufacturing
SIC 2024 Ice Cream & Frozen Desserts

311611 Animal Slaughtering
SIC 0751 Livestock Services, Except Veterinary
SIC 2011 Meat Packing Plants
SIC 2048 Prepared Feeds & Feed Ingredients for Animals & Fowls, Except Dogs & Cats

311612 Meat Processed from Carcasses
SIC 2013 Sausages & Other Prepared Meats
SIC 5147 Meat & Meat Products

311613 Rendering & Meat By-product Processing
SIC 2077 Animal & Marine Fats & Oils

311615 Poultry Processing
SIC 2015 Poultry Slaughtering & Processing

311711 Seafood Canning
SIC 2077 Animal & Marine Fats & Oils
SIC 2091 Canned & Cured Fish & Seafood

311712 Fresh & Frozen Seafood Processing
SIC 2077 Animal & Marine Fats & Oils
SIC 2092 Prepared Fresh or Frozen Fish & Seafood

311811 Retail Bakeries
SIC 5461 Retail Bakeries

311812 Commercial Bakeries
SIC 2051 Bread & Other Bakery Products, Except Cookies & Crackers
SIC 2052 Cookies & Crackers

311813 Frozen Bakery Product Manufacturing
SIC 2053 Frozen Bakery Products, Except Bread

311821 Cookie & Cracker Manufacturing
SIC 2052 Cookies & Crackers

311822 Flour Mixes & Dough Manufacturing from Purchased Flour
SIC 2045 Prepared Flour Mixes & Doughs

311823 Pasta Manufacturing
SIC 2098 Macaroni, Spaghetti, Vermicelli & Noodles

31183 Tortilla Manufacturing
SIC 2099 Food Preparations, nec

311911 Roasted Nuts & Peanut Butter Manufacturing
SIC 2068 Salted & Roasted Nuts & Seeds
SIC 2099 Food Preparations, nec

311919 Other Snack Food Manufacturing
SIC 2052 Cookies & Crackers
SIC 2096 Potato Chips, Corn Chips, & Similar Snacks

31192 Coffee & Tea Manufacturing
SIC 2043 Cereal Breakfast Foods
SIC 2095 Roasted Coffee
SIC 2099 Food Preparations, nec

31193 Flavoring Syrup & Concentrate Manufacturing
SIC 2087 Flavoring Extracts & Flavoring Syrups

311941 Mayonnaise, Dressing & Other Prepared Sauce Manufacturing
SIC 2035 Pickled Fruits & Vegetables, Vegetable Seasonings, & Sauces & Salad Dressings
SIC 2099 Food Preparations, nec

311942 Spice & Extract Manufacturing
SIC 2087 Flavoring Extracts & Flavoring Syrups
SIC 2095 Roasted Coffee
SIC 2099 Food Preparations, nec
SIC 2899 Chemical Preparations, nec

311991 Perishable Prepared Food Manufacturing
SIC 2099 Food Preparations, nec

311999 All Other Miscellaneous Food Manufacturing
SIC 2015 Poultry Slaughtering & Processing
SIC 2032 Canned Specialties
SIC 2087 Flavoring Extracts & Flavoring Syrups
SIC 2099 Food Preparations, nec

BEVERAGE & TOBACCO PRODUCT MANUFACTURING

312111 Soft Drink Manufacturing
SIC 2086 Bottled & Canned Soft Drinks & Carbonated Water

312112 Bottled Water Manufacturing
SIC 2086 Bottled & Canned Soft Drinks & Carbonated Water

312113 Ice Manufacturing
SIC 2097 Manufactured Ice

31212 Breweries
SIC 2082 Malt Beverages

31213 Wineries
SIC 2084 Wines, Brandy, & Brandy Spirits

31214 Distilleries
SIC 2085 Distilled & Blended Liquors

31221 Tobacco Stemming & Redrying
SIC 2141 Tobacco Stemming & Redrying
312221 Cigarette Manufacturing
SIC 2111 Cigarettes
312229 Other Tobacco Product Manufacturing
SIC 2121 Cigars
SIC 2131 Chewing & Smoking Tobacco & Snuff
SIC 2141 Tobacco Stemming & Redrying

TEXTILE MILLS

313111 Yarn Spinning Mills
SIC 2281 Yarn Spinning Mills
SIC 2299 Textile Goods, nec
313112 Yarn Texturing, Throwing & Twisting Mills
SIC 2282 Yarn Texturing, Throwing, Winding Mills
313113 Thread Mills
SIC 2284 Thread Mills
SIC 2299 Textile Goods, NEC
31321 Broadwoven Fabric Mills
SIC 2211 Broadwoven Fabric Mills, Cotton
SIC 2221 Broadwoven Fabric Mills, Manmade Fiber & Silk
SIC 2231 Broadwoven Fabric Mills, Wool
SIC 2299 Textile Goods, nec
313221 Narrow Fabric Mills
SIC 2241 Narrow Fabric & Other Smallware Mills: Cotton,
       Wool, Silk & Manmade Fiber
SIC 2299 Textile Goods, nec
313222 Schiffli Machine Embroidery
SIC 2397 Schiffli Machine Embroideries
31323 Nonwoven Fabric Mills
SIC 2297 Nonwoven Fabrics
SIC 2299 Textile Goods, nec
313241 Weft Knit Fabric Mills
SIC 2257 Weft Knit Fabric Mills
SIC 2259 Knitting Mills nec
313249 Other Knit Fabric & Lace Mills
SIC 2258 Lace & Warp Knit Fabric Mills
SIC 2259 Knitting Mills nec
313311 Broadwoven Fabric Finishing Mills
SIC 2231 Broadwoven Fabric Mills, Wool
SIC 2261 Finishers of Broadwoven Fabrics of Cotton
SIC 2262 Finishers of Broadwoven Fabrics of Manmade Fiber
       & Silk
SIC 2269 Finishers of Textiles, nec
SIC 5131 Piece Goods & Notions
313312 Textile & Fabric Finishing Mills
SIC 2231 Broadwoven Fabric Mills, Wool
SIC 2257 Weft Knit Fabric Mills
SIC 2258 Lace & Warp Knit Fabric Mills
SIC 2269 Finishers of Textiles, nec
SIC 2282 Yarn Texturizing, Throwing, Twisting, & Winding
       Mills
SIC 2284 Thread Mills
SIC 2299 Textile Goods, nec
SIC 5131 Piece Goods & Notions
31332 Fabric Coating Mills
SIC 2295 Coated Fabrics, Not Rubberized
SIC 3069 Fabricated Rubber Products, nec

TEXTILE PRODUCT MILLS

31411 Carpet & Rug Mills
SIC 2273 Carpets & Rugs
314121 Curtain & Drapery Mills
SIC 2391 Curtains & Draperies
SIC 5714 Drapery, Curtain, & Upholstery Stores
314129 Other Household Textile Product Mills
SIC 2392 Housefurnishings, Except Curtains & Draperies
314911 Textile Bag Mills
SIC 2392 Housefurnishings, Except Curtains & Draperies
SIC 2393 Textile Bags
314912 Canvas & Related Product Mills
SIC 2394 Canvas & Related Products
314991 Rope, Cordage & Twine Mills
SIC 2298 Cordage & Twine
314992 Tire Cord & Tire Fabric Mills
SIC 2296 Tire Cord & Fabrics
314999 All Other Miscellaneous Textile Product Mills
SIC 2299 Textile Goods, nec
SIC 2395 Pleating, Decorative & Novelty Stitching, & Tucking
       for the Trade
SIC 2396 Automotive Trimmings, Apparel Findings, & Related
       Products
SIC 2399 Fabricated Textile Products, nec

APPAREL MANUFACTURING

315111 Sheer Hosiery Mills
SIC 2251 Women's Full-Length & Knee-Length Hosiery,
       Except socks
SIC 2252 Hosiery, nec
315119 Other Hosiery & Sock Mills
SIC 2252 Hosiery, nec
315191 Outerwear Knitting Mills
SIC 2253 Knit Outerwear Mills
SIC 2259 Knitting Mills, nec
315192 Underwear & Nightwear Knitting Mills
SIC 2254 Knit Underwear & Nightwear Mills
SIC 2259 Knitting Mills, nec
315211 Men's & Boys' Cut & Sew Apparel Contractors
SIC 2311 Men's & Boys' Suits, Coats, & Overcoats
SIC 2321 Men's & Boys' Shirts, Except Work Shirts
SIC 2322 Men's & Boys' Underwear & Nightwear
SIC 2325 Men's & Boys' Trousers & Slacks
SIC 2326 Men's & Boys' Work Clothing
SIC 2329 Men's & Boys' Clothing, nec
SIC 2341 Women's, Misses', Children's, & Infants' Underwear
       & Nightwear
SIC 2361 Girls', Children's, & Infants' Dresses, Blouses &
       Shirts
SIC 2369 Girls', Children's, & Infants' Outerwear, nec
SIC 2384 Robes & Dressing Gowns
SIC 2385 Waterproof Outerwear
SIC 2389 Apparel & Accessories, nec
SIC 2395 Pleating, Decorative & Novelty Stitching, & Tucking
       for the Trade
315212 Women's & Girls' Cut & Sew Apparel Contractors
SIC 2331 Women's, Misses', & Juniors' Blouses & Shirts
SIC 2335 Women's, Misses' & Juniors' Dresses
SIC 2337 Women's, Misses', & Juniors' Suits, Skirts, & Coats
SIC 2339 Women's, Misses', & Juniors' Outerwear, nec

SIC 2341 Women's, Misses', Children's, & Infants' Underwear
& Nightwear
SIC 2342 Brassieres, Girdles, & Allied Garments
SIC 2361 Girls', Children's, & Infants' Dresses, Blouses, &
Shirts
SIC 2369 Girls', Children's, & Infants' Outerwear, nec
SIC 2384 Robes & Dressing Gowns
SIC 2385 Waterproof Outerwear
SIC 2389 Apparel & Accessories, nec
SIC 2395 Pleating, Decorative & Novelty Stitching, & Tucking
for the Trade
**315221 Men's & Boys' Cut & Sew Underwear & Nightwear
Manufacturing**
SIC 2322 Men's & Boys' Underwear & Nightwear
SIC 2341 Women's, Misses', Children's, & Infants' Underwear
& Nightwear
SIC 2369 Girls', Children's, & Infants' Outerwear, nec
SIC 2384 Robes & Dressing Gowns
**315222 Men's & Boys' Cut & Sew Suit, Coat & Overcoat
Manufacturing**
SIC 2311 Men's & Boys' Suits, Coats, & Overcoats
SIC 2369 Girls', Children's, & Infants' Outerwear, nec
SIC 2385 Waterproof Outerwear
315223 Men's & Boys' Cut & Sew Shirt Manufacturing
SIC 2321 Men's & Boys' Shirts, Except Work Shirts
SIC 2361 Girls', Children's, & Infants' Dresses, Blouses, &
Shirts
**315224 Men's & Boys' Cut & Sew Trouser, Slack & Jean
Manufacturing**
SIC 2325 Men's & Boys' Trousers & Slacks
SIC 2369 Girls', Children's, & Infants' Outerwear, NEC
315225 Men's & Boys' Cut & Sew Work Clothing Manufacturing
SIC 2326 Men's & Boys' Work Clothing
**315228 Men's & Boys' Cut & Sew Other Outerwear
Manufacturing**
SIC 2329 Men's & Boys' Clothing, nec
SIC 2369 Girls', Children's, & Infants' Outerwear, nec
SIC 2385 Waterproof Outerwear
**315231 Women's & Girls' Cut & Sew Lingerie, Loungewear &
Nightwear Manufacturing**
SIC 2341 Women's, Misses', Children's, & Infants' Underwear
& Nightwear
SIC 2342 Brassieres, Girdles, & Allied Garments
SIC 2369 Girls', Children's, & Infants' Outerwear, nec
SIC 2384 Robes & Dressing Gowns
SIC 2389 Apparel & Accessories, NEC
**315232 Women's & Girls' Cut & Sew Blouse & Shirt
Manufacturing**
SIC 2331 Women's, Misses', & Juniors' Blouses & Shirts
SIC 2361 Girls', Children's, & Infants' Dresses, Blouses &
Shirts
315233 Women's & Girls' Cut & Sew Dress Manufacturing
SIC 2335 Women's, Misses', & Juniors' Dresses
SIC 2361 Girls', Children's, & Infants' Dresses, Blouses &
Shirts
**315234 Women's & Girls' Cut & Sew Suit, Coat, Tailored Jacket
& Skirt Manufacturing**
SIC 2337 Women's, Misses', & Juniors' Suits, Skirts, & Coats
SIC 2369 Girls', Children's, & Infants' Outerwear, nec
SIC 2385 Waterproof Outerwear
**315238 Women's & Girls' Cut & Sew Other Outerwear
Manufacturing**
SIC 2339 Women's, Misses', & Juniors' Outerwear, nec
SIC 2369 Girls', Children's, & Infants' Outerwear, nec

SIC 2385 Waterproof Outerwear
315291 Infants' Cut & Sew Apparel Manufacturing
SIC 2341 Women's, Misses', Children's, & Infants' Underwear
& Nightwear
SIC 2361 Girls', Children's, & Infants' Dresses, Blouses, &
Shirts
SIC 2369 Girls', Children's, & Infants' Outerwear, nec
SIC 2385 Waterproof Outerwear
315292 Fur & Leather Apparel Manufacturing
SIC 2371 Fur Goods
SIC 2386 Leather & Sheep-lined Clothing
315299 All Other Cut & Sew Apparel Manufacturing
SIC 2329 Men's & Boys' Outerwear, nec
SIC 2339 Women's, Misses', & Juniors' Outerwear, nec
SIC 2389 Apparel & Accessories, nec
315991 Hat, Cap & Millinery Manufacturing
SIC 2353 Hats, Caps, & Millinery
315992 Glove & Mitten Manufacturing
SIC 2381 Dress & Work Gloves, Except Knit & All-Leather
SIC 3151 Leather Gloves & Mittens
315993 Men's & Boys' Neckwear Manufacturing
SIC 2323 Men's & Boys' Neckwear
**315999 Other Apparel Accessories & Other Apparel
Manufacturing**
SIC 2339 Women's, Misses', & Juniors' Outerwear, nec
SIC 2385 Waterproof Outerwear
SIC 2387 Apparel Belts
SIC 2389 Apparel & Accessories, nec
SIC 2396 Automotive Trimmings, Apparel Findings, & Related
Products
SIC 2399 Fabricated Textile Products, nec

LEATHER & ALLIED PRODUCT MANUFACTURING

31611 Leather & Hide Tanning & Finishing
SIC 3111 Leather Tanning & Finishing
SIC 3999 Manufacturing Industries, nec
316211 Rubber & Plastics Footwear Manufacturing
SIC 3021 Rubber & Plastics Footwear
316212 House Slipper Manufacturing
SIC 3142 House Slippers
316213 Men's Footwear Manufacturing
SIC 3143 Men's Footwear, Except Athletic
316214 Women's Footwear Manufacturing
SIC 3144 Women's Footwear, Except Athletic
316219 Other Footwear Manufacturing
SIC 3149 Footwear Except Rubber, NEC
316991 Luggage Manufacturing
SIC 3161 Luggage
316992 Women's Handbag & Purse Manufacturing
SIC 3171 Women's Handbags & Purses
316993 Personal Leather Good Manufacturing
SIC 3172 Personal Leather Goods, Except Women's Handbags
& Purses
316999 All Other Leather Good Manufacturing
SIC 3131 Boot & Shoe Cut Stock & Findings
SIC 3199 Leather Goods, nec

WOOD PRODUCT MANUFACTURING

321113 Sawmills
SIC 2421 Sawmills & Planing Mills, General
SIC 2429 Special Product Sawmills, nec
321114 Wood Preservation
SIC 2491 Wood Preserving
321211 Hardwood Veneer & Plywood Manufacturing
SIC 2435 Hardwood Veneer & Plywood
321212 Softwood Veneer & Plywood Manufacturing
SIC 2436 Softwood Veneer & Plywood
321213 Engineered Wood Member Manufacturing
SIC 2439 Structural Wood Members, nec
321214 Truss Manufacturing
SIC 2439 Structural Wood Members, nec
321219 Reconstituted Wood Product Manufacturing
SIC 2493 Reconstituted Wood Products
321911 Wood Window & Door Manufacturing
SIC 2431 Millwork
321912 Hardwood Dimension Mills
SIC 2426 Hardwood Dimension & Flooring Mills
321913 Softwood Cut Stock, Resawing Lumber, & Planing
SIC 2421 Sawmills & Planing Mills, General
SIC 2429 Special Product Sawmills, nec
SIC 2439 Structural Wood Members, nec
321914 Other Millwork
SIC 2421 Sawmills & Planing Mills, General
SIC 2426 Hardwood Dimension & Flooring Mills
SIC 2431 Millwork
32192 Wood Container & Pallet Manufacturing
SIC 2441 Nailed & Lock Corner Wood Boxes & Shook
SIC 2448 Wood Pallets & Skids
SIC 2449 Wood Containers, NEC
SIC 2499 Wood Products, nec
321991 Manufactured Home Manufacturing
SIC 2451 Mobile Homes
321992 Prefabricated Wood Building Manufacturing
SIC 2452 Prefabricated Wood Buildings & Components
321999 All Other Miscellaneous Wood Product Manufacturing
SIC 2426 Hardwood Dimension & Flooring Mills
SIC 2499 Wood Products, nec
SIC 3131 Boot & Shoe Cut Stock & Findings
SIC 3999 Manufacturing Industries, nec
SIC 2421 Sawmills & Planing Mills, General
SIC 2429 Special Product Sawmills, nec

PAPER MANUFACTURING

32211 Pulp Mills
SIC 2611 Pulp Mills
322121 Paper Mills
SIC 2611 Pulp Mills
SIC 2621 Paper Mills
322122 Newsprint Mills
SIC 2621 Paper Mills
32213 Paperboard Mills
SIC 2611 Pulp Mills
SIC 2631 Paperboard Mills
322211 Corrugated & Solid Fiber Box Manufacturing
SIC 2653 Corrugated & Solid Fiber Boxes
322212 Folding Paperboard Box Manufacturing
SIC 2657 Folding Paperboard Boxes, Including Sanitary

322213 Setup Paperboard Box Manufacturing
SIC 2652 Setup Paperboard Boxes
322214 Fiber Can, Tube, Drum, & Similar Products Manufacturing
SIC 2655 Fiber Cans, Tubes, Drums, & Similar Products
322215 Non-Folding Sanitary Food Container Manufacturing
SIC 2656 Sanitary Food Containers, Except Folding
SIC 2679 Converted Paper & Paperboard Products, NEC
322221 Coated & Laminated Packaging Paper & Plastics Film Manufacturing
SIC 2671 Packaging Paper & Plastics Film, Coated & Laminated
322222 Coated & Laminated Paper Manufacturing
SIC 2672 Coated & Laminated Paper, nec
SIC 2679 Converted Paper & Paperboard Products, nec
322223 Plastics, Foil, & Coated Paper Bag Manufacturing
SIC 2673 Plastics, Foil, & Coated Paper Bags
322224 Uncoated Paper & Multiwall Bag Manufacturing
SIC 2674 Uncoated Paper & Multiwall Bags
322225 Laminated Aluminum Foil Manufacturing for Flexible Packaging Uses
SIC 3497 Metal Foil & Leaf
322231 Die-Cut Paper & Paperboard Office Supplies Manufacturing
SIC 2675 Die-Cut Paper & Paperboard & Cardboard
SIC 2679 Converted Paper & Paperboard Products, nec
322232 Envelope Manufacturing
SIC 2677 Envelopes
322233 Stationery, Tablet, & Related Product Manufacturing
SIC 2678 Stationery, Tablets, & Related Products
322291 Sanitary Paper Product Manufacturing
SIC 2676 Sanitary Paper Products
322292 Surface-Coated Paperboard Manufacturing
SIC 2675 Die-Cut Paper & Paperboard & Cardboard
322298 All Other Converted Paper Product Manufacturing
SIC 2675 Die-Cut Paper & Paperboard & Cardboard
SIC 2679 Converted Paper & Paperboard Products, NEC

PRINTING & RELATED SUPPORT ACTIVITIES

323110 Commercial Lithographic Printing
SIC 2752 Commercial Printing, Lithographic
SIC 2771 Greeting Cards
SIC 2782 Blankbooks, Loose-leaf Binders & Devices
SIC 3999 Manufacturing Industries, nec
323111 Commercial Gravure Printing
SIC 2754 Commercial Printing, Gravure
SIC 2771 Greeting Cards
SIC 2782 Blankbooks, Loose-leaf Binders & Devices
SIC 3999 Manufacturing Industries, nec
323112 Commercial Flexographic Printing
SIC 2759 Commercial Printing, NEC
SIC 2771 Greeting Cards
SIC 2782 Blankbooks, Loose-leaf Binders & Devices
SIC 3999 Manufacturing Industries, nec
323113 Commercial Screen Printing
SIC 2396 Automotive Trimmings, Apparel Findings, & Related Products
SIC 2759 Commercial Printing, nec
SIC 2771 Greeting Cards
SIC 2782 Blankbooks, Loose-leaf Binders & Devices
SIC 3999 Manufacturing Industries, nec

323114 Quick Printing
SIC 2752 Commercial Printing, Lithographic
SIC 2759 Commercial Printing, nec
323115 Digital Printing
SIC 2759 Commercial Printing, nec
323116 Manifold Business Form Printing
SIC 2761 Manifold Business Forms
323117 Book Printing
SIC 2732 Book Printing
323118 Blankbook, Loose-leaf Binder & Device Manufacturing
SIC 2782 Blankbooks, Loose-leaf Binders & Devices
323119 Other Commercial Printing
SIC 2759 Commercial Printing, nec
SIC 2771 Greeting Cards
SIC 2782 Blankbooks, Loose-leaf Binders & Devices
SIC 3999 Manufacturing Industries, nec
323121 Tradebinding & Related Work
SIC 2789 Bookbinding & Related Work
323122 Prepress Services
SIC 2791 Typesetting
SIC 2796 Platemaking & Related Services

PETROLEUM & COAL PRODUCTS MANUFACTURING

32411 Petroleum Refineries
SIC 2911 Petroleum Refining
324121 Asphalt Paving Mixture & Block Manufacturing
SIC 2951 Asphalt Paving Mixtures & Blocks
324122 Asphalt Shingle & Coating Materials Manufacturing
SIC 2952 Asphalt Felts & Coatings
324191 Petroleum Lubricating Oil & Grease Manufacturing
SIC 2992 Lubricating Oils & Greases
324199 All Other Petroleum & Coal Products Manufacturing
SIC 2999 Products of Petroleum & Coal, nec
SIC 3312 Blast Furnaces & Steel Mills

CHEMICAL MANUFACTURING

32511 Petrochemical Manufacturing
SIC 2865 Cyclic Organic Crudes & Intermediates, & Organic
    Dyes & Pigments
SIC 2869 Industrial Organic Chemicals, nec
32512 Industrial Gas Manufacturing
SIC 2813 Industrial Gases
SIC 2869 Industrial Organic Chemicals, nec
325131 Inorganic Dye & Pigment Manufacturing
SIC 2816 Inorganic Pigments
SIC 2819 Industrial Inorganic Chemicals, nec
325132 Organic Dye & Pigment Manufacturing
SIC 2865 Cyclic Organic Crudes & Intermediates, & Organic
    Dyes & Pigments
325181 Alkalies & Chlorine Manufacturing
SIC 2812 Alkalies & Chlorine
325182 Carbon Black Manufacturing
SIC 2816 Inorganic pigments
SIC 2895 Carbon Black
325188 All Other Basic Inorganic Chemical Manufacturing
SIC 2819 Industrial Inorganic Chemicals, nec
SIC 2869 Industrial Organic Chemicals, nec

325191 Gum & Wood Chemical Manufacturing
SIC 2861 Gum & Wood Chemicals
325192 Cyclic Crude & Intermediate Manufacturing
SIC 2865 Cyclic Organic Crudes & Intermediates & Organic
    Dyes & Pigments
325193 Ethyl Alcohol Manufacturing
SIC 2869 Industrial Organic Chemicals
325199 All Other Basic Organic Chemical Manufacturing
SIC 2869 Industrial Organic Chemicals, nec
SIC 2899 Chemical & Chemical Preparations, nec
325211 Plastics Material & Resin Manufacturing
SIC 2821 Plastics Materials, Synthetic & Resins, &
    Nonvulcanizable Elastomers
325212 Synthetic Rubber Manufacturing
SIC 2822 Synthetic Rubber
325221 Cellulosic Manmade Fiber Manufacturing
SIC 2823 Cellulosic Manmade Fibers
325222 Noncellulosic Organic Fiber Manufacturing
SIC 2824 Manmade Organic Fibers, Except Cellulosic
325311 Nitrogenous Fertilizer Manufacturing
SIC 2873 Nitrogenous Fertilizers
325312 Phosphatic Fertilizer Manufacturing
SIC 2874 Phosphatic Fertilizers
325314 Fertilizer Manufacturing
SIC 2875 Fertilizers, Mixing Only
32532 Pesticide & Other Agricultural Chemical Manufacturing
SIC 2879 Pesticides & Agricultural Chemicals, nec
325411 Medicinal & Botanical Manufacturing
SIC 2833 Medicinal Chemicals & Botanical Products
325412 Pharmaceutical Preparation Manufacturing
SIC 2834 Pharmaceutical Preparations
SIC 2835 In-Vitro & In-Vivo Diagnostic Substances
325413 In-Vitro Diagnostic Substance Manufacturing
SIC 2835 In-Vitro & In-Vivo Diagnostic Substances
325414 Biological Product Manufacturing
SIC 2836 Biological Products, Except Diagnostic Substance
32551 Paint & Coating Manufacturing
SIC 2851 Paints, Varnishes, Lacquers, Enamels & Allied
    Products
SIC 2899 Chemicals & Chemical Preparations, nec
32552 Adhesive & Sealant Manufacturing
SIC 2891 Adhesives & Sealants
325611 Soap & Other Detergent Manufacturing
SIC 2841 Soaps & Other Detergents, Except Specialty Cleaners
SIC 2844 Toilet Preparations
325612 Polish & Other Sanitation Good Manufacturing
SIC 2842 Specialty Cleaning, Polishing, & Sanitary Preparations
325613 Surface Active Agent Manufacturing
SIC 2843 Surface Active Agents, Finishing Agents, Sulfonated
    Oils, & Assistants
32562 Toilet Preparation Manufacturing
SIC 2844 Perfumes, Cosmetics, & Other Toilet Preparations
32591 Printing Ink Manufacturing
SIC 2893 Printing Ink
32592 Explosives Manufacturing
SIC 2892 Explosives
325991 Custom Compounding of Purchased Resin
SIC 3087 Custom Compounding of Purchased Plastics Resin
**325992 Photographic Film, Paper, Plate & Chemical
    Manufacturing**
SIC 3861 Photographic Equipment & Supplies

325998 All Other Miscellaneous Chemical Product Manufacturing
SIC 2819 Industrial Inorganic Chemicals, nec
SIC 2899 Chemicals & Chemical Preparations, nec
SIC 3952 Lead Pencils & Art Goods
SIC 3999 Manufacturing Industries, nec

PLASTICS & RUBBER PRODUCTS MANUFACTURING

326111 Unsupported Plastics Bag Manufacturing
SIC 2673 Plastics, Foil, & Coated Paper Bags
326112 Unsupported Plastics Packaging Film & Sheet Manufacturing
SIC 2671 Packaging Paper & Plastics Film, Coated, & Laminated
326113 Unsupported Plastics Film & Sheet Manufacturing
SIC 3081 Unsupported Plastics Film & Sheets
326121 Unsupported Plastics Profile Shape Manufacturing
SIC 3082 Unsupported Plastics Profile Shapes
SIC 3089 Plastics Product, nec
326122 Plastics Pipe & Pipe Fitting Manufacturing
SIC 3084 Plastics Pipe
SIC 3089 Plastics Products, nec
32613 Laminated Plastics Plate, Sheet & Shape Manufacturing
SIC 3083 Laminated Plastics Plate, Sheet & Profile Shapes
32614 Polystyrene Foam Product Manufacturing
SIC 3086 Plastics Foam Products
32615 Urethane & Other Foam Product Manufacturing
SIC 3086 Plastics Foam Products
32616 Plastics Bottle Manufacturing
SIC 3085 Plastics Bottles
326191 Plastics Plumbing Fixture Manufacturing
SIC 3088 Plastics Plumbing Fixtures
326192 Resilient Floor Covering Manufacturing
SIC 3069 Fabricated Rubber Products, nec
SIC 3996 Linoleum, Asphalted-Felt-Base, & Other Hard Surface Floor Coverings, nec
326199 All Other Plastics Product Manufacturing
SIC 3089 Plastics Products, nec
SIC 3999 Manufacturing Industries, nec
326211 Tire Manufacturing
SIC 3011 Tires & Inner Tubes
326212 Tire Retreading
SIC 7534 Tire Retreading & Repair Shops
32622 Rubber & Plastics Hoses & Belting Manufacturing
SIC 3052 Rubber & Plastics Hose & Belting
326291 Rubber Product Manufacturing for Mechanical Use
SIC 3061 Molded, Extruded, & Lathe-Cut Mechanical Rubber Goods
326299 All Other Rubber Product Manufacturing
SIC 3069 Fabricated Rubber Products, nec

NONMETALLIC MINERAL PRODUCT MANUFACTURING

327111 Vitreous China Plumbing Fixture & China & Earthenware Fittings & Bathroom Accessories Manufacturing
SIC 3261 Vitreous China Plumbing Fixtures & China & Earthenware Fittings & Bathroom Accessories

327112 Vitreous China, Fine Earthenware & Other Pottery Product Manufacturing
SIC 3262 Vitreous China Table & Kitchen Articles
SIC 3263 Fine Earthenware Table & Kitchen Articles
SIC 3269 Pottery Products, nec
327113 Porcelain Electrical Supply Manufacturing
SIC 3264 Porcelain Electrical Supplies
327121 Brick & Structural Clay Tile Manufacturing
SIC 3251 Brick & Structural Clay Tile
327122 Ceramic Wall & Floor Tile Manufacturing
SIC 3253 Ceramic Wall & Floor Tile
327123 Other Structural Clay Product Manufacturing
SIC 3259 Structural Clay Products, nec
327124 Clay Refractory Manufacturing
SIC 3255 Clay Refractories
327125 Nonclay Refractory Manufacturing
SIC 3297 Nonclay Refractories
327211 Flat Glass Manufacturing
SIC 3211 Flat Glass
327212 Other Pressed & Blown Glass & Glassware Manufacturing
SIC 3229 Pressed & Blown Glass & Glassware, nec
327213 Glass Container Manufacturing
SIC 3221 Glass Containers
327215 Glass Product Manufacturing Made of Purchased Glass
SIC 3231 Glass Products Made of Purchased Glass
32731 Hydraulic Cement Manufacturing
SIC 3241 Cement, Hydraulic
32732 Ready-Mix Concrete Manufacturing
SIC 3273 Ready-Mixed Concrete
327331 Concrete Block & Brick Manufacturing
SIC 3271 Concrete Block & Brick
327332 Concrete Pipe Manufacturing
SIC 3272 Concrete Products, Except Block & Brick
32739 Other Concrete Product Manufacturing
SIC 3272 Concrete Products, Except Block & Brick
32741 Lime Manufacturing
SIC 3274 Lime
32742 Gypsum & Gypsum Product Manufacturing
SIC 3275 Gypsum Products
SIC 3299 Nonmetallic Mineral Products, nec
32791 Abrasive Product Manufacturing
SIC 3291 Abrasive Products
327991 Cut Stone & Stone Product Manufacturing
SIC 3281 Cut Stone & Stone Products
327992 Ground or Treated Mineral & Earth Manufacturing
SIC 3295 Minerals & Earths, Ground or Otherwise Treated
327993 Mineral Wool Manufacturing
SIC 3296 Mineral Wool
327999 All Other Miscellaneous Nonmetallic Mineral Product Manufacturing
SIC 3272 Concrete Products, Except Block & Brick
SIC 3292 Asbestos Products
SIC 3299 Nonmetallic Mineral Products, nec

PRIMARY METAL MANUFACTURING

331111 Iron & Steel Mills
SIC 3312 Steel Works, Blast Furnaces , & Rolling Mills
SIC 3399 Primary Metal Products, nec
331112 Electrometallurgical Ferroalloy Product Manufacturing
SIC 3313 Electrometallurgical Products, Except Steel

33121 Iron & Steel Pipes & Tubes Manufacturing from Purchased Steel
SIC 3317 Steel Pipe & Tubes
331221 Cold-Rolled Steel Shape Manufacturing
SIC 3316 Cold-Rolled Steel Sheet, Strip & Bars
331222 Steel Wire Drawing
SIC 3315 Steel Wiredrawing & Steel Nails & Spikes
331311 Alumina Refining
SIC 2819 Industrial Inorganic Chemicals, nec
331312 Primary Aluminum Production
SIC 3334 Primary Production of Aluminum
331314 Secondary Smelting & Alloying of Aluminum
SIC 3341 Secondary Smelting & Refining of Nonferrous Metals
SIC 3399 Primary Metal Products, nec
331315 Aluminum Sheet, Plate & Foil Manufacturing
SIC 3353 Aluminum Sheet, Plate, & Foil
331316 Aluminum Extruded Product Manufacturing
SIC 3354 Aluminum Extruded Products
331319 Other Aluminum Rolling & Drawing
SIC 3355 Aluminum Rolling & Drawing, nec
SIC 3357 Drawing & Insulating of Nonferrous Wire
331411 Primary Smelting & Refining of Copper
SIC 3331 Primary Smelting & Refining of Copper
331419 Primary Smelting & Refining of Nonferrous Metal
SIC 3339 Primary Smelting & Refining of Nonferrous Metals, Except Copper & Aluminum
331421 Copper Rolling, Drawing & Extruding
SIC 3351 Rolling, Drawing, & Extruding of Copper
331422 Copper Wire Drawing
SIC 3357 Drawing & Insulating of Nonferrous Wire
331423 Secondary Smelting, Refining, & Alloying of Copper
SIC 3341 Secondary Smelting & Refining of Nonferrous Metals
SIC 3399 Primary Metal Products, nec
331491 Nonferrous Metal Rolling, Drawing & Extruding
SIC 3356 Rolling, Drawing & Extruding of Nonferrous Metals, Except Copper & Aluminum
SIC 3357 Drawing & Insulating of Nonferrous Wire
331492 Secondary Smelting, Refining, & Alloying of Nonferrous Metal
SIC 3313 Electrometallurgical Products, Except Steel
SIC 3341 Secondary Smelting & Reining of Nonferrous Metals
SIC 3399 Primary Metal Products, nec
331511 Iron Foundries
SIC 3321 Gray & Ductile Iron Foundries
SIC 3322 Malleable Iron Foundries
331512 Steel Investment Foundries
SIC 3324 Steel Investment Foundries
331513 Steel Foundries,
SIC 3325 Steel Foundries, nec
331521 Aluminum Die-Castings
SIC 3363 Aluminum Die-Castings
331522 Nonferrous Die-Castings
SIC 3364 Nonferrous Die-Castings, Except Aluminum
331524 Aluminum Foundries
SIC 3365 Aluminum Foundries
331525 Copper Foundries
SIC 3366 Copper Foundries
331528 Other Nonferrous Foundries
SIC 3369 Nonferrous Foundries, Except Aluminum & Copper

FABRICATED METAL PRODUCT MANUFACTURING

332111 Iron & Steel Forging
SIC 3462 Iron & Steel Forgings
332112 Nonferrous Forging
SIC 3463 Nonferrous Forgings
332114 Custom Roll Forming
SIC 3449 Miscellaneous Structural Metal Work
332115 Crown & Closure Manufacturing
SIC 3466 Crowns & Closures
332116 Metal Stamping
SIC 3469 Metal Stampings, nec
332117 Powder Metallurgy Part Manufacturing
SIC 3499 Fabricated Metal Products, nec
332211 Cutlery & Flatware Manufacturing
SIC 3421 Cutlery
SIC 3914 Silverware, Plated Ware, & Stainless Steel Ware
332212 Hand & Edge Tool Manufacturing
SIC 3423 Hand & Edge Tools, Except Machine Tools & Handsaws
SIC 3523 Farm Machinery & Equipment
SIC 3524 Lawn & Garden Tractors & Home Lawn & Garden Equipment
SIC 3545 Cutting Tools, Machine Tools Accessories, & Machinist Precision Measuring Devices
SIC 3799 Transportation Equipment, nec
SIC 3999 Manufacturing Industries, nec
332213 Saw Blade & Handsaw Manufacturing
SIC 3425 Saw Blades & Handsaws
332214 Kitchen Utensil, Pot & Pan Manufacturing
SIC 3469 Metal Stampings, nec
332311 Prefabricated Metal Building & Component Manufacturing
SIC 3448 Prefabricated Metal Buildings & Components
332312 Fabricated Structural Metal Manufacturing
SIC 3441 Fabricated Structural Metal
SIC 3449 Miscellaneous Structural Metal Work
332313 Plate Work Manufacturing
SIC 3443 Fabricated Plate Work
332321 Metal Window & Door Manufacturing
SIC 3442 Metal Doors, Sash, Frames, Molding & Trim
SIC 3449 Miscellaneous Structural Metal Work
332322 Sheet Metal Work Manufacturing
SIC 3444 Sheet Metal Work
332323 Ornamental & Architectural Metal Work Manufacturing
SIC 3446 Architectural & Ornamental Metal Work
SIC 3449 Miscellaneous Structural Metal Work
SIC 3523 Farm Machinery & Equipment
33241 Power Boiler & Heat Exchanger Manufacturing
SIC 3443 Fabricated Plate Work
33242 Metal Tank Manufacturing
SIC 3443 Fabricated Plate Work
332431 Metal Can Manufacturing
SIC 3411 Metal Cans
332439 Other Metal Container Manufacturing
SIC 3412 Metal Shipping Barrels, Drums, Kegs, & Pails
SIC 3429 Hardware, nec
SIC 3444 Sheet Metal Work
SIC 3499 Fabricated Metal Products, nec
SIC 3537 Industrial Trucks, Tractors, Trailers, & Stackers
33251 Hardware Manufacturing
SIC 3429 Hardware, nec
SIC 3499 Fabricated Metal Products, nec

332611 Steel Spring Manufacturing
SIC 3493 Steel Springs, Except Wire

332612 Wire Spring Manufacturing
SIC 3495 Wire Springs

332618 Other Fabricated Wire Product Manufacturing
SIC 3315 Steel Wiredrawing & Steel Nails & Spikes
SIC 3399 Primary Metal Products, nec
SIC 3496 Miscellaneous Fabricated Wire Products

33271　Machine Shops
SIC 3599 Industrial & Commercial Machinery & Equipment, nec

332721 Precision Turned Product Manufacturing
SIC 3451 Screw Machine Products

332722 Bolt, Nut, Screw, Rivet & Washer Manufacturing
SIC 3452 Bolts, Nuts, Screws, Rivets, & Washers

332811 Metal Heat Treating
SIC 3398 Metal Heat Treating

332812 Metal Coating, Engraving , & Allied Services to Manufacturers
SIC 3479 Coating, Engraving, & Allied Services, nec

332813 Electroplating, Plating, Polishing, Anodizing & Coloring
SIC 3399 Primary Metal Products, nec
SIC 3471 Electroplating, Plating, Polishing, Anodizing, & Coloring

332911 Industrial Valve Manufacturing
SIC 3491 Industrial Valves

332912 Fluid Power Valve & Hose Fitting Manufacturing
SIC 3492 Fluid Power Valves & Hose Fittings
SIC 3728 Aircraft Parts & Auxiliary Equipment, nec

332913 Plumbing Fixture Fitting & Trim Manufacturing
SIC 3432 Plumbing Fixture Fittings & Trim

332919 Other Metal Valve & Pipe Fitting Manufacturing
SIC 3429 Hardware, nec
SIC 3494 Valves & Pipe Fittings, nec
SIC 3499 Fabricated Metal Products, nec

332991 Ball & Roller Bearing Manufacturing
SIC 3562 Ball & Roller Bearings

332992 Small Arms Ammunition Manufacturing
SIC 3482 Small Arms Ammunition

332993 Ammunition Manufacturing
SIC 3483 Ammunition, Except for Small Arms

332994 Small Arms Manufacturing
SIC 3484 Small Arms

332995 Other Ordnance & Accessories Manufacturing
SIC 3489 Ordnance & Accessories, nec

332996 Fabricated Pipe & Pipe Fitting Manufacturing
SIC 3498 Fabricated Pipe & Pipe Fittings

332997 Industrial Pattern Manufacturing
SIC 3543 Industrial Patterns

332998 Enameled Iron & Metal Sanitary Ware Manufacturing
SIC 3431 Enameled Iron & Metal Sanitary Ware

332999 All Other Miscellaneous Fabricated Metal Product Manufacturing
SIC 3291 Abrasive Products
SIC 3432 Plumbing Fixture Fittings & Trim
SIC 3494 Valves & Pipe Fittings, nec
SIC 3497 Metal Foil & Leaf
SIC 3499 Fabricated Metal Products, NEC
SIC 3537 Industrial Trucks, Tractors, Trailers, & Stackers
SIC 3599 Industrial & Commercial Machinery & Equipment, nec
SIC 3999 Manufacturing Industries, nec

MACHINERY MANUFACTURING

333111 Farm Machinery & Equipment Manufacturing
SIC 3523 Farm Machinery & Equipment

333112 Lawn & Garden Tractor & Home Lawn & Garden Equipment Manufacturing
SIC 3524 Lawn & Garden Tractors & Home Lawn & Garden Equipment

33312　Construction Machinery Manufacturing
SIC 3531 Construction Machinery & Equipment

333131 Mining Machinery & Equipment Manufacturing
SIC 3532 Mining Machinery & Equipment, Except Oil & Gas Field Machinery & Equipment

333132 Oil & Gas Field Machinery & Equipment Manufacturing
SIC 3533 Oil & Gas Field Machinery & Equipment

33321　Sawmill & Woodworking Machinery Manufacturing
SIC 3553 Woodworking Machinery

33322　Rubber & Plastics Industry Machinery Manufacturing
SIC 3559 Special Industry Machinery, nec

333291 Paper Industry Machinery Manufacturing
SIC 3554 Paper Industries Machinery

333292 Textile Machinery Manufacturing
SIC 3552 Textile Machinery

333293 Printing Machinery & Equipment Manufacturing
SIC 3555 Printing Trades Machinery & Equipment

333294 Food Product Machinery Manufacturing
SIC 3556 Food Products Machinery

333295 Semiconductor Machinery Manufacturing
SIC 3559 Special Industry Machinery, nec

333298 All Other Industrial Machinery Manufacturing
SIC 3559 Special Industry Machinery, nec
SIC 3639 Household Appliances, nec

333311 Automatic Vending Machine Manufacturing
SIC 3581 Automatic Vending Machines

333312 Commercial Laundry, Drycleaning & Pressing Machine Manufacturing
SIC 3582 Commercial Laundry, Drycleaning & Pressing Machines

333313 Office Machinery Manufacturing
SIC 3578 Calculating & Accounting Machinery, Except Electronic Computers
SIC 3579 Office Machines, nec

333314 Optical Instrument & Lens Manufacturing
SIC 3827 Optical Instruments & Lenses

333315 Photographic & Photocopying Equipment Manufacturing
SIC 3861 Photographic Equipment & Supplies

333319 Other Commercial & Service Industry Machinery Manufacturing
SIC 3559 Special Industry Machinery, nec
SIC 3589 Service Industry Machinery, nec
SIC 3599 Industrial & Commercial Machinery & Equipment, nec
SIC 3699 Electrical Machinery, Equipment & Supplies, nec

333411 Air Purification Equipment Manufacturing
SIC 3564 Industrial & Commercial Fans & Blowers & Air Purification Equipment

333412 Industrial & Commercial Fan & Blower Manufacturing
SIC 3564 Industrial & Commercial Fans & Blowers & Air Purification Equipment

333414 Heating Equipment Manufacturing
SIC 3433 Heating Equipment, Except Electric & Warm Air Furnaces

SIC 3634 Electric Housewares & Fans

333415 Air-Conditioning & Warm Air Heating Equipment & Commercial & Industrial Refrigeration Equipment Manufacturing

SIC 3443 Fabricated Plate Work

SIC 3585 Air-Conditioning & Warm Air Heating Equipment & Commercial & Industrial Refrigeration Equipment

333511 Industrial Mold Manufacturing

SIC 3544 Special Dies & Tools, Die Sets, Jigs & Fixtures, & Industrial Molds

333512 Machine Tool Manufacturing

SIC 3541 Machine Tools, Metal Cutting Type

333513 Machine Tool Manufacturing

SIC 3542 Machine Tools, Metal Forming Type

333514 Special Die & Tool, Die Set, Jig & Fixture Manufacturing

SIC 3544 Special Dies & Tools, Die Sets, Jigs & Fixtures, & Industrial Molds

333515 Cutting Tool & Machine Tool Accessory Manufacturing

SIC 3545 Cutting Tools, Machine Tool Accessories, & Machinists' Precision Measuring Devices

333516 Rolling Mill Machinery & Equipment Manufacturing

SIC 3547 Rolling Mill Machinery & Equipment

333518 Other Metalworking Machinery Manufacturing

SIC 3549 Metalworking Machinery, nec

333611 Turbine & Turbine Generator Set Unit Manufacturing

SIC 3511 Steam, Gas, & Hydraulic Turbines, & Turbine Generator Set Units

333612 Speed Changer, Industrial High-Speed Drive & Gear Manufacturing

SIC 3566 Speed Changers, Industrial High-Speed Drives, & Gears

333613 Mechanical Power Transmission Equipment Manufacturing

SIC 3568 Mechanical Power Transmission Equipment, nec

333618 Other Engine Equipment Manufacturing

SIC 3519 Internal Combustion Engines, nec

SIC 3699 Electrical Machinery, Equipment & Supplies, nec

333911 Pump & Pumping Equipment Manufacturing

SIC 3561 Pumps & Pumping Equipment

SIC 3743 Railroad Equipment

333912 Air & Gas Compressor Manufacturing

SIC 3563 Air & Gas Compressors

333913 Measuring & Dispensing Pump Manufacturing

SIC 3586 Measuring & Dispensing Pumps

333921 Elevator & Moving Stairway Manufacturing

SIC 3534 Elevators & Moving Stairways

333922 Conveyor & Conveying Equipment Manufacturing

SIC 3523 Farm Machinery & Equipment

SIC 3535 Conveyors & Conveying Equipment

333923 Overhead Traveling Crane, Hoist & Monorail System Manufacturing

SIC 3536 Overhead Traveling Cranes, Hoists, & Monorail Systems

SIC 3531 Construction Machinery & Equipment

333924 Industrial Truck, Tractor, Trailer & Stacker Machinery Manufacturing

SIC 3537 Industrial Trucks, Tractors, Trailers, & Stackers

333991 Power-Driven Hand Tool Manufacturing

SIC 3546 Power-Driven Handtools

333992 Welding & Soldering Equipment Manufacturing

SIC 3548 Electric & Gas Welding & Soldering Equipment

333993 Packaging Machinery Manufacturing

SIC 3565 Packaging Machinery

333994 Industrial Process Furnace & Oven Manufacturing

SIC 3567 Industrial Process Furnaces & Ovens

333995 Fluid Power Cylinder & Actuator Manufacturing

SIC 3593 Fluid Power Cylinders & Actuators

333996 Fluid Power Pump & Motor Manufacturing

SIC 3594 Fluid Power Pumps & Motors

333997 Scale & Balance Manufacturing

SIC 3596 Scales & Balances, Except Laboratory

333999 All Other General Purpose Machinery Manufacturing

SIC 3599 Industrial & Commercial Machinery & Equipment, nec

SIC 3569 General Industrial Machinery & Equipment, nec

COMPUTER & ELECTRONIC PRODUCT MANUFACTURING

334111 Electronic Computer Manufacturing

SIC 3571 Electronic Computers

334112 Computer Storage Device Manufacturing

SIC 3572 Computer Storage Devices

334113 Computer Terminal Manufacturing

SIC 3575 Computer Terminals

334119 Other Computer Peripheral Equipment Manufacturing

SIC 3577 Computer Peripheral Equipment, nec

SIC 3578 Calculating & Accounting Machines, Except Electronic Computers

SIC 3699 Electrical Machinery, Equipment & Supplies, nec

33421 Telephone Apparatus Manufacturing

SIC 3661 Telephone & Telegraph Apparatus

33422 Radio & Television Broadcasting & Wireless Communications Equipment Manufacturing

SIC 3663 Radio & Television Broadcasting & Communication Equipment

SIC 3679 Electronic Components, nec

33429 Other Communications Equipment Manufacturing

SIC 3669 Communications Equipment, nec

33431 Audio & Video Equipment Manufacturing

SIC 3651 Household Audio & Video Equipment

334411 Electron Tube Manufacturing

SIC 3671 Electron Tubes

334412 Printed Circuit Board Manufacturing

SIC 3672 Printed Circuit Boards

334413 Semiconductor & Related Device Manufacturing

SIC 3674 Semiconductors & Related Devices

334414 Electronic Capacitor Manufacturing

SIC 3675 Electronic Capacitors

334415 Electronic Resistor Manufacturing

SIC 3676 Electronic Resistors

334416 Electronic Coil, Transformer, & Other Inductor Manufacturing

SIC 3661 Telephone & Telegraph Apparatus

SIC 3677 Electronic Coils, Transformers, & Other Inductors

SIC 3825 Instruments for Measuring & Testing of Electricity & Electrical Signals

334417 Electronic Connector Manufacturing

SIC 3678 Electronic Connectors

334418 Printed Circuit/Electronics Assembly Manufacturing

SIC 3679 Electronic Components, nec

SIC 3661 Telephone & Telegraph Apparatus

334419 Other Electronic Component Manufacturing
SIC 3679 Electronic Components, nec

334510 Electromedical & Electrotherapeutic Apparatus Manufacturing
SIC 3842 Orthopedic, Prosthetic & Surgical Appliances & Supplies
SIC 3845 Electromedical & Electrotherapeutic Apparatus

334511 Search, Detection, Navigation, Guidance, Aeronautical, & Nautical System & Instrument Manufacturing
SIC 3812 Search, Detection, Navigation, Guidance, Aeronautical, & Nautical Systems & Instruments

334512 Automatic Environmental Control Manufacturing for Residential, Commercial & Appliance Use
SIC 3822 Automatic Controls for Regulating Residential & Commercial Environments & Appliances

334513 Instruments & Related Products Manufacturing for Measuring, Displaying, & Controlling Industrial Process Variables
SIC 3823 Industrial Instruments for Measurement, Display, & Control of Process Variables; & Related Products

334514 Totalizing Fluid Meter & Counting Device Manufacturing
SIC 3824 Totalizing Fluid Meters & Counting Devices

334515 Instrument Manufacturing for Measuring & Testing Electricity & Electrical Signals
SIC 3825 Instruments for Measuring & Testing of Electricity & Electrical Signals

334516 Analytical Laboratory Instrument Manufacturing
SIC 3826 Laboratory Analytical Instruments

334517 Irradiation Apparatus Manufacturing
SIC 3844 X-Ray Apparatus & Tubes & Related Irradiation Apparatus
SIC 3845 Electromedical & Electrotherapeutic Apparatus

334518 Watch, Clock, & Part Manufacturing
SIC 3495 Wire Springs
SIC 3579 Office Machines, nec
SIC 3873 Watches, Clocks, Clockwork Operated Devices, & Parts

334519 Other Measuring & Controlling Device Manufacturing
SIC 3829 Measuring & Controlling Devices, nec

334611 Software Reproducing
SIC 7372 Prepackaged Software

334612 Prerecorded Compact Disc , Tape, & Record Reproducing
SIC 3652 Phonograph Records & Prerecorded Audio Tapes & Disks
SIC 7819 Services Allied to Motion Picture Production

334613 Magnetic & Optical Recording Media Manufacturing
SIC 3695 Magnetic & Optical Recording Media

ELECTRICAL EQUIPMENT, APPLIANCE, & COMPONENT MANUFACTURING

33511 Electric Lamp Bulb & Part Manufacturing
SIC 3641 Electric Lamp Bulbs & Tubes

335121 Residential Electric Lighting Fixture Manufacturing
SIC 3645 Residential Electric Lighting Fixtures
SIC 3999 Manufacturing Industries, nec

335122 Commercial, Industrial & Institutional Electric Lighting Fixture Manufacturing
SIC 3646 Commercial, Industrial, & Institutional Electric Lighting Fixtures

335129 Other Lighting Equipment Manufacturing
SIC 3648 Lighting Equipment, nec
SIC 3699 Electrical Machinery, Equipment, & Supplies, nec

335211 Electric Housewares & Fan Manufacturing
SIC 3634 Electric Housewares & Fans

335212 Household Vacuum Cleaner Manufacturing
SIC 3635 Household Vacuum Cleaners
SIC 3639 Household Appliances, nec

335221 Household Cooking Appliance Manufacturing
SIC 3631 Household Cooking Equipment

335222 Household Refrigerator & Home Freezer Manufacturing
SIC 3632 Household Refrigerators & Home & Farm Freezers

335224 Household Laundry Equipment Manufacturing
SIC 3633 Household Laundry Equipment

335228 Other Household Appliance Manufacturing
SIC 3639 Household Appliances, nec

335311 Power, Distribution & Specialty Transformer Manufacturing
SIC 3548 Electric & Gas Welding & Soldering Equipment
SIC 3612 Power, Distribution, & Speciality Transformers

335312 Motor & Generator Manufacturing
SIC 3621 Motors & Generators
SIC 7694 Armature Rewinding Shops

335313 Switchgear & Switchboard Apparatus Manufacturing
SIC 3613 Switchgear & Switchboard Apparatus

335314 Relay & Industrial Control Manufacturing
SIC 3625 Relays & Industrial Controls

335911 Storage Battery Manufacturing
SIC 3691 Storage Batteries

335912 Dry & Wet Primary Battery Manufacturing
SIC 3692 Primary Batteries, Dry & Wet

335921 Fiber-Optic Cable Manufacturing
SIC 3357 Drawing & Insulating of Nonferrous Wire

335929 Other Communication & Energy Wire Manufacturing
SIC 3357 Drawing & Insulating of Nonferrous Wire

335931 Current-Carrying Wiring Device Manufacturing
SIC 3643 Current-Carrying Wiring Devices

335932 Noncurrent-Carrying Wiring Device Manufacturing
SIC 3644 Noncurrent-Carrying Wiring Devices

335991 Carbon & Graphite Product Manufacturing
SIC 3624 Carbon & Graphite Products

335999 All Other Miscellaneous Electrical Equipment & Component Manufacturing
SIC 3629 Electrical Industrial Apparatus, nec
SIC 3699 Electrical Machinery, Equipment, & Supplies, nec

TRANSPORTATION EQUIPMENT MANUFACTURING

336111 Automobile Manufacturing
SIC 3711 Motor Vehicles & Passenger Car Bodies

336112 Light Truck & Utility Vehicle Manufacturing
SIC 3711 Motor Vehicles & Passenger Car Bodies

33612 Heavy Duty Truck Manufacturing
SIC 3711 Motor Vehicles & Passenger Car Bodies

336211 Motor Vehicle Body Manufacturing
SIC 3711 Motor Vehicles & Passenger Car Bodies
SIC 3713 Truck & Bus Bodies
SIC 3714 Motor Vehicle Parts & Accessories

336212 Truck Trailer Manufacturing
SIC 3715 Truck Trailers

336213 Motor Home Manufacturing
SIC 3716 Motor Homes
336214 Travel Trailer & Camper Manufacturing
SIC 3792 Travel Trailers & Campers
SIC 3799 Transportation Equipment, nec
336311 Carburetor, Piston, Piston Ring & Valve Manufacturing
SIC 3592 Carburetors, Pistons, Piston Rings, & Valves
336312 Gasoline Engine & Engine Parts Manufacturing
SIC 3714 Motor Vehicle Parts & Accessories
336321 Vehicular Lighting Equipment Manufacturing
SIC 3647 Vehicular Lighting Equipment
336322 Other Motor Vehicle Electrical & Electronic Equipment Manufacturing
SIC 3679 Electronic Components, nec
SIC 3694 Electrical Equipment for Internal Combustion Engines
SIC 3714 Motor Vehicle Parts & Accessories
33633 Motor Vehicle Steering & Suspension Components Manufacturing
SIC 3714 Motor Vehicle Parts & Accessories
33634 Motor Vehicle Brake System Manufacturing
SIC 3292 Asbestos Products
SIC 3714 Motor Vehicle Parts & Accessories
33635 Motor Vehicle Transmission & Power Train Parts Manufacturing
SIC 3714 Motor Vehicle Parts & Accessories
33636 Motor Vehicle Fabric Accessories & Seat Manufacturing
SIC 2396 Automotive Trimmings, Apparel Findings, & Related Products
SIC 2399 Fabricated Textile Products, nec
SIC 2531 Public Building & Related Furniture
33637 Motor Vehicle Metal Stamping
SIC 3465 Automotive Stampings
336391 Motor Vehicle Air-Conditioning Manufacturing
SIC 3585 Air-Conditioning & Warm Air Heating Equipment & Commercial & Industrial Refrigeration Equipment
336399 All Other Motor Vehicle Parts Manufacturing
SIC 3519 Internal Combustion Engines, nec
SIC 3599 Industrial & Commercial Machinery & Equipment, NEC
SIC 3714 Motor Vehicle Parts & Accessories
336411 Aircraft Manufacturing
SIC 3721 Aircraft
336412 Aircraft Engine & Engine Parts Manufacturing
SIC 3724 Aircraft Engines & Engine Parts
336413 Other Aircraft Part & Auxiliary Equipment Manufacturing
SIC 3728 Aircraft Parts & Auxiliary Equipment, nec
336414 Guided Missile & Space Vehicle Manufacturing
SIC 3761 Guided Missiles & Space Vehicles
336415 Guided Missile & Space Vehicle Propulsion Unit & Propulsion Unit Parts Manufacturing
SIC 3764 Guided Missile & Space Vehicle Propulsion Units & Propulsion Unit Parts
336419 Other Guided Missile & Space Vehicle Parts & Auxiliary Equipment Manufacturing
SIC 3769 Guided Missile & Space Vehicle Parts & Auxiliary Equipment
33651 Railroad Rolling Stock Manufacturing
SIC 3531 Construction Machinery & Equipment
SIC 3743 Railroad Equipment
336611 Ship Building & Repairing
SIC 3731 Ship Building & Repairing

336612 Boat Building
SIC 3732 Boat Building & Repairing
336991 Motorcycle, Bicycle, & Parts Manufacturing
SIC 3944 Games, Toys, & Children's Vehicles, Except Dolls & Bicycles
SIC 3751 Motorcycles, Bicycles & Parts
336992 Military Armored Vehicle, Tank & Tank Component Manufacturing
SIC 3711 Motor Vehicles & Passenger Car Bodies
SIC 3795 Tanks & Tank Components
336999 All Other Transportation Equipment Manufacturing
SIC 3799 Transportation Equipment, nec

FURNITURE & RELATED PRODUCT MANUFACTURING

337121 Upholstered Household Furniture Manufacturing
SIC 2512 Wood Household Furniture, Upholstered
SIC 2515 Mattress, Foundations, & Convertible Beds
SIC 5712 Furniture
337122 Nonupholstered Wood Household Furniture Manufacturing
SIC 2511 Wood Household Furniture, Except Upholstered
SIC 5712 Furniture Stores
337124 Metal Household Furniture Manufacturing
SIC 2514 Metal Household Furniture
337125 Household Furniture Manufacturing
SIC 2519 Household Furniture, NEC
337127 Institutional Furniture Manufacturing
SIC 2531 Public Building & Related Furniture
SIC 2599 Furniture & Fixtures, nec
SIC 3952 Lead Pencils, Crayons, & Artist's Materials
SIC 3999 Manufacturing Industries, nec
337129 Wood Television, Radio, & Sewing Machine Cabinet Manufacturing
SIC 2517 Wood Television, Radio, Phonograph, & Sewing Machine Cabinets
337131 Wood Kitchen & Counter Top Manufacturing
SIC 2434 Wood Kitchen Cabinets
SIC 2541 Wood Office & Store Fixtures, Partitions, Shelving, & Lockers
SIC 5712 Furniture Stores
337132 Upholstered Wood Household Furniture Manufacturing
SIC 2515 Mattresses, Foundations, & Convertible Beds
SIC 5712 Furniture Stores
337133 Wood Household Furniture
SIC 5712 Furniture Stores
337134 Wood Office Furniture Manufacturing
SIC 2521 Wood Office Furniture
337135 Custom Architectural Woodwork, Millwork, & Fixtures
SIC 2541 Wood Office & Store Fixtures, Partitions, Shelving, and Lockers
337139 Other Wood Furniture Manufacturing
SIC 2426 Hardwood Dimension & Flooring Mills
SIC 2499 Wood Products, nec
SIC 2517 Wood Television, Radio, Phonograph, & Sewing Machine Cabinets
SIC 2531 Public Building & Related Furniture
SIC 2541 Wood Office & Store Fixtures, Partitions., Shelving, & Lockers
SIC 2599 Furniture & Fixtures, nec
SIC 3952 Lead Pencils, Crayons, & Artist's Materials

337141 Nonwood Office Furniture Manufacturing
SIC 2522 Office Furniture, Except Wood
337143 Household Furniture Manufacturing
SIC 2519 Household Furniture, NEC
337145 Nonwood Showcase, Partition, Shelving, & Locker Manufacturing
SIC 2542 Office & Store Fixtures, Partitions, Shelving, & Lockers, Except Wood
337148 Other Nonwood Furniture Manufacturing
SIC 2499 Wood Products, NEC
SIC 2531 Public Building & Related Furniture
SIC 2599 Furniture & Fixtures, nec
SIC 3499 Fabricated Metal Products, nec
SIC 3952 Lead Pencils, Crayons, & Artist's Materials
SIC 3999 Manufacturing Industries, nec
337212 Custom Architectural Woodwork & Millwork Manufacturing
SIC 2541 Wood Office & Store Fixtures, Partitions, Shelving, & Lockers
337214 Nonwood Office Furniture Manufacturing
SIC 2522 Office Furniture, Except Wood
337215 Showcase, Partition, Shelving, & Locker Manufacturing
SIC 2542 Office & Store Fixtures, Partitions, Shelving & Lockers, Except Wood
SIC 2541 Wood Office & Store Fixtures, Partitions, Shelving, & Lockers
SIC 2426 Hardwood Dimension & Flooring Mills
SIC 3499 Fabricated Metal Products, nec
33791 Mattress Manufacturing
SIC 2515 Mattresses, Foundations & Convertible Beds
33792 Blind & Shade Manufacturing
SIC 2591 Drapery Hardware & Window Blinds & Shades

MISCELLANEOUS MANUFACTURING

339111 Laboratory Apparatus & Furniture Manufacturing
SIC 3829 Measuring & Controlling Devices, nec
339112 Surgical & Medical Instrument Manufacturing
SIC 3841 Surgical & Medical Instruments & Apparatus
SIC 3829 Measuring & Controlling Devices, nec
339113 Surgical Appliance & Supplies Manufacturing
SIC 2599 Furniture & Fixtures, nec
SIC 3842 Orthopedic, Prosthetic, & Surgical Appliances & Supplies
339114 Dental Equipment & Supplies Manufacturing
SIC 3843 Dental Equipment & Supplies
339115 Ophthalmic Goods Manufacturing
SIC 3851 Opthalmic Goods
SIC 5995 Optical Goods Stores
339116 Dental Laboratories
SIC 8072 Dental Laboratories 339117 Eyeglass & Contact Lens Manufacturing
SIC 5995 Optical Goods Stores
339911 Jewelry Manufacturing
SIC 3469 Metal Stamping, nec
SIC 3479 Coating, Engraving, & Allied Services, nec
SIC 3911 Jewelry, Precious Metal
339912 Silverware & Plated Ware Manufacturing
SIC 3479 Coating, Engraving, & Allied Services, nec
SIC 3914 Silverware, Plated Ware, & Stainless Steel Ware
339913 Jewelers' Material & Lapidary Work Manufacturing
SIC 3915 Jewelers' Findings & Materials, & Lapidary Work

339914 Costume Jewelry & Novelty Manufacturing
SIC 3479 Coating, Engraving, & Allied Services, nec
SIC 3499 Fabricated Metal Products, nec
SIC 3961 Costume Jewelry & Costume Novelties, Except Precious Metal
33992 Sporting & Athletic Goods Manufacturing
SIC 3949 Sporting & Athletic Goods, nec
339931 Doll & Stuffed Toy Manufacturing
SIC 3942 Dolls & Stuffed Toys
339932 Game, Toy, & Children's Vehicle Manufacturing
SIC 3944 Games, Toys, & Children's Vehicles, Except Dolls & Bicycles
339941 Pen & Mechanical Pencil Manufacturing
SIC 3951 Pens, Mechanical Pencils, & Parts
339942 Lead Pencil & Art Good Manufacturing
SIC 2531 Public Buildings & Related Furniture
SIC 3579 Office Machines, nec
SIC 3952 Lead Pencils, Crayons, & Artists' Materials
339943 Marking Device Manufacturing
SIC 3953 Marking Devices
339944 Carbon Paper & Inked Ribbon Manufacturing
SIC 3955 Carbon Paper & Inked Ribbons
33995 Sign Manufacturing
SIC 3993 Signs & Advertising Specialties
339991 Gasket, Packing, & Sealing Device Manufacturing
SIC 3053 Gaskets, Packing, & Sealing Devices
339992 Musical Instrument Manufacturing
SIC 3931 Musical Instruments
339993 Fastener, Button, Needle & Pin Manufacturing
SIC 3965 Fasteners, Buttons, Needles, & Pins
SIC 3131 Boat & Shoe Cut Stock & Findings
339994 Broom, Brush & Mop Manufacturing
SIC 3991 Brooms & Brushes
SIC 2392 Housefurnishings, Except Curtains & Draperies
339995 Burial Casket Manufacturing
SIC 3995 Burial Caskets
339999 All Other Miscellaneous Manufacturing
SIC 2499 Wood Products, NEC
SIC 3999 Manufacturing Industries, nec

WHOLESALE TRADE

42111 Automobile & Other Motor Vehicle Wholesalers
SIC 5012 Automobiles & Other Motor Vehicles
42112 Motor Vehicle Supplies & New Part Wholesalers
SIC 5013 Motor Vehicle Supplies & New Parts
42113 Tire & Tube Wholesalers
SIC 5014 Tires & Tubes
42114 Motor Vehicle Part Wholesalers
SIC 5015 Motor Vehicle Parts, Used
42121 Furniture Wholesalers
SIC 5021 Furniture
42122 Home Furnishing Wholesalers
SIC 5023 Homefurnishings
42131 Lumber, Plywood, Millwork & Wood Panel Wholesalers
SIC 5031 Lumber, Plywood, Millwork, & Wood Panels
SIC 5211 Lumber & Other Building Materials Dealers - Retail
42132 Brick, Stone & Related Construction Material Wholesalers
SIC 5032 Brick, Stone, & Related Construction Materials
42133 Roofing, Siding & Insulation Material Wholesalers
SIC 5033 Roofing, Siding, & Insulation Materials

42139 Other Construction Material Wholesalers
SIC 5039 Construction Materials, nec
42141 Photographic Equipment & Supplies Wholesalers
SIC 5043 Photographic Equipment & Supplies
42142 Office Equipment Wholesalers
SIC 5044 Office Equipment
42143 Computer & Computer Peripheral Equipment & Software Wholesalers
SIC 5045 Computers & Computer Peripherals Equipment & Software
42144 Other Commercial Equipment Wholesalers
SIC 5046 Commercial Equipment, nec
42145 Medical, Dental & Hospital Equipment & Supplies Wholesalers
SIC 5047 Medical, Dental & Hospital Equipment & Supplies
42146 Ophthalmic Goods Wholesalers
SIC 5048 Ophthalmic Goods
42149 Other Professional Equipment & Supplies Wholesalers
SIC 5049 Professional Equipment & Supplies, nec
42151 Metal Service Centers & Offices
SIC 5051 Metals Service Centers & Offices
42152 Coal & Other Mineral & Ore Wholesalers
SIC 5052 Coal & Other Mineral & Ores
42161 Electrical Apparatus & Equipment, Wiring Supplies & Construction Material Wholesalers
SIC 5063 Electrical Apparatus & Equipment, Wiring Supplies & Construction Materials
42162 Electrical Appliance, Television & Radio Set Wholesalers
SIC 5064 Electrical Appliances, Television & Radio Sets
42169 Other Electronic Parts & Equipment Wholesalers
SIC 5065 Electronic Parts & Equipment, nec
42171 Hardware Wholesalers
SIC 5072 Hardware
42172 Plumbing & Heating Equipment & Supplies Wholesalers
SIC 5074 Plumbing & Heating Equipment & Supplies
42173 Warm Air Heating & Air-Conditioning Equipment & Supplies Wholesalers
SIC 5075 Warm Air Heating & Air-Conditioning Equipment & Supplies
42174 Refrigeration Equipment & Supplies Wholesalers
SIC 5078 Refrigeration Equipment & Supplies
42181 Construction & Mining Machinery & Equipment Wholesalers
SIC 5082 Construction & Mining Machinery & Equipment
42182 Farm & Garden Machinery & Equipment Wholesalers
SIC 5083 Farm & Garden Machinery & Equipment
42183 Industrial Machinery & Equipment Wholesalers
SIC 5084 Industrial Machinery & Equipment
SIC 5085 Industrial Supplies
42184 Industrial Supplies Wholesalers
SIC 5085 Industrial Supplies
42185 Service Establishment Equipment & Supplies Wholesalers
SIC 5087 Service Establishment Equipment & Supplies Wholesalers
42186 Transportation Equipment & Supplies Wholesalers
SIC 5088 Transportation Equipment and Supplies, Except Motor Vehicles
42191 Sporting & Recreational Goods & Supplies Wholesalers
SIC 5091 Sporting & Recreational Goods & Supplies
42192 Toy & Hobby Goods & Supplies Wholesalers
SIC 5092 Toys & Hobby Goods & Supplies

42193 Recyclable Material Wholesalers
SIC 5093 Scrap & Waste Materials
42194 Jewelry, Watch, Precious Stone & Precious Metal Wholesalers
SIC 5094 Jewelry, Watches, Precious Stones, & Precious Metals
42199 Other Miscellaneous Durable Goods Wholesalers
SIC 5099 Durable Goods, nec
SIC 7822 Motion Picture & Video Tape Distribution
42211 Printing & Writing Paper Wholesalers
SIC 5111 Printing & Writing Paper
42212 Stationary & Office Supplies Wholesalers
SIC 5112 Stationery & Office Supplies
42213 Industrial & Personal Service Paper Wholesalers
SIC 5113 Industrial & Personal Service Paper
42221 Drug, Drug Proprietaries & Druggists' Sundries Wholesalers
SIC 5122 Drugs, Drug Proprietaries, & Druggists' Sundries
42231 Piece Goods, Notions & Other Dry Goods Wholesalers
SIC 5131 Piece Goods, Notions, & Other Dry Goods
42232 Men's & Boys' Clothing & Furnishings Wholesalers
SIC 5136 Men's & Boys' Clothing & Furnishings
42233 Women's, Children's, & Infants' & Accessories Wholesalers
SIC 5137 Women's, Children's, & Infants' Clothing & Accessories
42234 Footwear Wholesalers
SIC 5139 Footwear
42241 General Line Grocery Wholesalers
SIC 5141 Groceries, General Line
42242 Packaged Frozen Food Wholesalers
SIC 5142 Packaged Frozen Foods
42243 Dairy Product Wholesalers
SIC 5143 Dairy Products, Except Dried or Canned
42244 Poultry & Poultry Product Wholesalers
SIC 5144 Poultry & Poultry Products
42245 Confectionery Wholesalers
SIC 5145 Confectionery
42246 Fish & Seafood Wholesalers
SIC 5146 Fish & Seafoods
42247 Meat & Meat Product Wholesalers
SIC 5147 Meats & Meat Products
42248 Fresh Fruit & Vegetable Wholesalers
SIC 5148 Fresh Fruits & Vegetables
42249 Other Grocery & Related Products Wholesalers
SIC 5149 Groceries & Related Products, nec
42251 Grain & Field Bean Wholesalers
SIC 5153 Grain & Field Beans
42252 Livestock Wholesalers
SIC 5154 Livestock
42259 Other Farm Product Raw Material Wholesalers
SIC 5159 Farm-Product Raw Materials, nec
42261 Plastics Materials & Basic Forms & Shapes Wholesalers
SIC 5162 Plastics Materials & Basic Forms & Shapes
42269 Other Chemical & Allied Products Wholesalers
SIC 5169 Chemicals & Allied Products, nec
42271 Petroleum Bulk Stations & Terminals
SIC 5171 Petroleum Bulk Stations & Terminals
42272 Petroleum & Petroleum Products Wholesalers
SIC 5172 Petroleum & Petroleum Products Wholesalers, Except Bulk Stations & Terminals
42281 Beer & Ale Wholesalers
SIC 5181 Beer & Ale

42282   Wine & Distilled Alcoholic Beverage Wholesalers
 SIC 5182 Wine & Distilled Alcoholic Beverages
42291   Farm Supplies Wholesalers
 SIC 5191 Farm Supplies
42292   Book, Periodical & Newspaper Wholesalers
 SIC 5192 Books, Periodicals, & Newspapers
42293   Flower, Nursery Stock & Florists' Supplies Wholesalers
 SIC 5193 Flowers, Nursery Stock, & Florists' Supplies
42294   Tobacco & Tobacco Product Wholesalers
 SIC 5194 Tobacco & Tobacco Products
42295   Paint, Varnish & Supplies Wholesalers
 SIC 5198 Paints, Varnishes, & Supplies
 SIC 5231 Paint, Glass & Wallpaper Stores
42299   Other Miscellaneous Nondurable Goods Wholesalers
 SIC 5199 Nondurable Goods, nec

RETAIL TRADE

44111   New Car Dealers
 SIC 5511 Motor Vehicle Dealers, New and Used
44112   Used Car Dealers
 SIC 5521 Motor Vehicle Dealers, Used Only
44121   Recreational Vehicle Dealers
 SIC 5561 Recreational Vehicle Dealers
441221 Motorcycle Dealers
 SIC 5571 Motorcycle Dealers
441222 Boat Dealers
 SIC 5551 Boat Dealers
441229 All Other Motor Vehicle Dealers
 SIC 5599 Automotive Dealers, NEC
44131   Automotive Parts & Accessories Stores
 SIC 5013 Motor Vehicle Supplies & New Parts
 SIC 5731 Radio, Television, & Consumer Electronics Stores
 SIC 5531 Auto & Home Supply Stores
44132   Tire Dealers
 SIC 5014 Tires & Tubes
 SIC 5531 Auto & Home Supply Stores
44211   Furniture Stores
 SIC 5021 Furniture
 SIC 5712 Furniture Stores
44221   Floor Covering Stores
 SIC 5023 Homefurnishings
 SIC 5713 Floor Coverings Stores
442291 Window Treatment Stores
 SIC 5714 Drapery, Curtain, & Upholstery Stores
 SIC 5719 Miscellaneous Homefurnishings Stores
442299 All Other Home Furnishings Stores
 SIC 5719 Miscellaneous Homefurnishings Stores
443111 Household Appliance Stores
 SIC 5722 Household Appliance Stores
 SIC 5999 Miscellaneous Retail Stores, nec
 SIC 7623 Refrigeration & Air-Conditioning Service & Repair Shops
 SIC 7629 Electrical & Electronic Repair Shops, nec
443112 Radio, Television & Other Electronics Stores
 SIC 5731 Radio, Television, & Consumer Electronics Stores
 SIC 5999 Miscellaneous Retail Stores, nec
 SIC 7622 Radio & Television Repair Shops
44312   Computer & Software Stores
 SIC 5045 Computers & Computer Peripheral Equipment & Software
 SIC 7378 Computer Maintenance & Repair '
 SIC 5734 Computer & Computer Software Stores

44313   Camera & Photographic Supplies Stores
 SIC 5946 Camera & Photographic Supply Stores
44411   Home Centers
 SIC 5211 Lumber & Other Building Materials Dealers
44412   Paint & Wallpaper Stores
 SIC 5198 Paints, Varnishes, & Supplies
 SIC 5231 Paint, Glass, & Wallpaper Stores
44413   Hardware Stores
 SIC 5251 Hardware Stores
44419   Other Building Material Dealers
 SIC 5031 Lumber, Plywood, Millwork, & Wood Panels
 SIC 5032 Brick, Stone, & Related Construction Materials
 SIC 5039 Construction Materials, nec
 SIC 5063 Electrical Apparatus & Equipment, Wiring Supplies, & Construction Materials
 SIC 5074 Plumbing & Heating Equipment & Supplies
 SIC 5211 Lumber & Other Building Materials Dealers
 SIC 5231 Paint, Glass, & Wallpaper Stores
44421   Outdoor Power Equipment Stores
 SIC 5083 Farm & Garden Machinery & Equipment
 SIC 5261 Retail Nurseries, Lawn & Garden Supply Stores
44422   Nursery & Garden Centers
 SIC 5191 Farm Supplies
 SIC 5193 Flowers, Nursery Stock, & Florists' Supplies
 SIC 5261 Retail Nurseries, Lawn & Garden Supply Stores
44511   Supermarkets & Other Grocery Stores
 SIC 5411 Grocery Stores
44512   Convenience Stores
 SIC 5411 Grocery Stores
44521   Meat Markets
 SIC 5421 Meat & Fish Markets, Including Freezer Provisioners
 SIC 5499 Miscellaneous Food Stores
44522   Fish & Seafood Markets
 SIC 5421 Meat & Fish Markets, Including Freezer Provisioners
44523   Fruit & Vegetable Markets
 SIC 5431 Fruit & Vegetable Markets
445291 Baked Goods Stores
 SIC 5461 Retail Bakeries
445292 Confectionery & Nut Stores
 SIC 5441 Candy, Nut & Confectionery Stores
445299 All Other Specialty Food Stores
 SIC 5499 Miscellaneous Food Stores
 SIC 5451 Dairy Products Stores
44531   Beer, Wine & Liquor Stores
 SIC 5921 Liquor Stores
44611   Pharmacies & Drug Stores
 SIC 5912 Drug Stores & Proprietary Stores
44612   Cosmetics, Beauty Supplies & Perfume Stores
 SIC 5087 Service Establishment Equipment & Supplies
 SIC 5999 Miscellaneous Retail Stores, nec
44613   Optical Goods Stores
 SIC 5995 Optical Goods Stores
446191 Food Supplement Stores
 SIC 5499 Miscellaneous Food Stores
446199 All Other Health & Personal Care Stores
 SIC 5047 Medical, Dental, & Hospital Equipment & Supplies
 SIC 5999 Miscellaneous Retail Stores, nec
44711   Gasoline Stations with Convenience Stores
 SIC 5541 Gasoline Service Station
 SIC 5411 Grocery Stores
44719   Other Gasoline Stations
 SIC 5541 Gasoline Service Station

44811 Men's Clothing Stores
SIC 5611 Men's & Boys' Clothing & Accessory Stores
44812 Women's Clothing Stores
SIC 5621 Women's Clothing Stores
44813 Children's & Infants' Clothing Stores
SIC 5641 Children's & Infants' Wear Stores
44814 Family Clothing Stores
SIC 5651 Family Clothing Stores
44815 Clothing Accessories Stores
SIC 5611 Men's & Boys' Clothing & Accessory Stores
SIC 5632 Women's Accessory & Specialty Stores
SIC 5699 Miscellaneous Apparel & Accessory Stores
44819 Other Clothing Stores
SIC 5699 Miscellaneous Apparel & Accessory Stores
SIC 5632 Women's Accessory & Specialty Stores
44821 Shoe Stores
SIC 5661 Shoe Stores
44831 Jewelry Stores
SIC 5999 Miscellaneous Retailer, nec
SIC 5944 Jewelry Stores
44832 Luggage & Leather Goods Stores
SIC 5948 Luggage & Leather Goods Stores
45111 Sporting Goods Stores
SIC 7699 Repair Shops & Related Services, NEC
SIC 5941 Sporting Goods Stores & Bicycle Shops
45112 Hobby, Toy & Game Stores
SIC 5945 Hobby, Toy, & Game Stores
45113 Sewing, Needlework & Piece Goods Stores
SIC 5714 Drapery, Curtain, & Upholstery Stores
SIC 5949 Sewing, Needlework, & Piece Goods Stores
45114 Musical Instrument & Supplies Stores
SIC 5736 Musical Instruments Stores
451211 Book Stores
SIC 5942 Book Stores
451212 News Dealers & Newsstands
SIC 5994 News Dealers & Newsstands
45122 Prerecorded Tape, Compact Disc & Record Stores
SIC 5735 Record & Prerecorded Tape Stores
45211 Department Stores
SIC 5311 Department Stores
45291 Warehouse Clubs & Superstores
SIC 5399 Miscellaneous General Merchandise Stores
SIC 5411 Grocery Stores
45299 All Other General Merchandise Stores
SIC 5399 Miscellaneous General Merchandise Stores
SIC 5331 Variety Stores
45311 Florists
SIC 5992 Florists
45321 Office Supplies & Stationery Stores
SIC 5049 Professional Equipment & Supplies, nec
SIC 5112 Stationery & Office Supplies
SIC 5943 Stationery Stores
45322 Gift, Novelty & Souvenir Stores
SIC 5947 Gift, Novelty, & Souvenir Shops
45331 Used Merchandise Stores
SIC 5932 Used Merchandise Stores
45391 Pet & Pet Supplies Stores
SIC 5999 Miscellaneous Retail Stores, NEC
45392 Art Dealers
SIC 5999 Miscellaneous Retail Stores, nec
45393 Manufactured Home Dealers
SIC 5271 Mobile Home Dealers

453991 Tobacco Stores
SIC 5993 Tobacco Stores & Stands
453999 All Other Miscellaneous Store Retailers
SIC 5999 Miscellaneous Retail Stores, nec
SIC 5261 Retail Nurseries, Lawn & Garden Supply Stores
45411 Electronic Shopping & Mail-Order Houses
SIC 5961 Catalog & Mail-Order Houses
45421 Vending Machine Operators
SIC 5962 Automatic Merchandise Machine Operators
454311 Heating Oil Dealers
SIC 5171 Petroleum Bulk Stations & Terminals
SIC 5983 Fuel Oil Dealers
454312 Liquefied Petroleum Gas Dealers
SIC 5171 Petroleum Bulk Stations & Terminals
SIC 5984 Liquefied Petroleum Gas Dealers
454319 Other Fuel Dealers
SIC 5989 Fuel Dealers, nec
45439 Other Direct Selling Establishments
SIC 5421 Meat & Fish Markets, Including Freezer Provisioners
SIC 5963 Direct Selling Establishments

TRANSPORTATION & WAREHOUSING

481111 Scheduled Passenger Air Transportation
SIC 4512 Air Transportation, Scheduled
481112 Scheduled Freight Air Transportation
SIC 4512 Air Transportation, Scheduled
481211 Nonscheduled Chartered Passenger Air Transportation
SIC 4522 Air Transportation, Nonscheduled
481212 Nonscheduled Chartered Freight Air Transportation
SIC 4522 Air Transportation, Nonscheduled
481219 Other Nonscheduled Air Transportation
SIC 7319 Advertising, nec
48122 Nonscheduled Speciality Air Transportation
SIC 0721 Crop Planting, Cultivating, & Protecting
SIC 1382 Oil & Gas Field Exploration Services
SIC 4522 Air Transportation, Nonscheduled
SIC 7335 Commercial Photography
SIC 7997 Membership Sports & Recreation Clubs
SIC 8299 Schools & Educational Services, nec
SIC 8713 Surveying Services
482111 Line-Haul Railroads
SIC 4011 Railroads, Line-Haul Operating
482112 Short Line Railroads
SIC 4013 Railroad Switching & Terminal Establishments
483111 Deep Sea Freight Transportation
SIC 4412 Deep Sea Foreign Transportation of Freight
483112 Deep Sea Passenger Transportation
SIC 4481 Deep Sea Transportation of Passengers, Except by Ferry
483113 Coastal & Great Lakes Freight Transportation
SIC 4424 Deep Sea Domestic Transportation of Freight
SIC 4432 Freight Transportation on the Great Lakes - St. Lawrence Seaway
SIC 4492 Towing & Tugboat Services
483114 Coastal & Great Lakes Passenger Transportation
SIC 4481 Deep Sea Transportation of Passengers, Except by Ferry
SIC 4482 Ferries
483211 Inland Water Freight Transportation
SIC 4449 Water Transportation of Freight, nec
SIC 4492 Towing & Tugboat Services

483212 Inland Water Passenger Transportation
SIC 4482 Ferries
SIC 4489 Water Transportation of Passengers, nec
48411 General Freight Trucking, Local
SIC 4212 Local Trucking without Storage
SIC 4214 Local Trucking with Storage
484121 General Freight Trucking, Long-Distance, Truckload
SIC 4213 Trucking, Except Local
484122 General Freight Trucking, Long-Distance, Less Than Truckload
SIC 4213 Trucking, Except Local
48421 Used Household & Office Goods Moving
SIC 4212 Local Trucking Without Storage
SIC 4213 Trucking, Except Local
SIC 4214 Local Trucking With Storage
48422 Specialized Freight Trucking, Local
SIC 4212 Local Trucking without Storage
SIC 4214 Local Trucking with Storage
48423 Specialized Freight Trucking, Long-Distance
SIC 4213 Trucking, Except Local
485111 Mixed Mode Transit Systems
SIC 4111 Local & Suburban Transit
485112 Commuter Rail Systems
SIC 4111 Local & Suburban Transit
485113 Bus & Motor Vehicle Transit Systems
SIC 4111 Local & Suburban Transit
485119 Other Urban Transit Systems
SIC 4111 Local & Suburban Transit
48521 Interurban & Rural Bus Transportation
SIC 4131 Intercity & Rural Bus Transportation
48531 Taxi Service
SIC 4121 Taxicabs
48532 Limousine Service
SIC 4119 Local Passenger Transportation, nec
48541 School & Employee Bus Transportation
SIC 4151 School Buses
SIC 4119 Local Passenger Transportation, nec
48551 Charter Bus Industry
SIC 4141 Local Charter Bus Service
SIC 4142 Bus Charter Services, Except Local
485991 Special Needs Transportation
SIC 4119 Local Passenger Transportation, nec
485999 All Other Transit & Ground Passenger Transportation
SIC 4111 Local & Suburban Transit
SIC 4119 Local Passenger Transportation, nec
48611 Pipeline Transportation of Crude Oil
SIC 4612 Crude Petroleum Pipelines
48621 Pipeline Transportation of Natural Gas
SIC 4922 Natural Gas Transmission
SIC 4923 Natural Gas Transmission & Distribution
48691 Pipeline Transportation of Refined Petroleum Products
SIC 4613 Refined Petroleum Pipelines
48699 All Other Pipeline Transportation
SIC 4619 Pipelines, nec
48711 Scenic & Sightseeing Transportation, Land
SIC 4119 Local Passenger Transportation, nec
SIC 4789 Transportation Services, nec
SIC 7999 Amusement & Recreation Services, nec
48721 Scenic & Sightseeing Transportation, Water
SIC 4489 Water Transportation of Passengers, nec
SIC 7999 Amusement & Recreation Services, nec
48799 Scenic & Sightseeing Transportation, Other
SIC 4522 Air Transportation, Nonscheduled
SIC 7999 Amusement & Recreation Services, nec

488111 Air Traffic Control
SIC 4581 Airports, Flying Fields, & Airport Terminal Services
SIC 9621 Regulation & Administration of Transportation Programs
488112 Airport Operations, except Air Traffic Control
SIC 4581 Airports, Flying Fields, & Airport Terminal Services
SIC 4959 Sanitary Services, nec
488119 Other Airport Operations
SIC 4581 Airports, Flying Fields, & Airport Terminal Services
SIC 4959 Sanitary Services, nec
48819 Other Support Activities for Air Transportation
SIC 4581 Airports, Flying Fields, & Airport Terminal Services
48821 Support Activities for Rail Transportation
SIC 4013 Railroad Switching & Terminal Establishments
SIC 4741 Rental of Railroad Cars
SIC 4789 Transportation Services, nec
48831 Port & Harbor Operations
SIC 4491 Marine Cargo Handling
SIC 4499 Water Transportation Services, nec
48832 Marine Cargo Handling
SIC 4491 Marine Cargo Handling
48833 Navigational Services to Shipping
SIC 4492 Towing & Tugboat Services
SIC 4499 Water Transportation Services, nec
48839 Other Support Activities for Water Transportation
SIC 4499 Water Transportation Services, nec
SIC 4785 Fixed Facilities & Inspection & Weighing Services for Motor Vehicle Transportation
SIC 7699 Repair Shops & Related Services, nec
48841 Motor Vehicle Towing
SIC 7549 Automotive Services, Except Repair & Carwashes
48849 Other Support Activities for Road Transportation
SIC 4173 Terminal & Service Facilities for Motor Vehicle Passenger Transportation
SIC 4231 Terminal & Joint Terminal Maintenance Facilities for Motor Freight Transportation
SIC 4785 Fixed Facilities & Inspection & Weighing Services for Motor Vehicle Transportation
48851 Freight Transportation Arrangement
SIC 4731 Arrangement of Transportation of Freight & Cargo
488991 Packing & Crating
SIC 4783 Packing & Crating
488999 All Other Support Activities for Transportation
SIC 4729 Arrangement of Passenger Transportation, nec
SIC 4789 Transportation Services, nec
49111 Postal Service
SIC 4311 United States Postal Service
49211 Couriers
SIC 4215 Courier Services, Except by Air
SIC 4513 Air Courier Services
49221 Local Messengers & Local Delivery
SIC 4215 Courier Services, Except by Air
49311 General Warehousing & Storage Facilities
SIC 4225 General Warehousing & Storage
SIC 4226 Special Warehousing & Storage, nec
49312 Refrigerated Storage Facilities
SIC 4222 Refrigerated Warehousing & Storage
SIC 4226 Special Warehousing & Storage, nec
49313 Farm Product Storage Facilities
SIC 4221 Farm Product Warehousing & Storage
49319 Other Warehousing & Storage Facilities
SIC 4226 Special Warehousing & Storage, nec

INFORMATION

51111 Newspaper Publishers
SIC 2711 Newspapers: Publishing or Publishing & Printing
51112 Periodical Publishers
SIC 2721 Periodicals: Publishing or Publishing & Printing
51113 Book Publishers
SIC 2731 Books: Publishing or Publishing & Printing
51114 Database & Directory Publishers
SIC 2741 Miscellaneous Publishing
511191 Greeting Card Publishers
SIC 2771 Greeting Cards
511199 All Other Publishers
SIC 2741 Miscellaneous Publishing
51121 Software Publishers
SIC 7372 Prepackaged Software
51211 Motion Picture & Video Production
SIC 7812 Motion Picture & Video Tape Production
51212 Motion Picture & Video Distribution
SIC 7822 Motion Picture & Video Tape Distribution
SIC 7829 Services Allied to Motion Picture Distribution
512131 Motion Picture Theaters, Except Drive-Ins.
SIC 7832 Motion Picture Theaters, Except Drive-In
512132 Drive-In Motion Picture Theaters
SIC 7833 Drive-In Motion Picture Theaters
512191 Teleproduction & Other Post-Production Services
SIC 7819 Services Allied to Motion Picture Production
512199 Other Motion Picture & Video Industries
SIC 7819 Services Allied to Motion Picture Production
SIC 7829 Services Allied to Motion Picture Distribution
51221 Record Production
SIC 8999 Services, nec
51222 Integrated Record Production/Distribution
SIC 3652 Phonograph Records & Prerecorded Audio Tapes & Disks
51223 Music Publishers
SIC 2731 Books: Publishing or Publishing & Printing
SIC 2741 Miscellaneous Publishing
SIC 8999 Services, nec
51224 Sound Recording Studios
SIC 7389 Business Services, nec
51229 Other Sound Recording Industries
SIC 7389 Business Services, nec
SIC 7922 Theatrical Producers & Miscellaneous Theatrical Services
513111 Radio Networks
SIC 4832 Radio Broadcasting Stations
513112 Radio Stations
SIC 4832 Radio Broadcasting Stations
51312 Television Broadcasting
SIC 4833 Television Broadcasting Stations
51321 Cable Networks
SIC 4841 Cable & Other Pay Television Services
51322 Cable & Other Program Distribution
SIC 4841 Cable & Other Pay Television Services
51331 Wired Telecommunications Carriers
SIC 4813 Telephone Communications, Except Radiotelephone
SIC 4822 Telegraph & Other Message Communications
513321 Paging
SIC 4812 Radiotelephone Communications
513322 Cellular & Other Wireless Telecommunications
SIC 4812 Radiotelephone Communications
SIC 4899 Communications Services, nec

51333 Telecommunications Resellers
SIC 4812 Radio Communications
SIC 4813 Telephone Communications, Except Radiotelephone
51334 Satellite Telecommunications
SIC 4899 Communications Services, NEC
51339 Other Telecommunications
SIC 4899 Communications Services, NEC
51411 News Syndicates
SIC 7383 News Syndicates
51412 Libraries & Archives
SIC 8231 Libraries
514191 On-Line Information Services
SIC 7375 Information Retrieval Services
514199 All Other Information Services
SIC 8999 Services, nec
51421 Data Processing Services
SIC 7374 Computer Processing & Data Preparation & Processing Services

FINANCE & INSURANCE

52111 Monetary Authorities - Central Bank
SIC 6011 Federal Reserve Banks
52211 Commercial Banking
SIC 6021 National Commercial Banks
SIC 6022 State Commercial Banks
SIC 6029 Commercial Banks, nec
SIC 6081 Branches & Agencies of Foreign Banks
52212 Savings Institutions
SIC 6035 Savings Institutions, Federally Chartered
SIC 6036 Savings Institutions, Not Federally Chartered
52213 Credit Unions
SIC 6061 Credit Unions, Federally Chartered
SIC 6062 Credit Unions, Not Federally Chartered
52219 Other Depository Credit Intermediation
SIC 6022 State Commercial Banks
52221 Credit Card Issuing
SIC 6021 National Commercial Banks
SIC 6022 State Commercial Banks
SIC 6141 Personal Credit Institutions
52222 Sales Financing
SIC 6141 Personal Credit Institutions
SIC 6153 Short-Term Business Credit Institutions, Except Agricultural .
SIC 6159 Miscellaneous Business Credit Institutions
522291 Consumer Lending
SIC 6141 Personal Credit Institutions
522292 Real Estate Credit
SIC 6162 Mortgage Bankers & Loan Correspondents
522293 International Trade Financing
SIC 6081 Branches & Agencies of Foreign Banks
SIC 6082 Foreign Trade & International Banking Institutions
SIC 6111 Federal & Federally-Sponsored Credit Agencies
SIC 6159 Miscellaneous Business Credit Institutions
522294 Secondary Market Financing
SIC 6111 Federal & Federally Sponsored Credit Agencies
522298 All Other Nondepository Credit Intermediation
SIC 5932 Used Merchandise Stores
SIC 6081 Branches & Agencies of Foreign Banks
SIC 6111 Federal & Federally-Sponsored Credit Agencies
SIC 6153 Short-Term Business Credit Institutions, Except Agricultural
SIC 6159 Miscellaneous Business Credit Institutions

52231 Mortgage & Other Loan Brokers
SIC 6163 Loan Brokers
52232 Financial Transactions Processing, Reserve, & Clearing House Activities
SIC 6019 Central Reserve Depository Institutions, nec
SIC 6099 Functions Related to Depository Banking, nec
SIC 6153 Short-Term Business Credit Institutions, Except Agricultural
SIC 7389 Business Services, nec
52239 Other Activities Related to Credit Intermediation
SIC 6099 Functions Related to Depository Banking, nec
SIC 6162 Mortgage Bankers & Loan Correspondents
52311 Investment Banking & Securities Dealing
SIC 6211 Security Brokers, Dealers, & Flotation Companies
52312 Securities Brokerage
SIC 6211 Security Brokers, Dealers, & Flotation Companies
52313 Commodity Contracts Dealing
SIC 6099 Functions Related to depository Banking, nec
SIC 6799 Investors, nec
SIC 6221 Commodity Contracts Brokers & Dealers
52314 Commodity Brokerage
SIC 6221 Commodity Contracts Brokers & Dealers
52321 Securities & Commodity Exchanges
SIC 6231 Security & Commodity Exchanges
52391 Miscellaneous Intermediation
SIC 6211 Securities Brokers, Dealers & Flotation Companies
SIC 6799 Investors, nec
52392 Portfolio Management
SIC 6282 Investment Advice
SIC 6371 Pension, Health, & Welfare Funds
SIC 6733 Trust, Except Educational, Religious, & Charitable
SIC 6799 Investors, nec
52393 Investment Advice
SIC 6282 Investment Advice
523991 Trust, Fiduciary & Custody Activities
SIC 6021 National Commercial Banks
SIC 6022 State Commercial Banks
SIC 6091 Nondepository Trust Facilities
SIC 6099 Functions Related to Depository Banking, nec
SIC 6289 Services Allied With the Exchange of Securities or Commodities, nec
SIC 6733 Trusts, Except Educational, Religious, & Charitable
523999 Miscellaneous Financial Investment Activities
SIC 6099 Functions Related to Depository Banking, nec
SIC 6211 Security Brokers, Dealers, & Flotation Companies
SIC 6289 Services Allied With the Exchange of Securities or Commodities, nec
SIC 6799 Investors, nec
SIC 6792 Oil Royalty Traders
524113 Direct Life Insurance Carriers
SIC 6311 Life Insurance
524114 Direct Health & Medical Insurance Carriers
SIC 6324 Hospital & Medical Service Plans
SIC 6321 Accident & Health Insurance
524126 Direct Property & Casualty Insurance Carriers
SIC 6331 Fire, Marine, & Casualty Insurance
SIC 6351 Surety Insurance
524127 Direct Title Insurance Carriers
SIC 6361 Title Insurance
524128 Other Direct Insurance Carriers
SIC 6399 Insurance Carriers, nec
52413 Reinsurance Carriers
SIC 6311 Life Insurance
SIC 6321 Accident & Health Insurance

SIC 6324 Hospital & Medical Service Plans
SIC 6331 Fire, Marine, & Casualty Insurance
SIC 6351 Surety Insurance
SIC 6361 Title Insurance
52421 Insurance Agencies & Brokerages
SIC 6411 Insurance Agents, Brokers & Service
524291 Claims Adjusters
SIC 6411 Insurance Agents, Brokers & Service
524292 Third Party Administration for Insurance & Pension Funds
SIC 6371 Pension, Health, & Welfare Funds
SIC 6411 Insurance Agents, Brokers & Service
524298 All Other Insurance Related Activities
SIC 6411 Insurance Agents, Brokers & Service
52511 Pension Funds
SIC 6371 Pension, Health, & Welfare Funds
52512 Health & Welfare Funds
SIC 6371 Pension, Health, & Welfare Funds
52519 Other Insurance Funds
SIC 6321 Accident & Health Insurance
SIC 6324 Hospital & Medical Service Plans
SIC 6331 Fire, Marine, & Casualty Insurance
SIC 6733 Trusts, Except Educational, Religious, & Charitable
52591 Open-End Investment Funds
SIC 6722 Management Investment Offices, Open-End
52592 Trusts, Estates, & Agency Accounts
SIC 6733 Trusts, Except Educational, Religious, & Charitable
52593 Real Estate Investment Trusts
SIC 6798 Real Estate Investment Trusts
52599 Other Financial Vehicles
SIC 6726 Unit Investment Trusts, Face-Amount Certificate Offices, & Closed-End Management Investment Offices

REAL ESTATE & RENTAL & LEASING

53111 Lessors of Residential Buildings & Dwellings
SIC 6513 Operators of Apartment Buildings
SIC 6514 Operators of Dwellings Other Than Apartment Buildings
53112 Lessors of Nonresidential Buildings
SIC 6512 Operators of Nonresidential Buildings
53113 Lessors of Miniwarehouses & Self Storage Units
SIC 4225 General Warehousing & Storage
53119 Lessors of Other Real Estate Property
SIC 6515 Operators of Residential Mobile Home Sites
SIC 6517 Lessors of Railroad Property
SIC 6519 Lessors of Real Property, nec
53121 Offices of Real Estate Agents & Brokers
SIC 6531 Real Estate Agents Managers
531311 Residential Property Managers
SIC 6531 Real Estate Agents & Managers
531312 Nonresidential Property Managers
SIC 6531 Real Estate Agents & Managers
53132 Offices of Real Estate Appraisers
SIC 6531 Real Estate Agents & Managers
531399 All Other Activities Related to Real Estate
SIC 6531 Real Estate Agents & Managers
532111 Passenger Car Rental
SIC 7514 Passenger Car Rental
532112 Passenger Car Leasing
SIC 7515 Passenger Car Leasing

53212 Truck, Utility Trailer, & RV Rental & Leasing
SIC 7513 Truck Rental & Leasing Without Drivers
SIC 7519 Utility Trailers & Recreational Vehicle Rental
53221 Consumer Electronics & Appliances Rental
SIC 7359 Equipment Rental & Leasing, nec
53222 Formal Wear & Costume Rental
SIC 7299 Miscellaneous Personal Services, nec
SIC 7819 Services Allied to Motion Picture Production
53223 Video Tape & Disc Rental
SIC 7841 Video Tape Rental
532291 Home Health Equipment Rental
SIC 7352 Medical Equipment Rental & Leasing
532292 Recreational Goods Rental
SIC 7999 Amusement & Recreation Services, nec
532299 All Other Consumer Goods Rental
SIC 7359 Equipment Rental & Leasing, nec
53231 General Rental Centers
SIC 7359 Equipment Rental & Leasing, nec
532411 Commercial Air, Rail, & Water Transportation Equipment Rental & Leasing
SIC 4499 Water Transportation Services, nec
SIC 4741 Rental of Railroad Cars
SIC 7359 Equipment Rental & Leasing, nec
532412 Construction, Mining & Forestry Machinery & Equipment Rental & Leasing
SIC 7353 Heavy Construction Equipment Rental & Leasing
SIC 7359 Equipment Rental & Leasing, nec
53242 Office Machinery & Equipment Rental & Leasing
SIC 7359 Equipment Rental & Leasing
SIC 7377 Computer Rental & Leasing
53249 Other Commercial & Industrial Machinery & Equipment Rental & Leasing
SIC 7352 Medical Equipment Rental & Leasing
SIC 7359 Equipment Rental & Leasing, nec
SIC 7819 Services Allied to Motion Picture Production
SIC 7922 Theatrical Producers & Miscellaneous Theatrical Services
53311 Owners & Lessors of Other Nonfinancial Assets
SIC 6792 Oil Royalty Traders
SIC 6794 Patent Owners & Lessors

PROFESSIONAL, SCIENTIFIC, & TECHNICAL SERVICES

54111 Offices of Lawyers
SIC 8111 Legal Services
541191 Title Abstract & Settlement Offices
SIC 6541 Title Abstract Offices
541199 All Other Legal Services
SIC 7389 Business Services, nec
541211 Offices of Certified Public Accountants
SIC 8721 Accounting, Auditing, & Bookkeeping Services
541213 Tax Preparation Services
SIC 7291 Tax Return Preparation Services
541214 Payroll Services
SIC 7819 Services Allied to Motion Picture Production
SIC 8721 Accounting, Auditing, & Bookkeeping Services
541219 Other Accounting Services
SIC 8721 Accounting, Auditing, & Bookkeeping Services
54131 Architectural Services
SIC 8712 Architectural Services

54132 Landscape Architectural Services
SIC 0781 Landscape Counseling & Planning
54133 Engineering Services
SIC 8711 Engineering Services
54134 Drafting Services
SIC 7389 Business Services, nec
54135 Building Inspection Services
SIC 7389 Business Services, nec
54136 Geophysical Surveying & Mapping Services
SIC 8713 Surveying Services
SIC 1081 Metal Mining Services
SIC 1382 Oil & Gas Field Exploration Services
SIC 1481 Nonmetallic Minerals Services, Except Fuels
54137 Surveying & Mapping Services
SIC 7389 Business Services, nec
SIC 8713 Surveying Services
54138 Testing Laboratories
SIC 8734 Testing Laboratories
54141 Interior Design Services
SIC 7389 Business Services, nec
54142 Industrial Design Services
SIC 7389 Business Services, nec
54143 Commercial Art & Graphic Design Services
SIC 7336 Commercial Art & Graphic Design
SIC 8099 Health & Allied Services, nec
54149 Other Specialized Design Services
SIC 7389 Business Services, nec
541511 Custom Computer Programming Services
SIC 7371 Computer Programming Services
541512 Computer Systems Design Services
SIC 7373 Computer Integrated Systems Design
SIC 7379 Computer Related Services, nec
541513 Computer Facilities Management Services
SIC 7376 Computer Facilities Management Services
541519 Other Computer Related Services
SIC 7379 Computer Related Services, nec
541611 Administrative Management & General Management Consulting Services
SIC 8742 Management Consulting Services
541612 Human Resources & Executive Search Consulting Services
SIC 8742 Management Consulting Services
SIC 7361 Employment Agencies
SIC 8999 Services, nec
541613 Marketing Consulting Services
SIC 8742 Management Consulting Services
541614 Process, Physical, Distribution & Logistics Consulting Services
SIC 8742 Management Consulting Services
541618 Other Management Consulting Services
SIC 4731 Arrangement of Transportation of Freight & Cargo
SIC 8748 Business Consulting Services, nec
54162 Environmental Consulting Services
SIC 8999 Services, nec
54169 Other Scientific & Technical Consulting Services
SIC 0781 Landscape Counseling & Planning
SIC 8748 Business Consulting Services, nec
SIC 8999 Services, nec
54171 Research & Development in the Physical Sciences & Engineering Sciences
SIC 8731 Commercial Physical & Biological Research
SIC 8733 Noncommercial Research Organizations

54172 Research & Development in the Life Sciences
SIC 8731 Commercial Physical & Biological Research
SIC 8733 Noncommercial Research Organizations
54173 Research & Development in the Social Sciences & Humanities
SIC 8732 Commercial Economic, Sociological, & Educational Research
SIC 8733 Noncommercial Research Organizations
54181 Advertising Agencies
SIC 7311 Advertising Agencies
54182 Public Relations Agencies
SIC 8743 Public Relations Services
54183 Media Buying Agencies
SIC 7319 Advertising, nec
54184 Media Representatives
SIC 7313 Radio, Television, & Publishers' Advertising Representatives
54185 Display Advertising
SIC 7312 Outdoor Advertising Services
SIC 7319 Advertising, nec
54186 Direct Mail Advertising
SIC 7331 Direct Mail Advertising Services
54187 Advertising Material Distribution Services
SIC 7319 Advertising, NEC
54189 Other Services Related to Advertising
SIC 7319 Advertising, nec
SIC 5199 Nondurable Goods, nec
SIC 7389 Business Services, nec
54191 Marketing Research & Public Opinion Polling
SIC 8732 Commercial Economic, Sociological, & Educational Research
541921 Photography Studios, Portrait
SIC 7221 Photographic Studios, Portrait
541922 Commercial Photography
SIC 7335 Commercial Photography
SIC 8099 Health & Allied Services, nec
54193 Translation & Interpretation Services
SIC 7389 Business Services, NEC
54194 Veterinary Services
SIC 0741 Veterinary Services for Livestock
SIC 0742 Veterinary Services for Animal Specialties
SIC 8734 Testing Laboratories
54199 All Other Professional, Scientific & Technical Services
SIC 7389 Business Services

MANAGEMENT OF COMPANIES & ENTERPRISES

551111 Offices of Bank Holding Companies
SIC 6712 Offices of Bank Holding Companies
551112 Offices of Other Holding Companies
SIC 6719 Offices of Holding Companies, nec
551114 Corporate, Subsidiary, & Regional Managing Offices
No SIC equivalent

ADMINISTRATIVE & SUPPORT, WASTE MANAGEMENT & REMEDIATION SERVICES

56111 Office Administrative Services
SIC 8741 Management Services

56121 Facilities Support Services
SIC 8744 Facilities Support Management Services
56131 Employment Placement Agencies
SIC 7361 Employment Agencies
SIC 7819 Services Allied to Motion Pictures Production
SIC 7922 Theatrical Producers & Miscellaneous Theatrical Services
56132 Temporary Help Services
SIC 7363 Help Supply Services
56133 Employee Leasing Services
SIC 7363 Help Supply Services
56141 Document Preparation Services
SIC 7338 Secretarial & Court Reporting
561421 Telephone Answering Services
SIC 7389 Business Services, nec
561422 Telemarketing Bureaus
SIC 7389 Business Services, nec
561431 Photocopying & Duplicating Services
SIC 7334 Photocopying & Duplicating Services
561432 Private Mail Centers
SIC 7389 Business Services, nec
561439 Other Business Service Centers
SIC 7334 Photocopying & Duplicating Services
SIC 7389 Business Services, nec
56144 Collection Agencies
SIC 7322 Adjustment & Collection Services
56145 Credit Bureaus
SIC 7323 Credit Reporting Services
561491 Repossession Services
SIC 7322 Adjustment & Collection
SIC 7389 Business Services, nec
561492 Court Reporting & Stenotype Services
SIC 7338 Secretarial & Court Reporting
561499 All Other Business Support Services
SIC 7389 Business Services, NEC
56151 Travel Agencies
SIC 4724 Travel Agencies
56152 Tour Operators
SIC 4725 Tour Operators
561591 Convention & Visitors Bureaus
SIC 7389 Business Services, nec
561599 All Other Travel Arrangement & Reservation Services
SIC 4729 Arrangement of Passenger Transportation, nec
SIC 7389 Business Services, nec
SIC 7999 Amusement & Recreation Services, nec
SIC 8699 Membership Organizations, nec
561611 Investigation Services
SIC 7381 Detective, Guard, & Armored Car Services
561612 Security Guards & Patrol Services
SIC 7381 Detective, Guard, & Armored Car Services
561613 Armored Car Services
SIC 7381 Detective, Guard, & Armored Car Services
561621 Security Systems Services
SIC 7382 Security Systems Services
SIC 1731 Electrical Work
561622 Locksmiths
SIC 7699 Repair Shops & Related Services, nec
56171 Exterminating & Pest Control Services
SIC 4959 Sanitary Services, NEC
SIC 7342 Disinfecting & Pest Control Services
56172 Janitorial Services
SIC 7342 Disinfecting & Pest Control Services
SIC 7349 Building Cleaning & Maintenance Services, nec
SIC 4581 Airports, Flying Fields, & Airport Terminal Services

56173 Landscaping Services
SIC 0782 Lawn & Garden Services
SIC 0783 Ornamental Shrub & Tree Services
56174 Carpet & Upholstery Cleaning Services
SIC 7217 Carpet & Upholstery Cleaning
56179 Other Services to Buildings & Dwellings
SIC 7389 Business Services, nec
SIC 7699 Repair Shops & Related Services, nec
56191 Packaging & Labeling Services
SIC 7389 Business Services, nec
56192 Convention & Trade Show Organizers
SIC 7389 Business Services, NEC
56199 All Other Support Services
SIC 7389 Business Services, nec
562111 Solid Waste Collection
SIC 4212 Local Trucking Without Storage
SIC 4953 Refuse Systems
562112 Hazardous Waste Collection
SIC 4212 Local Trucking Without Storage
SIC 4953 Refuse Systems
562119 Other Waste Collection
SIC 4212 Local Trucking Without Storage
SIC 4953 Refuse Systems
562211 Hazardous Waste Treatment & Disposal
SIC 4953 Refuse Systems
562212 Solid Waste Landfill
SIC 4953 Refuse Systems
562213 Solid Waste Combustors & Incinerators
SIC 4953 Refuse Systems
562219 Other Nonhazardous Waste Treatment & Disposal
SIC 4953 Refuse Systems
56291 Remediation Services
SIC 1799 Special Trade Contractors, nec
SIC 4959 Sanitary Services, nec
56292 Materials Recovery Facilities
SIC 4953 Refuse Systems
562991 Septic Tank & Related Services
SIC 7359 Equipment Rental & Leasing, nec
SIC 7699 Repair Shops & Related Services, nec
562998 All Other Miscellaneous Waste Management Services
SIC 4959 Sanitary Services, nec

EDUCATIONAL SERVICES

61111 Elementary & Secondary Schools
SIC 8211 Elementary & Secondary Schools
61121 Junior Colleges
SIC 8222 Junior Colleges & Technical Institutes
61131 Colleges, Universities & Professional Schools
SIC 8221 Colleges, Universities, & Professional Schools
61141 Business & Secretarial Schools
SIC 8244 Business & Secretarial Schools
61142 Computer Training
SIC 8243 Data Processing Schools
61143 Professional & Management Development Training Schools
SIC 8299 Schools & Educational Services, nec
611511 Cosmetology & Barber Schools
SIC 7231 Beauty Shops
SIC 7241 Barber Shops
611512 Flight Training
SIC 8249 Vocational Schools, nec
SIC 8299 Schools & Educational Services, nec

611513 Apprenticeship Training
SIC 8249 Vocational Schools, nec
611519 Other Technical & Trade Schools
SIC 8249 Vocational Schools, NEC
SIC 8243 Data Processing Schools
61161 Fine Arts Schools
SIC 8299 Schools & Educational Services, nec
SIC 7911 Dance Studios, Schools, & Halls
61162 Sports & Recreation Instruction
SIC 7999 Amusement & Recreation Services, nec
61163 Language Schools
SIC 8299 Schools & Educational Services, nec
611691 Exam Preparation & Tutoring
SIC 8299 Schools & Educational Services, nec
611692 Automobile Driving Schools
SIC 8299 Schools & Educational Services, nec
611699 All Other Miscellaneous Schools & Instruction
SIC 8299 Schools & Educational Services, nec
61171 Educational Support Services
SIC 8299 Schools & Educational Services nec
SIC 8748 Business Consulting Services, nec

HEALTH CARE & SOCIAL ASSISTANCE

621111 Offices of Physicians
SIC 8011 Offices & Clinics of Doctors of Medicine
SIC 8031 Offices & Clinics of Doctors of Osteopathy
621112 Offices of Physicians, Mental Health Specialists
SIC 8011 Offices & Clinics of Doctors of Medicine
SIC 8031 Offices & Clinics of Doctors of Osteopathy
62121 Offices of Dentists
SIC 8021 Offices & Clinics of Dentists
62131 Offices of Chiropractors
SIC 8041 Offices & Clinics of Chiropractors
62132 Offices of Optometrists
SIC 8042 Offices & Clinics of Optometrists
62133 Offices of Mental Health Practitioners
SIC 8049 Offices & Clinics of Health Practitioners, nec
62134 Offices of Physical, Occupational & Speech Therapists & Audiologists
SIC 8049 Offices & Clinics of Health Practitioners, nec
621391 Offices of Podiatrists
SIC 8043 Offices & Clinics of Podiatrists
621399 Offices of All Other Miscellaneous Health Practitioners
SIC 8049 Offices & Clinics of Health Practitioners, nec
62141 Family Planning Centers
SIC 8093 Speciality Outpatient Facilities, NEC
SIC 8099 Health & Allied Services, nec
62142 Outpatient Mental Health & Substance Abuse Centers
SIC 8093 Specialty Outpatient Facilities, nec
621491 HMO Medical Centers
SIC 8011 Offices & Clinics of Doctors of Medicine
621492 Kidney Dialysis Centers
SIC 8092 Kidney Dialysis Centers
621493 Freestanding Ambulatory Surgical & Emergency Centers
SIC 8011 Offices & Clinics of Doctors of Medicine
621498 All Other Outpatient Care Centers
SIC 8093 Specialty Outpatient Facilities, nec
621511 Medical Laboratories
SIC 8071 Medical Laboratories
621512 Diagnostic Imaging Centers
SIC 8071 Medical Laboratories

62161   Home Health Care Services
SIC 8082 Home Health Care Services
62191   Ambulance Services
SIC 4119 Local Passenger Transportation, nec
SIC 4522 Air Transportation, Nonscheduled
621991 Blood & Organ Banks
SIC 8099 Health & Allied Services, nec
621999 All Other Miscellaneous Ambulatory Health Care Services
SIC 8099 Health & Allied Services, nec
62211   General Medical & Surgical Hospitals
SIC 8062 General Medical & Surgical Hospitals
SIC 8069 Specialty Hospitals, Except Psychiatric
62221   Psychiatric & Substance Abuse Hospitals
SIC 8063 Psychiatric Hospitals
SIC 8069 Specialty Hospitals, Except Psychiatric
62231   Specialty Hospitals
SIC 8069 Specialty Hospitals, Except Psychiatric
62311   Nursing Care Facilities
SIC 8051 Skilled Nursing Care Facilities
SIC 8052 Intermediate Care Facilities
SIC 8059 Nursing & Personal Care Facilities, nec
62321   Residential Mental Retardation Facilities
SIC 8052 Intermediate Care Facilities
62322   Residential Mental Health & Substance Abuse Facilities
SIC 8361 Residential Care
623311 Continuing Care Retirement Communities
SIC 8051 Skilled Nursing Care Facilities
SIC 8052 Intermediate Care Facilities
SIC 8059 Nursing & Personal Care Facilities, nec
623312 Homes for the Elderly
SIC 8361 Residential Care
62399   Other Residential Care Facilities
SIC 8361 Residential Care
62411   Child & Youth Services
SIC 8322 Individual & Family Social Services
SIC 8641 Civic, Social, & Fraternal Organizations
62412   Services for the Elderly & Persons with Disabilities
SIC 8322 Individual & Family Social Services
62419   Other Individual & Family Services
SIC 8322 Individual & Family Social Services
62421   Community Food Services
SIC 8322 Individual & Family Social Services
624221 Temporary Shelters
SIC 8322 Individual & Family Social Services
624229 Other Community Housing Services
SIC 8322 Individual & Family Social Services
62423   Emergency & Other Relief Services
SIC 8322 Individual & Family Social Services
62431   Vocational Rehabilitation Services
SIC 8331 Job Training & Vocational Rehabilitation Services
62441   Child Day Care Services
SIC 8351 Child Day Care Services
SIC 7299 Miscellaneous Personal Services, nec

ARTS, ENTERTAINMENT, & RECREATION

71111   Theater Companies & Dinner Theaters
SIC 5812 Eating Places
SIC 7922 Theatrical Producers & Miscellaneous Theatrical Services

71112   Dance Companies
SIC 7922 Theatrical Producers & Miscellaneous Theatrical Services
71113   Musical Groups & Artists
SIC 7929 Bands, Orchestras, Actors, & Entertainment Groups
71119   Other Performing Arts Companies
SIC 7929 Bands, Orchestras, Actors, & Entertainment Groups
SIC 7999 Amusement & Recreation Services, nec
711211 Sports Teams & Clubs
SIC 7941 Professional Sports Clubs & Promoters
711212 Race Tracks
SIC 7948 Racing, Including Track Operations
711219 Other Spectator Sports
SIC 7941 Professional Sports Clubs & Promoters
SIC 7948 Racing, Including Track Operations
SIC 7999 Amusement & Recreation Services, nec
71131   Promoters of Performing Arts, Sports & Similar Events with Facilities
SIC 6512 Operators of Nonresidential Buildings
SIC 7922 Theatrical Procedures & Miscellaneous Theatrical Services
SIC 7941 Professional Sports Clubs & Promoters
71132   Promoters of Performing Arts, Sports & Similar Events without Facilities
SIC 7922 Theatrical Producers & Miscellaneous Theatrical Services
SIC 7941 Professional Sports Clubs & Promoters
71141   Agents & Managers for Artists, Athletes, Entertainers & Other Public Figures
SIC 7389 Business Services, nec
SIC 7922 Theatrical Producers & Miscellaneous Theatrical Services
SIC 7941 Professional Sports Clubs & Promoters
71151   Independent Artists, Writers, & Performers
SIC 7819 Services Allied to Motion Picture Production
SIC 7929 Bands, Orchestras, Actors, & Other Entertainers & Entertainment Services
SIC 8999 Services, nec
71211   Museums
SIC 8412 Museums & Art Galleries
71212   Historical Sites
SIC 8412 Museums & Art Galleries
71213   Zoos & Botanical Gardens
SIC 8422 Arboreta & Botanical & Zoological Gardens
71219   Nature Parks & Other Similar Institutions
SIC 7999 Amusement & Recreation Services, nec
SIC 8422 Arboreta & Botanical & Zoological Gardens
71311   Amusement & Theme Parks
SIC 7996 Amusement Parks
71312   Amusement Arcades
SIC 7993 Coin-Operated Amusement Devices
71321   Casinos
SIC 7999 Amusement & Recreation Services, nec
71329   Other Gambling Industries
SIC 7993 Coin-Operated Amusement Devices
SIC 7999 Amusement & Recreation Services, nec
71391   Golf Courses & Country Clubs
SIC 7992 Public Golf Courses
SIC 7997 Membership Sports & Recreation Clubs
71392   Skiing Facilities
SIC 7999 Amusement & Recreation Services, nec
71393   Marinas
SIC 4493 Marinas

71394 Fitness & Recreational Sports Centers
SIC 7991 Physical Fitness Facilities
SIC 7997 Membership Sports & Recreation Clubs
SIC 7999 Amusement & Recreation Services, nec

71395 Bowling Centers
SIC 7933 Bowling Centers

71399 All Other Amusement & Recreation Industries
SIC 7911 Dance Studios, Schools, & Halls
SIC 7993 Amusement & Recreation Services, nec
SIC 7997 Membership Sports & Recreation Clubs
SIC 7999 Amusement & Recreation Services, nec

ACCOMMODATION & FOODSERVICES

72111 Hotels & Motels
SIC 7011 Hotels & Motels
SIC 7041 Organization Hotels & Lodging Houses, on
     Membership Basis

72112 Casino Hotels
SIC 7011 Hotels & Motels

721191 Bed & Breakfast Inns
SIC 7011 Hotels & Motels

721199 All Other Traveler Accommodation
SIC 7011 Hotels & Motels

721211 RV Parks & Campgrounds
SIC 7033 Recreational Vehicle Parks & Campgrounds

721214 Recreational & Vacation Camps
SIC 7032 Sporting & Recreational Camps

72131 Rooming & Boarding Houses
SIC 7021 Rooming & Boarding Houses
SIC 7041 Organization Hotels & Lodging Houses, on
     Membership Basis

72211 Full-Service Restaurants
SIC 5812 Eating Places

722211 Limited-Service Restaurants
SIC 5812 Eating Places
SIC 5499 Miscellaneous Food Stores

722212 Cafeterias
SIC 5812 Eating Places

722213 Snack & Nonalcoholic Beverage Bars
SIC 5812 Eating Places
SIC 5461 Retail Bakeries

72231 Foodservice Contractors
SIC 5812 Eating Places

72232 Caterers
SIC 5812 Eating Places

72233 Mobile Caterers
SIC 5963 Direct Selling Establishments

72241 Drinking Places
SIC 5813 Drinking Places

OTHER SERVICES

811111 General Automotive Repair
SIC 7538 General Automotive Repair Shops

811112 Automotive Exhaust System Repair
SIC 7533 Automotive Exhaust System Repair Shops

811113 Automotive Transmission Repair
SIC 7537 Automotive Transmission Repair Shops

811118 Other Automotive Mechanical & Electrical Repair &
     Maintenance
SIC 7539 Automotive Repair Shops, nec

811121 Automotive Body, Paint & Upholstery Repair &
     Maintenance
SIC 7532 Top, Body, & Upholstery Repair Shops & Paint
     Shops

811122 Automotive Glass Replacement Shops
SIC 7536 Automotive Glass Replacement Shops

811191 Automotive Oil Change & Lubrication Shops
SIC 7549 Automotive Services, Except Repair & Carwashes

811192 Car Washes
SIC 7542 Carwashes

811198 All Other Automotive Repair & Maintenance
SIC 7534 Tire Retreading & Repair Shops
SIC 7549 Automotive Services, Except Repair & Carwashes

811211 Consumer Electronics Repair & Maintenance
SIC 7622 Radio & Television Repair Shops
SIC 7629 Electrical & Electronic Repair Shops, nec

811212 Computer & Office Machine Repair & Maintenance
SIC 7378 Computer Maintenance & Repair
SIC 7629 Electrical & Electronic Repair Shops, nec
SIC 7699 Repair Shops & Related Services, nec

811213 Communication Equipment Repair & Maintenance
SIC 7622 Radio & Television Repair Shops
SIC 7629 Electrical & Electronic Repair Shops, nec

811219 Other Electronic & Precision Equipment Repair &
     Maintenance
SIC 7629 Electrical & Electronic Repair Shops, nec
SIC 7699 Repair Shops & Related Services, NEC

81131 Commercial & Industrial Machinery & Equipment
     Repair & Maintenance
SIC 7699 Repair Shops & Related Services, nec
SIC 7623 Refrigerator & Air-Conditioning Service & Repair
     Shops
SIC 7694 Armature Rewinding Shops

811411 Home & Garden Equipment Repair & Maintenance
SIC 7699 Repair Shops & Related Services, nec

811412 Appliance Repair & Maintenance
SIC 7623 Refrigeration & Air-Conditioning Service & Repair
     Shops
SIC 7629 Electrical & Electronic Repair Shops, NEC
SIC 7699 Repairs Shops & Related Services, nec

81142 Reupholstery & Furniture Repair
SIC 7641 Reupholstery & Furniture Repair

81143 Footwear & Leather Goods Repair
SIC 7251 Shoe Repair & Shoeshine Parlors
SIC 7699 Repair Shops & Related Services

81149 Other Personal & Household Goods Repair &
     Maintenance
SIC 3732 Boat Building & Repairing
SIC 7219 Laundry & Garment Services, nec
SIC 7631 Watch, Clock, & Jewelry Repair
SIC 7692 Welding Repair
SIC 7699 Repair Shops & Related Services, nec

812111 Barber Shops
SIC 7241 Barber Shops

812112 Beauty Salons
SIC 7231 Beauty Shops

812113 Nail Salons
SIC 7231 Beauty Shops

812191 Diet & Weight Reducing Centers
SIC 7299 Miscellaneous Personal Services, nec

812199 Other Personal Care Services
SIC 7299 Miscellaneous Personal Services, nec,

81221   Funeral Homes
SIC 7261 Funeral Services & Crematories

81222   Cemeteries & Crematories
SIC 6531 Real Estate Agents & Managers
SIC 6553 Cemetery Subdividers & Developers
SIC 7261 Funeral Services & Crematories

81231   Coin-Operated Laundries & Drycleaners
SIC 7215 Coin-Operated Laundry & Drycleaning

812321 Laundries, Family & Commercial
SIC 7211 Power Laundries, Family & Commercial

812322 Drycleaning Plants
SIC 7216 Drycleaning Plants, Except Rug Cleaning

812331 Linen Supply
SIC 7213 Linen Supply
SIC 7219 Laundry & Garment Services, nec,

812332 Industrial Launderers
SIC 7218 Industrial Launderers

812391 Garment Pressing, & Agents for Laundries
SIC 7212 Garment Pressing & Agents for Laundries

812399 All Other Laundry Services
SIC 7219 Laundry & Garment Services, NEC

81291   Pet Care Services
SIC 0752 Animal Speciality Services, Except Veterinary

812921 Photo Finishing Laboratories
SIC 7384 Photofinishing Laboratories

812922 One-Hour Photo Finishing
SIC 7384 Photofinishing Laboratories

81293   Parking Lots & Garages
SIC 7521 Automobile Parking

81299   All Other Personal Services
SIC 7299 Miscellaneous Personal Services, nec
SIC 7389 Miscellaneous Business Services

81311   Religious Organizations
SIC 8661 Religious Organizations

813211 Grantmaking Foundations
SIC 6732 Educational, Religious, & Charitable Trust

813212 Voluntary Health Organizations
SIC 8399 Social Services, nec

813219 Other Grantmaking & Giving Services
SIC 8399 Social Services, NEC

813311 Human Rights Organizations
SIC 8399 Social Services, nec

813312 Environment, Conservation & Wildlife Organizations
SIC 8399 Social Services, nec
SIC 8699 Membership Organizations, nec

813319 Other Social Advocacy Organizations
SIC 8399 Social Services, NEC

81341   Civic & Social Organizations
SIC 8641 Civic, Social, & Fraternal Organizations
SIC 8699 Membership Organizations, nec

81391   Business Associations
SIC 8611 Business Associations
SIC 8699 Membership Organizations, nec

81392   Professional Organizations
SIC 8621 Professional Membership Organizations

81393   Labor Unions & Similar Labor Organizations
SIC 8631 Labor Unions & Similar Labor Organizations

81394   Political Organizations
SIC 8651 Political Organizations

81399   Other Similar Organizations
SIC 6531 Real Estate Agents & Managers
SIC 8641 Civic, Social, & Fraternal Organizations

SIC 8699 Membership Organizations, nec
81411   Private Households
SIC 8811 Private Households

PUBLIC ADMINISTRATION

92111   Executive Offices
SIC 9111 Executive Offices

92112   Legislative Bodies
SIC 9121 Legislative Bodies

92113   Public Finance
SIC 9311 Public Finance, Taxation, & Monetary Policy

92114   Executive & Legislative Offices, Combined
SIC 9131 Executive & Legislative Offices, Combined

92115   American Indian & Alaska Native Tribal Governments
SIC 8641 Civic, Social, & Fraternal Organizations

92119   All Other General Government
SIC 9199 General Government, nec

92211   Courts
SIC 9211 Courts

92212   Police Protection
SIC 9221 Police Protection

92213   Legal Counsel & Prosecution
SIC 9222 Legal Counsel & Prosecution

92214   Correctional Institutions
SIC 9223 Correctional Institutions

92215   Parole Offices & Probation Offices
SIC 8322 Individual & Family Social Services

92216   Fire Protection
SIC 9224 Fire Protection

92219   All Other Justice, Public Order, & Safety
SIC 9229 Public Order & Safety, nec

92311   Administration of Education Programs
SIC 9411 Administration of Educational Programs

92312   Administration of Public Health Programs
SIC 9431 Administration of Public Health Programs

92313   Administration of Social, Human Resource & Income Maintenance Programs
SIC 9441 Administration of Social, Human Resource & Income Maintenance Programs

92314   Administration of Veteran's Affairs
SIC 9451 Administration of Veteran's Affairs, Except Health Insurance

92411   Air & Water Resource & Solid Waste Management
SIC 9511 Air & Water Resource & Solid Waste Management

92412   Land, Mineral, Wildlife, & Forest Conservation
SIC 9512 Land, Mineral, Wildlife, & Forest Conservation

92511   Administration of Housing Programs
SIC 9531 Administration of Housing Programs

92512   Administration of Urban Planning & Community & Rural Development
SIC 9532 Administration of Urban Planning & Community & Rural Development

92611   Administration of General Economic Programs
SIC 9611 Administration of General Economic Programs

92612   Regulation & Administration of Transportation Programs
SIC 9621 Regulations & Administration of Transportation Programs

92613   Regulation & Administration of Communications, Electric, Gas, & Other Utilities
SIC 9631 Regulation & Administration of Communications, Electric, Gas, & Other Utilities

92614 Regulation of Agricultural Marketing & Commodities
SIC 9641 Regulation of Agricultural Marketing & Commodities
**92615 Regulation, Licensing, & Inspection of Miscellaneous
        Commercial Sectors**
SIC 9651 Regulation, Licensing, & Inspection of Miscellaneous
        Commercial Sectors
92711 Space Research & Technology
SIC 9661 Space Research & Technology
92811 National Security
SIC 9711 National Security
92812 International Affairs
SIC 9721 International Affairs
99999 Unclassified Establishments
SIC 9999 Nonclassifiable Establishments